JOHN SIMON ON THEATER

JOHN SIMON

ON THEATER

CRITICISM, 1974–2003

BY JOHN SIMON

INTRODUCTION BY JACK O'BRIEN

APPLAUSE THEATRE & CINEMA BOOKS ■ NEW YORK

John Simon on Theater: Criticism, 1974–2003
by John Simon
Copyright © 2005 by John Simon
All rights reserved

These reviews previously appeared in *The Hudson Review* and *New York* magazine.

Book design by Mark Lerner

Library of Congress Cataloging-in-Publication Data:
Simon, John Ivan.
 John Simon on theater : criticism, 1974-2003 / John Simon ; introduction by Jack O'Brien.
  p. cm. — (John Simon on—)
 Includes index.
 ISBN-13: 978-1-55783-505-5
 ISBN-10: 1-55783-505-5
 1. Theater—New York (State)—New York—Reviews. 2. Theater. I. Title. II. Series.

PN2277.N5S52 2005
792.9'5'097471—dc22

                    2005009983

British Library Cataloging-in-Publication Data
A catalog record of this book is available from the British Library

Applause Theatre & Cinema Books
19 West 21st Street, Suite 201
New York, NY 10010
Phone: (212) 575-9265
Fax: (212) 575-9270
Email: info@applausepub.com
Internet: www.applausepub.com
Applause books are available through your local bookstore, or you may order at
www.applausepub.com or call Music Dispatch at 800-637-2852

SALES & DISTRIBUTION
North America: Europe:
Hal Leonard Corp.   Roundhouse Publishing Ltd.
7777 West Bluemound Road   Millstone, Limers Lane
P. O. Box 13819   Northam, North Devon EX 39 2RG
Milwaukee, WI 53213   Phone: (0) 1237-474-474
Phone: (414) 774-3630   Fax: (0) 1237-474-774
Fax: (414) 774-3259   Email: roundhouse.group@ukgateway.net
Email: halinfo@halleonard.com
Internet: www.halleonard.com

For Pat,
supportive spouse,
consummate theatergoing companion,
manifold mentor.

And with thanks to Barry Boehm, who not only collected these pieces, but also offered helpful advice on which ones to include, there being no space for all.

Also thanks to the editors in whose magazines these pieces first appeared—especially the various editors of *New York* magazine, too numerous to name—and to Glenn Young, Michael Messina, and Kallie Shimek of Applause.

I ask the reader's forbearance for a certain number of repetitions in the following, written for different journals. Such overlapping seemed preferable to significant omissions, or to tampering with the original form of the pieces, which I wished to preserve.

AUTHOR'S NOTE

Times change, the saying goes, and we change within them. I have kept these reviews unchanged for historical reasons. But for the same reasons I must warn the reader that some of my present views have evolved in different directions. That change is reflected in certain later reviews, some of which did not make it into this book, and continues as I keep living and learning. Though I am no spring chicken, I hope Applause will someday bring out another collection before I am a dead duck, a book that might surprise the old John Simon no less than the old John Simon reader.

CONTENTS

Order of reviews and essays in each section is chronological according to the date it was originally published

Introduction

I don't, as a rule, hang with the critics. Not that there's anything wrong with them, mind you, but I've always thought best to keep my distance over the years, not putting too much stock in "the lions lying down with the lambs," and preferring to let the work speak for itself. Yes, all right, I'm a coward.

But as generations can be scarred by certain common experiences, or as trees are ringed by the years they have accumulated by simply standing in the forest, we of the theatre inevitably fall into a frame of reference pretty much dictated by the critic surveying and finally summing up our work. Max Beerbohm surely had his detractors as well as his enthusiasts, and, like the great G. B. Shaw before him, undoubtedly left some happier than others. But the likes of Shaw, Beerbohm, Harold Clurman, Walter Kerr, and Frank Rich all can draw a circle into which an entire range of artists can be gathered, collated, and finally succinctly objectified.

I myself am of the John Simon generation, if that means anything. I arrived in New York in the mid to late sixties, and began my association with Ellis Rabb's famed APA Repertory Theatre just about the time *New York* magazine was extricating itself from the moribund *Herald Tribune* to become the independent smart place either to park or pick up a quote.

None smarter than John's. And none whose quotes often smarted more, either. He was, perhaps, the first of the journalists to step completely outside what was understood as accepted journalistic

behavior and, taking aim, just let fly. We were aghast. We were titil-
lated. And, to be blunt, we lived in mortal fear of either being a target for this acid wit, or were incensed by the gaping wound he had
opened in a fallen colleague along the Great White Way. Whichever
way it went, the field was never to be the same again, and it was a
rare week that the spoken news from the Rialto didn't contain the
latest dart from that feared and fearless blowgun. Consequences
inevitably occurred, as famously when one evening at a party an
actress retaliated by intentionally dumping a plate of pasta upon
John's unsuspecting head. Still, it isn't that particular act that lingers
so much in memory. The pasta was merely a temporary distraction;
the reviews, however, survive.

You couldn't simply dismiss a Simon review if it were a pan, and
you couldn't smugly share in the joy, were it a rave. John was always
too far ahead of the class, outstripping everyone else in both knowledge, history, reference, and that one element without which any
critic can be dismissed as merely a "reviewer": he had standards.
Standards of authenticity, of beauty, of skill required, of pronunciation, grammar, even, God help us, line readings, all of which
he could summon up, rifle through, reference and apply without
hesitation and with an almost infuriating accuracy.

At the same time there seemed to run through his prose, especially during the earlier years of reviewing, a malcontent, a sim-
mering anger difficult to assess or explain at the time, but which
this generous if sadly incomplete collection of reviews helps clarify.
What often read as rage aimed at the occasional play, director, actor, or even an entire evening was not borne out of some rancor or
disappointment of Simon's with that particular theatre, but rather
stemmed from the fact that we were not attending to *all* theatre—
world theatre, as a matter of fact, rather than just American or British works, and certainly not with the same comprehension, respect
and appreciation he so passionately felt for the field in its entirety.
He was eager to take on giants of all walks—Spanish, Asian, East
European works, as well as O'Neill or Ayckbourn; he simply longed
for broader vistas to explore. For example, see him consider, in
this volume, Molière's *Le Misanthrope* in all its various reviews,
incarnations, and meditations, with an inexhaustible depth and understanding as well as an effortless mastery of French idiom and
nuance, and you will begin to understand how impatient he can be
with the paucity of wit and intelligence most of the rest of us happily settle for. Most reassuring of all he could be cranky, but never

a snob. The gift that awaits the reader is in the meticulous observation of performance, moments that leap to instant life, alongside of the unexpected appreciation and relish of pure trash he delights in as well as greatness. Finally, Simon simply loves theater. It was always its fools he could not suffer.

Simon has said repeatedly that a critic speaks merely for himself, for his own taste.

But what taste! What speaking! It's nearly impossible for anyone who cares about theatre to try casually flipping through the reviews which so eagerly crowd up to demand our attention in this collection. One is repeatedly caught, snagged, held by a paragraph, a reference, a celebration too stunning and original to begin quoting here, and, decades later, one turns once again to the top of the review to see, as we all once breathlessly parroted to each other back at the very inception, just "what it was that John Simon said!"

The heat cools on theatrical criticism nearly as fast as the ink dries, which is another reason I never write to critics, never complain, never take issue. By tomorrow, or perhaps the day after, the hubbub will have faded, the conflict forgotten, and the perceived injury a raw redness now, and nowhere near the humiliating wound one had originally imagined.

All traces of dumped pasta have been long ago laundered and shampooed away, and nothing of that original fury remains but what's finally left on the printed page. And here some thirty years later, thanks to this elegant collection of lucid, evocative writing, perhaps the most intriguing and, yes, even appalling revelation of all is the degree of accuracy with which, guns blazing, outrage unbound, whatever "Simon said" turned out to be right.

—Jack O'Brien
New York City
January 22, 2005

Criticism from
the 1970s

Candide

"A schoolboy jest," Voltaire called *Candide* when he tried to deny his authorship of it, and a jubilant schoolboy jape—a kind of musical *Ubu Roi*—is what the revised adaptation of *Candide* at Brooklyn's Chelsea Theater Center turns out to be. The 1956 musical, with lithely prancing melodies by Leonard Bernstein, and elegant pirouetting lyrics by Richard Wilbur (supplemented by John Latouche and Dorothy Parker), unfortunately also had a humorless book by Lillian Hellman and a top-heavy production under Tyrone Guthrie. There may have been excessive fear in those days of offending the Catholics, the Jews, and God knows whom else, and it is not by looking at imaginary censors that you leap into imaginative satire. The show flopped, as did a 1972 revival, despite the following the 1956 original cast album had built up. Now there is a new book by Hugh Wheeler; a new staging concept by Harold Prince in collaboration with Eugene and Franne Lee, the designers; and there are lyrical additives by Stephen Sondheim. Thanks be to all.

The new *Candide* lives precisely because of its preposterous, ubuesque quality. If musical comedy cannot match the clean, deep bite of Voltaire's satire—and it can't—then the schoolboy slingshot and campy outrageousness may be the best approximation. "In Morocco, a cruel war was raging between the black Moors and the less black Moors," is not quite Voltaire's way of putting it; "there are some of the holy brethren who still prefer the weaker sex," even less so; in their campy way, however, they are not bad at all. And having the Old Lady lean over the Jew's corpse rotting in the gutter (while the Inquisitor's was buried with great honors) and instruct it in the most maieutic tones, "There are advantages to being a Christian, after all," is pure camp, which, as it were, buggers description, but hits the target neatly in the rear. On the other hand, introducing old Voltaire himself as the narrator, instead of giving this role inappropriately to Pangloss, as Hellman did, is plain common sense.

The omission of some of the original songs saddens me, but the shifting around of others, with Sondheim additions, functions capitally—consider the scene built around the first (and new) use of "I Am Easily Assimilated," or the way the El Dorado song is cross-cut with the Old Lady's precarious misadventures. The concept of spreading the show over numerous acting areas, both conventional and bizarre, connected by ramps and drawbridges, while the audience, on bleachers and stools, is wedged in between—and the orchestra, split into sections, is stuffed onto and under the bleachers—creates just the sort of teasing, tingling disorientation that keeps one in a state of permanent, pleasurable surprise. And that network of ramps allows the endearingly informal choreography of Patricia Birch to look like a cross between a roundelay and a conga line, a madcap carnival that keeps circulating through the arteries of this environment like blood streaming through an exuberantly healthy organism.

Yes, it can be objected that the men's clothes are shedding all over, while the women's seem glued to the skins, but we must face the fact that few of the not-so-holy brethren who work in musical comedy still prefer the weaker sex. There is wit here—even in the way actors, who crawl over spectators or make them hold their props, politely apologize for the inconvenience—and verve, and invention. And if the present authors threaten to fly off into the tenuous, there is always Voltaire to bring them back into solidity. A young cast, mostly unknowns, works with an engaging mixture of innocence and proficiency, and two somewhat older hands, June Gable and Lewis J. Stadlen (the latter, perhaps, a mite too Jewish), dispense more sophisticated delights. "Charm," a term that defies definition, gets a tidy illustration from this *Candide*. Now if they would only put back those missing songs!

A Moon for the Misbegotten

It's hard to say whether O'Neill was created for Freud's benefit or Freud for O'Neill's, but these two support and complete each other like skeleton and flesh. It was O'Neill's greatest tragedy that he could not get out of the Oedipal stage: the women he loved, including his wives, appeared to him in the fluctuating forms of mother, virgin, and whore. But to sleep with mother was incestuous; with a whore, sinful and degrading; with a virgin, impossible. And so he was driven berserk by this love, and sex fixed his locus forever in an earthly hell.

This is why *A Moon for the Misbegotten*'s Josie, tough yet gentle, huge yet sensitive, stronger than most men yet not in the least mannish, either a virgin pretending to be a whore or a whore pretending under duress to be a virgin, possessed of an enormous frame that almost takes her out of the category "Woman" but endowed with a big maternal bosom to rest one's troubled head on, is O'Neill's ideal female. But because she is everything, she is too good to be true—certainly too good for the play's hero, James Tyrone, who is in most ways Eugene's drunken older brother Jamie, but also, in some ways, the playwright. *Moon* is a very sad play, for all its incidental humor; it suggests that there is peace only in oblivion, and that the little oblivions of drunkenness and sleep cannot hold a candle to the great forgetfulness of death. It is a play in love with death, and in it, more than ever, O'Neill is Hickey the Iceman, salesman of death.

Oddly, however, even for one who in no way shares O'Neill's obsessions, *Moon* succeeds; not so well as the two masterpieces, *Journey* and *Iceman*, but well enough, and better with each reseeing. The reason is hard to pinpoint. The language is never very distinguished, repetitiveness and tergiversation are everywhere, clichés are not always avoided, and the action proper is minimal. An incident related in Louis Sheaffer's important biography proved suggestive to me: already hit by the first effects of Parkinson's disease when, in World War II, the West Coast feared a Japanese attack, O'Neill taught himself to shoot, and "by holding the revolver with both hands, to offset his tremor, succeeded in hitting the target." So by clutching his characters stubbornly with both hands, by not letting go of their puny reversals, pathetic contradictions, fumbling verbalizations, footling flare-ups, and bone-crunching despair—by holding on to all this with two tremulous but compressed hands, the verbal and conceptual shakiness is overcome, compensated for by a sense of gigantic dedication, dogged sympathy for the characters, reverent nursing of mortal truth. You cannot move through this play without being ambushed by it; in the end, you forget about its foibles and eccentricities, and are aware only of the broad, common humanity by which the master playwright holds his characters and his audience, interpenetrating and dissolving in the same great sense of life's fleetingness, sorrowfulness, and nobility. To cavil with O'Neill, finally, is like trying to criticize an ocean.

The current revival is greatheartedly performed. Jason Robards reappears after a long and trying interval, more lined and chastened, an older and finer actor. The easy reliance on charming mannerism is all but gone, and what remains is a soul ravaged into purity. It may be that his Tyrone is not quite so dilapidated as he should be, but his flagging recalcitrance and despairing gallantry are consummate and moving. Colleen Dewhurst, though in many ways wrong for the virtually uncastable Josie, is as lucid and luminous, as unpoeticizingly poetic, as an actress can be in this part, and conveys uncloyingly the burning inwardness beneath the brash extroversion. The trio of leads is completed by a skillfully understated, deliberately offhand performance of Hogan by Ed Flanders: a wry, shrewd but feelingful, wisely contained obbligato against which the arias of James and Josie register their brave and piteous flourishes.

José Quintero's direction seems minimal, but, with these actors, that is enough. Ben Edwards's set is a disaster area: neither realistic nor evocatively exaggerated, it reeks of poverty without personal flavor, helpful neither to the actors who must play upon it nor to the spectators whose eyes starve on it. It includes the worst stage tree I have ever seen, but is, at least, atmospherically lighted by Mr. Edwards. Do not bypass this play; if catharsis through insight, empathy, and love is possible, the later O'Neill, as much as any dramatist ever, gives it to you with both his shaky, munificent hands.

Bad Habits

Bad Habits by Terrence McNally consists of two one-acters about unorthodox temples of mental therapy: Ravenswood, an expensive private sanatorium for couples, where a cynical doctor indulges his patients in their most exotic excesses; and *Dunelawn*, another haven of rehabilitation, where a beatifically smiling semicretinous doctor plies his patients with straitjackets and syringes until they are reduced to sweetly somnolent vegetables. Both plays go on a bit too long, and in both McNally succumbs to his chronic weakness, the inability to find the right ending. But this is not the amiably floundering McNally of *Tommy Flowers* and *Whiskey*; this is the McNally of *Next* and *Noon*, at his sick, mean, absurd yet purposive best, vicious crack topping vicious crack in the most demurely trotted-out fashion, like debutantes being presented at Court. For McNally, nothing has been desecrated enough not to deserve another friendly kick in the butt.

I could quote large chunks of devastating repartee, but would thereby shortchange the funniness of the plays as a whole, and the visual outrageousnesses that silently echo the verbal ones. No one is spared, except perhaps the most unpretentiously brutish, and the only virtue left standing is the forbearing acceptance of one's vices. It is a hopeless view of all therapy, moral as well as psychic, and a hideous estimate of mankind, but one that shoulders hideousness cheerfully and even with some pride in its magnitude. McNally, who was once Albee's protégé and disciple, has moved far beyond his now stagnating master, as if he had sucked him dry, and then some. You can call these plays unwholesome, inhuman—whatever you like—but not undazzling or unfunny. The production is, moreover, well designed, tidily directed by Robert Drivas, and acted by an octet of oddballs of whom each is very good in at least one play, and some triumph in both. My favorites are Cynthia Harris, mistress of slow burns and cuts to the quick, and Emory Bass, whose face radiates bitchiness at twice the speed of his sound. But even picking blindfolded you couldn't go far wrong.

Scapino

Question: What are the three famous dales of England? Answer: Its hills and dales, Chippendales, and Jim Dales. Q: But surely Jim Dale is unique? A: Yes and no. No, because these Jim Dales are a dancer, composer, singer, vaudevillian, classical actor, television host, and probably a host of other things I have overlooked, and all of them remarkable. Yes, because these Jim Dales are in fact the one and only Jim Dale, a singular manifold talent, from which it would be death to hide. Dale starred for Britain's National Theatre in *The National Health*, but a major national resource is what he really is. His appearances as Petruchio and Scapino with the Young Vic were among the highlights of the Brooklyn Academy of Music's British theater season; now the best of those programs, *Scapino*, is back at the Circle in the Square, and if you are even vaguely ambulatory, you owe it to yourself to see it.

Scapino is Frank Dunlop and Jim Dale's adaptation of Molière's *Les Fourberies de Scapin*, which genius has preserved fresher than cryogenics could these three centuries. The adapters have transposed it to the Naples of the post-neo-realist Italian film comedies, and added to it the spirit of British vaudeville and pantomime. But Molière is alive and well in this Neapolitan waterfront café where the action is now laid, and sometimes laid on with a trowel. For this is not a subtle play, nor an original one, Molière having ransacked Roman comedy, the Italian *lazzi*, and any number of his French contemporaries to compile this eclectic farce. Critics have found it wanting: "One of the least inspired of Molière's plays," Hofmannsthal wrote in his notebooks, and Boileau complained that in Scapin's ludicrous sack he could not recognize the author of *The Misanthrope*. But *Scapin/Scapino* is funny because it gives the director and actors full scope for weaving their grace notes and cadenzas around a simple, basic comic line: it provides archetypal characters and situations that coax the last drop of ingenuity from their interpreters.

I must honestly report that *Scapino* played better in Brooklyn. The acting area there was a huge triangle; here, the production suffers from a shrunken hypotenuse. There have also been cast changes. Christopher Hastings, the new Ottavio, is probably an improvement; and so, however slightly, may be Cleo Sylvestre, the new Zerbinetta—though a minimal chin has now been overcompensated for by hypertrophic feet. But Raymond Plait is a much less droll Carlo than his predecessor, and even sadder is the loss of Mel Martin as Giacinta. Miss Martin had very little to do, but she did it with grace and gusto, delicate sensuality and crystalline delivery, adding another dimension to the show. Her successor is Peter Ustinov's daughter, and a line in the play—"You're completely dependent on your father"—takes on devastating significance. The others, though, are the same enchanters as before, with Paul Brooke as Geronte my special favorite.

Carl Toms's setting and Frank Dunlop's staging continue to delight, but I must end as I began with Jim Dale: he is one of the five or six funniest comedians I have ever seen, and if I should be granted a dying wish, it would be for a command performance by him—so I could die laughing.

Short Eyes

Miguel Piñero's prison play, *Short Eyes*, has made it to the Vivian Beaumont, one of our larger and more elegant theaters. I worried about how it would adapt itself to the grand surroundings, but all is well: *Short Eyes* manages to live down that spacious stylishness. It remains effective theater, well put together, tightly acted, and staged with forcefulness and variety by Marvin Felix Camillo in David Mitchell's grimly telling set. I need not rehearse here the already well-known facts about Piñero's criminal youth, his redemption through participation in Camillo's drama workshop at Sing Sing, and his further development by joining The Family, a group of ex-convicts turned into an acting ensemble under Camillo's direction, and constituting most of the present cast.

However, since I wrote my original, rushed and somewhat laconic review, some noteworthy things have occurred. First, Walter Kerr printed a fascinating notice of the play, in which he graphically conveyed the carryings-on of the opening-night audience at Papp's Public Theater. More about this anon. Then Stanley Kauffmann published a challenging negative review in *The New Republic*, averring that most of this stuff has been told before "on TV, in the press, on film, and in other plays," and that Piñero "hasn't much skill in telling." "There is a strong irony," the critic continued, "but I'm not convinced that he's aware of it." Kauffmann pointed out that when the prisoners forget their racial and personal differences and, with the connivance of a white guard, kill the white man they all hate because he is a "short eyes" (prison slang for a child molester), they assert a badly needed superiority to someone—anyone. "But the inhumanity they then practice toward their 'inferior' is simply an extension of the very inhumanity, the social cruelty, that put them here in the first place. So, fundamentally, they are their own persecutors."

Kauffmann alone perceived this important truth, and he is probably right when he says the author leaves it "muzzy." For Piñero feels obliged to introduce a facile final irony, in which the police captain tells the prisoners that the dead man was innocent, and so leaves them prey to whatever pangs of conscience they are capable of. Still, we must not minimize Piñero's perception: Juan, the only prisoner who tried to prevent the killing, knows that the short eyes is guilty of *some* child molesting, even if he is probably innocent of the present charge. Yet Juan keeps silent, most likely because he wants the guilt of murder to have its effect. So Piñero must realize that there are certain things about which convicts can and should feel guilty; we should not blame him overmuch for not having reached, at 27, the deeper insight of an Oscar Wilde in *De Profundis*: "There are many things of which I was convicted that I had not done, but then there are many things of which I was convicted that I had done, and a still greater number of things in my life for which I was not indicted at all."

It is possible, surely, for a work to embody a greater truth than the author himself is aware of. One may then dispute exactly how much credit should go to the playwright; one cannot dispute the pregnancy of the play. Yes, these prisoners commit an act of ultimate swinishness, but are the people in the audience any less swinish? Kerr, in his account of the spectators' behavior, tended to absolve them; I, alas, lack his Christian charity. On two separate occasions, downtown and uptown, I watched an audience composed largely of blacks and Puerto Ricans, but containing also a goodly number of more or less hippified whites, behave with abominable inhumanity. The fact that they talked or shouted back at the stage (a barbarous habit, admired, oddly, by such different critics as Brustein and Barnes) is merely uncivilized. It does express involvement, but involvement that makes it impossible for others to hear, and for its exhibitor to stop and think, is imbecile, antisocial, and worthless. What truly appalled me, though, was the unbridled ecstasy with which these audiences savored—pealingly laughed, deafeningly cheered and applauded—the victim's being hung head down in a filthy toilet bowl, threatened with sexual assault, brutally hounded and mauled, and finally slaughtered. Similar ovations greeted other homosexual acts, fist fights, and even the least show of violence.

There is no excusing this on grounds of unsophisticated spontaneity, childlike identification, unconventionalized forthrightness. It is, I am afraid, bestiality, and though it may function also as catharsis, there remains the hideous underlying fact that any society that needs that much catharsis, of so gross a kind, can never get enough of it from the theater or other harmless sources, and is in grave trouble indeed.

And there is something else wrong with the play. A recent letter to the *Times*, from Jim Peck, a formerly jailed conscientious objector, objected most conscientiously to the depiction of "prison life as a frenzied interplay of personal conflicts... homosexuality and sadism... with never a dull moment. Actually, the outstanding characteristic of prison life is its unrelieved monotony, boredom and frustration." And Peck went on to wonder wisely whether this could be conveyed in a play. It is what Wilde described with "time itself does not progress. It revolves. It seems to circle around one centre of pain." In an interview in the *Times*, Piñero made it clear that he was aware of this phenomenon: "I saw all the loneliness there. Guys who didn't know how to read, just passing time, looking at the walls." If he can ever write *that* play, something much harder to do, it will have major dramatic and humane significance. Meanwhile, *Short Eyes* is a worthy preliminary sketch.

Camille: A Tearjerker

"It is not a drag show," said the efficient press agent for *Camille* to me on the telephone, and the same opinion is stated in Clive Barnes's review blown up outside the Evergreen Theater—though which of them got it from whom I cannot say. It seems to me however, that *Camille: A Tearjerker*, written, directed, and starred in by Charles Ludlam, and performed by his Ridiculous Theatrical Company is the very essence of a drag show; the difference is merely that the previous efforts of the Ridiculous were not even good enough for a good drag show; now, however, the company has progressed from the slime to the ridiculous.

Alexandre Dumas's *La Dame aux camélias* (or "*camilias*," as the current program would have it), from which the present *Camille* is "freely adapted," is a good bad play. Dumas *fils* based it on his own novel, which, in turn, was based on the real-life story of the courtesan Marie Duplessis, and in the process of all that basing, things got a bit debased. Marie Duplessis—or Alphonsine Plessis, which was her real, less euphonious name—was a girl who had started running away from home at twelve, was delivered roughly at that age by her father (her mother died years before) to a 70-year-old bachelor, from whom, however, she ran away. After several menial jobs, she became a kept woman by the age of fifteen, a courtesan at sixteen. Refined, beautiful, and extremely delicate (she was a consumptive, and died of TB in 1847, aged only 23), she became the mistress of a duke, who spent a fortune on her and disappeared. Many distinguished men admired or loved her, and Franz Liszt, who gave her piano lessons, considered her the first woman with whom he had been in love.

Earlier, she had met an elderly Polish baron, who treated her as his daughter, and tried to "save" her with a goodly, perpetual income. So she became chaste, and hoped for a respectable marriage. But, as she was to say, "I've loved… I've really loved, but no one has ever responded to my love. That is the real horror of my life." Soon she was back in prostitution. Yet she was no ordinary courtesan, but was invited to social functions, and sent opening-night tickets by the managers of the opera and theater, both of which she loved. Her conversation was charming and chaste, and, it is said, she never made grammatical mistakes. Her apartments were models of restrained sumptuousness, and her favorite flower *was* the camellia.

She compared herself to Manon Lescaut, and had a strong premonition of early death. From the other reigning courtesan of the day, she snatched away the young and wealthy Count Edouard de Perregaux, who married her, but they were soon separated. She was religious and also wild, wayward and quite witty. "I like telling lies," she once remarked, "because it keeps the teeth white." To Liszt she wrote: "Take me with you, take me wherever you want; I shan't be in your way. I sleep all day, in the evening you'll let me go to the theater, and at night you can do what you like with me." When she lay dying in a cheerless Parisian winter, the creditors were already pillaging her apartment. After the resplendent funeral, her possessions were auctioned off for fabulous prices, including "her brilliant feathered macaw, which repeated a rather sad little tune its mistress had taught it." She was herself rather like that bird.

Dumas's play (I haven't read the novel) makes Marguerite Gautier the heroine, into the charming, intelligent, and civilized person Marie Duplessis indeed was (quite an achievement considering her humble origins and no schooling), but, by romanticizing her, Dumas lessens her. Marie's tragedy was that, for whatever reason, she did not, could not, ever experience something she could call love (she was described as "adoring today what she hated yesterday, and vice versa"), and that there was no Armand Duval—or Alfredo Germont, in *La traviata*, based on the Dumas play—that she could make a supreme sacrifice for, and die in the arms of. *That* tragedy is no tragedy at all, thickly encased as it is in sugarcoating.

But whatever Dumas has or hasn't done to Alphonsine-Marie-Marguerite-Violetta, what Charles Ludlam has done to her shouldn't happen to a dog. I recall a Paris production of *La Dame aux caméllias* (I shall bypass the movie version, for I never had much affection for that sexless camp favorite Greta Garbo) in which the great Edwige Feuillère played Marguerite, and humdrum as the play is, the actress invested the part with such almost unbearable loveliness, such acute but unsentimental femininity: her love for Armand was not palpitations, yearnings, swoonings, merely the starkest, simplest need, like that of the lungs for oxygen. And when she died it was of consumption, not of a consuming passion—which made it more horrible. An otherwise healthy, sturdy woman, capable of total straightforward loving, was perishing stupidly of a blemished lung. I came out of the theater as shaken as when I saw Mme Feuillère in Claudel's *Partage de midi*, an incomparably better play.

Ludlam and his campy crew are funny at times, but in a destructive, unwholesome way. One hates oneself for laughing at Marguerite being travestied by a short, stocky, homely man in drag, who is outrageous even when by his or certain reviewers' standards he is playing it—you must excuse me—straight. Why doesn't Ludlam do something really daring—like camping up a play by a living author that virtually begs for it, say, *Tiny Alice* or *A Delicate Balance*? But poor, lovely, sad Marguerite! For his ruining her for people—or trying to—I shall not readily forgive Charles Ludlam.

Gypsy

About *Gypsy*, the good news first: Angela Lansbury is not Ethel Merman, and so much easier to look at. Now for the bad news: Angela Lansbury is no Ethel Merman, and thus much harder to listen to. But more about that later. The 1959 hit proves worthy not only of revival, but also of being the opening gala of the new season: the stuff of *Gypsy* shines through the somewhat humdrum staff of this production. To begin with, the music by Jule Styne is one of the most homogeneous and sustained scores to date, except for the rather routine and cloying "Little Lamb," sung by an inaudible singer to an intensely uncomfortable lamb. What makes the score particularly interesting is that half of its numbers seem to be made up not of notes but of echoes, and since one of the themes of the show is the unsentimental education of a young girl in vaudeville and burlesque, this amused allusiveness seems apt rather than derivative. A bit of a problem, though, might be the bald patches in some of the best songs, where the score is just a serviceable obbligato for the lyrics.

Yet since these lyrics are by Stephen Sondheim at his headiest—before his assurance began to smack of arrogance—the music can afford to mark time: the words sing out with verbal felicity and dramatic propulsion. When a stripper proclaims that, without a gimmick, "You can sacrifice your sacro / Working in the back row," there is more to this than an ingeniously ambushing rhyme. There is the word play on "sacrifice" and "sacro," suggestively coupling the sacred and the profane; the cozily butch irreverence of addressing the sacroiliac by its nickname; and, above all, the ambitiousness, perhaps even exhibitionism, with which a chorine jockeys for the front position. Again, when a quaintly named stripper sings, "Once I was a schlepper, / Now I'm Miss Mazeppa," this encapsulates her progress from, say, the Bronx to the Palladium, including plagiarism of the name of Adah Menken's most celebrated role, and the ethnic giveaway of pronouncing Mazeppa as "Mazepper."

The book by Arthur Laurents is very able as books for musicals go, but I cannot say how much of it is Laurents, and how much Gypsy Rose Lee's memoirs of her mother, Rose, her sister, June, and herself when young. Despite the titular bow to Gypsy, the protagonist here is Rose, the quintessential stage mother: dynamo, termagant, jokester, slave driver, pal, procuress, and beast. It is Rose's combination of resourcefulness and ruthlessness, courage and dementia, that the book concentrates on, making this mother-monster into one of the most realized and powerful characters in the American musical. When Merman played her, she was bone-deeply frightening, a fleshy monolith driven by a self-serving monomania masquerading as maternal love. Unfortunately, Miss Merman, while belting out home runs with virtually every note, was rather short on the appeal Rose must also have had. Miss Lansbury looks more believable: we can see a former *jolie laide* peeping through the comic garishness, and she moves and dances well: one more leap, and this woman could indeed have landed on the stage.

But, worse luck, the voice and the facial expressions won't do. As a singing instrument, the voice has no lower register, relatively little musicality, and a rasp over most of its range that is neither funky nor endearing—actually, it is in falsetto that it sounds best. I still hear Miss Lansbury in her first movie hit, *The Picture of Dorian Gray*, as a fallen waif pathetically shrilling out a sad song in a low dive; even her most determined present-day vocalizing reverberates with that staggering singsong. As a speaking instrument, Lansbury's voice has shaken off most of its Britishness, but hasn't acquired any American ethnicity, and so anchors Rose in a theatrical limbo.

As for Miss Lansbury's facial play, it consists mostly of turning down the corners of her mouth like a trained nurse making hospital corners on a bedsheet, and letting her eyes go either bulgily whirling (which, because of their closeness to each other, makes you wonder when they'll start caroming) or so narrowly slitty that you couldn't slip a calling card through their openings. Worst of all, though you get more craziness from Miss Lansbury than you did from Miss Merman, it is ludicrous rather than formidable.

The supporting cast is competent and undistinguished with two happy exceptions. Bonnie Langford, as Baby June, is the most fearfully accomplished child prima donna in years, if not decades. Although Arthur Laurents, who also directed, pushed her slightly too hard, she gives a most credibly incredible personification of the stage monster as child, and is closer to the essence of Rose than Miss Lansbury is. And as a sarcastic stripper, Mary Louise Wilson is so caustically irresistible that you don't know whether to hug yourself in doubled-up laughter, or her in sheer delight. That Rex Robbins is nowhere near Jack Klugman, the 1959 Herbie, is less of a problem than that Zan Charisse, though wistfully gawky enough as Gypsy, falls down badly in transit to raucous sexiness. A few glimpses of her understudy, Patricia Richardson, suggested rather more of the role's womanly prerequisites.

The sets by Robert Randolph and costumes by Raoul Pène du Bois have a perfunctory proficiency (though Robert Mackintosh has designed some more noteworthy albeit overrefined outfits for Miss Lansbury), and Robert Tucker re-creates faithfully the spare but inspired original choreography of Jerome Robbins. The show's first song is "Let Me Entertain You," and that—neither more, nor less—is what *Gypsy* will do for you. The darker implications are missed by this production.

Mack & Mabel

At the time of *Sugar*, I got more brickbats for liking the show than I usually get for despising one. I still think I was right, even more so after seeing *Mack & Mabel*, for which the same choreographer-director, Gower Champion, has worked more wonders yet. There are only three accredited thaumaturgists in our musical theater: Jerome Robbins, Bob Fosse, and Champion, to whom on the strength of what mediocre fare he has converted into stunning entertainment I am inclined to give the palm.

Lesser things first. Jerry Herman writes tuneful songs; that they are full of everybody's tunes, his own previous ones included, is not all to the bad. It is rather like falling in love with a former lover all over again years later: you don't know whether you relish that the old feels like new or that the new feels like old, but you distinctly enjoy getting two things for the price of one. At least, things sound different enough here—one or two songs even strive, with middling success, to crack the Herman mold. The Herman lyrics, which go in heavily for run-on lines, are unlikely to make Stephen Sondheim tremble in his elegant boots, but anything Sammy Kahn can do, Herman can do, do, do as well.

The book by Michael Stewart is a memory play: Mack Sennett, losing his studio in 1938, his two-reel silent comedies bypassed by the times and outtalked by the talkies, reminisces about his long career and his love for his leading lady, Mabel Normand. That love was like his movies: coming in short spurts consisting mostly of pushing her over into a pratfall into bed, and strictly without talking—without love-talk, anyway. Finally she left him, got involved in scandal and drugs, and received Mack's supreme love token too late: a sentimental joint comeback movie that never got released, which could not ward off her death approaching apace. It is to the book's credit that although it does embellish the tale, it doesn't over-romanticize it; it does, however, underdevelop it. The basically funny or touching situations and the moderately juicy dialogue are not underpinned by full-bodied characterizations; granted, it is not easy to give the two-dimensional folk of two-dimensional Hollywood a third dimension.

There is a strikingly effective all-purpose set by Robin Wagner, which achieves the neatest trick for unit sets: being able to look indoor or outdoor, as required. Patricia Zipprodt's costumes have the shrewdness of looking tastefully tasteless, and Tharon Musser's lighting has lost none of her lambent touch. Robert Preston may not change much from role to role, but he plays Preston superlatively. He abounds in gladsome surprises: when Mabel announces that the old routines are an insult to "my integrity as an artist," he responds with a "Your what?" without any of the dozen ways in which a lesser actor would have overplayed it. And he can, without the least loss of dignity, put more oo's into the word moooovies than anyone this side of Betty Boop. Bernadette Peters starts out overcute, but soon settles into a believable and winning Mabel Normand; her dancing may not be quite up to snuff, but her singing and acting easily make up for it. The book does rather shortchange her with emotional transitions, yet the purse of her lips is never short on dramatic suggestions. To lesser roles, Lisa Kirk and James Mitchell bring their customary expertise.

And over all of it hovers the great wizard, Gower Champion, tossing out more directorial and choreographic ideas per minute than most other directors per entire production. For openers, he truly makes theater move and behave like film, with all the dissolves, freeze frames, iris effects, and even, yes, superimposition, all of which is not just idle cleverness but a must in a musical about movies. One major problem remains: the violence of silent comedy needs the trickery of film, and though Champion has limited the slapstick to a necessary minimum, it remains, perforce, skimpy.

But otherwise, what plenty! Consider the quiet, dark opening of the show, reprised by the dark, subdued endings of both acts; after the frantic goings on, this melancholy coda explodes like a bomb of quietude. There are wonderful big effects: the boom on which Mack rides out over the spectators' heads, the firemen's pole along which the stars descend, the huge corkscrew slide down which the chorines spiral and sparkle, the massed forces on balconies and catwalks—some other fellow might have come up with these. But what about that large scrim on which scenes from Sennett films are projected and through which you can dimly discern Mack's defiant figure, and hear the song about his determination to make people laugh? What about extruding a corner of the stage into the audience, so that the bathing beauties can do their number in a breathtaking diagonal? What about the parasol that flies in between two dancers who seem to be merely its wings? And what of the ingenious way Mack sings his unromantic proposition inside a constricting Pullman sleeper, whereas for Mabel's reprise of the song, the railway car turns inside out, her romantic hopes soaring from a tiny lighted window out into the vastitudes of night?

And what of such fine little touches as Mabel's having to sidle past Mack in that train compartment to emphasize the tightness of space and situation? Almost any other director would have missed this psychologically pungent detail. When you see *Mack & Mabel*, observe silence for more than the music and words; quiet, please, for directorial genius at work!

Absurd Person Singular

The best kind of comedy, we know, has an underpainting of darkness; the comic mask resembles nothing so much as a grinning death's-head. Alan Ayckbourn's *Absurd Person Singular* is well aware of this: a witty and resourceful comedy that imperceptibly darkens into a dance—not of death, but of death-in-life. It is, then, the best kind of comedy, yet fairly far from the best specimen of its kind. Still, as commercial theater goes (and it goes farther than some highbrows and avant-gardists would have it), this British comedy is not inconsiderable; with more such plays around, the theater would be undergoing not exactly a renaissance, but a good prodding into action.

The play concerns three Christmas parties on three consecutive Yules, one per act. All three are seen from the vantage point of the kitchen, the soft underbelly of any party, where a household's guilty secrets are likeliest to hang out. The first pair of hosts, Sidney and Jane, are a sweatily-under-the-collar, upward-mobile couple, a tyrannical perfectionist of a little entrepreneur and his browbeaten wife whose sole escape is turning drudgery into a mystical cult, worthy of total dedication like the Eleusinian mysteries. The principal guests—Ronald, an abstracted fuddy-duddy of a banker, and Marion, his drunkenly patronizing malcontent of a wife; Geoffrey, a gallivanting architect better at beddings than buildings, and Eva, his depressive, suicidal wife—have nothing but contempt for their fussily meticulous, bumbling yet superefficient, hopelessly mediocre hosts.

By Act Two, in the architect's kitchen, things have changed. The professionally failing but promiscuously thriving Geoffrey is about to walk out on Eva, Eva is about to walk out of the window (or depart from life by any other emergency exit), a monstrous dog is biting or terrorizing the guests, the house is a shambles and chaos does not so much prevail as conduct a chamber ensemble for untuned and mismatched instruments. The old joke of failed attempts at suicide becomes a supremely funny running gag, gas oven, carving knife, overdose, window ledge, noose, live wire, and both the idiot doggedness with which it is pursued and the dogged idiocy with which it is fortuitously foiled, are among the more lacerating laughs of any season.

The third and crowning Christmas, at the shabby-genteel banker's—he befuddled and repressed, she besotted and irrepressible—is an artful blend of the tart and the bittersweet, the luridly laughable and quietly ghastly. It is as absurd and disturbing as an antimacassar made from a dead auntie's skin, and the final quasi-comic triumph of the first, arriviste couple has the laughs and lumps colliding in your throat. Eric Thompson has directed with unostentatious efficacy, and the performances are mostly good. Best is Larry Blyden, with the finest British accent ever to come out of Texas, and a kind of despotic aplomb and masterful gaucherie that should vault him to the top of our comedians' pile. Carole Shelley keeps up with him admirably, and Richard Kiley, though somewhat less than to the financier's manor born, trots out very fine bits. As his wife, Geraldine Page would be splendid if she could put a little more English into her vocal shots, and could get her admittedly riotous effects without having to overreach. Sandy Dennis as Eva is, of course, an expert at self-destructive dementia, and, in the second act, offers the added bonus of never opening her mouth, and thus sparing us the strangulated aspic of her voice. Tony Roberts does least for Geoffrey, but the part also does least for its interpreter. Theatergoers sluggishly avoiding this show would be singularly absurd persons.

Richard III

I dearly wish I had the sedative concession for Joe Papp's production of *Richard III* at the Newhouse Theater. I'm not sure exactly which barbiturates the protagonist and several other leading actors in Shakespeare's feistiest blood-and-thunder melodrama have ingested, but their consumption seems enormous—even contagious. Not only did Michael Moriarty walk through the title part in his

sleep (actually, he was supposed to limp, have a hump and a withered arm as well, but a somnambulist's being able to speak his lines
is remarkable enough in itself, and we must not be so insatiable as
to expect him to act as well), he even managed to put me to sleep
during the better—I mean, worse—part of his performance. And
he certainly elicited a good deal of slumber from his fellow actors,
too, most of whom made the *gisants* on a medieval tomb appear by
comparison a herd of rampaging elephants.

Of Moriarty's performance—and here the listless and unimaginative direction of Mel Shapiro must share in the blame—it can
only be said that it successfully rivaled its predecessor on the same
boards, the unforgettably abominable Macbeth of Christopher
Walken. Moriarty, who was so very fine in the execrable *Find Your
Way Home*, proves that even considerable training in classical acting at places like LAMDA and the Tyrone Guthrie Theater can leave
an able American actor stranded in Shakespeare. Richard III can
be a lot of things; Olivier has even made him almost more charming than monstrous (and if you have seen that great performance
on film, do not ruin your memories by seeing this one), but what
he cannot be is slow-witted and comatose—or shamble, stammer,
lumber, and mumble through what must be thought up, said, and
executed in a brilliant improvisatory flash. The effect is not that
of a Machiavellian monarch "in so far in blood," but of a hippo-
potamus in so far in mud as to make all movement and thought
unthinkable.

The women in the cast present a somewhat less slow-motion
problem. Marsha Mason, as Lady Anne, is merely ordinary, which
makes her look like some kind of a powerhouse, and poor Betty
Henritze, as mad Margaret, looks about as regal as a rabid mountain goat, which is probably why Shapiro has her leaping on every
table in sight, though why she must keep belaboring a toy drum,
except perhaps as a belated *hommage* to Günter Grass, remains a
mystery. Worse yet is the Elizabeth of Barbara Colby, whose acting
alternates between fishwifely rant and acute aphasia. Some sort of
booby prize must go also to Patrick Hines, who succeeds in making the cause of Edward IV's death appear to be some little-known
form of lethal imbecility.

A lot of young actors merely stand around trying to look as inconspicuous as possible, and it must be admitted that Santo Loquasto's dull scenery and John Conklin's monotonous costumes do
make it rather too easy for said actors to disappear into the staid

ambiance. Conklin's chiefly rust, gold, and black outfits seem all to be made from his grandmother's shawls. The one pleasant surprise of the production was Master Stephen Austin's little Duke of York; a decent child actor is about as hard to find in America as an acceptable Hamlet.

Equus

Peter Shaffer is a dramatist of talent and intelligence who has always delighted me with his smaller and zanier plays, like *The Private Ear* and *Black Comedy*, but left me hungry and disappointed with his mightier efforts, like *The Royal Hunt of the Sun* and *The Battle of Shrivings*. So I hoped that his new, serious, and, at the National Theatre of Britain, resoundingly successful play meant the breakthrough I awaited. Well, *Equus* has received wonderful notices; the audiences are lapping and clapping it up; Broadway has its new, much-needed dramatic hit; and I'm sure it couldn't happen to a nicer guy than Peter Shaffer. But to me the play is a bundle of anathemas.

First, *Equus* falls into that category of worn-out whimsy wherein we are told that insanity is more desirable, admirable, or just saner than sanity. At its lowest, this yields a film like *King of Hearts*; at its campiest, a farce like *Bad Habits*. Though much more sophisticated than these, *Equus* still asks us to believe that the crazed passion of a stableboy for horses, which, on the one hand, makes him create and fanatically worship a horse-god, Equus, and, on the other, drives him viciously to blind half a dozen harmless equines that witnessed his abortive love-making with a girl, is a fine and high-flown thing, a love that must be quashed because it is too grand, wild, and beautiful for the humdrum world of plodding humanity. To me, this is nonsense, and I don't for a moment believe the play's psychiatrist who is made to verbalize this bull (or horse); but, oh, how an audience of people who would consider anyone wearing a brown shoe with a black one a nut to be avoided stands up and cheers and makes cymbals of its palms to prove that it shares the playwright's noble and superior wisdom, and has all along lived by it, nobly and superiorly.

Next, and relatedly, the play asks us to believe that the psychiatrist who cures and "saves" this horse worshiper and blinder diminishes him: makes him plain, unpoetic, and common. Psychiatry, as its representative is made to confess, is a shriveler of souls. Now I hold no particular brief for psychiatry, having seen it not help about as many people as it has helped. But, fallible as it is—like all medicine, like all human endeavor—scoring facile points off it has always struck me as cheap and wrong-headed. I sympathize when a genius like Rilke or Ingmar Bergman refuses psychotherapy on the grounds that his greatness may somehow be lessened, that the achingly oversensitive artistic introspection may end up blunted. But what has this common stableboy to lose if, instead of naked nocturnal horseback-riding, and whipping himself, figuratively and literally, into a frenzy before a cloven-footed image, he makes love to a nice little girl, becomes a solid citizen, and occasionally wins or drops a few shillings at the races?

I particularly resent the further loading of the dice by making the psychiatrist, the spokesman for normality, an unhappily married man, his sex life with a dull and frigid wife completely atrophied, and his kicks coming from the perusal of illustrated tomes on Greek art. Not the goddesses of Phidias and Praxiteles, we are led to surmise, but the softly boyish *kouroi*, the charioteers and athletes of, say, Lysippus—after all, note the almost reverential ardor with which the psychiatrist treats and gazes at his ephebic patient's mind and body. Anthony Hopkins plays the doctor with an exacerbated tension, his words spat out overwrought, in acute but unanalyzed torment.

The play, furthermore, espouses the form of the case history, which, with the exception of the courtroom drama, is the most overworked and by now least imaginative form of theatrical offering. It is the difference between a great painting and its exploitation as a jigsaw puzzle: the art is no longer in the magnificent image, but in the fitting together of oddly shaped bits of wood. And then there is that obligatory (here not so obligatory) nude scene, in which cruel overhead lights are less than kind to Roberta Maxwell's physique, and in which the girl is, of course, the aggressor, causing a breach in the boy's equine fidelity. Then comes the grand nude blinding scene, showing off the boy's organ to best advantage, and all that, combined with the far-fetchedness of this whole notion of hippophilia, makes me agree with Martin Gottfried's view that what is really meant here is pederasty. In a season when every second new play seems to be frankly concerned with homosexuality, the love-that-dare-not-speak-its-name strategy of *Equus* strikes me as particularly jejune.

Lastly, we get that fashionably bittersweet semihappy ending: even if being cured is a cosmic cop-out, the boy, at least, will be cured—as if psychotherapy were such a simple matter: a little hypnosis here, a bit of abreaction there, and our hideously disturbed protagonist's mind is safely on the way to total recovery. But the final blow is the ordinariness of the play's language: "Without worship, you shrink, and I shrank my own life," declares the psychiatrist, hopping as nimbly from easy platitude to facile double entendre as a Cossack horseman from one galloping mount to another. The boy's mother, though a teacher, can come up with nothing better than: "He was my little Alan, and then the Devil came." And the key image is the doctor's, "I watch in a book Centaurs trampling the soil of Argos; and out in a field in Hampshire he is trying to become one!" What we need is more Lapithae, the mythic race who defeated the Centaurs and invented the bit and the bridle—only for horses, so far, but pretentious playwrights may be next.

The physical production of *Equus* is splendid in almost every detail, but no amount of external embellishment can overcome the hollowness within.

In the Boom Boom Room

It is good of David Rabe to rewrite *In the Boom Boom Room* so conscientiously, and of Joe Papp to put it on again so soon after its original failure. But the play has improved only very slightly, and the production at the Public Theater is a lot worse. Rabe, whose early plays dealt searchingly and searingly with the Vietnam war, is having (understandably) a much harder time dramatizing life in its fundamentals. His Chrissy, a troubled go-go girl scratching about for some meaning to her life, does not grow into the prototype of modern woman in search of her soul. Though some things about her ring touchingly true, she is inconsistent: sometimes too primitive, sometimes too sophisticated for the rest of her. Even her job is too specialized and quirky to anoint her readily as Everywoman; and the people she seeks comfort from are rather too spectacularly and excogitatedly unfeeling and exploitative. Many playwrights (e.g., Büchner, Chekhov, Brecht) have made their characters speak past one another, but here dialogue is too deliberately like blind men at target practice.

Despite moving and funny moments strewn throughout this shortened but still overlong play, the bulk of it is cards stacked too programmatically against the heroine, with failure, betrayal, madness, and degradation distributed premeditatedly and prodigally in all directions. Even the sense of time is faulty, with unhappy consequences for the logic of the play: in 1974, to dance barebreasted in a New York dive after having danced vaguely clothed in a Philadelphia cage is not the shuddering fall Rabe would have us believe; it may actually be a step up. Still, the dramatist commands respect for the insight and sympathy he lavishes on his heroine; such man-to-woman comprehension should give hope to the most embattled of radical feminists.

Chrissy is now played by a singer, Ellen Greene, who shows heartening potential as an actress, and needs only more experience and better direction. Here she mostly imitates Streisand, which is only a shade less disastrous than being Streisand. Even so she is far more real than Christopher Lloyd as her truck-driver lover, whose entire act is a George C. Scott impersonation; or Gwendolyn Brown as a hardened go-go captain and part-time lesbian, whose inaudible performance caves into itself; or Tom Quinn, who plays Chrissy's father with one stock gesture and one and a half expressions; or Helen Hanft, who plays a tragicomic mother with all the slickness of Off Off Broadway farce. The others flounder in various ways under Robert Hedley's indecisive and clumsy direction, which stays resolutely below minimal professionalism. The gifted David Mitchell's set is surprisingly unevocative, as is the trusty Martin Aronstein's lighting. For David Rabe it is definitely time for other rooms and, I hope, other voices.

All Over Town

All Over Town is, in one word, repellent. Murray Schisgal, whose up-and-down career I have viewed as a steady downward march since his one viable play, *The Tiger* (only half of an evening's fare at that), has now outdone himself with the opportunistic and vulgar drivel, that, in some quarters, passes for playwriting. How injudiciously some of my colleagues have here invoked Feydeau as ancestor. Feydeau always started and ended with a human reality, and what came in between was only a giant enlargement of the pettiest human foibles, not their falsification. Schisgal, conversely, exploits every crude and unrealistic longing of the moment. If whites want blacks to become amenable and even decadent (and thus doubly amenable), that is the kind of blacks he serves up. If blacks want, minimally, to make fools of whites some of the time, that is what Schisgal feeds them. If many men (especially of the theatergoing variety) are homely and undersexed, he purveys to them a supremely plain little fellow seducing women right and left, without even the benefit of playwriting that can make the improbable seem believable. But why bother, if even the reviewers will buy such wish fulfillment like hot cakes? If Jews are always a good *old* laugh for a New York audience, and the new cults of Oriental mysticism are the trendiest *recent* religious laugh, count on Schisgal to come up with a Yiddish guru, and, while touching every base, avoid grappling with the trickier basics of any.

All this might be overlooked if Schisgal were a born humorist, but, after a tremendous running, churning start, his leaps of wit are piddling. If it is not the verbal infelicities of "A word to the deficient should be sufficient," it is the wallowed-in puerilities of "I masturbate a dozen times a day." [Laughter from the audience.] "He's wonderful: he masturbates a dozen times a day." [Louder laughter.] "Any special way?" "No, the usual way: manually. [Frenzied and prolonged laughter.] I am right-handed." [Cataclysmically orgiastic laughter.] Cleavon Little, who plays the hero, now illustratively holds up his right hand (under Dustin Hoffman's desperate direction), and the laughter knows no bounds. Clearly, one word to the deficient is not sufficient, and Schisgal knows it only too disgustingly well.

Some of the performances, like those of Little, Pamela Payton-Wright, Zane Lasky, and Jim Jansen, manage to overcome this material; others, like those of William LeMassena, Carol Teitel, and Barnard Hughes, manage to diminish it further. However, the most pitiful display comes from Schisgal at the end, when he sends off each character with a mechanistic farewell line whose schematism is surpassed only by its witlessness. This is what you would get from someone who had taken one night-school course in playwriting—someone who should have stayed in bed.

The Ritz; Our Late Night

Terrence McNally's *The Ritz* was *The Tubs* until an Off Broadway cheapie, *Tubstrip*, encroached on its title. This is a farce about a New York homosexual bath house (pardon the pleonasm), where a fat, straight, middle-aged, Midwestern garbage man—he is quite high up in garbage, not working the streets—seeks refuge instead of refuse from a mafioso brother-in-law out to kill him for reasons too complicated, trivial, and insufficiently worked out by the playwright to go into. In this steam bath there is also an aging Puerto Rican singer, Googie Gomez, aspiring to be the next Bette Midler, and chasing after the hero, Gaetano, because she mistakes him for a producer. Then there is a private detective, hired telephonically by the villainous brother-in-law, Carmine, to ferret out Gaetano, but who mistakes Gaetano for Carmine. Then there is Chris, a somewhat overripe queen, whom Carmine mistakes for a detective: and a tiny homosexual with a predilection for obesity, a "chubby-chaser," who pursues both Gaetano, mistaking him for a "gay," and his subsequently arriving wife, Vivian, mistaking her for a man. And absolutely everybody mistakes Googie for a transvestite. We have, then, not so much a play of mistaken identity as a play-long identical mistake.

The entire charade is an uneasy tripartite alliance among homosexual-heterosexual confrontation gags, fey would-be Feydeau farce, and campy bitchinesses and in-jokes on the order of "I don't speak Spanish, so the Continental [Baths] is out," or "You know Ronald Reagan used to be lovers with John Wayne… That was just after he broke up with Xavier Cugat." Now there might be some kind of real comedy here if any one of the three aspects were fully and tellingly developed, but, in drama, three slapdash thirds do not add up to a harmonious whole. Lawrence King and Michael Yeargan's set is effectively three-tiered, but the triune plot is more trying than unified.

It is also fairly unfunny. The reason, I think, is that it tries too hard to remain a clean dirty joke, which, in my book, ranks in ignominy with the fig leaf in art and, in life, the see-through blouse worn with a brassiere. Just as you can't construct a play as a layer cake (which is different from making a single layer so rich that it takes on additional, symbolic meanings), you cannot have your jokes be both dirty and clean (not even a cake can be both eaten and had). McNally's intention is to dabble in religious, ethnic, and sexual humor without offending the most middle-class and middle-brow sensibilities. (In fact, the only person the play has offended so far is the CBS drama reviewer, but hers is an even lower sensibility.) Yet, whether you like it or not, a strong sexual, ethnic, or religious joke must offend some people—it is rather like eating garlic, acceptable only to fellow garlic eaters—and as for feeble jokes, they are now possible onstage only in such still, alas, underexploited areas as politics.

There are some funny bits in *The Ritz*, most of them provided by the talents of Jack Weston, Rita Moreno, Paul B. Price, and F. Murray Abraham, with some help from the director, Robert Drivas. The play itself is considerably less trenchant than McNally's previous offering, *Bad Habits*, and not even so outspoken as the above-mentioned lowly *Tubstrip*.

Seascape

Edward Albee's *Seascape* is the kind of play that can be loved only by God and Clive Barnes, at least one of whom doesn't exist. It concerns Nancy and Charlie, affluent middle-aged parents of three, bickering on a beach: she would like to become a beachcomber and have adventures; he just wants to rest and do nothing. As they review their uneventful lives and love lives, and become more acrimonious, two human-sized salamanders emerge from the sea. (Albee, like his characters, incorrectly refers to these amphibians as lizards, but that is the least of his catachreses.) There is reciprocal fear and curiosity, then the two couples—the salamanders have likewise been long married—exchange disa and data. The quadrupeds describe life in the sea, the bipeds life on land, and barring such footling differences as the number of their feet, the couples emerge curiously similar, down to their foibles and prejudices. But when Charlie scares the salamander wife by telling her about death, Leslie, her spouse, starts angrily back for the sea with her. Presto magico, Nancy and Charlie convince them to stay on, and shoulder our common duty, evolution. They even volunteer to coach the salamanders, who already speak good English, and, despite difficulties with words like *hand* and *finger*, can quickly annex terms like *evolution* and *aerodynamics*. "Begin!" says Leslie as the final curtain, under the weight of irony, descends. So what else is newt?

This simpleminded allegory can be interpreted in a dozen convenient, wishy-washy ways, the "lizards" standing for underprivileged minorities, upward mobility, *élan vital*, the instinctual, or whatever; the human beings for the bourgeoisie, the declining West, the Establishment, the victims of the superego, or whatnot. Or any other vague antinomies that must be reconciled so that some great, original philosophic maxim like "Life must go on" or "Life is a continual evolutionary process" might be derived from this splendiferous parable. Banal as all this is, a real artist might have breathed life into it; Albee endows it only with doughy verbiage, feebly quivering inaction, and grandly gesticulating pretentiousness.

There is a canard abroad, originated by Albee himself, that an Albee play has linguistic distinction. It has, to be sure, a style more literary than that of a play by Murray Schisgal or Neil Simon, but so has a sophomore term paper about William Faulkner. Here are some *Seascape* samples: "Continue the temporary and it becomes forever." "We've earned a little life, if you ask me—*ask me!!!*" "They don't look very formidable in the sense of prepossessing." "Nice, isn't it, when the real and the figurative come together?" "Sex goes, it diminishes—well, it becomes a holiday. Not like eating or sleeping; but that's nice, too—that it becomes a holiday." Notice what sorry stratagems are at work in these, for Albee, better-than-average lines. *Figurative* is, inappropriately, dragged in for *imagined* or *wished-for; formidable* is, inappositely, hauled out instead of *striking* or *impressive*. And so a platitude or triviality is supposedly ennobled by recourse to solecism. Epigrams like Albee's can be made with a cookie mold: "Continue the singular and it becomes the plural." "Continue not to conform and it becomes conformity." Continue piling up lines and it becomes a play. Ah, but you see, Simon and Schisgal would never use the word *figurative*, even thus incorrectly. This is the *je ne sais quoi* that makes Albee literature. (His *je ne sais*, by the way, extends to French, too; one of his characters is made to say *le petit mort* for *la petite mort*.)

Short as the play is, you feel it being dragged out desperately. If, for example, Charley tells Nancy to get a stick to fight off the sea creatures, she will ask, "What kind of stick?" and he retort, "A wooden stick!"—this followed by several more such witty lines about the stick. It is hard enough to strike a spark by rubbing two sticks together, but Albee's dramaturgy has, for years now, been trying to do it with one.

Yes, *The Zoo Story* and *Virginia Woolf* were plays; but how long will reviewers and audiences forgive such gaffes as *Tiny Alice*, *The Ballad of the Sad Café*, *Malcolm*, *Everything in the Garden*, *A Delicate Balance*, *Box Mao Box*, *All Over*, and now *Seascape*, this piece of flotsam washed ashore near Albee's Montauk home? To go on tolerating, however minimally, this proliferation of pratfalls is not to strike a blow for Albee so much as to strike a blow against euthanasia. Such incurable playwriting should have been put out of its misery sooner, while it still preserved a shred of dignity. But, I dare say, Albee is a playwright of ideas for people who have never had an idea.

Summerfolk

Have you ever looked for a perfect mind encased in an impeccable body? If so, you must have had many disappointments in life. But in the theater it occasionally happens that the lofty ideas of a playwright are given magnificent embodiment in a remarkable production. Such a wonder is on view—briefly—in Brooklyn, in the Royal Shakespeare Company's mounting of Maxim Gorky's *Summerfolk*. I have no idea how the Moscow Art Theater could originally turn down, or how the Anglo-American theater could remain so long in the dark about, what strikes me as one of those rarer-than-rare plays that successfully adapt the great and tempting but virtually inimitable examples of Chekhov to their own needs—for here Gorky, Chekhov's protégé, has actually managed to make the lessons of the master his own theatrical life's blood.

In 1899, Chekhov had written warningly to his admirer Gorky that his only fault was "lack of restraint and lack of grace. When someone expends the least amount of motion on a given action, that's grace. You tend to expend too much." By 1904, with a couple of plays, including that gloomy masterpiece *The Lower Depths* already behind him, Gorky was able to write *Summerfolk*, in which the motions are carefully contained, and the emotions rise through several cunningly gradated outbursts toward an astonishing climax, to drain away in a knowingly channeled denouement. Here Gorky, like Chekhov, has an exquisite sense of atmosphere, of a social and psychological climate conveyed neither through an unusual plot nor through a significant change in a principal character (although there is that, too), but through the subtle yet volatile interaction of a very considerable number of persons used like instruments in a concerto grosso. Each instrument—or character—is heard in solos and duets, smaller or bigger choirs, and as part of an orchestral *tutti*, thus simultaneously conveying individual problems and a joint societal destiny.

But that isn't all. Gorky is concerned with the lives and fates of that short-lived Russian bourgeoisie, the immediate descendants of newly liberated serfs or petty tradesmen, soon to be engulfed by the Revolution. These were people for whom the proletarian-intellectual-revolutionary Gorky had a great deal of feeling, but no political sympathy. He saw them as transitional figures, estival visitors vacationing in woodland villas: summerfolk who come and go during their one brief season, after which the land reverts to the peasants and workers, its year-round tenants. The metaphor is superbly carried out in the play's trajectory, and I only wish that the author had not felt obliged to spell it out in one of the speeches.

More important yet are the amazing changes of tone and mood that run through the play. Not only does the entire design hover between comedy and tragedy, but also the very scenes and individual speeches—sometimes even the shortest lines—have a way of jumping their tracks and landing in preposterousness rather than the heartbreak for which they were heading, or vice versa. And sometimes whole long passages casually straddle the sublime and the ridiculous, the hilarious and the shattering. This is partly the result of the dramatist's skillful checks and balances, but something beyond conscious artistry also makes itself felt: the heart-tugging tug-of-war in Gorky's unconscious between affectionate identification with these people and their condemnation on Marxist grounds. Indeed, the one fault of this lovely and potent play is the political partisanship operant in it; but it is a partisanship soft-pedaled and, for the most part, beautifully submerged in the music of people's utterances and feelings, their alternating upswings and dejection.

What I find finest about the work is the leisureliness yet thoroughness with which the characters disclose themselves, never as a simple note in music, but always as, at least, a double stop, a complex harmony or discord—even as the mysterious whistlings in the night, which so puzzlingly permeate the surrounding darkness of Act I, are eventually revealed as the whistles of the watchmen, the non-summerfolk—men of all seasons, and especially of that coming season of revolution. Yet unlike in his only slightly later play, *Enemies*, Gorky does not allow his politics to become simplistic;

the spirit that infuses *Summerfolk* is the one he later summarized in *My Childhood*, the first volume of his autobiography, as something more mystical than political: "Life is always surprising us—not by its rich, seething layer of bestial refuse—but by the bright, healthy, and creative human powers of goodness that are forever forcing their way up through it."

A play so rich in over- and undertones requires an expertly cogent and sensitive production, which is just what it gets from the RSC in the magisterial orchestration of David Jones, the director, who has found the unhurried tempos of speech and strategic deployment of actors with which to impart the sense of a great spaciousness suddenly cramped into cabals and confrontations, the sense of suspension in a timelessness crisscrossed nevertheless by spreading cracks of despair or sudden tremors of ominous merriment. He was greatly helped by the sensibly understated costuming and tantalizingly not-quite-naturalistic scenery of the husband-and-wife team of Timothy O'Brien and Tazeena Firth, the highly suggestive yet untricky lighting of Stewart Leviton, the unassumingly evocative music of Carl Davis, and the slightly ungrammatical but racy translation of Jeremy Brooks and Kitty Hunter Blair.

The final marvel, however, is the ensemble acting, in which fifteen principals and twelve subsidiary players combine in almost flawlessly unified performing. I am unhappy only about the needlessly exaggerated mugging and posturing of Susan Fleetwood's poetess, who, moreover, belongs strictly in Bloomsbury; the rather obvious effects from which Robert Ashby constructs the failed suitor and suicide, Ryumin; and the excessive one-sidedness with which David Suchet endows the lawyer-playboy, Zamislov. The others come up not only with splendid performances, but also a fascinating gamut of acting styles that become consonant and inextricably conjoined all the same. There are, for instance, very traditionalistic, classical performances from Sebastian Shaw, Tony Church, Lynette Davies, and Norman Rodway (the last-named leaning heavily but effectively on clowning); there is also the more spectacularly stylized work of actors like Ian Richardson, Mike Gwilym, and Patrick Godfrey (the last almost caricature, but brilliant); and then, again, such indescribably idiosyncratic performing as that of Margaret Tyzack and Janet Whiteside, two actresses who constantly astound you with their unpredictable choices that prove, on reflection, sovereignly right. And notice, please, how even a walk-on, Janet Chappell as a woman in yellow, creates a character out of two measly crumbs of dialogue.

The greatest tribute, though, is due to Estelle Kohler, a young actress who plays the difficult role of Varya, a many-sided, intensely internalized, Russian Nora Helmer, on whom Gorky's greatest hopes for humankind are centered. Miss Kohler gives a performance so delicately etched yet so powerful when necessary; so understated and ironic most of the time, yet so burning and finally cataclysmic; that she kept me in a state of growing wonderment and gratitude. She embodied perfectly the dramatically fertilizing duality, the tragic rift at the core of the play, and drew on seemingly exhaustless layers of ever deeper, ever more aching humanity, until that great hysterical scene that must stand as the ultimate in controlled unleashedness. I can think of no American actress of any age who could have equaled it.

Summerfolk is the one theatrical event of this season that even people generally indifferent to theater must see at least once, and that all our undisciplined, self-serving performers should be compelled to see again and again.

Private Lives

More and more I realize that certain plays are vehicles for the special talents of their interpreters, and that they depend almost entirely on their casting. Thus, if Noël Coward's *Private Lives* is cast properly, the rest will pretty much take care of itself. Unfortunately, the two performers of genius who, in a sense, were the play—Gertrude Lawrence and Noël Coward—are no more. What they did with it, even for someone who merely saw the photographs and heard recorded excerpts, was such perfection that no one else can quite replace it, any more, I imagine, than Chaliapin's Boris can be replaced, or Pavlova's Dying Swan. Which is not to say that Coward's comedy is the equal of Moussorgsky's opera (though it's much more alive than that Swan), but it demands as much style, charm, wit, and personality from its actors as many a greater work—probably more.

John Gielgud's mounting of it now on view here was just as surely lost in the casting as the battle of Waterloo was won on the playing fields of Eton. Maggie Smith was once a genuine actress, but she has become progressively more mannered—or perhaps, unmannerly—over the years, until, under all those affectations, one can no longer see a piece of acting, much less a flesh-and-blood woman. Moreover, Amanda and Elyot are, down to their manicured breath, upper-class creatures: elitists, snobs, spiritual aristocrats, as only someone like Coward, who successfully rose from the lower orders to become *plus royaliste que le roi* (or should I say *la reine*?), could conceive and create them. Their actual lines are, alas, not always witty enough, but their postures, gestures, and inflections are always the last word in blasé aristocratic elegance—which, dear Miss Smith, is not the same as mannerism!—so much so that they would prefer not to permit themselves the slightest emotional demonstrativeness (except when they fight like cats and dogs), and cloak their cravings for each other in triple understatement. When their yearnings do show through, it must be like a snowflake on a very dark night catching a stray light beam—something very delicate, fleeting, and almost heartbreaking.

Miss Smith, I fear, should never play anyone above middle station in life; her idea of a *grande dame* (see *Travels With My Aunt*) is quite vulgar, and her attempt at sophistication insufferably brittle. As Amanda, she exaggerates and coarsens whatever she touches, her chief device being a slow vocal rasp, rather like an arpeggio played on a comb, which may be funny once or twice, but becomes quickly irritating, and soon thereafter intolerable. She is not a very handsome woman, and the period hairdo makes her look like an upstart rooster aspiring to barnyard supremacy, which doesn't help either. Even so, she is preferable to the Elyot of John Standing, who is, above all other things, pudgy. Now Elyot Chase can have a variety of looks, but must never, *never* be pudgy, and to see him here looking like an elderly, deliquescent basset hound with a superfluity of female hormones and consequent adiposity, was, to say the least, disheartening, Worse yet, Standing's voice is thin, and his timing and emphasis frequently off: a line like the one about the Duke of Westminster's yacht (my touchstone for the actor playing the role) plummets full fathom five from his mouth. In fact, his name notwithstanding, Standing doesn't even know how to stand, and during his first-act scenes his second leg seemed to become a bothersome appendage, rather like a third leg or a tail, which he was at continuous but unsuccessful pains to dispose of. Finally, his performance was so lacking in any kind of virile charm that one could, at the utmost, see him playing Victor. But since the Victor of Remak Ramsey was roughly twice his size, Standing looked, in their third-act confrontation, downright puny, which, in turn, made his physical besting of Victor (not called for by the script) look totally ridiculous.

Victor and Sibyl must, at the very least, sound British, and though Ramsey can play a variety of Americans very well, he has lately had nothing but British parts on stage and screen, for which he is quite unsuited. And since he towers over the rest of the cast, Gielgud keeps having to position him at a distance, or making him inappositely sit down. Niki Flacks sounds better, but turns Sibyl into a caricature, which is dead wrong. The costumes are quite good, the sets tacky, and H. R. Poindexter's lighting cannot even suggest the essential moonlight. I found myself sitting through one of my favorite light comedies without laughing once.

A Doll's House

The entire seven-week engagement of Liv Ullmann in Ibsen's *A Doll's House* is said to be sold out. Good; then I can say my piece all the more easily, without robbing anyone of the pleasure of watching Miss Ullmann perform with a radiance that puts blinkers of light on our eyes and almost manages to white out the dark mess that surrounds her. And yet even that great actress is giving, beyond her personal charm, only a very good performance, not an outstanding one, and the first problem is to ascertain why.

Obviously to be encircled by actors who are dreadful must dispirit the ablest of performers, especially if, like Miss Ullmann, she is likely to be too loyal and kind to admit their dreadfulness even to herself. But, truly, what kind of *A Doll's House* is one in which, after the leading lady, only the nurse and the maid (Helen Stenborg and Judith Light) can be endured? Then there is the direction of the Norwegian director-playwright Tormod Skagestad, which is appalling. Granted, the thrust stage and theater in the half-round are not the proper setting for this play. So, for example, in the great closing scene, when Nora grows in stature even as Torvald shrivels, the only manner of conveying this properly is to have the two sit steadily together, and just talk or be still. For it is the words, the idea, that give Nora her greatness: the concept and realization of her independence. Jumping up and moving around would not express the spiritual quality of the idea. Here, however, Torvald gets up and, loudly remonstrating, circles around Nora, just so that Miss Ullmann's face should at least part of the time be visible to all—but it makes no dramatic sense; it actually endows him with a dominant energy when he should be sinking forlornly into himself.

Repeatedly, the director fails to find the proper movements, intonations, and stage images—not, I think, because of difficulties with English: Mr. Skagestad studied and taught here for two years. Thus, where Ibsen carefully does not let the Helmer children speak, Skagestad puts some of Nora's words into their oatmealy mouths and makes them perform extra business, needlessly and infelicitously incurring the results of the three tykes not being up to it. And how can he let, even with two such dismal interpreters, the scene between Krogstad and Mrs. Linde sag so completely that the play, at a crucial point, virtually ceases to exist?

Yet another problem may be either the director's or the diva's doing. When Claire Bloom recently played Nora, she did something very judicious. She made her, in the early scenes, not just a charming, innocent, harmlessly dissembling simpleton; rather, she displayed a certain slyness, a cunning gift for tongue-in-cheek role-playing. Such a Nora could, when sufficiently jolted, about-face totally, and resolutely—even sublimely—walk out on everything. Even so, by way of further precaution, Miss Bloom managed to suggest a gradual awakening. Miss Ullmann's Nora, however, is genuinely the naive, unreal plaything Helmer wants her to be; as long as she can get what she wants—which, in this case, is mostly money, a word the actress stresses almost distressingly—she is perfectly happy to be a skylark or squirrel or anything but a woman. Consequently, the nonappearance of the miracle, Torvald's ignominious lapse, must hit her over the head with a near-paralyzing thud to justify her leaving husband, children, and home in a sort of stunned, almost somnambulistic, trance. And that is how Miss Ullmann has to play it, and does with an admirably sustained, discolored dismay. But it makes for something less fine and, indeed, less believable.

To be sure, Miss Ullmann is playing in English, her third acting language, and is, moreover, repeating a part she has recently done in Norwegian, under a different director, and in a presumably somewhat different interpretation. All this must be confusing. And there is even something else, over which she has no control whatever: happenstance. We have all just seen and loved her in Ingmar Bergman's *Scenes From a Marriage*, where she was playing exactly a contemporary Nora Helmer; in the uncut version of the work, Bergman even incorporates an explicit *hommage* to Ibsen's play. On screen, in enormous close-ups, we saw Miss Ullmann's beautiful and supremely expressive face undergo similar crises and reversals as here: in fact, describe parallel parabolas. Watching her so soon again in a play, her verbal control, in English, a trifle diminished; her expressions, owing to poor sightlines, not always visible; her placement in space and time somewhat more distant—all this makes for a slight sense of anticlimax. Yet, for all that, how gracious and rewarding her performance is!

But, oh, for the others! Sam Waterston, I'm afraid, continues to be a pipsqueak. In a part where this works for him (Benedick in a farce version of *Much Ado*, Nick in a travesty of *The Great Gatsby*) he can be—or seem—quite effective; here, as husband to the vital (even when she is acting infantile) Miss Ullmann, his pip-squeakery reaches new heights. "Torvald may be a windbag," James Agate once observed, "but he should be a windbag of charm." Waterston squints out of slitty eyes; lets his voice come out as thin and flat as certain toothpastes used to (even they seem to have given it up) or else lets it sound sucked upon, as if his tongue were wrapped around a macaroon, and registers, to a varying degree, the selfsame brattish petulance posing pompously as injured pride. All we feel is that here we go round the same old mulberry bush once again.

It is overwhelmingly important that Torvald and Nora be evenly, interlockingly matched, for, as Frances Grain noted in an article (*Ibsenårbok* 1974), their marriage is "a collaboration of illusions." or what Oscar Wilde referred to, as the perfect marriage being based on a mutual misunderstanding. But *this* Nora could have seen through *this* Torvald even before she married him, and he, poor sap, would have been far too scared to take her on in the first place. Toward the end, when he gets really worked up, Waterston plays some kind of cheap melodrama, and it is on this plane, alas, that the rest of the main performers meet him.

Barbara Colby plays Kristine Linde as if she were doing Mrs. Danvers in some road-company adaptation of *Rebecca*. Her eyes glint malevolently, her mouth is distorted by a long-distance sneer, and her voice keeps bobsledding from a nasty squeak to a sarcastic growl several octaves below, or, inversely, shooting up like a javelin—always without cause, like the uncontrolled instrument it is. Not for a moment is she the harried woman, cheated by life, she is meant to be. As for the Dr. Rank of Michael Granger, he is

Rank in more ways than one, coming across rather like a Grand Street halvah vendor engaged in a mysterious vendetta and trying to disguise his fell intent with a ghastly hate-riddled grin. At times, he looked and sounded like Mel Brooks at his most outrageous. As for the Krogstad of Barton Heyman, his two characteristics are crassness and mean-spiritedness, which may, actually, be only one. It is astounding that Joseph Papp, after conceiving the bright idea of reviving his flagging operations by importing Miss Ullmann, should have ambushed her with such a cast; it is like setting a diamond solitaire in the tin ring off a Coca-Cola container.

Further things are wrong. The usually dependable Theoni V. Aldredge has designed costumes which, though tasteful, are far too opulent for the unwealthy Helmers; the upward turn in their fortunes occurred only a day or two ago, and there was hardly time to acquire such dazzling regalia: Torvald's fancy, scarlet-lined cape and emerald velvet dinner jacket; Nora's four, ever more gorgeous, costume changes. When she sets out in the end for an uncertain and toilsome future, she does so in a sumptuous red velvet gown, better suited for being presented at court. As for Christopher Hampton's translation, it continues to impress me as racy and easeful, but why does an Oxford graduate and talented playwright give us grammar like "doing it without him knowing it," "someone wants to take all the blame on themselves," "between the three of us," and other such lapses?

Two final points. How can those celebrated macaroons of Nora's—good-sized cookies—fit into a tiny paper bag barely larger than an ice-cream cone? Are those macaroons microroons? And when will an American production finally wake up to the proper title, *A Doll House*? The reference, after all, is to the miniature houses children play with, which, in Britain, are indeed called *doll's* houses, but are, in America, *doll* houses. The idea is not that Nora is a doll, and this is her house: rather, that here is such an unreal toy house in which two overgrown children, Nora and Torvald, play at living.

The Misanthrope

Updating a play is a lesser evil than cutting it, but still awkward, supererogatory, and a confession of impotence. If to enjoy Molière's *The Misanthrope* you must have it hustled from 1666 to 1966, you are like the fellow who cannot have sex with his wife unless she wears a different wig to bed every night. Moreover, certain things about the Sun King's France cannot be transposed unjarringly into De Gaulle's, and, besides, one of the major thrills of an old classic is to discover, under superficial, time-bound differences, the timeless truths. Put an eternal verity into contemporary clothing, and your very undue solicitude diminishes it; 50 million Frenchmen, or even one brilliant one, can be wrong; but a play that after three centuries doesn't look a day older, cannot. Nevertheless, even if he does not rate type twice as large as Molière's (as the program would have it), Tony Harrison, the translator-adaptor, deserves an accolade: his modernized *Misanthrope* is a clever conceit, and the National Theatre of Britain's fine production of it should be seen and savored first, and argued with only afterward.

The Misanthrope is one of that handful of plays that are not only incontestably great, but can even lay claim to perfection. It is, to begin with, flawlessly balanced on that microscopically fine line that separates comedy from tragedy, and the early productions (including Molière's own) that emphasized the former were as incomplete as subsequent ones that overstressed the latter. For the subject of the play or, rather, its related subjects, are not susceptible of solution—that is the very point—and the fact that this charming, witty, haunting, and heartbreaking play is neither comedy nor tragedy illustrates through its very form the insolubility of its problems. When François Mauriac wrote that "all the wretchedness of Alceste, the Alceste who is all of us, stems from that hunger for the absolute we bring to love, which is of all feelings the most relative," he was only partly right.

Alceste has three quarrels: with an unnamed adversary, a lawsuit; with Oronte, a wrangle about the latter's versifying; with his beloved Célimène, a constant discord about her inconstancy, shallowness, or, simply, insufficient love. These three seemingly unrelated but equally unhappy contests are, in fact, related: they demonstrate that the pursuit of absolute justice, absolute candor in social intercourse, absolute fulfillment in love are all equally quixotic, equally doomed. Yet they are the three aspects of the true idealist's aspirations: the quests for metaphysical, sociopolitical, and emotional-erotic perfection, as admirable as aims as they are unattainable as goals. And though their eluding us is tragic, our chasing after them is comic. Molière has put his finger on one of the quintessential contradictions of existence and, with all the graces of wit and all the gravity of underlying despair, written a play about it at which we cannot help laughing till we cry, and crying until we laugh.

The National Theatre-Harrison version emphasizes the laughter more than the tears, except in a totally inappropriate final tableau which, however theatrical, is quite misleading: we are not meant to concern ourselves with the abandoned Célimène, who is not the protagonist; whatever we feel must be about Alceste, and we must end by chasing after him, not dawdling over her. Such matters aside, the production, under John Dexter's self-effacingly canny direction (which is the best kind there is), manages to fascinate and absorb us steadily, and that, of course, is again, or still, the desert of Molière. In him, as Hofmannsthal justly perceived, "all torment, all endurance, all comprehension have become sheer spiritual strength and gaiety." But very much depends on how Alceste, in many ways the author's alter ego, and originally played by him, is enacted.

Alec McCowen is a marvelous actor in certain parts, but Alceste is only his second-best bet. That he produces vowel sounds tending to be too open, even diphthongized, is a footling idiosyncrasy; that he is of shorter stature than either his Célimène or Arsinoë is unsettling, but can be overlooked. More disturbing is that he is a bit too old for the part, a trifle too sophisticated even in his imbalance; one cannot but feel that Célimène may simply find him too old, and that his ranting and railing are the final exacerbation of world-weariness rather than the intractable intransigence of youthful perfectionism. Still, it is a most endearing performance in its playful enjoyment of its own histrionics while keeping its excesses well in hand, like a painter using only the boldest primary colors but applying them ever so sparingly and shrewdly.

As Célimène, Diana Rigg is better than I have ever seen her, but still not quite right. She has a way of protruding her face like a Ping-Pong paddle, while grinning vapidly or bursting into a whinnying laugh, and often even waggling her head as if it were not fully affixed to her neck. These may be the ways of a jolly milkmaid—especially one turned sassy barmaid—but not those of a refined, elegant, flighty aristocrat. Yet the actress is well-spoken, has a fetchingly predatory litheness, and is never dull.

The supporting cast is very polished, with only Albert Roffrano (a.k.a. Riggs O'Hara) out of place and faintly unsavory, and Gawn Grainger and Gillian Barge nothing less than superb. Tanya Moiseiwitsch's set is an ingenious blend of muted *grand siècle* opulence and brash modernity, though her costumes, trying for the same effect, succeed fully only for the women. The lighting and music are effective (the latter, at first, a mite overloud), and the translation, though lacking the consummate grace of Richard Wilbur's, is often devilishly clever. The attacks on its rhyming by Messrs. Barnes and Gottfried are ill-founded: *good* and *blood* can make it both as eye rhyme and as near rhyme, and *ought* and *sort* is a near rhyme which, in high Britannic, verges on a perfect rhyme. But, in any case, why should Harrison, whose ear is generally good, be denied his near rhymes, a practice dating back to Vaughan, and without which modern poetry from, say, Dickinson and Hopkins on would be unimaginable. I am more inclined to quarrel with his meter, which unduly lapses into trochaics (or catalectic iambs), but the actors navigate beautifully past these reefs. If they allow the clip-clop of the rhymed couplets to be heard faintly but persistently, that is as it should be; it is an adorable sound, like that of a far-off tennis game across a lazy summer afternoon.

A Letter for Queen Victoria

The season's scandal—if something that deadens you with its boredom more surely than Novocain could can still leave you with a sense of scandal—is Robert Wilson's *A Letter for Queen Victoria*. This is not quite so megalomaniacally absurd as Wilson's twelve-hour *Stalin* I languished through last season; here the nonsense words and nonsense action or inaction are spun out to a scant three hours. Though the work calls itself an opera, it is merely *tableaux vivants* done to monotonous nonmusic and accompanied by meaningless verbalizing and gyrations. The visuals are derived principally from Chirico, Magritte, and (except that they are nowhere near so heterosexual) Delvaux, and the words are Dada, but with the wit left out. That such things should succeed in a world that has lost all sense of what is art (to say nothing of all sense of what is sense) is not astonishing. But what is queer is that people who should know better, e.g., Jerome Robbins, should invoke the word *genius* for this mindless farrago.

What is truly pitiful, though, is that a fifteen-year-old autistic boy should be a kind of co-author and main performer here, his sad condition put on tasteless display. Wilson has worked with handicapped children, and his writing and cast may themselves be specimens of a dementedly self-induced autism, but all that does not justify having the poor boy whirl about like a deranged dervish and spout insensate and ill-articulated verbiage—even if Wilson proclaims it genius and matches it with similar cavortings and cacophony of his own. Unless we also bring back bearbaiting and visits to asylums for entertainment, this sort of thing, however cloaked in euphemism, is not to be countenanced. I am also leery of Wilson's making his grandmother, aged 88, stay up late and fatiguingly in order to perform in this and other Wilson works: it is one thing to give one's life for art, another for autism.

To reiterate, there is nothing here that hasn't been done already by Surrealism or Dada, *lettrisme* or *spatialisme*, which rules it out as innovation; *Letter* is, moreover, visually barren and aurally empty, which rules it out as theater and leaves only mindlessness. "If you try to think, to decipher meanings in the spectacle, you are missing the show," says *The Voice*. Says Clive Barnes: "Let the mind free-fall like petals floating down the Grand Canyon." Better yet, check your mind at the coatroom, or, best of all, do not bother to bring one.

P.S. Your Cat Is Dead!

There are dishonest plays and then there are ultra-dishonest plays such as *P.S. Your Cat Is Dead!* by James Kirkwood, whose previous gift to Broadway, UTBU, closed after one performance. The current play is made up of not so much two acts as two homosexual wish-fulfillment fantasies. In Act One, a bisexual burglar is overpowered by a disgruntled actor whom he tried to rob, tied face down to the kitchen table and has his trousers cut open and removed (ostensibly to allow him to urinate in the sink over which he is strapped), to be taunted and humiliated ad nauseam in his eminently sodomizable state. This is the fantasy of the middle-aged homosexual in which "a piece of rough trade"—the kind that often brutalizes and sometimes kills the client—is overwhelmed, immobilized, and tormented in turn. It is, in other words, a Steigian dream of glory infantile, homosexual style.

Act—or Fantasy—Two has the tied-down bisexual burglar being clever, charming, and persuasive, using all his wiles as well as his basic bonhomie to sweet-talk the heterosexual actor into having sex with him. Since this is a Broadway show in need of heterosexual patronage—though its primary purpose is clearly the delectation of homosexuals, as the vociferously responding, largely homosexual opening-night audience made manifest—it stops short of having him succeed. But the play is, if you'll pardon the word, open-ended: it concludes with Vito, the poetic burglar, spending the night on upright Jimmy's couch, and since Vito's acumen is inexhaustible, members of the audience who yearn for an unconventional happy ending are encouraged to assume one, while others can leave without their sense of decorum explicitly assaulted.

This second, then, is the ever-popular homosexual fantasy that any heterosexual is ultimately available for homosexual purposes. That was already a minor theme in *The Boys in the Band* (and, curiously, the actor who embodied it there appears again here as a heterosexual fascinated by Vito's bottom in bondage), and it is voiced repeatedly by Vito, who assures us that everyone swings a little: "*Queer* is a word like *tall*; everybody is a little bit tall—even midgets."

But these fantasies are only a liminal dishonesty, of the kind almost every Broadway play abounds in. A bigger one is the portrayal of Jimmy, the supposed archetypal straight, as someone who acts and talks like, at the very least, a latent homosexual. For seventeen months he has been living with Kate, who on this New Year's Eve is leaving him for a less cautiously constricted (for which read: less closet-queenish) man; now a deep-rooted hatred for her surfaces in invective that the premiere audience found absolutely delicious. The games Jimmy plays with Vito are distinctly homosexual-sado-masochist, and when Vito declares him "humpy in an offbeat way," Jimmy is taken aback at the *offbeat*, not at all at the *humpy*. Anyway, your ordinary heterosexual would simply turn the burglar over to the police. Not so Jimmy who, just to give you a taste of the taste-lessness of the play, plans to deliver him, bare-assed and neatly tied up, to a particularly pesky pederast who has been steadily chasing after Jimmy.

An even greater dishonesty tries to palm off these unsavory proceedings—e.g., when Kate asks what Jimmy intends to do with Vito, the actor replies, "Castrate him, maybe," and there is some suggestive business with a pair of scissors—as great good fun. Now it would be possible to present such goings-on seriously, as a study in pathology; or preposterously exaggerated into campy farce (and there is some of this in *P.S.*); but turning it all into jolly parlor comedy is as disingenuous as it is absurd. Yet the supreme dishonesty

lies in the treatment of women. Kate is a smart-ass, know-it-all su-
perbitch, and later we meet Janie, a "fag hag" of the most spaced-out
sort; both she and Kate react to the sick farandole around them with
exemplary unwholesomeness: either a prurient curiosity or a kind
of collusively fatuous nonchalance. Worse yet is Vito's former wife
whom we do not meet, but whom her ex-husband lovingly evokes
as a castrating gorilla. I hope the women's movement takes note of
how its brother-in-arms, gay liberation, portrays women onstage.

Kirkwood can write some funny lines, though more of them
are merely outrageous, and all of them are just enough for a nightclub act, which is, indeed, what he used to have. The staging by
Vivian Matalon is suitably slick, and the acting is much better than
the occasion warrants. Especially good is Tony Musante as Vito,
making one wish that his flexibility, variety, and subtlety were in
the service of something worthier. Not far behind are Keir Dullea
as Jimmy and Jennifer Warren as Kate. Miss Warren gives a most
compelling performance in Arthur Penn's forthcoming film, *Night
Moves*, which makes me regret her spoiling it for me retroactively
by appearing in *P.S.*

Henry de Montherlant, who, besides being bisexual, was a major
novelist, playwright, and essayist, wrote in *Notes sur mon théâtre*:
"When Mr. or Miss X puts on the cothurn or dons the peplum a
few hours after having incarnated the abject lucubrations of some
cinematic vaudevillian, he or she can go all out, yet I can go along
only halfway. It seems that if you pour, just once, inferior stuff into
a decanter that has hitherto held only good wine, the good wine
will henceforth always be spoiled." What a funny switch when appearing in the legitimate theater will start queering your cinematic
career. In one of his most applauded lines, Kirkwood compares life
to a shit sandwich: if so, what need to go to his play just to get a
triple-decker?

Bette Midler:
Clams on the Half Shell

A bunch of blacks are toiling in the shadow of a Mississippi steam-
boat and singing an almost unrecognizable arrangement of "Old
Man River" when some fishermen deliver a huge clam which, pres-

ently, opens and there, like the Hottentot Venus on a clam shell, is clamorous Bette Midler. Soon she is wiggling her scantily clad behind at the spectators, shrilling "Moon of Manakoora," and disbursing compliments to them: "We shaved, some of us even douched, and if that ain't an act of love, I don't know what love is." At the Minskoff, an exemplar of the eyesore school of architecture, we hurtle into a swamp of bad taste, to which Miss Midler's fans respond by clapping, hooting, shimmying in their seats or jumping out of them—a *Walpurgisnacht* worthy of the camera of Paul Morrissey, the brush of Richard Lindner.

Miss Midler is carried off as she came, but does not clam up for long. Soon she is back, telling jokes, bantering with the audience, belting out songs as blastingly as the audio permits, crooning sentimental ditties, or doing embryonic skits and dance numbers with her back-up group, the three Harlettes. There was a time when, even though one could perhaps not be sure of what constituted true art, one could be reasonably certain about what was kitsch, or bad art. Then came a series of manifestations culminating in pop art, which managed to confuse the issue thoroughly. Bad, non-, anti-, or pop art became enshrined as art and the kitsch-camp alliance triumphed. In *Kitsch: The World of Bad Taste*, Gillo Dorfles writes about "the vampire kitsch: all of us alive today are or can be its prey." Sure enough, the self-styled Divine Miss M. singing a torrid Latin number about having the clap in Rio ("What to do in Rio, / When you can't even pee-o?"), stood suddenly revealed as the Vampire Kitsch in person. Of course, no one who cracks jokes about Gerald Ford and Arlene Francis can be entirely bad, though she can be rather more forgettable than forgivable.

Miss Midler's Schleppin Fetchit routine, her walking like someone who has befouled himself and is trying to make the nearest bathroom without his shins ever touching his pant legs, could alone cause pains in healthy teeth. Her grin is infectious like the plague, and though her high notes may not exactly shatter icebergs, her voice could saw down all the forests of Alaska. She chokes the life out of a song, and the audience loves it; she tells dubious homosexual jokes, and the largely homosexual audience is in heaven; she insults the entire auditorium, and the very walls seem to reverberate with adoration. As Rex Reed, in a piece in which he dubbed Bette a "nymphet Lorelei," put it: "It's Mary Martin asking if we believe in fairies. Yes. We do. Clap harder." *Crede experto*: the ovation was like those felled Alaskan woods hitting the ground in unison. Miss

M definitely exudes an indefinable aroma, something like her own peculiar brand of patchouli—*Essence de Cloaque*, perhaps.

The show, *Bette Midler's Clams on the Half Shell*, has other attractions. There is also Lionel Hampton producing sounds on the vibraphone that remind me of those Amateur Hour contestants who played "Chopsticks" on water glasses; there is the Michael Powell Ensemble, a gospel group that cannot even preach to the converted; there are Tony Walton's sets, whose cleverness not even kitsch can diminish; and the direction and choreography of Joe Layton, as undistinguished as usual. But there is something else: most ingenious calculation. Exactly how many homosexual jokes we can have before we switch to Jewish jokes, how much cheap-shot satire before we shift to sentimentality, how much insulting of the audience before we change gears into universal accolades—Miss M, or her good fairy, has absolute control over the emotional calipers. If there is an award for mass manipulation, the Divine Miss M has amply deserved it. Let us, in fact, decree her the Order of King Kong first class and the triple fuchsia Lupe Velez ribbon.

A Chorus Line

A Chorus Line is a worm's-eye view of the American musical theater, but in this show the worm, the chorus line, has turned. It has turned into something with an individual as well as a conglomerate identity, something with egos and needs and dignity. Even if these boys and girls are only the worms with which the line is baited, they are still what finally hooks the big fish out front, for a musical, to a very large extent, not only sings and dances on its chorus line but also stands and falls on it. By examining the beings who, separately and together, make up a chorus, *A Chorus Line* does nothing less than zero in on such stuff as theater—and dreams—are made on.

"There is much of the actor about this author," Valéry remarked, rather contemptuously, of Stendhal. There is much of the actor, indeed of the chorus boy, about the principal authors of *A Chorus Line*: Michael Bennett, the director-choreographer-mastermind, began in the chorus; Nicholas Dante, the co-author, may still be there; and James Kirkwood, the other co-author, served long as an actor. I mention this anything but condescendingly: it is their know-how, coupled with ravaging frankness, that makes the show so authentic, interesting, and, finally, innovative. For *A Chorus Line* is something new and historic in musical comedy, the first *musical-vérité*. I allude, of course, to *cinéma-vérité*, the attempt to catch unmediated truth on film. To be sure, the show is staged *cinéma-vérité* (but, then, so is a good deal of *cinéma vérité* proper), staged not only in the sense that it is on stage, but also in that it follows a scripted book.

But this book is no ordinary musical book. It was clearly improvised in considerable measure, picking up real-life experiences of the writers and director, members of the cast (I would guess), and other theatrical and quasi-theatrical people. The framework is an audition: a Broadway show is being cast, and it requires a chorus of four boys and four girls. From an initial line-up of some two dozen, sixteen or so semifinalists have been chosen, and now comes the grueling whittling down to those final eight. The show's gimmick is that the director—a bit of a crud, but then, that's the way some of them are—is hurling questions at the candidates from the back of the house: hard, often psychoanalytical questions about their careers, backgrounds, personalities, motivation. I doubt very much whether such questions get asked of persons applying for anything short of the CIA, but it is a pardonable device in view of how well it works and how effectively it is executed.

There they stand, these sixteen; one at a time they are made to step in front of the white line—a line that becomes a veritable character in the show—each in turn spilling out his or her guts. The director's voice from the outer darkness is ruthlessly inquiring, with the insistence of a tongue on a sore tooth, of fingernails on a scab. And the victims of this inquisition sometimes tenderly, sometimes funnily, sometimes terrifyingly—lay themselves bare, in words, song, and dance. Their monologues are often interrupted, and we see them going on in pantomime, while other postulants speak, sing, or dance their thoughts on what is happening. These interior monologues are sometimes mere fragments, so that *A Chorus Line* goes from highly sculptured sequences for one performer to sudden mosaics—boisterous, rueful, or angry little fragments rattling their way into our notice. This musical never lets us forget that it comes at us out of a collective consciousness, that it is a polyptych, that behind the fierce or frightened solos there is a choral hymn of aspiration, anxiety, and hope.

The authors have tried, beyond evoking a situation in composite terms, to introduce bits of actual plot, such as the story of a featured dancer, former mistress of the rising, more opportunistic than dedicated, director. She missed out on stardom in Hollywood, and is now back on the chorus line, doggedly fighting for a fresh start, which her former lover would deny her for meanly selfish reasons. This "story" element is a little too shrill and contrived against the dispassionately documentary background. Again, the director's apparently more than just humane interest in a young Puerto Rican homosexual aspirant still struggling to find himself is either hinted at too insistently or not developed enough, An ad hoc existential inquiry in which all these contenders question one another about what they will do when they are too old to dance has something too deliberate and didactic about it. But these are footling flaws, easily absorbed by the overarching genuineness and polyphonic surge of the show as a whole.

My companion, being much more hard-headed than I am, found parts of the evening trashily sentimental; yet even she— once, briefly, a would-be actress—had to admit that of such is the theater made. For what the show captures admirably is the curious duality that makes this underbelly of show business at once exceedingly soft and hard as nails—very long, very scarlet nails. If one girl sweetly tells us that she started learning to dance after she saw, and fell in love with *The Red Shoes* and that glorious redhead in it, another girl will step forward to declare "Let's get one thing straight. I never saw *The Red Shoes*, I never heard of *The Red Shoes*, I don't give a fuck about *The Red Shoes*." This binary rhythm courses through the on-fire show, visually, aurally, philosophically. And so it should, for what is the theater if not, at the same time, the most cajolingly mendacious wish-fulfillment machine and the most mercilessly candid dispenser of devastating truths. In this respect, by the way, it is not unlike life, which is something else *A Chorus Line* is about.

There is ingenious yet feelingful direction and cannily emblematic choreography by Michael Bennett (although the solo for Donna McKechnie is perhaps a trifle under-imaginative), and excellent support from Robin Wagner's decor and Tharon Musser's lighting, both of which act up a storm. Marvin Hamlisch's score is derivative and pedestrian, but serviceable enough if you think of it as a kind of sonorous environment or underpinning, a trusty obbligato trailing after the drama with canine fidelity. There are good orchestrations and arrangements by several knowing hands, convincing rehearsal costumes for the gypsies (and some funky glitter for the final apotheosis) by Theoni V. Aldredge, and pretty decent lyrics by Edward Kleban.

Mostly, though, there is the cast, a cast of thousands of virtues. Once again, as in last week's *Rodgers & Hart*, the girls are better than the boys, but no one is wrong. It may be that Robert LuPone makes the director creepier than need be; everybody else is on the button. But, of course, not all buttons are genuine mother-of-pearl; so, cad that I am, I must single out Donna McKechnie, who makes the ex-girlfriend's interior contest of vulnerability and pluckiness into a superbly moving spectacle; Priscilla Lopez who has a way of making a song really happen, both to her and to us; and Carole Bishop, as an older, more experienced, more womanly candidate who can wield a mean monosyllabic line (In answer to "What would you like to be when you grow up?" "Young!"—said with a volume's worth of overtones) or polysyllabic look (her last, withering glance).

You can find faults in *A Chorus Line*, even incontrovertible and not inconsiderable ones. But, in the last analysis, they don't matter. The rhythm of the show carries you along—back and forth between sentiment and cynicism—like the systole and diastole of some huge, insolent yet innocent, invisible but all-embracing heart.

Chicago

Chicago has many of the ingredients from which a musical smash could be fashioned. There is some fascinatingly architectural scenery by Tony Walton, made out of mylar and vinyl and other members of the gaudy family of plastics, highlighted by neon, and covered with the hieroglyphs of Chicago in the twenties: there is the onstage orchestra on an elevated bandstand whose cylindrical pedestal opens up into an inner stage: there are wittily, impudently tasteless costumes by Patricia Zipprodt, which have a way of making a chorine's buttocks look most poutingly palpable. There is Bob Fosse's unearthly skill in turning the chorus line into undreamed-of phenomena: an invasion of humanoid fungi; a lava of lubricity spreading across the footlights; the innards of a giant kaleidoscope, anthropomorphized and rampaging; or simply dance routines that manage to outsmart almost anybody else's. And there is Fosse's happy directorial notion to make whatever happens only half an event—the other half being a circus or nightclub act mocking the first half. There is Jules Fisher's downright Machiavellian lighting that wrests shining little victories from the predominantly black set, then tosses them cavalierly back into the dark—only to lull it into a false sense of security, and ambush it with light from all sides.

But certain essentials are lacking. Fosse and Fred Ebb have not been able to come up with much of a book (out of a play by Maurine Dallas Watkins) about two rival murderesses in a Chicago jail who share the same hotshot lawyer (a kind of legal ménage à trois) and, after much infighting, discover that the road to survival is an uneasy sister act. The main troubles here are that the satirical bite is minimal, that the plot elements are achingly derivative, that so many conflicting styles—from Brecht to Tom Eyen, from Carlo Gozzi to Groucho Marx, from *Cabaret* to *Pippin*—have been pressed into unsmooth service. The burden on Fosse's cleverness is excessive, and though it gallantly rises to the occasion, it often looks out of place, like a great conversationalist at a Boy Scout jamboree.

Fred Ebb's lyrics are getting better with time, though they will probably never exult on the peaks of Sondheimian ingenuity or bask in the vale of quietly assured simplicity (e.g., Larry Hart's sad young woman singing "Only my book in bed / Knows how I look in bed"). But at least they do not fall into the cheap gags of the dialogue, e.g., "As they say in Southampton, 'You're shit out of luck!'" or "Life in jail?"—"Where else? Marshall Field's?" There are even genuinely ingenious ideas for songs, such as "Cell Block Tango" and "Class," where the lyrics, however, cannot sustain in detail the wit of the underlying conception. And here John Kander's music generally joins in the betrayal. It is all very well to have a period flavor for your melodies, but I doubt if that justifies a raid on all antiquarian shops. It is a neat though hardly novel idea to have a number of songs weave in and out of a saucy parlando, but when the time comes for an honest-to-goodness tune, it would be nice if it weren't like "Roxie," straight out of Jerry Herman.

And then there is the unkindness of age. Chita Rivera has somehow beaten the rap and, barring an occasional overfrill, glows on unabated and unabashed. But Gwen Verdon stands condemned to a creeping grandmotherliness of visage and sluggishness of demeanor that settle on the proceedings like coal dust on the lungs. Jerry Orbach does gamely by the legal beagle (actually more of a dachshund), but the part is lacking in dimension. In supporting roles, Mary McCarty and Barney Martin stoutly override the skimpiness or mawkishness of their material, and Cheryl Clark and Pamela

Sousa are chorines of exceptional charm. Yet in a stage line-up veering from senectitude to transvestism, from grayness to grotes-querie, one's eye was most often arrested by the dark, sulky, almost glowering beauty and intensity of Charlene Ryan, who, gripping as she was in the chorus and in a small part, almost demanded to have the whole show turned over to her. Unaccountably, it wasn't.

There is fun in *Chicago*, but, finally, there is almost invariably something second fiddle, or merely second city, about it. Still, like any spectacle that carries the Fosse signature, it demands to be seen. If only it could be cherished!

Death of a Salesman

Death of a Salesman has always struck me as an overrated play, and its current revival by the Circle in the Square does nothing to dispel that impression. My objections have never been political, nor was I much concerned with the once hotly debated issue of whether a little guy, Willy Loman (low man), was a suitable tragic hero. If Woyzeck could be both utterly low and transcendently tragic, why couldn't Willy? Only because Arthur Miller is no Georg Büchner. There is no poet in Miller (as there is, for instance, in Tennessee Williams)—not even a very clear thinker. But there is a dramatist of skill, who saw both the absurdity and the pathos of Willy's Brook-lyn-Jewish milieu, and reproduced the accents of its anguish with a fidelity learned from Ibsen.

The villain in *Death of a Salesman* is, of course, the American cult of success, dramatically exacerbated when the protagonist is a salesman—one who sells selling even more than material goods. The poignancy is enhanced by his being a Jew (which Miller never spells out, but abundantly suggests) who has to overcome addi-tional rootlessness and insecurity. Willy pursues the two-headed chimera of financial and social success—being rich and well liked (a near-contradiction in itself)—and how this delusory and ever more elusive aim lures him and his family to physical or moral disaster I consider a perfectly fit subject for tragedy. But, unfortu-nately, Miller himself is to a considerable extent the victim of the obsessions he sets out to expose, and cannot acquiesce in the no-tion that a desperate situation does not afford—somewhere, some-how—a solution.

Although trying to write the national tragedy of America, he must imply that it once could be deflected by the individualism of Willy's father or the buccaneering of his brother, Ben, and that even today it can be controverted by the enlightened nonchalance of a Charley, the love of work of a Bernard, or the facing up to truth and acceptance of failure of a Biff. But if there is to be tragedy, there must also be a greater sense of the inevitable, of why Willy could not have saved himself. Here there are too many open doors to make a stone wall loom as a tragic necessity. Worse yet is the grubby melodrama of making the catastrophe hinge not on life or society as it does, but on Biff's chancing on his father's extramarital dalliance with a female buyer to whom—to make matters even more unsubtle—he gives boxes of sheer hose while his poor wife is revealed piteously darning old stockings as frayed as Miller's symbolism. A darn shame!

If there is to be drama rather than tragedy, however, the minor characters have to come more cogently alive. Points then have to be made through texture, atmosphere, a sense of a multifaceted society jointly suffering and going under; in that case, the vignettes about the secondary characters are too sketchy here, too obvious or caricatured (the two floozies, the buyer, Howard with his wire recorder) to make the play's thesis come across as more than a thesis. Again, such feeble objective correlatives as Biff's kleptomania are not parlayed, either by poetry or by depth psychology, into the symbols they are meant to become. And the language is full of such blatancies as Willy's rebuking Biff for using the infantile word *gee*, only to exclaim promptly himself: "Gee, look at the moon." As for the attempt at heightened language in the closing "Requiem" section, it is for me one of the nadirs of modern drama—the salesman described, for example, as "a man way out there in the blue, riding on a smile and a shoeshine," and Linda sobbing out her repeated "We are free," fraught with elephantine irony. As Mary McCarthy wrote, "Still, *Death of a Salesman* is the only play of the new American School that can be said to touch home"—but don't miss the impact of that *still*.

George C. Scott has managed the physical staging well enough, but he blew it all on the casting. For one thing, he took out all the essential savor of Jewishness by almost perversely casting goyim; what is truly perverse, though, is making Charley and Bernard black, thus not only losing their right meanings but also obtruding others shriekingly false—historically, sociologically, and logically (a black will not be greeted with the remark that he is looking anemic). The supporting players range—with the pleasant exception of Chuck Patterson, however miscast—from undistinguished to bad, the Linda of Teresa Wright being most cruelly wrong. Miss Wright turns this painfully persistent, exasperatingly dedicated woman (a definitive performance by Mildred Dunnock in the original production) into a gentle Midwestern schoolmarm (shades of *Cheers for Miss Bishop* or *Good Morning, Miss Dove*), causing us to wonder whether Miller intended an attack on devious smarminess rather than a (perhaps naïve) tribute to bewildered devotion. James Farentino makes Biff look and act, and even walk, dumb, rather than tormented, while Harvey Keitel, superficially correct as Happy, has inexpressive eyes and an often inaudible delivery.

The one dazzler is Scott—an actor who can do more with a few strangulated monosyllables or an unfinished, aborted gesture than most others with whole tirades and choreographies. But Scott has two predominant characteristics, strength and violence, whereas Loman is all weakness and exacerbated good will. As Lee J. Cobb played him, the fluttering hands and vocal arpeggios conveyed a kind of lyricism of defeat; as the great but miscast Scott plays him, the soured dream has become a rage that could move mountains. A suicide? This Willy would become president of the company.

Laughter in the Soul: Molière's *Misanthrope*

It has become a critical commonplace that Molière's *Le Misanthrope* occupies the same place in Western comedy that *Hamlet* does in tragedy. When this remark is made casually, as it often is, it may be that the speaker is not even aware of what a great statement (in Goethe's famous phrase) he has calmly uttered. For although one could argue, for example, that *Tartuffe* and *King Lear* are even more extraordinary plays, the everlasting fascination of *Hamlet* and the *Misanthrope* lies in the infinite interpretations their respective protagonists have elicited, which is to say in the susceptibility of these protagonists to become emblematic embodiments of the various sensibilities of individuals in different eras, indeed of the collective sensibilities of those eras themselves.

Significantly, both the *Misanthrope* and *Hamlet* belong to two genres simultaneously: besides being a great comedy and tragedy, respectively, they are also problem plays leaving us with a great many more questions than answers. Thus at the end of *Othello*, for instance, we know well enough what caused the tragic outcome and how, but for human nature—or a particular kind of human nature—things could have turned out differently. In *Hamlet* we can have no such certainties, and the same is true of the *Misanthrope*, which, unlike other plays by Molière, comes to an open ending: Alceste rushes off to some unpeopled place to become a recluse, while Philinte and Eliante hurry after him to reclaim him for society. As Martin Turnell observed in *The Classical Moment*: "In no other play does Molière reveal such variety and complexity of feelings, but in no other does he show such reluctance to judge the individual or so marked a tendency to call in question all accepted standards and formulas."

The problem-play aspect of the *Misanthrope* lies, first of all, in that it works through indirection. The person who does not notice this will feel cheated, even if he is no less a man than Rousseau. "This," complained Jean-Jacques, "is not what we come to your theater to see; your misanthrope is not one perfect misanthropic crystal; on the contrary, he is changeable and his behavior is not consistently directed according to the principle of misanthropy." But Molière was, of course, no La Bruyère, and *vive la différence!* Rousseau's disappointment is based on a double misunderstanding: that the play concerns solely Alceste, and that misanthropy is a simple dislike of people.

There is in the *Aufzeichnungen*, the posthumously published jottings of Hugo von Hofmannsthal, a suggestive yet slightly mysterious passage about the play:

> In the *Misanthrope*, the entire dialogue is a critique, from start to finish: Alceste criticizes Célimène, or Philinthe [*sic*] criticizes Alceste, or vice versa, or Alceste criticizes the courtiers or an individual courtier, or the courtiers (together with Célimène) criticize absent persons, or Alceste criticizes them for their criticism; or Eliante criticizes Alceste's love for Célimène, or he himself criticizes his love; Arsinoé comes to criticize Célimène, and the latter returns her criticism, etc., etc. Criticism is but one of the forms of indirection.

The conclusion to this otherwise very useful observation is a bit gnomic, but it becomes clearer if we set it alongside a passage from Sainte-Beuve's essay on the death of Sir Walter Scott, in which the critic points out that Scott was not one of the greatest writers:

> Geniuses of this sort who have the gift of forgetting themselves and transforming themselves into an infinite number of personages whom they make live, speak, and act in a thousand touching and entertaining ways, are often capable of very ardent passions of their own, although they never express them directly. It is hard to believe, for instance, that Shakespeare and Molière, the two highest specimens of this class of mind, have never felt with a profound and sometimes bitter passion the things of life.

The *Misanthrope* strikes me as a supreme example of expressing such a bitter passion indirectly, so as not to appear very strongly to be saying it at all. The indirectness of its expression is explicable only partly, I think, by the natural fastidiousness of genius, which tends to clothe its absolutes in the garments of relativism because it is too perceptive to overlook what is particular, private, relative even in the most orthodox-seeming absolute (a cognizance whose lack makes Alceste look both ridiculous and pitiful); it is also, I believe, motivated by the necessity of caution in not-so-good King Louis's golden days—the desire, in short, not to fall into the same trap as one's protagonist.

I am inclined to disagree with Gide's argument in a lecture on "The Importance of the Audience," which runs: "'C'est une étrange entreprise,' said Molière, 'que celle de faire rire les honnêtes gens.'" A strange enterprise, and doubtless arduous, but to it we owe his masterpieces. And if Molière had aimed only at getting a laugh out of his cook, as is also alleged, we should have had further *Fourberies de Scapin* and a further *Monsieur de Pourceaugnac*—but I doubt if he would have given us the *Misanthrope*. These *honnêtes gens*, as Molière called them, equally distant from a court a little too rigid in its ways and a pit a little too free, were precisely what Molière regarded as *his public*; and this was the public to which he addressed himself. The court of Louis XIV represented formalism; the pit, naturalism; they represented *good taste*." I wonder whether Molière could trust even these sterling people or gentlefolk—or however *honnêtes gens* can best be rendered—to accept a view of society in which everyone is corrupt, or at least mildly hypocritical and ineffectual, like the worthy Philinte (a *raisonneur* much more ambiguous than Molière's other ones), or, at the very best, noble but ultimately passive, like Eliante.

Either there were not enough *honnêtes gens* around, or their perceptions were not quite up to the *Misanthrope*, for it was only a modest success, just a little better than a mild failure. Yet Gide may have been right in a sense different from the one he intended: Molière may have succeeded so well with this play *sub specie aeternitatis* precisely because, to entertain (or not scandalize) these good people, he encoded rather than made manifest his message. Accordingly, the play has been viewed in two principal ways. One might be called the romantic view, as expressed, say, by Mauriac in his "Alceste" (*Journal 1932–1939*):

> The comic in Alceste stems from the spectacle of a lover who collides everywhere with that brilliant and hard surface of mendacity, that mirror of the world, those formulas, gestures—all that protocol whose excuse for being is precisely to disguise the true thoughts, to withhold our spontaneous reactions, to interrupt our initial movement. But very early on these head-buttings of Alceste's no longer make the spectator laugh, because they correspond to a painful need to know at any cost whose torment almost all men have known—and it is for this reason that the two last acts of the *Misanthrope* give off a well-nigh tragic sound, it is for this reason that their beauty is sad.

What might be called the classical interpretation—which, officially, was also Molière's—perceives Alceste as an essentially comic character. This is stated by W. G. Moore in a somewhat more up-to-date manner in his *Molière: A New Criticism*:

> [Alceste] is ridiculous because he forgets that he is part of the picture. He is antisocial because he recommends on grounds of principle courses of action by which he stands to gain. It is one thing to reprove flattery and flirtation; it is quite another to insist that

one be preferred to all other suitors … what Alceste wanted, unbeknown to himself, was recognition, preference, distinction.

More traditionally, the classical view would hold simply that Alceste carries his virtues to the point of fanatical excess, which vitiates their value. In the notes to his Pléïade edition of Molière, Maurice Rat cites Lessing's dictum that a person can be ridiculous without being contemptible by way of summing up the funny but painful case of "this so naïve, stubborn young man who has the chimerical aim of wanting to correct the entire world."

But, as has more recently been pointed out by several commentators, the play, to be properly understood, must not be viewed merely as the story of Alceste. Indeed, it is hardly a story at all, for such action as there is consists entirely of arguments and more arguments, and a few revelations mostly through intercepted letters. Still, in W. G. Moore's apt formulation, "a canvas is rolled back, in conversations so momentous that they seem to be events." These conversations constitute the chain of critiques detected by Hofmannsthal; they are not only brilliant in themselves, they also add up to a magisterially orchestrated, sweeping attack on society as a whole. For Molière cogently interweaves several strands. There is, first, an assault on the lying and fawning of the age, the hypocrisy and sycophancy against which Alceste keeps inveighing, either in general terms or by adducing specific instances—it is in this context that the Alceste-Oronte quarrel takes on its symptomatic significance. We hear, next, of Alceste's lawsuit, which he stands to lose because he flatly refuses to call on the judges and sweet-talk them, and so the notion of sociopolitical injustice joins that of social dissembling. When Célimène appears, the theme of the devaluation of love into flirtatiousness and at least spiritual, if not sexual, infidelity is introduced. Over against these provocations for Alceste's understandable but immoderate philippics, we get the temperate voice of Philinte, soothingly counseling: "… faisons un peu grâce à la nature humaine"—advice that goes unheeded by our hero.

But Alceste is a complex figure despite his underlying predictability. When Philinte persuasively conveys to him that Eliante would suit him better than her cousin, he replies: "Il est vrai: ma raison me le dit chaque jour; / Mais la raison n'est pas ce qui règle l'amour." This is a dizzyingly complex statement. Yes, the perfectionist in Alceste knows that reason would opt for Eliante; but reason, he says, is not what governs love relationships. True enough, but true in the manner of old adages, folk wisdom, received knowledge; must he, the man who would change the whole world, acquiesce in such old saws? Certainly, if they serve his purpose, and the purpose of this rationalist-moralist-idealist is, at this point, to remain as self-deluded as, possible because his passion must be justified. Such self-contradiction would seem to be ridiculous, the matter of comedy—but hold! Is it really? After all, the universe Alceste wants is one of truth, honesty, and (as he keeps insisting in a way that must have seemed revolutionary to a century whose notion of nature—the pastoral—was the very paradigm of artificiality) honest-to-goodness naturalness. When he damns Oronte's sonnet it is primarily because "Ce n'est que jeu de mots, qu'affectation pure, / Et ce n'est point ainsi que parle la nature." And, surely, to love and desire simply, forthrightly, "naturally" a woman who happens to be Célimène rather than Eliante is not in itself unnatural, though it may be unwise.

Just what, however, is Alceste's idea of "the natural"? It is, among other things, the old song:

> Si le Roi m'avait donné
> Paris, sa grand'ville,
> Et qu'il me fallût quitter
> L'amour de ma mie,
> Je dirais au roi Henri:
> "Reprenez votre Paris,
> J'aime mieux ma mie, au gué!
> J'aime mieux ma mie."

If Molière is literally assigning this *vieille chanson* to the coarse but better (because not artificial) taste of *nos pères*, he is historically wrong; it has been shown that the King Henry in question is the second, not the fourth, of that name. But *pères* probably means forefathers, and what is being opposed here is the "méchant goût du siècle" with something that stems from the folk-mouth. Indeed, the song appears, *mutatis mutandis*, in Italy too, as Benedetto Croce reminds us: "*Se il papa mi donasse tutta Roma, / e mi dicesse: —Lascia andar chi t'ama— / io gli direi di no, Sacra Corona.*" Yet, we wonder, is this necessarily the language, the only language, of true love? Once a society becomes more complex—artistically, scientifically, culturally—cannot sensibility, and the language that expresses it, legitimately change into something more complicated, more stylized, but not ipso facto less real? And, in that sense, is Oronte's poem all that bad in the day of the metaphysical conceit, of Marinism and Gongorism and the not inconsiderable poetry they yielded? What Alceste is really after is simplicity. Call him misanthropist, purist, idealist, perfectionist, meliorist gone pessimistic, or what you will, above all other things he is a reactionary against the preciosity of the age, a back-to-naturist, an advocate of simplicity. But—and here lies his comic preposterousness and therewith his personal tragedy—he fails to understand that simplicity, at least when it is translated into utterance, is also a style, is also something arrived at with possibly much toilsome polishing. The author of the *ur-Si le Roi* may have had a highly turbulent and complicated love relationship with one or many women, and was surely not that Antoine de Bourbon, Duke of Vendôme and King of Navarre, who is its apparent speaker. What Alceste is after, then, is nothing more or less than a change of style, or, as Auden put it in the last verse of his quasi-sonnet: "New styles of architecture, a change of heart."

What makes Alceste touching—perhaps comically, rather than pathetically, touching—is that he is better, or, if you prefer, worse than his word: importuned by Oronte for a verdict on his sonnet, he first tries desperately to find ways of not having to give one, then to give it in the most indirect, general, tactful way possible. So we soon realize that Alceste's is a double-edged comedy (or, as always in this play where the two have a brilliant way of becoming one, double-edged pathos): it is not only that his position is exaggerated and intransigent, it is also that he himself cannot truly abide by it, either in social intercourse or in love. But besides this basic inconsistency, there is also the profound paradox inherent in misanthropy: such detestation for the ways of mankind must be a love turned to hate and, as such, has about it a ludicrous, as it were transvestite, air. The shrewd Célimène spots it when she retorts to Alceste's "Personne n'a, Madame, aimé comme je fais" with "En effet, la méthode en est toute nouvelle, / Car vous aimez les gens pour leur faire querelle." She is absolutely right, except that she has got it backwards: Alceste's love is not querulous; his querulousness is, in fact, his love.

If the misunderstanding of the relativity of simplicity is one of Alceste's problems, the other is a kind of orgiastic enjoyment of excess, especially excess that is damaging to himself—in short, spiritual masochism. I reject utterly certain neocritical attempts to make

Molière's drama into something formalistic and nonpsychological, as when Moore concludes:

> We should give "psychology" a rest in explanations of Molière's work… too many experts have assumed that Molière offers a realist set of characters… We know why the text was written: to provoke enjoyment by suggesting ridiculous ideas and postures. Is it not possible to do this without profound and accurate psychology? Some years ago the Abbé Bremond made a strong plea that Racine should not be thought of as primarily psychologist but as a poet. Just as he found the actions and reactions of Racinian characters neither very new nor very subtle, so might it be claimed that in the case of Molière we have too easily assumed that the skill must lie in the accuracy of character-drawing. But poets need not be, and are not, accurate…

As a corrective to an overpsychologizing view of Molière, this is a valid statement; but to throw out the psychologist in order to vindicate the poet is an egregious error, particularly since Molière's greatness lies in being supremely both, and in managing to fuse them so perfectly.

Now, this orgiastic self-destructive rage of Alceste's appears already in I, i: "Moi, je veux me fâcher, et ne veux point entendre." He *wants* to lose his lawsuit: "Je voudrais, m'en coutât-il grand-chose. / Pour la beauté du fait avoir perdu ma cause." He will elaborate on this in V, i, in a couple of tirades which, proceeding from "J'ai pour moi la justice, et je perds mon procès!" lead to the declaration that the case is to live for posterity "Comme une marque insigne, un fameux témoignage / De la méchanceté des hommes de notre âge." The cutting off of one's nose to spite one's face is gleefully evident here underneath the homily: "… pour vingt-mille francs j'aurai droit de pester / Contre l'iniquité de la nature humaine, / Et de nourrir pour elle une immortelle haine." Paradoxically, the advocate of nature has come full circle to an immortal hatred of nature, of which human nature is, inevitably, a large part. And these social excesses are matched by amorous ones. When Célimène's fickleness is already fairly evident, Alceste does two things. He first describes (IV, iii) with cold self-analytical accuracy what his procedure has

been: "Par ces fréquents soupçons, qu'on trouvait odieux, / Je cher-
chais le malheur qu'ont rencontré mes yeux." It is what the German
proverb calls *den Teufel an die Wand malen*—painting the devil on
the wall, and thus enabling him forthwith to appear in the flesh. But
while one part of Alceste's psyche wants to know the worst, even
to the extent of helping it into existence, the other half, only a few
moments later, wants not to know, even to the extent of suppress-
ing the evidence. He pleads with Célimène: "Efforcez-vous ici de
paraître fidèle, / Et je m'efforcerai, moi, de vous croire telle." This
Alceste, so far from being an oversimplification in the direction
of a nonpsychological comedic stylization (which, at other times,
he can fleetingly be), is here revealed as a human being of almost
Proustian complexity.

What is certain beyond all the ambiguities and contradictions is
a kind of arrogance, one that, again, is as pathetic as it is comic. Alceste may well be truest to himself when he exclaims, at the end of
IV, iii, that he wishes Célimène had neither rank nor wealth, so that
his own heart could with a splendid self-sacrificial gesture repair
the injustice of such a destiny, "Et que j'eusse la joie et la gloire, en
ce jour, / De vous voir tenir tout des mains de mon amour." Rightly
can Célimène snap back, "C'est me vouloir du bien d'une étrange
manière." But for Alceste the manner is not strange: for him there
is no *joie* without *gloire*, and if there is to be no glory of fulfillment, let there be glory in unflinching rejection. When, in II, iv,
Célimène, with fine brio, accused him of having to be "l'esprit con-
trariant" (premonitions of Goethe's Mephistopheles, *der Geist der
stets verneint*) who carries "l'honneur de contredire" to the point
of combatting his own sentiments, as she says, the moment he encounters them in someone else's mouth, Alceste still has a halfway
plausible comeback: "C'est que jamais, morbleu! les hommes n'ont
raison, / Que le chagrin contre eux est toujours de saison..." This
is particularly moving from someone who, trying to let Oronte off
easy, was willing (I, ii) to make excuses for mankind, pointing out
that "eût-on, d'autre part, cent belles qualités, / On regarde les gens
par leurs méchants côtés." But by the end of the play, as everything
collapses (V, iv), he can announce his final intention: "Montrer que
c'est à tort que sages on nous nomme, / Et que dans tous les coeurs
il est toujours de l'homme." The misanthropification, so to speak,
has become total. In I, i, the mortal malady had not yet reached
the heart: "Je veux qu'on soit sincère, et qu'en homme d'honneur
/ On ne lâche aucun mot qui ne parte du coeur." Now, frightfully,

the very heart has been infected by the disease of being human. This outcry, which might seem the last word in ludicrousness, is it so far removed from the mad—or not so mad—Lear's warning to the blind Gloucester about to kiss the hand he has recognized as his abused sovereign's: "Let me wipe it first, it smells of mortality"? For, surely, Lear's *mortality* is a synonym for being human, that fundamental *homme* that Alceste shudderingly perceives as the ultimate unprootable evil. There are, of course, always spectators who snigger when Lear makes that heartrending remark, though it is anything but funny; no more so is Alceste's *cri de coeur* against the humanness of the human heart. In this rockbottom revulsion from what is quintessentially human, which is as justified as it is unjust, as tragic as it is comic, comedy and tragedy meet and become one on ground that is, however, much closer to tragedy than to comedy.

If part of the *Misanthrope*'s greatness lies, then, in its pushing comedy as far in the direction of tragedy as it can go (so that it was hardly iconoclastic for Courteline, in his sequel, *La Conversion d'Alceste*, to bring back the reformed misanthrope from his self-exile, only to have him tragically discover Célimène in Philinte's arms, and so cry out in horror as the curtain descends—I quote from memory—"Mon unique amour! Ma seule amitié!"), another part lies in the play's not being the mere portrait of a person, and a rather special one at that, but, as I said before, the panorama of a society as well.

When Célimène and Arsinoé have at each other with faintly disguised ironies that tear great gashes in their egos, when Célimène and the two little marquis make devastating fun of any number of acquaintances, or when Philinte and Eliante court each other with a delicacy of tact carried to extremes, these scenes are not mere filler material: they show how beneath the elaborate courtliness of manners—sometimes, as in the Célimène-Arsinoé contest, reduced to a mere ridiculous shell; at other times, as in the obloquy trio for Célimène and the marquis, allowed naked expression behind the victims' backs—everything in society has become, at best, a polite mask; at worst, undisguised malevolence. Here we must again recall Hofmannsthal's observation that the play is an extended, multifaceted critique, and that this constant criticism is only an indirect way of—let me spell out what both Molière (out of prudence) and Hofmannsthal (in the shorthand of a diary) merely intimated—showing the fragility and impugnability of all human positions. Even Philinte, sweetly reasonable as he is, is too schematic, too academic in his approach, a fact he betrays when, without fully realizing its implications, he declares to Alceste (I, i): "Mon flegme est philosophe autant que votre bile"—a statement whose self-damaging impact is reinforced by its echoing Philinte's earlier reproof of Alceste: "Ce chagrin philosophe est un peu trop sauvage." Once it is codified into a philosophy, an emotion freezes into a defect. And speaking of defects, is it not typical of the rigidity of eminent scholars for the distinguished W. P. Ker to have said, in a lecture "On Comedy": "Would not one go to Plato or to Pascal, rather than to Menander or Molière, for the finest conversational humour, the true comic irony"? Such philophilosophy is *un peu trop acadèmique.*

That leaves only Eliante, who seems, and seems to remain, perfect. It would be good to know exactly what Molière intended with her. A way of showing Alceste's misguidedness in love? A reward for the tactful and loyal Philinte? A foil for Célimène? All of those, no doubt; but in so perfect a play we expect each character to have more than a merely passive importance. I would hazard a guess: as the only character who, even more than Philinte, has no effect on the play's happenings, she testifies to the fact that the thoroughly good and sensible person is a freak and outsider, as irrelevant to the vagaries of society as to the course of history.

Yet in the midst of all this fineness we must not forget the most astonishing fact of this play: that it accomplishes its revelations almost exclusively through language-as-character, and only minimally through plot. I am not referring here to the frequent sonorous felicities as in, for example, "Et jamais, quelque ap*pui* qu'on *pui*sse avoir d'ailleurs, / On ne doit se *brouiller* avec ses grands *brailleurs.*" I am referring, rather, to the way language is made to carry all kinds of content that could not have been put more palpably onto the seventeenth-century stage—sexuality for instance. It does not seem at all fanciful to me to argue that the great Alceste-Célimène scene (IV, iii), with its continuous reversal of positions, power, and control is a verbal equivalent for a sexual encounter, a figurative sexual act. That some such intention was conscious in Molière's mind is suggested even by the way the playwright cast the *Misanthrope.* Alceste was played by himself; Célimène by his wife, whose faithlessness caused him much chagrin; Eliante by Mlle de Brie, his mistress; and Arsinoé by Mlle du Parc, who rejected his advances. If one scrutinizes IV, iii, minutely, one can find, I think, the outline of a frenetic sexual bout starting in a jealous rage, climaxing in an orgasm of self-deception, and subsiding into postcoital sadness. But the language performs on other levels as well, not least on that of a very Chekhovian refusal of characters to understand or even hear one another and saying the self-revealing things without hearing what they themselves are saying—as when Célimène thinks she is merely deriding Arsinoé with "Ce grand aveuglement où chacun est pour soi," but is really passing judgment on herself, and on all the dramatis personae and the world they embody.

The foregoing meditation on the *Misanthrope* was prompted by its production by the National Theatre of Great Britain under John Dexter, which, on a guest engagement here, achieved some very fine things, but also missed some most important points. Fallible as it was—its fallibility emblematized by the Tony Harrison adaptation, which shifts the scene from the Sun King's Paris of 1666 to De Gaulle's of 1966, resulting in some unexpected felicities as well as expectable *contresens*—it was good to see the play on our boards. Already at the beginning of this century, the Austrian poet-playwright-essayist Richard von Schaukal noted that "we enjoy the theater of high style, say Molière, as an exquisite rarity such as a Meissen figurine in a glass case." It is useful that Dexter's production, whatever its shortcomings, brought the play nearer to present-day audiences. Martin Turnell was most likely right when he explained Molière's turning to lighter subjects by the assumption that "[the playwright] must have perceived that in the *Misanthrope* he had written something which was 'above the heads' of many of his audience." Yet even in its own time the play found true understanders, like that Donneau de Visé who, from being Molière's detractor, became his friend, even writing an introductory letter to the first edition of the *Misanthrope* (1667), in which he concluded that he found the comedy "all the more admirable for its hero's being its butt without becoming too ridiculous, and that he makes the *honnêtes gens* laugh without cracking dreary and low jokes, as one has become accustomed to in comic plays. Those of [the *Misanthrope*'s] kind seem more entertaining, even if one laughs at them less loud… they cause continuous laughter in the soul [*elles font continuellement rire dans l'âme.*]" Indeed, at one of Molière's opening nights that was proving to be a failure, someone called out from the audience: "Courage, Molière, c'est la vraie comédie!" And highly polished, refined, concentrated, and stylized as it is, the *Misanthrope* is also *la vraie vie*.

The Shadow Box

Last season, by some miracle, Broadway ended up in the black. Jubilation swept across the Rialto: the theater was saved and God (or Mammon) was in his heaven. Even assuming that one swallow makes a summer, and one Broadway a national theater—both preposterous assumptions—there remains the fact that the offerings that seem to have reversed the downward trend were in no significant way better than (or even different from) the shows that used to keep the Great White Way in the red. The inevitable conclusion is that the reason for the windfall is not intrinsic but adventitious—that it depends on some such extraneous factor as perhaps a bad year for the movies or an even greater dissatisfaction with television.

However that may be, the pathetic state of Broadway theater—and, for that matter, regional theater, inasmuch as the play I am about to mention had successful runs in Los Angeles and New Haven before coming to Broadway—is epitomized by the case of *The Shadow Box*. This alleged drama by the actor-playwright Michael Cristofer won both the Pulitzer Prize and Tony Award, and made a more than respectable showing in the voting for the third major award, given by the New York drama critics. It takes place in three cottages for the terminally ill on the grounds of a large hospital, in each of which an allegedly archetypal patient is dying in his or her own quirky way. To make things jazzier, one cottage represents all three cottages, the characters from one being largely confined to the porch; from the second, to the living room; from the third, to the kitchen. But there is also some actual interpenetration of the same space by all three groups, a device invented by Alan Ayckbourn in *How the Other Half Loves*, which may have worked once in a particular farce, but which is showing signs of undue proliferation—possibly because it saves space and additional set design and so cuts production costs.

In Cottage One, there is Joe, an average Joe from New Jersey, with his frustrated, griping wife who has never forgiven him for not making good, even though they have survived decently and have a guitar-playing son to prove it. In Cottage Two, there is a noble, intellectual homosexual flanked by his cast-off wife and picked-up hustler lover. Though the divorced wife has turned into a promiscuous playgirl and the hustler is in attendance mostly for the sake of an inheritance, the latter at least is converted by the homosexual's noble dying into a true friend and better person. In Cottage Three, a semi-demented, moribund crone is tyrannizing an unloved daughter who has been magnanimously writing her letters in the name of another beloved daughter, who ran away from home and hasn't been heard from since. The old woman, believing the factitious letters, keeps alive in the hope of her favorite's imminent return. Meanwhile the unloved daughter is slowly lapsing into bitterness.

The author could have more appropriately named these cottages instead of One, Two, and Three—Miller, Albee, and Williams Cottage. But perhaps his nomenclature was right after all, for this is certainly playwriting by the numbers. Not only is the action in each cottage a full-blown piece of eclecticism, but also the very dialogue is at best derivative, at worst garishly ostentatious. Moreover, the mentality displayed is unpleasantly misogynistic, what with the central female character in each cottage a bit of a beast, and the two principal men extremely decent fellows, joined at last in goodness even by the redeemed male whore. Mostly, though, the problem is that none of this rings true. The good are too good, the bitchy too bitchy, and I, for one, did not for a moment believe that the author has really comprehended the effect of oncoming death on any of his characters. He has made everything even more grandiose—and faintly obscene—by introducing The Interviewer, who is intended as a sort of cross between a staff psychiatrist and God. This character, who apparently listens in simultaneously on all three bugged cottages, is always there interrogating either the dying or their next-of-kin, sometimes over a loudspeaker, sometimes in person. The concept is doubly odious: first, because it is clearly a shabby shortcut for the author to draw out the characters in an essentially nondramatic way; secondly, because it suggests a hospital that surpasses even actual hospitals in inhumanity with a Big Brother always listening, watching, pestering with prying questions.

Gordon Davidson's direction, Ming Cho Lee's setting, and the acting by all but two or three cast members managed to be equally routine, with three performances especially offensive. But all this is unimportant; what matters is that a shoddy play meretriciously designed to strike critics and audiences dumb with awe before its Great Theme, did not begin to do justice to its subject. If *The Shadow Box* is the best dramatic fare it has to offer, Broadway deserves to die in whichever cottage it chooses.

The Elephant Man

The Elephant Man, by Bernard Pomerance, an American living in London, has won both the Drama Critics' Circle and Antoinette Perry (Tony) Awards for best play of the season, and, for all I know, some of those other, lesser awards that attach themselves to major-prize-winning plays, turning every theatrical meteor into a comet. The play is a decent effort to write something literate, symbolic, significant—Brechtian, yet more feelingful than the typical Brecht play, and the aim is, to some extent, achieved in the first act. In the second (and last), however, things fly apart; neither the center nor the periphery can hold.

The play is based on the real-life story of John Merrick, known as the Elephant Man. This victim of neurofibromatosis, a congenital disorder, was hideously deformed in almost every part of the body by that condition, which affected nerves, bones, and skin. Curvature of the spine and a lame hip further disabled him. As Frederick Treves, the brilliant surgeon who became his savior was to put it, Merrick was "the most disgusting specimen of humanity that I have ever seen." Despite his extensive experience with "deformities... mutilations and contortions," as the aging Treves was to write in a memoir of Merrick in 1923, he had never met "such a degraded and perverted version of a human being." Treves's description of Merrick, which Pomerance incorporates in his play, evokes an "enormous and misshapened [*sic*] head. From the brow there projected a huge bony mass like a loaf, while from the back of the head hung a bag of spongy, fungous-looking skin, the surface of which was comparable to brown cauliflower. On the top of the skull were a few long lank hairs. The osseous growth on the forehead almost occluded one eye. The circumference of the head, [though Merrick was a slight man] was no less than that of a man's waist. From the upperjaw there projected another mass of bone. It protruded from the mouth like a pink stump, turning the upper lip inside out and making the mouth a mere slobbering aperture... The nose was merely a lump of flesh... The face was no more capable of expression than a block of gnarled wood. The back was horrible, because from it hung, as far down as the middle of the thigh, huge, sack-like masses of flesh covered by the loathsome cauliflower skin." I will spare you the similarly nauseating description of the rest of the man, but two further things need mentioning: Merrick also exuded a dreadful stench, though that was later checked by regular baths; and, by way of a left-handed compliment from nature, his left arm and hand were delicate, almost girlish, and quite unaffected by his disorder.

John Merrick was abandoned by his family, grew up in the Leicester workhouse, suffered from impeded speech, was exhibited by showmen at various sideshows as far afield as Belgium, only to be rescued in the nick of time by Frederick Treves, who, with the approval of his committee chairman, Carr Gomm, put him up for life in 1886 at the London hospital in Whitechapel. Here Merrick spent his last years until his death at twenty-seven in 1890. By that time he was the celebrated darling of high society whose members visited him frequently and showered him with gifts. Within a week from publication of a letter to the *Times*, the British public contributed the money needed for his lifelong upkeep. The carnival freak who had been the object of jeers, laughter, and insults ended up well cared for, favored even by royalty. He had come to love the theater, into which he would be smuggled—masked and cloaked, through secret passages, and seated in the back of a box—through the kind offices of Mrs. Kendal, a gracious leading actress of the day. He read a lot, worshiped women from afar (his genitals, alas, were unimpaired), and built with his good left hand a very fine model of St. Philip's Church, an edifice he could see from his hospital window. According to Treves, he often repeated "I am happy every hour of the day." And yet he died by what was some sort of suicide. Because of the weight of his head, he could not sleep lying down, only propped up with pillows and with his brow resting on his raised knees. One day he elected to sleep as he frequently said he wanted to, like ordinary people. This caused rupture or compression of the spinal cord and death.

Pomerance has fashioned this material—which his brother found for him in Ashley Montagu's *The Elephant Man*—into a concise, fast-moving play—at least in its first act. In a prefatory remark, the playwright notes that Merrick's building of the model of the church should dominate the play and constitute its central metaphor. Moreover, "any attempt to reproduce [Merrick's] appearance and voice naturalistically—*if* it were possible—would seem... not only counterproductive, but, the more successful it was, the more distracting from the play. For how he appeared, let slide projections suffice." And an illustrated lecture by Treves forms, accordingly, part of the play. But here we run into a difficulty, especially as Merrick is portrayed on Broadway—by a very handsome, usually near-naked, actor, who merely muffles his voice slightly and sometimes assumes a twisted posture. We are, presumably, to see objectified the beauty of the man's soul. But this strategy puffs up the audience with a cheap feeling of superiority. *They* would not have, as parents, cast out the poor wretch; *they* would not have, as impresarios, subjected him to every sort of humiliation and stolen his last few shekels; *they* would not have, as policemen, reviled and brutalized him; *they* would not have, as trained nurses, run screaming from his room; *they* would not have, as hospital orderlies, come to gape at him with unholy curiosity. *This* Elephant Man, after all, is nothing short of a darling boy.

Pandering to the audience is bad enough, but Pomerance also leans heavily in the opposite direction. He minimizes or omits many of the decencies that were, in actuality, shown Merrick even by some very ordinary people, and he makes virtually all of Merrick's prosperous, highly-placed friends and patrons appear suspect: either they profit from the Elephant Man directly or indirectly, or they can project their private problems onto him and, seeing him cheerful in adversity, feel purged through him. The simultaneous sparing and not sparing of the audience gives the play an unpleasant having-it-both-ways character.

To drive home his antisocietal stance, the dramatist starts out with a Treves who is much more smug and Victorianly hypocritical than the real Treves was, and ends with a Treves profoundly shaken by doubts such as his real-life counterpart never had. This would, of course, be all right, if only the fictive Treves came by this transformation convincingly. In an early scene, Treves does not understand what Carr Gomm means when he refers to worldly success as a "consolation prize"; he sees himself as having "excessive blessings." But early in the second act Treves says of Merrick : "That, as he rises higher in the consolations of society, he gets visibly more grotesque is proof definitive he is like me. Like his condition, which I make no sense of, I make no sense of mine." (That last sentence does not parse, but never mind for the moment.) As the play progresses, Treves's hatred for social success, and thus also for himself, grows in intensity, till, toward the end, the man who taught Merrick that we live by rules, and that rules make us happy, laments: "I am an extremely successful and respected Englishman in a successful and respected England which informs us daily by the way it lives that it wants to die. I am in despair, in fact."

What has happened in the play to warrant such a change of attitude? Little if anything. At one point, Treves seems to have become
embroiled in the shady financial speculations of an aristocrat—Lord
John, an obviously fictitious character—who has feigned interest in
Merrick. All this is barely hinted at, yet it is meant to imply that
Treves has somehow abused his patient. Also, Mrs. Kendal, whom
Treves summons to bring feminine grace to the deprived Merrick,
becomes ever fonder of that gifted unfortunate. One day, during
one of her frequent, friendly visits, she feels so strongly for this
youth who worships women without ever having seen one of them
naked, that she lets down her hair and disrobes to the waist for him.
Merrick is ecstatic, but Treves enters and, scandalized, chases Mrs.
Kendal away. We don't know what would have happened without
this intervention; as it is, Mrs. Kendal never returns and Merrick
goes into a decline from which he never recovers. But are these
two lapses of Treves's enough, under any circumstances, to turn the
surgeon from a contentedly righteous, socially rising Englishman
into a bitter and desperate prophet of doom? In the kind of echo
effect Pomerance loves, Treves reaches out pleadingly to the same
Bishop How whom he has previously been mocking, and cries out,
"Help me!"—exactly as Merrick had clasped him, Frederick Treves,
five years ago, with the identical cry for help.

We simply do not see the reasons for Treves's moral and political
change, except that Pomerance obviously intends some kind of Hot-
spur-Hal relationship, whereby as Merrick rises, Treves sinks. But,
to complicate matters, Pomerance also wants to stress the parallel
between the supposedly normal and the supposedly abnormal man,
so that he must make Merrick's rise into a fall as well. Treves—or
Pomerance—worries about Merrick: "His heart won't sustain him
much longer… It is the overarc [*sic*] of things, quite inescapable that
as he's achieved greater and greater normalcy [again Pomerance's
bad English, a problem throughout] his condition has edged him
closer to the grave." But the play does not show him as visibly closer
to death; rather Merrick thrives on his improved conditions, and
there is no evidence that relative normality brings him an other
grief except, probably, that of never becoming a woman's lover. Is
this what finally kills him?

The cause of the Elephant Man's death seems to me the key problem of the play, yet it remains unresolved in a manner that does
not leave me with an aftertaste of provocative ambiguity but of depressing vagueness. Treves's just-quoted speech continues: "So…

a parable of growing up? To become more normal is to die? More accepted, to worsen? He… it is just a mockery of everything we live by." But, I repeat, the play fails to connect either growing up or increased normality with dying—unless maturity and normality mean making love to a woman. This is what Ross, the sleazy impresario who exhibited Merrick as a freak and even cheated him out of his measly earnings, cruelly implies in a scene in which Ross, dropping in on the now relatively prosperous Merrick, asks for a percentage of the emoluments the latter receives from his rich well-wishers. He claims to have discovered Merrick and helped him survive; he further claims that nothing has changed—that Treves merely exploits Merrick on a grander scale than he, Ross, was able to do. The dukes and fine ladies who come to see Merrick do so to "feel good about themselves by comparison" and John is still a whore, like most people—which is "no disgrace… Disgrace is to be a stupid whore." When Merrick protests that he is now a normal man, like others, Ross nastily inquires: "Had a woman yet? MER-RICK: Is that what makes a man? ROSS: In my time, it'd do for a start. MERRICK: Not what makes this one. Yet I am like others."

Well, is he or isn't he? When the author makes Merrick refuse Ross even a small handout—which the latter certainly does not deserve—is he making Merrick into one of the exceptional, truly just beings, or merely an ordinary practitioner of tit for tat, like most other people? And is it only Ross's taunt that stings him, in the very next scene, to play on Mrs. Kendal's sympathy (or is it something bigger?) till she undresses for him? And what would have happened if Treves had not burst in on that scene, which Mrs. Kendal describes as "For a moment… Paradise"? In an earlier scene she had described her glamorous persona as not truly herself but an illusion; would she now, revealing herself and saying, "No illusions!" (another Pomerantian echo effect), have gone all the way? From what we know of the highly respectable woman that the historic Mrs. Kendal was, even this much is inconceivable. But Pomerance's Mrs. Kendal is more equivocal. Yet whatever she might have done, such an act of alleged supreme kindness might be taken, by both Merrick and the rest of us, as a terrible piece of sexual teasing. With or without a *noli me tangere*, Merrick is raised to Paradise all too literally for only a moment, to be hurled back forthwith to a greater sense of deprivation than ignorance, even if it is not exactly bliss, could ever inflict. Mrs. Kendal, who goes a bit too facilely from her initial extreme actressiness to subsequent ripe femininity, is confirmed in her ambiguousness by her failure to see Merrick after the unfortunate incident. Is it the sense of guilt and shame or Treves's prohibition that keeps her away? Neither, under the circumstances, should be a sufficient deterrent. And why does Treves want to keep her from Merrick? Is it simple jealousy or an act of wise prescience? His stated motive, muttered to himself out of John's ear-shot is "because I don't want her here when you die." Yet how can he foresee a death that is essentially suicide? And, in any case, why should Mrs. Kendal not be a comforting presence at Merrick's end? We are clearly getting out of the realm of creative ambiguity into that of stultifying confusion. Even the character of Carr Gomm, the wise administrator, has a way of changing from his early cogency to later cynicism, further suggesting that the dramatis personae are too much at the service of the drama, and not enough at that of true personality.

To be sure, Pomerance can write nice lines and even good scenes. Take this bit of dialogue: "MERRICK:... Sometimes I think my head is so big because it is so full of dreams. Because it is. Do you know what happens when dreams cannot get out? MRS. KENDAL: Why, no. MERRICK: I don't either. Something must." The first sentence, largely because it was part of the play's publicity campaign, has become the most famous line from *The Elephant Man*; it is a good one, but I like what follows even better. The repetition of "Because it is" is child-like and touching, as is that hopeful-hopeless "Something must." But the dialogue can also get too good, as in the second-most-cited line of the play. Carr Gomm has just fired an orderly who, strict instructions to the contrary notwithstanding, has been gawking at Merrick. Treves explains to his patient that relieving him of importunate stares was a merciful act, even if the orderly was badly in need of his job. Replies Merrick: "If your mercy is so cruel, what do you have for justice?" That, first of all, is far too sophisticated a remark for Merrick so soon after his reclamation by Treves. What is worse, though, is that it corroborates a problematic attitude I have already mentioned: Pomerance's war against the upper classes, which is one of the main themes, but not really supported by the story, inasmuch as high society and the bourgeoisie did far better by Merrick than the lower orders from which he came, his own family included. Pomerance's dividedness is epitomized by such a line: are we to sympathize with Merrick's censure of society or with Gomm's act which was meant to be only just, not merciful?

We are now back to the split that runs through the entire work and sometimes leads Pomerance very far astray. Take the scene in which Merrick begins to win over Mrs. Kendal with his critique of *Romeo and Juliet*, which he has just finished reading. Had *he* been Romeo, says John, he would not just have held the mirror to Juliet's breath. To which the experienced actress, who has played Juliet, replies, "You mean the scene where Juliet appears to be dead and he holds a mirror to her breath, and sees..." "Nothing," interjects Merrick, who then proceeds to blame Romeo for rashly killing himself. He, Merrick, would also have taken her pulse, sent out for a doctor. Romeo, however, kills himself for an illusion, which "fools him because he does not care for her... That is not love. It was all an illusion. When the illusion ended, he had to kill himself." Exclaims Mrs. Kendal: "Why, that is extraordinary." And so it is—because nowhere in Shakespeare's play does Romeo hold a mirror to Juliet's breath which Mrs. Kendal, with Juliet in her repertory, must clearly know. (So, by the way, must our drama critics, yet none of them has commented on this oddity.) What is going on here? Pomerance obviously trying to make Merrick into a superior being, a romantic superman who out-Romeos Romeo. But in the process he unconsciously (I assume) rewrites Shakespeare's scene, perhaps confusing it with the one in which Lear holds a feather to the dead Cordelia's mouth. But in any case, should Merrick be so exalted and idealized, to say nothing of the literary legerdemain involved? Furthermore, the scene is forced into the "illusion" refrain that echoes all through the play: Mrs. Kendal's first description of her self as a stage illusionist, then revealing herself naked, without illusion. Here, in between those poles, we are reminded again that when illusion ceases, we must die—as Merrick, apparently, kills himself out of unrequitable love for the once unveiled Mrs. Kendal—which would make him a kind of Romeo after all.

Well, that is one of the big difficulties with the play: Pomerance does not quite know what Merrick means to him, or else he wants to make him stand for too many things. He is obviously the Beast in an updated version of the Beauty and the Beast fairy tale; he is also the Noble Savage, a concept too threadbare to stand further updating or even plain reiteration. He is, furthermore, the Artist in a mundane, materialistic society. Noticing the model of St. Philip's he is building, Mrs. Kendal remarks, "You are an artist, John, an artist." And presently Merrick declares that he did not start building until he "saw what St. Phillip's [*sic*, throughout] really was. It is not stone and steel and glass... it is an imitation of grace flying up and up from the mud. So, I make my imitation of an imitation. But even in that is Heaven to me, Mrs. Kendal." The artist, then, as imitator of the mystic or saint, and Merrick is indeed shown as a true Christian. Yet even here Pomerance is split, for he allows John to criticize the God who made him (with a wry allusion to the fact that he, Merrick, can use only his good left hand): "He should have used both hands, shouldn't he?" This is another echo effect recalling Carr Gomm's reply to Bishop How, who had proudly declared that *God* knew what to do with the Elephant Man even as Darwin did not; retorted Gomm: "He'd better, sir; he deformed him."

So we get Merrick the artist and believer amid a crass and unbelieving society. And there is, of course, Merrick the social, political, psychological scapegoat of the Establishment. "We have polished him like a mirror, and shout hallelujah when he reflects us to the inch," says Treves. "I have grown sorry for it." And as if all this were not enough, there is also a surreal use of Merrick in a dream sequence, where Treves is dreaming an inverted—as it were, mirror-world. Here a healthy and normal Merrick lectures about the merely allegedly normal Treves, and, using a travesty of the language in which Treves described the Elephant Man's anomalies to a medical gathering, turns Treves's so-called normality and adjustment into objects of justified scorn—Pomerance's social iconoclasm again.

If we now return to the crucial question of the cause of Merrick's death, we face the conflicting interpretations that the various symbolic meanings dictate. Here we must ask ourselves again about that liminal note in which Pomerance asserted that the: "building of [the model] constitutes the central metaphor. The groping towards the conditions where it can be built and the building of it are the action of the play." If this is true (and an author is not always the best judge of his work), the play is about artistic or civilizational fulfillment, which permits the incomplete being—Elephant Man or Everyman—to die in a state of completeness. But, then, what is all that stuff with Mrs. Kendal and the end of illusion—or love—about? Consider, furthermore, Merrick's words as he finishes the model: "It is done." Surely this is also the *Consummatum est* of Christ on the cross, which, in another display of the Pomerantian echo chamber, recurs at the very end. Treves, to Carr Gomm's routine inquiry whether he has anything to add to the obituary notice Gomm is sending to the *Times*, decides at first that he has nothing to add. In the very last exchange of the play, however, Treves announces, "I did think of one small thing," but Carr Gomm answers, "It's too late. It is done." *Consummatum est*, again. So we get Merrick as a Christ figure as well.

All rather confused, I am afraid, and not a little pretentious. For a play to be able to get away with such a load of ambiguity, it must, at the very least, have so poetic a diction that the language supplies its own certainties where human wisdom, knowledge, rational insight fail. How often have we found consolation in some little phrase we repeat to ourselves over and over in times of stress? Well, great poetry or prose works in a similar way: its lapidary precision, its suggestive resonance, its order imposed on disorder make up for the fact that it is not a poultice for uncertainty, suffering, transience. But Pomerance's language is often unintentionally ungrammatical, awkward, and, except in occasional felicitous stretches, less than incantatory or compelling.

Four further things disturb me. First, the scene (12) in which all the play's major characters file past Merrick and project, in rather schematic speeches, their own views of themselves onto him. This litany-like effect appears to me to derive too slavishly from Shaw's Epilogue to *Saint Joan*. Next, I could do without the portentous titles affixed to each scene, e.g., "Art Is as Nothing to Nature," "Mercy and Justice Elude Our Minds and Actions," "When the Illusion Ends He Must Kill Himself." Thirdly, and relatedly, there is a tendency to build up each of the play's twenty-one fairly short scenes toward a punchline that can be pungent or poignant, but is as often ponderous; in any case, the procedure palls after a while. A typical early scene, for example, ends as follows: "GOMM: So he [Merrick] will be like us. Ah. TREVES: Is something wrong, Mr. Gomm? With us?" Again, the otherwise apt and sparkling scene (9) between Treves and Mrs. Kendal ends with her discovery that the Elephant Man has a normäl penis because, as Treves explains awkwardly, there are no bones in that organ. "MRS. KENDAL: Well. Learn a little every day, don't we? TREVES: I am horribly embarrassed. *(He looks at Mrs. Kendal.)* MRS. KENDAL: Are you? Then he must be lonely indeed." And the lights fade on this rather too tidy, too facile summation. Or take the penultimate scene (20), which begins with Snork, a hospital orderly, reflecting to Merrick about the chanciness of life. Snork is looking for another, better word, but cannot summon it up. Later he enters triumphantly: "I remember it, Mr. Merrick. The word is 'arbitrary.' 'Arbitrary.' It is all so..." Whereupon he notices that the Elephant Man is dead and rushes out proclaiming the news. Blackout. Now, that sort of thing is just too pat. The, arbitrariness of Merrick's malformation and the arbitrariness of human existence are surpassed here by the arbitrariness of Pomerance's dramaturgy.

Finally, I must call attention to certain tendentious omissions from Merrick's story as Sir Frederick Treves told it in his last book, *The Elephant Man and Other Reminiscences* (1923). I find particularly fascinating the silver-fitted dressing-bag that Merrick asked Treves to buy him for Christmas. Neither the bag nor any of the elegant toilet articles in it could be of the least use to Merrick, who, for instance, could neither shave nor use an ordinary toothbrush, and certainly could not smoke the cigarettes in the silver case. But, as Treves notes, it "was an emblem of the real swell and the knockabout Don Juan of whom he had read. So every day Merrick laid out upon his table, with proud precision, the silver brushes, the razors, the shoe-horn and the silver cigarette-case.... The contemplation of these gave him great pleasure, and such is the power of self-deception that they convinced him he was the 'real thing.'"

This is very touching, but missing from the play. I suppose it would have seemed to Pomerance to reduce his hero's stature to something less superior to the rest of the world, something less heroic. Self-deception, as Pomerance wants it, is chiefly for the Establishment. And so he also neglects to analyze the true cause of Merrick's "suicide," and seems to settle for Treves's statement that it "was due to the desire that had dominated his life—the pathetic but hopeless desire to be 'like other people.'" But this runs counter to the nobler mold in which he has cast the rest of his hero's behavior—hence the Mrs. Kendal-unrequited-love motif, the artist-who-has-finished-his-work motif, and all the others. Still, to leave out the ritual of the silver-fitted dressing-bag appears to me to diminish Merrick rather than to magnify him. Arbitrary—the word is arbitrary.

Tartuffe

Like *The Misanthrope*, Molière's other masterpiece, *Tartuffe* is a comedy of an extremely serious sort; to play it as farce is to throw out the baby and keep the bathwater. Luckily for the Circle in the Square and its current production, Molière's bathwater is of the most aromatic and bubbling sort, and can, even without the baby, provide a cleansing and invigorating experience. So I can guardedly recommend this *Tartuffe*, even if Stephen Porter's staging has flaws ranging beyond what I consider a basically vulgar conception.

If the falsely pious Tartuffe has become the emblem of hypocrisy, it is surely not for being a kind of Groucho Marx travesty of a fake puritan. Orgon and his mother may be gullible ninnies, but we learn later of our hero's long and successful career in imposture, and so must assume that when it comes to deception, he is no piker. To allow him to be played as John Wood plays him, however dazzlingly, is to make the world we share with Molière a much simpler and sillier place—not a battleground where Vice allied with Folly might easily precipitate a debacle, but a sandbox in which the terrible tot who threatens to take away the model children's pails and shovels is promptly put in his place by a watchful nanny.

When you throw together a brilliantly headstrong actor and a not incompetent but less than forceful director, there is bound to be imbalance. With Wood at one end of the seesaw and Porter at the other, the evening becomes a plane so steeply inclined that the play pretty nearly slides off it. Still, let us not blame the actor more than the director: after seeing Porter's recent staging of *The Importance of Being Earnest*, and now this, I am more than ever convinced that his comic invention, though not inconsiderable, is arrested on the delightful but unprofound level of Coward and Feydeau.

It is, of course, very hard to cast a high, period, verse comedy with American actors whose training not only does not prepare them for this sort of thing, but also systematically incapacitates them for it. And, except for Wood, the cast is American, yet on the whole surprisingly good. To be sure, no director with any sensitivity to man-woman relations would have cast as Elmire and Mariane Tammy Grimes and Swoosie Kurtz, two actresses totally unsuited to these roles both histrionically and physically; their presence in the play upends virtually every scene they are in.

Miss Kurtz plays the conventional and weak-willed but presumably charming and attractive Mariane (there must be something about her to make Valère love and Dorine care for her) as a sulky, almost feelingless, sly little broad, middle-aged and mean-looking. As for Tammy Grimes, who, many years ago, was an interesting young actress with a slightly and pleasantly out-of-whack quality, she has unhappily evolved into a mannered, stilted "personality" who, so far from acting, merely turns every new assignment into an excuse to trot out her usual, campily self-serving act. As Elmire, she conjures up a college production in which it is considered an absolute scream to cast the captain of the football team as the leading lady.

To put it another way, Miss Grimes suffers from a prematurely developed Hermione Gingold complex, with which she begrimes the part of a delightful, sensible, normal woman. Looking in her period hairdo like a porcupine with frizzed quills, Miss Grimes bestrides the stage as if her voluminous skirt were the body of a horse and she one of those actors who have to impersonate simultaneously a rider and his mount; speaks her lines with her fake British diction as if every one of them were supposed to puncture a balloon at the other end of the auditorium, in a voice that seems to come from inside a beer barrel; puts in hammy pauses where fluency is needed; and turns Elmire into a female Tartuffe as scheming as her would-be seducer. Miss Grimes is the only actress to win the first annual Mayor's Award in Arts and Culture (1977). Let's hope it was for culture.

John Wood is a very funny fellow who properly acts with every part of the body, with his unspoken thoughts as much as with words—not least that delightful final snort he invents for an exit line. His vitality is boundless, and his rubatos and dynamic shadings prodigal and prodigious. But he does not seem to realize that *Tartuffe* was not written by Tom Stoppard, and he has allowed the director (whom in every other way he has under his thumb) to make him play the attempted seduction scene semi-disrobed on top of Elmire supine on a table in a style befitting *Deep Throat* rather than *Tartuffe*.

The rest of the cast, with the exception of Peter Coffield, who turns the wise Cléante into a soporific figure (surely *this* must be what is meant by the sleep of reason), is very pleasant indeed. Patricia Elliott is a buoyantly life-asserting Dorine (though I wish she were not at such pains to hide the rhymes); Stefan Gierasch is an admirably restrained Orgon, whose slow burns never char his lines and whose fine foolishness properly preserves the lineaments of rationality; Victor Garber is a droll Valère who maintains a certain sweetness and dignity in his vagaries; and Mildred Dunnock as Mme. Pernelle is, despite a certain shortage of breath, a model of anile pigheadedness, almost endearing in its poised complacency.

Zack Brown's set and costumes, though unexceptional, are also unexceptionable. And then there is Richard Wilbur's translation, so marvelous that it makes Molière into as great an English verse playwright as he was a French one. You may not always want to watch this *Tartuffe*, but you'll certainly enjoy hearing it.

Miss Margarida's Way

In *Miss Margarida's Way*, all the world (or at least all the theater) is a classroom, and we the eighth-graders in it. This temple of lower learning is presided over by a teacher, Miss Margarida, who harangues, hectors, harasses, cajoles, and terrorizes her students, the audience. She enters into a strange relationship with them: paternalistic, voyeuristic, sadomasochistic. She is also a narcissist, a pretentious fool, an ignoramus spreading bizarre misinformation. She is both authoritarian and helpless, sinister and finally pathetic. The play, by the young Brazilian playwright Roberto Athayde, is, we are told, an allegory of dictatorship. To me, it seems both a little more and a great deal less than that.

Miss Margarida may be the totalitarian despot, but, if so, who is the headmaster to whom she is accountable? And if so, why does she say things like, "Whenever you see a roach or a bug in your soup, don't be uneasy. Share your soup with them"? This play is really an absurdist farce much more than any sort of structured piece of symbolism. The author is far too undisciplined and, I am afraid, fuzzy-minded to give us anything so controlled as a tidily working satirical metaphor; which does not exclude, of course, croutons of political satire floating in his mess of pottage. Still, the occasionally funny and intermittently ominous two-act play would have profited immensely from being a highly concentrated half-hour curtain raiser, where the absurdities coming thicker and faster would have been more absurd for it—funnier, more frightening.

Among the nonsense sciences that Miss Margarida imparts to us, an occasional bit of witty wisdom falls pleasantly on our ears: "Biology is, of course, the science of life. No, the science of other people's lives. The science of our own lives is called medicine." The trouble with such diamond chips is that they are too small to make a gem of; still, they would glisten amiably if they were not intermingled with such unscintillating obviousnesses as, "We are extremely lucky in this class: every one of you is at least semiliterate." And, having learned his lesson from Beckett—a monologue play needs a little something or someone else to relieve its monotony—Athayde gives us a nonspeaking student planted in the audience, but this part contributes little to the evening.

What helps more is the performance of Estelle Parsons. The actress creates a blowsy monster, a cozy psychotic, a caricature larger than life-size yet real and forlorn enough for us to feel eventually a mite sorry for her. She wheedles as well as she fulminates, and she has an infantile aspect to her delivery, so that you begin to wonder—appropriately—whether the deleterious fairy tales she purveys are not meant to lull her own insecurities as much as her pupils' ignorance. Miss Parsons improvises amusingly with latecomers and those of the spectators who rise to the challenge to speak up or heckle. But this is where the playwright has made his worst miscalculation: by writing his play and, in his added capacity as director, staging it (with enough additional plants in the audience besides the main student to turn the auditorium into a veritable hothouse) so as to encourage audiences to improvise insults and witticisms at the teacher's expense, we get interjections that on both nights I attended (downtown and now uptown) made the worst lines of the play seem deep by comparison.

Perhaps that was his intention: to show us that we are stupid enough to deserve every Miss Margarida that comes our way. But by augmenting his own frequently feeble lines with the audience's many witlessnesses, he provides an event that sinks slowly but steadily into irredeemable inanity.

The Gin Game

Some plays are plays; others, merely vehicles. The Gin Game, a first effort by D. L. Coburn, is resolutely of the latter kind. It concerns two inmates of an old folks' home. The man, Weller Martin, lives for gin rummy now; the woman, Fonsia Dorsey (the names are better written than anything else), is willing to learn the game. They play, and miraculously—or contrivedly—she keeps winning. Through a series of gin-rummy sessions on the home's otherwise deserted back porch, the two oldsters play, grumble, become friends, quarrel, strip away each other's self-delusions, forgive and forsake each other, parted by the card game that brought them together. I think there is an allegory lurking in there somewhere; if so, I don't want to know it: the play is brittle enough without the added burden of pretentiousness.

The dialogue and characterization have their funny, or at least bittersweet-verging-on-wry, moments: "Do you like stewed tomatoes?... No." "I never talked to anyone who did." Or, better yet, "I don't take *my* medicine anymore. Only *our* medicine." But the card marathon drags on and on, with the author playing every deuce in his pack as if it were an ace or a joker. Pretty soon every line sounds like a repeat of a previous one or the verbalization of something we saw coming. *The Gin Game* feels like a prizewinning play in a provincial drama contest whose judges were Neil Simon, Robert Anderson, and Michael Cristofer.

It is staged, however, with almost indecent (because wasted) expertise by Mike Nichols, and acted to individual and joint near perfection by Hume Cronyn and Jessica Tandy. Miss Tandy plays it perhaps a shade too young, too fetching and sprightly. But her timing and emphases are magisterial, always managing to combine dead-center accuracy with a touch of the deliciously unexpected. Mr. Cronyn is a bit more conventional in his approach, but he is really old, with an easefully enacted excruciation, and he can make orneriness as touching as sweetness—more so, in fact. You could do worse than watch the chronic tandem of Tandy and Cronyn; after a while, you can even forget about the play and relax. And if your mind wanders, you can always relish the perfection in seediness of David Mitchell's set, pertinently lighted by Ronald Wallace.

Dracula; A Life in the Theater

There may be some little value in reviving *Dracula* straight; there is no good reason (though there is a bad one) for camping it up. If this half-century-old, rather silly boulevard play were mounted straightforwardly and done with the naive conviction with which it was originally performed, we could both smile at the innocence of past theater and reflect wryly on what most of today's hits will look like 50 years hence, should somebody choose to unearth them at all. But, for this effect, the material must not be kidded; everyone must be dead, or perhaps undead, serious.

Instead, the producers and the director, Dennis Rosa, have camped up the proceedings ferociously. We open, for instance, with a pantomime scene that cannot be in the Deane and Balderston original version, and is rather like a sophomoric parody of Noël Coward; presently, we are in the play proper, but with mugging and sashaying, quivering and quavering, and enough eyeball rolling to look like a bowling alley in miniature. And camp is there even before the actors commence: in Edward Gorey's sets and (though these are better) costumes. The scenery cheats shamelessly: rather than being the combination sanatorium and home of Dr. Seward and his daughter, it is riddled with bats and saddled with ghoulies (bat-winged putti!) as if it were Dracula's castle instead of the temple of Hippocrates. It is further misguided by being all black and white (except for a drop of red always—Oh, symbol-mindedness!), which is dull to look at; and it is all Gorey drawings—Gorey blown up to mammoth size. Now, Gorey drawings are fine in their proper place and format; here they look like postage stamps carrying on as if they were Picasso's *Guernica*—a sort of farcical megalomania that is the essence of camp.

It is all like having two fingers shoved into our solar plexus while being commanded to laugh. And the acting is likewise both nudging and inept. Dillon Evans, who plays Dr. Seward, should act only in plays with vividly colored sets; here, with Gorey's grays, he tends to disappear into the scenery. As his speciously endangered daughter, Ann Sachs is a curious ingenue indeed, looking 60 from some angles, like a boy from others, and from nowhere like an actress. Her performance is mostly mincing, as if she were portraying not Lucy but a Cuisinart. The lesser roles are performed in best summer-theater fashion, far too frail for autumn, Gretchen Oehler's bouts with cockney being particularly doomed.

As Van Helsing, the vampire slayer, Jerome Dempsey cuts a comic figure, all bloatedness and bombast, in a performance geared a little more at Macy's Thanksgiving parade than at the stage. As Dracula, Frank Langella is half right. His head does manage to look like a mummy's, he moves lithely, and he knows how to be menacing even while cowering. He also delivers some of his lines with appropriately acrid bonhomie. But he is not truly threatening, either sexually or murderously. There is no suggestion of lethal force or heterosexual fascination; moreover, there is a curious kind of narcissism here (abetted by the front-and-center staging)—as if, not being able to see himself reflected in mirrors, this Dracula desperately sought his image in the audience's rapt gaze.

But all this camp, as I suggested, does serve a purpose: not only bats but other flitty creatures as well seem to be irresistibly drawn to it. Personally, I found only one thing of interest: the charming and balanced performance, almost untouched by the wrongheaded direction of the personable Alan Coates as Jonathan Harker. If you have to see a *Dracula* of some sort, and if your intention is not to go on to the nearby Gilded Grape, you might as well catch the vastly preferable *Passion of Dracula* downtown—though even that is less than a must.

David Mamet is our current most promising playwright, following in the footsteps set down by John Guare, Israel Horovitz, and Sam Shepard before him. Let me hope that he will be better at keeping his promises than they seem to have been, and someday give us more than the pale fire his *A Life in the Theater* provides. We all know by now that Mamet can sail the currents and undercurrents of dialogue like an expert navigator; but for a playwright to become arrested on the level of the perfect ear is not enough. Neither through the world nor through the theater can you go as a giant, headless and bodiless, ear; and a play is not a come-as-you-hear party.

This is a series of vignettes, showing us an older, proudly de-clining actor and a young and ambitiously climbing one in their on- and offstage relationships. Each uses and abuses the other as best he can, with Robert, the descending one, in precarious control at first, gradually superseded and humbled by the ascending John. Vignettes etched in vitriol, then, recording every sentimental com-monplace of the theater as it happens during performance, in the wings, in dressing rooms, or on the darkened stage presided over by the little caged moon of the work light. Comforting platitudes, bur-lesque mishaps, grease-painted lies from among which a grinning truth now and then sallies on its deadly mission—all the love-hate of fellow actors is here in its gaudy sadomasochism, scarcely less lacerating for being platonic.

But Mamet gives away the show by the very fact that these, like almost all the scenes in every one of his plays, are duologues. Not dialogue, which any number can play, but duologues, with two—al-ways two—Mamet characters batting their slightly souped-up plati-tudes back and forth. We get tired of this Ping-Pong and yearn for a little verbal football or basketball, something more team-oriented and teeming with life, not always pared down to pairs by an author who is geared only to batting around words, rather than the battles and free-for-alls of larger issues and involvements. Is Mamet still waiting for Sophocles to introduce the third actor into the drama?

Beyond that, *A Life in the Theater* suffers from being, ultimately, only a compendium of all the timeless absurdities of the theater—old jokes to most of us, and fascinating only to the very sentimental or the very inexperienced and stagestruck. Neither actor is ever allowed to acquire a full personality, a life beyond that of lines in a graph, or a mannequin and mouthpiece for Mamet's jokey didacticism. Under their constantly changing costumes and civvies, Robert and John are merely people-shaped gags. Ellis Rabb plays Robert well if he is meant to be a fruity old ham or hammy old fruit, and Peter Evans is a good John if he is supposed to be amorphous under his ambitiousness—matters the author might have made clearer. John Lee Beatty's scenery, John David Ridge's costumes, Pat Collins's lighting, and Robert Waldman's incidental music combine expertly under Gerald Gutierrez's direction into genuine theatrical sleight of hand. But the writing remains too slight and offhand.

The Act

Imagine the incestuous marriage of TV and Las Vegas and, next, their idiotic progeny; you now have a perfect picture of *The Act*. If ever a supposed Broadway musical looked like a cross between a less than spectacular television spectacular and a dry-as-dust show at the Sands or the Desert Inn, this vulgar concoction, which comes to us burdened with disastrous out-of-town reviews, is it. After two dropped titles and one dropped director, after all kinds of cuts and redesigned costumes, *The Act* is here, and as welcome as an act of God—say, a drought or a hurricane.

Let us start with its main—almost its only—selling point: Liza Minnelli. I always thought Miss Minnelli's face deserving—of first prize in the beagle category. Less aphoristically speaking, it is a face going off in three directions simultaneously: the nose always en route to becoming a trunk, blubber lips unable to resist the pull of gravity, and a chin trying its damnedest to withdraw into the neck, apparently to avoid responsibility for what goes on above it. It is, like any face, one that could be redeemed by genuine talent, but Miss Minnelli has only brashness, pathos, and energy.

The brashness is of the manic variety, a mask for insecurity, self-doubt, hollowness; as such, it appeals to all fellow sufferers of inferiority feelings, deserved or not. The pathos consists of playing the waif, the lonesome offspring of famous and otherwise occupied parents; of being, when the time comes, an octogenarian orphan. The energy consists of belting out songs in the way inherited from Mother, though the fact that much of the show is lip-synced helps. Above all, there is a continuous playing up to the audience: love me, applaud me, cheer me on, sustain me, for without you I am nothing. But just how much more, I wonder, is nothing plus audience adulation?

The entire show, we learn gradually, is a Las Vegas act, during which the performer, Michelle Craig, relives her struggle to make it as a movie star, marriage to her debonair but always traveling producer-Svengali, cinematic success with his help, and emotional starvation. Then a miscarriage leading to barrenness—which, naturally in such shows, means utmost frustration; next, playing around with, and being abandoned by, an unworthy lover; divorce; career slippage; and, finally, at the concerned ex-husband's suggestion, a big nightclub act—this. And at the very end, of course, ovations, remarriage to ex-hubby, and blessedness forevermore. This is all enacted down front, between song and dance numbers, with the orchestra onstage; it is wrought by George Furth (author of the equally shallow book for *Company*) out of desiccated witticisms and overstuffed platitudes.

But this is not what matters here; what matters is that the whole show is conceived as a vast but facile ambiguity. Everything is so arranged that we should never be sure whether what is said and sung to us emanates from Michelle Craig or from Liza Minnelli. The character of Michelle is made to resemble as much as possible the persona Liza has been projecting, and whatever she says to the imaginary Las Vegas audience applies also to the people out front at the Majestic. If little things seem to go wrong onstage, the joke lies always in that this could be a spontaneous mishap rather than a scripted one. The air is heavy with carefully rehearsed improvisation—is this towel that a disembodied hand proffers from the wings offered to a sweat-drenched Michelle or to a dripping Liza, we wonder, while the show waits for her to wipe herself off?

At the very end, this namby-pambiguity reaches colossal heights. We think the show is over, as Liza goes up to the onstage conductor and introduces him to the audience by his real name, Stanley Lebowsky. Before that, she has made a superbly clichéd this-is-the-most-exciting-evening-of-my-life-thank-you-all-so-very-much speech at the Las Vegas cum New York audience. Now wonderful

Stanley Lebowsky moseys over to the piano and starts playing in a dim spotlight. Meanwhile Liza has ensconced herself on a modest chair she has dragged into a refulgent spotlight. She assumes a centripetal, scrunched-up position befitting an embryo or Judy Garland, and announces tremulously that she is now going to sing a very special song. There are more catches in her voice than in a standard old-time MGM contract.

With a sinking feeling we anticipate "Over the Rainbow," but no! It is to be a song by Nat Schreiber (a character in the show—a homosexual songwriter who adored Michelle so much that he worked himself, literally, to death over her act, expiring at the accompanist's piano during a rehearsal)—yes, part of the play, after all! But wait: they were not going to use it in the show, Michelle says, because she wasn't ready or grown-up enough for it (or some such drivel). But *now* she is. So it's really our own little Liza, who, *presto magico*, will change from girl-child into girl-woman before our very eyes. And, sure enough, the audience that has been giving Minnelli fragments of standing ovations (a few strategically planted claqueurs rise here and there in the auditorium, and dozens of true believers follow suit) after several numbers now loses all sense of proportion. "We love you, Liza!" and similar outcries are tossed stageward.

And there, ladies and gentlemen, is the end of theater. Theater which has labored long and hard to create illusions of reality for our edification and delight: theater which, through the art of the author and actor, has presented us with lives against which we can measure our own, is suddenly reduced to a cheap farce, a travesty of drama, a star turn, a nightclub act. What do the crowds roaring inside and thronging outside the Majestic Theater care about *The Act* or Michelle Craig, or anything except the blooming, bleeding, barnstorming ego of their darling Liza, Liza, Liza, a loud and barely talented near-nonentity, born to Judy Garland and Vincente Minnelli, and borne aloft by waves of bad taste that never ebb?

Ah, and speaking of ebb, there are the songs of Fred Ebb (lyrics) and John Kander (music), derivative when tuneful and tuneless when original; as for the lyrics, they come in two varieties: feelingful (e.g., "Someone to lean on. / Really rely on: / A shoulder to cry on") and witty (e.g., "Of course, I could be wrong, / But I think he comes on strong / Because his thing is not too long"). Then there are the sets by the usually impressive Tony Walton, which, though they move interestingly, are basically ugly, but with the built-in excuse that "this is Vegas, don't you know?" Worse yet are the garish

costumes by Halston, simplistic and blaring, progressively petrify-
ing into paillettes and vinyl, until the whole show seems laminated
and ready to be mounted as a relic in a rumpus room. And again
the crude inbreeding of an Ebb lyric that actually pays homage to
the costume designer by naming him.

Then there is the chorus line, consisting of four singularly unappealing boys and three equally unalluring blond girls (to make the
star stand out as a horse of a different color), and there can no longer be any doubt about the anti-aesthetics governing the show: no
patch of beauty must detract from the wonderful natural ugliness at
its center. Even the choreography, by that Vegas wizard Ron Lewis,
has less to do with dancing than with suggestive contortions and
the use of sundry props—sometimes quite ingenious, but almost
always relating to dance as the crasser kind of poster art relates to
painting. At its least tasteful, in "Arthur in the Afternoon," it even
becomes a male striptease.

The show was originally directed by Martin Scorsese, but the
out-of-town reviews that proclaimed his stage directing vastly inferior to his film work were unfair to him. Anyone who has seen *New
York, New York*, of which *The Act* is a spinoff, must recognize that
Scorsese's stage work is every bit as slick as his film directing. No
wonder Gower Champion was called in to redirect it, and I firmly
believe that the few touches of invention and grace that strayed into
the show are attributable to him.

There are also two quasi-acting roles in *The Act*. Arnold Soboloff
plays the undernourished part of the homosexual songwriter with
the appropriate anorexia; Barry Nelson, as the producer-husband
always on the move between London and Los Angeles, clearly considers his every scene a stopover between two connecting flights
that cannot connect soon enough. Always an exponent of the casual
school of performing, he now sprays his lines about as through a
built-in sprinkler system. At least someone had the good sense to
put the orchestra onstage; that way there is always something going
on. Whether it is worth the $25 top is, of course, another question.
Through most of the show I kept my courage up by thinking, Well,
at least she's not Barbra Streisand. Eventually, this changed to If only
she were Barbra Streisand!

Miss Sabina Harbison, upset by my review of Liza Minnelli in *The Act*, came to interview me about my critical tenets

Recently I had a visit from Miss Sabina Harbison, the well-known Patagonian press agent, who, having been upset by my review of Liza Minnelli in *The Act*, came to interview me about my critical tenets.

SABINA: First of all, I wanted to see what a chap who can find fault with a performer's face looks like himself.

SIMON: Much as I am dying to find out what you think, don't bother to tell me. A critic is not selling his looks on stage or screen as a performer is; so they are irrelevant.

SABINA: But, surely, Miss Minnelli is not selling her looks either. She is doing a part and should be judged on her performance alone.

SIMON: I don't think it's as simple as that. Would you say a performance includes the way an actress walks?

SABINA: Yes, but walking is something you learn—properly or improperly. It's a skill and, as such, fair subject for criticism. Whatever training can do, we have the right to expect from a professional.

SIMON: Agreed. Will you also concede that the objection to an ungainly walk is of an aesthetic order—just as your objection to ill-designed costumes would be?

SABINA: Certainly. But what have costumes to do with faces?

SIMON: Everything. I go to the theater to see beauty—in costumes, scenery, walks, faces, unless the situation specifically calls for something else. And if we are allowed to invoke aesthetic criteria where other things presented onstage are concerned, why should faces be taboo?

SABINA: You don't understand. If Minnelli is terrific in every other way, what do her ears or shoulders matter? Must every actress be beautiful?

SIMON: Of course, if you are a major talent, you rise above looks. Or, rather, you are able to *enact* them, just as you can act out clumsiness or intellectual passion. And I agree that the enactment of beauty is perhaps more thrilling to watch than sheer natural beauty, though I wouldn't sneeze at that either. Unfortunately, there are few performers around with that much talent, and Liza, in my view, is very far from being one of them. Furthermore, if a part does not call for good looks—if, indeed, it explicitly calls for the opposite—that's another matter. But there are not many such leading roles.

SABINA: Why do you say that? Where is it written that Michelle Craig, whom Liza portrays in *The Act*, is a beauty, or anything like it?

SIMON: I think that any leading man or woman, unless otherwise specified, should be attractive. There are several reasons for this. As I wrote in my book *Singularities*:

> Let us not speak slightingly of physical beauty just because there is something called spiritual beauty that is generally conceded to be a much finer thing. In any case, spiritual beauty is not all that useful to an actress: it is a slow worker, and in the two hours or so an actress holds the stage it might barely begin to make its presence felt. But physical beauty, as if aware of its transience, wastes no time in casting its spell.

You see, most heroines of plays markedly attract men. Michelle Craig, for instance, is a star, and has a husband, a lover, a principal dancer—even a homosexual songwriter—all gravitating toward her in various ways. So there is also the question of verisimilitude. But, mostly, I want to look at beauty, unless I'm watching a play about an ugly duckling; I want a total aesthetic experience.

SABINA: But those are *your* aesthetics. Minnelli and Streisand, both of whom you deplore, happen to be the two most bankable female stars.

SIMON: That is a sad comment on our society. Just think for a moment. Think of the leading actresses on whom Hollywood once based its reputation; but never mind Hollywood, let's stick with Broadway: how lovely in their various ways were Julie Haydon, Ethel Barrymore, Katharine Cornell, Lynn Fontanne, Laurette Taylor, Helen Hayes, and the rest.

SABINA: But those were dramatic actresses; Liza sings and dances.

SIMON: Very well, then, what about Gertrude Lawrence, not a pretty woman, but one whose exquisite charm and talent made everyone believe for decades that she was beautiful? And what about someone like Edith Piaf, whose outright homeliness was transfigured through sheer artistry of song and expression— without even moving about—into heartbreaking beauty?

SABINA: Let's say I concede your point for the sake of argument, but what about all those theatergoers who find Liza cute, delicious, sexy? Isn't it all just a question of taste?

SIMON: Yes—or of the lack of it. A critic speaks merely for himself, for his own taste. Then why is it all right to tell a writer that his play is trash? Critics, after all, can seriously affect an author's chances, but I doubt whether they have the slightest effect on a performer's love or sex life, no matter what they say.

SABINA: And I doubt that you turn away anyone from Liza's box office either, no matter what you say about her looks. The crowds who adore her will go on doing so, and just ignore you.

SIMON: Oh, absolutely. Most people do not read criticism, anyway; or only for the wrong reason: should I spend X dollars on this show or not? But no critic can tell them that. Even where a critic is generally agreed with, there is always a sense of letdown in specific cases. No, what a critic can and should do is make you think as you read him, develop your own ideas and taste in agreement or disagreement, or a mixture of the two.

SABINA: And how, pray tell, is an attack on a performer's physique going to make a reader evolve in his understanding of theater?

SIMON: In one of two ways. Either the reader comes to agree, however reluctantly, that a face and body are important aesthetic components of the theatrical experience; or the reader may reassert and strengthen his convictions that a performer's looks don't matter in the least. Personally, I have always considered the sensibilities of that princess who could feel a pea under all those mattresses enviably superior to mine. I, alas, wouldn't have been bothered by a watermelon.

SABINA: Suppose all were as you say; is there any need for a critic to be rude?

SIMON: It all depends on your notion of what is rude. If theater is profoundly important to you, a matter of aesthetic and spiritual survival, you do not want to see it polluted in any way. And you speak up in the least uncertain terms you can muster. Of course, it is a question of context. At a party, it would be bad manners to criticize a person's looks—the person isn't selling them on stage or screen as part of an aesthetic-artistic experience. Again, at a party I wouldn't care how much a surgeon's hands might shake. In the operating room, however...

SABINA: But everyone can see that a patient is dead. Doesn't it bother you that thousands, millions cheer Liza—as do many of your fellow critics?

SIMON: A large part of that is hype. If someone or something gets enough publicity in our society, it doesn't matter if the person is insignificant or if the thing causes lung cancer. He, she, or it fascinates, dazzles, and sells. Besides, people are both egotistic and insecure: they don't care what ferocious things you say about a playwright or director—after all, *they* don't write or direct plays. But they all have faces and can easily feel threatened by an attack on a face.

SABINA: Well, I'm sorry, but I still disagree. Liza looks just fine to me.

Knowing an impasse when I see one, I politely escorted Miss Harbison to the door. Though I noted her homeliness, I naturally said nothing. She was not selling her looks as an actress.

Uncommon Women and Others

Go tell it on the mountain, or at least on Mount Holyoke: two plays by Holyoke alumnae have opened in New York in as many weeks. Of the two, by far the better is *Uncommon Women and Others*, by Wendy Wasserstein, given a limited run by the Phoenix Theater. Although I suppose Carol K. Mack, the author of the other play, to have been a rather earlier Holyoke graduate, I like to imagine Wasserstein and Mack in the same classroom: the latter sedulously attentive, the former winging her way through on wit and bluff.

In any case, *Uncommon Women* begins with five Holyoke alumnae meeting in a restaurant six years after graduation. They comment on their respective development or nondevelopment, reminisce about absent friends and foes, and are presently transported back into their college days, only to return to the present at play's end. The prologue-play-epilogue construction is highly conventional, and, indeed, there is nothing uncommon about *Uncommon Women and Others*. In fact, Miss Wasserstein's problem is a very common one among young playwrights writing memory plays about themselves and friends when younger yet: nothing much has happened to them, and what has is far from unusual. Still, it matters to them, and they cannot see why it should not be equally fascinating to the rest of the world. But it isn't. When older authors, with more experience and greater perspective, look back at their pasts, they can find purposeful structures along with universal significance that would have eluded their less mature and distanced selves.

Miss Wasserstein has a chortlingly mischievous sense of outer and inner dialogue, of what these collegians said or merely thought; and she observes her characters, one of whom must be herself, with a nice blend of sympathy and unsentimentality. But there is no shape, no sense of direction, no purpose here, except recording something for memory's sake, which is all too private a pursuit. These girls, giggling, straining, wisecracking, or brazening their way through college and the last remnants of their childhood, are recognizable and likable creatures, but, give or take a bit, we know them already too well—even their existential surprises hold little dramatic surprise for us.

Yet the dialogue is brisk and sassy, the characters are mettlesome, giddy, and richly absurd. Only Susie Friend, the goody-goody one, and Carter, the weirdo, are exaggerated—though this may be more the director's doing than the author's; the others ring true, individually and together, but no larger, collective truth emerges. There is also a certain fuzziness about period: anachronisms pop up here and there. What is greatly to Wasserstein's credit, however, is that Mrs. Plum, the housemother, does not come out as a caricature: while kidding her, the playwright does not rob her of her humanity. And Josephine Nichols plays her to perfection, funnily but not ludicrously.

Almost all the acting is a joy. Mind you, most of these characters do not require immense imaginative leaps by their interpreters; still, how often do we not see actors unable to play even closer roles? Swoosie Kurtz is marvelous as the comic hedonist, an oversexed hellion not without the pathos of oversexed hellions. Her quizzical inflections and out-of-left-field timing are a delight. Jill Eikenberry, as the stunner and overachiever who is basically insecure, is superb. It is not easy to embody smoothly contrary extremes, but Miss Eikenberry, one of our loveliest and most gifted actresses, does it with a tremulous, humorless assiduity that is just right and obviously requires a great deal of humor and intelligence to achieve.

Everybody else is good, too, though I was especially pleased with Ellen Parker and Ann McDonough, both of them new to me, and both very able to infuse considerable refinement into parts that lent themselves to obviousness. Would that Steven Robman had directed with a slightly more acute sense of pacing, but no matter: the fun, though small-scale, was genuine.

Cold Storage

If *Cold Storage* had a second act up to its first, it would be one hell of a play. But even if the first act were no better than the second, you could still do a lot worse than see this show. Ronald Ribman is one of our most interesting wildly uneven playwrights: at his worst, he'll drive you up the slipperiest wall in no time; at his best, as in the first act of the present play, he can keep you laughing and thinking simultaneously, which is one of the better stunts in a playwright's bag of tricks. *Cold Storage* is about two men in the cancer ward of a Manhattan hospital. Parmigian, a veteran of six months' dying, is really proficient at it—not so much because of the experience he has acquired as because of his inquiring spirit and irrepressible gallows humor. Landau, a new arrival, won't even face up to lethal reality; a civil but withdrawn man, he insists that he is only in for something exploratory.

The two men cross verbiage in the roof garden, which Parmigian, an Armenian fruit dealer who says he has read all the books (and may indeed have read a few crates of them), has all to himself—the other patients can't stand his wildly inventive but sardonically unsettling banter. Landau, defying hospital rules, in a Bloomingdale's robe, and refusing to settle into the sort of wheelchair Parmigian has made himself a nest of, has ventured into the garden unaware of the combination vaudeville, psychoanalysis, and outright provocation the older man will subject him to. Landau endures Parmigian's ribald and prying shock treatment, but his skeptical wit enables him to give almost as good as he takes.

Landau is an investment adviser in the fine arts; he has a job, wife, and children to whom he wants to return as fast as possible. But he also has something gnawing on his insides: a secret that is worse, perhaps, than cancer. With teasing, badgering, and sometimes insults, Parmigian worms it out of him. Landau's parents and sister perished in the Holocaust; they saved him at a supreme cost to themselves, and his survival is now a pall of guilt to him. Here, I think, Ribman is at his least convincing. Altogether, the Holocaust as a dramatic device may need to be laid to rest next to the atom bomb; it has served, both well and badly, in too many plays, novels, and films, and, for a while at least, has exhausted its potency. It is now too much like a medal from several wars ago pinned to a bulging, bourgeois dinner jacket. And Ribman doesn't even manage it well; he seems to me to have his facts about wartime Portugal wrong.

There are other facts he certainly mangles. The entire art world appears to be alien to him. What kind of an art adviser, for instance, would not know the difference between Pieter Bruegel (whom Len Cariou, who plays Landau, totally mispronounces; but, then, he doesn't do so well even with cloisonné) and Jan van der Heyden, born more than a century after Bruegel, and not resembling him at all? And what kind of an arts department (a rather vague term, by the way, for Landau's place of work) would have half of its members getting the hots when a pretty woman bends over? The arts department in which heterosexual males are not a modest minority hasn't been invented yet. Even about hospital matters Ribman is a bit shaky: one does not get a stomach x-ray on a full stomach in the evening, but in the morning, on an empty one.

I am not convinced, either, by the rather too facile bit of therapy with which Parmigian exorcises Landau's trauma; but I am moved by the revelation that Parmigian, the seemingly self-assured joker, needs someone else—be it only the evasive Landau—in the end. And most of the interplay between the two men does ring true: I can believe both the play's rowdiness and its gentleness. Unlike, say, *The Shadow Box*, in which neither death nor life rings true, *Cold Storage* succeeds in doing justice to both.

As Parmigian, Martin Balsam gives a stunning performance that does not minimize the man's exasperating officiousness, yet allows him to be all the more authentic, and even winning, for having his flaw. I don't know whether the character he creates is as Armenian as he seems Jewish, and whether he is not written a little too cleverly for what he is meant to be. But the man is truly unforgettable: He has both bulk and grace. His bulk repels the indignities of illness, hospitalization, and hopelessness; his grace enables him to swim rather than sink into oblivion.

Len Cariou is compelling as Landau as long as he is tense, superior, and unwillingly amused by Parmigian; when he has to turn irate and agonized, however, his ire emerges a bit too loud, his agony a trifle too mechanistic. As a nurse, Ruth Rivera is less interesting than Julie Carmen was in the original American Place Theater production, since which, though, the author has wisely excised a supererogatory prologue, although his other changes may be less felicitous. Frank Corsaro's direction would be fine but for some hyped-up movement: those are, after all, wheelchairs, not bumper cars. And how can Parmigian sip forever from one little hospital bottle without a refill?

Karl Eigsti has designed the very best in hospital roof gardens (I can't help preferring Kert Lundell's more depressing set for the APT); William Mintzer's lighting is very finely modulated. But what really lights up the evening is the playful intelligence of the writing, and the articulate energy of the performances.

On the Twentieth Century

On the Twentieth Century is a real musical comedy: it has pizzazz and razzle-dazzle, bursts of energy and invention, music and laughter, and good, expensive production values. It does not go in for that dubious kind of innovativeness that, on Broadway, usually means no more than cutting corners—say, with a clever little unit set that, by means of projections or dismantling and reassembling, becomes transformed. Instead, there are real, lavish sets in grand, gratuitous excess.

This, then, is to musicals what a movie-movie is to films; but, somehow, musical-musical has no ring to it, which *On the Twentieth Century* certainly has. It is a musicalization of the well-known Hecht-MacArthur play that gave rise to the well-known movie (with Lombard and Barrymore), which brought about the well-known Broadway revival (with Swanson and Ferrer), which may have led to this musical that will become well known—but perhaps not *very* well known, for want of a more consistently good first act and slightly more consequential music.

The plot concerns—as any man whose soul is not dead, and who can still breathe despite the air pollution, will recall—Oscar Jaffee, a now rich, now broke, lovable rascal of a Broadway producer, escaping from a Chicago flop and his latest batch of creditors on the Twentieth Century Limited, the crack train to New York (the time is the early 1930s). He finagles his way into getting the stateroom next to that of Lily Garland, his onetime discovery and mistress, now a big Hollywood star and Jaffee-hater. The trick is to cook up a project, get Lily to put her gilt-edged name on the contract, and raise money on that. (Steps two and three are reversible.) On Jaffee's team are Owen and Oliver, his two trusty, but by now disconsolate, henchmen; on Lily's team are her latest cardboard lover (the aspiring movie star Bruce Granit), a sassy maid, and a rival producer named Max Jacobs. Two shrewdies, then, are plotting and counterplotting; caught in the middle are various passengers and personnel of the New York-bound train.

There are comic encounters and farcical twists; there are also jolly flashbacks to Oscar and Lily's past history, and fantasy sequences about what might happen in the future. The way it is all written, directed, and acted, it falls somewhere between high and low camp; let's call it middle camp. It is always brash, often funny, sometimes vulgar, occasionally inspired, and, for a stretch in the first act, flaccid. But this good, though not great, musical has atypically a better second act than first—one that goes from strength to strength, and merely ends limply. It is possible not to enjoy the show enormously, but even Queen Victoria would have been amused by much of it. The Betty Comden-Adolph Green lyrics are always civilized fun, and if the Cy Coleman tunes are less than memorable, they are at least musical, which cannot be said for many other current scores.

Harold Prince has provided lively direction, well spiced with the salt of old gags and the pepper of newish ones. Robin Wagner, who once before charmed us with his train sets for *Sugar*, has come up with even grander designs, showing the train from all angles and various distances to create the effect of a film with fast cutting. There are also rousing simulations of train movement, suggestions of the black but light-studded night that covers the travelers from (telegraph) pole to pole, and a joyous evocation of Art Deco wherever possible. To all this, Florence Klotz's costumes and Ken Billington's lighting lend enthusiastic support. There are also decent but sparing dances from Larry Fuller, and good and raucous orchestrations from Hershy Kay.

As Oscar Jaffee, John Cullum gives his best performance to date. If it does seem, consciously or unconsciously, derivative of John Barrymore's, that is a good source to draw from, and Cullum contributes his own nice timing and verve. He may not look quite old and battered enough for the part, but in a musical version this matters less than it would in a production of the play. As Lily, Madeline Kahn is rather too campy for my money both in appearance and in demeanor (I would love to have seen what Marcia Rodd or Blythe Danner could have done with the part), and in her first flashback scene she is downright offensive. But she gets better as she and the train hurtle along; if she did not indulge in periodic campy gurgling and shrilling during the songs—thereby losing the odd lyric—she would probably do. Still, it would be nice if Broadway leading ladies could occasionally represent the heterosexual image of women.

The religious fanatic has been turned into a woman here, perhaps to oblige Imogene Coca. Miss Coca is an acquired taste that I never quite acquired; but her numerous fans in the audience were lapping her up like cola. Supporting parts are all well handled, and Kevin Kline as Bruce, Lily's Errol Flynnish paramour and parasite, very nearly steals the show. The part depends heavily on pantomime, pratfalls, twistings and turnings, double-jointedness—it is almost danced rather than acted—and Kline proves himself the worthy heir of the silent-screen comedians. Bravo! The Twentieth Century may have been Limited, but there is limitless exuberance to *On the Twentieth Century.*

Deathtrap; *Museum*

How do you write about Ira Levin's new thriller, *Deathtrap*, without spilling the beans, which would be unsporting as well as unhygienic? It concerns a formerly successful, now burnt-out mystery playwright; a young disciple who sends him a play clearly destined to become a Broadway smash, for which the older man resolves to kill him; and the stale playwright's disapproving wife, who has strong scruples and a weak heart. At this point—which, mind you, is very near the beginning—twists and reversals relentlessly take over, and giving them away is neither cricket not criticism. Though, truth to tell, you wouldn't buy any of these peripeteias, and some of them I couldn't even give away.

To complicate the reversals, we have also a Dutch psychic inhabiting the one neighboring house—the scene is a section of Westport, Connecticut, apparently as isolated as the least chic part of the
Gran Chaco—for reasons as unconvincing as everything else about
the play. She keeps rushing over to stick her ESP into other people's
monkey business. The fifth character, or wheel, is a family lawyer
with dramaturgical aspirations. The play that the disciple has allegedly written is also called *Deathtrap*, and also has five characters: I
trust you perceive the symbolic parallel. Only the inner *Deathtrap*
is said to be a sure hit, which is where the parallel ends.

The plot, in short, is impossible. Are the characters less so? The
only figure even slightly more complex than pulling out the spout
of a box of granulated sugar is the fading writer, Sidney Bruhl. Although there is no sign in Sidney Bruhl's window, there are some
signs of wit in his lines. That, however, is not enough to make him
remotely believable: his switches from ordinariness to Machiavel-
lianism, diabolic cleverness to ineptitude, hetero- to homosexuality,
are far too meteoric.

Nevertheless, he does have a few good laugh lines, and even the
less clever characters are allowed their quota of chuckles. Moreover, Levin is at times successful in topping his laughs. After Bruhl
remarks about his acolyte's play, "Can't miss—a gifted director
couldn't even hurt it," he asseverates that nothing could go wrong
with a play that will clearly star Liv Ullmann and George C. Scott;
"Trish Van Devere?" his wife shyly interjects (referring to Scott's
less-talented but usually nepotistically cast wife). There is quite a
bit of this sort of thing throughout—not bad as far as it goes, save
that you can't make a suit out of wadding.

Bruhl is played by John Wood, the excellent British comedian,
whose intensely British accent in Westport is limply explained by
one Canadian parent. Although Wood deploys a prodigal excess of
technique, the result is not convincing, merely faintly unappetizing.
His tearing into, then slowly masticating, indeed worrying each
superficial retort or spurious epigram suggest not so much great
acting as nasty eating habits. The other cast members do what they
can with not very rewarding material. Though Marian Winters's
Dutch accent sounds rather too Norwegian, this is more than made
up for by the general double Dutch.

There is, of course, a basic problem with the comedy-mystery
genre, wherein the laughs are supposed to lull you into a false security the chills can all the more scarily dissipate. Often, alas, the

comedy just makes the terror look less real, whereas the violence, if staged realistically (as it has to be), ends up looking unduly brutal in a context of frivolity. Some writers have mastered this complicated process of fusion, but they are usually from England, where there still survives a sophisticated cynicism that can accommodate weapons as disparate as the epigram and the revolver.

Robert Moore's staging is competent, and there are solid production values. But I wish that Levin, instead of writing a play about how one writes, or doesn't write, a mystery play, had written such a play. Or abstained.

Museum, by Tina Howe, at the Public Theater, is a civilized little play that accomplishes a good deal in a casual manner, with an irreverence whose surface is so glossy that it almost blinds us to the deeper, satirical intent—which may be a failing, but a venial one, surely. We are given a museum gallery where an avant-garde show is in its last day. We are also given a rogue's gallery of museum visitors, guards, curators, artists. The play is both a medieval *theatrum mundi* and a wry view of modern art. Miss Howe has a wicked ear for the clichés of art talk, as we get them from cocktail-party pundits and (virtually identically) from current art criticism. With admirable equity, she reduces people and paintings to compatible smithereens.

But her characters talk about other things as well, and, all together, constitute a composite portrait of human gullibility, obtuseness, pseudo-sophistication, and befuddlement. It is an urbane spoof, powerfully abetted by Robert Yodice's devilishly authentic museum setting, complete with phony art that no expert could distinguish from the equally phony real thing. The large acting ensemble, most of whom are double-cast, perform with skill and taste, especially Larry Bryggman and Lynn Milgrim. Max Stafford-Clark has directed with deftness and wit, and Jennifer Tipton's lighting captures the fishbowl quality of museum light. The play is recommended to theater lovers, contemporary art haters, and all other decent folk.

Dancin'

Dancin' is a musical without book, scenery, or a final "g." To dispense with the first two is possible; with the third, fatal. It indicates a forced casualness or arch folksiness—both forms of talking down—that may please a lot of audiences but costs Bob Fosse the difference between a mere crowd pleaser and a success of a higher order.

Fosse has picked music from all over: the score goes from Sousa (though not Persepolis) to (Melissa) Manchester and Bach, with stopovers at Varèse, Cohan, Cat Stevens, and various other whistle-stops. For this olio, Fosse has devised a heterogeneous choreography ranging from classical ballet through modern dance to every form of showbiz and disco dancin'. Some marriages are made in heaven, but others were clearly invented by the divorce courts; the blood wedding of ballet and popular dance has always gone a-courtin' disaster. It is different, of course, when a ballet choreographer absorbs, say, jazz idiom into the classical vocabulary; what doesn't work is the two side by side, like internecine Siamese twins. The proximity of popular dance gives ballet an air of pretentiousness; ballet retaliates by making pop dancing look facile and tawdry.

This is too bad. First, because Fosse, for all his specialization in the popular forms of dance, has clear talent for the other as well; second, because both idioms have their different but distinctive merits. But constant slipping from one into the other cheapens even the choreographer; it is as if he had to resort to the other when he runs out of ideas in the one. Yet ideas are precisely what Fosse has aplenty; he scatters them prodigally, with always yet another spare cornucopia up his sleeve or trouser leg. Some are, or seem, new; others are familiar, only because he invented or evolved them to perfection. Yet even the oldest come freshly alive as Fosse serves them up: a soft-shoe can look airier, wispier, softer as he frames it; a knee slide can, in context, take on the reverence of prayer.

But a unifying style, if not a book, is needed to keep a musical from splintering into a chaotic tug-of-war. Actually, though, *Dancin'* is not exactly bookless; the underlying book would seem to be the *Kama Sutra*, or some such sex manual, whose positions Fosse has choreographed. Whereas much of our dance invention has been tending toward the patently homosexual, Fosse carries heterosexuality to aggressive, obsessive, excessive lengths. This lands him, not infrequently, in sexuality left crudely untransfigured by art, as in a number set to a Bach chaconne during which a bumpkin of a ballet student has an orgiastic fantasy about his girl neighbor at the barre, and copulation thrives. Here, as elsewhere, Fosse also obtrudes spoken words on what should have been a show majoring in dance with a strong minor in singing. These words, written and sometimes spoken on tape by Fosse himself, are always supererogatory and often shy-making: good enough for a choreographer, perhaps, but not for a writer.

Dancers, like choreographers, should be seen, not heard. Thus when Charles Ward concludes a splendid bit of dancing by piping up in a reedily underdeveloped voice, anticlimax reaches a new, high-pitched low. This is not necessarily true of dancers' singing, some of which is quite creditable here although Wayne Cilento, for example, has a voice of shreds and tatters that lets a tune drop right through. Thus the potentially fetching "Mr. Bojangles" number—a good idea developed by Fosse with uncharacteristic schematism—ends up exasperatingly. Here the arrangement is also to blame; in fact, when Gordon Lowry Harrell and Ralph Burns, the arrangers, are not being overfancy (the only instrument they seem to have overlooked is the theorbo), they opt straightforwardly for piercing your eardrums.

But to get back to the sexiness. Fosse has picked women dancers, all of whom are gifted, and some of whom are also stunners. We all know what Ann Reinking can do with her swaggeringly sensual impudence of look and movement, and relish her aura of an A student in Sex Education with a lot of useful extra fieldwork under her belt; but here, too, is another sinuous and opulent temptress in Sandahl Bergman, who can curve her very feet with a fine surfeit of erotic abandon; and here, above all, is Vicki Frederick, who from her filigree nose to her magnanimous hips exudes a unique mixture of gamine and *femme fatale*, always at the service of a talent that puts emotional meaning into the meanest little choreographic commonplace.

Unfortunately, the men, though excellent dancers, tend to lack that indispensable gratuity (oxymoron intended!) of innate good looks. Cilento and John Mineo in particular lack visual charisma. But there is sassy sexual bravura in Willa Kim's costumes (when they do not go overboard); Peter Larkin's minimal décor twists itself into richly suggestive shapes; and Jules Fisher's lighting, particularly a sunset glow the like of which, even in nature, I saw only on a rainy evening in Florence, will leave you blinking with cozy disbelief. *Dancin'* is sheer perfection for the vulgarians, anathema for the purists, and a mixed bag for the overwhelming rest of us. There are tasty morsels like "Joint Endeavor," a Schnitzlerian *Reigen* in dance, and such crowd-pleasing tastelessnesses as that chaconne. Well, *chaconne à son goût*.

Catsplay

If Broadway producers had any sense at all, they would have snapped up *Catsplay*, which they could have caught either at Washington's Arena Theater or at the Guthrie in Minneapolis. Written by the Hungarian novelist-playwright István Örkény, it is artistically accomplished and meltingly humane; it cries out for the biggest and best exposure. Failing that, it is good of the Manhattan Theater Club, in conjunction with the New York Shakespeare Festival, to bring it to the premises of the former if only for a limited run, which may yet inspire some producer with even a limited intelligence to perceive the work's unlimited potential. Meanwhile, the present production is quite good enough to convince me that this is the best new play of the season.

The form is a seemingly novel one, epistolary drama. Epistolary novels are anything but novel, of course, and Örkény's work started out in that form; the transfer to drama is not entirely smooth. The action, sometimes a bit inactive, stems from the correspondence between two sisters. One is Erzsi (widow of Béla) Orbán, the concierge in what used to be her family's house in Budapest. The other is Giza, paralyzed from the waist down, and living as comfortably as one can in a wheelchair off her wealthy German industrialist son. Erzsi is the grasshopper, Giza the ant, and most of the time it looks as if the fable were once again to be proved right. Now well into her sixties, Erzsi loses her first and only love all over again; gets nothing but censure from her own antlike daughter; and lives in a world so petty and puny that even fantasies are miniaturized by it, such as playing at being a pair of amorous tabbies with Mousie, a dim, unfeline neighbor woman. But Erzsi survives in battered splendor because, in the words of Hungary's greatest poet, Endre Ady, she is one of those "unkissed ones who live in kisses."

Basically, this is a wonderfully old-fashioned play that deals in such antique commodities as sympathy for all of its characters—well, almost all; the eternal fascination of memories that, however uncertain and elusive, are yet life-sustaining; the glory of even the most foolish passion in an old woman who loves with the dewy-eyed incontinence of a schoolgirl; the defiances a gallant spirit hurls at the encroachments of mortality. How nice to see the problems of elderly people (Örkény himself is 66) depicted with the dignity and freshness usually reserved for the tribulations of the young or middle-aged. And all this with a humor grafted on sadness that produces a new tree: a laughing willow. *Catsplay* is full of aching laughter and mocking heartbreak, both equally exhilarating.

A play, then, about life that refuses to capitulate to any sort of betrayal—by friends, family, lovers, or even common sense. Erzsi can outwit swollen ankles just by trading in ugly orthopedic shoes for precariously dainty high heels; she can make reason armed with incontestable proof withdraw before her indomitable lies; and she can survive even suicide. Yet she is also capable of deviations into unblinking truth; she is, in short, Don Quixote and Sancho Panza rolled into one. And she is superlatively embodied by Helen Burns.

Miss Burns is a small, dumpy Englishwoman, neither young nor pretty. But these strictures are meaningless. As well chide the moon for being rotund when it is bursting its seams with radiance. The actress is all wily, crotchety life affirmation; all devious passion posturing as collectedness. The spirit of a slim gazelle leaps out of her bulbous body; her eyes are ceaselessly cajoling, conning, browbeating the world. She walks across level ground as if conquering a mountain peak, her face leaning into the winds of opposition, whether they are there or not. Her voice can go from bullying to wheedling within a fragile phrase; the diction is always exemplary, but without the elocutionist's smarminess. Before the evening is half over, she has become immense and beautiful through the sheer power of her performing.

There is other good acting, too. Katherine Squire brings great finesse to Giza, not allowing her cool reasonableness to freeze over, and not letting her ultimate confession of impotence play unduly on our sympathy. She and Miss Burns, despite obvious physical and psychic differences, convey true sisterhood—a lovely joint achievement. Bette Henritze is dead right as the meek little Mousie, who nevertheless nurtures seedlings of grandeur in the recesses of her insignificance. And Charles Mayer is fine as an aged waiter, his old-world serviceableness undimmed by the New Order. Susan Sharkey, a charming actress, has trouble with the part of the charmless daughter but does well enough, as does Eleanor Phelps, who is a bit too regal for an unregal part. Alas, Jane Cronin lapses into caricature, Robert Gerringer gives his customary stock performance, and Peter Phillips is simply inept.

Lynne Meadow has directed with economy and purposefulness in John Lee Beatty's modest but apt set. Jennifer von Mayrhauser's costumes are droll but uncondescending; Dennis Parichy's lighting is cannily inconspicuous. Especially gratifying is Clara Györgyei's translation, which never smacks of translation, and errs only once, with a "disinterested" for uninterested. Do not impoverish your year by missing what, though not a work of genius, will do nicely until one comes along.

The Best Little Whorehouse in Texas

Does the notion of a musical situated in a brothel make you grin from ear to ear? Does the idea of a kindly madam with strict rules against kinkiness and slovenliness set your heart going pitty-pat? Do you believe that if there is anything nicer than a whore with a heart of gold it is a whole whorehouseful of whores with hearts of gold? Or are you a Texan? In all the above cases you will love *The Best Little Whorehouse in Texas*; in all others, not.

Frankly, I find attempts to squeeze salaciousness out of a bordello setting at this late stage rather repellent, not because of the setting but because of the squeezing. It is like trying to squeeze blood out of stones: if you can do it, you're a thaumaturge deserving of our wonderment; but if you can't, and just stand there huffing and puffing, you're a damned fool. Every variation on the brothel theme has been worked into the ground—except in certain money-rich but culture-poor areas like Texas, where every day something new is discovered that is elsewhere a putrescent platitude. As the play's dreary jokes about whores and their clients, or the old jokes about crooked politicians, or (worst of all) the pathetic jokes depending on schoolboy scatology dribbled off the stage, the audience greeted them with salvos of sophomoric laughter.

It was an audience such as I had never seen at a Broadway opening night before. (Although the Entermedia Theater is actually Off Broadway, its considerable size makes it more like Broadway's best little house away from home.) There were ten-gallon hats galore, outlandish garb beggaring description, and faces that seemed never to have seen the inside of a theater before. And there was Liz Smith in what looked like a Nieman-Marcus cowboy suit with Texas catchwords colorfully embroidered on its white silk shirt.

Well, this audience responded with hoots and hollers to every G-rated naughtiness and Z-grade joke that threatened to make the Entermedia collapse like the Mercer Arts Center.

Let's take it from the top. The book is by Larry L. King, who wrote the original article about the Chicken Ranch brothel, which all the good Texans in and out of office tried to keep running until a meddlesome hypocrite of a reformer with a TV program forced the slippery governor to instruct the two-faced mayor to command the jovially foulmouthed, laissez-faire sheriff to order the nice Madam Mona to close her joint down; and by Peter Masterson, actor and member of Actors Studio, who persuaded his fellow Texan, King, to collaborate with him on a musicalization of the article. It is a book that once seems to have contained a good deal of plot, remnants of which still float around here and there—something about a whore who has a sweet child back home to whom she places loving long-distance calls, and about the Sheriff and Madam's romance back when Mona was just one of the girls working her way up—but now contains mostly gags on the order of "I'm gonna flatten him so he has to roll down his socks to shit!" or "I kin tell when someone's pissin' on mah boots an' tellin' me it's a rainstorm."

The score is by Carol Hall, another Texan, and it is about what you would expect: undistinguished country-and-western stuff, with one better than average number in it, "Hard Candy Christmas." The dances are by Tommy Tune, and they have a couple of moments, though their best invention is a gimmick: a chorus line of cheerleader-Angelettes—of whom two thirds are artificial dolls and one third living dolls. The difference is that the living dolls can almost answer simple questions, whereas the artificial dolls move with greater springiness. The staging is by Masterson and Tune, and it keeps the action moving along the multi-level, minimally attractive set by Marjorie Kellogg. Ann Roth's costumes and Dennis Parichy's lighting are functional enough, but the performances are mostly perfunctory.

In the leading role of Mona, Carlin Glynn has the advantage of being Texan, but the disadvantage of being rather colorless. Henderson Forsythe is fine as the Sheriff, but renders—or rends—his one song so pitifully that you wish he had appointed a deputy to sing it. Pamela Blair is as good as the part of the working mother permits, and Susan Mansur gets the most out of a waitress's song that should have been much better written. Clinton Allmon and Don Crabtree are dull, and Joan Ellis and Delores Hall gross, in parts that could use polish; J. Frank Lucas and Jay Garner deliver competent caricatures. The whores remain indistinguishable one from the other, although Lisa Brown and Donna King are at least attractive. All in all, *The Best Little Whorehouse* is a clean dirty joke, which is the worst kind there is.

The 5th of July

Lanford Wilson's *The 5th of July* is a pretty good Chekhovian play written too late. There must be any number of contemporary musicians who could compose a pretty good piece of Mozart, Chopin, or Brahms; and we know that there have been painters in our midst who could turn out pretty good Matisses, Modiglianis, and Chiricos, even if they had a little trouble with Vermeer. All but the greatest masters can be imitated—later—consciously or unconsciously; the fact that the fakes may not fool a few experts is less important than the fact that they can take in the rest of the world.

In drama, the situation is somewhat different. You are not dealing with sounds or pigments or even mere words, but with climates of thought and feeling that, however skillfully replicated, have a way of emerging skewed from a later sensibility. Perhaps the most spectacular imitations in English drama are the quasi-Jacobean plays of Beddoes; even they err, however, by being more Jacobean than the Jacobeans'. Wilson's Chekhov does not out-Chekhov the originals; it is merely out of place in its anachronistic garb, like people in nineteenth-century attire in a Danish-modern living room.

Actually, we are far from Danish modern here—on a ramshackle farm near Lebanon, Missouri, on Independence Day, 1977, and the following day, when the second-rate fireworks are over. We meet Ken, Gwen, John, and June, Ken's sister, who were all involved with one another—ideologically or physically, homo- or heterosexually—in their antiwar, pro-hippie sixties' student days at Berkeley. Now Gwen is a nutty millionairess trying to become a Nashville pop star, and is living with the opportunistic John, who manages her affairs and satisfies her complex libido. Ken, who loved and was let down by both of them, has lost his legs in Vietnam, and is now an English teacher living with gentle Jed, a dedicated botanist. Jane has an illegitimate daughter (by John, if I follow the play's convolutions correctly), and, with her promiscuous days behind her, has turned into a cynically wisecracking mother and intermittent homebody. Shirley, the daughter, is a bright but foolish teenager, a movie buff aspiring to greatness of an as yet unspecified sort.

There is also Aunt Sally, a jovial, mild eccentric who carries about (and sometimes misplaces) her husband's ashes in a candy box, and cannot quite resolve to scatter them as she was instructed to do. And there is Weston Hurley, Gwen's country-music writer from New Jersey, a guitar-strumming simpleton who is the butt of everyone's jokes when not telling preposterous stories that make him his own patsy.

Put all these people together on Ken's inherited farm that Gwen wants to buy and convert into a recording studio—an unlikely plot device but needed to keep the characters spinning in the semblance of a non-vacuum—and you have a clash of remembrances, recriminations, interests, and expectations. What you do not have, however, is dramatic development: a forward movement of a significant sort, a true change of human dynamics, despite not one but two switcheroos thrown in at the end. There are small conflicts, less than shattering revelations, and, mostly, people persisting in their old semi-impotent, semi-resigned ways.

All that is very Chekhovian—this sense of *plus ça change*, these people loving and hating one another to a stalemate, this blasé and cunning chatter that cannot keep the wolf of reality from the door, this getting nowhere even when one is most on the go, the very business of selling a house (*Cherry Orchard*) or planting for the future (*Uncle Vanya*) or yearning for other places (*Three Sisters*). But it doesn't work, for two reasons. It looks, sounds, and feels like a copy, however witty, wistful, and exquisite; and all that aimlessness, frustration, and failure does not have a compelling substratum of loss. In Chekhov's Russia, there were intimations of a collapsing empire, of a social order headed for bloody extinction; in Wilson's world, there is only the sense of the departed sixties, with their feeble political and sexual protests coming to an end. That is the implied fifth of July: the post-activist, post-coital, post-holiday depression.

Within this somewhat less than weighty framework, the individual moonings and moanings are also, unsurprisingly, trivial. But Wilson writes intelligent, amusing, racy dialogue, and is able to create lively albeit minuscule confrontations. The play is never uninteresting; it is merely, in the most profound sense, unsatisfying. It is accorded a fine production, though, under Marshall W. Mason's skilled direction, which errs only in trying to be too fast, too manifold, too clever. There are some perfect performances: Joyce Reehling, as the drolly disillusioned June; Helen Stenborg, as the modestly heroic aunt; Nancy Snyder, as the tumultuous, outrageous, disenchanted yet still hopeful Gwen; and Danton Stone as the Garden State musician who cultivates his country-and-Western.

Almost as good are William Hurt as Ken, if only he did not turn every line into a throwaway one; Jeff Daniels as Jed, if only he were not quite so uniformly subdued; and Jonathan Hogan as John, if only he exuded a little more sexuality. As the messy adolescent, Amy Wright overacts shamelessly, and gives the one poor performance in a production whose scenery by John Lee Beatty, costumes by Laura Crow, and lighting by Marc B. Weiss make no false moves. What it all lacks, however, and desperately, is a little urgency.

Ain't Misbehavin'

It was with trepidation that I confronted *Ain't Misbehavin'* on Broadway: would the slapdash playfulness, the lovable smallness of the show survive the lure of self-aggrandizement? Nothing to worry about; they did. John Lee Beatty, the set designer who specializes in thinking small and cheap—albeit with taste and imagination—has added suggestions of a nightclub with a proscenium arch whose lights permit themselves a modest trick, but nothing assertive. Randy Barcelo's costumes have a few sassy surprises—not so much up their sleeves as in the brims of their hats—but they never presume. A sixpiece band has been discreetly conveyed to the back of the stage, where it remains mostly hidden by a scrim. When it does glide forward and gets all lit up, it still keeps its sonorous place largely as a backup for Luther Henderson's piano, which still does most of the accompanying in fine, Wallerian style. This piano has now become peripatetic and will sashay around the stage, but at least, unlike a strolling violin, it never mingles with the audience.

True, the Longacre, however intimate, is not so touchingly hole-in-the-wallish as the space at the Manhattan Theater Club, where this concatenation of songs by Fats Waller first saw the light of klieg. But the delicious songs by Waller and his friends, suggestively lighted by Pat Collins, continue their joyous renaissance under Richard Maltby Jr.'s canny and easeful staging, with Arthur Faria's fetching mini-choreography. Luther Henderson's orchestrations and William Elliott and Jeffrey Gutcheon's vocal arrangements manage to be both imaginative and homey, and it's wonderful that Maltby and Murray Horwitz had the idea in the first place and also wrote lively additional lyrics.

Now that—whew!—I have discharged my other obligations, allow me to rave incontinently about the cast of five that works together as nimbly and wickedly as five fingers in a piece of sleight of hand. Above my praise for them individually, I must set my admiration for them as a protean ensemble that, subdividing and coalescing into any number from one to five, is always gloriously one.

There is, in this quizzical quintet, Ken Page, a corpulent but lightsome man, who has that extraordinary quality I associate with children, idiots, and great performers: absolute spontaneity. Performers, unlike the other two groups, have to fake it, and Page does this with such guileless conviction going from seignorial indignation to irrepressible roguery as only the most untampered-with children and divinely inspired idiots could match. When, for instance, he throws back his head to emit a very nearly endless note, and we feel drenched by that warm geyser of sound, we would swear that his gleeful surprise is as genuine as our own.

Then there is Armelia McQueen, a red-hot mama that can turn into a milky baby or anything intermediate in rather less than a trice. Imperious or mellow, she cajoles or commands, and floats her imposing girth on the air like the zippiest of zeppelins. The beautifully trained voice rides the octaves like a surfer, and when, for example, she stretches an imaginary stocking between ineluctably diverging hands, the gesture is so real that you tremble for the meshes of the hose.

Andre De Shields is next, the epitome of suave rascality. A fellow of slides and slithers, his very voice handles the staff as if it were a greasy pole; his snippy words and snide looks are worthy of a French pastry cook caught among Bronx bagel bakers. Even when he stands still, he seems to undulate; you just know that his suit is filled not with a body, but with lizards of both the lounge and leapin' varieties.

Charlaine Woodard, who reminds me of Shelley Duvall, can make dopiness look like a privileged state, and generally carries on like a very hip sleepwalker. When she throws herself into a dance movement, she knows no more than we do where a given foot or elbow of hers might end up; when she recovers her balance, she beams incredulously, like someone whose wallet is returned intact by a passing gypsy. In song, notes take off from her cantilevered lips for unknown destinations, and seem to hit home quite accidentally. She is also very, very sweet.

But the most miraculous finger of this hand is the fat little thumb called Nell Carter. Looking like a slightly larger-than-life eight ball with a pert face painted on and four clothespins added for limbs, she is simply immense. She has, in fact, every attribute of a giant-ess, except the size. On exaggeratedly dainty feet, she moves like someone who would brook no contradiction from a bulldozer, if there were one rash enough to cross her path. Though she can leap up as lyrically as Wordsworth's heart to a rainbow, she is more likely to cock her head, latch on to the ground with her feet, and, arms akimbo, either charm the birds out of a tree or wither the tree itself with a glance. Her voice, which by itself should win acting awards, ranges from soprano sax to bass tuba and can thunder, wail, flicker, and put away a note with a marvelously smug little click.

Yet the ultimate hero of the evening is the man who either sang and popularized or actually wrote these gorgeous songs: Thomas, or "Fats," Waller. I almost believe that under yet another first name he wrote one of the finest English lyrics, "Go, Lovely Rose."

Wings

The second and last Yale offering was Arthur Kopit's *Wings*, origi-nally a radio play, but cleverly recast for the stage. Emily Stilson, an elderly ex-aviatrix and stunt flier, suffers a stroke. Brought to a hos-pital, she and its staff move at first through bewilderingly different, noncommunicating worlds. Gradually, through the cool efficiency of the doctors, fumbling goodwill of the nurses, and dedicated min-istrations of Amy, a sympathetic therapist, the aphasia that reduced Mrs. Stilson to a confused thinker and wretched, at first only sub-liminal, speaker, begins to subside, and she seems on the way to full communication. But death woos her more potently; despite Amy's urgent summoning, Emily flies off into the ultimate darkness.

The language of the mind losing hold of words as it drifts off to sleep was first explored by Joyce in *Ulysses* at the end of the Ithaca episode. But it was Beckett who, in his plays and novels, evoked states bordering on, or representing, aphasia, albeit not literally reproducing clinical cases. Kopit pushes farther in that direction, but for all his research into and re-creation of actual defective speech by patients, he too keeps the verbiage within literary boundaries. Thus the work's master metaphor is wings, flying—symbolizing both speech winging its way from person to person and the psyche setting forth on perilous voyages into life and, eventually, out of it.

The play has many virtues. The opening scene, which evokes a stroke by the simple flickering of lights and fading of sounds (the ticking of a clock) until there is both terrible silence and frightening clatter, is magisterial. So too is the use of several revolving black panels—now transparent, now opaque—combined with mirrors that distort and mislead to suggest the labyrinthine world of hospitals, sickness, inability to understand and be understood. By various verbal and visual means, Kopit achingly conveys the humiliations of a disability that isolates a mind from its peers and makes of cross-purposes a spirit-breaking cross to bear. He gives us both charmingly wistful moments where patient and therapist become fellow ignoramuses before the mystery of words, and moments of nervous humor when a speech-therapy group session yields funny contretemps amid tentative successes.

But, finally, the language of the play, especially in its supposedly most rapturously acrobatic moments, does not quite sustain the poetic flights and dramatic impact demanded from it. Moreover, the tragic conclusion, after strong promises of recovery, seems, though clinically possible, dramatically forced. Most serious of all, the several implications of the "wings" image never interlock completely with the blessed click of everything falling into place. Still, there is the Emily of Constance Cummings, so precise yet lyrical, so various yet consistent, so cleanly able to convey the most enormous strivings of mind and body as to be immensely moving without ever losing her hold on the role's firm, intellectual progress. This superb achievement is condignly backed up by a flawless supporting cast, headed by the fine Marianne Owen.

For the direction by John Madden, set by Andrew Jackness, costumes by Jeanne Button, lighting by Tom Schraeder, sound by Tom Voegeli, and music by Herb Pilhofer, I have nothing but praise. I hope that the two weeks at the Public Theater will not be the end of this lovely, collaborative effort.

Eubie!

Eubie! is another musical with an exclamation point in its title, which, except in the case of *Oklahoma!*, has always proved a bad omen. Actually, this old-fashioned revue contrived from the songs of Eubie Blake is only once unpleasant, in a Japanesey number called "Oriental Blues," but almost equally rarely outstanding. The best thing about it is the dancing—tap and otherwise—of the Hines brothers, Maurice and Gregory. Gregory, moreover, is a splendid comic actor, and whatever he does (even the semipermanent wink of the left eye while the right beams ahead ingenuously) is touched with the comeliness of total, easeful assurance.

Something good can be said about each of the dozen performers, except for the unfunny comedian, Jeffery V. Thompson, and some are particularly appealing. Janet Powell can make a movement simultaneously seductive and witty, and Lynnie Godfrey and Ethel Beatty can sing with aphrodisiac raucousness. My favorite among the women, though, is Terry Burrell, who, inexplicably, is given the least to do. Built rather like Tenniel's Alice in the process of becoming alarmingly elongated, Miss Burrell sings, dances, and, yes, even mugs with a certain rapturous commitment enhanced by her eccentric good looks.

The show, however, exudes a music-hall proficiency that is the product of calculation rather than imagination. Eubie Blake's music, although easy to listen to, is no less easy to forget; even if the many hands responsible for the orchestrations and vocal arrangements have labored to good effect, there are only two first-rate songs: "I'm Just Wild About Harry" (which, however, gets milked shamelessly) and "Memories of You." The various dance routines (other than the Hineses') and production numbers are merely competent rehashings of old standbys, sometimes huffing with strain, and one bit of vaudeville centering on a park bench is downright lamentable. I don't know who among Julianne Boyd, Henry LeTang, and Billy Wilson is accountable for what here, but I cannot imagine any of the cooks wishing to take credit for this broth.

Karl Eigsti's scenery and Bernard Johnson's costumes are what one would expect from a better nightclub, which is not quite good enough for Broadway, and William Mintzer's lighting is equally predictable. One number, "If You've Never Been Vamped by a Brownskin…" appears both in *Eubie!* and in *Ain't Misbehavin'* (don't ask me what that means), with which the present show must, to its disadvantage, be compared. Those truly concerned with musical theater should see both and note conclusively the difference between competence and inspiration. Still, I am convinced that there is a sufficient number of theatergoers whose demands are not rigorously exacting and who would find *Eubie!* as enjoyable as a very successful family picnic at which weather, food, and spirits (in both senses) collaborate perfectly. It is at them that the show is geared, and they will not be disappointed by it.

On opening night something quite marvelous did happen: Eubie Blake himself, 95 years old and in need of supporting when he walks, came up on stage for the curtain calls. When the old trouper felt the boards underfoot, he revived like Atlas when his feet touched Mother Earth. He moved springily, chatted sassily with cast and audience, and even danced a little. The accumulated razzle-dazzle of 76 years in show business transfigured him and communicated to all present the joy of making music and theater. If only *Eubie!* could incorporate this in every performance.

Ballroom

Ballroom is a touching show. It is also human, life-enhancing, and droll. It is also flawed, the way seconds are in a very nice resale store: if you don't look hard, you probably won't notice the imperfections. The story, based on Jerome Kass's television musical, *Queen of the Stardust Ballroom*, is deceptively simple. Bea Asher, a Bronx widow who runs a lackadaisical jumble shop with her hard-bitten sister-in-law, Helen, is expected by her family to turn into a wallflower on her husband's grave. Angie, a raucous but good-natured friend, persuades Bea to start living again at the Stardust Ballroom. Reluctant at first, Bea goes there tentatively, and, after a rough start, meets Alfred Rossi, a mailman who is one of the regulars. The regulars are, in fact, one big, happy, hopping and gliding family, and soon Bea and Alfred are tangoing steady.

With scrupulous slowness, Bea and Alfred become lovers; unkindly, however, life has equipped this amiable mailman with a wife he cannot leave. But Bea is happy and is willing to settle for a 50-percent solution. Helen starts raising bloody hell, and for a while it looks as if Bea's grown children will also side against their mother.

But, like Helen's husband, Jack, they end up approving of Mother's transfiguration. Bea is elected Queen of the Stardust Ballroom, she and Alfred love each other, and life, a bit limpingly, dances on.

I give away the plot for two reasons. First, because it is not good enough to sell, and, second, because it is better for your enjoyment of the show to concentrate on other things. Those, by the way, are neither the tunes by Billy Goldenberg, which he may have gotten from a jumble shop, nor the humdrum lyrics by Alan and Marilyn Bergman, which prove not in the least arresting, except for the development of the story, whose points they keep needlessly reiterating. But if the Goldenbergman score is negligible as invention, it does have a seedy authenticity that makes it at least bearable. Just about everything else, though, is a pleasure.

The book by Jerome Kass, as doctored by Larry Gelbart, is unpretentiously engaging. It allows the principal characters a great deal of palpable personality, and it permits even some of the most peripheral figures to flit by as flesh rather than shadows. There is both wit and pathos here, blended in knowing proportion—perhaps a bit too knowing, but, then, symmetry is to minor art what asymmetry is to major. All I know is that I laughed quite a bit and cried not a little, and, in between, was not bored. Perhaps the story was a mite slow getting started, but once under way, it got to its destination as dependably as *my* mailman. Now let me tell you about what Michael Bennett has done—and it is not, primarily, choreography or even, strictly speaking, direction. It is, first of all, casting. I can't remember when I last saw a Broadway show in which every part, down to the least nonspeaking one, was so perfectly cast— well, maybe Howard Parker, who plays Angie's partner, is a bit too patently young. But of the ballroom's other denizens, some are actually middle-aged, and all of them look it. They also look sweet, ridiculous, preposterous in appearance and demeanor, and fiercely believable. True, there is one couple that looks a bit too young, or elegant, or handsome for the Stardust, but I can see why Bennett put them there: Svetlana McLee Grody and David Evans are so splendid that they act as a yardstick by which to measure the deviation of the others (although Adriana Keathley is quite lovely too).

The others are mostly off, but ever so endearingly. And they can act. Lynn Roberts and Bernie Knee, as the Stardust's band singers, are, if anything, more real than reality. But everyone is devastatingly right. Let me single out the Angie of Patricia Drylie, who is one of the most lovable, wise jerks anyone ever had for a best, bossy friend; Sally-Jane Heit, who does not turn the unlovable Helen into someone lovable (bravo!) and whom you listen to with interest and sympathy (double bravo!); and the extraordinary John Hallow, who makes her husband—a part that could have easily lapsed into caricature—into someone as quirkily real as an itch in an unreachable part of your back. Assembling this flawless cast is worthy of the Nobel Prize for chemistry.

But Bennett has also choreographed some delightful dances, perfectly poised on the razor's edge between what the Stardust's clients could manage and what only a shrewd, skillful choreographer could create. I am sorry only that at the end Bennett did not see fit to transcend reality, to give us a burst of glorious exaggeration; but never mind—there has been enough pleasure to waft us out of the theater contented. To this Robin Wagner's cunning set design, Theoni V. Aldredge's spunky costumes, and Tharon Musser's rhapsodic lighting contribute expertly, as does the rest of the technical staff. And then there are the two principals.

Vincent Gardenia is everything the man in the street (and hallways) could possibly be: he makes ordinariness, homeliness, and a kind of soft-edged cockiness into great, shining virtues—no, into small, shining virtues, just the right size to be portable without strain. And Dorothy Loudon—has anyone ever gotten more out of shyness, tentativeness, even a self-effacing way of bending the body this way and that, as though a straight posture were an unexampled piece of ostentation? She delivers not only dialogue and songs to unassuming perfection, but also silences, thoughts, changes of heart. Thanks to her, you feel as well oriented inside Bea Asher as inside your own skin, and quite a bit safer, as one always does inside true artistic creation. Oh, there are some false steps in *Ballroom*, but who can tell the stumbles from the dance?

They're Playing Our Song

This always happens at a Neil Simon show. All around, there are people burbling, gurgling, giggling, guffawing; "fabulous... fantastic," "marvelous" balloon out of their throats right during the play, loud enough to be disturbing if one cared about missing a soon to be duplicated line or two. And you sit there smiling occasionally, laughing once or twice, and wondering the rest of the time whether you are from the same planet, nay, galaxy. Even on the lines the crowd doesn't laugh up, there is often someone in some distant part of the house to let out a solitary laugh, like the cry of a passing loon over a hushed landscape. What is there to laugh about? Only the loon knows.

Some of these people are downright touching. The man in front of me at *They're Playing Our Song* often began laughing five or six seconds after I had dismissed the joke as too easy, too predictable, or too dragged-in-by-the-shorthairs. But the spectators laugh explosively, and they cannot all be backers, relatives, or friends—or can they? "You can't sit in a dentist's chair nowadays without hearing one of your songs," or "I was going to take a Valium, but I couldn't get my teeth unclenched," or "A smile—small victory for Sonia Walsk!" … "No, I just had my teeth cleaned, and I don't want to waste it" (to choose three from the dental domain) are funny enough, but they are not organic. They could be said by either person in this two-character comedy with songs (not quite a play, not quite a musical, but teamed up like the sturdy blind man with the sighted lame chap on his back), and at almost any point; they do not come out of a human being's individuality, and most of the plot is there only to set them up. Yet few people seem to worry about such things.

They're Playing Our Song is the story of a famous work-obsessed tunesmith—a wisecracking, Jewish-style urban neurotic—to whom comes, for purposes of collaboration, a not yet famous young woman lyricist—a wisecracking, Jewish-style urban neurotic. When he is nervous (about his work, his wife, or just because the author wants him that way), he confesses to his tape recorder; when she is nervous (about her work, her poverty, or Leon, the lover with whom she keeps breaking off but who clings to her like a psychic leech, as we learn from her tales of woe and his importunate phone calls), she is late for appointments or totally discombobulated. She means to be adulatory but ends up being patronizing, he wants to sound businesslike but comes out overeager and vulnerable. And full of one-liners like this morale booster: "We're not going to write the score for *The Gulag Archipelago!*"

The rest is mere arbitrary maneuvering to make the collaboration and concomitant Leon-crossed love affair conform to an updated, post-Freudian version of tunesmith meets lyricist, tunesmith loses lyricist, tunesmith wins lyricist. It appears that in some ways Simon is really a wasteful playwright: after having named his hero Vernon Gersch, why didn't he just use the leftovers of those two celebrated songwriters' names and call the heroine Wynn Duke? I guess that would have sounded too Aryan, so she became Sonia Walsk. In other ways, though, Simon is thrifty: everything he writes these days comes from his family's or surrounding lives. Thus *Chapter Two*, it was announced, was the story of Simon's courtship of Marsha Mason; this show, as the program declares, is "loosely based" on the affair of its composer and its lyricist, Marvin Hamlisch and Carole Bayer Sager. After autobiography and biography, what is left? Maybe hagiography.

If I were Hamlisch or Sager, I wouldn't particularly relish or savor a show that, even with that "loosely" thrown in, turned my love life into a series of ludicrous entanglements and pseudo-portentous partings no more significant than the tergiversations of two dust particles in a random light beam. But, then, as Vernon and Sonia are afflicted with those delusions of grandeur that—since they start from Tin Pan Valley and aim no higher than Tin Pan Mountain— scarcely deserve the term megalomania, so their prototypes, too, may be micromaniacs.

At any rate, on their first night out, Vernon and Sonia go to a discotheque where, whenever a song by one of them is played, he or she goes into a song and dance of self-exaltation that makes the dance of the chosen maiden in *The Rite of Spring* look like small capers, never mind potatoes. Perhaps because of its tang of veracity, this is one of the two best numbers in the show, and certainly the one for which Hamlisch—a composer always at a disadvantage when his music is not being written by Scott Joplin—comes up with anything resembling a tune. Luckily for the relationship (assuming that, like Vernon and Sonia's, it endures), Sager's lyrics are no better; if anything, worse. The other good number has Vernon's singing and dancing alter egos (yes, he has three of them, as Sonia has her three; they are what provides the show with a comic mini chorus line) appear in the hospital room where our broken-legged-and-hearted hero is in traction, and sing and dance while accompanying themselves on tinkling toy pianos.

There are other nice production values. Douglas W. Schmidt's sets and projections are as cute as they are clever, which is appropriate; Tharon Musser's lighting is inventive as always; and then there are the costumes. Sonia, as a recurrent gag would have it, gets her clothes from terminated stage shows, and keeps appearing in something out of Off Broadway Chekhov or road-company Maugham. The joke is harped upon so relentlessly that it comes across less like a running gag than like a case of the runs, but the costumes it elicits from Ann Roth are a joy. Patricia Birch is an expert at devising artful dance numbers for nondancers, and here she is again up to her very considerable snuff. Robert Moore's direction is, perhaps needfully, overemphatic, though I wish it had curbed Robert Klein a bit.

Klein is a truly funny comedian, but he does have an isotopic way of turning light comedy into heavy comedy; a little less would have been more, though possibly not Moore. I am of two minds about Lucie Arnaz, whose raspy speaking voice is off-putting but whose raucous singing voice is rousing, whose performance is efficient but a bit mechanical, whose looks and comportment have a way of slipping from alluring into feral. She emerges as a kind of sheep in wolf's—or Desi in Lucille's—clothing. There were three able orchestrators at work on Hamlisch's music; when any of it is played, these three alter egos can rightfully exclaim: "They're playing our song!"

Sweeney Todd, the Demon Barber of Fleet Street

You have to give *Sweeney Todd, the Demon Barber of Fleet Street* an A for intelligent effort. Now, effort may not be worth much, but intelligent effort is; the only thing it is worth less than is success. This musical melodrama—based on Christopher Bond's recent play version of the old story—has a book by Hugh Wheeler, music and lyrics by Stephen Sondheim, and staging by Harold Prince. By now you must know that it concerns a barber condemned to long penal servitude because a crooked judge coveted and ravished his pretty wife, and how the vengeance-bent barber escapes from Australia, returns to London, and teams up with Mrs. Lovett, who runs the worst pie shop in Fleet Street. Not content with slitting the throats of the guilty judge and his beastly beadle, Todd gives super-close shaves to most of his customers (in a corrupt society there is nothing like an overincisive razor to provide redeeming social content), who end up inside Mrs. Lovett's suddenly hugely popular comestibles, making her the sweetheart of stigma pies. There is also a love story involving Sweeney's daughter—the rotten judge's ward and intended bride—and the gallant sailor who saved Sweeney's life; a further subplot about a somewhat benighted apprentice boyishly enamored of Mrs. Lovett; and, of course, comeuppance for the bad and everything coming up roses for most of the good.

As Grand Guignol, this is all very well, but does it call for ultrasophisticated musicalization distinctly aspiring to opera? True, there are many great dramas and operas in which corpses drop like bowling pins, but their tone is consistent, not a *mélange des genres*. There are ways of treating profuse demises—either steady seriousness or black comedy—but *Sweeney Todd* is like a mad dinner party at which the dessert interrupts the hors d'oeuvre and the pousse-café is poured into the soup. What we have here is neither fish nor fowl but a clear case of what T. S. Eliot called dissociation of sensibility.

Not that the score itself is very consistent either. The lyrics, as always with Sondheim, are cleverer and more razor-sharp than anybody else's today; only when trying for heartwarming directness do they have a way of ringing a mite excogitated and self-conscious. There is, of course, something showy about the cleverness too; but, then, pyrotechnics are supposed to be pyrotechnical. Significantly, it is in the ballads that awkwardnesses occur—as in the very title of "Green Finch and Linnet Bird": linnet bird is a rank pleonasm. And, finally, is it really necessary to have a four-letter word—in rhyming position yet!—recurring in a lyric strong enough without it?

But what of the music? Since the time I wrote about my surprise at his unfamiliarity with some of the greats of our musical theater, I have been delighted to glimpse Sondheim at operas by Janáček and requiems by Britten (no causal relationship implied), and, inevitably, his musical idiom has grown in various directions. *Sweeney Todd* contains a great deal of *Peter Grimes* and *Mother Courage* (critics who cited Weill seem to me mistaken; it is the fiercer Brecht collaborators, Dessau and Eisler, who are overheard here), and that expectant or minatory *sordino* rumble for orchestral underpainting of spoken dialogue, which can be found in any number of modern theatrical composers. The way "The Ballad of Sweeney Todd" recurs, piece by ominous piece, as incremental repetition throughout the show suggests the sea interludes in *Peter Grimes* and, in its stern melody and aggressive orchestration, the opening and closing number of *Mother Courage*.

Expanding your musical range is fine, and even a certain derivativeness is no capital offense, but your reach should not exceed your

digestion. Here the foreign matter often sings out like the swallowed critters from the belly of Peter's wolf. Moreover, whenever
the score threatens to sound too serious, there is a jejune retreat to
tried-and-true show-biz razzmatazz, as in numbers like "Pirelli's
Miracle Elixir," "A Little Priest," and "By the Sea," which, though
good, sound either dragged in by the hair or out of sync with the
grander aims of the rest.

Still, in trying to stretch the vocabulary of the Broadway musical, Sondheim & Co. are surely on the right track, even if in the
end Sondheim should prove more a precursor than an achiever.
The *mise en scène* here is similarly grandiose and likewise eclectic, with the enormous architectural set—like giant beehives and
rabbit warrens erected along the side walls of Victoria (or is it
Charing Cross?) Station—deriving in part from Richard Foreman's concept for *The Threepenny Opera*. Although Eugene Lee's
construction and backdrop—not to mention the corrugated-tin
patchwork quilt that alternately hides and reveals a panorama of
cacopolitan London—are vastly imposing, they tend to dwarf the
bits of movable scenery on which most of the action takes place,
besides providing tantalizing labyrinths that never live up to their
sinister promise, as a versatile catwalk cum crane cum Bridge of
Sighs, for instance, does.

Harold Prince has evolved into an extremely able director of
musicals, and all past reservations I may have had no longer apply.
Even so, he has not solved the probably insoluble problem of how
to make the numerous throat slittings, if not less gory, at least less
repetitious. My only serious quarrel, however, is with the staging
of the Bedlam scene, where the silhouette technique, not exploited
imaginatively enough, ends up looking like a gratuitous intrusion.
All else is cogent and sturdily managed. Franne Lee's costumes,
though perhaps not hewing strictly to period, are good enough to
illustrate Mayhew's London, or to hang in the sauciest of rogues'
galleries. Ken Billington's lighting is his best to date, and Jonathan
Tunick's orchestrations are as diverse, different, and suggestive as
the occasion demands.

The performances, alas, are uneven. As Mrs. Lovett, Angela Lansbury is a pie-faced wonder. Looking in her funny period hairdo like
Winston Churchill disguised as a snail, she carries the show as said
mollusk does his house. Undaunted by elaborate stage business that
might give a decathlon champion pause, she simultaneously sings,
dances, acts, and toils away exultantly, yet without ever hogging

the stage. Never have so many owed so much to one. Len Cariou, though he works earnestly and often effectively, is outclassed, perhaps because of a basic colorlessness that is hard to overcome even when it almost (but not wholly) fits the part. For the rest, Merle Louise, Jack Eric Williams, and Ken Jennings are outstanding, while the others—especially the young lovers—disappoint. Never mind; *Sweeney Todd*, even if it is more spectacular and provocative than finished and satisfying, has to be seen. It is a historic event on Broadway, and it is history's privilege to overwhelm without quite fulfilling us.

A word about miking. Granted that the Uris Theater is cavernous and less than benign in its acoustics, it won't do to have part of Cariou's biggest aria snuffed out by body-mike static. Suggestions, anyone?

Zoot Suit

One doesn't want to act superior to Los Angeles and the theatrical hits that, front time to time, it sends us. Yet if these exports continue to be more or less in the class of *Zoot Suit*, which is only slightly below the grisly norm, what else is one to do? Written by Luis Valdez, the director of El Teatro Campesino, the show may have worked as agitprop performed in the fields and on street corners to enhance Chicano pride; now, rewritten and (I gather) bloated, it rattles around the huge Winter Garden like—to borrow a phrase from E. E. Cummings—"a fragment of angry candy" in a large tin box.

The phrase is uncannily appropriate. *Zoot Suit* is angry about the way Chicanos were treated during World War II, notably at the time of the Sleepy Lagoon murder case, on which the play is very loosely based, and about how, to some extent, they may still be treated. Hence its Mexican Americans are all fearless, intelligent, and witty—as well as justifiably angry and violent. Concomitantly, every Anglo (I'll come to the two exceptions presently) is a sneering or snarling Chicano-hating beast. *Zoot Suit* is also candy-coated: we are treated periodically to exuberant but largely irrelevant and uninspired dance sequences by Patricia Birch, to music chosen, and occasionally written, by Daniel Valdez—Luis's brother and one of the principal actors. The music, moreover, is canned, which, in a big theater, always has a deadening effect. The whole thing falls absurdly short of its vast subject—racial injustice.

The characters are caricatures drawn by blind hate or blind love; the action is spasmodic, inconsistent, and clobberingly obvious. Stylistically, we are treated to inferior poster art (like the vulgar Zoot Suit poster) with some overlays of Brecht and a pretentious set of alternative endings. There is also an imaginary character, El Pachuco (the symbol of the Chicano spirit), who may derive from the Ardell of David Rabe's *Pavlo Hummel*, or from any number of other sources. Yet the supreme failure of *Zoot Suit* lies in its language—and not just the Spanish and *caló* dialect words that litter the text (though they, too, seem untenable on any level beyond agitprop), but also and particularly the general banality and bathos of stuff like "I don't pretend to know how you feel, but let me say we've just begun to fight" or "It leaves us rather lonesome, with the empty feeling of being alone."

But if the production drips with well-meaning ineptitude, it is not free from unappetizing calculation either. I don't mean only the choice of a grandiose theater and the ruthlessly hard-sell advertising; I mean especially the concept of the two only sympathetic Anglos: the lawyer who defends the seventeen young Chicanos accused of murder and the leftist newspaper editress who runs the campaign for their release—the former implicitly, the latter explicitly, Jewish. Although all kinds of people rallied to the cause of the 38th Street Gang, the only ones depicted here are Jews—on the assumption, I daresay, that most of our theatergoers are Jewish and that buttering them up is good for business.

To espouse the terminology of *Zoot Suit* (a lengthy glossary of *caló* is provided by the program), I can describe the cheap set by Thomas A. Walsh and Roberto Morales only as *Que desmadre!*, though the costumes of Peter J. Hall rate a guarded *Orale!*, whereas the staging by Luis Valdez is as *pinche* as his dramaturgy. The acting is hard to evaluate, since the writing is mostly *pendejadas*, although an audience of theatrical *verdolagas* (many more Hispanics than *gabachos*) lapped it all up as if everyone on stage were a *chingón*. I myself could latch on to merely one line in all this *puro pedo*, the newspaperwoman's encouragement to the imprisoned hero: "Henry, we are all in jail, only some of us don't know it." This must be scant consolation to a fellow ostensibly in for life, but it strikes a sympathetic chord in anyone condemned to sitting through *Zoot Suit*. A program note refers to the play as "a dramatization of the imagination," which may be a subliterate way of saying "imaginary drama."

Bedroom Farce

What makes Alan Ayckbourn's *Bedroom Farce* so utterly captivating is not any one thing but that joyous mix of quasi-mystical elements that makes soufflés rise, parties come off, and audiences leave a theater in a state of euphoria. The stage represents three bedrooms. On our left, that of the aging Ernest and Delia, for whom the filigree of humdrum problems and puny satisfactions is completely absorbing. In the middle bedroom are Malcolm and Kate, a couple bursting with bounce—practical jokers who stuff the marital bed with everything from shoes to saucepans. The right-hand bedroom is that of Nick, a snippily self-satisfied businessman now bedridden and groaning with a backache. Jan, his capable, independent-spirited wife, was once the girl of Trevor, Ernest and Delia's oddball son.

The absurdly self-absorbed and clumsy Trevor and his spouse, Susannah—insecure, awkward, and given to hysteria—have no visible bedroom. But, unhappy in their own, they turn everyone else's into a battlefield too. Invited to a party of Kate and Malcolm's, they wreck it with their internecine intemperateness, which radiates misery in all directions. The boudoir ceases to be, as traditionally in bedroom farce, the locus of illicit sexual mischief, and becomes instead the place where licit relationships are most sorely tested. Yet neither relationships nor tests are of a particularly sexual sort; the hotbed of errant eroticism has become the cold bed of marriages settled into routine and gamesmanship that can all too easily be disrupted by the most inconsequential turmoil from without.

The bedroom, then, as the soft but not especially lusty underbelly of everyday conjugality: resigned on the left, edgily witty on the right, and coyly playful in the middle—all strategies meant to mask the naked unease exhibited by Trevor and Susannah's portable and contagious bed of pain. Yet the old couple are viewed more positively than the younger ones—perhaps because they hark back to a less sex-tormented era—and their use of the bedroom as a conversation pit for reviewing the day's trivia comes across as a sensible, though Pyrrhic, victory. Consider Delia, who, exuding equanimity, tells her distraught daughter-in-law, "My mother used to say: if s-e-x ever rears its ugly head, close your eyes before you see the rest of it."

That remark is typical of Ayckbourn's people: it is, like them, both silly and wise. They are neither unduly clever nor outrageously dim-witted, but of average intelligence and average stupidity in a sturdy amalgam. And they can make fools of others and themselves with equal ease, thanks to either quality. They are funny not because they are smarter or more foolish than the rest of us, but because they are exactly like us, only in a slightly tightened, sharpened version, to make a particular brand of lopsidedness reveal its bias more theatrically. Yet unlike, say, Neil Simon, Ayckbourn does not make neuroses and deficiencies appear more cutely epigrammatic, more wittily seductive, than they are. We do not have our egos stroked, only our noses rubbed in the truth—but rubbed jovially, as Eskimos allegedly rub their noses together by way of kissing.

And when Ayckbourn turns serious, he does not go preachy on us. When things in the end do not work out after all—as so often in Ayckbourn plays—Trevor and Susannah fail in a farcical way; the drama rolls in without a portentous shift of gears. So, too, when Kate reveals to Malcolm that he does not fully satisfy her in bed, this essentially sad revelation is kept well within the comic register. Ayckbourn extends the range of farce, without cheating, to cover situations that are not farcical—the fibrillations of the heart under the feverish laughter. And he keeps his characters characters, not walking stacks of interchangeable jokebooks. No one in *Bedroom Farce* could make someone else's quips or gaffes.

Particularly handy is the sense of rhythm—the way the action shifts among bedrooms 1, 2, and 3 unpredictably yet satisfyingly in scenes of unequal length—sometimes hardly more than a subliminal flash in, say, bedroom 3, antiphonally interlarding the comedy in bedroom 2. The secret of this is dramatic timing, which must be taken up and elaborated by the timing of the direction and performances. The very melody of British English, with its crispness and rubatos, is exploited to the utmost.

Ayckbourn and Peter Hall, who co-directed this production originally for Britain's National Theatre, have worked out every aural and visual detail to perfection. The way a bit of physical space is filled or a bit of conversational space is left empty is calculated to provoke maximum hilarity, but the calculation always wears the happy disguise of absolute spontaneity. And the British cast performs understated wonders. Malcolm and Kate, whose practical joking cloaks an emotional lacuna, are embodied by Derek Newark, who deserves the grand prize for shouting through clenched teeth, and Susan Littler, whose slow-motion facial play and time-bomb delivery are irresistible. Polly Adams's Jan bustles and bullies with sweetly exasperating efficiency, while Michael Stroud's Nick turns the spasmodic locomotion of a backache sufferer into a sublimely grotesque angular choreography.

As Susannah, Delia Lindsay suggests the subcutaneous hysteria of a neophyte lion tamer, and her nightmare scene in her mother-in-law's bed is a comic jewel. As Trevor, Stephen Moore ably conveys wall-to-wall off-the-wallness, but lacks that modicum of charm that would explain his appeal. Best of all are the oldsters: Michael Gough's Ernest, a semi-deflated blimp whose crustiness is mitigated by surges of childlike joy, and whose slowness and blinkeredness are ways of keeping chaos at bay; and Joan Hickson's Delia, perhaps a shade too lower-class, but equipped with facial expressions and verbal deliveries that squeeze the last bit of comic juice from a line, only to hit us again playfully with the remaining skin.

Whereas at your typical successful comedy I tend to laugh intermittently—and then inwardly, inaudibly—at *Bedroom Farce* my laughter was a veritable chain reaction, the characters and situations being so funny that I laughed even in between the jokes.

Faith Healer

Brian Friel, the able Irish playwright whose first work, *Philadelphia, Here I Come!*, remains one of my happier theatrical memories, though his later plays have all proved more or less flawed, has come a long way in search of the new with *Faith Healer*. A long way away from theater. For *Faith Healer* consists of four monologues: the first by Frank, the itinerant Irish faith healer, half mountebank, half miracle worker; the second by Gracie, his long-suffering upper-class wife; the third by Teddy, Frank's Cockney manager, who traveled with the couple, to both of whom he was devoted in a funny, carping way; and the fourth by Frank again.

This could have made a splendid novel; indeed, the script reads like a four-part novella of genuine albeit somewhat attenuated merit. But a play whose characters never confront one another? True, there is interest in the fact that the monologues cover roughly the same events from different perspectives and are a sort of Irish version of Akutagawa's novel and Kurosawa's movie—call it *Rash O'Mon*. But here the versions are not truly different; only the emphases and a few details diverge, proving that each person understands the others better than himself. Frank, the faith healer, is gradually revealed as an alcoholic weakling; a philandering husband; a man unsure of his powers, which mysteriously come and go; an "artiste" who drives his manager crazy even as his manager bugs him; and someone who can find certainty only in his abandoned homeland, which is both Ireland and death.

The work proceeds along three levels. It is a look at the nature and meaning of faith, though on this plane it says nothing startling. It is also a study of the artist, of the price he pays for his gift and its ambiguous value to him and those around him. Finally, it is an examination of the curious symbiosis that holds a performer, his dedicated wife, and the manager, who, apparently incapable of physical love for either man or woman, finds fulfillment in platonically loving this strange, squabbling, yet interdependent couple. For, peccant and often hateful as he is, Frank is still what sustains Gracie and Teddy—even as they provide him with resented but needed sustenance. Still, interesting as Friel's verbal fugue is, the lack of direct interaction among its characters removes it from the realm of drama into that of the novel or short story; the stage becomes an internment camp for displaced genres.

Yet though *Faith Healer* has as many holes as Swiss cheese, it also has as much good cheese. Even at its least dramatic, Friel's writing has its share of Hibernian gusto and is food for the life of the mind. Intelligence and craftsmanship are always in evidence, even when the shadow of tedium falls across them. And there are people here—people who suffer and inflict suffering as much out of love as out of lack of it. The exploiter and the exploited not only need one another, they generally cannot even tell which of them is which. Surely this is the stuff of drama, save only its all-important form.

The Teddy episode, moreover, is extremely funny. No one has ever stated the case against the brainpower of actors more wickedly, wittily, and, I fear, compellingly than Friel through Teddy's mouth. The parable of Teddy's two dogs does for actors what the parable of the Prodigal Son does for sinners—and for fatted calves. As delivered with superlative timing and dynamic shading by Donal Donnelly, this is one of the current theater's comic highlights—suffusion with pathos only makes the humor shine forth more dazzlingly.

James Mason may, even in a dressed-down, almost drab version of himself, still be too worldly, ironically superior, *distingué* for
Frank; but he does hold you with that wearily flickering eye of his,
that voice too much experience has exacerbated into querulousness. And then, superbly, something darts into life under all that
jadedness. Clarissa Kaye (Mrs. Mason) reveals herself as an awesome technician: She has the control over intonation and expression of a great *lieder* singer. The voice and face have perfect pitch
and can modulate or wrench themselves into antithetical states with
magisterial assurance. And Donnelly, I repeat, is enchanting. Jose
Quintero's subdued direction embraces the play without violating
it; Marilyn Rennagel's lighting performs more like a musical score:
you can virtually hear its moody permutations harmonize with the
spoken word. Flaws be damned; *Faith Healer* is well worth experiencing.

Whose Life Is It Anyway?

Once a television play, always a television play. If you like TV drama
at its best, which is roughly like boulevard theater at its second best,
Whose Life Is It Anyway? is your thing. Brian Clark's play concerns
the efforts of Ken Harrison, a young sculptor whom a car accident
paralyzed from the neck down, to get discharged from an English
hospital and, ipso facto, die a swift, fully human death rather than
live as a mere head: a thinking, yearning, jeering, cursing, and ultimately inhuman head. The chief doctor, Emerson, and those of his
persuasion, use all their institutionalized might to keep him alive;
others, gathered around the pretty and sensitive Dr. Scott, who falls
into something like love with Harrison (*amour de tête?*), and Philip
Hill, Ken's doughty lawyer, try to help him win his desired death.
The contest, in which medicine, psychiatry, and the law vie with
one another, is resolved by judicial decision.

Everything is tidily crafted, craftily tailored to the public taste.
Every character is allotted his redeeming grace or humanizing
foible; every sleeve has a nifty little surprise stitched into it. The
comedy carries with it a carefully meted out dosage of pain; the
sadness is liberally doused with belly laughs. Dr. Scott must un-
professionally allow herself to be drawn to Harrison as a woman,
while also suggesting a future involvement with Hill, Harrison's

operative alter ego. Kay Sadler, the sweet young nurse, though also taken with Harrison, must become the girlfriend of John, the West Indian orderly—who, as a black, is, naturally, a free spirit and, as such, yet another alter ego of Harrison's.

Harrison is one raging lust for life and lust for sex, and so propels the play along an endless course of sick and sex jokes, thwarted longing turning in its impotence into an inky spray of black humor. But *Whose Life Is It Anyway?* is not a true black comedy, only a gray one painted black. Nor is it a tragicomedy in the true sense, for the laughter, the gimmickry, the manipulation allow no room for authentic tears. You can get rid of the accumulated sadness through your nose, with one hefty blow. It is a cleverly constructed work, but, precisely, one that is more constructed than written.

There is much technical polish in the production as well, starting with Alan Tagg's neat, no-nonsense scenery and Tharon Musser's lucidly methodical lighting. Michael Lindsay-Hogg's staging is crisp and cogent, and there is a welter of fine supporting performances, notably by Kenneth Welsh as Hill, Beverly May as a stern but (needless to say) human head nurse, and Pippa Pearthree as the ingenuous but (of course) not silly young nurse, Kay Sadler. The trouble, if any, is with the three leads. Tom Conti must have been splendid in the early months of his performing Ken Harrison in London (though his Ken is scarcely different from, say, his Norman in *The Norman Conquests*); by now, everything he does has about it a blinding high gloss that is the opposite of freshness. This is also a performance too aware of its charm, which makes it a bit less charming; and, on opening night, Conti was given to cutting off his fellow actors. Still, something worth experiencing. As Dr. Scott, Jean Marsh is a mite too cutely unphysicianly; in fact, her whole approach to the part, though smooth, remains superficial. Yet it is only the dependable Philip Bosco, as Dr. Emerson, who is downright disappointing, giving us a typical, somewhat over-oiled robot, where more humanity would have balanced the play better. And after years of performing Britishy parts, Bosco still manages only an upper-American unctuousness.

To be sure, there are the jokes. Some of them are highly competent, like "KAY: Would you like some more [drinking] water? HARRISON: Yes, please, since you went to all the trouble of heating it up." One joke, in fact, is inspired. When Harrison asks the shuffling-in lawyer, "How are you?" Hill replies with healthy hypochondria, "So-so." Looking at Ken, he realizes his absurdity, and freezes into superb ludicrousness. But a lot of the play is just jokey, on the "Did you hear about the plastic surgeon who melted before the fire?" level. I wonder whether a plastic playwright would have fared much better.

The Misanthrope

Comedy of manners and comedy of humors, romantic tragicomedy and philosophical facetiae, speculation on the social contract before Rousseau, heartwarming and heartbreaking—what isn't Molière's *Misanthrope*? It is one of those few plays that submit to and survive every sort of interpretation and misinterpretation; its very protagonist, Alceste, has been played in almost the full range from tragic hero to buffoon. No one production can exhaust the play's possibilities, and about the only thing concerning the work all scholars and critics can agree on is its greatness. The current production, which the Comédie Française has brought briefly to BAM, is extremely elegant, intelligently conceived, and, on the whole, well acted and directed; if it does not quite catch fire, neither does it allow one's interest to cool. And, most uncommonly for our times, it does not take a single outrageous liberty.

Pierre Dux, once a great leading actor with the Français, has remembered that this is Molière's own house, and has even given us a traditional Alceste: essentially comic, but shot through with moments of pathos. Personally, I would have preferred it if Alceste's seriousness had been hinted at a little earlier, and if the grave moments did not stick out quite so gloomily from the others; yet Dux has wisely controlled the characterizations that most easily get out of hand (Acaste, Clitandre, Oronte), and it is only Alceste whom he has orchestrated with insufficient subtlety. Or it may be that François Beaulieu, who plays him—not at all badly, but without either comic or tragic grace—can be led only so far by any director. The pacing and blocking—especially the marshaling of various mute servants as they mingle with the speaking characters—are a delight to both the mind and the senses.

There are some splendid performances—from Michel Duchaussoy as a Philinte whose elocution, deportment, and general interpretation of the part are exemplary; Guy Michel as a lusciously saucy and hedonistic Acaste; Bérangère Dautun as a rich-voiced and far from obvious Arsinoé; and Bernard Dhéran as an Oronte who is, sagely, not so great a fool but that he may deserve the praise Alceste gives him before the Marshals' Tribunal. The Célimène of Béatrice Agenin is a little lacking in energy, but otherwise nicely balanced between wit and folly, femininity and frivolity. The Eliante of Fanny Delbrice, though vocally a bit uneven, manages the difficult (because almost out of character) speech in II, v, with more appropriateness than usual—to which Dux's staging thoughtfully contributes.

Jacques Marillier's scenery, subdued but evocative, and costumes, mostly in muted colors, are both wonderfully apt. It is one of those cases where understatement does not have a trace of self-consciousness about it, and where the shapes of the costumes speak as eloquently as the colors. Alain Margoni's demure music is similarly tasteful and tactful. This *Misanthrope* is recommended to one and all; for the Peter Brooks and Andrei Serbans of this world, it should be compulsory.

Talley's Folly

Lanford Wilson's *5th of July*, a good play, turns out to be the first part of a cycle of which the current, even better, *Talley's Folly* is the second. The latter takes place, however, more than 30 years earlier, in July 1944, when Aunt Sally—who in the former play had such difficulty in disposing of the ashes of her beloved husband, Matt—is being wooed and won by Matt Friedman, the enthusiastic, fast-talking Jewish accountant from St. Louis. The place is a farm near Lebanon, Missouri; specifically, an old boathouse that is also a gazebo, built in lovable folly by an eccentric Talley ancestor. It is now Sally's secret stronghold. Here Matt, the son of Jewish war victims, started romancing the 31-year-old (but going on 27) Sally the previous summer; here he returns to win the heart of this reclusive, half-spinsterish, half-passionate nurse. Some dark secret keeps her from him, as does also her formerly mill-owning family, now rich only in prejudices against Jews, foreigners, Matt Friedmans.

The play is a duologue between Matt and Sally, from sundown through moonrise and thence to the start of three decades of married happiness. In the distance there is occasional band music holding out promises, but also the barking of threatening dogs of the kind that tear Tennessee Williams heroes into Orpheus-like pieces. Nearer by is the croaking of frogs, a discreet natural obbligato against which Matt and Sally can play out their duet of pursuit and evasion, hopefulness and disillusion, until revelations of their pasts to each other bring better understanding, absolution through mutual compassion, and final tremulous affirmation of love. It is a curious love that slowly emerges from a protective husk of banter, teasing, even pugnacity. Once out, however, it can match the moon in its zenith—hold its own even under the coming scrutiny of long sunlight.

Gradually, with the double assurance of a master of psychology and dramaturgy, Wilson unfolds not so much a series of events as a conversation that will last two joint lifetimes. Matt and Sally indulge here in some funny little sublunary capers, but mostly they abandon themselves to a river more movemented than the one flowing past the boathouse—the river of their talk. Into its eddies, sluggish spots, whirlpools, and ultimate torrent, their diverse but kindred beings slowly, haltingly, ineluctably dissolve. Wilson has written some of the most tender, wisely funny, chargedly understated dialogue I have heard from a stage in many a moon, dialogue fraught with the essence of the greatest drama on earth: that of two pitiful yet glorious human beings clumsily and splendidly staggering toward each other.

It is dialogue that, like most exalted stage dialogue, skirts the ridiculous only to stumble triumphantly onto the sublime. Says Matt: "We are so much alike to be so different, aren't we?" It sounds almost like nonsense, yet its seeming awkwardness stems only from its pressing through to the limits of the articulable; it is about that strange paradox that can make two people with identical needs and yearnings the most skittishly skirmishing antagonists. After explaining his undue tarrying by the emptiness of his car's gas tank, Matt finally confesses: "This car isn't out of gas." "What is it out of?" "Hope. The car is out of hope." The statement neither anthropomorphizes a machine nor reifies the human beings implied by the image; it simply suggests that the whole world, from a dumb engine to an overcomplicated psyche, requires the same spiritual essence to move forward. (How wise, by the way, are the French to call gasoline *essence*!)

Lanford Wilson understands the interplay of the absurd and the miraculous—indeed, their very identity—and how it sustains life. Matt mockingly and lovingly sings "Lindy Lou" to his girl. Shrinking, she protests, "Don't sing to me, Matt. And my name isn't Lindy Lou, it's Sally Talley." Then she gasps, and they laugh. The prosaic truth is imbued with preposterous poetry—doggerel that needs only a little love to change into lyric immortality. When, in 1944, Matt, the signal victim of Nazi persecution, tries to amuse Sally with a comic German accent, the young Protestant woman shudders, "No, don't! That's creepy." Matt responds with the gentlest and saddest of ironies: "Yeah. You should only know."

I could go on quoting and extolling—which in the case of *Talley's Folly* are near-synonymous—forever. But that would delay your getting to the Circle Rep and finding out for yourselves. In John Lee Beatty's grandly ludicrous set, under Dennis Parichy's realistically fairy-tale lighting, and with Marshall W. Mason's direction as inventively true to the text as a Balanchine choreography to its music, two actors whom I have tended to disbelieve in the past perform wonders of persuasion. Judd Hirsch makes Matt's likableness that plods on in walking-wounded fashion, the Semitically self-depreciating wit, and the moments of morbid apocalypse, come to unerring life—as full of warts as the croaking toads, and as crazily, left-handedly, poetic. Trish Hawkins accomplishes the even harder task of turning an overgrown hoyden masquerading as a sturdy loner into someone who wins us over not by spurts of facile sentiment, but by letting the roughnesses, jaggednesses, unsurenesses themselves convince us of their primordial humanity.

Wilson is the only American playwright I can think of who is steadily growing, improving, paring himself down to essentials. *Talley's Folly* is—in range, mood, scope—a minor work, although a broad social background is suggestively sketched in; but the fineness of its details makes up in penetrancy and pervasiveness for what it may lack in weight and impact. Its small, insistent truths, like sand in a beach house, seep into every cranny of our awareness.

Getting Out

It is gratifying to have that remarkable play, Marsha Norman's *Getting Out*, with us again, this time not for a severely limited run. I have written about its many astounding virtues in *New York* (November 13, 1978) and, again, at greater length, in the current *Hudson Review*. But oh, what bungling before this revival came to pass! After the splendid reviews garnered by the Phoenix Theater production, it was imperative to transfer the play immediately to Broadway, to which it is preeminently suited, as was done, for instance, with *The Elephant Man*. This would have allowed the Off Broadway notices to reverberate freshly in the ears of interested parties unable to catch the minuscule initial run, while also generating the excitement attendant on a transfer from Off Broadway to Broadway—as thrilling to the public as a commoner's marrying royalty.

Unfortunately, the neophyte producers who were going to mount *Getting Out* on Broadway overextended themselves and, after gumming up the works for a good while, had to relinquish it. Further delays, as I understand, were caused by the temporary unavailability of one of the leading actresses. Finally, the new producing team decided to bring the play into a house one of its members owns, the Theater de Lys, a less good showcase than the Marymount Theater, where it was originally on view. Here the set, which represents four locales simultaneously, is unduly cramped—not to mention a noisy air-conditioning system and the rumble of passing subway trains.

Even so, under Jon Jory's wisely plotted and unerringly paced direction, the play is still a must. The past and present of the heroine—Arlene, as she calls herself now, and Arlie, as she was known then—continue to simmer and sizzle respectively. At the center is Arlene, the presumably reformed parolee with nothing much to look forward to yet loath to look back at her fascinating and repellent former self, Arlie, who burns up the edges of the acting area even as she has scorched Arlene's memories. Arlie is almost always hovering around the periphery: maltreated, full of hate, suffering and inflicting violence, punished and rebellious, in and out of prison, in and out of Arlene's haunted brain. *Getting Out* is about more than one kind of imprisonment: a tyrannical family circle, an impersonal school system, cramping economic conditions, jail, inadequate opportunities for rehabilitation, and the past that does not let one go.

Yet the marvelous balance of *Getting Out* is such that the play neither preaches nor sentimentalizes; least of all does it offer easy solutions for problems that seem all but insoluble. Keeping its sense of horror and sense of humor equally to the fore, it points no accusing fingers and hands out no facile accolades. There is pity for all—even for the repulsive mother and the contemptible pimp—but no whitewashing. Above all, there is understanding of every sort. Every impulse and revulsion, every overreaction and impassivity, every murderous urge and unfathomable softening is fully realized from within. No gesture is arbitrary, no syllable rings false. The language is the play's greatest asset: coarse-grained, unvarnished, often hateful, sometimes fumbling for tenderness, funny yet beyond laughter (except the hysterical kind), heartbreaking yet a stranger to tears. And always frighteningly true.

The miracle is that *Getting Out* was written by a thirtyish Louisville newspaperwoman whose only concrete experience with the lower orders and criminality was some work with severely disturbed children, and who had never written for the stage before. Originally produced by the Actors Theater of Louisville, this is still substantially its production. The supporting performances range from satisfactory to just barely adequate, but no matter: the two leads are sublime, and carry Marsha Norman's play securely.

As Arlie, Pamela Reed is the exploding embodiment of thwarted innocence, of youthful enthusiasm turned to hatred, of pain hardened into brutal defiance. Miss Reed can squeeze beauty and wit out of total aggression and never loses the child that cowers inside the monster. As her older and soberer self, Arlene, Susan Kingsley is perhaps even more soul-wrenching. Such contrary states as determination and puzzlement, eagerness and exhaustion, nascent trust and invincible suspiciousness, unforgiving rancor and the need for re-attachment fight it out in her face, body, voice. The entire woman is a constantly riven battleground, except when the inner violence temporarily subsides into a barbed no-man's-land where past grief and grievance rest up for renewed outbursts. These, more muted and abrasive than Arlie's eruptions, are, if anything, even more chilling. Bring on laurel wreaths for the Misses Norman, Kingsley, and Reed.

Happy Days

When Samuel Beckett's *Happy Days* first appeared on the stage, I did not yet love it, but at least I liked it more than either Kenneth Tynan or Robert Brustein did. Since then, however, my admiration and affection for the play have steadily grown, and I am now con-

vinced that all it needs to be a resounding success is a good actress
with no ax to grind, a director who does not place himself above
the author, and an audience with some brains in their heads. Such
requirements may, of course, be progressively harder to meet, and,
certainly, the current revival of *Happy Days* at the Public Theater
fails in at least two of them.

The play, as you should know, concerns Winnie, waist-deep
in the sod at the center of a mound overgrown with withered
grass; and then, in the second act, chin-deep. While she still can,
she spends her days fussing with the toiletries in her large bag,
a parasol, and, occasionally, her husband, Willie. He lives in a
hole on the other side of the mound, is still fully mobile but extremely uncommunicative. Mostly he reads his newspaper, mutters to himself, and now and then says a word or two to Winnie.
She, however, is cheerful—insanely cheerful under the circumstances—and keeps up a steady patter of observations, reflections,
recollections, and sometimes even snatches of half-remembered
poetry and songs. She has a gun in her satchel, but suicide is out
of the question; even when she is in it up to her head, even when
Willie can no longer climb the mound to touch her, she goes on
contentedly, garrulously, gossipily, ecstatically jabbering about the
infinite mercies of existence.

Happy Days is both a masterly literary metaphor and a powerful
stage image. An image, moreover, that sustains itself through a series
of small but brilliant variations for one and a quarter hours—the
duration of the play and, it would seem, of human life, with which
it manages to become co-extensive. This is not the place—and decidedly not the space—for a full discussion of the play, but I must
quote two magisterial moments from it. The first occurs in Act I
when, describing how an ant disports itself, Winnie elicits Willie's
pun, "Formication." Blissfully, she exclaims: "How can one better
magnify the Almighty than by sniggering with him at his little jokes,
particularly the poorer ones?" A whole world view, a philosophy of
life, a theology even, are encapsulated in that remark.

Then, in the even bleaker, but still comic, Act II, there is the moment when Winnie tries to convince herself that she has not yet lost
her reason: "Not yet. *Pause.* Not all. *Pause.* Some remains. *Pause.*
Sounds. *Pause.* Like little… sunderings, little falls… apart." This,
to me, appears infinitely heroic, endlessly moving. Beckett's best
plays, like this one, are great because they are free of every vestige of
that dramatic provincialism that addresses itself to specific aspects

or problems of life. They are, instead, about life itself: all life, and nothing but life.

And also about what keeps life going: sounds. And words, which are also sounds—"Ah yes, great mercies, great mercies." Which is why Walter Kerr strikes me as dead wrong when he writes in *Journey to the Center of the Theater*, his new book, that in Beckett's plays "if existence [has] any meaning… it [is] not going to be conveyed to us in language." Winnie's words Kerr found to be "pass-the-time words, pretty flights into futility. They accomplished nothing on the arid desert she inhabited; the sand would soon reach her mouth, it was silence that was coming." Well, what greater achievement is there in life, as Beckett, the lapsed Catholic (as opposed to Kerr, the practicing one), perceives it, than keeping one's courage going by passing the time through hearing and emitting sounds, by glorying in the word, which was in the beginning, and accompanies us, sheltering, to the end? Surely Beckett is not one of Kerr's silent comedians but the one dramatist who has written a play (*Not I*) about a mouth—just a mouth that doesn't stop talking. And what else is the series of novels Beckett has written—all of them straining toward, and some attaining, the condition of monologue—except words that make the inevitable flight to futility at least pretty, sometimes actually beautiful?

As the editors of the invaluable *Samuel Beckett: The Critical Heritage* remind us, Winnie is "considered one of the greatest and most challenging roles in the dramatic repertoire." Unfortunately, the lovely, always fine and often magnificent, Irene Worth fails to meet that challenge. I don't know to what extent the failure is hers, and to what extent that of Andrei Serban, the director she seems to trust, but whom I trust as far as I can throw the Empire State Building. The attempt seems to have been to render Winnie (also Willie, also the play) as comical as possible by making Miss Worth carry on as brashly, ribaldly, coquettishly, and scatter-brainedly as can be. Those qualities are, most assuredly, parts of Winnie, but they must not obscure a basic quality of touching, childlike courage—of brave, tragicomic whistling in the dark.

All previous Winnies I have seen kept, in their different ways, that quality to the fore. The superb Ruth White did it through a touchingly dumb, almost bovine, confidence; the highly accomplished Jessica Tandy, through a brittle worldliness that is the very mask any frightened girl-child is likeliest to assume; and the incomparable, the sublime Madeleine Renaud, through charm—the charm of child, woman, crone, artist, and, above all, chatterer who

knows that only this verbal chatter can stave off the other, more terrible chatter of teeth at the approach of annihilation. Miss Worth,
however, gives us—or is directed to give us—speech so full of accelerandos, rallentandos, unnecessary crescendos, capricious di-
minuendos, and all sorts of rubatos that one feels in the presence
not of a real human being but of some dreadful talking or singing
doll out of E. T. A. Hoffmann or Pierre Boulez's underground electronic hell's kitchen. Still, Miss Worth has some fine moments, but
the human and artistic greatness of the play is severely impaired.

Matters are not helped by the presence of George Voskovec as
Willie, a small and easy role that requires ungiftedness and un-
charmingness as bottomless as Voskovec's to ruin it. Here, again,
Serban, by making the actor growl and grunt lines that should be
spoken, and by choreographing at the end a whole clown show
complete with Willie's repeatedly butting the ground with his head,
has made a bad thing worse. Moreover, Voskovec's ugly Czech accent, so incommensurate with Worth's melodious strains, inflicts
further uncalled-for cacophony.

Michael Yeargan and Lawrence King's set is impressive, although
perhaps a bit too grand; Jane Greenwood's costuming is correct,
though a trifle too arch; Jennifer Tipton's lighting is flawless. But,
for me, Serban has diminished *Happy Days* to about 40 percent of
its potential; I can recommend this production only to those who
already know the play and are interested in comparisons rather
than discoveries.

Richard III

Richard III, starring Al Pacino, disproves two charges frequently
brought against American companies in Shakespearean productions: that they cannot do accents and that they are incapable of
ensemble work. In this *Richard III* there are accents aplenty—every
kind of accent you have ever heard in your life, except one that has
anything to do with Shakespeare. As for ensemble work, everyone
from star to walk-on—absolutely without exception—manages to
give a bad performance. Such unheard-of consistence does make
for an ensemble: an ensemble of horror, but an ensemble. Actually,
Pacino has a few good moments, but what are they as against entire
scenes mangled or merely thrown away?

What Pacino seems to be playing most of the time is Rumpel-
stiltskin, the mean, foot-stamping dwarf—except in one scene,
where, unaccountably sporting a beret, he may think he is doing
Toulouse-Lautrec. He frequently walks with a cane that, more often
yet, he tosses at the bystanders, who may toss it back at him—perhaps because he is considering, if his bid for kingship fails, juggling
as an alternative profession. With the young princes, when he must
keep his menace down to loaded ironies, Pacino is very effective,
as he is also in one or two other instances, but in such scenes as the
opening monologue (Gloucestershire, if not Yorkshire, ham), the
wooing of Lady Anne (leaden), and the departure for battle at Bosworth Field (clownish—he starts out to the left, only to be pointed
to the right), and in many others, he is ludicrous.

His greatest problem—after mood—is vocal. Pacino wallows
in the Bard's verbiage like someone who has just inherited a fortune in syllables and wants to squeeze every sinful delight out of
spending it. "Lass-civvy-ous," he will say, or "desk-ant"; he will even
misaccentuate a word in his dogged pursuit of pentameter: "The
idle pleasures *of* these days..." hitting that "of" as if Shakespeare's
scansion were metronomic. And the pauses! "Dive... thoughts...
down to my soul... Here... Clarence... comes," by which time, in
any sensible production, Clarence would be gone. (Indeed, despite
heavy cutting, this *Richard III* lasts as long as any normal uncut version.) Otherwise, Pacino gives us speech that is the flattest Amur-
rican ("Stayanley, wot's de noose?"), except when he opts for a bit
of falsetto in imitation of Olivier's marvelous Richard, or when,
in a scene with Jaime Sanchez's Ratcliffe, he falls into the latter's
Hispanic singsong.

I shall spare you the misery of reading about the rest of the
cast—apparently handpicked for their one talent: the ability not
to give the star any competition whatsoever. But I must voice my
utter consternation at Penelope Allen's Lady Anne. This part (remember how superbly touching Claire Bloom was in the excellent,
still underrated movie *Richard III*?) virtually cannot fail, though
even Miss Allen's appearance goes a long way toward achieving
the impossible—she looks like the ghost of Sir Cedric Hardwicke,
dentures and all, gotten up for the part of Sir Andrew Aguecheek.
But oh, the performance! A face frozen into ghostly absence, the
movements and gestures of a constipated arthritic, and the toneless speech of an ill-taught deaf person talking by guesswork. It is
almost enough to make Linda Selman's Bronx fishwife of a Queen

Elizabeth, who keeps giving us the finger, look good.

The staging by David Wheeler—who is a friend of mine but probably won't be hereafter—is either totally gray or given to pseudo-ideas, such as having Richard strangle his own henchman Catesby on Bosworth Field. Richard, incidentally, fights bare-handed against Richmond's armed followers. What is this? A last-minute plea for sympathy for the devil? An allusion to Elizabethan bearbaiting? Sheer directorial madness? Michael Langham and Ed Gilbert are known to have lent a hand or foot to Wheeler, and it is just possible that every scene was directed not by a triumvirate but by a stalemate. Or else the star may have supplied his own Pacinoid direction.

Tony Straiges, the gifted set designer, has come up with the most unevocative scenery of his short but distinguished career; Jeanne Button's costume design is totally schizophrenic, with the women's costumes some five centuries behind the men's—perhaps to explain how feminism came about. Even the worthy Thomas Skelton's lighting for once goes in for crude, monochromatic effects: entire scenes are all green or all red, as if the show were lit by traffic lights. "Dogs bark at me as I halt by them," says Richard at one point; if they were admitted to this production, they would hardly stop at that.

The audience aimed at—and obtained—was one of teenyboppers in fact or spirit. Most of the time I heard gum-snapping from the row behind me, and my companion overheard the prize remark in the ladies' room before the show began. Said one nubile thing to another: "See you at halftime!" Still, there is one great moment when Pacino, the spittingest actor I've ever seen (he creates a Scottish mist around him wherever he moves), gets Lady Anne to expectorate in his face. It is a perfect case of spit for spat and provides us with the only true catharsis. But this happens early in the play; after that, we are left high and dry.

Peter Pan

"Above all she had the touch of heartbreaking tragedy that is there in the story or fable from beginning to end…" "He was a tragic and rather ghastly creation who knew no peace, and whose soul was in torment… a bogey of fear who lives perpetually in the grey recesses of every small boy's mind." These perceptive evaluations of how the hero and villain of J. M. Barrie's *Peter Pan* were, and had to be, played were, alas, not written about Sandy Duncan and George Rose in the current Broadway revival of the musical-comedy version. The first eyewitness account—from Denis Mackail, Barrie's biographer—concerns Nina Boucicault, the original Peter Pan of the 1904 premiere; the second—from Daphne du Maurier—concerns her father, Gerald, the original Captain Hook. I derive both quotations from Andrew Birkin's *J. M. Barrie and the Lost Boys*, one of the most remarkable biographical works I have ever read.

Just as Barrie is a much more important playwright than his current neglect indicates, *Peter Pan* is a much deeper, darker, finer play than this insipid revival of its blandly boring, bowdlerized musicalization suggests. As Max Beerbohm wrote in his penetrating review of 1905: "Mr. Barrie is not that rare creature, a man of genius. He is something even more rare—a child who, by some divine grace, can express through an artistic medium the childishness that is in him." Barrie was a complex and contradictory talent; to this day experts debate whether he was impotent, homosexual, a sadist. Certain facts are incontrovertible. He did declare that "nothing that happens after we are twelve matters very much," and a large part of his life and work confirms this assertion. His greatest horror as a young man was the thought of marriage and having to make love to a woman—it was a recurrent nightmare that had him waking up screaming. In his notebooks we find things like "Grow up & have to give up marbles—awful thought."

Yet Barrie did love pretty women and kept having platonic romances with many of them, especially actresses. One of these he married, but whether the marriage was consummated is unclear; certainly there were no children. For her tenth wedding anniversary, Mrs. Barrie extracted from her husband the promise not to be pawed and kissed good-night any more; eventually, and fairly scandalously, she divorced him. Yet there is no plain evidence of homosexuality, at least of an active sort, even though there was Barrie's overinvolvement with his mother, into whose childhood he kept wanting to withdraw. The real problem may have been his short stature: Barrie measured only five feet three. In a 1931 letter, Barrie wrote that at six feet three "I would not have bothered to turn out reels of printed matter. My one aim would have been to become a favorite of the ladies..."

He fell, as it were, in love with five young children, the Llewellyn Davies boys, and the stories they told one another gave rise to *Peter*

Pan. When the Davies boys were orphaned, Barrie became their de facto guardian; it was the tragedy of his life that his two favorites among them died young: one in World War 1, the other drowning at Oxford with a fellow student, possibly in a homosexual suicide pact.

I dwell on all this to indicate what serious and fascinating problems underlie that spellbinding play *Peter Pan*, with which this shortened and shallow musicalization of 1954, tailored to the ambiguous talents of Mary Martin and Cyril Ritchard, has relatively little to do. The songs, whether by Carolyn Leigh and Mark Charlap, or by Betty Comden, Adolph Green, and Jule Styne (whose "additional songs" constitute half the score) are undistinguished—though I rather like "Hook's Waltz," which George Rose renders now as if he had swallowed his own hook; the dances by Jerome Robbins, at least as rechoreographed by Rob Iscove, who also lamely directed, are uninspired. It is typical of this feeble version that it opts for the syrupy ending Barrie added for one performance only in 1908, rather than for the much tougher and funnier one in the printed text. In any case, what we see at the Lunt-Fontanne Theater has nothing to do with Barrie's own 1922 notebook entry that sums up the play: "Long after writing 'P. Pan' its true meaning came to me—Desperate attempt to grow up but can't." We get barely a hint that mixed in with the jollity of eternal childhood is a terrible pathos.

Sandy Duncan would be a charming and convincing Peter but for two things: she has an uninteresting voice, and she is dreadfully, dreadfully American in a play whose Britishness is of the essence. There is something specific and splendid about British children that has to be captured here before one can reach for the universal. A Peter Pan who, more than once, says "Yeah!" is an aberration. But the whole production is recast in the mold of Middle America. The sole major exception is George Rose, who, however, turns Captain Hook into a campy Punch looking for a Jude rather than a Judy. No child could recognize its fears in him, no adult find the deeper meaning in that performance.

The others, especially the two Wendys (child and woman), are best ignored altogether. Peter Wolf's scenery fluctuates between attractiveness and garishness; Bill Hargate's costumes are mostly shoddy or sleazy. Tinker Bell has become a laser beam—well, at least she isn't a hologram. In the flying sequences, the wires show overmuch. But the audience minds no more than it does that the meaning doesn't show at all.

Evita

"He looted the country," the great writer Jorge Luis Borges said to Paul Theroux about Juan Perón. "His wife was a prostitute. A common prostitute." Or, you might say, a whore with a hoard of gold. Is that a fit subject for a musical or pop opera or whatever *Evita* is? Perhaps, if the work had an intelligent—or at least clear—point of view. But Tim Rice and Andrew Lloyd Webber have taken Eva Duarte Perón—this whore, dictatress, and hypocritical pseudo-saint—and turned her into something mighty like a heroine. It is hard to say from their trashy work whether they actually admire her, which would be reprehensible, or are merely exploiting, without any moral point of view, her sensational story which is, if anything, more loathsome.

The most charitable guess is that they admire her but lack the courage of their convictions—note how much more likable they make her than they do Juan Perón, whom they clearly despise. They even make her arch-enemy, Ché Guevara, concede: "She had her moments. She had some style." Otherwise, this fictionalized Ché acts as a highly critical commentator, a mocking and damning chorus. He is supposed to represent the voice of reason, of humanity, undercutting the Perón lies and underlining the Perón crimes. But that, for the authors, is having it both ways: relishing every bit of Eva's scheming and ruthlessness while conveniently setting up a cardboard figure to castigate them. Moral judgments issuing from a figment—for this Ché is only a ghost, a stage device—cannot carry the same conviction as the resourceful and irresistible rise of a real figure. The stage Evita comes out ahead of the stage Ché by being more substantial, historic, alive. In a play about Ché a disembodied Evita would, of course, finish second.

So it is perfectly useless to say that Evita is not held up for approbation; a protagonist who displays cunning, energy, wit, and, above all, phenomenal success will always seduce the unthinking masses, whether they be shirtless Argentines or bedizened Broadwayites. What the real-life Eva accomplished on a large scale the stage Evita reproduces in miniature, but stench is stench on any scale. I am not arguing, of course, that anyone seeing *Evita* will rush out and do likewise, but I am saying that a show like this ends up glorifying a base opportunist and Fascist, just as certain books by Capote and Mailer end up magnifying and dignifying murderers.

It is particularly melancholy to note the number of Jews involved in the producing of *Evita*, starting with its director; how would these people feel about a musical whose protagonist was Stalin, Hitler, or that other Eva, Braun—even assuming that the show would include a choric Mandelstam or fictionalized Einstein to berate that protagonist?

The answer to that question, I am afraid, is available in the movie *The Producers*, in which a crazy Nazi writes a passionate tribute to his idol that as a gimmicked-up Broadway musical, *Springtime for Hitler*, has, theatergoers laughing their asinine heads off and becomes the hit of the town. I should not at all be surprised if this "Springtime for Evita" (as even Clive Barnes saw fit to dub the blatantly pro-Evita London version) ends up doing just as well. Let no one doubt the ability of life to imitate anti-art.

There are, to be sure, other problems with *Evita*. In a real opera, the simplicities or melodramatics of the typical plot are compensated for by the music and singing. It sometimes positively helps that a libretto is only a set of static but emotion-charged situations—like those flashy stills from a movie displayed outside the cinema—on which the composer and singers can work their wonders. In *Evita*, however, you have Lloyd Webber's junky tunes (except for two or three that are quite nice although derivative) and Rice's either strained or flat lyrics, and, instead of singing, electronics. Abe Jacob's sound comes across as if it comprised stationary mikes, body mikes, even soul mikes—no mere human sound is allowed to besmirch this triumph of technology.

You look, then, for an inventive story line, for the battle of wits and words, for character development; in *Evita* there is none. Responsible for this is in part the quasi-operatic form and in part the lack of ideas in the authors' heads. Granted, there are a couple of clever touches. Evita's rise is embodied in a number in which a revolving panel spews out a long line of ever fancier lovers even as, after each turn of the panel, Evita is revealed in a more resplendent dishabille. And Perón's coming to power is conveyed by a game of musical chairs in which Juan defeats the other colonels. Very nice, but hardly enough to hang a whole musical on.

Other clevernesses abound, but these, I am fairly sure, are due to the various designers, the director, and the choreographer. Well, not so much the choreographer, Larry Fuller, who is mostly copying the styles of others, notably the devices of Michael Bennett. But Timothy O'Brien and Tazeena Firth have used something like a giant Erector Set and a huge screen that rises, descends, approaches, and recedes to good effect; David Hersey has done all kinds of innovative things with lighting, especially using light from below with dramatic eeriness, and Harold Prince has orchestrated newsreel clips, slides, banners, placards, torches, and large numbers of extras in sculptural masses most tellingly. He has shrewdly perceived that the thinness and sleaziness of the material can best be disguised by turning it into a three-ring circus. Quite literally, few are the times when the principals are not doing one thing, the dancers quite another, and the overhead screen a third. As it happens, the documentary footage about the Peróns is much the most interesting element, and Prince wisely allows it to usurp our attention at the slightest possible opportunity.

The three principals are surprisingly good; I say surprisingly because I have never much cared for any of them heretofore. Patti LuPone's lupine presence and barnstorming antics are an apt replica of Eva Perón's looks and methods. Miss LuPone is neither charming nor attractive, and her voice, whenever volume is required, goes harshly metallic over and above the ministrations of microphones. But she acts very persuasively, sings and dances hard yet without visible effort, and in all ways gives of herself unstintingly, thus overcoming her natural disadvantages. Bob Gunton struts and postures with a nice blend of Perónian obtuseness and menace, and his coprophagous smile may well be the most appallingly apt histrionic element in the show. As Ché, Mandy Patinkin sorely lacks the original's grace and good looks, but he shows a variety and flexibility I would not have suspected in him and does convey the multiplicity and ubiquity we want from a one-man chorus. Jane Ohringer seems appealing as Perón's child-mistress thrown out by Evita, but in such a relatively sympathetic role, and with one of the show's better numbers to sing, it would be hard not to score.

In the end, we must concede to the show what the lyrics say about its heroine: it has its moments, it has some style. It even has lots of style or, in view of its eclecticism, styles. But I must come back to the moral issue: what sorts of chaps are these authors who can exalt with equal enthusiasm Jesus Christ the last time round and Eva Perón this time? The two had nothing in common except that both died at 33. To Rice and Lloyd Webber, however, they seem equally suitable for enshrinement: Jesus, they tell us, was a superstar; Evita, as one of her lyrics drives home, had star quality. The star of Bethlehem or the star of Buenos Aires can pay off equally well for our star-struck authors. If you want to help fill the coffers of these two amoral, barely talented whippersnappers and their knowing or duped accomplices, by all means see this artfully produced monument to human indecency. The bad taste of the offering should linger in your mouth.

Sugar Babies

Vulgarians of the world, unite and rush off to Sugar Babies; you have nothing to lose but the last shred of good taste that may fortuitously adhere to you. If there is such a thing as consummate bad taste, Sugar Babies has it, and anyone concerned for his aesthetic health is herewith urged to switch to Sweet 'n Low. Conceived by Ralph G. Allen and Harry Rigby (conception is a blessing, but not as they conceive), the show is a glorification of burlesque without a jot of leavening satire or a tittle of brazen honesty (to evoke burlesque without including the artists of the G-string is like paying tribute to the symphonic orchestra without including a string section). Now, I can imagine (though not condone) an homage to something as vulgar as burlesque on a modest scale, preserving the crudity and raunchiness of the original even in its shabby format. But I am appalled by the use of one of Broadway's biggest and best-appointed theaters, by the spending of much money and effort in 1979 to the apotheosis of the most primitive, mindless kind of spectacle that ever muddied the boards. That some prominent reviewers could rave about this exhibition is nothing short of disheartening.

Well, this is where the unholy alliance between vulgarity and sentimentality, between senile nostalgia and ever-fresh bad taste, comes in. There is nothing wrong with sexual humor, scatological farce, flashy and fleshy display, if there is demonstrable wit, some form of visible or audible originality, about it. Making pigs of ourselves (s'encanailler, as French so neatly puts it) is profoundly human, so long as the redeeming aspects of creative imagination are present—if the jokes are new and inventive, if the lewdness has levity, if the Flesh is offered by the Devil (who is also a gentleman) rather than by graceless peddlers. In Sugar Babies, the obscenity is obsolete, the bawdry tawdry, and the wit nit. It all appeals only to inane nostalgia, bathing gook in the golden glow of idle reminiscence. To recall affectionately our youthful innocence is one thing;

to crawl back into our crassest immaturity, quite another. Where is the slush of yesteryear? At the Mark Hellinger Theater.

I am sorry that among those whose songs have been used or reused there should be the names of Jimmy McHugh and Dorothy Fields, even if they are represented mostly by their lesser efforts; what the others have contributed is abysmal. Raoul Pène du Bois has come up with perfect costumes and scenery, and Gilbert V. Hemsley Jr.'s lights are equally right. Ralph G. Allen's sketches, "based on traditional material," are as base as the traditional material and, by now, old enough to know better. The eponymous Ernest Flatt's choreography, like his and Rudy Tronto's staging, labors under the advantage that, in this kind of venture, ineptitude is appropriate. The supporting cast is amply suited to the aforesaid traditional material, and the chorus girls really look as if they had gotten their minks the way minks do.

Mickey Rooney looks and does everything a burlesque comic can be expected to look and do; he may not be a Bert Lahr or a David Burns, but he comes within croaking distance of both. At a mere 59, he manages to look like a sassy 68 and move like a nimble 72, although his rendition of "I Can't Give You Anything but Love, Baby" (a good song, that) gives us also a sufficiency of false and cracked notes. A balding, bulging bundle of brashness, Rooney is truly a hardy perennial. Ann Miller, at a mere *je ne sais combien*, manages to move even better, her brand of stale dancing unwithered by age; her legs are still fine, and her figure (though not her face) still squeezable into shape. But whereas Rooney's personality continues to be that of a small-time winner, Miss Miller's remains that of an all-time loser, her every (only?) expression oozing vapidity.

There is one oasis in this desert of degradation: Bob Williams's reverse dog act, with the dog pathetically flubbing or funking everything while the trainer covers up with heroically smiling-through-the-tears patter. I have seen this thing done even better, at the Lido in Paris last year, but it is, as Williams and friend do it, still funny, touching, and good. At least *Sugar Babies* sports a nice dog-within-a-dog.

The Jail Diary of Albie Sachs

The Jail Diary of Albie Sachs, which David Edgar has fashioned from the prison memoir of a young Jewish South African lawyer, Albert Sachs, is by its very ominous understatement one of the most powerful stage works to come out of South Africa, that cradle of social injustice and extraordinary playwriting. It is pitiful that it should take the brutality of apartheid to produce some of the most haunting drama of our time, but inspiriting that such drama gets written, whether or not our audiences want or deserve it. Those at the Manhattan Theater Club are particularly crass and unruly. Take the young couple that came in just as the play began: swathed in furs and carrying brimful glasses, they proceeded to undress, drink, rattle ice cubes, and chatter inanely through the most moving scenes, not to mention their trampling on my feet. They were, however, a useful reminder that the scandal of South Africa could happen here.

Albie Sachs, jailed under the preposterous "90-days law," which allows the government to arrest and detain people without trial for indefinitely renewable three-month periods, was held in solitary confinement for nigh on six months, during which he was dragged from one jail to another, almost released only to be thrown back in, sometimes accorded a few comforts (books, writing materials) and sometimes not, and never tortured except by utter isolation. He was not quite a hero: though long refusing to answer questions, he did make some concessions at last to get out. Rearrested two years later, he finally left the country in self-defense. Nevertheless, his stalling game did help others, and even his partial, as it were Brechtian, heroism inspired friends and confounded enemies. At one point in the play, Albie lies down on his cot and lets us stare in absolute silence at bare cell walls. Even this little proves acutely painful; then what about six months?

Sachs does not hate anyone: not a former Nazi prison commander who shows him some kindness, not various more or less obvious brutes merely executing orders, not the hand that holds the whip, even though he cringes hearing another, presumably black, prisoner being flogged next door. He hates only the whip itself and racism. Of such material, you cannot make heroes, only saints. But Albie is too sensual and unfanatical for a saint. Yet by hanging on to humor, sanity, and humanity under extremely trying circumstances, he proves himself something as good: a full human being. This brings this documentary drama that much nearer to us; so too does its humor, from black to childish but all of it invigorating and elating.

As Albie, Brian Murray gives a complex, munificent, subtly chiseled yet ultimately towering performance. This Albie is faintly fatuous even at his best; his defiance is humpbacked, his brave words a bit buffoonish. But Murray conveys intelligence in action: thoughts watching themselves being hatched and taking wing; the mind forced to be both performer and spectator and enjoying both. When he cannot pad a harsh, cement wall with sensuous bonhomie, he plays a kind of mental squash against the naked hardness. But when he cannot even play this squash, and squashes fists of flesh against metal doors, he makes us feel his physical defeat and pain as keenly as his intellectual victories. Particularly moving is the way he regresses—becomes more childish, clownish, sluggish as confinement corrodes him—and how, when he cannot bounce, he crawls back. The role (as long and arduous as Hamlet) demands nonstop mental and physical energy, which Murray rises to with superb pacing, shading, shaping.

Although this performance alone makes the play a must, there is also uniformly fine supporting work from the entire cast, the cogent direction of Lynne Meadow, the set design of John Lee Beatty, and Jennifer Tipton's lighting. If there is one flaw, it is that the last scene, though philosophically needed, is dramatically anticlimactic and should have been boiled down to one speech. No matter. *The Jail Diary of Albie Sachs*, though no circus, is as necessary as bread.

Night and Day

Rumors from England reported that in his new stage work, *Night and Day*, Tom Stoppard, like Prospero at the end of *The Tempest*, abjured his magic and returned to solid dramatic humanity. There was still plenty of cleverness, we were told, but it was not what the play was about: the tricks, the verbal bravura, the visual pyrotechnics were subservient to something bigger—though I don't recall anyone's telling me what this bigger something was. Last week we found out. When the staff of acrobatic rhetoric is buried and the book of dramaturgical tricks drowned, when all that is *mere* cleverness is peeled away, there remains—more cleverness.

Let me not put cleverness down, at least not when it is as erudite, intricate, various, original, and witty as Stoppard's can be. Compared to his product, Ayckbourn's is (usually) Brand X; Neil Simon's, Z. But though you can heighten ordinary crossword puzzles into the London *Times* kind, double your crostics, and three-dimensionalize your ticktacktoe, you cannot deepen mere cleverness into genuine art. Stoppard gives the best interviews within recent and not so recent memory; his party conversation—I was privileged to hear it on a few occasions—is glittering; I have sat agape at any number of his plays ("How does he think up those things?"); the only trouble is that I never was—and this does not follow as the night the day—moved by him.

The point is that comedy—which is what Stoppard writes even when, as in *Night and Day*, someone gets killed—can be moving in its particular way. In Shaw's *Man and Superman*, for instance, John Tanner's ludicrous nonwooing of and conquest by Ann Whitefield is finally moving as well as funny. Even in a Feydeau farce there is something touching when things sort themselves out at last and revert to a frail, precarious—human—order. The playwright whom—in his literacy, wit, farflung fantasy, ability to use the stage as a picture book of wonders, and weaving of verbal magic carpets—Stoppard most resembles is Jean Giraudoux. Yet Giraudoux has something that sets him entirely apart from and above Stoppard. It is an indefinable something that goes by various names—"poetry," "feeling," and "soul" leap to mind—but that can at least be described as the quality almost entirely absent from Stoppard's work. Did you feel anything for the deaths of Stoppard's Rosencrantz and Guildenstern? Did you give a hoot if Cahoot's *Macbeth* could not be performed at Prague's National Theater? Did it make even a Hecuban difference whether that eponymous Free Man entered or exited?

In *Night and Day*, the author, according to his statements in a *New York Times* interview, discovered that two plays he had been thinking about could actually be the same play. One was a love story, the other a play about journalism. "The arcs intersected," be told the interviewer, and he wound up, he hoped, "with more than the sum of two parts." As I see it, it is three plays that intersected, and what Stoppard wound up with is less than the sum of one part.

Briefly, Geoffrey Carson is a British mine owner and a key figure in the imaginary but all too imaginable African country of Kam-

bawe, where Colonel Shimbu has revolted against President Mageeba. Carson's country house is to be the meeting place for secret
negotiations between the two adversaries; because it has the only
unnationalized Telex, it is also where Dick Wagner, star reporter,
and George Guthrie, ace photographer, of the London *Daily Globe*
foregather, and where Jacob Milne, the quixotic free lance who
scooped them, shows up in due time. This, naturally, gives rise to
lengthy discussions of what journalism is or should be ("I am with
you on the free press—its the newspapers that I can't stand!"), a
debate in which President Mageeba joins in, punctuating his repres-
sive views with a blood-drawing riding crop.

But the house also turns into a trysting place. Ruth, Carson's
wife, who is devoted to her husband yet also has a penchant for
one-night stands, has just returned from London, where she once
bedded Dick Wagner ("twice" would make her "a tart," according to
her code; what happens once in hotel rooms doesn't count because
"they are a separate moral universe"). She is horrified to see Dick
pop up for what she erroneously takes to be a second helping, and
becomes all the more waspish because she has just begun planning
another dalliance, with Jacob. Incidentally, an appreciable part of
the play consists of monologues and dialogues inside Ruth's head;
these strange interludes are often, deliberately but confusingly, difficult to distinguish from what goes on outside.

So, you see, there is this African civil war, then the inquiry into
the nature of journalism, and, thirdly, the love story diversified with
interior monologues. The war is extremely hard to follow because
huge quantities of imaginary facts and invented, outlandish names
are hurled at you at break*head* speed. The debate on journalism
is not illustrated by the story: the ideas and actions of the various
journalists are neither fully embodied nor significantly belied by
their respective destinies; everything remains random and rather
chaotic. As for the love story—what love story? Ruth's patronizing affection for her husband? Her fly-by-night affair with Dick
that might or might not be extended by one more night and day?
Her fantasized fling with Jacob? Or perhaps (especially in Maggie
Smith's narcissistic performance) her infatuation with herself—her
cleverness with words and parallel lives and loves?

Stoppard's notion of dramatic intersections proves even more
perilous to the playwright than real ones to speeding drivers: his
stories do not so much intersect as collide. In any case, should plots
intersect? Shouldn't they rather intertwine, fuse, and reinforce one

another? What they certainly must avoid is what they do here: keep bombarding us with triple but not triune sets of information. The spectator's brain is caught in a cross fire of complex pseudogeographical and pseudohistorical data and relentlessly clever verbiage in elaborate syntactical garb. It is worse than watching a three-ring circus; it is like *being* in all three rings simultaneously.

However, so much cleverness cannot come entirely to nothing. There are substantial stretches of laughter-begetting repartee, verbal and visual inventions to take one's breath away, and ample opportunities for the director, actors, and set and lighting designers (Carl Toms and Neil Peter Jampolis, and bravo to both) to work their stunts and spells. Most of them do. As Ruth, Maggie Smith is a superior ham; if that is your dish, you can feast on it here. No one can toss her head in more directions at once; no one can stretch timing out farther and still make the point, in the nick of time, snap into place; no one can offer you a better roller-coaster ride on her voice; and no one can better persuade you that the work of a master choreographer has gone into mere lounging and skulking. Still, ham is ham, and, in the theater, I am with the orthodox Muslims and Jews. And, by the way, someone should tell Miss Smith that "slavering," according to the Oxford English Dictionary, rhymes not with "wavering" but with "have a ring."

Paul Hecht is a splendidly idiosyncratic Wagner, Dwight Schultz a laconically incisive Guthrie, Joseph Maher an assuredly efficacious Carson (if the part contained more comedy, he'd be better yet), and Peter Evans, whom I used not to like, pleasantly surprised me with the range of his Jacob. Clarence Williams III does the black menace he specializes in yet again; his Mageeba is on target, but what could the Caliban this dictator played back in his English school days have been like? Clumsy, I suspect. The accents are all well managed under Peter Wood's inventive and well-paced direction; the visual elements range from fine to spectacular. But there remains that great emptiness where the play's depth ought to be—where the poetic, emotional, moral universe should take over. Perhaps Stoppard's plays are all written in hotel rooms.

Bent

Martin Sherman, the author of *Bent*, tells us about the research he did in London's Wiener Library: reading dozens of books about Nazi Germany and the plight of homosexuals under Hitler. Actually, the only prerequisites for the writing of *Bent* that I can detect are three movies: *Cabaret*, *Seven Beauties*, and *The Damned*. And even out of that, a better play could have been fashioned. Perhaps Mr. Sherman spent his time at the Wiener reading smuggled-in copies of Kerouac and Rechy.

There are two main troubles with *Bent*: it is melodrama—bad enough—worsening into mushiness in Act II, and it is all utterly ahistorical and preposterous, a kind of combination homosexual wet dream and Steigian dream of glory. In the first, or melodramatic, act, there is still some competence; at least Sherman knows how to keep the story moving along, how to cut his scenes short to achieve a nervous hurtling forward, and how to sprinkle the proceedings with the pepper of violence and the salt of tearfulness. But credibility goes out through the fourth wall from the outset.

We are presented with a shabby pad shared by a homosexual couple: Max, the canny dope pusher and make-out artist, and Rudy, the sweetly compliant and gently nagging dancer in a homosexual nightclub. It is the morning after an orgy, and forthwith, naked and menacing, Wolf appears at the bedroom door. He is a storm trooper well into S&M and stupidity who, even in these skimpy quarters, still believes Max to be a baron who will drive him out in style to an opulent country house. We are supposedly in the Berlin of 1934, though the characters and dialogue might as well be out of today's Holly- or Isherwood. (You might have to substitute Hell's Angels for the SS, that is all.) Now two SS men with submachine guns burst in, having previously knocked patiently on the door half a dozen times, so that Sherman can have his characters and us believing that it is Mr. Rosen, the landlord, in quest of his rent money. The troopers slit the throat of Wolf, who is nothing less than the lover of the leader of Berlin's storm troops, because he resisted arrest—tell *that* to Hitler's horse marines.

Meanwhile Max and Rudy escape to the homosexual nightclub where "Greta" is doing his pseudo-Dietrich drag act in a rosy swing. Later, in the dressing room, "Greta" reveals that he is a solid, straight paterfamilias doing this work merely for money—an equal opportunity policy doubtless obliges the club to hire a quota of straights for its drag queens. He has nothing but contempt for "queers" and was, in fact, the one who betrayed Wolf's whereabouts to the SS men. These totally unscrupulous murderers rewarded "Greta" with a thick wad of bills for the information (!), which he, for all his loathing, fairly readily surrenders to the hunted and powerless Max and Rudy to help them escape!! Why? Because he has made pots of money "off your kind." Some fake transvestites, it seems, are true gentlemen underneath.

By this time, our disbelief, though suspended more firmly than "Greta" in his swing, comes tumbling down; the next scene, where Max refuses a passport and ticket to Amsterdam, proffered by a kindly homosexual uncle, because Rudy could not survive alone, shoves the dropped disbelief right through the floorboards. Henceforth absurdity jostles absurdity, and any attempt at full itemization would result in a Homeric catalogue. But let me stress that every Nazi (or is it heterosexual?) shown in *Bent* is a fiendish, ravening, unmitigated monster, whereas the homosexuals, with the exception of Wolf, are basically decent human beings capable of love and sacrifice, their little shortcomings only making them human to a fault. Now, I am perfectly willing to believe in diabolic Nazis and homosexuals only a little lower than the angels, but a play made up of only these forfeits all claims to serious art and aspires at best to slick commercialism.

Bent, however, fails even in those terms. In Act II, Max and Horst, his new love, are in Dachau, obliged to pile up rocks on the left, then lug and heap them up on the right—back and forth, ad infinitum, ostensibly to drive them crazy. Under close surveillance, they nevertheless manage to, talk, argue, shout, occasionally even touch quasi-accidentally; we are no longer even in the realm of the absurd but in that of lubricious fantasizing. Surely, in Dachau, inmates were put to other uses, but if rock toting there was, would the wily Max, who wheels and deals with the guards, have chosen that job for himself and Horst? And not even the Nazis could make men do this backbreaking work for twelve hours a day, with only three-minute hourly breaks to be spent standing at rigid attention, without losing them well before they could be driven off their rockers.

On this rocky road to romance, Horst converts Max back to humanity and true love by having them spend those breaks of three minutes (which in the play last at least nine) standing a couple of yards apart, looking straight ahead, talking explicit sex about organs in each other's mouths and anuses, until orgasm—whether literal or figurative is not clear. It may be one way of getting your rocks off, but, beyond its incredibility (in Dachau, you worried about survival, not sex), this is also distasteful. Not because it is homosexual, but because this kind of brute sex talk eludes the powers of even the greatest writers (from whom Sherman is several light-years away) to make it compelling, and defies the skills of the finest actors to make it anything but embarrassing when delivered straight (or bent) from downstage center into the auditorium. However, even this is not the chief fiasco of *Bent*; that is attained in Max's narrative of how he proved his heterosexuality to the Nazis (which I'll spare you) and in the final scenes of sentimental heroics worthy of Hollywood at its worst.

Robert Alan Ackerman's staging, as well as all the visual aspects, can be commended for sturdy professionalism, and most of the performances are as good as the material allows. David Dukes is splendid as Horst, and David Marshall Grant very good in the easier part of Rudy. Richard Gere, a thoroughly competent but unproven actor, does better than I expected as Max; still, I would have vastly preferred seeing Ian McKellen, who, by all accounts, was magisterial in the London production. Either way, *Bent* deals with something too deep and difficult to be entrusted to hack writing.

Criticism from
the 1980s

Betrayal

With *Betrayal*, Harold Pinter has committed the strategic error of writing a comprehensible play. When—once or twice—he flirted with perspicuity before, it was in one-acters and television playlets, where contingency could be invoked as excuse. Never before in a full-length stage work had Pinter deviated into sense, and thus into that manifest triviality, if not vacuity, that the percipient few had unfailingly noted, drowned out though their dissenting was by the din of hosannas. Rightly was Noël Coward an early defender of Pinter's: underneath the third-rate imitator of Beckett, there always lurked a second-rate Coward clone.

Betrayal, which might be more aptly entitled *Self-betrayal*, is Pinter's most Cowardly play, but with only a fraction of Noël's wit. It deals with a classic crypto-homosexual motif: the sharing of the same woman by two close friends. This *topos* figures prominently in Pinter's *oeuvre*—in *The Basement* and *No Man's Land*, for example; even Pinter's best play, *The Homecoming*, is an extended, exaggerated variation on it. In *Betrayal*, there is an added device: the story proceeds widdershins. From a bittersweet postlude to an adulterous affair, it moves through breakup, climax, rising action, back to an impetuous beginning. In the closing stage image, Jerry, the literary agent vinously aroused to venery, grabs the arm of Emma, the wife of his best friend, Robert, a publisher; for seven years, past or to come, he won't let it go.

The notion of making the clock go backward is almost a literary commonplace; Anatole France, in *Le Jardin d'Epicure*, daydreamed about living all life backward, from creaky eld to a glorious youth further enriched by experience—going from wizened caterpillar to blissful, but also wise, butterfly. Let's give Pinter his due: two hacks aside, no serious dramatist has written a play in reverse. Yet it is, finally, only a gimmick—one that the movies have often used for a funny sequence or two but that Pinter prodigally expands over two acts. Needless to say, things do look strange in reverse: An upside-down face, a glove turned inside out, "Pinter" spelled "Retnip," give pause. (Even front to back, Pinter gives pauses, but more about that anon.) And, yes, this rheumy crone was once a burbling baby; that muddy river, once a bubbling spring. Ex-lovers filled with melancholy, rancor, or remorse began as impassioned arm grabbers. So what else is new? The difference between a gimmick and an idea is that whereas the one merely titillates, the other changes our vision.

Oh, there is another device or two at work in the play. Things recollected turn out to be imperfectly, distortedly so; certain asseverations are revealed as untruths. And, of course, the audience can feel cheaply superior to the characters: it knows how things will really turn out. But these characters are so mundane and banal that feeling superior to them is a shabby triumph indeed. The real superiority fulgurating here is that of the author: Jerry is only an agent, Robert only a publisher, Emma only an art-gallery owner—all middlemen, culture brokers, parasites; while Pinter, as we all know, is an Artist and Creator. Here, by the way, is the Creator talking, in a segment from a *Times* interview with Mel Gussow (December 30, 1979), all of which is a model of how to answer questions with non sequiturs, self-contradiction, evasion: "M.G.: Did you make any changes in *Betrayal*? H.P.: In rehearsal in London, I did three things. I cut one word, 'please.' I also took out a pause and inserted a pause. M.G.: And that made all the difference? H.P.: That made all the *damn* difference."

Like all Pinter plays, this one is full of pauses and longer silences. But a technique that worked, up to a point, when pauses cropped up amid troubling enigmas fails when they are dropped into the middle of simplicities or platitudes. Here they do not fill up with mystery, menace, or suggestiveness; they only add a more literal kind of emptiness to what is already vacuous enough. They attenuate thinness into exiguity. So the characters stand fully unmasked in their flimsiness and unoriginality: Jerry in his expansive fatuity, Robert in his self-despising sardonicism, Emma in her bourgeois unfulfillment, her *bovarisme*. There are few surprises and fewer insights; even Robert's almost tacit acceptance of the affair can be readily explained by his own infidelities and self-loathing.

What could have made *Betrayal*—this story of a protracted, querulous, loveless love affair, which might *more* aptly be entitled *The Seven-Year Bitch*—interesting would have been a keener portrayal of the publishing world, of the way art and intellect are exploited as commodities, and of the mixture of glowering wit and boisterous self-depreciation that, especially in London, characterizes a milieu of mock-heroic hucksters. A modicum of this does come through, notably in Robert's tragicomic confession of his hatred for novels. Alternatively, the play might have explored its clandestine sub-theme: the homoerotic attraction between friendly sharers of one woman. "Maybe I should have had an affair with [Jerry] myself!" exclaims Robert to his wife. And when the fleetingly jealous husband goes sour on his crony, Jerry expostulates: "That's what you are banishing me to: a state of catatonia." But the play does not scrutinize this, either; in its general listlessness and crawling pace, it might be more aptly entitled *Homage to Catatonia*.

Incidentally, both remarks I have quoted are, instead of being left tersely alone, followed by feeble and tautological expatiations. It would seem that Pinter's ear and eye are deteriorating "Have you ever been to the Sahara desert?" someone asks redundantly; a restaurant whose menu names it as La Spezia features a painting of Venice rather than of that equally picturesque spot on the gulf that engulfed Shelley. Matters are worsened in the present production by the fact that the American cast—particularly Raul Julia, who, both as an actor and as an early enough transplant, should by now have managed to control his Hispanic accent—are ill at ease with Pinter's British intonations, hesitations, idiosyncrasies.

Julia, in fact, is deplorable as Jerry—is, I have come to realize, a hopeless actor altogether. His youthful Puerto Rican charm has yielded to a smug puffiness of aspect and demeanor, a self-inflation from ill-deserved acclaim that makes him wallow in every expression, welter in every drearily drawn out syllable, like a porker in particularly luscious mud. He brings to every part he plays a mindlessness that only an even more unthinking audience can mistake for ingenuousness. As Robert, that valuable actor (see what he can do for *All That Jazz*) Roy Scheider is miscast, but still succeeds in fusing outrage and irony, aggression and defeat, into one round-eyed stare.

What finally makes *Betrayal* endurable is Blythe Danner, the most underrated and underused major leading lady of our stage and screen. With a barely expressed expression, a slight rift in her voice or posture, a hopeful gaze that breaks into smithereens, Miss Danner conveys more than most others with a steamer trunkful of Actors Studio tricks. With three strangulated sobs, she can move us *beyond* tears; with the nervous wiggling of the toes of her left foot (the right, though doubtless equally inspired, was not visible from where I sat), she wittily transmits the rising tide of panic. That Meryl Streep should have become an instant idol while Blythe Danner is still in limbo after years of no less unfaltering excellence is a cruel testimonial to critical and public obtuseness.

Peter Hall has directed with his customary—and here also apposite—slickness, and the production was designed by John Bury with his usual resourcefulness and elegance: even the way in which the scenery shuttles between similar yet different boxes in exaggerated perspective underlines the sterile to-and-fro of the plot. If *Betrayal* registers at all, it is only because nothing, not even human mortality, is quite so unutterably sad as the dying of love, whether traced forward or backward.

The Lady From Dubuque

In *All Over*, Edward Albee wrote about a man dying offstage; in *The Lady From Dubuque*, he writes about a woman dying more or less onstage. Otherwise, there is not much difference: *All Over* was the worst play about dying until Michael Cristofer's *The Shadow Box*; *The Lady From Dubuque* is the worst play about dying since *The Shadow Box*. It is also one of the worst plays about anything, ever.

Jo is dying of cancer as her valiant husband, Sam, stands lovingly by. This Saturday night in their living room they are playing Twenty Questions with their four best friends: the dependable Edgar and his well-meaning but dim wife, Lucinda; the boozing and brawling Fred and his fourth wife presumptive, the ignorant but jolly Carol. For much of the first act the game and drinking take us through that heavily worked-over Albee territory, the closed circuit bitchery he steadfastly puts into the mouths of his married and unmarried

couples, and that several critics have identified as homosexual back-
(and front-) biting in heterosexual drag. What had some freshness,
acerb wit, and propulsion in *Who's Afraid of Virginia Woolf?* is here
the ultimate in witless nastiness, gratuitous offensiveness, and, above
all, psychological nonsense and verbal infelicity. For example, when
it emerges that Sam, in Twenty Questions, is a pair of famous people—perhaps a homosexual couple—we get the following: "Marx and
Engels!... Oh, were they queer?... You know, Marx and Engels—the
Kaufman and Hart of their day."... "I don't know any of these people."
"Don't worry. You wouldn't have liked them." If you can laugh at this,
you can probably laugh at cancer, too.

Indeed, Albee turns cancer into a sort of sick joke. Apparently
privileged by the fact that she is dying, Jo is beastly to everyone:
patronizing to Edgar, sarcastic to Carol, blatantly contemptuous to
Lucinda, and continuously needling to Fred, who, quite arbitrarily,
won't provoke in Act I and, equally arbitrarily, does nothing but
provoke in Act II. Now, there is no need for someone doomed and
in pain to be that bestial to everybody, or for everybody to tolerate
and thus encourage it, but it permits Albee to practice his only skill,
however moribund—insult comedy. There is no reason either for
everyone to dwell on Lucinda's being awful when she is not much
dumber than the rest, and a good deal nicer; nor is there much
reason for all to turn on Sam in Act II and keep him tied up with
a leather strap most of the time just for insisting on an obvious
truth. But all this feeds Albee's penchant for hostility, spitefulness,
perverse lashing out at decency—a quality he regularly manages to
equate with stupidity or weakness and decks out with a sandwich
board reading, KICK ME!

Anyhow, after much multidirectional animosity and nonstop
imbibing (in a drawing-room comedy—or tragedy—by Albee, the
Bar should automatically get top billing), Jo, in acute pain, is carried
upstairs to bed by Sam. Forthwith, an elegant, elderly woman in a
red coat arrives in the company of an elegant, middle-aged black;
we don't know who they are, how they got in, and why, but they
seem to know exactly what is going on and take possession of the
place as the curtain falls. In Act II, Sunday morning, Sam comes
down in his nightshirt (no man in New York with a Jasper Johns
on his wall puts a nightshirt on his back, but what is a little unreality more or less to Albee as long as it allows him another jibe or
two?) and, understandably shocked, asks the intruders who they are
The woman launches on an interminable, teasing tirade with which

she evades the question, while Sam asks a dozen times. "Who *are* you?"—a variation, I suppose, on Twenty Questions. Then the black joins in in a game of sadistic obfuscation until it finally dribbles out that the woman, Elizabeth, is Jo's mother, unheard from for years, and Oscar, the black, her "friend."

Sam, whom Jo has told that her mother is a tiny New Jersey woman with pink hair who never lived on a farm, naturally rejects the notion that Elizabeth, who claims to have raised Jo on a farm near Dubuque and does not fit any part of the description, can be Jo's mother. After much palaver during which Elizabeth and Oscar give each other some skin each time they score a biggie and generally camp it up, last night's friends troop in again: Fred and Carol to announce their impending wedding, Lucinda and Edgar to patch up yesterday's quarrel. Sam demurs that this is not Jo's mother and gets knocked out and tied up for his pains; Jo comes down in a kind of trance, heads for Elizabeth as if hypnotically drawn to her, and is rewarded with an embrace that puts her gently to sleep on the couch.

Fred is perfectly disgusting to all, especially to Carol, who nevertheless will marry him. Oscar changes into Sam's nightshirt and carries Jo off upstairs to peaceful death. The harrowing account from Act I about the horrors of slow dying has been wiped out by an Elizabeth and Oscar *ex machina*. Everybody leaves, and Elizabeth tells Sam a dream of hers about a series of distant, silent atomic explosions. When Sam identifies this as the end of the world, Elizabeth notes they had been talking about nothing else all along.

So ends the play, and Albee's last claim to being a dramatist, but no significant part of the world. *The Lady From Dubuque* is a lot of desperate pretensions and last-ditch attitudinizing about nothing, borrowed for the most part from previous Albee catastrophes. Let me enumerate the strategies for stretching out nothing into two acts. (1) Repetition. Roughly one fourth of the dialogue is multiple repeats, e.g., "I suppose you should know... I suppose I should know... I suppose you should." Second billing, after the Bar, should go to the Echo. (2) Asides. After a character has spoken to another, he will repeat the same point to the audience, thus: "I like your friends. *(To audience)* I like his friends." About one thirteenth of the play is redundant asides. (3) Not answering simple questions. This, drawn out beyond endurance, supposedly creates suspense. (4) Irrelevant but grandiose political or metaphysical mouthings. So Marx and Engels are trotted out repeatedly, or America is told:

"We're too moral for 'immoral'—it hardly matters to survive; a real Nixon will come along someday if the Russians don't." If Albee has read even one chapter of *Das Kapital*, I'll eat the others. (5) Obscenity. When all else fails, bring on the four-letter words. Albee, apparently, takes this to be still daring; but, then, he is always a couple of decades behind. Which leads to (6) *Ex post facto* liberalism. Oscar revels in ironies at the expense of racism as if they were boldly new; they have been heard on Broadway (and elsewhere) for 30 or 40 years. (7) Running gags that, though unfunny, keep running; thus variations on "No offense!… None taken!" pop up a half dozen times. (8) Mystification. Is Elizabeth Jo's mother, or are she and Oscar angels of death? Obviously Albee himself doesn't know; he has publicly stated that they are not, yet how else—except perhaps as master burglars—could they get past the locks of an expensive Manhattan apartment? But mystification obviates the need for characterization, which is beyond Albee. Besides, as we are told in one of the deepest lines, "Everything is true—therefore, nothing is true." Still, I'll tell you: Elizabeth is really Tinier Alice (as Albee says about Jo, and perhaps about himself, "Each moment she becomes less and less"), and Oscar is really Wilde through a glass, darkly.

One last point. Albee is sometimes described—most often by himself—as a word-wizard, a stylist. No. He shares his characters' subliteracy. In the play, we hear such offenses against grammar as "tear up a few mutual tufts" and "we need a circus to bounce it all off of." In a recent *Times* interview, Albee said, "exchanged mutual hostages" and "to keep everybody's mind off of Jo's dying." For the record: Maureen Anderman, Celia Weston, and David Leary perform heroically; Frances Conroy and Earle Hyman, badly; the rest, indifferently.

Clothes for a Summer Hotel

With *Clothes for a Summer Hotel*, Tennessee Williams has finally written a play that, unlike its eight or ten predecessors, is not embarrassing. Neither, however, is it good. It starts out promisingly enough, as an overworked Scott Fitzgerald, himself in precarious health, comes from Hollywood to call on his allegedly cured wife— soon to die in a fire—at an Asheville mental institution. The asylum is atop a windswept hill and guarded by ominous German nuns in Draculaesque capes. But soon we switch to the overillustrative reminiscences of one or the other tormented mind, to the wheezing symbolism of fire and salamander tropes, and hindsight-burdened colloquies in limbo between omniscient ghosts. A program note by Williams calls this "a ghost play," and adds defensively: "In a sense all plays are ghost plays." Especially, I daresay, when written by ghost playwrights.

Sadder—as well as duller—as it gets with each repetition, it has to be said yet again: Williams has long since written himself out, and this unfocused, meandering, unnecessary play—for all that it is a short step up—merely reconfirms the obvious. *Clothes* shuttles not so much between Scott's and Zelda's fantasies and recollections as between two already published works: Nancy Milford's *Zelda* and Hemingway's *A Moveable Feast*. Almost everything of interest and value in the play is contained in one or the other of those books, and is better in its original form.

I reiterate: there is nothing necessary about this ghost play, nothing that needed saying in *this* world. Williams's Zelda is yet another precious lost soul, driven by her frustrations into lyrically foul-mouthed dementia—just like all those other Tennesseean Ophelias, e.g., Alma (Winemiller), Blanche (DuBois), and Catherine (Holly) from the standard Williams ABC. As for Scott, he functions mostly as a straight man to Zelda, except in a scene with Hemingway, where both his straightness and his talent are questioned by a callous competitor who protests too much. The remaining roles are indeed disembodied wraiths, and it does seem rather a pity to haul in Gerald and Sara Murphy, Mrs. Pat Campbell, and several others as little more than window dressing for an undertaker's parlor. It takes a lot more living than these characters do to make even a funeral home.

There is, moreover, a curious textbook quality about much of the writing. Thus Scott will say things like "… My novel, *The Last Tycoon*, which I must live to complete," to which Zelda responds with "You have your notes, and Bunny Wilson will complete it—not quite in your style, of course." Be it said for Williams that he has no one interject, "Bunny? Oh, you mean *Edmund* Wilson"; he does, however, give us such anachronistic language as "counterproductive" and "a meaningful conversation." If, as he puts it in the play, "words are the love acts of writers," he is clearly suffering from lovelessness, if not impotence.

Occasionally a bit of the old Williams wit resurfaces. When Edouard, the dashing French flyer who has just had sex with Zelda
in a cheap hotel and is worried that Scott may have tracked them
down, exclaims, "He may have recognized your cries," Zelda answers, "How could he have, having never heard them before?" The
clever old hand reasserts itself, but the ear is failing; surely no one
between any sheets except those of a book would use that participial
construction, especially with "have" and "having" clumsily jostling
each other. But perhaps the play is merely a first draft for a screenplay in the Hollywood that Williams (through Fitzgerald) describes
as a place where "people pretend to feel, but… don't feel at all."

Under the circumstances, José Quintero's direction does whatever flesh and blood can do for a ghost play, and Oliver Smith's
scenery is nicely evocative—creepy or nostalgic, as the particular
scene requires. Theoni V. Aldredge's costumes and Marilyn Rennagel's lighting discharge the flashy demands made on them, and
Anna Sokolow's "dance consulting" gets the cast to sashay around
appropriately to Michael Valenti's suitably unoriginal "original music." But, perhaps understandably, the acting falters.

Kenneth Haigh does intelligent, conscientious work as Scott (although no writer would turn "plagiarize" into a four-syllable word),
in an underwritten part for which he is not quite suited physically
or vocally. Still, this is nothing to be ashamed of—which is more
than I can say for Geraldine Page's Zelda. Miss Page gives what she
has doubtless been encouraged to view as a virtuoso performance
oozing technique from every syllable, movement, and pore. But
technique—particularly when it is of the affected kind—can be that
multitude of trees for which one cannot see the forest. Consider the
sheer inhumanity of her voice, which here sounds mostly like the
meowings of a sick cat gallantly trying to be coquettish. The mannerisms never abate—not even in the scenes in which Zelda is supposed
to be anything but mad. Thus, time after time, Miss Page builds to a
major outburst, only to peter out at the last moment into a dying fall.
Quite effective once or twice, but not when it is as recurrent as the
design in wallpaper. And all that making like a sculpture gallery with
the body—truly, we are left in a daze of whines and poses.

Yet if Miss Page has turned an act into a jag, the blame must be
shared by the director, who must also be castigated for casting David Canary and Marilyn Rockafellow in key roles that they manage
to trivialize. Especially unsatisfactory is Robert Black's (physically
right) Hemingway—with whom, incidentally, Williams practices

his typically gossip-mongering approach when he has someone remark on (I haven't got this down verbatim) "Ernest's somewhat too carefully calculated cultivation of the prizefight, the bull ring, and the man-to-man attitude derived from Gertrude Stein." There is, however, very sound work from Michael Connolly as Gerald Murphy, from Mary Doyle as a lesser madwoman, and (though she is miscast) from Josephine Nichols as Mrs. Campbell.

In one scene, Williams articulates the not entirely novel notion that Fitzgerald jealously sabotaged what might have turned out to be his wife's superior talent for writing. If that had been the main thrust of the play, the result might have been, however unfounded as literary criticism, something of greater dramatic and human interest.

Children of a Lesser God

Children of a Lesser God does for deaf-mutes what *Whose Life Is It Anyway?* did for those paralyzed from the neck down. It is as if some papal demarcation line had allocated human affliction below itself to Brian Clark and above itself to Mark Medoff. I do wish that only genuine artists were allowed to deal with major afflictions, while the Medoffs and Clarks of this world were allotted the full spectrum from chilblains to psoriasis.

Children, alas, is as unable to sound the depths of human suffering as it is to ascend the heights of poetic expression. If it were willing to settle for melodrama and tearjerking, its diction and dramaturgy might almost pass muster. It insists, however, on tackling grave issues, on searching souls, on going spelunking with one soggy book of matches. It is just barely possible that it sincerely believes itself to be advancing the cause of humanity by examining the problems in and around the marriage of James Leeds, a teacher in a total- and partial-deaf-mute school, and Sarah Norman, a young woman of rare intelligence whose hypertrophic pride restricts her to working as a maid at the school, while carrying on with the instructors as she once did with a passing parade of men her unimpaired sister would rustle up for her.

Sarah has been discarded as a retardate by her perfectly civilized mother (which I find hard to believe); out of fierce pride, she has refused to learn to speak imperfectly (which I can believe)

and rejected the halfway house of lipreading (which is, again, hard
to believe). So she just sweeps up and sleeps around, while sticking to signing (the manual sign language). James is atoning for his
father's warmongering military career by having joined, first, the
Peace Corps and now the faculty of this special school. As written,
James is indeed intelligent, charming, witty, and a bit unstable—a
fellow who might have, as he says, single-handedly rehabilitated
Ecuador just as he now signs away with magnificent, two-handed
proficiency. But why would this bright, sunny chap take on—not
just as student, but also as wife—the deeply troubled, bitter, self-
sabotaging Sarah? Only God and Mr. Medoff know, but the former
will not, and the latter cannot, tell.

Just look at the adventitious complications the playwright feels
obliged to toss in. There is the delinquent mother who—suddenly
and unconvincingly—becomes all supportive understanding. There
is an angry male student, Orin, who seems to be organizing Deaf-
mute Liberation and hires a lawyer to sue the principal for not engaging people with impaired hearing or speech as faculty, but who
is really a pussycat. There is Lydia, the sweet, girlish student, who
keeps brazenly chasing after James even after he has married Sarah.
There is Mr. Franklin, the principal, who throws monkey wrenches
into romance and roadblocks into worthy causes, but who is a jolly
decent fellow in his ornery, cynical way. And there is Edna Klein,
the lawyer, hired to prosecute Orin and Sarah's suit—a perfect blend
of gaucherie and heartfelt helpfulness. Medoff has the unfortunate
virtue of trying so hard to create black-and-white human beings
rather than black or white clichés that he ends up with consummate
clichés of black-and-whiteness—and many more problems than his
makeshift plot can bear.

Makeshift indeed! *Children* was a laboratory experiment in play-
making, with Phyllis Frelich (who plays Sarah) and her husband,
Robert Steinberg (who understudies James)—she a deaf-mute actress, he an actor and stage manager without impairments—telling
Medoff about their marriage, which seems to be a fine and successful union. But that, for Medoff, was not dramatic enough, and
he had to pump it full of conflict, bit by disconnected bit. There is
enough spurious confrontation, prefabricated anger, and bargain-
basement misunderstanding here to keep your average soap opera
foaming for months. Yet, of course, there is also the deaf-mute language, signing, which the author perceived as particularly theatrical: a steady stream of manual subtitles while someone gifted with

speech (usually James) delivers the spoken equivalent for those who cannot read fingers, At first, this does create a lively visual image; eventually, though, one feels trapped in one of those ghastly television commercials whose simplistic message is both written on the screen and intoned in stentorian voiceover.

However, Gordon Davidson has directed with great verve and inventiveness, filling Thomas A. Walsh's unattractive skeletal set with a continuous flow of shapely movement that, at climactic moments, freezes into expressive tableaus. To this, Tharon Musser's lighting adds an appropriately sculptural dimension; one feels that here the lights are the scenery. Nancy Potts's costumes are properly unobtrusive, and the acting is uniformly of the highest caliber. But there is a problem. Although Phyllis Frelich is splendid in every other way, she is neither young nor alluring enough for Sarah. (Admirably, Miss Frelich considers her real-life affliction not a handicap but a separate but equal culture, thus requiring no patronizing critical concessions.) This is too bad, because John Rubinstein is not only a histrionically and humanly winning James, but also a young man of great good looks. The juxtaposition does not convince.

It might, to be sure, if Medoff had written a better play—not a set of acting and playwriting exercises. If you want a true insight into the problem discussed, you can get it far better from a poem, "Mutterings Over the Crib of a Deaf Child," by James Wright, who just died, tragically prematurely, of cancer. With typical manipulativeness, Medoff opts for one of those currently fashionable, neither happy nor quite unhappy, endings; he has James and Sarah reaffirm their love, only to have her declare that they cannot cohabit in either her world of silence or his world of speech, but must find a third world to live in. *Children of a Lesser God* (the very title is pretentious) neglects to tell us whether this is Africa or Heaven.

Morning's at Seven

Why exhume a piece of boulevard theater that should be decently allowed to decompose in peace? In his *American Drama Since World War II*, Gerald Weales observes that *Morning's at Seven*, "which was first presented unsuccessfully in 1939, jumbles together enough clichés of situations and language to provide Inge with material for four or five plays…" Paul Osborn's play possesses every hallmark of craftiness and craft, but not a trace of genuine art. This is the story of four elderly sisters: Cora, wanly married to bluff Thor, a retired businessman; dim Ida, married to depressed Carl, who dreamed of dentistry but settled for carpentry; spunky Esty, married to misanthropic David, a disgruntled professor who opted out of academia, if not of life itself; and Arry, who, for love of Thor, never married and has become the resident albatross in Cora's house.

Cora's and Ida's backyards occupy one half of the stage each; between them, you can just glimpse the 1922 midwestern town where, down the road a piece, is Esty and David's house. Ida's 40-year-old son, Homer, still lives with his parents; as the play opens, he is bringing Myrtle, with whom he has been going for the last eleven years, home for the first time. The reason for the belated visit is not that Homer has made up his mind, but that his mother has become worried over a movie in which someone as old-bachelorish as he comes to a sticky end.

Morning's at Seven saddles us with nine characters who are, or soon will be, urban counterparts of Grant Wood's *American Gothic*. All of them—even the quasi-intellectual David, who considers the rest morons—are egregious fools in one way or another, carefully designed to enable the most mindless spectator to feel at least slightly superior to them. As Weales writes, "Osborn... although he occasionally reaches for a pathetic moment, presents the whole thing as wry comedy, almost a parody of lonely lostness in the Midwestern backyard."

Calculation and manipulation are the coefficients of Osborn's dramaturgy. When facile laughter has reached its nadir (say, after Carl walks off in a daze, is missing, and elicits Ida's "If they could only drag the river," to which Esty replies, "There is no river around here!"), we are given a bit of equally premeditated pathos. When a character has seemed smarter and more independent than the rest for a while, he is forthwith revealed as dependent and not so smart. When a character has seemed less juicy than last year's orange rinds, he promptly gets a touch of a surprisingly sexual past or present. When things are heading for a sharp climax, count on a blunt anticlimax—or vice versa. Every character has his little shocker, equidistant from the previous and following characters.

The audience loves it—at least the kind of audience I saw it with. The kind that, when a character has answered "Yep!" three times in a row, anticipates him with a loud "Yep!" the fourth time round; that applauds thunderously for a joke worth a despairing smile; and that, when a sister expresses the wish that another sister would die, produces a gasp powerful enough to vacuum a five-room apartment. But this is not my idea of "wry comedy." If people—even in 1922, even in the Midwest—could really be this stupid, the author, instead of grinningly accepting it, should have written a tragedy, and we should all go and blow our brains out. If, on the other hand, the author is overstating out of anger, contempt, or horror, he should rouse us to creative indignation rather than to orgies of guffawing condescension or smirking complacency. There is something nauseating about a play that not only panders to the lowest common denominator but also remains so aloof that you cannot even tell what its attitude toward it is.

I am not sure whether, by squeezing every crowd-pleasing drop out of the material, the production makes it better or worse. Certainly William Ritman's contiguous backyards are as cheerfully benighted as anything out of D. W. Griffith or Norman Rockwell, and Richard Nelson's lighting and Linda Fisher's costumes abet the atmosphere manfully and womanfully. Vivian Matalon has directed to a fare-thee-well, if not beyond: every bit of timing, blocking, emphasis or de-emphasis is perfectly adjusted to the audience's tempo of digestion, not overlooking the occasional jolt to produce a burp. Given the manifest aim not to leave Rockwell enough alone, the acting is horribly accomplished, with Elizabeth Wilson, Nancy Marchand, and David Rounds leading the way to deadly accuracy, or deadly something-or-other A vote for *Morning's at Seven* is as good as a vote for Ronald Reagan.

Barnum

It is slight, slapdash, and without a book. (It had a book once, but providently lost it.) And it works—my, how *Barnum* works! Call it a *capriccio* in the manner of Jacques Callot, a fantasy on the career of P. T. Barnum, an illustrated disquisition on the nature of humbug—or, best, an evocation of sideshows, freak shows, human shows (in Thomas Hardy's sense), the life of the circus and the circus of life. It is so simple and virtually eventless that it ought to be static; yet, as Galileo remarked in a somewhat different context, it moves. In more senses than one.

Barnum is a little like *Stop the World*, etc., a little like a Robert

Altman movie, and mostly like itself. Time goes by in it, yet also stands still; people are gulled, humbugged, conned out of their money and emotions, yet they all leap back with a tumbler's bounce. It is all a circus act: the actors clown, juggle, walk the high wire, swing from trapezes. And it is all not quite a circus: the animals, for example, are only faked in. It is, however, theater, in which characters that are scarcely more than cutouts come to biochemically verifiable life. The damned thing buoys your spirits, lifts up your heart, and *lives*.

Obviously, the real Barnum was no British actor, pop singer, and music hall performer such as Jim Dale (of course, nobody is like Jim Dale, and I wonder how even he can manage all that charm, wit, energy, multiplicity, Jimdalishness nonstop); but, then, neither was Barnum what he said, thought, or wrote he was—in that autobiography of which David Grimsted has written that, like Barnum's career, it was "a combination of piquant reality and genial fraud welded seamlessly into amusing myth." Not a bad description, incidentally, of the show itself.

Cy Coleman has composed one of those scores of his in which every song reminds you of some other song, but just distorted and askew enough to wiggle into a nice near-originality. Michael Stewart's lyrics are always crunchily appetizing, and Mark Bramble's book (as mentioned) has been, for the most part, salutarily jettisoned. David Mitchell has designed a fluidly circusy setting that flexibly converts into more or less flamboyant environments, as required. From the world's most elevated elephant to its minutest midget, everyone is there—not literally, but through suggestion, imagination, taste. And Joe Layton, a director-choreographer whose work I have not previously admired, has here swept me along with directorial legerdemain worthy of its subject.

The cast is doubly right. The supporting parts are not only well taken, they are also filled with performers who manage to look more like people than like actors, and Marianne Tatum is a delicious Jenny Lind; she sings almost well enough for Lind, and if she isn't the cat's pajamas, she is certainly the nightingale's nightie. Glenn Close, an actress about whom I tended to have reservations, is a splendid Mrs. Barnum, with the ambiguities of a passionate Puritan etched into the wily, pinched prettinesses of her face, her very presence exuding the sour-sweet joys of circus lemonade. Theoni V. Aldredge's costumes trustily abet these actresses' assets, and all the other technical contributions come through in fine fettle. As for

Jim Dale, from high wire to low comedy, from his summer sunrise smile to the sovereignty of his hand movements this prodigy does everything a bit more lustrously than it could possibly be done. If Barnum was "the Prince of Humbugs," Dale is the king of comedians; I would not be surprised if he could even do the Prince of Homburg.

A Day in Hollywood/A Night in the Ukraine

It would be nice to have *A Day in Hollywood* without *A Night in the Ukraine*, but if you left this "musical double feature" at the intermission, you would miss Tony Walton's set for the co-feature: a wonder of false perspective and genuine trompe l'oeil. And, at the prices one has to pay these days, it's hard to walk out on anything; so, I guess, *A Day in Hollywood/A Night in the Ukraine* it will be—half charming and half disenchanting.

A Day in Hollywood is a cunning little musical revue made up of a few passable new songs and a lot of memory-gilded oldies, presented ostensibly by the ushers and usherettes at Grauman's Chinese Theater. One of them plays the piano (abetted, in the best tradition, by an invisible orchestra) while the others sing and dance, as well as caper, cavort, cut up in more ways than anyone could conceive—anyone except Tommy Tune with his choreographic invention that is like champagne that never goes flat. Walton has designed a miniature Grauman's Chinese lobby with a row of swinging doors in the back wall, each with a porthole in it. The number of uses to which Tune has put these doors and round windows borders on infinity, but that is only the beginning.

Above this level is a sort of transom extending the width of the stage; here two pairs of legs are carrying on as only disembodied legs and feet can. Since we don't see what happens above hip level, anything can happen: legs literally fly, feet hover in mid-air, there are acrobatic contortions that are obvious cheats, but the sweetest, most fairytale, least earthbound cheats ever perpetrated by two pairs of legs and feet. (They belong to Niki Harris and Albert Stephenson, and I hope that someday their upper halves will get equal time.) There is a veritable parade of famous legs, celebrities from the hips down being obtainable at half price, and sometimes, by a kind of pedal meiosis or mitosis, we get three pairs of legs that split up into ménages à trois.

The whole people below perform with equal grace, especially Priscilla Lopez, Peggy Hewett, and Frank Lazarus, who finally made clear to me what is meant by "tickling the ivories." Lazarus, a South African who wrote most of the new music and presumably chose the rest, does not play the piano: he plays with it. I virtually saw (in one number, *actually* saw) the keys of the piano come to insanely giggling life under his digital cajolery, and the resulting music proved as exhilarating visually as aurally.

But then comes the takeoff on Chekhov's *The Bear* cum *The Sea Gull* as a Marx Brothers movie, a kind of neo-Marxist Sea Bear called *A Night in the Ukraine* that is as endless as the Arctic night. As Samovar, the crooked lawyer, David Garrison creates a very persuasive—somewhat less gruff but amusingly fey—Groucho; as a Jewish-Italian footman, Frank Lazarus is a Chico who puts his foot in it with great suavity. The others are not so interesting: Priscilla Lopez, as a less than entrancing transsexual Harpo; Peggy Hewett, as the rich Widow Pavlenko, whose house is being turned topsy-turvy and who is only a skittery foothill to Margaret Dumont's mountain of injured respectability; and several amiably forgettable others. There are some jokes in the songs and in the book by the Anglicized American Dick Vosburgh; however, the Hasty Pudding would have made it all less slow, and the Triangle Club less square. And, there being no choreography, only staging, even Tommy's instrument was untuned.

Mass Appeal

Likableness is one of the minor virtues, but, as these go, surely the best. *Mass Appeal*, by Bill C. Davis, has not only all the likableness you could ask for but also other merits. It is about something—a recognizable, human something; it has an inexhaustible supply of humor-leavened moral purpose; and its economic two characters, along with the very real offstage personages, delineate and develop a conflict, create a tangible world, and leave your mind with something to chew on all the way home and beyond.

Mass Appeal concerns a jolly Irish priest in an average upstate-

New York town. Father Tim Farley is a trimmer, one of those who, in Dante's words, are *sanza infamia e sanza lodo*—neither reprehensible nor praiseworthy. He preaches sermons (the play begins with one of them) that do not rock the pews, consoles his parishioners by aggrandizing their standard griefs into pinnacles of suffering, and receives regular donations of sparkling Burgundy that, along with his Mercedes, assure his creature as well as spiritual comforts. But the dreary Monsignor who runs the nearby seminary upsets Father Farley's righteous routine by sending over a troubling seminarian, Mark Dolson, a fellow of tough questions and high demands, who sees Catholicism as an arduous climb to salvation rather than a warm bubble bath that must eventually go down the drain.

The Monsignor knows Father Farley for the sort of epicurean, worldly-wise compromiser just right for taking the lion out of Mark, a chap who opposes the Monsignor's decision to rusticate two seminarians suspected of homosexuality yet would preach brimstone sermons against blue-haired old ladies. During a "dialogue sermon" Mark embarrasses Father Farley in front of his flock with a potent argument for admitting women to the priesthood; later, in the priest's study, he launches on the long debate that will gradually widen the ideological gulf between them while, paradoxically, tightening the emotional bond. There ensues an agon between a goner and a comer—but which is which?

Now, you might find this a bit schematic, even stereotyped, this contest between a bibulous priest and an intransigent seminarian. But Davis coaxes new life into and out of the old antinomies. Mark had a genuinely perplexing childhood and a sixties rebelliousness that led him into bisexual excesses from which he now seeks shelter; his ministry of defiant challenge is a roundabout plea for love that is not altogether unlike Father Farley's basking in acceptance. Meanwhile Farley's and Mark's reciprocal feelings evolve: from canny teacher and bright but bristling student, the men become grudgingly affectionate father and son, and, eventually, platonically homoerotic lovers. It is all chaste, comical, and poignant, full of quaint reversals, sudden victories and defeats, and honest befuddlement.

I can't tell you more of the plot because the surprises really matter here, which may be proof that *Mass Appeal* is not the best kind of playwriting. But it is second-best in such an intelligent, magnanimous, stageworthy way, and so passionate and funny! Why, Mark wonders, does Father Farley put up with him.? The answer is wonderfully complex and right: "Because you're a lunatic! And the church needs lunatics. The only problem with lunatics is that they don't know how to survive. I do." Note the slight but significant change in tone from the earlier "Mark, your sermon sucks!" "You haven't heard the rest of it." "The rest of it could be the Sermon on the Mount—after two minutes they would turn off." But it is not yet the Farley who will go to bat for Mark against congregation and Monsignor, lest a young man lose his vocation and the church a brilliant priest.

The proof of the pudding is that you care not only about two persons and their precarious relationship but also about the entire parish, the seminary, the future of Catholicism, even if you are not a Catholic and not in the least religious. As it happens, my companion at the play was one of the first woman ministers of the Episcopal church, and she found most of the details of clerical life, *mutatis mutandis*, accurately captured; the correctness, however, extends to more important domains of human interaction. True, Davis tends to steer toward slightly oversimplified comedy (but funny!); yet this very strategy makes the moments of impassioned audacity and sickening failure stand out all the more movingly or sorrowfully—and not just stand out but also blend into the true texture of existence.

Much of this is due also to the acting and staging. Milo O'Shea resists, for the most part, his tendency to juice things up, and achieves a comely blend of cynicism and vulnerability, boldness and deflation, fading manipulativeness and growing humanity; were *he* in the pulpit, I might be converted to churchgoing. As for Eric Roberts, his Mark, despite a few lapses into overacting, is achingly felt and firmly conveyed; the performance has range and richness of shading. Moreover, seldom have two actors looked so right. They have been shrewdly paced and held neither too tightly nor too flaccidly by Geraldine Fitzgerald's wise and generous direction, in which even the most complicated, knockabout stage business is executed with startling spontaneity and without a hitch. The physical production, though modest, has the warmth of an adequate little red wine.

There are moments in the second act that become a bit too consciously theatrical; for the rest *Mass Appeal* (an appeal made during Mass) infuses a potentially special-interest topic with genuine but unvulgar mass appeal. I can't be sure whether this is one of those gripping bits of autobiography of which certain authors, *hominess unius libri*, have one, and only one, specimen in them, or whether Bill C. Davis is an authentic dramatist who can go from this to other strengths. Be that as it may, *Mass Appeal* will delight you, disturb you, and unstintingly entertain you.

The Marriage Dance

Even if you are fastidious about your laughter—if *Sugar Babies*, for instance, is more apt to make you cry about human tastelessness—you can laugh your head off at *The Marriage Dance*, upstairs at BAM. The 21-year-old Brecht's *The Wedding* (*Die Kleinbürgerhochzeit*) is coupled with the ripe Georges Feydeau's *The Purging* (*On purge Bébé*—both original titles are better), and though the BAM Theatre Company production is, like most marriages, imperfect, these rarely seen plays are so thoroughgoingly the stuff of life and staff of comedy that Brooklyn should seem nearer than ever.

The Wedding is one of those darkling comedies in which tragedy is barely avoided from moment to moment as the uproarious action lurches ahead heedlessly, like a novice slalom racer knocking down flags right and left. We witness a wedding dinner at which the bride, gibbous with advanced pregnancy, flirts brazenly with the groom's best friend; the bride's father keeps telling funny stories that range from the lugubrious to the funereal; a battle-scarred husband-and-wife pair of wedding guests add another bloody chapter to their internecine marriage; the bride's silly sister and her amiably imbecile swain disport themselves clumsily; and things all around keep collapsing.

For Brecht has found a superb objective correlative for this crumbling world of feral lovers and spouses: the furniture that the young couple carefully built themselves, and in which they take appropriate pride, proceeds to come slowly, hilariously apart, harmonizing with the dissolution of human gentility. When the older husband, exasperated by his wife's provocations, plucks one of the few remaining legs off the festive table, to hurl it at his prostrate spouse, the casual, ghastly logic of that gesture and the compliance, indeed complicity, with which that leg comes off, propel an already riotous play to the summit of comedy. Not even my telling you about it here can dim the true, painful comicalness of that moment one whit.

Unfortunately, a stylistic unsureness runs through all levels of the production. The otherwise smooth translation by Richard Nelson (with Helga Ciulei) misses, perhaps inevitably, the ludicrous aping of stiltedly upper-class German by inept plebeians; but, surely, it could have avoided present-day coarseness. Thus Brecht ends with "*Es macht nichts*" ("No matter!"), which is here rendered by an obscenity. Seldom does the director, André Ernotte, even try for the moods, gestures, and manners of 1919 Germany, which, by anchoring the production in the specific, would have provided a jumping-off point into the universal. The acting is similarly anachronous, and the company lacks homogeneity of speech and acting technique. Even so, no one is outright bad except for Norman Snow as the groom's friend—an actor uniquely gifted in making whatever he does simultaneously heavy and hollow.

The Purging is from 1910, by which time Feydeau had already fled his family abode, driven out by Mme Feydeau who, eventually, drove him to divorce, and perhaps also helped drive him out of his mind. The play is as good a letter of farewell-cum-vengeful satire as anyone wishing to remain within the bounds of French gentlemanliness and Gallic wit could possibly contrive. In life, Marianne Feydeau doubtless had her own side of the story; but in art, the playwright has the last, monstrously funny, tragicomic word. Considering his sad end—premature death in a mental institution—the poor fellow deserves it.

With exquisite tact and modesty, the madman Feydeau imagined himself to be, not the great Napoleon I, but little Napoleon III; with the same tact, the methodical artist Feydeau makes his quasi-autobiographical hero, the chamber-pot manufacturer Follavoine, as ridiculous as he is put-upon, as foolishly self-serving as tyrannically henpecked. Mme. Follavoine simultaneously ruins two marriages: her own and that of M. Chouilloux of the Ministry of War, who might have made Follavoine's fortune by appointing him supplier of chamber pots to the French army. And she continues to spoil Baby, her rotten son, even further, while causing two healthy stomachs to become assaulted by the purgative constipated Baby is allowed to shirk. Even the mere process of finding the Azores in a dictionary can provide Feydeau with enough comic ammunition to supply the French army with jokes for a goodly period.

But André Ernotte has again directed without sufficient sense of place and time; a Belgian, his stagings fall, like Belgium, between the two stools of Germany and France. The supporting roles are poorly taken, but Guy Michaels is a properly odious Baby, Roxanne Hart a charmingly maddening Mme Follavoine (though why imitate Roberta Maxwell's voice?), and Brian Murray, as Follavoine, perfection itself. Here is impeccable timing of speech and gesture, comic exaggeration that is nevertheless under utter control, and a flawless period sense. For this performance you should go to Timbuktu, let alone Brooklyn. Peter Barnes's adaptation of the text is fine, too, and the visual elements for both productions (sets by Heidi Landesman, costumes by John David Ridge, lighting by F. Mitchell Dana) are on the beam. This show will end the season for you with a comic bang.

Look Back in Anger

We cannot help looking at *Look Back in Anger* as we would at a baby shoe, with a mixture of tenderness, amusement, and sadness. The text of our meditation could be either "My God, how fitting it was once, and how tiny it seems now," or else "What connection is there between today's unwieldy lummox and the lovable cherub who once wore this little shoe?" John Osborne's play, which in 1956 magisterially summed up—or appeared to sum up—what had happened to post-war Britain (and even, to a lesser extent, the world), is now a museum piece. But don't get me wrong: a museum piece is in a museum because it is worth preserving and because, at least from time to time, it is worth looking at. And looking back through.

On the surface, Jimmy Porter was the smart lower-class young man who finds, as his class has come nominally into power, that power is not so easily grasped and, even if grasped, not all that satisfying. Underneath, Jimmy is still the product of the old dispensation, envious of the seemingly natural privileges and old Tory values of Colonel Redfern, his father-in-law, for whom he feels a troublesome sympathy that is inchoately reciprocated. Still deeper down—where Osborne never bothered to dive—Jimmy is a crybaby, a neo-Jacobean malcontent, a ranter about society who harbors a psychic tapeworm that neither overindulgence nor even self-indulgence can ever wholly satiate.

And there is something deeper than that. Quite clearly, neither of the two intelligent, attractive, thoroughly worthy young women in love with Jimmy—his well-born, forbearing wife, Alison, or Helena, her overbearing and equally upper-class friend—can satisfy him, except as a target for the sly little darts of his teasing or the great envenomed arrows of his invective. He seems much more at ease with his friend Cliff, the assistant at his candy-stall (can three people really make a living off it?). I have no doubt that some sort of latent, rarefied homosexuality (which, thanks to the English public-school system, flows wide and deep over Albion) is clandestinely in effect here; why else would Cliff have no private life beyond sitting around Jimmy's one-room flat? Oh, he does side with the injured Alison against Jimmy, but ever so ineffectually—almost out of a passively homosexual self-identification with woman's role and lot.

I mention all this to suggest that the play holds interest beyond its particular moment in social history. It never amounted to all that much in that department, anyway—its most profound insight along those lines being Alison's remark to her father, a retired Indian-army colonel: "You're hurt because everything is changed. Jimmy is hurt because everything is the same. And neither of you can face it. Something has gone wrong somewhere, hasn't it?" Something, certainly, the way the kick has gone out of the booze in Eugene O'Neill's saloon; but what, and where? To begin with, in Osborne himself, who kept turning out, with diminishing returns, plays in which an authorial mouthpiece spews forth streams of rhetorical aggression with steadily increasing bitterness and incoherence. But locating the problem in the author's jaundiced world view does not do away with it, or make it less challengingly symptomatic and worth speculating about.

Such speculation is made especially fruitful because the play is generally perceptive, witty, well constructed dramatically, and psychologically convincing in all but one major point. Helena has no business giving up so easily, killing her love for Jimmy in the cradle just because Alison has lost her baby and walks shakily back into Jimmy's life. In fact, Helena's allegedly strict, old-fashioned morality is never made believable, especially in view of the alacrity with which she flings herself at her dear friend's husband. But the rest works—and nobody ever accused Osborne of not knowing how to write stinging tirades, of which this play provides God's, or Satan's, plenty.

The production is more than respectable and less than compelling. Only Malcolm McDowell is up to the lancinating impact of the original production spearheaded by Kenneth Haigh. To be as good as Haigh was, and that in a different way, is no small achievement. Haigh played Jimmy with a more unrelieved, more lachrymose underlying violence; McDowell preserves a residue of cheerfulness. Haigh was a relentlessly smoldering volcano, whereas McDowell is a jauntily perking pot with a seriocomically jiggling lid. But that approach, at the present remove, makes good sense, particularly because when the lid does blow off, it does so with smashing (in both senses) explosiveness. With McDowell we enjoy the actor's control over the very rampages of the character: with Haigh, the fascination lay in the crack-up that, from moment to moment, threatened to overtake the performer himself. Although McDowell has grown a bit older and, to my view, a shade less dashing, my companion found him overwhelmingly to her taste.

The women are both competent or better, but suffer from being neither so brilliant nor so British—nor indeed anywhere near so beautiful—as were Mary Ure and Claire Bloom in earlier versions. Lisa Banes is a credible, if at times almost too stolid, Alison, and Fran Brill, after a pallid start, gets better and better. I am not quite sure whether it helps or distracts that Miss Banes reminds one of Meryl Streep and Miss Brill of Liz Ashley. Raymond Hardie is more than creditable as Cliff, perhaps a shade too soft in places, but decidedly appealing. What does drag the show down several notches is the Colonel Redfern of Robert Burr, an actor who seems to me to have made it on vaguely resembling, vainly imitating, and once actually understudying Richard Burton. Here he makes hash of his role: bewilderment emerges as benightedness, trigness as muscle-boundness, Colonel Blimp as a Blimpieburger.

Roger Mooney's set, even if curiously off-center, fits the characters; A. Christina Giannini's costumes and Dennis Parichy's lighting (though not his best) fill the bill. Ted Craig, an Australian, has directed with a shrewd eye for detail, although Alison's luggage, surely brought along from her paternal home, should be of much better quality. *Look Back in Anger* will hold your attention and reward your attendance with more food for the mind and heart than most current offerings can rustle up; even fading has proved as becoming to it as it is to blue jeans, ancestral photographs, and unduly shrill voices.

Last Summer at Bluefish Cove

Last Summer at Bluefish Cove, by Jane Chambers, concerns one summer, seven lesbians, and one wavering straight at a lesbian beach colony. This is very much the female counterpart of Mart Crowley's *The Boys in the Band*, what with a serio-comic cross section of homosexual types accidentally invaded by a straight outsider who is absorbed by the group. Though Chambers can write, she gives us more ideology and propaganda than dramaturgy and artistry.

This regrettably uncompelling work displays manifold strategy: (1) Give the straights a nice, prophylactic view of lesbianism, with lots of all-girl fun and *just* enough minor nastiness characteristic of heterosexual lives and soap operas. (2) Add a major, socially redeeming theme—in this case a promiscuous but lovable lesbian, doomed by cancer, finding one last fulfilling and emotionally exalting experience with a naive, formerly dissatisfied, heterosexual divorcee whom she converts to the joys of Sapphic love. (3) Make your homosexual audiences happy with little lesbian in-jokes and the implication that straights are mostly closet inverts just waiting to be brought out by truly liberated homosexuals (the same fantasy as in *The Boys in the Band*). (4) Make your heterosexual audiences happy by showing the straight emerging from the closet as a very fine person who loves and supports her dying lover and ends up as a mature woman free to choose any kind of sexuality (but leave the ending prudently open). (5) Show just enough lesbian sexual interplay to titillate all audiences, but not enough to jolt any but the staunchest puritans—i.e., the old, reliable, jejune strategy of the clean dirty joke. Clearly, a play so elaborately programmatic, for all its possible commercial future, has little artistic present.

Aside from the absence of any point worth making, *Bluefish Cove* suffers from a hobbling inconsistency of tone: the drama of the dying heroine and the light comedy of lesbian couplings and infighting do not blend into a unified whole. Chambers displays wise self-irony about lesbianism ("There is nothing more disgusting than a male-chauvinist dyke!") and a laudable curb on sentimentality (e.g., the simplicity of "Dykes are women, too!"), and there are none of the maudlin self-incriminations of Mart Crowley. Yet the play remains—for me, at any rate—both unenlightening and uninvolving: Jane Chambers can surely do better.

In the last respect, the cast is also to blame (it is no longer quite the original one, incidentally). As the heroine, Jean Smart is alternately excellent and perfunctory; as the *raisonneuse*, Aphroditi Kolaitis (though she has a tendency to lead with her head) starts out with real gusto and persuasion, then runs out of steam. The others are uniformly uninteresting and, in the cases of Dolores Kenan and Elizabeth Wingate, downright poor. Nyla Lyon has ably directed a production that suffers from cramped quarters and a shoestring budget.

Richard III

Should not the law protect a dead genius as much as it does a living nonentity against assault and battery? In the present instance, it is Shakespeare's *Richard III* that is being beaten to a pulp with a blunt weapon, the weapon in question being Michael Moriarty's mind. Moriarty, who once looked like a promising actor, has become one of the most sinister influences in our theater, having, among other things, contributed heavily to the ruining of the play *G. R. Point* and the movie *Who'll Stop the Rain*. This sort of thing goes beyond lack of talent and must have to do with some amalgam of arrogance and benightedness, lack of taste and abysmal lack of common sense. This *Richard III* is the worst major Shakespearean production I have ever seen, and it is not merely bad—it is swinish.

Once before, at Lincoln Center, Moriarty, out of something bordering on imbecility, chose to play Richard as a flaming homosexual. Marsha Mason played Lady Anne, and it was so that a flagrantly pederastic Richard got to be parodied in Neil Simon's *The Goodbye Girl*. Richard Dreyfuss reduced this interpretation to ultimate ridicule, and anyone with an ounce more intelligence than Moriarty would have gotten the message and left bad enough alone. But no, he is back with a Richard who, besides having nothing to do with Shakespeare, is some sort of combination of the male whore Moriarty played rather well in *Find Your Way Home* and Oskar Matzerath, plus four feet and minus a tin drum. If you can imagine a particularly backward baby stretched to over six feet and cavorting insanely while also rattling away so fast in a voice so thin as to be incomprehensible—though it can shatter glass—you've got yourself this Richard.

This Richard, by the way, has no hump. The hump, miraculously, has transmigrated onto Burke Pearson's King Edward, a performance that would have been quite dismal enough even without a hump. Neither has Richard a clubfoot—it is there when he remembers it, but does not prevent him from bounding about like a randy gazelle when it suits his purposes, and could best be described as a galloping limp. His defects are thus reduced to grotesquely nonflexible index and ring fingers on the left hand and a totally nonfunctioning brain. The Matzerath aspect comes in in peculiar hops, unaccountable rages, breakings out in a child's version of an Indian war dance, repeated beatings of the forehead with the hand, and, especially, quite arbitrary singing of some of the lines of dialogue. This is a totally tuneless singsong, as by someone who cannot carry a tune any more than the world on his back but nevertheless wishes to sing you a favorite aria. So "My kingdom for a horse!" is sung a cappella and to a ghastly nontune, turning that dramatic moment into a horse operetta.

This Richard III is also afflicted with what I take to be obscene adolescent (Oskar Matzerath again?) sexuality. In two separate scenes, Moriarty sticks a sword or dagger to his crotch and dances around with it, much to the delight of an imbecile audience. When Queen Elizabeth leaves to win over her daughter to marry the murderous Richard, she suddenly rushes back, grabs him by the penis, whereupon he turns away, cowering in shame. Elizabeth, however, holds up two fingers about two inches from each other, to indicate the puny size of the royal organ, and breaks into hysterical laughter. As she runs off guffawing ghoulishly, the P.A. system joins in with a chorus of hags cackling in stereophonic cacophony. In a moment of despair, Richard is about to seek consolation from oral intercourse with Ratcliff, but settles for squeezing his head against Ratcliff's genitalia.

I shall give you only two more examples of the evening's nonstop absurdities. At Bosworth Field, though Richard has a sizable army, Richmond (Michael O'Hare, made up and behaving rather like David Bowie—snow-white face and scarlet lips) is entirely alone and unarmed. Richard conveniently drops his sword—by the sound of it, it must weigh at least an ounce or two—and this is picked up by Richmond, who proceeds to run Richard through, very palpably between the right arm and the torso, as if he were saying, "Do you mind holding this sword for me while I adjust my makeup?" (When Clarence is murdered, even before the dagger touches him, oodles of blood spout in all directions, though other slayings, like this one, are rigorously dry.) Richard now staggers up a flight of stairs (unlikely on Bosworth Field) to his throne on top of them (unlikelier yet on a battlefield) and dies there. On his way, however, he stops twice to spit at Richmond, which the latter takes with exemplary equanimity.

The production begins with a sleeping Tyrrel on the ground, aroused by Richard's coming. It ends with Richmond falling asleep in much the same position, aroused by the coming of a mysterious figure: it is Richard III or Moriarty II with his hair slicked back like an apprentice butcher's and wearing a World War I army greatcoat. This figure now wakes up, in dumb play, the sleeping Richmond, who, likewise in dumb play, registers fright. So ends this supremely dumb play.

I cannot begin to describe the horrors and idiocies in which this production abounds. Though it is nominally directed by the Belgian André Ernotte, I cannot imagine a Walloon touring company exhibiting such incompetence—although there is a profusion of highly static tableaus, as if the cast were posing for a court painter to do their group portrait, which may be Ernotte's contribution—and so I must assume Moriarty's hand in most of the staging. This execrable actor even had the nerve to start a Shakespearean company called Potter's Field, which, as you may know, is the sort of cemetery with unmarked graves where actors and other derelicts used to be interred. Moriarty's company, many of whom appear in this production, deserve to be buried in the nearest one—alive.

With the exception of Robert York, who plays the younger prince badly but sweetly and innocently, there is not a bad performance in this large cast. All the performances are at the very least rotten; at worst, loathsome. Viveca Lindfors plays mad Queen Margaret with twitches and tremors, as if she were suffering from terminal fleabites. Her gown seems to be always in danger of slipping off and receives more attention than her characterization, which consists mostly of letting her arms and hands behave as if they were Geiger counters that have just hit upon a vast uranium cache. She delivers her lines as if they were written by a typewriter that lost its space key and most of its consonants: we get an endless, undifferentiated outpouring of vowels as diphthongs in some regional Swedish accent that occasionally seems to border on English, but not often enough to yield apprehensible meanings.

As Buckingham, David Huffman portrays an ill-spoken, childish-looking lout who might be a down-on-the-charts rock singer and surely cannot speak his lines. As Hastings, Geoffrey Horne looks all right but cannot act at all, until his final tantrum on the floor when facing death, at which point he snivels with style. Philip Casnoff's Clarence is an emaciated punk who speaks in a thin, edgy, ignoble voice and dies with a paroxysm worthy of a decapitated chicken. Denise Bessette's Lady Anne—looking, walking, and talking like a twelve-year-old fishwife—would be the laughingstock of an intelligent high-school production; Robin Bartlett, as Queen Elizabeth, has a voice, movements, and face of surpassing jerkiness and vulgarity and should never be cast as anything but an itinerant gefilte-fish vendor with a serious nervous disorder.

As Rivers, Jay McCormack looks and acts like a second-rate Osric in *Hamlet*; as Tyrrel, Richard Seer convinces as Richard's probable catamite, but as not much else. When he relates the killing of the little princes, he suddenly sounds like someone describing a gourmet meal at Lutèce, with saliva cascading through his mouth. Jason Scott, as Prince Edward, does not suggest a brave boy so much as a mummified elder actor, his face and voice practically reeking with formaldehyde. Donald Linahan's Bishop seems to have been rushed over from a drag-queen contest, with the cassock mistakenly grabbed instead of a Mae West outfit. Even Anna Galiena, who plays the interpolated part of Jane Shore (couldn't the production have derived something more relevant from Olivier's magnificent movie version of *Richard III*?), wearing the same nightgown night and day, manages, without opening her mouth to strike more phony attitudes than a fashion model doing a Richard Avedon spread.

Ann Emonts's costumes are passable, but was it Ernotte's crazy notion to do *Richard III* in Directoire outfits? Nothing about that period corresponds to the *modus operandi* of the Wars of the Roses. Less fortunate even are the vermilion and turquoise stairs of the set by Bill Stabile, who might want to try mobiles next. Marc B. Weiss's lighting does some interesting things, but they are wasted on a production more deserving of being swallowed up by eternal darkness. Most shocking, however, was the audience reaction. Although I heard a few "terrible"s here and there, and noticed a number of walkouts, a goodly showing of folk stayed to give Moriarty a thunderous ovation. An elderly woman, recognizing me in the intermission, avidly asked me what I thought of the show. I said it belonged in a pigsty. "Why," she said, "because you can't hear what the actors are saying?" "No," I said, "because you occasionally can."

One of the big problems with the training of American actors is that they are not taught to speak verse. An even bigger problem is that they are not taught how to speak. Some of the lesser actors in *Richard III* you would not have been able to understand even at a medium-noisy cocktail party. But not one of them knows how to enunciate and project properly; unlike the great English actors who could make the telephone book sound like poetic drama, these Potter's Fieldhands and the rest can make Shakespeare sound like the Brooklyn phone book read over a bad connection. In a recent interview with *Theater* magazine, Eric Bentley, the distinguished critic, said, "We live in a miserable world and we have a miserable theater to match it." Truer words were seldom spoken. If a new Scipio decides to treat the American Shakespeare Festival like Carthage—raze it to the ground and pour salt over it—I'll gladly contribute my salt shakers.

42nd Street

At the end of the much delayed premiere of *42nd Street*, David Merrick came onstage to announce to a flabbergasted cast and audience the death that afternoon of Gower Champion. It was, like the show itself, something out of the movies. I was reminded of Anton Walbrook's announcement of Moira Shearer's death in *The Red Shoes*. Unlike a ballerina's, a director-choreographer's death does not stop the show, and it went on—to re-establish Gower Champion at the forefront of his profession. For a while, poor basic material, such as *Rockabye Hamlet* and the badly dated *Irene*—despite his handsome contribution to the latter—had somewhat dimmed Champion's star; how unjust to have to die on the day when it was so gloriously relumed.

42nd Street, based on the 1933 Warner movie, is a musical that moves along the parallel lines of nostalgia and camp, which, though they will meet in infinity, are still obdurately separate by 11 PM. The old songs, whether from this movie or other film scores by the team of Harry Warren and Al Dubin, supply most of the nostalgia; the camp comes chiefly from the book (so foreshortened as to be aptly dubbed by Merrick "Lead Ins and Crossovers") of Michael Stewart and Mark Bramble, which, while retaining much of the original silliness, adds a little contemporary bitchiness of its own. Though nostalgia and camp do not blend, there is an overarching element that bridges the gap: Gower Champion's choreography, every bit as lavish and original as what Busby Berkeley did for this film and others like it, but with an added fineness of detail, and justness of overall conception. The staging—not only of the dances but also of the entire show—has an intensity and sweep that transcend both nostalgia and camp. It grabs you by the throat or entrails—sometimes, indeed, by the heart—and carries you beyond razzmatazz, beyond even pizzazz, into elation.

The story is one of your archer archetypes: aging prima donna's rich Texas lover foots bills for musical that will mark comeback of distinguished but fading director; sweet girl from the sticks gets spot on chorus line as the feud of director and star is exacerbated by presence of latter's real heartthrob, a two-bit thespian and ne'er-do-well. Star breaks ankle, and chorine learns the part in 36 hours and turns show into hit; herself a bright new star, she and director head for romance. Stewart and Bramble sometimes retain the original's ingenuousness, as when the previously beastly star tells her replacement, "Get out there and be so swell to make me hate you!" At other times, they add such daring new humor as this description of the star as a good sort who, "on her first show, made 30 bucks a week and sent a hundred back to her mother." It's a hodgepodge, but, happily, there's not much of it; the musical numbers promptly preempt the stage.

And marvelous they are. For example: Peggy Sawyer, the heroine, has just been hired and hasn't mastered the routines yet; in "You're Getting to Be a Habit With Me," she stumbles, skids, shoots all over the stage in desperate search for her partner and always pops up in the wrong place—getting to be a habitual nuisance. The choreographic mishaps are plotted so resourcefully that her misplacements are the visual equivalents of, say, the wrong notes in a song like Bernstein's "Wrong-Note Rag"—tart discords more piquant than most harmonies. Or take "Dames," in which Robin Wagner's ingenious scenery turns itself inside out and, again, outside in with a difference, making the whole world one kaleidoscope that spews forth girls, girls, girls in Theoni V. Aldredge's snappy yet also slightly screwy costumes; and then as mirrors open up further hallucinatory dimensions and swirling vistas, magic seems only a little farther than your fingertips. One more example: "We're in the Money," in which four down-at-heel girls find a dime and, forthwith, Depression and repressions vanish. Enlarged dimes become a cross between Amazons' shields and G-strings, as chorines parade on behind them; placed on the floor, they are platforms for the girls to spin on. At the center, a bigger, silver dollar of a platform has the lead girls tapping and spinning; in the background, skyscrapers rise, made of dimes and dollars. All this, as in a dream, proliferating from that initial dime—truly, a wonderful dime had by everyone.

42nd Street cost upward of two million dollars' worth of dimes, and, to its credit be it said, you can see where every dime went. But there is also a debit side that is, along with the book, headed by Tammy Grimes. That she can ruin everything respectable, from Molière to Turgenev, everyone but the New York reviewers seems to know by now. Yet one might have thought that she could at least play an aging, non-dancing, insolent musical-comedy star, simply by using what God has withheld from her. Not so. Here is the old, amateurish imitation of W. C. Fields coming from a face like a blasé butcher block. Frail consonants fall prey to distended vowels; entire words are snorted up by the nose and remain unintelligible. Such acting comes by the yard or pound, and when you consider a display of femininity worthy of a drill sergeant, you wonder what even that Texas millionaire sees here—except perhaps, myopically, an oil derrick.

As the veteran Broadway director, Jerry Orbach has found a role in which his blend of cuteness and sleaziness can be put to best use. Danny Carroll, Carole Cook, and Joseph Bova perform neatly in supporting roles, and Lee Roy Reams, as the innocently swaggering tenor, treads winningly in Dick Powell's shoes. Karen Prunczik is properly brash and trenchant-voiced in the role created by Ginger Rogers; James Congdon, though, is nowhere near so paradoxically oily *and* wooden as George Brent was—but, then, who is? What is exhilarating is the large chorus, dancing and singing to well-honed, smartly tuned perfection, making even the one or two derivative numbers (e.g., the opening, out of *A Chorus Line* via *All That Jazz*) a pleasure to watch.

I cannot convey in a short space the mixture of judiciousness and dazzlement that go into Robin Wagner's sets and Tharon Musser's lighting, with Theoni V. Aldredge's costumes only a short step behind. And, as Peggy Sawyer, Wanda Richert, a relative newcomer, is glowingly right: a fine amalgam of naïveté and determination, backcountry wholesomeness and show-biz éclat, she dances, sings, and emotes to a fare-thee-well. But the greatest hail—like the greatest farewell—must go to Gower Champion. He has turned out work here that would be a fitting climax to any two careers and that gives the American musical comedy that look of opulence and high gloss combined with purposefulness and efficacy (invention for the sake of the show rather than mere showiness) for which the world's eyes have always been directed to Broadway. I hope that dance notation will reconstruct and perpetuate some of Champion's previous choreographies and that this one will be filmed for the joy and wonder of future generations.

The Suicide

Nadezhda Mandelshtam, in *Hope Against Hope*, evokes the sad picture of Nikolai Erdman in internal exile: living in "a poky little hole," drinking, and, literally and figuratively, falling silent. After the great director Vsevolod Meyerhold scored with Erdman's first play, *The Mandate*, he spent eighteen months preparing *The Suicide*, the second and better one, only to have it banned after the dress rehearsal in 1932; it still hasn't been performed in Russia. Its hero, Senya, after toying with the idea of suicide, elects to live; Erdman, too, chose life at the cost of artistic suicide enforced by Stalin's henchmen. Someone ought to write a play about the 38 years of lying low that remained to Erdman; it would be fraught, I am sure, with more drama and gallows humor than *The Suicide*.

Senya, unemployed and despondent, has to contend with the pity of his wife and the pitilessness of his mother-in-law; aside from such daymares, he also has nightmares. When his scheme to set himself up as a tuba virtuoso catches crabs (in blowers' parlance), he announces his intention to end it all, Forthwith, every joker who wants the suicide note to represent his or her interest—the State lends an ear only to criticism from suicides—starts wooing him for his or her crackbrained cause. Workers, writers, intellectuals, faded beauties—everyone wants to be the beneficiary of a ringing suicide note. Yet despite a grand farewell banquet and an efflorescence of eulogies, Senya chooses survival—in the present production, it would seem, out of sheer cowardice. But the director has taken many liberties with the text (which, unfortunately, I have been unable to examine), and it may be that Erdman was after something bigger: what makes people, even under totalitarianism, decide, to quote Mrs. Mandelshtam, "to go on living even though everything [is] pushing… to suicide."

For its time and place, *The Suicide* was a remarkably brave, outspoken play, and it is astonishing that it got as far as a dress rehearsal. Its closest competitors in social criticism—plays by Bulgakov, Evgeny Shwartz, and one or two others—contain nothing so overtly stinging as "Tell me, Yegor, is there life after death?"—"There may be now, but there won't be under socialism." Unlike Meyerhold and Osip Mandelshtam, however, Erdman was not a fighter and fell silent in exchange for mere life. Perhaps he knew what the characters of *The Suicide* do not: that even suicide notes do not speak all that loudly to deaf ears. About this play, though, at least in its present version, I must regretfully agree with one of my least favorite drama critics, Josef Stalin, who wrote Stanislavsky that he did not have "a very high opinion" of it.

Jonas Jurašas, who directed, was, so we are told, a leading director in the Soviet Union before his emigration. He has, I gather, considerably refurbished the play. Thus the Gypsies, who, in the original, have a much smaller role, now become a sort of surreal chorus popping up everywhere to comment on Senya's dreams and act out his nightmares. Again, the way in which Jurašas ends the play allows us to view all of it as a single nasty dream of Senya's. With his scenic designer, Santo Loquasto, the director has worked out a huge, as it were, Constructivist set that spills out into the auditorium and provides the cast with more of a workout than Jack LaLanne could. They run along vertiginous catwalks, climb up forbidding ladders, and plummet down firemen's poles; at the very least, they dash in and out dozens of doors that jostle one another seemingly all the way into infinity. Sometimes they have to deliver speeches swinging from these doors. Even a much stronger play might not survive so much body-building.

Still, *The Suicide* is lucky in its leading man, Derek Jacobi, who, visually and vocally, is flexibility itself. With a face that can hurtle from nondescript to tragic, from nonplussed to exultant, in a matter of fractions of a second, Jacobi is a comic Everyman and then some. His succulent British accent is lower-middle-class with an upward mobility that can quickly become recidivous and lapse into one of those Eliza Doolittle whines that drove Henry Higgins to choice fulminations. Jacobi's performance is perfectly centered between slyness and fatuity, enterprisingness and cowardice; even when silent and immobile, this worthy actor provides his colleagues with as many platforms and perches as the scenery does to strut their wares from.

What are their wares? John Heffernan, looking once again not like a mere unmade bed but like a whole dormitory in disarray, is a wonderfully up-in-the-clouds and down-at-heel intellectual. John Christopher Jones, wisely refraining from some of the others' rash, fake-Russian stage accents, makes a maniacal Marxist quietly believable and funny. The rest, however, seem to have been chosen for either their lack of looks or lack of talent—or, most likely, both. There are particularly squirm-making performances from Angela Pietropinto, Grayson Hall, Clarence Felder, David Sabin, Chip Zien, Leda Siskind, and William Myers, with the others not far ahead. For this, the director must shoulder some of the blame. And having two faded beauties played by Laura Esterman and Mary Lou Rosato may be a joke, but not a very good one. The Lithuanian director's English is, I hear, good enough to rule out linguistics as an excuse. But Jurašas may not be aware of how much Jacobi's Britishness, cunningly though it is pitched on the social scale, jars against the lingo of the rest.

Santo Loquasto's set and costumes are impressive albeit fulsome, and F. Mitchell Dana's lighting is sturdily effective. As for Richard Weinstock's music, we can perhaps derive some consolation from assuming its vulgarity to be deliberate. Enough is going on in *The Suicide* to keep your attention engaged and coax the occasional laugh from you; your deeper levels, however, are likely to remain disengaged.

The Seagull

Andrei Serban's mounting of *The Seagull* for Joseph Papp comes a step or two nearer what Chekhov has written than did the Romanian director's version of *The Cherry Orchard* four years ago. At the rate Mr. Serban is progressing, it should take him only 96 more years to realize Chekhov's intentions, and, the way he is being indulged by Papp and others, he might just live, and direct, that long. The only problem is that Chekhov would have to have written 30 full-length works instead of five or six—unless Serban were to keep redirecting the same plays.

The Seagull is the first of the great foursome of truly Chekhovian tragicomedies, the one in which the gears still mesh with an ever so slight harrumphing. Certainly, the ponderous symbolism of the shot seagull is troublesome, even if it is not Nina, the obvious analogue to the floppy symbol, who shoots herself. She hangs on to a dubious future, whereas Konstantin, the seagull killer, shoots himself. The question raised by the play is: between putting an early end to it or eking out a wretched life on the edge of insanity and prostitution, which is worse? (Which is better is not the question.) From what Konstantin says about Nina's acting—and surely he bends over backward—there can be no hope that Nina will be saved by her vocation, as some critics have supposed.

That, precisely, is the point: we live between the devil and the deep blue sea—or, in this case, lake: the lake that serves as background for Konstantin's playlet, though in this production it seems at first to be in the auditorium and then to move around like the rest of Serban's shifty topography. (Thus piano music comes from different directions, sometimes suggesting that there is a Bechstein grand parked somewhere on a raft.) In any case, nobody in the play gets what he wants: Dr. Dorn, well traveled and beloved of women, is just as foiled by the uncreativity of his life as is old Sorin, the civil servant who never loved or (he feels) lived, but whose declining years are snugly wrapped in a blanket of self-pity and fussed over by the household. For ever failure in *The Seagull* there is a corresponding, equally acrid-tasting success.

Yet we do not get crudely obvious counterparts but vaguely parallel lives that flow along with only an eddy of bravado here, a brief whirlpool of gratuitous passion there. Underneath the frustrations and self-dramatizing, the ludicrous yearnings and emotional pratfalls, however, there is genuine misery, worthy of our best compassion; but the fastidious author uncovers it only sparingly, leaving the rest to our empathetic imagination. So, too, the director must keep everything under seemly control, bearing in mind Chekhov's extraordinary delicacy of spirit. As the Soviet critic K. Zhukovsky has noted, Chekhov was perhaps the only man who apologized to his friends for *not* borrowing any money from them.

Serban, contrariwise, would sell whatever he has by way of soul for theatrical effects. From his skillful designer, Michael H. Yeargan, he has elicited a set that is based on wonderfully polished boards that form, in the first two acts, a kind of peninsula in the lake (no waterlogging here!), in back of which arches a similarly constructed parallel bridge of sighs across which all of the characters must, most of the time, make their entrances and exits. This can be quite ridiculous when, say, a character downstage left does not exit by a convenient minibridge leading directly to the left end of the bigger bridge but first crosses all the way to the right, then goes up the right minibridge, and then trudges the full length of the big bridge back to more or less where he came from, making his exit conspicuous enough to detract attention from what's happening downstage. To an only slightly lesser degree than in his *Cherry Orchard*, Serban has contrived a separate, supererogatory scenario for the upstage area to run concurrently with the legitimate action down front.

The staging is, typically, overfussy about details and blithely neglectful of deeper, subtler, more affecting albeit elusive matters. Several characters, for instance, have arbitrary quasi-choreographies: Sorin tends to do a fidgety little two-step, sometimes even while sedated; Arkadina will burst into a waltz on "I feel as light as a bird," and something between a farandole and a fandango on "It's so boring"; Masha expresses her repressed love in a spiritedly foot-stamping flamenco. When Konstantin tells of Nina's downfall, all pull up their chairs around him as if for a long winter night's gossip session, and the lights dim as though he were about to favor us with a torch song. Against such harebrained whimsies there are spells of clanking literal-mindedness. Let a character talk about being torn apart, and forthwith the director conjures up for her an unlikely piece of cloth she can rip to her heart's content; let someone mention the restlessness of the dogs, and promptly the stage fills up with enough offstage baying and howling to drown half a page of dialogue. In a quaint slipup, however, when someone mentions sugarplums, Serban (because of inadequate English?) produces a basket of garden-variety plums.

Most of the performances are misdirected or naturally poor. Thus the dashing but thoroughly decent Dorn emerges as a smarmy Levantine rug merchant (F. Murray Abraham) whom you would not trust as far as you could throw a Bukhara the size of a mosque. Masha (Pamela Payton-Wright) either prances with a cornhusk pipe in her scrunched-up face, like some demented Mammy Yokum, or else squats silently like an Indian squaw. Michael Egan is a sullen, barely effusive Shamraev; as Paulina, Joyce Van Patten thinks she is doing *The Perils of Pauline*. The accomplished and dependable Rosemary Harris has been directed to play Arkadina as a woman unable to utter a sincere syllable or make a natural gesture; as Konstantin, Brent Spiner looks too comically homely even for that unheroic part, emits a squeezed-out, nasal voice, and, despite some good moments, suggests a bedazzled high-school student adrift in a college production. Christopher Walken goes through his usual backpack of tricks as he gives us a hippie Trigorin alternately coked-up and zonked—at one point he even seems to chew gum. Kathryn Dowling, though fetching and touching for three acts, cannot get closer to the fourth-act Nina (thanks in part to capricious direction) than a minor possessed nun from *The Devils*. When she proclaims her intention of going to what she pronounces as Yale-etz, I can merely assume that the place has a famous drama school. Only George Hall's not overpathetic Sorin and Richard Russell Ramos's castrated bear of a Medvedenko register fully and appropriately.

A Lesson From Aloes

A Lesson From Aloes is yet another earnest, compassionate, great-heartedly dedicated play by Athol Fugard about the miseries of apartheid—the devastation it works on South Africans of every stripe. Here we have Piet, a decently concerned Afrikaaner who failed as a farmer and now does odd jobs around Port Elizabeth. His wife, Gladys, of English descent, suffered a breakdown when the police confiscated her intimate diaries; she has been released from a hospital after prolonged shock treatments. For years now. Piet has been friend to and fellow activist (on a small scale) with Steve Daniels, a "colored" bricklayer who did six months in jail for infringing a banning order. The mental tortures there, plus the prospect of enforced joblessness for himself and his family, have induced him to leave in hate the land he onesidedly loved. Fearfully, he is setting out for England with wife and children.

Somebody had apparently betrayed Steve to the police, and everyone, even his own wife, suspects Piet of being the informer. When Steve comes to say good-bye, Gladys, in one of her hysterical outbursts, accuses Piet in front of Steve. Piet, stunned, refuses to defend himself. Steve, in a state of uncertainty, leaves thoroughly demoralized; Gladys, broken and possibly even more embittered than Steve, seeks refuge in what may be permanent institutionalization; a solitary Piet is left to contemplate his beloved aloes: unprepossessing plants with bitter, prickly leaves that somehow manage to endure in poor soil with scant watering.

Fugard's commitment to his suffering country is exemplary, and he writes about the national pain with commendable restraint and subtlety. In this, as in most of his plays, he avoids representing extremes of brutality and terror and manages to convey the widespread wretchedness all the better for it. Yet there is a cost: the play has visually no other dimensions than those of fear, frustration, isolation, and hopelessness, and there are not even bursts of major violence to induce catharsis. In this instance, moreover, there is a serious shortcoming: for the sake of concentration on the central problem and the resultant confrontations, too much background material is left unfilled-in. Just how neurotic was Gladys to begin with to make the diary incident send her over the brink? How did she and Piet come to marry and live until then? What possible gain or other motive could have made Piet turn traitor? And why would everybody's suspicion necessarily descend on him? What sort of work does Piet do now, and what did Gladys do when she was better? Why is the disturbed Gladys allowed possession of so many pills? There is a certain existential thickness missing from the play, a broader actuality in which to situate the specific conflict. Exile, madness, lonely brooding: to prevent these terrible solutions from adding up to agitprop, more fleshing out is needed—more characters, perhaps, or even a touch of humor beyond the running gag of Piet and his unceasing quotations.

Symbolism, too, weighs crunchingly on the play: not only the aloes (whose lesson of flowering in a desert, incidentally, seems to have little relevance to Piet and none to the others) but also roses that refuse to grow and a new diary that Gladys fusses over but whose pages turn out to be blank. Moreover, Fugard's language is a trifle prosaic, only seldom rising to the heart-searing poetry of Gladys's cry to Steve: "They have burned my brain as brown as yours!" And yet there is much beauty here: the beauty of friendship, decency, love, trying to assert themselves against impossible odds; the beauty, also, of small people being so used by life that they acquire the smoothness of worn utensils, the sheen of threadbare clothes. And Fugard never tries to squeeze pathos out of them; he merely lets them slowly, sadly fill up with it.

Under the author's simple, dignified direction, the cast performs with authority. As Piet, Harris Yulin is better than I have ever seen him: even his ponderousness serves him in good stead here. Maria Tucci, though perhaps a trifle unrelieved in her anguish, is steadily compelling. And James Earl Jones, though up to his old vocal tricks (strange, arbitrary changes in volume), exudes a moving array of contradictory feelings. Susan Hilferty's costumes are plain and good, but William Armstrong's lighting could be more evocative, as could be, even on an obvious shoestring, Michael H. Yeargan's décor. *A Lesson From Aloes* is the only uncompromisingly honorable drama on Broadway today. For all its singlemindedness, it finely allows its characters some ambiguities, a core of mystery; you will come from it feeling that you haven't wasted your time and money, and especially not your brain.

Amadeus

Not unlike *Equus*, Peter Shaffer's *Amadeus* is a goddamned middlebrow masterpiece. (It is also God-damning, as the hero-villain, Antonio Salieri, discovers that God does not reward virtue and piety with immortality—something he could have found out from going to see Shaffer's Royal *Hunt of the Sun*.) It has every ingredient the middlebrow hungers for: great historic names, the debunking of great historic names, the debunking of the debunking of great historic names. As in *Equus*, there is a bit of sexual titillation, a bit of dressing down of the audience (the middlebrow loves to play *hypocrite spectateur* as long as the famous author assures him of being *mon semblable, mon frère*), a bit of barbershop metaphysics—a quarrel with God is particularly salable as long as it need not be taken seriously—and a lot of striking production values. Throw in a couple of British stars and loud reports of a huge London success, and the soufflé rises to the skies. But imagine now that the principal characters are called not Mozart and Salieri but Smith and Jones, or even Porto-Riche and Capus, and what have you got? What indeed.

Shaffer has taken grains of truth from the lives of Mozart and Salieri and secreted a tissue of shoddy invention around them— roughly the reverse of the process by which oysters make pearls. For example, we know from the published letters that Mozart was fond of baby talk and bawdry; so Shaffer gives us a Mozart who spews ridiculous filth all over the place and a Wolfgang and Constanze who wantonly welter in public while emitting streams of the stickiest verbiage. Salieri was, apparently, envious of Mozart and bore him ill will; given his favored position at court, he may well have done him damage. But out of this Shaffer fabricates a fanatical hatred that sometimes verges on love-hate, and an argument with God of such grandiosely outrageous dimensions as would have required a much grander Salieri than the mediocrity he was and as most of the play represents him.

Given the feebleness and obvious jokes of the writing—not the least offensive of which is the sight gag that turns Mozart into a hopping, skipping, fright-wig-wearing, self-promoting popinjay— one is less than eager to indulge in speculation about Shaffer's purpose. Still, is he trying to tell us that it is a curse to be a mediocre artist? That genius is roundly misunderstood? That one can be a great creator and still a mundane human being? That one can be a mediocrity, yet so appreciative of greatness that one's envy of it can be inspired, almost partaking of genius? The first three are pretty obvious; the fourth is desperately farfetched. Mediocrities generally do not appreciate greatness—it's part of what makes them mediocre. To keep myself entertained during the rather long stretches between selections from Mozart's music, I tried to guess which of his main characters the author identified himself with. Does he see *Amadeus* as a sort of O'Neill and Shaffer, or as a Shaffer and Martinus Scriblerus? Or does he perceive himself as capaciously, magnanimously containing both?

There is theatrical know-how in some of this, an undeniable coup de théâtre or two, along with such cheap tricks as having the emperor repeatedly say, "Well there it is!"—shade of the father in *Equus* with his "if you perceive my meaning"—and all those cutesy conceits about how this or that famous aria was engendered. There are gimcrack epigrams, such as "What use, after all, is man if not to teach God his lessons?" (I myself prefer Wilde's version: "An honest God's man's noblest work of art"); and coy role reversals, as when Salieri, who narrates the story in flashback to us, the unborn generations, brings down the first-act curtain on the excuse that he has to pee and winks at the audience: "The bladder being a human appendage, it is not something you ghosts need concern yourselves with."

Peter Hall has directed with all his customary shrewdness and showmanship, and John Bury's scenery, costumes, and lighting couldn't be more apt and inventive. If arresting stage groupings and movements and tastefully controlled scenic panoply are what you're after, you won't be cheated here. Tim Curry is as good a Mozart as the odious conception allows; Jane Seymour is a lovely, saucy, and spirited Constance; Nicholas Kepros a splendidly cunning fool of an Emperor Joseph II; and the entire supporting cast more than satisfactory. I was, however, somewhat disappointed in Ian McKellen as Salieri. As an old wretch reminiscing, he is a poor man's Roy Dotrice doing John Aubrey; as Salieri in his splendor and misery, he resorts far too many times to expressing torment by speaking ever so slowly in a gray, toneless little head voice while rolling his eyes upward in reproof of the Creator. McKellen always struck me as a very good technician but a not quite true artist—a kind of toned-down Peter O'Toole. Nothing to sneeze at, mind you, but if there is real greatness in him, I have yet to experience it.

If you want a genuine imaginative re-creation of Mozart, I recommend Mörike's novella *Mozart on the Journey to Prague*. However, the opening-night audience ate up *Amadeus*. And what got the biggest laugh? Mozart telling a fat antagonist, "You look like a toad." Now, there is true wit for you, on both sides of the footlights!

Nowhere in the western world, I daresay, do the classics fare as badly as in our theater. I don't know whether it is the teaching or the learning—more properly the lack of teaching and the unwillingness to learn—that is to blame. In any case, American theater seems to be equipped only for the latest American plays; there is no sense of other times and other places—as what follows shockingly demonstrates.

Crimes of the Heart;
True West

From time to time a play comes along that restores one's faith in our theater, that justifies endless evenings spent, like some unfortunate Beckett character, chin-deep in trash. This time it is the Manhattan Theatre Club's *Crimes of the Heart*, by Beth Henley, a new playwright of charm, warmth, style, unpretentiousness, and authentically individual vision.

We are dealing here with the reunion in Hazlehurst, Mississippi, of the three MaGrath sisters (note that even in her names Miss Henley always hits the right ludicrous note). Lenny, the eldest, is a patient Christian sufferer: monstrously accident-prone, shuttling between gentle hopefulness and slightly comic hysteria, a martyr to her sexual insecurity and a grandfather who takes most of her energies and an unconscionable time dying. Babe Botrelle, the youngest and zaniest sister, has just shot her husband in the stomach because, as she puts it, she didn't like the way he looked. Babe (who would like to be a saxophonist) is in serious trouble: she needs the best lawyer in town, but that happens to be the husband she shot. Meg, the middle sister, has had a modest singing career that culminated in Biloxi. In Los Angeles, where she now lives, she has been reduced to a menial job. She is moody and promiscuous, and has ruined, before leaving home, the chances of "Doc" Porter to go to medical school. She made him spend a night with her in a house that lay in the path of Hurricane Camille; the roof collapsed, leaving Doc with a bad leg and, soon thereafter, no Meg.

The time of the play is "Five years after Hurricane Camille," but in Hazlehurst there are always disasters, be they ever so humble. Today, for instance, it is Lenny's thirtieth birthday, and everyone has forgotten it, except pushy and obnoxious Cousin Chick, who has brought a crummy present. God certainly forgot, because he has allowed Lenny's beloved old horse to be struck dead by lightning the night before, even though there was hardly a storm. Crazy things happen in Hazlehurst: Pa MaGrath ran out on his family; Ma MaGrath hanged her cat and then hanged herself next to it, thus earning nationwide publicity. Babe rates only local headlines. She will be defended by an eager recent graduate of Ole Miss Law School whose name is Barnette Lloyd. (Names have a way of being transsexual in Hazlehurst.) Barnette harbors an epic grudge against the crooked and beastly Botrelle as well as a nascent love for Babe. But enough of this plot-recounting—though, God knows, there is so much plot here that I can't begin to give it away. And all of it is demented, funny, and, unbelievable as this may sound, totally believable.

The three sisters are wonderful creations: Lenny out of Chekhov, Babe out of Flannery O'Connor, and Meg out of Tennessee Williams in one of his more benign moods. But "out of" must not be taken to mean imitation; it is just a legitimate literary genealogy. Ultimately, the sisters belong only to Miss Henley and to themselves. Their lives are lavish with incident, their idiosyncrasies insidiously compelling, their mutual loyalty and help (though often frazzled) able to nudge heartbreak toward heart-lift. And the subsidiary characters are just as good—even those we only hear about or from (on the phone), such as the shot husband, his shocked sister, and a sexually active fifteen year-old black.

Miss Henley is marvelous at exposition, cogently interspersing it with action, and making it just as lively and suspenseful as the actual happenings. Her dialogue is equally fine: always in character (though Babe may once or twice become too benighted), always furthering our understanding while sharpening our curiosity, always doing something to make us laugh, get lumps in the throat, care. The jokes are juicy but never gratuitous, seeming to stem from the characters rather than from the author, and seldom lacking implications of a wider sort. Thus when Meg finds Babe outlandishly trying to commit suicide because, among other things, she thinks she will be committed, Meg shouts: "You're just as perfectly sane as anyone walking the streets of Hazlehurst, Mississippi." On one level, this is an absurd lie; on another, higher level, an absurd truth. It is also a touching expression of sisterly solidarity, while deriving its true funniness from the context. Miss Henley plays, juggles, conjures with context—Hazlehurst, the South, the world.

The play is in three fully packed, old-fashioned acts, each able to top its predecessor, none repetitious, dragging, predictable. But the author's most precious gift is the ability to balance characters between heady poetry and stalwart prose, between grotesque heightening and compelling recognizability—between absurdism and naturalism. If she errs in any way, it is in slightly artificial resolutions, whether happy or sad.

Melvin Bernhardt has staged it all with the same affectionate, incisive attention to detail with which John Lee Beatty designed the kitchen set, Patricia McGourty the mundane costumes, and Dennis Parichy the lighting. As for the cast, it is a dream ensemble, with only Peter MacNicol a trifle overstated as Barnette (but very good all the same). Perfection is the word for Mia Dillon's Babe, Mary Beth Hurt's Meg, Stephen Burleigh's Doc, and Julie Nesbitt's Chick; as for Lizbeth MacKay's Lenny, she goes beyond that, into the miraculous.

I have only one fear—that this clearly autobiographical play may be stocked with the riches of youthful memories that many playwrights cannot duplicate in subsequent works. I hope this is not the case with Beth Henley; be that as it may, *Crimes of the Heart* bursts with energy, merriment, sagacity, and, best of all, a generosity toward people and life that many good writers achieve only in their most mature offerings, if at all.

Whereas no one expects much more from the author of *Postcards* and *The Last of Mrs. Lincoln*, one does expect a great deal more from

Sam Shepard, one of our best playwrights, who only recently gave us the startling, demonically hallucinated *Buried Child*. The gifted but erratic Shepard has let us down before, but never so gracelessly, completely, and unforgivably as with *True West*. Granted, both he and his favorite director, Robert Woodruff, who withdrew from the production, have hurled anathemas at Joe Papp, who recast and partly redirected it, and at the new actors, who, allegedly, changed and subverted the text.

Yet even assuming that the worst havoc has been wreaked on the play, this cannot account for the lack of a single idea, a single line worth committing to paper. The whole thing is a feeble imitation of Pinter, without even Pinter's ability to suggest that his meaninglessness might conceal meaning. This tale of two brothers—one a petty crook, the other a petty screenwriter—who gradually reverse roles only to become more than ever locked in irreconcilable antagonism, steadily suggests less than it says, which itself is pretty close to nothing. Even the sight gags, involving the laying waste of an orderly bourgeois house by anarchic littering and destruction, was done more pungently and suggestively in *Buried Child*.

As cagey an actor as Peter Boyle cannot find ways to build the criminal brother into a figure of more than routine smarminess and menace; Tommy Lee Jones's screenwriter is only a hopping, blithering pipsqueak. I could believe that almost anyone from a commercial-jingle writer to an overindulged schoolboy wrote *True West*, only not that it was written by Sam Shepard. Why, the imbecile scenario that the burglar brother dictates to the writer brother sounds no different from the rest of the play. As for the satire on the Hollywood producer (Louis Zorich), *Really Rosie* does that better, and it's kid stuff, for gosh sakes.

Still Life

In *Still Life*, Emily Mann, who wrote and directed, places three people on a platform at a speakers' table. There is Mark, a Vietnam veteran, who seems to be excessively controlled, self-accusing, and at home with his misery; Cheryl, his wife and mother of their small son, who seems insane enough—though calmly, ever so calmly— to be put away; and Nadine, a somewhat older woman—unhappy wife, mother of three girls, photographer, feminist, and Mark's current lover. Mark, apparently, is a photographer too, but he also runs some sort of store; he seems to be separated from Cheryl, though also somehow living with her. They appear to be all right financially, though there often isn't enough to eat. Cheryl, though quite mad, seems to be coping; Nadine, though quite sensible, is nutty—keeps perceiving herself as a plunger, worries about not being depressed enough, thinks that Mark's having killed a family of five in Vietnam may somehow help her psychic equilibrium.

Where are these people who are often directly addressing us and often merely monologizing into space? Is this a talk show? A symposium? Group therapy? A meeting of Maniacs Anonymous? Beckett's Hell, only with no giant jars encasing the trio? Sometimes the three seem unaware of one another; sometimes they interact. Mark interrupts the proceedings to show some preposterous Vietnam slides, including one of a sweet, well-fed puppy that is supposed to have started devouring its master the moment his head was blown off. Whereupon Mark shot it, incurring guilt feelings maybe worse than from killing that family of five. Nadine tells us how incredibly gentle Mark is; Cheryl, how incredibly violent he is, what with that gun of his. Mark tells us how his mother, the day he came back from the war, told him not to drink so much coffee. And how his parents promptly went off to a party. And how he needs his gun.

One or another character suddenly goes backstage, and may be heard shouting "Wow!" They may be taking in liquids, or letting them out. Mark plays a tape of an anti-genocide song, and everyone strikes suitably distraught poses. Cheryl won't let Mark drive. (How does he get to his store?) He starts getting violent and banging the table. There is much talk about sex, kinky and otherwise. Also drugs. Mark wanted Cheryl to make love to a girl in Hong Kong. Shocking! Yet lesbianism makes sense, given what men are like these days. The war was terrible—people get killed in wars!—and we are all responsible. Also, it seems, for the fact that these three for whom Emily Mann's 28-year-old heart bleeds (the play, it appears, is largely based on their true stories) are so stupid, crazy, odious, and boring.

O my dear liberal, radical, feminist, juvenile Emily Mann! These people would be just as dreary and hopeless if there had been no Vietnam, and it would be just as much of an imposition to spend 90 minutes in their company—or yours, to the extent that these stories could not be this preposterous historically, clinically, humanly, without your having doctored them. This play is all nostalgia for the sixties, all radical chic: bourgeois radicalism that any true-blue Red—or genuine theater lover—must deplore. The actors—John Spencer, Timothy Near, Mary McDonnell—are convincing enough to make us want to run from them, but not so fast as from their pretentious author.

The American Place Theater, where *Still Life* is playing, has for a long time been unable to find a stageworthy offering. *Really Rosie* is only renting space there; other works of modest interest were part of special projects, not on the main stage. To forestall losing another needed institutional theater, a dramaturg of talent is urgently required—one with a better nose for what constitutes a good play than the present management can collectively muster.

Undiscovered Country

How often in a season, a decade, a lifetime can you see a work of genius on a nearby stage? A work of genius, moreover, that you did not even know existed? Such a play is Arthur Schnitzler's *Das weite Land* (1911), which the Hartford Stage Company is now performing in the Tom Stoppard version entitled *Undiscovered Country*. Even if you saw this powerful, insinuating work at Britain's National Theatre, there are many reasons for seeing it again in this production; if you didn't, Hartford shouldn't be too far to go, even on foot, for a treat as rare as this.

Not for nothing did Freud view Schnitzler, with a mixture of reverence and pique, as his secular alter ego; I know of no playwright or fiction writer (Schnitzler was, superlatively, both) who understood the vagaries of love, sex, and obsession—the topography of the generally triangular area stretching among those points—better than this still underrated Austrian giant. A physician-turned-writer, he had the most uncannily penetrating, witty, and tragic view of every cranny of man-woman relations, and expressed it with a kind of ruthless lyricism. It is Freud translated into a highly poetic, easefully musical prose; it is what you might get from a stethoscope that can hear the unconscious, a stethosocope that can sing.

Undiscovered Country is a series of concentric circles. There is the story of Friedrich Hofreiter, a prosperous Viennese businessman, charming hedonist, and faithless husband; Genia, his lovely, loving, faithful, confusedly suffering wife; and Otto von Aigner, an innocent, generous young naval lieutenant. Beyond that, there is the estrangement of Otto's parents, the worldly hotelier Dr. von Aigner, and his divorced actress wife. Beyond that, there is the strange marriage of Friedrich's banker, Natter, and his frivolous spouse, Adele, Friedrich's former mistress. And beyond that is the recent past, in which a brilliant young pianist killed himself out of unrequited love for Genia, and the near future, in which twenty-year-old, headstrong Erna may become Friedrich's next mistress, thus foiling the marital hopes of Friedrich's physician and best friend, the decent and sensible Dr. Mauer. Weaving in and out among these principals is a host of lesser figures, swelling an already rich complement into a swirling constellation of idle, intriguing, tormenting and tormented humanity, playing the not dissimilar games of tennis and life, inflicting and enduring spasms of love, and, for all their cleverness, not fathoming what any of it is about.

Schnitzler's play keeps you on the tenterhooks usually reserved for thrillers. It is written not so much in lines as in beams of ironic light, each wickedly or wistfully illuminating some further human insight or folly, or hopeless tangle of both. It is so wittily cynical yet also achingly compassionate that it keeps you excitedly spinning between hilarity and heartache as you follow this saddest, funniest, truest of commentaries on the hell of loving and the hell of not loving. Tom Stoppard's occasional additions do not help, nor is his translation (and, alas, abridgment) up to the refinement and opulence of the original. But it is sound, stageworthy English, and takes fewer liberties than you might expect from the author of *Travesties*.

The Hartford Stage Company production, though respectable enough and sufficient to convey the work's greatness, has serious lacks as well as solid virtues. Mark Lamos's direction starts out inauspiciously: in the early scenes, Lamos fills the large and sparsely furnished stage with a nervous, arbitrary, overelaborate, much too geometrically patterned choreography that is stilted as well as distracting. But, after a while, the staging settles down to judicious movement, cogent pacing, and generally laudable restraint. David Jenkins's scenery, mostly projections but also some hazily discernible papier-mâché cascades of blossoms, cannily conjures up the stifling lushness of Klimtian gardens. Pat Collins's lighting casts a faintly chilling dazzlement that perfectly externalizes the inner atmosphere of the principals' souls. And there are some stirring performances. Keith Baxter's Friedrich is an incisive rendition of a reckless sensualist, amoral but not willfully evil, lucid yet repeatedly self-blinded, destructive and also pitiful. Baxter treads a masterly middle path between self-dramatizing theatricality and a sense of inner emptiness, bravado and pathos. No less superb is Barbara Bryne, as the lonely, aging actress whose worldly wisdom and kindly understanding are not proof against ultimate delusion and bereavement. In supporting roles, there is admirable work from Ruby Holbrook, Mark Capri, Nafe Katter, William Wright, Jerry Allan Jones, Mary Munger, and one or two others; though too old for Dr. von Aigner, Stefan Schnabel invests this jaded yet not invulnerable *raisonneur* with a fine acerbity gentled by amusement.

Unfortunately, Lowell Detweiler's costumes are on the drab side, and some key performances fail, partly or wholly. Jennifer Harmon's Genia is commonplace, with that manneredly actressy, rasping voice and no emotional depth; James Phipps is a callow, silly Otto; Davis Hall, though not exactly bad, is too puny, unprepossessing, unmoving as Dr. Mauer; Mary Layne, as Erna, has good moments, but exaggerates the girl's hoydenishness and affectations; as Adele, Carol Fox Prescott is ratty and inept. Still, do not let any of this deter you from a unique and ineradicable experience.

One final pleasure of *Undiscovered Country* is that, though emblazoned with revelations, it also maintains a little twilight of mystery and ambiguity—allows room for the indefinable where your imagination must grope its way toward hypothesis. Across the aisle from me, the night I was there, sat that master of shallow overexplicitness, Arthur Miller. My companion wondered, "Do you think he'll go home and break his quill?"

Lolita

Vladimir Nabokov's *Lolita* was not so much adapted as debased to the stage by Edward Albee. How do I reprehend it? Let me count the ways. I don't happen to think that the novel is a total masterpiece or Nabokov an unqualified genius. But he was a man and writer of immense culture, erudition, complexity, refinement, and endless (though one often wished for an end) verbal invention. Albee, on the other hand, is a playwright who twice, long ago, was touched by inspiration and produced a brace of clever, effective, sometimes even moving plays, and then staggered from bad to worse, ruining along the way even other people's novels and plays by adapting them. (One definition of a hack is a fellow who thinks a major novel can be worthily adapted for the stage—who does not know that form is content.)

The Albee who has depraved Nabokov's novel is an ignoramus, a vulgarian, a hack who falls back on hoary stage devices that he cannot even handle with consistency and assurance. Thus the writer-narrator (Albee, surely, not Nabokov!) whom he puts continuously and obtrusively on stage can talk to Humbert and Quilty but not to the other characters he created; his control over the action comes and goes with no inner logic. The feeble excuse that characters can get away from their author is not really developed with any intelligence and conviction; everything here is mindless, arbitrary, and tastes of device like a public swimming pool of chlorine.

The rich, textured prose of Nabokov, the many-layered irony, the social criticism, the learnedly literate references that situate Humbert and his guilty passion in an old, exquisite, perhaps doomed culture, the wit (sometimes labored, but never coarse), the urbanity—all this is marred, polluted, gone. Here is a skeleton plot decked out with Nabokovian tatters swathed in burlap updating; a plethora of obscenities, cheap sexual innuendos, pitifully unfunny byplay between the narrator and Humbert. Everything is spelled out in block capitals and repeated; Albee's words mingle with the remnants of Nabokov's like garishly bedizened gatecrashers invading a royal ball.

And there is something else. Lionel Trilling describes a passage in Nabokov's novel as "one of the few examples of rapture in modern writing." Though Lolita is only twelve or thirteen, she is in many ways grown-up; it is Humbert who, in various respects, is the child. The relation is bizarre, but it is—on his side, anyway—passionate and heterosexual. The play version is not only not heterosexual, it exudes low homosexual camp. Charlotte Haze is turned into a huge, unsightly grotesque; other women are pushy, silly, laughable, obnoxious. Humbert's passion for Lolita is not only trivialized by Albee's dreadful dialogue, especially in the love scenes, but also overshadowed by the curious relationship between Humbert and the narrator. The way they banter and cavort with, tease and wink at, each other—the anthropomorphized author always voyeuristically present and practically sharing Lolita with Humbert—suggests at least a latent homosexual relationship, if not two male lovers camping it up together. Repeated references to pedophilia (a word that Nabokov, as far as I recall, eschews) reinforce the change in atmosphere. Now, I have nothing against homosexual drama; but I do not approve of sneaking a cuckoo's egg into a nest of a different feather.

Under the circumstances, you cannot expect much from the acting. Donald Sutherland, who has just done restrained and humane work in *Ordinary People*, here reverts to his wonted blatancies: externalized emotions, overripe surfaces cradling an inner vacuum like a penniless dipsomaniac nursing his last drink, unnatural gestures with cupped hands and self-consciously discordant fingers, no Old World comportment, and speech that uneasily combines fruitiness and crispness—a papaya trying to make like zwieback. Blanche Baker, 24, is eminently competent as a Lolita of, say, sixteen but not twelve, and lacks the mystery that, I assume, is the very ichor of a nymphet.

Ian Richardson makes the narrator unpleasantly fey and patronizing, and Shirley Stoler tops her physical overabundance with a skimpy talent. Clive Revill revels indecently in Quilty; but that is pretty much what the text demands and perhaps what Frank Dunlop, the director, wanted. William Ritman's décor matches Albee's imaginative bankruptcy every inch of the way, and is the ugliest scenery to hit Broadway since *Onward, Victoria*, another Ritman effort. It is mostly a pack of movable panels that change color and configuration, but remain obstinately prosaic. Neither Nancy Potts's costumes nor David F. Segal's lighting adds any Nabokovian style. If Nabokov were alive today, this *Lolita* would surely finish him off, except that he doubtless wouldn't go near it—an example I would advise you to follow.

Woman of the Year

It is not entirely clear what the source of *Woman of the Year*, the musical starring Lauren Bacall, is. Is it the 1942 Tracy-Hepburn movie, on which Peter Stone has based his book, or is it headlines, gossip columns, and cocktail-party chatter about such things as the Russian dancer Aleksandr Godunov's recent defection? For there is something consistently second-best about almost every aspect of the show, and a pervasive feeling that what ought to be the blueness of a diamond has been yellowed over by emulation, doggedness, slickness—everything short of true inspiration.

The book is a Stone throw from the old plot (itself no marvel), but not necessarily in the right direction. The sportswriter hero has become a cartoonist, the political-columnist heroine has turned into a high-powered television anchorwoman and interviewer, which in itself may indicate some shrinkage. The device by which the two are brought together—Tess Harding's televised attack on "the funnies," as our heroine calls them, and our hero, Sam Craig's, putting her into his cartoon about Katz, the cynical New York cat, as Tessycat, the calculating feline temptress—is not particularly felicitous, but the book's main difficulty lies not there. The trouble is that this is yet another extended excursion into the alleged humor of name-dropping—mentioning name-brand products and people in arch contexts, or any context at all—that Woody Allen's recent movies have pretty much run into the ground.

Thus we have Tess talking on the phone to a telephoney parade of assorted celebrities, e.g.: "Do you think the opening of the Knesset was the right moment for playing *Scheherazade*? *(Pause)* Zei gezund, Zubin! *(Hangs up)*." We are here dropping such name products as *Scheherazade*, Zubin Mehta, and the Israeli parliament; the Jewish context is supposed to provide humorous discrepancy: an Indian-Arabian faux pas in Israel, and then the Yiddish greeting that picks up an earlier quasi-joke about everyone in New York, even the Puerto Ricans, sounding Jewish. None of this is intrinsically apt—the least of Mehta's problems being his programming—but the mere allusions to such things as Knesset and Zubin are meant to make you feel like an insider and dissolve in knowing laughter. Yet here at least the honorable comic strategy of discrepancy is used, however desultorily.

But when we get a running gag in which Tess's co-anchorman repeatedly promises his audience appearances by X, Y, and Marvin Hamlisch, there is at work only recognition, repetition, and the suggestion that Hamlisch may be less talented than pushy. The fact that the last reference to Hamlisch adds the ironic epithet "multitalented" does not significantly heighten the wit. Compare the brilliant comic changes that Christopher Durang rings on *Equus* in his *Beyond Therapy*. And now take the comic nadir—yet another telephonic snippet, from Tess to Björn Borg: "I told you there was more to life than top spin." This is the kind of humor where, for Borg, you can substitute the name of any celebrity and then add, on the dotted line where it now says "top spin," whatever is the suitable *terminus technicus*.

Better than the book is John Kander's music, which, though also somewhat formulaic, manages, with the help of Michael Sporn's able orchestrations, to sound at least pleasingly warmed-up, if not freshly cooked. And there are four or five songs that definitely bear rehearsing. Fred Ebb's lyrics have a distinctly tidal quality: in the first hour of the show, they are decidedly low, but become progressively higher thereafter. There is a serious drawback to Tony Charmoli's choreography, which looks like not quite successful evocations of movie musicals imperfectly caught on television; we seem to be watching "Singing in the Drizzle," "Flying Down to Cuzco," and "Babes in Goyland." The worthy Tony Walton has provided his second-best décor, the esteemed Theoni V. Aldredge her second-best costumes—except those for Miss Bacall, which are smashing. Marilyn Renagel's lighting isn't even second-best; with Robert Moore's comic staging, though it is his very best, we are back to second-best again.

Lauren Bacall is, as always, suave, sparkling, cool, and ironic—a very rich cat (not necessarily Tessycat) that has swallowed an inexhaustible array of canaries. This persona, or stance, goes a long way, but it isn't quite enough for the marathon that is a musical lead. When the glitter has to become a warm glow, when the dancing has to go beyond agile stylishness, when the performer has to give generously rather than just exude urbanity, Miss Bacall fails us. When the lid should be off, the curled lip is on; we get a delectable Lauren Bacall, not an unforgettable Tess Harding. Harry Guardino is an extremely accomplished and appealing Sam Craig, and there is first-rate supporting work from Roderick Cook, Eivind Harum, and a few others. There is brightness, shrewdness, and measured invention throughout *Woman of the Year*; what is missing is that spark that would make it all catch life.

Translations; March of the Falsettos

Translations, by Brian Friel, is a transitional play. It takes place in Ireland in 1833, when the discriminatory laws against Catholics have been repealed, and hedge schools—young people learning not only the three R's but also Greek and Latin in clandestine classrooms—are no longer needed. But another calamity, the potato blight, is only a dozen years away. Master Hugh's hedge school in Baile Beag, the scene of the action, teaches peasant youths and maidens such esoterica as the Greek and Latin authors, but the basic language is Irish; English is studiously ignored. Along comes an English regiment in charge of producing a reliable map of Ireland, and with it is Lieutenant Yolland, a decent, easygoing chap who is put in charge of transliterating Irish place names into something Englishmen can read and pronounce.

As the very title of the play indicates, the subject is language—or, rather, languages: the cleavage between people caused by unshared speech and the problems caused or exacerbated by their mutual incomprehension. Translation itself is a sort of transition: the bridge between sequestration and communion. But it is a bridge where structural weaknesses cause disturbances, from traffic bottlenecks to total collapse of the bridge, from comic mishaps to tragic misunderstandings. It is a fascinating subject, and Friel plays imaginatively with more forms of translation and mistranslation than you can shake a shillelagh at—even such translations as a foolish dreamer's translating himself, with the help of that great interpreter, poteen, into the age of Hellenic myth, and fancying himself Pallas Athene's bridegroom.

The major dramatic thread concerns Yolland's love for Maire, a local girl, claimed by Manus, Hugh's impoverished son and assistant teacher. The embittered girl, all set to emigrate to America, in turn falls for the lieutenant, who, with the help of Owen, Hugh's other son, who has made good in Dublin, is working away on standardizing the nomenclature while yearning to learn the Irish language and settle down with Maire here in Baile Beag, which has already become Ballybeg. Maire, conversely, wishes she had been taught English, to make the union easier. But, as one of these barefoot Latinists might have said, *dis aliter visum*—it was not meant to be. The second act of *Translations*, whose haunting highlight is the scene in which Yolland and Maire make verbal love with the only words they have, and cherish, in common—Irish place names—is altogether engrossing. But it, too, is only a transition between the humdrum exposition of Act I and the deliberately low-key non-resolution of Act III. A splendid middle, then, flanked by unsatisfying extremities, the last scene even unpleasantly reminiscent of an O'Casey ending: little people drunkenly or self-absorbedly unaware of the tragedy in their midst.

There are fine ironies scattered throughout the play, and the concentric translation metaphors expand with powerfully poetic impact. If only people learned a common language instead of wallowing in parochialism, or studying luxuriously useless dead languages (like the Irish peasantry), or not even studying them (like the English conquerors). For even a shared dead language could palliate the need for translation. Add to this the magisterial drama- turgic device of having Irish represented by English spoken with a brogue, while English is represented by brogueless English. Thus two people can talk at each other in essentially the same language (humanity) and not understand, while the audience is privileged to grasp both sides of this noncommunicating and realize how rec- oncilable the differences might be but for the linguistic wall. Still, the play feels far too much like a fragment from a novel, with too much missing at both ends to yield a fulfilling entity.

The Abbey Theatre's Joe Dowling has guest-directed competently a cast that, despite some linguistic problems of its own, is generally good. There is first-rate work from Daniel Gerroll as Yolland, and spirited acting from Ellen Parker as Maire, though the fact that both her fellow students (Valerie Mahaffey and Lauren Thompson) so far outshine her in looks rather militates against the verisimilitude of Yolland's falling in love with *her* on first sight. The excellent Bar- nard Hughes does what he can with Hugh, a fairly standard slinger of fanciful blarney, and there is particularly interesting work from Stephen Burleigh and Jarlath Conroy as his sons. Only Jake Dengel, as the beautiful dreamer, gives a nightmare of a performance.*

March of the Falsettos is an attractive mini-musical that augurs well for its sole author, William Finn. It is the second musical tale of Marvin (I missed *In Trousers*, the first), a young father who would like to keep the loving friendship of his sympathetic ex-wife, Trina, and the total love of his son, Jason, while living in homosexual bliss with his spiffy lover, Whizzer. Meanwhile, Trina has gone to Men- del, Marvin's psychiatrist, and been promptly promoted from pa- tient to mistress. The 70-minute musical without spoken dialogue concerns the interaction of this voluble quintet, and Finn, with the help of the extremely clever staging of James Lapine, puts them through some swiftly shifting combinations and permutations.

And there is the trouble. These are less people than they are a rapidly shuffled deck of cards; no character has a chance of evolving

---

*P.S. 2005: What a difference a production can make! Some years later, I saw Sam Mendes's mounting of *Translations* at the Donmar Warehouse in London and was swept away. This is a very great play indeed, and my cavils fell away like autumn leaves. A still later Broad- way production, directed by Howard Davies, was, however, a total disaster.

beyond a well-observed but minimal identity. The music is heavily derivative from Stephen Sondheim, but it is intelligent, well-crafted music, at times capable of transcending its mold. Finn is particularly good with reprises, letting them spring up naturally and assume piquantly new significance. His lyrics are uneven, but never contemptible, and there is a commendable integrity to the whole enterprise despite a certain lack of integration. Thus two of the best numbers, the introductory "Four Jews Bitching in a Room" and the title song, do not fit easily and logically into the proceedings.

The cast is able, especially the Whizzer of Stephen Bogardus and the Mendel of Chip Zien; only Michael Rupert's Marvin could be more appealing. The Spartan production values are put to shrewd maximum use, and the small band under Michael Starobin performs stylishly. *March of the Falsettos* should be seen in part for what it is, and in much larger part for what it promises.

A Taste of Honey

Consider the revival of Shelagh Delaney's A *Taste of Honey*, performed at Roundabout II, compared to which your average hole in the wall is the theater of Epidaurus. It is a play whose first version was written by a seventeen-year-old girl; produced in 1958, it is as alive and moving and real today as it will be forever. It concerns Helen, a semi-floozy mother, who goes off to marry her latest beau, a much younger, shiftless operator, while Jo, her teen-age daughter, stays at home (when she doesn't work in a bar) to give birth to a child by a black sailor who has abandoned her. She is attended in her pregnancy by a touching outcast, Geof, a sweetly motherly homosexual art student. A real tearjerker? Not at all!

It is a gutsy play, full of rowdy impertinence and genuinely comic indignation. Its characters, even the weakest, have enough spine for a brontosaurus, which doesn't stop them from getting temporarily discouraged and bitter. But their sense of humor prevails, and their loving quarrels with life and one another are full of wry, understated heroism. Helen's ghastly hats are worn as bravely into the fray of scrambling ahead as Achilles's helmet was to the Trojan battlements. Jo's rough-hewn, slightly dented innocence shines with tomboyish dauntlessness: this kid is fierce and funny, rolling her vulnerability into a ball and bouncing it off anything and anyone.

Even Helen's worthless Peter is as absurd as he is mean and menacing, and can be cut down with a sharp laugh. Geof is too intelligent to become maudlin, but his cleverness is only a jump ahead of his loneliness; still, that jump makes all the difference. Only the black sailor is a somewhat shadowy figure, but even he has a simplicity that is not simplistic or a piece of authorial patronization.

And how good the writing is! "I don't care for the cinema any more," grumbles Helen; "it is getting more and more like the theater." Such an unassuming line, yet it contains a critique of film, theater, Helen herself, and a funny joke at the playwright's own expense. "Oh well," says Geof, his marriage proposal rejected by Jo, "you need somebody to love you while you're looking for someone to love." Note how heartbreaking that statement is, yet with what casual gallantry it is tossed off. And note how, by using the longer, heavier "somebody" to describe himself, and the lighter, more discardable "someone" to designate the future successful lover, Geof betrays his unconscious attempt to salvage some dignity and importance for his generous but thankless role. And when Jo, uncharacteristically anguished, exclaims, "And me, I'm contemporary. I really am, aren't I? I really do live at the same time as myself, don't I?" this moving *cri de coeur* is sheer poetry. There is the growing urgency of the progression from "me" to "I" to "myself"; there is the shortness of the sentences, made more jagged by the questions appended to their ends; and there is the powerful image of split personality expressed in the plainest and starkest words.

Add to this a flawlessly directed production (by Tony Tanner), good design (especially A. Christina Giannini's costumes), and all-round fine acting. Particularly right are Amanda Plummer's unsentimental Jo, Keith Reddin's self-effacing yet also assertive Geof, and Valerie French's Helen, always somewhat out of it, which is exactly in keeping. *A Taste of Honey* is everything *Light Bulb* is not: honest rather than stagy, forthright rather than would-be-symbolic—in short, pungently, poignantly, unself-consciously human.

The Little Foxes

The Little Foxes is Lillian Hellman's best play, alas. It is a sobering realization that work of this caliber can earn you a major reputation in the American theater. Writing about a revival of *The Children's*

Hour, Eric Bentley aptly noted: "There is an absence of genuine passion not only in the individual characters but in the whole production, and nothing in its place but the hard humorless drive of the authoress's will-power." That applies equally to the current mounting of *The Little Foxes,* a lackluster and tedious enterprise that marks Elizabeth Taylor's premature Broadway debut. At 49, Miss Taylor is not yet ready for the legitimate theater.

But, first, the play. In Volume 8 of *The Revels History of Drama in English,* Walter J. Meserve speaks of it as "making use of the trappings of melodrama." It does not make use of melodrama; it is it. The term, which for me is always pejorative, means essentially static characters, emphasis on a drastic plot at the expense of more artistic elements, and language that remains stubbornly earthbound. True, the daughter, Alexandra, evolves; but since she is such an ancillary, undernourished character, the change seems simply pasted on, not developed. As for the others, they just keep scheming along, with an occasional contrived deviation into nonchalance that vainly attempts to humanize them. Humor, of course, would help; but this is a boon Miss Hellman has very little of, and then usually of the most primitive sort—as when Addie, the black servant, remarks, "You ain't born in the South unless you're a fool." Miss Hellman should know: she was born there.

What makes the play better than other Hellman efforts is that it deals with greed—the fight for money—a subject apparently close to the playwright's heart; at any rate, Hellman writes much more compellingly about it than about, say, politics in *Watch on the Rhine* or sexual deviation in *The Children's Hour.* But since the theme is monolithic, with virtually no relief from subplots, orchestration becomes the primary requirement, and this is where Austin Pendleton, the director, fails miserably. Instead of finding a proper rhythm and dynamic variety for the play, he dumps us almost immediately in a hubbub of Hubbards, and can go only from crescendos to chaos, forfeiting what might have been a musical structure. Even the scene wherein Oscar Hubbard worms the truth about the safe-deposit box out of his son, Leo, is paced and blocked so ludicrously as to suggest a routine from a minstrel show.

Pendleton has also cast every character perversely against the dramatist's specifications. Thus Birdie has "a pretty, well-bred, faded face," but that is exactly what Maureen Stapleton hasn't (any more than a Southern accent), except perhaps the "faded," though even that is subverted by fleshiness. Horace is a tall, formerly good-looking man, whereas Tom Aldredge, besides being an iffy actor, has neither stature nor looks. Alexandra must be, as stipulated, pretty and delicate—these are actually plot elements—but Ann Talman is bovine of face and figure, besides not being able to act. Her only qualification is that she studies with Mr. Pendleton, who provides for his own. As for Miss Taylor, she looks not like "a handsome woman of 40," but like an overstuffed 50 with absolutely no class.

The only dignified presence and performance comes from Novella Nelson as Addie; except for Anthony Zerbe (Ben), no one in the cast can even sound Southern. Sadly schematic monotones issue from Dennis Christopher (remember Dan Duryea's Leo?) and Joe Ponazecki, good on other occasions. And then there is Liz. Though she sometimes forces it into a lower register, her voice generally continues to be squeaky and infantile, her movements lack grace and even maturity, and her entire performance, in contradistinction to her appearance, lacks weight. Watching her on the stage, I became more aware than ever of the magic wrought by the motion-picture camera. Andrew Jackness's set is conventional, Florence Klotz's costumes would look better on hangers, and Paul Gallo's good lighting merely illuminates a place as depressing as an elephant graveyard.

Cloud 9

Cloud 9 is a cheeky view of British sexuality during the last century. In Act I, we are in the colonial Africa of 1880, where some proper Victorians are having a hard time keeping the natives down, their moral pretenses up, and a stiff upper lip in place. Adultery, homosexuality, and lesbianism pullulate in Clive's—the good British hero's—family and entourage, and there is even bustling activity under the neighboring landowner's, Mrs. Saunders's, bustle, as Clive knows full well. He is there; he is the activity. This must be the first theatrical sex scene in which the man remains completely hidden inside the woman's skirt throughout.

Betty, Clive's wife, is played by a man; Edward, his incipiently homosexual son, by a woman; Victoria, his daughter, by a much-tossed-about doll. Clive's best friend, the intrepid explorer Harry Bagley, is carrying on with Betty; also with Joshua, the black house servant; and ditto with Edward. Victoria's nanny is in love with Betty, and is promptly married off to Harry, for the sake of appearances. And more, much more: everyone pretends, and suffers for it gallantly.

In Act II, we're in London in 1980, though for the family it is only 25 years later. (Don't ask me how that is possible; maybe they were all born on February 29.) Edward, now played by a man, has become a homosexual gardener maltreated by his youthfully ruthless hustler lover, Gerry. As Edward fondles his unhappily married sister's breast, he and Victoria both enjoy it, and Edward concludes that he must be a lesbian. Victoria leaves her well-meaning but smug and hopelessly heterosexual husband, Martin, and moves in with a young lesbian mother, Lin; they are joined by Edward in a ménage à trois. Betty, now played by a woman, has left Clive, masturbates profusely, is becoming liberated, and tries to pick up Edward's faithless, feckless Gerry. Lin's little daughter, Cathy, played by a man, is a monster of aggression who keeps shooting off her toy gun. It seems unlikely, though, that she will reconquer Africa for the Crown.

Cloud 9 may sound preposterous, sophomoric, and dull. Actually, it is absurdist, sophisticated, a bit too long, but not really boring. At first only spottily funny, it becomes a bundle of merry mischief, and, toward the end, fleetingly but genuinely touching. Betty's soliloquy in praise of onanism, magnificently delivered by E. Katherine Kerr, actually wrests lyricism from an unlikely subject; even Gerry, the male hustler, has his amiable side—conveyed, however, without any sentimentality.

The play is the work of Caryl Churchill, an Englishwoman who has been active in fringe theater and BBC radio and TV, but who was not previously represented over here. Though the subject is not particularly original—the Victorians, who wouldn't let it all hang out; the moderns, who won't zip it up for a minute—Churchill treats it with a flair: a mixture of brattish ingenuousness and malicious charm. How else describe Clive's declaration of love to Mrs. Saunders: "Caroline, if you were shot with poisoned arrows, you know what I'd do? I'd fuck your dead body and poison myself." Somewhat less purply, Harry, back from an expedition, tells Betty: "You've been thought of where no white woman has ever been thought of before." And Betty's mater declares: "Young women are never happy. Then, when they are older, they realize they were ecstatic."

Particularly well handled are the transitions from the anodyne to the outrageous, and the prickly area between the two. Says Betty, the Victorian wife, "I don't think mother is on a visit. I think she lives with us." That is still genteel humor. But soon Mother, obtruding on Betty's outdoor tryst with Harry, is told: "Why don't you go back to the house, Mother, and rest your insect bite." That's beginning to be rude. When Clive, who has been pawing Harry in best buddy-buddy fashion, discovers Harry's bisexuality, he exclaims in horror: "You've been away from England too long!" Wonderfully double-edged, that: Clive is unwittingly absurd; the author, wittingly wicked. And here is Betty, now middle-aged, confronting her daughter's self-proclaimed lesbianism: "I think I have known for some time. But I don't usually think about it, so I don't know whether I know or not." That is beautiful British befuddlement, and you watch it disappear at play's end with a twinge of regret.

If there is anything wrong here, it is the strong suggestion that straights have the worst time of it, are the biggest fools. Must larky homosexual propaganda necessarily turn into anti-heterosexual dialectics? And there is something a mite schematic, geometrical—as well as overlong—about the naughtinesses portrayed. Otherwise, though, there is poignant characterization mixed in with the absurdist slapstick, and one is allowed to feel a little as well as laugh quite a lot, which is nice. The acting is good enough: everyone gets to play at least two characters, and plays at least one of them very well. Only Concetta Tomei has difficulties with both her absurdism and her Britishness, and Don Amendolia is a bit too gross for little Cathy, though right as the jokily ominous Joshua. Jeffrey Jones is an endearingly fatuous Clive, Nicolas Surovy a hilariously bifurcate Harry, Željko Ivanek a good young Betty and better Gerry, Veronica Castang a tangy Lin, and E. Katherine Kerr both a ripping Mrs. Saunders and a splendidly riven older Betty.

The transformations, though sometimes arbitrary, contribute to the fun, and the flashbacks from Act II to Act I add a quaintly wistful dimension: the past is not exactly recaptured, but keeps playing tag with the present. Tommy Tune has directed with the same precision and brio he brought to his dancing and choreography, and is developing into a fine farce director. All visual aspects are handled with engaging modesty and appositeness, and Lawrence Miller's scenery achieves a good deal with fetchingly unassuming means. *Cloud 9* may be small potatoes, but they are whipped up into a toothsomely fluffy purée.

American Buffalo

By now you must know that David Mamet's *American Buffalo* concerns Donny, a middle-aged junk-shop owner; Bobby, a slow-witted youth with whom he has a faintly paternal and perhaps incipiently or latently homosexual relationship; and Teach, a probably psychopathic petty criminal. The three are variously involved in the projected stealing of a coin collection belonging to a man who bought an Indian-head (buffalo on the obverse) nickel from Donny. The robbery never gets off the ground: another accomplice fails to show up, the men fight among themselves, Bobby is fairly seriously injured by Teach, and the other two, instead of heading for lucrative loot, merely transport Bobby to the hospital.

When the play was done on Broadway, reviewers vied with one another in unearthing profound significance in it. The American buffalo, naturally, became a symbol of diverse things; fly-by-night crooks talking of themselves as businessmen turned the play into an allegory of American capitalism; Mamet's games with language opened up vistas on semantics, semiotics, and sociolinguistics. Not that Mamet did not intend to portend heavily; but what he contrived seems to me no more than a stew of upside-down Saroyan, thirties gangster movies, Pinter, and a dash or two of Beckett. And, of course, a large dose of scatology and obscenity to lend contemporary relevance.

Occasionally the characters are funny, but it is the funniness of stupidity trying to outsmart even greater stupidity, which I place fairly low on the scale of humor. And, I suspect, Mamet cheats, by allowing Donny and, especially, Teach bits of rather too fancy lingo, which he then undercuts by making them use it inappropriately or incorrectly. What cleverness there is in this tends to get swallowed up by straining toward allusiveness, suggestiveness, import—but import that remains unrealized because the characters are too dim, too puny, too repulsive.

Nevertheless, *American Buffalo* is a field day for actors, and, under Arvin Brown's shrewd and assiduous direction, the performers lay about them with a fervor that shades by pawkily calculated stages into ferocity. Thomas Waites is a splendidly befogged Bobby, who can make stubbornness and stupidity almost appealing, but precisely without quite letting them drift into likableness. His is merely a meanness. Still in its infancy, cute in the manner of baby wolverines. Clifton James is perfect as Donny, a fellow whose very moments of friendliness have a soiled, greasy, untouchable quality, and whose layers of viscous cunning are piled on a solid base of obtuseness.

But the star turn is the role of Teach, and Al Pacino lets loose with an almost blinding array of histrionics. The main strategy is letting the eyes go dead while, around them, the face, the limbs, the body, the voice twitch away in a barely contained (but still, precariously, controlled) St. Vitus's dance. Yet, on closer inspection, the eyes aren't exactly dead either: they are humorless, undeterrable leeches that fasten onto their object of scrutiny and suck it dry. There is madness and menace about this Teach, but also a certain charm: an endless choreography of tics, kinks, mannerisms (could someone, please, count the crotch pattings for me?)—epic idiosyncrasies that make the monster ludicrous, and thus seemingly pettable. Finally, though, the panoply of physical and vocal devices (the latter including moments of complete etiolation of the voice) becomes burdensome—indeed exhausting, when one recalls the countless other times Pacino has trotted it out. There is, however, undeniable ensemble work here, with shabbiness, shadiness, shiftiness tossed like so many balls from player to player. Marjorie Kellogg's set, Bill Walker's costumes, Ronald Wallace's lighting make cogent contributions, and one is not bored. Even so, regardless of how many buffaloes can dance on an Indian's head, don't take a wooden nickel for art.

The Tempest

The Tempest is very possibly Shakespeare's most poetic play, but what Lee Breuer and his wife, Ruth Maleczech, have inflicted on it in Central Park under Joe Papp's aegis should not have been done to *Titus Andronicus*, his crudest. Breuer and Maleczech are leading lights of Mabou Mines, an avant-garde outfit that specializes in elaborately gimmicky but basically hollow theater pieces of the multimedia type, though it has on occasion done well by Beckett. But there is a certain critical awe before avant-garde offerings, so that Mabou Mines can get roughly the same good reviews for an intermittently clever piece of antinuclear propaganda such as *Dead End Kids* and for a humorless parody of private-eye thrillers such as *Wrong Guys*, with its tacked-on attack on capitalism to make the counterculture happy.

What Mabou Mines does with its own silly concoctions, such as Lee Breuer's abominable *Sister Suzy Cinema*, is its own affair, but when these people are turned loose on Shakespeare's sublime lyrical-philosophical masterpiece, they do it unconscionable, unforgivable harm. All kinds of cheap sight gags, stupidly irrelevant anachronisms, vulgar electronic devices have been hurled into the play, and it hurts me even to have to enumerate them. To begin with, Breuer and Maleczech have dropped an atom bomb on Shakespeare's language.

Thus Raul Julia does Prospero with his usual inappropriate and comic-sounding Hispanic accent (to say nothing of the dumb facial expressions accompanying it), while Jessica Nelson, as Miranda, speaks in a colorless, badly enunciated mid-American, where "sea storm," for example, becomes "cistorm." Members of the courts of Naples and Milan speak in exaggerated Spanish, Southern-white, Southern-black, and flat American accents. Caliban speaks cockney, Trinculo (here a woman—the absurd Lola Pashalinsky from the Ridiculous Theatrical Company) is done as Mae West, Stephano mouthed as W. C. Fields, and the numerous small children in the cast emit a barely comprehensible baby talk. And David Marshall Grant, as Ferdinand, sounds like a robot dispensing only vaguely humanoid tones, whose inventor should be sent either back to the drawing board or to Siberia. No one speaks Shakespearean verse.

You will have gathered that the play has been updated. On an empty stage (there was, originally, a set by the excellent David Mitchell, but it either died of shame or was removed by the directors as too good for the rest of the production), we see, to begin with, Prospero performing some sort of voodoo ritual.

He is wearing one of Carol Oditz's preposterous costumes—part timeless white shepherd's garb, part contemporary beach outfit, the whole thing topped by a woman's skull-hugging purple angora cap. Two tiny tots (they are Ariels, this production having twelve Ariels of all ages and colors—black, brown, white, and one beefy Japanese wrestler—speaking alternately or in unison, or together with their own or other voices on the P.A. system) come on with a toy phonograph that plays "Whistle While You Work." Later, there will be Balinese gamelan music, and then Brazilian music by the Samba Ensemble.

Prospero plays with a toy helicopter while a real helicopter

circles above. He throws the toy down a trapdoor while the P.A.
system blares hideously, a few garbled bits of the shipwreck scene
decipherable amid the cacophony. Then some men in white pilot
uniforms run pell-mell across the stage, and that is Act 1, Scene 1. I
could go on listing, bit by painful bit, every insult, rape, imbecility
perpetrated on the defenseless play. But what's the point?

Should I tell you about the ridiculous uses to which the turntable
is put throughout? About the mock hara-kiri performed by various
cast members? About the arrows with which Cupid-Ariels shoot
Ferdinand front and back? (Why not Sebastian, while they're at
it?) Or the cigarette that Barry Miller, the Caliban in torn fatigues,
smokes while saying "by Sycorax, my mother" in such a way that it
sounds like "buy cigarettes, my mother"? Or the demitasses proffered by disembodied hands to Sebastian and Antonio (Bill Raymond and Steven Keats, and both terrible) to sip from while they
plan mayhem? Or about Ferdinand playing with one light bamboo
rod when supposedly lugging heavy logs? A bamboo that promptly
turns phallic? Or about other cheap sexual jokes Breuer and Maleczech insert, as when Caliban is made to say leeringly, "I'll show thee
every fertile inch" as if he were about to drop his pants, then wait
for several beats, and add "of the island"? But why go on?

This production is nauseating in every respect, from beginning
to the midway intermission, during which, holding my stomach, I
left. The pathetic thing is that, although quite a few people departed
early on, many more stayed, a lot of them laughing, clapping, enjoying themselves. (Others, to be sure, sat in glum silence.) Now, I have
no objection to people having any kind of good time, except when
the joke is at Shakespeare's expense—when people are being given
stones and told they are bread. The fact that a good many devour
these stones either in the name of culture or because they cannot tell
the difference between stones and bread does not exculpate anyone.
Least of all Joseph Papp, who invited these tasteless shenanigans in
the first place and allowed them to go on in the second.

Do Breuer and Maleczech have any zany new ideas? The sad
truth is that they are foisting onto Shakespeare not even fresh tricks
but the same old ones that they have been using on their Mabou
Mines theater pieces. Like so many other avant-gardists of today,
they have a small stock of theatrical trumpery with which they imprint or bedizen whatever they touch. Shame on everyone, including the actors! Were I one of them, I would rather drive a cab, wait
on tables, be out of work even, than lend a hand to this debasement

of beauty. *The Tempest* will survive, but can participants in such a sinister farce preserve a clear conscience?

My Fair Lady

What can a critic give to a show that has everything? And that has had its praises sung, deservedly, backward and forward? *My Fair Lady* continues—despite the current revival—to be one of the rare perfect musicals; if it has a blemish, it is the one noted by Ken Tynan long ago: Henry Higgins, that incomparable linguist, should not be made to utter the illiterate "she should be hung" and "I'd be equally as willing… than to…" where the "as" is clumsily superfluous and the "than" barbarous. If Alan Jay Lerner really cared about "the cold-blooded murder of the English tongue," he would long since have fixed those lyrics; by way of encouragement, let me remind him that Brecht and Coward were not above reworking their famous lyrics years later.

Anyway, *My Fair Lady* is still a rewarding show, weighted down though it is now by heavy burdens. First, there is the Eliza of Nancy Ringham, who at the penultimate minute replaced Cheryl Kennedy, whose vocal cords have, apparently, become frayed. This is one of those even rarer cases where the understudy goes on on opening night and proves a perfect dud. Though Miss Ringham, a Minnesotan who has studied and worked in England, is statuesque, touchingly eager, and possessed of vocal cords in mint condition, she cannot phrase in musicianly fashion, time her lines, express feeling, walk, stand, do Cockney or upper-class English—or anything else—with assurance, presence, or an ounce of charm. Indeed, she cannot even make us take note of her entrance in a Cecil Beaton gown at the top of a staircase—which, to me, spells gilt-edged failure. Ezra Pound, in a letter, spoke of another Doolittle, Hilda, as having the prairie winds in her underwear; Miss Ringham cannot even lay claim to that—only to the Minnesota dairy farms and cornfields in her entire performance.

Then there is—or was—Rex Harrison. His Higgins, at 73, has to be approached with an archaeologist's spade. One can still see the remnants of a once great performance under the literal and figurative flab, but one is, as it were, obliged to dig out that proverbial thin man said to be lurking inside every fat one. The face now often

droops into expressionlessness, the voice (despite the gross amplification at the Uris Theater) cackles unduly or peters out, the movements are often unsteady. Bernard Levin, the English critic, once
asked me how he would make out in Los Angeles without knowing
how to drive: could he ride the freeways on a bicycle? He was pretty
good on the straightaway, he said, but had some trouble with the
turns. Conversely, Harrison still manages turns rather deftly, but on
the straightaway he is apt to falter or buckle, and even just standing, he sometimes lists peculiarly. I am sorry to have to report this,
but stage traffic is almost as demanding and dangerous as the L.A.
freeways, and tough on vintage bicycles.

Even sadder, alas, is the presence of the formerly wonderful
Cathleen Nesbitt, now 93, as Mrs. Higgins. One now has to wait
for her every line and fear for her every move; the best I could do
was to tune out and remember that she was once the beloved of
Rupert Brooke. As Freddy, Nicholas Wyman bellows unmusically
and overdoes the callowness; Jack Gwillim is a handsome Picker-
ing, but not a moving one; Milo O'Shea is a nimble and spirited
Doolittle, but his Cockney gives way to a brogue, and he too often substitutes pixieish cuteness for comic dignity. I liked Marian
Baer's understated Mrs. Pearce, but found the singing and dancing
ensembles a bit raggle-taggle and, at Ascot and the embassy ball,
downright infra dig.

I don't know whether it is storage, the passage of time, or cheaper
ingredients, but something has even attacked Beaton's marvelous
costumes, though they are still smashing. Some of Oliver Smith's
décor (though impeded by Ken Billington's lighting) is still fine,
and Hanya Holm's pleasant dances are still pleasant as restaged by
Crandall Diehl. Patrick Garland, who has done yeoman's work in
drama, seems less at ease directing musicals—the movements are
sometimes stilted or rudimentary—but Shaw, Lerner, and Loewe
are still out there in full force and effulgence: splendid individually
and miraculous in concert. It's still a pretty fair *Fair Lady*; too bad
it isn't a great one.

Othello

In some ways, *Othello* is the most unsatisfying of Shakespeare's
tragic masterpieces. The murderous jealousy of the hero does not

seem sufficiently credible; the malice of the villain is too sketch-
ily and self-contradictorily motivated. But such is the poetic heat
generated by an efficacious staging and enactment of the play that
we do not expostulate with it any more than we would with a laser
beam. And even if the production is inadequate in other ways, a fine
Othello, Iago, and Desdemona should suffice to make it work. In
the current American Shakespeare Theater mounting at Stratford,
Connecticut, two thirds of that bottom-line requirement are, by
and large, met; the third third, however, is a catastrophe.

An Othello by James Earl Jones and a Iago by Christopher Plummer is a fascinating conjunction, not only because of the intrinsic
worth of those actors, but also because it brings together top-notch
talent from the United States and British spheres for a kind of theatrical summit meeting. And, truly, both actors give performances
that seldom if ever relax their grips on our attention, even though
both are, finally, miscalculated.

There are, as far as I can see, only three ways of making Othello
believable. He is either laboring under repressed feelings of inferiority, as a Moor among racially intolerant Venetians; or he is, despite other strengths, a man undermined by barbaric superstitions
or tribal notions of women's frailty and untrustworthiness; or he
is, quite simply, stupid. The third choice, clearly, does not make for
high tragedy and is thus scarcely an option. The first is hard to make
consonant with the text, and uncongenial to present-day audiences.
That leaves the second, which Jones seems to have gone for.

He plays a powerful, self-assured, enormously dignified leader
of men, with a voice that could move mountains (and which Jones
here commands with greater sureness than, to my knowledge, ever
before), but who has some primitive traits: faith in the totemic force
of the handkerchief, rubbing index fingers together to convey time's
mockery (even though the text speaks of "his slow, unmoving finger"), sticking his tongue out twice before the exclamation, "Goats
and monkeys!" To convey this better, a few more such hints would
have been useful—a few more warts on the heroic stature. Yet this
is a minor cavil in view of Jones's ability to astonish us with the
underplaying, to greater effect, of lines that are usually thundered
out, with the often tremendous impact of anguished self-control.

In the final scenes of murder, agonized repentance, towering
love, and suicide, however, Jones does not scale the supreme pinnacle of tragedy. Here the actor needs a special reserve of energy,
invention, emotional largesse with which to surpass all previous cli-

maxes, and this Jones fails to summon up. Indeed, there are periods during which he goes almost blank, which may make psychological sense but is dramatically deficient. Still, this is a much finer Moor of Venice than Jones has given us previously, and is the best American Othello I am aware of, Paul Robeson's not excluded.

Yet if Jones, at the last skimps a little, Plummer is overgenerous with his Iago. The play, after all, is not the tragedy of Iago—Iago is not its eponymous protagonist—though Plummer, at times, would have us believe it so. It may be that the one thing that stands between this actor and greatness is his inability to efface himself when that is called for; under the direction of Peter Coe, whom I sense to be too weak to contain Plummer, we get a Iago who even has the last, albeit unspoken, word in the play: quite illicitly, the wounded, prostrate Plummer half raises himself and shakes a triumphant fist at the world, his face gloating with what we are made to feel is his victory in death.

Nor is that all. Plummer—a devastatingly handsome, elegant, beautifully spoken, and agile actor—virtually sings and dances his way through the work, sometimes we feel that we are witnessing the ballet *The Moor's Pavane* or the opera *Otello*. Looking like the Hapsburg hero of *Mayerling*, Plummer dominates people and actions like some diabolic saint. Thus when, on two occasions, he gets slapped by Roderigo—an unconvincing pair of directorial conceits—he endures it with such superhuman self-restraint that we feel he could accomplish anything; in no way could this man, at his age, remain a mere, mean ensign. And when, later on, he suddenly kisses Desdemona smack on the mouth—a directorial and histrionic absurdity—we wonder why she doesn't respond with something warmer than amazement, and why he bothers, even for a second, to look shocked by his own temerity. The performance is too big, too central; this Iago is played not wisely, but too well.

As for the Desdemona of Shannon John, it is rather less effective than if the pinch-hitting stage manager, script in hand, were to walk through the part. Looking like a vapid starlet on the beach at Malibu, cursed with a voice as infantile as a moppet's whose only modes are utter flatness or singsong, Miss John must have been a huge success the last time she acted for Peter Coe, when she portrayed Anne Baxter's autistic daughter, though that seems insufficient reason to repeat the characterization here. Miss John, the program says, has studied acting with Herbert Berghof, and it is more than likely that she is entitled to have her entire tuition refunded.

Unfortunately, the supporting cast is scarcely, if at all, better, except for Aideen O'Kelly's very respectable Emilia. It is hard to conceive of the foolish Roderigo, the straightforward Cassio, the marginal Gratiano, Lodovico, and Montano played with anything worse than a passive badness; here, however, it manages to be active. As for David Sabin's Brabantio—what daughter wouldn't run off with the Fuller Brush man to getaway from him? And just because Bianca is a strumpet, must Geoanne Sosa (a graduate of the *Billy Jack* films) play her less well than would any Times Square prostitute?

When Coe leaves the play essentially alone, the direction can pass muster; once, he even has a very good idea. After the handkerchief scene between Bianca and Cassio, he has Othello and Iago sit down to the left and right of the palace door—alone in space, as it were—and stare obliquely into the distance. Each is in the vise of such cosmic evil or folly that this stylized, depersonalized reading of the lines climaxing in "The pity of it, Iago" best renders the unconscionableness of it. Other Coe inventions, however, prove injudicious if not inept, e.g., Othello's stabbing as well as choking Desdemona (as though she were Rasputin), then castrating Iago before committing hara-kiri himself. The potentially most daring device—having the action freeze for a cinematic stop-shot while someone monologizes—might have worked better if used more consistently instead of being timidly hauled out only twice and thus looking self-conscious and self-defeating.

Robert Fletcher's set, clearly the recycled décor of Stratford's earlier *Henry V*, is unprepossessing and at times even unsuitable; nothing becomes cardboard less than its trying, vainly, to impersonate marble. Fletcher's costumes, though uneven, are much better, sometimes genuinely appealing, though often, in their materials, forced to reveal the tight hand on the purse strings.

There are, nevertheless, a few unforgettable moments in this production: the way Iago, early on, spits a geyser's worth at the mention of Othello; the manner in which Othello, in a transcendent rage, wipes up the floor with Iago. If only this mighty pair did not have to teeter over a hole where Desdemona ought to be!

Nicholas Nickleby

The typical Dickens novel has three layers. There is the plot, which in the early works tends to be a fairy tale. Good people, mostly young, struggle, are set upon by evil wizards and witches, but, partly through their own efforts and partly through the help of good fairies, end up triumphant, while the wicked tormentors get their just deserts. Wilde may have been thinking of Dickens when he made Miss Prism say about her three-volume novel, "The good ended happily, the bad unhappily. That is what fiction means." Over this fairy-tale layer stretches a layer of description: people in their settings, customs, and manners; the look and feel of a place and period. This is what Walter Bagehot appreciated about Dickens: "He describes London like a special correspondent for posterity." The third layer is the social commentary: the author's noble philippics against every iniquity, whether caused by political systems or human nature.

Now, a stage version of *Nicholas Nickleby*, even one that lasts eight and a half hours, as does the one adapted by David Edgar for the Royal Shakespeare Company, can do scant justice to the second and third layers because, except in very small doses, they are fictional devices—they don't "play." That leaves the fairy-tale plot, which the stage, with some abridgement, can render beautifully. And since Dickens's imagination was matchless, an uncommon wealth of characters pours, hurtles, slithers, skulks, and trips across the stage in a veritable Dance of Life. They speak with succulently individual voices, have oversimplified but attention-grabbing and memory-hugging traits, and are interwoven throughout the work in deliciously dizzying patterns.

The foreshortening of the stage version may even help in some cases. The amiable fools, adorable do-gooders, and pathetic victims tend to prattle on boringly in Dickens; in the novel *Nickleby*, we get the endless blather of Mrs. Nickleby, the long arias or duets for one or two Cheerybles, and the heart-rending utterances of Smike, all of them drastically and salutarily shortened onstage. But all the good points earned for decimating, say, Mrs. Nickleby are lost by the dramatization of Smike.

In the novel, Smike is a somewhat mentally deficient youth with a limp, but otherwise lean and tall, very good at household and garden tasks, and speaking plainly and coherently. In the play, he

becomes a ghastly victim of something like cerebral palsy—disfigured, brain-damaged, deformed in body and limbs—a junior-ver-
sion Elephant Man. Moreover, his pathetic condition is milked in
every way: scenes or acts repeatedly end with Smike dragging himself off, or being dragged or carried off by others; indeed, the entire
play concludes with Smike's phantasm (no such thing in Dickens)
coming out of the grave to sing a mournful ditty and be held up
once again by Nicholas amid the universal jubilation, apparently to
make all of us feel guilty of the existence of cerebral palsy—or TB,
of which Smike actually dies.

This is not at all in Dickens's spirit, which strives for reconciliation even at the price of cheating. That David Edgar and the RSC
have taken other, lesser liberties doesn't seriously bother me. I can
forgive that foolish Lord Verisopht is upgraded into a clever financial avenger at the end, that Sir Mulberry Hawk plays out a silly,
melodramatic scene at Madeline's thwarted wedding, that Kate's
presence is added to Smike's Devonshire deathbed, that contemporary references are smuggled in (e.g., about how much money
can be got from American audiences—a proleptic allusion to the
present $100 tickets; or about an actor from Crummles's company
defecting to a theater near Waterloo Bridge—a gibe at someone's
leaving the RSC for the more heavily subsidized National Theatre).
But the change of Smike is gross. Dickens's propensity for tearjerking with pathetic characters is notorious, yet not even Little
Nell and Jo the crossing sweeper combined are as arrant a piece
of heartstring tugging as Edgar's Smike. Is the assumption that we
have become such brutes that unless a character is paralyzed from
the neck down or monstrously misshapen, he can no longer elicit
pity?

And while I am carping, I must question two other aspects of
this dramatization. Though using all the cast members as a composite narrator speaking bits of exposition from various parts of
the stage—a sort of aural mosaic—is an amiable variation on stage
conventions and quite welcome, the switch toward the end of the
play to highly expressionistic devices—notably, turning the actors
into houses anthropomorphically defying Ralph Nickleby—smacks
a little too much of trickery, of theatricalizing material that was
written theatrically enough to begin with, of failure of nerve, and,
finally, of prettification. Ralph's death—particularly since he is also
made to pronounce repentantly some of Smike's expressions (which
he couldn't have known)—becomes both too expiatory and too pic-

torial. Dickens, to do him justice, made Ralph's death no finer than his life.

Second, there is the taint of serious anachronism. Thus Kate and Madeline, those typically Victorian heroines who are really walking tear ducts, have been modernized into much more sturdy, self-reliant creatures; correspondingly, the assaults on Kate's chastity by Sir Mulberry have become infinitely cruder than conceivable in 1838. This is a disservice to the historical worth of the novel, too valuable to be sacrificed by way of pandering to present pressures.

When all this is said, however, there remains very much about *Nicholas Nickleby* that is good theater in many more ways than Broadway audiences usually get, and that shows off splendidly the versatility of British acting and the inventiveness of British staging. Thirty-nine actors create circa 150 roles and display marvelous variety and no less marvelous unity. There is only one performer, Suzanne Bertish, who grated on my nerves, whether she was playing Fanny Squeers, Miss Snevellicci, or Peg Sliderskew (not even hamming her Juliet in *Romeo* convincingly—perhaps because she is so hammy when not trying to ham); and some actors were better in one role than in another (Christopher Benjamin as Crummles rather than Bray, Christopher Ravenscroff as Lenville rather than Frank Cheeryble).

There was also some minor miscasting. Mrs. Nickleby (Priscilla Morgan, a replacement, and not very good) should be more of a *grande dame* on the surface, for better comic effect; Miss La Creevy should be somewhat younger and more vulnerable; and, both as Mrs. Squeers and as Mrs. Crummles, Lila Kaye should be a shade or two less obvious. As opposed to this, however, there are so many superb performances that, at the risk of slighting scarcely less deserving ones, I must single them out: Janet Dale as Miss Knag and Mrs. Wititterley, Cathryn Harrison as Tilda Price and Miss Petowker, Alun Armstrong as Squeers, Edward Petherbridge as Noggs (not quite what Dickens wrote, but just as magnificent), Patrick Godfrey as Kenwigs, and Bob Peck as a perfectly contrasted Browdie and Hawk. Roger Rees makes a handsome and sensitive Nicholas, though he relies too heavily on a voice strangulated with emotion; and Emily Richard and Lucy Gutteridge, albeit not fragile and exquisite enough, are pleasing as Kate and Madeline.

Trevor Nunn and John Caird have directed with great resourcefulness and a keen eye for both majestic sweep and incisive minutiae. They have converted the theater into a near-total acting area (with some activity even during intermissions), made sovereign use of catwalks and platforms, got maximal suggestiveness out of minimal scenery, found ways of making crowds both grotesque realities and menacing or wretched abstractions, created a variety of conveyances and even horses out of people plus a few props, kept everything moving at a brisk, fluid pace without slighting the savory detail or eloquent pause, and put such cinematic techniques as crosscutting, dissolves, and superimposition to canny theatrical application. The scenery (John Napier and Dermot Hayes), costumes (Napier), and lighting (David Hersey) are a world of wonders, and Stephen Oliver's songs and background music are apt, tasteful, and handsomely executed. The production thrills with a combination of éclat and restraint, a seemingly improvisatory exuberance that yet remains within the bounds of disciplined integration.

Ultimately, though, for all its rococo embellishments (defended by Edgar Johnson, the Dickens biographer, but questioned by me), the novel is markedly superior to the play, simply because, as Geoffrey Tillotson put it with only slight exaggeration, any page of Dickens's contains more things than any page by another writer—so that, for example, those acutely vivid minor characters emerge shortchanged on the stage. Yet even the novel has too many of those mannerisms of which Freud complained in Dickens (by a curious coincidence, Freud was 26 when he wrote this—Dickens's age when writing Nickleby):

> ... those flawless girls, selfless and good, so good that they are quite colorless; then the fact that all the good people immediately become friends as soon as they meet and work together throughout the whole book; then the sharp distinction between virtue and vice which doesn't exist in life (where should I be, for example?); finally his easy toleration of feeble-mindedness, represented in almost every novel by one or two blockheads or crazy people, who belong to the side of the "good ones," and so on. Oh, I had almost forgotten the philanthropist, who has such a frightful lot of money and is available for any noble purpose.

Nicholas Nickleby, the play, has much narrative excitement and technical brilliance, but it is a middlebrow enterprise.

The Dresser

Three Broadway plays this week and one Off Broadway one last week deal with the symbiotic relations of two men. Whether it is a tightrope walker and the chap he carries piggyback, a famous playwright and a great actor, a ham actor and his dresser, or a priest and a seminarian, in each nexus there is a seemingly homoerotic undercurrent that remains, conciously or unconsciously, unexplored. I cannot say whether this is the new trend that is replacing all those incurably ill and paralyzed or dreadfully disfigured characters we were getting previously; conceivably the authors merely wish to exalt friendships between two males. In either case, however, the quiddity and existential meaning of these deep-seated relationships remain woefully underanalyzed.

Ronald Harwood used to be the dresser and an actor in the company of Donald Wolfit, the last of the legendary British actor-managers whose companies mainly rattled around the provinces, often under grueling circumstances. In Sir Donald's companies the gruel was particularly thick, and Harwood has since put his recollections of it to twofold use: in the biography *Sir Donald Wolfit* (1971), and now in the play *The Dresser*, about a semi-imaginary, dour, barnstorming actor known as "Sir" (as Harwood always addressed Wolfit) and his quirky, mother-hennish, likable dresser. Of the two endeavors, the book is by far the more interesting, showing how much more food for thought there can be in a loose, complex life than in a carefully trimmed, arbitrarily reordered composition.

Sir, and the play about him, are a good 60 percent Wolfit, his wife (the actress Rosalind Iden), and other figures from their world, although rearranged in time and space; Norman, the dresser, does not, however, seem to be a portrait of Harwood. In the play, Sir, having just suffered a minor nervous breakdown, escapes from the hospital to play Lear for the (I think) 247th time, though he cannot even remember his first line. Moreover, this is a wretched provincial theater during an air raid in 1942; not only the performance but also the whole joint may bomb. Norman, who lives largely through and for Sir, puts him miraculously back together; with a little further help from the old gray magic of the theater, a Lear arises from the ruin of a man and the near-ruin of a building.

Sir and Norman emerge as a real-life replica of Lear and the Fool, a point the playwright belabors with a jackhammer, but which, for all that, fails to illuminate anything. The play is too short and sche-matic and gimmicky to allow for character development, and by picking up Sir at the frayed end of his career and Norman well past the sozzled midpoint of his, it does not, despite some retrospective monologues, allow us to share sufficiently in the evolution and dis-solution of the principal relationship.

What makes the book so much more absorbing is that Wolfit was an immensely richer, trickier, more contradictory, but finally posi-tive character than this Sir, who actually mouths or mimes some of Wolfit's prejudices, absurdities, and outrageous remarks, but lacks the passion, incidental decencies, life force, and large though un-wieldy talent that animated the real-life actor. In fact, Wolfit con-sidered it his mission to bring theater, and particularly Shakespeare, to remote audiences, and cared almost as much about his public as about his ego. Sir, contrariwise, considers the theatergoers (along with the critics, whom Wolfit both hated and revered) "swines." Is it Harwood, Sir, or Paul Rogers, who plays him, that foists this incorrect plural on us? Wolfit, who was briefly a teacher and loved the language, would no more have committed the solecism than harbored the feeling.

Still, *The Dresser* is clever and articulate as well as simplistic. We get Sir and his unhappy actress wife (the real Wolfits' marriage was idyllic), Sir and his clumsy and trembling yet sometimes rebellious company, Sir and a pretty ingenue, and Sir and Norman, bicker-ing, fussing, embracing against a background of all sorts of cute and melancholy backstage and onstage contretemps. Harwood has a jolly way with both authentic and invented anecdotes, but it all smells first of greasepaint, then of midnight oil, and only in the last place of life. Thus in the book he tells us of Wolfit's hatred of homo-sexuals but also of the allowances the actor-manager made when he liked a pederast in his company. Norman, written and played as a repressed homosexual, seems to wince at Sir's mocking of "nancies," while thriving on his grudging crumbs of affection, but the essence of this relationship is never pushed through to.

Yet the production and acting make the play eminently worth attending. Michael Elliott, the manifestly able director, actually di-rected Wolfit and Tom Courtenay (who plays Norman and whom Wolfit admired) in *Ghosts*. Courtenay gives a grandly exaggerated, appropriately mannered, clucking, and comically plangent perfor-mance, which matches the likewise hypertrophic, in its different way equally fruity one of Paul Rogers, who rises, as Lear, to truly flyblown majesty. There is racy supporting work from all others, notably Rachel Gurney, Marge Redmond, the impishly sorrowful Douglas Seale, and the fetching Lisabeth Bartlett. The visual, aural, and lighting effects could not be seedier, zanier, or more hilarious, and the fine acting carries us past much of the patness and unearned pathos. Behind the physical papier-mâché of *The Dresser* lurks the psychological papier-mâché, but also enough raucous bravura for an evening of roisterous delights.

Merrily We Roll Along

Merrily We Roll Along, the new Stephen Sondheim (music and lyrics) George Furth (book) musical, is loosely based on the 1934 Kaufman and Hart play of the same name. That was no great blessing, either, and depended chiefly on a gimmick the musical retains: the story is told backward, mostly from the point of view of a successful (in this version) songwriter and producer looking back at how his present embarrassment of material riches and artistic mediocrity evolved, step by step, from initial poverty, idealism, and talent. So the only thing that differentiates this show from the other trash that has been coming at us in big waves lately is that instead of desperately waiting for it to end we wait desperately for it to begin.

What with caricatures of the likes of Dorothy Parker and George Gershwin, the play at least exhibited faint traces of idiosyncratic identity; in George Furth's book, the three central characters are watery show-biz clichés drained from hundreds of leaky, old vehicles and expected to be held together by a grid of second-rate one-liners that proves as supportive as a sieve. Franklin Shepard was a young composer of talent, good-looking and a Wasp, and so, naturally, sold out; Charley Kringas, his librettist and lyricist, is funny-looking and Jewish, and so, of course, remains the soul of honesty. Mary Flynn, the roly-poly novelist-turned-film reviewer, always silently in love with Frank, remains a faithful buddy to both until dipsomania gets the better of her and she becomes disgustingly outspoken at an opening-night party, only to be unceremoniously ejected. And that, believe it or not, is the grand climax to which the show builds up, or, rather, from which it builds down. Unless you count Frank's even earlier speech to the graduating class of his old school, in which he seems to advocate compromise. When, at the end—or is it the beginning?—we return to this speech, it seems to advocate idealism. Inconsistent? In a show without any consistency, substance, or meaning, who cares? Certainly not the authors.

Back in 1934 Kaufman and Hart thought at first of calling their play *All Our Yesterdays*, and that is pretty much what Sondheim, Furth, and Harold Prince, the director, have given us. There are plot, staging, design, music, and dance concepts from just about all their previous shows cluttering up the stage: rehashed, warmed-over, or half-baked. Thus we get the interweaving of two song numbers, progression by alternating fits and starts in book and score, present and former selves interacting (*Follies*), movable platforms of different levels (*Company*), closely packed human blocs dancing as a viscous mass (from Prince's *Evita*, likewise choreographed by Larry Fuller), and reams of music and lyric writing that broken-wingedly take off from, or are takeoffs on, former Sondheim songs. No wonder audiences applaud bits of the overture as they ordinarily do only at revivals: they are welcoming back old Sondheim melodies even if they sound older and leaner after a long absence of invention.

I cannot begin to tell you how poor this music is: only one number, "Old Friends," reprised as it is, sticks in the memory as a song; the rest are only battalions of black ants scurrying all over, under, and behind the staves in the hope of hitting upon a formation that would read like music. The characters in the show usually wear T-shirts that label them EX-WIFE, EX-EX-WIFE, SECRETARY, and so forth; if only the tunes could have worn T-shirts with TUNE written on them, maybe they would have impressed us as such. But, come to think of it, no: the device does precious little to make even the characters cohere and register. Yet if Sondheim has been erratic as a composer before, this is the first time that his lyrics, too, seem to drag their feet; thus they will stoop even to the mere marking of time, literally and figuratively, in the repetition, ad nauseam, of "Day after day after day after day." If it is imitation Sondheim one wants, there are now Sondheim imitators such as William Finn who can do the job better than Sondheim himself.

And why must a large cast of young unknowns be as histrionically unpersuasive and physically unprepossessing as this bunch? I could not find a single winning combination of performance and presence. One of them at least has the excuse of being the director's daughter, but what can the others claim for themselves? Indeed, one performance is almost a sick joke: Terry Finn's Gussie is the blatantly misogynistic homosexual's idea of a predatory female. Finally, Eugene

Lee's sets and Judith Dolan's costumes are so prosaic that not even David Hersey's lighting can coax a spark of poetry from them.

The one feeble, tired notion the show keeps belaboring is summed up in this exchange, "FRANKLIN: Why do I have to be poor to write music? CHARLEY: Because once you're rich, you never will." I don't see why this has to be true, but it does rather look as if the *Merrily* makers had concentrated their entire effete energies on proving it so.*

Torch Song Trilogy

Kenneth Tynan created a stir some years ago by asserting that the two principal types of humor in the American theater were the Jewish and the homosexual. If this is so, and it well may be, the good news is that the two strains have been successfully crossbred in Harvey Fierstein's *Torch Song Trilogy*, which is a very amusing as well as moving affair for whose enjoyment, be it said right off, neither Jewishness nor homosexuality is a prerequisite.

This trilogy of shortish plays that lasts, all told (and is all ever told!), a little over four hours is about half the length of *Nicholas Nickleby*, but has at least twice as much to tell us about the way we live now. And when I say *we*, I mean people, any people, except perhaps those living in an offshore lighthouse or in the very buckle of the Bible Belt. Fierstein wrote, and performed the lead in these three plays one at a time, but it is much better to see them as they are now: the long acts of one extended but not excessive work that gathers meaning as it progresses until, at last, all parts of it resonate in the mind in a bittersweet harmony made of dissonances, pain, resignation, and a little daredevil hope.

Arnold Beckoff, the protagonist, has all the earmarks of a stylized projection of the actor-author himself, yet even though one feels this potentially stifling closeness, one is not, or not for long, an embarrassed voyeur. Buttonholing immediacy is transmuted—by wit, irony, fair play to one and all—first into a bearable distance, then into a sense of wonder. For Beckoff-Fierstein emerges at the far end of identification in a state of liberated semi-detachment that is not quite so good as serenity but that will—will have to-do.

In the first play, Arnold, a drag queen, is either backstage at the

---

*P.S. 2005: Sorry. This is a much better show than I realized at the time. Some of it was the production's fault, much of it mine.

nightclub where he performs (a performance we do not see—an unfortunate evasion), or at a gay bar called the International Stud, which gives the play its name, or in his apartment, when not in that of his new lover, Ed, a bisexual who is also involved with a young woman called Laurel. The themes here are Arnold's drifting into the orgiastic back rooms of gay hotspots versus his yearning for a solid relationship, Ed's shuttling between two kinds of sexuality and styles of life, and the difficulties with commitment to anything, even noncommitment. In dialogues, monologues, phone conversations with a homosexual friend, Arnold reveals himself and his world with a sweet campiness, an outrageousness whose bark is worse than its bite, an arrested development that does not preclude perceptions of devastating lucidity. "I always thought of myself as a kind person," says Arnold; "not small, but generous in a bitchy sort of way." Or: "To me a lap in bed is worth three in a [gay] bar, because deep down I know they don't marry sluts." Or: "That's really hitting below the belt: appealing to my Susan Hayward fantasies!"

Now, these lines may not be funny out of context, and they lose a lot on paper, without Fierstein's engagingly abrasive presence: the face of a weather vane whirling between corruption and innocence; the movements of an overgrown, precociously epicene baby, and the mind of a tirelessly impudent, lubricious wit that can instantly switch to self-mockery and comic Weltschmerz enunciated with a provocatively rasping voice that seems to be picking away at existential scabs on the self, on others, on the world. An upside-down world that one meets with tragicomic defiance: "I could make love to an 80-year-old woman. I could probably make love to an 80-year-old camel. I could make love to an 80-year-old anything as long as it kept its mouth shut."

In the second play, *Fugues in a Nursery*, it is a year later in the upstate farmhouse shared by Ed and Laurel, now living together and playing weekend hosts to Arnold and his new lover, Alan, a very young male model. Fierstein situates the entire action in an enormous symbolic bed in which the two couples talk, argue, copulate, and crisscross both emotionally and sexually. The writing is in the form of a fugue, which is clever, but also means something: the overlapping, intermingling dialogue, in which we are often not sure about who is talking to whom, conveys thought-provoking parallels between homo- and heterosexual relationships—though the captious might argue that Ed's bisexuality muddies the analogies. In any case, *Fugues* is an extremely droll and ingenious scrutiny of sexual politics whose humor, honorably, never hides the underlying cruelty or, still deeper down, the underlying pathos. With gallant gallows humor, Arnold wonders about this foursome: "If two wrongs don't make a right, maybe four do?"

It is the last play, *Widows and Children First!*, that rises to true heights and ties all the foregoing together. Ed is unhappily married to Laurel, has had a fight with her and is temporarily bunking *chez* Arnold, after whom he still hankers; Alan, who had been living with Arnold, has met a horrible, homosexual death; Arnold is trying to adopt legally a problem teenager, David, a tough, street-wise, homosexual kid, chock-full of precocious knowledge and sarcasm, but not without a touching residue of childishness. Into this *ménage*, on a visit from Florida, comes Mrs. Beckoff, Arnold's widowed mother. She knows about her son's homosexuality, but cannot really accept it, and keeps needling him. Mother and son try to love each other, but cannot quite make it; their defense, which is also an offense, is wit: her Jewish wit against his homosexual one. While they fumble for each other's affection out of one side of their mouths, they cleverly lacerate each other out of the other side. The combat, fought with bare tongues and occasional desperate gestures, is verbal Grand Guignol of matchless humor and horror.

It turns out that the two widowed creatures, mother and son, are, except for their different sexualities, deeply alike down to their very jokes. The Jewish ones, to be sure, suggest a sad, lonely stand-up comedian resorting to an almost metaphysical sardonicism; the homosexual ones suggest a sarcastic masquerader, flamboyantly theatricalizing everything. But they climax in a very similar, murderous and suicidal, bitchiness: envenomed chicken soup against poisoned paillettes. When mother accuses son of not knowing how to bring up David, Arnold answers: "What's there to know? Whenever there is a problem, I simply imagine how you would solve it… *And then I do the opposite!*" But in fact—and here lies the play's subtlety—Arnold does the same, or nearly. And sometimes he realizes it. Reminiscing about Alan, he says: "It's easier to love someone who's dead. They make so few mistakes. MOTHER: You have an unusual way of looking at things. ARNOLD: It runs in the family."

All values are inverted and subverted. "ARNOLD: What would you say if I went out and came home with a girl and told you I was straight? MOTHER (*patronizingly*): If you were happy, I'd be happy." There are ironies within ironies in this, a whole topsy-turvy world. And alongside the mother conflict are, cunningly and touchingly orchestrated, the David problem, the Ed problem, and even the Laurel problem. The author's ultimate achievement is the perfect blend of hard justice and warm empathy with which he embraces all characters, his own alter ego included. The performances by Joel Crothers, Diane Tarleton, Paul Joynt are very fine; more remarkable yet are Fierstein's Arnold, Matthew Broderick's wryly abstracted David aroused to sudden spurts of insistence, and Estelle Getty's quintessential Jewish mother.

There are flaws. Arnold's source of income grows unclear. Could a drag-queen single parent adopt even as unwanted a kid as David? Alan was presented as a fling in the second play, the third makes him out to have been a beloved spouse. No matter. Peter Pope's staging and the production values are good; the play is better. What are you waiting for?

Dreamgirls

If you look past book, lyrics, and music, you might easily perceive *Dreamgirls* as a great musical. There is a splendid concept behind it, resplendent technology worked by prodigious designers in front of it, and a consummate magician, Michael Bennett, hovering above it. But at the center of all this invention and activity—where the substance ought to be—there is something perilously close to nothing.

The ingenious concept is twofold. First, the story is told almost entirely in musical, quasi-operatic terms: much that might be spoken in a standard musical comedy is here sung. Particularly clever is the way certain songs do double duty: as set pieces performed in some show-within-the-show and as plot elements of *Dreamgirls*—expressions of the feelings and situations of the characters. This doubleness may be concurrent or consecutive. Even reprises are usually more than just that: ironic commentaries on the past in terms of the present, or vice versa. Second, the story unfolds in cinematic style, with virtually every device known to the movies translated into theater in a display of fluidity, simultaneity, and variety that is awesome.

To achieve all this, the computer had to become coequal with the designers. The main scenic elements are metallic towers and bridges, carrying either massed spotlights or people, and moving in a ghostly choreography flesh-and-blood dancers might envy. The towers revolve around their own axes while gliding into ever shifting positions; the bridges soar or sink to reveal, for instance, a payola pantomime in which slinky silhouetted figures on several levels are greasing the palms of numerous shadowy disc jockeys in front of a solid wall of muted blue reflectors. It is a multilayered frieze to make the blood freeze. A scarcely less telling effect occurs whenever, in the process of revolving, a spotlight-laden tower briefly casts its beams into our eyes, and being blinded by show-biz razzle-dazzle turns from metaphor into acute reality. The scenic units move along eighteen miles of cable; the technology and inventiveness that sets them in motion is many more miles ahead of current theatrical practice.

Adding to the cinematic effect is a complex schema of spotlighting from unprecedented angles, which helps create elaborate fades and dissolves. Further, there are quite a few dressers hidden onstage helping cast members to make lightning costume changes and reappear within a couple of seconds from another direction in new outfits and wigs as transformed personalities. This, again, makes palpable the transmutations, not always salutary, wrought by show business on its eagerly malleable pawns. And, thanks to the computer, lights on an object or subject are altered with an eerie, insidious gradualness, as if it were happening from within, or else with crashing abruptness; meanwhile a curtain or sliding panel materializes out of nowhere, propelled by no human agency, and everything as Yeats said in a rather different context—is changed, changed utterly. It is as if the entire enormous stage were a plaything in the hands of some invisible giant coolly, continuously juggling with it. This giant has four heads: Robin Wagner's for sets, Theoni V. Aldredge's for costumes (and what stunners they are!), Tharon Musser's for lights, and Michael Bennett's for heading them all in the right directions.

Unfortunately, there is also the writing. Tom Eyen's book is full of commonplaces, contradictions, and confusion as it recounts a story that is both too close and not close enough to that of the Supremes and one or two other figures from the world of black popular music. One problem is too many plots, subplots, and overplots jostling one another and getting short shrift. Another is no hero or heroine one can sufficiently feel for: I am in favor of subtle shades of gray rather than black and white characterizations, but in a musical, where characters must be evoked with a few bold strokes, such subtlety is

devilishly hard to achieve. Still another is the prolonged collaboration of the entire cast on the shaping of the book; this worked in
A Chorus Line, where everyone drew on his life story, but doesn't
work here, where actors must invent characters, for which they
would have to be writers. Eyen's lyrics are no better than the book;
especially annoying is one in which the facile rhymes *there*, *where*,
and *share* (plus a little *air*) are milked to a fare-thee-well.

As for Henry Krieger's music, which must convey the contest
between Motown and soul, between plumbing the gut and climbing the charts, it doesn't manage to sound very memorable—or
even very different—in either mode. Always serviceable, it is also
instantly forgettable. The one exception is the rejected lover's, not
lament but defiance, "And I'm Telling You I'm Not Going," a high-
gospel number shatteringly delivered by Jennifer Holliday; yet that
is more a performing than a composing triumph. There is good
work also from Cleavant Derricks, Loretta Devine, Sheryl Lee
Ralph, Deborah Burrell, Ben Harney, and some others, but there is
no part capacious enough to hold one of these effusive talents. Still,
the way the two Michaels, Bennett and Peters, have moved them
all around in a constant quasi-choreographic flow elicits admiration if not involvement. *Dreamgirls* is a nonstop geyser of visual
originality; perhaps it is just as well that there is no content for all
this form to detract from.

Come Back to the 5 and Dime Jimmy Dean, Jimmy Dean

Why does a play like *Come Back to the 5 and Dime Jimmy Dean,
Jimmy Dean* get mounted on Broadway in a fancy production? If
it went back to some theatrical five-and-dime store—say, a little
theater in Whitefish or Waco—to be done in a modest production
giving a batch of budding actresses a chance to be seen, who could
object? It concerns a bunch of Frank Capra-ish little people in a tiny
Texas town, not far from where *Giant* was shot, and where these
mildly amiable and mildly obnoxious losers started the Disciples of
James Dean club, of which Mona, who is the mother of the eponymous and pleonastic Jimmy Dean, Jimmy Dean—a twenty- year-old
whom we never get to see and who may or may not have been sired

by the movie star during a one-night stand—is the president. The play takes place on September 30, 1975, during the club's twentieth reunion, and also two decades earlier, on the night when Dean's demise was broadcast to the world. The scene is the local five-and-dime, where Mona, Sissy, and Joe (a Deanish-looking, effeminate youth who is the club's vice-president) all work under Juanita, the Bible-thumping, fly-swatting proprietress. The back wall of the stage is a trompe l'oeil mirror, in which, with slightly distorted sound, the events of the past take place. But past and present are otherwise as intertwined as the braid of an epaulet, giving the director a chance to strut his stuff—which, presumably, is where Robert Altman, perceiving a chance for bravura staging, came in. Among the other major characters are Stella May, now a fat, tough-talking, hard-drinking, childless married woman, and Edna Louise, now as before a wispy waif, although pregnant with her seventh offspring.

There is no growth whatsoever in any of these characters: in '75 they are the same dwarfs they were in the shadow of *Giant* in '55. True, one of them has had a double mastectomy, one has undergone a sex change, one has produced a child that may or may not be a moron, and one, for very uncompelling reasons, seems to lose her faith in the Bible and thereupon takes her first swig of bourbon; but we are not even made to feel that there is that much difference between the Old Testament and Old Crow. What we are made to feel, however—though it's not in the script—is that Mona has undergone a lobotomy, because of the way Sandy Dennis plays her. The play is full of supposedly portentous revelations that—perhaps because the dramaturgy is as flat as the Texas landscape—you can see coming a mile off, but the more things change in these Texas trilogies or monologies, the more they are the same shows.

Altman is undeniably clever. Thus he begins the show with the present and the past literally coexisting as world and mirror-world; after that, the characters merely slip upstage for the electronically slightly distorted past or downstage for the existentially slightly blighted present. And David Gropman's ingenious and evocative set design serves Mr. Altman admirably. But what director in his right taste would choose Ed Graczyk's inconsequential, manipulative, and quite unnecessary play, and what director in his right mind would let Sandy Dennis make rancid mincemeat of the key role?

True, Mona is a disturbed woman. But does that mean that her

lines should run on in defiance of all logic, emotional sense, intel-
ligibility, and punctuation, with pauses only where they most surely
sabotage the meaning? Must the tone of voice almost throughout
be as dead as the sound of a sewing machine in the next apartment? Must the eyes be as blank as those uninked pages of the *New
York Times* we keep getting with ever more frustrating frequency?
Must the actress also flash on and off, almost irrelevantly, a smile
that is barely distinguishable from the effect of swallowing a fish-
hook? Miss Dennis seems to be playing not Mona but Heisenberg's
uncertainty principle. And you expect the play to change, at any
moment, into the last scene of *Streetcar*, with two men in white
carting her off.

The funny thing about our theater is that, as William Goldman
pointed out years ago in *The Season*, there are some totally unpalatable actresses who become critics' darlings, and who are forthwith
encouraged to indulge themselves in their worst excesses to ever
greater critical acclaim. Indeed, Miss Dennis started out as a seemingly normal actress years ago, but then switched to a kind of kooki-
ness that, being rabidly praised by Walter Kerr and others, rapidly
changed into this irreversible and always identical stage persona of
someone hanging on by her teeth to the last fraying shred of sanity.

But consider this now: why are a good many actresses allowed,
indeed encouraged, to make such painful exhibitions of themselves,
but actors almost never? There certainly is no male counterpart of
Sandy Dennis in the American theater—at least not one steadily
employed and applauded. It almost makes one suspect that there is
a force loose among either the public or the directors and reviewers,
or both, that wants to see women look sick, demented, deprived
of their healthy sexuality, humiliated in public. Think back, if you
can, to the theater of the thirties and early forties and find me an
equivalent there of this type of leading lady.

As Sissy, the optimist full of sometimes false bravado, Cher gives
a perfectly agreeable and believable performance, though she lacks
vocal projection. Karen Black is, on the other hand, militantly unsubtle, but has good elocution. Kathy Bates would be a credible
Stella May if she could sound Texan; the defensive brashness and
monumental self-unawareness are compellingly conveyed. Edna
Louise is the ultimate wimp, and offers nothing to Marta Heflin,
who repays her in kind. Mark Patton does well enough by what little
there is to Joe. By far the most unassailable performance, though, is
Sudie Bond's Juanita: there is exemplary tact here about how far you

can go to get everything out of a rather cliché role without lapsing into cheap farce, pathos, or mannerism. Miss Bond does nothing to make Juanita likable and everything to make her precise and real—and that is what does make her, finally, likable.

Scott Bushnell's costumes are to the point, Paul Gallo's lighting is extremely tricky, and Richard Fitzgerald delivers the somewhat peculiar sound effects demanded of him. Altman is better with the graphic deployment of his actors than with finding the tight tempos, and, as in his movies, speech sometimes gets wantonly blurred. Although the play becomes a little less boring in the second act, it is too little and too late, and at the cost of some whopping improbabilities. Hit-or-miss directorial bravura and an expensive production are not enough to justify so much ado; you will not find a million-dollar baby in this five-and-ten-cent store.

The Dining Room

That stimulating writer A. R. Gurney Jr. has come up with *The Dining Room*, in which an elegant, old-fashioned (though not genuinely antique) dining room serves as the real and symbolic setting for countless, not directly related lives—or, rather, telltale fragments of them—forming a passing parade of Wasp America—preppie, post-preppie, and anti-preppie—from its heyday to its present, precariously eked-out survival. The dining room is the scene of much more than merely eating-of assorted fun, sadness, contentment, and rebellion—as a modus vivendi goes from viable to friable.

One problem here may be excessive trickiness. In Thornton Wilder's *The Long Christmas Dinner*, from which this play seems to derive, there is, although stylized and accelerated, a consecutive progression and confinement to one family. Gurney, however, jumps back and forth in time, around in place (this only *seems* to be the same dining room), and ever onward with new dramatis personae. Moreover, we get double exposure, as one unrelated episode slowly dissolves into another. And the director, David Trainer, uses his cast of six in a deliberately unsettling way, so that at times an older actor will play a child and a much younger one the parent. All this proves more alienation than the material can bear, especially since the writing does not maintain its marvelous half-wistful, half-ludicrous trenchancy.

Even so, *The Dining Room* moves so fast under Trainer's inventive direction that if you find one course insipid, the next one, much more delightfully pungent, is already being served. Loren Sherman's set, Deborah Shaw's costumes, and Frances Aronson's lighting are all tasteful and exact, and the six actors playing many roles are better in some than in others, but never less than palatable. There is no denying that Gurney has been in better form before—notably in the not dissimilar *Scenes From American Life*—yet even at his second best he is observant, thoughtful, and, when most unflinchingly satirical, still unabatedly humane.

"Master Harold"... and the boys

Except for the over-explicit title, all is well with Athol Fugard's *"Master Harold"... and the boys*. Fugard has now perfected his way of writing plays about the tragedy of apartheid; he avoids the spectacular horrors and concentrates instead on the subtle corrosion and corruption, on the crumbling of the spirit for which the cure would be heroic action that may not be forthcoming, and which the blacks try to assuage with the salve of dreams, the whites with the cautery of oppression. For Fugard, the ultimate evil is the weakness, the cowardice, that is one of the constituents of so much human nature. When, rarely, unalloyed nobility does occur, its chances of prevailing are slim. Yet it exists, and its mere existence is reason enough for not wiping the name of mankind off the slate. The play springs two wonders on us: it is devastating without being depressing, and it is pungently specific without any loss in universality.

The sixteenish son of white parents who own a tearoom in Port Elizabeth in 1950, "Master" Harold has a tricky, touchy relationship with Sam and Willie, the two black employees. Sam is wise, even philosophical, and hopes for a better world; although Harold has passed on some of his book learning to him, Sam has been more of a father to the boy than his real father, a physical and moral cripple. Willie is a simple soul, seemingly content with funny-sweet fantasies of winning in a ballroom-dancing competition. Not only are the relations between the white boy and the black men who helped him grow up an intricate network of generosities and withholdings, of frustrations and humiliations (not entirely one-sided, though the boy is selfish and the men are a trifle, just a trifle, too good), but even the interaction between Sam and Willie has its curious yet credible complexities. The psychological sharpness, dramatic scope, and existential suggestivity that Fugard wrests from humble but never trite ingredients are a precious, precarious compensation for the ills of being. The author cannot legislate justice for South Africa or the rest of the world, but his plays are among the few small, doughty justifications for carrying on.

The two black actors are exhilarating. Danny Glover, as Willie, demonstrates with thrilling straightforwardness that the unlikeliest beings can harbor staunch talents for learning and endurance; his movements are patience translated into motion, his eyes teem with dormant ardor. As Sam, Zakes Mokae gives a performance stripped of everything that smacks of effect, technique, acting; the only reason for calling it a performance is that life can hardly be that undiluted—that sheerly, overwhelmingly to the point. Only Lonny Price is disappointing as Master Harold, as young Hally vindictively wishes to be called; his effects are big, but seldom let you forget that they are effects.

This production—originally by the Yale Repertory Theatre—has correctly self-effacing scenery by Jane Clark, costumes by Sheila McLamb, and lights by David Noling. And Mr. Fugard directs with the same insight and control with which he writes. There is, despite the noble metaphor of life as ballroom dancing, a certain dearth of language here: these characters, almost by definition, cannot talk poetry, which only a few masters, such as Beckett, have been able to extract from rock-bottom prose. O'Neill, for instance, never quite could, yet it did not finally keep him from greatness. What Fugard offers is wave upon wave of comprehension, compassion, and achingly autobiographical honesty that create a poetry of their own.

Nine

Nine, the musical into which Federico Fellini's film *8½* has shrunk, is a curiously titillating, enervating, engaging, and frustrating piece of work. It displays much talent, some genuine achievement, equal amounts of intelligence and foolishness, a lot of vulgarity, and more than a little grace. You want it to be much better than it is because you can sense the wherewithal for distinction; you wince at opportunities let slip and false steps taken, but you never quite give up on it. In the end, you are left in a state of mixed excitation, unfulfilled expectancy, and mild revulsion, wondering whether you are sorry you came or sad at having to go.

I was never a great admirer of *8½* (as I had been of most earlier Fellini), but there is no denying that the musical's book (if that's the word for it—a few scattered and randomly reassembled signatures would be nearer the mark) is an impoverishment. The movie's Guido Anselmi was a film director and lecher who also had problems with religion, mysticism, cultural politics, high finance, fathoming his childhood, and coping with his dreams; the musical's Guido Contini has real difficulties only with his women and his writer's block. Thus in Arthur Kopit's book, based on a previous version by Mario Fratti, elements that in the movie found their places among many other contrasting, reinforcing, and range-extending ones balloon into overinflated, repetitious triviality. There are also such witless lines as "A cantaloupe is a genius compared to Guido Contini" and such flatfooted lyrics (by the composer-lyricist Maury Yeston) as "When he was working on a film on ancient Rome, / He made the gladiators take the slave girls home."

Yet right away, too, we see and hear real ideas. The white, black-striped building blocks and black latticework of Lawrence Miller's set have their cool handsomeness; the half-moon-shaped orchestra pit with a runway for a lip neatly suggests a spa (where we are); the Canalettoesque backdrop that, under Marcia Madeira's sure lighting, modulates picturesquely from day to night and back, practically smells of Venice (where we also are); and the whole stage maintains a feeling of striated oddity befitting Guido's inner landscape (where we are most of all). Against this dominant whiteness, a black-clad Guido is surrounded by 21 women in black (the costumes by William Ivey Long, already striking and multiform, will later explode into orgasms of color and architectural structure). Guido squats silently while the women shower him with adoring movement and sound; presently he rises to conduct them in a lush cantata profana that, as they sway and warble ever more lustfully, swells into a veritable whoratorio.

Yet even the exploration of the director-and-womanizer's anxieties is trifling; still more so is the dipping into his past via his mother, his wife, and his childhood self. These remain from the movie, as do the voracious mistress, Carla, and the voluminous tart, Saraghina, and a few minor Fellinian figures. Mostly, though, we get verbal, musical, and choreographic dallying on and around those

black-striped white polyhedrons. From these, the ingenious director-choreographer Tommy Tune does conjure up canals, lagoons,
gondolas, beaches, and more, but, finally, this unit set, despite the
director's and designers' magic, becomes confining, monotonous,
arid. The stage show merely conveys the mind's elegant prison; the
movie, with its frantic agitation across shifting scenery, could show
us life, the world, movement itself becoming a cage.

There are, moreover, two enormous lapses. One is the lack of
balls as this supposedly macho, frenziedly heterosexual carnival is
swathed in a flagrantly homosexual sensibility. Women are dressed,
made up, made to behave in ways that reduce them to subaltern or
threatening grotesques or succubae; and though there was some
of this in *8 1/2*, there, at least, they didn't come across as female
impersonators. Consequently, we get no contest between love and
lust, only shadowboxing between oversimplified stick figures and
bloated travesties. Yet even in this there is enough invention and
skill to alleviate some of the sham and campy crudity.

The other lapse is the Guido of Raul Julia, or an excess of balls.
For Julia's acting consists chiefly of rolling his large eyeballs around
in his head, like two billiard balls caroming off an invisible third,
presumably in back of them, where the brain should be. Julia gives
a completely unthinking façade of a performance, which he coats
with a layer of limacine charm indistinguishable from castor oil.
Could there be 21 women in the world—much less on one stage—
who would swoon for him? Is this really a great movie director
or, more likely, a gofer or a grip? His heavy Hispanic accent plays
havoc with both his Italian and his English; but worst of all is his
wildly off-pitch croaking that mangles the intricate melodic lines.
At times, my companion and I had to cover our ears.

Several others, however, are wonderful, though many have
problems with Mr. Yeston's demanding tessitura. Thus the stylish,
aristocratically restrained, and vocally sophisticated Karen Akers
has trouble—as Luisa, the wife—with the lower register; the stunningly sensual Shelly Burch, slinkily kittenish and coltishly long-
legged—as Claudia, the star—thins out and quavers at the top. But
there is vocal and kinetic witchery from Liliane Montevecchi, pure
but not unironic sweetness from Taina Elg, and nicely barkless bite
from Stephanie Cotsirilos. As Carla, the mistress, Anita Morris is
an all-round prodigy: she manages to be simultaneously a flawless singer, actress, gymnast, and contortionist, and does not even
wholly succumb to the extreme tastelessness of some of her chores.

And as the boy Guido, Cameron Johann acts with naturalness and sings blessedly on pitch.

Which brings us to the very pleasurable music that bespeaks both Mr. Yeston's having studied at the B.M.I. Workshop and his teaching music theory at Yale. For there is something of the student's derivativeness as well as of the instructor's learnedness about this score, which makes up in musical erudition what it lacks in natural originality. But eclectic or not, the music is seldom less than ingratiating, and the composer's vocal arrangements, like Jonathan Tunick's orchestrations, are zestfully idiosyncratic. Yeston's lyrics, alas, are less good, relying overmuch on trite ideas and rhymes, e.g., "only-lonely" and "scheme-dream-theme." Kopit's dialogue does rouse itself into some tart and telling exchanges, and Tommy Tune's staging, within the above-mentioned limitations, is endlessly resourceful. The conclusion is an even worse cop-out than Fellini's, but there are visual effects to rival those of the movie in opulence and inventiveness, and bright little touches of sassiness or sentiment pop up with pleasing frequency in the unlikeliest crannies. The core of *Nine* may be hollow or even rancid, but the surface it dazzlingly dressed to the nines.

Geniuses

The characters in Jonathan Reynold's *Geniuses* (at Playwrights Horizons) are in equal measure geniuses and maniacs, which is what makes them so amusing, endearing, scary, and related to us. The scene is a village hut 200 miles north of Manila and considerably closer to nowhere, a locale that stands in for Angola, about which the boy-wonder movie director Milo McGee McGarr is shooting a multi-million-dollar war epic, *Parabola of Death*. Though this title leaves the dramatis personae hilariously befogged, the audience should have no trouble recognizing *Geniuses* as mocking the making of *Apocalypse Now*.

What we get is a thoroughly funny farce about Hollywood away from home, when it tends to behave even worse; about the sensitive but absurd writer, Jocko Pyle, whose highbrow East Coast values are in acrimonious conflict with those of the West Coast Eldorado, off which he is trying to make some bittersweet bucks; about the broader clash of East and West, as the movielanders confront and all but founder on the chaotic but cunning ways of the Filipinos, only partially embodied in Winston Legazpi, a willing but fallible bodyguard and rascal; about the power plays in the realms of fame, wealth, and sex that sap the churning out of this lagging superproduction. Lagging indeed, because Jocko tears up sheets of manuscript as fast as he can type them, and sometimes, in despair, even before he has typed them. Lagging also because in a particularly costly battle sequence none of the Philippine army helicopters was in frame, the appropriate palms (the greedy, not the leafy, kind) having been left ungreased. And about to lag even more because a typhoon is bent on destroying the sets built by the irascible and sadistic Eugene Winter—a typhoon that also threatens Eugene himself, Jocko, Winston, the ace makeup man Bart Keely (who is sometimes—most often by himself—mistaken for Hemingway), and Skye Bullene, the blond sexpot, former Playboy playmate, current McGarr bedmate, soon to be a 30-second nude walk-on in this major movie. All of them are sardined, or piranhaed, together in this hazardous, typhoon-battered hut, into which the odd, peremptory radio message from Milo in his private helicopter penetrates to spread further disarray. Milo himself doesn't alight till Act III, but then with enough ominous *désinvolture* to put a basilisk on his guard.

Reynolds has wrought a highly civilized satire that stays almost consistently in high gear, even while its freewheeling ways manage to roll over and flatten everything from est and its likes to the prose style of Papa Hemingway. But it also has more serious implications as it chronicles the rise to power of Skye Bullene from sexy blonde, cultureless and cultist ("If it's been worshiped, I've done it!"), to impending movie mogul, or examines the wising up of Jocko Pyle, from sarcastically compulsive truth-teller to (at least partial) accepter of the world as it is and of cookies as they crumble you. Sometimes, as at the end of Act II, the play becomes a bit too straightforwardly grave for its devious levity, but comic disorder is soon enough restored.

There are moments of letdown: New York-versus-Los Angeles jokes, for example, have a way of sounding tired even when they are freshly and adroitly minted, as when the shortness of the Los Angeles roadway named after Nixon elicits Jocko's comment: "That's the way L.A. deals with everybody. Lose a little popularity and they cut off your freeway." A little of this auto route goes a long way, but Reynolds can drive along it as obsessively as a Joan Didion heroine.

Yet all is forgiven when such rollicking characters as Skye take over, or Bart, the wizard of many-hued bruises and wounds, who measures the artistry of a film in the number of gashes, slashes, and gory demises. Milo, however, for whom the only real filmmaking thrill is the Deal and whose getting and spending lays waste merely the powers at Paramount, suffers from the wrong actor: David Garrison is not commanding enough, either in caricature or in charisma, and certainly not Hibernian. Likewise disappointing is Michael Gross as Jocko. Though he has the requisite technique and sprightliness, he lacks the charm that would make this smartass likable and give the play a sturdy center.

But the rest is all for the best. As Bart, Kurt Knudson kneads woolliness, bonhomie, and a not entirely requited self-love into a spicy meatball; as Eugene, David Rasche nicely balances his egomania between the laughable and the sinister, as Winston, Thomas Ikeda tastes as good as his dubious food does to desperate palates. Sensational is the word for Joanne Camp as she peels off layer after layer of Skye's phony tinsel, genuine tinsel, wistful dimwittedness, and several more down to a fundamental shrewdness, all with exemplary nuttiness, charm, command—truly an onion that makes you cry, laugh, and fall utterly in love with her. And let's not forget the steady flow of beguiling sight gags, in which our author is abetted by his wily director Gerald Gutierrez, and the magisterial special-effects team of Esquire Jauchem and Gregory Meeh.

Add to this Andrew Jackness's beautifully seedy set, Ann Emonts's canny costumes, James F. Ingalls's smart lighting, and B. H. Barry's chilling or comic fights. "We are in hell!" is the last line of one of Jocko's endless attempts at an ending, after which the hapless scenarist reads out: "Dissolve to the Holocaust. THE END." In *Geniuses*, we too are in a hell of predatory proximities, mitigated however by peals of parabolic laughter; no cure, but the loveliest of palliatives.

Little Shop of Horrors

Anyone wishing to do an update of Susan Sontag's notorious piece on camp (heaven forfend!) could proceed from two current musical specimens of low camp. High camp is to be found in the low to middle reaches of playwrights such as Joe Orton and Caryl Churchill. Fictional examples are *Myra Breckinridge* and the novels of Ronald Firbank; in verse, there are the Ouijaboard poems of James Merrill. Low camp is a sort of outrageous farce with few artistic pretensions, frequently but not always of homosexual coloration, and displaying a voluptuously iconoclastic flippancy toward most things, love and heterosexual sex in particular. Conversely, it can also be extremely sentimental (sadism and sentimentality constitute a notorious partnership), but the hand on the heart is undercut by the tongue in the cheek.

To start with the nastier of the two endeavors, *Little Shop of Horrors* is a musicalization of a 1960 Roger Corman horror film, so jejune even by the standards of its lowly genre as to appear neither in Carlos Clarens's *An Illustrated History of the Horror Film* nor in Leslie Halliwell's compendious *Film Guide*. This esoteric choice is campy but also practical: few people are likely to know the ur-text well enough for invidious comparisons. I would guess that the musical, such as it is, is an improvement, the film's inadvertent humor probably falling short of the show's advertent kind. It has also had the benefit of some intervening horror films to draw on or allude to; thus the man-eating plant has a maw out of *Jaws*, and the heavy is a sadistic dentist extracted from *Marathon Man*.

Yet whatever else a musical may or may not have, a decent score is a *sine qua non*, and that is precisely what this *Little Shop* lacks—unless we are meant to count the score as one of its horrors. Howard Ashman (book, lyrics, direction) is new to me; Alan Menken (music) is remembered chiefly, if at all, for *God Bless You, Mr. Rosewater*, which is best forgotten. Knowledgeable sources tell me that any number of rock groups have been despoiled by Mr. Menken; my untutored ears caught only a fairly undifferentiated shuttling between cacophony and monotony. The Ashman lyrics tend to self-destruct, inducing, on the relatively rare occasions when neither their delivery nor the accompanying din obliterates them, instant oblivion.

Mr. Ashman has done better by the book, though, which contains some genuinely funny ideas, even if often insufficiently developed, and some clever lines well handled by a cast in which only Franc Luz (in a number of roles, all of which he makes pretty much identical) fails to satisfy. The story concerns a down-and-out flower shop on skid row, whose Jewish florist, Mushnik, *kvetches* while his masochistic salesgirl, Audrey, nurses various debilities inflicted on her by her dentist-cum-Hell's Angel lover, and while Seymour, his nebbishy factotum, breeds a small new plant that, out of hopeless love for Audrey, he names Audrey II. The plant begins to grow at a spectacular rate, making Seymour famous and Mushnik rich, and Audrey, though still manhandled, happier. The catch is that the plant craves meat, preferably human, as it presently announces in a jivey bass. The dialogue can stoop to Seymour's rejoinder to Audrey II's importunate "Feed me," "Shut your flytrap!," or rise to his declaration of love to Audrey I: "I always knew you were a nice girl underneath the bruises and the handcuffs."

The best performance comes, expectably, from the plant itself—as it grows in size, viciousness, and lethal appetite; as it is designed, with satanic bonhomie, by Martin P. Robinson; and as it is enacted kinetically by Mr. Robinson and vocally by Ron Taylor. But there is excellent work also from Lee Wilkof as the schnooky Seymour with ten green thumbs, Hy Anzell as the greedy Mushnik, and Ellen Greene as Audrey, though in her laudable effort to stay in character when singing—as a cross between a sotto voce Monroe and a Jewish-accented Judy Holliday—she often lets her lyrics become undecipherable. As the chorus, a trio of skid-row ethnics, Jennifer Leigh Warren, Sheila Kay Davis, and the improbably named Marlène Danielle are fun, although it wouldn't hurt if at least one of them were a looker.

There are sound production values from Edward Gianfrancesco (set), Craig Evans (lights), Sally Lesser (costumes), and Otts Munderloh (sound); only Edie Cowan's musical staging is lackluster. Ashman has directed competently; if only amid all that low camp there were an occasional bit of pointed parody, pertinent satire, or more offbeat wit!

A Midsummer Night's Dream

A Midsummer Night's Dream is customarily a one-ass comedy. In Central Park, the director, James Lapine, has upped the ante and encouraged or allowed *three* actors to make asses of themselves, while most of the others, including Bottom, emerge half-assed. Mr. Lapine has the kind of sensibility that accords well with, say, *March of the Falsettos* and his own rather fey *Twelve Dreams*, but the more resolutely heterosexual temper of the *Dream* does not seem congenial to his approach.

No male or female in this production appears to have a genuine (i.e., noncampy) craving, or even love-hate, for his or her opposite number, but there are strangely homosexual touchings, rubbings, and gropings scattered throughout the action. The play was, after all, a kind of epithalamium written, most likely, for a high-born wedding, with Elizabeth I (not just any old queen) in attendance, yet nowhere here is a nuptial spirit discernible. Theseus and Hippolyta are seen as less at court than in a divorce court; Oberon and Titania seem to inhabit different mythologies; and the four Athenian lovers, though eventually dressed (like everyone else) in white *Star Trek* outfits, might be contemplating not marriage but a puckish round-robin tennis tournament. The period, incidentally, is no period at all: modern, Elizabethan, Rombergian, and (in the case of Oberon, who looks like a sixties Chingachgook), some Haight-Ashbury version of Fenimore Cooperland.

There are liberties taken with the text, but that's the least of it. What, for instance, is the purpose of having an already naturally homely actress (Marcell Rosenblatt), made rock-bottom repellent by makeup and costume, play Puck as a hee-hawing, bowleggedly scurrying, misshapen imp, propelled, it would seem, by bursts of flatulence issuing from his mouth and delivering lines as if spitting out beer gone flat? (Ass No. 1.) Why have Oberon (William Hurt), looking like the least of the Mohicans, act zonked out of his mind, spacing out his poetry with rampantly ornery pauses and asinine snorts or hisses, and throwing in capriciously meaningless emphases like a backfiring Yamaha while pounding the ground with his feet? (Ass No. 2.) And why should Hermia (Deborah Rush) be played as a croaking hillbilly, mindlessly braying out her verse—clearly a straggler from *Pump Boys and Dinettes*? (Ass No. 3.)

Many others are almost as hard to take. Philostrate (Ricky Jay), the majordomo, is turned into a mountebank performing conjuring and juggling tricks for a director who clearly does not trust (or fathom) Shakespeare's magic. (Mr. Jay, too, indulges in a constant neighing laugh.) Theseus (James Hurdle) is listless and lackluster, Egeus (Ralph Drischell) merely routine. Demetrius (Rick Lieberman) is a silly lout with pimples all over his performance; Lysander (Kevin Conroy), though much better looking, sounds and acts only slightly better. Bottom the Weaver (Jeffrey DeMunn), looking, along with the other mechanicals, like a cross between a factory worker and a hippie, is played broadly but without true humor, let alone pathos, as if in fear of offending the textile workers' union. Flute,

Snug, and Snout lack all distinction, and Michele Shay is, despite a pretty face, an inept Titania who speaks unpoetically (and with strong remnants of a black accent), moves awkwardly for a fairy queen, and conveys little feeling, human or fairyish.

That leaves, on the credit side, only the following: Christine Baranski, whose Helena is deeply, easefully funny yet also touching, even if, in the later scenes, she becomes repetitious and overdone; Steve Vinovich, whose Quince, humdrum at first, turns hilarious during the play within the play; J. Patrick O'Brien, whose nicely crapulent and befogged Starveling becomes, as Moon, a oneman syzygy; and Diane Venora, whose handsome Hippolyta triumphs, with poise and dignity, over Lapine's absurd staging, most notably when she must cavort semi-nude with Oberon (?!) through Hermia's dream (no doubt something to do with Lapine's sophomoric Jungianizing). Miss Venora, moreover, exhibits a speech free from both regionalism and fake Britishness, admirably suited for American Shakespeare.

There are other virtues. Heidi Landesman has designed—or, rather, landscaped—the stage into an enchanted glade with real flowers on grassy knolls, a bubbling mere, ground fog, and, farther off, real shrubs and trees in nature's own sweet, casual disarray; and Frances Aronson has lighted it well enough to be fit for a *féerie* at the Sun King's Versailles. Allen Shawn has composed atypical yet delightfully apt music, somewhat less good vocally than orchestrally, but nice enough all round, albeit not served impeccably by either orchestra or singers. Less felicitous is Graciela Daniele's choreography, which, though devised for nondancers, may carry nondancing too far. Worst is Randy Barcelo's costuming, about as magical as an end-of-summer sale at an unchic junk shop, and with fairies gotten up (and directed) as something out of not *A Midsummer Night's Dream* but *Marat/Sade*.

Chalk up most, if not all, the blame to Mr. Lapine. Herewith three samples of his crassness. When Puck first sees the sleeping Hermia, he exclaims, "Pretty soul!" Lapine has Puck lift Hermia's skirt, seemingly examine her pudenda, and then intone his (her? its?) "Pretty soul!" While watching from the sidelines what fools these mortals be, Oberon and Puck assume a few select positions from the *Kamasutra*. When Flute starts to speak Thisbe's lines in his usual voice, Quince promptly squeezes his testicles and out comes a perfect castrato's falsetto. This is the level of much of the directorial invention. And, oh yes, the hunting hounds brought on are not, as

is customary, an elegant brace of greyhounds but a couple of wad-
dling bassets. Another low trick.

Ghosts

"In none of my other plays," wrote Ibsen in a letter of January 6,
1882, "is the author such an outsider, so entirely absent, as in this
one." The play was his new *Ghosts*; what he meant by his absence
was that he did not have a spokesman in it, that he did not take
sides—a manifest lie, as Strindberg lost no time pointing out in one
of *his* letters: "Isn't Ibsen being a coward in his explanation?" Obviously, Ibsen was against the bourgeois and religious constraints
and hypocrisies, high and low, whether Pastor Manders's or Jacob
Engstrand's; obviously, he was for the emancipation Mrs. Alving
and her son, Oswald, tried to fight for, only to be defeated: she by
the role of wife and mother, he by his diseased body and mind.

But in a deeper, unintentional sense, Ibsen was blurting out the
truth: *his* genius is almost totally absent from *Ghosts*. Among his
major plays it is the weakest: there is no real conflict in it; the real
action it mostly in the past and also in the future, but hardly in the
present; the exposition with which Ibsen ingeniously suffuses the
early parts of his plays here eats up virtually the whole work; there is
no clear protagonist and antagonist or set of antagonists; everything
is as fanatically compressed and speeded up as in an old Hollywood
two-reeler, only these problems do not lend themselves to acceleration. Tragedy cannot be played in farce tempo.

Yes, *Ghosts* is an important play, but its importance is socio-
historic rather than literary and dramatic. The problems of repres-
sive societies, marriages of convenience, libertinism, inherited
syphilis, euthanasia, and prostitution (Engstrand's sailors' hostel
will, in fact, be a brothel) are fundamentally human, but they are
crammed into the play pell-mell, they are fudged with allusiveness and circumlocution because of contemporary censorship and
prudery (and still they got Ibsen into trouble), and they prevent
the play from having a center, a central theme, central action, even
central characters. For, in a sense, Regina is just as tragic as Mrs.
Alving or Oswald, yet she hardly gets a chance in the writing. And
there is no real showdown between Pastor Manders and Mrs. Alving, only a gap that extends across the decades.

But, alas, it was typical of Roger Stevens to pick a man like Ralph G. Allen as his artistic consultant at the Kennedy Center, and for the two of them to pick *Ghosts*. (Allen conceived and wrote most of *Sugar Babies*, which makes him eminently qualified to be the arbiter of culture.) If we had a lot of good Ibsen going, *Ghosts* would earn its niche; but what about the remarkable new translation of the sublime *Brand* by the distinguished poet Geoffrey Hill—*Brand*, which has never been done professionally hereabouts? We haven't even had a decent production of Ibsen's supreme masterpiece, *The Master Builder*, in a troll's age. And when was the last serious try at *Rosmersholm*?

All right, however—*Ghosts* it is. Do we then get, Liv Ullmann to play Mrs. Alving? The actress has been superb in Swedish films by Ingmar Bergman and Jan Troell, two of the world's great directors. But her American movies (save *Zandy's Bride*, for Troell) were disasters, and all her American stage appearances have been, to put it mildly, mistakes. Is it that Miss Ullmann needs a genius director? Is it that she is less effective on the stage than on the screen? Is it an English-language problem? To an extent, certainly. We cannot have Mrs. Alving speaking in a pronounced Norwegian accent when Manders deploys fancy British stage English and the other actors range from high to low American. The five players of *Ghosts* must be an ensemble: imagine a hand whose five fingers came each from a different animal. At times, Miss Ullmann can barely be understood.

Or is the part wrong for her? At 43, Miss Ullmann is old enough to have *been* Mrs. Alving, but perhaps not old enough to play her. The actress has a light, girlish quality, wonderfully suited to reveal underlying patches of moving womanliness, but she seems unsuited to convey an older, dry, strong woman who has turned her repressed femininity into efficiency and achievement, though always letting her husband take the credit—and here, by the way, Ibsen is no great help, for there is much *talk* of her efficiency, but what we *see* is a woman with no head for business.

In any case, Miss Ullmann is best at portraying either wide-eyed peasant innocence, as in the three films she did for Troell, or troubled modem young womanhood, beset by fears, uncertainties, neuroses—and sometimes succumbing to them—as in the Bergman films. None of this has any bearing on Mrs. Alving. Ullmann-style, she emerges cute, coquettish, audience-ogling, or merely bewildered; this is not a woman whom self-denial has whittled down to bone-hardness. We do not get the irony-coated desperateness and the last hope for fulfillment through her son, whom she overindulges and idealizes. And given her present hairstyle, costume, and makeup, Miss Ullmann forfeits even most of her good looks.

John Neville, who also took over the direction, is a polished, extremely wellspoken Pastor Manders, perfect for regional repertory in Nottingham or Halifax (Canada), where he scored some of his major successes. He turns Manders, who must embody the sinisterly oppressive forces of Lutheran piety and Nordic bourgeois propriety, into a kind of Canon Chasuble, full of funny singsong and amusing hesitancies, as well as drolly histrionic gestures, but no strength or bite. There is no sense of the unyielding antagonism that, under the civilized conversation, pits him against Mrs. Alving's progressive ideas. We get no sense of powerful ideologies locked in a combat of strong but flawed wills; instead, an invisible stream carries along the grotesque husk of a Manders and the toy paper boat of a Mrs. Alving—the one gliding laughably, the other wistfully bobbing up and down.

Edward Binns turns Engstrand, the expansive but slimily manipulative carpenter, into a merely irritating nonentity, and a very contemporary New York one. Kevin Spacey makes a good stab at Oswald, but there is far too much of a nice, healthy, sane American youth about him, and little of the doomed artist, the victim of his father's venereal disease, burning up and out before our eyes. As Regina, Jane Murray is on the right track, but has difficulty finding the proper blend of peasant shrewdness and acquired ladylikeness: the true coarseness, fake submissiveness, and veneer of sophistication are all there, but fail to coalesce. She also lacks that ineffable quality that would make us really care. And Arthur Kopit, in his otherwise impressive and highly actable adaptation, has erred by giving her too many French tags and thus making her ridiculous.

The play was initially directed by John Madden, a gifted young director, and his being supplanted by Mr. Neville speaks, I suspect, poorly for the person or persons responsible for it. What we have now is typical provincial-rep blocking and pacing (some of Mrs. Alving's countercrosses are downright embarrassing), without the slightest originality or distinction. And, this once, even the excellent Theoni V. Aldredge was, so to speak, asleep at the swatch: her costumes vainly try to be both inconspicuous and arresting. Kevin Rupnik's set has the unfortunate quality of looking too much like a set and nowhere near enough Norwegian, moody, handsome, besides not even making good use of space. Equally bad is Martin Aronstein's lighting, which cannot even make a devastating fire or an even more terrifying, cruelly ironic sunrise seem the least bit painterly, poetic, or dramatic, all of which Ibsen requires.

The production was a tremendous hit in Washington, which doesn't surprise me at all. What we've got is a good new version; what we need is someone to produce, design, direct, and play it.

A Doll's Life

Here is what happened to Ibsen's Nora afterward. When she slammed that door on the uncomprehending Torvald, she apparently developed this thing about doors. Or, more precisely, about slamming them behind her. First she took up with an impecunious musician, Otto, who was also the composer of the great unproduced Norwegian opera *Loki and Baldur*, and worked as a waitress to support them. But all the time, in the miserable garret they shared, he had her eye on this very substantial door. When, through the good offices of Johan, a barrister and a client at her restaurant, she managed to get an audition for Otto's opera and her lover gives her only 5 out of the 50 kroner he receives as an advance, she exclaims, "Scratch the artist and find a Torvald!" and gets down to the real business of voluptuously slamming that door behind her.

She is next seen working under harrowing sweatshop conditions in a foul herring cannery (when not being jailed for making feminist speeches), but Johan comes through again and gets her out of it and into the bed of Eric, a cannery owner, shipping magnate, and millionaire roué. Though she relishes him sexually, she also uses him to learn about becoming a tycoon, while also getting him to make the sweatshops less sweaty. But, mostly, Eric has this tall, magisterial, spoiling-to-beslammed door on which Nora has her eye. So, when Eric comes up with an additional mistress, the perfumery salesgirl Jacqueline, and announces that he wants Nora to be "decorative, amusing, and compliant," Nora can exultantly do her thing and slam his door behind her.

She and Jacqueline start their own perfume business with Johan as a silent partner—Johan who has already helped her in a number of legal and business ways; money starts pouring in, and the freshly divorced Johan is openly pining for her. After a brief misunderstanding, during which Johan is forced into kissing the arms of a certain Camilla, Nora and Johan start keeping company, though we never get to see his door, and all goes well until Johan, a champion of men's liberation *avant la lettre*, starts cooking dinner, offering to fetch Nora's slippers, and proposing marriage. At this point Nora yearns to be with her children, and maybe with Torvald, all over again—in fact, to revisit the first door she slammed, the kind of thing a liberated woman never forgets.

So, even though she does not exactly slam Johan's door—leaving it, rather, with an equivocal quasi-promise, expectantly ajar in a sort of exitus interruptus—she rushes back to her husband and kids, who, initially wary, begin to warm to her. As the stage lights dim—obligingly expunging that fatal door from Nora's purview—Torvald and Nora settle down to a spotlighted table with a "We must talk!" uttered portentously as they embark on the great male-female dialogue leading to a more equable future. Concomitantly, I think, they may discuss therapy for her portophilia. So ends the new musical *A Doll's Life*, contributing handsomely to making a critic's existence a dog's life.

Betty Comden and Adolph Green, a usually talented pair of collaborators, have written the presumptuous and execrable book and the scarcely better lyrics, which include things like (I quote from memory, my hands having trembled too much) "Who is this elf / Who inhabits my body? / I know now it's myself." Then there is the music by Larry Grossman, which is like two bars of Sondheim stretched on the rack. It proceeds by quaint little premonitory lurches (another Sondheim device) that irrupt on the dialogue and gradually coalesce into a treacly texture that is then used over and over again until you cannot tell a new song from a reprise.

I forgot to mention that the whole thing is awash with watered-down Pirandello, what with a cast of present-day actors rehearsing *A Doll House*, which then turns into *A Doll's Life*, but with whatever actors are temporarily sidelined by the plot often becoming a commenting chorus, sometimes in period, sometimes in modern dress. To add further enriching complexity, Harold Prince, the director, and Larry Fuller, his choreographer, have devised a dance ensemble of three women (one in white, one in black, one in red) and one man in black who are meant to look madly Munchian and punctuate the ends of many scenes with something between dancing and posturing, though much closer to the latter.

The gifted partners in design, Timothy O'Brien and Tazeena

Firth, have come a cropper for the first time within memory with rather atrocious sets built around an Art Nouveau catwalk bisected by an Edvard Munch gazebo against a cyclorama of expressionist waves in *fauve* colors. The catwalk may be a legacy of *Sweeney Todd*—Mr. Prince does not let go of an idea lightly. Ken Billington has tried hard to make his lighting interesting, managing mostly to call undue attention to it. Prince's direction is routine, except for one clever idea (again involving doors!) whereby an opera is seen from the vestibule of a set of boxes, and whenever a loge door opens for a few seconds, the ludicrous operatic dumb play becomes, yet more ludicrously, audible. A swell idea that palls somewhere around the eighteenth time.

Nora is mugged by Betsy Joslyn, who is too cute by half for even the macaroon-munching Nora, much less the liberated career woman. She has a way of leaning forward into her lines, or into the audience, of moving with a dumpy gracelessness, and of not so much singing as stridulating into the portals of our ears. She is also gifted with a large, flat, round, and exceedingly smug face that mostly smiles and smiles, like a happy dishpan in a Brillo commercial. In the triple role of an actor-director, Torvald, and Johan, George Hearn does better, without exactly becoming a triple threat. Edmund Lyndeck is suitably repellent as the icy Eric, but Peter Gallagher carries Otto's oafishness too far. (The authors' operatic parody, by the way, must rank among the rankest spoofs ever.) The others go through the motions, with only Penny Orloff's fine voice occasionally cutting through the tedium. *A Doll's Life* is the kind of show that could make passionate door-slammers of us all.

Cats

If you like lavishness, if you like opulence, if you like kitty-litterature at its grandest, *Cats* is surely your thing. The moment you enter the Winter Garden, you are transported into a world of junk sculpture by the cubic yard under a dome of many-colored stars that glitter on and off, viridescent cat's eyes emblazoned on the dark, a Spielbergian flying saucer of colored lights rising slowly above the stage, a semi-abstract townscape backdrop featuring a huge (and soon to be revealed as Jellicle) moon, Andrew Lloyd Webber's brashly sassy overture pouring at you from an invisible orchestra, and from every part of the theater (high and low) cats, cats, cats scampering, scurrying, scrabbling, and slithering across the auditorium and onto the stage (though there is scarcely a difference between those two areas, the whole world being a catwalk).

Somewhere between $5 million and $7 million dollars (we hear) has been spent on creating this ambience that can vie with the Place de la Bastille on July 14 and the carnival in Rio, and, presto magico, the fur is flying. As you know, the words are from the verses of T. S. Eliot, with some additions by two lesser poets, Trevor Nunn, the show's director, and Richard Stilgoe. As you also know, these are mostly Eliot's Practical Cats poems, slight but endearing, plus a few similarly whimsical pieces from the *Nachlass*, and the already famous "Memory," concocted from various early poems with some questionable additives. But Nunn, Lloyd Webber, and the rest have molded this material into a semblance of a plot full of Christian esc(h)atology as it might have been preached in the catacombs.

The show has apparently gained in grandeur since its London version, but it has lost one thing: the English accents. That old Tom from St. Louis always strove to out-British the British, and these verses fitted themselves to the British scene and the British tongue. They are somehow less funny with genuine American or fake British accents, though, with one or two exceptions, the New York cast, even when dancing up a cataclysm, manage to enunciate Old Possum's verses with exemplary elocution, and Lloyd Webber and David Cullen have toned down the orchestrations so as not to drown out the words.

And what of the tunes? In his usual fashion, Lloyd Webber has contrived melodies that vary from the catchy to the merely serviceable, from the vaguely Puccinian to the less categorizably derivative, but very much—including even the mercilessly milked hit, "Memory" purrloined. Never have I had such a yen to hire a private tune detective to track down the provenance of these songs, but mongrels though they be, they manage to work as a score. They blend in with John Napier's splendid scenery and costumes, Gillian Lynne's unspectacular but adequate choreography (particularly as executed by some lightsome, high-flying dancers), David Hersey's endlessly imaginative and show-stopping lighting, and Trevor Nunn's canny and effervescent direction into a delightful albeit trivial *Gesamtmostkunstwerk*.

You will enjoy scenic effects to elate you, stage (and auditorium) movement to keep your eyeballs rolling every which way, talented players galore to thrill you (only one obnoxious performance, by Wendy Edmead), and sundry cunning devices to keep you eagerly expectant, with your expectations almost always astonishingly gratified. But there is, finally, too much dazzlement. As (in a chorus from "The Rock") Eliot himself said: "In our rhythm of earthly life we tire of the light." Too much insubstantial smart-aleckiness, too much costly gimcrackery, too many sequined inventions and spangled conceits, and all those orgasms of light all around us—for the first time in my life I found myself agreeing with Jerzy Grotowski's notion of a "poor theater." As on certain jukeboxes of yore you could buy three minutes of silence, I yearned to purchase a square foot of ungimmicked-up austerity.

Cats, Sheridan Morley has written, "is about the possibilities of theater," and with such a caressingly, insinuatingly, ferally feline cast, the pussybilities, at any rate, are limitless. I must single out as my particular favorites Donna Ming, Harry Groener, Bonnie Simmons, and Stephen Hanan, though there are at least half a dozen others who are scarcely behind them. Betty Buckley, as the aging beauty Grizabella, keeps the pathos within bounds and sings "Memory" (damn it, where was that tune lifted from, anyway?) with commendably understated wistfulness. And Ken Page, as Old Deuteronomy (the song about him is the best in the score), manages to be as massive as Blake's God and is nicely balanced by Timothy Scott's winsomely whirling devil of a Mr. Mistoffelees (consistently misspelled in the program).

There is something for everyone—even dog lovers—in *Cats*: a kind of whiskered Disneyland full of sound and furry. You may justly feel that it is slight and overblown, that it is wasteful (the money spent on it could have kept all the starving cats of China in heavy cream for a century or two) and terribly arch, but you cannot help experiencing surges of childish jubilation, as cleverness after sleek cleverness rubs against your shins.

Plenty

David Hare once observed that his plays were intended as puzzles for the audience to solve. And what good fun it was to puzzle out the meanings of such enigmatic but amusing works as *Slag* and

Knuckle, or even the less successful *Teeth 'n' Smiles*. But *Plenty*—
which reaches us four years after the London premiere—though far
more disciplined than his previous offerings, is not a conundrum,
merely a jigsaw puzzle with the pieces all too knowingly scrambled.
In the end, after milking this purposive disarray for its maximum
ironic value, Hare himself unriddles everything for us. We are left as
spectators of not so much a play as a display: impressed, sometimes
entertained, often dazzled. But quite unmoved.

Susan Traherne, the heroine, was a wartime hero at seventeen,
doing undercover work for Britain in occupied France. Men she
loved were tortured and disappeared. Yet a great hope was being
bravely hatched: a future of plenty, a cornucopia of justice and well-
being. But bourgeois plenty is moral poverty, and it drives Susan
crazy. A try at an illegitimate child by the solidly working-class
Mick fails; he becomes a liability, and she almost shoots him. Raymond, a young man in the foreign service, whom she met in Belgium during an amorous holiday with a fellow wartime hero that
ended bizarrely, straightens out her problems and, out of gratitude,
she marries him. But she has been institutionalized, and her madness—even if largely a passion for a better world and a nostalgia for
the idealistic past—is still a madness and, over a fifteen-year period,
drags the decent Raymond down with it.

There is much more to *Plenty*, of course, and a variety of minor
characters more or less integrated into the proceedings. Yet the
point is not so much the story as the cunning way in which it is
fragmented and skips back and forth in time. Some of this is to keep
us guessing, surprised, and a bit bewildered; some of it is to underscore, often heavily, certain ironies about Britain's history, betrayed
aspirations, and decline. As in all his plays, Hare keeps, directly or
indirectly, jocularly or bitterly, excoriating his country; here it is
chiefly done by canny juxtapositions that, alas, come at the expense
of cumulative strength: too many fragments, too much empty space
around them, and a disorienting inconsistency of tone.

For we go from documentary realism to fanciful satire, from
scenes that are pure drawing-room comedy to others that drip
with gall. Absurdism waits in the wings, sometimes letting its
toes protrude; ironically understated faces stick out a homilet-
ic tongue. Finally, it is Hare's virtue that does him in: the cool,
cerebral sardonicism that unpassions both the attacks on post-
war "normality" and Susan's "abnormal" reactions becomes, in
the end, self-defeating. Somewhere between Shaw and Osborne,

Pinter and Rattigan, the play's backside lands on the floor.

Moreover, I am tired of the axiomatic, unanalyzed proposition that a bad society causes individual insanity. True, Hare at last permits the long-put-upon Raymond a denunciation of Susan's selfishness and living in the past, but it's too little and too late. Worse yet, the exhilaration of the war years is presented in terms of an Errol Flynn movie—insufficient counterweight to all that postwar indignation. Yet it must be conceded that Hare knows how to write a scene, a line, an epigram, and that his darts—hurled at a variety of figures chiefly from the diplomatic world—are not merely poisoned but also go straight to the mark.

As his own director, Hare sensibly provides a somewhat static, abstract, pictorial quality, not unlike the famous artworks blown up to huge, even cycloramic, size that his splendid designer, John Gunter, places behind the actors. Life becomes a sequence of moral tableaus—perhaps Hogarthian etchings—to be indelibly imprinted on our minds. Here it would help if the entire cast were authentically British, even though the American contingent struggles valiantly to stiffen its upper lip and Anglicize its utterance. Kate Nelligan, repeating her London performance, is a very fine Susan, a role that, unfortunately, would need genius to redeem it. Her best support comes from Ellen Parker, as an off-the-wall friend, and George Martin, as a tragicomic diplomat. Both Edward Herrmann (Raymond) and Daniel Gerroll (Mick) are winning, but without that extra something that makes a performance definitive. Some of the lesser parts are handled inadequately by Bill Moor, Johann Carlo, and Dominic Chianese.

Gunter's ingenious set design (I won't give away its plot) is condignly supplemented by Arden Fingerhut's lighting and Jane Greenwood's costumes. Nick Bicht supplies an interesting background musical assemblage. Interesting, in fact, is the word for *Plenty*: it tickles our funny bone, nerves, and sense of the theatrical; too bad that the heart—and sometimes even the head—remains unengaged.

Edmond

Edmond is Probably David Mamet's best play in quite a long time, which may not be saying all that much but at least proves that there is life in the young fellow yet. Edmond Burke (named so, presumably, to establish his ultraconservativeness) walks out on his wife, with whom he has become "spiritually and sexually" bored, and proceeds to become engulfed in a cross between a binge and a nightmare. He has numerous encounters—mostly unpleasant, if not downright vicious—with pimps, whores, shills, sleazy hotel porters and pawnbrokers, and other assorted lowlifes. Foiled, swindled, robbed, and beaten up, the worm turns, and Edmond wallops a black pimp who threatens him with a knife. He then accompanies a waitress home, has sex with her, and, exasperated by her delusions of being an actress and unwillingness to face the truth, works himself up into homicide with a knife he bought for "self-defense."

Edmond winds up in jail, where his cell mate, a brawny black, forces him into oral and passive anal intercourse. Rejecting the cold comfort of the prison chaplain and scorning God, Edmond embraces his imprisonment and sexual slavery with the first happiness we see him achieve, and we leave him, in the double-decker bunk with his lover and master, hopefully confronting existential and eschatological problems. The philosophy of this double-dyed bunkum is summed up in Edmond's repeated "Every fear hides a wish." The two things our hero was most afraid of, loss of liberty and blacks, have turned out to fulfill his deepest cravings. A dubious lesson from Freud, still more dubiously applied, *Edmond* fails as a play because it cannot make us experience and share its thesis. But, except when its dialogue Pinterizes blatantly, it works scene by scene, thanks to harrowing spareness, eerie exoticism, and the odd patch of racily dim-witted dialogue.

This Goodman Theatre-of-Chicago production, starkly staged by the group's director, Gregory Mosher, has traveled well. Colin Stinton is sublimely average—and, therefore, flawless—as Edmond; the others are not only good but also adept at handling several parts each. Costumes and scenery are rightly inconspicuous, but Kevin Rigdon's lighting is a powerfully felt presence. This is the third not uninteresting play in three weeks to come to us from Chicago, proving there's life in the old city yet.

Quartermaine's Terms

Quartermaine's Terms, by Simon Gray and now at New Haven's
Long Wharf, is a wonderfully restrained, irreverently humane,
wryly tender play. A mixture of wild but not rudderless humor
and wrenching but comedically muted pain, it is the kind of work
that, if only there were more of its kind, could help the commercial
theater out of its present slump. Gray can reconcile the needs of
large, uncerebral audiences with the requirements of a discriminating, even finicky, enclave of selective theatergoers. Just as the play
keeps us suspended between laughter and melancholy, so does it
meld primal (almost primitive) emotions with fastidious speculations about the compromises, contradictions, numbing paradoxes
of existence, and allows each spectator to enjoy the show according
to his intellectual means.

St. John Quartermaine is the worst but most amiable teacher at
a seedy but undaunted school of English for foreigners in Cambridge, England. A chap who distinguishes himself from the wallpaper chiefly by speaking now and then, he uses his commonplace
words and deeds as a ludicrous and wistful way to meet every blow
life metes out with equanimity. Quartermaine's slow but unstoppa-
ble slide into inefficiency, loneliness, nullity takes place in the staff
room of the Cull-Loomis School, where the other teachers jokily
patronize, cheerfully exploit, and ultimately ignore the poor fellow.
No doubt about it, his endless decency is very nearly matched by his
obtuseness, but what of his gift for reinterpreting slights, slaps, and
catastrophes (and there are plenty of them, on- and offstage) as footling stumbling-stones to be serenely risen above—if not, indeed,
blessings in disguise? By lifting myopic meliorism to the level of
quixotic magnanimity, Quartermaine, though no Cambridge don,
becomes a sort of greater, Cervantian, Don.

Gray's fineness is encapsulated in the play's very title. St. John
(pronounced Sinjohn) Quartermaine gets his name—not entirely
ironically—from both the desert saint and Rider Haggard's explorer
hero; he is followed through five or six terms of teaching, including
the term, or termination, of his career. But we are also offered his
character in terms of his terms: his language, with its insipidly jovial
banalities, and his stipulations vis-à-vis the world—his trading of
empathy and obligingness for general forbearance, his gratitude for
the space of one staff-room armchair in which to luxuriate in life's

meager handouts. His colleagues—an assortment of self-serving mediocrities and self-dramatizing neurotics, ranging from unloved wife and mother-hagridden spinster to deluded would-be novelist and accident-prone eager beaver—condescend to him, unaware of how necessary he is to their delusions of superiority.

Fairest to our hero is Eddie Loomis, who, with his lover, the always offstage Thomas Cull, runs the school as a reasonably enlightened fief, balancing despotism with exasperated tolerance for Quartermaine—unlike the seemingly sympathetic colleague, Windscape, who, upon succeeding Eddie as headmaster, begins by having St. John's head. Eddie is, by the way, a most compassionate treatment of an aging, fussy homosexual; but Gray brings like comprehension to all his characters, and the funny-sad ironies in which they are mired. Take this exchange between two dissimilar teachers who both happened to spend some vacation time in Sheffield: "We were doing a tour of out-of-the-way urban domestic architecture. What were you doing there?" "I was attending my aunt's funeral, as a matter of fact." A happy occasion for Meadle, the second speaker, who also found Daphne, his future wife, there. Surprising everyone for once, Quartermaine inquires if she has good legs. To which Meadle, huffily: "Daphne's legs happen to be my sort of legs," as St. John stares, puzzled, at Meadle's trousered limbs. We're in the hands of a true dramatist.

Under Kenneth Frankel's uncannily—or just cannily—right direction, all perform handsomely in the good design of David Jenkins (set), Bill Walker (costumes), and Pat Collins (lights). Dana Ivey, Anthony Heald, and John Cunningham are perfect, with Caroline Lagerfelt next. And crowning all is Remak Ramsey's flawless Quartermaine; if his and Gray's understatedly heartbreaking ending does not get you where you live, either you or I don't know what theater—and art—is.

A View From the Bridge; Painting Churches

What's all the fuss about *A View From the Bridge*, the play and its current revival, brought to Broadway from New Haven's Long Wharf, where, it must be assumed, they know all about longshoremen? Arthur Miller's play was first produced as a one-act tragedy in 1955 (complete with vestigial tragic chorus in the person of a lawyer, Alfieri, bearing the name of Italy's greatest tragic dramatist), then painfully stretched to a full-length play in 1956. The grandiose choric passages, which proved an embarrassment, were pared down; even so, Alfieri has to be the voice of history, the voice of poetry, and the voice of legal advice when he finally gets off his cothurnus and into the play. And what actor can sing trios with himself?

Eddie Carbone (black as coal?) is a Brooklyn longshoreman who, childless, has brought up Catherine, the orphaned niece of his wife, Beatrice, as his own daughter. Now that she is seventeen, he at first—stubbornly—refuses to let her take a good job, wear high heels, go out on proper dates, and—finally and frantically—to marry Rodolpho (the Italian spelling, of course, would be "Rodolfo"), who, with his elder brother, Marco, is a "submarine" (illegal immigrant), secretly sheltered by and working with Eddie, a distant relative of the Calabrian brethren. Rodolpho and the paterfamilias Marco are manifestly fine fellows, and the only reason Eddie opposes the marriage, and goes to absurd and ridiculous lengths to make Rodolpho out to be an opportunist and a homosexual, is that he himself unconsciously lusts after Catherine, as everyone in the play could have realized long ago, except that without this dread and drawn-out revelation there wouldn't be any play. Eddie betrays the submarines to the Immigration Service, and when, on top of that, he tries to knife the vengeful Marco, kills himself in the scuffle. Everyone else's life, we are to infer, is in ruins. The play, certainly, is a shambles.

Like *Death of a Salesman*, this is no tragedy—any more than lusting for your wife's niece, as the play keeps portentously hinting, is incest. That a middle-aged man, unfulfilled in marriage, should harbor a yen for his pretty young ward is, at best, the stuff of drama, and even that only if the author's talent can make it so. For tragedy, in any case, a writer needs a powerful philosophical vision and an exaltedly poetic language. Miller has neither, only some vague sympathy for "common people" who cannot express themselves properly (a most understandable fellow feeling), and Eddie's lingo consists chiefly of confusing "who" and "which" and mangling relative clauses. The best Miller can do by way of poetry (confined, incidentally, to the mouth of Alfieri) is to say that Eddie's eyes are like tunnels, though, oddly, it is Miller who has the tunnel vision.

Heroic stature? If Willy Loman was too short, Eddie Carbone

is positively a pygmy. Nothing he says or does shows particular insight, depth of feeling, nobility of aspiration, originality of vision, lyricism of utterance. He is not even heroic in reverse: satanic, Sadian, Machiavellian, a supermadman. He is, however, notably obtuse; if he were an angle, he'd have easily 179 degrees. Tony Lo Bianco, who plays him, and Arvin Brown (artistic director of the Long Wharf), who directed him, elected to solve the problem by turning Eddie, especially in the first half, into a figure of farce—an Italian Archie Bunker. Lo Bianco, a good comedian in real comedy, carries on like something between a man bitten by a tarantula and a wind-up toy that won't wind down. Not stopping for a fraction of a second, he blithers, blusters, jigs, and jerks; the arms never cease sawing the air, while the footwork would be the envy of a jittery boxer. This performance makes St. Vitus's dance look, in comparison, like a slinky tango.

Of course, it doesn't work. If the poetry isn't poetic, the tragedy isn't tragic, the Italians aren't Italian (no priests, religion, large families), must the hero even be deprived of intended heroism? Miller has called him in some ways "wondrous and humane" (would any good writer use "wondrous" seriously?) because of his "sacrifice of himself for his conception, however misguided, of right, dignity, justice." Other interpreters have tried to play Eddie as seriously and dignifiedly as possible, with small but at least some returns; as a manic marionette, he is merely a poor, if not indeed ethnic, joke. Even Lo Bianco's accent carries Italianese to ludicrous heights, and when the actor and director finally try to shift gears, the result is only a kind of melodrama verging on slapstick.

Brown's direction is disastrous throughout: schematic, rhythmless, flatfooted. For instance, when extras appear onstage, they do so not like people behaving naturally, with the asymmetry of spontaneity, but like actors coming in from their backstage poker games to preordained positions in unison, and cursing their lot as walk-ons under their breath. Stage movement is either minimal or stilted, and even the big homosexual kiss is delivered in a crouching position for minimum efficacy, with the three actors forming a schematic straight line downstage.

There is fine work from Rose Gregorio as Beatrice and James Hayden as Rodolpho. As Catherine, Saundra Santiago tries desperately hard, but is utterly charmless throughout. As Marco, Alan Feinstein is fake through and through, even his silent fury emerging somehow cutesy, to say nothing of his Russian accent. As Alfieri,

Robert Prosky begins by underplaying sensibly, but ends up pulling as many stops as anyone. Hugh Landwehr's Red Hook and Brooklyn Bridge look neither truly seedy nor oppressive, only like cheap scenery; Bill Walker's costumes and Ronald Wallace's lighting are adequate. But where is there anything remotely tragic in all this? Perhaps in Miller's intentions deluding themselves into believing that they are gloriously arrayed in tragedy, poetry, significance, when they are merely pitiful figurines gesticulating in their underwear.

   Painting Churches, by Tina Howe, is as surprising as its title. The Churches being painted turn out to be Gardner and Fanny Church, a Boston Brahmin couple. He is a distinguished poet sliding into dotage; she, his eccentric and giddy, but still fundamentally sane, wife. They have sold their Beacon Hill house and are packing up to move into a small Cotuit cottage. The painter is their reasonably batty daughter, Mags, who is beginning to make it as an artist in New York. She will do one last double portrait in the bare living room—wintry, though outside it is spring—and help with the packing. Before the inevitable "exeunt severally," there is to be some drinking and fighting, and quite a bit of reminiscing and mutual revelation. It is an old story, but, among these bluebloods and artists, it takes on an odd slant, more wistful and extravagant, that points private truth toward universality.

   Miss Howe, with all that authentic background behind her, with wit, sympathy, and a kind of devil-may-care *désinvolture* to spare, shows how curiously brilliance and naivety, politeness and intransigence, magnanimity and cattiness can cohabit in these three beings who exacerbate and sustain one another with their tenuous, inexact yet loving, outreach. In the first half, a comic, even absurdist, abandon prevails, with the emphasis on the trio's dottiness. Then, as Gardner becomes more senile and sweetly pathetic (as well as difficult) by the minute, the women reveal the strength beneath their bizarreness, the endurance under the flutteriness. The author has demonstrated in previous plays her ability to meld the grotesque and the touching; here the fusion glistens with the pride of a successful alloy. Occasional longueurs and exaggerations disappear into the overall iridescence; these gallant, outlandish people are irresistible.

   Thanks to good writing, sound casting, and unostentatiously sensitive direction by Carole Rothman, an inauspicious-seeming cast works victoriously together. As Gardner, Donald Moffat puts his stiffness to excellent use. Getting mad at sheafs of his papers dropping from his hands, laughing at old family jokes or dubious fellow Bostonians, berating his helpmate for mistreating his precious books, producing cocktails with sheepish glee, or reciting famous poems blissfully unaware they are not by him, he is by turns aware, semi-absent, or totally out of it with equal grandeur. Marion Seldes may dither a bit too much at first, but she soon infuses Fanny's flightiness with fortitude and a lover's bitterness that are finely wrought and greatly moving. And Frances Conroy is a believable Mags, adroitly juggling neuroses and determination, and keeping the least dashing role from becoming stagnant.

Modest but first-rate scenery by Heidi Landesman, lighting by Frances Aronson, costumes by Nan Cibula help make this Second Stage production an altogether rewarding event. There are depths in the seeming vagaries of *Painting Churches* undreamt of in the solid bathos of *A View From the Bridge*.

Moose Murders

The theater being in the sad shape it is in (and I don't mean this season only), selective patrons cannot even imagine what horrors reviewers are exposed to, night after nightmarish night. St. John of the Cross may have had an inkling when he wrote of the dark night of the soul, but even that was, for him, a *noche dichosa*; there was nothing lucky about the night (actually afternoon) on which I saw *Moose Murders*, which is as close as I ever hope to get to the bottomless pit. We critics tend to console ourselves during what seems less and less aptly named the intermission—"remission" would be nearer the mark—by bringing up (so to speak) the titles of earlier all-time lows. On this occasion, such previous contenders as *Marlowe* and *Cleavage* were cited, but the few hardy survivors of those disasters pronounced them painless compared to even the first act of *Moose Murders*. And none of us then had a notion of what the second act held in store.

This abysmally imbecile comedy-thriller takes place (took place—it closed after one supererogatory performance) at the Wild Moose Lodge, in a part of the Adirondacks located somewhere between the Himalayas and Patagonia, on a furibundly thunderstormy night with all bridges down and all communication with the civilized world, or mere sanity, severed. The lodge is run by one solitary Indian, Joe Buffalo Dance, who speaks pure Tonto, except when he takes off his braided Indian wig, at which times he lapses into his allegedly natural speech, a brogue so thick that the Gate Theatre wouldn't wish it on the Abbey. Stranded here is a husband-and-wife musical act: Snooks Keene, short of stature, skirt, and talent, who sings and wisecracks, and her blind husband, Howie, who accompanies her on the hand organ. They are strident, out of tune, and totally inept, but at least they didn't write *Moose Murders*. She jokes ("Go peel a scab!" she'll tell Nurse Dagmar, but I'm anticipating) while he falls all over the furniture. There being no trace of guests at the lodge, the act must have been hired to entertain the stuffed moose heads, which proliferate in all sizes from deer to elephant. There is also a non-eponymous stuffed goose, but then "Goose Murders" would read less well on a marquee.

The lodge has been acquired by the millionairess Hedda Holloway, who arrives with her entourage. Her husband, Sidney, who, since a fall from the roof, has become a total paralytic, swathed, mummy-like, in bandages from top to toe, and pushed about in a wheelchair when not forgotten outside in the pouring rain; his nurse, Dagmar, a huge, Nazi-style virago, in audacious front-and-rear décolletage; son Stinky, a brain-damaged dope fiend, whose one aim is to sleep with his mother, at whom he keeps lunging; Lauraine, the fluttery and anorectic elder daughter, accompanied by Nelson, her sad-sack, chip-on-the-shoulder husband; and, lastly, little daughter Gay, who, when she can briefly be prevented from tap-dancing, is told that her father is a vegetable (what did she think he was, blancmange?) and exclaims, "Like a lima bean? Gross me out!" It gradually emerges that there are three different cabals among these good folks, each hell-bent on liquidating the others for the sake of the Holloway fortune. And in mid-storm, the dismissed Buffalo Dance returns disguised as a moose, to join in the murderous fun.

In the course of an evening during which blind Howie gets a gun and shoots to kill and the mummy rises from the wheelchair to kick the moose in the privates, where two others have already kicked him, I naturally turned sleuth; to track down the perpetrators, I cannily scanned the program credits. The author is one Arthur Bicknell, "probably best known for *My Great Dead Sister...* produced... by the Production Company and directed by Norman René." That was a potent clue: over the years, there has been a steady stream of malodorous junk emanating from the Production Company and its artistic director, Norman René. *My Great Dead Sister* was a flop, but *Masterpieces*, a play for which Mr. Bicknell is probably less well known, will soon be revived by his alma mater, Ithaca College, and those of you who missed his work here might well consider catching that one, there.

Moose Murders, which featured Lillie Robertson, was directed by her husband, John Roach, rather the way a blind director repeatedly kicked in the groin might stage it. Mr. Roach, who is president of The Production Company, looms equally large in Force Ten Productions, which, besides producing *Moose Murders*, claims among its previous ventures *Paradise Alley* (a dog for which it did receive screen credit even though its contribution was tenuous and Sylvester Stallone had banned Roach and his partner from the premises) and a film with Karen Black no one I know has heard of. And so on through the program notes (and behind them), in dizzyingly incestuous spirals. Backing all this, I learn, is Texas oil money; and sitting in front, on the afternoon I attended, were creatures if not from the black lagoon, surely from the neighboring gutters. One enormous, pear-shaped individual, arriving late with vomit down his shirtfront, smelled so bad that he sent three nearby critics and their companions scurrying for the back of the theater, and, by intermission, had emptied out several rows around him. *Moose Murders* is the only stage play I ever saw in stereo-odoriferous Smellorama. So what is ailing Broadway? Rank stupidity.

Brighton Beach Memoirs; 'night, Mother

Brighton Beach Memoirs is Neil Simon's *Long Day's Journey Into Night*. Simon is the world's richest playwright and he even owns the Eugene O'Neill Theater, but though you can buy the name, you cannot buy the genius. Actually, rather than into one night, the play takes us into two consecutive Wednesday evenings in 1937 (when Simon was ten rather than, as in the play, fifteen), but the pseudo-autobiographical hero is actually called Eugene, and there is an ostensible scraping off of layers of patina to get at the alleged truth; if no one takes dope, there are plenty of dopes around, not least the author, who, like all those comedians wanting to play Hamlet, imagines that he can write a serious play.

The first problem with *Memoirs* is that it has no intention of being truthful. In a *Times* interview with Leslie Bennetts, Simon tells of a father who would disappear for months, years, finally forever, and who'd have terrible fights with his wife. In the play, Jack Jerome is the most responsible, wise, and generous man alive, and his wife, Kate, heroically coping with the deprivations of the Depression, is not a jot behind him in magnanimity. Her one true fight is with her widowed sister, Blanche, who, with her daughters Nora and Laurie, has been living with the Jeromes for years, working herself blind to earn her keep, but a drain nevertheless. Otherwise, the fights are harmless ones between various parents and children—a sort of *Life With Father* Jewish, but not too Jewish, style—and even the children's missteps are footling if not laudable: Nora's wanting to accept a role in a Broadway musical and quit school, elder brother Stanley's near loss of his job when he sticks up for a black handyman abused by the boss. Oh, hoping to make extra money for the family, Stanley does once gamble away a week's salary and run off intending to join the army; but he soon returns, makes back most of the money, and gets closer to Dad than ever.

Then why, you ask, the comparison to O'Neill's play? Because Eugene is a budding playwright with problems (not TB, to be sure, only puberty and lust for his cousin), there is a serious money shortage, there is near tragedy in the house across the street, there is the Depression and the threat of Hitler to Jewish relatives in Europe, there is Father's losing one of his jobs and getting a minor heart attack, there is everyone's hurting everyone else's feelings and apologizing profusely and making up. What there isn't, though, is honesty. The first act is typical Simon farce cum sentimentality, and the better for it; the second, in which ostensibly grave themes and conflicts are hauled out, is fraught with earnest speechifying, ponderous and platitudinous moralizing, and heartwarming uplift oozing all over the place, with everybody's soul putting on Adler Elevator shoes and ending up closer to heaven. The dramaturgy itself becomes woefully schematic: every character gets his tête-à-tête with every other character who has taken umbrage, and all ends in sunshine—even for the endangered relatives in Europe.

If all this were presented as farce, it might work. If it were honestly and painfully told, it might work. But Simon, who has also filled the play with those odious clean dirty jokes, wants to have his pain and let everybody eat cake, too. So everyone is funny and noble and ends happily, and Neil-Eugene—who is also a good student and obedient son—is funniest and noblest of all, even if given to somewhat excessive masturbation. Actually, the masturbation is more joked about than real—except, of course, in the playwriting. Simon is a reverse Antaeus: the closer his feet get to touching the ground of reality, the weaker his writing becomes. And, as a final dishonesty, his Jewish family talks and looks as un-Jewish as possible (through the writing, casting, and directing), so that Wasps should not feel excluded, let alone offended. In fact, the Irish family across the way though drowning in drink and filth—are, we are sanctimoniously informed, very nice people indeed.

Gene Saks has directed adroitly and vivaciously; Patricia Zipprodt's costumes and Tharon Musser's lighting can nowise be faulted, and even a second-best set from David Mitchell is quite good enough. The cast is uneven: Željko Ivanek (Stanley) is marvelous; Matthew Broderick (Eugene) fine, but too young to begin doing shtick; Mandy Ingber (Laurie) a perfect stage brat, which, however, is not the same as a real kid; Elizabeth Franz (Kate) commanding but out of character; Peter Michael Goetz (Jack) given to breaking up his speeches nonsensically, and dull to boot; Joyce Van Patten (Blanche) nondescript to the point of vanishing; and Jodi Thelen (Nora) simperingly tremulous to the point of being sickening. Still, the man behind me was convulsed with laughter; if you like commercial theater at its most mercenary, you should love this one.

A mother and divorced daughter live in symbiosis somewhere in middle America. The house on a country road is new and mediocre; the relationship between the women, which may or may not have been love once, has gone rancid. Thelma Cates can live with the humdrumness, pettiness, pointlessness of it all, particularly with daughter Jessie to take care of her. But Jessie has had enough. The father she loved is dead; the husband she loved left her; her son—whereabouts unknown—is headed for a life of crime; she herself is fat, unattractive, epileptic, and surpassingly bored with it all. She has a gun and, as she calmly tells her mother, will use it on herself in a couple of hours. She has ordered all her mother's affairs as far ahead as possible, and merely wishes to go over them and a few fundamental matters in a good closing talk.

Thelma, at first, is incredulous. Then she brings out her entire repertoire of tendernesses, coaxings, resentments, angers, revelations, and beseechings. But Jessie stands pat. She tries to explain as best she can what perhaps cannot be explained. The rest of the play is an agon between these two women with unequal resources: Jessie has the greater intelligence and resolve, but Thelma has her little blandishments, surprises out of the past, emotional projectiles. Yet Jessie says "'night, Mother," literally and figuratively, and Thelma, in the last stretch, almost enjoys all those final plans and instructions. Is this some sort of victory for the suicide?

Whatever else it is, it is Marsha Norman's new 90-minute, intermissionless play, 'night, Mother: honest, uncompromising, lucid, penetrating, well-written, dramatic, and as unmanipulatively moving as we expected from the author of the remarkable Getting Out. Though there are many laughs, I cannot tell you that the play isn't, as the popular parlance has it, "depressing." But I can tell you that it gleams with wisdom, reeks of observed and comprehended reality. That it is something to feel, think, and talk about; that it will force you to examine and re-examine new and old beliefs, fresh and stale convictions. That it will relentlessly confront you with your own and other people's humanity; that it will do what only the profoundest things—philosophy, religion, and art—can do for human beings, which may not be much but is all there is.

The play combines the lucent objectivity of a case history with the sublime subjectivity of language, style, art; it does not wrest forced, factitious tears from you, and it scrupulously, fastidiously refrains from telling you what to think. The subjects are suicide, love, and the meaning of life—as huge as they come; but they are treated with the specificity of threading a needle or choosing the right breakfast for your needs. Humor and pathos pop up as naturally as wild flowers or fences by the roadside; there is devastating psychological accuracy and nothing seems contrived; and there is that bustle of minutely perceived existential details that bespeak the master. The imminent suicide, from force of habit, puts lotion on her hands after doing the dishes; the mother, told by her daughter to keep washing a dirty chocolate pan after the shot rings out from behind the locked door for as long as it takes for the police and relatives to arrive, tries to assert her independence by saying she'll just sit and wait—yet as she goes to the phone after the gunshot, she already clutches the pan.

Believers and atheists, Freudians and anti-Freudians, rationalists and idealists, Marxists and capitalists, parents and children—everyone will have his or her interpretation of 'night, Mother. I think I know what Miss Norman really meant by it, but so will you, and your meaning, I wager, will be different. Good! Perhaps even great. Certainly great is the acting of Anne Pitoniak as Thelma and Kathy Bates as Jessie. The greatness is not only in their speech and moves, it is also, superlatively, in their repertoire of facial expressions, changing through subtle gradations, splintering brusquely, or hinting at double and triple bottoms. It is hard to say what exactly Tom Moore's direction contributed, but it looks masterly. So does Heidi Landesman's quintessentially middle-class set, and James F. Ingalls's cogent lighting. Miss Norman may not provide answers, but anyone who can serve up questions so brilliantly—in language that is only slightly, but finally appositely and awesomely, heightened—has more than earned that right.

The Man Who Had Three Arms

What can I say about Edward Albee's *The Man Who Had Three Arms* that I haven't said about some dozen of his preceding offerings? The author of two good plays, Albee has written nothing of merit since *Virginia Woolf*. Here he has concocted a monologue in lecture format for the hero (the two other actors, in a variety of small roles, might as well be part of the unimaginative slide projections meant to juice up this lectern drama), a man who once sprouted a mysterious third arm on his back, and so became famous, rich, and sought after; but now that it has vanished, he ekes out a measly existence from $500 lectures (overpriced, if the play is a fair sample) in the course of which he tells his life story, blames everyone else for his troubles, viciously insults the audience, and indulges in pitiful verbal games that insult the intelligence.

In other words, Himself, as the monologist is called (Albee regularly eschews anything as unsymbolic as a name), is Albee himself, who briefly displayed talent; he acquired fame, wealth, easy sexual conquests, and now berates the world for withdrawing these gifts whereas it should be blamed for having proffered them prematurely and excessively. Accompanying the invective is an obbligato of whining self-pity: as the audience is being baited and verbally booted out of the theater, it is also begged for compassion and companionship. The play snarls and snivels alternatingly or even simultaneously, has no dramatic invention or introspective honesty, and is as abject as it is vile.

In addition, it is humorlessly foulmouthed, pretentiously would-be-cultured, crammed with every conceivable desperate pun on arms, and, despite protestations of heterosexuality, full of venomous misogyny, campiness, and an acrid degradation of sex that I do not perceive as particularly heterosexual characteristics. The verbal wit is on the level of "not a situation most people come face to face or crotch to crotch with," and the culture scales the heights of a Piaf tag in French and a slight misquotation of two of E. E. Cummings's best-known lines, "how do you like your blueeyed boy / Mister Death." Albee's English is, as, usual, poor, though no worse than his ethnic jokes. Given all this, Robert Drivas's performance is a piece of heroism, but as misplaced as swimming the Hellespont with two arms tied behind your back.

My One and Only

Too many cooks are said to spoil the broth. Was that the case with *My One and Only*, a musical on which everyone from dead geniuses to past and present *Wunderkinder*, from the heart of show-biz-oriented academia to the grand masters of Broadway glitz, seems to have contributed? Over a year in the making and heaven knows how long in the planning, having undergone some three versions, used up several creative staffs, acquired almost more producers than performers, postponed its opening two or three times, this particular concoction seems never to have been much of a broth, though it does have by way of pivot that six-foot-six tap-dancing broth of a boy from Texas, Tommy Tune, who appears to be the main director, choreographer, and star of the venture. I wouldn't call it exactly spoiled, only so thin an aquatic and aerial extravaganza that, under the waves of razzle and clouds of dazzle, there is nothing for the spirit to latch on to. Unserved guests at the feast for the eyes and the ears, the head and the heart sit there, hungry and disconsolate.

What we get here is a randomly assembled George and Ira Gershwin score, vaguely based on *Funny Face*, with a new book by Tim Mayer rewritten by Peter Stone, about a barnstorming Texas pilot, Captain Billy Buck Chandler (Tommy Tune), who wants to be the first American to fly nonstop to Paris, but meets, falls for, and pursues Edith Herbert (Twiggy), the English champion Channel swimmer and aquacade star, which slows down his flying plans. Edith is under the blackmailing power of her manager and ex-lover, the alleged Prince Nicolai Erraclyovitch Tchatchavadze (you'd think a phony Georgian would be more careful to get the name right), who is really a Soviet agent as well as Edith's Svengali; Billy has a devoted female mechanic, Mickey (who is really a fed out to nab Prince Nikki). There is also a bogus black bishop, whose mission is "apostolic by daylight and alcoholic after dark," when he runs the illegal Club Havana (it's 1927 and Prohibition), as well as Mr. Magix, a black fairy godfather, who transforms the not-quite-hick-but-merely-hayseed (the joke is the show's, not mine!) into a suave suitor for Edith.

I think this is more than enough of the plot, which is meant to be elemental, what with Billy (air) wooing, winning, losing, and regaining Edith (water). Unfortunately, the book sorely lacks a little solid earthiness as its generally wan or worn one-liners try hard to parlay themselves into honest laugh getters, which a few of them actually are. And the romantic leads, even more cripplingly, fail to catch fire. This is not the fault of Twiggy, who has a muted, overcast but then, suddenly, sunny charm, and who dances, sings, and acts both vivaciously and wistfully, and, finally, winningly. Alas, she is deliberately overshadowed by a staging that favors the director-choreographer-star, who, for all his fine dancing, is out of tune with romance and electricity, and, given his six-foot-six-inch frame, with the rest of the cast.

Mr. Tune would make a dandy second-story man—in fact, he is one already, his head inhabiting some kind of mezzanine while the rest of the show struggles on on the ground floor. He is a sort of vertical version of an old comedic device, the horse made up of two performers, one the front-, the other the hindquarters. The person doing Tune's lower half performs with rippling agility, but the midget doing the upper half lets the operation down with his "aw, shucks," "gee, whiz," "I'll be hornswoggled" brand of naiveté that never becomes truly lovable, charismatic, or just persuasive about winning the girl. The love numbers, though sometimes childishly energetic, like the one danced barefoot and splashily in a shallow pool, never yield erotic combustion, and other relationships, e.g., the shortchanged comedy couple, Nikki and Mickey (Bruce Weill and Denny Dillon), have much less of a chance and no more pizzazz. There is also a geriatric barbershop quartet, a gaggle of not untalented white female dancers not big on femininity, and a bunch of extremely nimble black male dancers not big on masculinity, as well as a transvestite routine completing the counsels of despair.

And the score? The glorious old Gershwin songs, cut loose from their moorings, come across as resplendent ocean liners adrift on a sewage canal; *My One and Only* just doesn't have enough character to supply them with a vital new context. Thus the wonderful "Soon" is used as a throwaway song by Tommy Tune for the sake of a feeble gag later on; thus the witty and enchanting "How Long Has This Been Goin' On?" is forced into the inappropriate role of final romantic duet for the lovers and further undercut by squeezing Twiggy, who sings most of it, against the proscenium arch while Tune emotes (or demotes) stage center. There are, however, some genuine highlights, notably a quiet tap duet for Tune and the venerable Charles "Honi" Coles and a rousing free-for-all to "Kickin' the Clouds Away," to which the company cuts loose and, by way of kicking away the clouds, dances up a storm.

Notable in the cast is Roscoe Lee Browne, an irrepressible comedian absent too long, but the role of the bishop makes little dramatic sense under the sly, pungent delivery he gives it. There are amusing sets by Adrianne Lobel (refurbished by the uncredited Tony Walton), and there are jocund choreographic and directorial touches by some combination of Tommy Tune, Thommie Walsh, Mike Nichols, and Michael Bennett (the last two uncredited), but none of them so splendid as to make us sweat to unscramble Tommy from Thommie, Michael from Mike. Marcia Madeira has lit it all stunningly, Rita Ryack has designed at least one smashing, Paco Rabanneish bathing suit for Twiggy, and there is lively orchestral sound credited to four gents along with vocal arrangements credited to no one. *My One and Only* manages to glitter and be gay in more ways than one, but it whirls off in too many directions from no solid center.

Private Lives

Noël Coward's *Private Lives* was one of the most coruscating comedies in the English language, and will be so again starting July 18, or whenever Richard Burton and Elizabeth Taylor are through playing it. Actually, that's not what they're really playing. Miss Taylor is, all too palpably, repeating her imperious, dying millionairess, Mrs. Goforth, from *Boom!*, Joseph Losey's even more dreadful movie version of *The Milk Train Doesn't Stop Here Anymore*. What Burton is doing is less clear; it would seem to be some combination of a robot from Čapek's *R.U.R.*, an impression of Terry-Thomas as a shell-shocked colonel in an Ealing comedy, and blind Captain Cat in *Under Milk Wood*, which, being a radio play, requires little movement and less facial expression. The celebrated star couple, a mini-constellation, are both on stage at the Lunt-Fontanne (what, alas, is in a name?) Theater, but they are not in the same play and not playing opposite, but against, if not past, each other.

The Elizabeth (it looks more like Hackensack to me) Theatre Group, headed by Zev Bufman and Miss Taylor, plainly chose this property for Burton and Taylor for its fan- or gossip-magazine value, and for a clientele that approaches theater in such a spirit, that's the ticket. At a reputed weekly $70,000 each, the couple cannot lose; still, considering their age, ailments, and various current injuries that curtail if not cripple them, David Storey's *Home* might have made a more suitable vehicle, albeit lacking the spicy parallel between the twice-married, twice-divorced Burtons and Coward's Elyot and Amanda, who can't live with or without each other. But it's not so much life as publicity that's imitating art here, and doing it badly.

Private Lives has become as sacred as a profane text can, so that it's *lèse majesté* to make even slight, unseemly changes and interpolations, and not so slight and odious cuts. And then, with all those cuts, to drag out this brief, breezy play to over two and a half hours, what with marathon intermissions for our stars to regain their breath and not much shorter pauses between, or within, their lines. Still, one thing is achieved here: to anyone with an eye, ear, and brain in his head, it is conclusively demonstrated that Miss T.'s short list of talents does not include acting, even if certain audiences may accept as a substitute a collection of smirks, sneers, poses, vocal ritards, sledgehammer emphases, inaudibilities despite miking, arm flailings, leg twitchings, and the rest. (Her entire film career is clearly attributable to her former face, her former directors, and the cutting room.) And since she evidently cannot sing, a dance has been substituted for her on the unfounded assumption that she can do that.

In fact, a number of line changes must exist merely to accommodate Miss T., who does not, either by physical girth or by technical dearth, belong on the stage—call her E.T., the extraterritorial.

Thus "Don't say any more; you're making me cry so dreadfully," with which Gertie Lawrence, even on a recording, could wring our hearts, is apocopated into "Don't say any more," because Miss Taylor cannot cry. Elyot's first-act line about what the pair will do if discovered by their new spouses—"Run like stags"—now goes "If he comes near me, I'll run like a stag," presumably because the idea of Miss T. running like anything faster than a sumo wrestler is inconceivable, even if the change turns Elyot unpleasantly into a (lower case) coward. In Act II, Burton must stop at "Come and kiss me, darling, before your body rots"—and jettison "and worms pop in and out of your eye sockets," no doubt because the mere thought of those famed violet orbs becoming worm food is wormwood to the mind.

Richard Burton, even before he started laying waste his sizable talent, was not much for comedy. Here, while his ex-wife keeps her gaze blissfully riveted on the packed house while serving up yummy double entendres, he seems to have affixed his beclouded stare to the vision of the weekly paycheck, which, like Macbeth's dagger, looms before his eyes. Though his voice is still that superbly muted funeral trumpet of a majestically dying swan, the rest of him seems pickled in a laboratory jar. The actor cares so little about what he is doing that he will mangle a famous lyric ("True to the dream I am dreaming" becomes "Dreaming the dreams I've been dreaming") and even lose a natural laugh when identifying that sempiternal yacht as "The Duke of Westminster's, I expect. It always is" by running the two sentences together. With all those unwarranted pauses yawning about, why stint on a needed one?

Often, though, it is his co-star who leads him to ruin, either by not giving him anything to play off or by seducing him into misreadings. Thus the manifestly anxious, indeed heartbreaking, repetition of "In love all over again, aren't we?… Aren't we?" is fish-wifed up by her as "Aren't we?… *Aren't we??!!*" This induces Burton, a bit later, to append to "You love me, too, don't you? There's no doubt about it anywhere, is there?" an extra, shrily overemphatic "*Is there?*" And whoever came up with the totally uncharacteristic and anachronistic "You're nothing but a rampaging gasbag"—as out of place as the filter-tipped cigarettes and Burton's high-heeled boots—should have that bag over his or her head.

Though Milton Katselas (a singularly wrong-headed choice) is credited with the directing, which unnamed others have refurbished, it is manifest that not much direction was taken. The fights, wittily choreographed in Coward's stage directions, are paltry and arthritic—and, when Miss T. starts bumping Burton with her bosom and he bumps back, tasteless; the pacing and blocking are inert and inept. Even David Mitchell's set design may have been constrained by the cast: the partition between the two Deauville terraces has been virtually (and improbably) eliminated, because no hurdle is low enough for some stags to clear. But the worst torture must have been inflicted on the capable Theoni V. Aldredge, who couldn't have designed the geometric progression of horrors that pass for Miss T.'s costumes. Every outfit has a deeply slit skirt, revealing legs that generations of Hollywood directors toiled to keep out of sight; one dress, low-cut and laced across the back, produces almost as much dorsal as frontal cleavage; and the last, black-and-white number had me, for a moment, mistaking Miss T. for the frumpish maid in some outlandish uniform.

John Cullum, as Victor, is pompous and dithering beyond the line of duty; as Sibyl, the usually able Kathryn Walker makes a complete visual and histrionic fool of herself. As Louise, the maid, Helena Carroll adds a number of lines to her part in a French as inauthentic as the rest. I wish I could say that something of the play survives Miss Taylor's form and Mr. Burton's formaldehyde, but no such luck. One moment, however, may live forever in my memory, alas: Burton, presenting a drink to Taylor, simultaneously tweaks her left breast. Done with even vestigial eroticism, it might have been questionable but rowdy fun; executed with no more feeling than the turning on of a bathroom tap, it managed to turn my stomach.

Passion; Egyptology (My Head Was a Sledgehammer)

Passion Play, by Peter Nichols, which, for reasons of titular conflict, is called *Passion* on Broadway, needs its British title desperately. The story of James, 50, a distinguished art restorer and expert, and his wife, Eleanor, likewise 50, a voice teacher and concert chorister, and of James's slowly aroused but then unquenchable passion for Kate, an amoral photographer in her early twenties, it rings every change on "passion" and "play," as well as on the medieval, religious meaning of "passion play" and all its conceivable contemporary lay equivalents. Life, according to Nichols, is a hectic mixture of, or contest between, passion and play: marriage, love affairs, casual sex, work, religion, creation, recreation, everyday existence—all of them are a sort of, usually warring, aggregate of passion and play. The difficulty lies in sorting them out; the impossibility, in reconciling them. The history of this conflict is the record of an agony, a crucifixion: the love life, or just plain life, of an ordinary human being.

Kate was the mistress of Albert, James's friend and coeval and a famous crusading editor; for her, Albert left Agnes, his fiftyish wife and friend to Eleanor. But Albert died, and at his funeral, where the promiscuous Kate wore an expensive outfit meant to intoxicate James, that solidly married father of two grown and gone daughters began to fall for her. The rest of the play—and this is as much as I can divulge of a plot that depends all too much on surprises—concerns the permutations of this passion, which, unlike Freud's sexual act ("a process in which four persons are involved"), according to your mode of counting, involves three or five. That is because, alongside the basic trio, we get from Nichols the inward (or private, secret, unvoiced) selves of James and Eleanor, to wit, Jim and Nell. On stage, Jim and Nell are made to resemble their outward selves, but their words and actions express the hopes, longings, fears, and thoughts that James and Eleanor leave unexpressed.

The device has a long theatrical history, dating back, as I wrote in another context, "at least as far as Jean-Victor Pellerin's *Intimité* (1922), and conceivably even to the two angels in *Doctor Faustus*." It is best known hereabouts from Brian Friel's delightful *Philadelphia, Here I Come!*, but Nichols is much trickier than any of its previous users. At carefully calculated intervals, he springs on us, first, Jim, then, quite a bit later, Nell. (Where was she until then?) Thereupon he has Jim (who, by rights, should remain invisible and inaudible to anyone but James) anticipating some of James's doings, even calling up Kate on the phone. When the novelty of this wears off, Jim actually *becomes* the outward self, interacting with Eleanor, while James seems to become the inward one. After a while, Nell similarly takes over for Eleanor in a psychiatrist's office. This can be rationalized as the unconscious self receiving therapy; but Jim's taking over from James in the middle of nowhere would require reams of casuistry to defend.

Thenceforth things become Gordianly entangled. You never

know any more which is the outer, which the inner, self, with every self apparently interacting with every other one. (If that is the point, it is not susceptible to lucid dramatic realization.) As the stage action also frequently takes place in two different locations simultaneously, with one minor speaking character and six all-purpose mumbling extras likewise involved, the proceedings become so chaotic that I got more—though not much more—from a subsequent reading of the play than from seeing it. Yet since *Passion* is so plainly geared to enactment, to being visual fun (otherwise, why bother with the doubling device?), it is self-defeating: less clear and effective in the mode in which it wants to be more so. Two equally grave flaws are that it works up to an ending that is totally opaque, explicable in any number of ways, all equally unpersuasive; and that, as it proceeds, it does not shed much new light on marriage and adultery, monogamy and polygamy, fidelity and infidelity—passion and play.

It also cheats. For whereas James and Eleanor are made—thanks to their hidden alter egos, who are, as is the wont of hidden alter egos, more interesting than the public egos—into dizzyingly complex persons, poor Kate is given an only quasi-artistic profession (photography) and a name that is already a nickname and diminutive, and denied a private Katie or Katelet. This is grossly unfair: as a major part of the plot and even of a kind of subplot, or pre-plot, involving Agnes, Kate is jolly well entitled to her own private self. But the author, male and middle-aged, patronizes Kate into a pornographic fantasy figure: a girl of the mindless, unbridled younger generation, scarcely interested in anything but sex, and always ready to have it, straight or kinky, with any passing, passable stranger. Although a playwright can, and must, be selective, such tendentious oversimplification strikes me as dishonest and unworthy of the author of *Joe Egg* and *The National Health*.

The production further undercuts the play. Marshall W. Mason is a very clever director, and, therefore, perfect for a splendid but not primarily clever dramatist such as Lanford Wilson. He is, however, at the very least redundant for a play that is already too clever by half, and onto which he grafts his own, in this case not even related, brand of cleverness. In the event, a three-ring circus becomes the tower of Babel. Equally culpable is the set by John Lee Beatty, which reduces a potentially absorbing stylized space to an unconvincingly and flatly realistic one, and then tries to overcompensate by adding, in the rear, an irrelevant Magritte element. Neither Jennifer von Mayrhauser's excellent costumes nor Ron Wallace's superbly designed (though, when I saw it, malfunctioning) lighting can counteract all that. Bob Gunton looks much too young for James, and acts without discernible depth, charm, or finesse. As Agnes, Stephanie Gordon is a total loss; as Eleanor and Nell, Cathryn Damon and E. Katherine Kerr are decent without being outstanding. Frank Langella is a most amusing and nimble Jim, though I am not sure that the character was meant as a takeoff on Gore Vidal. Roxanne Hart, as Kate, is, in this sexpot's favorite word, right—absolutely right.

Passion is an unsatisfactory play by an intelligent and gifted playwright, and so contains lines and passages of poignancy and grace. But it also has a great deal of manipulativeness and pretension, what with, for example, Mozart's *Requiem* and the *Saint Matthew Passion* (yes, I know, it's a passion play) being pumped into it periodically, along with Beethoven's Ninth, discussions of Christianity versus paganism, classical versus modern art, psychotherapy versus the right to refuse it, and sundry other topics not immiscible with the matter at hand but inadmissible when so self-consciously and perfunctorily dragged in and surrounded by all that gimmickry. We watch with an initially amused bedevilment that subsides into frustrated lassitude.

Not so much about Richard Foreman, who continues to be the scandal of mindless derivativeness he has always been. Whereas Mabou Mines, likewise sponsored by Joe Papp, tries, however fallibly, to use the performance piece as a means of communication, Foreman's Ontological-Hysteric Theater remains the same splashy means of masturbation. In *Egyptology (My Head Was a Sledgehammer)*, Foreman merely continues to hammer away at our heads: visually, with his hysterical dadaist-surrealist images, and aurally, with his vapidly ontological, tautological, and illogical verbiage and din, the one no more meaningful than the other.

The set, by Foreman and Nancy Winters, is a moderately amusing jumble of hospital ward, horror-movie attic, and the Cairo flea market. And the costumes by Patricia McGourty (who is steadily improving) look like a droll sublimation of a drag party with an Egyptian motif. But what goes on is merely the backwash of dada and surrealism, attenuated and 70 years too late. To assume that this is avant-garde, as the Foremaniacs appear to do, is like trying to compose Haydn symphonies or paint Vermeer interiors in 1983 and calling it art. As a send-up, it's like spoofing McKinley in the reign of Reagan; but it isn't a send-up, only self-indulgence.

The actors—or cutups—represent an aviatrix who crashes in a moth-eaten antiques-shop version of Egypt, where she contends frantically and anachronistically with B-movie Egyptian barflies, whores, jackal-headed gods, evil nurses, carnival strong men, and Louis XIV, who seems to figure as an *hommage* to Foreman's former mangling of a play by Molière. The stage is, as usual, crisscrossed by meaningless wires, and there are the customary explosions of sound alternating with scratchy recordings of old pop tunes, while everyone careers, cavorts, and camps around to his, her, or Foreman's heart's content. Props and people are wheeled on and off, and while, for instance, some interchangeable character intones, "Immediately I thought of pushing you around with my inheritance of cultural expectations," a phalanx of performers brandishing ice-cream cones menacingly advances on the aviatrix, who responds with tricks of her own, such as phoning Louis XIV for help.

No genuine acting is possible amid these cultural expectorations, though I must stress that the nonstop whine affected by Foreman's on- and offstage leading lady, Kate Manheim, is barely less grating than the machine-made cacophony. Foreman himself seems to attend all performances of the show: to have written and directed it argues a man a charlatan; to watch it more than once proves him certifiable.

Orgasmo Adulto Escapes From the Zoo

I am not very fond of one-man plays, or one-woman, one-trained-seal, one-anything plays. When I think how hard Aeschylus, Sophocles, and Euripides must have labored to add another actor, and yet another, to the initial one, it seems to me a bit of a crime when one author or one performer—or, more often, one author-performer—tramples on all that hard-earned progress to indulge his ego and his producer in the least costly, and sometimes cheapest, exhibition. Surely drama was meant to be conflict—good, solid, dialogue-packed and action-studded conflict—and putting it all inside one mouth, even with the customary devious support from telephones, offstage noises, changed voices, invisible interlocutors, the odd doll impersonating an infant, and the rest of the bag of tricks, does not diminish our sense of deprivation. Generally speaking, there is something demoralizing about going to theatrical solos—like being invited to dine off paper plates.

There are, however, exceptions: if the performer is great, the material is marvelous, or the situation, though dramatic, calls for a monologue—say, the story of Jonah. A little of all three of these conditions obtains in *Orgasmo Adulto Escapes From the Zoo.* (Please don't ask me to explain the title; I could do it, but it would take more space than the explanation is worth—besides, the original Italian title is *Tutta casa, letto e chiesa.*) Anyway, *Orgasmo* is two evenings' worth of dramatic monologues—four playlets per performance—by Franca Rame and Dario Fo, who are a famous Italian husband-and-wife playwriting-and-acting team; their works are social and political satires, and are, I am told, best when performed by the authors themselves. I say "I am told" because, though some of their plays have infiltrated the U.S.A., their bodies have not got past our State Department's nylon curtain thus far: it seems Fo and Rame are Communists and could easily overthrow our government with a few well-chosen one-liners.

Well, these eight plays are definitely not Communist propaganda; they are feminist propaganda. They are monologues for women, and are performed here by Estelle Parsons, who also slightly adapted them and (with the help of friend or Fo) considerably translated them, but not entirely, there being a lot of simple, quotidian Italian words left macaronically lying about for the sake of local *colore.* The direction is by Rame and Parsons, along the lines of the original Rame-Fo staging. There are three incidental male roles, but they are non-speaking, because the men are dumb in every sense, as well as deaf to reason. Actually, three is an overstatement. In one playlet, the man consists of a mere arm that has penetrated past the chain of the woman's front door (more often the penetration—simulated, of course—is of a different kind); in another, he is just the cloddishly sleeping extremities of a husband protruding from opposite ends of a blanket. These roles, or fractions thereof, are played by John Masterson with as much animation as is consistent with what must be a great though unvoiced self-abnegation.

And what are the eight playlets about? *Waking Up* is about a comically beleaguered housewife who has a job at the factory but must also, unpaid, work as a wife, mother, and housekeeper, and has grown so befuddled that she can't remember anything and very nearly rushes off to work on Sunday. *A Woman Alone* is about a wife put upon by a husband who is a lousy lover and petty tyrant, and by his brother who is a randy paraplegic with just one big, mobile, horny hand. She is caught in an affair with a young boy, is locked into the apartment every day by her husband, spied on by a voyeur from the building opposite, harassed by an obscene telephone caller, besieged by her naked lover trying to get into the apartment (the aforementioned arm), until She takes comic-violent vengeance on all these men. *Contrasto for a Solo Voice* is about a peasant lass who contrives, for one night at any rate, to take (I am using a euphemism; the plays revel in obscenity and scatology) her lover rather than be taken by him. *The Freak Mamma* is about a crazy-seeming mother who enters a church and goes to confession in the hope of escaping the pursuing cops, and tells of a series of transformations she underwent while watching over her Red Brigades son, which took her from Communism to Maoism, from punk to radical feminism.

These are the chiefly comic plays. The more serious ones include *We All Have the Same Story*, a symbolic fairy tale about the dual nature of woman as factitious angel and repressed hellion, and about how she must come to terms with her suppressed rebelliousness by releasing and digesting it before she can be whole. *Monologue of a Whore in a Lunatic Asylum* is the extorted confession of a factory-worker-cum-whore much abused by men, whom a woman doctor has strapped into a sort of psychiatric electric chair that, with mild shocks, forces her to tell the story of her politicization into a violent anarchist feminist. *It Happens Tomorrow* offers the immobile, spotlighted face of a woman, while her impersonal voice on tape relates her torture as a political prisoner, resulting in near-death. *Medea* is an alleged rural Italian version of the story told by Euripides, often couched in words closely approximating the original but placing the emphasis on a more contemporary feminist interpretation of the celebrated infanticide.

As feminist agit-prop for the Italy of the seventies (when most of these pieces were written), this may have been pretty incendiary stuff; for today's America, it is rather passé. Though anti-E.R.A. women may still find it shocking, the rest will consider it mild and obsolescent, as flat as yesterday's beer or yesteryear's revolutions. The men in the audience, being of the kind that frequent such entertainments, find the anti-male jokes and tirades (many of them deserved) hugely amusing, especially if they have a simplistic sense of humor. The more serious playlets (each evening contains two), which have moments of wry merriment, tend to be more interesting because they function more clearly on two levels. Though the comic ones, in turn, have some serious elements in them, these are not enough for an added dimension. On the whole, the satire—sexual or political—is broad and sophomoric; still, there are flashes when something happens: a joke comes alive, a homely truth hits home, an absurdist situation takes on a hallucinatory, surreal reality. But, alas, what vastitudes of stale cake between the raisins d'être.

Estelle Parsons seems to have written the introductory material to the playlets, and it is, by and large, no worse or better than the rest. This shows, according to how you look at it, how literary Miss Parsons is, or how histrionic the authors are. As an actress, Miss Parsons is both energetic and versatile, both gifted and excessive. She manages—with help from Ruth Morley's evocative costumes and from some lively wigs, but more through her own flexibility and range—to be as different in each piece as the writing permits, and her throwaway lines and subtler effects work as well as her exaggerated comic turns. She has many moods and voices and accents, and can, not quite consistently but more than sporadically, be surprising.

Yet she does sometimes stoop to vulgarity—always prompted by the material, to be sure, but with a little more wallowing and exultation in it than seems strictly necessary. Of course, one could argue with some justification that without this extra fillip, the vulgarity might be less supportable yet. (But one could also argue, with equal justification, that perhaps this entire trip wasn't necessary.) Oddly enough, though her voice is more a comic than a tragic organ, Miss Parsons does handsomely by Medea—possibly because this is a very active, country Medea, and because she also switches to being the chorus leader with a different voice. In any case, her one short Medea is easily worth three long ones by Zoë Caldwell. But her voice disappoints in It Happens Tomorrow, in part, perhaps, because it is on tape, but more so because it lacks grandeur. She rehearses the horrible tortures with the proper unhistrionic matter-of-factness, but that is precisely why innate vocal beauty is needed to move us despite the required flat delivery.

And another problem. Miss Parsons keeps shuttling between acting and clowning. She does both well, but they have a way of tripping each other up. I dare say the writing is largely, or even wholly, to blame; yet a very great actress would have found a way to bridge the impossible, to reconcile the irreconcilable, to transcend. There are fleeting instances when Miss Parsons does so, and there is always something spirited, enterprising, and likable about her: even when she makes a fool of herself, she does it gallantly and endearingly. And she can do wonders for a good line, such as the anguished question of a woman who has just given birth: "Is it a boy? No? What is it then?"

But, seriously, dear Franca Rame and Dario Fo: one-character plays—is that what theater is fo'?

La Cage aux Folles

The best way to enjoy La Cage aux Folles is with earplugs. You can then see the luscious sets by David Mitchell, whose gliding, flying, gyrating is as thrilling as their design. You can see how Jules Fisher has lit them, making the waters of St. Tropez truly liquid, the sky above truly skyey. You can see the sumptuous and inventive costumes of Theoni V. Aldredge, tasteful even when they are conjuring up the outré. You can see, even without having to hear them, how good are the performances of Gene Barry, as Georges, the homosexual owner of the Cage aux Folles nightclub, and of George Hearn, as Albin, his lover and, under the name Zaza, the club's transvestite star. You could, unfortunately, not avoid seeing the rest of the cast or the strenuous but unrewarding choreography of Scott Salmon, but was there ever a perfect solution to anything?

And, conveniently, earplugs are removable. For the three or four better songs Jerry Herman has written, you could take them out; for the others and for the reprises with which the show is awash, you could stick the plugs back in. You would certainly want to keep them in for the dialogue, whether it comes from the play by Jean Poiret (who also wrote the movie version) or whether it was contrived by Harvey Fierstein in what he may or may not perceive as the spirit of the original. I had precious little use for the film, but at least it was authentically French rather than Brooklyn with a few n'est-ce pas added, the points were made with a trowel rather than a sledgehammer, and the dinner scene was genuine farce. It also had such fine supporting actors as Michel Galabru as the girl's father.

I suppose there is no one left in America who doesn't know the story, and readers of this magazine recently had it rehearsed for them in Ross Wetzsteon's panegyric. It is, in its way, a remarkable concoction, cadging or coercing sympathy on various levels with the most meretricious premeditation. That homosexual relations are grossly oversimplified and sugarcoated in *Cage* is no hanging matter; heterosexual relations have been similarly falsified in musicals since the year one—a very good year for cheap muscatel. But what we have here is the something-specious-for-everybody mentality at its apogee. For the affluent, middle-class, middle-aged theatergoer there is a chance to feel wonderfully tolerant toward homosexuals, and tolerance is, of course, a good thing, though in this simplistic presentation it becomes really blindly patronizing smugness. This adorable, happily married homosexual couple of two decades' standing, and their sudden problem because "their" son is about to marry into a reactionary, anti-homosexual family (translation: Jewish into Christian or vice versa, rich into poor or vice versa, enlightenedly liberal into conventionally conservative or what have you), is the very stuff of which facile viewer self-righteousness is made. After all, this is a homosexuality where drag merely means cute, marital fidelity between two men comes easy and lasts forever, and an S&M bullwhip is only a snappier kind of bongo drum.

For homosexuals, this, even more than *Torch Song Trilogy*, is the Broadway legitimization of their modus vivendi, all the way from respectably bourgeois to outrageously transvestite, via a budget of $5 million. That the homosexual couple is played by eminently heterosexual actors, that discrimination against them is represented by paper mice (not even tigers), that Fierstein's (or perhaps Poiret's) values are seemingly no different from Neil Simon's with one set of genitals changed, that if this were a musical based on the "threatening" work of a gifted and candid homosexual such as Jean Genet or Djuna Barnes, there would be not standing ovations by the end of Act I but a stampede for the exit does not trouble them at all. Frills, fantasy, factitiousness are there in abundance, and as these have worked for benighted heterosexuals, they'll work no less well for benighted homosexuals.

But there is worse: *Cage* plays into the hands of homophobes. No "right-minded" antihomosexual (and which two-bit fag-baiter doesn't consider himself rightminded?) would identify him- or herself with the heterosexual characters of this *Cage*. Crude, stupid, unprepossessing—or, in the case of the young lovers, smarmy and untalented (John Weiner looks and acts like a TV weatherman from Albuquerque; Leslie Stevens is a five-and-ten-cent baby in a million-dollar store)—these people are not "us," say the sons and daughters of Anita Bryant as they march mulishly on.

But, someone tells me, aren't you forgetting that this is only a musical—just entertainment? Well, as just entertainment it is fair to middling, as noted above. Arthur Laurents has directed with a mixture of obviousness and ingenuity (the latter, alas, often derived from sources as various as Gypsy and *Dreamgirls*); the sights are stunning and you can amuse yourself by following, not the predictable plot and feeble gags, but the itinerary across the stage of that $5 million, so well marshaled that you can see where every C-note went; and Barry and Hearn are truly accomplished and touching. The rest is as phony as the name of the transvestite chorines at the club, Les Cagelles, which is about as French as "usherette."

However, the sanctimonious piety with which this show is being hailed, in standing ovations, critical hosannas, bourgeois self-congratulation, and homosexual ecstasies—the first-act curtain number, "I Am What I Am," Albin's defiant self-assertion as drag queen and surrogate mother to young Jean-Michel, is being touted as the new "gay anthem"—forces one to take it more seriously. I fully expect straight couples to wear the ticket stubs of *Cage* as goody-goody-conduct medals on their chests. And take that "I Am What I Am": it is a fair enough show song, cleverly integrated into the plot, strategically positioned, and superlatively delivered by George Hearn. But put it alongside the proud cocotte's *chanson* by Jacques Prévert and Joseph Kosma, "Je suis comme je suis"—which has been translated and adapted by Eric Bentley into the song of a 42nd Street male hustler—and you can see the difference between true lyricism, honesty, art and a deftly posturing placebo.

Though considerably better than, say, *Porky's*, *La Cage aux Folles* is equally beyond criticism; far be it from me to try to prevent its watered-down felicities from reaching their own level. And, after all, *Cats* misrepresents felines, too.

Uncle Vanya

Andrei Serban refers to his staging of *Uncle Vanya* as his most naturalistic mounting of a Chekhov play, and what we see in the huge, sprawling acting area of La Mama Annex is indeed natural wood:

lots and lots of wood carpentered into three runways or catwalks on different levels, surrounded by fences, platforms, stairways, sunken conversation—or should we say dialogue?—pits, etc., the whole thing looking like a cross between a temporary jungle gym for foolhardy kids and a fun-house maze for infantile adults. Occasionally an actor loses his footing during one of the more hazardous trajectories, but it hardly matters in a production that hasn't the slightest idea of where it is going anyway.

Rhythm, tempo, stretches of aching rallentandos and wry accelerandos—all that makes a Chekhov play so close to a musical composition—are completely garbled here into a viscous mass, within which, on some misbegotten aleatory principle, the actors improvise recklessly according to their private and discordant styles, or lacks of style. In what seems like an attempt to compensate for the loss of the Chekhovian music, Serban pumps into the proceedings a good deal of irrelevant Italian opera blared out by the P.A. system, but the one useful thing this could accomplish—the drowning out of the actors—occurs only intermittently.

The casting, never Serban's strong suit (but, then, what is?), hits a new low. The touching Vanya, a man of great wasted intelligence and tragicomic passion, is played by Joseph Chaikin as a small, rather badly carved marionette (its features rushed over or skimped on), whose strings have a way of getting entangled, which makes the puppet's movements needlessly jerky. This explains the mild irritation with which it stumbles or staggers through the great emotional climaxes, or, for that matter, the more ordinary scenes, the difference between the two remaining minimal. The voice is puny—maybe *it* should be piped in instead of all that Bellini—and has an inappropriate lower-class accent. The only time Chaikin, a well-known avant-garde actor-director, comes to cheerful life is during a scene he is unaccountably made to play sitting in the lap of Professor Serebryakov, the object of his hate. But this derives more from Edgar Bergen and Charlie McCarthy than from Chekhov, so the lively vocalizing may actually be ventriloquism.

Not, however, by James Cahill, who plays Serebryakov. Cahill, whom I consider easily one of the least talented actors in the New York theater, but who never stops working, seems to have made it largely on his tallness, which apparently passes for comic gawkiness, and a voice for which "fruity" would be an understatement; it is more like a rancid banana split. He turns the subtly hateful professor into a harmless (except to Chekhov) oaf, which robs the play of one of its motors. Equally preposterous is the Yelyena of Diane Venora, who plays a bored, frustrated nineteenth-century Russian aristocrat as a contemporary East Village neurotic who giggles, weeps, drops to her knees, camps around for no reason— unless it's drugs. As the nanny, Shami Chaikin, a woman to whom cuteness comes about as easy as to Henry Kissinger, tries to be cute, which is wrong anyway and which she makes horrible. As Telyegin, Mohammad Ghaffari does a fairly convincing impersonation of a whirling dervish, with Near Eastern accent, costume, and some sort of outlandish instrument he strums away at to the greater glory of Allah. Beatrice Manley-Blau makes Mrs. Voinitsky so inconspicuous, she is hardly there; yet what little is left of her is not convincing enough for a ghost.

The only passable performances come from F. Murray Abraham and Frances Conroy. But for all his ability to toss off lines with offhand rapidity and his possession of a number of somewhat mannered devices for sounding and acting different, and thus, presumably, appearing "real," Abraham lacks that warmth or charm or enthusiasm with which Dr. Astrov gets women as different as Sonya and Yelyena, each in her own way, to fall for him. As for Miss Conroy, she is good while the going is relatively easy but cannot move us with the ultimate zeal for self-abnegation with which other Sonyas could make stones—and, no doubt, even wood—weep. Santo Loquasto's costumes are uneven, but his carpentry is, as noted, compelling, though not exactly scenery. Thus the "set" obliges Astrov to bid Vanya and Sonya a long good-bye from a platform that is actually functioning as the top of the desk where, in the pit, the two are working. The effect is bizarre, but no more so than one of Serebryakov's exits along an endless runway, during which the professor executes three pirouettes to the right and one to the left. The only thing that holds up in this Vanya is Jennifer Tipton's thoughtful, diverse, always idiomatic lighting.

And what of Jean-Claude van Itallie's "new English version"? When v. I. first did a "new version"—of *The Cherry Orchard*—it was substantially the same as Ann Dunnigan's translation in Signet Classics. This resulted in a settlement in which v. I. paid legal costs and agreed to stop further printing or producing his "new version." That, however, did not deter him from several other "new versions" of Chekhov. Should we then not look more closely at these new bottles for traces of old wine?

Heartbreak House

There is no doubt in my mind that *Heartbreak House* is Shaw's masterwork. A four-hour play when uncut—not a minute should be cut—it contains a whole dying world along with inklings of another, better one trying to be born. It is a play that bears its historical context (England in World War I) and its autobiographical content (Shaw at 60, beginning to feel old) not lightly, but bravely, wittily, often profoundly, and sometimes even with a bittersweet lyricism all too rare in Shaw's oeuvre. A symbolic play, but one whose symbolism is magnanimous rather than constricting, for it applies to all societies in transition, all doomed social orders, all individuals who, while the ground is sliding under their feet, try to make the best of it by philosophizing, clowning, cursing, or inveighing—all good or at least pardonable ways of dealing with a landslide and the stumbling and tumbling it induces. The only ones whom Shaw will not forgive are the chiselers and snivelers, one of whom the production at the Circle in the Square unforgivably eliminates: Billy Dunn has been cut from this version, pared down to three hours (including two intermissions), which, to anyone who loves this marvelous play, must feel like fingernails bitten to the quick.

Next to the scissors, the biggest culprit is that miserable invention theater-in-the-round. The set must represent a country house built in the shape of a ship, not only to endow the proceedings with Captain Shotover's omnipresent eccentricity, not only to convey the metaphor of the ship of state, not only to suggest an ocean journey on a vessel out of control, but also and above all to provide an aura of quirky unreality in which everything is possible—as, say, in the Forest of Arden—so that the most outrageous tomfoolery and the most poignant poetry can converge, collide, and blend into one. Marjorie Bradley Kellogg has done the best she could to make an arena seaworthy, but it just isn't shipshape.

Anthony Page's direction is not much help. There is something mechanical about most of it, and the mechanism is rickety at that. To be sure, this is no play to be raced through, but neither is it to be dawdled over as so often here. And the cast or, to remain nautical, crew is a motley one indeed. Captain Shotover is 88, but Rex Harrison plays him as if *he* were that old. This is an interesting idea and pays off now and then; but, essentially, Shotover should be the peppiest, pepperiest, youngest and most rousing person present, and Harrison's somnolence, miserliness with the decibels, letting a third of his speeches dribble into his beard, are on balance ill-conceived. Granted, individual lines are well delivered, there is more spirit gum than spirit to this captain.

Rosemary Harris, however, is a most plausible, buoyant Hesione (though I imagine her as an even better Ariadne in the recent London production), incipiently blowzy but not overblown, exasperating (as she should be) but bewitchingly so. Even if Amy Irving does not quite manage to make Ellie's dizzying transformations entirely credible, she has a fine, poised, forceful way with the part: graceful, dignified, and slightly frightening. As Boss Mangan, Philip Bosco has himself a high old time with a nonstop high dudgeon, and though his tricks are old, there's no one like Bosco to take to and energize a stage without hogging it. And what a sublimely ridiculous haircut he sports! Dana Ivey, a wonderful actress, is miscast as Ariadne. Her accent and pacing are perfect, but she is playing mostly Miss Prism and sometimes Lady Bracknell, never Lady Utterword.

Stephen McHattie is a lackluster Hector Hushabye (which takes some undoing) who, except in the neatly executed imaginary duel, lacks charm, dash, bravura, and has a voice that is both gravelly and strangulated, like a call for help from someone buried alive. Jan Miner is not stout enough for Nurse Guinness, Bill Moor is a garish and effete caricature of a Randall, and the utterly un-British William Prince turns Mazzini Dunn into a fruitier but less tart Virgil Thomson. The last two are disastrous. Jane Greenwood's costumes are uninspired but inoffensive, and Paul Gallo's lighting is spot-on. A *Heartbreak House*, in short, too short and short on excellence; yet so superior a play in a nugatory season mustn't be shunned.

Bertolt Brecht once answered a magazine inquiry about when he had laughed loudest with "when I heard that Shaw was a Socialist." Yet as this play demonstrates with its eloquent plea for an end to idleness, for the right people to grab hold of the helm instead of lulling themselves into indolent sleep (Hushabye), spouting obsolete verbiage (Utterword), or overshooting the mark (Shotover), he was a more responsible Socialist than most, Brecht included.

Noises Off

Critics, deludedly assuming everyone tries to divine their reviews, tend to internalize their reactions. But at Michael Frayn's *Noises Off*, my colleagues and I were laughing loudly and helplessly, all caution flung to the gales of laughter around us. The play is so funny that it had me guffawing not only *on* the many bowling-over laugh lines and sight gags but also *around* them; it creates an atmosphere so charged that sparks whiz about everywhere, detonating hilarity even *between* specific laughs. In some of Act I, more of Act III, and all of Act II, *Noises Off* is as sidesplitting a farce as I have seen. Ever? Ever.

Noises Off starts with a program-within-a-program you must giggle over in your playbill. It is for a typical moth-eaten British sex farce, *Nothing On* (note the symmetry of the titles), presented by a cast of no-talents at the Grand Theatre, Weston-super-Mare. What we watch onstage is the final, faltering run-through of this threadbare frolic, in which an aging but still randy comedienne, Dotty Otley, plays a maid in a supposedly vacated country house, where the renting agent, played by Garry Lejeune, a vacuous *jeune premier*, has brought a dumb blonde, played by Brooke Ashton, a dumb blonde, for an assignation. The owner of the house, a playwright played by Frederick Fellowes, a third-rate method actor with madness in his method, arrives with his gung ho wife, played by Belinda Blair, the cast gossip. The owners are trying to evade the tax agents, for whom they promptly mistake the illicit lovers. Soon matters are further complicated by a burglar, played by Selsdon Mowbray, who has two afflictions: galloping deafness that comes and goes and steady dipsomania that comes and comes. There is also a pair of stage managers: Tim Allgood, who doubles as a rich Arab wanting to buy the house, and Poppy Norton-Taylor, who understudies Brooke in life as well as in art.

Just as *Noises Off* echoes, *Nothing On*, life, if you can call it that, imitates… whatever it is—certainly not art. Lloyd Dallas, who is directing *On* in *Off*, is also having concurrent affairs with Brooke and Poppy. An unflappably solicitous hack, his affability stuffed with ice (that good actor Brian Murray does not quite manage the Baked Alaska quality), he is losing his grip on his lousy actors just as on his messy philandering. Almost everyone in the production is involved with almost everyone else in sex or vengeance or both—there is sabotage and mayhem onstage and off. And Selsdon's affair with the bottle and consequent disappearances and last-minute retrievals spread panic among all. Enough plot; let me add only that all three acts of *Off* concern the first act of *On*: the Weston-super-Mare dress rehearsal onstage; a matinée, next month, backstage at Goole; and another performance, another month later, onstage at Stockton-on-Tees, where the last shred of precariously maintained discipline disintegrates and the actors improvise preposterously—except for Brooke, who stupidly sticks to the script with equal disastrousness—and though Chaos is restored, the great Anarch won't even let the curtain fall.

I doubt whether Frayn has written anything else as funny, but, then, very few people have. The way the ludicrous theatricality of shoddy lives and the shoddy ludicrousness of lifeless theater interpenetrate so that all boundaries yield to universal havoc—universal *comic* havoc—is endlessly funny and even a trifle melancholy. Thus the actors, both on and off, exhibit the full spectrum of human gullibility, folly, incompetence, and imbecility, and yet, absurdly, muddle through. And Lloyd, the director, who comes nearest to being a man of sense, finds himself being sucked into incoherence, even unto declaring that doors and sardines—both of which figure ubiquitously in *Nothing On*—are what theater, farce, and life are all about. A demented remark, but, in a condignly crazy way, the play bears him out. Sardines are for indulging our appetites and doors are for escaping into privacy, but the sardines keep vanishing and some unbargained-for Other is always lurking in the haven behind each door. Which is what the farce of life and the farce of theater are all about. And in this life as in this theater, we are never sure which is onstage and which backstage, which is presumable play-acting and which putative reality. It may even be that doors become sardines and sardines doors. Certainly Lloyd, just griping about a calamitous *Richard III* he is directing back in London, turns, unconsciously and hilariously, into Richard III. So tragedy pops up in farce, and kippers become portals. And Frayn becomes a superior Alan Ayckbourn.

Michael Blakemore, who triumphantly directed the show in London, repeats his assignment here—abetted by Michael Frayn's cuts, additions, and revisions—with even greater choreographic splendor. For example, one thing the play lacked over there was a cactus; this lapse has here been pointedly rectified. Another thing it lacked was an ending; now it comes closer to having one. It still has risibly apt sets and costumes by Michael Annals (amazing what three Michaels can do for a play!) and a cast that is largely lovely. Victor Garber, Deborah Rush, Linda Thorson, Jim Piddock, and Douglas Seale are at most a hairbreadth from perfection, and Paxton Whitehead is even closer than that. Brian Murray, fair in Act I, becomes delightful in II and III. Alas, Dorothy Loudon hams it up foolishly and destructively, only to settle down a bit in Act III; Amy Wright looks right but acts, if she acts at all, wrong.

There is something exhilarating about the rehabilitation of a genre. Scholars have lately been extolling the importance and dignity of farce, but where were the contemporary farces that could corroborate them? In *Noises Off* we have the pleasure of seeing a once thriving but lately moribund genre come alive again to shake us with laughter and even, improbably, shake us up into a little peripheral thought. I call that exciting.

The Real Thing

The playwright hero of Noël Coward's story "The Wooden Madonna" has been called by critics "a second Somerset Maugham," "a second Noël Coward," and "a second Oscar Wilde." I am sure that Tom Stoppard has been hailed as all that and more, and with some justification, even though unlike those three he is heterosexual. Surely his new play, *The Real Thing*, is as literate (barring the occasional grammatical lapse), witty, and dizzyingly ingenious as anything you will have seen in a long time, except for *Noises Off*, which, however, is farce rather than high comedy. In fact, Stoppard is as clever a playwright as you can find operating today in the English language. Therein lies his strength and also, I am afraid, his weakness. But do not let anything I am about to say deter you from seeing the play happily, profitably, gratefully.

In Stoppard's novel, *Lord Malquist & Mr. Moon*, there was a question so urgent that it had to be italicized: "*That's what I'd like to know. Who's a genuine what?*" In the intervening seventeen years, things have become more complicated, and the question is not only *who* but also *what* is a genuine what. It is as if *The Real Thing* took place entirely between two facing mirrors, Life and Art, reflecting what they see back and forth to infinity (mirrors playing an endless game of Ping-Pong), except that one cannot be quite sure which mirror is which. And in trying to establish what they are reflecting with any certainty, one is forced to keep turning one's head from one mirror to the other; yet the final answer resides in the last image, the one in infinity, to which neither the dramatis personae nor the audience will ever penetrate. So both have to settle for accepting one uncertainty as a working hypothesis. But which one?

I am giving away an open secret when I say that the play begins with a scene of marriage and infidelity. Or, rather, illusory marriage, for this is a scene from *House of Cards*, a play by Henry Boot, the hero of *The Real Thing*—and illusory infidelity, for the adultery in question, we later learn, was merely putative. The actors are Charlotte, Henry's real-life wife, and Max, their real-life friend, who is married to Annie in real life (I am speaking, of course, as if *The Real Thing* were real life, and as if real life existed), who, however, is in love with Henry, as he is with her. But "real life" is also a house of cards, and soon marriages collapse—painfully for some, happily for others—to re-form in different configurations. Will *they* last?

For example, Annie, likewise an actress as well as a militant pacifist, has, after her marriage to Henry, met on a train from Scotland a simple soldier called Brodie—himself, it seems, an ardent pacifist. Upon setting fire to a wreath on a militaristic monument, he gets six years in jail for arson. To help release him sooner, Annie persuades him to write a play about what happened, a play that, being plain reality, is so bad that the extremely reluctant Henry has to be argued into rewriting it, i.e., putting enough illusion into its bare, rude truth to make it artlike, performable, real. ("I tart up Brodie's unspeakable drivel into speakable drivel," Henry says.) Aside from being debated acrimoniously enough to break up a marriage, this train ride with Brodie will be seen, at least in part, enacted as it might have happened, as Brodie wrote it, as Henry rewrote it, and as, presumably further revised, it was done on TV. And this isn't even the main plot of *The Real Thing*, though it impinges on it, or vice versa. Which mirror are we looking at? The events of life are reflected, somewhat distorted, in art; the events of art, somewhat travestied (or more tragic?), are echoed by life. And, of course, affairs and adulteries and marriages are everywhere, but which, if any, are real? Not necessarily the real ones.

Even the recorded music, classical or popular, that gets played on phonographs or radios extends this state of reflections, echoes, multiple bottoms on and on. A trio from *Così fan tutte* comes from an opera about infidelity that proves not infidelity—unless, of course, semblance or intention equals reality. Also there's a bit of *La traviata* on the radio, about a formerly light woman who now pretends to be unfaithful—actually is unfaithful—but only because she believes it will benefit the one man she adores and keeps adoring. All of which comments on the action of the play. And so on. If this makes your head spin, rest assured that in watching *The Real Thing*, the head-spinning is greatly assuaged by spectacle and mitigated by wit—more wit than you can absorb, but what you can is amply sufficient. There is also something from time to time approaching real drama, real feeling, but this is not quite the real thing. Never mind, though; it, too, fascinates.

Yet, undeniably, there is loss. Cleverness, when it is as enormous as Stoppard's, can become a bit of an enormity, especially when it starts taking itself too seriously—either because it is too clever or because it is, after all, not clever enough. Wilde, you see, had the cleverness in *The Importance of Being Earnest* (from which an earlier Stoppard play, *Travesties*, takes off) not to take anything in it remotely in earnest. Congreve, in his differently but scarcely less clever *The Way of the World*, which does have serious overtones, had the good judgment not to make all the characters, situations, and speeches clever or funny. There is genuine dumbness, oafishness, evil in it. Conversely, Pirandello, the grand master of illusion, often isn't being funny at all. But Stoppard's hurtlingly, and sometimes hurtingly, funny cleverness is an avalanche that sweeps away even the chap who started it.

In *The Real Thing*, the semiautobiographical Henry Boot and, in life, the unavoidably autobiographical Tom Stoppard state or have stated their inability to come to grips with and write about love. Yet here, even more than in *Night and Day*, a less successful work, the subject is largely love, and though Stoppard has some pertinent things to say about it, his pertness militates against the pertinence. Take a woman's complaint that so much has been written about the misery of the unrequited lover "but not a word about the utter tedium of the unrequitee," where, as so often here, the very diction undercuts the *cri de coeur*, sometimes, but not always, intentionally. These characters go about their infidelities—really testimonials of love meant to make the other person feel—in a jokey context, with anguish ever ready to melt into epigrams. In *Peter Hall's Diaries*, Sir Peter attends a performance of Shaw's *Pygmalion* with Tom and Miriam Stoppard, and carps that this play is "love without pain." In its more serious moments,

The Real Thing seems to be pain without love and, finally, pain without pain.

And remarkable as the wit is, one gasps for respite. Must even a very young girl have adult wit? Must even a common soldier be a laughing philosopher? Must one wife be more clever than the next? And though much of the wit is golden, e.g., "You're beginning to appall me—there's something scary about stupidity made coherent," there is much that is merely silver and tarnishes in the open air. Thus there is rather too much of what I'd call the joke of the displaced or vague referent. For example, a wife says she deplores all this humiliation, and when the husband says he regrets its being humiliating to her, she rejoins, "Humiliating for you, not for me." If her father worries about daughter Debbie's being out late in a part of town where some murders have been committed, Mother quips that Debbie is not likely to kill anyone. The archetypal form of this occurs in: "I'm sorry." "What for?" "I don't know."

Still, it is all civilized and much of it scintillating, even if Stoppard's heart seems mostly in the unfeeling jokes such as the diatribe against digital watches—a long tirade whose every barb works like clockwork—than in the more feeling ones such as "Dignified cuckoldry is a difficult trick, but I try to live with it. Think of it as modern marriage." (I may have got this slightly wrong, but so has Stoppard.) The play has been greatly rewritten since it left London and is, I am told on good authority, much improved here. Certainly the production could scarcely be bettered. Any laugh that Stoppard might have missed, Mike Nichols, the ingenious director, has quietly but dazzlingly slipped in, and Tony Walton's sets are charming and suggestive, and can be changed with a speed that redounds to their glory and the play's efficiency. Anthea Sylbert's costumes look comfortably lived in, and Tharon Musser's hard-edged lighting matches the author's wit.

I have never before liked Jeremy Irons, but here his wimpy personality and windy delivery work wonders for him in creating a Henry who can rattle off jests at breakneck speed, then put on the brakes to achieve heartbreaking slowness. Weakness of aspect and personality become touching, and there is throughout a fine blend of shrewdness and fatuity, irony and vulnerability. Despite his musical illiteracy and assorted pip-squeakeries, this man, in Irons's hands, makes you believe that he is an artist of talent, and that under the flippancies, deep down in his flibbertigibbety soul, he cares about something. As his two wives, Glenn Close and Christine Baranski are both highly accomplished comediennes, who can get under the skin of comedy as easily as under that of another character. Close's English accent is better, but both look very much like English actresses, which is both apposite and aesthetically unfortunate. As Debbie, Cynthia Nixon manages to be precocious without being obnoxious. Kenneth Welsh is a marvelous Max, wonderfully different on stage and on stage-within-stage. As the young actor Billie, Peter Gallagher slips superbly from difficult accent to accent, and combines pliable ease with solid manliness. In the only somewhat underwritten role of Brodie, Vyto Ruginis nevertheless creates a fully fleshed character.

The one problem with the play is that those two mirrors are so damned clever they can reflect away even with nothing between them. That would make Stoppard another Wilde—not bad. Now how about trying for another Molière?

Old Times

In a theater full of phonies, there is, I believe, none bigger, none more pervasive, none phonier than Harold Pinter, whose terminally specious *Old Times* is being revived at the Roundabout, insofar as a corpse can be revived. That he has taken in a large segment of the so-called literate world is only a depressing comment on that world—literate, semiliterate, pseudoliterate, or illiterate, with the boundaries as blurred as those between Third World countries. If there is one thing that distinguishes the culture consumers of this century from those of previous eras, it is that if people in the past did not understand an alleged artwork, they tended to think it was bad. In our century, if something is not understood, the tendency is to deem it deeper, subtler, finer for that. Both attitudes are wrongheaded, but the second is by far the more deleterious and culturally deadening.

A good work finally establishes itself even in the teeth of critical and public incomprehension. The only sad part is that, in the past, very often the author had to die before recognition came—think of Büchner, think of Kleist. Nowadays, however, any clever faker in any art—any dog—has his day, which, having been enshrined by "experts" in books, museums, concert halls, and duly seconded by a public of culture vultures and me-too sheep, may extend into decades, even a century, before the crust of undeserved adulation can be scraped off it. There are whole movements, such as Abstract Expressionism and a great deal of post-Webernian music, that must be flushed down the drain before true art can have a chance and humanity recover its aesthetic sanity. The reasons for the triumph of sham are too numerous and complex to be gone into here, but two major contributing factors can be cited. One is poor education, which begets gulls and charlatans, who interbreed and reproduce in geometric progression; another, general loss of self-confidence (despite that sublime cautionary tale by Hans Christian Andersen), whereby people dare no longer say, "I don't care what anybody claims, shouts, semiologizes, or deconstructs, this stinks, and no one can tell me otherwise." No; one tries to score points by discovering virtues where none exists, or dumbly believes what the media have trumpeted at him. And so a piece of theatrical trash, whether it's called *La Tragédie de Carmen* or *Old Times*, some eye-assaulting daub by Motherwell or Rauschenberg, or putrid cacophony by Penderecki or Nono, passes for pristine art. And where large financial investments or professional reputations are at stake, reassessments are likely to come with agonizing slowness.

I said just about everything I have to say about *Old Times* when it appeared on Broadway a dozen years ago, and you can find my evaluation in my book *Uneasy Stages*, pages 380–384. Here, with infinite distaste, I go again. Deeley, apparently a filmmaker, and his wife, Kate, manifestly nothing, inhabit a converted farmhouse, where they play host to Anna, an old friend of Kate's, now married to a rich Italian and revisiting England for the first time in twenty years. To quote from my book:

> We care neither about the characters nor about the issues. It appears that there may have been a lesbian relationship between the two women when they were roommates. There also seems to have existed a struggle for dominance between them, and perhaps an exchange of identities, which manifested itself in Anna's stealing Kate's underwear. Deeley and Kate met in a suburban cinema where both of them were seeing, apparently for the first time, *Odd Man Out* (note the title!), after which they struck up a conversation; later it emerges that Kate and Anna had seen the film together beforehand. It emerges also that, at a party, Deeley once stared up the skirt of a woman

wearing his future wife's underwear... There may, in fact, have been something between him and Anna, and Kate may have married him on the rebound, after she was rejected by Anna. And so on, through a set of imperfectly remembered or wishfully imagined incidents. What is Anna up to now? Has she come to reclaim Kate? Or would she rather snatch Deeley from her? Or does she intend to subjugate both? But of what consequence are these shadow-boxing shadows? Why should anyone give a tinker's damn about such nebulous figures with wispy, indefinable, and probably illusory problems?

The very opening device of *Old Times* betrays its utter dishonesty. While Deeley and Kate discuss the not-yet-arrived Anna in their living room, a tenebrose figure, her back turned to them and us, skulks in the upstage shadows. After a while, the lights come up full blast, the figure swivels; she's Anna, and she's here—a piece of cheap trickery leading some critics to theorize that Anna isn't there at all, except in Kate's and Deeley's minds. This is rubbish, but no more so than any other interpretation of this play, which is a set of Rorschach blots onto which you can project anything you like. (An old trope, this, but let's use it once more for *Old Times'* sake.)

Even from the standpoint of quantity, *Old Times* is a cheat. A supposed two-act, full-length play, it runs some 80 minutes including intermission, endless Pinterian pauses, and two lengthy passages in which the characters do nothing but sing snatches of supposedly suggestive golden oldies. Sung badly and without much purpose, they are no more golden than Pinter's silence, and they reduce the play to some 50 minutes. There are those who will defend all this as the mysterious workings of remembrance and forgetting. Again I quote:

> Memory and oblivion... do not work in this way. Typically, someone will declare: "I was interested once in the arts, but I can't remember now which ones they were." This gets a cheap laugh out of an absurdity that has no bearing on human reality. You might say that Pinter is not trying to write realistic dialogue. Yet even if absurd, or absurdist, the statement must have some human relevance. The joke

here is purely verbal, based on the fact that "arts" is a plural noun, requiring [a] "they" that in this context falls estrangingly, comically on our ears. If the line were deprived of its grammatical idiosyncracy and ran, "I had an artistic interest once, but I can't remember what it was," most of the humor would be gone, and most of the pseudo-meaningfulness as well. Now, when Beckett's Estragon answers Vladimir's question about what to do while they are waiting with "What about hanging ourselves?" the remark is certainly absurdist, and the humor lies in the casual formulation of so dread a notion. Yet there is human truth in this: people have killed themselves out of sheer frustrating ennui.

And that's just it: Pinter was, is, and always will be an actor who turned—not playwright, but imitation, enacted playwright, a Beckett travesty. There is wit sporadically in Pinter, but much more sheer nastiness, and still more vagueness and deliberately self-contradictory mystification. His plays—with the exception of the simpler television ones—are labyrinths without issues, leading from the excogitated to the preposterous. "Maze" and "amaze" come from the same root, but a good maze is one whose exit or meaning, can be, astonishingly, puzzled out. In a bad one, we are simply, dismally stuck. As I wrote:

> But what about the language? Pinterites will ask... Like Albee, Pinter is linguistically *nouveau riche*. Anna uses the word "lest" and Deeley is startled: "The word 'lest.' I haven't heard it in a long time." Later, there is a similar reaction: "Gaze?" "The word 'gaze.' You don't hear it very often." Accordingly, we get a certain overwriting whose verbosity is supposed to impress the audience as much as the dramatis personae; it may take any form from euphuism to bureaucratic jargon. While Kate is taking a bath, Deeley expatiates to Anna: "She gives herself a very good scrub, but can she, with the same efficiency, give herself a good rub?... I have not found this to be the case." The purpose is to create an aura of enticing sexuality for three (i.e., Which of us gets

to dry that lovely body we both desire? Couldn't we perhaps do it together?), but the mock-serious grandiloquence about trivia is only a verbal trick, not worthy of being—as, alas, it is—one of the comic mainstays of Pinter's oeuvre.

In the London premiere and the subsequent Broadway one, at least the production values were splendid. Peter Hall directed with uncanny inventiveness in John Bury's scenery bristling with slight, unnerving distortions. In New York, Mary Ure, Robert Shaw, and Rosemary Harris gave solid though unspectacular performances. Now Marjorie Bradley Kellogg has designed a set that conveys nothing (apt, perhaps, but not helpful), and Kenneth Frankel's staging, even with Pinter's help, merely approximates, instead of surpassing, Hall's. Although both Anthony Hopkins and Jane Alexander are convincing, Marsha Mason (Kate), despite a creditable British accent, isn't. Aside from other flaws, she exudes a smugness that, when uncalled for, is histrionic suicide. There is high-style costuming by Linda Fisher and high-key lighting by Judy Rasmussen, but what Pinter needs is a dressing-down and a blacking out.

The Rink

Circumstances beyond my control compelled me to see *The Rink* at its antepenultimate preview, though nothing much could have changed between Monday and Wednesday, when most of the critics went. Advance rumors, which one cannot help hearing in this business, were abuzz with references to "The Rank," and I even heard that certain people couldn't wait to read me on *this* one. I was as prepared for anything as the most dedicated Boy Scout, but—I'm sorry if this comes as a disappointment to "certain people"—*The Rink* is not really rank, only long, intermittently tedious, fairly cliché-ridden, and lacking in any sort of urgency, even the musical-comedy kind. But it has its points, is never unbearable, though rather overpriced at $45 for a rear mezzanine seat, which is all we could get for February 6. However, the sound (by Otts Munderloh) was very live up there, and I could see everything as plain as the nose on a performer's face.

The Rink is another pseudosignificant, comi-tragi-sentimental

tale of a long and supposedly complex mother-daughter relationship in the manner of *Terms of Endearment*. Here Anna, the mother,
is selling the Antonelli roller rink, somewhere on a doomed eastern
boardwalk sometime in the seventies, just as Angel, her 30-year-old
hippie daughter (29, according to Anna: "I'm your mother—there's
no way I have a 30-year-old daughter!"), makes one of her rare
return visits from her roamings, this one meant to be permanent:
"I can't run any more, Ma. I'm tired. I'm real tired." Since Grampa
Antonelli, disgusted with his son, Dino, left the rink to Anna and
Angel, Dino's wife and daughter (or, respectively, Chita Rivera
and Liza Minnelli), the daughter could legally stop the wreckers,
who have already begun moving everything out of the rink, which
served also as the Antonelli residence. Even Angel's beloved glitter-
ball seems gone, soon to be replaced by a ball of greater militancy.
Will Angel be able to stop this? Will Anna finally shake the years of
unhappiness with Dino and after Dino, and go off with "good old
Lenny," a devoted but unglamorous suitor of many years, to Rome,
freedom, and not quite marriage, because "at our age, people don't
get married; they just set up light housekeeping and wait for the
Social Security checks to start coming in."

The book is by Terrence McNally, who has written plays with
plots, but don't go to *The Rink* expecting a working story. As the
time frame keeps fluctuating between past and present, and often
fuses the two, there is no coherent, credible action, only clichés
and crises, one after another after another. But McNally can create amusing situations and write funny lines, and there are some
of the former and quite a few of the latter floating around. There
are also some unintentionally funny lines, such as Miss Minnelli's
repeated complaint to Miss Rivera, "You never once told me I'm
pretty!" The score, by John Kander and Fred Ebb, is in their usual
vein: music generally pleasant but awesomely derivative, and the
two best songs ("After All These Years" and "What Happened to
the Old Days?") sounding almost interchangeable; lyrics always
adequate and seldom exciting. Too bad, because the one number
that takes chances, "Mrs. A.," shows that the team could do more.
And too bad also that the cleverest lyrics (in "Don't Ah Ma Me")
get the most tuneless tune.

Graciela Daniele's choreography may be her best yet, which
places it somewhere near the top of second-rate choreographies.
But when it tries to be serious, as in a gang rape, that is no more
compelling than the show's other crises. The title number, per-

formed on roller skates, is jolly and deftly executed. Then there is extremely effective, evocative, and versatile scenery by Peter Larkin, with genuinely painterly qualities and that fish-eye-lens perspective one finds in such paintings as Robert Delaunay's *St. Séverin*. This is helped enormously by Marc B. Weiss's imaginative lighting, which makes the tawdry look poetic and neatly undercuts the lush with a tinge of irony. It is not Weiss's fault if the clever final *coup de théâtre* is also rather mushy.

Opportunities for the costume designer to shine are limited, but Theoni V. Aldredge has had—and conveyed—fun wherever possible, as in the compilation of not-so-glad-rags in which Angel turns up, eliciting Anna's "You know certain outfits trigger me. Did you have to wear all ten of them?" A. J. Antoon has directed fluidly and inventively, and must be credited with the effortless blending of disparate elements. The stage space is used well, and movement is not allowed to stall or to become excessive. But before I can discuss the performances, a preamble is required.

The cast, besides the Misses Rivera, Minnelli, and one standard little girl, comprises six men—a kind of barbershop, or hair-salon, sextet—who play all the other parts, starting with the wreckers and including various girls and women of diverse ages and conditions. And *The Rink* makes *La Cage aux Folles* look like *Oklahoma!* There is, of course, nothing wrong with a show on a homosexual subject looking and sounding homosexual (*La Cage*, incidentally, seems nowhere near forthright enough). But we have here an ostensibly heterosexual show being, in halfway-in, halfway-out-of-the-closet fashion, homosexualized in sundry ways. Not only could the men in drag have been more suitably replaced by women, but even the two leading roles seem at times to be played by men. Here the direction errs, but much of it has to do with acting styles and writing. For instance, would a mother trying to encourage her shy teenaged daughter to be bolder with the boy she fancies say, "I could go for him myself. See the ass on that kid?" In fact, the entire Anna-Angel relationship comes across more like an endless lovers' quarrel than a mother-daughter imbroglio, which may resemble the former but not that closely. Especially when you consider how pallid and amorphous the Anna-Dino and other heterosexual relations are, not to mention that campy mixture of exaggeration and winking at the audience with which much of the show is played.

And the sell-out audience picked up on the innuendos and kept falling into hysterical ecstasies. The theater was awash with subtexts that had nothing to do with the avowed text. In this light, Miss Minnelli's and Miss Rivera's performances are knowing and efficiently executed, though Miss Rivera's is far more proficiently multifaceted. Miss Minnelli can belt out a song in her plangent, vibrato-laden voice, and she does more than justice to the childish eagerness of the adolescent Angel as well as the sense of rejection of the older one. What she lacks is something beyond the floppy-toy and tearful-clown qualities, beyond the painted smile and the hangdog pathos. Conversely, Miss Rivera—who, to be sure, has the better part—is an able singer, authoritative dancer, and clear enunciator, with an emotional range that has gradations as well as extremes, and a projection of gags with a certain zing—more vibration than punch—that is idiosyncratic and winning.

The six men perform with dextrous flexibility and blend into a suitably diversified yet harmonious ensemble. Rightly, no one here is stellar and no one lets the group down in any of his several supporting roles, although Scott Holmes lacks the magnetism to make the weakly conceived and underwritten part of Dino take on incremental life. For the record, be it noted that Miss Minnelli receives a rare double opening ovation: applause when the lights go on revealing her from behind, and more applause when she turns to face the audience. It is nice when your back hand is as strong as your fore hand.

Cinders

In E. E. Cumming's play *Santa Claus*, there is an endemic disease named cinderella wreaking its devastation; in Janusz Głowacki's play *Cinders*, cinderella is both a disease and an opiate in present-day Poland: a play put on by girls in a reform school, enacted listlessly to show how much grimmer than the Grimms is Socialist reality; a peg on which a swinging young Polish film director can hang his documentary about crime and rehabilitation; a fantasy, about a girl like themselves who marries a rich American, with which the inmates while away nocturnal hours when they ought to be sleeping, because a communal daydream is preferable to individual nightmare. As Głowacki says in a program note, there are many versions of the Cinderella story, and the main plot of *Cinders* is yet another, tragic one. Indeed, the hope of the lowly and downtrodden to be rescued by a prince on both the personal and political levels makes Poland a palimpsest of Cinderella stories.

Głowacki is a provocative writer, as his screenplay for Andrzej Wajda's underrated comedy, *Hunting Flies*, demonstrates. There is similarly wry to bitter humor in *Cinders*. The contribution of Communist governments to their respective literatures is the Kafkaization of much of the writing; ironically, Kafka's only partly antibureaucratic satire swathed in more private obsessions has become the chief mode of encoded opposition to the political and social conditions. True, Poland had earlier produced such notable neo-Kafkans as Bruno Schulz and Witold Gombrowicz, though the latter (in his journal) claimed to be bored by Kafka.

The very opening scene of *Cinders*, in which the decent but weak principal of the reformatory is informed by an inspector that a filmmaker wants to make a documentary about the *Cinderella* dramatization the girls have performed, is supremely Kafkaesque. The inspector loathes equally theater, the Cinderella tale, and avant-garde filmmakers, but is no less loath to commit himself, being a consummate fence sitter, the Communist-bureaucratic model of the medieval stylite. The wretched principal is reduced to trying to unscramble the secret meaning of the inspector's gnomic utterances and to figure out the correct response. Everything the inspector says is a test, though even the tester isn't sure what the right answer is; the hapless examinee does not even understand the questions. While the mindless inspector strives to read the principal's mind, that mind is so frantically busy trying to read between the inspector's lines as to lose all decipherable identity. It is a cat-and-mouse game as comic as it is scary, and George Guidall (Principal) and Peter McRobbie (Inspector) play it with a sure sense of its vertiginous absurdity and lurking danger.

Soon a third player is added: the deputy principal, a perfect apparatchik with nary a scruple and a kind of shrewdness that borders at one end on stupidity and at the other on dementia. He embodies that odd mixture of ludicrousness and menace that, by means of imbecile faithfulness to a cause, enables such nonentities to tyrannize their inferiors and threaten their immediate superiors while enhancing their self-importance. Thus the deputy principal clearly has his eye on the principal's job and will use any tool, from lies to double-talk, from groveling humility to sneaky undermining. Meanwhile, the director wants to make a searing documentary that will wow them in the West, which means that the *Cinderella* sequences have to be interspersed with wrenching self-revelations by each girl; these the deputy principal proposes to elicit. If necessary, the girls' TV will be confiscated. But, the perplexed director remonstrates, "there's no television in the rec room." "You're right," comes the deputy's answer, "we'll have to give them one, then take it away." The trick is to invoke "certain measures. Sanctions. We'll terrify them. Gently."

The director is a swine of a different color. He lives in Western-style comfort and makes deliberately ambivalent films that please the Polish authorities with seeming flattery while they are also winning prizes at Oberhausen, where they look like daring exposés. He purports to care about the girls, to want to improve their lot, but except for willingness to join the deputy principal in having sex with one or another of them, his real purpose is cinematic exploitation. His interest focuses on the girl playing Cinderella, who, despite a beastly background that drove her to crime, has true nobility and heroism. While the other girls either cravenly confess for the camera merely to play ball with the deputy (even though they stand to be stigmatized forever by the revelations perpetuated on film), or else concoct lurid pasts more criminal than the truth to delight the director, Cinderella refuses to talk. She will act her silly role but not spill her guts for her tormentors. This, though she is the best actress in the lot and the best teller of tales—clearly, the artist—as well as the protector of weaker girls against the bullies.

The chief bully is the bruiser who plays the Prince. A kind of androgyne, very probably a lesbian, totally ruthless, she is the ringleader, sadistic to her fellows, yet a toady to the authorities. In due time, the principal, whom Cinderella pities and even helps with his crumbling marriage, will be made to seem to let her down (being himself outwitted and overpowered), and she will be surrounded by enemies from above and below as her fellow inmates are made to think her a stoolie. After a gallant fight, the artist-heroine succumbs in a defeat that is also a victory, but mostly a defeat.

This is where Kafka has it all over his current, politicized disciples. He wrote fantasies that, despite symbolic overtones, were not mere allegories, but achieved, through ambiguity and indirection, a wider range. Głowacki, however, like so many others, offers pure political allegory, with every major character an archetype. Though his writing is peripherally splendid, the center lacks multiple resonance, and there is finally something simplistic about

Cinders, as in the work of such other Polish dramatists as Mrożek and Różewicz.

But the message does not always win out over artistry. The already cited opening scene; another in which Cinderella tries to straighten out the principal's home life; still another in which the deputy principal, while seeming to endorse the protest song of the girls, makes them, by insidious degrees, rewrite it into a hymn to things as they are, an ode to oppression—these and a few others are strong, funny-frightful stuff. Still others, however, are monochromatic and schematic, and there are inconsistencies in the writing, as when the girls, at one moment not to be fooled by the deputy principal, walk into a similar trap the next. And Cinderella, though properly hardened and suspicious, may still be too brave and noble, too much like the heroes of Romantic dramas by Krasiński and Słowacki, who uncompromisingly wanted everything or nothing.

Still, while Głowacki sticks to understatement and irony, there is much to admire. To a man's offer, "I'm going to help you," Cinderella replies, "Aren't you frightened someone will walk in?" Such things dazzle in Christina Paul's excellent translation, though the current production, at the Public Theater, tries to be over-American, turning zloty into dollars, and Polish girls (sometimes) into creatures of S. E. Hinton. But John Madden has directed magisterially (how the space teems with life!) in Andrew Jackness's minimal but deftly depressing décor, to which Jane Greenwood added costumes exuding squalor. Besides the already praised Messrs. Guidall and McRobbie, there is Robin Gammell's tremendous deputy principal, superbly pitched between the serpentine and the vermicular, and Lucinda Jenney's marvelous Cinderella, humane without letting up on her toughness, touching without any false pathos. Christopher Walken, playing the director, is good and creepy, as is Dori Hartley as the Prince. Among the other, somewhat underwritten, girls, Anna Levine makes the most of her part. Add to this haunting music by Richard Peaslee and highly dramatic lighting by Paul Gallo, and you have a flawed but worthy play, with plenty of diamonds among its ashes.

Death of a Salesman;
Glengarry Glen Ross

One of America's two or three contributions to mythology is the figure of the salesman. From the serpentine snake-oil seller to the horny depredator of farmers' daughters, from Flannery O'Connor's lecherous Bible peddler to E. E. Cummings's "it that stinks to please," he skulks and scampers through American literature and lore, the wily Odysseus who sailed west "to seek a newer world." From 76 trombones to one Brooklyn Bridge, there is nothing he cannot sell to the U.S.A. (the Unwary Suckers of America), and if, in the sentimental play whose eponymous hero he is, he commits suicide, no matter—there is one reborn every minute.

The current revival of *Death of a Salesman* makes woefully clear what a confused piece of goods this supposedly supreme American tragedy is. Arthur Miller apparently meant to show us a sympathetic fellow, the salesman Willy Loman, destroyed by his materialistic values, by capitalism's fiats. This, as Miller tells us in an essay, "is the tragedy of a man who did believe [why not "believed"?] that he alone was not meeting the qualifications laid down for mankind by those clean-shaven frontiersmen who inhabit the peaks of broadcasting and advertising offices." But, as he says in another essay, for a play to be a tragedy, "the joy must be there, the promise of the right way of life must be there." Leaving aside the questionableness of this definition, where is that promise in *Death of a Salesman*? It may be brother Ben, who struck it rich in Alaska and South Africa's jungles (though what jungles there may be there, only Miller knows); but he, with his fortune in diamonds, is as much of a materialist as Willy, merely a bolder one. Or it may be that the supersalesman David Singleman, who at age 84 could still conduct successful business in 30 cities without leaving his hotel room, and who died the death of a salesman in his green velvet slippers in a railway smoker and had hundreds of salesmen and buyers at his funeral. But his values were no different from Willy's, either, only he was better at implementing them. So puny Willy is further diminished by having been outsmarted by Ben and outsold by Dave.

That leaves Biff, whose "self-realization" is meant to be, Miller says, "the counterbalance to Willy's disaster." Well, Biff is one hell of a confused and ineffectual counterbalance. To the extent that he stands for anything, it is for the recognition of failure: his father's as "a hard-working drummer who landed in the ash can," and his own as a dollar-an-hour toiler who is "nothing!" And his solution? To buy a farm out West for which he either doesn't have the money or else can get it only from the insurance payment if the company swallows Willy's suicide as an accident, an outcome about which Miller remains vague. Some joy, this, in either case; some promise of the right way!

I shall not elaborate again on what I have written so many times: that Willy is a fool without redeeming virtues who browbeats his wife, raises his sons to be either horrible failures or still more horrible successes, cheats with other women, lies about his past successes, accepts handouts from his friend Charley but turns down Charley's offer of an honest job. Is this a tragic hero? Or is Biff, whose disintegration absurdly hinges on discovering his father *in flagrante*, but who already before that could not pass a high-school math test even with a friend cheating for him, and who becomes a petty thief? And what of Miller's language? Though he can replicate Willy's Jewish speech well enough (without the honesty, however, of admitting the character's Jewishness), other forms of diction here, especially the stabs at poetic heightening, are pathetic—not even tragic—fiascoes. And what about such nonsense as much of the melodrama's hinging on the discovery of a bit of rubber hose attached to the stove, with which Willy thinks of gassing himself? How would *that* look like an accident? Are insurance companies idiots? Or is Willy one? Can an idiot be a tragic hero?

I firmly believe that what made the success of the original *Salesman* was the production: Lee J. Cobb's spectacular performance and several other fine enactments, Kazan's staging, and Jo Mielziner's set. Here Ben Edwards's scenery, though clever in part and well lit by Thomas Skelton, is far less poetic; Michael Rudman's direction, though unfussy, ranges from uninventive to pedestrian; and the acting is uneven. Dustin Hoffman is an honest, proper Willy, with perfect Jewish intonation and cadences and all the pettiness and volatility Miller has written into the part. But it took Cobb's larger-than-life persona, the music of that voice, the kinetic sculpture of those gestures, the beauty of that face, and the power of that frame to make Willy, however illegitimately, transcendent. Cobb was the tragedy.

As Linda, Kate Reid is magnificent but totally un-Jewish, which is aurally and visually off-putting; yet what honest and intelligent acting! John Malkovich, who was so splendid in *True West*, is dreadful here. It is just barely possible to play Biff as a latent homosexual, but not as a midwestern one with grindingly monotonous delivery and gestures. As a result, Stephen Lang, who is a pungent, vital Happy, emerges as the more interesting son, which totally unbalances the play. And these Lomans are in no sense a family, especially with Louis Zorich, abysmal as Ben, affecting an accent that may at best be Martian. The others, with the exception of Kathy Rossetter, are good, and David Huddleston, as Charley, is outstanding. Good, too, are Ruth Morley's understatedly graceless costumes. But the play, with every new revival, creaks more and more unto heaven.

I take this opportunity to correct a serious misquotation that crept into my obituary for Tennessee Williams (*New York*, March 14, 1983). I there gave the most famous line from *Death of a Salesman* as "Attention must be paid to such a man," though it reads, in fact, "Attention, attention must be finally paid to such a person." Actually, I think my version is an improvement, but since I used the line to demonstrate the unwarranted presence of blank verse in Mr. Miller's prose, I must withdraw the example. The piece of prose in question is not blank verse, merely blank.

The dead Willy Loman, this time unsentimental and sleazy, rises again as a bunch of cunning hucksters in David Mamet's *Glengarry Glen Ross*, about a Chicago real-estate office (part, of a larger concern, in both senses of that word) whose four salesmen and manager hustle worthless Florida land with such prestigious monikers as Glengarry Highlands and Glen Ross Farms to gullible dolts whose hearts are in peculiar highlands with palm-studded beaches. Mamet spent a year as assistant manager of a Chicago real-estate office and says he loved it; he now gives us a systematic survey of the trade's outer and inner workings. The first act of this rather short play takes place in a Chinese restaurant that is both refuge and surrogate office for the salesmen. It is in three scenes, three archetypal confrontations: an aging salesman who has lost his grip is trying to buy the help of a ruthless young office manager; a highpowered, sinister salesman attempts to suborn an insecure colleague into ransacking the office files for hot leads to sell to the competition; a swaggering, cunning young salesman cons a poor slob into buying a piece of Glengarry, a bit of real-estate moonshine masquerading as bonded scotch.

In Act II, the files have been robbed, the office is a shambles, and a detective abetted by the manager is questioning the employees, one by one. There is multifarious intramural collusion and backstabbing, and the play becomes a sort of thriller, although the incident that topples the culprit does not ring true. Nevertheless, this act has far more dramatic life than the first as it switches from toned-down Pinter to souped-up Hecht and MacArthur. The characters are now less dependent on that Pinterian wordplay that glitters with dazzling nastiness or glaring stupidity, but that is really just an authorial trick of verbal one-upmanship or one-downmanship. Consider the casuistic combat in this exchange: "The thing we are talking about... We are *speaking* about it." The substitution of a synonym is supposed to chop the other fellow down to kindling, yet fails by being too clever for the speaker (or talker) and too facile for the author. Line after line is both too clever and not clever enough, e.g., "The broads all look like they just got fucked with a dead cat."

In the second act things get appreciably livelier. "When I talk to the police, I get nervous," complains one grilled salesman. "You know who doesn't?" responds a jaunty colleague. "Thieves!" Or take this advice from a scoundrel on how to talk to the cops: "Always tell the truth. It's easier to remember." Two funny lines, though unfortunately, they cancel each other out. Still, as in Miller, we get here the exhilaration of selling, but without Miller's sentimentality. Yet here the trouble is that the author enjoys his characters too much, that he revels in their brazen, agile crookedness. This strikes me as reprehensible, immoral. It would be all right in a totally cynical work such as *Volpone*, where the victims are merely inept versions of the villains; but the dupe in *Glengarry* is a pathetic nonentity, which makes the others monsters.

Finally, I question the contention of Mamet's champions that the merciless profusion of four-letter words is skillfully turned into a litany, a poetry of the obscene. I may be an unpoetic clod, but I must confess to not being swept away by this cloacal lyricism, which sounds to me no more convincing than Miller's attempt to drink shallowly from the Pierian spring. The obscenities are not transmuted by sufficient originality and wit as they are, say, in Jarry and Apollinaire. Nevertheless, *Glengarry Glen Ross* is a better play than *American Buffalo*, though in both the absence of women creates a lopsided world.

This is substantially the production of Chicago's Goodman Theater, directed more than adequately but less than rivetingly by Gregory Mosher, with a rather skimpy look to it that is entirely apposite.

The acting is always competent, with Joe Mantegna, Robert Prosky, and James Tolkan better than that. Several reviewers called this the best American drama of the season, and on Broadway, where its only competitors were a couple of outright flops, it certainly is.

Sunday in the Park With George

Sunday in the Park With George is, I am afraid, as clever a show as you are likely to see. There is some sort of concept, invention, originality, trick in every square inch and unsquare moment of it (well, in the first act, anyway), but the trouble with these concepts, inventions, etc. is that they are all clever rather than penetrating, revealing, exhilarating, moving, or anything else that ingenuity alone, without thoughtfulness and feeling, cannot be. It is a meal made up exclusively of fancy hors d'oeuvres; better yet, it is intricate sculpture in ice: instead of melting your heart, it melts itself. And while it lasts, it does not touch the soul with any kind of warmth, though it makes gestures in that direction; in fact, it feels icy to the touch. Not for nothing does it play in a theater adjacent to the one housing *The Real Thing*. Except that it has music—if that's what that is—it is the same kind of heaping up of dazzlement with, and frustration by, cleverness.

It would, however, be wrong to underestimate that cleverness just because the show's creators so patently overestimate it. To take Georges Seurat's famous painting *La Grande Jatte*, and coax it to life bit by bit on the stage complete with the imaginary identities and relationships of the people depicted in it, and to introduce some of Seurat's ideas about art even as bits of scenery—and, as it were, bits of plot—float down, pop up through slots, slide in, glide about, appear and disappear all over the stage… this brings into play oodles of theatrical and technical ingeniousness. Thus, because Seurat was (in a term he repudiated) a pointillist, the music will, as he paints, go staccato. Thus, if he is painting a scruffy mutt and an effete lapdog, he will sing about it in a song that barks and yaps, growls and whines. And the lyrics are, as always with Stephen Sondheim, at best infernally, at worst doggedly, clever. "What's the matter with the middle? / That's the puddle where the poodle did the piddle," even if there is no poodle among the dogs. And, as so often with Sondheim, the repulsive is at the heels of the clever: "Piece of pastry, piece of chicken, / Here's a handkerchief somebody was sick in." And, as usual with Sondheim, the composer lags behind the lyricist.

The music here is, in a sense, pointillistic throughout. There are bits of modernism—superficial borrowings from a variety of serious composers along with devices from such modish minimalists as Glass and Reich—splintered and thrown together with bits of standard Sondheimisms that here, however, sound like mere riffs. This mixture allows for some bizarre and sometimes striking effects—especially in the fetching part writing for chorus and the frequently unusual chamber instrumentation by Michael Starobin; finally, though, there is nothing to sink your teeth in, nothing with a genuine musical profile. Strictly speaking, this is a musical without a single song in it.

And what is James Lapine's book trying to impart? Something about the choice the artist must make between his art and human fulfillment (Yeats's "perfection of the work" versus "perfection of the life"), something about the envy and resentment that are the great man's lot, something about the hopelessness of a simple woman's trying to love a genius, something about unfulfilled yearnings and mutual misunderstanding. It's both too much and too little, too old and too scattered among the clevernesses of bringing *La Grande Jatte* to life; there is no time, in the one act they get, to come to know these characters except insofar as they are clichés, and surely no chance to become involved with them. "Connect, Georges, connect!" Seurat says to himself, vaguely echoing E. M. Forster, but the flecks refuse to coalesce.

The second act features a new bunch of characters. The time is today, and George, an American avant-garde artist who is Seurat's putative great-grandson, is showing his latest work, a piece of laser art entitled *Chromalume #7*, to an invited audience at MOMA. The demonstration is preceded by a slide lecture about Seurat given jointly by George and his grandmother, the baby in *La Grande Jatte*, begotten by Seurat on his mistress and model Dot. This is followed by a typical museum-opening party; then back to France and the now very changed island of Grande Jatte, where George is to create a new work at the invitation of the French government, but fears that he is going stale. Dot (whom Lapine invented along with the rest) appears to George, and there is a bittersweet, ghostly romance in which the past is relived and its wounds are healed. Or something like that; the whole confused second act seems to exist only for Bran Ferren's nifty laser show, and because Broadway musicals are expected to have two acts.

There is adorably cunning scenery by Tony Straiges, cannily Seuratian costuming by Patricia Zipprodt and Ann Hould-Ward, and spectacular lighting by Richard Nelson. There are some fine performances, notably from Bernadette Peters, Barbara Bryne, and Mandy Patinkin (though the part of Seurat is undemanding except when it goes canine); for the rest, cleverness is all. Thus some of the figures in the show are cardboard cutouts that contribute almost as much as the allegedly noncardboard ones. Even the mistress's name, Dot, is a pun on the painter's style, though in France only a dowry is called *dot*. Why not have named her, even more aptly, Dotty? There is something crazy about spending this much money and effort on mere cleverness.*

Balm in Gilead

Lanford Wilson's plays come mostly in two modes: sweet with tough overtones or harsh with an undercurrent of sentiment, indeed sentimentality, each susceptible of almost infinite variety within its perimeters. *Balm in Gilead* (1965), with its despairing, Old Testament title, is of the latter sort, and good. It has been revived with some minor changes by the author and additional concepts by the director, in a fascinating co-production by Wilson's home company, Circle Rep. and Chicago's Steppenwolf Theater. The cross-fertilization is most heartening, with one small reservation: there are a few Chicago accents where there ought to be New York ones.

The action, somewhat updated to 1972, takes place in and around an all-night coffee shop on upper Broadway, superbly designed and lighted by Kevin Rigdon. There are 25 characters: two countermen, a waitress, and assorted bums, whores, pushers, addicts, transvestites, lesbians (some categories overlap), and, at the end, even a few children celebrating Halloween. At the center of this series of conversations, monologues, and fights are Joe, a young middle-class New Yorker who has been sucked into drug pushing, and Darlene, a very young, dumb, rather too innocent drifter from Chicago, who

---

*P.S. 2005: In this and other reviews of Sondheim's music, the passage of time, repeated exposure, and my own maturing have proved me wrong.

briefly find and lose each other in a magma of anomie, crime, flare-ups, and aimlessness under the sad and angry bustle.

Wilson wants us to perceive the group as a complex unit, a representative cross section: "the scum, the lost, the desperate, the dispossessed, the cool"; their dialogue, like their lives, is made to overlap, creating discontinuous or semi-obliterated verbiage rather than communication and solidarity, but also a certain dimly sensed complicity that sometimes elicits a flutter of fellow feeling before a conflagration of rage or the hoarfrost of apathy takes over. We get, as always with Wilson, a rare understanding (or minutely diverse lives, some of them so crumbled into triviality and non sequiturs that one wonders by what heroic patience and compassion he could focus on them long enough even to notice them, let alone comprehend, absolve, and love them.

And this is the rare dramatist who is both witty and humorous, both empathetic and impartial, both brutal and delicate. He is as apt at rapid-fire exchanges as at long, funambulistic, breathtakingly sustained monologues, and he sees all his characters from the inside. Take the scene where Darlene, the still untainted future whore, tells about how she almost got married to Cotton ("They called him an albino; you know what that is?" "Yes." "It's a kind of horse.") to Ann, a former teacher but already a hardened prostitute, who, nevertheless, slowly warms to the girl's absurd and absolutely boring story. Darlene rattles on into some sublime stupidity above and beyond her words, while Ann, with minuscule interjections and one tiny action, conveys a fleeting recognition, a flurry of sisterliness.

Or consider the moment when Joe and Darlene leave the coffee shop for their first, tentative yet grasping, sexual encounter in her pad across the street. "I haven't seen the neighborhood at daytime yet," says she. And he: "Neither has anybody else." A world of implications underlies a funny line—lives whose daylight side is completely divorced from their night side. Or this exchange between Ann and John, the counterman: "I made a hundred tonight. [In the 1965 version, only "sixty," but inflation has upped many figures in the dialogue.]" "Hundred scores or hundred bills?" "Four scores—ha!—and 38 cents. I always end up with odd change; never can figure out where the hell it came from." Those 38 cents are the difference between routine competence and art, between a play accosting life and life itself trapped in a play.

John Malkovich has directed with vaulting imaginativeness and dedicated accuracy, but also with too much of a muchness. In this he may have been abetted by Gary Sinise, his fellow actor-director from Steppenwolf, who plays the bum Dopey, a bit of a *raisonneur* even in the text, who here, however, becomes compère, magician, even Demiurge, governing lights and music, pulling the invisible strings whereby human marionettes are activated or made to subside. There is now a *Nicholas Nickleby*ish scenario before the play proper begins, and an expressionist lighting plot that makes massive, perhaps over-explicit statements. Though fine, a little less would go farther.

Most of the acting is first-rate. There are spectacularly delivered comic monologues by James Pickens Jr., and a no less tellingly rendered interior monologue, externalized and scattered in fragments throughout the play, by Terry Kinney. As Ann, Glenne Headly is an arresting mixture of flintiness and remnants of complaisance. Paul Butler and Zane Lasky make two very different but equally convincing countermen. As a pair of lesbians and probable prostitutes, Karen Sederholm, zonked, and Charlotte Maier, terrifying, are remarkable. As Xavier, Tom Zanarini (his lines now much improved by the author) makes a tiny part memorable, as Bruce McCarty does one whose lines, moreover, are mostly in Spanish.

Laurie Metcalf could be a magnificent Darlene—her enormous monologue is a treasure trove of deliciously dippy details—if only she did not overdo her dithering, were a bit less mannered. Also attractive, as the part explicitly calls for. As Joe, Danton Stone is even more miscast; something piddling and gristly about him makes him better in supporting parts. And Gary Sinise is directorishly self-conscious as Dopey. But Miss Headly earns further praise for her wonderfully idiomatic costuming. "Is there no balm in Gilead? Is there no physician there?" In life, perhaps not; in Lanford Wilson's art, decidedly.

Hurlyburly

After *Goose and Tomtom*, I feared not just for David Rabe's talent, but even for his sanity. With the current *Hurlyburly*, however, the author of the deservedly acclaimed Vietnam trilogy reclaims, and even adds to, his reputation. The increments are chiefly in the area of humor; though Rabe has been funny before, I doubt if his previous work possessed such passages of sustained comedy, verbal and visual gags topping one another in a riotous *gradus ad Parnassum*. True, there are fairly painful longueurs in the more than three hours of this dark comedy, yet there is also some sort of payoff even in the overlong stretches. And although *Hurlyburly* emerges (unintentionally) as a play more or less about nothing, that nothing ascends, in its better moments, to a philosophical nothingness, which has a sorry dignity of its own. Unfortunately, the play also tries, or seems to try, to become seriously concerned—it is extremely hard to distinguish between irony and naïveté in some of its passages—and this does not work at all.

Eddie and Mickey are two young casting directors sharing a good-humoredly ramshackle house in the Hollywood Hills. They are close friends (though this has to be taken on faith), even if Mickey is a casual cynic and Eddie is a more sensitive, introspective type who has been hurt by life and is, accordingly, played by William Hurt. One regular visitor is Phil, a cloddish, macho actor, half ludicrously pontificating slob, half short-fused and sadistic maniac, and altogether obsessed with promiscuous sex, although married and the father of a baby girl. Another is Artie, a small, unsightly, middle-aged, Jewish hack screenwriter, similarly obsessed. For all four the goal is Making It, which subdivides into making money, making a name for yourself, and making women. The chief aids along the way are liquor, cocaine, and conversation (which last, in turn, subdivides into airheaded and heavy); the obstacles are those demanding bitches who are always separated or divorced from one, or else leaving or being left by one—and perhaps also one's inveterate lack of talent. And then there is the whopping dissociation of sensibility between what one thinks and says, or says and does, or does and is.

As for the women, they, too, suffer from a detached retina of the inner eye. There is Donna, a fallen yet innocent teenager who seems to live in a hotel elevator and has only one treasured possession: Willie Nelson's Stardust album, about which she rhapsodizes with touching, transcendent imbecility. She is brought to Eddie and Mickey by Artie as "a CARE package, so you don't say I never give you nothin'." They can "keep her and fuck her" if they want to, "just to stay in practice in case you meet a woman." When the boys express some doubts about her, Arnie exclaims: "What do you want from me? A guarantee? She worked the last time I used her." Mickey and Phil, who has just beaten up his wife for interrupting his "Far East theory—you know, it's a complex fucking idea," promptly go to it.

Then there is Darlene, a pseudosophisticated photojournalist. Eddie and she fell for each other, but then Mickey took her out for dinner and, because their vibes proved right, did not come back till around 6 A.M., so, as Eddie bitterly notes, "the dinner must have been successful." But upon realizing that Eddie's need is greater, Mickey, a true Pythias, cedes Darlene to his Damon. The pair fall to it in a wildly comic scene in which they dither about commitment and the rest of the jargon even as Eddie's head is already bobbing away under Darlene's skirt. Later, things will bog down between them because Eddie theorizes at length that just as she doesn't care about which of two restaurants he'll take her to when she is starving, she cannot decide which of two men to go to bed with. Poor Darlene, who says things like "I got myself semi-straight—I was semi-functional anyway," is now in danger of being driven wholly bananas.

Lastly, there is Bonnie, who does exotic dances clad in a balloon, performs fellatio on visiting firemen in the back of cars while her six-year-old daughter is regaled with fairy tales in the front seat, and is game for just about any game in town except for some misgivings about Phil, whom the boys fix up with her. Phil, for no reason, wallops her and throws her out of her own car, and when she shows her horrible bruises to Eddie, Eddie's sympathy is all for Phil. As Mickey later rebukes Eddie, "This investment is very safe, because no matter how far you fall, Phil will be lower." Bonnie, at any rate, keeps some horse sense and wry humor, though she, too has to delude herself manifoldly to keep going.

It is true, as has been noted, that the play's first half is better, mainly because it does not drag in quasi-serious philosophizing, Still, it is not as if all *Hurly* were good and all *burly* bad. Snappy bits keep surfacing throughout, and the ending is even moving in its emotionally twisted, strangulated way. In fact, only one long scene involving anagrams tries one's patience beyond endurance. There are, however, problems with language as well—several characters, but especially Eddie, speak in too long sentences with overassertive paragraph structure. But the chief difficulty is Eddie himself: Rabe seems to be divided, indeed riven, about him. To the extent that he is part of the ghastly Hollywood scene, Eddie is guilty; but to the extent that he is Rabe's alter ego, he is meant to be deeper, more sinned against, more likable. The split is beyond mending, and with Eddie in patches, the play, too, falls apart. In the end, we can tell no more than Rabe can whether we are beholding shallowness posturing as existential trauma or stature eroded by parental, societal, political iniquities.

Yet the production is a wonder. The amusingly apt scenery of

Tony Walton, the subtly satirical costumes of Ann Roth, the down-right analytical lighting of Jennifer Tipton provide a perfect setting for Mike Nichols's magisterial direction. This is, in fact, more like a cross between choreography and painting, always with something kinetically or pictorially challenging to delight us—though, at times, I did feel suffocated by cleverness. And then there is that dream of ensemble acting come true.

William Hurt is not quite up to the near-superhuman task of making complete sense of the fragmented Eddie, but he comes impressively close, and such a scene as the one in which he talks back at his TV set is as fine a piece of acting as you can see anywhere *off* TV. Harvey Keitel (Phil) is awesomely right and can even gain some legitimate sympathy for a sick brute; Judith Ivey (Bonnie) is so phenomenal that she can play table tennis with your heart and be at both ends of the table simultaneously. Christopher Walken (Mickey), his irritating mannerisms seemingly forgotten, is as good as he was in his early days, which is superb; Sigourney Weaver (Darlene) plays a tall woman with filigree adorableness, an emotional cliché-monger with a sprig of fresh mint in every platitude, and benightedness with consummate intelligence—than which no one could want more. As Artie, the Jewish leprechaun, Jerry Stiller radiates gnomic wisdom—watch him parry "Just because you're Jewish doesn't make you Freud" with "And just because you are whatever the hell you are doesn't make you what the fuck you think you are!" And—as Donna, Cynthia Nixon plays the cherubic child-whore with perfect, unself-conscious asepticism; if she doesn't reach into your marrow with her last two lines, you must have been deboned.

Rabe has been accused of misogyny in this play, and his men are indeed beastly to and about women. Yet if *Hurlyburly* has any Pyrrhic winners in it, it is the women who, as mothers and daughters, wrest a tiny victory from their defeat as lovers and wives.

Benefactors

Before Michael Frayn, the author of *Noises Off,* became a playwright and novelist of distinction, he was a sometimes delightful, sometimes devastating (and often both) satirical *feuilletoniste* for the *Guardian* and *Observer*. In one of his columns, he noted, "I'm not entirely sure

with what motive the other cheek is not only turned but so relentlessly hammered against one's fist"; in another, he declared himself
"a bureaucracy-loving socialist... who believes that people... should
have all their decisions made for them by... so-called experts who
think they know what's best for everyone." Mainly, though not wholly, out of these concepts, he has written a play, *Benefactors*, which,
while probably not the best, is surely the most provocative drama I
have seen in years. Playing at London's Vaudeville Theatre, it can be
described as a strangely unsettling, tragic vaudeville.

David Kitzinger, an architect working for the city of London,
is planning the redevelopment of the not quite slum but "twilight
area" around Basuto Road, a name with significantly Third World
associations. David is an enthusiastic do-gooder, but a bright, tasteful, cultivated one—just like his wife, Jane, an anthropologist who
works for him, now chiefly by interviewing folks in "Basutoland"
about the sort of housing they would prefer. The Kitzingers have
smart children whom we never get to see. But we do get to see their
untidy neighbors, Colin and Sheila Molyneux, whom the Kitzingers
have all but adopted (David and Colin were university friends) and
whom they are dragging into respectability; we do not get to see
their unsmart children. Colin, a brilliant, bitter classics scholar, now
edits a dubious women's magazine and an encyclopedia; on a Swiss
vacation, he married a sweet but dopey ex-nurse, Sheila, whom he
loved for three months in Lugano and one in London, and never
again—her or anyone else. He brims with cynical ill will toward all,
and toward David, his chief benefactor, in particular.

The Molyneux depend on the Kitzingers for numerous benefits—from meals through child care to family outings—yet when
David gets truly absorbed with building ultramodern housing in
the Basuto Road, Colin fights him, mostly out of pristine spite. Of
course, he makes a grand crusade of it, pretends to help people preserve what they are used to and love. David, his hands full of—and
usually tied by—bureaucratic red tape, nevertheless forgives Colin
his destructive, and largely successful, campaign against him. By
this time, Colin has left his job and family to become a rabble-
rousing derelict. The useless Sheila has become a valuable, though
costly, assistant to David, with whom she is unrequitedly in love.
Jane, in whom Colin claims to perceive a certain kindred blackness,
has gone to work for an organization defending old housing, which
supports Colin, whom she hates, and undermines David, whom she
loves. And she becomes bossy.

Don't think I have given away much of the plot. First, because there is a good deal more; second, because *Benefactors* is not about plot, but about ideas and counter-ideas, theories and counter-theories held, consciously or unconsciously, by its four characters. Consciously or unconsciously, they help or hinder one another, never quite knowing which is, or will turn out to be, which. Most plainly, *Benefactors* is about change, about how people, circumstances, and history change, or don't change, or both do and don't, with everyone evaluating this differently, contradictorily and even self-contradictorily, and being both right and wrong, though exactly how nobody knows—not the characters, not the audience, not the author. It is also a play about good and evil, about what people want or do not want, and about whether they have to be told what they want before they can start wanting it. It is about the way private and public issues intermesh and interact, about how there are at least two bedeviling sides to absolutely everything, about what (and whether) happiness is, and about the sadness or funniness of it all, if one only knew which. But mostly, and obsessively, it is about change—about whether everything or nothing changes, or whether, perhaps, change is the ultimate changelessness. The only thing about which it is *not* is adultery, and that in itself should clue you in on how original it is.

Benefactors, finally, is a play about everything, by a man who undertakes to be Heraclitus, Thomas Love Peacock, Shaw, Chekhov, and Anouilh; if he is a bit less good than any of them at their specialty, he is a match for all of them in this pentatholon. My companion disliked but respected the play, and got an understandable headache from it. I found it highly intelligent but unlikable after Act I, extremely ingenious and troubling by the end. Which was only the beginning. I had no peace until I had bought and read the text, only then to be properly haunted by its artless-seeming wit, harmless-looking subversion, lucid insolubility. Creepingly, imperceptibly, it overpowers you.

Michael Blakemore has directed with a disarming straightforwardness made of slyly concealed cunning in Michael Annals's suitably stripped-down design. The cast—Patricia Hodge, Brenda Blethyn, Oliver Cotton, Tim Piggot-Smith—goes about its work with a quiet efficiency that gradually reveals shattering booby traps of perfection. *Benefactors* is a problem play with a vengeance, but, as someone in it says, "if you don't like problems... don't take up living."

After the Fall

Arthur Miller's *After the Fall* is a moral and artistic embarrassment. Coming close on the heels of his ex-wife Marilyn Monroe's suicide, and not so very much after the HUAC fiasco, it was an attempt, in 1964, to show that Miller's political nobility, patience with two difficult wives, willingness to try marriage again with a third, more than compensated for his running out on his humble background and warring parents, his occasional coldness toward his women, and his intermittent (very brief) losses of courage. No justification or apology is tendered, however, for, Miller's dreadful writing, for his pompousness, pretentiousness, and formlessness, for his actionless wordiness, and for the dismalness of those endless words. For the insult to the intelligence that is *After the Fall*, there is indeed no forgiveness.

The very first statement of the text, dutifully reprinted in the program of the current revival, declares: "The action takes place in the mind, thought, and memory of Quentin," Miller's thin, and thinly disguised, lawyer alter ego. As I wrote in my review of the original production, "Though *mind* would seem to cover the whole thing very nicely, one might, pedantically, wish to throw in *memory*. But what on earth is that pleonastic *thought*, for? To satisfy Miller's need for self-magnifying grandiloquence: damn the tautologies, full speed to the stars." Miller has cut his play down from three and a half hours to a little over two and a half, which is still roughly two and a quarter hours too long. About fifteen minutes of a confrontation between Quentin and Maggie (Miss Monroe, in a blatant indiscretion that the brown hair of her present interpreter is perhaps meant to mitigate) can pass for drama; the rest is an interminable monologue into whose interstices—as Richard Gilman rightly noted in 1964—some "wind, shadows, and purple smoke" have been allowed to seep.

It is interesting to reread what some of the better critics wrote about *After the Fall* after the premiere. "Not even a simulacrum of drama," wrote Gilman of the play, calling it "a process of self-justification which at any time is repellent but which becomes truly monstrous in the absence of any intelligence, craft or art..." What made this "endless sophomoric revery about meaning... so stupefying" was that its "observations are so unutterably pompous and flaccid, that they compose a rhetoric of such hopeless banality and adolescent mutterings, that whatever might have been palpable and actual is converted into gas." Robert Brustein referred to "a shameless piece of tabloid gossip… shapeless, tedious, overwritten, and confused." Its "characters are too shallow to be plumbed," and so dishonest was the play that "while Mr. Miller is eager to scourge himself for his inability to love, he is still conducting a vendetta against the former objects of his love: there is a misogynistic strain in the play which the author does not seem to recognize, nor does he recognize how much self-justification is hidden in his apparent remorse." For more details, I urge you to read the sections on *After the Fall* in Brustein's *Seasons of Discontent* and Gilman's *Common and Uncommon Masks*.

I myself, in a review reprinted in *Uneasy Stages*, noted the self-serving arrogance of this play, and the still greater arrogance of the playwright's comments to the press about it. Said Miller: "*After the Fall* is experimental in any terms. It involves what is not a new theatrical style so much as a new style of thinking about the world, the unification, the synthesis of individual psychology and social and moral considerations to make a moral biology on the stage. Instead of having a work concentrate on one element of man, I have tried to put him on in totality." Remarking on this total put-on, I wrote:

> This about a play that has for its sum total of newness a narrator who comments on or steps into remembered events—muddying their sequence and creating formlessness—and that has for its only solution to all the injustice, lovelessness, cruelty, loneliness, disaffection in this world an utterance made by the character representing Miller's new wife to the effect that "one must finally take one's life in one's arms" and "kiss it" even though it has the "dreadful face" of an idiot child. *O altitudo!* The playwright is requested kindly to refrain from making a moral biology on the stage—or on the rug, either.

Here was a play in which, I observed, "Quentin-Miller's humdrum peccadilloes are played out under the gaze of a Nazi death camp," where the character of Maggie inconsistently "hurtles from a paragon of healthy sexuality to a pathetic, abject, neurotic bitch" and where the poor taste of badmouthing one's former wives is topped by the canonizing of one's present spouse, chiefly for her "self-abnegation—the key to a woman's success with Mr. Miller." I went on to point out the poverty of language, deficiency of grammar, and general humorlessness.

But seriously, folks, what are we to make of a playwright who can write such things as "Maybe it's not enough to know yourself. Or maybe it's too much"? I think the answer is somewhere in between, as Mr. Miller might discover were he to attempt to find it. Instead, we are given self-adulation, as when other characters gush about Quentin's "brief" (i.e., *Death of a Salesman*): "This is superb! It's hardly like a brief at all [that much is certainly true]; there's a majestic quality, like a classic opinion!" Or, when Maggie raves about Quentin's footgear: "I love your shoes. You have such good taste." Truly, a man of distinction from top to toe. And how does he express his love? "You're so beautiful it's hard to look at you." And what about all that prose poetry: "How few the days are that hold the mind together like a tapestry hung on four or five hooks." Anyone want to go for six hooks? And what about the philosophical profundities: "The evidence is bad for promises. But how else do you touch the world except with promises?" And the grammar? We get "I sat by the park for a while," which can perhaps be excused as a Yiddishism (though, if that is the case, why is there only one?) and, inexcusably, "I cannot make a decision any more without something inside me sits up..." Something inside *me* throws up.

Miller, I repeat, has cut and rewritten quite a bit. But certain softenings, attenuations, eliminations cannot save the unsalvageable. In the current revival, moreover, the main roles are glaringly miscast. Frank Langella lacks the Jewish self-hatred continually turning into self-absolution and back again that informs Quentin despite his deceptively Wasp name, and his often comedic approach to supposed high seriousness is misplaced, though it may make the proceedings more bearable. Dianne Wiest is too old, too plain, too unsexy for Maggie, who is incessantly hailed as a sex goddess. Worse, she condescends to the part, as if to say, "Please observe the intelligence with which I portray this woman's silliness"—which destroys everything.

The others are either miscast or bad, with the exception of Mary-Joan Nigro, who dares make the first wife genuinely abrasive yet preserves some sympathy for her. But among the bad performances some are conspicuously awful; still some of Mr. Miller's nobility has rubbed off on me, and I refuse to name names. John Tillinger, an able director, has been disabled by the play, with which even

Kazan came to grief. And such good designers as John Lee Beatty and Dennis Parichy fall flat with set and lighting, respectively. But after the initial fall of the writing, caducity is everywhere. The characters of the play, isolated from one another, at least reverse the old formula: they stand alone and fall together. With the death of Lillian Hellman, the mantle of America's most overrated playwright descends on Mr. Miller's stalwart shoulders.

Cyrano de Bergerac; Much Ado About Nothing

The Royal Shakespeare Company's *Much Ado About Nothing* and *Cyrano de Bergerac* are a triple triumph: for the RSC, which displays such versatility; for England, which can boast such theatrical culture and fertility; and for theater itself, which proves here how much feeling, thought, humanity, it can dispense. Before you even go on to reading the next paragraph, pick up your phone and order tickets to *both* productions—you would not want to see just one panel of a diptych.

Cyrano de Bergerac may well be the most theatrical play ever written; it is, in any case, the perfect fairy tale for adults. Other fairy tales are preponderantly for children, but Rostand's heroic comedy, by embracing adult characters and adult problems and then projecting them into glorious, all-encompassing exaggerations, enlists the fantasies and yearning of grown-ups in much the same way the Grimm brothers get kids where they live or want to live. What man would not wish to be as brave, pure, noble, brilliant, witty, literate, loving, and invincible as Cyrano, possessed of a panache compared to which the driven snow is slush? And what is his tragicomic flaw—other than excess honesty? A footling, or noseling, trick played on him by nature—the sort of absurd accident we all like to blame our setbacks on. And Roxane? A bluestocking at first—which translates into liberated female intellectual, in feminist parlance; then loving, resourceful, courageous inspirer of two grand passions (three, counting De Guiche's) that defy death for her; and despite all that, a virgin to her dying day. Ah, love divorced from the chicaneries of the flesh! If nymphomaniacs have pinups, they must be nuns.

Yet if Cyrano is hokum, it is the grandest hokum there is; on that

lower level where perfection is possible, it achieves the kind of consummation that, on the highest rung, often eludes even a Sophocles
and a Shakespeare because they are only human. The wonder of it
is that while it plays brazenly on every conceivable emotion and
wish-fulfillment fantasy, it maintains the dignity of graceful writing
and unerringly shapely stagecraft. This is why it was presumptuous
of Anthony Burgess to rewrite the play for the 1971 Tyrone Guthrie
Theater version; luckily, however, his good angel or Terry Hands,
joint artistic director of the RSC, who staged this *Cyrano*, prevailed
upon him to return to the original. The result is a literate and satisfying English version; if it does not as thrillingly as Richard Wilbur's
Molière read as if the author had written in English, it suggests, at
any rate, a collaboration between Rostand and Burgess, like the
work of an English Labiche and Martin or Flers and Caillavet.

Hands and the RSC have practiced thaumaturgy. Using black flats
and drapes as a background, Ralph Koltai has created scenery consisting of large sculptural elements ranging from the realistic to the
semi-abstract and kept relatively sparse. In this way, it is the bustle
of human bodies, their kinetic and verbal interaction, that really fills
the space. This enables scene shifts to be swift and kaleidoscopic,
the visible onslaught of stagehands echoing the rush of life. And the
way in which every set trails off into dark emptiness suggests a stark,
cavernous Beyond, a void of indifference to be lit up by the fireworks
of the heart. And then there are Alexander Reid's costumes, marvels
of understated elegance and persuasive functionalism. Roxane's outfit
on the battlefield, for instance, is the perfect midpoint between cheerfulness and sobriety, and fetching to boot.

No less imposing is Terry Hands's lighting. It is most unusual
for the director to serve as his own lighting designer, but it makes
as excellent sense as for a composer to conduct his own music.
At the theatricals in the Hôtel de Bourgogne, for example, larger-
than-life shadows festoon the walls; at Ragueneau's pastry shop, the
lights seem to be made of flour; Roxane's balcony is a floating island
of luminescence between earth and heaven; at the siege of Arras,
the brave Gascon cadets become a living frieze on a wall of white
cannon smoke; in an autumnal cloister garden, the disembodied,
burnished crown of an oak sheds dying leaves and dying light on an
undying love. Hands's lighting always manages to bring out something unexpected, an epitome or symbol, without, however, stealing
the lightning from the drama and poetry.

Hands's direction is similarly spectacular. It is bouncily physical, with action permeating the remotest corners of the stage, but always providing a harmonious accompaniment, not interference, to the soloists up front. One is tempted to see the play again just to watch these complementary, marginal activities, yet even a second seeing wouldn't suffice to reveal all that throbbingly jostling existence. Bodies and objects hurtle through the stage space, people and things collapse over or under one another—the whole world seems to be stitched together with a zest for motion; just the way the Gascon cadets make their feast disappear in a trice so as not to share it with De Guiche is like a magic trick performed in concert by a regiment of magicians.

All the acting is good, much of it wonderful. Derek Jacobi is in many ways the definitive Cyrano, with a playfully ferocious range from indomitability to pathos, from iridescent bravura to dusky self-abnegation. With his large but not preposterous nose, Jacobi takes on a curious resemblance to Robert Donat or Roger Livesey— unsightliness makes him handsomer. His voice is as agilely athletic as his body, and he has the gift of commanding attention with his very immobility. He peoples the stage with as many Cyranos as his famous tirade postulates noses, and as his stature grows, his nose seems to shrink. Only in his death scene can he not quite transcend technique into art, but by this time we care enough to forgive. As Roxane, Sinead Cusack is greatly appealing and accomplished, though her bluestocking may be a mite kittenish and her maturation into womanhood a trifle too slow. This Roxane is more bouncy than intellectual, but on its own terms the performance works and may even bring the character closer to American audiences.

The true marvel, though, is the large supporting cast, in which no performance grates, and in which many a cameo etches itself into our awareness as memorably as a lead. I was particularly taken with the subtle degrees by which John Carlisle transforms De Guiche into fineness, with Pete Postlethwaite's balancing of Ragueneau between lovableness and loutishness, and with Tom Mannion's making Christian pungently idiosyncratic rather than the customary pallid cliché. Add to this a magisterial score by Nigel Hess, which knows how to stay in period and still sneak in hints of modernity, and also knows exactly when to desist, and you have a *Cyrano* that your memory will uncork and inhale for years to come.

Visually, *Much Ado About Nothing* is even more astonishing. Darkling, polished floors and glossy Lucite partitions with trees and such painted on them, walls that suddenly sprout tall windows with silhouette's flitting behind them, a gently hilly horizon with stars and mysterious red lights playing above it—everything here is sheen, reflection, translucence, diaphaneity. But suddenly a change of lighting can make everything opaque, or maintain the transparence but tint it red or grisaille or zebraed chiaroscuro. Will-o'-the-wisps dance in our gaze like motes in moonbeams, and partitions pop up or vanish to make the space protean. And when Reid conjures up an inexhaustible array of unostentatiously sumptuous costumes, Koltai's décor and Hands's lighting evoke a survey of Renaissance painting. Now it is a Caravaggio that sucks us in, now a Ribera, now a Pieter de Hooch. Crosslighting brings out the sculpturalness of the figures as we glimpse them on the oblique between history and art. And here Hess's music is even more insinuating and rapturous—though still controlled—until we no longer know whether we are in a theater, a concert hall, or an art gallery.

Much Ado is a shrewd play in which comedy and near-tragedy chase each other like a kitten and its tail until they are revealed to be the same organism: the scheme of things as they are. Villainy is all but motiveless and joy very nearly accidental; intrigues are defanged into pranks, and bumblers set the world aright: "What your wisdoms could not discover, these shallow fools have brought to light"—foolish goodness muddles through to save learned folly from itself. With what ingenious directorial touches—except for the odd bit of overfussiness, as in Benedick's eavesdropping sequence—the messiness of Messina is given its chaotic shape. The yeomen of the guard persist in considering Conrade the main culprit and barely bother with Borachio; when a chain of men doff their hats, the last one is sure to don his; when Benedick and Beatrice have finally staggered into their happiness, we can still see them sparring in dumb show.

Though perhaps more tomboyish than blue-bloodedly disdainful, Sinead Cusack is a crunchily delicious Beatrice, the honeyed huskiness of her voice harboring stingers in unexpected syllables. Clare Bryan Shaw remarkably coaxes mature poise out of Hero's fluff, and Christopher Bowen finds just enough personableness in the callow Claudio. Ken Bones is a touching Don Pedro, lonely beneath his authority; John Carlisle is an amusingly diabolical Don John, employing unusual stresses and pauses to tickling effect—indeed, the entire cast is expert at rubatos to put new mettle into old lines, but Carlisle excels them all. The elderly brothers Leonato and Antonio (Edward Jewesbury and Jeffrey Dench) are superb individually but even better as carriers of sibling rivalry into its terminal phase. Hero's ladies-in-waiting are nicely differentiated, and as the hog-tied Conrade, John Bowe is hopping-mad with style. The guard is absurd without excess, and Dogberry (Christopher Benjamin) is adorable as he wields his stupidity as if it were sweetest reason; Verges (tiny Jimmy Gardner) is the small dogged shadow of that lucent lunacy.

Derek Jacobi's Benedick is a bit of a problem. Once again there is dazzling technical prowess, but the actor seems neither aristocratic nor scholarly enough for the part, and becomes effete when overexcited. Sometimes he is too broad, as in the eavesdropping scene (one of two or three scenes that Hands overdirected into camp), and without his impressive Cyrano nose he looks a bit too commonplace. But out of oddball intonations he wrests a good deal of offbeat humor. To think that the RSC has two solid companies in England and still enough talent left over for this American tour. And after some eighteen months the performances are still as pristine as if factory-sealed and unwrapped by us for the first time. Let the American theater establishment look at this and weep—and try to do better.

Whoopi Goldberg

The eponymous and pseudonymous Whoopi Goldberg begins her show of monologues with a number in which Fontaine, a black dope addict and thief, flies to Europe (how did he get a passport?) and is jolted out of his hipsterism by the memory of Anne Frank at her museum in "Amsterdam, Amdam, Goddamn." The show ends with a tiny curtain speech in which Miss Goldberg, who is black, thanks the audience and tells how much her being on the Great White Way—"no joke intended"—means to people across the country who are living through her. In between, she does another monologue by a white, thirteen-year-old Valley Girl who, being pregnant, is tossed out by her mother. (How shocking, think Mr. and Mrs. Broadway in the audience, but how bravely this little girl walks down the beach with nothing but a suitcase and a zygote to her name.) Then comes a monologue about a horribly deformed cripple who nevertheless finds romance because "normal is in the eye of the beholder." (How touching, think Mr. and Mrs. B., and how lucky that we aren't cripples, but if we were—in the mind, say—no matter, for brains are in the eye of the beholder.)

After intermission, Whoopi does a Jamaican woman imported to the U.S. by a lecher of 85, who, while feebly trying to have intercourse *a tergo*, dies and leaves her a house and $62 million. (How nice, think the B.'s, that this should be a land of opportunities for black immigrants.) Next, Whoopi is a nine-year-old black girl dreaming of being a white, blonde TV star and making herself blonde by covering her hair with a white skirt. (How sweet, think the B.'s, she may at least grow up to be Whoopi Goldberg.) Lastly, we get a Bowery bum panhandling quarters from a willing audience—this money is later refunded—while telling tales of dancing with the Nicholas Brothers. (How wonderful, rejoice the B.'s, that he accepts our charity instead of mugging us.)

How can an act that appeals so calculatedly to middle-class whites, any-class blacks, cripples, and pubescent unwed mothers, as well as catering to other forms of pious condescension, fail on Broadway? No way, considering that the only object of cheap sympathy it misses is Native Americans, and it's a long, long way to the reservation.

My point is that Whoopi Goldberg, whom Mike Nichols discovered in a theater workshop and supervised and sponsored on Broadway, is as phony as a three-dollar bill or, to use a trope more appropriate to what Mr. Nichols collects and cashes in on, a three-legged racehorse. His others, to be sure, have four; this one, though, sorely misses a leg to stand on. Actually, Miss Goldberg—as she chooses to call herself, presumably as a sop to the largest and most bread-buttering segment of her potential public—is an accomplished nightclub comedienne with good timing, lively facial expressions, considerable flexibility in her impersonations, and real skill with accents. What she doesn't have is material worth doing in a better cabaret, let alone as a full evening on Broadway. Much of it is routinely foulmouthed, sniping at facile targets such as airline food and Bergdorf Goodman punkers, and all of it only very sporadically funny or relevant or containing deeper artistic truths.

There is something disturbingly specious about these numbers and the number Miss Goldberg does on the audience. To begin with, her true name is neither Whoopi nor Goldberg, and she makes a big mystery of her identity—though that is the least of it. We are told she has a repertoire of seventeen routines, though everyone I have talked to has seen the same six. She plays on the audience's fears—"I'd just as soon cut your throats as look at you"— and then sleazily allays them by having Fontaine remember Anne Frank when next he mugs someone: "I will remember there is still some good in that person, and that will save their life." Later, as she compares her dreadlocks with those of a plant in the audience, she assures us that they are not even dreadlocks, only "doo-doo" braids. And why does she fall out of character to giggle along with the audience? And why does a professional like Nichols let her do this, as well as let her numbers run on way too long? And how cricket is it for Nichols the producer to make up a quasi-critical statement comparing Goldberg to, among others, Ruth Draper, and have this statement run in the ads? (Ruth Draper, by the way, was about something, and far above the stuff of *Whoopi Goldberg*, as Mr. Nichols ought to know.)

The greatest mystery, however, is why a large audience of glittering names will turn up for this mediocre event, and why so many people laugh what passes for their heads off at absolutely nothing. Or is Whoopi-Fontaine's answer to a supposedly snooty stewardess who tells him to fasten his seat belt—"Fuck you!"—a cause for rolling in the aisles? Is it the adulatory article in the Sunday Times or is it just Mike Nichols's magic name that accounts for turning this first draft into a second coming?

Einstein on the Beach

I clearly lack the space to do justice to *Einstein on the Beach*, an alleged opera in four acts lasting 70 minutes apiece, or one act of ignominy lasting over four and a half hours. What in 1976 was the emperor's not-so-new clothes is in 1984 the tattered rags of inane avant-gardism. Although Robert Wilson has a certain gift for creating stage images, jauntily enhanced by his and Beverly Emmons's lighting, there is no excuse for making these pictures last hours; in a few minutes of your time, a de Chirico or Magritte can do them better. The text of scant words endlessly repeated is sheer nonsense; though it required the combined wits of Christopher Knowles, Samuel H. Johnson, and Lucinda Childs, any half-wit could have done as much by himself. The minimalist choreography, presumably for people who abhor dancing, is by Miss Childs; the music and lyrics are by Philip Glass.

To take the lyrics first: they are either the names of the near-identical note sequences relentlessly repeated, e.g., "Sol, si, do, fa, sol, si, fa, do," or sequences of numerals, e.g., "two, two, three, three, four, four," chanted ad nauseam. Anyone who can take credit for solfège and kiddie maths as lyrics has, evidently, neither a sense of words nor a sense of shame. That he is an utter no-talent is confirmed by the similarly misnamed "music." This is music either for musical ignoramuses or for people who will get on any trendy bandwagon, even if the band is mostly a synthesizer and the wagon hardly moves. It must be best for the completely stoned. In fact, *Einstein on the Beach* is a four-and-a-half-hour masturbatory daydream for people too unimaginative to have their own daydreams and too lazy or impotent to masturbate.

The usual defense of *Einstein* is that "it turned me around" or "it completely changes your sense of time." But although I fervently champion art as an eye-, ear-, mind-, and soul-opener, I see no point in changing our sense of time. Our great problem is that we do not sufficiently understand and appreciate the shortness of our time, that we do not (and, apparently, will not) comprehend how much great art of all kinds there is in this world in which our time is so short that we can explore only a fraction of its wonders. Hence it is stupid and vicious to entice people into wasting hours of their brief span on minimalist drivel nauseatingly repeated until they feel—as if under the influence of drugs—timelessly afloat in some nihilist nirvana. As it is, many in the audience kept going out into the lobby to eat, drink, socialize, i.e., be seen, rather than watch the show. Many others sensibly "turned around" early and simply left. Ask yourself how much Bartók, Berg, Stravinsky, and Janáček you have listened to before you waste your time on Glass; how much real theater, ballet, and art you have seen before you hypnotize and heroinize yourself into Robert Wilson's solipsism.

Thus, did you attend one of the two performances in Carnegie Hall of *Jeanne d'Arc au bûcher*, the dramatic oratorio by Arthur Honegger on a text by Claudel? This 1938 work was stirringly performed by Ozawa and the Bostonians; well sung by choruses and soloists, among whom only the execrable tenor (and French) of John Gilmore proved jarring; and movingly enacted by Marthe Keller, Vernon Dobtcheff, and the great Georges Wilson, who also directed. This was music and drama that turned you, not around, but inward and, thence, forward.

As Is

Hooray! Circle Rep is itself again after months of floundering, and William M. Hoffman's *As Is* is as good a play and production as we have come to expect from this talented organization in past years. It is quite clear that *As Is*, a play about AIDS, the mysterious and lethal disease that threatens homosexuals especially but has also claimed victims among heterosexuals, deals with something everyone in this production has strong comprehension of and concern about. The 90 uninterrupted minutes of the show are redolent of the same passionate involvement that characterized the work of such ideologically committed organizations as the Group Theatre and the Berliner Ensemble.

Rich, a young Wasp fiction writer beginning to have real success, is breaking up with Saul, his longtime lover, who is a Jewish photographer. Saul still adores Rich, who, however, has become involved with Chet, a young, handsome, empty man, and is impatient and cruel with Saul as they're dividing their communal property. Even though some of what is to be divvied up is very much in the homosexual domain, e.g., "the world's largest collection of Magic Marker hustler portraits," the situation is similar to the breakup of a heterosexual marriage. Rich is guilt-riddenly, defensively aggressive, and Saul is ironically, lovingly counterattacking. The scene is charged with recrimination, witty retaliation, and melancholy, and it is both very specifically 1980s Greenwich Village and timelessly, universally human.

There is a prologue, a soliloquy in which a woman hospice worker sets the scene with a poetic but not, as so often with this kind of thing, inept or irrelevant monologue. She expresses the pity of it all, as she will also in a complementary epilogue. In between are a number of scenes in which there is simultaneous dialogue in several playing areas—one of the few departures from conventional, realistic dramaturgy, among which must also be counted a chorus of doctors surrounding the panickily questioning Rich with the reiterated utterance, "The simple fact is that we know little about acquired immune deficiency syndrome." For, at the end of the initial breakup scene, Rich reveals that he has come down with AIDS. Henceforth, the play shifts swiftly backward and forward across widely varied patches of time and space, recounting stages in two homosexual liaisons, depicting a number of homosexual milieus such as an S&M metal-and-leather bar and an AIDS clinic (whose one patient is female), to progress ineluctably toward the hospital room where Rich is in the grips of the first virulent attack of the disease, and where much of the later action, including a touching reconciliation with a straight brother, takes place.

The extremely effective direction by Marshall W. Mason owes something to John Malkovich's staging of *Balm in Gilead*, though there the polyphonal approach was more appropriate because the play depends more on mood and atmosphere than on plot and character development, and a few missed words don't matter. My program is remarkably free from jotted-down quotations because this dialogue is so good, the action so gripping, and the spectator's attention so constantly stretched to the utmost by having to follow the verbal counterpoint or synchronicity. But just as several things are often interwoven dramatically, so there is an almost constant— and admirable—interpenetration of emotional and intellectual states ranging from the fiercely comic through the soberly reflective to the achingly resigned. *As Is* has a range of feeling to match its shifts of time and locale, but what makes it particularly persuasive is that the feelings are not merely juxtaposed or superimposed but actually blended in a complete musical harmony.

At almost no moment are you allowed to laugh unequivocally—though there is a great deal of first-rate comedy here—just as at almost no moment are you at liberty to yield to total dejection, because even in the most tearful moments there is a resilience, a vitality, a refusal to knuckle under to either the cessation of life or the end of love. Saul's love for Rich struggles on against crushing odds just as Rich, finally, fights back against the implacable, perhaps undefeatable, foe. *As Is* is not only about AIDS but also about the aids and comforts of courage and devotion. Yet these virtues are never made to seem sudden, uncomplicated, unearned.

Let me cite two skillful scenes. One is predominantly comic—in the S&M bar—yet it never elides a necessary undertone of dismalness. The other—in an AIDS hot-line center—has two telephone operators deal with desperate callers and situations, yet manages to be every bit as hilarious as grave, and this without cheating. What helps throughout is the quicksilver nature of homosexual wit, which shuttles dizzyingly between bitchy outrageousness and tragic laughter. It is your basic black humor accented with strands of oversize, jangling artificial pearls. And it creates its effect.

The acting is unified and remarkable, especially that of Jonathan Hogan, Jonathan Hadary, Lou Liberatore, and Claris Erickson. With impeccable décor, lighting, and costumes, this is the best new play of the season.

Biloxi Blues

By George, He's done it! Incredible as it may seem—to me, anyhow—in *Biloxi Blues*, Neil Simon has written a play that is not a farce, not mostly one-liners and two-dimensional characters, nor one of those maudlin stabs at high seriousness such as *The Gingerbread Lady*, part of *Chapter Two*, and Act II of *Brighton Beach Memoirs*. Rather, he has given us pungent characters we keep wondering about, jokes that interact with other jokes to erect comic structures, humor that is relatively free from both self-aggrandizement and self-pity, an underpainting of seriousness without which the final coat of comedy wouldn't take, and a sense of the dignity of otherness in the characters around the author's alter ego that shields them from condescension or sentimentalization. Best of all, Simon allows his characters the privilege of his not understanding them down to the last detail—or, at least, not explaining them. Like all real Others, in literature as in life, they have those secrets they do not tell even themselves, much less divulge to a mere scribbler.

Biloxi Blues is also a "chapter two," this time the sequel to Simon's fictionalized autobiography begun, or re-begun, in *Brighton Beach Memoirs*. If that play concerned chiefly Eugene Morris Jerome's growing pains, this one deals with his pains (and pleasures), if not exactly full-grown, at least resolutely crescent: bigger than a bread basket but packable into a new kit bag—for Eugene is in the army, in Biloxi, in 1943. He and a bunch of fellow recruits from the tri-state area are about to be whipped into shape by tough, southern Sgt. Toomey before being shipped off to battle in Europe or Asia. Yet these recruits are not simply raw: they carry within them civilian anomalies that are well done, even overcooked. The army, here subsumed by Toomey, will have to outsmart them by devious logic, by an almost Zen cunning. True, some of the youths can be out-bullied or outwitted, but some must be practically out-Wittgensteined. And Sgt. Toomey, that fox in wolf's clothing, is the drillmaster-dialectician to do it.

He is, however, up against stiff opposition. The huge, thick, perpetually tumescent Pvt. Wykowski may be a minor problem, but Pvt. Carney, a heap of pondered irresoluteness who sings in his sleep, is a bigger one. Even if Pvt. Selridge's drolly belligerent benightedness is a pushover that can be bested by push-ups, Pvt. Hennessy's straightforwardness that cloaks his vulnerability is an emotional stumbling stone. The real tough ones, though, are the two Jewish boys. Eugene is bad enough: innocent yet clever, canny yet naïve, a mass of guileless guile. And, hardest of all, the wimpy, bespectacled, stomach-troubled, intellect-tormented Arnold Epstein. At home in Tolstoy as in the Talmud, he is so weak in the flesh that he has to be a karate champion of the spirit, his acrid humor a black belt, his hands deadly weapons even if, as it were, tied behind his back. He engages Toomey in a comic-Dostoevskian duel of wills that lifts both of them to dizzyingly absurd heights.

That these young men are in the shadow of combat and death makes them touching; that their main concerns are licking the army and getting laid makes them amusing; that they are, even in their simpleness, unpredictable makes them human. Actually, Eugene has three ambitions: to lose his virginity, to fall in love, to become a writer. For the first, there is the jovial Rowena—a semipro who is a whore only on weekends; for the second, there is Daisy Hannigan, a nice Catholic girl who grooves on Jewish imaginativeness and has a journalist father, which brings her closer to Eugene, who keeps a journal. And for the third, there is *Biloxi Blues*. What makes this play better than any previous effort by Simon is his splitting himself up into Eugene and Arnold: looking at the world with four eyes instead of two, he sees more, and more variously. We are told at play's end what became of the other characters, and it is not quite what we expected. We are not told what became of Eugene, because we know that, like Antoine Doinel, who grew up into Truffaut, he turned into Neil Simon. But that, too, on the evidence of his latest play, is a surprise. And a happy one.

Happy, too, is the whole production: Gene Saks's flawless staging, David Mitchell's delectable scenery, Ann Roth's knowing costumes, Tharon Musser's multifaceted lighting. And then there is the stunning ensemble acting in which everyone does disciplined wonders, though, as Eugene, Matthew Broderick somewhat undercuts his excellence with a slight leaning toward shtick. It would be hard to improve on Randall Edwards, Penelope Ann Miller, Matt Mulhern, Alan Ruck, Geoffrey Sharp; and Brian Sadler (Toomey) and Barry Miller (Arnold) are even more prodigious, probably because their parts are more complex. Whatever they do is a bit different and absolutely on the nose, than which there is no better. But don't get me wrong: Simon has not yet become Shaw, Pirandello, or Chekhov; he has, however, barring a few obvious or exaggerated moments, written a play that rings with a newer, deeper, sweeter truth.

Big River; The Normal Heart

We've all heard the one about the musical you leave humming the scenery; well, *Big River* is the one from which you emerge hurrahing the sets. Heidi Landesman has done yeoman's work on and off Broadway, and a terrific *Midsummer Night's Dream* in Central Park, but in this musicalization of *Huckleberry Finn*, she gets her first chance to cut loose in a big, Broadway manner, and two splendid things happen: she doesn't lose control and go hog-wild; and she comes up with a style that (though remotely related to Wilford Leach's) is redolently, ebulliently, enchantingly her own. From the moment the lights go down, your heart leaps up as you feel enveloped by a master of ambience, atmosphere, and sheer prettiness, who, with the expert assistance of Richard Riddell's insinuating lighting and Patricia McGourty's bouncy costumes, carries you along as adventuresomely as ever the Mississippi did Huck and Jim. But don't expect me to describe this décor; I'd as soon give away the outcome of a particularly daedal thriller.

I'll come to the other virtues of *Big River* presently, but the score, I fear, is not one of them. Granted, I have no use for either country or gospel music, but I doubt if this is the best of either kind, kinds that, in any case, sound relentlessly alike from top to bottom. Amplification only exacerbates matters; the main problem, though, is the timidity, uninventiveness, boredom of this music and these words by Roger Miller, no matter how heavy a burden of Grammy Awards his mantels may groan under, how many guests he can serve chicken-fried steaks to off his Gold Records. Call it generation gap, call it cultural barrier, but my River—insofar as I make any claim on it—will always be "Ole Man" rather than "Big." Let me add that for all the efforts of Daniel Troob (musical supervision), Steven

Margoshes (orchestrations), and John Richard Lewis (incidental music/dance arrangements), this stuff is to my idea of show music what hog calling is to poetry.

The book by William Hauptman has excellent features as well as expendable ones. The former can be described as Mark Twain, the latter as William Hauptman, and never the twain do meet more than casually, uneasily, labilely. This at least allows us no doubt about when we need attend and when we can cheerfully drift along the scenery—but not only the scenery. For there are also vastly enjoyable performances under Des McAnuff's visually fulfilling, sculptured and rhythmic, direction, which wisely makes as much of quiet moments, dying falls, and silences as it does of the rowdiest hustle and most rollicking bustle.

The two leads leave little to be desired. Daniel H. Jenkins is the quintessential Huck: ingenuous but not cloying, mischievous but not smartass, boyish but neither callow nor infantile, winning but not precious. Even his voice flirts delightfully with the enticements of roughness and squeakiness without ever yielding to them; altogether, he is America's answer to Peter Pan, unaffected and unselfconscious. As Jim, Ron Richardson is a fine blend of browbeatenness and nobility, temerity and fearfulness, benightedness and shrewd intuition. His acting is economical and hits home without broad effects; his singing is velvety or stentorian as required. Hard as it is for a modern black to squeeze himself into Jim, Richardson achieves it with only minimal lapses.

There are other gladdening performances from Patti Cohenour (Mary Jane), John Goodman (Pap Finn), a somewhat overwrought René Auberjonois (Duke), a welcomely restrained Bob Gunton (King), a not exactly Twainian but still most proficient John Short (Tom Sawyer), and a variety of authenticity-exuding townsfolk, rustics, slaves, and onstage musicians. Only Jennifer Leigh Warren overdoes her caterwauling; she could take lessons from Carol Woods in *Grind*, who achieves much more with less.

But, finally, is this musical trip down the Mississippi, fun as it frequently is, really recessary? Rereading a few random pages of the book, I was tickled and shaken as I seldom, if ever, was by the show. As T. S. Eliot noted in his introduction to the novel, there is a River God in it, and it is Man's subjection to him "that gives to Man his dignity." Nothing in *Big River* is that big, that divine; and, to go on with Eliot, "Without some kind of God, Man is not even very interesting."

Conversely, what makes Larry Kramer's imperfect *The Normal Heart*—the second play this season about AIDS—so compelling is its sense of urgency, necessity, a cause. Like William M. Hoffman's *As Is*, it is written out of an inner compulsion that goads it on, rushes it over and past minor and not so minor flaws, makes it stick in the craw if not the heart—though sometimes in that, too. This is no more or less artful transposition of somebody else's Mississippi, but generates its own river of indignation and anger, fear and love, sometimes incontinently overflowing its banks, sometimes bogging down at mudbanks, but generally sweeping us along with it.

Kramer's play—probably more autobiographical, informed, and data-filled, but also more intemperate and biased—is less literate and poetic than *As Is*, but more rousingly polemical, more politically and morally challenging. It concerns, first, the troubled involvement of Ned Weeks, a writer, with an AIDs-crisis organization he helped found but that eschews his confrontational tactics and eventually dumps him. It concerns, second, Ned's love affair with Felix, a *New York Times* fashion reporter, who comes out of the closet for Ned even as Ned comes out of emotional lethargy for him. There is, third, Ned's tricky relationship with his heterosexual lawyer brother, made trickier by their Jewishness. Fourth, there are the efforts of Dr. Emma Brookner—a smart, tough, tireless doctor confined to a wheelchair by polio—to combat AIDS, succor the victims, and mobilize the purblind or adversary medical powers that be. Lastly, there is the complex interaction—or inaction—of city and federal governments; the vagaries of the heterosexual and homosexual press; public opinion or apathy or hostility; and violently conflicting views and plans of action in the crisis center.

The play's most original contribution is its examination of the relationship between promiscuity and AIDS, a certain swinging homosexual life-style and the spread of the disease. Although the author's preference is for loving monogamy, persuasive spokesmen for a whole spectrum from abstinent celibacy to extreme indulgence as a supposed homosexual hallmark are given hearing. As a result, what could have been a mere staged tract—and, in its lesser moments, is just that—transcends often enough into a fleshed-out, generously dramatized struggle, in which warring ideologies do not fail to breathe, sweat, weep, bleed—be human. Despite some awesome self-importance, there is also a leaven of humor and self-criticism, and language that can rouse itself out of a tendency to creak into moving arias and duets of passion.

The production sagely espouses simplicity. Eugene Lee and Keith Raywood's set is spare if not downright stark, Natasha Katz's lighting is duly untender and enlightening, Bill Walker's costumes are pointedly minimal. Michael Lindsay-Hogg has directed with pared-down directness in which every detail gets its exact due: we can choke back our sobs over a gallant death, but cry rightly over a carton of spilt milk. I admired the performances of Brad Davis, William DeAcutis, Philip Richard Allen, and several others, but was bowled over by those of D. W. Moffett and Robert Dorfman. Only Concetta Tomei, as the solid rock of a doctor, seemed more mineral than human. If you ask me which of the two plays about AIDS you should see, I can only say, "Both!"

Aren't We All?

July 16, 1967: Noël Coward confides to his diary (about the revival of Frederick Lonsdale's most famous play), "The opening night of [*The Last of*] *Mrs. Cheyney*… was fairly dreary. Freddie Lonsdale's dialogue sounds curiously laboured and dated." July 26, 1927: Arnold Bennett, for whom, a week earlier, Lonsdale gave a "very merry" party at the Garrick Club, notes in his journal about F.L.'s second-most-famous play, "… Lonsdale's *On Approval* at the Fortune Theatre. Not a bad first Act in a very old-fashioned 'smart' way, with some very good jocular lines." June 1978: J. C. Trewin revises Allardyce Nicoll's classic *British Drama*, and writes, "Lonsdale spent his time in the stage Dukeries (every peer, it was suggested, but Southend), freely conferring titles and earl-and-the-girl witticisms. His work has been much revived, for epigrams, eighteen-carat or rolled-gold, must always have their place in the theatre; Lonsdale was a far better craftsman than Wilde (*The Importance of Being Earnest* apart). Still, we must doubt how much his work will be durable."

April 29, 1985: Lonsdale's first hit, the 1923 *Aren't We All?*, opens in New York after a successful London run, again starring Rex Harrison and Claudette Colbert. I think Lonsdale's work (even—if Coward, a friendly rival, felt sour about it in '67; and Bennett, a friend with a lower-class orientation, found it old-fashioned at its very inception) will prove modestly, marginally durable. The present production has trimmed the play—whether for the better,

I cannot judge, never having seen another production, and one doesn't *read* Lonsdale—but it seems to capture its spirit faithfully and handsomely under Clifford Williams's winsomely idiomatic, undawdling direction. It is somewhat lighter than a puffball, but the deftly sportive cast manages to volley with it effortlessly, providing tennis for anyone, spectators included.

We begin in the Mayfair house of the Hon. William Tatham, where Willie hasn't heard in twelve days from his wife, Margaret (Margot), off on a trip to Egypt. (In the text, the hiatus is only of eight days' duration, but the mail service between Egypt and England, like that between New Jersey and New York, has become so much worse that the ante had to be upped by four days.) Since even his cables to Margot have remained unanswered, Willie may be almost justified in becoming slightly enmeshed with the bewitching Kitty Lake, an actress temporarily plying her seduction offstage. All the more so since Willie is the son of the elderly Duke of Grenham, a widowed peer peerless in the pursuit of young shopgirls, whom he likes to take to the British Museum, because, as the widowed Lady Frinton, bent on hooking him, observes, "He knows perfectly well that only an air raid could drive members of his class into it."

But, unheedful of his father's precepts—"The British Museum is much more interesting than it looks from the outside"—Willie is on the drawing-room sofa, in a passionate clinch with Kitty, when Margaret arrives unannounced in flight from Egypt. This allows Lord Grenham to remonstrate with those who identify Willie as his father's son, "No, it's the opposite: he's been found out." But he nevertheless devises a scheme to confront his unrelenting daughter-in-law with her own fallibility. Here I interrupt this account to point out what a sweetly innocent play *Aren't We All?* is to begin with. The British Museum may be a fine and, if you're a peer of the realm, all but private place; but few, I think, do there more than embrace. The indiscretions in this play—and there are several, either in the plot or in casual references—are essentially innocuous: as in a Feydeau farce, so in this drawing-room comedy, affairs remain unconsummated. Whether on the playing fields of Mayfair, in the gardens of Alexandria, or among the sarcophagi of the British Museum—and especially, I suspect, in the theater—this was an age of innocence, whose very interruptions were precoital.

What was uninterruptus, however, was the flow of language, the spray of verbal wit that even such second-rate playwrights as Lonsdale could muster in an era when words still issued with style, a turn of phrase could almost be observed pirouetting in the air, and talk still aspired to the state of conversation. One recalls Colley Cibber writing in his Apology, a couple of centuries before, about Sir John Vanbrugh that "his most entertaining Scenes seem'd to be no more than his common Conversation committed to Paper." This is the feeling one gets from *Aren't We All?*: what a nice age in which common conversation shimmered along like that, and even dullards fulfilled exemplarily the roles of straight men to those cleverer than they were.

And so here—among sets by Finlay James and in costumes by Judith Blandin, in both of which quaintness, graciousness, and luxury live in a happy ménage à trois—are actors young or uneroded by age being silkenly silly or waspishly wise, who, when the author's invention flags and dialogue sags, breathe into it the needed artificial inspiration, the kiss of not quite life but of its agreeable simulacrum. Rex Harrison mumbles a bit and, at the first preview, was a mite prone to dance around his lines and gradually sidle up to them; but when he did hit them—often enough—there was the youthfully beatific deviltry polished to a fare-thee-well by age-old cunning. And Claudette Colbert—as unwitherable by age as the Cleopatra she once played—proves his equal in sagacious roguery, her eyebrows arching heavenward even as her voice scoops up wood shavings from an imaginary barroom floor. How inspiriting to see these two old-timers who do not go quiet into the good-night kiss, but rail against the failing of the glands.

As the feuding and loving Tathams, the alluringly aristocratic Jeremy Brett and Lynn Redgrave manage the not inconsiderable feat of being both romantic and funny, liberally scattering charm and comedic technique without losing a certain decorous equipoise. George Rose and especially Brenda Forbes are on hand to provide expert farcical relief from all that highish comedy, and the rest—with the exception of Ned Schmidtke, who is neither very attractive nor very Australian—come through well enough, especially the sexy Leslie O'Hara as the siren-dipitous May. *Aren't We All?* may not be much, but I welcome a little gloss and froth in an age of carefully cultivated dregs and dross.

The Lisbon Traviata

Terrence McNally's plays have usually been maliciously funny, and generally more out of the closet than those of his contemporaries. This was most overtly true of *And Things That Go Bump in the Night* and *Noon*, somewhat less obviously so of several others. With *The Lisbon Traviata*, McNally brings into the uptown venue some of the most floridly flagrant excesses of a group of homosexuals whom Julius Novick, in his *Village Voice* review, correctly termed "opera queens." In the first act, Stephen, in whom we are to recognize a stylized self-portrait, and Mendy (who, until he was fired by the director, was played by Michael "Mendy" Wager—clearly, this is a *pièce à clef* in more than the musical sense) are two opera fanatics and old friends relentlessly oneupmanshipping each other with operatic trivia. Stephen, whose roommate and ex-lover Mike is using their apartment to consummate a new relationship, has forgotten to bring along to Mendy's the newly available recording of Maria Callas's Lisbon *Traviata*, which Mendy slavers for with the kind of craving for instant gratification it took this baby over half a century to perfect. His most outrageous maneuvers to obtain it fail, however, as he and Stephen have at each other verbally.

This first act is extremely funny if you know anything about opera. It is all bitchiness, which, however, like jazz, can range from hot to cool, from the scatological and obscene to the epigrammatic. But the second act, in which Mendy dwindles to a voice on the phone or answering machine, changes gears completely. Some wit remains; the rest is pure acid and venom. Stephen, next morning, discovers Mike, whom he still loves (or merely craves) with a "trick"—actually, a nice young man—and proceeds to torture them both. Homosexual sex is graphically evoked, shocking at least two of my colleagues audibly. The conclusion may seem tragic to the author but, with its unearned violence, strikes me as only melodramatic and extraordinarily sadistic.

The Lisbon Traviata, unbalanced as it is in more ways than one, offers insight into a type of homosexual psyche in its ripest confusion, at the level where both characters and author lose control, and we get a glimpse into the abyss that is sharp but uncathartic. Consider some key lines, most of them uttered by the author's alter ego. "People who don't like opera, don't like life." This is meant as irony, most opera being a kind of hyperbole antithetical to everyday reality, and *wor-*

shiped by some (as opposed to *loved*) precisely for its unlifelikeness. "What's wrong with quiet [without an opera record playing]?" "You have to listen to yourself think." No comment required. A sudden outburst against Maria Callas, the most melodramatic of divas, who until then has been idolized by the play's characters at the expense of other divas: "That woman's fucked up my life! Piano legs! The myopic cunt!" Now excessive, operatic violence begins to be imitated by life. Finally—and in the context of murder, irony fades—this about the Humming Chorus from *Butterfly*: "Sometimes I think this is the most beautiful music ever written. Christ knows it's the most banal." The supreme beauty of banality? This is camp sensibility carried to its horrifying pinnacle. True, the protagonist is half mad by now, yet his murderous act is being justified in strange ways. If the banal can be beautiful, then the unworthy can be sublime, the operatic perfectly normal, and murder just a part of life. So what was initially treated as a joke has become at least half accepted as the truth—as Cio-Cio-San's seppuku becomes equated with the stabbing of Mike. Someone, on- and offstage, has been fucked up here, but not, I think, by Maria Callas.

Benjamin Hendrickson, Seth Allen, Steven Culp, and especially Stephen Schnetzer give fine performances under John Tillinger's knowing direction in good sets by Philipp Jung. The first act, because it knows what it's about, is cannily funny; the second, because it doesn't, is uncannily revealing.

The Mystery of Edwin Drood

There is something heartbreakingly beautiful about the last, unfinished work of a great artist. I would give anything to hear what Mahler would have made of his Tenth Symphony, or Bartók of his Viola Concerto: the completions that other men wrought on them strike me as, axiomatically, not quite satisfactory. I don't think that Charles Dickens's last, broken-off novel, *The Mystery of Edwin Drood*, would have been one of his best, but it would surely have been better than what any of the completers (some of them distinguished authors in their own right) were able to summon up. The true mystery of *Edwin Drood* is not whether the eponymous hero was killed, and, if so, by whom; rather, it is what the genius who, after the fifth installment, disappeared—less prematurely than

young Drood, but, at 68, still far too early—might have committed
to paper and posterity: a greater awareness of the dark side of life,
perhaps even a truer understanding of evil, whose real nature had
always eluded him.

Yet there is also a unique nobility about an unfinished work,
beyond the mere pathos of its fragmentariness. One perceives it
as that archaic torso of Apollo that, to Rilke, spelled the need to
change one's life; one searches in it for an ultimate vision of truth
as it might be revealed only on death's threshold (whether or not
the author was aware of his fatal whereabouts); one feels in it the
unyielding dedication of the artist who kept on creating, defying
the unvanquishable enemy with the last stirrings of his imagination. It is thrilling that on the final page of *Drood* Dickens wrote
of how morning infiltrates the gloomy cathedral of Cloisterham
(Rochester) symbolizing Resurrection and Life, of how "flecks of
brightness dart into the sternest marble corners of the building,
fluttering there like wings." Surely it was better for him to die with
the creative juices still flowing, and better for us to know that it is
possible for an author not to capitulate, but let some other, superhuman, hand write *finis* on the middle of the page.

When you approach *The Mystery of Edwin Drood* with the reverence due to it, the pleasantly silly musical comedy (yes, comedy)
Rupert Holmes has whittled from it must appear a minor sacrilege—not so much spitting as pitching horseshoes on Dickens's
grave. But if you are willing and able to overlook that *Drood* was
not just a mystery story but actually a book as concerned as any of
its author's with the human condition, you can have some modest,
relaxed fun with *The Mystery of Edwin Drood* the musical. Using
the rather tired conceit of a troupe of thespians performing a musical stage version of Dickens's unfinished novel at the Amusement
Pier of Greater Dorping-on-Sea, Holmes affords us a not unamus-
ing, though certainly not peerless, spectacle in which everything is
guyed jovially without excess of camp. If there is no ravishing tunefulness or sizzling humor, there is at least seldom-flagging, cohesive
professionalism, not all that frequent of late in Joe Papp's Central
Park Shakespeare Festival offerings.

The production values are decidedly pleasing, with a mostly
tasteful gloss to them. Wilford Leach, some of whose recent stagings have left much to be desired, here conjures up cannily the
pinchbeck atmosphere of the Victorian music hall, the histrionic
prowess and trappings of a company not unrelated to that of Mr.

Vincent Crummles, so vividly resuscitated for us by Trevor Nunn's mummers in the RSC's *Nicholas Nickleby*. A profusion of onstage life spills over into adjacent areas unforcedly and infectiously, and any number of moribund theatrical devices, such as silhouettes projected onto a screen by backlighting, are infused with fresh deviltry. Leach has blocked so well that his characters describe patterns to gladden the eye that deciphers them, and he seldom runs out of fetching felicities of sight and sound as the show skips along with only minor sags.

He is stoutly helped by the choreography of Graciela Daniele, whose work has often been too minimalist or derivative for my taste but who here comes up with decorative curlicues of dance that seamlessly blend into the calligraphy of the staging, so that we are at a loss to say where direction leaves off and choreography begins, and vice versa. And while the dancing is distinctly tongue-in-cheek—and, in the opium-den scene, borderline lubricious—it always swerves away from vulgarity.

Bob Shaw's sets could not be more helpful. They have a sort of adult-storybook quality that prevents the whimsical from becoming cute. Each set is a toy, but a toy for grown-ups that children may also fancy. And the transformations of one set into the other are like sleight of hand performed by a giant's palms. Yet none of this seems unduly gimmicky, and if it is precious, it is more so in the sense of endearing than that of recherché. Much the same can be said for the costumes of Lindsay W. Davis, which strike a cunning middle path between the eccentric and the engaging. As for Paul Gallo, he is one of our most unassuming lighting designers, who quite unostentatiously makes the stage as glowingly alive as a Holbein portrait.

The weakest thing about *Drood* is Holmes's music. His book, for all its non-Dickensianness, and his lyrics, despite such gaffes as "Betwixt our hearts let nothing come between," have a sprightliness with which the tunes have difficulty catching up. Not that the melodies are bad, or even unoriginal; it is just that they all have a certain facile noncommittalness, except for the genuinely toe-tapping (but also more conventional) "Don't Quit While You're Ahead." The orchestra, under Michael Starobin, is neatly controlled, pulsating without being pertinacious, but there are, what with overzealous amplification, some words that are hard to unscramble, some sounds that are hard to endure.

The performances are, down to the smallest parts, uniformly

polished and winning. There is very good work from Howard Mc-
Gillin, Larry Shue, Betty Buckley, Patti Cohenour, John Herrera,
Jerome Dempsey, Don Kehr, and the indomitable Cleo Laine. As
narrator, compere, and, when needed, actor, George Rose expertly
holds things together with the Crazy Glue of his guileless guile.
But I must confess to a runaway predilection for the Helena of Jana
Schneider, who exudes a blend of seduction and irony that keeps
your emotional reactions on exquisite tenterhooks throughout.

The show leans heavily on audience participation. Not only are
the spectators encouraged to clap and, at times, even sing along,
they are also allowed to vote on the identity of the murderer and
on which two characters should end up happily united. Not that
any choice greatly affects the concluding material, so crafted as to
fit all contingencies with minimal adjustments. And there is no
danger that the audience's solution will be much of a competition
to those already offered by such illustrious scribes as J. I. M. Stewart
("Michael Innes"), C. Day Lewis, and several others.

Although this *Mystery of Edwin Drood* does not finally arouse
us more than any reasonably well crafted piece of trivia, it does
prove how much better our actors, directors, etc. are at Holmes or
Gilbert and Sullivan than at Shakespeare, the ostensible purpose of
"Shakespeare in the Park." The reason is obvious: this stuff is much
easier to do. Should leaden Shakespeare then be phased out in favor
of such trippingly performed fluff? The answer to that is shrouded
in greater mystery than anything in *Edwin Drood*.

This, after all, is the oldest dilemma, the prime pons asinorum
in life as in the arts: is something always better than nothing, or are
there times when nothing is better than something? My guess is
that one has to keep trying, and that, like one swallow, one Shakespeare does not make a summer.

Song & Dance

In 1932 Jean Cocteau wrote the monodrama *La Voix humaine*, about
a rejected woman convulsively trying, over the telephone, to cling
to her lover, who is about to marry another. Though bordering on
the sentimental, it was a dazzling display piece for a great actress
who could wring any heart with it, as Berthe Bovy, I gather, did. In
1959, Francis Poulenc, by turning it into a 40-minute mono-opera

and getting the incomparable Denise Duval to sing it, made something gloriously vocal and human out of it. It is surely from this that
Andrew Lloyd Webber, who never had an original idea, musical or
otherwise (consider, for instance, his pastiche *Requiem*), got the
notion for a 40-minute mono-musical in which an Englishwoman
sings about her generally unhappy love affairs with a potpourri of
American men. Entitled *Tell Me on a Sunday*, it was a concert hit in
1979, and Lloyd Webber decided to attach it to his orchestral work
Variations (on the Paganini A minor Caprice), written the year
before, which lent itself to being danced to.

In 1982, this glued-together apple and orange became a London
musical, *Song & Dance*, and a palpable (though, to my mind, neither watchable nor listenable) hit, with lyrics by Don Black, known
chiefly for supplying title songs for James Bond movies, and orchestrations by Lloyd Webber and David Caddick. Now Richard Maltby
Jr., one of the creators of *Ain't Misbehavin'* and *Baby*, and the New
York City Ballet's Peter Martins have rethought and more idiomatically Americanized a work whose America, initially, was about as
authentic as that of *Mahagonny* (though there the similarity ends).
By all accounts, what is now at the Royale surpasses its previous
avatars, but that, folks, still isn't much.

The *Song* part now tells the story of Emma, an English hat designer in her early thirties, who journeys to New York, then Los
Angeles, then back to New York, drifting wherever her sundry
love affairs take her. There is, first, Chuck, the pop musician whom
Emma leaves by more or less mutual accord; then Sheldon Bloom, a
producer who whisks her off to L.A. and there abandons her; then,
back in New York, Joe, a young Nebraskan, of whom we learn only
that he lives in the Village with a roommate named Dwight and
wears red cowboy boots—which makes him sound like an unlikely
prospect for any girl. Yet he turns out to be Emma's one true passion (why?), then dumps her, and not, as she would have preferred,
on a park bench on a Sunday afternoon, which, since Emma is
played by Bernadette Peters, recently of the Sondheim opus that
still hangs in a few doors down, is one of the few things that would
make sense here.

Emma now turns to Paul, a married man, from whom, when
he leaves his wife and children for her, she proceeds to disengage
herself. In the end, like the Marschallin in *Rosenkavalier*, she looks
into the mirror to observe the changes time has wrought in her,
and determines either to accept her new, hardened self or to try

to regain her former, innocent one. Owing to the quirks of the amplification and acoustics, I'm not sure which, though frankly, I don't give a damn.

The obvious trouble with all this is that not only do the unseen men remain nebulous and unreal, so, too, does the seen woman. This Emma could be Emma Hamilton, Emma Woodhouse, Emma Bovary, or even that concept envisioned by the poet Christian Morgenstern when he wrote that all seagulls look as if their name were Emma. One moment she is mad as a hatter, another moment as insipid as a midinette, but never—unlike Cocteau's heroine, who epitomizes every jilted lover—does she stand for anything. And neither in word nor in song can she convey—Lloyd Webber and Black have seen to that—what makes the shadowy Joe more important and lovable than the equally wraithlike other men. There is, however, one—and only one—smashing song in the score, "Capped Teeth and Caesar Salad," which should rightfully be enshrined as the anthem of Hollywood and which, orchestrated by Lloyd Webber and David Cullen with (I believe) additional lyrics by Maltby, is an unqualified delight, especially as performed by Bernadette Peters.

Miss Peters is an unimpeachable peach of a performer who does so much for the top half of this double bill as to warrant its immediate rechristening as *Song of Bernadette*. She not only sings, acts, and (in the bottom half) dances to perfection, she also, superlatively, *is*. For there are moments in any show, even far better ones than this, where the author and director have not provided for the performer—black holes that he or she must fill out simply by being there. And when it comes to being there, no one, not even Martin Heidegger, could have been more ontogenetic than Miss Peters is here; if nothing else, we can watch her face luminesce and the down on it tremble. Into everything she injects life and projects it—even into this.

In the *Dance* half, however, things go from bad to worse. This, it appears, is the story of the aforementioned Joe, who also has to undergo some sort of transformation to become, in the end, reunited with and worthy of Emma. Since she is now a successful and prosperous milliner, the conversion smacks of self-interest. But exactly what goes on in Peter Martins's choreographic tale remains swathed in murk, even as the stage, moodily lighted (or darkened) by the masterly Jules Fisher, represents nocturnal New York only eventually breaking into a diaphanous dawn, to which Robin Wagner's gossamer yet strongly evocative scenery handsomely contributes.

There is an unlikely street-corner exchange of clothes between Joe and a young black who may be Dwight, after which Joe enters a bar and flirts with some girls with greater confidence. Yet it is upon seeing (perhaps in a beatific vision) a fashion show of Emma's that he resumes his Nebraskan attire and, ostensibly, wins the heroine.

Martins's choreography consists chiefly of emulating *Fancy Free*—or, if you prefer, *On the Town*—while making every effort to avoid outright plagiarism. Actually, what we get is an overextended version of all those dance sequences from countless shows about New York in which we see New Yorkers going about their daily business or nightly leisure in dance terms—in fact, I kept waiting for the obligatory subway straphanger sequence, which, in a unique stroke of originality, Martins managed to forgo. Musically, the Paganiniana of *Dance* is no better than the cavatinas of *Song*, so that Lloyd Webber's *Cav* and *Pag* are not likely to inspire a choreographer. Even so, there are moments when Martins rises from farrago to a jolly fandango, and his highly gifted dancers, among whom the sexy Mary Ellen Stuart is particularly eye-catching, are able to cut loose with boisterous brio.

Still, by far the most enthralling element is the tap sequence performed—and, doubtless, choreographed—by Gregg Burge. His tapping subsumes everything from ballet to soft-shoe, from the flight of birds to the undulations of water snakes. Even standing, he dances with his facial expressions; when he starts moving, Burge burgeons, flowers, erupts, and conquers. Yet the entire ensemble enchants, with the fetching Miss Stuart followed closely by Cynthia Onrubia; only the talented Gen Horiuchi gets a bit lost in the shuffle. No matter. Over all is spilled the cornucopia of invention that is Willa Kim's wildly exuberant costuming, which, like the indefatigable dancers, never relaxes.

But whereas *Song* can rely on the unwobbling pivot of Miss Peters, *Dance* has no such prop in the Joe of Christopher d'Amboise. A fine dancer, a chip off the old block with remarkable *ballon*, he can effortlessly execute every chore of the choreography. Yet he is, physically as well as artistically, bland, lacking in personality, hollow. His looks and deportment vie in characterlessness, and he makes the mystery of Emma's obsession even less scrutable. And when it comes to singing, d'Amboise doesn't even try. For the rest, everything in *Song & Dance* is tried, even if little is true.

The Iceman Cometh;
A Map of the World

When the Moscow Art Theatre finally came to New York in 1968, I experienced one of my great theatrical disappointments. This dreary, musty, mummified museum piece was supposed to be *The Cherry Orchard* as performed by the theater for which it was written? Some thing not altogether unlike my feeling then—and equal nausea—overwhelmed me at the current revival of *The Iceman Cometh*, which turns a great play about death in life or life in death into one of sheer death: a deadly bore conceived in unimaginative dutifulness, executed with lifeless languor, to be consumed in a reverential stupor.

In 1956, the director José Quintero and the actor Jason Robards Jr. revived O'Neill's masterpiece, which had been received with respectful unenthusiasm at its 1946 premiere, and made a hit out of it. At 36, Robards was younger and much more handsome than the Hickey O'Neill had envisioned; Quintero, who never struck me as a good director, had then a youthful élan to mitigate his mediocrity. A solid cast was assembled at the old Circle in the Square—thus the matricidal Don Parritt was played (brilliantly) by a promising newcomer called Robert Redford—and, for once, a theater in the round and, more particularly, a shabby one, really helped: the acting space looked, felt, perhaps even smelled like a cheap run-down saloon, and you could, from that floor plan, re-create the flophouse above—*ex ungue leonem.*

My, how it all worked; three decades later, I can still recall Roberts Blossom doing a superlative Willie Oban; any number of characterizations, in fact, survive in my memory as safely as an old film in an up-to-date *cinémathèque.* Perhaps most wonderful was Robards's song and dance, for his speech had the rhythms and melodies of a wild yet honeyed music (Scriabin, maybe?), and his footwork and gestures were the stuff of which Nijinskys are made. There was poetry in the air; in no play since *King Lear*, perhaps, had despair sung out so seductively, had human misery had so many funny-sad changes rung on or wrung from it, had hopelessness become as heroic as the self-delusion in Harry Hope's saloon.

The current revival lasts an unconscionable four hours and 50 minutes with three brief intermissions; for the premiere production (as Louis Sheaffer reminds us), the author obtained a 7:30-to-11:20 duration with, among other things, "fifteen minutes cut from the original running time by quickening the pace." There is no quickening of anything in the stuffed dinosaur Quintero has lugged onto the Lunt-Fontanne stage, apparently mistaking it for the American Museum of Natural History. In the first act alone, where the mostly sleeping derelicts create a nearly overmastering urge in the audience to follow suit, he has carefully surrounded what dialogue there is with enough pauses for an audience to circumambulate every line as if it were an excavated antique sculpture that needed to be experienced from every angle. And Thomas R. Skelton's skimpy pools of light make sure the stage is engulfed in enough darkness to allow any actor not actually speaking a snooze as undisturbed as that of many a spectator. The play might as well have been called *The Sandman Cometh.*

In the second act, things do pick up a bit, but not much. The pacing throughout remains lethargic beyond the legitimate needs of the play. Though Quintero had managed to block *Iceman* passably in the round, behind a proscenium he cannot make the stage livelier than a crumbling frieze with an occasional lizard scrabbling across it. Torpor, of course, is appropriate here, but a double order of rigor mortis is not. In the hands of a great director near-inertia can have a rhythm, a fluidity of its own; here, petrifaction is occasionally upgraded into ossification.

With some exceptions, the performances range from impossible to acceptable. It is at the lower end, regrettably, that we find Jason Robards, who seems to have lost just about everything losable: energy, elegance, speed of reaction, vocal flexibility, that fevered elasticity of being and springiness of soul shared by salesman and actor that made Robards's 1956 Hickey archetypal; now, the kick has gone out of Hickey, even as it has at one point out of Harry Hope's booze. Nor does it help that the wending among the various tables Quintero has devised for Hickey during his monumental monologue (which worked well in central staging) now seems arbitrary and constrained; has the space shrunk or Robards overexpanded? He's now a slalom racer doing the course without skis.

The next-best part—arguably the best—is that of Larry, the *raisonneur*, the appraiser, the author's mouthpiece. This role is almost surefire, and Donald Moffat, looking as gaunt as a desert father in a year when locusts are scarce, starts out promisingly. His anchorite's voice seems tailored for jeremiads, and from behind his Michelangelesque eyebrows emerge looks to smite the Philistines and make true believers quake. Here, you think, is a man who, while refusing to judge, does something weightier yet—comprehends. But the performance does not change, grow, or even significantly shrivel at the end; it merely peters out into the same Larry in slow motion and finally in a freeze frame. Not so much a convert to nihilism as a frozen grimace, Moffat is the only Larry ever to end up boring me.

With Barnard Hughes's Harry, I have the opposite trouble. Hughes is too good and complaisant a comedian to be, or allow himself to be, genuinely pathetic—if not tragic—and his Hope elic- its laughs both where they work and where they detract. Moreover, he rather overdoes the Irishness; surely we should think of him less as Hibernian than as human. The fourth major character is an absolute disaster: Paul McCrane plays Parritt as a scurvy little rat exuding loathsomeness and self-loathing from the outset. We assume the worst right off, and he can neither surprise nor sadden us, neither decline in stature nor grow in pathos.

John Pankow does Rocky, the bartender-pimp, with a nice com- bination of deviousness and stupidity, but as his colleague, Chuck, Harris Laskawy is both wooden and attitudinizing. The best among the minor characters are James Greene, whose Jimmy Tomorrow is flawless in look, sound, and gesture; Roger Robinson, who needs only a little restraint to make a definitive Joe Mott; and Natalia Nogulich, who among an adequate trio of tarts is just a little more adequate. While some of the others can at least be overlooked, the aggressive oiliness of John Christopher Jones's Willie, the not even English-sounding actorishness of Bill Moor's Captain, and the rockbottom incompetence (including almost total incomprehen- sibility) of Leonardo Cimino's Hugo are so many wrecking balls hurled at the play's edifice.

Ben Edwards, a designer specializing in seediness, has outdone himself here by making the squalor of the set not even theatrically interesting; Jane Greenwood's costumes will please the less fashion- able thrift shops, which is as it should be. This so-called American National Theater Production of *The Iceman Cometh* goeth before a fall and bespeaks not a "National Theater" but a provincial barn.

David Hare boasts three qualities admirable in a playwright: literateness, social awareness, and a willingness to try new forms rather than safely repeat himself. Literateness is always safe; the danger of social awareness is uncritical radicalism (which, in *Plenty*, becomes a frenetic shadowboxing); the danger with innovation is gimmickiness, from which his genuinely arresting new play, *A Map of the World*, is not wholly free.

We are in Bombay in 1978 at a UNESCO conference on poverty, but if the participants don't stick their noses too far out of the luxury hotel (by Indian standards, to be sure) in which they are housed, they need not be reminded of the gap between speechifying and reality. Here we have a twofold confrontation between Victor Mehta, a major Indian-born novelist—an arch-conservative of biting brilliance—now living the country squire's life in Shropshire with his English wife and child, and Stephen Andrews, a young, left-wing, intellectual British journalist, as hopefully and perhaps naïvely idealistic as Mehta is sardonically and perhaps justifiably cynical. Not only do they lock horns ideologically, they are also pitted against each other by Peggy Whitton, a gorgeous young American actress of dubious talent, who is making a movie in India. Though Peggy has spent a happy night with Victor, she is willing to switch to Stephen should he win the private political debate she instigates between them, to be adjudicated by Elaine Le Fanu, a sophisticated, indeed jaded, black American TV commentator covering the conference.

This device smacks of contrivance; what does ring true is that the delegate from Mozambique, a Communist who nevertheless needs help from Western capitalism, threatens to wreck the conference if Mehta gives the speech he was invited to deliver, unless, to defuse its rightist politics, he prefaces it with a statement that a novelist perforce perceives reality from a fictional point of view. What rings false again is that this disclaimer should have been co-drafted by Stephen, and that it should be so humblingly worded that no serious writer, let alone one modeled (however loosely) on the prickly and arrogant V. S. Naipaul, would consider delivering it.

You would think, in any case, that this ideological and sexual jockeying and jousting would be more than enough to fill out a play, but Hare adds another level—the present, when a mediocre film director is making a commerical movie based on Mehta's novel about the aforementioned events (Mehta would never have allowed this), and the real-life Mehta and Peggy, now his consort, arrive at the studio to complicate matters. Supererogatory as all this is, it doesn't even elicit more than perfunctory writing, and actually undercuts the efficacy of the main action as each character turns into the actor portraying him, and the locale into a movie set. A few facile ironies may be gained—as well as some facile sentimentality improbably imputed to Mehta—but the loss is greater.

Nevertheless, *A Map of the World* is distinguished by being a genuine play of ideas in the Shavian mold, and by, Shavianly again, doing justice to both sides of the—possibly irresoluble—argument and not loading the dice on the side of Stephen, author's alter ego though he be. As minor perquisites, there are amusing observations on any number of subjects, everything from the absurdity of international conferences to the sexual *démarches* of American women.

Some of the minor characters are trenchantly observed—thus Martinson, the senior diplomat in charge of the conference, and M'Bengue, the delegate from Mozambique, as well as a number of movie people. However, Elaine does not come across sharply enough, perhaps in part because of Alfre Woodard's poor performance, all empty posturing. The excessively juvenile Peggy of Elizabeth McGovern is scarcely better, but at least her legs are unquestionable works of art. Richard Venture and Ving Rhames are equally fine as Martinson and M'Bengue and as the actors enacting them; as the actresses playing Elaine and Peggy, Woodard and McGovern are tolerable. In the extremely tricky part of the film Mehta, the actor playing Mehta, and the real-life or meta-Mehta, Roshan Seth, repeating his London performance, is often startlingly right, and as often merely right enough. Superb, however, is Željko Ivanek, a young actor whose range on stage and in movies seems limitless, and who delivers both Stephen and the actor playing him with precocious mastery. And I think no other American actor could render so perfectly an Oxford-bred yet faintly lower-class English accent.

Good scenery (Hayden Griffin), costumes (Jane Greenwood), lighting (Rory Dempster), music (Nick Bicât), and the author's didactic direction further enhance a play that, flaws and all, entertains almost as much as it instructs.

Aunt Dan and Lemon

Some wicked fairy must have presided over the birth of Wallace Shawn's *Aunt Dan and Lemon* (at the Public Theater). She must have decreed, "Thou shalt have neither language nor structure, neither shapeliness nor significance, neither wit nor good sense. Be thou bereft!" And so there is this poor, unappetizing worm wriggling around the stage and pretending to be an iconoclastic play though merely offending against taste, intelligence, and basic hygiene as it waits for someone to step on it and put it and its captive audience (no intermission, of course!) out of their misery.

Lemon, to call it by its rightful name, opens with an anemic, anorectic young woman, Leonora, nicknamed Lemon, soliloquizing in her dingy London flat about the uneventfulness, lovelessness, drabness of her idle, reclusive life. Subsisting mostly on a variety of juices although juiceless herself, she thrives on her reading, mostly books about the Nazis, who fascinate her and whose Holocaustal practices she recites with awe and, as we gradually realize, approval. Presently Lemon introduces us to her past. We meet her American father, Jack, a businessman, who promptly gets down to soliloquizing. There is relatively little dialogue in the play, and what there is is usually only thinly disguised monologue: someone is feeding someone else cues for disquisitions, lengthy reminiscences, elaborate plummetings of fancy in language to make Iowa, by comparison, seem Alpine.

Jack discourses on his harshly practical work ethic, whence we move to a family dinner scene, where Susan, Lemon's English mother, worries tearfully about her little daughter's non-eating, whereupon Jack, in a combination breakdown and temper tantrum, bawls out Susan. We are, next, given a friend of the parents, Danielle, the youngest American don at Oxford, whom Lemon turns into her beloved Aunt Dan. Dan is an ardent Kissinger fetishist, and explains in interminable, incomparably boring monologues why we need servants and such to do our dirty work, and how Kissinger is just a grave, brave man doing what is distasteful to others but needs doing. Eventually Dan and the liberal Susan, totally incapable of defending her position, part for good; Lemon and Dan continue their discreetly lesbian-tinged friendship until the latter's death. Presumably Lemon's pro-Nazi sentiments stem from Dan's Henryolatry, as the play concludes with Lemon soliloquizing again: though we may be repelled by our squashing of a cockroach, she suggests, we are also fascinated by its death throes; similarly, we would kill criminals if large groups of them were taking over. And if we vindicate American settlers who decimated Indians, we must also, however uneasily, find the Nazis' extermination of Jews remarkable in its efficacy and ideological consistency.

Even while educating Lemon politically, Dan broadens her sexual horizons. So she introduces her to the friends she voluptuously
admires: Mindy, a call girl who, for money, does everything, even
kill; and Andy, a cynical roué whose life is all laughs and lechery.
The point, I suppose, is that sexual amorality leads to ideological
immorality. But Shawn has neither Shaw's wit nor Shaw's intellect
with which to interweave plot and subplot dramatically and make
antithetical positions come equally alive as they clash and give off
sparks. We are tempted to conclude that the supposed intellectual
challenge, like the sexual provocation, is only the game-playing of
a prurient and presumptuous little boy, egged on by a number of
indulgent reviewers.

Max Stafford-Clark's directing impresses me less the more I see
of it; the design in this Shakespeare Festival-Royal Court co-production is serviceable but undistinguished. The two worst and un-
sightliest performers, the author and Linda Bassett, are given three
parts each, even though they haven't enough variety for one. Larry
Pine (Andy) and Lynsey Baxter (Mindy) are satisfactory though
unmemorable; the dwarfish Linda Hunt (Dan), though competent, does not grow from part to part. But there is one spectacular
performance from Kathryn Pogson as Lemon, who is able to coax
variety from monotonous writing, intensity from inertia, iniqui-
tous charm out of blather without, however, doing violence to the
author's intentions. These are sometimes defended with the excuse
that Shawn presents only the seamy side of an argument so as to
force the audience to think and take the other. If the antidote to
an author's asininities is left to audiences such as I am usually surrounded by, heaven help us all!

Lillian

Take, if you will, or must, Lillian Hellman, one of the least pleasant persons and most mundane writers who ever made it big in
American theater and letters; add Zoe Caldwell, an actress who
has become less and less an interpreter of roles and more and more
an exuder of a specious *grande dame* quality; put them both into
that most factitious and undramatic medium, the monodrama, and
what have you got? *Lillian*, by William Luce, a gratingly unnecessary piece of Hellman hagiography cum Caldwell self-promotion

that, as reverently and confiningly directed by Robert Whitehead, Miss Caldwell's husband, might as well have been housed in a Saks or Henri Bendel window.

First, monodrama. If it can work at all, it must be either a real play or a set of varied monologues, perhaps culled from the writings of a manifold, witty, challenging writer or, at the very least, a canny eccentric such as John Aubrey. If, however, your sources are the autobiographical writings of Lillian Hellman, augmented by a profile of her by a Texas TV station, you get the trivial, dishonest, and self-aggrandizing natterings of a stylistically undistinguished author, who, moreover, was humorless and megalomaniacal enough to slap a libel suit on a fellow author, Mary McCarthy, for saying on a TV talk show that she did not even trust the truthfulness of Hellman's *the*'s and *and*'s. In short, as something to make a play from, Miss Hellman's autobiographies rank just ahead of the Congressional Record and cigarette commercials.

Let me be specific. Hellman could write the occasional lively sentence, such as this, about her childhood: "To be an orphan seemed to me a self-made piece of independence," though even here one might point out that what Hellman really meant was not "self-made" but its opposite, "ready-made." Most often, though, she will give you mildly amusing but essentially inconsequential reminiscences on the order of her father and mother's debate on whether it was Dad or Lillian who was "considered the sweetest-smelling baby in New Orleans." Or you'll get: "Tallulah was sitting in a large group giving the monologue she always thought was conversation." The audience I saw the play with burst into gales of laughter at this, much to my companion's and my amazement. Time and again, ancient, feeble witticisms—"I also saw Norma Shearer, her face unclouded by thought"—would send the spectators into ecstasies, and we were sadly reminded of how polarized our world has become, that there are now theatergoers to whom this sort of thing is novel, funny, perhaps even literature.

Next, the play. William Luce specializes in one-woman-writer shows: Emily Dickinson, Charlotte Brontë, and now Hellman have been subjected to his zeal. His dramatic construction is minimal. Here he has Hellman sitting in a hospital room adjoining the one in which her beloved Dashiell Hammett lies dying. She is drinking tea and chain-smoking furiously while mellowly delivering her personal recollections to—whom? There is something faintly distasteful about rehashing these self-indulgent trivia while your lover is expiring, but even more so is Luce's device for stirring up (as he thinks) periodic drama whenever the anecdotes wear too thin by having the lighting suddenly come horizontally and stridently from the sickroom and having Lillian get up and cross to the door to peek in at Dash, mumble something to the comatose novelist or to an invisible nurse, shed a few tears, fight back others, and launch into yet another anecdote about her relatives, her faithful black retainers, or herself.

But there is nothing about what it was like to be married to a writer, Arthur Kober, and very little about living with another, Hammett, except for some oft-rehearsed incidents grown shopworn. Nothing about what it is like to be a writer oneself, or about how one evolved one's politics, and just what they were. Nothing about Russia, very little about Broadway and Hollywood, and not much about literary and other friendships and enmities. A lot of this has to do with Hellman's own omissions, but a lot also with Luce journalism, which consists of—besides the oft-told HUAC-Hellman conflict—mostly footling tales favorable to our heroine. The harshest bit of self-criticism is an understatement such as "Alexander Woollcott once said I looked like the prowhead on a whaling ship." But there is no mention (how could there be, given the source?) of Hellman's mean-spiritedness, tightfistedness, litigiousness, desperate derivativeness in her later playwriting, and, worst of all, her politics, which caused her to remain an unreconstructed though unavowed Stalinist well after her onetime fellow Communists were giving up even on milder forms of Marxism. None of which prevented her from posing for an ad in Blackglama mink, possibly the most counterproductive effort in the history of advertising.

My point is not to make Hellman look odious—she did that far better herself. I am merely suggesting that whereas a warts-and-all theatrical portrayal might have some ornery life to it, Luce's kitschy portrait of Hellman is fit only for hanging on a wall full of Ertés and René Bouchés.

Lastly, the performance. Miss Caldwell is a highly polished actress, but also a glibly external one. It wasn't always so—I can recall fine work she did for Tyrone Guthrie in Minneapolis; latterly, however, she depends solely on technique and attitudinizing. Note, for example, the rubato with which she mouths "the morning paaay-ppper" or the downward glissando and slow dissolve she puts into "How childish!" Or the pose she strikes (not for the first time) on the line "The audience was yelling 'Author! Author!'"—a cross between something out of Jaques Dalcroze and a freeze-frame of a fireman sliding down his pole. It is all so artfully modulated, calibrated, calculated, and as spurious as Hellman herself. The makeup is compellingly Hellman-like, but even Miss Caldwell's genteel stage English is nothing like Lillian's edgy tough talk.

Ben Edwards's set looks penurious even by the standards of this notoriously shoestring designer, and David Gooding's music is merely distracting; Jane Greenwood's suit and Thomas Skelton's lighting are apt. If you want to spend an evening with the sweetest-smelling Broadway baby, Lillian may be your dish; if you are looking for truth and enlightenment, art or beauty, forget it. By not helping to prolong the show's run, you may even save the relentlessly smoking star from lung cancer.

Caligula

Talk about turning a play into something else: Circle Rep has turned *Caligula* completely upside down, anagrammatizing (Albert) Camus into (Yma) Sumac. I wish I could call this adaptation by Marshall W. Mason and Harry Newman, as staged by Mason, something as harmless as inept or bad; it is, at the very least, demented.

As Camus wrote it—starting in 1936, revising as late as 1959, and probably leaving it unfinished at his accidental death in 1960—*Caligula* is a potentially brilliant play, patched together from snatches of greatness that do not quite coalesce and lack the ending to properly cap them off. All along, there was a dichotomy in the conception. *Caligula* began as a wish-fulfillment fantasy: The 25-year-old author, in precarious health and fearing death, was expressing through the hero his own passion for living to the utmost at the expense, if need be, of everyone else. But along came his disenchantment with the Communist party and his horror of Stalin and Hitler; presently Caligula became also a portrait of a contemporary dictator. How could one protagonist embody two such contradictory concepts? While the play started out close to Suetonius, successive versions departed further and further; it is unfortunate that Circle Rep worked not from the last available French text but from Stuart Gilbert's considerably earlier English adaptation.

The worst possible idea was to update the play and put it in modern American dress, with everything from tautological closed-circuit-television screens to a whole punk-rock video sequence, from American Express cards to submachine guns. The play is about modern times—no fool can miss that—but it needs the quasi-Roman look and sound as a distancing device, as an incentive to us to work out the parallels and discover how far we have not come since the maddest and most murderous of imperial tyrants. That Caligula still manages to move us, and is in many ways more impressive than his victims and adversaries, is a further comment on the paltriness of our times. But to turn, say, the poets of Rome, meant as a takeoff on real contemporary art, into cretinous rock and country musicians (played by some truly grim-looking specimens) is to miss the point of Camus's satire. So each bit of modernization proves either a vulgarization or a trivialization of the author's intentions.

Even the technical aspects are appalling. Mason's staging tries to stylize while everything else aims at realism: a cut-rate high-tech set by the good John Lee Beatty, ragtag costumes by the fine Jennifer von Mayrhauser, crass lighting by the subtle Dennis Parichy—I blame them all on the director. The platitudinous musical score plods from Albinoni's Adagio to equally banal pop selections. Every cheap trick is dragged in, from turning the lights up on the audience as Caligula shouts "You're all criminals!" to letting us hear every last sound of an offstage rape. And the adapters' language is of a piece with all this, e.g., "Death is like a bus ride to a small midwestern state..."

As Caligula, Ken Marshall tries gamely, but cannot summon up the twisted poetry, the crystalline logical insanity of an angelic actor such as Gérard Philipe, who must have created the role with scalding impetuousness. And Jay Patterson makes a credible Cherea. The rest, with one or two minor exceptions, range from ludicrous to loathsome. The only thing worse this company could have done than so to butcher Caligula would have been to murder, in full view of the audience, a herd of moose.

Loot

Most people know that satire must be funny; many, that it must hurt; but few realize that it must also display superior intelligence as its right to mock the world. In these debased times, when an alleged satire such as the movie *Down and Out in Beverly Hills*, made of stale mush, can be a success, I fear for *Loot*, which admirably meets all three prerequisites.

Joe Orton, who was murdered at age 34 by his lover, was 33 when he wrote *Loot* (1966), his funniest play. It is informed by a magnificent indignation against government, Catholicism, women, male and female authority figures (e.g., parents)—indeed, humanity in general—surpassed only by its hatred of hypocrisy. It unfurls its faintly absurdist story with enormous wit, but never becomes incoherent with hate or soft with optimism about some hidden, underlying human goodness. Rather, it goes about its sacred mission of a total demolition job with unfailing good humor, reveling in its cool unraveling of the social fabric. Evil gets away with everything, without even the familiar cop-out of its having to live with pangs of conscience or an enervating satiety amid its ill-gained wealth.

But to get away with this, Orton not only had to be unremittingly funny, he also had to convince us of his intellectual right to his bleak misanthropy. In the play, language is bandied about, bent into every sort of paradox and play on words, twisted into sidesplitting non sequiturs of impeccable pseudo-logic: "It will put Paradise to shame." "Have you ever seen Paradise?" "Only in photographs." By his command over his medium, Orton asserts his right to his somber vision: this jaundiced view wears that difficult color, yellow, with such sovereign style that it persuades us that to discriminate against humanity spells a discriminating palate, ultimate good taste. Besides, if your lover kills you, the man he loves, out of sheer envy, doesn't that rather prove your point?

Loot concerns that good citizen, father, and Catholic Mr. McLeavy, who is mourning his dead wife awaiting interment. With him is nurse Fay, who eased Mrs. M. through her last illness by poisoning her, and who, having killed seven husbands in ten years for their money, now has her eye on Mr. M. The McLeavy boy, Hal has just pulled off a bank robbery with his friend Dennis, who works for the undertaker burying Mrs. M. and is in love with the murderous nurse. A semi-demented police inspector, Truscott of the Yard, is snooping around, and the boys don't know where to hide the loot. That is about as much as you need to know—except that this is not a play for those easily offended or lacking a sense of humor, like those subscribers to the Manhattan Theatre Club I saw leaving in disgust or, worse yet, incomprehension.

Orton was, clearly, a follower of Oscar Wilde, and *Loot* is arguably the twentieth-century *Importance of Being Earnest*. It is instructive to study how well the lesson of the master has been digested by the disciple. Compare the scene near the beginning of *Loot* where Fay questions Hal about, among other things, Dennis with Lady Bracknell's first-act examination of Jack: "FAY: Have you known him long? HAL: We shared the same cradle. FAY: Was that economy or malpractice? HAL: We were too young for malpractice, and economics still defeat us." And further: "FAY: You will be forced to associate with young men like yourself. Does that prospect please you? HAL: I'm not sure. FAY: Well, hesitation is something to be going on with. [Cf. Lady Bracknell on ignorance.] We can build on that. What will you do when you're old? HAL: I shall die. FAY: I see you're determined to run the gamut of all experience. That can bring you nothing but unhappiness." This may be merely funny when read; well acted on stage, it is a bloody riot.

The production couldn't be better. Željko Ivanek (Hal) is an uproarious combination of stupidity, cunning, and compulsive inability to lie in a performance that heroically refuses to pander to the audience with the least cuteness or self-indulgence. As his chum, Dennis, Kevin Bacon is almost as good, which is to say very. As McLeavy, Charles Keating is the image of honest befuddlement, in his firm belief in Church and State, the infallible formula for self-destruction he pursues with adorable idiocy. As Fay, the personification of female rottenness, Zoë Wanamaker is pursed and poised to perfection, overacting genteelly in a way that proves just right. As Truscott, the embodiment of male corruption, Joseph Maher portrays an idiot savant with sublime near-rationalness that turns the world irretrievably topsy-turvy as he makes madness and evil seem endearingly quixotic. In the small part of a bobby, Nick Ullett does yeoman's work.

John Tillinger has directed ebulliently, though I wish he had not let the delirium slacken somewhat toward the end. Highly proficient scenery (John Lee Beatty), costumes (Bill Walker), and lighting (Richard Nelson) help make *Loot* a hoot. It is subversive humor, of the sort homosexuals are particularly brilliant at. In Orton's play, we get a world where goodness is doomed, intelligence merely low cunning, and stupidity abject. The revival follows appropriately on the heels of *It's Only a Play*, by Terrence McNally, Orton's chief American emulator. But Orton's blackness is thicker, funnier, deeper.

Hamlet; Execution of Justice

The good news from the Public Theater is that Liviu Ciulei's *Hamlet* is the best Shakespeare ever presented at Papp's downtown emporium; the bad news is that it's still pretty bad. I sincerely hope that the Romanian director does not speak good English; otherwise, there would be no excuse for the way the poetry is mangled here, even granted that to American actors verse is about as foreign a language as Romanian. But this does not explain why so many roles are so badly filled, whether by domestic ham or by Romanian pastrami.

Ciulei has not cut the text overmuch, yet some of his cutting is bizarre: a friend of mine rightly missed such a line as "I'll lug the guts into the neighbor room," and there were even more perplexing lacunae. At least the director resisted, on the whole, the current directorial mania to rewrite the play. Such a conceit as having the players make up on one side of the stage while the court paints and bedizens itself on the other and Hamlet puts on a clown face is, though supererogatory, a relatively harmless way for a director to call attention to himself. Still, it wastes time better used on more text merely to explain the obvious. To have Ophelia go crazy at a kind of Mad Hatter's tea party is more questionable. And it is surely ill-advised to set the play too close to our own time, and thus intensify anachronism without achieving contemporaneity. Then, as William Ivey Long's costumes can't decide whether they are Victorian, Edwardian, or Georgian, confusion spreads further.

Nevertheless, Ciulei indisputably knows how to direct a crowd, and, with the help of B. H. Barry, the fight scenes are particularly exciting. The trouble is with his direction of individuals. Although he thinks up interesting business, as when the "mad" Hamlet squats relaxedly in midair beside a couch or when he wiggles a seemingly boneless index finger to convey Polonius's wormlike nature (in which Kevin Kline's physical agility is of inestimable help), he has some mighty queer notions of how the main characters should look, speak, and behave. He will even permit Laertes to sound British while most of the others cannot even sound mid-Atlantic; and several characters, notably Ophelia, walk all wrong.

On the other hand, Bob Shaw's scenery—a slightly forward-slanting white backdrop on which a sky is occasionally and discreetly projected, and a few angular, metallic-seeming pillars that can be smoothly and artfully shifted to convey very different spaces—

couldn't be more economically evocative. Jennifer Tipton's highly dramatic lighting, very often oblique, knows how to jolt and dislocate without losing credibility. And there is something to be said for the absence of background music. What cannot be condoned is the absence of acting. Most of the performers belong to what I'd call the Romanian National Theater of America; they have been circulating among the productions of Liviu Ciulei, Lucien Pintilie, and Andrei Serban, and seem a little out of place this side of Bucharest.

Hamlet asks Ophelia, "Are you honest? Are you fair?" What he should ask is "Are you for real?" Harriet Harris, an appalling actress, plays Ophelia as a bag lady in the making. Flat- and pasty-faced, head-wobbling and gawky, convulsed with weird and extraneous movements, her expression hysterical from the outset and her voice unfocused, she is ghostlier than a ghost and not half so much fun. But ghostliness seems to run in the family: David Pierce's Laertes is wimpy, wispy, wan almost to the point of transparency, and seems to be not so much acting as hallucinating. As for papa Polonius, the way that ill-favored and ill-spoken, and infinitely plebeian, actor Leonardo Cimino plays him, he is no majordomo—barely a court jester.

And what a court, from top to bottom—or, rather, from bottom to bottom. Harris Yulin's Claudius is a crude, smug vulgarian; Priscilla Smith's Gertrude, when she's not sleepwalking, joins her spouse in butchering Shakespeare's poetry: her "willow" speech about the drowned Ophelia could dry up a fountain. Richard Frank's Horatio starts pleasantly, but looks and sounds out of place and time and keeps getting worse. Mario Arrambide's Marcellus, David Cromwell's Guildenstern, Lynn Cohen's Player Queen, Ron Faber's Voltemand, and Peter Crook's Fortinbras are simply scandalous; by being merely mediocre, Randle Mell scores as Rosencrantz. By far the best work comes from Jeff Weiss, an actor-playwright who has never been seen off Off Off Broadway (where he has poured out endless plays in one of which I was the villain), and who not only manages to be totally different as Ghost, Player King, and Osric, but also remains restrained, dignified, compelling in parts all too easily hammed up.

And the Hamlet? Kevin Kline is an adroit, likable, intelligent actor, often terrific in swashbuckling or comic roles (a good Richard III even, and an estimable Henry V), but he cannot hack Hamlet. He prosifies the soliloquies, trying to make up with eccentric changes in dynamics for the lack in poetics; he fails at anguish and suffering; and never, never does he break your heart. He moves lithely and strikingly, though, and handles the comedy very well—too well, perhaps, as he threatens to turn the Prince of Denmark into the Pirate King. What he finally lacks most is a musical voice and sufficiently expressive eyes. As a mountain guide, he'd be jolly good on the plateaus but no match for the peaks.

Much as I would like to like *Execution of Justice*—because it deals with a gross miscarriage of justice, and one, furthermore, for which our glorious jury system and those twelve solid, ordinary, wonderful citizens and peers are largely to blame—it is hard to do so. Emily Mann, who put together and directed this docudrama, has underwritten and overdirected, so that much that should be in clear focus remains fuzzy, and much that should be simply stated and directed is gussied and gimmicked up into shrillness and garishness.

To be sure, the San Francisco trial of City Supervisor Dan White for the shooting of Mayor George Moscone and Supervisor Harvey Milk is not, in the truest sense, stageworthy. The lawyers were not mental giants giving us a gripping intellectual duel, nor were they great demagogues bringing a host of histrionic emotions into epic play. Of interest here were either tiny technicalities or enormous legal, social, political issues; the former are too small for the stage, the latter too large for a mere documentary play and would require the resources of a major poetic and philosophical dramatist freely interpreting. Yet be it said for Miss Mann that, though a known radical, she has tried to be fair to both sides and all individuals—or at least so it seems to one who hasn't followed the case closely. But much of what she has done is puzzling.

Thus she prominently displays Sister Boom Boom, a San Francisco transvestite who affects nun's garb, whom she identifies as a "political activist." Yet as shown, S.B.B. is a grotesque derived from Genet, occasionally pertinent but mostly campy, outrageous, obfuscatory. He/she can be viewed in various ways, but we get no clues, and since this ambiguous character is not germane to the trial, it all seems so much mystification. Again, the prosecutor is presented as a bit of a buffoon. Was he? Or is the actor overacting? Or overdirected? Or doesn't Miss Mann see the buffoonery? Questions like these beset us all along the way, yet because they are not profound moral or intellectual universals but only footling particulars, they don't make for creative ambiguity, merely for distracting murkiness.

What is certain, however, is that *Execution of Justice* is overdirected and overproduced. There are film projections on an overhanging cube wherein the real-life people alternate with the actors performing them, superimpositions or fancy counterpointings of several sets of unrelated utterances, occasional games with chronology, elaborate choreographies for the attorneys every time they rise and move about, several performances whipped up to fever pitch, photomurals of San Francisco and literal-minded background music, an intrusion into the courtroom of outside events (the candlelight march with added gestures, a police counterattack with deafening explosions and blinding lights), and so on. How I yearned for the simple, bare facts consecutively and clearly enacted! Or even a few judicious comments from experts on jurisprudence, sociology, psychiatry—other than the mostly preposterous psychiatrists giving expert testimony, easy targets for the author's ironies.

As for the acting, it can hardly be judged under the circumstances, though John Spencer (White), Nicholas Hormann (D. A. Freitas), and Adam Redfield (Harvey Milk's lover) seem to be doing the right things, and Marcia Jean Kurtz and Lisabeth Bartlett seem to be doing the wrong ones, while the rest fall somewhere in between. But it is worrisome when such fine actors as Peter Friedman and Donal Donnelly appear to be overreaching. The White case is so important that the play is not without fascination, but I wonder whether it is a good thing when an audience is impelled to applaud a suicide, even if it is Dan White's?

Long Day's Journey Into Night

Whoever butchers *Long Day's Journey Into Night* isn't merely slaughtering hogs or cows; he is slaughtering the greatest play written by an American. This squarely places Jonathan Miller, the British director of the present revival, into the category of master butcher extraordinary. I have seen bad productions of this towering masterpiece, but none that so ingeniously and incontrovertibly totaled it. If the butchers' guild of Nuremberg competed for a prize, Miller could be their Walther von Stolzing.

His perversity (and his entire career as a director is founded on it) is threefold here. First, the pacing. Miller has manifestly aimed for the equivalent of the four-minute mile: a running time of under three hours (including one intermission) is, in fact, considerably better than four minutes for a miler, and worse than anything for

O'Neill. The actors were clearly goaded to deliver most of their lines (occasionally also trimmed and fiddled with) as if trying to outdo one another at tongue twisters or practicing to narrate the tango in the Sitwell-Walton *Façade*, the speed of delivery enough to daunt a Chuck Yeager; it is murder for the moods, meanings, and implications of O'Neill's masterwork. What should brood, bubbles; what should sing out, rattles on; what should groan or cry out in pain, motorcycles and machineguns along.

Next, the overlapping. Miller, who also directs opera, frequently has two, three, or four characters talking, shouting, or muttering simultaneously—God knows how they can respond to statements they could not possibly have heard—so that much of the time we're listening to something like the sextet from *Lucia di Lammermoor* without the music. As an experience, this ranks somewhere between the fingernail on the blackboard and Chinese water torture. Further, it guarantees that goodly chunks of the play go directly down the drain, and even the parts that you miraculously manage to unscramble or catch on the supersonic wing cannot begin to sink in and reverberate in the soul. If the record-breaking time is meant to make it easier for an audience to sit through this long, difficult work, the result is the exact opposite: whereas O'Neill can rivet us for hours at a normal speed and without aural smog, miler Miller mangles our ability to concentrate and loses our attention.

Third, some of the casting. As Jamie, Kevin Spacey does the best one can if forced to play a falling-down drunk delivering complex speeches at breakneck speed with impeccable diction; it is a sorry miracle, but a miracle nonetheless. Even better is Peter Gallagher, who, as Edmund, actually manages to convey the illusion of a deliberate, spacious delivery while coerced to keep up with the pack. However, as Mary Tyrone, Bethel Leslie is the second-greatest piece of miscasting in recent theatrical history. Though she can fire off lines even faster than the rest without losing clarity of diction, and her readings have moments of cogency and aplomb, she is basically an overage soubrette: a light-voiced, lightweight actress, not without charm, but hardly the ravaged wraith, the noble ruin she is meant to be—indeed, she even looks too young and insouciant. As Cathleen, a formerly surefire part, Jodie Lynne McClintock proves that no role is foolproof.

Now for the greatest piece of miscasting: Jack Lemmon as James Tyrone. Lemmon is an amiable and accomplished movie comedian, with shtick amusingly coming out of his ears. Here he plays Tyrone as if he were doing burlesque or, at best, a Billy Wilder movie with every lovable old trick and comic mannerism unleashed on O'Neill's tragedy. Not that the part, or play, is without humor, but you cannot do James Tyrone looking like the Kentucky Fried Chicken Colonel, and doing a cross between Alan King and Professor Irwin Corey, with cacklings and croonings and rubbery expressions reminiscent even of—of all people!—huggable old Jack Lemmon. Even his walk is absurd: a shuffling, shambling octogenarian's rather than that of a 65-year-old young for his age. O'Neill's Tyrone, the archetypal matinee idol, wasted his life touring in *The Count of Monte Cristo*, Lemmon's Tyrone must have been touring in *Abie's Irish Rose*. And I wish he wouldn't commit the ghastly (and anachronistic) mistake of saying "Keep your dirty tongue off of [*sic*] Ireland."

Miller has committed lesser errors as well, such as keeping the cast busy with clever but often extraneous business that further distracts from the text. And he has made (or let) Tony Straiges design a house that looks like a provincial funeral parlor, only less cheerful, surrounded—and even invaded—by palpable blackness. As Richard Nelson (no doubt at Miller's behest) has unlighted it, morning looks like midnight, and midnight like Tartarus. Willa Kim's desperately white costumes seemed to be designed solely to catch every last bit of available night. Uncalled for by the stage directions, a grand piano has been put on the stage. Though the brothers occasionally chase each other around it, it serves no real purpose until near the end, when the drugged, time-tripping Mary wistfully picks out a few nostalgic notes on it with one hand. That is as much as Miller's tinkering gets out of the sublime and awe-inspiring music of O'Neill's drama.

Mistero Buffo

To be funny, Dario Fo need only be. Others must do or say things; enough for him just to stand there with his canny, capacious face, those eyes and that mouth that have seen and tasted everything. And is it indeed necessary to utter the ludicrousness of existence when we are all party to it, or isn't it enough for Fo to roll his eyes and curl his lips in sardonic silence? And in red socks, which are the only conspicuously tendentious element in his otherwise sober yet casual attire.

A great gift, this humor of the unstated, the potential, because what actually gets written for a performer (sometimes even by himself if, like Fo, he happens to be also a playwright and monologuist) is not always that funny. Yet Fo does proceed to interact with the audience in various joshing, conspiratorial, verbal ways, and, once off on one of his monologues, makes you feel in the hands of a great *improvvisatore*. The art of improvisation consists of making an absolute minimum of improvisation and maximum of premeditation emerge as the acme of spontaneity, which, furthermore, could not have happened without our inspiring collaboration. And that's what Fo offers, with the able assistance of Ron Jenkins—comedy-scholar, clown, and co-translator with Stuart Hood of some of Fo's writings—who stands there self-effacingly smiling, but delivers one hell of a running, racing, rollicking translation, occasionally kidded by Fo.

Mistero Buffo (Comic Mystery) is an updated version of the work of those medieval itinerant mountebanks known as *giullari* (Italian), *jongleurs* (French), or, in plain English, jugglers, who not only juggled but also (the word comes from the Latin *ioculari*, to jest) told pointed jokes. Now the portly but agile Mr. Fo can leap about as eloquently as he can sling words through the air—as if they were so many rotating dinner plates, only saucier. In a trice, he goes from medieval and other historic matter to present concerns—political, philosophical, religious, social, or simply sundry—either explaining or demonstrating. Moreover, Fo is an expert at what he calls *grammelot*, an adaptable double-talk that can sound like a variety of languages and dialects, and does indeed contain a few actual words (these are projected, in English, onto a screen), but the double-talk is double-bottomed so as to smuggle in a lot of common sense.

A typical monologue, involving a great deal of gesture and body movement, characteristically combines past and present by being both about Boniface VIII, a pope Dante hated so much he consigned him to hell while still alive, and John Paul II, a pope so beloved by all he is already seen enskied and sainted. Centering on the assassination plot against our pope, this skit (it really is more than a monologue) is as funny as anything. In his delicious (alas, untranslated) book, *Un paese senza*, Alberto Arbasino wonders, "Perhaps not even King Ubu of Poland foresaw a Polish pope, nor did the Brecht of *Puntila* foresee a Pope Wojtyla." It takes Fo-sight to envision it in all its ramifications (no pun on Franca Rame, Mrs. Fo, intended), and you must see it to believe it fully and hilariously.

Unfortunately, the alternating program, in which Miss Rame performs a selection from *Tutta casa, letto e chiesa* (*It's All Bed, Board and Church*), is much less satisfying. Though a competent actress, Miss Rame is not an inspired clown; the acts are not quasi-improvisational commentaries but scripted monodramas (by Rame and Fo), and less amusing—you can't even get Reagan into them; the feminist themes, though perhaps still pertinent in Italy, seem dated here; and, above all, a fuller selection from this material has already been performed, ably and in English, by Estelle Parsons. By the time you read this, both shows will have departed; but now that the Fos are no longer denied U.S. visas, they should be frequent visitors, so be sure to catch the next go-around.

Me and My Girl

The new Marquis Theater has opened with a show about a reluctant earl, and we can count our blessings. *Me and My Girl*, the 1937 London musical—variously refurbished but redolent of that time, that place—is seldom less than likable and often downright adorable; so, averaging in the sporadic dull spots, let's settle on lovable. It has all the aroma of a less complicated period of history and show business (soon to be swept away, which only adds to its aura), and is revived in a way soundly resisting camp, condescension, or an excess of nostalgia. Reassembled with loving meticulousness under the supervision of Richard Armitage, son of the composer, Noel Gay (pen name of Reginald Armitage), it includes a few songs from other shows by Gay, indulges in a few playful anachronisms, invents a couple of new production numbers, simplifies a thing or two for American audiences, but never betrays what I take to be the spirit of the original: a sly innocence, a sentimentality leavened with wryness, and a love story that finds a core of believableness in a swirl of fantasy.

Hareford Hall and the earldom that goes with it are to devolve on the offspring of the late earl's ephemeral love match: Bill Snibson, a jaunty cockney, insolent but true-blue, whom the family may reluctantly accept provided he gives up his girlfriend, Sally Smith, and marries someone suitable—presumably the calculating Lady Jaqueline, who has been giving her cousin and intended, the silly but amiable Gerald, a royal runaround. Determined to make a real

Hareford out of Bill is crusty old Maria, Duchess of Dene (who is not without her sense of humor, however); leading the anti-Snibson forces is her lifelong suitor, the snobbish, besotted Sir John Tremayne, who finally sprouts some sense and decency. It is all poppycock, of course, but quality poppycock, with a tongue in the cheek for every tear in the eye, and a hundred tricks up the sleeve for one heart on it.

Noel Gay was one of the most popular composers of the period, and this was his biggest hit. Richard Armitage, the son, and his two sons enlisted Stephen Fry as adapter, and together they tracked down the lost L. Arthur Rose-Douglas Furber book and lyrics, which required detective work almost as thrilling as the show itself. Similar ingenuity and persistence had to go into rounding up some of the music and reconstructing the staging. Here—besides the memories of surviving fans—Mike Ockrent, the present director and contributor to revisions, must have proved of invaluable help. The end result, though an elaborate patchwork, emerges hearteningly of a piece. It is a double Pygmalion story—with a handsome bow to G.B.S.—where both hero and heroine take turns at being Pygmalion and Galatea. And if, in the present version, we can glimpse proleptic reminiscences of several later musicals and movies, no matter: the patchwork becomes a bit of latticework, and no one the worse for it.

Actually, part of the fun in watching *Me and My Girl* comes from trying to guess what in this marriage of true minds is old, what new; what borrowed, and what a touch more blue than the Lord Chamberlain countenanced in 1937. (He even blue-penciled the word "sissy.") But for all its new sauce, the old sauciness retains its innocence. Such an uproarious scene as the one in which Lady Jaquie tries to vamp the new earl, whose faithfulness to Sally is like a rock even as his flesh weakens and his bones turn to rubber, is endearing, not raunchy. The way Robert Lindsay, as Bill, tosses, twists, winds, and uncoils himself—lunges, falls, bounces back only to sprawl again—is a major delight. In scene after scene, Lindsay's flexibility, verbal as well as physical, extends to a whole spectrum of accents between low and posh along which he slithers, to madcap juggling with every part of his body, to uncanny timing in facial expressions as well as line delivery, to a whole parade of comic-balletic walks. The performance owes an obol or two to a number of famed dancers and comedians, but the seamless, personally enriched synthesis is Lindsay's own. And when you consider that these breathtakingly acrobatic shenanigans are being performed by an actor equally adept at playing a splendid Edmund to Olivier's Lear, your pleasure is enhanced by amazement.

The star is surrounded by an American cast that, to its great credit, does not let him down. As Sally, Maryann Plunkett has the right blend of sweetness and spunk, reasonableness and romance; she conveys the basic cockney homeliness of the character as faithfully as its glossier singing and dancing aspects; and indeed, her rendition of the touching "Once You Lose Your Heart" (twice) is a model of reigned-in pathos, no-nonsense staunchness. As the purposeful duchess, Jane Connell, always fun to watch, adds a new and welcome note of restraint to her rollicking repertoire. The scrumptious George S. Irving, after a somewhat uncertain start as Sir John (sure to be firmed up in time), proves himself yet again a champion at instantly deflatable bearishness. Nick Ullett is a Gerald irrepressible even in adversity; and though the talented Timothy Jerome's solicitor may be, as directed, a shade too oily-D'Oyly Carte, it is nevertheless a cherishable creation. There is, in fact, solid work from all, even if Jane Surnmerhays is a trifle more lurid than a Mayfair Messalina may fairly be. And for once it does not matter how effete the chorus boys are and how horsey the chorines—we are in England, aren't we?

Modestly, miraculously, everything works: Martin Johns's fast-changing, stylishly sappy décor; Ann Curtis's truehearted costumes, Chris Ellis's bubbly lighting, Gillian Gregory's ironically tacky choreography, and, best of all, the steadfastly appealing score. Even when the lyrics become a mite too knowingly naïve, the tunes steer the shortest route to the ear, heart, and—in the case of a couple of such rousing numbers as "The Lambeth Walk"—feet. Some scenes do go on a bit, notably a history lesson made up of almost sadistic puns (although elsewhere the punning can be quite pungent), but the show invariably straightens itself out. This is in no small part owed to Mike Ockrent's direction, which somehow manages to be both unflagging and relaxed. A winsome old show niftily mounted in a spacious yet cozy new theater—who, in the dead of August, could reasonably ask for more?

You Never Can Tell

I beg your indulgence if I overuse words like "adorable" in this review of *You Never Can Tell* (1896), Shaw's most enchanting comedy,
which is being given, in most respects, a highly respectable revival
at Circle in the Square. Shaw numbered it among his Plays Pleasant,
but that is an understatement; it is a Play Delicious, a Play Exquisite,
a Play Adorable. (I won't say it again, I promise.)

It takes place by the seaside in Devonshire within one day,
between a painless matutinal tooth extraction by young Valentine—performed on his first patient for the first five shillings he
has earned in the six weeks since he hung up his shingle—and a
late-evening free-for-all that charms the heart out of any spectator's
breast. Besides Valentine, the innocent rake and cool duelist of sex,
there is the girl he falls in raging love with at first sight: Gloria, a
beautiful, even cooler feminist, whom her mother has shaped into
the New Woman, and who will not hear of love—and is an immediate goner.

There are also Gloria's mother, Mrs. Clandon, author of many
books of humanistic and feminist theory, who must finally confront
life; the twins, Dolly and Philip, Gloria's younger siblings, a pair
of dazzlingly voluble, volatile creatures, precocious and spoiled,
and spankingly, spankably clever; the Waiter, who goes by various names and is the epitome of tact, providing food for body or
thought exactly as required, knowing when to materialize to save
a situation, when to make small talk or philosophize, and when to
efface himself discreetly and vanish. And there are also a bristling
landlord and a couple of lawyers: a solicitous solicitor and a formidable barrister.

I'll say no more for fear of spoiling for you an experience that
hardly needs any comment beyond the urgent plea that you catch
it. If you like, I will add that it is Shaw's most Wildean comedy; take
this line: "In a seaside resort there's one thing you must have before
anybody can be seen going about with you; and that's a father, alive
or dead. Am I to infer that you have omitted that indispensable part
of your social equipment?" Isn't that redolent of *The Importance of
Being Earnest* (1895)? But Shaw goes Wilde one better by giving his
comedy solid philosophical underpinnings, which, however, never
hamper the fun—in fact, they heighten it. You will be amazed that
even this frothiest and close to earliest of Shaw's comedies contains

insights of the utmost relevance to our time, uttered with a lightness
that nowise diminishes their acuity.

The cast contains one glory, several greater and lesser delights,
and one disaster. Philip Bosco crowns a long career of playing Shavian roles with perspicacity and suavity by giving a performance
that is unsurpassable, unforgettable, and, well, uncanny. His Waiter
is good enough to eat, yet completely unfattening, containing no
excess of any sort, only lean, sweet perfection. Fine as Leo G. Carroll was in the part in 1948 (can you believe that this play was absent from Broadway for 38 years? of course you can, that's what's
killing Broadway), Bosco is better yet—sublime. Not far behind is
the marvelous Valentine of Victor Garber, in whom wit and folly,
callowness and wisdom are blended into a package of consummate
charm, and of a Britishness few American actors could match. Uta
Hagen, though she neither looks nor sounds right as Mrs. Clandon,
manages a performance of considerable intelligence and humanity, perhaps a bit too much of the latter; the sharp haughtiness of
Frieda Inescort in 1948 was more appropriate. Nice, mellow work,
though.

Very good, too, is Lise Hilboldt, an actress I have had problems
with before, but whose Gloria has lovely dynamic and emotional
shading. She plays true double stops: two different strings bowed
simultaneously into quivering harmony. Gordon Sterne is most enjoyable as the trusty solicitor, and Stephen McHattie gets the awesome creepiness of the barrister. Stefan Gierasch is a bit obvious
as an embittered rich man, but only a bit; and John David Cullum
is an adequate Philip. But then there is Amanda Plummer's Dolly.
This smart, pert, garrulous, fetching yet trying young thing must
be kept only fleetingly exasperating. Miss Plummer promptly esca-
lates the exasperating into the insufferable, and proceeds from there
to dizzying heights of manic self-indulgence. Expert at portraying misfits (and nothing else), she piles on tics, quirks, vocal and
gestural paroxysms that would burst the seams of Grand Guignol,
and thickens her words into a glutinous paste of impenetrability. It
is Shaw's supreme triumph that some of Dolly's lines survive even
this wanton destruction.

Stephen Porter's staging is consistently resourceful and elegant,
animated but never hectic. Thomas Lynch's modest scenery nevertheless evokes an ambience, Richard Nelson's lighting is astute, and
Martin Pakledinaz's costumes get progressively comelier. One final
warning: do not expect a barrage of belly laughs. Though *You Never*

Can Tell has its share of uproarious passages and even scenes, the humor is generally inward, contained; it makes you beam rather than guffaw, and is the better for it.

The Colored Museum

The Colored Museum is a near-musical revue that is young in spirit, gifted in most aspects, and black. Written by George C. Wolfe, with music by Kysia Bostick and direction by L. Kenneth Richardson, this is a sophisticated, satirical, seriously funny show that spoofs white and black America alike. It is remarkably unafraid of lampooning black foibles, which is a sign of artistic maturity. We come of age—all of us, black or white—when we can laugh at ourselves.

Not all the numbers are equally funny and mordant, but the best ones are mightily both. We start with a bang: in "Git on Board," the smarmy stewardess on a Celebrity Airlines flight to Savannah takes the passengers through three centuries of black-American history, from slavery to the ambiguous present. At takeoff, the passengers are urged to fasten their shackles; on arrival, to take all their belongings, because everything left on board will be instantly trashed. Danitra Vance makes a fine, solicitously despotic stewardess. In "Cooking With Aunt Ethel," Vickilyn Reynolds, rolypoly and mischievous, is a mythic Aunt Jemima, stirring a bubbling cauldron whose contents will be something to contend with through the ages.

Though "The Photo Session" and "Soldier With a Secret" are less fully realized, they do make pointed comments. "The Gospel According to Miss Roj" presents, performing in a nightclub, a glitzy black transvestite whose monologue blending past and present as well as two put-upon minorities is witty and feral, pathetic as well as frightening. Like the Socratic aporias, it forces us to reconsider our preconceptions, and Reggie Montgomery plays it achingly close to the bone. In "The Hairpiece," Danitra Vance is a young woman at her makeup mirror in a quandary between two wigs, an Afro and a Euro, that comment tartly on her tergiversations. The skit, like several others, would profit from being played less stentorianly; much gets lost in the shouting.

Even funnier and more ferocious is "The Last Mama-on-the-Couch Play," which starts as a deadly satire on *Raisin in the Sun* and proceeds to make mincemeat of every type of black theater and its white audience. In "Symbiosis," Tommy Hollis is splendid as an assimilated young black careerist in the process of discarding the treasures of his youth over the protests of Reggie Montgomery as his former self. Everything must go into an elegant trash can, from *Soul on Ice* to an early Michael Jackson album that "proves he had a black nose." But can one eradicate one's origins?

The same question surfaces in "LaLa's Opening," where Loretta Devine is smashing as LaLa, a Frenchified, Josephine Bakerish song-stress trying to Franglais away her poor-black beginnings. She'll say things like "I told him my name, whatever my name was back then," but she cannot lose the little-girl-lost she once was, who comes back to haunt her. That little girl blends into a somewhat older girl (Danitra Vance), who, in "Permutations," gives illegitimate birth in a literal and figurative closet. This number, championing the prolif-eration of all-but-doomed babies, strikes me as unsound as well as maudlin. In the final number, "The Party," Vickilyn Reynolds enacts the symbolic acceptance and transcendence of the past.

Aside from a slight structural flaw—two contradictory framing devices, a plane flight and a museum (the skits arch their way in on a turntable, like art exhibits)—it all works well against a dazzlingly white, high-tech set by Brian Martin, on which the highly polished cast performs its bright material to a fare-thee-well. And to a hail and well met.

Coastal Disturbances

To classify Tina Howe's *Coastal Disturbances* as a slice-of-life play would be as niggardly as it is truthful. For although Miss Howe is expert at using public places—a restaurant, museum, or, in this case, a beach—for crossroads and cross sections of humanity, she does not stop there. We do not find out merely how various people react to art or food or lolling about on a beach (and swimming and tan-ning seem to be distinctly secondary here to lolling); we learn about people *in extremis*. Because in Miss Howe's only slightly intensified world, confronting art and dinners out, or shedding some clothes and running about barefoot in the sand, can be quite enough to bring out both the best and the beast in us. And, above all, the real in us—the silly, pathetic, gallantly pretending, fragile truth of us.

The play begins slowly and modestly, slicing away at life manually rather than with some fancy Cuisinart. Exercising in the
sand or posing on his perch is Leo the lifeguard, the cynosure of
women's fantasies and a sort of latter-day Hal from Inge's *Picnic*,
but more truthfully observed. He surveys a bit of sandy, New Eng-
landy beach, sheltered and aseptic, onto which people drag their
diversely messy or resignedly understated lives. There is Faith Bigelow, the youngish banker's wife, proud to be pregnant at last after
a long wait, and her brattish adopted child, Miranda; there is her
friend and houseguest, Ariel Took, just out of an institution after
a garish divorce and the discovery she can bear no more children
and barely cope with her precocious, uncontrollably high-spirited
ten-year-old, Winston. Insecure and emotionally starved, she's
always on the edge. More controlledly edgy is Mrs. Adams, M.J.,
who, after decades of marriage and children, has not forgiven her
husband, Hammie, a retired and irrepressible eye surgeon and
lothario, who lends a studiously deaf ear to her genteel carping.
She ends up taking out most of her frustration on her quite good
beachscapes—watercolors, of course.

Into it all walks gorgeous young Holly Dancer, a kind of holy
fool dancing through life, a photographer caught between talent
and neurosis, between sex and shrinking from sex, between a disastrous affair with a slippery New York gallery owner (who strings her
along about putting her show on and getting his divorce) and a nice,
quiet nervous breakdown at the beachside house of a sturdy Massachusetts aunt. Leo is smitten and Holly is tempted, as the other
women watch with mixed emotions. But fear not, the developments
will not be obvious, or, at least, no more so than in life. And they
will be acted out, observed, and commented on with that poetic
freshness, slightly crazy honesty, and lovableness bristling with terror that are Tina Howe's very own way of decorating life—not to
make it less true, mind you, only more livable.

What makes the play so exhilaratingly and painfully believable
is that the author puts a part of herself, or a part of the people she
has known and absorbed into herself, into all her characters, so that
she has a personal stake in all the little successes and gaffes, miseries
and releases from misery, occasional highs and absolute hells with
which the beach is awash. Everyone is felt from within; no one is
patronized, simplified, rejected. But this wouldn't be enough if she
didn't also possess the loupe of loneliness, the magnifying glass a
shy but feelingful person holds over everyday events until, under

the beams of her scrutinizing, they flare into poetry. Miss Howe's people either speak trivialities—but desperately suffered or acutely enjoyed trivialities—or they launch into bizarre, lyrical monologues, utterly fanciful and ferociously right for them. It all ends as a mosaic whose tesserae are of wildly uneven sizes and do not properly fit; but even the gaps between them sing out and a picture does emerge: lopsided, ludicrous, and heartbreakingly sweet.

The characters speak, pell-mell, to, at, through, or past one another, often in cacophonous simultaneity as active misunderstanding and passive misunderstoodness wistfully overlap. Not only words, actions, too, are non sequiturs—and hardly a one that doesn't beget laughter or honest anxiety. The words tend to be, deliberately and appositely, inadequate to the sensations; the happenings, achingly or uproariously, inadequate to the words. On the simplest level, this, after a sliver of glass has been extracted from a child's foot: "How in hell does a piece of broken glass get on *our* beach?" "You're not safe anywhere any more. A friend of mine went to a birthday party in Ipswich and found a razor blade in the chili." What foolish pride, self-absorption, irrelevant madness in that sliver of nonconversation! But it is the lengthier arias that best convey Miss Howe's music, bittersweetly mocking or extravagantly aquiver, terrified of succumbing to silence.

As Howe wrote *Coastal Disturbances*, and Carole Rothman brilliantly staged it, the brief stillnesses are only lacunae between hectic romps and staggering contretemps: there is enough action in this sand to fill a Roman arena on a slightly off day. The sand itself participates, as things and people get buried in it, or as it spews up remnants of childhood and reminders of death. Tony Straiges's nicely minimal but maximally alive set provides enough infinity for the actors to yearn toward. And not only can everyone act here (although Ronald Guttman does not project), but everybody, young or old, is also comely. It may be cheating a little, but how our theater can use such legerdemain! As the young lovers, Annette Bening and Timothy Daly are as smashing visually as histrionically, and the rest are scarcely less involving. The vibrant Joanne Camp makes the most of the anxiety-laden but somewhat underwritten Ariel; the stately Rosemary Murphy and handsome Addison Powell, as the civilized bickering Adamses, use finely suggestive understatement: Heather MacRae, serenely gravid, nevertheless conveys an undercurrent or two; Ronald Guttman is slick and sexy; and Jonas Abry and Rachel Mathieu are deliciously exasperating children.

There is one flaw in Dennis Parichy's otherwise lovely lighting, when shadows appear on what should be space; Susan Hilferty's costumes are pungently to the point. Just as Holly wants to switch from nudes to deeper penetration with X-ray photography, Miss Howe has looked deeper into the soul even than in *Painting Churches*, and brought us images that are entertaining, scary, and beautiful.

Wild Honey

Whichever way you slice it, *Wild Honey* is a play divided against itself. Written by Chekhov at, apparently, age 21, it was posthumously discovered in a manuscript without title page or title but with numerous corrections. The fair copy was destroyed by the author when the diva to whom the work was dedicated rejected it. Huge and unwieldy, *Platonov* (as it is usually called) has been cut and adapted for production before, but never more boldly than by Michael Frayn (who, by the way, knows Russian), under its present, more erotic title. *Wild Honey* falls midway between not-quite-ripe *Cherry Orchard* and less joyously noisy *Noises Off*, and is, for all its faults, the best thing Fraykhov ever wrote: charming, funny, and deeply melancholy. But in the New York production, the elements do not blend even as much as they did in London; watching it is like dining on good food off a badly wobbly table.

The complete text of *Platonov*, as translated by David Magarshack, immerses one in 200 turgid pages, twenty confusing characters, and two different plays. There is the social play, about the bankruptcy of the landed gentry, the dilettantism of the intellectuals, and the boredom of provincial life only fitfully mitigated by grandiloquent small talk, joyless carousing, and dalliances ranging from the platonic to the scandalous. And there is the more intimate tragicomedy of Platonov, potentially a second Byron, turned village schoolmaster and reluctant Don Juan. He is, to quote a title of Drieu La Rochelle's, *l'Homme couvert de femmes*, or, more precisely, a man drowning in the adoration of four women: his homely, devoted, forgiving, but finally distraught wife, and three very different malcontents driven by the same demon. This tragi-farcical private hell resounds, even in the unformed voice of young Chekhov, with comic despair.

But the two plays, and their variously satirical and wistful, outrageous and agonized tones, do not mesh into what was to become

Chekhov's way, succinctly defined by Peter Szondi as a "resignation in which yearning and irony combine into a middle position." Nor could the adaptation, however ingenious, bridge the gap without wholly discarding the Chekhovian blueprint or forgetting all Frayn has digested—from Feydeau to the theater of the absurd—for the sake of a lost, by now inconceivable simplicity.

Still, if only the New York mounting were up to the London one of 1984, which it means to duplicate. The stage, the auditorium, the acting at the National Theatre—all were more congenial. Though Ian McKellen, the sole holdover, was already overdoing Platonov, three years of overdoing and an underdone Broadway supporting cast have driven him over the edge. Even so, McKellen's storm in a samovar is fascinating: all that madness, and nothing but method in it! McKellen mugs, struts, fidgets, prances, erupts, and shrivels expertly, and his vocal music can do—and does—everything from Gielgud to a sewing machine. It is almost as impressive as it is self-conscious and self-applauding, but oh, what a drop of sincerity could do in that ocean of technique.

It is hard to assess what is most to blame for the rest: Christopher Morahan's pumping up his own direction for Broadway, a general lack of period and place sense common to American actors, or just poor performances. Sullivan Brown is droll as Dr. Triletzky, an overgrown baby trying to leap into any cradle; Kate Burton, relieved of her usual burden of being a delicious ingenue, does well by Sasha, the plain, kind, put-upon wife. Although Kathryn Walker imbues Anna—the lusty, youngish widow who hopes to escape boredom and bankruptcy in the arms of Platonov—with plenty of presence, her work is unvaried and vulgar, pitched too close to Tallulah Bankhead. Kim Cattrall looks pretty as Sofya, the young wife espousing adultery with the loftiest of ideals, but her performance seldom rises above the dutiful. As Marya, the hysterical chemistry student besotted with Platonov, the usually much better J. Smith-Cameron seems to have her Bunsen burner stuck on high.

Among the men, three made me positively squirm—Stephen Mendillo, Jonathan Moore, and Frank Maraden. And, as noted, Morahan has staged much of *Wild Honey* as if it were Woody Allen's *Midsummer Night's Sex Comedy*, with a spectrum of jarring accents from high British through middle Canadian to low U.S. But John Gunter's sets manage to be detailed and atmospheric without excessive literal-mindedness, and Deirdre Clancy's costumes are handsome or desperate as need be.

And there is Frayn's way with words. Chekhov has Platonov say, "Only those novels have happy endings in which I'm not the hero." Not bad, but how much better is Frayn's "The only stories that end happily are the ones that don't have me in them." Again, trying to ward off Anna's advances, Chekhov's Platonov concedes, "We may perhaps meet again many, many years hence, when both of us will be able to laugh and shed senile tears over these days." How much stronger is "… when we're both old enough to laugh together and shed an ancient tear or two over the past. As the present will mercifully have become." Fraykhov is not nearly so good as the mature Chekhov, or even as Frayn without Chekhov (though there is much funny stuff here that is pure Frayn and not in the original), but there is also a civilized, weary, heedless poetry that flashes forth from time to time with a brightness way beyond a Neil Simon's.

On the Verge, or The Geography of Yearning; Hunting Cockroaches

Eric Overmyer achieves something quite remarkable with *On the Verge, or The Geography of Yearning*: he takes a fantasy full of fantasy beings and fantasy words, and somehow gives it all flesh. The play, presented by the Acting Company, is about three American woman explorers, circa 1888, jointly conquering the last *Terra Incognita*, which starts out as just another (although funnier) jungle, just another (although trickier) set of Himalayas, and ends up becoming the Future. For what could have been left for the primly midwestern Fanny, the Brahminishly Bostonian Mary, and the flakily word-besotted Alexandra to explore but the uncharted, unconscionable future?

At first, these Victorian ladies in their fulsome traveling regalia stir up a mere passel of conventional hilarity as they hack their way through not very triste tropics or hoist themselves up unmenacing mountain walls while one-upwomanshipping one another with tales of past exploits. They are mere comical speaking diary entries. Thus Fanny: "I introduced croquet to the headhunters of the headwaters of the Putamayo… Of course, I insisted they use only regulation wooden balls... The rascals were always batting their latest trophies about. I was strict. They respected me for that." Or Mary: "The bane of my travels in the tropics is a bland, mucilaginous paste called manioc... [It] tastes, in the best recipes, like the bottom of a budgie's cage, and is more suited for masonry than human consumption." And on and on races the manioc fun.

But slowly the women are exposed to an infestation by the future in appropriately schlocky forms. On the ground, they find such artifacts as eggbeaters and I LIKE IKE buttons; in their heads, there pop up such inexplicable vocables as "Red Chinese," and "Mr. Coffee." They also encounter natives: at first, fairly sensible ones such as aviator-eating anthropophagi and cuddly-abominable snowmen; then weirder ones such as a man in white, who may be Mr. Coffee, Bebe Rebozo, or even God, followed by a leatherjacketed toll collector, the Bridge Troll, part pop songwriter, part Method actor. And then the 1950s are upon them in full, junky efflorescence.

The gallant adventurers respond differently to future shock. One "embraces [the future] with all [her] heart," one accepts it like "cyclones, pit vipers, and bad grammar," and one pushes on, scientifically intoxicated, into the future's future. They are all, like the author, obsessed with words as much as with things, whether they despise those words as slang, appropriate them for jingle and rock-lyric writing, or use them as a ladder to scale the galaxies of the unknown. But the wonder of *On the Verge* is that these women (complemented by one actor in various, mostly male, guises) become distinct characters we care about, even hate to part with. Whether you take the work as sardonic cultural history couched in voluptuous wordplay, as the story of women's liberation perceived as our seriocomic destiny, or as merely jaundiced time-tripping and star-trekking, it draws you in, affectionately and mischievously, and, just possibly, wisely.

The production is very nearly optimal. Garland Wright's staging is a tongue-in-cheek audiovisual tongue twister, John Arnone's sets are a semi-abstract demi-paradise rapturously nuzzling the infinite, Ann Hould-Ward's costumes skip along from stuffy to funky without skipping a comic beat, and James F. Ingalls's lighting could educate everyone from rock-concert designers to glowworms. The three actresses prove delicious: Lisa Banes and Laura Hicks immediately and steadily, Patricia Hodges gradually. As all the men, Tom Robbins also delights—intermittently. *On the Verge* left me euphoric: satiated, but far from surfeited.

I wish *Hunting Cockroaches*, by the Polish émigré playwright Janusz Głowacki, were as good as it is sassy and likable. Głowacki's last play hereabouts, *Cinders*, was a dazzling piece of current Polish reality viewed in all its absurdist glare. The new work sees the Lower East Side life of a struggling Polish playwright and his ex-actress wife in similar fashion, but the absurdism is too winsome, anodyne, good-natured for the weight of hurt and deprivation it aims to carry. This Polish play is too much of an American joke.

The beginning is smashing. Anka, the wife, emerges from the bathroom in her flannel nightgown and woolly bobby socks, walks across the ruinous apartment to the kitchen, and hangs up some used tea bags to dry, while Jan, her husband, pretends to sleep on a battlefield of a bed. All through this, Anka recites Lady Macbeth's sleepwalking speech, then explains to the audience the sag in her post-Polish acting career: "They say I have an awful accent," she burbles in an accent thicker than her socks. Then, after an expectant pause, sweetly and awfully: "Do I?" There is something heartbreakingly funny about this scene, which the play fitfully recaptures. The rest of the time it is only funny, or slightly wearying.

It is a play, essentially, about insomnia and the dreams, or fantasies, it begets. For most of the two acts, Jan and Anka Krupinski are in their sprawling, disheveled bed that serves all kinds of purposes except sex and sleep. There are elaborate rituals of wooing Morpheus, also Anka's yearnings for a baby, for Jan to stop gazing at the fearful symmetry of a map of America and start writing something ("We'll move uptown, to 4th Street!"), and for herself to act again. There are Jan's ripostes and rationalizations, his accounts of stabs at making it here without a sincere smile (because "in Eastern Europe no one has a sincere smile, except drunks and informers"), his versions of hopeless, Polish hope. And there are the skittering multitudes of cockroaches that one studies, analyzes, and swats with a shoe on what is the ceiling of the apartment below, eliciting retaliatory bangs from the downstairs tenant, on what is one's floor.

Also, there are the apparitions that crawl out from under the bed: humorously harrowing figures from the real or imagined past, Polish and American. These chronic nonsleepers' nightmares range from Polish secret police to prying American immigration officers, from clinging bums in the park to patronizing Park Avenue liberals who pursue the Krupinskis with clammy kindnesses.

There are wonderful moments: trying to phone friends in Po-

land, but having to eliminate, for political reasons, all but the
Warsaw time service; or, conversely, becoming enraptured when a
Polish commissar hot for the Krupinskis' Warsaw apartment urges
them to emigrate: "The CIA finances the whole thing: all the Scotch
you can drink, lunch with Susan Sontag…" Or when Jan is urged
to write with "a more complex view, a darker view if you will" and
eagerly responds, "I will, I will!" But, hang it, something more is
needed. When Anka reproaches Jan for not having written even
one sentence a day since they've lived in that apartment—"939 sentences, this makes at least the first act of a play, no?"—the answer
is, indeed, no. The sentences are here, often uproarious; but where
is the act?

As Anka, Dianne Wiest would be splendid if she didn't play up
to the audience and herself quite so much: she has a puppyishness
whose fey slobberings need a little demoisturizing. Ron Silver admirably avoids cuteness as Jan, but neither he nor Miss Wiest can
wholly convey the exquisite horror of a Polish accent. Most of the
supporting parts are well handled, especially by Joan Copeland and
Larry Block, and Arthur Penn has directed Jadwiga Kosicka's fla-
vorous translation with condign pungency. Heidi Landesman's set,
Rita Ryack's costumes, Richard Nelson's lighting all artfully juggle
grotesquerie and grime, but the play just tickles and tickles until it
trickles away.

Les Misérables

There is no way a critic can affect a popular hit of two continents
with an $11-million advance sale in New York alone. Fully aware of
the unimportance of this action, I put pen to paper to say that *Les
Misérables* is a mixed bag, with an interminable-seeming first act
in which, musically and dramatically, little ignites, and a second
act that is appreciably better and contains undeniably stirring moments. Since the show has an arresting look, one powerful performance, a couple of catchy songs, over three hours' duration, and
plenty of uplift and advance publicity, who, in a lean season, would
turn thumbs down on it?

Surely everyone knows what Victor Hugo's enormous 1862 novel
is about without (unless he had it thrust on him in school) having
read it. I myself have always been content with a few bravura pas-

sages from this Christian epic and social document, supplemented by the great performances of Fredric March and Charles Laughton in the 1935 movie version. Similarly, almost everyone knows that Claude-Michel Schonberg and Alain Boublil, assisted by Jean-Marc Natel, first turned their musicalization of it into a record, and only then into the hit of the Paris stage. Here, it was embraced by the producer Cameron Mackintosh, who convinced Trevor Nunn and John Caird of the Royal Shakespeare Company that this would be a worthy follow-up to their *Nicholas Nickleby.* Englished by Herbert Kretzmer, who, along with the French creators and James Fenton, supplied additions as well as subtractions, the show became, despite mostly poor notices, the hit of London. Polished and tightened for America, it was a success in Washington despite troubles with the giant turntable, and arrived in New York, where, after technical difficulties that delayed by some 45 minutes the preview I caught, it will, presumably, proceed without a hitch. Whew!

There is no escaping the feeling that the action of this almost completely sung soft-rock musical (there is no real dancing or dialogue) is a rapid tour through a very long novel. Especially in the first act—as we track the unhappy Jean Valjean, freed after nineteen years of unjust penal servitude but still followed by prejudice and the unrelenting policeman Javert, who does not believe in redemption—the show seems not so much aswirl on a mighty turntable as trudging along a treadmill. Famous episodes pop up like specters in a Disneyland tunnel ride as episode jostles choppy episode, and the score, with its monotonous beat and near-doggerel lyrics, seems to keep recycling the same couple of tunes.

John Napier, the *Nickleby* designer, has, however, created simple but highly evocative sets of a dark, this time French rather than English, squalor, and David Hersey again applies lighting skills so ingenious they can almost do cross-hatching with lights. Add Andreane Neofitou's costumes, and you have stage imagery that soars while the show trundles. Yet that trundling is always bolstered by Colm Wilkinson as Valjean. Looking somewhat like Anthony Hopkins, this is one Irish tenor who acts as well as he sings, which he does ravishingly, and that without the slightest loss of spontaneity or stamina after a year and a half in such a relentlessly demanding role. Would that the mostly American cast around him were fully up to him.

In the second act, when both the 1830 Revolution and the love story get under way, and Javert's hounding of the parole-breaking

Valjean reaches new heights as well as reversals, the music also begins to take off. Although the show's hit song, "On My Own," nicely sung by the spunky but a trifle too cute-voiced Frances Ruffelle as Eponine, leaves me cold, things pick up with rousingly militant or wistfully reminiscing numbers, to culminate in "Bring Him Home," superbly sung and crooned by our hero over the prostrate form of the gallant student Marius, lover of Jean's adopted daughter, Cosette. From this resounding climax, the show proceeds handily and relatively tunefully, without even seeming excessively episodic. But there are problems with the cast.

Terrence Mann is no Javert for me. The former Rum Tum Tugger of *Cats* sports an inescapably comic-juvenile face. However stiffly he tries to embody an inexorable sense of the Law, his visage, like his voice, maintains an inchoate sneer, the vestige of a snicker. There is something brittle about this Javert, and, unlike Valjean, he does not seem to age. Even his obsession has something perfunctory about it. As the tragic Fantine, reduced to prostitution to support her daughter, Randy Graff gives a remote, inexpressive performance; she sings adequately, though with excessive vibrato, and only her pallor keeps her from blending into the dusky background. As that daughter, Cosette, Judy Kuhn sings prettily but lacks sufficient style and comeliness for a heroine. David Bryant, though he puts his big solo across creditably, is equally uncharismatic as Marius. Leo Burmester does almost too much with the comic villainy of Thénardier and sings—especially that amusing waltz of his—with raucous deviltry. As his spouse, Jennifer Butt falls behind.

The tall Michael Maguire is altogether commanding as Enjolras, the revolutionary leader, and two children are winning: Donna Vivino, as an adorable though not entirely audible Young Cosette, and Braden Danner as the feisty Gavroche, even if I could not make out his defiantly shouted dying utterance. Nunn and Caird have directed with their customary panache, even if the ensemble works less dazzlingly than in *Nickleby*. There are some great tableaux, such as the dead sprawling across both sides of the barricade, or the ghosts of his dead comrades haunting Marius. Despite a noble effort, the sewers of Paris don't quite make it (although John Cameron's perky orchestration is particularly resourceful here), but for this you need the movies—or Victor Hugo's words. The final scene is too inspirational by half for my taste, which brings me yet again to *Les Misérables'* being half good. But a hefty half it is.

Fences

Fences, by August Wilson, is a dignified, understatedly eloquent, elegant play. "Elegant" may be an odd term to apply to a piece about an underprivileged, oppressed black family precariously surviving in a northern industrial city during the late fifties, with backward glances to a worse past and forward looks at a strenuous uphill path. But "elegant" is the word for a work that tries to make sense of a predicament in which race is subsumed by humanity, in which black color is no more defining than the blue collar, and whose ultimate pigmentation is the black and blue of bruises—not so much on the body as on the soul.

Elegant for another reason as well. Because the play is constructed in a way both naturally fluid and artfully controlled, both improvised like the riffs of a jam session and thought-out like the development in sonata form. Paradoxical as it may seem, Wilson has achieved (to change metaphors) the lepidopterological miracle of mounting a butterfly as an exhibit and still keeping the creature alive. How? With a very long, very fine pin that goes not only through the moth but also through us; it may be our sympathetic trembling that makes the creature seem aquiver, our tears that make it shimmer with aliveness.

But alive it certainly becomes. Troy Maxson is an ex-con and ex-baseball pro and present garbage collector; a steady provider for his wife, Rose, and his son Cory; a man of boundless energy and boisterous bitterness. He has been frustrated all along: first by a stern, overbearing father; then by racism in the baseball world and elsewhere; finally, by economic straits that drove him to crime. A semisolid citizen now, he is still plagued by illiteracy, unfair employment practices, threatening indigence, drink, and a sexual drive his overworked and emotionally unfulfilled wife cannot quite satisfy. A difficult husband, he was once an abused son, which makes him an uncaring father to Lyons, his musician son by a former wife, and an overexacting, seemingly unfeeling father to Cory, his athletically gifted son by Rose, for whom he does care. His attitude toward his brother, Gabriel, a brain-damaged World War II vet, is similarly ambiguous: though he is caring and protective of Gabriel, he also exploits him. Perhaps his purest, least ambivalent feelings are for Bono, a longtime friend and colleague; yet even with him, when the shared alcoholic haze lifts, a bristling wariness sets in.

Out of these relationships, and others with offstage characters, Wilson has fashioned a comedy-drama that, in its first act, is well-nigh flawless. Although its four scenes covering one week in 1957 are of necessity episodic, the episodes flow into one another. Fantasy, mostly in Troy's accounts of his wrestling with Death and the Devil, good-humoredly reverts to reality, with Rose as the pungent catalyst. Levity, no less imperceptibly, turns sour or grim, particularly when Cory is accosted right-headedly but wrongheartedly by his canny but confused father. Life, in all its bittersweetness, fills the stage—to be faced with gallant affection or fierce animosity.

In the second act—partly because the temporal gaps are greater, partly because problems are ticked off a bit too hastily and schematically—there is some loss in the spontaneity, dovetailing, and free breathing of the five scenes. But this is always offset by intelligent stating of the dilemmas, assured use of language, unponderous handling of symbols (baseball tropes, fences, Gabriel's horn), and refusal to lapse into either shrillness or sentimentality. Pain and anger are balanced by humor and common sense, and both passion and compassion are played on a muted trumpet that insinuates rather than insists. *Fences* marks a long step forward for Wilson's dramaturgy.

Lloyd Richards has directed with sage understatement, keeping outbursts to a minimum and allowing strangulated, internalized grief to speak all the louder. He has put the relatively small acting area of a backyard and alley to excellent use, showing how confinement can teem with pointed and pointless activity, but without turning animation into mere theatricality. He is greatly aided by the hemmed-in, shabby-genteel set of James D. Sandefur, the exiguous yet jaunty or grave costuming of Candice Donnelly, and the broodingly lifelike lighting of Danianne Mizzy, marred only by a burst of symbolic dazzlement near the end, probably a directorial miscalculation.

As Rose, Mary Alice is simply—or complexly—perfect: the strong black woman holding the family together with pliancy and compliancy, but also with a concealed fund of stubborn probity and courage. James Earl Jones is consistently good as Troy, and downright astonishing in moments of quiet pugnacity, amusing swagger, and forlorn tenderness; only his patches of crushed, impotent suffering fail to ring quite true. As Cory, Courtney B. Vance gives a remarkably calibrated and compelling performance, and there is solid support from Ray Aranha, Charles Brown, Karima Miller, and

especially Frankie R. Faison. My only quarrel was with the audience, which, by laughing, cheering, applauding in the wrong places
(e.g., when a put-upon wife finally hits her husband—no cheerful
triumph for her, but a tragedy for both), often shattered a finespun
mood. But *Fences* is good enough to survive that too.

Driving Miss Daisy

There is a kind of play as redolent of the good old days as 5-cent
beer and about as likely to make a comeback. What a sweet surprise,
then, to find *Driving Miss Daisy*, a two-and-a-half-character play by
Alfred Uhry (author and lyricist of *The Robber Bridegroom*, which
I missed), at the tiny upstairs theater of Playwrights Horizons; it
is full of an old-style unpretentiousness, coziness, and—despite
genuine emotions—quietude. It concerns Miss Daisy Werthan, a
crotchety, parsimonious, monumentally stubborn 72-year-old Atlanta widow, who, while insisting she can still drive, has to bow to
the combined wills of her son, Boolie, and all the insurance companies in the land and accept a black chauffeur, Hoke, whom Boolie
has hired for her.

Hoke is delighted that the Werthans are Jews, whom, in the past,
he has found much easier to work for than Baptists. But he has
never met the like of Miss Daisy for taciturn intractability, almost
whimsical orneriness. He himself is a proud and determined man,
respectful but never servile, possessed of amusingly ingenious ways
to drive an iceberg as well as a car. The play covers, in bright but
unflashy episodes, 25 years in these two lives, with Boolie providing an intermittent, droll or exasperated, obbligato to a duet that
progresses from discord to close harmony in small, credible steps.

It is to Uhry's credit that there is no cheating. Miss Daisy, in
her prosperity, never forgets her hard, impecunious childhood and
struggling schoolteacher days; though she is not exactly a champion
at the other virtues (except perhaps at propriety), in the generosity
sweepstakes she was left at the starting gate. Her always-offstage
maid, Idella, has come to terms with this; Boolie, who pays Hoke
out of his pocket ("highway robbery," Daisy calls his modest salary),
plays along with it; it is Hoke who, slowly, goodhumoredly, disman-
tles Daisy's suspiciousness and isolation, even if he can never quite
get her ungivingness to give. Still, Daisy teaches Hoke to read and

write even as he teaches her about human rights and wrongs, and a prickly (on her part) and wary (on his) affection develops between them, the limits of which she will not overstep even after she, well into her nineties and after many changes in cars and conditions, declares him her best friend. Even more than a delicate miniaturist's talent, the playwright exhibits tact: he milks neither the sentiment nor the humor of the situation, and also resists, without avoiding the issues of racism and anti-Semitism, giving us a social tract. Neither the bombing of the synagogue to which Hoke has been regularly driving her nor the testimonial dinner for Martin Luther King Jr. that, despite her son's cautious abstention, she insists on attending can induce Miss Daisy to accept Hoke as her equal in every way.

The dialogue is savory and spirited, and although not a moment of *Driving Miss Daisy* becomes momentous, not a minute of its 80 is boring. Even the predictable, in Uhry's hands, manages to be idiosyncratic enough to be palatable, and connoisseurs of filigree pleasures should feel snugly ensconced here. Those pleasures are vastly enhanced by a tastefully trimmed-down production, smartly and unfussily directed by Ron Lagomarsino and designed with elegant economy by Thomas Lynch (scenery), Michael Krass (costumes), and Ken Tabachnick (lights). But the evening's jewel is the acting. Dana Ivey, in splendid command of the accent, gives a performance exemplarily clean of outline yet rich in detail. I am not wholly sure that (without a chance for elaborate makeup) she really reaches 97 in the end, a feat even more rare on the stage than in life. And Ray Gill infuses the almost incidental role of Boolie with uncommon restraint and suggestiveness.

Primus inter pares, however, is Morgan Freeman. A specialist in tough, violent, often malign parts, he plays Hoke with an easygoing steadfastness both ironic and overwhelmingly humane. His pliability is strength in action, his sarcastic muttering cauterizes as much as it cuts, his wry warmth is as devoid of self-abnegation as of self-righteousness, and his overarching shrewdness is always clearly at the service of decency and good sense. I cannot think of another actor who could get such emotional variety from mere "Yes'm"s, or whose last-ditch self-assertion could be more quietly commanding. A magnificent performance.

Les Liaisons dangereuses

Cholderlos de Laclos's world-class masterpiece, *Les Liaisons dangereuses* (1782), which the *Times* called "an obscure French epistolary novel," is as familiar to the literate as *Tristram Shandy* or *The Sorrows of Young Werther*. Ernst Jünger should have included it among his "gruesome books," with Sade's *La Philosophie dans le boudoir*, but, unlike the Divine Marquis, the artillery officer Laclos was, at least on this one occasion, a genuine writer. The novel is a psychological and philosophical horror story wherein the irresistible seducer, the Vicomte de Valmont, and the supreme seductress, the Marquise de Merteuil, former lovers and now companions in nefariousness, plan and execute the seduction and downfall of two young women: the married Présidente de Tourvel, 22, a woman of matchless beauty, piety, and virtue, and Cécile Volanges, 15, a lovely, spirited, innocently sensuous girl.

Their motive? Vanity and Don Juanism on Valmont's part, vanity and vengefulness toward an ex-lover Cécile is to marry on Mme de Merteuil's; but also, and especially, the Iago-like pursuit of the pleasures of evil. For *Les Liaisons* is far more metaphysical than physical, and not in the least prurient; to oversimplify, it is the destruction of a noble soul and the corruption of a sweet child for the joy of wreaking havoc, for the glory of conquering impregnable purity and unsoiled adolescence, for the titillation in proving a seraph and a cherub no match for two collusive demons. There are sensual gratifications, but they pale before the planting of Satan's flag in God's territory.

Christopher Hampton's stage adaptation of *Les Liaisons dangereuses* is not only a trivialization and vulgarization of the novel, but also a fatuous and unappetizing play in its own right. Unlike many colleagues, I believe that an adaptation of a major work of art, if it commits the artistic gaffe of transposing the work into a medium where it cannot properly function, should at least strive for the same level of seriousness as the original. But the play neither can nor cares to operate in that realm. Laclos, by using the slow, discursive epistolary form, was able to convey the gradual erosion of Mme de Tourvel's resistance, as well as analyze in clinical and moral detail the spread of a poison. In this, he approximates the *moralistes*, such as La Bruyère and Joubert, and, more important, extends into prose (as Jean Giraudoux has shown in a penetrating

essay) the style of Racine's dramatic poetry. For the novel is written in the sparse, translucent diction of Racine, with all the equili-
bristic elegance of neoclassical syntax, and thrives on the powerful
clash between moral disruptiveness and formal control. Hampton
has deracinated the work, reducing its icily burning Frenchness to
ribald English badinage; instead of Racine, he gives us not even
Congreve, but Wycherley.

One of the strengths of Laclos's epistolary strategy is—besides
allowing various correspondents to report the same events differently—the letter writer's ability to frame his accounts of mock sincerity and fake passion with monstrously lucid, cynical comments
to his or her correspondent and accomplice. A letter thus becomes
a double-bottomed construct, and theater can't duplicate this: Valmont can undercut his eloquent pursuit of Mme de Tourvel only
with winking asides to the audience or with jeering notes in his
romantic cantilenas. The former instantly remove the sense of tragedy, the latter turn the victim into a susceptible idiot and likewise
undermine the tragedy.

But there is a device that even the play could thrive on—dramatic irony. As long as we know from his confidences to Merteuil
what Valmont is really up to, he can play his wooing of the confused
Tourvel and seduction of the unsuspecting Volanges absolutely
straight with startling effect. Yet as written by Hampton, directed by
Howard Davies, and performed by these RSC actors—notably Alan
Rickman as Valmont—the fascination of doubleness and ambiguity
is lost, as are the growing frenzy and the ultimate despair. When the
stage version tries, near the end, to shift gears into tragedy—albeit
of a social and historical sort, not Laclos's dialectical and transcen-
dental kind—it's too late: there is no way for Pulcinella's removed
mask to reveal a tragic penitent.

Essential to the novel's drama is the *beauté du diable* of its villains
and the exquisiteness of its victims. Valmont is clearly a man of
extreme virility, handsomeness, and manly grace; Mme de Tourvel
is the consummate challenge to him of angelic loveliness blended
with voluptuous femininity. Alas, Alan Rickman, though rich-
voiced and well-spoken, gives us a quite unaristocratic, rather oily
histrion, midway between a fop and a jackanapes. His favorite maneuver is to close his already slitty eyes entirely while soulfully part-
ing his lushly damp lips, which makes him look like a fish trying to
sing a passionate aria. His gestures are excessive and his footwork
is skittish; this Valmont would seem to be a greater threat to her

footman than to Mme de Tourvel. As for the lady, Suzanne Burden turns her into a husky-voiced, angular tomboy with a lopsided face and unfeminine coiffure; she is raw, rawboned, and incipiently querulous, and Hampton unhappily tunes in on her story when she is already half hooked on Valmont. The character is thus deprived of both her womanly and her angelic nature.

The most highly touted performance in London was Lindsay Duncan's Merteuil. Miss Duncan is an accomplished technician with a pleasing countenance and the ability to convey breeding and temperament; she also sneers well—too well. She has some of the less fortunate features of sundry British actresses: something rheumy about the eyes, nostrils that outflare a coney's, an overweening upper lip, and a slightly pinched, high-pitched voice. They do not add up to a strongly sexual—or even Gallic—presence. This lack, to be sure, is symptomatic of the production, which reeks of stout and Earl Grey rather than of burgundy and champagne. Among the rest, only Beatie Edney, as Cécile, scores: she evokes a wholesome but corruptible teenager with an endearing eagerness to yield, and if her hairdo is out of period (like so much else here, deliberately or otherwise), it at least suggests, like her general appearance, one of Balthus's favorite models.

The scenery by Bob Crowley makes the most of economic constriction. It's a unit set in brown, cream, and beige tones, all wooden slats, brutalized bureau drawers with necklaces hanging out like ravaged intestines, and swirling draperies spreading their florid disarray into the auditorium. But when his costumes repeat these wan vanilla and sober earth tones, with only the merest hint of peach or rose, the effect is, inappropriately, of a movie in sepia tone. Chris Parry's lighting is excellent, but for what I take to be an intrusion of Beverly Emmons, his American associate, in the form of varicolored stripes of light shakily projected onto a whitish jacket of Valmont's. Ilona Sekacz's updated period music, which disintegrates into a fine harpsichord hysteria, is good, save when it tries to convey electronically something snapping in Valmont.

The gifted Christopher Hampton has fallen into lesser errors as well. He has studded his text with fairly explicit overtones of perversion that, in Laclos, are hardly a whiff. There are solecisms ("intriguing" for "fascinating," "general factotum," "the reason was because") of the sort Laclos was incapable of. Worst of all are the smug anachronisms, verbal and visual, heralding the Revolution. These are almost as lip-smacking in their irrelevant politics as the endless sexual puns, the very thing Laclos execrated in a footnote. Thus Valmont, of Cécile: "I found her very open to persuasion"; or Valmont, in an ardent letter to Mme de Tourvel, which he writes using the naked back of a concubine for his desk, "I have just come—to my desk... The position in which I find myself as I write" etc. This incident, rating in Laclos a throwaway line or two, is drawn out into a lengthy scene, in which the courtesan absurdly holds a bedsheet against her body and Valmont doesn't undress at all.

Some of these drawn-out unsubtleties must be chalked up to the director, a great rubber-in of things that were better erased. But we are back to the basic unstageworthiness. The novel speaks mightily to the imagination, which fills the interstices with a terrible beauty; the play, spelling things out, does not cast the spell of the unspoken and unspeakable. The artillery officer Laclos, a specialist in fortifications and their conquest, wrote one of the most terrifying accounts of the duel of the sexes. Hampton, Davies & Co. have turned this design for human casemates and cannons into a tonier and naughtier Tom and Jerry cartoon.

Beirut

As a piece of theater, Alan Bowne's *Beirut* is without any merit; as a piece of dishonesty, it is very nearly incomparable. Anyone wishing to write pretentious, posturing, vacuous, manipulative, and tasteless trash—of the sort that gets good reviews and foundation grants—would do well to study *Beirut* and such other Bowne works as the repugnant *Forty-Deuce* carefully. Not for nothing does Bowne come out of the filmmaking stable of Paul Morrissey, who, in turn, emerged from the art-sty of Andy Warhol. *Beirut* is all exploitative titillation and a veritable anthology of dishonesties. Herewith the salient ones.

Dishonesty 1: The play exploits the AIDS crisis, but without naming the disease. We're in New York in the near future, and all suspected carriers of the unnamed plague are branded on their buttocks with a large P for "positive," though, as you'll see, other meanings present themselves. Positives are sequestered in the East Village, now dubbed Beirut. Vicious guards inspect them daily for sores; at the first sign, the P's are executed, and their bodies are burned in Tompkins Square. (No health hazard?) By not calling

this AIDS, Bowne reaps the benefits of alleged timelessness and seriousness, while playing fast and loose with symptoms and consequences, and so spreads hysteria without shedding light.

Dishonesty 2: Bowne has not thought out a plausible and consistent dystopia, though he poses as a liberal castigator of our "fascist"
government. There are glaring improbabilities and impossibilities
throughout this 59-minute play. Intercourse is prohibited, even between spouses; surveillance devices in every room (and, presumably, every bush) make sex impossible. Yet when the heroine, Blue, a
young Negative from Queens, sneaks into the basement room—private and spacious, albeit disgusting—in which her beloved Torch,
a young Brooklyn Positive, is kept, she allows as how if they can
only make it to New Jersey, they'll be safe. Does the plague abhor
bridges and tunnels? In New Jersey, however, Torch might *have* to
drop his pants sometimes, he remarks, and another set of devices, it
seems, will pick up the P on his backside! In New York, even department stores and discos are closed, we learn, because the plague can
be communicated through public sweating. (P for "perspiration"?)
Bodies of Ns who tried to sneak in to see Ps are strung up all along
14th Street, yet Blue had no serious problem joining Torch and even
sending advance notice of her coming. Her aim is to get him into
bed so she'll have to stay with him and share his fate; gallantly, he
keeps refusing even as she is practically raping him.

Dishonesty 3: The plague is orally transmissible, and Torch
knocks a can of juice he drank from out of Blue's hands. Later,
Blue drinks from it, but nothing further is made of this dishonest
suspense in which the play abounds. Thus Blue, who doesn't even
know on which buttock to paste her fake P (right for women, left for
men—why?), nevertheless improvises a prisoner number credible
to the guard who catches her with Torch.

Dishonesty 4: The play is founded on absurdities. Blue and
Torch—a womanizer—met at a disco, but have never even kissed.
Bowne needs Blue's *intacta* status to magnify her sacrifice in coming to Torch. But would a woman risk a hideous death for someone
she's barely met and not so much as kissed? She keeps insisting that
only in the compound, where doomed Ps are allowed to fornicate
(the Ns obviously haven't discovered condoms), is love still possible. And though she talks a lot about love, all she keeps wanting
is sex. Clearly, Bowne thinks the two identical.

Dishonesty 5: There are two strongly S&M scenes. In one, the
guard compels Torch to bare first Blue's breasts, then her crotch; he

leaves, threatening worse. In the other, Torch forces Blue to kneel and crawl for him. Further, both main characters are near-naked throughout, with occasionally bared behinds. The play is pornography, without the honesty to admit it. Oh, *Beirut*! Oh, Calcutta!

Dishonesty 6: To make a grim subject more commercial, Bowne slips in cheap jokes, such as malapropisms for both main characters.

Dishonesty 7: *Beirut* seems to me a homosexual play in disguise. It makes much more sense if P stands for "pederasty." For Blue (funny name for a girl), read a boy, as in Little Boy Blue; for discos, read the baths; for this fully heterosexual plague, read AIDS, etc. There is, of course, nothing wrong with a play being homosexual, unless it misleadingly pretends to be straight. And unless, like this one, it's lousy. Curiously, Walker Hicklin gets costuming credit for two pairs of standard underwear; even so, his contribution to costumes may be greater than the author's to drama.

Burn This

Lanford Wilson seems to me at present our soundest, most satisfying dramatist. He is more disciplined and dependable than Sam Shepard; more various and productive than Tina Howe, Marsha Norman, David Rabe; less autobiographically obsessed than any number of others; and far less quirky, mean-spirited, puny than David Mamet. He writes with a humanistic concern for all kinds of people, the ability to absorb and convey all manner of vocations and activities, a true curiosity about life, and no discernible fixations clouding his vision. To people who want eccentricity or mania from their playwrights, he may seem a bit bland; to those who value comprehensiveness, comprehension, and compassion, his preeminence is perspicuous.

In recent years, there have been three Off Broadway Wilson revivals so good and so well done that they deserved to reach Broadway, if only Broadway deserved them: *Serenading Louie, Balm in Gilead*, and *Lemon Sky*. Wilson's latest work, *Burn This*, has every ingredient needed to make it a commercial success on Broadway, which is the very thing, I'm afraid, that makes it a much lesser play. The customary Wilson blend of humor and seriousness, of bristliness and pathos is there all right, but so is a conscious or uncon-

scious desire to offer something for everybody, to make everyone
go home well fed, well edified, and thoroughly unchallenged. For
almost three hours, Wilson gives us facets of insight and fascination
that do not coalesce into a hard diamond of truth and revelation,
as in so many of even his second-best plays.

The aim is to show two complex persons with serious impedi-
ments to feeling and commitment groping toward each other. One
is the dancer and fledgling choreographer, Anna; the other is Pale,
the weird and violent brother of Anna's apartment mate and dance
partner, who, with his male lover, has just died in a freak accident.
As the play opens, Anna and her other roommate, the homosexual
adman Larry, have just returned from the midwestern funeral,
where the dead young man's family provided material for oodles
of wry jokes, which they now share with Burton, Anna's very rich,
cynical screenwriter boyfriend, who has rushed over to comfort the
badly shaken young woman. She, by the way, is the only character
with a last name, Anna Mann, which makes me wonder whether
it is a pun on Anyman and the play an updated morality; but this
line of inquiry is not encouraged by the proceedings.

We have, on the one hand, a triangle play—Anna, Pale, Burton—
and, on the other, a study of odd, contemporary people interacting
suspiciously, jokily, vehemently. What diminishes the piece is that,
for once, Wilson offers us only incidental, casual glances into the
worlds of the characters: dance, restaurant management (Pale's job),
screenwriting, advertising, and homosexuality. There are flashes of
comic perception, but they are a far cry from the illumination Wilson has achieved elsewhere with a highly charged, poetic empathy.
Thus Larry is not even allowed any homosexual involvement, and
serves only as a charming, wisecracking sideliner and occasional
plot device.

Furthermore, we do not really get to understand why Anna chooses Pale over Burton. The problem is partly that their main attraction
is sexual, something very hard, if not impossible, to convey as drama,
rather than soft-core porn. We do not see them evolve and grow
toward each other with any compelling dynamic; indeed, the scenes
that bring Pale onstage are mostly showcases for his bizarre and contradictory personality, and here John Malkovich, who portrays him,
may do more harm than good. Long-haired and always at odds with
his unruly tresses, gun-toting and irascible but also tender and intui-
tive, illiterate yet composing tone poems in the shower in the style
of Shostakovich, hating his wife, who left him long ago taking along

their two children, but struggling against his anger to humanize his feelings for Anna—this Pale is not easy to embody.

But Malkovich, oozing a zonked sensitivity or sensitive zonked-ness, gives at least one and a half performances where one would do, expertly wallowing in all conceivable and several inconceivable mannerisms. His pauses, sudden changes of tempo, eerie inflec-tions, tigerish pacing and pouncing, explosions followed by cata-tonia, though of considerable histrionic, and even greater clinical, interest, are not so much an enactment as a manhandling and maul-ing of the role. This is Steppenwolf theater bordering on werewolf. By contrast, Joan Allen is wonderfully various and unstinting with-out losing control and, though rather too tall for a ballet dancer, possessed of all the true dimensions of humanity. Jonathan Hogan's blondined, lemon-voiced, tentacle-fingered, cadaverous Burton is not my idea of jaded yet self-assured virility; but Lou Liberatore, an easeful and endearing Larry, under perfectly timed one-liners, conveys something deeper.

Marshall W. Mason has directed with equally cogent attention to detail and overarching shape, and is guilty only of tolerating Mal-kovich's excesses. John Lee Beatty's loft is marvelously archetypal and is, like Laura Crow's careful costumes, enhancingly lighted by Dennis Parichy. But Lanford Wilson has not fully worked out his characters—how could the feckless, combative Pale hold down a tyrannically demanding, vacationless, seventeen-hour-a-day job for eighteen years?—and has settled for a handsome crazy quilt of jokes, some troubled atmosphere, and abrasiveness tear-jerkingly drifting into mellowness in what is really *The Voice of the Turtle* for the eighties. I don't begrudge Wilson the success he'll doubtless reap, but I wish it were with a play other than *Burn This.**

Mahabharata

Indian mythology has never appealed to me: too many races, tribes, religions spewing up too many conflicting tales; divinities with too many faces, eyes, limbs; too much of a muchness. It is, in the words of the *Larousse Encyclopedia of Mythology,* "an inextricable jungle of luxuriant growths [where] you lose the light of day and all clear sense of direction." The *Mahabharata,* one of the two great Indian epics,

---

* P.S. 2005: He didn't.

consists of 100,000 lines in eighteen books, about eight times the length of the combined *Iliad* and *Odyssey*. The other, the *Ramayana*, is a mere 24,000 stanzas in seven books. It comes as no surprise that Peter Brook, the director with the most epic ego, picked the much longer *Mahabharata* for dramatization. The other Saturday, it began with an introductory speech by Brook a little after 1 P.M. and ended with a curtain speech by him shortly before midnight.

There were two intermissions, of 20 and 50 minutes more or less, but that still allowed well over nine hours for the audience to expiate their love of culture by sitting on scantily padded benches, one of the nastier forms of minimalism. The site was the BAM Majestic Theater, which, at a cost of over $5 million, was refurbished so as to look like a gaudy ruin, thus replicating Brook's Parisian shrine of the arts, the Bouffes du Nord. Artificial ruins were popular in the eighteenth century (most of Brook's innovations are resolutely backward-looking), when they graced the formal gardens of the rich and cost the taxpayers nothing. This publicly funded, expensive Temple of Dilapidation in an impoverished neighborhood that could have used the money better will be there after Brook majestically returns to Paris; who and what can be fitted into it then?

But back to the *Mahabharata*, which evolved between 400 B.C. and 600 A.D. though it took Brook and his favorite scriptwriter, Jean-Claude Carriére, a mere ten years to boil it down (in much the same way they decimated *Carmen*) to a prose text of fewer than 150 pages. This could, to be sure, be performed in much less time than nine hours if it weren't garnished with all kinds of stage hocus-pocus (some of it quite effective), and if the actors, either deliberately or out of incompetence, did not deliver many of their lines at a snail's or a Pinter's pace (none of it effective).

These actors are recruited from the first, second, and third worlds, and some of them from out of this world. They dedicate long hours and years to acquiring the Brookian style, which means that they are either fanatical cultists or unemployable anywhere else. How they sound in French at their headquarters I don't know, but in English, they enrich Hindu mythology with the story of the Tower of Babel, what with accents ranging from the opaque to the inscrutable and, even when scrutable, often cacophonous.

Excuse me for not trying to summarize the plot, which concerns the struggle of the five Pandavas with their cousins, the hundred Kauravas, for supremacy, and enlists men, spirits, and gods in sexual and marital, conspiratorial and martial tangles and conflicts, culminating in a bloody war that exterminates most, if not all, humankind. There are philosophical and theological discussions, and the action shifts from this world to one or two next ones, with good and bad guys not necessarily getting their just rewards, though the Brook-Carriére version takes some liberties and fudges the eschatology. "What is not in the *Mahabharata*," says the text of the poem, "is not to be found anywhere else in the world," which, on reflection, is a good thing, or life would be even longer and drearier.

This is largely visual theater, and Brook has combined strategies from sundry Eastern theatrical traditions with some of his own, making him the true *macher* of *The Mahabharata*. The large circular acting area is covered with reddish sand and has a pool down front and a river upstage, containing genuine water. There are ladders going up a sort of mid-stage proscenium, as well as iron brackets up the back wall. These allow for spectacular gymnastic displays, occasionally with a remote bearing on the action. Luscious carpets and straw matting are intermittently spread on the sand, and a variety of artifacts from chariot wheels (without chariots) to barricade-like screens made of (mahabha)rattan are rolled or brandished about. A band of peripatetic musicians with Oriental instruments pop up in likely and unlikely places to play discreetly disorienting music. Fires, equally ubiquitous, snake across the stage, encircling the actors as if they were so many Brünnhildes.

The trouble with this visual theater—everything from jiggling puppets to clouds of arrows crisscrossing the sky—is that it is all too often interrupted for what seems like, or is, hours of logorrheic theater—great philosophic-poetic palaver, worthy of Gurdjieff or Kahlil Gibran, Carlos Castaneda or Shirley MacLaine. I find a hero gnawing at the bowels of his enemy as edifying as a totally miscast Krishna instructing the great archer Arjuna that it doesn't matter who lives or dies in the battle to come, because all will end up in the "Inconceivable Region" of eternity, of which this nine-hour-plus *Mahabharata* gave me a rather too convincing foretaste. In the *Times*, Frank Rich styled Brook "one of the great theater minds of our time"; too bad it is cracked.

Sarafina!; Frankie and Johnny in the Clair de Lune

Sarafina! is infectious—not like a disease, but like health when it bubbles with enthusiasm, humor, righteous anger, passion, and unquenchable hope. This musical about black South African high-school children has some undeniable flaws, but also the strength, spirit, and savvy with which to overcome them exultantly.

Written and directed by Mbongeni Ngema—who gave us *Asina-mali!*—with songs by Ngema and the trumpet wizard Hugh Maseke-la, it is a predominantly musical celebration of the power, courage, and endurance of adolescents tragically catapulted into bloodily engulfing adult history. And a celebration, too, of mbaqanga the rocklike music that electrifies and sustains the black townships. These young students were the core of the 1976 Soweto uprising, when 200,000 of them gathered and marched forth from Morris Isaacson High School, where the action of *Sarafina!* is mostly laid. It is performed by the Committed Artists, founded by Ngema—spe-cifically by eleven girls and nine boys, a couple of grownups, and a seven-piece band who also take the parts of the South African army and police.

The young people, whom Ngema chose from all over his country, are an undiluted joy to watch and listen to. They were given, Ngema says, eight months' training in singing, dancing, and acting, and the glory of it is that they combine the artistry and discipline of a time-tested ensemble with the idiosyncratic sparkle of amateurs bursting into unrehearsed fire. Ngema calls some of the girls world-class beauties; to my view, the beauty of it all is in how ordinary everyone looks, how plainly representative of a large and gallant segment of oppressed humanity whose eventual triumph seems to be happen-ing in flash-forward on the Mitzi Newhouse stage.

I don't want to oversell an essentially modest show, intimate de-spite its big cast and bigger cause. Yet, though I have scant use for rock, I found this *mbaqanga* an engaging and often elating music, zestily orchestrated and compellingly performed by the musicians and singer-dancers alike. In fact, the music is so good that it dwarfs even further the rudimentary book, partly about the horrors of South African history, partly about the Morris Isaacson students enacting a school show about those horrors under the eye of their beloved schoolmistress, who then joins in it. What emerges is perfunctory, indeed awkward—those good musicians cannot properly double as murderous police; part of the bandstand should not look like a funny mock-up of a tank—and lengthens the show unduly. The narration of a cruel incident is less potent than the prowess of these kids and this music, which communicates even with the non-English lyrics, let alone the sweetly or stirringly folklike English ones.

In the second act, we become aware of longueurs, even of a certain sameness in the songs, which may or may not be avoidable. Yet there are high points in this act as well, as when a robust, seemingly crew-cutted young woman with extraordinary vocal and physical expressiveness renders a song that creeps into every part of one's body and soul. There are superb touches—for example, in the way Sarah Roberts's costumes gradually transform the kids from somewhat comically Europeanized schoolchildren into liberated Africans in warm-colored, free-swirling native garments. Or, again, in the way Mannie Manim has lighted the show to give it the sense of emerging and burgeoning sculptural masses, a throbbing three-dimensionality for which Ngema and his co-choreographer, Ndaba Mhlongo, must no less be praised.

Now and again, *Sarafina!* slips into cliché, as even that unnecessary exclamation point after the heroine's name betokens. Yet it offers, aside from the obvious pleasures, incidental ones, too, such as the way these kids speak the English language. Thus Leleti Khumalo, as Sarafina, has something like a warbling trill to her r's, which puts a delightful ritard into words containing that often slurred phoneme. Altogether, English takes on a new lilt here, even as the musical numbers, except for one or two unduly showbizzy ones, transmute sounds we distantly associate with something familiar into something quite unfamiliar yet surprisingly close.

Terrence McNally's *Frankie and Johnny in the Clair de Lune* is highly commendable in its aspirations and disappointing in what it delivers. It is heartening when a dramatist who is most successful at homosexual plays (e.g., the uproarious first act of *The Lisbon Traviata*), plays with a homosexual ambience (*The Ritz*), and plays that gleefully skewer their subjects (*Bad Habits, It's Only a Play*) attempts to write a two-character piece—no easy thing—about a voluble man and a wary woman footing the slippery path toward each other.

To put it most simply, McNally is aiming to get down to jovially heterosexual basics, which—to use a simile from his beloved realm of music—is rather like John Cage trying to write for the charts. He wants his hero and heroine blue-collar, presumably for the sake of universality, and so gives us the first night together—after a first date—of Frankie the waitress and Johnny the short-order cook, who work at the same eatery. When the opening scene, played in near-Stygian darkness, consists of the prolonged sounds of sexual grunting as it shrills toward climax, I sense oncoming trouble: this is not the way to make heterosexuality palatable to anyone but rank groundlings or worse.

Soon, more serious troubles arise. McNally is too devious and sophisticated to write straightforward, down-to-earth characters. So he makes Johnny into a kind of idiot savant: someone who, from reading Shakespeare and the dictionary, and from listening to classical music, has acquired almost McNallian repartee and flights of fancy, which the author periodically interlards with blatant lapses to bring him down: "I guess Bach was Jewish—those Goldberg Variations." Frankie, with her guardedness, skepticism, practicality, and craving for good sex and midnight snacks, is, although a mite schematic, a more believable creature, but even with her McNally cannot resist bits of cynical smartness that are off pitch, as when Johnny refuses to get out of her apartment, and she exclaims, "This is worse than *Looking for Mr. Goodbar*," or when, asked whether among her previous men there was "anyone serious," she retorts, "Try terminal."

The madcap enthusiast—Johnny proposes marriage immediately in bursts of baroque magniloquence—versus the cautious debunker, and how the former manically tramples down barriers only to trip himself up occasionally (e.g., the obligatory sexual fiasco the second time round), is an old story: the courtship of the grasshopper and the ant. But it can still hit pay dirt, as it occasionally does here among much more that is merely dirt. And it does not help that some things ring patently false: the announcer on an all-night classical-music station taking phone calls and playing requests (even encores) like a pop D.J.; Frankie, a seemingly normal woman, succumbing to watching the couple across the street practicing advanced S&M, and being able to see acts they perform on the floor.

Paul Benedict has directed decently enough, and Kathy Bates and Kenneth Welsh are both highly skilled actors. I consider it unfortunate, however, that Welsh, who looks just right for an average guy, should play opposite an actress who, even for a midnight snacker, is enormously overweight. Frankie need not be alluring, let alone slender, but Johnny is not one of those men described in a recent *Times* article as "fat admirers"; or, if he is, that would call for a much different play from the determinedly wholesome one McNally is at such pains to contrive and, for intermittent moments, able to achieve. I do, however, strongly protest the device of a series of cutesy coincidences and parallelisms supposed to bind these lovers together, on the whole; ropes or chains would have been more persuasive.

Into the Woods

Once upon a time, fairly long ago, a little musical seedling started germinating. It was called *Into the Woods* and was to be a deconstruction of the Grimm brothers' fairy tales. There was to be cruelty and bloodshed, some of which is also in the tales collected by the brothers, but also bitchiness, camp, and a great absence of happily-ever-after, which were to be the contributions of the parents—James Lapine, the book writer, and Stephen Sondheim, the lyricist-composer. The zygote began as a reading at Playwrights Horizons; then, as an embryo, it became a full-scale flop at San Diego's Old Globe Theatre. It spent its fetal days as a workshop at 890 Broadway; and now, after two years' gestation, which is enough to bring forth an elephant, it emerges at the Martin Beck as a ridiculous mouse.

We get three main fairy tales: a revisionist "Cinderella," a revisionist "Jack and the Beanstalk," and one that is grim with one *m* only, "The Baker and His Wife"—out of Lapine, alas, not Marcel Pagnol. Sporadically, we also get bits of Rapunzel, who is now the Witch's daughter, and Little Red Ridinghood, who is now an arrogant pip-squeak (out of, say, Molly Ringwald) for whom a wolf is no more than a windup Pluto. Way at the periphery, there are Snow White and Sleeping Beauty, but merely as devices for Cinderella's prince (hereinafter Prince C.) and Rapunzel's prince (hereinafter Prince R.) to cheat on their wives with. And then there is Lapine's mismatched couple, the nerdy baker and his bossy wife, who desperately want to have a baby but can't unless they supply the Witch with the four things she needs for her rejuvenation: a slipper like Cinderella's, a cape like Ridinghood's, a cow like Jack's, and gold tresses like Rapunzel's.

Cinderella is now scarcely better than her sisters, only shabbier and prettier, and hell-bent on posh parties and upward mobility. Rapunzel is a silly narcissist infatuated with her hair; neither girl cares much about her jaded or loutish prince. Cinderella's family is even more trivial than loathsome, though that too. Jack with his toy cow is a good-natured dimwit; his mother, a nagging termagant. The Witch is a mere crotchety crone who enjoys hurling thunderbolts at men's genitals even more than at women's wombs, though that too. However, she is really sweet Bernadette Peters, the Star in temporary Halloween drag, as Miss P. won't let you forget, and not especially menacing.

The menace devolves on a giantess we see only as a shadow and, later, as a bashed-in head (*caput mortuum*, as they say in Stravinsky's *Oedipus Rex*); she is the widow of the giant Jack slew, and out for revenge. Earlier, we've had the cutting off of the odd toe or heel, the blinding of Prince R. by his falling into thorns, the pecking out of the wicked sisters' eyes, and the disemboweling of the wolf; now the real bloodletting begins. Jack's mom and the baker's wife are offered up to the giantess (whose voice is that of Merle Louise electronically turned into a castrato's), who squashes them like bugs. Rapunzel has been banished to the desert by her witch mother, where the girl bears the prince's twins and goes crazy; she occasionally runs across the stage babbling or shrieking. Cinderella's mother's ghost, who lives in a tree, is dematerialized when the tree is blasted.

As a woman friend points out, there is something sinister about this show, which hypocritically celebrates the importance of children and our caring for them, yet punishes every childbearing woman with madness or death. Only the virginal tomboy Ridinghood and the neglected and childless wife Cinderella are spared. This tells us something about the self-contradictoriness of this oft rewritten show, and even more about the unconscious matricidalness that informs it. But, then, James Lapine is a lost cause. His first play, *Table Settings*, was a cheapshot satire—a Jewish American Prince Charming's modish kvetching about his family. Then came his pretentious piece of Jungian maundering, *Twelve Dreams*, proving yet again that a little learning is a dangerous thing. And then the book for *Sunday in the Park With George*, the mature Sondheim's weakest show until *Into the Woods* came along.

The dialogue, except for the odd bitchy or campy joke, is a sorry mess. There are long stretches—especially in the worse second act, but also in the bad enough first one—during which the actors stand about disconsolately mouthing platitudes or vacuities, as if anxiously improvising while they wait for the messenger to arrive with the script. They might as well be waiting for Godot. What does come is yet another waspish—or gnattish—one-liner, and we're off and limping again. Thus, about the dead giant: "Do you think it was a picnic, disposing of [his] remains?" Or Jack, about his squashed mother: "I buried her in a footprint." Or this feeble epigram from Prince C.: "I've been raised to be charming, not sincere."

But what of the score? Sondheim's early, show-bizzy, relatively unself-conscious phase yielded some captivating tunes, but the rivulet quickly ran dry; in the later, grander, more studied phase, when Sondheim started ogling modern classical composers, the music turned into high-sounding nothings worthy of Philip Glass or Steve Reich. By *Sunday in the Park*, it was all tuning up, getting revved up; but no melody really took off. *Into the Woods* is even more desperate: endless introductions to songs, and by the time we cry, "Enough of this foreplay!" the thing is over—that intro was the song. Jonathan Tunick does what he can with the orchestrations, but how do you embroider without thread? A late addition to the score (the show was being revised up to the last minute), "No One Is Alone," comes closest to being a tune, but, unfortunately, the tune of Sammy Davis Jr.'s hit "Candy Man."

Yet that Sondheim can no longer write melodies is old news; the new news is that he is even losing his touch with his forte, lyrics. Here he grinds out the most mechanistic rhyming-dictionary stuff—long, boring series of rhymes on the same word, or clichés such as "kiss me" rhyming with "miss me." Also such glib vulgarities as (about the cow) "There are bugs on her dugs / There are flies in her eyes." And such trite goody-goodiness as "You are not alone, / No one is alone" and, worse yet, an unironic echo of an irony from *Candide*: "Things will come aright now, / We can make them so." Furthermore, there is no integration of book and score: hardly have Jack and the Baker finished singing "Witches can be right, / Giants can be good," making us hope for reconciliation, before they've clobbered the giantess to death. Oh, and did I tell you about the tired device of the Narrator, played with total lack of charm by Tom Aldredge? He comes back as a character, to no better effect.

Succinctly put, *Into the Woods* is an uneasy mixture of camp for a large part of the Broadway audience and sentimental twaddle for another. The true message may be the line "Stay a child while you can be a child," a skill the authors seem to have developed to perfection. And, for once, even Tony Straiges's scenery is only so-so, either a slavish copy of standard fairy-tale illustrations or an enchanted forest begotten by an interior decorator or a window dresser. It took two designers, Patricia Zipprodt and Ann Hould-Ward, to come up with the forgettable costumes, but Richard Nelson's lighting does achieve haunting effects. The sad thing is that this musical, which ought to have all the splendor of the fairy tales, looks impoverished beside one about French proletarians and another about English alley cats.

Under James Lapine's intermittently frenzied but mostly lethargic direction, no actor achieves wonders. Joanna Gleason, as the Baker's Wife, is her usual toughly smart self, and Chip Zien is an amiable Baker, but surely of nothing beyond bagels. Ben Wright is a likably fullthroated Jack, and Kim Crosby a pretty and musicianly Cinderella. All the mothers and both princes are mediocre—Chuck Wagner as Prince R. and Pamela Winslow as Rapunzel, worse than that. And this is the first show in which our Bernadette becomes a mere exponent of the Peters Principle, cutesy and smug. But she is no worse than the show she inhabits, one of whose best lines— would you believe it?—is "If the end is right, it justifies the beans." What it does not justify is the dollars they exact for admission; the box office, I am informed, does not accept beans.

The Phantom of the Opera; The Cherry Orchard

To look on the bright side first, *The Phantom of the Opera* is a terrific technical achievement. If you want scenery and costumes, sight gags and sight thrills, they're all there—$8.5 million worth of them—on the aptly named Majestic stage. And who doesn't want to see candles sprout all around an underground lake (even if it does not make technological sense) and a giant chandelier almost crash onto the audience below (even if it looks more like a giant balloon changing courses in midair)? It is good, mindless fun, and costs less than a trip to Disney World. One of the Phantom's ominous lines runs, "Remember, there are worse things than a shattered chandelier!" Quite. The question here is, are there better ones?

Maria Björnson's costumes are plentiful and lavish, and in surprisingly good taste. Her décor is equally copious, always cunning and sometimes compelling, even if it is not so painterly (e.g., Christian Bérard) or sculptural (e.g., Theo Otto) as great scenery can be. But it is scenery that performs stunning tricks, and in a much nicer setting than the circus. The lighting, by Andrew Bridge, slithers expertly from bewitching to spooky. And there is the direction of Harold Prince, sometimes buttressed by the musical staging and choreography of Gillian Lynne, to provide stylishness and razzmatazz, ingenuity and wit.

The only areas in which *The Phantom of the Opera* is deficient are book, music, and lyrics. To be sure, the 1911 potboiler by Gaston Leroux, on which the show is based, had a solid theme in the Monster's impossible love for the Girl, which served both fairy tales and authors as diverse as Victor Hugo and Gerald Du Maurier tidily. If it's not so romantic as Beauty and the Beast, not so epic as Esmeralda and Quasimodo, not so suggestive as Trilby and Svengali, and not so titillating as Sarah Brightman and Andrew Lloyd Webber, it is nevertheless within strumming distance of the heartstrings. But the way Richard Stilgoe and A.L.W. have adapted it, it is hard to follow and harder to care about: Tonto and the Masked Man generate as many sparks as the chorine Christine Daaé and her Phantom. There is nothing here to make us care whether this Keane oleograph of a Christine ends up with the horribly disfigured sub-Mandrake the Magician Phantom or with the clothing-store-dummy Vicomte Raoul de Chagny. Lacking are genuine emotion, sensitivity, soul.

The lyrics, by Stilgoe and Charles Hart, are as good as your average rock lyrics. They are mostly on the level of "You'll curse the day you didn't do / All that the Phantom asked of you." Or, more unrhymed but no more original, "Share each day with me, / Each night, each morning..." And then, regrettably, there is the music, made up in equal parts of syrup, saccharin, and synthesizer. It's not so much that Lloyd Webber lacks an ear for melody as that he has too much of a one for other people's melodies, especially Puccini's. The result here is a fourfold mixture: disco, operatic parody, attempts at genuine opera (mostly *Turandot* and *Manon Lescaut*), and soup. The critic John Rockwell thinks that A.L.W. is the chap to bring off the wedding of musical comedy and opera, but some marriages are better left uncontracted: can you imagine the nuptials of Neil Simon and William Shakespeare?

The additional problem for the book, score, and choreography is that the inclusion of so much dramatic, musical, and balletic pastiche tends to push the entire work toward the put-on—an intermittently witty parody of opera, ballet, and classier musicals. The thing that Lloyd Webber, with his classical-music background, seems most to lust for is to be taken seriously as a composer, but, on the evidence in thus far, I predict that Gershwin and Rodgers, let alone Puccini and Ravel (another of his magnets), have nothing to fear from him.

But back to the confusions of *Phantom*. The show strives for a protagonist simultaneously a brilliant scientist, a master magician, and a suffering, all-too-human monster. To say nothing of credibility (how many chandeliers' worth of disbelief can we suspend?), there is the simple clash of these aims to inhibit any identification. If you never know whether to admire the hero's scientific acumen, be tickled by his magicianly razzle-dazzle, or feel pity for his miserable condition, you're likely to end up not feeling anything. The obvious clue is the not-so-minor character of Meg, the *rat d'opéra*, who serves no better end than to fulfill whatever disparate and trivial purpose the moment spews up. Similarly, the scenery subserves mostly adventitious, tricksterish needs, as when the gilt figure atop the Opéra's proscenium is lowered a few feet when the action shifts to the roof, and an object still within the sightlines is needed for the Phantom to pop out of. But any illusion of a façade is shattered.

The best things about *Phantom* are its balletic and operatic spoofs, but even they are too numerous, too long-winded, and not quite inventive enough. Prince's pacing and stage pictures, however, work handily, although the director is not quite so successful with actors. Michael Crawford, the Phantom, proves again that he is an agile and graceful performer who uses his body, hands, and speaking voice to good effect. That it is scarcely a singing voice does not much matter in a show so tinnily overmiked that it seems to be issuing from an opera-sized can of sardines. And an actor is severely limited if much of his face is covered by a mask or monster makeup; on film, with closeups, one eye and half a mouth can still do things; on stage, they can only get lost.

Sarah Brightman, as Christine, contributes mostly a dazed waif- or clown-face, a voice that ranges from pleasantly amplifiable to unpleasantly amplifiable, and an acting ability that remains totally masked from view. Her casting is the triumph of uxoriousness over common sense. In supporting roles, Judy Kaye, Cris Groenendaal, and Nicholas Wyman do nicely (but David Romano doesn't); as the dashing Vicomte Raoul, Steve Barton would carry the fashions in Macy's window better than he does his role. None of this is to say that on some mundane level *The Phantom of the Opera* can't be enjoyed, but it helps if you go expecting the best little opera house this side of Paris rather than, say, *Guys and Dolls*.

What Peter Brook may lack in dependable artistry, he very nearly makes up for in shrewdness. The good thing about his mounting of *The Cherry Orchard* is that neither his sundry quirks nor his sporadic clevernesses get in the way of Chekhov, so that BAM is now offering, shortcomings be damned, an honorable incarnation of a great play. I regret Brook's decision to race through its two-and-a-half-hour duration without intermission, thus making immoderate demands on the audience that would never have occurred to the author. I think that the passage of time and a delusory change of direction in the action are felt more acutely if there is an interval at least at the end of Act II; the human behind, after sitting on those Spartan seats, would also be grateful. But Brook is clearly a director who wants the audience to suffer for their (his?) art.

I realize, further, that elaborate scenery would suit neither Brook's traveling company nor his concept of a deep and wide acting space. Very well, but even so, I am dubious about using only a few sticks of scenery (mostly screens) and keeping even that celebrated bookcase illogically under wraps most of the time Gaev is apostrophizing it. More problematic is the covering of the entire large stage with the fancy Persian rugs Brook is so fond of as if the action took place in an Einstein Moomjy showroom. This is especially troubling during the outdoor act, and deprives the closing one, despite a partly rolled-up carpet, of the feeling of emptiness Chekhov wanted.

Still, these matters are more or less compensated for by Brook's imaginative blocking and subtly shifting tempos, as well as by Chloe Obolensky's elegantly understated costumes and Jean Kalman's correspondingly delicate lighting. It is equally heartening to report that Elisaveta Lavrova's translation feels idiomatic and unfussy, and rolls as neatly into the ear as one of Gaev's imaginary billiard balls into the designated pocket. If Charlotta's magic tricks are more amateurish and amateurishly executed than usual, that does not harm the scene. And that the music is sparing and apposite is a further blessing. Where I do have real difficulties is with some of the performances and some interpretations—the two being, of course, things apart.

The problem is, first, linguistic. It grates on my ears to have an extremely close and similar pair of siblings in which the brother, Gaev, has a thick, sometimes barely scrutable Swedish accent, while the sister, Lyubov, has a high British one. Add to the distress a basically lackluster Yepihodov (Jan Triska, whom I have yet to see give a good performance) with a heavy Czech accent. Firs is redolent of New England, Pishchik is from Chicago, and Anya sounds plebeianly New Yorky. Lopakhin is altogether too American; but Charlotta, who is German, speaks mid-Atlantic English. This would matter less if the play did not call for homogeneity and close-knit ensemble acting.

More dubious yet is Brook's insistence on monochromatic, or monolithic, characterizations. So, that fine actor Erland Josephson turns Gaev into a mere defeated baby, whereas the part can be much more interestingly played with surface luster and bravado, and the lost child gradually peeping through. Likewise, Natasha Parry (Mrs. B.) plays Lyubov with the right faded good looks and intense theatricality, but all too much on the same note of near-unchecked hysteria. The perpetual student, Trofimov, is a naïve idealist, but Željko Ivanek (in his first unexciting performance ever) never lets him achieve his modicum of visionary dignity. Varya, whom Chekhov himself described as a fool and a crybaby, is played by the too handsome Stephanie Roth too grandly, almost for tragedy.

That always reliable actor Brian Dennehy is made to take Chekhov's description of Lopakhin too literally, and waves his arms about as if trying to fly into the flies. And he is allowed to stray too far from his solid decency when he grovels on the floor toward Lyubov's hem or, elsewhere, becomes excessively mean. Linda Hunt (Charlotta) is a painfully repetitious actress, always flashing the same superior smile and extruding the same genteel orotundity. But the one rotten performance is the Dunyasha of Kate Mailer (Norman's daughter), who mugs and simpers and seems forever on the verge of petit, or even grand, mal.

On the other hand, though he doesn't quite convey a man of 87 years, Roberts Blossom is an irresistible Firs, touching in his very straightforward way of fussing over his master. David Pierce, whose limpness and pallor I have deplored on other occasions, here manages to make his atypically pasty-faced, more smarmy than arrogant Yasha absolutely right. And Mike Nussbaum gives us a thoroughly diverting Pishchik, as likable as obnoxious, the actor's best work to date. The other famous author's daughter, Rebecca

Miller, is both talented and attractive, and should, after shedding her accent, do all right for herself.

And, for once, the BAM Majestic Theater—yet another Majestic!—expensively restored to a semiruinous state, works very well in context: the Gaev-Ranevsky estate might just be in this stage of creeping dilapidation. I suppose that when a theater can become an ambience, the gain is considerable.

Without wishing to detract from Peter Brook's genuine accomplishment, I must nevertheless point out the built-in asset of any but the feeblest production of *The Cherry Orchard*—the marvelous play itself. Between the superficial majesty of a *Phantom of the Opera* and the majestic, soul-searing simplicity (and, again, complexity) of Chekhov's comedy-drama—both aspects well captured by Brook—there is an abyss greater than a thousand underground lakes. O, to live in a city, a society, in which such works, unsullied by deconstructionist stagings, would be our staple diet.

A Streetcar Named Desire

Some things went terribly wrong with the Circle in the Square production of *A Streetcar Named Desire*, and though some of the errors are easily traceable, others challenge the nosologist's ingenuity. It is, in any case, unfortunate that one of our finest plays should have fallen into the wrong hands, especially since intellectuals of the more captious sort still tend to be sniffy about it (e.g., Mary McCarthy in "A Streetcar Called Success," reprinted in *Theatre Chronicles 1937–1962*). Yet, though they have made good points against it, it remains a solidly stageworthy, funny, and gripping—above all, true—play, which finally knocks out the very people who have scored those points.

Typical objections focus on the character of Blanche, as when McCarthy writes: "It is not enough that she should be a drunkard (this in itself is plausible); she must also be a notorious libertine who has been run out of a small town like a prostitute, a thing absolutely inconceivable for a woman to whom conventionality is the end of existence; she must have an 'interesting' biography, a homosexual husband who has shot himself after their marriage, a story so patently untrue that the audience thinks the character must have invented it; and finally she must be a symbol of art and beauty... [and] she must [also] be given a poetic moment of self-definition..." This, clearly, is quite a load for any character to bear, but, well cast, Blanche works and moves us.

She is a composite. One part of her is a genteel, aristocratic southern woman in decline, and Williams, I fear, knew few if any such ladies, which gives Blanche a fetching touch of romantic idealization. But he did know all kinds of parvenue, nouveau riche southern women: much-divorced, hard-drinking, fast-living, who, when heterosexual men (unjustly) started turning their backs on them, would become reckless companions to homosexuals. Blanche is a bit of that, but she is also Williams himself: the middle-aged homosexual (unjustly) no longer attractive to younger homosexuals, unless his fame or wealth seduces them. As Flaubert said, "Madame Bovary, c'est moi," Williams could—and did—say, "Blanche is me." So there are three heterogeneous elements making up Blanche, but because great actresses and directors thrive on paradox, and because Williams's language and insight were here still in the ascendant, she is a character who, by her very opposite pulls, conveys the taut, tormenting contradictions of the human soul.

Unfortunately, Blythe Danner, good actress though she is, fails here, partly because hers are a droll, slightly clownish face and a coltish, humorous personality—lovableness rather than vulnerable delicacy, tragic self-destructiveness, or even a cerebral or poetic streak. Such words as "Della Robbia blue" and "Rosenkavalier" do not glide insouciantly off her tongue; the monologue about her dead poet husband accords ill with her fundamentally uncomplicated nature; poetic one-liners such as "Sometimes—there's God—so quickly!" and "I have always depended on the kindness of strangers" do not issue from her with the right, heart-stopping music. She does, however, discharge Blanche's comic and outrageous business well, and manages the edginess and anger. Only the lyrical, tragic center is missing.

Partly, too, it's a matter of accent. To her credit, Miss Danner provides a southern accent that is, if anything, too good—more Tallulah Bankhead or Carrie Nye than Mississippi; but she is left high and dry by the total un-southernness of Aidan Quinn (Stanley), Frank Converse (Mitch), and, except very fitfully, Frances McDormand (Stella)—to say nothing of the secondary players, of whom even little may be too much. Thus her performance often seems exaggerated through the failure of the others to meet her halfway.

Partly—indeed, largely—there is also the problem of the staging.

Nikos Psacharopoulos is an essentially flimsy and unimaginative director who has made his reputation (chiefly as the head of the Williamstown Theater) by means of some very real talents, although, unfortunately, not of the artistic kind. His *Streetcar*, which he has done more than once, is consequently better than many other of his productions, but still not good enough to help Miss Danner to a persuasive performance. What, for example, are we to make of the rape in Scene X, which is now played as if Blanche were asking for it? Is this sheer directorial incompetence or some sort of misplaced feminism, according to which a woman of Blanche's stature would not allow herself to be degraded without some consent? Or, heaven help us, is this some sort of misplaced Freudianism?

In any case, such staging deprives Blanche of the chief motive for going over the edge, and so gravely undercuts the play. But lesser directorial errors do their share of damage, too. How could Psacharopoulos allow the generally uninspired costumer, Jess Goldstein, to dress Blanche in bright red in Scene IX and so ruin the dramatic and symbolic effect of Stanley's scarlet pajamas in Scene X? And how could he permit Mitch himself to snuff out the candle (as if he were Laura Wingfield) at the end of Scene VI, thereby canceling out the kiss on which the scene—and, in this version, the whole first act—should conclude?

Some of the problems have to do with mounting plays in a theater-in-the-round, a deadly concept for which Circle in the Square will be paying as long as it lives. Because of this, and because John Conklin's otherwise evocative set is rather cluttered (Conklin is a devotee of clutter), all the peripheral, atmospheric bits evoking New Orleans street life fall, curiously for a play done in the round, flat. There is just the narrowest pathway circumscribing the main playing area, thus leaving scant room for Williams's fairly elaborate subsidiary scenario—which may also require more walk-ons than the producers wish to pay for. And between scenes, when much of this street life takes place, you sometimes cannot tell the extras from the stagehands—except that the latter, because of lighting that hits them through slats, appear to be fugitives from a chain gang.

Some roles have been given the stamp of definitiveness by their creators, which is surely the case with the Stanley Kowalski of Marlon Brando. I pity any actor who must follow in those footsteps: he is damned if he imitates and damned if he doesn't. But Aidan Quinn is a singularly poor choice for the part. Exceedingly Irish-looking for a Pole, not especially winning of face or athletic of build, a competent but uncharismatic actor, he neither charms nor threatens, and is too babyish to boot. Meant to embody the "rough trade" one part of Williams seems to have hankered for, Quinn instead suggests more the young collector of Scene V than the perilous Stanley.

In theory, Stanley and Mitch should be coevals, but in practice they seldom are: Karl Malden was by nine years Brando's senior, and Frank Converse is middle-aged. Mitch, moreover, is meant to be unprepossessing, a mother's boy, perhaps even a crypto-homosexual, and thus more pathetically Blanche's last chance. Converse does his best to meet those requirements but remains too virile and good-looking for the part. No actress, provided she can act at all and look presentable, can mess up Stella—a part in which Williams was not very interested, and which he left vague enough to fit just about anybody. Frances McDormand does more than acceptably by it.

What, then, do we have here? A perfect *Streetcar* for an audience such as I saw it with, in which one woman asked her escort to translate "Voulez-vous coucher avec moi" for her, and another exclaimed loudly, after the play's most celebrated line (about the kindness of strangers), "What did she say?" (But it is also true that some of the actors, because of the venue and their diction, are at times inaudible.) For the sophisticated, this *Streetcar* is vehicular suicide.

M. Butterfly; Joe Turner's Come and Gone; Julius Caesar

There is a marvelous play in the true story underlying David Henry Hwang's *M. Butterfly*, but Hwang lets it slip through his fingers. A French diplomat in Peking conducted a twenty-year affair with a star of the Peking Opera specializing in female roles. Without leaving his wife, he set up clandestine housekeeping with the actor, a Maoist spy, who gleaned some confidential materials about the Vietnam War. The actor even produced a blond baby he claimed to have borne the diplomat. The Frenchman was eventually transferred back home; the actor, during the Cultural Revolution, spent four years in a labor camp. Then, however, he was sent to Paris to continue his love affair-cum-spying. The diplomat took him back and divorced his wife. Discovered and tried, he was sent to prison. Through all this, he insisted that he never realized his lover was a man.

Can love be *that* blind? Can wish-fulfillment fantasy be *that* strong? Can a diplomat stationed in Peking not know that all roles in the Peking Opera are taken by men? Could the French, who were *au courant*, not have known that the Chinese would not have allowed a lesser foreign diplomat two apartments? Why was there no suspicion of espionage until much later? What really went through the French wife's head? What became eventually of the actor and the Eurasian child? And if it was all just to mask a homosexual affair, exactly how did that work? No real answers.

Hwang is rightly interested in both the sexual and political implications, both the private and public problems. He is curious about the borderline between sexualities and the games people play in that no-man's—or no-woman's—land. Also about the lies one lives because of social, moral, religious, and political pressures. The troubled relationship of East and West obsesses him. The son of affluent Chinese Americans, he has scores to settle with both America and the new China, the former for making him embarrassed about his ethnicity, the latter for repudiating his bourgeois status and Armani suits. Not quite in tune with either culture, he lets loose genuine indignation, which gives the play what life it has.

But Hwang is unwilling or unable to explore the deeper workings of the central relationship. For psychology, he often substitutes one-liners and posturing; for tormented poetry, angry rhetoric. On the political side, he tries to squeeze far too much mileage out of *Madama Butterfly* to convey male fantasies at the expense of submissive women, Occidental fantasies at the expense of a conquered Orient. But it doesn't really work, because René Gallimard and Song Liling keep reversing roles, with the passive Song often in active ascendance, exploiting Gallimard, yet in the end affirming his lasting love. It barely works on the personal level, much less the symbolic.

Unfortunately, potshots, sarcasms, double entendres (e.g., the comical female commissar, out of some kind of *Stinkweed Drum Song*, admonishing Liling, "You represent our great Chairman Mao in every position you take!") are no substitutes for making us care and leave with more understanding than we came in with. This has much to do with authorial laziness. Anyone willing to name his French hero

after the best-known Parisian publisher, and the chief French diplomat after one of France's main military ports (M. Toulon, indeed!),
has scant respect for the sensuous quiddity of details. But the real rub
is that Hwang brings in too many schematic issues and underdeveloped secondary characters, and the principals are not alive enough
to excuse all this blurring at the margins. When the commissar, later,
says, "You go to France and be a pervert for Chairman Mao," this is
not only crude and preposterous in the light of Maoist policy toward
homosexuality, but also the same joke milked.

Another bad sign is that the five minutes during which Song
wordlessly removes his female makeup and garb and changes back
into a man are among the most theatrically effective; I mistrust a
play in which so long an absence of dialogue comes as a relief. Nevertheless, Hwang does have some good lines, as when Gallimard
tries to explain his alleged blindness with "Happiness is so rare that
our minds can turn somersaults to protect it." That, to me, would
have been a play: two creatures artfully and desperately deluding
each other and themselves to maintain a consuming illusion; the
sexual and international politics could have arisen organically out
of that *folie à deux* of which Hwang gives us too little. We could have
been spared such cardboard characters as a Danish girl and Marc,
a sort of jock and frat brother of René's, who says things like "One
night can we just drink and throw up without conversation?" How
un-French can you get? No talk?

John Dexter has directed adroitly but overfussily: René is always changing jackets or pushing screens around, bouncing and
scurrying about. John Lithgow is an invaluable actor with range
and charm, but he is (no pun intended) a single-bottomed one.
He does what a part calls for, provided it is clear-cut, but ambiguities are not right for him, any more than Frenchness is. His Gallimard is apple pie, not *tarte aux pommes*. But, then, the others
aren't French, either—not Rose Gregorio, John Getz, or George
N. Martin. As Liling, B. D. Wong is fine and self-contradictory as
intended, and makes a very feminine woman, though not, alas, a
bewitching one.

The unqualified success of *M. Butterfly* is in its look and sound.
Eiko Ishioka provides a modernistic version of the curving ramp of
Eastern theater (spiraling from very high up down into a vomito-
rium) against which she places evocative fragments of scenery and
gorgeously ornate Eastern or strikingly simple Western costumes,
the latter often in truculently primary colors, the whole thing fur-

ther enhanced by Andy Phillips's sly lighting. The blend of taped Puccini and Lucia Hwong's onstage Chinese music is likewise piquantly suggestive. But, unlike Chinese food, Hwang's play leaves you hungry for less—a better-thought-out and more penetratingly felt less.

August Wilson's earnest dedication and historic vision, his forays into humor and poetry, are all manifest in *Joe Turner's Come and Gone*. Yet the play doesn't work for me. It is set in 1911, in a Pittsburgh boardinghouse run by Seth and Bertha Holly, both thoroughly northernized blacks (he also a tinsmith vainly struggling to expand his business) who have misgivings about southern blacks' coming North in droves and gumming up the works. One boarder, Bynum—a "binding man"—dabbles in voodoo but, as a transitional figure between witch doctor and therapist, helps people find their "song," which will fulfill them.

The other boarders, and the owners, are a bit schematic: the restless young man with a guitar, always on the make; the passive young woman, abandoned by her husband and attaching herself to whoever claims her; the headstrong and promiscuous but sassily savvy adventuress; the comically carping Seth and the shrewd and patient Bertha, preparing hearty meals. There irrupts Herald Loomis, forbidding and foreboding, a shabby ex-deacon wandering with his small daughter in search of Martha, the wife who left him when Joe Turner, the legendary plantation owner, impressed him into seven years of labor. Herald must find Martha before he can begin again.

Bynum has had an awesome visionary experience related near the start; at the end of the overlong first act, Herald, in a paralytic seizure, blurts out his own frightening one. Against the more mundane concerns of the others, and triggered by the final arrival of Martha, who has chosen Pentecostal Christianity, Bynum's and Herald's visions fuse into an understanding of the past—African and slave—as a guide to the future. But there are structural problems: Herald's Act I seizure is more of a climax than his reunion with Martha; the secondary characters verge on the perfunctory; a romance between two children is unconvincingly tacked on. Cross section and panorama overpower individuality; the play dawdles and lurches more than it builds and deepens.

The production is unimpeachable. Lloyd Richards has directed both sturdily and sensitively, and the cast, headed by Delroy Lindo and Ed Hall, could not be better. Still, I couldn't rid myself of the nagging suspicion that *Joe Turner's* worthiness is greater than its worth.

There's nothing redeeming about Joe Papp's *Julius Caesar*, the second item in a six-year complete Shakespeare cycle that promises to be as artistic as a seven-day bicycle race. I would call this production calamitous if it weren't too depressing for such a charged word. Although nominally directed by Stuart Vaughan, a once and future Shakespearean (albeit of no great vision), it is tailored to Papp's specifications like the Barneys suit he is currently advertising—only less elegant. In a *Times* piece, Papp answers "Must actors be Shakespearean when performing a Shakespeare tragedy?" with "Absolutely not."

That is like saying you don't have to be Shavian when playing Shaw, or Williamsian when playing Tennessee Williams. Just imagine *The Glass Menagerie* with Bronx accents in the manner of Odets, or *Arms and the Man* performed as if it were by Osborne or Pinter. There are various approaches to Shakespeare, but they cannot bypass poetry and homogeneity. You cannot speak verse either as prose or as a semi-literate person imagines verse: and even though all roads may lead to Rome, all kinds of jumbled accents do not. Papp boasts that he won't cast English actors in his Shakespeare project because he wants "the plays to be accessible to everyone." But what kind of audience from any part of the English-speaking world would have found the likes of Gielgud, Richardson, and Olivier inaccessible? Especially since Papp goes on to say, "You don't have to be educated in Shakespeare to enjoy [this] play." Well, if you credit the audiences with so much on the one hand, why assume that they are imbeciles on the other?

British English having more of a melody, and British actors having (at least until recently) more training, good British Shakespeare sounds better than the best American. Nevertheless, there was a time when America had something called stage English that was a serviceable vehicle for almost anything, Shakespeare included. The trouble with this *Caesar* is, to begin with, that everyone is doing his own incompatible thing. Roman patricians, like Roman plebeians, had a common denominator in speech and bearing, which has to be found; here, no one even seems comfortable in a toga.

We get the Cassius of Edward Herrmann, a Connecticut clubbie arguing the merits of various golf clubs; the Caesar of John McMartin, with that amusingly insidious whine of his, great for *Sweet*

Charity but unlikely to con a single legionary across the Rubicon. We get the Brutus of Martin Sheen, whose performance is mostly in his bouffant hairdo (does he think he is playing Samson?) and who rattles through the part like an old sewing machine about to conk out. And, most unspeaking and unspeakable, there is the Mark Antony of Al Pacino.

Pacino now looks like a shrunken little old man with cavernous eye sockets and grimly forward-teased hair. Generally sallow and surly, he is unable to negotiate more than four or five of those strenuous, consecutive words without having to take a break in mid-speech. And all this in the accent of a Brooklyn mafioso, with much toe-wiggling (sandals can be treacherous) and eyeball-rolling. Pacino has justified his speech with "You don't need to be German to play Bach." No, but a little German helps in *singing* Bach: Antony is not played on an accordion, although as you listen to Pacino, you wish he were. He tends to mouth without understanding: in "I come to bury Caesar, not to praise him," he accentuates "Caesar," not "bury"; next, it's "the *copse* of Caesar." Or is it the cops?

Yet the moment the lights go up on Bob Shaw's dreary set and Lindsay W. Davis's routine costumes, we know we're in trouble: two hacks are delivering the lines of the tribunes to a Roman crowd that strikes textbook poses and makes desultory moves as we get our first whiffs of Lee Hoiby's score tootling and churning away. Let me cite only two examples of the direction. Cinna the conspirator and Cinna the poet are played by the same actor, whereas the whole point is that the maddened crowd will kill an obviously different man merely because of homonymy. Again, when the mob does in Cinna, it needlessly displays his heart skewered on a dagger. This prompted a woman near me to exclaim, "Is that his liver?" Then, in an accent worthy of this *Caesar*, "No, it's his hort."

The Gospel at Colonus

There is a desparate urge afoot to prove that we are all alike, all members of the same Family of (as it used to be called) Man. Differences cause trouble, so let's wish them away. Hellenism, Hebraism, black Pentecostal Christianity—they're really all the same thing, aren't they? They're not. We must respect the plurality of human religions, myths, beliefs: consider each in its individuality before we draw universal conclusions.

Whatever the similarities, Oedipus is not Job any more than he is Lear. The choir at a Pentecostal service is not a Greek chorus: a visiting revivalist draws no sermon from "The Book of Oedipus" any more than he becomes a Sophoclean messenger. Gospel music does not lend itself to Sophocles' choric songs, even if the honorable Fitzgerald translation is mauled and whittled down by Lee Breuer—book writer, lyricist, and director of *The Gospel at Colonus*, where we hear Oedipus say, "I'm an old, messed-up man." The language of the streets is not Sophoclean poetry; *The Gospel at Colonus* is no *Oedipus at Colonus*, it's a travesty and a mess.

This sorry mythcegenation is the brainchild of Lee Breuer, a co-founder of Mabou Mines, from whom I have had nothing but wretched evenings in the theater, whether *Sister Suzie Cinema*, a doo-wop musical, or *The Tempest* (staged for Papp in Central Park), a throw-up spectacle. A hate letter Breuer sent to a colleague of mine was subliterate, yet its author held the Beckett Chair at Dublin's Trinity College and is co-chairman of the Yale Directing Department. Well, perhaps he knows something about chairs. The composer Bob Telson, his frequent collaborator, has some impeccable credentials (Harvard, Nadia Boulanger) and some peccant ones (Philip Glass, Tito Puente); here, he has written pseudo-gospel music that is not folk material rethought in the manner of a Bartók or a Janáček, only a pastiche souped up by synthesizer and spread out to some two and a half hours. Monotony never had it so good.

The nobility of Sophocles' tragedy about the death of Oedipus lies in its tremendous dramatic confrontations, in its sublime poetry, and in its scrutiny of guilt, expiation, and salvation—which, however, differ significantly from their biblical counterparts. To chop up this text, coarsen its language, drop in bits from the other Theban plays, rearrange the snippets so as to omit or truncate the great choric songs and agons, and give it all a faux-naïf, gospel-service veneer is vulgarization of the crassest kind. Thus Polyneices' "Why are you so silent?" is answered by the congregation with "Because you're evil"; a little girl's question about Oedipus, "Was his death a painless one?," elicits from a pastor "He was taken without lamentation, without suffering. I think I feel like saying this again." Various ministers, members of the congregation, and the congregation as a whole, present the story of *Oedipus at Colonus* as a gospel service. To complicate matters needlessly, we get one speaking

Oedipus (Morgan Freeman, as a visiting pastor) and six singing ones (Clarence Fountain and the Five Blind Boys of Alabama), two Antigones, and other reduplications, so that identical bits are often repeated by widely scattered speakers or singers who, with the help of merciless miking, keep us guessing about who is saying what to whom. There is a retractable staircase, a white piano that sinks and re-emerges (the black one stays put), a black-leather-coated Polyneices rushing in through a fire exit, Oedipus making his final departure up the stairs and out through a door from which pour blinding light and fake smoke (is he in Heaven, is he in Hell?), and a few more such tragical tidbits.

The sundry musical groups—including Bob Telson himself at one of the pianos, and a real-life minister as Theseus—perform as well as this hodgepodge can be performed, and Morgan Freeman even rises above it with his unforced dignity of voice and bearing. But what grossness in Alison Yerxa's décor, which includes Doric columns worthy of an automobile showroom, and a cyclorama depicting night and day, mountains and waterfalls, one mammoth hornet and a host of naked, androgynous angels, flying or falling like demented Icaruses, all in a style like an amalgam of Salvador Dalí and LeRoy Neiman. Add to this condignly garish costumes by Ghretta Hynd, flashy lighting by Julie Archer, and, especially, static, uninventive direction that makes a long event seem even longer, and you'll have ample reason to curse the notion of those two white boys, Breuer and Telson, to colonize the gospel. Perhaps they think they are DuBose Heyward and George Gershwin. Not so.

Carrie

The Authors of the musical *Carrie* claim as their source of inspiration Berg's *Lulu*, which is rather as if *Leave It to Beaver* traced its pedigree to *Moses und Aron*. At best, *Carrie* is a lower-, or lowest-, case lulu. A musical based on a sleazy movie made from a cheap thriller need not be awful, especially if Terry Hands and the Royal Shakespeare Company joined hands with the makers of *Fame* (of movie and TV fame) in creating it. One would have hoped for something spectacularly weird, dementedly arousing. Instead, we get an unstable mixture that crumbles on exposure to the stage, almost every disparate part of it unappetizing enough to stick in our craw.

Though Lawrence D. Cohen's screenplay for De Palma's *Carrie* crawled with too many self-contradictions and improbabilities even for a horror film, Cohen's book for the musical isn't content to crawl with them—it pullulates. Here, things go directly from left field into foul territory, and even the one interesting idea, telekinesis—the repressed heroine's power to move objects by mental concentration—is put to minimal dramatic effect. Everything that in the movie was, however bogus, a climax is omitted, toned down, or thuddingly flubbed. Carrie's blowing out a bulb early on is more effective than the supposedly staggering conflagration she wreaks at the prom, which is nothing more than the laziest of laser shows, for which a provincial rock concert would blush.

Indeed, *Carrie* yields even the dimmest meaning only to the extent one can recall the movie, something one would happily have forgotten. As things stand, Cohen (book), Michael Gore (music), and Dean Pitchford (lyrics) have labored for seven artistically lean years to come up with this, their sixth draft of *Carrie*: and with the help of their director, Terry Hands, they have manifestly restructured the show several times since the initial Stratford-on-Avon mounting. But all this is merely grist for the archaeologists who will tell you that some plastic wall that still survives once served to keep the audience from getting hosed down by Carrie. Since the hose, however, bit the dust long ago, the wall serves at best as a conversation piece.

Carrie is still a mystery, though not quite as intended. Now you have such things to puzzle over as what the final stairway-to-the-stars set means; why Betty Buckley, who plays Margaret, the religious-fanatic mother, is often barefoot for no good reason; or why, lonely man-hater that she is, she will wear a sexy negligee. Or, again, why Carrie, in a black-light sequence in which her shoes, hairbrushes, powder puff, and prom dress are dancing with her (something that belongs in *Carnival*), ends up wearing a quite different dress to the prom, which, incidentally, she seems to go off to in her nightgown. And how would Carrie, over her mother's veto, acquire such a wardrobe? If by practicing telekinesis on J. C. Penney's, which would make quite a nice scene, we don't see it.

There are further mysteries. Why does the gym teacher, Miss Gardner, wear a cocktail dress to gym class? Why does a strictly PG-13-rated shower scene have to rise several yards into the air on a platform? Why do high-school kids at a disco wear identical inappropriate costumes (and at the prom, near-identical ones)? Why does the bad Chris make one of her entrances through a trapdoor; why does a pig's blood fill only a small spill-proof bucket from which Carrie is bedaubed slowly and carefully, as if a makeup person were powdering a star between takes of a movie? There are also less important questions. Why does the bad Sue suddenly get nauseatingly good, to the point of giving her beloved boyfriend to Carrie? Does that boy, Tommy, really fall for Carrie or only pretend to? Why does Sue's astral body attend the prom—are we sinking so low as to crib from the abject *Romance, Romance*? Why does the nice Miss Gardner have to perish along with the wicked Chris? Why is Margaret sometimes hateful, sometimes loving, without appropriate transition? What in hell (or heaven) happens in the end?

Perhaps the only thing about *Carrie* that works is Terry Hands's powerfully sculptured lighting, which manages to be more three-dimensional and various than any lighting within memory, thereby reducing the later laser show to an anticlimax. Ralph Koltai's sets are nervy, but their highly kinetic high-tech sleekness has little to do with establishing a realistic ambience from which the supra-real goings-on could startlingly take off. Hands's direction is zealous but inconsistent, sometimes even clumsy, and Alexander Reid's costumes are more distinguished for their transcendent vulgarity than for their sense. Debbie Allen's choreography is enthusiastic but repetitious—which brings me to the score. This is the most arrant rehash of terminally exhausted fifties pop, with its lyrics maundering on about being alone until they start maundering on about not being alone or how painful it is to be strong. (Earlier, it was painful to be weak.) Not a single song registers in this flavorless fricassee—only endless reiteration of the words "Carrie" and "Mama."

It was a nice idea to have a half-British, half-American cast (though Equity's generosity might have been better used elsewhere), even if most of them are only half-noticeable. Thus Darlene Love (Miss Gardner) can sing, period; Gene Anthony Ray (bad Billy) can dance, period; Paul Gyngell (good Tommy) looks right, period. Neither Charlotte d'Amboise (bad Chris) nor Sally Ann Triplett (good Sue) stands out, though both might make good stand-ins; and Betty Buckley, with no help from the script, is unable to make a cohesive whole out of Margaret. As Carrie, Linzi Hateley is talented and affecting; she can act and sing and be appealingly awkward with equal skill, but the part has nowhere to go. Those of us who, over the years, have sadly learned how to leave a musical humming the scenery will now have to learn how to hum the lighting. Carrie, a gutless shocker, is not even up to "Little Lulu."

The Film Society

Jon Robin Baitz, the author of *The Film Society*, is 25 years old and, though American, lived some half dozen years in South Africa from age ten on. I imagine that the play's Blenheim School in Durban is some version of the once respectable but tottering institution he attended there. What is immediately arresting about his play is that none of the characters is a pupil: five are teachers, the sixth is the autocratic mother of one of them. Baitz has drawn on his past without indulging himself in autobiographical maunderings. There are no blacks to be seen, either, yet we sense their suffering even as we see the whites' stifled aspirations and stunted growth.

Jonathon Balton, who was a student at Blenheim, is now a junior master as well as head of the film society: a weak, well-meaning chap, he'll get a print of *Touch of Evil* when he orders *That Touch of Mink*. He wards off as well as he can the politely domineering headmaster, Neville Sutter, and the bullying blowhard of a history master, Hamish Fox (dying of cancer), while adoring the two young, liberal teachers, Terry Sinclair and his wife, Nan. Terry, the black sheep of a respected conservative family, is a fighting radical (the time is 1970) whom his patient, put-upon wife tries to moderate. But in the wake of a disastrous incident, Terry is fired; the school, now viewed as a hotbed of anti-apartheid, is slowly going to seed and heading for bankruptcy.

Since Mrs. Balton, Jonathon's mother, is a rich widow, she could bail the school out. But she will do it only if Sutter, who has already promoted the ineffectual Jonathon to assistant head, resigns in favor of her son. Jonathon hates his mother and doesn't want the job; he also desperately wants to keep on Nan, in danger of being sacked like her husband. What gives all this the fascination of an internecine anthill is that Blenheim—such a tiny operation run by scions of families that have been friends and neighbors for decades—is riddled with animosities, intrigues, and paroxysms of doomed solidarity, as if it were South Africa itself. And, *in parvo*, it is.

Young Mr. Baitz knows how to write scenes for loving spouses lashing out against each other, for elderly fellow oligarchs *realpoliliki*ng against one another, for the prematurely un-young hero trying to hold on to obsolete loyalties and a crumbling status quo that he would glue together with wheedling smiles and hopeful handouts. And Baitz brings to life (and death) even the offstage blacks. True, the play is slow to get going and has its longueurs; sometimes the shadow of Simon Gray looms too large; Jonathon's big, symbolically reminiscing monologue is provocative but does not knock your socks off—at most, it loosens your shoelaces. The grammar is sometimes distressing ("the both of you"), the humor at times forced (Jonathon, like his mother, refers to this or that "thingie"; eventually, a boat becomes a "dinghy thingie"). But there is exacerbated reality here: good people with unraveling lives or goaded out of amiable inefficiency into fear-maddened beastliness.

Best of all, there is love of language: It is not always as poetic or muscular as it wants to be, but it is real language, fitted to each character—moving, ravening, or rueful as needed. "Tell them to go fuck themselves, Neville." "I'd never be so socially unattractive." Or: "My eyes continue to go out on me." "Well, there's eyes for you." The tone is unostentatious but trembling with the unstated.

Dillon Evans is a bit shaky as Fox, and Daniel Gerroll, as Terry, is getting too metallically twangy, too manneredly audience-courting. But the others do very well under John Tillinger's direction. As Jonathon, the fine Nathan Lane weakens merely in his monologue, with schematic pauses after almost every initial "And"; Laila Robins's Nan subtly grows in stoic stature; and William Glover's Sutter is splendid, with understatements that slice your heart to ribbons. Good set and lighting by Santo Looquasto and Dennis Parichy, respectively; slightly less on-target costumes by Candice Donnelly. Though it's riskier to gamble on writers' futures than on pork bellies, I would invest in Jon Robin Baitz.

Waiting for Godot

Beckett's *Waiting for Godot* is the tragedy of man comically told. Mike Nichols's *Godot* at Lincoln Center is the tragedy of an American theater turned into shtick. With this fractured *Godot*, Nichols proves yet again (as if it were necessary) that he is one of the greatest directors of mediocre material. Not content with finding mediocrity where it so plentifully exists, he must create it where it isn't: in the heart of a masterpiece.

The reason Beckett is execrated in Communist countries and trivialized in capitalist ones is that neither ideology can accept his stance: a heroic negation of any kind of salvation, so monumental as to dwarf the myths of redemption according to Marx, Mammon, or the Judeo-Christian God. The only way man can endure his mortality and assorted miseries is with an epic vaudeville act: you only laugh when it hurts—and it hurts all the time. The sole surcease is death, the classic case of a cure worse than the malady. This is a laugh, all right, but not one that leaves the throat unlacerated.

So let me make one thing clear right away: what you can see at the Mitzi Newhouse if you are able to get in (even many subscribers have been denied tickets) is not *Godot* but some rowdily performed piece of paltry burlesque dipped in a Beckett sauce. *Waiting for Godot* is a tragicomic masterwork; wading through this *Waiting for Godot* is a passable pastime, a good enough way of avoiding a confrontation with the essential.

To start with, the ecumenical is consistently shrunk to the American, rather like turning the universe into the Universal back lot. Tony Walton, an expert in glamour and glamorized poverty (consider his set for *The House of Blue Leaves*), has given Nichols a jaunty sandbox filled with American bric-a-brac, from a rusty Nevada license plate (remember where atom bombs are detonated?) to a picturesque coyote's skull and other bones, from trendy sunglasses (Gogo goggles?) to a hubcap to play with, but, in view of the size of the stage, no Frisbee.

The play has new lines written into it, all vulgarisms and quite uncalled for. Many are spoken by Vladimir and Estragon during Lucky's monologue to discourage the speaker. Coyote jawbones become a movie clapper in Estragon's hands, or Yorick's skull as this gung ho Gogo, Robin Williams, mutters a Hamletic "Alas!" He also wields a large bone with words appropriate to an Oscar presentation, and goes through his usual vocal routines, doing a buzzer on a TV game show, a takeoff on the *Twilight Zone* menace music, and all sorts of trick voices, as if this were *Good Morning, Godot*. Steve Martin, as Vladimir, takes fewer liberties, but his repertoire of reactions to the slur "Crritic!"—which includes a sort of death on the installment plan along with jack-in-the-box revivals—would feed an entire family of clowns for one solid engagement. And we get added dialogue like the archly and invidiously contemporary "You're a *liberal?!!*" And so on.

And on. According to a program note, this stuff is from a brand-new version of the play, to be published by Faber and Faber in London. But what Faber and Grove Press are publishing is Beckett's *Theatrical Notebook* for the Berlin production (1975), with addenda from its San Quentin revival (1984)—unlikely to contain references to the recent presidential race. I think we are being gulled by Greg Mosher of Lincoln Center and Nichols with his directorial tricks.

Didi performs his morning ablutions with his own matutinal spittle, catches a few lice on his belly, and waves off an extruded fart with a lighted match. Beckett? Surely not. Steve Martin? He has some decency. Nichols? You betcha. Anyone who can have the barren tree, which in Act II sprouts "four or five leaves" and prompts Vladimir's "It's covered with leaves," display only one leaf—thus changing a pathetically hopeful remark into an imbecile one—has no feeling or understanding for the play. (And don't tell me that Beckett himself rewrote the number of leaves!) Nichols's scenario of gimmicks obliterates the text.

Pathos is now almost completely missing; what little is left is mostly in Jennifer Tipton's literally stunning lighting: her sunset is what Jules Laforgue must have envisioned with "*un coucher de cosmogonies.*" And Martin-Didi's repeated message to Godot, "Tell him you saw us" (later reduced to "saw me"), is quietly affecting—as so much else ought to be. But the trouble with casting Williams and Martin in these roles is that they make too young, too well-fed, too famous a pair. Instead of conveying half a century's struggling and starving, they suggest a "Fifty Years of TV Comedy" retrospective at the Museum of Broadcasting.

As Pozzo, F. Murray Abraham is better, but the actor has such a common face, voice, and accent that he does not embody a usurping upper class. He exudes mafioso nastiness; conversely, Kurt Kasznar, in the Broadway production, scored with a genial look and sound belied by evil words and actions. Much the best is Bill Irwin as Lucky, speaking as well as miming expertly, but looking too much like a nice Ivy Leaguer of bygone days, his crew cut inexplicably dyed white. Lukas Haas makes a decent Boy. And, I repeat, Martin has good moments; only Williams (who even eats that last carrot as if it were a chic hors d'oeuvre) and Nichols are unpardonable. The audience at the first critics' preview laughed itself silly. Yet if theatergoers are really so benighted that only this kind of *Godot* can reach them, they are not worth reaching. Beckett's God, or Godot, is absent; Nichols's *Godot* is dead.

Coriolanus

It takes remarkable perversity to entrust (as Joe Papp has done) the direction of *Coriolanus* to Steven Berkoff, an English actor-author-director specializing in low-life stories and characters. In his plays, he may retell a classic myth in terms of East London deadbeats (*Greek*) or evoke the grubbiest types with vulgar ethnic stereotypes (*Kvetch*). In the movies, he is best known as the bald heavy in *Octopussy*. *Coriolanus*, whose hero is the supreme aristocrat, falls rather outside his purview.

For several decades now, *Coriolanus*, one of Shakespeare's finest but most forbidding plays, has enjoyed a certain popularity for the wrong reasons. Leftists and rightists of every stripe have seized upon it to prove the vileness of their political adversaries. I perceive Shakespeare to be neither the enemy of the people nor the defender of some sort of oligarchy, merely one who laments a worthy patrician's inability to deal with a populace manipulated by demagogues. I have no doubt as to whose side he is on, but sides matter less than the gap between them. What the play says clearly is that the perfectionist disastrously cannot accept compromise, however expedient; in this, Coriolanus is to tragedy what Alceste is to comedy.

Nor do I see much virtue in the Freudian interpretations with which the play has become encrusted: Coriolanus's bowing before the joint pleading of mother, wife, and child, but especially mother, is merely good Roman *pietas*. Repressed incest is an arbitrary superimposition, just like Garry Wills's recent comparison (in the *Times*) of Coriolanus to a rock star. The exact opposite of the rock star, he refuses to curry favor with those who must be bid "to wash their faces and keep their teeth clean" and told what to think by others. One cannot help admiring—however one judges him—the man who refuses to seek votes by baring his battle-scarred chest to the plebs, who must leave the room during the recital of his heroically earned praises.

But should such a man be portrayed by Christopher Walken, a specialist in modern neuroses and psychoses in middle- or lower-class figures? Yes, if we are to believe the rock-star analogy; one of Walken's best performances was as Kid Champion, the rock-star hero of Thomas Babe's play. No, if dignity and hauteur, upper-class speech and bearing, or even hairstyle, have anything to do with it.

Walken rattles off most of his speeches as if he were tossing loose change to beggars; he comports himself like Mick Jagger in his heyday being asked to perform gratis at a railway-brakemen's benefit.

What is the period here? In Martin Pakledinaz's extremely gauche costuming, eras jostle one another. Thus one tribune is a George Raftish gangster, the other a collegiate Malcolm X. The Roman matrons are dressed (mostly) like Norns in ballet slippers; the Roman senators live and fight in all-purpose basic black—Walken in a double-breasted suit and black (Fascist?) shirt. Menenius gets a Sol Hurok-style fur-trimmed overcoat and silver-topped cane. Volumnia ages so that she wears different wigs and, finally, none; the others remain unchanged. The nine-man all-purpose ensemble switches from plebs to senators to soldiers, either Roman or Volscian ("Volsci," by the way, is pronounced here to sound like "Bolshie")—including a messenger in cyclist togs and cap. They always wear the same impeccable boots, even when they are the starving mob whose (well-cut) jackets are torn improbably, as if by a tailor for basting purposes. And Aufidius sports an African jewel-encrusted cap and wristlets along with glossy fatigues: the style is early Idi Amin.

As usual at Papp's emporium, blacks and whites are cast indiscriminately and illogically; more troubling, though, is the inconsistency of speech and style. In contrast to Walken's anti-poetic hero, there is Moses Gunn's Cominius, all rhetorical singsong and plangent quavers (with appropriate gestures) worthy of a nineteenth-century barnstormer. Even the good Irene Worth, as Volumnia, has been conned into a delivery fluctuating between the grand style, which she does so well, and some kind of nutty declamation verging on *Pierrot Lunaire*. The only effective performances are those of Keith David as a powerful Aufidius (he could blow away this Coriolanus) and of Paul Hecht as an urbane Menenius, nicely balancing power politics with principle.

But what can actors—often miscast, such as the flimsily nerdish Thomas Kopache as the Roman general Titus Lartius—do under such direction? Berkoff stages some scenes realistically, some in slow motion, others as vaudeville (the tribunes, with dancers' canes, doing some of their lines as patter while the plebs, in funny hats, become a chorus line), still others in pantomime, as when Volumnia picks flowers from an invisible arbor, which, when she no longer needs it, she simply drops. Ashley Crow is a wraith as Virgilia (when she mimes embroidering, she never looks at her work), and

Sharon Washington, as Valeria, mostly grins inanely. The ensemble scurries about relentlessly.

Coriolanus and mother do a bit of a waltz together, and he and the senators sometimes sashay oddly onto the stage—they're on horseback, though this is neither consistent nor historical. Loren Sherman's black-and-white unit set, with Giacomettian chairs that the characters keep rearranging, is all right; Larry Spivak has recorded some music on tape that, from a platform above the actors, he accompanies in one-man-band fashion on a number of drums and other strikables. Some of this works, though there is also a steady, ominous hum of which it is hard to say whether it is music or the airconditioning. Whoever wrote in a line for Aufidius at Antium to regale his guests with—"So I said, 'For 50 ducats, I want to see her naked'"—should be strung up by all his thumbs. In fact, the person who comes off best in this production is Young Marcius: he has been cut out of the play entirely.

Our Town

There are a few truly indestructible plays, though indestructibility, incidentally, shouldn't be confused with perfection. Thornton Wilder's *Our Town* is guaranteed 100 percent actor-, director-, critic-proof; but that does not make it a masterpiece, any more than the chair that is hardest to break is necessarily the best or most beautiful. To survive a million militantly amateurish high-school productions as well as—more amazingly—the impenetrable, pedantic praise of a structuralist critic (i.e., Peter Szondi, in his *Theorie des modernen Dramas*) is quite an accomplishment. But that doesn't make *Our Town*, despite its valiant efforts, either Georg Kaiser or Chekhov.

Wilder the dramatist (the novelist, though neither better nor worse, is a somewhat different story) is a curious specimen. A second-rate artist with a genuine flair for borrowing other people's ideas—which, in the theater, has proved an established practice—he did manage, in *Our Town* and *The Skin of Our Teeth* especially, to make something idiosyncratic out of his annexations. In *Skin*, the source was chiefly Joyce; in *Our Town*, it seems to be mainly Norman Rockwell.

I have not read Wilder biographies or critical studies, so I don't know what he admitted, but *Our Town* strikes me as a somewhat jaundiced, patronizing view of American small-town life straining to remain objective. That, in itself, would not be achievement enough; but Wilder had also to resist a contrary pull toward nostalgia about the past—or, more precisely, sentimentality about a fantasy past—and that represents an estimable artistic, intellectual, and human effort, one that cannot be denied appreciation and respect.

What saved Wilder from becoming Norman Rockwell or Frank Capra was, in the first place, his cosmopolitan outlook and European orientation; in the second, his homosexuality, which he could not bring out into the open. It is this, I am sure, that made Wilder a heavy drinker, irascible to the point of pugnacity, and, finally, interesting. He could not keep Daumier out of his Rockwellizing, or Preston Sturges out of his Capricity. And so much the better.

Our Town (1938) is a piece of grassroots Americana subjected to a kind of alienation effect more Pirandellian than Brechtian. I myself heard Wilder at Harvard (in 1950 or '51) crapulously insulting an audience for giggling at an abominable student play, which he defended for its grass rootiness, something it may not even have had. In *Our Town*, three characters, in differing ways, detach themselves from the basic, idealized Tarkingtonizing. They are the Stage Manager, with his intellectual but unsnobbish superiority and "creatorliness" (as playwright and God figure); Emily, the pure maiden who becomes a saint as beloved-wife-dead-in-childbirth, with death allowing her the perspective unavailable to those in the mainstream; and Simon Stimson, the organist and social outcast (or, at least, eccentric) of Grover's Corners, i.e., Wilder. But, of course, all three are Wilder.

Stimson, driven to drink and misanthropy, is the disgruntled artist and homosexual in a town without either (it is not for nothing that he is an organist, one of the two or three professions that were always enlightenedly welcoming to homosexuals). He rings the one wry note in this radiant little town, and—along with the godlike creator and the sainted and wised-up dead—provides the leavening that (if you'll allow me a mixed metaphor) keeps the thing from going flat and treacly. By giving the work a Beckettian production, the director, Gregory Mosher, has helped to restore the balance Wilder was striving for, and thus to rescue it from the highschoolishness it can drown in. Though, to be sure, it succeeds even when drowned in tears, which the last act of this acerb production still managed to be: the sniffles all over the Lyceum could not be ascribed to the unseasonably mild weather.

The even more minimal than usual nonscenery by Douglas Stein, the strictly puritanical costumes by Jane Greenwood, and the soberly restrained lighting by Kevin Rigdon contribute stylishly to the overarching austerity of the production, which Mosher has paced sensibly and cast very well, with three big exceptions. Spalding Gray plays the Stage Manager as a young, countercultural smart-ass who might have wandered in from one of Gray's own dreary monologues, and is unsettling in his inappropriateness and charmlessness; James Rebhorn makes Dr. Gibbs boringly stiff, without any added dimension; and Marcell Rosenblatt overacts, and with the wrong ethnicity at that, as Mrs. Soames, the town gossip.

But many of the others range from fine to remarkable, notably W. H. Macy, Frances Conroy, Roberta Maxwell, Peter Maloney, and Jeff Weiss as Stimson. And especially heartwarming is the work of the two young leads in roles that can, in the wrong hands, almost break this unbreakable play. Yet Eric Stoltz is a naturally natural—as opposed to studiedly and coyly natural—George; and Penelope Ann Miller's Emily is close to marvelous. Although not totally up to the demands of the last act, this Emily, while still alive, is both innocent and knowing, always a step ahead of George, as she should be. Eyelashes have seldom been batted so perfectly (a thousand!), the simplest word rarely been given more pregnant timing and emphasis with Stradivarian vocal cords, so that a mere "What, George?" hits you right in the solar plexus and soul.

"Do any human beings ever realize life while they live it?" asks the dead Emily. "No," says the Stage Manager, "the saints and poets, maybe—they do some." Here is your chance to join them—some.

Legs Diamond

For what, I wonder, will *Legs Diamond* be remembered, in the unlikely event that it will be? Perhaps for being the only musical whose book was co-scripted by a ready-to-wear designer (Charles Suppon) who won a Coty Award for his women's wear. But, unfortunately, the show lacks consistency. The other half of the book should not have been by Harvey Fierstein but by a prizewinning interior decorator. The score should not have been by Peter Allen but by a prizewinning window dresser. And the star should not have been Mr. Allen but an award-winning hairstylist. Although all concerned did their level best to make it look as if such was the case, you somehow can't beat the genuine article.

The beginning is promising enough, which is why I can't describe it; *Legs Diamond*, whose rest doesn't matter, may be the one show where you mustn't give away the beginning. I will say, however, that this beginning involves life-size dummies simulating the show's chorus boys and girls, only ever so much prettier. So *Legs Diamond* may be the big Broadway musical with the worst-looking chorus line within memory. There, now I have run out of distinctions.

There is no real book, only random incidents, set mostly in a nightclub (the most hackneyed venue for a musical), relating to the self-proclaimedly untrue story of the bootlegger and nightclub owner Legs Diamond, legendary for being legendary. But these incidents cannot even decide exactly what tone to assume; thus no story and no tone. There are, however, numerous scenes in which Allen as narrator (which he is) or actor (which he isn't) along with other actors can be seen standing around trying to be funny. The standing around works; the other doesn't: some defeated-sounding verbiage is nudged on by people who seem aware that the stuff isn't funny but who can't afford to get out of their contracts.

Actually, the show suffers from a twofold identity crisis. It is not only always identical to itself (same level of invention and energy, no variety or progression) but also identical, bit by bit, to bits from more other musicals than I have room to mention. There is hardly a scene but makes you feel nostalgic for the same scene in an earlier show, where it worked better. And there isn't one character you care a rap about. Or even half a rap.

Yet the thing isn't truly unprofessional or incomprehensible or totally off-the-wall—it has, in short, none of those redeeming vices that could make us forget about virtues. What could have helped it is magisterial direction (Robert Allan Ackerman's is lackluster) or, better yet, a charming cast. But that is the last thing it has. Allen sings in the manner that nowadays passes for singing—and, with the elephantine amplification it gets, may even surpass it; and he dances acceptably, though without a dancer's pleasing body. His acting consists of a utility smile, precautiously stapled to his face, and of punching every line, not too hard, but *equally* hard, which is just as bad. Yet he does exude some hand-me-down chutzpa.

Then there is Julie Wilson, as an aging chanteuse, nightclub manager, and former song-and-dance partner of Diamond's. She is a fine performer in a nightclub—I mean a real one, not one in a musical—but she does not know how to deliver dialogue, carry herself, act. As Arnold Rothstein, the big-time gang boss Legs horns in on, Joe Silver is one-note creepy where two notes might not have been excessive. As the flighty young songstress who greedily shuttles between Arnold and Legs, Randall Edwards is all right, but how many knockoffs of the archetypal ungolden-hearted blonde can we take? Of the three Rothstein henchmen, Christian Kauffmann is fun, Raymond Serra passable, and Jim Fyfe nowhere. Pat McNamara, as a crooked cop, and Brenda Braxton, as a spunky showgirl, did nothing for me and very little for themselves.

The good set designer David Mitchell has a few bright new ideas here, but mostly recycles his old ones; the gifted costume designer Willa Kim gives us sartorial potluck; and Jules Fisher, the lighting designer, has had better nights and seen better days. Whatever Allen has seems to be catching: the melodic and verbal malaise of his score has been passed on to all. The choreographer, Alan Johnson, has distinguished himself with specials for Shirley MacLaine, Ann Reinking, Ann-Margret, and the like. I guess *Legs Diamond* wasn't special enough for him.

Eastern Standard;
Heathen Valley

It's possible for yuppies to have problems, I daresay, and it's okay to write plays about them, though a glut may be imminent. It's permissible to make the principals of *Eastern Standard* liberal dogooders, who also have their problems. And it is nice to have a playwright deal simultaneously with a heterosexual and a homosexual love affair and, though clearly more interested in the latter, be eminently fair to the former. There is concern here for many (too many) of the troubling issues of the eighties, and there is a tart intelligence at work observing them. The only thing missing is a play.

Richard Greenberg is so with-it, so cool, so consistently witty in exactly the same way for several characters, and writing so detachedly from so many directions, that there is no point of view, no gutsiness, no passion. Stephen, the rich young architect, can rusticate comfortably in his Long Island villa while wrestling with his artistic, social, and emotional problems. The canny young Wall Street broker, Phoebe, can join him in his prolonged estivation, despite the fact that her boss and lover, Loomis, has been charged with insider trading, which may implicate her; she can agonize at leisure about whom she loves more, Stephen or Loomis.

Phoebe's brother, Peter, a liberal TV producer and homosexual playboy, has contracted AIDS and anxiously searches for a way to cope with this; Stephen's best friend, the homosexual painter Drew—the cleverest person onstage and the author's spokesman— falls madly in love with Peter and cannot understand why his love is both encouraged and kept at arm's length. (Needless to say, these two are also spending the summer *chez* Stephen.) Along, too, is Ellen, a would-be actress who waits on tables and who lies in wait for Stephen, whom she ever so innocently tries to snatch from Phoebe; Ellen, in turn, has brought May, a bag woman whom they are all trying to redeem.

Ellen allows the author to make jokes about actors; May permits him to be at once scabrous and concerned about the homeless; Stephen enables him to mock postmodern architecture; Peter lets him make fun of television's hypocrisy while also waxing serious about AIDS; Drew, the raisonneur, empowers him to be perceptive, epigrammatic, charming, mildly self-critical, and to take swipes at postmodern painting. As you may gather, this is like trying to cram an athlete's foot into a baby's sock. Worse, issues such as AIDS and the homeless are too serious to be dealt with in sentimental pieties alternating with sly humor, neither of them an adequate mode and each giving the other the lie. Which brings me back to Greenberg's facile idea-mongering that neither wit nor up-to-date smartness can mold into a continuous action. The courage to take a position—any position—would help, but it might also offend someone and so prove uncommercial. Yet spinelessness, too, may offend—especially with the all-round happy ending the play hastily settles for without suitable preparation.

Seeing *Eastern Standard* for the second time, and remaining mostly unengaged, I could concentrate more on the acting. Peter Frechette continues to amaze me as he did at the Manhattan Theatre Club: his Drew is perfection, about which one can either go on at inordinate length or leave it at that. As Phoebe, Patricia Clarkson is neither youthful nor dazzling enough but, after a slow start, does yeoman's work; Dylan Baker is a believable Stephen. As Peter, Kevin Conroy is schematic, but Barbara Garrick is a finely molded and modulated Ellen. Anne Meara handles the unconvincingly written bag woman persuasively, and Michael Engler has staged the whole thing expertly. There is good design from everyone, though Philipp Jung's scenery worked better at the MTC. Given the state of Broadway, we should be grateful for this much; but let us not be too liberal with our gratitude.

We must, however, be truly grateful for Romulus Linney, even when, as in *Heathen Valley*, he gives us his second best. He is one of the few playwrights left who are not afraid of being unclassifiable. He writes neither smart-ass eighties comedies nor sitcomatose TV fare masquerading as theater; neither the last, indeed posthumous, gasps of jazzy absurdism nor any of the varieties of liberal breast-beating. Here he writes about life in Appalachia in the 1840s (not so different from today) and about the efforts to sustain and contain the arid and ferocious lives of those whom civilization has forgotten.

Heathen Valley, which Linney adapted from his first published work, a 1962 novel, concerns North Carolina mountain people who have neither the church nor the law to hold on to, and live barren lives studded with superstition, vendetta, incest, with only a midwife to tend them in childbirth, sickness, and death. Some form of Christianity would be helpful, but can it be the orthodox Episcopalianism the Bishop wants to force on them? Or should it be the rough-hewn kind that Starns—a man of the people who has served time in jail and worked since as a church caretaker, offers?

Three men head for the valley ensconced in the Appalachian Mountains: the Bishop, Starns (his newly appointed deacon), and Billy, the orphan avidly searching for a home—a youth who appreciates both the valley's people and Starns's way with them and serves as the play's narrator. And there's the rub: *Heathen Valley*, conceived as a novel, is harder to convert to drama than those cussed, ornery mountain people to Episcopalian orthodoxy. We get something between a church pageant and story theater, and only intermittently a play.

This is so partly because it is all done on a shoestring: bare platform, drapes, a few lights, and a cast of six often addressing invisible others who may be fellow townsfolk or spooks. Add (or subtract) weak actors, from whom only the excellent Scott Sowers stands out as Starns, and no wonder that Linney, as his own director, can bring only half of it to life. But that half has pungent humanity and idiosyncratic vision going for it.

In a Pig's Valise

Raymond Chandler was a remarkable writer who, more than anyone (and that includes Hammett), set the tone for American detective fiction. It is a genre so yummily plummy as to warrant the parody with music *In a Pig's Valise*, book and lyrics by Eric Overmyer, music by August Darnell, a.k.a. Kid Creole, some of whose Coconuts occasionally drop into the action from the balcony where they are playing the score. It is an amusing evening, as charming as it is clever. The title, by the way, comes from Chandler's novel *The Little Sister* and is a synonym for "in a pig's eye." I am happy to report that a pig's valise holds more than its eye: this show might just be your overnight bag.

Overmyer has two (in both senses) precious gifts: he spins words dizzyingly and is equally deft with genre. In *On the Verge*, he gleamingly parodied the writings of Victorian women travelers and much more besides; in a less happy play, *In Perpetuity Throughout the Universe*, he took on the clichés and stereotypes of right-wing paranoia. Now he goes all the way from Chandler to *Chinatown*, from Hammett's fat Mr. Gutman, here called Gut Bucket (the bigger of the evil Bucket brothers, the smaller of whom is Shrimp Bucket), to that great spiller of guts Mickey Spillane. He manages both the baroque Chandlerian tropes (at a floor show: "Do I have to sit this close? I'll get sequin burn on my retina") and the steely, staccato stichomythia ("It's a free country!"—"Don't kid yourself"). He is a good punster (a gangster vocal quartet is "the four horsemen of the a cappella lips") and a fine twister of other people's platitudes (a blind sax player is "visually challenged").

The plot concerns the aforementioned Bucket brothers, who run the Heartbreak Hotel, at the corner of Neon and Lonely, in front of which a funny, chubby shamus, James Taxi, stands "loitering with intent to meet some mysteriosoette," who duly appears in the person of Dolores Con Leche, a torrid tamale of an ethnic dancer. She auditioned for the job of the vanished lead dancer in the Heartbreak's floor show, Mitzi Montenegro, was hired by Shrimp Bucket, the show's choreographer, and given a room and a knockout pill.

Then, by means of a sinister Bucket invention, her dreams were stolen from her to be marketed on CD-like discs. She engages Taxi to recover her purloined oneiric images; he declares, "We'll look into this dream snatch."

Taxi also acts as the narrator between episodes, enabling Overmyer to be even more overtly parodic of the Chandlerian style, to which his own can well hold a candle. The raunchy music of Kid Creole and the Coconuts—reggae and rap, funk and rhythm and blues—fits in W. C. Handily, and Overmyer's lyrics are only slightly less jolly than his dialogue and monologues. I am a sucker for such a bit as this between Dolores and Taxi: "Mitzi Montenegro is my sister, my kid sister." "Say no more. Where I come from, that counts for something." Or this, when Taxi, disguised as an Indian nabob who might finance the dream-stealing machine, is being entertained by the Buckets, and their black bouncer, the Bop Op, is serving him a whiskey: "What's the brand?"—"Heart of Darkness, the white man's bourbon."—"How does *he* get all the good lines?"—"Affirmative action."

The songs are not only fun in themselves but are also sassily choreographed by Graciela Daniele, who directed the entire show with jauntily spoofing humor. Bob Shaw's set design has well-nigh Shavian wit, Jeanne Button's costumes are bright as a you-know-what, and the lighting, by Peggy Eisenhauer, befits the general mood. The performances, though, are a mite uneven. Nathan Lane is pleasantly goofy as the fleet-footed flatfoot (but no Peter Sellers when it comes to Indian accents), and Ada Maris is equally apt as actress, dancer, and looker as Con Leche, often nuttily mispronounced as Con Leechee. As her backup dancers, the Balkanettes, the Asiatic Lauren Tom is delightful, the black Dian Sorel dull. Of the Bucket brothers, Michael McCormick's Shrimp pushes too hard, but Jonathan Freeman's Sydney Greenstreet-ish Gut is splendid, even if in his other role as the fake-French concierge, Zoot Alors, Freeman, too, is too, too outré—though his waggish wig saves the day. So pack up your troubles in a pig's valise and enjoy a show in which Mickey Mouse's three-fingered glove is thought to belong to someone "digitally challenged."

Shirley Valentine

Willy Russell's *Shirley Valentine* is a friendly puppy dog of a play that, all floppy ears and sloppy paws, jumps all over you, yapping and slobbering. Who could find enough hardness in his heart to kick it away just because it is an Old English sheepdog, unaware of its weight and muddiness, rather than a play? I suspect even of those great baby-and-dog-hating curmudgeons of the W. C. Fields school that their bark is worse than their kick.

Shirley Valentine is a one-character play (I don't think that inanimate objects, however frequently apostrophized but failing to respond, count) in which a 42 year-old middle-class housewife of that name—by now, actually, Shirley Bradshaw, housebroken mother of two grown children—soliloquizes about the middling woes and minuscule pleasures of Liverpudlian married monotony. She is preparing dinner for her husband, Joe, with some cooking wine of the kind that goes not into the dish but into the cook. She especially needs the sustenance today, when Joe, who expects the usual steak at the precise usual time will have to make do with eggs and chips: Shirley, gave away the steak to a dog whose owners raised him to be a strict vegetarian. She just wanted the pleasure of seeing the expression on the dog's face as he discovered his true culinary heritage.

Shirley, you see, can still be whimsical. Commenting about a say-it-with-chocolates commercial, she muses: "Cadbury's would go out of business if women didn't hold out a bit." She remarks about her best girlfriend that "she found [her husband] in bed with the milkman; from that day forward Jane was a feminist." She is also philosophical in a nice, tart way: "I always thought of leaving Joel when the kids grew up; but by the time they grew up, there was nowhere to go." Again, "Marriage is like the Middle East, isn't it? There's no solution." What she isn't any longer, though, is the free spirit she once was, jumping off (low) roofs and such. And suddenly, at 42, she is handed this airline ticket by Jane and the invitation to come share a fortnight's holiday in Greece. Will Shirley have the courage to go despite the undoubted indignation of her smug husband, selfish daughter, and all those others who will assume that the only thing two middle-aged women would go looking for in Greece is, of course, sex?

I am giving away nothing if I tell you that the second act takes place not in the Bradshaws' crisply sterile kitchen but on a Greek island where our heroine is deliciously baking on a rock in the Aegean sun. What we want from the worm-will-turn plot is not suspense but the satisfaction of our appetites for the liberation of some and the comeuppance of others. *Shirley Valentive* delivers these in a manner to thrill matinee ladies without unduly disturbing their complacent spouses.

For this is a feminist play that does not offend anti-feminists, and at times even an anti-feminist play that doesn't offend feminists. It is an anti-British play that had the British guffawing wholeheartedly, and a hymn to unconventionality that holds out hope even to the most hidebound. Prudes can smile at its sex jokes, slaves and slave drivers share a laugh at its advocacy of liberation. It is a play not written, like true comedies, in a mixture of soap bubbles and bile but propelled instead by a moist, warm puppy nose nudging you to do right by yourself and, coincidentally, the world.

Nothing reprehensible about that, but nothing remarkable either, especially when this is only a one-character play—the best way of shirking the real confrontations of drama—and when you consider that Russell has written it once before: *Shirley Valentine* is a sort of *Educating Rita* twenty years later. This said, I must add that it is acted by the coruscating Pauline Collins, directed by Simon Callow, and designed by Bruno Santini and Nick Chelton to a fare-thee-well. It may even be that two weeks in Greece for all concerned parties might end the Middle East crisis—but, somehow, I doubt it.

Jerome Robbins' Broadway

The art of embalming has received a shot in the arm, so to speak, from cryogenics. Not since ancient Egypt has it thrived as it does nowadays, and never before, I daresay, has the embalmer embalmed himself. That is the miracle of *Jerome Robbins' Broadway*, which, as corpses go, dances pretty well.

This anthology of some of Jerome Robbins's favorite things from his two-decade Broadway tenure (1944–1964) has to be seen in two perspectives. It is manifestly one thing for people who saw the first runs of the musicals from which these dance or song-and-dance numbers were culled, and another for folks to whom they are new—although some of them come from shows that have been fairly steadily revived. The problem for viewers from column A is that they remember the originals and are likely to prefer their memories, only partly out of nostalgia. More important, these sequences were, or seemed, innovative then; they were part of a context from which they drew much of their strength; and they were performed better than they are now.

The problem for younger theatergoers (but not children) is that, while their eyes may be opened to the splendors of the past, it may all be too much of a muchness or not-enoughness. Fourteen numbers from ten shows bombard the inexpert sensibility and confound it. These viewers from column B may be thrilled, but I wager that they do not recall what they have seen for very long, except as a pleasantly gaudy blur. For this is not a full-bodied musical revue blending songs, skits, and dances; it is Robbins and more Robbins.

As for me, I have never relished anthologies, though they do have their uses. Like all compromises, though, they frustrate more than they satisfy. So these are the raisins, you say to yourself, but what was the cake like? How did these excerpts enhance and become enhanced by the context? What happened before and after this? Even the worst coitus is interruptus only at one end; these numbers have incompleteness in their very beginnings.

Even so, there is one good and important thing about *Jerome Robbins' Broadway*: it reminds us that musicals of yore did not disguise human beings as cats or roller-skating locomotives, did not apply choreography to computerized scenery or create a *son et lumiére* show that makes the human presence redundant. They did not even spend hundreds of thousands of dollars on gutting a theater so as to turn it into a mere environment. And Robbins's choreography was always savvy and often captivating, even if not meant to fill out a whole evening. Personally, I would have preferred to see more stuff from unknown sources, represented here by the interesting "Mr. Monotony" number, cut successively from *Miss Liberty* and *Call Me Madam*; or from little-known or forgotten ones, such as the here-included "Charleston" from *Billion Dollar Baby*. But except for the lengthy and overfamiliar material from *West Side Story*, *The King and I*, and *Fiddler on the Roof* nothing actually made me impatient.

Well, yes, the narration. Ploddingly written by Jason Alexander (an actor aspiring to become a writer, always a risky proposition) and smugly delivered by himself (an actor good enough for the modest ambience of *Forbidden Broadway* but not for a forbiddingly overblown *Jerry Robbins' Broadway*), it provides a lamely uninventive continuity charmlessly spoken. And when Alexander performs in some of the numbers, he is equally lackluster. Which brings me to the second major problem of the show: that none of the performers manages to make you forget, even for a moment, the one who created the part—or, in the case of Peter Pan, even the first re-creator, Sandy Duncan.

To be blunt about it, there is no one here the like of Zero Mostel, Mary Martin, Joan McCracken, Sono Osato, Maria Karnilova, Nanette Fabray, Chita Rivera, Adolph or Mitzi Green, and sundry others I remember vividly from the original productions; their memories do not get effaced, but are in some cases defaced, by the incumbents. In the present cast, Michael Kubala, rangy and goofy, has much of the old-time nimbly poetic zaniness, both in the numbers from *On the Town* and in "Comedy Tonight" from *A Funny Thing Happened on the Way to the Forum*, which may be the most successful sequence of this show. There are nice moments also from the sprightly Scott Wise, the stylish Jane Lanier, and the funny Faith Prince. Charlotte d'Amboise is better as Anita than as Peter Pan, and Debbie Shapiro is a good belter but an unwinning presence. And Robert La Fosse—who, with Jason Alexander, has star billing—continues to be a solid but unexciting dancer, as he is at the ballet: when he smiles, he is too cute; when he is serious, his prettiness defeats him.

The orchestra, except for a shabby sounding overture with piped-in chorus, does well by the trusty old orchestrations faithfully re-created, and it is heartening to see sets by Oliver Smith and Boris Aronson, costumes by Irene Sharaff and Alvin Colt, bestride the stage once again in devout replication. But, ultimately, what the show lacks among the ensemble members perhaps even more than among the leads is that pristine glow that musical-comedy performers used to have. They strutted, they sparkled, they had presence; you sat up, noticed, were infected with their radiance. However proficient and determined this cast may be, the high gloss is missing. To realize that Robbins—uniquely on Broadway—got the kind of unlimited rehearsal time Brecht arrogated to himself and his fanatically drilled Berliner Ensemble, and then to have to pay a very un-Brechtian $55 top seems a bit high for medium-high gloss.

For the last scene, from *On the Town* again, Robin Wagner, who coordinated the scenery, designed a "Broadway at Night" set displaying marquees lit up with the names of Jerry Robbins shows stretching from here to eternity, but there is a bit of cheating: *West Side Story*, *Fiddler on the Roof*, and *Peter Pan* appear twice. Perhaps it would have been seemlier for Mr. Robbins to do a few more musicals before publicly canonizing himself. Still, *Jerome Robbins' Broadway* may run forever, not so much for what it is as for what it isn't: no choo-choo, pussycat, or phantom getup to mask and minimize human communication. But even that is only a negative virtue, more manner than matter.

Ubu

If Alfred Jarry had not rewritten, edited, or just published under his name (we'll never know which) a group effort of his own and his classmates' at the lycée of Rennes, he would now be a near-forgotten *décadent* of the *fin de siècle* such as Jean Lorrain or Marcel Schwob. Though some critics rate him higher, and I myself have an irrational fondness for him, it is he, rather than Oscar Wilde, who could have said that he put his genius in his life and only his talent in his works. The exception is that remarkable piece *Ubu Roi* (*King Ubu*), which began as a series of pasquinades by fifteen-year-old schoolboys against an inept physics teacher, M. Hébert, whom his pupils satirized as Père Heb or Hébé (it was Jarry's later masterstroke to turn this into Ubu). Whatever classics the boys were reading supplied, in travestied form, further epic or dramatic misadventures for the hapless pedagogue.

Eight years later, eking out a hand-to-mouth literary existence in Paris, Jarry, the paradigm of the brilliantly eccentric artist, hit upon the idea of turning these scattershot writings into a single play. And so, in June 1896, *Ubu Roi* appeared in book form to good reviews; on December 11 of that year, it was mounted for what turned out to be a single tempestuous evening, at the distinguished Lugné-Poe's Théâtre de l'Oeuvre. It created the biggest scandal since Victor Hugo's *Hernani* and made theatrical history. For all practical purposes, the modern theater (whatever exactly that may be) was born.

Ubu Roi is a marvelous thing, despite its deficiencies as a play. It combines amoral, childish humor with what the French call,

untranslatably, *une humeur tracassière*—a pestering, cantankerous, curmudgeonly disposition and the nagging wit it begets. It
comprises scatology and persiflage (being, in many ways, a parody
of *Macbeth*), absurdity and even bits of harmless tomfoolery. It incorporates much of what Cubism, Dadaism, and Surrealism were
to capitalize on, and what, channeled through the declared Jarryite
Antonin Artaud, became the fountainhead of modernist playwriting from the Theater of Cruelty to the Theater of the Absurd. Jarry
systematically transformed himself into a real-life version of the
comically inhuman super-puppet Father Ubu and died young of
drink, drugs, and TB. Ubu, however, who even became a word in
the French—indeed, world-language—*ubuesque*, lives on forever.

I tell you all this so you can appreciate the full injustice of what
Lincoln Center Theater has perpetrated at the Newhouse under the
title *Ubu*. The sunscreen Bain de Soleil lists among its sundry virtues its "non-comedogenic" quality, which it explains with "won't
clog pores." Well, the Lincoln Center *Ubu* is strictly "non-comedio-
genic," which I define as generating absolutely no comedy, whatever
it may do to the pores. (I wouldn't be surprised if it clogged them.)
If you have ever sat through the lengthy telling of a funny story by
a person lacking the tiniest sliver of a sense of humor, you may have
some inkling of what this misbegotten *Ubu* is like.

To be sure, *Ubu Roi* does not translate easily, if at all. Take the
first word of the play, so shocking to contemporary theatergoers,
Ubu's stentorian "Merdre!"—which is, of course, the basic French
curseword with an added "r" for good, or bad, measure. Scatology
had never been heard on a stage before, not even with an extra
phoneme to soften it into a kind of baby talk. But whereas it is only
near-impossible to re-create this vocable in English—the present
adaptation by Larry Sloan and Doug Wright from a literal translation by Jacqueline de la Chaume uses "shittr," which doesn't work—
it is utterly impossible to bring back the innocent time when that
or any word uttered by an actor could give offense. So how, with its
many puns and other linguistic games, and with its unresurrectable
timeliness, can this work be done here, and now?

I suspect that, unless some compatible genius could rethink it
completely—but would it still be *Ubu Roi* then?—the only thing to
do is to get a better translation by someone bilingual and re-create the staging of 1896, as a historic document or museum exhibit.
And why not? Wouldn't you like to see the 1606 *Lear* or the 1666
Misanthrope reproduced exactly, if such a thing were feasible? The

Ubu sets and costumes by Jarry, Bonnard, Vuillard, Sérusier, and Toulouse-Lautrec (not a bad team) could be reproduced, as could the music by Claude Terrasse. There are so many accounts of the acting that even the performances could be approximated.

Larry Sloan's direction is completely witless, and Douglas Stein's set, which looks like a fancy college swimming pool with the water drained out of it—or simply transferred to the adaptation—makes no sense, let alone inspired nonsense. Susan Hilferty's costumes sadly display a few traces of their prototypes in watered-down versions, and Stephen Strawbridge's lighting would be more suited to an operating theater. Most distressing is the acting, except for that of Christopher Durang (who quit early) as Ubu's conscience, a role grafted on from one of Jarry's weaker sequels, *Ubu cocu*. Durang has amusingness built into his very being; you can no more resist smiling at him than at a Saint Bernard puppy, and few puppies have his talent. In the lackluster cast, Oliver Platt, as Ubu, is poorest: no comic heft, no vermiculate grandeur, no arias of sneaky bestiality—only oily sniveling and inapposite boyishness.

The Lady in Question

Charles Busch wrote *The Lady in Question* and, as is his wont, plays the female lead. The offering is co-produced by Kyle Renick, of the WPA Theatre, and the show's director, Kenneth Elliott, who also plays one of the male leads and, as an old college friend, was co-founder with Busch of Theatre-in-Limbo. He directed their first production, *Vampire Lesbians of Sodom*, now in its fifth year. The actors in *Lady* are all members of Theatre-in-Limbo; there is a care-free cottage-industry spirit informing the proceedings.

The plot is a takeoff on old Hollywood melodramas about Nazism. It concerns the great actress Raina Aldric ("all dreck"?), ill, wheelchair-ridden, and imprisoned by the Nazis, who want to destroy her because of her appearance in an anti-Nazi play. Professor Mittelhoffer and his nubile daughter, Heidi, are trying to rescue her, but they need the aid of someone in Baron von Elsner's *Schloss* in the Bavarian Alps: its underground passages connect with the prison whence Raina is to be sprung. Baron von Elsner (Kenneth Elliott) is himself a Nazi, albeit rather less redoubtable than his cigar-chomping, termagant mother, Augusta (Meghan Robinson, who doubles as Raina), or his vicious little blonde-pigtailed niece, Lotte (Andy Halliday, in the other drag part). To complicate matters, both Heidi (Theresa Marlowe) and Lotte are in love with Karel (Why not Karl? A Sudeten German?) Freiser (Robert Carey), an S.A. man by the looks of his rather fanciful uniform.

Fresh from the United States is Professor Erik Maxwell (Arnie Kolodner), who seems to profess nothing more than perilously loudmouthed hatred of the Nazis. He is Raina's son, long separated from his mother and eager to help in her escape. He gets himself invited to the baron's *Schloss* along with two American women traveling in Bavaria: Gertrude Garnet (pronounced "Garnay" and played by Busch), a renowned pianist on a concert tour, and her wisecracking companion, Kitty, Countess de Borgia (Julie Halston). In truth, they are ex-vaudevillians, except that the former Gertie Garnet (pronounced "Garnett") has become a genuine concert pianist, whereas Kitty is a distinctly fake countess. (On the other hand, she's a real woman.) The time is 1940, but actually the timeless time of drag shows, which, in one guise or another, have thrived ever since guys would be dolls.

The plot, need we say, chronicles the awakening of Gertrude from a vain, selfish, loveless artist into a freedom fighter, Erik Maxwell—lover and *mensch*, to use a Bavarian term. The production is neither quite high nor quite low camp—perhaps middle camp, some of the performers putting it on pretty thick while others lean toward thin. The verbal humor is meager: Gertrude's asking the baron to show her his magnificent *schlong*... er... *Schloss* is a fairly typical example. There is a trifle more humor in Busch's and Halliday's female impersonations. Busch calls his Garnet "Norma Shearer with a little bit of Greer Garson thrown in for affectation"; I see it more as Joan Crawford with a little bit of Lynn Bari thrown in. Andy Halliday, who is not very feminine, is amusing partly because of that and partly because of his role and getup, which make of him Patty McCormack with a little bit of Jane Withers thrown in for affection.

The spectators, mostly men with other men, have a ball. Some of them, I observed, were rocked by transports of footstomping ecstasy; others talked back at the stage, like the youth behind me, who, upon Gertrude's line over the prostrate Baron, "And before him trembled all of Schaffhausen," gasped "Tosca!" It is certainly one happy audience, moved by that emotional unison Jules Romains called *unanimisme*. It makes one wonder: is this kind of commu-

nal joy to be had nowadays only in minority theater? Homosexual
audiences at drag shows, black audiences at plays by blacks, and so
on? No harm in this, except that I miss the grand old function of
theater: the uniting of all sorts of people in their shared humanity,
transcending factions. Or was there never really such a theater, save
in our wishful thinking and self-deceiving memories?

To me, the most interesting thing about *The Lady in Question*
is a device used by almost all the performers: that of suddenly and
gratuitously becoming hysterical and yelling, hissing, shrieking
out a few lines. Theresa Marlowe does this most often and, to my
taste, least appetizingly. It does suggest, though, that underlying
the relatively decorous surface—the hero and heroine never even
kiss—there is something else. Anger? Contempt? A need to pretend
to lose control for the sake of at least mild outrageousness? In Busch
himself, this takes a somewhat different form: he does not become
frenetic so much as simply drop the pretense of femininity and
turn—fleetingly, incongruously—male. The trouble with all this is
merely that both performers and audience seem to accept it as the
supreme form of wit.

Privates on Parade

What a marvelous play—musical—show Peter Nichols's *Privates
on Parade* is, and how nearly impossible to get across to a standard
American audience. It is so full of English history, theatrical history, and social commentary, of army slang and other Britishisms,
that it would tax even the most sophisticated New York theatergoers, let alone the good folks who subscribe to the Roundabout. No
wonder a number of them walked out during the second act (if not
sooner), yet what a fine thing they were missing! My heart goes out
to everyone: to the Roundabout, which cannot really be blamed for
the incurable acoustics of its theater; to the cast, doing its damnedest with those difficult accents; to the absent playwright, who has
written such a smashing play only to lose much of it in transit; to
the befuddled viewers, even though some audibly enjoy themselves;
and to myself, trying to sell this show to you while having to admit
how hard it is to follow.

I wonder how many people in the audience understand the double entendre in the title (which is not the one, by the way, Nichols

would have chosen) *Privates on Parade*, i.e., "genitals on display"? In any case, this is the story of a bunch of men and one woman civilian in an entertainment unit of the British army in Singapore, 1948. That was the beginning of the Malayan Emergency, a run-through for the Vietnam war, during which British and colonial forces tried to hold the Malayan peninsula and Singapore against some 5,000 Chinese Communists, who managed to harass them until the Communist state of Malaysia came about.

Here, then, are Major Giles Flack, an eccentric army regular; Acting Captain Terri Dennis, an unemployed pantomine actor and self-styled raving queen; Sergeant Major Reg Drummond, ex-bobby, bully, secret trader of arms and supplies to the Communists, pimp of young Malayan boys to army personnel, and lover of the aforementioned civilian, Sylvia Morgan; Sylvia herself, an Anglo-Indian dancer, also a part-time prostitute, and more British than the king; Private Steven Flowers (the author's stand-in), a twenty-year-old virgin and nice small-town boy, who wants to become a teacher, has been transferred here from an Intelligence unit, and is suspected by Reg of spying on his activities, even though Steven, a former clerk, wouldn't begin to know how.

The group further includes Leading Aircraftman Eric Young-Love, bespectacled, homely, and yearning for his fiancée in Blighty, Corporal Len Bonny, accordionist turned quartermaster, an army regular with a wife back home; his lover (Len likes to be taken care of), Lance Corporal Charles Bishop, a confirmed homosexual but, unlike Terri, a guilt-ridden one; and Flight-Sergeant Kevin Cartwright, an ordinary sort of bloke who has had a number of women but never a white one. Two native servants, Lee and Cheng, perform a variety of roles, including some that are scary. Red, brown, yellow, white, and true-blue in skin and/or ideology, they are a motley crew, and Nichols, who served with such a unit, fashioned them in part out of observed reality.

Privates is about the everyday interaction of these characters, which includes Steven's initiation by Sylvia into love and sex; about what happens to all of them in what is, after all, a war; and about the musical numbers they put on for mighty strange audiences, not least a regiment of Gurkhas who don't understand beans. Nichols achieves—comically, gravely, brilliantly—the total interpenetration of routine army life with its absurdities, army shows with their sentimental escapism and transvestite humor, and the reality of war with its maiming and dying. Metaphors become real: the *warfare* of love, the *theater* of war, the brave *show* put on in life as on the stage. It's more than Pirandellian: illusion and reality don't merely get mixed up, they lose all meaning in a world where craziness enfolds craziness, chaos without end.

It's amazing how little it takes Nichols to create a character: a couple of sentences, a gesture or footling action, an attitude, and, presto magico, there's a person—and one to care about. If only the production, estimable as it is, were better yet. The main problem is the Roundabout's budget: though not a great deal of scenery is required, even the modest demands remain unmet—no fault of that good designer Loren Sherman. The costumes, by Lindsay W. Davis, should be tacky, and are; Denis King's zesty music is performed plausibly. Larry Carpenter has directed well on the whole, although some moments could register more strongly. Jim Dale does splendidly by Terri Dennis's funny and outrageous sides, less well by his heart. Simon Jones's fine Major Flack could have, for my taste, a touch more lunacy, as John Cleese's did in the excellent movie version. The rest are solid, especially John Curry (Charles) and the invaluable Donna Murphy.

Love Letters

The epistolary novel having existed all along, it is scant surprise that epistolary plays should pop up now and then. What could be more appealing to an actor and actress than, wearing their own best clothes on a nearly empty stage, with nothing to distract the gaze from them, to read an exchange of letters between two articulate epistolists? True enough, if the correspondents are, for example, Bernard Shaw and Mrs. Pat Campbell or Abélard and Héloïse (even though their letters are forgeries, they're good ones). It is nice, too, for us to get at other people's private letters without having to steam them open.

But the letters, whether historic or fictional, have to be written by persons or characters with lively enough minds to scratch onto paper things more profound or passionate, more intense or revealing, more exquisitely phrased, than oral utterance could muster. If it is an epistolary novel, let it be as racy as, say, *Humphry Clinker* or *Les Liaisons dangereuses*, the second of which was fairly effectively posted to the stage. Always, though, the letter must do something more than the speaker could or would; in A. R. Gurney's *Love Letters*, the missives seem often to accomplish less.

This is the story of Andrew Makepeace Ladd III and Melissa Gardner from our own Gothic North, who meet in second grade at a New England school; marry or bed others, except for one brief but significant interlude; keep yearning, consciously or not, for each other; and exchange letters, letters, letters. Andy comes from a good but not wealthy family; Melissa's folks are immensely rich. He goes to boys' schools he thrives at, culminating in Yale and Skull and Bones; Melissa kicks around a variety of girls' schools and junior college, all of which she hates. In her letters, she keeps teasing Andy about favoring institutions where he can be off with the boys; she does this with particular gusto when those institutions become the Navy and U.S. Senate. That persistent, mocking leitmotiv can be quite a bore.

This is not to suggest, however, that Gurney is anything less than a pro. His Melissa, drinking too much and moderately promiscuous, is recognizably and believably the poor little rich girl we have recognized and disbelieved in life; his Andy, the determined Wasp without much sting, the busy bee rather short on honey, we have known and shaken our heads over. But there are elements in their story that jibe neither with their characters nor with the laws of probability, lax as these have become. When Andy finally leaves Japan and the Japanese woman he very nearly married, it seems incredible that he wouldn't visit Melissa Stateside, but rush instead into marriage with someone else. It is no less hard to accept that he—no professional writer of any kind—would be so fanatical about letter writing, even finding various excuses for bypassing the phone, Melissa's protests notwithstanding. There are, in short, too many instances where the author or the form dictates to the characters rather than, as in the best works, the other way around.

But then, for all its humaneness, intelligence, and judicious blend of gaiety and gravity, *Love Letters* is not so much a play as a capital exercise for actors. Accordingly, a number of luminaries have already had a crack at playing these parts during the show's intermittent previous performances; for its current eight-week run, eight starry couples have been engaged, each for one week. I caught the opening team, Stockard Channing and John Rubinstein. The director, who remains the same, is John Tillinger, and he has cleverly seated the pair next to each other at a weighty hardwood table in massive armchairs—rather than, as customary, at slightly angled music stands on opposite ends of the stage. Thus, while artfully appearing to be reading from their scripts, they are always in full simultaneous view, and we can delight concurrently in action and reaction.

There are many pregnant silences, too—enough to provide a whole directorial obbligato, and Tillinger has orchestrated them soundly. I only wish he could have talked Gurney out of the last bit, where one of the correspondents chatters on posthumously. It may have worked for Thornton Wilder and a couple of others, but in this context it rings distressingly cute. Are there to be no more unhappy endings anywhere except in real life?

John Rubinstein gives a thoroughly decent performance, helped greatly by that neither-young-nor-old quality enabling him to span the decades with pleasing plausibility. Stockard Charming, however, is magnificent, with her dancing eyes, her mouth as moldable as Plasticine, her desperate hopefulness and disconsolate humor. Still, given the tour-de-force nature of the show, I couldn't help wishing to see all eight pairs of actors the same night for about fifteen minutes apiece.

Orpheus Descending

No sooner have folks finished doing in Tennessee Williams with his terrible late plays than, doggone it, they start digging up his terrible early ones. Peter Hall launched his new bi-continental acting company with Vanessa Redgrave in Williams's *Orpheus Descending*, and having scored with it in London, where it must have made it on its crazy southern exoticism, decided to bless New York with it next. I wonder what freighter or cargo plane was sturdy enough not to sink or crash under the weight of all that symbolism, under which the stage of the Neil Simon Theater risks imminent collapse.

A reworking of *Battle of Angels*, which failed in 1940, *Orpheus Descending*, which failed in 1957, was a favorite of Williams's, to be tinkered with for seventeen years if you count only the rewrites, for a lifetime if you count all the recyclings of its plot and characters. The story is archetypal Williams: how quick, bright things come to confusion in this merciless, materialistic world in which "there's just two kinds of people, the ones that are bought and the buyers," as Val Xavier, the itinerant musician and Jack-of-all-trades-and-

Jills, tells Lady Torrance, the young-middle-aged wife of a vicious dry-goods-store owner dying upstairs of cancer. But perhaps there is a way out: maybe "there's a kind that's never been branded," or a beautiful, tiny, light-blue bird, diaphanous enough for hawks not to see it and so airy that it doesn't have legs with which to alight on earth—it just sleeps on the wind.

Such winged, legless creatures are "the fugitive kind," like Val, like Lady's image of herself, like rich, aristocratic Carol Cutrere, no longer in the first blush of nymphomania, who drives up and down the Dixie Highway, "juking" all night. They know that there is "something wild in the country"—or was, before the country "broke out sick with neon": wild things that leave their "clean skins" and "white bones" behind, to pass on to other fugitive kinders, even though they, like all of us, are sentenced "to solitary confinement inside our own lonely skins." The play is awash in this sort of overwrought, overloaded imagery; why, that light-blue bird alone alights on the dialogue some half-dozen times—not bad for a legless metaphor. But the metaphors are as nothing to the symbols: beautiful sky-blue automobiles with jammed steering wheels that skid all over the stage and collide like bumper cars. There's Val, who is Orpheus descending into hell with his guitar to rescue Lady, and also Christ (Xavier = Savior) dying on Easter Saturday to rise again in every other Williams play. Like Orpheus, he is torn to shreds by yapping women; like Christ, he is hounded to death by wicked men with dawgs and blowtorches, who, lest we miss the point, keep shouting, "Christ!" There is bird symbolism and snake symbolism (the latter only skin-deep); there is light and dark symbolism, fire and blowtorch symbolism, orchard and vineyard and (so help me!) barren-fig-tree symbolism. There is fruitful-womb and abortion symbolism, birth and rebirth symbolism, clown and conjure-man symbolism—exactly how much I can't tell you because I forgot to take my abacus along to the theater.

Mostly, though, there is overripe, hothouse, southern-gothic atmosphere with sexy men to die for and evil men to die from, with sex- or God-crazed women, gossiping banshees and knife-wielding goons, all in a viscous mass of poeticism, southernisms, sadomasochism in which a couple of soiled but innocent, lurid but lyrical, proletarian but poetically articulate lovers trash about but with their heads in—nay, above—the clouds. In Tennessee's best plays, this hellish-heavenly brew is sparingly indulged in; in the rest, there is enough of it to bog down a herd of rampaging buffalo.

To give Peter Hall his due, he might well have altered or short-ened some things—as Harold Clurman did in 1957, though with no great luck—but there is always that Lady (St.-Just, not Torrance), Tennessee's executrix, to overrule anyone who would drop a com-ma, let alone change an iota. So we get all those switches to ghostly lighting as characters start monologuizing at the audience, all that elaborate choreography outside the store windows that, given the set and lighting design, gets lost in the shuffle anyway. And all those invisible hounds obligingly baying transitions between scenes, and such absurdities as when Nurse Porter looks at Lady—or not even at Lady but at Val—and promptly pronounces Lady pregnant, thereby putting rabbit-test-makers out of business.

For good measure, though, Hall adds mistakes of his own, e.g., showing the men rousted out of their beds to chase Val in full KKK regalia, letting Miss Redgrave don a monkey mask or doff her clothes for a mini-nude scene. And Hall insists on all the minor characters' simply reeking of local color. There is also an ugly set by Alison Chitty with a cloud-striated sky between two skeletal poles, like a zebra skin hung out to dry; and a snakeskin jacket for Val (costumes likewise by Chitty) that looks like a begrimed bit of fabric torn off a Las Vegas lounge chair.

There might have been some real interest had Sir Peter's London company been brought over intact; but Miss Redgrave, apparently, insisted on American actors, though why she was willing to make an exception where she is concerned remains unclear. Her perfor-mance, fine actress though she is, is a mess. Too tall, too much a British schoolmarm, too well coiffed and gowned; too hard and brittle, too knowing in her comic delivery, too absurd with her musical-comedy Italian accent (a southern one may have been too difficult); too actressy for the plodding American cast that flaps around her ankles like a dropped skirt—Miss Redgrave trails the play behind her like clouds of shredded glory. It is a grand perfor-mance, but of the wrong part in the wrong play.

Kevin Anderson—baby-faced, baby-voiced, and as sexy as a toddler in a pram—is totally miscast as Val. He gives a dutiful per-formance that exudes no sex, no charm, no magnetism—not even animal litheness; but he does at times leap into the air or have a wall-banging fit in the best Steppenwolf acting style. I presume that he was cast either because he is the only young actor tall enough for Miss Redgrave or because he was good in *Orphans* and it was assumed that he would be as good in all plays containing the mystic tetragrammaton O-R-P-H. As Carol, Anne Twomey, always with a feather sticking out of her hair or hat (another legless bird?), is far too robust and invulnerable to be one of the fugitive kind, except perhaps from a chain gang. As Vee, the sheriff's visionary wife, Tammy Grimes is deranged enough, though unfortunately not in the Vee manner but in that of every other Grimes performance. In an otherwise undistinguished cast, Brad Sullivan, as Jabe, attracts attention with his ineptitude, Sloane Shelton, as Beulah, with her surprising believability.

Even the sound and light effects (by Paul Arditti and Paul Pyant, respectively) are desperately hyped-up. When a truck passes the Torrance store, it's like the Nazi invasion of Poland with tanks and flamethrowers. Worse yet is the electronic score by Stephen Edwards, which underlines specious poetry with fake music; oh, for the good old days when the likes of Paul Bowles and Ned Rorem scored Williams! Who would have thought that Orpheus could descend *this* low?

The Threepenny Opera

That modern classic, *The Threepenny Opera* of Brecht and Weill is changed, changed utterly in its present, supposedly faithful revival. Even the title, no doubt to oblige the poster designer's whim, has been turned into 3 Penny Opera, a piece of cheekiness to be ignored. To be ignored, too, is the rest of this Threepenny, whose only asset is Georgia Brown as Mrs. Peachum; the rest is very far from ginger- or Georgia-peachy.

The return to the original 1928 text is a good move; Brecht was a pathological diddler with his own works, and his rewritings—almost always substituting ideological gamesmanship for inspiration—are regularly for the worse. But the production's intended fidelity has been subverted in two ways. First, Julius Rudel beefed up the music from the original for eight-piece band to a less mordant, soupier and syrupier, Broadwayization for fifteen players. (Weill's own concert-hall suite for seventeen has no singing and is not meant for the theater.) Second, the text was cut, either lest suburbanites be inconvenienced by a late curtain or lest comfortable middle-class sensibilities be offended by, say, the gory details of how fake beggars play on the factitious generosity of liberal-capitalist humanitarians.

But there is worse. John Dexter, an often compelling director, strikes out here; for some reason, neither his head nor his heart seems to have been engaged. Back in 1956, Brecht congratulated Giorgio Strehler on the "fire and coolness" of his Milan production; here, everything is room-temperature. There is no inventiveness in the use of space, and there are such distracting curlicues as Ethyl Eichelberger's camping up of the Ballad Singer into something by Charles Ludlam out of Charles Busch, and Peter Gennaro's hapless choreography, which has Macheath in his cell carrying on like Baryshnikov as Gregor Samsa changed into a bug.

What few ideas there are feeble. The New York homeless emerging from and fading back into their crates is a far less powerful image (even if it were more forcefully executed) than some of Brecht's details of begging, criminal, police, and business activities—all ultimately interchangeable—that the production skimps on or whittles away. And although Jocelyn Herbert's notion of a skeletal set is sound, a skeleton wearing the Brighton Pavillion for a hat is sartorially incorrect. The lights (by Andy Phillips) are better, but can be only as good as the actors they illumine. And except for Miss Brown, who, abandoned by all hands, goes down like a gallant captain with the ship, the raggle-taggle cast is not worth the wattage expended.

My heart goes out to Nancy Ringham, though; having once replaced Rex Harrison's last Eliza at the eleventh hour, she now had to jump into the breach for Maureen McGovern, who, we learn, injured her throat singing these undemanding, abundantly miked numbers. Though Miss Ringham is hopeless as that iron butterfly, Polly, she has a pleasantly apple-cheeked voice that outstrips Sting's bland five-note vocal exercises all the way. With the cops after him rather than police backing him up, MacSting is a musical and histrionic zero. The brio, hauteur, menace, sinister charm that make up Mackie are all missing; instead, there is pallor, stiffness, inconspicuousness: Sting could give chameleons lessons on how to disappear into their surroundings. When he must plumb his private hell, he gives us no more than Morpheus descending. "Sting" should be pronounced with something a little harder than a G.

Equally devoid of personality is the Tiger Brown of Larry Marshall, a usually lively performer, who here comes across as a catatonic puppet anxiously scanning the horizon for a puppeteer. Worse yet is the Peachum of Alvin Epstein, an actor who always struck me as his own overeager understudy. He now croaks like a raven, struts like a pouter pigeon, and looks like an albino puffin—a performance of purely ornithological interest. As Lucy, Kim Criswell, though alive and kicking, exhibits vulgarity unredeemed by style. From the general torpor of Macheath's gang, only Josh Mostel (Matt) salvages a little spunk. The most mindless performance is that of Suzzanne Douglas, who confuses condescension with personality and would parlay a passel of pouts into Jenny's archetypal whoredom. As for the good Georgia Brown, her particular timbre suffers most from miking that pretends to discretion but is often aggressive.

Michael Feingold's translation is to be commended for trying to capture the spirit of the original, and chided for little liberties, cutenesses, and a smirking smuttiness replacing Brecht's visceral one. And it cannot resolve the real difficulties; thus Mackie's climactic "*Gerettet!*" (an amphibrach) that Blitzstein rendered with the flat-footed "Reprievèd!" now becomes the downright lame "rescùed!" More and more, I feel that Brecht's German, like Janáček's Czech, cannot be properly Englished, least of all if every cast member has a different accent. For this *Threepenny*, I wouldn't give you tuppence.

A Few Good Men

If you just let A Few Good Men wash over you, which seems to be its sole aim, you will be left constantly atingle, as by a first-rate shower head. A largely but not entirely fictitious story, it concerns the death of a Marine private at the U.S. Naval Base at Guantanamo Bay, Cuba. He may have died as part of the internal, illegal but traditional, disciplining of a sloppy soldier by his fellows. Or because he had been sending complaining letters to influential outsiders asking for a transfer, the disciplining order may have come from higher up. Or the corporal and PFC who worked him over, and are about to stand trial, may have wanted, or been ordered, to kill him.

A young Navy lawyer, Lieutenant J. G. Kaffee, has been appointed to the defense (perhaps because he is inexperienced) over the head of sexy and smart Lieutenant Commander Joanne Galloway, another lawyer, itching to get the case. In the event, she and Lieutenant J. G. Weinberg, a brand-new father, end up assisting Kaffee, a fox in sheep's clothing. There are flashbacks, trips to the camp, the Washington court-martial, and behind-the-scenes intrigue aplenty.

For a 28-year-old novice playwright, or anyone else, Aaron Sorkin has done a bang-up job, even if you allow for the substantial help he got from his director, Don Scardino, and a battery of experienced producers. Although everything is calculated for maximum effect, I hesitate to call it manipulative. Some of the characterizations are oversimplified, some of the plotting mechanistic, but a dose of human juice is there, too, and the tension is niftily interwoven with humor. There may, in fact, be too many, often very fetching, wisecracks—as if no one could qualify for armed service without passing a stand-up-comedy exam.

When, however, you consider how flawlessly the large cast interacts (well, maybe Geoffrey Nauffts overdoes the dumbness of a corporal on the witness stand), how utterly effective are the leads (Tom Hulce, Megan Gallagher, Stephen Lang, and Mark Nelson), how purposeful are Ben Edwards's plain scenery and Thomas R. Skelton's tricky lighting (with John Gromada's potent sound effects), how magisterially Don Scardino has directed every last little—or big—thing, you will concede that a few good men and one good woman have joined up to give us three cracklingly good hours of theater.

Yet a bad taste lingers in the mouth: it is all too neat, too comforting, too untrue. In what court-martial involving higher-ups has this much justice been done? When have all—prisoners, witnesses, lawyers—got exactly what they deserve? The play comes up with a dangerously reassuring solution that recent military and political history has given the consistent lie to. Good commercial theater, yes; truth, no. Art we must not even invoke.

The Circle

There are two qualities even more precious than intelligence, wisdom, and beauty: sense of humor and charm. Though—in the theater, at any rate—the former survives, however precariously, the latter is practically extinct. Charm, like poetry, cannot be defined; it can only be pointed to. So let me point to Somerset Maugham's 68-year-old comedy, The Circle. That is what charm is.

Let it be understood: charm is not a moral virtue or a guarantee of literary greatness; it is, however, a major aesthetic value. And it's elusive. In real life, it seems, Maugham had very little of it; but in a play such as this, which also has a sufficiency of humor and wit, the charm is superabundant. Some would-be witty lines, e.g., the one about Barbados "sound[ing] like a cure for flat feet," fall flat; some of the humor, say of Arnold Champion-Cheney M.P.'s compulsive repositioning of a chair that has been minimally displaced, is ridden too hard. But the charm never fails; you luxuriate in it as in a bath in a perfectly appointed tub, where the bubbles take the place of bons mots.

Stuffy Arnold and effervescent Elizabeth have been married three years. They live at Aston-Adey, their gorgeous house in Dorset, without children but with a butler and footman; it is 1921, and the century has come of age. Coming, too, are Lady Kitty, Arnold's delicious mother, who ran off to Italy with a lover when Arnold was five; and that lover, Lord Porteous, a most charming man, once prime minister presumptive and the immediate superior and best friend of Clive Champion-Cheney, the injured spouse. Elizabeth has invited them unbeknown to her husband, who hasn't seen his mother in 30 years; also at Aston-Adey is Clive, staying at the guest cottage. And there is Edward "Teddie" Luton, a young businessman now living in Malaya and clearly enamored of Elizabeth, who just may be reciprocating.

This is as much as you need to know. The story is slight and ever so fragile, but it has enough of everything save depth, weight, and consequence—the potential enemies of charm. Yet if you look and listen, you'll realize that under its airy inconsequentiality, it is not without lightly worn wisdom, casually sketched in but evergreen verities. Not for nothing did some of the most dazzling lights of the British theater appear in its various productions: Ernest Thesiger, Fay Compton, Leon Quartermaine, Celia Johnson, Nigel Playfair, Athene Seyler, John Gielgud, Yvonne Arnaud, and Leslie Banks constitute but a partial list.

The present revival, under Brian Murray's canny direction, respects that—and every other—tradition. Except that some of the parts are played by actors older (but not less charming) than called for, everything is in its place, like Arnold's furniture. This includes Desmond Heeley's set, Jane Greenwood's costumes, and John Michael Deegan's lighting; we might be back at the Haymarket in March 1921. Which means, first and foremost, the performances—every last one of them as fresh as a spring day in a sun-and-nostalgia-drenched yesteryear.

We should all of us be (though very few of us will) as endearingly sly, spry, and spiffy as Rex Harrison is at 81. He still moves like the most debonair of bon vivants, flashes that sweet-and-sour smile of his (equally good for seduction and sarcasm), and utters his lines as trippingly as a skilled child skipping rope. Only the walk is a bit slower, but is a leisurely stroll worse than a brisk constitutional? Glynis Johns, who used to bubble like champagne, now warms our palate like vintage wine—a fair trade-off—and doesn't just deliver her dialogue but also savors it, as we do. If she can't quite make us believe she is the age she's meant to be, she makes us believe something better—that irresistibility knows no season. My one cavil is that where Maugham correctly wrote "*as* I should have done," she allows the contemporary corruption *like* to creep in. Good grammar is grace under pressure.

The slight surprise and great joy of the evening is Stewart Granger's Clive: someone who was always a solid movie actor proves positively enchanting on the stage. At 76, he has stepped out of retirement as sparkling as a jet-setter off the Concorde, and the best I can say for him is that he earns the right, if Equity would allow it, to revert to his real name, James Stewart: he is easily as charming as Jimmy, and he doesn't write doggerel. Equally right is everyone else—well, the good Arnold of Robin Chadwick might be a bit more attractive. Harley Venton is a handsome, sturdy, impassioned Teddie, and the adorably husky-sounding Roma Downey reminds me of the young Glynis Johns—is there higher praise?

There is one minor quarrel I have with Murray's otherwise impeccable staging. Both Harrison and Granger indulge in mannerisms easily removable. Sir Rex has a way of putting a hand to his face in mock despair; Granger tends to extend a didactic index finger with which to impale his interlocutor. It's surely not too late for Murray to clean up two such splendid performances.

Criticism from
the 1990s

The Merchant of Venice

When the Prince of Aragon arrives to woo Portia by trying to choose the one among three caskets that has her picture in it, his minstrels, in this production of *The Merchant of Venice* by the Peter Hall Company, wear the oddest costume. It is the ludicrous garb the Spanish Inquisition inflicted on the heretics it burned at the stake, dunce cap and all, but with the added bizarreness of large red tongues of flame forming an ornamental border around the hems of their white penitential gowns. Not only is this concept disgusting in its decorative cruelty, it is also dumb: why would a suitor remind Portia of the horrors being perpetrated in his country, as if they were a tourist attraction?

It is in such stupid clevernesses that Peter Hall's mounting of Shakespeare's fairy-tale comedy—with serious overtones—abounds. For example, whereas this *Merchant*, as initially presented in London, contained only two spittings (Antonio on Shylock and, later, vice versa), it is now a four-and-a-half-spit play, the half a particularly gross and loud summoning up of spittle in somebody's throat that, finally, does not get disgorged. Or consider how, after Chris Dyer's ingenious sets have duly dazzled us by the speed, cunning, and handsomeness with which they transform the stage from austere Venice to idyllic Belmont and back, they come a cropper when they should rise to a climax. Lorenzo is about to launch on his great "How sweet the moonlight sleeps upon this bank" speech and introduce one of Shakespeare's most poetic and rapturous nocturnes.

The scenery, which has thus far worked its magic by things sliding in and out of the wings, now pulls a switch: the entire back flies up to reveal—a plain blue backcloth. No starry sky, no vegetation, and certainly no bank to sit on. So the actors must join the sweet-sleeping moonlight on the bare floor.

That is perverse, like so much else about this production, which, granted, does not indulge in the major current aberration of setting the play in the calculatedly most unlikely time and place but makes up for this with a barrage of minor absurdities, such as turning Portia into an experienced, almost phlegmatic, woman of the world, and Bassanio into a green Venetian schoolboy with canals not in his ears but behind them. Again, it has been growingly irritating to watch Shakespearean casts dash onto and off the stage at ever more athletic clips: here it is as if the entire company were practicing for an Olympic relay even when merely moving from one part of the stage to another.

Ideas are spewed up with great rapidity, and equally quickly forgotten. Thus Antonio is turned into a Christ figure in hairstyle, clothing, demeanor (the way he bares and offers his chest suggests Christ the Pelican proffering his breast to his offspring to feed on), and Shylock becomes an image of the Jews clamoring for the blood of Jesus. This is not followed through, however, any more than is, for example, the by now commonplace suggestion of homosexual love between Antonio and Bassanio. But it is with Shylock that the production crumbles.

The only way one can explain Shylock is that Shakespeare set out to write a typical Jewish villain of the kind that kindled the audience imagination primed by contemporary political and literary analogues. But, being Shakespeare, he came to understand the humanity of the Jew and the inhumanity of the Christians' treatment of him, so that he produced something much more moving than intended, even if inconsistent. Dustin Hoffman and Peter Hall stress Shylock's differentness; he is a decent person whose woes stem from his being a despised outsider condemned to the hated trade of money-lending. They tend to overlook that Shylock is also a comically villainous figure, and that his mode of retaliation is no better than his provocation. In this grotesquely dog-eat-dog world, the Christian curs and the Jewish mongrel are equally, though diversely, reprehensible—and also, thanks to Shakespeare's humanity, forgivable.

Hoffman has never played an unsympathetic role. His characters may achieve lovableness late in the game, but achieve it they must (think of *Midnight Cowboy* or *Rain Man*); otherwise, it is no go. And given the troubled history of *Merchant* (banning in some American schools, protests against various productions), it is safer, with an eye to the box office, to present a Shylock driven to terrible extremes, suffering indignities with scarcely more than a grapefruit-in-the-face smile, and attaining at least comic grandeur as a redoubtable knife sharpener.

As John Palmer has written, the play "suggests for the first time on any stage that the Jew has a case." For something more, a sage and noble Jew, one had to wait close to a couple of centuries for the work of a German: Lessing's *Nathan the Wise*. But to judge from overheard comments, the audience still perceives the play as anti-Semitic and Dustin Hoffman's vocally undernourished performance as capital.

When it comes to problems of voice and demeanor, the curiously skulking, listing, and singsong Antonio of Leigh Lawson, too, has plenty of those. Geraldine James is a strong, commanding Portia, so much so that her tender feelings, insofar as she will muster them, ring almost false. Her arms, moreover, are given to sawing out a pound of air at moments of excitement. Nathaniel Parker's Bassanio is merely boyish, but Richard Garnett's callow Lorenzo is a near-nonentity. Francesca Buller is a diminutive but perky Jessica, much preferable to the bouncy-butterball Nerissa of Julia Swift. The Gobbos, young and old, are dutiful and dull, but Michael Siberry is a full-bodied Gratiano, loutish and impressive at once, the most striking presence here.

In the vastly exaggerated casket scenes, Michael Carter manages an amusing Aragon; Herb Downer, a merely risible Morocco. As the Duke of Venice, the seasoned Basil Henson is bigger than the sum of his part. Robert Lockhart's music is hell-bent on being different, dramatic, and various, at all of which it succeeds, though less so than at sounding ugly. There remains, however, the music of Shakespeare's language, clearly enunciated by a mostly British and duly trained cast, an all too rare pleasure hereabouts.

Lear

What would you cast a small, obese, unsightly, classically untrained, moderately untalented, ill-spoken actress who says, "I don't like Shakespeare's plays, they don't interest me as an actor [note the masculine gender]" as? Why, naturally, as Lear. You would, that is, if you were Lee Breuer, one of the most pretentious and ungifted writer-directors in America, and if said actress—oops—actor were your wife, Ruth Maleczech. The reason for this *Lear* was that, as R.M. puts it, "Lear's language seduced me." But is that any reason, I ask you, for raping Shakespeare?

Because none of the actors in the Mabou Mines company, among whose founders are the Breuers—and none of the pickup actors from other, similarly inspired, companies—can speak Shakespeare's language or enunciate properly, two remedies were found: the scene was shifted to rural Georgia, circa 1959, and the actors wear microphones that, being of the cheap kind, look like life-support tubes stuck into their noses. As these assorted no-talents whisper or shriek into their microphones (you never know who is speaking), the moribund production makes at least a fairly compelling argument for euthanasia.

A few little changes had to be made in this "light" adaptation, as the Mabous call it. All the male characters had to be switched to females, all the female ones turned into males. The Fool has become a transvestite in a mink coat and carries a hand mike shaped like a penis (or "penile," as a cultural reporter in the *Times* calls it, though civilized dictionaries do not admit the word) and keeps referring to his "dildo"—not, of course, in the "lightly" adapted original text. Other changes in this "light" adaptation excise all references to kingship and substitute ones derogatory to capitalism, under which Mabou Mines has been thriving (grants from both public and private sectors, workshops at prestigious institutes and colleges, you name it). As Breuer puts it, "We're always learning new things about Shakespeare. It doesn't matter whether they are true or not, it matters whether they turn on my imagination." Some things are better left turned off.

The Georgia farm country of the late fifties is an ideal place for Mabou to indulge its camp sensibilities. The dresses, shoes, coiffures, cars (two automotive replicas rattle around the stage) of the period are, of course, sheer heaven, and the presence of such Ludlamite actors as Lola Pashalinski and Black-Eyed Susan elicits squeals of ecstasy from the audience.

Breuer explains that he was trying to show "the relationship between love and power as it confronts women in America today." But how does that apply to rural Georgia in '59? No big mamas there, like this Lear, without their big daddies; no mixed black-and-white families (a bow to the current fad for nontraditional casting); no mink-coat-wearing transvestites in the service of big mamas, etc. And how does all of this relate to "America today… with men as colonists and women as the colonized"? If anything, this dictatorial female Lear is the colonist bossing around her sons; for women feeling colonized, you would have to go back to a play called *King Lear*, by W. Shakespeare.

The acting is execrable throughout, on a par with the rest of the invention. At the first intermission—which, alas, didn't come till Act III, I beat a salutary retreat. From what I read about the production, four years in the uxorious Mr. Breuer's making, I passed up many wonders—for example, the scene where the poor Fool is hanged by Georgia rednecks ("hung," as the aforementioned *Times* cultural correspondent puts it). So, too, I missed the scene on the "deserted pitch 'n' putt range" and the final one at a "trash dump," though I hope someday to find the entire production there. Lear's knights, by the way, have been "lightly" changed into dawgs here, Ma Lear being a cynophile. Some three or four canines are actually yapping around (along with the odd woolly doggie Lear carries in her bosom—I expected a line such as "How sharper than a mongrel's tooth…" but was frustrated even in this modest wish), these mutts being the only natural actors here, and the only ones whose bark carries without amplification. They also look better than the rest of the cast.

It is comforting to know that this garbage has received grants from the Rockefeller Foundation, the Wexner Center, the Jerome Foundation, the Reader's Digest/Wallace Fund, Philip Morris, the National Endowment for the Arts (Jesse Helms, where are you when we need you?), and the New York State Council on the Arts. And especially from AT&T, which has funded some of the choicest trash in recent years and has been running huge ads with Ruth Maleczech's gussied-up visage, the copy stating that this is "the latest example of our 50-year commitment to the arts." I'm afraid AT&T would not know an art if it fell over it.

Sex, Drugs, Rock & Roll

Eric Bogosian and his monologues, entitled this time *Sex, Drugs, Rock & Roll*, are a phenomenon in the process of becoming an institution. We expect them as we do the annual concert of some beloved singer, the yearly book of some favorite fertile novelist. Is Bogosian the Pavarotti of the nonmusical theater or the Ed Doctorow of the boards? Or is he simply the updated reincarnation of Lenny Bruce?

Greatly and bilaterally talented, Bogosian writes as well as he acts, acts as sharply as he writes. Finally, you don't know whether a brilliant piece of business—the way one of his characters scratches himself: where, for how long, in what sort of counterpoint with his talk—is acting or writing. Or when another character tilts his head at a special angle (is there a storyboard for this?), the shape of the accompanying silence, its reflection on what was or is about to be said—is this acting or a smartly written stage direction?

Clever and often devastating as is the dialogue, in which we hear one speaker and divine the other, you can't quote it without the expressions, inflections, movements that go with it. Bogosian is a one-man band whose instruments are pen, visage, voice, body, and space—the locales the monologues carve out of it: the edge of a costly swimming pool over which its arriviste proprietor brandishes his Havana cigar; the scatter-pillowed den on whose floor a yoga-positioned pseudo-artist bogarts his joint as he propounds his paranoid philosophy about computers taking over; the sky-high-tech office in which a monstrously upward-mobile businessman handles with versatile disingenuousness the variety of calls stacked on his phone like inbound planes at an international airport. Always the character comes complete with, captured inside, his framing ambience.

Even if Bogosian gives you no story, his gallery of characters—all male, but telling us not a little about their women—proves a living tapestry with no shortage of figures in the carpet. The range is not enormous: from a smug British rock singer being interviewed on television to some two-bit disk jockey flipping out into his mike, from a homeless panhandler to an irate bag man, from a vaunting sexual athlete to a brash tycoon, from this shabby loser to that shady winner, the distance is not great, and has been covered by Bogosian before. Yet it is amazing how much of our society he can squeeze into it, ever new or at least newly horrible.

But what is almost more astounding than the deadly accuracy of these honest poison-pen sketches—the amount of piercing detail is dizzying—is the ability of the performer to transform himself utterly into another character in the twinkling of a merciless eye. This is a quick-change artist working entirely without costumes—well, he may take off a jacket or roll up a sleeve—but the essential transformation is in the voice clambering up or skidding down octaves and changing accents along the way, in the eyes caving in or bulging out, in the drawstrings of the mouth pulled viciously taut or slackened to cretinous looseness. A new man emerges from the ashes of the previous one, flares up for his brief moment, and is flicked back to ash as Bogosian chainsmokes his creations.

What makes these characters particularly arresting is our not knowing what to make of them. Is the author mocking them and enlisting our mockery in support? Or is he mocking us, for presuming to feel superior to them? Is he endorsing their "Fuck you!" (often voiced, sometimes mute) flung at the world? Most likely it is love-hate for them, for us, even for himself (for bothering) that motivates this protean protozoan. This is no gently ribbing Ruth Draper, no mischievously crowd-pleasing Lily Tomlin; this is Eric Bogosian, spiky, stinging, caustic without cauterizing.

And funny. Take his southern-accented barfly Casanova, who tells us in one unblinking word where his strength lies: he's "endowed." The dimension and duration of his performance devastates women with pleasure; other men's dream is his quotidian reality. His hunting grounds are the tony financial-district bars with those sexy Wall Street women, good from their big bow ties all the way down to their Adidas footgear, who provide strange beds in which he (and they) come to two hours later, transfigured by transient bliss. The women may end it the next day (he's not ashamed to admit it), or *he* may a few days later. Some are inconsolable. One of them is even supposed to have drowned herself, though he can't say for sure—he wasn't there. The macho monster has his craftsmanly conscientiousness about his work, a pride neither falsely modest nor falsely immodest.

John Arnone's minimal but crafty set helps, as does Ian Kroeze's lighting, which limns a face angrily or bathes it in acquiescence. Though a director (Jo Bonney) is credited, the rest is Bogosian or, rather, that battery of multiform Bogosians battering down whatever delusions and self-deceptions we may still have clung to until his command: cling no more!

Prelude to a Kiss

When in the opening scene of a play the middle-aged host and hostess copulate on the floor and no one pays the slightest attention, we know that reality is not where it's at. When the heroine is almost always needlessly barefoot in Act 1, and always shod in Act II, we know that some sort of fancy stylization (perhaps directorial) is afoot. But when throughout no one drinks just beer but always only Molson's, and, furthermore—in a bar, at home, anywhere—never out of a glass but straight from the bottle, we suspend our belief, not our disbelief.

Craig Lucas's *Prelude to a Kiss* is a fantasy, which is fine (think of *Peter Pan*, for example), but it is a mendacious, meretricious fantasy, which is bad. Even the title lies: the play is the postlude to a kiss, but that would not jibe with what Ella Fitzgerald is singing in the background (an elaborately captious score often drowns out the actors). If the play were an honest fantasy, I wouldn't divulge certain plot points—you'd never learn from me whether Tinker Bell lives or dies—but when the author counts on gentlemanly silence from the critics to get away with his unscrupulousness, I say the hell with that.

In *Prelude*, a sick old man with only months to live stumbles onto a suburban wedding, kisses the bride, and forthwith exchanges inner identities with her. Much to the bewilderment of Peter, the groom, Rita, the bride, behaves queerly during their Jamaican honeymoon; back in New York, through a number of slips, Rita betrays her true identity: she is the Old Man in Rita's body—he wanted to enjoy youth and passion once more before dying. Eventually, the real Rita, in the Old Man's shape, moves in with Peter, and they have a pretty nice marriage going, but—as is protested a bit too coyly—no sex. There's more, but this is quite enough.

The Old Man, though it is never stated, is homosexual, else he would become Peter, so as to enjoy Rita's lovemaking. (Note, by the way, that "Rita" and "Peteah" rhyme, so as to enhance the confusion of genders). Instead, he/she goes on a honeymoon with handsome Peter (Alec Baldwin), buys herself expensive trinkets charged to Rita's father, and proves only too willing to give up his/her job as a bartender and let Peter bring home the bacon. (But why would the educated, comfortably middle-class Rita have worked as a barkeep in the first place?) The fake Rita self-betrayingly refers to her dentist father as a surgeon; why, having boned up on the real Rita's diaries, would she make such mistakes? The answer here, as elsewhere, is that this is a logicless play for an MTV audience that never connects the dots between dotty moments.

A hokey charade, then, whose chief purposes are to mock heterosexual relationships and to satisfy cravings for the unobtainable heterosexual male, without concern for minimal structural consistency. Thus Peter says to Rita (who now inhabits the Old Man's body) that he misses her "little white feet"; whereupon the Old Man (i.e., Rita) holds up his and inquires cutely, "What? You don't like these?" Yet if that seeming Old Man were really Rita, she/he would say something like "So do I." But Lucas has no intention to be anything but cutely mischievous all the way, without even making fantasy-sense. Again, would the fake Rita (if there were no hidden agenda) give "herself away by discussing with Peter how she prefers the term "hole" to "crack," adding that she really likes "hole and dick," then consider his suggestion, "slit," only to exclaim, after some reflection, "Tool I like"?

Norman René, Lucas's longtime collaborator, piles his directorial archness on top of the text's. In the Jamaica scene, he introduces a static but suggestive nonspeaking baler; into an ordinary bar scene, he sticks a conspicuous and gratuitous transvestite; throughout, there is a campily trompe-l'oeil window with a repertoire of irrelevant, off-the-wall prospects. Yet he does not see fit to make the "male" Rita's manner any different from the female one's. Granted, the actress playing Rita would make this difficult: pretty Mary-Louise Parker has developed a goony, bug-eyed look, a toothily sheepish grin, an anserine waddle, and a sort of deliquescent baby voice that make her weird right from the start.

Baldwin is good as Peter, but the author has him incessantly addressing the spectators—sometimes in the middle of a speech to another character—a hoary device that has been milked to death in recent dramaturgy; it serves mostly to help lazy playwrights over scenes that would take real ability to dramatize properly. Barnard Hughes enlists his considerable skill and charm to make the Old Man as sweet as possible; Debra Monk, Larry Bryggman, and John Dossett do nicely in supporting parts, unconvincingly written and directed though they be. The production values, notably Loy Arcenas's décor, are as accomplished as usual at Circle Rep.

The climactic piece of dental-dramatic advice is the Old Man's Parthian shot: "The next time, floss!" Indeed, flossiness is all, and if you enjoy two and a half hours of smart-ass chatter and campy subversion—e.g., the honeymoon lament "It's a real busman's holiday with you around: you could fuck up a wet dream!" this may be your cup of… whatever. What is fantasy for? Presumably to fulfill some innocent universal yearnings: to fly like the other Peter and never grow old, to be fabulously wealthy and work philanthropic wonders with your money, to live on a desert island in harmony with a loved one. But what kind of wholesome longings does *Prelude to a Kiss* satisfy?

The Grapes of Wrath

The Grapes of Wrath, in Chicago's Steppenwolf production, has at last reached New York; may it be received more hospitably than Steinbeck's Okies were by California. My reservations should not keep anyone from treading to these grapes.

It is, of course, a bit cheeky to turn a well-known novel into a play, and downright insolent when that book has been turned into a beloved, unforgettable film. It can be countered that few today read books, and that Frank Galati's stage version sticks closer to Steinbeck's novel than did John Ford's movie. Whereupon it can be argued that the multitudes that don't read books are probably the same ones that avoid serious theater, and that, however faithful, an under-three-hours play cannot but decimate a hefty novel. Still, there must be enough people left who want to see a play that has something to say and knows how to say it. I hope so; I do hope so.

The key to this enterprise, which Galati also directed, is understatement. Scenery is sparing, music is functional, emotions—as far as possible and perhaps further—are reined in. The Joad truck may be emblematic: basically realistic, it is nevertheless foreshortened, and its wheels do not touch ground. Nothing in this production is fundamentally unreal; and it is (perhaps owing to the unions' prohibitive price for overtime) rather too short; but, oh, how it soars! Although there is much humor, this is a play about deprivation, anguish, suffering; yet these characters have no more learned how to wallow in emotions than they have learned courtly etiquette or correct grammar. All they have—in great, stammering tongue-tied excess—is rending humanity.

Kevin Rigdon's scenery sovereignly conveys the four elements.

Actual water and fire are put to magnificent uses; air and earth are evoked less literally, by highly suggestive abstract design. But it is with his lighting that the excellent Rigdon really scores: other designers light people and objects; he manages also to light space. Erin Quigley's costumes look acutely right; Rob Milburn's sound is exemplary. And Michael Smith's music, besides being good country music, shifts scenery, produces sound effects, creates a landscape, and furthers the plot.

Even though some roles are no longer filled by Steppenwolves, the large company is an ensemble with only two weak links. Mark Deakins does not quite succeed in limning the underwritten part of Connie Rivers, and Robert Breuler's Pa both looks and sounds soft and flabby, which is at least one soft flabbiness too many. But there is extraordinarily satisfying, stripped-to-the-essentials work from Rick Snyder, Nathan Davis, Jeff Perry, James Noah, Jim True, Francis Guinan, and all those others. And Sally Murphy is a most appealingly mousy Rose of Sharon.

The three principals—Gary Sinise (Tom), Terry Kinney (Preacher Jim Casy), and Lois Smith (Ma)—are all remarkable; but it is devilishly precarious going up against our memories of Henry Fonda, John Carradine, and Jane Darwell. That they come off as well as they do in their distinctively distinct ways is no small achievement. *The Grapes of Wrath* is a lesson in history, stagecraft, and truth that we cannot afford not to learn.

Lettice & Lovage

Peter Shaffer would be a more useful playwright to have around if he did not so often reach beyond his true *métier*. At first, when he turned out *Five Finger Exercise, The Private Ear & The Public Eye*, and such, he was that always welcome commodity the solid *boulevardier*, the master of urbane laughter and eyelash-lubricating tears. This is an endangered species, like writers of *vers de société*, yet needed to make some rough corner of America briefly, breezily Gallic. (Hence the italicized words in this paragraph.)

Ill-advisedly, though, he keeps trying to be profound, as in *Equus* and *Amadeus* (he should be restrained from plays whose titles end in -us). These three-dollar-bill plays have doubtless earned him millions, and if their motive were merely cynical acquisitiveness, one could dismiss them and forget. But in them, as also in *The Royal Hunt of the Sun* (which should really be called *The Royal Hunt of the N-us*), he strives for high art and falls flat (his future autobiographical play should be titled *Icarus*), and ludicrousness, however clad in greenbacks, the Muses and posterity will not forgive.

Happily, in the current *Lettice & Lovage*, Shaffer has not written an overreaching -us play (it's *Lettice*, not lettuce), but has, unhappily, become an underreacher. This play is not even superior, civilized situation comedy to manicure the mind; it is (to use its characters' favorite slur) a *mere* vehicle for two brilliant performers to strut their wares in. And so tremendous are the two Maggies or Margarets, Smith and Tyzack, that the thing works up considerable, but still ephemeral, steam. *Lettice & Lovage* is a two-act play in three acts: two contrived but pleasant; the third, for lack of honesty to the characters, pure nothingness.

Let me explain. Lettice Douffet is a sort of actress-cum-writer without portfolio; being Too Much for either stage or story, she settles for being a tourist guide, assigned by the Preservation Trust to Fustian House, Wiltshire, of all England's historic houses the unstateliest and dullest. So Lettice starts to embroider her spiel, and in the first four delicious scenes, she progressively improves on historic truth, much as if Trevelyan were being rewritten by Poe. Though some tourists are thrilled, others complain; eventually, dour Lotte Schoen from the Preservation Trust—of Germanic descent and bureaucratic disposition—descends on Lettice like the avenging goddess of historicity, unmasks her, and summons her to the London office, there to be formally fired. The firing scene, in turn, provides high-caliber farce.

Act II still manages, sort of. Miss Schoen, though girdled with righteousness and girded with the sword of justice, falls prey to the impractical but infectious flamboyance of her victim (a typical Shaffer motif), and seeks her out in her wretched but unhumble basement abode to offer her alternative employment. The two women exchange life stories, and theatrical Lettice, through a drink spiced with the herb lovage and seemingly having Wagnerian potion-power, loosens up puritanical Lotte into a mensch. Here, however, the author falters. What ought to become a sweet lesbian love story turns, from lack of nerve (another Shaffer trademark), into fanciful dust. For Act III reveals that Lotte has been steadily visiting Lettice in her basement apartment for the past six months and that they have been playing peculiar games together, but not the implicit truth of such an intimacy.

But the Shaffer formula, such as it is, consists of writing from the point of view of the apparent winner (Pizarro, Dr. Dysart, Salieri), who envies and ultimately succumbs to the seeming loser (Atahualpa, Alan Strang, Mozart). Here Shaffer reversed the angle and wrote from the vantage point of Lettice, rather than that, more congenial to him, of the excluded, romance-starved rationalist yearning for Dionysus. Had he not shifted into reverse, he would have had to make this a love story between two women, which, I assume, he found too outspoken, too commercially risky. Actually, Broadway is quite ready for any sort of homosexuality, especially if treated in Shaffer's glossy manner.

Well, there remain the acting and the staging, and the scattered undeniably funny bits: above all, that luminous brace of actresses. Make no mistake: in the much less thankful, rather underwritten role of Lotte, Miss Tyzack is every bit as dazzling as Miss Smith in the stellar part. Just as the play's will-o'-the-wispy fantast and the earthbound sourpuss—the Yea and the Nay—need each other, neither actress could shine so starrily if the other's light were less diamantine. You'll have no difficulty admiring Miss Smith's razzle-dazzle, but consider no less Miss Tyzack's concentrate of deflation, her horrifiedly acerb reactions, her eventual blushing conversion. This requires actorly invention equal to the Smithian comic bravura, campy bravado, and thespian theophany. These two great artists give, in a way, a single, not-to-be-missed performance.

There is substantive supporting work from Bette Henritze, Dane Knell, and the here somewhat overheated Paxton Whitehead; but the third gold star goes to Michael Blakemore, who yet again proves himself an endlessly resourceful director (which is lovely) and one who calls attention to the play rather than to himself (which is sublime). I can't think of an American trio that could make as polished chamber music as Smith, Tyzack, and Blakemore.

Aspects of Love

Alex sleeps with Rose, his uncle, George, sleeps with Giulietta. Rose sleeps with George and eventually marries him. Alex sleeps with Rose again. George sleeps with Giulietta again. Giulietta sleeps with Rose. Rose sleeps with Hugo. Alex finally gets to sleep with Giulietta. George and Rose's daughter, Jenny, wants to sleep with Alex, and he with her, but she is barely fifteen. So Alex goes off with Giulietta, but will, three years after curtain time, sleep with Jenny. Everybody gets his or her ass pecked in *Aspects of Love*, a truly happy show.

Well, not quite everybody. In real life, young David, son of those eminent literati Edward and Constance Garnett, worked as a conscientious objector during World War I on the farm of Vanessa (Mrs. Clive) Bell and her homosexual lover and fellow painter, Duncan Grant. Soon after begetting a daughter, Angelica, Grant went back to being a full-time homosexual, though the ménage continued untroubled, with Clive periodically dropping in. David Garnett fell in love with Vanessa (Virginia Woolf's sister) but was rejected by her and had an affair with Duncan instead. (This is the part that's missing from *Aspects*.) Eventually, however, he settled into full-time, even overtime, heterosexuality, vowing, however, that little Angelica, whose growth from the cradle on he watched over, would someday become his wife—as, indeed, she did. This was his way of settling the score with Vanessa and Duncan.

This grotesque tale can be had straight from Angelica Bell Garnett's autobiography, *Deceived With Love*. It can be had fictionalized from Garnett's 1955 *Aspects of Love*, an artificial, arid novella dedicated to Angelica, who was to divorce David. And it can now be had, tarted up grossly and ridiculously, in Andrew Lloyd Webber's musical of that name. It can also, with impunity, be bypassed altogether. That is, if you don't mind missing Maria Björnson's scenery, which is imaginative, eye- and breath-catching, and harder-working than any scenery I know. If it were human, I'd fear it might rupture itself. It does, in fact, split laterally, to spectacular effect.

Elaborate in detail yet simple in impact, both painterly and functional, this décor is continually on the move without tiring the eye or mind, unlovely only in one night sky with red clouds that hurtles into an Expressionism too close to poster art. Still, if one could see these sets without the show, *Aspects* would earn my kudos. Why, the scenery even displays—discreetly—posters that recapitulate the glory days of the French cinema, not a bad lagniappe.

But, alas, the "book adaptation" by Andrew Lloyd Webber, the lyrics by Don Black and Charles Hart, and the music by A.L.W. are also there to muddy the waters. Not to mention the dances by Gillian Lynne, which achieve what seems to have been her goal all along: the choreographic nadir. Still, the prize goes to the "libretto" of this through-composed musical: it fails on all counts. Wit: "If you can't keep your tongue still, / You will have the face of Edith Sitwell," which has neither rhyme nor reason. Urbanity: "You could teach George Bernard Shaw / A thing or two!" / "I had a go…" / "You've dined with Garbo…" / "Only twice." Profundity: "A memory that is best forgotten / That's what this ugly scene should be. / Life goes on, / So must we…" (All those sophomoric ellipses, by the way, are part of the text.)

Unfortunately, you cannot sing an ellipsis, but even the rest of this drivel is pretty hard to set to music. Lloyd Webber comes up with soft rock made softer yet and sounding like two dozen hurdy-gurdies electronically amplified. It is short-breathed, squeezed-out music, with brief phrases repeated over and over with minimal variation, adding up to four or five melodies (some of them borrowings, notably from *Evita* and *Les Mis*)—a matter of setting tripe to treacle and teeth on edge. It is the sonorous equivalent of dousing an unsightly body with cheap perfume: You take dialogue such as "You are the man, / I understand, / Who can clear my expenses, / Here they are: / Thirty thousand lire!" drench it with tonal patchouli, and redrench it the moment evaporation sets in. Menotti, the putative father of this sort of operaticized badinage, has much to account for.

The actors, less agile and resourceful than the scenery, wear themselves to a frazzle chasing after it. In the part of Rose Vibert, a French touring-company actress who becomes a star of stage, screen, and sheets, the aptly named Ann Crumb turns the game of love into a love game. Actually, she gets fifteen points for singing but is a total loser in looks, acting ability, bearing, personality, speaking voice, and French pronunciation. As Giulietta Trapani, the bisexual sculptress and free spirit, Kathleen Rowe McAllen, another American, is better but not memorable. Except that he can make his gravelly voice even hoarser as his character ages (Rose and Giulietta, dishonestly, grow no older in seventeen years), Kevin Colson contributes little: his George does not convince me of irresistible charm, sophistication, savoir-vivre. As the twelve- and fourteen year-old Jenny, Deanna and Danielle Du Clos will do, though the fact that the latter is taller and sturdier than her would-be lover, Alex, undermines the message.

As Alex, Michael Ball has a fine tenor voice but looks less Bloomsbury than Pillsbury Doughboy, which, although suitable in some ways, doesn't make for a charismatic hero. Walter Charles is un-French and insipid as Marcel, the actormanager; and Don Goodspeed, though he does look like a gigolo, does nothing for

Hugo, a lousy role anyway. As Elizabeth, the faithful retainer, Suzanne Briar is an embarrassment. Whatever he may have done for the show's logistics, Trevor Nunn was none too clever with casting. Even the excellent Miss Björnson, having depleted her imagination with the sets, did rather less well by the costumes.

Save for the scenery, then, picturesquely lighted by Andrew Bridge, there is little to recommend here. Perhaps the most ludicrous aspect of *Aspects of Love* is the way it telescopes into a speeded-up farce events that should be allowed breathing space. As in a Disney True-Life Adventure, where the life cycle of a plant is compressed into ten seconds, everything rushes forward on the double, halving its humanity. *Aspects of Love*, which could give sentimental trash a bad name, is a memory that is best forgotten.

The Piano Lesson

The fourth play to reach Broadway in August Wilson's decade-by-decade survey of black lives in twentieth-century America, *The Piano Lesson* also happens to take place in the century's fourth decade. It's 1936 in Pittsburgh, where the widowed Berniece lives at her uncle Doaker's with her daughter, Maretha, eleven, and that precious eponymous piano, into which a slave ancestor carved much of the family history. Berniece's brother, Boy Willie, who owns half of the piano, has just driven up from down South with his friend Lymon to sell a truckful of watermelons and the piano; the money, added to his savings, will enable him to buy some of the land his forebears worked as slaves and sharecroppers.

Most of the play concerns the debate between Berniece, who toils as a domestic but will not sell that tradition-steeped piano, and Boy Willie, the agrarian worker to whom land, that land, is dearer than any piano, no matter who wept and bled for it. Observing this battle of wills are Doaker, a railroad man, essentially neutral but more sympathetic to Berniece; Lymon, wanted back home by the police, and eager to settle in Pittsburgh and start chasing after its women; and Wining Boy, another uncle, a musician turned gambler, footloose and irresponsible, and thinking of heading south with Boy Willie.

Someone else, too, is hovering over the piano: the ghost of James Sutter, whose ancestor bought the piano from another white man for one and a half slaves—Boy Willie and Berniece's great-grand-mother Berniece and her nine-year-old son. It was that first Berniece's husband who carved his lost family into the master's piano. James Sutter has recently drowned in his own well, pushed in, it is believed, by the ghosts of the *Yellow Dog*, the train on which Boy Willie and Berniece's father, who stole the piano back from the Sutters, was fleeing a lynch mob that eventually burned the railroad car with him and three hoboes in it. They became the Yellow Dog Ghosts, drowning guilty parties in their wells, it seems.

Various members of Berniece's family have seen and been scared by James Sutter's ghost, which sometimes even plays the piano. Aside from this ghost subplot, there is also another about Berniece, whose husband was killed stealing wood with Boy Willie and Lymon three years ago, and her suitor Avery, an elevator operator who got the call in a dream and is about to start his own church; he wants the reluctant Berniece to marry him and play the piano for his future choir. Berniece, who keeps putting him off, has a near-fling with Lymon—an episode I don't believe at all. And this still doesn't account for Wining Boy, the ne'er-do-well uncle, who comically gets in the way of Berniece as, in a tense scene, she threatens to shoot Boy Willie, who is trying to make off with the piano. The farce and drama mix poorly.

And there is yet another subplot about a swinging young woman, Grace, with whom both Boy Willie and Lymon try to get involved, but whose husband... oh, well, that's enough plot to confuse you, just as it does most of us in the audience. Wilson's play won the Pulitzer Prize even before it opened in New York; myself, I see *The Piano Lesson* as desperately in need of soft-pedaling. It is sincere but overcrowded, overzealous, and, without quite knowing where it is headed, repeats everything three or four times.

It is, in fact, three plays: first, a drama about the conflict between the brother who wants to sell the past for the future, even if farm work may itself be a thing of the past, and the sister to whom the family past is sacred, even though she hates its symbol so much that she won't play it, and lets her daughter do so only at the cost of keeping the piano's tragic history hidden from her. But this battle of ideas is too limited, too repetitive. It does not fan out enough, does not sufficiently involve the others in it, does not provide the audience with surprises and complexity.

Second, it is a play of the supernatural, in which Berniece and Boy Willie, each in his own way, must battle Sutter's ghost. But although it provides the otherwise divided siblings with a common enemy, this aspect of the play remains underdeveloped and serves mostly as a splashy first and second-act curtain. And not only is the ghost stuff tacked on and uncompelling, it is also contradictorily presented. Whereas the characters see the ghost clearly, the audience gets only a light effect, a wind effect, and piano keys playing by themselves, This is too much for an imaginary ghost and too little for a real one; and why, in this day and age, bring in ghosts at all?

Third, it is a Broadway entertainment with situation comedy, musical interludes (singing, piano playing), halfhearted melodrama (Berniece's gun, promptly dropped), mostly detracting from the real drama. And even that element, the best, is often mishandled. If the piano represents a bitter past that must be remembered and honored, why would Berniece conceal it from Maretha rather than reverently instruct her in it? This further weakens Berniece's case for keeping the piano, a case strengthened only by S. Epatha Merkerson's superb portrayal of the woman; but that is not a moral argument.

Indeed, far too much of the play's strength resides in the acting, under Lloyd Richards's thoughtful direction. I cite Carl Gordon's repressed yet imposing Doaker, Rocky Carroll's sweetly befuddled Lymon, Tommy Hollis's naïvely fervent Avery, and Lou Myers's feckless, laughing yet defeated Wining Boy. Miss Merkerson handles strangulated monosyllables and wordless passion with wrenching intensity; Charles S. Dutton (Boy Willie) blends humor, rage, and boundlessly bounding energy into a charming cross between a lion cub and a tornado. But it's not enough: the writing, the construction, is a three-legged chair, always wobbly in one direction or another.

Perhaps the play's long gestation, including two years of testing and rewriting at five leading university and commercial theaters, was a mixed blessing. Though it afforded Wilson and Richards opportunities unavailable, I believe, to less favored, non-minority practitioners, it also makes the play come across as a palimpsest, with earlier versions distractingly discernible underneath. The most disturbing ghosts in *The Piano Lesson* are those of its former selves.

Hamlet

Shakespeare's two greatest plays—and, therefore, the world's—are *Hamlet* and *King Lear*. They complement each other as the supreme leaps of the poetic imagination into the existential and into the essential. Shakespeare encoded this distinction for us: In *Hamlet* we read, "the readiness is all"; in *Lear*, "Ripeness is all." Readiness is the ability to act, the chief existential problem; ripeness is the ability to feel and understand—the essence of living. *Lear* is a lesson in comprehension; *Hamlet*, a lesson in behavior.

But don't expect even this rudimentary sort of insight from Joseph Papp's Shakespeare Marathon *Hamlet*, which relies mainly on adventitious curiosities. Kevin Kline is re-creating the role he played at the Public in 1986, and this time also directing, a rare feat for a young actor. Even rarer is the coup of Diane Venora; she, too, played the prince at the Public, in 1982, and now essays Ophelia. How many Hamlets to make an omlet?

Peter Brook has claimed that two trestles and a board are enough to make theater, but the good Robin Wagner's minimal scenery for this *Hamlet* puts a dent in that contention. Two black columns framing a painted-backdrop sky, said sky bisected by a red velvet curtain descending from on high and hiding a door, as well as the odd concealed actor, are all there is. And, without great acting, it's not enough. Jules Fisher's lighting works heroically overtime, but it cannot create battlements, halls, bedchambers, a seacoast, a graveyard, and all else in Elsinore.

When Kline, as director, finally does provide a bit of scenery, a dais with an espalier of candelabra for the play within a play, he perversely puts the royal spectators, not the players, upon it. And if Kline does poorly with convexity, he does worse with concavity: he cannot provide any burial holes for Yorick and Ophelia; a wheeled-on wheelbarrow for a grave is not a pit but the pits. And he cannot fit a convincing duel into the confines of the Anspacher: courtiers watching the Laertes-Hamlet bout seem to be in as much danger as Brünnhildes at the Met.

A further problem is Martin Pakledinaz's careless and unsightly costuming. Modern dress is fine, but not if it has Horatio wear a sport coat and heavy wool shirt at a court function. And not if Hamlet and Laertes, at different times, appear in mod shirts and tapered pants like waiters in our trendier restaurants. Poor Ophelia must, when she is not barefoot as Hamlet and Gertrude are at other times), wear the most unbecomingly sensible loafers; Gertrude's negligee is scarcely different from the one formal gown she wears for coronations, fencing displays, funerals, and, for all I know, coffee klatches. Polonius, for some reason, is the nattiest dresser around. No better than the costumes is Bob James's no-account music, but at least there is less of it.

When Kline last did Hamlet, he had a director. This time round, he has only himself, which proves considerably worse. As of now, Kline is only a comic actor, and though a not unimportant part of Hamlet is indeed comical, a much greater portion isn't. Kline the director (K1) was unfortunately unable to teach Kline the actor (K2) any new tricks—or, rather, avoidance of tricks—and so K2 is wholly unable to eschew bizarre, exaggerated, hammy readings in both the soliloquies and the serious moments of the dialogue. There is a great deal of physical and vocal attitudinizing: crescendos and decrescendos (especially stage whispers, which K1 seems to have inflicted on other actors as well), the very kinds of strutting and posturing that Hamlet warns the players against. As K2 carries on, there's not a moist eye in the house.

Take the line "Wherein I'll catch the conscience of the king." It's possible to accentuate either *catch* or *conscience* for heavy irony (probably misplaced here), even *king*. But K2, perhaps because he is narcissistically enamored of the phoneme K, stresses all three, reducing the line to meaningless bluster. Or he delivers the "To be or not to be" soliloquy as if he believed himself to be mad, lamenting his own ineffectual histrionics. KI must know that one interpretation of the prince is that of a man unable to act; K2 tends to reduce him to an actor unable to.

Yes, in some of the witty moments, K2 is good, though less so than some other Hamlets; among American ones, I recall with special pleasure George Grizzard for Tyrone Guthrie in Minneapolis. Even in looks, the handsome Kline did better for Liviu Ciulei; now, with a fluffy coiffure, he looks rather like Mark Linn-Baker at his cutest and nerdiest. Having no doubt read about Olivier's great backward fall as Coriolanus, Kline gives us two backward falls here, but no interpretation. This is sometimes the Oedipal Hamlet, sometimes the procrastinator, sometimes the bedeviled intellectual, sometimes the out-of-joint extrovert (as when he performs a quaint dance of vengeance behind the praying king), but never the great Dane—at best, a yapping Yorkie.

Granted, there are few actors for him to bounce off here. Brian Murray is a slow, heavy, Colonel Blimpy sort of Claudius; Dana Ivey, an obvious Gertrude, shrill and incomprehensible when loud; Peter Francis James, a well-spoken but inept and soporific Horatio, who sings the prince, and everyone else, to rest well before those flights of angels get a crack at it; Michael Cumpsty, another well-spoken but dull actor, is a routine Laertes. The languidly fluttery Philip Goodwin and mindlessly trumpet-voiced Reg E. Cathey are an ill-assorted R & G; Clement Fowler is a worse hack than any Player King on record (the scenes with the players are particularly botched by K1), etc., etc.

However, Macintyre Dixon is a jolly Gravedigger, Robert Murch a dignified and beautifully articulated Ghost, Josef Sommer a sensibly understated Polonius (but must he say "affectchion" and "directchion"?), Don Reilly a believable Fortinbras. And despite poor direction, which either misdirects her or ignores her miscalculations, Diane Venora is a fascinating Ophelia. She plays her tougher than usual, older and more knowing than Ophelia has any business being, and she does whisper a lot. But she *feels* everything she is saying and doing; there is nothing phony about her. In an otherwise point-of-viewless production, she is the only one who moves us: a loving woman, scorned and hurt, whose retaliatory madness is as genuine as Hamlet's is feigned.

Six Degrees of Separation

Herewith the ingredients of John Guare's new, 90-minute comedy, *Six Degrees of Separation*. I list them in alphabetical order, but can't vouch for the completeness of the list.

Art sales, millions of questionable dollars in; Cézanne's paintings, unfinished patches in, as symbol; doormen, humanity of; doormen, loathing of rich tenants by; guilt, Jewish; guilt, parental; guilt, white liberal; gullibility, lower-class; gullibility, upper-class; homosexuals, brazenness of; homosexuals, humor of; homosexuals, pathos of; imagination, as source of vulnerability; imagination, as weapon; Kandinsky, two-sided painting by, as symbol; marital unfulfillment, comedy of; marital unfulfillment, wistfulness of.

Also: naked man, popping out on stage, daring effect of (cf. *Lisbon Traviata*); pink shirt, as status symbol; pink shirt, as sunburst, poetic but not status symbol; Poitier, Sidney, alleged paternity of, used as confidence trick; resentment, children's toward parents, undisguised; resentment, parents' toward children, semi-disguised; resentment, whites' toward blacks, disguised; rich people, ludicrousness of; rich people, secret pain of; separation, six degrees of between everyone and everyone else; sociopathic con man, devilish cunning of; sociopathic con man, poor lost soul of underneath.

Further: South Africa, problem of; suicide; theatrical aspirations, of kids coming to New York from Utah, absurdity of; theatrical aspirations, of kids coming from Utah to New York, pathos of; uncertainty, as device in penultimate scene; uncertainty, as device in ultimate scene.

There you have it: 35 degrees of manipulation, cunningly executed, seemingly seamlessly joined, interlarded with clever one-liners, alternating comic situations with mildly disturbing ones, drenched in social significance, sprinkled with poignancy. *Six Degrees of Separation* is a play about everything, with something in it for everyone, and with enough Cézannian empty patches into which you may project your own particular thing in the unlikely case that Guare overlooked it.

The play is not uninteresting: cleverness, however dishonest, provided only that it is diabolical enough, never bores. Take this, from a South African millionaire: "One has to stay there to educate the black workers, and we know we've been successful when they kill us." Liberals can laugh at this for liberal reasons; conservatives, for conservative reasons; blacks, for black reasons. Again, the con-man antihero who pretends to be Poitier's son tempts his white victims with the possibility of bit parts in *Cats*, the movie, which his father is directing. Says the ever-enjoyable Stockard Channing, as one of the victims, "It seems the common thread linking us all was our overwhelming need to be in the movie *Cats*." What joke is more ego-enhancing than one enabling us to laugh superiorly at a show we inferiorly relished.

Need I add that Jerry Zaks has directed perkily, that the seventeen-member cast is (with only a couple of exceptions) up to big roles in *Cats*, and that the Lincoln Center production has high gloss? (The better to bamboozle you with.)

Falsettoland

William Finn, the young composer-lyricist who made a name for himself with *March of the Falsettos*, continues now with a sequel, *Falsettoland*. There was an even earlier installment in this so-called "Marvin Trilogy," *In Trousers*, as well as a catastrophic sidestep, *Romance in Hard Times*. But it is here, as his characters march ever farther into Falsettoland, that Finn seems most at home.

The falsettos, if I understand him correctly, are people who sing in a different voice and march to a different drummer; they croon a bit higher and swoon a bit deeper. They may be off pitch and out of sync, but they "take a stand" in Falsettoland. To be more specific, the dramatis personae—male and female, adults and children—are either Jewish or homosexual, or, more often than not, both.

In this third part of the "Marvin Trilogy," we have Marvin both without his departed lover, Whizzer, and without his wife, Trina, who, when Marvin took off with Whizzer, took up with and married Marvin's shrink, Mendel. So, at the end of *March*, Marvin was left both Whizzerless and de-Trinated but still in a nice relationship with his twelve-and-a-half-year-old son, Jason, who was no longer averse to growing up just like dear old Dad. *Falsettoland* begins shortly thereafter. It is hung, as it were, on three hooks: sports, i.e., baseball and racquetball; Judaism, i.e., Jason's approaching bar mitzvah; and AIDS, of which Marvin's regained Whizzer will die, with ominous signs for Marvin.

The sports motif centers first on Jason, as his family and friends watch him play baseball: "We're watching Jewish boys / Who cannot play baseball / Play baseball." Who should show up, at Jason's invitation, but Whizzer, who, as a goy, can give Jason useful pointers. In the process, Marvin and Whizzer are reunited. Together, they play racquetball. In an early bout, Whizzer outplays Marvin; in a later one, the score is reversed because our champion is already racked by AIDS: sports as an index of adjustment or maladjustment, power or powerlessness.

The bar mitzvah—is Jason going to have it or will his parents' bickering over it make him not want it?—brings in the motif of Judaism, of spiritual values versus social ones; it becomes a battleground for divorced parents and an arena for filial rebellion, a sport at which Jewish children are markedly superior.

As for AIDS, when Jason, deeply moved by Whizzer's illness,

decides to turn his bar mitzvah into a bedside party in Whizzer's hospital room to be attended also by Mendel and Dr. Charlotte and Cordelia, "the lesbians from next door"—all the characters and themes converge. For the lesbian lovers, Charlotte and Cordelia, are also, respectively, Whizzer's physician and the kosher caterer of the bar mitzvah. But how, you ask, do sports fit into this confluence of themes? Well, love is a game, life is a game, a sport: harder for some than for others, and unpredictable for all.

It might all hang together if only the words and music were better than they are. Notice that Finn is trying something ambitious here: a 70-minute through-composed musical encompassing the full range of dramatic expression from farce to tragedy. This would be a tall order for the most far-reaching talent; if Finn could swing it, he would have something to crow, as well as sing, about. But once *Falsettoland* moves into AIDS territory, it seems hopelessly inadequate to its subject, both musically and verbally.

Even here, he pulls off one number, "Unlikely Lovers," in which the male and female homosexual couples harmonize at Whizzer's bedside. But this is promptly undermined by the next number, Jason's prayer to "Mister God" to save Whizzer in exchange for his, Jason's, agreeing to get bar mitzvahed. This would be "the miracle of Judaism," which Danny Gerard keeps pronouncing "Judyism" (Who is this Judy, anyway?) And the next number, Whizzer's aria of resignation, "You Gotta Die Sometime," may be the nadir: "Life sucks. / People always hate a loser. / And they hate lame ducks. / Screw me and shucks, / That's it... / That's the ball game. / It's the chink in the armor, / The shit in the karma, / The blues."

As if these blues were not enough, we also get black and white: "[Death] lifts me in his arms and tells me to embrace his attack. / Then the scene goes to black." Finally (after we've also had "When [death comes] screw the nerves, / I'll be eating hors d'oeuvres"), "[Death] puts his arms around my neck and walks me to the bed / He pins me against the wall and kisses me like crazy. /... Delight. / And the scene turns to white." After this, and more like it, we feel like reversing Dylan Thomas's famous advice and suggesting, "Oh, do go silent into that good night!"

But if Finn's lyric writing is not improving (any more than his English, wherein we are subjected to "I had a wife. She I divorced," a woman referring to herself as a "lout," "pathetical error," "I can't help but feeling I've failed," and other such pathetic errors), his tunes, gratifyingly, seem to be. Whereas, at his best, Finn used to sound like a Sondheim clone, now, at his worst, he sounds only like a Sondheim epigone. At his best, however, as in Mendel and Jason's duet, "Everyone Hates His Father," he manages melody that is both personal and tuneful. But here, again, the lyrics! God says, "Moses, everyone hates his parents. / That's how it is," to which Finn, as Mendel, adds, "And God knew / Because God hated his."

James Lapine's staging, however, is ingenious to the max, even if some of the touches may be excessive, as when Marvin, in bed with the sleeping Whizzer, sings about his bliss and, at one point, lifts the covers to run his gaze appreciatively over what is, after all, size rather than quality. Douglas Stein's minimal scenery is tasteful, and Michael Starobin's arrangements and conducting are to the point. Michael Rupert (Marvin) and Stephen Bogardus (Whizzer) are best in a cast in which the gifted Faith Prince overemphasizes the comic in Trina, and the unappealing Chip Zien misses the psychiatric in Mendel. Janet Metz's shrill voice is too grotesque for Cordelia, but Heather MacRae (Charlotte) and Danny Gerard (Jason) are thoroughly competent.

Our Country's Good

Something life-enhancing is afoot in *Our Country's Good*, which Hartford Stage is presenting through November 3 and which is worth catching if transportation to Hartford is not a major problem. I have no idea just how to apportion the praise for Timberlake Wertenbaker's adaption of *The Playmaker*, a novel by that leading Australian fictionist Thomas Keneally, which I haven't read, and which, in turn, may be derived from actual events in Sydney, Australia—here, in 1788 and 1789, the colony of New South Wales. In any case, the idea is wonderful: convicts enacting Farquhar's *The Recruiting Officer* under the guidance of a progressive young officer, supervised by an even more farsighted governor.

There is irony galore as mostly recalcitrant riffraff, some of them illiterate and one or two in the shadow of the gallows, reluctantly coalesce into an acting ensemble. "Actors," we are told, "can't behave like normal people—not even like normal criminals." With the help of Second Lieutenant Clark (Michael Cumpsty), they learn not only to act, more or less, but also to act as human beings; they are supported by the governor, Captain Phillip, R.N., and Captain Collins of the Royal Marines (Richard Poe and Sam Tsoutsouvas), but impeded by the ranking officer, Major Ross, and Captain Trench (Adam LeFevre and Gregory Wallace), both Royal Marines and soulless martinets.

The actors (and some actresses) who play these and other officers also play various convicts who, in the play within the play, enact characters much nearer to the officers than to themselves. So we get ironies within ironies, perhaps not pushed quite far enough but rich and resonant anyway. Faint echoes of *Marat/Sade* are not really bothersome; that a good many characters have to be made to matter in relatively short stage time is more of a problem. On the whole, though, Miss Wertenbaker, an American living in England, rises gallantly to the challenge, and what rough spots there are might be glossed over by one of those polished British casts not available here.

Only Cumpsty is British, and he is very fine; but so, too, are a number of Americans, notably Richard Poe, Sam Tsoutsouvas, Helen Carey (as a tough, withdrawn convict), and Tracey Ellis (as a delicate, near-virginal one). Superb scenery (Christopher Barreca), excellent lighting (Mimi Sherin), and almost as good costumes (Candice Donnelly) combine under the direction of Mark Lamos, who is not quite in his spectacular top form here, but more than estimable all the same. What I find especially exhilarating is the belief in the therapeutic powers of theater, the redemptive forces of art. Whether or not this is strictly true, someone—Keneally, Wertenbaker, history, or, most likely, the trio—makes a plausible, stirring case for it, even in a somewhat ragged production.

A Bright Room Called Day

Our theater needs bigger topics, freer play of ideas, a more cosmopolitan approach, and language disenthralled from the mundane tongue and ear. Tony Kushner's *A Bright Room Called Day*, at the Public, meets all these requirements—ineptly. The work of a literate young man who wants to make important as well as poetic statements, the play concerns a group of spouses and friends—artists, theater people, radicals—caught floundering in the late days of Weimar and early days of Hitler. If these not unenlightened bohemians could have unselfishly banded together, they could, it seems, have stopped Hitler before he fairly got started.

It is doubtful that such marginal figures could have made much of a difference. But at least Kushner should have tried harder to dramatize his point, rather than leave much of it to capsule information projected onto two screens, the audience being unhappily confined to two facing areas with the stage shoehorned in between. These projected texts keep coming, and with a teasing gradualness at that, like demented surtitles for an opera that can do without them. Even so, they are preferable to a dragged-in ghost (a mysterious old slattern symbolizing a mysterious old slattern), poetic apostrophes to her right and left hands by the heroine, and lurching tropes such as "the moon was huge and rusty like an infected eye."

Worst, however, is the attempt to make it all relevant to Reagan-Bush America via a silly (though supposedly canny) Jewish Long Island woman who inexplicably haunts Berlin in 1990 and pontificates to an incomprehending German gigolo about how today's America is the same as Hitler's Germany. And as if that weren't enough, the part is played by the performance artist Reno, proving only that performance art is, after all, a slightly lesser evil than Nazism. Still, Kushner should be encouraged, though not quite to the tune of all the grants, prizes, sinecures, heaped on him. Michael Greif's staging is at least better than David Greenspan's might have been, and there are good performers (notably Frances Conroy, Ellen McLaughlin, Joan MacIntosh, and Angie Phillips) superbly lit by Frances Aronson.

Assassins

The most interesting thing about *Assassins*, the Stephen Sondheim-John Weidman musical whose limited run at Playwrights Horizons was sold out long before it began, is not visible on stage. It is in the heads of its creators: what the hell were they thinking when they came up with this idea for a show?

Sondheim has told us that he was haunted by the title of someone else's bad play, *Assassins*. The word stuck in his memory, and when John Weidman, who had written the book for *Pacific Overtures* (one of the worst books for a Sondheim musical), came around for another shot at a collaboration, Steve tossed that unforgettable title, *Assassins*, at him. It might as well have been *Mudlarks* or *Appendec-*

tomy for all the good it did. We have here a case of the old story of the man who finds a button in the street and has a suit made to go with it. It's usually better the other way round.

Assassins gathers up the men and women who have killed or tried to kill American presidents and aims to figure out what they had in common, what made them do it. The answer seems to be that they were all losers of one kind or another, genuinely deprived or imagining themselves cheated by society, and bent on getting even or somehow making a mark. So what else is new? To be sure, one could write a searching, perhaps even moving, show concentrating on one such person, but it would have to be compassionate, analytical, philosophical. *Assassins* is none of these.

The motivation behind the show is specious; it seems to be an uneasy amalgam of bleeding-heart liberalism and high camp. Here, for instance, are these immigrants who had a terribly underpaid job and shot William McKinley; unsatisfied delusions of grandeur and shot James Garfield; a gnawing stomach ailment they could not afford to cure and so took a potshot at F.D.R. Well, we might feel sorry for them if they were treated with pity and true understanding, but not if we are to evince knee-jerk sympathy for them as victims of an evil capitalist society. Or we might be amused, if the humor were less flimsy than Charles Guiteau, slayer of Garfield, alternately intoning a silly hymn, "I'm Going to Meet the Lordie," and doing a soft-shoe routine up and down the steps to the gallows as he sings a Sondheim patter song.

The show is particularly condescending to the little Jewish fellow, Samuel Byck, who tried to crash a commercial plane into Nixon's White House, and to the two women, Lynette "Squeaky" Fromme and Sara Jane Moore, who attempted to shoot Gerald Ford. Fromme's humor lies in her sexual enslavement by Charlie Manson, and Moore's in the number of times she says "Shit!" as she rummages for her gun in her overstuffed pocketbook or accidentally shoots her lapdog. There is camp humor also about John Wilkes Booth, a poor actor, apparently, who could not remember cues and kept getting poor reviews, as one lyric wittily rhymes it. Booth, by the way, is meant to be the armature that holds the show together. He incredibly inspires the other assassins, eggs on Zangara to shoot Roosevelt, and, in one wholly preposterous and tasteless scene, talks Lee Harvey Oswald, a harmless would-be suicide, into becoming a president slayer, even supplying him with a high-powered rifle with a telescopic sight.

Yes, there is the odd bit of drollery in Weidman's dialogue, and Sondheim has written two pretty good songs and five indifferent ones in what is, qualitatively and quantitatively, his poorest score. Jerry Zaks, a funny director, has knocked himself out in search of clever tricks, and some of them, indeed, are. There is amusing scenery by Loren Sherman and lively costuming by William Ivey Long; Paul Gallo's lighting is, as always, expert. But even such old hands as Paul Gemignani on percussion, Michael Starobin at the synthesizer, and Paul Ford on the piano cannot replace a genuine orchestra with full-bodied orchestrations, and D. J. Giagni's nice choreographic hints are not real dancing.

Some of the performers are fine, notably Patrick Cassidy (Balladeer), Terrence Mann (Czolgosz), Annie Golden (Fromme), Eddie Korbich (Zangara), and William Parry (Ford). Victor Garber (Booth), Lee Wilkof (Byck), and Debra Monk (Moore) are either miscast or given material that lets them down. Greg Germann is a dull John Hinckley, Michael Shulman an unfortunate child actor, and Jonathan Hadary, as Guiteau, unspeakably dreadful. He may actually nab the hotly contested laurels for worst actor in New York.

But a show that begins with a fairground shooting gallery in which you get to knock off U.S. presidents, and does not go appreciably uphill from there, would be in poor taste anytime and is much more so now. When the terrible events in the gulf began, Sondheim & Co.—all affluent folks in no great need of turning a buck—could have done the gallant thing and shut down, or shot down, their not very viable brainchild. I would personally have handed them a cigar.

Dead Mother or Shirley Not All in Vain

What prompted Joseph Papp to fish the profoundly untalented and deeply incoherent David Greenspan out of the morass of the fringe (lunatic fringe, that is) theater, name him one of his heirs, and throw open the resources of the Public Theater to him? *Gonza the Lancer*, his previous contribution to the Public, was an ugly dismantling of a Japanese classic, which I walked out on in disgust. Now we get

Greenspan's own *Dead Mother or Shirley Not All in Vain*, a special blend of homosexual provocation, Jewish self-hatred, and brazen self-display. Talent and taste I would not expect from Greenspan, but here there is not even sense. This belongs either at the HOME (which is not a house) for Contemporary Theatre, which spawned Greenspan, or on a psychiatrist's couch. And it should be covered only by the politically correct reviewers from the *Village Voice* and *American Theatre*, who wallow in this sort of stuff.

The current work, written by David Greenspan, directed by ditto, and starring ditto, is in five acts and lasts two agonizing hours and 40 suffocating minutes. It is about a Jewish family with one homosexual son, Harold (Greenspan), and one heterosexual son, Daniel (Ben Bodd). Harold is married to Sylvia, although (as far as I could make out the nonlinear writing and inept delivery) Daniel had to consummate the marriage for him. To extract permission to marry, Harold had to disguise himself as Shirley, his mother, and crawl into bed with his half-asleep father, Melvin, and brainwash him.

Now Daniel wants to marry Maxine, who insists on meeting his mother first. However, Shirley has since died. So Harold must be pressed into service again to impersonate his mother, which he does in Charles Ludlam–Charles Busch style, only with less ability and more screaming. When his nerve runs out, he hides in the john, whence Daniel must coax him out.

Greenspan is fond of bathroom scenes. There was one in his biblical-autobiographical epic, *2 Samuel 11, Etc.*, at the HOME, in which he also masturbated on the toilet, or so I was told by the *Voice* reviewer, who trumpeted the work as a masterpiece.

We get also Maxine's wheelchair-bound and brain-damaged granduncle, Saul (Ron Bagden), who can only grunt, though he later gets to regurgitate the interminable monologue a black female dental technician (unseen) had recited while cleaning his teeth. When Harold, still in discreet drag, emerges from the bathroom as Shirley, there is Melvin, and an awkward confrontation ensues, allowing Greenspan to indulge in further hysterics. Before that, however, Mary Shultz, a favorite actress of Greenspan's, has delivered an endless speech in the breathless, dementedly grinning manner that is de rigueur for actresses in the low-camp theater. But Greenspan has his ready-made audience that grooves on his nonsense. At the words "to have children," they get a hand gesture for intercourse and dissolve in guffaws; "after my parents were killed in a hijacking" elicits even louder laughter; and at "his head was chopped off," the hilarity peaks.

There follows a series of mythological vignettes whose chief purpose is to get easy yaks by camping up myths acted out in outrageous garb. Thus Zeus, flaunting his godfatherly (fake) phallus, says of his progenitor, "I threw the goddamn fucking bastard into the underworld and he never since troubled me." (Gales of laughter.) Here the clever designer, Elsa Ward, supplies costumes travestying male and female sexual organs, and Greenspan hits the jackpot as Eris, getting to wear both real female undies and mock male genitals, though no myth makes an androgyne of Eris. Paris, however, gets the biggest ithyphallic rubber appendage, which Mary Shultz, as an Aphrodite in dark glasses, flicks or massages. Earlier, Paris the shepherd was buggering one of his sheep as he soliloquized. It's only a wooden sheep, but you can't have everything.

After the mythological interludes, Granduncle Saul gets to deliver the aforementioned dental discourse, which is all about microbes, bacteria, and "Rinse, please!" While he delivers it, Greenspan the actor stands gazing at him, listening in silent rapture to the words of Greenspan, the author, his half-profile bathed in a halo of half-light.

Came, finally, an intermission, and I got the hell out, narrowly missing a shrink-bashing scene in which the four male actors, seated behind music stands, jeeringly read from the works of several psychiatrists not politically correct on the subject of homosexuality. And more, much more. Once again I raise the question: why does Papp put on, with taxpayers' money, *Dead Mother or Shirley Not All in Vain*, by the author of, among other classics, *Dig a Hole and Bury Your Father*? Note that, far from discouraging you from seeing this play, I strongly urge you to catch it and send me your reply to the above question. There will be a modest cash prize for the best answer.

La Bête

CLAUDINE: Off to the playhouse! Would you tarry yet,
  Oreste? The town's abuzz about *La Bête*.
ORESTE: I saw it, gritting my teeth through every scene;
  As foul a play as ever was, Claudine.
CLAUDINE: Two million dollars' worth of rhyming verse,
  The lightest footwork and the heaviest purse

In town. A work that has the graceful air
Of Richard Wilbur translating Molière.
Would you dismiss such daring, put a curse on
A golden-tongued young playwright, David Hirson?

ORESTE: I would, Claudine. And being an old codger,
I can recall the bombs his father, Roger,
Wrote long ago. Pretension seems to run
Amok among the Hirsons, father and son.
And what's so great about its being in rhyme?
Pastiche for its own sake is the cute crime
Of every sophomore who's spent some time
In college drama classes, though few had
A Stuart Ostrow who'd produced their dad—
Writer of turkeys and the book for *Pippin*.

CLAUDINE: Come now, admit, you must have found it gripping
When clever words from fleet tongues come a-tripping
In a tale of theatre intrigue that, though set
In bygone France, speaks to our problems yet.

ORESTE: That among actor-playwrights there are bores
Who, having mighty patrons, can find scores
Of fools to laugh at their poor jokes? It's true—
The herd of giggling fops proved it anew.
But that's old stuff. When rhymed and spoken fast,
Banalities may sound like gems that last.
The only thing that came across the ramp,
In Richard Jones's staging, was pure camp.
Such ceaseless flutter, fey posturing, no rest
For eye or ear, all swish and swirl…

CLAUDINE: Oreste,
You are unfair. And Richard Hudson's sets:
That chandelier, those busts with turning heads!

ORESTE: They seem to have turned yours. The chandelier
In *Phantom* did something at least, but here
It's only gimmickry, like all the rest.

CLAUDINE: But surely Tom McGowan's acting's the best
Bravura seen on staid Broadway in years.

ORESTE: Well, if you like swinging from chandeliers
(Figuratively speaking). A monologue
Of half an hour may leave the crowd agog,
But what's it say? If you want camp, why bother?
You can get it cheaper downtown in *Dead Mother*.

There is some wasted talent, yes: James Greene,
Michael Cumpsty, Dylan Baker. But Claudine,
What tripe they're made to utter—with duds on
To make you puke, likewise by Richard Hudson.
Itr's all pretense, down to the title. At least
They could have called it honestly *The Beast*.
And, speaking of beasts, there is onstage a bird
That comes off best—by not speaking a word.
(This staunch defense of art against ersatz
Was co-produced by Lloyd Webber of *Cats*.)

The Two Parts of Henry IV

When Joyce's Stephen Dedalus said, "History is a nightmare from which I am trying to awake," he meant history, not Shakespeare's Histories. But that is only because he did not have the benefit of seeing JoAnne Akalaitis's production of Joe Papp's (formerly Shakespeare's) *The Two Parts of Henry IV*.

Suppose the Devil decided to destroy that most divine of dramatists, William Shakespeare, utterly, starting in America. First, he would create an impresario from Hell and make him supreme purveyor of the Bard for this country. It is, I suppose, touching that a semi-literate person should have worked his way up, through promotional and self-promotional but strictly nonartistic skills, to this position. But it is only politically touching; although art can be political, politics is never art. This obvious truth is, alas, beyond the comprehension of the politically correct powers that have taken over much of American theater; if you don't believe me, pick up the February issue of the highly subsidized rag aptly named *American Theatre* and check out especially (but not exclusively) the cover story on *The HipHop Waltz of Eurydice*.

The Devil would next have Papp appoint as his heir apparent JoAnne Akalaitis, a typical countercultural pseudo-artist with all the right credentials in her background (Mabou Mines, Richard Serra, Philip Glass) but who didn't discover Shakespeare until relatively late in life, when Papp had her direct *Cymbeline*, a triumph in the pages of *American Theatre*, a partial success in those of the *Village Voice*, and a fiasco just about everywhere else.

Next, the Devil would see to it that government grants and many other types of funding make nontraditional casting de rigueur. This is the equivalent of affirmative action in the theater, which stipulates that companies unable to survive without subsidies can get them only by casting persons of color, of the wrong gender, with physical handicaps, etc., in parts for which they are totally unsuited. It means defying logic, historical and social authenticity, biological credibility, thus making the theater a political battleground at the expense of artistic integrity and efficacy.

This has nothing to do with democracy or dramatic enrichment: ancient Greece, the cradle of both democracy and theater, recognized excellence as being the only artistic criterion. But in our present populist society and multicultural theater, with the fanatical support of Actors Equity (which, let's remember, is only a labor union having no more intellectual authority than other labor unions, viz. those that by various maneuvers keep persons of color out), such strategies as Akalaitis's casting two brother English princes (in *Cymbeline*) with one white, one black actor are applauded, as was, at the recent conference of the Modern Language Association, a paper arguing that in *The Tempest*, a play about colonial oppression, especially of women, Caliban should be played as a black lesbian. In our theater as in academia, which abets it, common sense is just a vile hang-up of the prevailing but dying Europhallocentric mentality.

These ideas (ideas?) are hatched by the various special-interest groups (under the aegis of knee-jerk liberalism) for whom Shakespeare, theater, art, genuine education are of no concern whatever. A Shakespearean production is merely a political arena in which members of *our* group (whichever it is) should be prominently cast, never mind whether they are right for the parts, never mind whether they can act. And under the leaky umbrella of JoAnne Akalaitis, Joe Papp, and his casting director, Rosemarie Tichler (who believes that classically untrained actors are best for Shakespeare, and that poetry must never be spoken as poetry), anarchy holds sway. At least the old-style anarchists did not ooze hypocritical pieties; their bombs were honest-to-goodness bombs, not Shakespearean productions.

Quite aside from everything else, these procedures miseducate American youth about Shakespeare, unless they turn it off him altogether. And untalented directors who use "good citizenship" to cover up their bad workmanship are usually forced also into ever more crazily sensationalistic stagings, as further means of deflecting attention from their basic incompetence.

Thus, equally disastrous as the Mabou Mines type of nonsense that Akalaitis imposes on the *Henrys* (which makes them, especially Part II, look like *Marat/Sade* performed not only about but also by and for madmen) is what happens during the plays' quieter moments. When Akalaitis cannot jazz up a scene with masturbating zanies to the left, interracially fornicating zanies to the right, and someone juggling with dead rats in the center, while Pistol, down front, first sniffs then tosses about the turds from an offal bucket, she is left stranded in her ineptitude. A great confrontation, such as that of the dying Henry IV with his repentant son, Hal, which does not allow for gimmickry, gets lost in the indifferent acting, inhospitable stage design, and limp directing.

But never mind intimate scenes; even group ones are beyond Akalaitis when, as in the opening of Part I, no violent activity is called for or artificially inducible. She simply does not know how to devise quiet movements, changes in pace and position, vocal variety. Such scenes lie there, as inert as something in a patriotic pageant.

Next to lack of true feeling—how flat Hal's final denial of Falstaff falls!—there is the complete absence of a genuine sense of humor. Tossing around rubber chickens, masturbation with roast capon legs, men with bare behinds and green-paper pubic hair, people scratching their privates, everyone in the tavern trembling in unison (D.T.'s, Saint Vitus's dance, or just having fun?)—these are not real humor. And how pitiful is the concept of Shallow and Silence acted as amateur clowns by amateurish actors!

I am not sure whether the endless string of gross anachronisms (telephones, cigarettes, fluorescent lights, mopeds, baseball caps, bottled soft drinks, etc.) is meant to be humor or relevance to our time (as allowing a Hispanic actor to burst into Spanish surely is): either way, it is bankruptcy of the imagination. And so is the constant attempt to startle us, as when those two aristocratic wives, the Welsh Lady Mortimer and the English Lady Percy, are played, respectively, by an Asian American actress of no distinction and a black actress who repeats in every vocal and behavioral detail her performance as a floozie in *The Piano Lesson,* presumably all this Juilliard graduate (the second such in two weeks) can do.

But from neither the many misplaced ethnics nor the many flatly American-accented whites is there anything resembling poetry to be had; only one performance in a cast of 35 lingers pleasurably in my memory (where many remain as thorns): that of Traber Burns as a subtly oily and vinegary, and lavishly orotund, Glendower. Louis Zorich is a one-dimensional Falstaff: Jared Harris, a grating-voiced, mush-mouthed, and psychotic Hotspur; Larry Bryggman, a boring, plebeian Henry IV; Thomas Gibson, a wobbly Hal (sometimes good, sometimes crass); Ruth Maleczech, a broad Mistress Quickly indistinguishable from the actress's recent Lear; Arnold Molina, a wimpy John of Lancaster; Caris Corfman, an oafish Rumor; and so on and on.

Philip Glass's music has a few nice quiet moments but is largely a droning nuisance when not an all-obliterating catastrophe. Jennifer Tipton's fine lighting is mostly wasted on George Tsypin's sets, good only where they ape John Piper, a much better designer and artist. John Boesche's projections, including floral tents and battles in palimpsest, are merely distracting. Gabriel Berry's costumes are creepy, David S. Leong's fights undistinguished. Even a dwarf, preposterous as Peto, is untalented; no Michael Dunn or Hervé Villechaize he, though tinier than either. But Miss Akalaitis's intellectual and artistic dwarfishness is gigantic.

A Room of One's Own

"The easiest of Virginia's books," Quentin Bell calls *A Room of One's Own*, in his fine biography of his aunt, Virginia Woolf. "The argument is developed easily and conversationally, striking home in some memorable passages, but always lightly and amusingly expressed. It is that rare thing—a lively but good-tempered polemic..." This last point was aptly elaborated on by Mitchell A. Leaska: "The militant feminist is as incapable of producing worthwhile fiction as the male chauvinist, precisely because her artistic powers are forever inflamed with ill feeling."

Leaska goes on to summarize *A Room*: "Great artists, asserted Virginia Woolf, are androgynous... But androgyny can flourish only when one has intellectual freedom, and that freedom depends upon... five hundred pounds a year and a room of one's own." Those last five words are the title of the book version of two 1928 lectures given by Woolf at a couple of women's colleges, a book about which, with characteristic diffidence, she felt less than wholly sanguine: "A brilliant essay?—I daresay: it has much work in it, many opinions boiled down into a kind of jelly, which I have stained red as far as

I can." Thus in her diary for May 12, 1929. But by August 19, she laments, "As usual much is watery and flimsy and pitched in too high a voice."

Latching on to the easy conversationalism of the book, Patrick Garland has adapted it for the stage, abridging and kneading it, but nowise betraying its essence and tone; and in Eileen Atkins, Woolf has found an embodier to squeeze out the wateriness and flimsiness from the work and pitch the voice considerably lower, without, however, changing the melody. It's the difference between a Brecht-Weill song rendered by the young soprano Lotte Lenya and by the maturer mezzo Lotte Lenya: good either way, but it's the lower register that really grabs you in the gut.

Eileen Atkins does not look like Virginia Woolf, save that she, too, has the long, somewhat angular face of many British women, which the unsympathetic call "equine" and the aficionados "strong." Otherwise, Miss Atkins, sturdier by far, could have blown Mrs. Woolf with one breath from Bloomsbury to Billingsgate. But make no mistake: that Miss Atkins is tougher does not mean she gives a performance all muscle and bounce and no sensitivity and soul. Far from it: she has created a marvelous, vital, and energizing entity; call it Virginia Atkins or Eileen Woolf. I call it simply magnificent.

The actress takes us, step by intelligent step, through the historic, social, and emotional background of women's liberation, so slow and painful, but inevitable and triumphant; the liberation that writers such as Aphra Behn, Jane Austen, the three Brontës, the two Georges (Eliot and Sand), several others mentioned here, and not least Woolf herself helped bring about. Woolf, by leaning with radiant irony on Trevelyan's *History of England*—one of the few onstage props Miss Atkins uses—takes us through the history of patriarchy: repression in life and idealization (another form of repression) in literature. The Woolfian irony is wielded no less potently by Miss Atkins: a vorpal blade, it glints in her eye and voice—but only for a flash, a snicker-snack; already the face has grown mock-innocent, impassive, and the voice has turned blandly dulcet or fallen silent. But the cut was lethal.

Under Garland's apt direction, this true-blue actress delivers that reddest of red jellies Woolf was after. The blood of all squelched, trampled-on women, writers and nonwriters, courses through this evening and keeps us, women and men, laughing blithely, compassionately, androgynously. At times Miss Atkins may be a shade too didactic, with effects a pennyworth or scruple too heavy, pauses a mite too conspiratorial. But this is only a mole on a beloved face, not so much black mark as beauty mark.

Woolf knew what today's feminists don't: that humor and wit are more powerful polemics than shrillness and fanaticism. And Miss Atkins's performance—down to those unforgettable reined-in tears and choked-back sobs near the end—is a labor of artistry, love, and creative lightness. This is the only show, on or off Broadway, that combines great ideas, inspired acting, and a helluva good time.

The Substance of Fire

Publishing, though perhaps not so exciting as some bigger businesses, has the artistic and intellectual cachet (earned or not) to make it interesting—as are also the social and economic changes that have affected it since the mid-century. As more and more publishing houses become part of huge, faceless and soulless, conglomerates, and family businesses with colorful, idiosyncratic, sometimes even highbrow heads are becoming extinct (like readers of real books), publishing becomes dramatic. Death throes play.

So we have just read about the imminent passing of North Point Press, as intelligent and tasteful a small publisher as you could ask for, and about the death of its co-founder from cancer—perhaps aggravated by heartbreak? And so we have just seen a picture in the *Times* of the staff of a new subdivision of a large publishing house: the sassily stylish female head surrounded by four young and pretty assistants dressed and posed with studied casualness, looking for all the world as if what was being pushed was not books but the latest couture concepts in bohemian chic.

Suddenly we realize that a play cannily, incisively, and artistically addressing changes on the American publishing scene might have uncommon interest: aesthetically, politically, culturally, and philosophically. And Jon Robin Baitz's *The Substance of Fire* is such a play—almost.

The 29-year-old playwright made a stunning New York debut a couple of seasons ago with *The Film Society*. No less catchily, *The Substance of Fire* begins with a stockholders' meeting at a fine but troubled family publishing house whose autocratic head, the widowed Isaac Geldhart, may be superseded by his elder son, Aaron.

Backed by Japanese interests, Aaron wants to make the house less elitist and more profitable. Isaac's repressed and patronized aide, he is now plumping for a flashy, potentially best-selling novel; Isaac, however, plans to bring out a six-volume history of Nazi medical experiments in the camps instead.

Already the issue is falsely posited. No commercial publisher would want to, and no university press could afford to, bring out such a work in six volumes; in one or two, yes. Again, Isaac ridicules all three of his children: Aaron is a mere "accountant" to him; Martin, the younger son, a Rhodes scholar and professor of landscape gardening, "an assistant gardener"; and Sarah, an actress, who has flown in from the West Coast for the meeting, "a hired clown," because she is a regular on a children's TV show. So far, so good; but must Isaac have been, among the older Geldharts, the sole—possibly craven—survivor of the Holocaust? Must Aaron have had a homosexual college affair with the author of that potential bestseller? Must Martin, in our age, still be a 1968-style hippie? Must Sarah have a positively awesome repertoire of Hollywood-airhead mannerisms? And must Baitz then leave all these splashy elements unexplored?

There is genuine intelligence, wit, and skill at work here, but also clumsiness. Thus the play has no middle: we neither know how the story progressed from Act I to Act II (three and a half years later) nor believe the few unpersuasive hints tossed out. Why should changes that ought to have made the firm solvent have bankrupted it? How can Isaac, in his current position, think of buying it back? Or is he mad? Martin clearly doesn't believe that, yet Aaron has called in a psychiatric social worker, Miss Hackett, to assess their dad's sanity. What's been going on here? Aaron and Sarah are no longer on the scene, Martin barely. And Miss Hackett: if she is a major character, there ought to be more of her; if a minor one, less.

There are other problems. A hand-painted postcard by the young Hitler is made to bear a burden of symbolism either too heavy or imperfectly integrated into the play. Isaac's European social background is fudged (perhaps not so much by the writing as by Ron Rifkin's otherwise excellent performance): was it upper- or lower-middleclass? Slippage of focus prevents a civilized and arresting play from attaining indelibility. And from moving us.

Daniel Sullivan's staging is on the button, though, as are John Lee Beatty's terrific scenery and Arden Fingerhut's sympathetic lighting. Ron Rifkin is a tightly wound, stinging, often devastating, yet never less than human Isaac; as Martin, Patrick Breen, a personable actor, equally compellingly embodies his version of familial guilt; Jon Tenney is a letter-perfect Aaron; and the always enjoyable Sarah Jessica Parker, although perhaps a touch excessive as Sarah, is once again fun. Years ago, that cosmopolitan and flamboyant man of letters Niccolò Tucci invited me to his place for a spaghetti lunch and informed me that I would be a swell critic but for a terrible blind spot where the talent of his daughter, Maria Tucci, was concerned. Well, now that she no longer plays adorable ingenues or lambent leading ladies, Miss Tucci finally gets my vote, not goat: her oddball, frumpy Miss Hackett is up to snuff. Despite its youthful flaws, despite my aforementioned reservations, I recommend *The Substance of Fire* for its verve and heat, if not quite fire.

Miss Saigon; I Hate Hamlet

Butterflies were free; now they are rampant. First there was the Madama butterfly (*Papilio Pucciniensis*); then came the savvier Em butterfly (*Lepidopter Hvangianus*); and now here's the sappier Missaigon butterfly (*Helicopter Boublilii*) of gargantuan dimensions. But, speaking either entomologically or theatrically, big is not better. Big is not necessarily beautiful, either. But big sure is big.

Alain Boublil and Claude-Michel (the wrong) Schönberg, who shrewdly concocted *Miss Saigon*, as they did the earlier shrewd *Les Misérables* (misery loves company, so *Les Miz* is recycled as *Miz Saigon*), know the power of miz, or myth. In their first smash, a generous fellow whose life is all misery dies a happy man, having made a brighter future for his daughter. In their current (presold and gilt-edged) smash, a generous girl whose life is all misery dies a happy woman, having made a brighter future for her son. Such a formula cannot fail if you pepper it with enough war, revolution, social injustice, racial inequity, and, above all, self-sacrifice: make every mother (father) and mother's son (father's daughter) in the audience feel holier than hell, and you have the makings of a gold mine. But heart is not enough: you've got to have glitz, lots and lots of glitz.

How is Miss Saigon mythic? Why, it's the central station for all incoming and outgoing myths: the East-Is-East-and-West-Is-West myth, the Submissive-Oriental-Girl myth (you haven't had sex until you've, etc.), the Shed-Tears-for-the-Underdog (But-Put-Your-Faith-in-the-Dollar-or-Yen) myth, the Lovely-Young-Girl-Who-Must-Endure- Countless-Trials myth (Cupid and Psyche, Cinderella, the Little Mermaid, etc.), and more. But carefully calculated as it is to touch every conceivable soft spot (mother love, save the children, expiate your wealth, grovel about your Ugly Americanism, etc.), it is so much by the numbers as to be more than mythic—mathic.

And what better way to exploit middlebrow pieties than with the, sort of story and music that has worked for David Belasco, Giacomo Puccini, and Andrew Lloyd Webber? The formula is simple:

> Unearth some form of tried-and-true schmaltz and give it a contemporary coating—in this case, disco, soft rock, whatever goes in our tonier cocktail lounges and toned-down jukeboxes. Although for climactic moments Schönberg will trot out a bit of *Turandot*, he mostly leaves Puccini to Andrew. His soft-core filling is, of all things, Albert William Ketèlbey, composer of "In a Monastery Garden… In a Persian Market," and now—as it were, posthumously—"In a Saigon Hellhole," "In a Bangkok Brothel," and "In a Nostalgic Nowhere."

Though the surface sound is vaguely with-it and tough, underneath is the smoothly through-composed, quasi-operatic pretension, the fake gentility of our composer's published comment about a news photo reproduced in the program, showing a child being snatched from a Vietnamese mother: "This photograph was, for Alain and I, the start of everything." That ghastly genteelism (whether Schönberg's own or translated by one of his associates), "for Alain and I," tells it all: *Miss Saigon* is a show for people who say "for you and I," but not for me. Understand: I am not sneering at genuine human misery, only at its overinflated and underfelt commercial exploitation.

Which is not to say that *Miss Saigon* doesn't have its clevernesses, though not in its music or English lyrics, as translated from Alain Boublil's French and supplied with additional material by Richard Maltby Jr. (who continues to fiddle with them since the London cast album was released), lyrics that are either *faux naïf* or falsely sophisticated, and always inauthentic. No character expresses himself as an American soldier, Vietnamese bargirl, Eurasian pimp, and so on would, but always in dismal clichés from all over, copulating in the same second-best show-biz bed. Thus, "You are sunlight and I moon / joined by the gods of fortúne" (less for tune than for rhyme) or "We can't forget / Must not forget / That they are all / Our children too." The lyric that Ellen, the hero's American wife (i.e., Kate Pinkerton), sings after meeting Kim (i.e., Cio-Cio-San) is, like several others, so bathetic that it had many in the audience groaning or sniggering.

But the production values are there. John Napier's décor is, as always, spectacular; David Hersey's lighting, if possible, even more so. The Neofitou-Benzinger team's costumes are, as required, garish or grubby to a fault. And Bob Avian's polished musical staging combines neatly with Nicholas Hytner's proficient direction. Everyone in the cast works hard, and Lea Salonga, as Kim, manages to be moving despite, not because of, her material. As the Engineer, Jonathan Pryce is in a special class: though foolish political correctness has deprived him of the needed Eurasian makeup, and he emerges as English as Monty Python, his is one of musical comedy's supreme star turns, in a league with, say, Robert Preston's in *The Music Man*. Without him, there would be no show.

Largely because of Pryce, there is one number that really works: "The American Dream." But a satire on capitalism using all the conspicuous spending of current main-stem-musical concepts achieves the opposite of what it purports to do: it ends up glorifying rather than castigating the American Dream, and leaves the audience not shaken but slaphappy.

It would be pleasant to be able to hail *I Hate Hamlet* as a good old-fashioned Broadway farce. Andrew, a youthful TV star whose series has been canceled, reluctantly agrees to play Hamlet for Joe Papp in Central Park. His girl, Deirdre, a rich, flaky would-be actress and 28-year-old virgin, plays a bit part in *Hamlet* but a large one in Andrew's sex-starved misery, compounded by his hatred of *Hamlet*, which he could never finish reading, and his inability to act. But his new, palatial Greenwich Village apartment is haunted by its former owner, John Barrymore, come back to Earth to make a true Prince out of Andrew.

The premise, like Andrew's new premises (lushly designed by Tony Straiges), has possibilities, especially when you add a real-estate agent who dabbles in spiritualism, an actors' agent who once had an affair with Barrymore, and a Hollywood TV producer come East to coax our budding Hamlet back West with a $3-million contract. Paul Rudnick, the author and (like several others associated with this venture) Yale Drama School product, is witty and has a way with a wayward situation or line. But, like so many other young playwrights, he cannot construct a whole with a shape to it, in which the parts build toward a mutually sustaining climax.

It's nice to have two female agents in one small play, but they should be allowed more interaction. It's nice to have a television producer who says such things as "Maybe I should leave Hollywood and just produce, direct, and write Shakespeare," but he shouldn't be as predictable as this Gary Peter Lefkowitz character. And Barrymore's ghost, even if Nicol Williamson is good at delivering zingers, shouldn't get all the best ones.

Michael Engler, the director, does not squeeze as much humor out of the play as a more experienced hand could, and the casting is disastrous. Adam Arkin is a credible Lefkowitz, and Jane Adams, as Deirdre, gives the most genuine and winning performance of all. But Caroline Aaron contributes a bare minimum to one agent, and Celeste Holm rather less to the other. Williamson seems bored much of the time (understandably), but the real catastrophe is the Andrew of Evan Handler. Needed here is a Kevin Bacon or Sean Penn, not someone who looks like a young Jackie Mason and sounds like a stale Woody Allen. Neither television nor even Papp would want this plangent, homely schlepper, and a 28-year-old virgin given him as an alternative would opt for 28 more years of abstinence. There are funny lines, granted; but it takes more than that to make a true comedy.

The Will Rogers Follies

"They call that town Nice," says Will Rogers from the Ziegfeld Follies stage in *The Will Rogers Follies*, pronouncing it correctly as *neece*, "because the French don't have a word for 'nice.'" Well, if they don't, they'll have to invent one when they see this show. There are pretty girls, costumes, and scenery—nice. Pretty dances, music, and words—nice and old-fashioned. Pretty orchestrations, light effects, and performances—nice and... heck, just plain nice!

It all comes down to how much *nice* you can stomach. The scenery is no problem. What Tony Walton has designed is absolutely delicious and right: different, yet also in period; exaggerated, but with a sense of humor, the rope motif snaking its way through everything from runways to telephones, shapes and colors spinning in and out of one another as if the entire stage, or world, were the trick of that great Rope Twirler in the sky. There is no end to the twists Walton can think up, aided by Jules Fisher's lighting, which conjures up a pageant of insubstantial marvels, as Tommy Tune moves his dancers all over that quintessential staircase, and magic ambushes you everywhere.

To this, Willa Kim's costumes contribute unstintingly. They, too, have a period sense while being thoroughly original—a bit vulgar at times, as under Ziegfeld, but with a controlled vulgarity that sneaks into elegance, a gaudiness with style. And again, Tune finds ways of converting those costumes into visual music, even into dance, as when the chorines, gotten up as heifers, hunker down and let their rope-made tails perform a soft-shoe of their own, caressing the floor as sassily as any dancer's feet. There are ideas everywhere, genuine showbiz razzle-dazzle, sometimes a mite prurient, but who's complaining?

The entertainer's story is told in revue numbers, or as song cues, tableau cues, production-number cues—for this is also the story, partly, of Florenz Ziegfeld and his Follies or follies, Will having been one of Flo's headliners. Peter Stone's book is in fact a giant song cue, or picture frame, for the show: Will Rogers's life pared down to storybook essentials barer than, with one brief exception, the showgirls themselves. Those essentials are then playfully gussied up and mythicized, but no matter: no one wishing to study Will Rogers's work and life would dream of using this show as a research library. There are sweetly tickling touches of humor scattered throughout, though least so in the part of Clem, Will's father, with whose unfunny jokes Dick Latessa struggles gallantly. And there are also those homespun, rope-spun truths over which the show seems to stop for a moment while it licks its chops; but mostly, it is nice, wholesome, retrospective fun.

Cy Coleman seems to be recycling his own and everybody else's good old tunes, but as rehashings go, this one is succulent, with a melodic flavor appropriate to the heyday of Ziegfeld and Rogers. But unlike the design, which manages to fuse the old and the new, the music, studded with Betty Comden and Adolph Green's equally proficient lyrics, sticks to the old. Nicely, gracefully old, and vastly preferable to what sputters from most of today's musical stages, but strictly uninnovative. And a bit anonymous, like this entire Will Rogers story, which could, with a few modest modifications, be anybody's life: mine, yours, your grandmother's. It leaves you purring rather than elated.

Keith Carradine, a trifle too boyishly good-looking for Rogers, is an utterly amiable compère and accomplished leading man—rope-swinger, word-slinger, pop singer, and even guitar-strummer—as witty and wise as anyone who never met a man he didn't like and wasn't liked by in return. It is to Carradine's great credit that his Will doesn't drown himself and us in all that goodwill. Dee Hoty, as Betty Blake (later Mrs. Rogers), whose role is scarcely more than straining to keep her roaming spouse tethered, takes a while to warm us up to her, but succeeds in the end. And these Rogerses, together or apart, can really rope you in with a song.

Only one other role matters, that of a ubiquitous blonde labeled Ziegfeld's Favorite, who serves a variety of functions and, thanks to the leggy, sexy, cheekily droll Cady Huffman, serves them well. But most of the show's brio devolves on the singing and dancing chorus, and with Tommy Tune's flair for idiosyncratic choreography and kaleidoscopic picture-making, it all hurtles at you out of a fancy that never takes five, as startling as a singing telegram, only much more delightful.

Still, there are moments of depletion, but at such times, out comes a wonderful dog act or a sensational rope twirler (Vince Bruce), or the recorded voice of Gregory Peck pretending to be Ziegfeld issuing commands from his glass booth in the Palace Theater's upper reaches, though we know—almost as well as Peck—that it's God speaking from his even higher Heaven. Ziegfeld, after all, must have sounded more like William Powell.

Lips Together, Teeth Apart

The temptation in discussing Terrence McNally's latest, *Lips Together, Teeth Apart*, is to say that it contains everything but the kitchen sink. This would be unfair, however: it contains the kitchen sink too. Chloe Haddock, who with her husband, John, is spending the Fourth of July weekend on Fire Island in the beach house of Sam and Sally Truman, is a compulsive nurturer, and we often see her, through the screen door, busying herself in the well-appointed kitchen. The house used to belong to Sally's brother, David, who recently died of AIDS and, unaccountably, left it to his sister rather than to his devoted black lover, Aaron. Sally's husband, Sam, is Chloe's brother, which is why this (as we shall see) troubled foursome is together in the first place. If at this point you were to guess that *Lips Together* is McNally's version of *Who's Afraid of Virginia Woolf*, you'd be painfully right.

But McNally has crowded much more into his play about two unlikely couples together than his former mentor and friend Edward Albee did into his. In *Lips Together*, in which we also keenly feel the presence of the unseen homosexuals inhabiting the neighboring houses—we are awash in their music, hear the onstage characters make small talk with them, listen to Sam describe how two of them copulate in the bushes, watch their streamers fly in during the July 4 fireworks—we get a veritable encyclopedia of social, marital, sexual, and ideological data about the way we live now and wish to hell we didn't.

Herewith a partial table of contents: a marriage, formerly lusty, now lethargic; another marriage, a one-sided business (Sally never loved Sam); lovemaking, heterosexual; lovemaking, homosexual (not seen, never fear); hints of kinky sexual practices; suggestions of quasi-incestuous closeness between Sally and her late brother; views of excessive closeness between Chloe and her living brother; AIDS as the cause of David's death and possible motive for the suicide of the handsome young man (unseen but fulsomely dwelt on) who waves at Sally, then swims out into the ocean mother-naked, to come back as a bloated corpse; AIDS as a possible source of contamination of the water in the onstage swimming pool (did they, for sentimental reasons, keep it unchanged since David's death?), water that various characters malignly splash on the others, or drink, or try to drown themselves in.

Further: adultery between John and Sally, with John still lusting but Sally rejecting; the other spouses' awareness of said adultery and fear it might recommence; potential dying from an incurable disease (not AIDS) by one character, this possible demise contemplated by one and all with, successively, fear and trembling, fervent optimism, and sardonic amusement. Also male-bonding between heterosexuals, who really hate each other, and occasionally try to break each other's bones; suspicion of latent homosexuality in these (and, by extension, all other) heterosexual males—a favorite Mc-

Nally topos; social, sartorial, and existential differences between a couple from New Jersey and one from Connecticut; the financial basis for divergent philosophies of life; the games (mostly hostile) people play; music of various kinds, but chiefly operatic, ad infinitum; and more, much more, which generally proves less.

Be it said that when it comes to witty, often bitchy, dialogue, McNally is a past master. Be it further said that he sometimes surprises us with a searing insight, phrased with terse, epigrammatic, downright marmoreal perfection. Moreover, he is adept at blending two actions, or several monologues or dialogues, into one stage picture. But, on the debit side, he can be crassly arbitrary, as when a ring is accidentally swept into the pool in Act One and not retrieved until two acts later, when it provides a convenient opportunity for attempted (or merely symbolic?) murder and suicide. He has no respect for minimal consistency of character and plot, as when someone who all through her youth splashed about in swimming pools is said to be allergic to the chlorine in this one, or a longtime actress in amateur musicals cannot tell *Gypsy* from *Annie*. So, too, we gather that it was David's lover, Aaron, who faithfully tended him to the end, only to be told later that it was Sally who lovingly helped David die.

An even graver problem is the language. Though an expert at repartee, McNally understandably wants to write lyrically as well. So he introduces brief monologues in which a character expresses his innermost, unspoken thoughts in very fanciful language. Later, however, when the spoken dialogue is meant to acquire a deeper, more poetic quality, he cannot find a way of keeping monologue distinguishable from dialogue, and we are repeatedly left having to puzzle out whether something is being said or merely thought. And McNally seems to have only a very foggy notion of what heterosexual love talk sounds like; in the last act, he goes from clinker to clinker. Tiresome, too, in the long run, is his ceaseless foisting of his passion for opera on us, whether his characters are opera queens or short-order cooks. And all those cute in-jokes, such as naming the black lover Aaron, after Shakespeare's lesser Moor.

John Tillinger has directed resourcefully and suavely on John Lee Beatty's wonderful set, but his casting is problematic. Christine Baranski and Anthony Heald, the Haddocks, make a fishy-looking couple, and Nathan Lane and Swoosie Kurtz, the Trumans, look even more mismatched. Again, when brother and sister (Lane and Baranski) dance together, the dialogue calls for a sensuously compelling spectacle; what we get instead is grotesque. There is intermittently good acting from everyone, but only Miss Baranski is consistently, hilariously, heartbreakingly fine.

McNally has once again come up with a promising and, for a while, absorbing situation; for an act or so, he carries the ball, then fumbles it. You would think Scott Fitzgerald had him in mind when he said there were no second acts in American lives.

Othello

In *Othello*, Shakespeare created a most unusual triangle: the Beast, the Fool, and the Sacrificial Lamb. The idea was to show how, for lack of critical intelligence to challenge it, evil prevails against goodness. Iago, the cerebral Machiavel, meets no match in either Othello's genuine but unintellectual nobility or Desdemona's patient, loving innocence. That in the end Iago, too, comes to unrepentant grief is no compensation for the deaths of Othello, Desdemona, Emilia, and even silly Roderigo, not to mention the hairbreadth escape of valiant Cassio.

Much ink has been wasted on the alleged motiveless malignity of Iago, the Moor's possible cuckolding of him and Cassio's unquestionable promotion over him being insufficient cause for so much diabolical disaster inflicted on the wholly or relatively blameless. But that, surely, is the point: not that Iago's evil was totally unmotivated but that there is wickedness abroad for which slight provocation is enough to set in motion horrendous retaliation. Hitler was right about Germany's being shortchanged at Versailles; he was monstrously wrong about how he chose to even the score.

But for *Othello* to work in the theater, that triangle has to be perfectly cast: Iago must be a subtle, charming, credible villain; Othello has to be a noble, heroic fool; and Desdemona must be believable in her shattering resourcelessness. In Joe Dowling's Central Park production for Joseph Papp—not dreadful, but lacking the necessary dread—the mishandling of those main roles (along with some lesser flaws) allows the play to lapse into insignificance, almost as if the moral were "Do not lose a precious handkerchief, lest you also lose your life."

Probably the ablest member of that peccant trio is Christopher Walken, but his Iago, much as he delighted the opening night crowd, is also the most erratic. He plays the ensign—and the director allows this—as the heavy in a C-grade biker movie, complete with up-to-date leather jacket, slovenly diction (although he can do much better), ludicrously cut purple punker hair, and two expressions: sneering or zonked. No matter how big this goes over with an uninformed audience, it is a terrible waste of genuine talent, to say nothing of Shakespeare's play.

Even Bernard Shaw, who was temperamentally ill equipped to appreciate much of Shakespeare, understood that the character of Othello is "magnificent by the volume of its passion and the splendor of its word-music." And these are the respects in which Raul Julia fails. Though he has a powerful physique and a strong voice, he looks dopey in this part—brutish and befuddled, not a great man of action outfenced by sly innuendo; and he goes down vocally because of his slow, lumbering or blustering, readings, further hampered by a marked Hispanic accent. When Olivier played Othello with a Caribbean accent—also questionable—he at any rate knew the meaning of what he was saying; he was not your modernist painter distorting the human body without having learned anatomy and figure drawing.

Desdemona is a hard part for today's actresses and audiences: how does one make the loving and obedient wife, who even covers up her own murder by her lord and master, palatable? Here again Shaw's remark about Maud Jeffries is to the point: "Her voice was so pathetically charming and musical, and she is so beautiful a woman, that I hasten to confess I never saw a Desdemona I liked better." Kathryn Meisle's voice and delivery are too angular, too bold for the part; her looks, too robust and sporty. She might make a good Beatrice or Portia, but Desdemona, no.

By far the best work here comes from Mary Beth Hurt as Emilia: she takes that relatively short and often colorlessly played part and turns it into a fully rounded human being, playful and serious, giddy and compassionate, always involved in other people, in lived life. Good, too, is Miriam Healy-Louie as a flighty but spirited Bianca, but the others are undistinguished when not poor, like Michael R. Gill's softly oozing Cassio, or Daniel Oreskes's appalling Gratiano, who can flub a line even before he opens his mouth.

Where in all this is the director? Joe Dowling, formerly of Ireland's Abbey Theatre, proved his mettle here with *Juno and the Paycock* and *Translations*, both Irish plays. But *Othello* is not *O'Thello*, and evidently not his cup of tay, as his indulging the caprices of the not ungifted Frank Conway, his set designer, confirms. So we get a giant head of Aphrodite cluttering up the place to indicate that the location is Cyprus (the goddess's birthplace); later it is toppled over, to indicate that things won't turn out well. Dowling also permits Jane Greenwood to come up with some peculiar costumes, not least of all those men's leggings cross-laced up the rear. And he lets the worthy Richard Nelson bathe Iago in ominous flat white light for soliloquies and longer asides, to let us know these are unvoiced thoughts—as if shortfalls in acting could be fixed by bringing on the lighting designer.

Post-Post Porn Modernist

Miss Annie Sprinkle has arrived with *Post-Post Porn Modernist*, a monologue, monodrama, illustrated lecture, and photo session. On a set representing the boudoir of a porn queen, she rehashes her life—from chubby middle-class West Coast Jewish girl Ellen Steinberg, through sexual performance artist Annie Sprinkle, to her currently evolving self as Anya, a sexual mystic. Her twenty-year career includes periods as a professional prostitute and as a monogamous matron, married to Willem de Ridder, her current director.

The show credits a spiritual adviser, but Miss Sprinkle, for all her spirituality, is also a thriving businesswoman, doing brisk mail-order trade in her pubic hair, urine, and soiled underwear, the price of the last-named having just gone up to $100, it being an article not easily mass-produced. During intermission, you can have your Polaroid picture taken with, as the program says, "Annie's tits on your head," more impressive than such traditional photographic headgear as Mickey Mouse ears or a Wagnerian horned helmet.

Act I features precious implements from Annie's "toy chest," with accompanying encomia; the "Transformation Salon," slides of some plain women who pose as porn stars, with capsule biographies, e.g., "Denise Coffee studies Hassidic Judaism in New York," then, with the next slide, "She is also Blondie Bazooms." There is the "Bosom Ballet," in which the aforementioned appendages display their terpsichorean endowments; and a "Public Cervix Announcement," wherein Miss Sprinkle inserts a speculum and invites the audience to inspect her cervix as spectators' cameras flash like sheet lightning and she salutes "those big, hard Nikon lenses."

Miss Sprinkle was discovered by Professor Richard Schechner—head of Performance Studies at New York University, who brought her act to his Performing Garage—and she has appeared in various NEA-subsidized spaces. She is also a renowned supplier of videotapes for connoisseurs of cunnilingus. Her motto is "Let there be pleasure on earth, and let it begin with me." And, charismatically, she gets the audience to chant along with her such sonorous vocables as "vaginal canal" and "Fallopian tube."

Act II begins with answers to questions from the audience. Replying to one, she admitted that "my rhythm isn't all that good; I'm more of a creative and conceptual lover." One of her creations is the "valley orgasm" of fifteen minutes, though her ultimate aim is the hour-long one. The self-proclaimed "bisexual lesbian feminist" disburses such apothegms as "in an ideal world, men will not ejaculate, and women will." In "The Men I've Loved," we are shown slides of her many lovers who died of AIDS, with tributes to their prowess. Only in the last part of her program, when, to dreary "mystical" music, she performs Anya's endless religious-erotic ritual, does Miss Sprinkle's drizzly talent sadly dry up.

Dancing at Lughnasa

Near the end of Brian Friel's *Dancing at Lughnasa*, Michael, the narrator, says of a haunting recollection, "in that memory, atmosphere is more real than incident, and everything is simultaneously actual and illusory." That pretty much sums up the play, its characters, and—very nearly—Brian Friel's playwriting. More important than people's actions are their emanations, their unvoiced interaction, the charge that circulates among people. What happens is less important than what has happened, what ought to happen, and what, whether the characters know it or not (some do, some don't), never will.

Such an atmosphere cannot help being several things: wistful, tender, insinuating itself into our sensorium by some sort of capillaries, and Chekhovian. Friel once actually gave us an "Irish translation" of *The Three Sisters* (no, not Gaelic), but much of his work is more Chekhovian than *any* translation could be—which is intended as high praise. It is the art of making unfulfillment fulfilling.

Lugh is the Irish name of the pagan god of harvests, whose August festivals survived until very recently on hilltops and by lake and river shores. This festival, or Lughnasa, involved various rituals, including bilberry picking and a great deal of dancing. The bilberries are in the play, too, but the dancing is pervasive. When the narrator, who is the grown son of one of them, remembers the five Mundy sisters who are the play's collective heroine, they seem to be swaying to a music half heard, half imagined, in rhythm with its mood rather than its beat. As you watch and listen to *Dancing at Lughnasa*, you yourself are caught up in a gentle undulation, a dance more within than with the body, which may be no more than the oscillations of the soul between gaiety and despair.

The time is 1936, early August, as remembered by Michael, then seven. The locale is Donegal, Ireland's most poetic county, near the village of Ballybeg, which Friel's imagination has affixed to the map of Ireland more compellingly than any cartographer. The sisters are Kate, 40, a schoolteacher, earnest and the one real money-earner; Maggie, 38, housekeeper and family humorist; Agnes, 35, the quietest and most repressed, who takes in knitting; Rose, 32, another knitter, much livelier but mentally not quite there; and Chris, 26, Michael's mother, in love with Michael's father, the Welsh traveling salesman Gerry Evans, whom she won't marry despite his steady wooing, because he is emotionally and economically unsafe. But, like Chris, he dances magnificently, with body and soul.

The males, then, are Gerry, a dreamy drummer; Michael, who sometimes impersonates his boyhood self, but discreetly from the sidelines, leaving his center-stage presence visible only to his fellow players; and Father Jack, 53, the Mundy sisters' brother, who has come back from a quarter century's missionary work in Africa under a cloud—a very funny one at that. And there is an inanimate character of importance: the radio, a sickly contraption that works only intermittently, either filling the air with wonderful thirties dance music or sputtering into silence and filling the characters with frustration. And another, albeit unseen, presence: the date itself, 1936, a kind of summer festival in the history of Europe—a garden party or *thé dansant* on the way to disaster.

The interaction, I repeat, is exquisite in this tremulous play, which wouldn't be Friel, wouldn't be Irish, if it were not poetic, eloquent, flowingly verbal even in its condemnation of words as troublers of stillness, and sad-funny when not funny-sad. Last summer in London, it did not quite get through to me, jet-lagged as I was only a few hours after arrival. (What did seem better in London was Joe Vaněk's lyrical set, perhaps because the stage there had a different configuration.) There, the play felt a bit talky and bland, though the equally fine cast was rather less subdued. On present viewing, the longings and privations, jokes and outcries of these characters—all of them cheated out of something essential—appear strong enough to accompany us well beyond the theater and the playing time.

Though the men in the cast—Donal Donnelly, Robert Gwilym, and Gerard McSorley—are all fine, they are (rightly, perhaps) outshone by the women. Bríd Brennan, Catherine Byrne, Rosaleen Linehan, Dearbhla Molloy, and Bríd Ní Neachtain perform miraculously, though some have roles that are not palpably striking. Thus Agnes, the most hemmed in and self-denying of the sisters, is portrayed by Miss Brennan in the homeliest, most understated mode. But watch her carefully: she exudes wonders. Yet the ultimate wonder is Friel's central image, the dance, which never stops during this restrained feast of a play. It is always there in one of several forms, a dormant volcano of passion always ready to erupt, and, when it does so, eliciting pure awe.

In the Jungle of Cities

In the Jungle of Cities, formerly by Bertolt Brecht, must now be ascribed to Anne Bogart, whose total distortion of it is on view at the Public Theater. Even as we mourn the death of Joseph Papp, whose loss will loom larger with every passing year, we must save some space in our hearts wherein to greive for what Miss Bogart has perpetrated against Brecht, the theater, and—to the best of her abilities—mankind. For what the director offers us has only incidental bearing on Brecht's interesting but immature, veiledly autobiographical third play (1927 in the revised version, used and abused here.) The text has been cut and otherwise meddled with— the translator's name isn't even in the program—but that is the least of it. After some 45 minutes, and the departures of several spectators, I, too, left; a longer stay would have been unendurable.

Miss Bogart paints the faces of every character a different color—red, green, yellow, etc., some of them even two-tone—seemingly without, or against, any rhyme or reason. Actually, it is partly to be facilely avant-garde, partly to be stupidly politically correct. Since the villainous Shlink and some of his henchmen are Malays of the Peter Lorre variety, the work might be foolishly viewed as anti-Asiatic rather than, correctly, as a macabre pseudo-Hollywood fantasy laid in a mythic Chicago. So Shlink is made up to be the whitest person on stage; siblings are played by a black and white, the black in red makeup (a Native African American?) and so on to further confuse the issue. Gabriel Barry's costumes carefully avoid any collective sense, and are often out of individual character. Donald Eastman's set, the Potemkin façade of some sort of warehouse that doesn't change, has little bearing on the changing action. Heather Carson's lighting, however, does keep changing—unmotivatedly.

This is a New York Shakespeare Festival and Mabou Mines co-production (note that JoAnne Akalaitis, NYSF's new artistic director, is a product of Mabou), and these standard Mabou actors must be reckoned as some of the worst that can be scraped up in New York. Two of the characters are named Baboon and Worm; perhaps taking this as a cue, the cast is a menagerie of untalentedness and ugliness to whom "ensemble acting" would seem to be a dirty term. Here one person does nothing but an unconvincing shuffle, another mumbles deliberately (a particularly unhappy choice in a cast not distinguished for elocution), someone else does an old-style nancy-boy routine, and yet another merely grins and grins. And Ruth Maleczech, the Mother Outrage of Mabou Mines, plays two roles here—including one that Brecht never wrote.

The misdirector comes up with all sorts of stylized movement and business—if sheer ungainly and arbitrary busyiness constitutes enough style to merit the name "stylization"—and, lest any of Brecht's surviving meanings come through, has the sound level of Judson Wright's wretched music up high enough to drown puppies, never mind words. I am very far from demanding naturalism from drama, but where a text has all the antirealism you could ask for built into it, to try to cram in, contradictorily, more is not just to paint the lilly, it is to defoliate it.

Anne Bogart has previously endeared herself to me by placing the action of *Spring's Awakening* on a spaceship and that of *South Pacific* in a disabled veterans' ward; she endeared herself to Providence's Trinity Rep (which, having read the raves she gets in certain publications, hired her as artistic director) to the point where they encourage her to leave at the first opportunity. Her work strikes me as absolutely mindless, untheatrical.

Moreover, Bogart turns the 102 minutes of running, or crawling, time into one claustrophobic act, hoping to forestall a mass exodus. So don't just take my world for it; do check out the horror, but be sure to ask for tickets on the right, i.e., entrance and exit side, of the house. The exit on the far (left) leads to a blind alley, and my companion and I very nearly had to climb a fence to escape.

Blue Man Group

Blue Man Group comprises three madcaps who, though mad, wear no caps—not even hair on their shaven heads, which they paint blue. No robin's-egg blue, as might befit these glabrous ovoid craniums, because the trio doesn't want to represent a specific group, not even robins. Cobalt blue then, making Matt Goldman, Phil Stanton, and Chris Wink look like men from Mars, except that Mars is the red planet.

What do they do? Easier to tell you what they don't do. They don't do a play. They don't talk, save sometimes through running electronic displays or stacks of schizophrenia-inducing posters. They don't do magic tricks. And they don't make sense, only a very special kind of nonsense. It would make sense to a clever child, to Lewis Carroll and to Edward Lear, to Yves Klein, *le monochrome*, who painted solid blue canvases. But not to Gainsborough, *The Blue Boy* notwithstanding, because he painted neatly. When Blue Man Group paints with it mouths (spitting colored food onto a canvas), with other people's bodies (painted blue and rolled onto a canvas), with spouts in their jackets gushing blue, red, and yellow, it paints sloppily. That is what makes a frenetic action painting look like modern art. It may even *be* modern art; it is certainly the merriest performance art I know of.

BMG likes paints and foods best, because with them you can make the most massive messes. But it can wreak sloppy havoc with less condutive materials; computers, camcorders, drums, strobe lights, and endless rolls of paper in which it wraps the audience. (Eat your heart out, Christo, though you could never make as big a mess of it as the blue men make of three boxes of Cap'n Crunch, and an audiovisual mess at that.) BMG also makes music on weird organs made from plastic plumbing tubes (hence the show is called *Tubes*), tubes that take on a riot of colors until they look like a designer bowel organ, perhaps a Versacephone. There is also backup music from another trio who (we see them dimly in blue light) may be men with blue guitars. Wallace Stevens would have liked them. *I* did.

Mad Forest; Marvin's Room

The music seemed to have deserted Caryl Churchill in her recent work; with *Mad Forest*, however, she is out of the desert, and a light is shining at the Perry Street Theater. Shortly after the execution of the Romanian dictator Nicolae Ceausescu and his equally awful wife, Elena, in late 1989, Romania was struggling (mostly unsuccessfully) toward democratization in a mass of burning but unanswered questions, recrimination, and a slew of new difficulties, some of them indistinguishable from the old. Miss Churchill and her director, Mark Wing-Davey, together with ten drama students, went to Bucharest and London. Truthful, pointed, and poignant, it applies to all our worlds. Here too, it should provide entertainment as liberally as education.

The author has shrewdly constructed a work in three acts: before, during, and after the overthrow of the Ceausescus and their dread secret police, the Securitate. The second act, delivered in Romanian accents (not especially consistent or convincing), is based on interview tapes in which various Romanians spell out what happened, or appears to have happened, during those bloody but almost inscrutably opaque days in late December 1989. The accents represent the English in which the Romanians spoke to Miss Churchill and her team. To this, the author prepends a first act about two fictional families, the quasi-proletarian Vladus and the more intellectual, quasi-bourgeois Antonescus, and their interaction during the Ceausescu era. Repression is dramatized in many terrible ways, most tellingly by interminable silences, or by the radio blaring while people whisper so as not to be overheard, or by loud voices barking official lies while communication proceeds by silently exchanged notes or bank notes.

If this silence is scary in Act One, the uncheckable, vindictive garrulity after the so-called liberation is, in Act Three, even scarier. Everyone suspects everyone, old wounds fester, a new regime proves as harsh as the one before, nobody knows who is a friend or foe, jobs are imperiled, ingrained ethnic hatreds resurface and proliferate. Babble unleashed leads to blows, a wedding party becomes a hailstorm of fisticuffs. Rampant aggression is no better than cramped repression.

Beyond this realistic triptych, Churchill introduces a Fascist archangel (the misguidedness of religion) and an opportunistic bloodsucker of a Dracula (capitalism? the West? the symbolism is vague), and a speaking dog (the desperate urban-underdog riff-raff), which adds a bit of metapolitical theatrical bravura to the proceedings, as well as biting humor. So, too, interpolated snatches of Romanian dialogue and blatant officially approved music intensify the perplexing political smog. The Romanian set-and-costume designer Marina Draghici and the American lighting designer Christopher Akerlind combine their powerful talents to make a small stage become as large and threatening as life itself. And under Wing-Davey's strikingly risk-taking direction, a cast of eleven plays a multiplicity of roles with precision and persuasiveness. A few longueurs aside, *Mad Forest* is absorbing, disturbing, and brutally amusing enough for all audiences.

American playwrights tend to reduce social and political horror to the merely personal. It is not that sickness, infighting, and death in the fmily are subjects unworthy of drama. On the contrary, they have proved too worthy for too long and are, in less than expert hands, losing their edge. When this problem is compounded with AIDS, but AIDS as a plague that dare not speak its name, a play can become both unfocused and sullen as unredeeming farce is gobbled up by unremitting gloom. That Scott McPherson, the author of *Marvin's Room*, has lost his lover to AIDS, and has himself tested HIV-positive, hovers like a black cloud over the play as the attempt to crossbreed Larry Kramer with Ionesco results in something self-contradictory and, ultimately, numbing.

Bessie, the heroine of *Marvin's Room*, is a middle-aged spinster who has sacrificed her life to caring for her sick and senile father, Marvin, dimly discernible and sometimes inchoately audible in a back room, letting his death-in-life seep onto the stage and into Bessie's selfless existence. But now Bessie herself is diagnosed—by a ludicrously incompetent doctor—as gravely ill with leukemia and in need of a bone-marrow transplant. The donor could be either her harried, truculent sister, Lee, or one of Lee's sons. The college-age, bitter Hank, however, is an arsonist confined to, and only provisionally released from, a mental institution; the high-school-age Charlie is a nice bookworm, hard to pry loose from printed matter. This trio from Ohio descends on Bessie in Florida, dimly trying to help out, but really creating even greater havoc in her precarious life.

There could be a real play in this if McPherson could find the right tone. It is, in theory, commendale that, by not writing about himself and his lover more overtly, he tries to universalize his losses and problems. Likewise, choosing absurdist comedy as the basic vehicle for one's grim talk is an understandable strategy in a culture that wants to amuse itself to death with escapist fare. But the exact tone, however hard to achieve, is indispensable; the British Miss Churchill has managed it in *Mad Forest*. In *Marvin's Room*, things begin in a funny-grim way (which is effective) but quickly progress to grim with only an intermittent rude joke (still workmanlike), then hurtle into grimmer than grim, undercut by the aura of earlier grotesquerie, to end up neither funny nor sad, but merely distasteful. Too bad, because David Petrarca's canny direction and the generally good cast—in which Laura Esterman, Lisa Emery, Mark Rosenthal, and Alice Drummond are outstanding, and only Shona Tucker is too obvious—deserve better. As do we.

Two Shakespearean Actors

Is it wholly bad that theater cannot provoke the kind of tumult sometimes encountered at sports events? Of course it is terrible that some twenty people died and many more were wounded in the Astor Place Riot of 1849, when the English Shakespearean William Macready played Macbeth concurrently with the native favorite, Edwin Forrest, in New York City. But might it not mean that people really cared about theater then? Alas, no; the rioting was social and political: rich people's imported theater versus poor folk's domestic stuff; Britain, the traditional enemy, versus America; highbrow versus any other kind of brow.

It was an epic event, though, and to do it full justice a movie would be needed. Richard Nelson, who wrote *Two Shakespearean Actors* about it, is one of our most—forgive the weasel word—interesting playwrights. Having lived both in America and in England, he has acquired a sort of mid-Atlantic accent in his writing. This equips him with both dryly English quips and juicy American humor. Although his plays, especially the more serious ones, have a way of not quite coming off, they show a concern for the world that few American plays do, and they command attention through sheer intelligence when not through dramatic tension. Moreover, the plays stay with you: they say something even well after the last actor has stopped speaking.

Nelson's concern here is, first and last, with the life of the theater and the lives in the theater. How do British and American actors and acting differ? How did Macready's *Macbeth* look and feel; how did Forrest's? Just what were the strengths and weaknesses of each? Clearly, both his Macready and his Forrest are what Cocteau aptly dubbed *monstres sacrés*: sacramental nuisances, holy terrors. They are obnoxious and lovable, impossible and necessary, and always larger than life-size. These two are sworn rivals, yet also friendly enemies, brothers under the greasepaint if not under the skin.

In 1849, Macready was 56, Forrest only 43; much is made of the patronizing tone of the older man, the arrogance of the younger. The English actor's private problem is homosexuality; that of the American, adulterous philandering. Macready's main pitfall is jadedness; Forrest's, crudity. But both captivate and conquer their audiences, even as they tend to make life miserable for their fellow actors. Both are affectionately drawn here with perhaps only cursory historic, but genuine histrionic, veracity. Surrounding them is a gallery of American and English actors with their absurdities but also their appeal. When Forrest says, "Life is not half so much fun as the theater," you believe him, not on faith, but on the evidence of what Nelson has put rambunctiously and endearingly before you.

The author tells us no less about theater through the figure of Dion Boucicault, the facile playwright married to a charming, all-comprehending (though not necessarily all-forgiving) actress. His farcically compulsive womanizing is contrasted with Forrest's melodramatic infidelity vis-à-vis a desperate, hysterical spouse. There is also Macready's fellow actor and traveling companion, John Ryder, the play's most arresting character, whose loyalties are divided between Macready who enjoys him and Forrest who employs him. He, above all, reminds us of the perplexity and pain that also figure in the repertoire of a theatrical life.

The large cast has been incisively, strikingly directed. True, there was a Royal Shakespeare Company production before this one, and Jack O'Brien, the present director, may have seen it in England. But you cannot get from another production something so keenly and intricately ensconced in the here and now, something that flows so naturally with *these* actors, on *this* stage. O'Brien, who does splendid work at his Old Globe in San Diego, proves conclusively what a loss to New York the intervening distance presents.

Two Shakespearean Actors is a longish play, and it sags a bit just after the middle; also, as already noted, having to keep the climactic rioting offstage slightly mutes the effect. Still, this is an evening that also boasts David Jenkins's leanly functional sets, Jane Greenwood's spirited costumes, and Jules Fisher's canny lighting. Brian Bedford's Macready combines quizzical condescension with yeomanly sanguinity in an utterly cherishable performance. The often terrific Victor Garber is a trifle short on bravura as an otherwise proficient Forrest; a touch of Kevin Kline could have helped here. Željko Ivanek is a marvelously torn Ryder, wallowing in a homemade brew of insecurity and swagger, eagerness to please undercut by unquenchable outspokenness.

Frances Conroy gives her patented unhappy-wife performance, but always makes it freshly wounded and wounding. Jennifer Van Dyck plays her rival for Forrest's libido with great, perhaps too great, assurance. Laura Innes is as deliciously sardonic as she is toothsome as Mrs. Boucicault; Katie Finneran is persuasive as an overingenuous ingenue. Tom Lacy has a hilarious bit as a waspish actor who goes up on his lines, and Eric Stoltz does capitally by the doltish Boucicault. It's great to hear him boozily ask Judy Kuhn (the one loose cannon in the ensemble), "Whish wish… which witch" she plays.

When Forrest brags of doing research in mental institutions, Macready retorts, "We're different actors. You study asylums and I study the play." Spectators no less antithetical should find pleasure here, provided only that they love theater.

Sight Unseen

You should certainly catch, for all its imperfections, the exciting *Sight Unseen*. This is by far the best play Donald Margulies has yet written, and its flaws are tactful enough never to interfere with what, indisputably, is there.

Jonathan Waxman, once a devout Jew and promising painter, has become a huge, affluent success, though as fishy as any Fischl or Schnabel. He was always drawn to shiksas, but eventually jilted his first and best one, Patricia. Fifteen years later, she is lovelessly married to Nick, an odd, able, semi-impoverished British archaeologist, but finding life in archaeology and chilly England Spartanly bracing. Jonathan, married to another shiksa too pregnant to travel, comes to London for his first European retrospective. His father has just died; he no longer wears either the yarmulke of his youth or the red bandanna of his art-school enthusiasm, when he and Patricia shared bed and ideals. Cocky on the outside but lost beneath, he calls Patricia from London and goes up-country for an overnight reconnoitering of her and Nick's and his own embattled lives. The visit turns nightmarish as Nick displays sardonic hostility, sneering both at Waxman's and all modern art, while Patricia, still secretly in love with Jonathan, proves bitter and vengeful.

Margulies ingeniously flashes forward to scenes in London with Grete, a smart young German art critic interviewing Jonathan and asking sincere but wrenching questions about his commercialism, his betrayed roots, his compromised art; questions he construes as anti-Semitic, which they may even be, and yet… Finally, the play flashes back to when Jonathan and Patricia were lovers and she posed for the nude that now hangs over her and Nick's fireplace, obsessing her with nostalgia and Nick with jealousy. This nude is one of the key symbols; the other is a later Waxman painting hung in the show, which is socially, politically, and artistically incorrect.

The problem with *Sight Unseen* (a reference to the way rich collectors buy as-yet-unpainted Waxmans, and to the commercialization of art and life) is that it tries to deal with too many big themes hard to make cover one another neatly like those triangles in geometry. There is the loopy love triangle, the renegade Jew in the shadow of the Holocaust, the artist as victim or con man—runaway horses in a troika that end up upsetting the apple cart.

Bit by bit, however, the play fascinates. The dialogue is abrasive and unsettling; the situation fraught with potential mayhem; the predicament human. Margulies manages to write a Pinter play better than Pinter. He is helped by Michael Bloom's staging, full of sinister rubatos; nervousmaking lighting by Donald Holder; no-frill but great-skill scenery by James Youmans; and remarkable acting.

Dennis Boutsikaris is able to do justice to Jonathan's multiple convolutions, past and present, and to make him clever, horrid, pitiful, and one of us. Jon de Vries is an astounding Nick: both lumbering and lightning-quick, turning squinting humility into a sudden stiletto, making servility ooze venom. As the earnest yet insidious journalist, Laura Linney is dead on in looks, accent, gesture, and timing. Only the excellent Deborah Hedwall disappoints a little: her Patricia is too raw, too bristling, too weird, depriving the play of the sympathetic center it needs. But what a play—I haven't even mentioned how funny much of it is. Seriously.

Crazy for You;
The Baltimore Waltz

One of the more agreeable forms of the musical is the silly-sweet one, with nothing on its mind, and happy to pass its lighthead-edness on to you. Of course it has songs and dancing and gags and scenery and costumes galore, and also romance whose path is roughened a bit before it is allowed to run smooth. But mostly there is the atmosphere of beatific tomfoolery, enabling us to thumb our noses at reality for a while—make merry Mardi Gras before Ash Wednesday overtakes us. Crudely put, it is escapism.

Yet escapism can look pretty appealing when, as in *Crazy for You*, it admits to its friendly fakery, even calls attention to it at every possible turn, then charms us anyway. Purists, to be sure, have every right to be offended. The show, based on George and Ira Gershwin's *Girl Crazy*, could just as well have been revived straight, without evoking unhappy memories of the bootless tinkering in *My One and Only*. There was no need to drag in songs from elsewhere and make us think that the Gershwins stuck "Someone to Watch Over Me" into everything they wrote. There was no need to have Ken Ludwig write a new book if that meant kicking out some good old songs and hauling in some dubious old jokes, many of them recycled from Ludwig's *Lend Me a Tenor*.

And yet… If you enjoy chomping on corny one-liners off the cob of nostalgia, if you're amused by a new old-style book and an old old-style book does not strike you as sacrosanct, if you're not all that fussy about which Gershwin songs you are getting (less well-known ones from the original or wholly unknown ones from God knows where), and if you thrill to the fledgling efforts of a future major choreographer (Susan Stroman) whom you can watch grop-ing her way to greatness; if, further, you can have fun with tongue-in-cheek scenery (Robin Wagner), impudent costuming (William Ivey Long), and spectacular lighting (Paul Gallo), *Crazy for You* is sure to keep your feet and spirits on tappytoes.

Yes, the Ludwig tale of slick Eastern lad and plucky Western lass in love against the let's-put-on-a-show background, complete with a parody of Ziegfeld Follies (and Ziegfeld's personal folly) and a re-enlisting of *Lend Me a Tenor* mistaken identities, creaks out of every crevice—and still manages to amuse. And yes, neither Harry

Groener nor Jodi Benson is an ideal lead: she sings well, but lacks looks and charisma; he dances nicely but not effortlessly, and is more effective disguised as the formidable impresario Bela Zangler than undisguised as the tenderhearted playboy Bobby Child. And true, the chorines dance a lot better than they look. And also true, the chief comics, Bruce Adler and Jane Connell, are not notably funny. But there are compensations.

The second leads, John Hillner and Michele Pawk, are very much on target, she in particular. William D. Brohn's orchestrations and Peter Howard's arrangements strike all the right notes. Even if he lets some routines run on too long, Mike Ockrent has directed flavorously, with always new surprises up his capacious sleeve. And, above all, there is the ceaselessly inventive and superabundant choreography of Miss Stroman, whose only problem is that she has too many swirling ideas and does not yet know how to leave well enough alone. But already she dazzles with sheer imagination and, better yet, the ability to tell a story in dance, to further rather than arrest the plot while displaying more originality than anyone since Tommy Tune. When the great American musical-comedy tradition is perilously close to total eclipse, *Crazy for You* lights a small but gallant and inspiriting candle.

There are plays that are merely bad, and others that are downright repellent. Paula Vogel's *The Baltimore Waltz* establishes itself firmly in the latter category. The author, who teaches drama at Brown and has garnered more grants and awards than a black sofa gathers lint, informs us that her brother Carl, after being fired from his elementary-school teaching job for flaunting his homosexuality, wanted her to take a trip to Europe with him. Not knowing that he had tested HIV-positive, she declined for reasons she now rues, and Carl, without getting his trip, died of AIDS in their native Baltimore. The dedication of the play reads, "To the memory of Carl—because I cannot sew." The reference, of course, is to the AIDS quilt. Miss Vogel is being unduly modest: I am sure she sews at least as well as she writes plays.

The piece is a fantasy trip to Europe. In this fantasy, the author calls herself Anna, a first-grade teacher dying of ATD (acquired toilet disease), something that attacks young, unmarried female grade-school teachers who, as her comic physician explains, use "the johnny in the classroom to make wawa." Carl, Anna's brother and colleague, cashiered for teaching lewd homosexual songs to his tiny wards, is taking Sis to Vienna for treatment by the celebrated Dr. Todesröcheln (German for "death rattle"), "a specialist in uritosia." "He writes poems about urine?" Anna inquires. "No," Carl explains, "he drinks it." He also, as we see later, lets the patients indulge.

So off to a fantasy Europe they go, Carl making arrangements with an old school friend now living in Vienna, Harry Lime, whose former address was *The Third Man.* "There is something up," he tells Harry over the phone; "no, *that* hasn't been up for ages." It is Harry who recommended Dr. Todesröcheln, and who, in a blond fright wig, proves to be Dr. T. But let's not anticipate.

As they set off, Anna announces, "In whatever time is left, this teacher means to fuck her brains out," and so she does, with any waiter, bellhop, or other comer. Typical scene: a bed, presented vertically (this is avant-garde theater!), with Anna and a Parisian waiter under the sheets. Anna's voice, in a crescendo, repeats, "Oh, yes!" The garçon's voice, likewise crescendo, repeats, "*Ah, oui!*" Carl and Anna picked him up in a bistro (stuffing herself is her other indulgence) "where Hemingway threw up all over Fitzgerald's suede shoes, which really *was* a moveable feast."

While Anna's heterosexual escapades are shown bluntly enough, Carl's homosexual ones are rendered metaphorically. Wherever he goes, Carl carries his floppy toy bunny. Fishy-looking men (all minor parts are played by the same unappetizing actor, Joe Mantello) emerge periodically from odd places; each carries the identical floppy bunny, to be furtively exchanged for Carl's in dark nooks or crannies. Why are homosexual encounters treated in this oblique fashion? The bunny trope, moreover, does not work. Whenever the siblings go through Customs, Anna must hold Carl's rabbit, lest the Customs officers, suspecting it of harboring contraband, tear it apart. First, women carrying bunnies can be just as suspected of smuggling as men. Second, there are x-ray machines expressly designed to protect bunnies from needless disembowelment. Third, how do you hand over your homosexuality to your sister during inspections? The floppy metaphor flops.

Other devices similarly misfire, e.g., the slide show of their trip Carl puts on for Anna, where the slides turn out to be seedy locations around Baltimore. Throughout, the relationship between brother and sister gets closer and stickier; then Vogel pulls her dramatic flip-flop and reveals that it is really Carl who is dying—but not until Dr. T. and Anna, as it were, toast each other with urine. Carl dies, and Anna performs a pas de deux with his corpse, which adds incestuous necrophilia to the repertoire of tastelessness. In the final scene, the dead Carl reappears in full Austrian guardsman's dress uniform, and waltzes the swooning Anna around to the music of Strauss—something out of *The Chocolate Soldier* coated with bittersweet incest.

I would not dwell on *The Baltimore Waltz* at such length if it had not earned widespread critical praise and a major grant from AT&T (which does not stand for acquired toilet & trough disease), ensuring it productions at four reputable theaters across the country. I daresay AIDS plays nowadays command Pavlovian adulation, especially if by espousing absurdist technique they awe both sponsors and spectators. But some subjects, such as AIDS and the Holocaust, are not laughing matters, and should be protected from the likes of Paula Vogel. Be it said, however, that the Circle Rep production—condignly directed by Anne Bogart, who can be entrusted only with this kind of play—is efficient in most respects, and that Richard Thompson is good as Carl, and Cherry Jones remarkable as Anna.

Death and the Maiden

Ariel Dorfman, the Chilean writer, brings us his *Death and the Maiden*, a drama set in a country that, the program coyly tells us, "is probably Chile." A long era of dictatorship has yielded to a new democracy, and Gerardo Escobar, a lawyer, has been appointed to the presidential commission investigating political crimes. Driving back to his beach house, he blows a tire and, having neither a spare nor a jack (much is made of these two unconvincing circumstances), gets a stranger, Dr. Miranda, to give him a lift home. By an even less persuasive device, Miranda drops in after midnight, and Gerardo's wife, Paulina, recognizes him (or so she thinks) as the man who, fifteen years ago, participated in torturing her and repeatedly raped her. But she keeps mum.

Miranda accepts Gerardo's invitation to spend the night (more stretching of credibility), and while he sleeps, Paulina knocks him out, drags him into the living room, ties him to a chair, and gags him. In the morning, she is seated beside him with a gun. She tells her flabbergasted husband that they will hold a trial; Gerardo is to be the defense, Paulina the witness, prosecutor, and judge. Miranda, when he does get a chance to speak, flatly denies being *that* doctor. Paulina, we gather, has been mentally unbalanced since those terrible events: Is she capable of determining what's what? And how will she deal with Miranda if he is found guilty?

But we do not get enough of the Escobars' home life to infer just how crazy Paulina is. Or enough about this society to deduce whether Miranda's loving Schubert's famous quartet and quoting (or misquoting) Nietzsche constitute enough grounds for identifying a person. We don't even know what to make of the fact that former evildoers are to be ferreted out but granted amnesty. Yet these are small matters compared to the basic insufficiency of reducing a national and individual tragedy to a mere whodunit. For despite the little grace (or disgrace) notes of humorous squabbles and troubled personal relationships, the play is really all is-he-or-isn't-he, did-he-or-didn't-he: too trivial for the amount of suffering on which it is predicated. Can you imagine *Hamlet* if its only real concern were whether Claudius did or did not poison his brother?

Yet even as a whodunit, *Death and the Maiden* fails because it avoids coming satisfactorily to grips with the one question it raises. Would Agatha Christie leave a murder unresolved and then pride herself on her ambiguity? And it isn't as if the wit, pathos, or language here were good enough to carry the play or even a half-pound paperweight. Mike Nichols's direction does not seem to achieve more than anyone else's would, and the acting does rather less. Gene Hackman is a believable Miranda, perhaps because he is spared the excesses of Dorfman's fancy writing. But Richard Dreyfuss's lawyer is only Richard Dreyfuss, take it or leave it. As for Glenn Close, she is not exactly bad but seems, as usual, miscast. For Miss Close is almost always a bit too much this or not enough that; with rare exceptions, her performances leave you undernourished or overstuffed. Personally, I would have loved to see Mary Beth Hurt or Laila Robins in the part, or indeed Lizbeth Mackay, Miss Close's talented standby.

Curiously, Tony Walton, perhaps having shot his wad on *Baboons*, has under-or misdesigned the scenery, which is sparse and a bit bewildering. And Jules Fisher's lighting (no doubt at Nichols's behest) turns illicitly stylized for a naturalistic play. But Ann Roth's costumes are suitably understated. Last time, I reviewed a terrible play by Richard Caliban. Here, despite an Ariel and a Miranda, things are not appreciably better.

Guys and Dolls

There are only a very few musicals where everything blessedly works. Of this hot little handful *Guys and Dolls* is sweatily, coolly, gorgeously one. The current revival is not consistently top-notch, but has enough excellence—and where not that, solid competence—to give you a lasting high. More I cannot wish you.

Let's get the few, nonfatal lapses speedily out of the way. As Adelaide, the ebullient Faith Prince goes over the top. She must do *something* every second, like a demented Method actor gone campy, unaware of the sometimes urgent need just to be there and, for a brief breathing space, do nothing. Even the greatest music needs an occasional pause—think Stravinsky. Miss Prince would be much truer and funnier if she weren't so relentless. Still, she has many rich moments, and in these Nathan Lane beautifully abets her. Lane himself is not quite the right Nathan here; as that beleaguered bantam gangster, he is a bit too winsome, too wistfully mellow, too lovably Lane for Detroit. But, unlike Miss Prince's, his wrongness is easeful, and his rightness, when it comes, sublime.

Another problem is the Sarah of Josie de Guzman, the standby who, at the eleventh hour, replaced Carolyn Mignini. Miss de Guzman is not the "mission doll," the upper-class ice maiden in need of—seemingly impossible—melting. She is a real singer and natural actress, pleasantly ethnic and amiably mundane. Yet there is no miracle, no marvelous meltdown. But at least also, thank God, no Mignini. And good as Walter Bobbie is as Nicely-Nicely—yes, I have learned from Frank Rich that Runyon made him thin—once you've seen the immortal Stubby Kaye, it becomes lèse majesté not to make him fat, if only the better to rock the boat.

And now an end to grievances. The Frank Loesser score, the Swerling-Burrows book, the Damon Runyon characters are as intoxicatingly irresistible as ever, and there are things here even finer than in the fabled original production. Take the Sky Masterson of Peter Gallagher, who acts, sings, and looks better than the formidable Robert Alda did. Gallagher creates a quieter, more introverted and complex Sky. He is not just a dashing leading man; there are things going on under his assurance. Or take such a relatively minor figure as Lieutenant Branigan, whom William Ivey Long, whose costumes carry sassiness to heroic extremes, has decked out with the perfect musical-comedy version of the movie *Dick*

Tracy: a canary-yellow trench coat and a *clashing* muddy-yellow hat. And the actor, Steve Ryan, is equally long on humor. A flatfoot ballooning into exuberance, Ryan—helped by his coat, hat, and wit—levitates.

Jerry Zaks's staging has many a high point, e.g., the way sitters bounce when Harty the Horse plunks himself on their bench, and the way their tamed men appear in the leading ladies' illustrated imaginings during "Marry the Man Today." Even lovelier, perhaps, is Christopher Chadman's choreography, which, buoyed by the splendid likes of Scott Wise and Gary Chryst, soars, bounces, and slides to new heights of musical-comedy dancing, yet is always securely grounded in character.

But the absolute peak here—complementarily and superlatively lighted by Paul Gallo—is the set design of Tony Walton. Taking his cue from such salon painters as the airy Dufy and breezy Van Dongen, Walton seems also to have absorbed (not copied!) the art of such tangy minor masters as the illustrators Dignimont and Touchagues, both also ace stage designers. The forms here are whimsical, the hues insolently oversaturated, the contours slightly blurry, as in an expansive alcoholic vision. And Walton's sewer set, with the fish-eye perspective of a Delaunay cathedral, is a masterpiece.

Given all this, and then some I have no space for, I can only reprise, More I Cannot Wish You. This *Guys and Dolls* is permanently floating, and you'll swing with it like a bell.

Jelly's Last Jam

If you want a musical that combines much of what is good about the old with annunciatory touches of something mindstretchingly new, I commend to you *Jelly's Last Jam*. Using some of Jelly Roll Morton's fine old tunes with worthy new lyrics by Susan Birkenhead, George C. Wolfe (with a healthy musical assist from Luther Henderson) has undertaken to blend the story of Ferdinand Le Menthe Morton with that of the birth of jazz, and both with the racial problem within the black race: the light-skinned Creoles' intolerance for the darker-skinned.

A tall order for one musical to deliver, and *Jam* may be excused for not entirely succeeding. No matter how cleverly Wolfe has condensed, there are elements here that cry out for more detailed attention. Such things as the central relationship between the Roll and the singer and café owner Anita need more development than they get here. The exact function of the Other Man, Jack—Morton's companion, colleague, and both victim and involuntary victimizer—remains underexplored. And Jelly's later life is overelided.

On the other hand, what achievements! The format is Jelly's trial on the night of his death before the Chimney Man (a.k.a. Death, as a sinister song-and-dance man), assisted by a group of girl singers, the three Hunnies, as Jelly's life is being rerun to determine the nature of his afterlife. This is *Everyman* set to music, but what makes it startling is that here it is blacks who assess a black antihero.

How dazzling are the tap duets between the young Morton (Savion Glover) and the adult Morton (Gregory Hines), as choreographed by Hines and Ted L. Levy. How stunning the Mardi Gras atmosphere, not just aesthetic but also fraught with social and historic insight. How exciting the birth-of-jazz numbers in which African roots are evoked, with, the help of such mighty performing talents as Mary Bond Davis and Ruben Santiago-Hudson. How aptly satirical the dance number in which Tin Pan Alley and the Roll do not roll happily in the hay together. How effectively sinister (and prophetic!) the scene on Central Avenue, Los Angeles, in which Jelly is gang-stabbed by fellow blacks.

Best of all is Scene 6, Chicago, where Jelly and Anita meet musically and carnally, going from mutual provocation to cohabitation and collaboration, and where the marvelous Tonya Pinkins encapsulates Black Women's Lib. Here writing, direction, design, and acting combine to make the scene a touchstone of musical comedy as *Gesamtkunstwerk*. The great Morton song "Lovin' Is a Lowdown Blues," further galvanized by the new Birkenhead lyric, has Anita and Jelly making out in a four-poster that keeps symbolically turning as an epic mating game is enacted, with Chimney Man and the Hunnies singing, dancing, and commenting from the sidelines. As stingingly choreographed by Hope Clarke, this becomes a sexy, funny, thrilling bit of social history—if not, indeed, moral philosophy.

Once again, the droopy-faced Gregory Hines proves the consummate leading man. Acting, dancing, singing, or just standing in emotion-filled stillness, he puts into this Jelly Roll a part of himself that is deeper than the part. And he is backed up by the complementary talents of Keith David as the most awesome of levelers; Tonya Pinkins as a woman who goes smoothly from sultry arrogance to earthy humaneness; Savion Glover as a young Morton, warm of heart and hot of foot; Ann Duquesnay as the formidable grandmother who traumatizes the boy; and Stanley Wayne Mathis as the touching loser—or is it winner?—Jack.

Jules Fisher demonstrates that he is the fountainhead of new concepts in lighting design, while Toni-Leslie James's costumes manage the minor miracle of controlled flashiness. In his scenery, Robin Wagner—like a juggler who can make ten balls look like one, and one like ten—plays with the shapes of space, making concrete look didactically abstract, and abstract become glowingly concrete. The smart supplementary music by Luther Henderson, King Oliver, and Anonymous perfectly enhances that of Jelly Roll, whose last jam—thanks to George C. Wolfe, who also directed—may well be his best.

Richard III

A tricky thing, modernization; it has to be consistent and cannot be a patchwork of Then and Now that works now and then. This is one of several problems with the *Richard III* that Britain's Royal National Theatre has brought to BAM, where it explodes with a big bang, proving, alas, that dazzlement is not necessarily enlightenment, and that a bombshell is also something that self-destructs. There is much wrong with a *Richard III* in which the little princes arrive on a model train, but Richard and Richmond fight their final duel with broadswords and in full armor.

The name of the ruse is gimmickry; but call it ingeniousness and it smells no sweeter. Place the action in the thirties, give Richard an accent modeled on Edward VIII's, fill the air with hints of an English Hitler, and what have you got? Confusion. If the aim, rightly or wrongly, is to lure young people into the theater, are the thirties any less remotely and inscrutably the past to them than the Wars of the Roses and the Swan of Avon? When art has to change its tune to be heard by contemporary ears, it is surely singing its swan song.

Take Richard's vocalization (e.g., "beautah" for beauty), modeled, as Benedict Nightingale tells us in a Times piece, on Edward's speech of abdication "for the love of Wallace [*sic*] Simpson"—and here I had always thought that Wallis Simpson was a woman! Why compare the coldly efficient Gloucester to the tepidly ineffectual future Duke of Windsor? And why display two thirties-style micro-phones when these look as strange to modern eyes as medieval musical instruments? And why affect an accent that hampers communication, especially on tour in non-English-speaking countries?

I endorse modern dress if timeliness is of the essence and is used consistently; but if we are reaching back, why not go all the way—to Shakespeare? A parallel is far more effective if our noses are not being rubbed in it and we can all discover the internecine relevance to ourselves in the turmoils of York and Lancaster. Well, perhaps not the woman in green at the Brooklyn premiere: seeing the name EDWARD IV projected onto the backdrop at the start (another gimmick: each section of the play is emblazoned with the name of the then-ruling monarch), she remonstrated, "I thought we were seeing *Richard III!*" Still, an audience is supposed to have its imagination stretched, not its ego massaged. Yet even though Richard Eyre, the director, admits in a program note that the production makes interpretive cuts and additions, the star, Ian McKellen, declares in his note that "our production is not an adaptation—not even an interpretation."

What then is McKellen's noninterpretative interpretation of Richard? His visual symbol is a man almost bald on one side, with corresponding slight curvature of spine, limpness of arm, and lameness of foot. But on his other side, fullness of hair, nimbleness of limb, fairness of countenance. This would be a useful conceit if Richard, either for Shakespeare or for McKellen, were half angel, half beast. But no, for both of them he is pure evil, bold and cunning, mitigated only by a certain charm, and wildly, viciously successful until the end. McKellen performs some fiendishly clever physical business and has a plethora of pawky vocal tricks. But the opacity of accent and some excesses of archness are unhelpful.

I imagine that it must have been at least partly McKellen's idea to turn Richmond into a pipsqueak (McKellen even pronounces his name in mocking French fashion, "Richemonde"), making the play's heroic figure into a silly boy who can conquer Richard only with the help of a killer squadron (like Achilles and his Myrmidons in *Troilus and Cressida*) and who ends the play with a proto-Fascist salute much like Richard's. Yet the last thing Shakespeare had in mind here was that royal power of necessity corrupts. And the Walpurgisnacht-like dream sequence at the end creates further confusion in the guise of shallow theatricality.

But there is also *good* theatricality here—a royal dinner party, for instance—and Bob Crowley's scenery is simple but highly effective, even if his costumes, other than the military uniforms, are mostly garish. Jean Kalman's lighting is persuasive, except for the bathing of an assassin in satanic red light. Dominic Muldowney's music is evocative though merely functional, and Richard Eyre's staging is aptly pointed, with perhaps a slight tendency toward unduly horizontal lineups. The real problem, though, is the supporting cast.

Nothing is gained by Terence Rigby's obesity and crassness as Buckingham, even if it allows the self-indulgent McKellen to call him "Bucking-ham." Malcolm Sinclair's Clarence remains singularly unmoving; indeed, among the men, only Richard Bremmer's Neville Chamberlainish Stanley really scores, with David Beames and Tristram Wyniark also notable for not playing Catesby and Ratcliffe as obvious villains. But all the women are weak, with Antonia Pemberton's Margaret and Anastasia Hille's Anne especially wanting. Still, the women's protracted curses and lamentations are particularly hard to stage, and Eyre may be excused for failing with them, given the absence of great actresses. Yet he is to be blamed for flashily dragging in executions that Shakespeare wisely left offstage—the more so since the text speaks of headsman's blocks but Eyre gives us the garrote.

Salome; Fires in the Mirror

In 1893, Oscar Wilde published his first major play as *Salome: A Tragedy in One Act*. The *Salome* at Circle in the Square is an amateurish farce. Properly produced, it could have been a milestone for the English language, for poetry in prose, and for genuine sensuousness and sensuality, something our alternately prurient and preachy, pornographic and AIDS-obsessed theater could well have used.

To start with, everyone mispronounces the name of the prophet Jokanaan. The chief mangler is Salome herself, who calls him "Your Carnin," though the rhythm clearly demands the proper stress on the double a. As for the Princess, her name should have nothing to do with sausage. Not that Al Pacino, as Herod, actually says "salami," but he does, like a good Italian, say something like "salame."

Sarah Bernhardt, who was rehearsing the lead in the aborted 1892 premiere, rightly perceived the play as a stylized heraldic fresco, in which "the words should fall like pearls on crystal." In Robert Allan Ackerman's staging, they fall like saliva into a spittoon. Wilde viewed this, his favorite play, as turning the objective, genre drama into something as personal as a sonnet: "The recurring phrases in *Salomé* that bind it together like a piece of music with recurring motifs are... the artistic equivalent of the old ballads." Here they are the equivalent of what you hear at such temples of art as the Port Authority Bus Terminal and Yankee Stadium. Everyone speaks in his own contemporary and unorchestrated idiolect, and, with one exception, no one knows how to speak verse. And there is no unified acting style—if, indeed, there is any.

Jokanaan seems to have been cast not for his electrifying voice or awesome looks but for his buttocks, which are grandly displayed. Otherwise, nothing about Arnold Vosloo explains Salome's passion, unless she has a thing about South African accents and fancies the mispronunciation of "limned in color" as "limed in color."

Sheryl Lee may have been a marvelous corpse for *Twin Peaks*, but for Salome more animation is required. It's a difficult part: the Princess of Judea has to be both nubile virgin and Walter Pater's primeval, amoral Mona Lisa. As Max Beerbohm put it, reviewing the 1905 English premiere, Salome has to be "impersonated by an actress of mysterious charm and force, an actress vibrating with as much sense of beauty as power for horror." Miss Lee does not vibrate; she hardly even acts. She mouths Wilde's prose poetry dutifully, like a schoolgirl reciting her lesson, her looks of a perfect Wisconsin dairymaid unenhanced by the unseductive costuming of Zack Brown. (His set, as lit by Arden Fingerhut, is rather more effective.)

The dance of the seven veils, which strips Salome naked, is as sensual as the peeling of an onion. Richard Peaslee and Hamza El Din may have come up with authentic Casbah music, but Richard Strauss read Oscar's mind much better. And Lar Lubovitch's choreography would not do a Tenth Avenue belly dancer proud. No one here has grasped that Wilde's play takes place neither in ancient Judea nor in some modern Mediterranean seaport dive, but in a Yellow Nineties or Art Nouveau poetic never-never land.

Al Pacino renders the Tetrarch as a self-indulgent homosexual who is not very lustful about Salome, not very frightened in the end, and not above playing most of his role for cheap laughs. Pacino's drawl is Higher Slobovian delivered at a very low speed, with Peculiar breaks, as in "Think you I'm like the King of Egypt who gives no feast... to his guests but that he shows them a corpse?" There are problems with syntax, as in "I'm not one of those who breaks their oaths." And the articulation can collapse, as in "I will pay thee, Reilly," which turns out to mean "royally."

The director is no help. Though there is a huge moon on the backdrop, he has the characters addressing some other moon in front of them; perhaps he thinks the locale is on Saturn. He lets the executioner, who should be standing discreetly in the back, loll about the steps to the throne, and get a better and comfier view of Salome's crotch than the Tetrarch himself. He turns Tigellinus, the Roman ambassador, into an effeminate stripling. He stages the internecine squabbles of Jews and Nazarenes for facile yoks. He casts the Page of Herodias as a big, strapping fellow, larger than the Captain of the Guard, whom he worships. He begins the play with a strange sexual huddle between a soldier and a male slave. He has one of Salome's slave girls, an oafish white woman, disport herself like a society matron; she is also Salome's understudy. Meanwhile, the other slave girl, a stunning black woman (Tanya M. Gibson), much more like a Salome than Sheryl Lee, is made nothing of.

The only solid performance here is the Herodias of Suzanne Bertish. Her usually annoying smugness for once fits the character. More important, the actress, though half American, has trained and worked in England. With impeccable diction and fluent ease with poetic language, she is far more commanding than Herod or anyone else. If the other roles were cast as aptly, this might have been a *Salome* to remember for things other than its ludicrousness.

Fires in the Mirror does very well by my least favored genre, the one-person show. Anna Deavere Smith has conducted interviews with many figures—famous, notorious, obscure, anonymous—who have some kind of relevance, often distant but never far-fetched, to the deaths of a black child and a Hasidic scholar visiting from Australia in Crown Heights, Brooklyn, in August 1991. The swerving and death-dealing car of the Lubavitcher *rebbe*, and the alleged preferential treatment given the driver by a private Lubavitcher ambulance, the retaliatory stabbing of the young Hasid by black youths, and the subsequent litigation and turmoil are what Miss Smith sets out to elucidate.

She has chosen highly suggestive selections from those interviews with a cross section of blacks and Jews, who shed light either on the specific events of Crown Heights or on various aspects of their lives that provide the tinder for such traumatic incidents. She is a first-rate journalist who, through often offbeat snippets, spirals toward the core of the problem, while remaining scrupulously impartial throughout.

Her presentation, featuring telling titles in slide projections, very few props, excellent body language, and a fine sense of running order, has but one minor shortcoming. Miss Smith does not do voices and accents compellingly, and her statement that she does not do impersonations is otiose; the moment you change your sound and looks for each character, you are an impersonator, like it or not. Still, through 90 firmly packed, fair-minded yet unsettling minutes, she creates a powerful piece of lived and felt history.

The Sisters Rosensweig; The Destiny of Me

The Sisters Rosensweig is Wendy Wasserstein's most accomplished play to date. It is through-composed, with no obtrusive narrator haranguing us. Its central, but not hypertrophic, character is the eldest sister, Sara Goode, divorced from her second husband. An expatriate in London, she is celebrating her fifty-fourth birthday, for which her younger sister Gorgeous Teitelbaum has flown in from Boston, where she dispenses personal advice over the airwaves. From farthest India, the youngest sister, Pfeni Rosensweig, has jetted in; now a travel writer, she is shirking her mission, a study of the lives of women in Tajikistan. Equitably, all three sisters end up sharing center stage, both literally and figuratively.

Gorgeous, who, we are told, is happily married with four children, is group leader of the Temple Beth-El sisterhood of Newton, Massachusetts, on a visit to London. Pfeni is here to touch base with her lover, the famous stage director Geoffrey Duncan, whom she has converted to heterosexuality and may soon be marrying. Here, too, is a friend of Geoffrey's, the New York faux furrier and genuine mensch Mervyn Kant. Rounding out the cast are Tess, Sara's precocious teenager; Tom Valiunus, Tess's dopey but good-natured punker boyfriend, with whom she is planning a political-protest trip to his ancestral Lithuania; and Nicholas Pym, a British banker, stuffed shirt, and suitor to Sara.

This is the stuff of Anglo-American comedy, more specifically Anglo-Jewish-American drawing-room comedy, in which some related but diverse mores and some diverse but trying-to-become-related people are playing off one another. Sara, a banker herself, is high-powered, smart, and sex-starved. Pfeni and the ebullient but labile heterosexual Geoffrey are having difficulties, And the ostensibly contented Gorgeous is there to stick her bobbed but nosy nose into everybody's business.

A seasoned theatergoer may well guess several plot developments, though there are also a few surprises. But plot is far less important than character and dialogue, both of which Miss Wasserstein does handsomely and humorously. She is surely one of our wittiest one-liner writers, but under the bubbles and eddies of her wit are real people in deep water, resolutely and resonantly trying to keep from drowning. And she is able to orchestrate the interaction of her disparate characters into a complex, convincing polyphony. There may be a touch of the arbitrary here and there; mostly, however, the play flows, entertains, and liberally dispenses unpompous wisdom about ourselves.

Particularly pleasing is that *Sisters* manages to be both of its time, 1991, and of all time, unless human nature changes radically, which for these 5,000 years it hasn't. The three Rosensweig sisters are by no means unworthy descendants of a famed earlier sisterly trio, to whom an occasional quotation in the text alludes. If I have any problem with the play, it is that several of its characters have a propensity for bursting into song and dance at the slightest, or even no provocation. In a straight play, this can be as unsettling as long spoken passages in a musical.

It is to the skilled cast's credit that every last drop of humor is extracted easefully, even as the no-less-germane modulations into seriousness are achieved with gear-shifts a Lexus or Infiniti might envy. Jane Alexander's Sara is one of the most memorable of this stylish actress's creations; here is perfect timing backed up with the subtlest changes of intonation and incomparable facial play. Without effort or undue emphasis, Miss Alexander's diaphanous face reveals the playground of ideas and battleground of emotions; it is as if the countenance itself had repartee, soliloquies, and tirades at its wordless disposal.

Madeline Kahn, as Gorgeous, is once again her special blend of philosopher and fool, shrewd observer and egocentric, outrageous jokester and wistful waif—a ditsy Diotima whom none could improve on. Frances McDormand is saddled with the autobiographical character whom most playwrights either overwrite or, as in this case, slightly underwrite. But she does Pfeni gamely and touchingly, opposite John Vickery's dazzlingly campy and exquisitely English-theatrical Geoffrey. Robert Klein's Mervyn is all we expect from this sovereign clown: exuberantly wisecracking, irrepressibly amorous, impudently ingratiating. And Patrick Fitzgerald's affably preposterous Tom has no lack of assurance and authenticity.

I am less taken with Julie Dretzin's Tess and, especially, Rex Robbins's Nicholas, but they do not gum up the works. Daniel Sullivan's direction is as painterly as it is musicianly: everything in the right place and tempo. John Lee Beatty's set is devilishly right, and Pat Collins's lighting and Jane Greenwood's costumes collude with it cunningly. You will not be bored here.

In *The Destiny of Me*, Larry Kramer has written a worthy sequel to *The Normal Heart*, his autobiography as Ned Weeks, writer and gay activist. In this long but absorbing play, Kramer superimposes Ned's battle with AIDS at the National Institute, under a scarcely disguised doctor figure, on his own growing up as Alexander, a precious adolescent in a middle-class, Depression-and-Holocaust-era Jewish family. The heterosexual older brother, Ben, and the somewhat flighty mother, Rena, are tolerant enough of Alexander's incipient homosexuality; but the father, Richard—a Yale graduate, minor bureaucrat, and professional failure—brutalizes the boy for his addiction to musical comedy, dressing up in his mother's clothes, and "sissy" personality. As Ned and Alexander interact, flow into each other across the years, and separate again, we get, in ingenious double exposure, a coming-of age and a coming-of-AIDS play, a kind of—and this is meant as praise—Jewish-homosexual *Long Day's Journey Into Night*.

What Kramer captures expertly in the past is family relations in their ambiguities, hostilities, and reconciliations, with the brothers' love for each other finally overcoming all differences. And almost equally skillfully in the present, the bristling relations of patient and doctor, patient and nurse (who happens to be the doctor's wife), against a background of embattled gay activists whom Ned himself organized, but toward whom, with his strength now sapped by illness, his attitude has become ambivalent. But not hostile—as it is toward the doctor and sassy nurse, with both of whom he engages in a medical-political battle of wits, even as they, to the best of their belated abilities, try their utmost to save him. Yet this is deemed inadequate by both Ned and the loud and destructive—perhaps self-destructive—protesters, heard but not seen.

Under Marshall W. Mason's superlative direction, Kramer's characters always engage our attention, and often our feelings; what is lacking is language, the flare of poetry. It's like an Arthur Miller play trying to hoist itself into a Tennessee Williams one: we hear the straining bootstraps snap. The role of Ned fits Jonathan Hadary like a rubber glove; but while he is persuasive, John Cameron Mitchell, as Alexander, is something even better: compelling. Fine, too, is Oni Faida Lampley as the nurse; the others—Peter Frechette, Piper Laurie, Bruce McCarty, and David Spielberg—are okay, where more would be better. Except for one improbable conversion, the play makes no false move, and impresses by its ultimate fairness to all parties. Though it falls short of the higher reaches of art, it may be the most comprehending, and is certainly the most comprehensive, AIDS play so far.

Oleanna

Although I am not in the habit of quoting myself, in reviewing David Mamet's *Oleanna* I must repeat something from my *National Review* movie column about Mamet's *Glengarry Glen Ross*: "His view is not darkly tragic, or even darkly comic; his concern is to render everything as glossily black as the best-shined shoes. I remain unimpressed by an author who tries to dazzle me with the sheen of his footwear." And so it is again in *Oleanna*.

To start with the title: I gather that it refers to a song about a nineteenth-century Norwegian American utopian community in the Midwest, on whose site young Mamet once went camping. He loved the word *Oleanna* and vowed to use it someday, somewhere. So, rather campily, he entitled his play, in which a student called Carol accuses a professor called John of sexual harassment, *Oleanna*. He could just as well have called it *Oleomargarine* or *Tasmanian Devil*. And the title is no more arbitrary and unreal than the play.

In Act One, the professor has summoned the failing student to his office. She has trouble with the textbook (which he wrote) and with the entire course. Asked what she didn't understand, Carol, who sounds like a robot with a limited vocabulary, replies: "Any of

it. What is everybody talking about? What does it mean?" John offers to assist her with special tutoring; he pities such a Platonic idea
of a nincompoop. When he uses the word *indictment*, Carol needs
to have it explained to her; but then she herself uses such words as
recant, impinge, and *hierarchy*.

In truth, the language of the play is totally synthetic. John speaks
mostly in pedantic convolutions, Carol in echoing vacuities. There
is no drop of human reality anywhere. Deliberate? Maybe, but to
what end? To generate sympathy? It doesn't. Antipathy? Why would
one want to? For roughly a third of Act One, John is on the phone
with his wife or his Realtor or lawyer about a house he is buying;
the negotiations have hit a snag. The real-estate maneuvering (a
leftover from *Glengarry*?) has almost nothing to do with the matter
at hand, but goes on endlessly, right in front of Carol, even though
John could hang up and phone back later. In Act Two, when the
situation is truly desperate, he is still taking interminable calls in
front of Carol. A strange hang-up, this inability to hang up.

In an attempt to make Carol relax, John tells a mildly off-color
joke and once, paternally, puts an arm around her shoulder. By
Act Two, Carol has alerted the faculty committee that was ready
to grant John tenure that she has been sexually harassed. Not only
won't he get tenure, he may also be fired. By the end of the play,
she is slapping a lawsuit on him for attempted rape. His house will
be lost, too; his wife and child will suffer. But the Carol of Act Two,
who is backed by and represents an undefined "Group," has become
vengefully articulate, indeed glibly eloquent. Was her near-imbecil-
ity in Act One—and throughout the course she was flunking—an
elaborate act of entrapment? Or is she a genuine idiot savant whom
the Group has coached in some fancy lingo? Or is Mamet simply
playing fast and loose with authorial responsibility? A characteristic
sentence of John's, if diagrammed, would look like two Christmas
trees engaged in unnatural practices. Carol's blatant dumbness and
sudden, frightening fluency are even less persuasive.

I have no idea whether Mamet thought he was making out a
balanced case, with each character having genuine claims to credibility, or whether we are to root entirely for John. Certainly Carol's
having a snit over his referring to the faculty committee that has a
couple of women on it as "good men and true," and her reprimand-
ing him for calling his wife "baby," are not calculated to win friends
for her. And her dress and hairdo, making her look like a candidate
for an advanced degree in frumpishness, would guarantee even the

most purblind professor's picking some other student for the object of his extracurricular lust. And what kind of dramatist wastes
one full act—half his play—on tedious, creaky exposition? But why
care about any of this? Mamet has created two wooden dolls and
pumped some Martian dialogue into them. The topic is relevant;
the play is a piece of refuse.

Very remotely, *Oleanna* resembles Ionesco's *The Lesson*. That is
an absurdist play, its teacher and pupil behaving and speaking sur-
really. But because the characters are imbued with wild fantasy, the
language sparkles with zany poetry, and a genuine sense of tragicomic despair hovers over the proceedings, Ionesco's play towers
over Mamet's, especially as directed by Mamet himself and performed by his wife, Rebecca Pidgeon, and one of his favorite actors,
W. H. Macy. Neither actor is a star, the scenery consists of a few
sticks of used office furniture, and the theater is Off Broadway; yet
it took thirteen producers to mount this play. That in itself should
tell you something.

Someone Who'll Watch Over Me

Some plays are too good for note-taking. I had resolved to jot down
some of the witticisms in which *Someone Who'll Watch Over Me*
abounds, but promptly realized that there was too much going on
every instant—verbally, visually, emotionally. At Frank McGuiness's
comedy-drama you don't want to miss a line, a facial expression, a
single silent beat.

The three hostages in the play, chained to separate walls of a
Lebanese basement room serving as their cell, are as remote from
one another as can be; not quite a cross section of humanity, they
are nevertheless a constant reminder of the variety, hostility, and
ultimate harmony human diversity can give rise to. The starkness
of the wall space framing these inmates effectively displays their
quirks and touches of genius, their zesty individuality and kindred
vulnerability. Their positioning, with a chain gripping each of them
at one ankle and granting them only a puny radius of activity, shows
off each as perfectly as a picture hung in a well-curated exhibition. And never has the lack of the fourth wall seemed more apt:
that invisible wall becomes the one to which you, the viewer, are
chained—riveted by the play yet imprisoned in your existence.

First, we see two chained men. Adam is a black American doctor who has clearly had an arduous rise from a limiting background and seems most likely to survive under hardships; as a physician, he will conserve his physique with exercise and maintain a sound mind in a bound body. One can imagine how hard it must have been for this determinedly goal-oriented young man to be stuck with a fantastical Irishman for a cellmate.

Edward is a journalist, married and with children, by turns enthusiastic and cynical, feckless and devoted to his family, and, above all, gorgeously gabby. But he could not have survived had his confinement remained solitary; such a born comedian needs an audience, which Adam, whom he teases and humors, provides. Of course, Edward exercises nothing but his tongue, which comically lashes out at Adam's calisthenics and just about everything else. Yet he is warmhearted and giving, his wit naughty rather than nasty.

This twosome is joined by a third captive, at first in a comatose sleep on the paltry mat, as thin as cushions in a sports stadium, which, along with an individual water bottle, is all the comfort the jailers will grant. Michael proves to be a college English instructor, a fussy, middle-aged closet homosexual, haunted by memories of his deceased wife. A mother's boy, he is concerned most about whether his Arab captors have informed his mother back in England of his relative safety. Predictably, this fussbudget will emerge, in many ways, the bravest of the trio. Predictably, because such a play in which, obviously, there cannot be much overt action needs a switcheroo. But just because something is predictable does not diminish its dramatic value when it is emotionally exhilarating.

There is something especially endearing about the way Michael quotes and paraphrases medieval English literature. You'd think that a poem such as "The Wanderer" wouldn't have much to say to these motion-starved men, but it does. Therein lies the glory of McGuinness's invention: it draws its substance from every part of the geographical, historical, cultural map; it welds disparateness into solidarity; it compensates for the fettered body with a larkingly unfettered spirit. Black American savvy, Irish wit, and English humor come together in a play that, both as drama of ideas and as sheer entertainment, outstrips all current competition.

As the three little Indians dwindle dismally to two, and are further reduced—liberatingly as well as sadly to one, we experience their most minute loss or gain as our own. Some may find the second act slightly anticlimactic, but I am not of their party: something is always happening in this play, even if it takes the mind's eye to detect it. There may be a temporary slackening toward the end, when understatement borders on ordinariness, but not for long. There come, at the very last, a few words and one gesture (the latter aptly and ecumenically harking back to ancient Sparta) that make everything resoundingly right again.

From the strictly naturalistic, logical point of view, you can find a few flaws. And though I do not mind the physical absence of the captors (a clever stroke), I chafe, as usual in such cases, at the absence of women. But they *are* present here by that very absence, by the way they are missed and recalled. Besides, there is something so rich about the performances that they transcend mere maleness into spiritual androgyny. James McDaniel commandingly turns Adam into a man both strong and scared, his steadfastness perforated by breakdowns (such as the other two also experience), but whose bouncing back proves as comforting as a dependable thermostat.

Stephen Rea may be the most dazzling addition to our histrionic horizon. Catch him playing the exact opposite role in the movie *The Crying Game* and then, having seen him as Edward, tell me if this young Irishman doesn't create the strongest possible effect with the most economical means—and if that isn't great acting, what is? As for Alec McCowen as Michael, watch this consummate artist turn prissiness into self-respect, fuddy-duddiness into grandeur, and intellectual elitism into true, sharable wisdom. His way of rattling his chain, like Rea's of wiggling his toes, is pure characterization. In McCowen, McDaniel, and Rea we have an ensemble as unbeatable as a violin, a viola, and a cello.

Let's not overlook the ingeniously angled set, starkly yet suggestively painted by Robin Don, an oubliette enveloped between scenes by the great, star-twinkling firmament; or the lighting by Natasha Katz, which fills this windowless space lit by one chary lamp with that borderline gloom between hopeful fantasizing and harrowing reality. And let's thank Noel Pearson, the producer who so seamlessly follows up *Dancing at Lughnasa* with this languishing in Lebanon; and the splendid director, Robin Lefèvre, who can make men chained beyond one another's reach become movingly conjunct in a pas de trois of their longings. How proper that the author, who hails from that most Hibernian of counties, Donegal, should be a lecturer in English. His life, like his play, illustrates what can be gained from crossfertilization by seeming opposites.

Jeffrey

If you got your fill of the depressive from Miller, it is to Paul Rud-nick's *Jeffrey* that you must repair to regale yourself on the manic. This is a prime specimen of a rising new genre, the AIDS comedy (cf. *The Baltimore Waltz, Falsettos, Marvin's Room*, parts of *The Destiny of Me*), which may eventually lead to a new formula for shows: boy meets boy, boy gets AIDS, boy loses boy. (With, of course, minor variations.) Rudnick's play blends reasonably skillfully comedy, se-riousness, and surrealism, so that it is not the mélange that proves tiresome but the components.

The opening—the most ingenious scene—shows Jeffrey in bed with a succession of bedmates, all of whom prove variously unsat-isfactory. Finding himself accosted in a gym by yet another man, Steve—and, further, finding himself going wobbly over the tall, muscular Steve's advances—Jeffrey, haunted also by the specter of AIDS, settles on what is unarguably safer than safe sex: total absti-nence. A free-lance waiter, Jeffrey plies his trade at various posh functions, at all of which Steve pops up as a fellow waiter (though he haunts him in other places, too), to tempt him with ever more insolent allurements, until Jeffrey considers even that most desper-ate of remedies, leaving New York and rejoining his parents in the Midwest.

We follow our hero as he rattles about town, often in the com-pany of his best friends: Sterling, a successful and snootily aphoris-tic interior decorator, and Darius, his boyfriend, a dancer now (but not forever) in *Cats*. They meet up with a variety of folks mostly form the homosexual world, played by three actors, and one actress in a number of parts each. There are even some surreal (or super-natural) encounters. Probably the funniest part, after the opening scene, is one in which Jeffrey goes to Saint Patrick's Cathedral to pray, only to be sexually accosted by a priest. This brings out some choice Rudnickisms, e.g., "You are some sort of lunatic in a priest suit." "Isn't that redundant?" And, by way of penance, "Say six Hail Marys and bring me your shorts." Never fear that I am spoiling your fun; there is plenty more where these come from.

Your enjoyment of *Jeffrey* will depend on how cherishable you deem dialogue such as "All gay men aren't crazy about sex; all *men* are crazy about sex. All gay men are crazy about opera." I must warn you, though, that Rudnick cheats. He allows persons to fall out of character, and situations out of any sense, to get his laughs. But he has a fine cast working under Christopher Ashley's appropriately manic direction, with John Michael Higgins (Jeffrey), Edward Hibbert (Sterling), and Darryl Theirse (sundry roles) especially amusing. Yet a spectator has ample time here to wonder at what point does absurdism become merely absurd.

Angels in America; Kiss of the Spider Woman

How nice it would be to have stumbled upon *Angels in America* on some far-off stage in London or Los Angeles, unemcumbered by the hurrahing heralds of "Genius'" or the demurring trumpeters of "Trumpery!" One could then have mused, "Who would have imagined that Tony Kushner the author of the grandiosely vacuous *A Bright Room Called Day*, would make such progress? At least now he is writing from the inside out rather than, wrongly, the reverse." But before we elevate *Angels in America* to the rank of masterpiece, we must ponder both its surtitle and its subtitle.

The surtitle, *A Gay Fantasia on National Themes* should remind us that this effort to be national or ecumenical is, after all, a minority report. Not so much a minority of one, which the true artist always rightly is, as a minority of one percent (if we espouse the latest official figure) or 5 to 10 (the proposed counterfigures for homosexuals in America), which is both too much and too little. It is dangerous for the playwright to speak chiefly and tendentiously for such a social minority. And the subtitle, *Millennium Approaches*, literally a reference to the year 2000, should alert us to the second half of *Angels*, entitled *Perestroika*, still only approaching, as it is being revised by the author for an autumn opening. When we have both parts in tandem or in repertory, we shall be better able to determine whether the American theater has achieved a milestone, an artistic millennium, or just another, longer and more pretentious, *Jeffrey*.

Angels, Part One, is an attempt to encapsulate the Reagan-Bush era in the story of two families or quasi-families. One is the Mormon and seemingly heterosexual couple, Joe and Harper Pitt—joined later by Joe's mother, Hannah—who come east from Utah, to play out a kind of return of the pioneers to New York and Washington.

The other is the more complicated ménage of Louis Ironson and Prior Walter, a homosexual couple, in which Prior falls prey to AIDS, and Louis to cowardice. Louis, a clerical worker, drifts, like Joe, into the orbit of Roy Cohn, the play's devil figure (although Mr. Lies, the spirit of drugs and thus a fake travel agent, is another, lesser, one). Cohn aspires to crooked control of New York, Washington, and the country by creating a fake family of filial acolytes, who are to be his spies and agents in the centers of power. He is, moreover, so evil as to deny his homosexuality and AIDS.

To complement the eastward journey of the Mormons (significantly known as Latter-day Saints), there are two westward journeys: that of Louis's ancestors, the European Jews, one of whose last true representatives, a grandmother, is eulogized at start of play as (significantly for Kushner's thirst for ecumenism) the Last of the Mohicans. And that of Prior's Anglo ancestors, ghosts who go west to haunt their scion, although his business is really with the future, with the angel of death and the afterlife—perhaps even God, the good father, unlike Roy, the bad one.

But it is too early to talk extensively and conclusively about a play that, however long, is only half a play. To be sure, it is also unfair to open such a half-play without its second part, especially when one hears from the West what a mess *Perestroika* was there. So, are the Salt Lake City real-estate agent and the Bronx bag woman, who now seem obtrusive danglers, essential to the grand plan? Are Harper's Valium-induced gibberings about Antarctica and the ozone layer germane to what follows? Are those biblical references—Lazarus resurrected, Jacob and the angel—to become properly integrated symbols? And, apropos integration, will the black homosexual Belize and his argument with the Jewish Louis give rise to a reconciliation of blacks and Jews? Will, as the title *Perestroika* implies, Europe join America in the action? Will the fact that some male roles are played by a woman assume valid meaning? Tune in next fall.

George C. Wolfe has directed with almost too much inventiveness, while Robin Wagner's scenery and Jules Fisher's lighting perform what they are supposed to—miracles. Only the costumes and music fall rather short. Ron Leibman is more Roy Cohn than Cohn himself ever was, even though many of his lines are (unacknowledgedly) taken directly from Cohn's dicta. Joe Mantello is properly slippery as Louis—all honor to Kushner for not making his alter ego more appealing. As Prior, the excellent Stephen Spinella is spindliness incarnate (or disincarnate), the most frighteningly real onstage AIDS patient; I hope this good actor doesn't starve himself for his craft. Good, too, are David Marshall Grant as a saint uneasily heading for the gay life, and Jeffrey Wright as a philosophical black drag queen.

Marcia Gay Harden's Harper is a lot less moving than she might be; Ellen McLaughlin and Kathleen Chalfant truly manage only one role each, though the variety demanded from them may be excessive. The two most important things about *Angels in America* are both good news and bad. The good is that, for all its three and a half hours, the play doesn't ever bore you; the bad is that it is unfinished, and that it is hard to see how Kushner—or anyone—could pull such far-flung ambitions, such heterogeneous though homosexual strands together into one tightly knit, ravelproof whole.

In my review of the movie version of Manuel Puig's novel *Kiss of the Spider Woman*, I called it "the reduction of a fairly clever piece of high camp to a cross between substandard Hollywood and rather low camp." Camp (think Charles Ludlam) can be quite amusing, but must be very careful about what it is camping up: Aeschylus, yes; Auschwitz, no. This story of a Marxist revolutionary and dragqueen window dresser thrown together into the same cell of a barbaric Argentine prison, there to find their true selves amid betrayal, torture, poisoning by warden's orders, could have made an opera in the hands of a major composer; otherwise, it should have been left alone—certainly not camped down even lower than the movie. Its painful subject has been reduced to painfully bad taste.

By keeping his own voice strictly out of the novel, Puig stimulatingly had us trying to figure out which of his two main characters is saying what part of that dialogue, or thinking those interior monologues. Puig made you think—just what the Kander and Ebb musical with Terrence McNally's book strives to make unnecessary. It does, however, want to have a tough edge, and so bits of torture steadily recur. The result shortchanges both human dignity under stress and uninhibited Broadway razzmatazz. The show's motto could be a line from one of the lyrics: "Whatever was grim is going to be grand." The impossible transformation is neither grim nor grand, though, only queasy.

You may recall that Molina, 37 and given eight years for "molesting a male minor," eases his own, and eventually Valentín's, pain by telling his firebrand cellmate in phenomenal detail the stories of movies he kept seeing and reseeing all his life, most of them escapist fantasies.

"It doesn't matter that the way of life shown by Hollywood is phony," Puig once stated; "it helped you hope." Puig the fantast felt closer to Molina, but yearned to be also the heroic Valentín. Yet the musical trivializes both the revolutionary and his idea of *revolución*, presumably because those do not fit in with McNally's brand of humor and a musical audience's need for escapism. It does not even convey what, as Pauline Kael noted, Puig called for: the delirium of excess. The delirium of mediocrity is a sorry sort of delirium.

In the novel, the Spider Woman is a minor character, chiefly a symbol for the allurements of death, with perhaps further symbolic ramifications. In the musical, she crawls all over the place and merges with the character of Aurora, the movie star Molina draws sustenance from, thus achieving the non-Puigian and self-contradictory message that what gives hope and life is also what gives death. Both women are, of course, portrayed by Chita Rivera. Yet the image on the musical's logo is that of a young woman, beautiful and sexy. Miss Rivera is—well, Miss Rivera. She has been outfitted with a Louise Brooks bob, enough makeup to feed the faces of all the uncosmeticized girl children of China, and costumes by Florence Klotz in which that fine designer has clearly squelched her good taste. Miss Rivera looks as if she were playing Norma Desmond in *Sunset Boulevard*, which, for all I know, she may be doing. She sings well, has unimpaired diction, and, if the casting call went out to Gray Panthers only, may well have outdanced all others.

Brent Carver is a first-rate Molina, though as un-Latin as they come. He negotiates the role's exacting and contradictory demands with stylish finesse, and avoids countless lurking pitfalls. Anthony Crivello, however, is a charmless Valentín, although he sings nicely. He has been changed from upper-class to lower-class either because middle-class theatergoers can more easily accept hungry revolutionaries or because Crivello can't manage upper-class. Herndon Lackey and Kirsti Carnahan are quite undistinguished as, respectively, the evil warden and Valentín's girl, and Merle Louise is ludicrous in the risible part of Molina's mother, dragged in chiefly to countenance her son's uncloseting himself with the sappy "You Could Never Shame Me."

Though Kander's music impartially recycles his own and everyone else's, it is catchy enough, even if Ebb's lyrics tend to let it down. Vincent Patterson's choreography, even augmented by Rob Marshall, is unable to tell movie plots as it is meant to. Jerome Silkin's basic set is either a very chic prison or Philip Johnson's State Theater atrium, which comes to the same thing. The Silkin projections, mostly spiderwebs or lush tropical vegetation, work well enough in their overexplicit, overassertive way, making it hard to assess Howell Binkley's lighting.

Harold Prince, a hands-on director if ever there was one, leaves his imprint on much of the show's swift pacing and bracing bravura. Yet, in places, his usual good judgment fails him. The "Morphine Tango," wherein a hospital emergency room becomes a tango palace, is one such; another is the Saigon-chief-of-police-style execution of Molina; and the worst is the *Broadway Melody*-ish concluding musical number, which impossibly tries to be both satirical and feelgoodish. Still, lovers of Hal Prince and Chita Rivera may not feel cheated by this cell-blockbuster musical.

Let's face it, though, the person who'll get the most out of this is Gerard Alessandrini. Just wait until the next edition of *Forbidden Broadway*!

Peer Gynt

Great men can err greatly. No one admires and respects Ingmar Bergman more than I do, but his *Peer Gynt* at BAM struck me as a disaster. "The theater calls for nothing," Bergman has declared. "TV includes everything, film includes everything, there everything is shown. Theater ought to be the encounter of human beings with human beings and nothing more. All else is distracting." It is apparently on this principle that this *Peer Gynt*, his second, has been constructed. But not all plays will submit to such Spartan, indeed Procrustean, treatment. Ibsen was not Brecht or Beckett.

Peer Gynt was conceived by Ibsen as a poem, not initially intended for the stage. It was to encompass one man's life from boyhood to death, a life that was to be an exemplar. Peer is the *homme moyen sensuel*: attractive, imaginative, variously gifted; but also craven, dishonest with others and himself, and ludicrously megalomaniacal. A sometimes loving son to his adoring mother, Åse, he is perfectly horrid to Solveig, the good and lovely woman who selflessly loves him. Created as a companion piece to *Brand*, the story of an inflexible idealist, *Peer Gynt* was to show man the compromiser, temporizer, and egoist—at best one of Dante's trimmers, "displeasing to God as to his enemies."

When Ibsen adapted his "poem" for the stage, he asked Grieg to write music for it, and the composer responded opulently: Ibsen was even willing, in the interest of brevity (a complete *Gynt* runs to at least five hours), to let Grieg's music replace the entire fourth act. Far from wanting a minimalist production, Ibsen aimed for something large-scale, sensuous, awesome. Peer is man projected onto the entire globe; we need, not necessarily elaborate sets, but scenery that will convey North and South, mountains and desert, land and sea: churning ambition trying to encompass all. Peer wants to be nothing less than emperor of the universe. Lennart Mörk's shabby permanent set of black walls with squiggles painted on them, with a bare platform in the middle that can be variously tilted, raised, and jiggled, does not do the trick. I realize that Bergman originally staged this in a small theater, but still!

Nor does Mörk's costuming of, for example, all the peasantry at the Haegstad wedding in near-identical shades of red create the right kind of atmosphere, especially if all these reddlemen and women must do their dancing in narrow areas on each side of the platform, as if they were rival folkdance troupes from hell and not merrily uninhibited revelers. Of Donya Feuer's choreography, the less said, the better.

Ever since I first experienced Börje Ahlstedt as the lead in *I Am Curious Yellow* and *I Am Curious Blue*, he has been to me a crude lout. That worked for Vilgot Sjlman's films, but subsequent sightings of Ahlstedt on stage and screen did little to dispel that early impression. Nothing about his voice, looks, and demeanor could explain to me his evident popularity in Sweden even in non-oafish roles. Now in his early fifties, he suggests a heavyset, beer-bloated burgher or a prosperous peasant, but not the Everyman figure of at least glib appeal, someone who can steal a bride from her wedding with her own hearty cooperation, or make the innocent and endearing young Solveig fall instantly into lifelong love with him—a love that defies abandonment without consummation and decades of absence without communication. Yet faithfully she waits in her cottage for Peer to slink and shuffle back to her, an old man on the verge of perdition, trying to placate Death the Buttonmolder with the one good testimonial on which his salvation depends.

Such a Peer must have something warmly winning about him, as Richard Thomas did in Mark Lamos's far more satisfying production for Hartford Stage. Ahlstedt is not even able to suggest a youth in the beginning and then gradually age as the play progresses.

Equally bizarre is the casting directing of Bibi Andersson as Åse, his mother. The actress looks as young and beautiful as ever and, with her tomboyishly husky voice and shag haircut, suggests nothing so much as Peer's sophisticated, urbanized daughter. Lena Endre is a striking and almost too heroic Solveig, but better to err on that side; Therese Brunnander, as the runaway bride, and Gertie Kulle, as the Troll King's daughter, are no slouches, either. There is only one blot on the large, often doubling, supporting cast: the unsightly Anitra of Solveig Ternström—what irony that Solveig's amoral opposite number should be played by an actress named Solveig!

Bergman has staged a *Peer* indebted to the "poor theater" of the wretched Grotowski: everything is shabby, grotesque, deflatory. Everything, that is, except an adorable ostrich that once sashays across the desert scene, much to the delight of the spectacle-starved audience, to whom the droning voices of the four translators in their transistors are scant compensation. And if the skimpy score was to be drawn from the works of the excellent Bohuslav Martinů, the overfamiliar and underappropriate Charleston from *La Revue de cuisine* should surely have been sidestepped. The *Peer Gynt* one should have seen is Bergman's 1957 Malmö version, with Max von Sydow, Gunnel Lindblom, and Ingrid Thulin, one picture of which talks louder than this entire mounting.

Madame de Sade

Everything that miscarried in Ingmar Bergman's *Peer Gynt* works beautifully in his mounting of Yukio Mishima's *Madame de Sade*. Here the pared-down approach comes into its own, for this sensual play is not at all sensuous. In Mishima's austere exercise, we are in a landscape of ideas; events take place mostly beyond the cyclorama or in the past or future. Onstage there is a situation, with people speaking out more than acting out. In the course of three acts, a dozen years go by; but what's that *sub specie aeternitatis*? Only the moment and eternity count.

Mishima wrote the play to figure out "why the Marquise de Sade, after having demonstrated such absolute fidelity to her husband during the long years in prison, should have left him the moment he was at last free." A nice conundrum, to which the answer may be more complicated than what he comes up with. But the handful of women debating the Marquis's merit and meaning raises enough questions to keep the mind occupied and makes dispensing with final answers easy.

There is Renée, Mme de Sade, who stands by her husband through all the ignominies heaped on her by him, and all the ignominies heaped on him and her by others. True, he does not seem to have practiced the extremes of his sadism on her—"I don't know whether it is a sign of his respect or his contempt," she muses. Or, at times, he may have, as her mother, Mme de Montreuil, contends. It was she who saw to it that her son-in-law be kept in prison, whence only the Revolution at long last sprung him, and whither Napoleon, a scant seven years later, reconfined him for life. There is also Anne, Renée's younger sister, who runs off with her brother-in-law on a spree to Venice: "*une petite pensionnaire rebelle,*" Maurice Heine, Sade's biographer, rightly called her. Recklessly infatuated with Sade, Anne taunts her sister, who, for various selfless reasons, accepts and even promotes the affair.

Then the three women whom Mishima invented. The Countess de Saint-Fond is a kind of female Sade, loosely modeled on Sade's triumphantly evil heroine, Juliette; she acts throughout the play as an agent provocateur and disciple and defender of the "divine Marquis." Her antithesis, the Baronne de Simiane (note the simian name!), is a pious woman who becomes a nun, and whom Mishima—as Sade would have—uses, to ridicule religion. "Are you implying that God is an old dog?" "Yes, and also a lazy one," we hear, much as we do in José Rivera's current *Marisol*. Lastly, there is Charlotte, the housekeeper, through whom Mishima shows how the servile underdog, come the Revolution, becomes an even worse top dog.

In the difficult and somewhat arid genre of the play of ideas, *Madame de Sade* is good but not outstanding. It is always intelligent, often witty, and, above all, literate. Depends on how you feel about such lines as "Even the tortures of hell can be transmuted by a woman's hand into roses." This is a defiant, romantic poeticization of Sade. In truth, Renée was writing her jailed husband to send her his dirty, cast-off underwear, no doubt to transmute it into smelling like roses. But the play does contribute to the ongoing rehabilitation of Sade as a Nietzschean philosopher, Freudian analyst, and psychological novelist way ahead of his time.

What makes Bergman's production so inventive and enriching is the director's insight into the play's universality. By various subtle means, he makes the play—visually, vocally, kinetically—at once French, Japanese, and Swedish. He has, for example, the characters moving in ways suggestive of both Kabuki and the minuet. Some of the scenery and costuming is Japanese, some Scandinavian modern, the rest classical French. Movement, though stylized and controlled, is also freely choreographic and abundantly animated. The avoidance of all furniture is a fine touch, as are the sparse but well-employed props (fans, letters, a riding crop). The spare, Japanese-style background music by Ingrid Yoda (note the hybrid name!) is a subtle asset. Charles Koroly's understated scenery suggests both modern picture windows and eighteenth-century pavilions and arcades.

The final glory is in the performances. No one, not even George Cukor, from whom Bergman admits learning a lot, has directed actresses as well as Bergman. Take Anita Björk, one of Sweden's greatest actresses, as Mme de Montreuil. Far from a stock villain, she is a strong woman of principles, possibly misguided, but upheld with Metternichian vigor and Machiavellian skill; we never lose our grudging sympathy for her. As Renée, Stina Ekblad is magnificent. Her face, even in repose, conveys a woman torn in sundry directions, a wife sundered from sex and suffering from it, a lover whose fanaticism has penetrated deeper than ever plummet sounded.

Agneta Ekmanner, a former model and charming comedienne of stage and screen, has been aptly described by Peter Cowie as Sweden's "woman of today." As Saint-Fond, she oozes provocation with her lissome body, smirking voice, and incendiary smile. The strikingly beautiful, viola-voiced Marie Richardson finds the perfect blend of innocence and experience for Anne, and Margaretha Byström combines the stolid strength and ultimate helplessness of Mme de Simiane. As Charlotte, Helena Brodin embodies both the docile present and the volcanic tomorrow. Under Bergman's guidance, this sextet raises ensemble acting to new heights.

She Loves Me

Let's reach for all those approbative words that have been gathering dust on the shelf: charming, lovable, touching, delicious, heartwarming. And this one: enchanting. It's been a long time since we could put them to work again, especially for the musical theater. But now that *She Loves Me* is here, we need them all. And then some.

Back in the thirties, there was a winsome play on the Budapest stage, *Kispatika* (Small Perfumery), by Miklós László. Orson Welles once said, "My favorite people in the world are the Hungarian Jews—all those clever, charming, warm, and witty men, like Molnár and Alex Korda." László was, clearly, of their company. No wonder that Ernst Lubitsch seized on this play for one of his most ravishing screen comedies, *The Shop Around the Corner* (1940). Then, in 1963, along came the Broadway-musical version, *She Loves Me*, with lyrics by Sheldon Harnick, music by Jerry Bock, and direction by Hal Prince, and God was truly in his heaven.

The story of the sweet and smelly shenanigans in and around a small Budapest perfumery is the most endearing, enduring mix of the innocent and the savvy. Joe Masteroff's masterly book simplifies some things and expands others, but stays admirably within the scented, sentimental world of the original. Here are Georg Nowack and Amalia Balash (names and spellings are always slightly off, but so what?), the sparring clerks who, unbeknown to themselves, are love-smitten pen pals spoiling for the day when they'll have the nerve to meet face-to-face. Here are Steven Kodaly and Ilona Ritter, another pair of employees, and what a pair! He, dapper Lothario, cheats whenever he can; she, sassy soubrette, sulks and grouses, but puts up with it. There is also Sipos, the humble but droll family man, bent on keeping his job, and Arpad, the bike-riding errand boy with upward as well as lateral mobility. And there is the owner, Mr. Maraczek, a decent man whom an anonymous letter warns of his wife's waywardness with one of his clerks, but who suspects the wrong fellow.

Out of these ingredients and a few peripheral others, the creators of *She Loves Me* have fashioned the perfect intimate musical. (Perfect? Yes, damn it, perfect.) Every marvelous song works equally as a musical number and as a piece of plot and character development. And however frenziedly convoluted a modest production number in a café for lovers—with an imperious headwaiter, harried busboy, and unleashed couples—may be, it, too, is both comic and moving, the humor and pathos inextricably, ineffably blended. (But why remove Amalia from the midst of that maelstrom, and why, a bit later, cut the irresistible "Tango Tragique"?)

Both the main plot and the various subplots coalesce with a dramatic and romantic inevitability that leaves one pleasurably gasping for breath. And for more. If I may use one last olfactory metaphor, this perfumery reeks of humanity. I can never listen to the original-cast recording without growing teary; though almost no one in the cast of the Roundabout revival is quite as apt as his or her unforgettable Broadway prototype 30 years ago, the production is good enough—and the show great enough—to leave the heart thumping, the eyes aglitter with tears.

Scott Ellis has directed a bit too flashily in places (as well as anachronistically: Scotch tape in the workroom, a hospital chair on casters), but there is no disputing the liveliness of his approach. The scenery cannot quite disguise the limitations of budget and space, but Tony Walton invests them with prankish resourcefulness and impeccable taste, helped along by Peter Kaczorowski's insinuating lighting. David Charles and Jane Greenwood's costumes may be a bit too drab here, a bit too grand there, but they are worn with exemplary conviction.

There is only one real blemish on the casting. Louis Zorich plays Maraczek without a shred of charm, emotional appeal, or the flavor of Mitteleuropa (think how well the equally American Frank Morgan managed it in the movie), but then, his wife's company gave the director his first break. Judy Kuhn sings and looks Amalia to a fare-thee-well, and you can almost see the bouquets of audience empathy flying toward her. Boyd Gaines is a rather too boyish Georg, and is overdirected in his big moment, the title song, which he delivers like an uncaged gazelle. But his genuine sparkle and judicious imitation of Jimmy Stewart in the role carry the day.

Howard McGillin, one of my favorite performers, sings Kodaly splendidly, but is rather miscast. There is such an ingrained niceness about him that he apparently cannot even conceive of, let alone convey, sleaziness. Moreover, he is up against the late Jack Cassidy, whose original Kodaly was an epochal event in our musical theater. Sally Mayes is not quite the comedic Ilona most of us envision, yet she executes her straighter version with verve and savoir-faire, and looks more Hungarian than anyone else on stage. Lee Wilkof is a canny and enormously engaging Sipos; Brad Kane's Arpad can pedal his way into the hardest heart. Jonathan Freeman's snooty headwaiter exudes comic condescension, and Joey McKneely, who sometimes seems to dance on his mcknees, is the epitome of beleaguered busboyishness.

So all you have to do is learn to look around and past Zorich, and all will be more than well. I can't remember when I have encountered such deep-felt (as opposed to merely Pavlovian) audience enthusiasm. This is measured not so much by thunderous applause as by electric silence. All through the two most infectious numbers, "Vanilla Ice Cream" and "She Loves Me," in which Amalia and Georg, respectively, acknowledge their love, I could feel audience involvement building to fever pitch way before its release in thunderclaps. It was more than an ovation—a transport. And here let us also tip our hats to Todd Haimes, Roundabout's artistic director, who has felicitously restored Broadway to itself.

Sunset Boulevard

The movie *Sunset Boulevard* (1950) was well defined by David Shipman as "classic but not a masterpiece." As such, it is prime material for a stage musical: if your adaptation fails, you are not quite a vandal; if it is only mediocre, it can still be propped up by everyone's presumed recollection of and affection for a classic. There has been talk periodically about turning the film into a musical, but it was not till 43 years later that Andrew Lloyd Webber, Don Black, and Christopher Hampton slithered in where angels fear to tread. But then, multimillionaire that he is, Sir Andrew (with a little assist from Paramount Pictures) has no need of angels.

But there is another reason for him to be attracted to Billy Wilder's movie: both he and Wilder are men working between two stools. Dwight Macdonald observed, "Although Mr. Wilder is considered a very cynical fellow in Hollywood, he seems to me not bitter enough; he uses bitter chocolate for his icing, but underneath is the stale old cake." Or, as David Thomson put it, Wilder "is eventually chicken-hearted; the scathing survey of foolish characters never exceeds a melodramatic approach.... Although he believes the worst of people, Wilder lacks the will to make it credible." And as Wilder was caught between satire and commercialism, so A.L.W. gesticulates frantically between Puccini and pop, not quite having the will for the latter or the talent for the former. The new musical *Sunset Boulevard*, which opened in London July 12 (Los Angeles in December, New York next fall), brandishes its spurious brio all over the place, but is, to quote Stevie Smith, not waving but drowning.

Built into the movie was an essential lack of point of view. The not-so-very-young down-and-out screenwriter Joe Gillis, escaping the car repossessors, drives right into the estate of Norma Desmond, an aging ex-film star now living in seclusion. She is trying to write a screenplay about Salome, with which to make her stellar comeback. A stridently demanding woman but infantile underneath, she is lovingly watched over by Max von Mayerling, one of Hollywood's former top directors, who made a star of her, and was her first husband, but now is her faithful chauffeur and lackey. (Believe that one if you can, though in the movie, the magnetism of Erich von Stroheim helped.) Norma engages Joe as her script doctor, and, being still vaguely seductive as well as rich, turns him into her lover and kept man.

Joe has another life, too, with a young crowd, and sneaks out of Norma's palazzo, where he is now a captive, to work on a script of his own with a delightful young woman, Betty, the lover of an absent friend of his, and soon to become his own. Caught between the faded glamour of Norma's gilded cage, for which he feels too good, and Betty's youthful freshness, for which he feels not good enough, Joe tells both women the truth, with disastrous consequences all around. Norma, rejected and humiliated, shoots him, then goes totally insane herself. Joe is discovered at the start as a corpse floating in Norma's swimming pool, yet the story is narrated by him. The show ends, as it begins, with a corpse, only this time it is its own.

The movie, which Wilder co-wrote with Charles Brackett and D. M. Marshman Jr., depended chiefly on atmosphere and reasonably witty dialogue. Norma Desmond's wealth and eccentricity were shown in picturesque detail, as was the Hollywood scene, and all sorts of former movie greats and near-greats studded the supporting cast, And there were film clips of Norma Desmond (i.e., Gloria Swanson) from her glory days. You could do this in Hollywood then, with the camera as your aide; in today's West End or Broadway, you are hampered by the space limitations of the stage, which a few flabby projections do not conquer, and by the Grim Reaper's preempting the services of your supporting cast. Even the dialogue's space is usurped by the songs that, with Don Black and Christopher Hampton's pedestrian lyrics and A.L.W.'s no less pedestrian music, get nowhere in a Hollywood where you are lost without wheels. The music seems to be vamping, vamping endlessly until it finally works up the nerve to accost a tune. And then it sounds like something recycled from former A.L.W. shows, or scooped up from Sir Andrew's cutting-room floor. There is not a song here that is—never mind memorable—a song. The lyrics are paltry stuff, and though Black boasted in a newspaper interview about the purity of his rhymes—citing *brochure* and *kosher!*—what about *palazzo* and *terazza*, or "Of course, there's bound to be a little gaffing, / Eternal youth is worth a little suff'ring"? The playwright Christopher Hampton was unable to enliven the book, even with borrowings from Oscar Wilde, e.g., "Who is Norma?" "I don't usually read private cigarette cases."

The musical outdoes the movie in lack of point of view. Neither the "modern" world of Betty and her friends nor the Jurassic one of Norma, Max, and the rest (but where is the rest, where are the movie's colorful fossils?) is anything to involve us. And when the authors outlandishly keep hitting the first syllable in *boulevard* (it's always SUN-set BOU-levard), you feel that the sorry scansion is wagging the dog.

Patti LuPone is less grotesque than grotesquely miscast as Norma. The book has lowered her age to 50, but being and looking fortyish, she does not for a moment convey the sumptuous past she is supposed to be trailing behind her. Sitting next to Gloria Swanson in her late seventies on a talk show, I was more enthralled. Trevor Nunn has directed LuPone to swish and sway and talk like Tallulah Bankhead, but it all sounds forced, amateurish, desperate. She can sing well enough in her somewhat adenoidal voice, but is further undercut by Anthony Powell's *outré* costumes, one of which makes her look like a cross between a rooster and a bellhop, another like a Bedouin chief crossed with a zebra.

The Kevin Anderson who plays Joe is the wrong Kevin Anderson; it should have been the gifted, golden-voiced, and handsome singer from the New York City Opera, not the pouty, pudgy-faced lout from Chicago's Steppenwolf Ensemble. Good at what he can do, here he comes across as a youthful Hollywood hanger-on, much too green to have written several screenplays, been through the mill, and become disenchanted and cynical. How well William Holden was able to convey in his dealings with Norma "the mixture of pity and guilt and nausea" (Pauline Kael's phrase); Anderson merely suggests slightly curdled milk. As Max, Daniel Benzali impersonates a Stroheim made of straw, and the insipid Meredith Braun must have been cast as Betty mostly for looking even homelier than Miss LuPone. The rest haven't got a chance under Nunn's no-account direction.

But there is that one marvelous piece of scenery, Norma's living room, the epitome and apotheosis of all those neo-Egyptian old-style cinema palaces in all their magisterial bad taste, sover-

eignly conjured up by John Napier and lusciously lighted by Andrew Bridge. It can even be hydraulically hoisted halfway to heaven,
so that two contrasting actions can proceed simultaneously one
above the other. But the other sets have been skimped on; even
C. B. deMille's *Samson and Delilah* soundstage looks sadly shorn.
And those unfamiliar with the movie may often not know what is
happening: a blue-lit man suspended in midair may strike them
not as a corpse in a pool but as a Kushnerian angel descending on
America.

The Madness of King George III

The Madness of King George III presents us with two years in the
reign of Britian's Farmer King, who lost the Colonies and, for part
of his life, his reason, but not the sympathy of his people. Great figures such as Pitt the Younger, Fox, and Burke buzzed around him,
Whig and Tory rivalries flared up in the House of Commons, across
the Channel there was a revolution that would affect the future of
the world. But George had his fifteen children (though some died)
by his homely queen, muddled through his "madness" as best he
could, survived a battery of doctors even more dangerous than his
illness, to succumb to a malady at last and spend his final decade
blind, deaf, and deranged in an isolated suite in Windsor Castle.

The court of George III was the stodgiest in Europe, but the king
had a sense of humor that drew Alan Bennett to write this play. As
you watch it unfurl its historical panorama, you feel that you are
witnessing something enormously civilized and civilizing, without
being able to pinpoint its exact purport. Before you is the essence
of a country's politics, the uneasy division of power among king,
cabinet, and parliament, the story of a not quite happy and not quite
unhappy royal marriage, and the detailed account of tortures to
which ignorant physicians can subject a patient, helpless even if he
is king. Also the machinations of the Prince of Wales to appropriate the throne, the comic conflict of rival schools of medicine all
equally benighted, the intrigues for preferment granted or withheld—but what does it all mean?

Strangely, the lack of a clear contour and unequivocal aim does
not come across as a drawback. Bennet has the gift of creating arresting characters and absorbing situations out of a couple of ex-

changed sentences here, a short speech there, and a stage image or two, and these jockeyings for inside tracks become your very own horse race. And you are kept continually guessing: is this comedy, farce, satire, drama, or tragedy? All are present, and it is a wonder how they all cohere. The look is that of a set of Rowlandson caricatures come to fantastic yet fully believable life.

The king suffered from a then undiagnosable and still not fully understood hereditary metabolic disorder called porphyria, which makes the skin hypersensitive, the mind unstable, and the urine blue. Its coming and goings are ungraspable, and though its symptoms resemble dementia, it is not that. Curiously, Porphyria is also the name of the heroine of one of Browning's most romantic poems. There it is a blonde, blue-eyed beauty; here an itchy blue-urined illness: what's in a name? Such odd coincidences (although not this specific one) thrive in Bennett's mind, and what finally makes his play so endearing is that an eccentric author and an eccentric protagonist are playing games with each other across the chessboard of history.

What do you make of a remark such as "the bloom has at any rate gone off the Queen's ugliness. Since she fell from her carriage and broke her nose, she is quite handsome"? Or this, from George's most demonic doctor: "The state of monarchy and the state of lunacy share a frontier. Some of my lunatics fancy themselves kings. He is King, so where shall his fancy take refuge?" Or this query from George, unable to recollect his weird actions after regaining his senses, to a lady-in-waiting: "Did we ever forget ourselves utterly, because if we did forget ourselves, I would so like to remember"? I like it.

What the play may really be about is what theater can do when an actor such as Nigel Hawthorne plays George and he is surrounded by an ensemble in which no one takes one false step, even though the great staircase, the raked floor, the intricacies of the dialogue and stage action might easily trip one up. Hawthorne himself is irresistible (except when he talks impenetrably mispronounced German). There is a twinkle in his eye, voice, entire frame when he is cheerful; when things go wrong, and his doctors apply gruesome treatments, the empathy he elicits is so potent you can barely look at the stage. He conveys superlatively the joy a true actor gets from his craft; that sense of pleasure that encircles his entire performance like a halo.

The simplicity and fluidity of Nicholas Hytner's direction, the spareness and suggestivity of Mark Thompson's scenery and costumes, the rapidity with which everything moves and the intensity with which Paul Pyant has lighted it—all this helps you experience another people's past as keenly as if it were your own present. And how sly Bennett is to cut off the story, where he does, in 1789, so he can give you, however tricksily, the happiest of endings! He and the Royal National Theatre of Britain, whose production this is, are bringing a feast to Stamford, Brooklyn, Baltimore, and Boston, where the show is or will be on view. Partake of it wherever you can.

Pterodactyls

How would you feel about a new play by one Nicky Silver, whose previous works include *Fat Men in Skirts*, *Free Will and Wanton Lust*, *Wanking 'Tards* (whatever they are), and *My Marriage to Ernest Borgnine*? A play whose logo is a young man dressed as a chambermaid, his genitals being groped by a male hand? Good, you say? Very well, then, you are ready for *Pterodactyls*, something that resembles *The Twilight of the Golds*, except that it is a hundred times worse.

Here, too, we have Father, Mother, Brother, Sister. But we begin with a nonsense lecture given by Brother (to whom?) about dinosaurs. Then he comes home after five years of studying sculpture. Sister, who is in love with a mildly cretinous Waiter, feels too tight inside her skin, and forgets everything. She does not recognize Brother, claims she never had one, and takes him for a rapist. He did in fact play one at age 10 in a Pinter play; the night before the performance (flashback), Mother wakes him up at 2:30 AM, wanting to be cradled in his arms. When Sister announces she is marrying Waiter, Mother pays no attention: "I need a hot drink and a cold bath, or vice versa," she says, and a minute later: "I need a quick drink and a slow bath, or the other way around."

Mother engages Waiter to replace their missing chambermaid, and he promptly reappears in uniform. Brother announces repeatedly that he has AIDS, but Mother won't hear it. Later, when Sister discovers her fiancé-chambermaid kissing Brother, she goes deaf and hears nothing. Brother discovers dinosaur bones at the bottom of his garden, and starts reconstructing a *tyrannosaurus rex* skeleton in the living room. Father always calls him Buzz, though his name is Todd; they compromise on Buzz-Todd. Later, Brother gives Sister a huge handgun as a wedding present. She proceeds to use it lethally forthwith.

And so on. In the first few scenes, everyone talks very fast. In later scenes, David Warren, the director, has them talk very slow. Everyone gets to soliloquize at length, though the one-liners are even worse: "So a dog buried bones." "We don't have a dog." "Maybe your sister." Kelly Bishop (Mother) is best. Hope Davis (Sister) looks oddest: her nose is in Act Two when her chin is still in Act One.

I appreciate homosexual humor, Jewish humor, and a combination of the above. But is that all there is going to be on our boards from now till doomsday? If our playwrights did not have their eyes glued to their navels, they might notice a world out there. Why is there no play about Bosnia, Somalia, or Haiti? Or about poverty here, or the failing of our education, where multiculturalism comes ahead of learning something? Were plays being written about real problems—and they could still have wit—the theater might at last become ecumenical and have a genuine future.

Desdemona: A Play About a Handkerchief

Having heartily disliked Paula Vogel's previous, highly touted offerings, I was pleasantly surprised by her latest: *Desdemona: A Play About a Handkerchief* is no mere piece of Kleenex. It is, to be sure, a genre I don't much care for: the play that parasitically lays its eggs in the host body of a classic, in this case *Othello*, a play about the profoundest human emotions. The model may have been Stoppard's *Rosencrantz and Guildenstern Are Dead*. But whereas *R & G*, a much cleverer work, fits its story seamlessly into the interstices of *H*, providing a backstage view of that masterpiece, *Desdemona*, a backstairs view of the story of O, takes the kinds of liberties that make it rather more travesty and persiflage.

Or, rather, revisionism. We have here the spoiled Venetian aristocrats' daughter, Desdemona, an imperious, promiscuous, scheming minx, of the kind that could not have fooled the noble Moor were his perception twice as dark as his skin. This Desdemona has a proto-lesbian affection for the whore Bianca, with whom she has even traded places in bed in one of her brothel's darkened bedchambers; conversely, she treats the faithful Emilia (well, yes, she snitched that hankie, but quite guilelessly) with condescension and inconsistency. To her husband, she is an utter hypocrite; why, she even had, and intends to resume, a steamy affair with cousin Lodovico. You might say this Desdemona is her own best Iago and deserves what she will get. Vogel's play, then, is a tabloid version of *Othello*.

The language, moreover, is macaronic mock-Elizabethan, Irish, cockney, current British and American slang pell-mell, for no compelling reason. And either the author or the director has seen fit to punctuate (or puncture) the proceedings with brief freeze-frames accompanied by a clash of cymbals, followed by blackouts, after which the action continues where it left off, or with the actors moved to different positions. This is amusing a few times, and futile from, say, the tenth time on. What is left after these strictures? Quite a lot, actually.

A rare thing these days, the play is not boring. It may have little to say, but it goes briskly about its business of letting three juicy characters interact for 80 idiosyncratic minutes, and if its sassiness seldom makes it into wit, it still crackles along cheekily, with incontestable vitality. Vulgarity even, which sometimes becomes sophomoric but affords us a wallow in a nice mud bath. Best of all, three sparkling actresses and a scintillating director treat us to a fizzy verbal and visual light show.

I wish J. Smith-Cameron were a bit prettier and less mannered as Desdemona, but she has energy and efficacy to spare, and does convey the intended girl-woman quality. The always enchanting Cherry Jones offers a lusty yet also innocent Bianca, bursting with sensuous cherry-ripeness but awesome when aroused. Fran Brill's Emilia is a cannily layered, intricately insinuating performance of effortless complexity. And Gloria Muzio, the director, proves again how graphic she can be with wordplay, how pictorially precise with her blocking. Here she has also elicited resourceful scenery from Derek McLane, translucent enough to allow Michael Lincoln's lighting novel ways of suffusing the scene. Feminists will undoubtedly find deeper meanings in this play; the rest of us can have a shallow good time with it.

Perestroika

After an intermission of six months, and with more delays than a
NASA launching, Part Two of *Angels in America, Perestroika*, has
finally opened. Tony Kushner might have continued fiddling with
it even longer, except that Frank Rich, an *Angels* enthusiast, is quitting his post as chief drama critic of the Times, and his successor
is said to be an only lukewarm Angelist: hence the need to catch
Rich before he leaves. Actually, and not altogether surprisingly, the
best assessments of *Angels in America* so far have come not from us
drama critics but from outsiders: Andrew Sullivan, the homosexual
editor of *The New Republic*, in his column of June 21, 1993; and the
psychiatrist Yale Kramer, in a penetrating analysis in last July's issue
of *The American Spectator*. More on this later.

Continuing where Part One, *Millennium Approaches*, left off,
Perestroika supplies the same virtues and vices. Kushner is a funny
fellow, and there is both nicely elaborated humor and rapid-fire wit
throughout much of the three-and-a-half-hour span. When Hannah Pitt, the Mormon mother, her burlap hair in a shopworn bun,
confronts her son's lover's lighter-than-air ex-lover, Prior Walter,
who has just corroborated his homosexuality, she leaps to the en-
thymeme "Are you a hairdresser?" "Well," he answers, "it would be
your lucky day if I was." Later, when Prior finds being a prophet
onerous, he asks Hannah, who knows her Bible, what God does
with prophets who refuse their vision. She replies, "He feeds them
to whales." But, of course, the jokes get nastier, as when the clue
in a guessing game, "New York's No. 1 closeted queen," elicits the
response "Koch" and huge audience laughter.

Further, Kushner handily sustains interest not only with his dialogue but also with artful construction, as he shifts among his three
main stories: the affair of the AIDS-crossed lovers, Prior and Louis
Ironson (the author's alter ego); the latent-homosexuality-and-ram-
pant-dementia-crossed Mormon spouses, Joe and Harper Pitt (note
the wife's masculine-sounding name); and the dying Roy Cohn and
his circle. That circle includes Joe, chief clerk to a high-ranking
judge and Louis's current lover Belize, Roy's black male nurse and
verbal sparring partner, who was Louis's lover before Prior: and the
ghost of Ethel Rosenberg. If all this sounds a bit contrived, well, it
is. Yet even as the overlapping or simultaneous scenes can add zest,
they can also spread confusion; moreover, they unduly protect the

author from committing himself to any one of his characters.

The play aspires to epic status and, with its free-ranging action and propulsive energy, does approach it. Yet epic has to sweep across a more representative canvas. Here the straight characters are few, and either mad or marginal. And whereas the author of this "Gay Fantasia on National Themes" has the right to his limitations, he must also bear their consequences, all the more so since even his homosexual figures are confined to certain types while excluding others.

Lastly, Kushner has written good parts for the actors, indeed challenging multiple roles for most of his cast of eight. (Sometimes, when he arbitrarily casts women as men, he overdoes it.) With snazzy direction from George C. Wolfe, Kathleen Chalfant, David Marshall Grant, Marcia Gay Harden, Ron Leibman, Joe Mantello, Ellen McLaughlin, Stephen Spinella, and Jeffrey Wright perform impressively, supported by the witty sets of Robin Wagner, cheeky costumes of Toni-Leslie James, and well-nigh gestic lighting of Jules Fisher. Only Anthony Davis's music misses.

But the fact remains that *Angels in America*—and especially Part Two, from which we expect a resolution—goes nowhere. Great drama need not provide answers (and seldom does), so long as it raises the right questions; *Angels*, for all its attitudinizing, may not raise any. On the most mundane level, it dodges the issue of AIDS; though Prior is dying of it for seven hours, the final tableau implies full remission—or, at any rate, denies us the dramatically necessary impact of his death. On the most metaphysical level, Prior is proclaimed a prophet by the visiting angel and even mounts to Heaven, where a conclave of angels, in a particularly ill-written scene, grants him return to Earth. Why?

Kushner doesn't tell and, as usual, hedges his bets. In this June-moony Heaven (the act is titled "Heaven, I'm in Heaven"), Prior meets Harper, who is there for no better reason than that she has experienced a long-delayed orgasm. Kushner wants to have things both ways: either to play it safe, or so as not to have to know what he is talking about.

In the aforementioned essay, Yale Kramer showed in great and compelling detail, that Kushner is pleading not just for homosexuality but also and especially for transgression, a life-style of flouted complaisance and flaunted socially unacceptable excess. And Andrew Sullivan argued that "gay life—and gay death—surely awaits something grander and subtler than this," for "the script never ascended... above a West Village version of Neil Simon." To which I would add that even the play's central concept of the homosexual hero as prophet and consort of angels was long ago anticipated by Rimbaud, who pronounced himself angel and seer. And I mistrust any writer who (in a Sunday piece in the *Times*) commits the pleonasm "from whence." Granted, this was acceptable in Shakespeare's day, but we've come a long way since then—grammatically up, and dramatically down.

All in the Timing

An original turn of mind is to be saluted in our tired theater. There is no lack of slick competence, but a playwright with ideas—his own ideas—in his head is relatively rare. Such a one is David Ives. *All in the Timing*, his bill of six snappy one-acters, is idiosyncratic, perky, quirky, and astringent. Situated on the border between playful fantasy and baleful absurdity, it sometimes verges on the cleverly sophomoric—but so does some of Beckett and Ionesco. Sometimes the playlets go on a little too long, but only by one or two hairbreadths. The laughter at Primary Stages, where the show is playing, is steady and has an educated ring.

Five of the pieces have been seen, separately, before; but the one premiere is probably the best, which is good news indeed: the already accomplished author is getting better yet. What he so sparklingly exhibits is an awareness of language, which, coming from our playwrights, is not a truism. Most of them use language as if it were a pair of comfortable old shoes to get them where they are going, and, as such, to be taken for granted. To Ives, however, language is a playground, a battleground, a testing ground: the confines within which we are grounded or, worse yet, ground to dust. Unless, that is, we can use it as a trampoline to the stars. Language, for Ives, is not a means to an end, but what makes a play a play and life life.

You might argue that language is equally crucial to a Pinter or a Mamet. But these men deconstruct language. They put it at the service of inarticulateness, of prosaic power plays, of anomie and entropy. In Ives, too, this is sometimes the case. Yet there is a sense that even when it turns, quite literally, into monkey business or is fraudulently re-invented by a charlatan, it carries in itself—in itself alone—the possibility of salvation. If, as in *Sure Thing*, you can keep rephrasing your errors, the maze will turn into amazement; if, as in *Variations on the Death of Trotsky*, you can play word games with death, you may squeeze comedy from your dying.

In *Sure Thing*, a young man accosts a young woman at a café table for a seat; she is reading and ostensibly waiting for someone, but lets him sit down. A conversation staggers into being, but keeps foundering on invisible reefs. At every faux pas, a bell rings, and the fumbler gets a second chance. After many an errant trial and trying error, the two finally connect. You can read this playlet as an anthology of pathetic pickup ploys, as a satire on postlapsatian conversation, as a utopian fantasy on infinite renewal, as a fugue for speaking voices in lieu of musical instruments, as a sketch of two ordinary human beings engaged in the bizarre business of living.

Words, Words, Words has three monkeys typing away at their respective typewriters for Professor Rosenbaum of Columbia University. The room they are kept in also contains food (bananas) and recreational facilities (a rubber tire on a rope to swing on). If they keep at it long enough, the trio, as the saying has it, is supposed to come up with *Hamlet*. The three simians—named Swift, Kafka, and Milton—are trying to figure out just what this *Hamlet* that is expected of them might be, even as they keep stumbling upon bits of it and of other famous literature. This is a sketch in which the verbal and visual are hilariously mated, and, in the cast, Nancy Opel shines at monkeyshines.

In *Unamunda*, a shy young woman shows up for instruction in that universal language, in which *English* is *Jonklese* (i.e., John Cleese), *squeegee* is "Excuse me?" and "I am speechless" becomes "Iago arf spinachless." Made up of proper names, trade names, near-homonyms, and sheer absurdities, the language keeps turning into rap and doo-wop. When the inventor-teacher admits to being a swindler, the student eggs him on to greater nefariousness. Just as the previous skit was, on a deeper level, a satire on today's literary establishment, this one sends up both Esperanto and Academia. It is a jauntily jaundiced view of both communication and education.

Philip Glass Buys a Loaf of Bread presents a simple human transaction involving Glass, the baker, and two other customers. This evolves into Glass music transmuted into common speech, even as mundane behavior is acted out as if staged by Robert Wilson. By this type of translation or analogy, the musically absurd and theatrically preposterous are revealed in their full ridiculousness.

Next, *The Philadelphia* shows us how people can fall into a particular pocket of existence—a black hole, if you will—from which communication with others becomes impossible. Physically, they may be in New York, but metaphysically they are "in a Philadelphia," the town that invented "the cheese steak, something that no one in his right mind would eat." Such a person asking a drugstore clerk, newspaper vendor, or waitress for something perfectly ordinary, is up against a brick wall. But there are other, even blacker holes, such as being in a Cleveland, which is "like death, without the advantages."

Finally, in *Variations on the Death of Trotsky*, the bell from *Sure Thing* appears again, the one bit of duplication in an otherwise unique evening. But the skit is still scrumptious. Mrs. Trotsky has discovered in a 1992 *Britannica* that Leo will be killed on this very day—indeed, a pickax is already lodged in the back of his head. I'll let you experience this choice bit of mockery unprepared for; it could, however, use a bit of tightening.

The cast, besides Miss Opel, includes Daniel Hagen, Wendy Lawless, Ted Neustadt, and Robert Stanton, all good, and is directed by Jason McConnell Buzas with an exquisite feel for inflections and tempos. *All in the Timing* is never less than funny, and sometimes a good deal more. Eccentric and idiosyncratic as he is, David Ives may yet become the Charles Ives of our theater.

The Government Inspector

Just when you thought it was safe to go back to the National Actors Theatre, along comes its recidivous *The Government Inspector*, and it's back to square one. Here is Nikolai Gogol's foolproof satire that's been wowing them worldwide since 1836; the adaptation is by Adrian Mitchell, an experienced hand; and Michael Langham, who steered the last two NAT productions out of the doldrums, is back at the helm. So what could go wrong? Everything.

The play concerns a corrupt backwoods Russian town that mistakes an idly traveling minor civil servant, Khlestakov, for a government inspector—or inspector-general, as the Russian title, *Revizor*, is sometimes rendered. Whereupon all the slatternly, inept, and bribable town officials, not to mention various landowners and merchants, vie with one another as to who can bribe the fellow more bounteously, entertain him more lavishly, and shower him with more servile adulation. Grasping gradually the nature of their error, Khlestakov becomes ever more grasping, and obtains, along with money and goods, the mayor's daughter's hand offered in marriage and the promise of the mayoress's extramarital favors. Vastly enriched and entertained, Khlestakov spins out spectacular lies about his life and position in Saint Petersburg, then takes a providential powder. A letter of his, exposing the town to a journalist, gets opened and read aloud to all and sundry, leaving them reeling; then the real inspector-general arrives, leaving them in speechless dismay.

For starters, Langham's production turns the play into a piece of absurdism. That may, to be sure, have been inevitable with the 23-year-old Khlestakov played by Tony Randall, old enough to be his grandfather. Moreover, Randall plays him as a 73-year-old pretending to be 23, which concentrates the ludicrousness not where Gogol intended it. Altogether, the heavily italicized acting bypasses what the author wrote: a triumph of realism that would never have been passed by the censor, had not the czar read and loved the manuscript. True, the twin figures of Bobchinsky and Dobchinsky are absurdism *avant la lettre*, presaging Dürrenmatt's Toby and Roby in *The Visit*, but even their interchangeability need not be overemphasized. The corruption and idiocy of these people should be brought closer to us by realism, not distanced by puppetry. Which brings us to the second missed opportunity: to make the place and people look more like our milieu, like us. Nabokov warned that "it is as useless to look in [Gogol] for an authentic Russian background as it would be to try to form a conception of Denmark on the basis of that little affair in cloudy Elsinore." A daring production would have, without quite leaving Russia, brought the play home to America.

Foreseeing the ravages of rampant Randallism, Gogol warned: "The less an actor works for laughs, the funnier his part will be." Randall, funny when properly cast, is here a melancholy phenomenon. Trying for rakish youth, he concentrates on being dapperly Machiavellian, which Khlestakov is not: "He talks and acts without any reflection," Gogol insisted. Randall gives us a deliberate intriguer, a provincial Casanova, a kind of Gogol au go-go instead of the author's "brainless ninny." Even his occasional endearing moments would work better were they less endearing. Similarly, Peter

Michael Goetz as the mayor (here, in a misplaced bid for authenticity, called the police governor) turns the character into something rather too grand, almost heroic.

When Langham tries to be extra clever, he usually outsmarts himself. Thus he has the maid, Avdotya (Elizabeth Heflin), speak her lines in Russian, which serves no useful purpose I can decipher. Thus, too, he employs stereophonic sound, as when the harness bells of a departing troika can be heard, as it were, circling the auditorium, the kind of excess better left to *Perestroika* or Walt Disney. But Langham's chief error is the tempo. If the production did not move at a pace befitting the peripatetic philosophers teaching as they were walking, a few comic sparks might have been struck even by this noncombustible cast.

Most of the acting could pass for government-inspected ham, and is not worth singling out even for pillorying. Still, mention must be made of Lainie Kazan's vulgarity as a concupiscent matron and of Nicholas Kepros's grossly caricatural Khlopov, who could not pass for a school superintendent even in New York City. Douglas Stein's sets look like the backs of flats used in other productions (and probably are), and Lewis Brown's costumes are humorless when not downright inappropriate. Particularly aberrant are a flouncy pink dress for the mayor's daughter, and a final gendarme's uniform befitting Lord Nelson. Richard Nelson's lighting, however, is imaginative, as is Stanley Silverman's music. "Ah, shit, it's great to be a general," the mayor says. But not, at least here, an inspector-general.

Hello Again

Michael John LaChiusa's musical *Hello Again* is labeled in the program as "suggested by the play *La Ronde* by Arthur Schnitzler," even though the play (unlike the mediocre French movie based on it) is called *Reigen*, and the only thing Schnitzler might have suggested to LaChiusa is to go soak his head. *Hello Again* is dismal enough in its own right, but as a version of *Reigen*—which, like it or not, it is—it falls somewhere between tasteless maundering and moral turpitude.

Schnitzler's play is a masterpiece of sensitive, speculative realism. It is a sad, comic, profound look at the social, psychological, and philosophical components and implications of human sexuality, but the one thing it is not at all concerned with is the sexual act as such, indicated in the text by hyphens and on the stage by a blackout. The concern is with what leads up to the act and away from it. It is, on an earlier and far deeper level, a study of the six or more degrees of separation between everyone's being in bed with everyone else, figuratively and even literally. The interest lies in the sexual roles people play, and in their mutability according to who the partner is, which is why each character is shown in two very different relationships. Sex is what goes and comes round—hence *Reigen,* a round dance—leveling social and cultural differences with the thoroughness, though not the finality, of death.

To turn this play about the life force in its manifold ramifications into a campy but simpleminded exercise in capriciousness is tantamount to reducing, say, *King Lear* to *Angels in America.* Indeed, the term *angel,* a favorite homosexual symbol, is almost as frequent in LaChiusa's musical as in Kushner's play. But the musical, even though it turns two of Schnitzler's heterosexual encounters into homosexual ones, is scarcely more heterosexual in spirit in the remaining eight. Moreover, to indulge LaChiusa's subaltern whimsy, it leaps back and forth across the decades of our century for no better reason than to accommodate pastiches of different types of music from operatic to operettic, from torchy to twitchy, from swing to rock.

By splitting up its characters in time and place (thus the Husband's first episode is in the 1950s, the second—in which he dies—in the 1910s), it makes two different persons of each character, or, more precisely, two shadowy, sketchy half-characters. And by hip-hopping from one era and society into another, it destroys the original's circularity and meaning while shamelessly keeping patches of actual Schnitzler dialogue, now out of context, debased, and pointless.

What is most likely to fool people is that *Hello Again* looks different from the typical musical, and that our sensation-hungry age mistakes difference for originality. Squiggles are different from circles and triangles, but whereas the latter are geometry, the former are nothing. The different, self-deludedly posturing as the new, makes it only on its easy recognizability: change is self-evident; recognizing quality requires taste, discrimination, thought. The typical reaction, overheard in the ladies' room at *Hello Again,* was "I loved it, but I'll have to wait for the reviews to find out what it was about." It is better not to love something until you do know what it is about.

And best not to depend on the reviewers to explain it to you: that is putting too much faith in their mystagogic skills.

LaChiusa's music is, except in a couple of places, perfectly tuneless, but such is the talent of Michael Starobin, the orchestrator, that he can disguise with a prodigality of sonorous and rhythmic spice the dearth of melodic meat. Graciela Daniele's staging and choreography are similarly scattershot and arbitrary, assuming that random assertiveness, especially if coarsely eroticized, will pass for invention—which, nowadays, it often does. Asked for a glass of water, the Nurse holds it close to her crotch, eliciting from her postulant, the College Boy, an eloquent "Yum!" Greater depths of sleaziness are achieved in a movie-theater scene, where the Young Wife twice administers oral sex to the College Boy as if this were standard behavior in regular movie houses. Discretion and understatement are conspicuously missing from LaChiusa and Daniele's repertoire.

Too bad that a number of gifted performers should be mired in this mess. Donna Murphy offers a well-sung and -acted Whore, touching precisely because she does not play on our sympathy. The gifted Judy Blazer almost succeeds in humanizing the cardboard part of the Nurse—but what is a full-time nurse doing in the house of a college boy who may or may not have sprained his ankle? Carolee Carmello is an evocative and provocative Young Wife, and Dennis Parlato a smoothly devious Husband. John Cameron Mitchell is crisp and droll as the Young Thing, though hardly someone to steer a first-class passenger off-course into steerage. Michele Pawk does her sinuously seductive best in the ill-written part of the Actress, and John Dossett unwraps an impressive singing voice in the even more leadenly written role of the Senator.

The others, though less good, will do. Toni-Leslie James's costumes are properly stylish or suggestive, and Derek McLane's décor wryly minimal. It leaves setting the scenes mostly to Jules Fisher and Peggy Eisenhauer's lighting, which carries out the task with fine painterly fettle. But production values cannot validate a production. *Hello Again* is the sort of thing that could give camp a bad name.

Three Tall Women;
Damn Yankees

Few playwrights have had such a spectacular rise and fall as Edward Albee. The celebrated author of *The Zoo Story* and *Who's Afraid of Virginia Woolf* turned into the execrated perpetrator of *The Lady From Dubuque* and *The Man Who Had Three Arms,* and landed somewhere between obloquy and oblivion. If someone had told me how good his *Three Tall Women* (1991) is, I wouldn't have believed him; I hardly believed my own eyes and ears.

The play is said to concern Albee's mother, but that is almost as irrelevant as that he was an adopted child who subsequently became estranged from his family. At most one could say that this allowed him both a special closeness to his protagonist and a certain distance, both of which he has turned to good advantage. In Act One, he views his nonagenarian heroine, A, from the outside, dispassionately. In Act Two, as she lies dying, he creates her passionately from the inside. From the outside, A is a bit of a pain both to B, her hired companion, and to C, the woman lawyer whom B has called in to straighten out A's finances. From the inside, Albee splits the woman into three selves—the young, the middle-aged, and the old (the actress playing C becoming the first of these; the one playing B, the second) and brings them on in a three-way conversation to sort out the salient facts about her life and other lives intertwined with hers.

If this is a gimmick, it is an inspired one; the change of perspective is no more unsettling than reversing a reversible raincoat, and much more rewarding. Because B and C become different persons in the process, a double perspective operates for them, too: the tough, cynical C becomes the 26-year-old, naïve A, a woman sexually and existentially confused as marriage beckons; the hunched-over and subservient yet also saucy companion, B, becomes the fiftyish A, at the height of her rich woman's powers but also confronted with the setbacks a mediocre marriage and aging flesh are heir to. As for A, she is now no longer the dotty crone, a nuisance in her dotage, but the shrewd old lady with many a penetrating insight. And all this is played out against the background of… but no, I must leave room for surprise.

If you think I have revealed too much as is, I ask how else I could have conveyed the canniness and multivalence of Albee's construction. I do not share Albee's worldview—a kind of scurrilous bonhomie or amused contempt that sometimes parts to reveal better and worse things behind it—but no one can question its personal validity and dramatic efficacy. Especially noteworthy is the author's ability to keep the three women in Act Two both different and identical, the markedly diverse phases of the unmistakably same being. The three tall women of Act One become one tall woman in quirky triplicate, but in both acts, the tallness is not merely physical. Even senile or servile, stooped with age or inferior rank, these women retain proud vestiges of a shady, ambiguous grandeur.

What Albee has wrestled down here is his self-contradictory tendency toward attitudinizing hauteur and lowdown nastiness; to the extent that rudiments of both are still there, they have been polished and domesticated: there is no longer the freakish feel of a keyboard being played only at its two extremities. And he has been staunchly supported by his director and cast. Lawrence Sacharow moves his three women around as much as decently possible, avoiding both statically talking heads and arbitrary, gratuitous choreography. B's crouch in Act One may seem a bit B-movieish, but it works, and the use of the few but good props is telling.

As A, Myra Carter is A-1 in my book. She prattles on or zeroes in with equal command, and negotiates the terrain from Alzheimer's to zippiness with roguishly sportive ease, even when lightning U-turns are required. As B—indeed, as both Bs—Marian Seldes gives the performance of her lifetime: there is spice to her obsequiousness, bite to her throwaway lines, bemusement in her self-possession. As C—or the two Cs—Jordan Baker is not quite in the same league, but more or less holds her own. These three are not a crowd; they are a company.

The new production of *Damn Yankees* deserves the usually usurped honorific "revival." To revive is not just to make something conscientiously like the original, or self-consciously unlike it, but to make it live again with its own singing, dancing, and breathing life. Richard Adler and Jerry Ross's show, with a book by George Abbott and Douglass Wallop, is now 39, the awkward age for a musical: too young for a golden oldie, too old to slide smoothly into contemporary consciousness. So its director, Jack O'Brien, has deftly updated the book: the Faustian story of a middle-aged real-estate man who leases (rather than sells) his soul to the Devil to regain his youth and lead the cellared Washington Senators into taking the mickey out of the royally mantled Yankees.

Joe Boyd, once scouted for Kansas City, is happily married to Meg, who, however, becomes for six months of the year a baseball widow. Fuming as he watches on TV the Senators lose again, he declares he'd sell his soul to the Devil for a good longball hitter. Promptly Mr. Applegate appears, and a deal is made: Joe will be 22 and infallible, and will lead his team to pennant victory by the 25th; but he extracts an unprecedented safety clause: he has until 9 P.M. on the 24th to revert to his old self. Joe hopes to clinch the pennant by then, and return to his dear Meg, whom he must abandon without leaving so much as a farewell note. To ensure Joe's remaining in the fold, Applegate summons Lola, his chief temptress, from hell. If she doesn't pry Joe from Meg, the sexy Lola will revert to what she was before the Devil's ministrations: the ugliest woman in Providence, Rhode Island.

Jack O'Brien developed this show at San Diego's Old Globe, whose artistic director he is, under the watchful eye of 106-year-old George Abbott; it is a remarkable case of modernization without anachronism. The many new jokes about everything from Joe Mc-Carthy to Arthur Murray, Edsels to Eleanor Roosevelt, are never out of time, but would, in their time, have seemed out of place. So when, in this version, Applegate and Lola watch the great dead lovers being blown about Limbo (very Dantesque, this), he points out Tristan and Isolde, Paolo and Francesca, and, after a little squinting, J. Edgar Hoover and Clyde Tolson. Such sharp-sightedness requires the Devil's eye; also that of a 1990s adapter.

This now slicker show presupposes a more sophisticated audience. Thus when Lola's seduction routine in the great tango "Whatever Lola Wants (Lola Gets)"—please don't ask me to explain the parentheses—fails to win Joe Hardy, which is Joe Boyd's nom de guerre or bull-pen name, Applegate sarcastically berates Lola, "Bizet cut that out of Carmen, honey!" Again, when he balefully invokes Milton (dismissed by Lola as "some guy on television in a dress") with an allusion to *Paradise Lost*, he taps into realms undreamed of by 1955 musical comedy.

Damn Yankees, based on a novel by the aptly named co-librettist Douglass Wallop, was the first musical to successfully unite the national pastime with the national art form; onstage, it seems, diamonds were for never. But in the Eisenhower era, when the country and Broadway espoused an enforced innocence verging on infantilism, Lola could not be a real Lilith or Helen of Troy, and Joe, the all-

American Adam, could not even come close to falling. This allows the story much sporting, but little sportive, urgency. The Devil is permitted to smack of Mark Twain and Machiavelli, Fred Allen and Oscar Levant; but Lola, except in the musical numbers, is left with a rather flat persona. Granted, in a musical, the contest between sacred and profane love is not likely to leave you in great suspense about its outcome; even so, it should not be a case of no contest.

By 1955 standards, as Richard Adler writes in his autobiography, *You Gotta Have Heart* (named, you guessed it, after the musical's showstopper), "baseball and love and Faust made an unpalatable stew." What went a long way toward palatabilizing it was Gwen Verdon, the dancer-actress-singer who had, on top of her other talents, a vulnerability rare in that type of performer. The current Lola is Bebe Neuwirth, who once portrayed my mother in a skit of the revue *Upstairs at O'Neal's*. I trust I will not be accused of filial impiety if I aver that Miss Neuwirth does not quite have that moving fragility; but the new book downplays that aspect of Lola, and, when she really needs it, Miss Neuwirth manages it handily.*

Hers, to be sure, is a different Lola: blonde, petite, sassy—not the full-bodied redhead of Miss Verdon. But whatever Bebe wants, Bebe gets: this Lola is a mischievous gamine, a concupiscent Kewpie doll, and a terrific comedienne on top of her nimble dancing and frisky singing. Whether assuming a droll Latino accent or using her own spoken contralto drawl and twirly girlish croon, Miss Neuwirth has timing, inflections, shading, and emphases to elicit frissons of delight as she plies her special brand of pliant implacability. The next key role is Applegate, and Victor Garber's new one is even more different from Ray Walston's prototype. Walston was a national Devil; Garber is a megalopolitan one. Walston was folksy and seemingly forthright; Garber is dapper and debonair. Walston was an apple-for-the-teacher Applegate; Garber is a Big Apple Applegate. A hellishly good actor, Garber falls just one tenth of a point short of a helluva Devil: it may be excess campiness, or some tiny aspect of face, frame, or hairstyle. Still, if not quite up to Scratch, he is pretty much up to snuff, especially when foiled, at which times his dither is as consummate as his blither.

As Joe Hardy, a kind of bat-wielding Andy Hardy, Jarred Emick is archetypally right. Gifted with a fine, symmetrical, slightly an-

---

*P.S. 2005: In this skit about drama critics' mothers, mine included, Miss Neuwirth actually portrayed the mother of another critic. Memory plays strange tricks—especially when Miss N. is involved.

gular face, he springs out of our classic comic strips, looking like Joe Palooka, Li'l Abner, and Clark Kent rolled into one. With or without song, he conveys exemplary boyish bewilderment and boy scout fervor, not to mention the exquisite melancholy when, having become his anxiety-ridden wife's boarder, he must bolster her ego without revealing himself. As Meg, Linda Stephens is no less perfect, and that not only in her singing and acting, but also in a quintessential dignity and grace, enabling her to play the dated figure of a meek hausfrau in a way that even militant feminists would greet with a tear of sympathy, not rage. In the less grateful role of the middle-aged Joe, Dennis Kelly, too, acquits himself admirably.

As the team manager, Dick Latessa has the proper lovable bluster; as a nosy reporter, Vicki Lewis, her profile all proboscis, is irrepressible. And the Senators themselves could scarcely be better as acrobatic dancers, full-throated singers, and ball-playerishly virile comedians. I myself would designate Gregory Jbara and Scott Wise *primi inter pares*, but you can take your pick. That brings us to Rob Marshall's exhilarating choreography, which tips its hat to Bob Fosse's hat-tipping style (to name but one of its hallmarks), yet remains resplendently idiosyncratic as it finds individual vocabularies for each dancer without neglecting a marvelous ensemble spirit.

Douglas W. Schmidt's tongue-in-cheek and often worm's-eye-view scenery, David C. Woolard's sweetly saucy costumes, David F. Segal's rousing lighting (abetted by Gregory Meeh's satanic special effects) all add to the merriment. The sundry orchestrators and arrangers shine, as does the orchestra under David Chase's sprightly baton. But the final tribute must go to Jack O'Brien's direction, whose visual touches are as quotably witty as his additions to the dialogue. The recasting of the bluesy duet "Two Lost Souls," now for Applegate and Lola, provides the demonic duo with a much-needed number to share, and turning the duet "Near to You" into an emotion-laden trio for Meg and her two Joes makes it, as staged and performed, into one of the highlights of my musical-going life. Altogether, this revival contrasts hearteningly with the concurrent one of *My Fair Lady*: it refurbishes rather than disfigures.

In his Fosse biography, Martin Gottfried writes: "Sooner or later, most of the creators of *Damn Yankees* would apologize for it." That no longer holds true. Both the surviving original creators and the stunning re-creators need feel nothing other than pride.

Carousel

The oldest joke about poor musicals is that you exit humming the scenery. *Carousel* is anything but a poor musical, yet from Nicholas Hytner's production of it, which had all London on its ear, you still emerge humming the scenery. Bob Crowley's sets are gleamingly stylized by a skillful eye and hand, as if the Saint-Exupéry who illustrated *The Little Prince* had suddenly discovered Lyonel Feininger. Everything from a perfectly hemispherical grassy knoll to a delightfully cartoonish New England church, from an Amarcordish ocean-liner side view to an Erector-Set Heaven, from meandering picket fences to serpentine beach-framing walls of reeds, from large toy houses busting out with little ones to a stage floor that (with the help of Paul Pyant's miraculous lighting) convinces you that it is shimmering water, works its canny magic. The rest of the show resists the magical to espouse the mediocre.

Reports from London extolled the "dark" quality of this *Carousel*. Compared with the original production, now almost a half-century ago, it may indeed have some added cross-hatching. But as against Molnár's *Liliom*, on which it is based, it is still on the lighter side, although Hytner's way of constricting most of the group scenes to a huddle, with space looming all around, does achieve suggestions of something lowering out there. But the principal innovation is multiracial casting, with two major and many minor and chorus parts played by performers of color. This directorial choice (which also makes one of the heavenly messengers a woman) in some ways militates against the meaning of the work. For if a small nineteenth-century New England fishing town was so liberal and liberated, the contrary carnival barker Billy Bigelow, who at best is a bit of a rebel without a cause, is diminished into an almost totally gratuitous malcontent.

The production has one other substantial asset in the late Kenneth MacMillan's last choreography, its rapturous second-act ballet danced incandescently by Sandra Brown and Jon Marshall Sharp. Even here, though, Agnes de Mille may have, in 1945, caught something of the *genius loci* that has eluded Sir Kenneth. Yet the real loss is in the performing. Michael Hayden, an American hailed in London by all and sundry as a revelation, does not impress me with his Billy. A thoroughly competent chorus-boy type with boyish good looks, he offers passable acting and just-possible singing; his rather too youthful, unweighty presence belies the character's vast stock of existential and amatory experience, as a sense of social injustice dwindles to pouting petulance. As the loving Julie, Sally Murphy is adequate in every way and outstanding in none. Eddie Korbich's Mr. Snow (played, conversely, by a black actor in London) may be a shade nerdier than is needed, but is otherwise effective; Audra Ann McDonald's Carrie (played, conversely, by a white actress in London—O fearful symmetry!) sings well, but is militantly charmless. As Jigger, the puny Fisher Stevens rasps his way through his songs, but as the maternal Nettie Fowler, Shirley Verrett finds a neat musical-comedy niche for her formerly operatic voice. The others manage to be almost extraordinarily ordinary.

Crowley's costumes, with too many unwarranted red highlights, are not up to his sets but will do. Hytner's direction is accomplished, yet seems forced at times—nowhere more *voulu* than in Billy's death scene on Crowley's almost too spectacularly Felliniesque wharf, where the chorus hovers in fear, frozen into a too architectural frieze. Hammerstein's language has often seemed wobbly to me, folksiness slipping into literariness, as in "He don't say much, but what he do say is awful pithy." And the ending, as always with Mr. H., has enough uplift for ten pairs of Adler Elevator shoes. But the R&H's songs, with Rodgers at his most tuneful, remain, even with imperfect delivery, special.

Medea

"One must be absolutely modern. This is what Euripides was, as he still is," writes our premier classical scholar, Bernard Knox (with an acknowledged assist from Rimbaud), in his absorbing new book, *Backing Into the Future*. In a letter of May 17, 1948, our still undervalued poet-playwright Robinson Jeffers, who wrote his version of *Medea*, declares, "There is much in any Greek play that would seem dull or absurd to anyone but a classical scholar." Which statement is true? Both.

Any new production of *Medea* must come to grips with the fact that although Euripides speaks as one of us, much of his technique strikes us as dated, though less so than that of his fellow Greek dramatists. This *Medea*, originally produced at London's Almeida Theatre, has many features to its credit, most notably that its director, Jonathan Kent, is aware of this *aporia* (as the Greeks would call it) or hot potato (as we would): Euripides today is both necessary and impossible. So Kent pawkily tries to steer a course between these infernal Symplegades (or a rock and a hard place).

The first and worst problem a director of a Greek drama now faces is what to do with the chorus. In the case of Medea, Jeffers reduced it to three women, as Grillparzer did before him; Anouilh, in his version, eliminated it altogether. Kent, too, retains three women, but then what? How should they look? Since Paul Brown's costumes here are modern, but with classical Greek overtones, Kent picked something resembling contemporary Greek folk dress, but with distinct echoes of a Melina Mercouri movie. It doesn't look quite right, but what would? Next, how to explain the chorus's very presence? "It is hard to imagine fifteen women standing by while a mother murders her children," wrote Moses Hadas, the late, great classicist. *Three* women standing by doesn't make it much easier. For this, Kent has no solution. But by assigning the roles to three actresses of very different ages and types (the eldest coming across like a man), he achieves a nice, stylized effect—something like the Three Ages of Woman.

The Greek chorus sang and danced; so Kent lets his women do some singing and dancing. For the former, they are usually backed up by an invisible choir, which makes for a bizarre but not uninteresting effect. The dancing, such as it is, is pretty ludicrous, but one admires Kent's guts for risking it at all. And there isn't much of it. The next problem is what kind of décor to use, other than the standard all-purpose Greek-drama set (Woolworth Hellenic), of which everyone is heartily sick. With the help of his set designer, Peter J. Davison, Kent came up with an imposingly monumental solution, which, along with the scenery for the current *Carousel*, raises the troubling possibility that British set design has way outstripped ours. What we get makes scant sense architecturally but is fiercely theatrical. Two tall, asymmetrical facades intersect at right angles; they are seemingly made of large square bronze sheets, artfully imbricated, with rivets displayed. In the lesser façade, stage right, is an empty doorway revealing some mighty girders. The main façade has, among other things, a picture window that sometimes lights up to reveal, say, Medea a shut-in in her palace, or hovering over her slain children, something the Greeks would never have shown. There is also a functioning, likewise square, onstage well. And in the end, the set does something sensational that you have to see for yourself.

Jonathan Dove's music is, in the spirit of the show, neither modern nor antiquarian, sometimes haunting and sometimes, alas, banal. More interesting sounds are produced by carefully calibrated bangings on the walls. The acting, by a low-profile British cast (save for the star, about whom more anon), is generally solid, distinguished by elocution American actors should envy. The diction of John Turner (Creon)—a tall, imposing man in a fuzzy black greatcoat for which numerous sheep must have been left shivering—is so good I felt virtually impaled by his consonants. I liked Tim Oliver Woodward's Jason, a fellow with one foot in tragedy, the other in trashiness, paltry one moment and deeply pitiable the next.

Diana Rigg's Medea is seldom absolutely right, but always hugely watchable. She, I think, suffers most from the directorial ambivalence: one moment a Mycenean lioness, she turns Mayfair hostess in a twinkling, her tigerish stalking yielding too readily to a kittenish purr. With her back frequently against the wall, her regal figure and darting eyes, she looks part caryatid, part Fury. In this she is superbly abetted by Wayne Dowdeswell's lighting, which uses horizontal and diagonal shafts of light to mesmeric or hallucinatory effect.

And yet Miss Rigg's disciplined and highly cultivated tones, and her fine sense of humor (which she has manifestly been urged to indulge), have a way of making this a thoroughly modern Medea, one eliciting too many knowingly deliberate laughs. Miss Rigg is, rightly, more sensual than her New York predecessors in the role, Judith Anderson and Zoe Caldwell, but they were, rightly, more terrifying. And for all that she looks sexy in red and marmoreal in discreetly blood-spattered white, she seems, like those others, a bit overmature for the role.

Why is Medea always played by an actress of a certain age, whom a man, fickle wretch that he is, might easily trade in for a newer model? This tragedy, about more complex issues, must not have that mundane, trumpery look of an Ivana being swapped for a Maria, which greatly lessens its impact. I do, however, owe Miss Rigg an apology. Years ago, when she played a nude scene in a play about Abelard and Heloïse, I described her as "built like a brick basilica with inadequate flying buttresses." (This was subsequently often misquoted, initially by Miss Rigg herself in her witty book *No Turn Unstoned*, as "a brick mausoleum.") Well, though there is no nude scene here, I can declare Miss Rigg's figure now generously buttressed.

All in all, this is a production that deserves to be seen—as well as heard, in Alistair Elliot's wonderfully colloquial yet not unpoetic translation—even if its split personality militates against full impact. It is rich in ideas in its every aspect, including Miss Rigg's performance, and ideas, even intermittently misguided ones, are precious in our theater so habitually short on thought.

Beauty and the Beast

For their production of *Beauty and the Beast*, the Disney people have wisely abolished the Broadway rule "No one under 5 admitted." They should have been consistent, though, and stipulated "No one over 5 admitted" as well. What's the point of antagonizing the adult part of your audience? America has manifestly produced a breed of millionaire toddlers, kiddies who can afford $65 tickets (phooey on those $20 ones in the balcony), and who, if told that they needed an adult to accompany them, would simply cut off their parents' allowance. So the audience for *B & B* will dismiss my strictures as the ravings of an old fogy, which is fine with me: who would want Mickey's millions withdrawn in a huff from reclaiming 42nd Street, Disney's other, and worthier, theatrical project?

There is a lot of amazing hocus-pocus at the Palace Theatre, not the least astounding being the question of authorship. Even the smarter 5-year-olds are unlikely to believe that the story was simply dreamed up by the book writer, one Linda Woolverton, holder of a master's degree in children's theater from Cal State, Fullerton. Yet you scour the program in vain for mention of Madame Marie Leprince de Beaumont, who, married unhappily in 1743, was divorced in 1745, and left for London to become a governess and eventually write *La Belle et la bête*, which, in 1946, inspired Jean Cocteau's most magical movie. In 1991 came the Disney animated feature *Beauty and the Beast*, for which the new Broadway show seems to be a belated infomercial.

But, surely, the folks at Disney are no fools and wouldn't put the horse quite that far behind the cart? After all, right after papal infallibility comes the Eisner/Katzenberg kind. Which would be challenged if 12 million bucks (conservative estimate) were blown on a flop. So, if *Beauty and the Beast* isn't magical in the least (no, that isn't one of the show's lyrics, though it might as well be), it does, however, bristle with magic tricks. But are we to judge *B & B* on how closely it replicates the movie? On how dazzling its trickery is? On how sweetly it brings back our childhood? Or are we to review it as a Broadway musical?

Frankly, it doesn't matter. This is the sort of show that makes it on entirely other considerations than its reviews. So I'll say it honestly and without fear of being banned from Disney's forthcoming renovated New Amsterdam Theater: *B & B* bored the pants off me. But only the show; some of the special effects are first-rate.

The problem is that the technique of animation has become so good that whereas cartoons no longer have the slightest difficulty looking like people, people still find it dauntingly difficult to look like cartoons. This may prove the downfall of *Beauty and the Beast*, the musical: the live actors straining to re-create their drawn alter egos end up less than drawn and more than quartered. Poor Madame de Beaumont obviously wrote her fairy tale in response to her unhappy marriage: in reality, her brute of a husband had refused to become princely, so she spun a therapeutic fantasy in which he did. Perhaps the musical should have snatched the opportunity to tell the story of how the love of a good feminist turns a wife-beater into a Prince Charming, or some such contemporary fairy tale. But that way it might have failed as an infomercial.

So the performers are in trouble. Dear little Susan Egan manages to look reasonably like the cartoon version of Belle (at least she is in the ball—or theme—park), and sings quite winningly. Acting, evidently, wasn't called for. Terrence Mann, as the Beast, looks like a more soulful version of Tim Curry or, during tantrums, like a bigger, prettier Eric Bogosian. He is never very frightening, what with that wistful gaze and velvety voice (amplified, like everything else here, into the bestially inhuman), and for all those fangs and claws and horns, he looks at the most like a Cowardly Bison. Of course, that's still better than his looks as the restored Prince, but then, Hugh Grant can't be in everything. Too bad that even the augmented Alan Menken-Howard Ashman-Tim Rice score sounds like an uneasy ménage à trois, the Menken-Ashman songs coming off somewhat better than the Menken-Rice ones.

Burke Moses makes such a fine, fatuous Gaston that his arrogant, blustery songs seem better than they are. Similarly, Beth Fowler and Gary Beach, as, respectively, an anthropomorphic teapot and candelabra, manage to heat up and brighten their material. Tom Bosley is wasted on the no-account part of Belle's papa, and, among the rest, only Stacey Logan, as Babette the feather duster, flutters fetchingly.

But let's get to the crux: the illusions. The boy Brian Press is a most convincing teacup, his seemingly trunkless head an eloquent piece of crockery; and though Matt West's strictly Vegas-style choreography does not flatter the dancing flatware and kitchen utensils, it blends smoothly with the giant champagne bottles luminously popping their corks, although this might be too racy for small children. (The 34 phallic candles popping up in a sort of serial erection are distinctly too priapic for the under-5 crowd.) The Beast's transformation into the Prince while he is levitating in midair, wrapped up more thoroughly than Tutankhamen's mummy, would have made Harry Houdini salivate. The only real downer is the pack of wolves the Beast fights to save Belle's life: there's many a New York household that can boast fiercer-looking cockroaches.

Ann Hould-Ward's costumes are zestily fanciful and actually make the humans look progressively more thinglike (creeping reification?), which is more than I require: I am willing to take my human teapots on sight rather than on the installment plan. Natasha Katz's lighting works its spell in tandem with Jim Steinmeyer and John Gaughan's illusions. But Stan Meyer's sets, although they move about as restlessly as dromomaniacs, are an aesthetic disaster, looking like picture postcards in a provincial drugstore. Only the puns in Linda Woolverton's dialogue can equal their crudity. Robert Jess Roth, the director whose biggest successes were in "creating and directing shows at various Disney venues," has effectively removed all the moving, as opposed to mobile, parts of the story.

In fact, the entire production should be shipped over to Euro Disney (where the French, who love their fairy tales unadulterated, would enjoy using it as a shooting gallery) to recoup the losses of that failing venture. But the musical may be just a stopgap measure until the already heralded *Beauty and the Beast* ice show skates into town. In a piece of sublime (and cost-cutting) illusionism, the currently underemployed Tonya Harding might play both leads—one of them to perfection.

Broken Glass;
An Inspector Calls

Arthur Miller may be the world's most overrated playwright, but even he could not have served up the jagged shards of *Broken Glass* without some hidden agenda, some secret scenario under the banal plot and shoddy dialogue. I'll take a stab at unscrambling it after I tiptoe warily across the sliverlike scenes of *Broken Glass*, which gives the epithet *shattering* a theatrically new, and wholly undesirable, meaning.

Brooklyn, 1938: Sylvia Gellburg, a middle-aged Jewish housewife (Amy Irving, fine but saddled with a dreadful wig), loses control of her legs, to the dismay of her stuffy but not unloving husband, Phillip (the talented Ron Rifkin in a sadly mechanistic performance). Dr. Harry Hyman, a generalist who diagnoses the paralysis as hysterically induced but who admits to scant knowledge of psychiatry, nevertheless administers psychotherapy to Sylvia. Hyman (David Dukes, in a sincere but flavorless performance) spares no amount of time questioning Phillip, Sylvia, and her sister, Harriet (Lauren Klein—with a good but very broad piece of acting), in an effort to crack this medical mystery, to the extent that one wonders how much time he has left for other patients. He is assisted in his etiological endeavors by his *shiksa* wife, Margaret (Frances Conroy, in what has become her signature, or rote, performance), who helpfully putters around his office. The dramatis personae are rounded out by Stanton Case, the millionaire-yachtsman head of Brooklyn Guarantee [*sic*], where Phillip is the only Jewish employee. Case (the excellent George N. Martin, doing his level but losing best) is a patronizing, unconscious anti-Semite, and a stick-figure knockoff of Howard Wagner in *Death of a Salesman*.

We are to be absorbed by the allegedly riveting quest for the correct diagnosis and cure. Sylvia may have lost her mobility from the shock of reading in the papers about Nazi cruelty to Jews, including photographs of bearded patriarchs forced to scrub sidewalks with toothbrushes, and Jewish store windows being smashed on Kristallnacht (the eponymous broken glass, which here has also deeper, or more splintered, meanings). Or she may have suddenly realized that Phillip's entire life has been an effort "to disappear into the goyim," even to the extent of forcing an entirely un-Jewish army career on their son, so that she has gone lame with resentment. Or, most daring (and predictable) of revelations: it may all have to do with Phillip's not having had sex with her in twenty years; she now even develops a crush on Dr. Hyman, who, during house calls, is troubled by her advances but gently fends them off.

Since the audience is always at least one jump ahead of these discoveries, something else—to stay within the play's leggy metaphor—may be afoot. Miller is remasticating his perennial theme, sometimes disguised, sometimes flaunted: the Wandering Jew as a floating island of raw sensibility in a sea of goyish uncaring, battered but uneroded by the billows of disparagement. In *Incident at Vichy*, we heard: "Jew is only the name we give to that stranger, that agony we cannot feel, that death we look at like a cold abstraction. Each man has his Jew; it is the other. And the Jews have their Jews." Now a new spin is put on this trusty conceit: "Everybody's persecuted. The poor by the rich, the rich by the poor. The black by the white, the white by the black, the men by the women, the women by the men, the Catholics by the Protestants, the Protestants by the Catholics—and of course all of them by the Jews." Victimization is what makes the world go round, and so we find Phillip and Sylvia as each other's victims and victimizers—an idea long ago done up brown by Strindberg and Bergman, here rendered in washed-out sepia tones.

The minimum requirement for a good play is that it be written out of some inner necessity rather than sheer velleity. Yet the printed text of *Broken Glass* (Penguin Books) and the since revised stage version display, among many others, a fundamental difference. In the book, what makes Sylvia walk again is her loving concern for her stricken husband. At the Booth Theatre, she rises from her wheelchair to exult in her deliverance as Phillip dies of a heart attack. An author who can (to please today's audiences more comfortable with a feminist than with a patriarchal message?) change his meaning by 180 degrees is to my mind not an artist. Can you imagine Miller's model, Ibsen, rewriting *The Master Builder* so that Solness falls off his steeple into Hilde's loving arms? Or O'Neill having Mary Tyrone kick her morphine addiction and take up jujubes instead? Tennessee Williams, to be sure, sometimes bowed to directorial editing, but then spent much of his life trying to get his original versions restored. Yet Miller's ultimate failure is his language: tone-deafness in a playwright is only a shade less bad than in a composer. Here is Harry to Sylvia in a rapt moment: "Listen to me, I haven't been this moved by a woman in a long time." Or, even more moved: "The depth of your flesh must be wonderful." Or this from Phillip: "I got a… a big yen for her. She's even more beautiful when she sleeps. I gave her a kiss. On the mouth. She didn't wake up. I never had such a yen in my life." Or Harry, an opera lover, demystifying opera to Sylvia: "There's nothing to understand; either she wants to and he doesn't, or he wants to and she doesn't. Either way one of them gets killed and the other one jumps off a building." With lovers like these, opera needs no enemies. Whatever else John Tillinger, the director, may not have done, he seems to have been instrumental in ridding the text of some linguistic anachronisms and grammatical lapses, though others remain.

Santo Loquasto's scenery, surprisingly, is crudely schematic, perhaps taking its cue from the text. William Bolcom's overamplified offstage cello riffs—the text, pretentiously and hackneyedly, calls for an onstage cellist, mercifully spared us—are sorry stuff, but even sorrier is Tillinger's use of a turntable on which one frozen scene revolves into darkness as another one whirls into the light. Sorriest, though, is the spectacle—visible to the mind's eye—of Miller thrashing about desperately in search of a plot. But, as noted earlier, it may all be a *pièce à clef.* Could the offstage Allan Kershowitz, a crafty fellow, stand for the great litigator who brought chutzpah to the Harvard Law School? Could the sexy, dedicated, empathetic Dr. Hyman stand for the author? And could Sylvia's condition allude to the play's having no legs?

Several of J. B. Priestley's plays are thrilling; *An Inspector Calls* is merely a thriller. But a good one: psychological, socially critical, and even metaphysical. Yet its metaphysics should come as a final surprise. The Birlings, an affluent Yorkshire family, are celebrating in 1912 the engagement of daughter Sheila to the even more affluent Gerald Croft. Papa Arthur blusters a bit, brother Eric hits the bottle a mite heavily; otherwise all is well with the world. Into their postprandial calm intrudes Inspector Goole, announcing the horribly painful suicide of a pretty, unemployed young woman in whose death, as he proceeds to demonstrate, the entire family, including mother Sybil and prospective son-in-law Gerald, is deeply implicated.

Things unfurl in the manner of an intelligent and effective thriller against the background, as written, of a very brummagem drawing room in the fictional town of Brumley, until something bursts the surroundings and opens up the play to cosmic dimensions. But for that astounding extension to work, what precedes it must be staidly mundane. The 32-year-old British director Stephen Daldry has recast the work in an Expressionist mold, as if reconceived by Kaiser or Toller for Berlin, 1920. Right off the bat, some children seem to crawl out of the ground and play games with the fringes of the curtain and an abandoned but functioning radio. When the curtain teasingly rises, a curtain of rain takes over, so convincingly that it discreetly sprayed us in row H.

Against an odd, semi-dilapidated, almost surreal townscape, a Schiele-esque toylike house on stilts looms large stage center, just big enough for five actors to be glimpsed talking behind its slitty windows. (This house will later undergo some extraordinary permutations.) Meanwhile, one or two inscrutable characters, a crone who may be a parlormaid and a little boy who may be the kid from *Waiting for Godot*, flit about mysteriously. Much later, a whole crowd of extras will, silently and ominously, stalk into view. All this against an enormous sky aswirl with clouds that can turn into a storm or part for a dazzle of eerie nocturnal sunlight. In short, Daldry and his able designer, Ian MacNeil, *begin* with the portentous, which makes its final, called-for appearance woefully anticlimactic.

I was tickled most by the rich Birlings' only telephone being in a near-collapsed outdoor public phone booth with broken glass (has Arthur Miller been here?). The scenery, lighting, special effects, and supernumeraries form a separate show, very enjoyable but totally divorced from the play. And given such a precocious production, it may be unsurprising that the older actors—Rosemary Harris, Philip Bosco, Kenneth Cranham—are unremarkable, whereas the younger ones—Jane Adams, Aden Gillett, and Marcus D'Amico—shine. In particular Miss Adams, who is spectacular.

Passion; *Grease*

Stephen Sondheim's new musical, *Passion*, starts *in medias res* with a vengeance. Two young lovers, naked in bed, are enjoying a moment of postcoital bliss, giving the lie to the medieval adage about *animal triste*. They are singing their brains out (it would be their hearts if the score were by someone else), as the extremely pretty adulteress, Clara, displays a torso to rhapsodize over, and her lover, Giorgio (a captain in less than mufti), soon flashes by in the altogether.

A flashy beginning, then, but one that already displays what will be a singularly passionless score. There have been musicals about which the complaint was that all the songs sounded too similar; this one goes a step further: all the songs sound the same. The score is a glutinous mass; although there are ample passages of dialogue, it comes across as through-composed. There are no high and low points only a rather undifferentiated continuum that could be the outtakes from previous Sondheim shows. Jonathan Tunick's woodwind-rich orchestrations help, especially in the unsung passages, with their chamber-music effects. And Sondheim restrains his cleverness in the lyrics, but then lacks the passion to put in its place. I think what he had in mind was emulating contemporary opera. But most contemporary opera, with its endless, tuneless recitatives, sets a pernicious example.

Those half dozen Americans who have read *Fosca*, the 1860s novel by Iginio Tarchetti, and the few hundreds who have seen *Passione d'amore*, the mediocre movie Ettore Scola made from it, will recall that this is the story of Giorgio, a handsome captain posted to Parma, a sleepy army outpost, and thus forced to leave his beloved but married Clara in Milan. At mealtimes in Parma, he is seated beside Fosca, the commanding officer's cousin. She is a homely woman, made uglier by a packet of maladies both physical and mental that manifest themselves in hysterical howls in her upstairs room and sudden collapses at the dinner table.

Fosca falls into unbridled love with the unresponsive, indeed repelled, Giorgio. Abject and demanding, wheedling and peremptory, she becomes his pathetic, platonic succubus. Yet Giorgio, despite periodic leaves spent with Clara, falls more and more prey to this unblushing Parma violet, until… Watching *Passion*, an even creepier show than *Assassins*, is like watching the mating dance of a pair of snakes, an image solicited by the show's logo, in which the title's second capital S is reversed, so that the two serpentine letters look like facing adders joined at the crotch.

Matters are made ghostlier by duets constantly turning into trios, as whichever woman is currently absent comes onstage singing a letter she is writing or reading; *Passion* is to a large extent an epistolary musical. There is also much musical crosscutting, a plethora of stops and starts, and the unsettling intrusion of soldiers, officers, parents, and chambermaids chorically repeating verbatim the intimate outpourings of individual lovers. And James Lapine, the librettist and director, desperate for bits of choreography other than marching soldiers, has the officers filing in and out of the mess (the dining room, not the show) with arm movements befitting some outlandish military drill.

For additional activity, the scenery is seldom allowed to stand still. Adrianne Lobel uses minimalist scrims and curlicue-covered, terra-cotta-colored sliding panels—for indoors; for outdoors—deliquescent landscapes in sepia washes—she overleaps the ottocento to plunge us into the world of such Italian modernists as Ardengo Soffici and Carlo Carrà. Beverly Emmons's lighting is suitably romantic; Jane Greenwood's costumes for the women, paragons of tasteful opulence.

Marin Mazzie couldn't be lovelier as Clara—vocally, visually, and histrionically; Donna Murphy is almost too spookily perfect as Fosca, with a thrilling singing voice, albeit a somewhat affected speaking one. But the man they contend for is a disaster: not only is Jere Shea totally un-Italian (Giorgio of Hollywood?), he is also undashing, untouching, more hulk than hunk. The supporting cast is solid, save for Gregg Edelman as the commanding officer, and Matthew Porretta as an Austrian baron, both of whom strike one as kids playing adults. Yet even if everything else were equal, a musical-comedy book, unlike a novel or a movie, would be too cramped a space in which to develop so radical a psychic change as *Passion* hinges on.

In 1972, only a half generation after the fact, the way for *Grease* to recycle fifties rock and roll was nostalgia. Now, more than a whole generation later, how do you revive *Grease* and recycle nostalgia? The answer is travesty, camp. A neverland becomes a never-never land, middle America becomes Vegas, lost innocence becomes pseudo-innocence, a spoof becomes a cartoon. The new *Grease* is neither wholly faithful nor wholly unfaithful to the old *Grease*: still, if there is such a thing as a *Grease* purist, he or she will mind. But for the younger crowd, the ones for whom the fifties might as well be the fifteenth century, this show should feel rampagingly right.

For the loss in authenticity, there is a gain in tolerance. The smart high school set of '59 would not have admitted blacks, fatties, and more than one nerd to sneer at. As the show's archetypal high school, Rydell High, rides high again, it has two blacks, three obese persons, and a whole nest of twittering song-nerds. It has also acquired some political correctness (though not so much as the original touring version or the badly bowdlerized movie); thus the greaser's dream car is now a dragon wagon, not a pussy wagon. Well, win some, lose some.

I don't see anyone in the present cast quite the equal of the spunky Adrienne Barbeau, the adorable Carole Demas, and the witty Barry Bostwick, Walter Bobbie, and Timothy Meyers. But I may be proved wrong by the passage of time and a new wave of nostalgia. Certainly Susan Wood is a fetching and spirited Sandy, Megan Mullally makes a mettlesome Marty (and what legs!), Ricky Paull Goldin's Danny looks like John Travolta, and Sam Harris (Doody) and Billy Porter (a black Teen Angel) sing delightfully. There is much vivid dancing, most notably from Sandra Purpuro as Cha-Cha, and the part of the teacher, Miss Lynch, has been beefed up—sorry, cowed up—for Marcia Lewis, who milks it merrily.

Several of the Jim Jacobs and Warren Casey songs hold up pleasurably, and Jeff Calhoun has directed and choreographed this *Grease*-for-today with inventiveness and zest. The new concept places most of the action on an elevated inner stage that creates the effect of looking into a multiple-bottomed box. It makes the show more like a play-within-a-play—Brecht comes to Rydell High—but, hey! why not? The heroes here are the design team: totally crrrazy costumes by Willa Kim, fantabulous lighting by Howell Binkley, and neon-studded, comic-book-come-alive scenery by John Arnone. My only problem is with Rosie O'Donnell: she delivers her lines with the proper deadpan hauteur, but a fat Rizzo? As soon have a lean Zero Mostel.

Show Boat

What do you say to bliss that is coming your way? You say, "Hello, *Show Boat!*" and you rush to the box office for tickets to the Garth Drabinsky production that first sailed into Toronto but has now cast anchor by a wharf known as the Gershwin. There is levity on the levee, as well as heartache and tears, with music and lyrics by Jerome Kern and Oscar Hammerstein II, and on the stage, 71 performers 71. Acting, singing, dancing come gloriously together. The show, as I had already reported from Toronto, was very fine there. A further year in which to get the barnacles off was well spent: this *Show Boat* is now a dreamboat.

With most old musicals, the problem is how to flesh them out: there were fewer songs than we now expect, and most books have dated badly. No such difficulty here. As there were several productions during the authors' lifetimes, and several movie versions, additional material kept accruing. The complete studio recording of every scrap of *Show Boat* on EMI runs to 3 hours, 41 minutes, and 36 seconds. And since the show was based on Edna Ferber's sprawling novel, there is plot enough to burn.

The director who undertakes a revival need not borrow, say, from other Kern shows and hire a librettist to fill out or spruce up the story; he'll have more use for pruning shears than for tuning forks. But cutting isn't easy when what you must throw away is as good as what you end up keeping. The fact is that the American musical had three undisputed peaks—*Show Boat*, *Porgy and Bess*, and *Oklahoma!*—on the way to realizing its potential. There have been others as good since then, but these three set the tone. Coming in 1927, *Show Boat* was the first to turn its back on the mindless extravaganzas and help create a full-fledged American genre: inheriting something from operetta and ogling opera out of the corner of its eye, the modern musical was born.

Because it covers three generations of show folk, because its, action spans four decades, because it shuttles between steamy Natchez and boreal Chicago, and because it touches on such varied subjects as race relations and the dispersal of families, *Show Boat* is usually described as having epic sweep. In a production such as this, certainly.

Eugene Lee has constructed the scenery mostly out of real materials, e.g., wood, metal, clapboard, burlap; by a charming paradox, the solidity and weightiness contribute to the flow of the story: you believe that this *Cotton Blossom* will stay afloat for decades, that this revolving door to the Palmer House will serve as turnstile to generations. Moreover, Lee has made the set as nearly monochrome as possible. Even the river is not your usual swirl of blues and greens but a scintillant sepia, a river from old photographs and etchings, encrusted with the past. Yet the scenery allows uninterrupted forward movement by novel devices I leave it to you to discover.

Against this daguerreotype background, Florence Klotz has designed a passing parade of costumes, a survey of a goodly chunk of the history of clothes. Most wonderful is her color sense: she knows exactly when the self-effacement of pastels is called for, and when to hit you in the eye with flame red or canary yellow. Bustles decrease and vanish, hemlines keep rising, Army and Navy uniforms evolve. And Richard Pilbrow's lighting not only shows the succession of oil, gas, and electricity, but also conjures up southern and northern climes and one of the best stage storms you have ever seen. You get in equal measure lived life and felt life, the outside and the inside of reality.

Harold Prince, the director, has extended the stage beyond the proscenium arch to the right and left. This is the Mississippi flowing on and on, but it is also the horizontality of everyday existence. He has seen to it that there is real water under the stage, to reflect upward with that restless kaleidoscope of glimmers that reminds us that all stasis is illusory: reality is flux. Against this agitated flatness, the love story of Gaylord and Magnolia strikes some stunning verticals with, first, her a level above him, then him a level above her, until they finally meet on the empty top deck against the night sky, level with each other, equal in love.

There are some problems with the plotting, but Prince's staging moves so swiftly and involvingly that there is no time for questions. Degradation and redemption are the stuff of life, and at least both Julie and Gay sink with a gallant gesture. There is talk that Prince has darkened the story, yet the chiaroscuro was always there, and the truthful director merely looks at it squarely. How stoically this Magnolia grieves; how warily she and Gay accept their final reunion!

Prince makes sure that the songs register properly. Thus when the already alcoholic Julie rouses herself to put across "Bill" for the nightclub owner for whom she works, the club's maintenance staff is at work dusting and polishing, and a bunch of chorines are lolling about between rehearsals. Gradually the cleaners stop working and the chorus girls are shocked out of their idling: all are sucked into the song and Julie's emotions. Since the workers are black and the chorines white, we are drawn back into a like breakdown on the levee, where Julie sang a similarly self-sacrificing and all-enduring woman's love song, "Can't Help Lovin' Dat Man." And Prince has Joe walking periodically across the scene, intoning snatches of "Ol' Man River," to remind us of the persisting social predicaments.

The director is seconded by his choreographer, Susan Stroman, who with this effort surges to the forefront of Broadway dance creators. Her two dance montages—one for the worsening fortunes of the Ravenals, and one for the passage of American decades and the co-optation of the Charleston from black street performers by white show biz and society—achieve what has often been claimed but never fully delivered: the enabling of the stage to do all that the movies can.

The cast here is a true constellation. John McMartin's rubber-legged, fluttery-voiced, always genially bemused Cap'n Andy is mated with the starchy, beady-eyed Parthy of Elaine Stritch, whose maternal and grandmotherly instincts flicker behind the triple brass of termagancy. Though Rebecca Luker's pretty and sweet Magnolia has much of her father's softness, the firm, pentagonal face and survivor's tenacity derive equally clearly from her mother. Mark Jacoby's Gaylord Ravenal is the slippery river gambler who may after all be a scion of the Tennessee Ravenals: the persuasive and the suspect in him are beyond anyone's disentangling, including his own. When he and Miss Luker join in "You Are Love," one of the greatest love duets, their shimmering voices and rapt personalities blend with the full moon and the stars into what may just be the music of the spheres.

Michel Bell's Joe has the monumental yet caressing voice of a true basso cantante and the human presence to match; he is well paired with Gretha Boston as his no-nonsense wife, whose rendition of the great "Mis'ry's Comin' Aroun'," backed up by the ubiquitous and superlative choir, sends shivers into the listening heart. And Lonette McKee's penetrantly sung Julie is also shatteringly acted: she unravels before our eyes with minimal posturing. As the comedy couple, the chirpy Dorothy Stanley and superbly agile Joel Blum are—like everyone else—right on the money. And speaking of money, sure, *Show Boat*'s prices are the steepest on Broadway. But is even a $75 top too much for three hours of perfect bliss?

Love! Valour! Compassion!

When, over three centuries ago, John Dryden initiated heroic drama, he declared that "love and valour ought to be the subject of it." To this program, Terrence McNally has added compassion and three exclamation points. Thus we get *Love! Valour! Compassion!*, a long play about three long weekends (Memorial Day, Fourth of July, Labor Day). Encapsulating the lives of eight homosexuals, two of them played by the same actor, it means to be memorable, forthcoming, a labor of love.

The locale is an isolated Dutchess County lakeside summer

house, where Gregory, a famous but fading choreographer, is struggling with a new ballet while also planning a drag version of *Swan Lake* for an AIDS benefit. His lover, the blind and boyish Bobby, is seduced by the naughty Hispanic dancer Ramon, who is the boyfriend of John Jeckyll, a nasty British rehearsal pianist, who hides a Hyde just under his skin. His twin, James, however, is the sweetest of dithering queens, liked by everybody, but dying of AIDS. The gang's cutup is HIV-positive Buzz, who designs costumes for Gregory. Fat, loverless, and yearning, Buzz is a wizard at musical-comedy trivia and a wellspring of campy jokes. Representing non-show business are Arthur and Perry, an accountant and a lawyer, married to each other for fourteen years. Perry is the raisonneur of the group, though he is scarcely less campy than Buzz.

These are not wholly carefree holidays. Ramon's fling with Bobby stirs up trouble for himself with the vindictive John, and for Bobby with the heartbroken Gregory. Even the motherly Arthur evinces a yen for Ramon, especially when, both naked, they share a raft on the lake. Tempers flare and taunts are taunted. Defiance circulates among the group. John reads and reveals Gregory's private diary. Somebody gets spat at. Somebody's sister dies in India. The group goes skinny-dipping. Two guys hide in a closet to watch two others carry on. Buzz and James find each other. John plays classical piano music, giving McNally a chance to show off his knowledge of serious music, even as Buzz's show-biz jokes allow him to parade his musical-comedy erudition. It rains a lot, but there is also smooching in the moonlight. And a few comic dance turns.

There is no denying that McNally can write funny lines as well as anyone. Often they are catty, but sometimes actually human. Buzz complains about his room: "That little horror under the eaves—I call it the Patty Hearst Memorial Closet." He gripes, "I'm sick of straight people. There's too goddamn many of them... They're taking over, I'm telling you!" Or "I'm so intense. I need someone like Dennis Hopper." Someone asks, "Is there no British equivalent to *machismo*?" "No. None at all," affirms James, adding the ruminative topper: "Maybe Glenda Jackson."

Sometimes, however, he overreaches. "'Nocturnal emissions' is so much nicer than 'wet dreams.' It made me think of Chopin: Nocturnal Emission in B-flat." The joke falls (non-B) flat. Someone is called a kibitz. "What's a kibitz?" asks Ramon. "A kibbutz is a place where old gay Jewish couples live." Somehow the kibitz-kibbutz homophone gets in the hair of those "old gay Jewish couples," which is itself stretching things a bit. And almost all the jokes are, one way or another, sexual. Is there no other kind of humor?

A bigger problem is McNally's waxing poetic every so often. There is intrinsically nothing wrong with waxing poetic, except when the waxing is more like a waning. For example, Perry has a habit of saying when the situation gets hairy, "Anyway." It is an aposiopesis all pick up and play variations on. The device is harped on until it loses its poetic charm and becomes a sweaty factotum, having to provide even the curtain line. No way. Also, I find kissing a relative stranger's AIDS lesion more frivolous than Franciscan.

What is McNally trying to say with this play? True, ever since he burst on the Broadway scene with *And Things That Go Bump in the Night*, he has been gnawing away at the closet door, which, finally nibbled away, reveals even the various ways three parallel gay couples are entwined in their sleep. (No differently from straight ones.) But, surely, there must be more to it, otherwise why the grandiose title? Though, frankly, I don't see much compassion here, and still less valour, with or without a "u."

Erich Kästner once published his poems as an anthology, *Lyrische Hausapotheke* ("Lyrical Medicine Chest"). In the index, he listed all possible emotional disasters, along with the page numbers for the poems that might soothe those ills. McNally may be trying for something similar. If so, his situations are not quite inclusive enough, his solutions not sufficiently solacing. But perhaps he is just giving us a slice of life, or two, or three. Anyway....

Joe Mantello has directed knowingly amid canny scenery by Loy Arcenas, superb lighting by Brian MacDevitt, and mischievous costumes by Jess Goldstein. I was unconvinced by Stephen Bogardus (Gregory), Justin Kirk (Bobby), and John Glover's British accent, though the rest of Glover's performance(s) are fine. As were those of John Benjamin Hickey, Stephen Spinella, Randy Becker, and Nathan Lane, our favorite teddy bear, as Buzz.

Vita & Virginia

It is not clear what went on physically between Virginia Woolf and Vita Sackville-West. Virginia, as Nigel Nicolson, Vita's son, puts it, "was sexually frigid." Vita, in Virginia's words, was "a pronounced Sapphist," though she was actually bisexual. Vita herself wrote to her tolerant, homosexual husband, "I *have* gone to bed with her (twice), but that's all." And also, "It is a fire with which I have no wish to play." As Roger Poole writes in *The Unknown Virginia Woolf*, "[Her] anaesthesia in sexual matters was proportionately relieved in the context of beautiful and talented women." Or, as Quentin Bell has it in his biography of his aunt Virginia: "What was, to her, important was the extent to which she was emotionally involved."

And emotionally involved the two women writers certainly were. Nicolson quotes Vita as leaving a lunch with "my head swimming with Virginia." And Bell notes that Virginia "could believe in [Vita] as a Kentish nymph, a blue-blooded dryad, an aristocratic goddess," but not as a literary equal, which prevented her from fully giving herself to one who wrote, she felt, "with complete competency, and a pen of brass." But to Vita (as to others), Virginia was a genius. The result was a touching *amitié amoureuse*, which you can savor deliciously and absorbingly in *Vita & Virginia*, the dramatic duologue Eileen Atkins has extracted from the women's letters, and in which she enacts the virginal Virginia, with Vanessa Redgrave as the vitality-exuding Vita.

The four women on the Union Square Theatre stage are enchanting, irresistible, and frequently sublime. I say "four" because to disentangle the writers from the actresses is hardly possible and quite unnecessary: you will find it easy to gather into your hearts Vita, Virginia, Vanessa, and Eileen in a delirious *ménage à quatre*, for all four of them are articulate charmers, perceptive and impassioned, witty and mischievous, and damn good company. Virginia, a prickly coquette, was full of sass and irony; Vita, for all that Virginia condescended to her intellectually—"a mind that, if slow, works doggedly"—was full of pert, sophisticated savvy. There was in them great warmth for each other, and the occasional umbrage taken only led to closer harmony. A niece, Angelica Garnett, mentions "Virginia's excited and unbridled accounts" of her flirtations, and unbridled excitement we get here. We also get what Angelica has to say about Virginia's relations with the woman dearest to her, Angelica's mother: "Communication was a luxury to which no effort attached."

Effortless luxury best describes these performances, by turns thrilling, hilarious, and wrenching, as we follow almost two decades of correspondence and friendship. Like the two writers, the two actresses are perfect foils for each other: Miss Atkins sober yet quizzical, disapproving yet indulgent, both doting mentor and (though ten years older) awed younger sister; Miss Redgrave, enraptured hero worshiper yet also teasing mother, allowing Virginia to preen prankishly in her adulation. It is a privileged symbiosis, and the very voices of the actresses blend entrancingly: Miss Atkins's higher, like a crisply snippy glockenspiel; Miss Redgrave's like dark velvet caressed against the grain, sexy and tenor-saxy.

Besides acting with body and soul, these great artists play gorgeously with the English language. How flat American speech sounds compared with the sinuous or supercilious assurance with which Atkins and Redgrave bat at each other the exquisite tones of Bloomsbury salons and centuries-old aristocratic ancestral homes, respectively. To hear Vanessa and Eileen intoning the intoxicating speech melodies of Vita and Virginia is a musical pleasure running parallel to the dramatic.

Zoe Caldwell has directed simply yet stylishly on Ben Edwards's English-countryside set, centering on one of those lushly Britannic hedges, while John Gromada's soundtrack features the magically multifaceted birdsong of that green and pleasant land. Costumed with droll authenticity by Jane Greenwood, here is Vita in her coltish elegance, Virginia in her perky dowdiness. But the stage is also peopled with a gallery of the famous and infamous who impinged on Vita and Virginia, and were impinged on right back in spades. Don't assume this to be an academic exercise about two literary lesbians; it is the glowing conjuration of a world of love and wisdom, banter and profundity, sunlight and sadness.

The final images, vocal and visual, of Virginia's death, and of how loss is reclaimed by immortal poetry, are as moving as anything I have ever experienced. This is that rare evening in the theater of which I can affirm that those who miss it shall, in Will's words, "think themselves accursed they were not here." The others will have had an adventure in beauty to draw on joyously as long as heart and memory endure.

The Merchant of Venice

John Gross's magisterial monograph *Shylock: A Legend and Its Legacy* concludes, "I do believe that the ground for the Holocaust was well-prepared, and to that extent the play can never seem quite the same again. It is still a masterpiece; but there is a permanent chill in the air, even in the gardens of Belmont." The play, of course, is *The Merchant of Venice*, and, as revived at the Public Theater, it does not merely cast a chill; rather, it makes you wonder how Barry Edelstein could so miscast and misdirect the work as to make a total shambles of it.

The politically correct worriers are here, as usual, in error. If the Holocaust casts its shadow on *Merchant*, or vice versa, this (*pace* John Gross) is not a cause for worry. What is is the assumption that sweeping under the carpet, censoring, or expunging is the way to deal with history. Without reiterating the overexposed Santayana dictum, I ask: how can we learn from history if we eradicate it? The play depicts a state of affairs that was, in many ways still is, and—given the fallibility of human nature—is likely to persist. Instead of ignoring it or, as in the present case, fiddling with it, let us squarely confront it.

Edelstein has no clear position about the Shylock question. His Venetian Jews wear a yellow circle on their clothes (as, at certain times in Venice, they did), but even that interests him only to the extent of having Shylock draw a similar circle on Antonio's chest to outline the incision he prepares to make. That you could scarcely get a pound of flesh from that is the least of our problems. Edelstein's portrayal of anti-Semitism is promptly undercut by his casting so many black and Hispanic actors as Venetian patricians, some even saying things like "a hangman's nyoose," under the illusion that this is upper-class English. This negates the notion of a monolithic—anti-Semitic and xenophobic—Venice. That this city-state is also anti-black is clear from Portia's comment when the Prince of Morocco chooses the wrong casket: "Let all of his complexion choose one so."

Edelstein's choice—which is no better—is to make the men of Venice flagrant or closeted homosexuals. (Perhaps pink triangles could have been artfully intermingled with the yellow circles.) This thread runs through the entire production, whether Salerio and Solanio avidly kiss in the piazza, or Lorenzo forgets about Jessica the moment they hit Belmont (the great, lyrical moonlight scene is one of this version's lowest points), or, at the happy resolution, Antonio and Bassanio go off arm in arm as Portia, abandoned, stares mournfully into the distance. Even if it could be demonstrated that this was Shakespeare's subtext, a subtext should not be turned into the text. A touch of bitters enhances a cocktail; bitters alone are unpalatable.

While all the men here are awful—some merely miscast or misdirected, others fundamentally bad—the women are surprisingly good. Laila Robins, one of our very best young actresses, manages to get a great deal out of Portia despite every kind of sabotage, not least from Catherine Zuber's costuming (why must Venice always be visualized in Pietro Longhi's eighteenth-century terms?), which renders her ridiculous in male drag. Gail Grate is a saucily sophisticated Nerissa, of keen timing and wit; Nina Landey, a most appealing newcomer, would be a fine Jessica if the director had allowed her to lighten up in places. These three manage to make this *Merchant* watchable—no mean achievement.

That good scenic designer John Arnone has, for once, made a botch of things, using gloomy or washed-out colors and having horse troughs stand in for the canals of Venice. Mimi Jordan Sherin's lighting scores a few good effects, but Michael Torke's music is, as ever to my ears, appalling. Which brings me, reluctantly, to Shylock. Ron Leibman has always been more like a force of nature than an actor, and has, with minuscule variations of degree, always given the same performance. It may have seemed logical to progress from *Angels in America*'s Roy Cohn to Shakespeare's Jew—from shyster to Shylock—but his work here does not find the right gradations even in excess. A hurricane without conviction is no hurricane at all.

The Heiress

How little it takes for a great evening of theater! A brilliant novelist, Henry James, to write you a story; a clever husband-and wife team, Ruth and Augustus Goetz, to adapt it for the stage; a director like Jed Harris; and a pair of actors like Wendy Hiller and Basil Rathbone. Of course, that was in 1947, when literate stuff still sold on Broadway, though even then the producers nearly wrecked it by, at first, insisting on an unconscionable happy ending.

And now, in 1995? You needed the smarts of André Bishop and Bernard Gersten of Lincoln Center Theater to realize that a play about basic, eternal human problems—even without reference to racism or AIDS; even without nudity, male or female—could make it, as *The Heiress* must if there is anything resembling a civilized theatrical audience left in New York.

Since many of you have seen the movie, you may think you know the story; but it is far, far stronger on the stage. Austin Sloper, a wealthy Washington Square physician, cannot forgive his loving daughter, Catherine, whose birth caused the death of his beautiful wife, and who, on top of that, turned out to be "an entirely mediocre… creature without a shred of poise," as he sees it, little realizing that her shyness, if not her plainness, was caused by his frigidity. Morris Townsend, a young man of good looks, great charm, and poor prospects, arrives on the scene, and instantly he and Catherine fall in love.

It is certainly love on the love-starved girl's part, but is it on his? He is a cultivated butterfly, now living off his widowed sister, whose five needy children he never helped while spending his modest inheritance on travel and luxuries. Dr. Sloper is right to see him as a fortune hunter. But poor Catherine is equally right to want to marry such a spirited suitor. And even Morris, craving Catherine's money and house as much as he does her, is not entirely in the wrong: with him, the wallflower would bloom—if not forever, for a glorious day.

This is where the work's mastery asserts itself. None of these main characters is entirely right or wrong. Dr. Sloper is a cold and even cruel fish, but he sees much of the truth about Morris, even if he is purblind about Catherine, whose hidden toughness greatly resembles his overt strength. And though Morris is no good at earning, he may, with his talent for spending, at least be more liberating in the short range than some sedulous dullard. So Catherine is almost right to demand her happiness: better to pay the Pied Piper someday, or even now, than never to have danced to his heady music.

Thus everyone is both right and wrong, and we have a story that, though amusing in places, is ultimately as lean, stark, and fateful as Greek drama. And for this we needed a gifted director such as Gerald Gutierrez, not afraid to take chances on letting people just sit and talk, on enveloping the stage in darkness when that is called for, on letting retards into the propulsiveness where rubatos are helpful. We needed a Dr. Sloper who, like Philip Bosco, knows how to use irony as a weapon with the supreme swordsmanship that allows him to dismiss Catherine's goodness with "You're good for nothing unless you are clever." The actor has a way of being engagingly brutal, humanely forbidding: his Sloper is wise and fallible, strong and pathetic, in seamless oneness.

We needed a Catherine like Cherry Jones, whose long-shining, awesome talent should finally be obvious even to the most dense.

She can turn as translucent as John Lee Beatty's fine, diaphanous set, and so let us see into her innermost self, where conflicting impulses nag away at each other until repressed but luminous humanity bursts dazzlingly forth, only to be finally and irrevocably squelched. Miss Jones does wonders with the minutest movement, the subtlest inflection, and can act even with her cheekbones. Just her range of "yes"es is prodigious and shattering; not since Joyce's Molly Bloom has anyone got such mileage out of that humdrum monosyllable. This is a performance to feast on.

Jon Tenney dexterously maintains the ambiguities of Morris in steady motion, never letting the character shed his genuine complexity, and always keeping us guessing. Frances Sternhagen is delicious in her chaffering-starling way, and Lizbeth Mackay is deeply touching in her tormented silences. The others, too, are fine; only Michelle O'Neill is a bit too commonplace. Also contributing gallantly are Jane Greenwood's tastefully eloquent costumes and Beverly Emmons's thoughtful lighting.

How ironic that the dearly sought theatrical success that always eluded James the playwright should have come to a number of dramatic and operatic adaptations of his fiction. Anyway, *The Heiress* has a wealth of treasures to bestow; it would be foolish to abstain from one's share in them.

Arcadia

"Its ingenuity is stupendous," wrote Harold Hobson in the London *Sunday Times* about Tom Stoppard's first hit, and so is that of his latest, *Arcadia*: stupendous and sometimes, I'm afraid, stupefying. To say that Stoppard is the cleverest playwright active in English is probably a platitude. But cleverness engenders its own problems: it is almost as hard for a clever playwright to create an unclever character as it is for a plodding playwright to create a clever one.

But some characters, even in a Stoppard play, cannot be clever. The only way the author can manage this is to make them into fools or near-mutes. There is nothing in between, where most of the real world situates itself. This, to be sure, is also true of Oscar Wilde, Stoppard's inspiration; there are passages in *Arcadia* that are distant but distinct echoes of *The Importance of Being Earnest*. Wilde, however, did not cheat: he would not have an Englishman in 1809 use the Yiddishism *tush*, or have two characters—Including the 13-year-old Thomasina—Interpret Poussin's famous *Et in Arcadia ego* ("I too have lived in Arcadia") as being spoken by Death, i.e., the skull in the picture, a theory first proposed by Erwin Panofsky a century and a half later.

Arcadia takes place—first alternatingly, then simultaneously— in 1809 and today. The constant is a garden room at Sidley Park, the Derbyshire manor of Lord and Lady Croom. Their daughter, Thomasina Coverly, is being tutored by a young scientist, Septimus Hodge, a classmate of Lord Byron, who is visiting at Sidley Park. Lady Croom, whose other child is the tongue-tied Augustus, is witty and imperious, and has a yen for the handsome Hodge. Also present are Richard Noakes, the landscape architect (who is striving to convert the classically natural gardens into picturesque Gothic), and Ezra Chater, the resident poetaster (who is married to a beautiful flirt with whom Hodge, like Captain Brice, Royal Navy, her ladyship's brother, has an affair). The catch is that we are shown some of the less interesting characters (the foolish Chater, the brainless Brice) but not some of the more promising ones (Mrs. Chater, Lord Byron).

In the modern scenes, we get the three young Coverlys of today: Valentine, a mathematician in love with Hannah Jarvis, the author of a book about Lady Caroline Lamb, Byron's mistress; his younger brother, the autistic Gus, also taken with Hannah; and their sister, Chloë, a flighty young woman with a crush on Bernard Nightingale, a literary don doing research on Byron at Sidley Park. And we get Hannah herself, doing research for her next book on the life of the mysterious hermit of Sidley Park, and thus on the entire Coverly clan.

There are all kinds of parallels and divergences between the "old" story and the "new"; also some curious misreadings of the past by the present-day researchers, which contrast with the true story as we see it unfurl. The concinnity with which the two stories correspond or don't (with interesting insights into the triumphs and fiascoes of scholarship), and the way past and present—even if only figuratively—finally intermingle, are almost fiendishly crafty. But in the end, Stoppard—who never went to university and has an autodidact's infatuation with his homemade erudition—overdoes it: there are goodly chunks of the play that seem to have been written for the delectation of graduate students in literature and science, and you often wish Stoppard would rein in his parade.

Take this, for example: "English landscape was invented by gardeners imitating foreign painters who were evoking classical authors. The whole thing was brought home in the luggage from the grand tour. Here, look—Capability Brown doing Claude, who was doing Virgil. Arcadia! And here, superimposed by Richard Noakes, untamed nature in the style of Salvator Rosa. It's the gothic novel expressed in landscape." And then all those references to Francis Jeffrey and *The Edinburgh Review*, Southey's verse epics, Fermat's last theorem, iterated algorithms, etc., etc—some of which was cut from the New York production, but much of which remains *pour épater les bourgeois*. Stoppard may end up like the man, cited by the physicist, philosopher, and wit Georg Christoph Lichtenberg, who "had so much intellect [*Verstand*] that he could be put to almost no earthly use."

In the London production, the much finer English cast (having, moreover, no problems with accents) just about managed the almost impossible task of making these distilled, volatile words become flesh; under the same canny director, Trevor Nunn, the American cast finds it a lot harder to cope. Blair Brown, Robert Sean Leonard, and Peter Mahoney hold their own, and Billy Crudup, as Hodge, is a revelation—even better than his British counterpart, Rufus Sewell. But Lisa Banes, Victor Garber, and Haviland Morris attitudinize horrendously, and as the delightful Thomasina, Jennifer Dundas is a grotesque disgrace.

Mark Thompson's set and costumes, Paul Pyant's lighting, and Jeremy Sams's music continue to coruscate, and no sophisticated theatergoer will feel that he has wasted his time here; but I actually think that, at least in New York, *Arcadia* makes better reading than seeing.

Travels With My Aunt

Novels make poor plays, right? Usually, but not in the case of *Travels With My Aunt*, as adapted and directed by Giles Havergal of Glasgow's Citizens' Theatre. Graham Greene's less-than-best effort made an even weaker film, with Maggie Smith braying away in the title part as though she were really in Robert Louis Stevenson's *Travels With a Donkey*. But this stage version is something else: an exercise in high camp so inspired as to be quintessential theater. For what is high camp if not mummery carried to such giddy heights as to become, bypassing literature, the essence of playfulness, sheer riotous theatricality? I haven't laughed this sweetly since I watched Letterman make the ass he is out of himself at the Oscars—only there I laughed *at*, here I laughed *with*.

You may recall this as the story of Henry Pulling, a dried-up retired bank clerk devoted to tatting and growing dahlias, who at his mother's funeral meets his aunt Augusta (an obvious *hommage* to Oscar Wilde) and is taken under her fabulous, fluttery wing. Aunt Augusta is a glorious hybrid; black sheep, bird of paradise, and gilded butterfly, she is a mid-septuagenarian with the frivolity of a dippy debutante and the wisdom of Solomon. She believes in travel, adventure, sex, and life as a fiesta. She dallies with her gigantic black butler, Wordsworth, and eventually marries an Italian con man, Visconti, as the action shifts from Brighton to Istanbul to Paris to Paraguay. Repressed bachelor Henry progresses from shocked befuddlement through grudging admiration to enthusiastic abandon as he leaves dahlias for dalliance, emotional parchedness for Paraguayan exuberance.

But the full excitement comes from the amazing, absurd, wicked, and irresistible characters who pop up all over: efficacious spies and ineffectual policemen, too-faithful retainers and too-loving pen pals, not-so-secret agents and damsels of distressing dizziness, opportunists who can climb the greasy pole of success with one hand and busybodies with a hand or nose in everything. These and more, plus a hilarious dog that comes to an epic end, are brought to pullulating life by a quartet of dream zanies to tickle you pink and turn a couple of your hours as golden as the shower that impregnated Danaë.

What four comedians! They play many different characters, or take turns playing the same one, or can even be Henry in quadruplicate, with the tiniest, delicious variants. You are left just enough time between gales of laughter for gasps of astonishment at so much versatility. There is Jim Dale, who is mostly an exquisite Aunt Augusta, not in vulgar drag but in an impeccable gray suit (except when it turns impeccably white), with gestures and inflections suggestive but never obvious. There is Brian Murray, who is mostly Henry (but also a lot of others), and is surely one of the supreme comic actors of our day, at his finest when he is aghast, his eyes popping out of his head.

Martin Rayner, an actor new to me, works his own wonders,

whether when, small and white as he is, he turns into a giant black man, or switches from accent to accent as an aural quick-change artist, or is just a one-man barrelful of monkeys. And despite his tiny role, Tom Beckett is right up there with the rest, especially unforgettable as Wolf, a dog whose pranks and demise he—no lesser word will do—immortalizes. Add to this Havergal's magisterial direction, the ingeniously ecumenical set by Stewart Laing, extravagantly lit by Gerry Jenkinson, and you can have yourself a ball at this ballsiest, totally uneffete evening of sky-high camp. I discovered only one minute lapse: the Italian paper *La Repubblica* spelled with one *b*; otherwise, perfection from A to Z.

Indiscretions

In the preface to *Les Parents terribles*, Jean Cocteau wrote, "I wished to attempt a drama that would be a comedy whose core would be vaudeville if the action and characters were not those of drama." In the stage directions, he added, "One obligatory detail: the very realistic scenery must be constructed solidly enough to allow doors to be slammed." In Sean Mathias's disastrous staging, now entitled *Indiscretions*, the scenery is surrealistic, there is only one door slamming, and the characters are grotesquely dehumanized caricatures.

True, no masterpiece has been desecrated; though well written line by line, this 1938 play was dated at its inception—the plot too artificially excogitated, the characters too weather-vanish, the dialogue too rhetorical. Even so, Cocteau tried to write about people: disorderly ones versus orderly ones. Mathias and his adapter—Jeremy Sams, better known as a composer—have done everything in their power to turn the play into low camp, the kind of travesty that, in the heyday of gay-bashing, homosexuals in bars perpetrated to get even with the Establishment.

George, the father, is a second-rate inventor; Yvonne, the mother, is a neurasthenic who hardly leaves her bed and harbors a pathological love for her 22-year-old, presumably virginal son, Michael. The three lead messy lives in an apartment as untidy as a Gypsy caravan (*roulotte*, which Sams translates incorrectly), where only Leonie, Yvonne's unmarried sister, manages to impose some order. Leonie, who lost George to Yvonne, has been living with them these

23 years and keeping the household afloat on her modest inheritance. Still secretly in love with George, she looks after his son better than either parent does.

The initial brouhaha over a 22-year-old fellow "sleeping out" (how to translate the French *découcher*?) makes little sense today. But when it emerges that—by one of those tricks of fate more favored by playwrights than by fate—George and Michael have been carrying on unawares with the same 25-year-old woman, Madeleine, the story gets rolling with theatrical, if not quite psychological, conviction. And what does Mathias do to it?

Item: son is jumping up and down on Mother's bed as on a trampoline while Dad imitates him from the floor, as both indulge in rooster imitations as if trying out for a production of *Peter Pan*. Item: mother and son are not just snuggling up on her bed but rolling around in it like the lovers in the obligatory sex scene of today's movies. Item: dad, out of a clear blue sky, kisses son hard on the mouth, perhaps on the assumption that, in France, every kiss is a French kiss. Item: to coerce Madeleine into lying to Michael, George pins her down on the floor, then sticks his hand up her skirt and does something that instantly subdues her. Item: At the play's end, where a line states that things have returned to order, the set, contradictorily, comes apart before our eyes. Why? It's the modish thing for sets to do, cf. *An Inspector Calls*.

In the cast of five, four are—or act—the wrong age. And everyone speaks with a different accent. Yvonne, a part created on the Paris stage by the unforgettable Germaine Dermoz (and in the movie by the racy Yvonne de Bray), is mauled here by the unmentionable Kathleen Turner. If you haven't seen Miss Piggy as Miss Havisham, Shirley Temple as Tallulah Bankhead, or Goldie Hawn as the lion dancer in Kabuki, Miss Turner's Yvonne is your next-best bet. As father and son, Roger Rees and Jude Law give identically hysterical, over-the-top performances, each more delinquently juvenile than the other. Eternally teenagerish Cynthia Nixon tries valiantly to be three years older than her lover, and is particularly abused by the director when made not to walk up a gigantic spiral staircase but to climb up a jungle gym inside that staircase (this defies description!) so as to stare up Eileen Atkins's skirt.

As for Miss Atkins, one of our supreme actresses, she has been directed to play not a sensible, bittersweet old-maid aunt but the lesbian warden in a women's-prison movie, unaccountably bedizened in Chanel and Schiaparelli. Even so, some of her greatness flickers through. The sets and costumes by Stephen Brimson Lewis brim over with cutesy absurdity (why would an inventor, even if unsuccessful, dress up as a World War I fighter pilot, goggles and all?) to overshadow all the rest. We have left many a poor musical humming the scenery; this is a first for a straight (or, at any rate, straight-bashing) play.

The Mountain Giants

Although Luigi Pirandello was only 69 when he died, his last play, *The Mountain Giants*, is the work of a *vecchiardo*, an annoying old man. It remains incomplete, finished by his son Stefano from an outline Dad told him on his deathbed. There is a sense, though, that even the finished play might have felt unfinished. The aging master clearly wanted to recapitulate and epitomize all his previous writing and thinking. This was to be a poetic-philosophical summa, a tough trick to pull off, especially if you are given to long interruptions and radical revisions. "With *The Mountain Giants*," Pirandello wrote his Beatrice, Marta Abba, "I shall go down, all the way down into the very bowels of despair."

Yet what the play lacks is guts of its own. It is all wearyingly cerebral and minimally dramatic. And that the great director Giorgio Strehler has kept rethinking and restaging it—this is his third version—adds to the unspontaneity, the sense of something pondered to death. What has been called Pirandello's "most consciously dialectical play" is essentially a debate between Countess Ilse, who leads a troupe of touring players to the Villa della Scalogna (Villa Jinx), and Cotrone, a magician who presides over its hard-luck inhabitants, A debate about the relation of art to life ensues, with Cotrone improvising art out of happenstance, while Ilse wants life to conform to her high standards of art, exemplified in her production of a play by a young poet who died for love of her. There is also a tertium quid, the actor Cromo, who espouses commodity theater.

Interspersed with this are the marital difficulties of Ilse and her husband, and, finally, Ilse's defiance of her audience, the servants of the Mountain Giants, themselves too busy to attend the theater. The servants want to be entertained; when Ilse defies them, they kill her. A crude synopsis, this, but the play itself is schematic, what with puppets that behave like humans, and humans who might as well be puppets. And always the "overly abstract quality" that Eric Bentley complained about in the late Pirandello.

Strehler's staging is itself barren. A few ramps, platforms, chairs; some slides; a lot of severe underlighting. Hardly the way to animate windy philosophizings on the order of "You are everything and nothing... you are nothing and everything." Perhaps *halfway* down to the bowels of despair would have been a better vantage point. The manifestly competent actors do what they can, but only the Ilse of Andrea Jonasson (Mrs. Strehler) achieves true dramatic stature, with Franco Graziosi a nice but uncharismatic Cotrone. And when the unfinished part of the play is done as a wordless *lazzo*, a middling pantomime to mediocre music, *The Mountain Giants* (seen briefly at BAM) shrink to molehill Pygmies.

Sylvia; 2: *Göring at Nuremberg*

The difference between an artist and a hack is one of itinerary. The artist proceeds from a vision to its realization; the hack reverses the direction, going from a precalculated effect to its systematic elaboration. *This* gag or punch line is sure to make you laugh, *this* twist guaranteed to make you reach for your hankie; the trick is merely to set up the surefire joke, the surefire tearjerker. The one-gag substance of A. R. Gurney's self-styled "romantic comedy" *Sylvia* is to make an actress play a dog—do all the canine things Fido, Rover, or, in this case, Sylvia would do—but at the same time endow her with human wit, wisdom, and waywardness and allow her to communicate with her master and mistress, and vice versa.

Greg picks up the bitch Sylvia in Central Park; or, rather, Sylvia, as a tag designates her, picks him up. He takes her home and, over the desperate protests of his English-teacher wife, Kate, keeps Sylvia and lavishes increasingly demented love on her. His wife of 22 years feels cruelly neglected, his office job is ignored and lost, his less besotted friends are sent screaming out of the house, his psychotherapist is driven bonkers. The marriage is on the rocks as Greg and Sylvia conduct a love affair that, except for physical consummation, is a textbook case of pathological zoophilia, a.k.a. zooerastia.

Naïve and purblind souls will, of course, perceive Sylvia as a fantasy; but a true fantasy is poetic—think of all those charming and lyrical plays by James Barrie. Gurney remains doggedly prosaic. Dog lovers will believe *Sylvia* to represent with delicious insight the very essence of canine-human relations. But real dogs do not quote Homer and Tennessee Williams, do not sing pop songs in close harmony with their owners. The great poet Rainer Maria Rilke once aptly rebuked the young writer Friedrich Huch, who sent him his novel about children: "You have done an injustice to childhood," he wrote to him, explaining that he had turned children, illicitly and demeaningly, into miniature adults. Gurney has turned the anthropomorphic Sylvia into Greg's mistress, Kate's triumphant rival. If dogs had an official organization, they would picket the Manhattan Theatre Club.

Artists may be clever; hacks have to be. Gurney has minutely figured out his effects. Thus lovable Sylvia is also irritating enough to please the cynophobes in the audience. And the play is self-contradictory enough to make its heroine both a philosopher and a human actress who repeatedly jumps up on other actors, dryhumping them and sending the primed-for-fun audience into gales of Pavlovian laughter. If an artist such as, say, Gogol or Ionesco had written *Sylvia*, it would have ended as a comedy so black as to be indistinguishable from tragedy. Gurney has Kate preposterously accept Sylvia as man's *and* woman's best friend, and Greg, Kate, and the bitch end up blissfully wallowing in a menagerie à trois.

Sarah Jessica Parker was born as well as bred to play a dog; never before, to my knowledge, has she so perfectly embodied a part. As Greg, Charles Kimbrough is the very model of an obsessed zooerast, and the delightful Blythe Danner lavishes her talent and loveliness on making Kate almost believable. Playing a macho male dog owner, a bitchy female dog hater, and a flightily androgynous psychotherapist is the gifted Derek Smith. That all three (or is it four?) sexes should be enacted by the same actor conveys the play's mendacious subtext (or is it text?) that everyone—man, woman, or beast—is interchangeable. John Tillinger has directed with condign cynicism, and John Lee Beatty's sets and Jane Greenwood's costumes err only in being cleverer than the dialogue. *Sylvia: A Romantic Comedy*? "Oh, sure," as its heroine says in a skeptical moment, "and I am Marie of Romania."

2: Göring at Nuremberg, by Romulus Linney, is a play good enough to make you wish it were better: a little more, and it would be a major historical drama. The production it gets at Primary Stages is also less than it might be. Too bad for *2*; but, for us, still a boon in an unbounteous season.

2 is more than a docudrama (e.g., *Having Our Say*) that merely plunks a set of actual events on a stage. Although it relies on and incorporates things said and done at the Nuremberg trials in 1945–46, it is also an inventive, cannily speculative inquiry into Hermann Göring and what human nature is capable of: the weird amalgam of high intelligence and low cunning, perverted loyalty and obtuse heroism, shrewdness and crassness that can both animate and animalize a human being. The Göring whom Linney evokes for us is an extreme example of the two-faced Janus head found atop many a neck; in a milder form, we can see it in our workplaces and residences, our streets and mirrors.

Linney has imagined much of what might have happened behind the scenes of the Nuremberg Palace of Justice, but in a way that searches for truths rather than merely toys with suppositions. Here is the American commandant of the prison housing the top Nazis, a sarcastic martinet whom Göring knows how to manipulate. Here is the southern captain, a passionate hunter, with whom Göring goes on imaginary hunts, and whose racist patronization of his black sergeant he fans and exploits. Alternatively, he plays up to the sergeant, the son of a black minister who inculcated his love of Cranach's religious paintings in him. Göring has shadily acquired some Cranachs from conquered museums, and describes them glowingly to the sergeant, while also seemingly commiserating with him about the captain's contumely. He cannot make much headway with the Jewish army psychiatrist assigned to him, so he contents himself with getting his goat.

There is also the court-assigned German defender, whose attitude to Göring changes from admiration to shock as the two are compelled to watch films of the Nazi atrocities that leave his client unflinching. Finally, though, the lawyer reverts to grudging respect for Göring's intellect, however misguided. Briefly, too, we get Göring's devoted actress wife, and the young daughter who blindly loves on. But mostly there is Göring himself, the eternal Two to Hitler, but now Numero Uno, who can accept being shot but not being hanged (or "hung," as Linney unfortunately has it). Göring now feels himself to be the leader of his fellow prisoners, and fights against being sequestered from them. You need not approve of him to be impressed by his ingenuity, tenacity, and brave though misplaced loyalty to Hitler when all it can do is harm him. If only the play did not lack that touch of greatness that would lift it into literature. Perhaps it would have to show more aspects of the

protagonist than it touches upon; perhaps it requires a stronger antagonist. Perhaps some of the relationships, notably with the family,
need fuller development; perhaps the language does not quite rise
to the occasion.

Clarence Felder, under Thomas Bullard's direction, makes
Göring rather too cartoonish, and certainly less grand a presence,
mentally and corporeally, than the playwright had in mind. Yet he
has his moments when he manages to confound our feelings and
induce a moral uncertainty, something like the ironic aporia with
which Socrates leaves the Sophists at the end of a Platonic dialogue.
Matthew Lewis lacks the taut *Junker* elegance the defense counsel
ought to have; but the rest acquit themselves solidly enough. There
is food for thought here: not fast food or junk food but substantial
nourishment for the mind.

The Tempest

George C. Wolfe's production of *The Tempest* is a willful misreading
of the play that turns a supreme poetic masterpiece into a circus,
without a morsel for the mind to feed on. *The Tempest* is really
three plays in one: a metaphysical meditation on the nature of the
universe; a highly lyrical, romantic pastoral; and a masque with
music, singing, and dancing. It is only the last and least aspect that
Wolfe begins to do justice to, and even that with more brio than
taste. This elegant, tragicomic fairy tale becomes a crowd-courting
extravaganza: brash, loutish, and irredeemably vulgar.

We have here a case of multiple mistaken identities. In Wolfe's
staging, there are maybe three minutes in which one might recognize a semblance of verse. Prospero hacks the pentameter to bits,
with a pause after every two or three words; Ariel and Miranda
turn poetic sentiment into cloddish farce; others display voices and
accents inimical to Shakespeare; still others are total nonentities.
Egged on by Wolfe, they mistake the music of the spheres for the
parlance of the gutter.

Wolfe systematically mistakes the nature of the dramatis
personae because he's evidently indifferent to the meaning of the
play. Thus Prospero (Patrick Stewart), the dispossessed duke turned
benevolent magician (God, the Poet, the Playwright), becomes here
a huffing and puffing Calibanish creature out of *Star Trek*, gruff

and crass, his English accent at odds with the surrounding Babel of tongues—everything from Broadway to black and Spanish Harlem. As Miranda, the epitome of lyrical girlishness, the able Carrie Preston has been coiffed, costumed, and coerced into a quasi Ariel: a cavorting tomboy who turns her most lyrical utterances into raucous laugh lines.

Ariel himself can be Played by an ephebe or a boyish actress, but not as Tondelayo in *White Cargo*, for whom Wolfe has mistaken him. Aunjanue Ellis, black, female, and sexy, with a mediocre speaking and singing voice, moves well and has spunk but suggests only that this Prospero, a British official in Graham Greene's Africa, has got himself a native mistress to exploit. Caliban is played by the well-spoken Teagle F. Bougere, whose shaved and red-dyed head conveys the original inhabitants of Bermuda, where Wolfe has laid the action. Just because a Bermudan shipwreck provided Shakespeare with a few ideas does not prevent the play's imagery from being Mediterranean and English. But Wolfe seizes on the chance to make the masques, dances, and songs Caribbean, everything from calypso to rap, with Carlos Valdez composing a crudely obstreperous score that drowns Shakespeare's ethereal lyrics full fathoms five in impenetrable clangor. And what characters: the nobles—led by Larry Bryggman and Macintyre Dixon—could not be mistaken for Shakespearean actors; Nestor Serrano (Antonio) at least could. As the clowns Stephano and Trinculo, John Pankow and Bill Irwin manage a few droll moments. But the worst case of mistaken identity is the Ferdinand of Kamar de los Reyes, who last played a Hispanic boxer for Wolfe and whose sweet prince is—in looks, speech, and demeanor—a pugilist who kayos every syllable he mouths.

Besides the poetry, Wolfe discards the metaphysics of the play, which does not interest him. Instead, his emphasis is on stilts, puppets, endless masks, saucy costumes, colored cloths frenetically waved about, shadow play, light effects well executed by Paul Gallo, good sound effects by Dan Moses Schreier, and lots of camp, notably in the ludicrous shipwreck scene, which should have been in earnest, to set off the subsequent magic.

But magic is what Wolfe dispenses with most. *The Tempest* is about all kinds of magic: the magic of poetry, music, romance, wisdom, love, and a divinity that guides our way. Prospero should be full of spells; not, as Stewart plays him, devoid of charms in both senses of the word. Riccardo Hernandez's set is no help, either, unless you want your enchanted island to be a round sandbox in which actors kick up cloudfuls of dirt. Toni-Leslie James's costumes range from grandiose to garish; Barbara Pollitt's puppets are striking but, like the handlers running around with them, irrelevant clutter. Hope Clarke's choreography is perfunctory. This *Tempest* is not recommended to anyone, least of all to young people eager to encounter the Bard: the Wolfe is at the door and the way to Shakespeare is barred.

Betty Buckley

I have now caught my third and best Norma Desmond in *Sunset Boulevard*: Betty Buckley. Thanks to her, we finally have a show on which the sun also rises. In the original, London production, Patti LuPone's Norma was a tough gutter sparrow, a mettlesome American Edith Piaf. She sang and belted well, acted hard as nails, and was solidly of a piece. But of a small piece, because Miss LuPone is short of stature, and stature is what Norma Desmond, the fire-breathing silent movie star who fell prey to sound, has to have. If you tell me that Gloria Swanson, the movie Norma, was also short, I reply, "Remember Alan Ladd!" The movies can manufacture tallness out of anything: camera angles or orange crates. Onstage, you have to have at least one foot on the floor; in the old movies, this was required only in the bedroom scenes.

So, Miss LuPone's all-important staircase scenes—regal descents and scurrying ascents—fell flat. If you are petite, barely jutting over the balustrade, you simply can't staircase the joint. And what a joint! John Napier has designed a palazzo horrendously opulent and huge enough that it could easily have been shared by the Gaekwar of Baroda and the Grand Mogul of Lahore. It made Miss LuPone look less like the chatelaine than like the domestic help.

Along came Glenn Close, as the Los Angeles and New York Norma, tall and commanding. Close, but no cigar. Her Norma looked like a cross between a cigar-store Indian and a cathedral gargoyle, enough to scare the bejesus out of any man she'd want to drag into her lair—Joe Gillis, the down-on-his-luck screenwriter, no exception. The way Miss Close hammed and mugged would have put the old-time Hollywood vamps to shame: there is, after all, such a thing as too much vamplitude. On top of which, she couldn't really sing.

Trying to follow one of her songs was like attempting to complete a connect-the-dots drawing with several numbers missing.

Then there was the problem of the rest of the New York cast, a hand-me-down from L.A. Alan Campbell, the Gillis, was a rather too ordinary Joe. Neither as handsome nor as ambiguous as William Holden in the movie, he had something tentative, not to say chorus-boyish, about him. Still, he was an acceptable preliminary sketch, and he has improved with time. Now I can believe him and, more important, feel for him. I had more trouble With Alice Ripley, as Betty, the sweet 22-year-old fiancée of Joe's friend Artie. An aspiring screenwriter herself, she collaborates with Joe on developing one of his short stories into a screenplay; the two fall in love, with dire consequences. Miss Ripley was competent but smug; she lacked the superficial invulnerability but underlying fragility of the adorable American ingenue.

The other consequential roles were decently handled. George Hearn—as Norma's discoverer, former director, first husband, and now devoted butler—sang well and acted right but without the wonderful creepiness with which Erich von Stroheim stamped the role of Max von Mayerling. As Cecil B. DeMille, Alan Oppenheimer was probably better than DeMille himself: tough in a likable way, dishonest only to be kind. The others didn't matter, and still don't.

Oh, but the scenery! In New York as in London, I was overwhelmed by Norma's pleasure dome, and the way it moved hydraulically down and up, allowing for a horizontally bisected stage, the equivalent of a split screen. Above were the lonely, sclerotic doings in Norma's xenophobic Xanadu; below, the cheerful New Year's Eve conviviality among a bunch of Hollywood hopefuls. As a result, I underrated the no smaller virtues of the other sets. And then the breathtaking, mind-boggling, almost show-stopping costumes of Anthony Powell, worthy of that series of novels by his literary namesake. A dance to the music of time, indeed. These costumes are a ritual dance of bygone splendors, and a funeral dance for the Theda Baras and Clara Bows never to be seen again.

Less successful are the somewhat uncomfortably through-composed score by Andrew Lloyd Webber and the book and lyrics by Don Blake and Christopher Hampton, based on the Billy Wilder film. A lot of high camp here: what else to make of a steal from Oscar Wilde ("I'm sorry, I don't usually read private cigarette cases") followed closely by one from Noël Coward ("Mad about the boy")? There is some fun left in the words, as also in Trevor Nunn's sporadically inventive staging, but it is all a bit like an out-of-focus projection of the movie. The songs have that slightly overripe, vaguely cloying syncretism that Lloyd Webber specializes in, but with it an undeniable professionalism and hummability. They sound especially good when sung by someone such as Steven Stein-Grainger, George Hearn's temporary replacement, a trained operatic singer with an exceptionally fine head voice. His Max, however, lacks age, histrionic authority, and *cojones*.

But never mind: there is Betty Buckley, whose presence appears to have rewritten, recast, and redirected the entire show. Unlike previous Normas, she abounds in childlikeness, girlishness, womanliness, and age-old humanity—the whole spectrum. Whereas other Normas made me laugh and shudder, this one also made me smile and cry. Moreover, she brings attractiveness and sexiness to the role. At last, Joe Gillis has a believable and disturbing dilemma. To be this Norma's kept man could give gigoloism a good name; no wonder Joe isn't that eager to throw it over even for a young, bright, and pretty all-American girl.

Most important of all, Miss Buckley can sing. Every note is in place, and you can hear the pianissimos as clearly as the fortes. And not only is it musical singing, but it is also musical acting. She knows how to characterize with her singing voice, how to make an emotion *cantabile*. And if in her speech she sometimes affects a certain petulant baby talk, her singing is flawless. It moves you as much as her acting in what is a seamlessly compelling musical-comedy performance.

Still, the original, more straightforward London ending was better, with Miss LuPone unafraid to make craziness scary. The rewritten, prettified ending shortchanges the horror, try as Miss Buckley does to make it ring true. But her basic genuineness heightens everyone else's acting while giving us a Norma who will remain the norm. With the radiant Buckley in residence, 10086 Sunset Boulevard has become as important a number in musical annals as 1066 in English history—that of the Norma(n) Conquest.

The Food Chain

Kenneth Tynan famously observed that the two kinds of humor dominant in the New York theater are the Jewish and the homo-

sexual. He did not, however, elaborate on their essences and differences. Examined more closely, Jewish humor usually revolves
around family plotting, infighting, colorful figures from the world
of business or show business indulging in chicanery, or romances
between persons of different social backgrounds. Homosexual
humor tends to involve groups of unrelated (except sexually) individuals practicing clever put-downs on one another; absurdist
farce with strong sexual situations (hetero- or homosexual, or the
latter disguised as the former); and, lately, attempts to laugh its way
through the AIDS crisis. You might say Jewish comedy is basically
kvetching; homosexual humor, fundamentally insult comedy. Each
can be hilarious.

But these contours have become blurred with the prevalence
of playwrights who are both Jewish and homosexual, so that the
respective motifs have become entwined—indeed, Siamesely
twinned. How this will ultimately affect the theater remains to be
seen. My guess: not much; there'll still be one successful comedy in
20 or 30 tries. But it may lessen the variety of available humor. Or
it may create strange dichotomies within individual playwrights as
disparate traditions end up sharing the same dramatic bed.

A case in point is Nicky Silver's *The Food Chain*, which is evenly
divided between the comedy of dysfunctional families and the comedy of lovers who have become strangers tormenting each other. In
fact, the three-scene layout here is paradigmatic. Scene I, "Amanda,"
features the heroine, whose husband has disappeared a few days
into their marriage, frantically seeking help from Bea, a Jewish cri-
sis-center switchboard operator who finds her own problems far
more fascinating. The resemblance to Nichols and May dialogues
further underlines the Jewishness of this comedy. Scene II, "Otto,"
takes us to the pad of Serge, a runway model awaiting his latest
lover while being besieged by a cast-off one—the wheedling and
haranguing Otto, an obese ex-salesman simultaneously pleading
and plying himself with junk food. The dialogue here characteristically evokes Albee and Terrence McNally. Scene III, "Fatty and
Skinny Lay in Bed," brings both plot strands and types of humor
explosively together.

Silver is a funny writer who, even in this less-than-best effort,
prodigally fires off prize one-liners. But a play can no more subsist
on these alone than a human being on nothing but dessert. The
jokes stampeding the play cause its collapse. The skin of verbiage
needs the skeleton of story and the flesh of character to hold it up.

Robert Falls's frenetic direction may be appropriate, but seems at times as overwrought as the compulsory car chase in current movies. Hope Davis is pungently goofy as Amanda, Tom McGowan's fatso is a bit thin on charm, and Rudolf Martin could make the mute husband a mite more eloquent. But Patrick Fabian convinces as the model, and Phyllis Newman brings needed understatement to the uncompassionate Bea. Thomas Lynch's sets are witty; William Ivey Long's costumes, apt; Kenneth Posner's lighting, stylish. But the author should remember that all that is Silver is not all gold. Under his glitter, as of now, there is only more glitter.

Funnyhouse of a Negro; A Movie Star Has to Star in Black and White

What does the playwright Adrienne Kennedy have going for her? First, she is black. Second, she is a woman. Third, she writes symbolism, lousy symbolism, but anti-realistic, which, to impressionable and politically correct souls, spells Magic Time. Boldness, originality, poetry—all this from a black woman from Cleveland. Oh, the wonder of it! In an interview, Miss Kennedy remarked, "The white male writer… stand[s an] 80 percent greater chance of getting his writing career to pay off." I don't think Miss Kennedy was ever more mistaken—except when she sits down to write one of her plays. Signature Theater Company, temporarily housed at the Public, is devoting its entire season to Miss Kennedy's work, starting with the double bill of *Funnyhouse of a Negro* (1964) and *A Movie Star Has to Star in Black and White* (1976), the very titles exuding the pretentiousness that is the author's hallmark.

Not much goes on in *Funnyhouse*, or indeed in any of Kennedy's plays. The author, who here goes by Negro-Sarah, is a young black would-be playwright who—unhappy with her lot—projects herself onto other characters: Queen Victoria Regina (a bit redundant, that), a Duchess of Hapsburg (spelled "Dutchess" in the program), Patrice Lumumba (spelled "Lamumba"), and Jesus. Each of these is styled "one of herselves," and each is a crashing bore. Other characters are the mother, who runs around barefoot in a shift cursing her husband;

the Landlady-Funnyhouse Lady, Sarah's white landlady; and Raymond Funnyhouse Man, her white Jewish lover. The play blathers on as Sarah, "a child of torment," feels "trapped in blackness."

Rather incoherently, Miss K. explains, "When I made the breakthrough where the character could have other personas, the images seemed more indigenous." Indigenous to what? Anyway, the drama here consists of recurrent violent knocks on a door, presumably from the evil father, though it is a suited Lumumba and a T-shirted Jesus who emerge, to little or no effect. And the knocking continues. Bits of monologue spoken by one character are repeated by others, over and over in a verbal circle jerk. All of them laugh a lot, though they (or the author) will not let us in on the joke, if there is one.

Of prime interest here is a headless gypsum statue of Queen Victoria with books piled on its plinth, a perfect symbol of the author. Second most interesting is the complaint of several characters that their hair is falling out in clumps. And third is Sarah's revelation that her father "hung" himself. If Miss Kennedy can't make sense, couldn't she at least manage grammar?

The second play, *A Movie Star*, is introduced by the Columbia Pictures Lady, holding her torch aloft and spouting, like everyone in the play, a lot of dates that are doubtless deeply significant to the author but meaningless to us. The first scene unfolds simultaneously in a hospital lobby and in the famous cigarette sequence from *Now, Voyager*; the second, in the room of Clara's comatose brother and the bedroom scene from *Viva Zapata!*; the third, in the old room of Clara, the heroine, and the rowboat scene from *A Place in the Sun*. The men (Paul Henreid, Marlon Brando, Monty Clift) speak no more than the comatose brother; the women (Bette Davis, Jean Peters, Shelley Winters) bubble over with authorial gush and guff. What these parallel movie scenes have to do with Clara's failed marriage to Eddie is anybody's guess.

The writing is desperately poetic—e.g., "I call God, and the owl answers. It haunts my tower, calling." (Another Kennedy play is *The Owl Answers*; a great recycler, our Miss K.) The brother dies discreetly, without disrupting the flow of Sis's verbiage. It all might have been more fun had Miss K. chosen other movies—to project herself onto, say *Ben-Hur*, *Metropolis*, and *Duck Soup*. And you can always spot pretentiousness by a mood-setting cello; but a cello throughout is pretentiousness cubed.

Victor/Victoria; Hello, Dolly

One way or another, *Victor/Victoria* will make history. Like a karaoke record, it's got everything minus one: a true star, a solid cast and ensemble, savvy staging and choreography, lush scenery and costumes and lighting, a funny (or at least doggedly farcical) book—everything but one really good song. This will be the test: can a Broadway musical make it without a score?

Wearing my other hat as film critic, I was unimpressed by the 1982 movie *Victor/Victoria*, which was based on an old German film. Aside from other problems, there was too much special pleading. The message? "Scratch a macho man, and he is either gay or susceptible to acting or seeming gay. Let's cheer whenever a he-man kisses another guy." Such sentiments are by no means unconscionable, but let's not be bowled over: propaganda is the end of art. Not that there is much art in *Victor/Victoria* to begin with.

Blake Edwards's musical book is no worse or better than the original screenplay, which he also directed, and here, once again, is Julie Andrews to hoist it over many a hurdle. After a 30-year absence, she is as here as if she'd never left. True, there are a few times when she is on automatic pilot: for the rest, it is stunt flying of a high order. T. H. White, upon meeting the future Mrs. Edwards in 1960, wrote to David Garnett about "flirting with Julie—who is a *honey*." And so she still is—without, perhaps, the italics: a look, voice, and personality that live in perfect harmony with one another, whether she is singing, dancing, acting, or just being.

Tony Roberts, as Toddy, has the thankless task of following in Robert Preston's ineffaceable footsteps but manages to be entirely engaging. The delicious Rachel York is overdirected into an excess of slapstick vulgarity but salvages as much as is humanly possible; Michael Nouri provides handsome and amiable, though rather bland, romantic interest; the others fall neatly into place. And what a place! A Paris designed by Robin Wagner to be as piquant, seductive, and opulent as the real thing, and twice as resourceful. Not to be outdone, Willa Kim's costumes start high and keep surpassing themselves. The Jules Fisher-Peggy Eisenhauer lighting, which uses neon as a *ne plus ultra*, works white, black, and polychrome magic. Rob Marshall's choreography gambols freshly and friskily, and Edwards pulls directorial aces from both his sleeves.

But there is—or rather, isn't—the unrelievedly second-rate music of the late Henry Mancini, augmented by three songs from Frank Wildhorn, which blend in seamlessly, alas. All the lyrics are by the once capable Leslie Bricusse, now given to such stuff as "Paris is so sexy / Riding in a taxi [texi?] / Gives you apoplexy." And though Billy Byers's orchestrations and David Krane's dance arrangements perform heroically, even "Le Jazz Hot," the nearest thing to a hit, is at most a near miss. Still, *Victor/Victoria* may be the best unmusical musical you are ever going to see. Question is, is that enough?

When *Hello, Dolly* was first done in 1964, it starred Carol Channing sounding like a Carol Channing with a frog in her throat. Now, 31 years later, it stars a Carol Channing sounding like a frog with Carol Channing in its throat. Either way, it's a phenomenon. Or better than that: a monument, a landmark, an institution. You do not criticize the Astrodome, you don't argue with the Eiffel Tower, you don't question the Carnaval in Rio. Miss Channing is as *there* as Mount Everest; it is hard to say whether she is most famous for Dolly Levi and Lorelei Lee or whether they are most famous for her. I first saw her in her debut show, *Lend an Ear*, in 1948, and, while lending an ear, happily gave her my heart.

At 74, Miss Channing has slowed down a tad, but everything else is the same, and what is more inspiring than a triumph over time? Her widow Dolly Gallagher Levi—a matchmaker who resolves to marry herself off to the miserly millionaire merchant Horace Vandergelder, come hell or high dudgeon—is one of those creations that transcend the part, the show, and the roof of the theater where they're playing. Miss C. scoops up the audience in her arms like a rag doll, and transports it to a hearth of well-being whose fires are never banked. Just the way she coos (croaks?) "Horace Vandergelder" could melt an icecap or two. Johann Nestroy's 1842 Viennese comedy lost a good deal turning into Thornton Wilder's *The Matchmaker*, and still more becoming Michael Stewart's book for *Hello, Dolly!* But it gained Carol Channing—a fair exchange.

The present revival wisely strives to replicate the original production. Gower Champion's debonair dances and Oliver Smith's airy scenery seem pretty much intact, and the current costumes (Jonathan Bixby) and lighting (Ken Billington) do not stray far from the originals: the director, Lee Roy Reams, has seen to that. The supporting cast is not all that it might be, though Florence Lacey is a cherishable Mrs. Molloy, and Michael DeVries sings impressively as Cornelius Hackl. But no matter: Jerry Herman's better songs remain easy winners, though I wish there were a couple more of them; the rest is Miss Charming. It suffices.

Master Class

Maria Callas, or at least callasomania, elicited the best work from Terrence McNally in the first act of *The Lisbon Traviata*. He returns to the charge with *Master Class*, wherein the Greek-American soprano is the actual heroine. Having lost her voice rather soon in her career, Callas, among other things, gave master classes at Juilliard in the early seventies, classes that are the subject of an entire book by John Ardoin, and were (it seems) attended by McNally. Callas was a figure almost as tragic as the ones she portrayed, with a voice that had its imperfections and an acting ability unmatched in the Italian repertory. Beyond that, Callas was the diva with whom homosexuals (a huge percentage of operagoers) empathized to an unparalleled degree, perhaps because, as Wayne Koestenbaum put it in *The Queen's Throat*, "she was a mess *and* she was a goddess... Her operatic performances seemed real; her real life seemed operatic."

McNally imagines a series of coaching sessions with, respectively, a sweetly naïve and klutzy soprano, Sophie; a callowly complacent tenor Tony: and an overzealous, aggressive soprano, Sharon. In between, there are reflections on art and artists by Maria, and her Olympian banter with Manny, the pianist; with a sullen stagehand; and with the master-class audience, namely us. So far, so good. But McNally in his cleverness or ambition may go too far: he must bring in Maria's troubled emotional life with her solicitous husband, G. B. Meneghini, and her domineering lover, Aristotle Onassis. So he has two flashbacks in which the set, a rehearsal studio, becomes through projections the auditorium and, later, the stage at La Scala, and Callas, in monodrama, acts out scenes from her past, assuming also the voices of the main men in her life. It is a daring conceit, but I find it an unfair oversimplification and put-down of the men, as well as a facile plea for sympathy for Maria. It also feels inappropriate to hear her describe herself as a *monstre sacré*. She was one, but it is not for her to say it.

To have taken an essentially nondramatic situation and given it such body and heft is nevertheless an achievement—a more than usually forceful tour de force. Much, to be sure, depends on the leading actress. The only person who could have really played Callas is Maria Callas; had she lived longer, or had the play been written earlier, I have no doubt she would have. As it is, Zoe Caldwell does a wonderful second-best job. She does not quite look or sound (in speaking—she, rightly, doesn't even try to sing) like Callas, but that is unimportant. She has technique, artistry, boldness, and éclat to spare; what she doesn't quite have is sensual appeal. Callas, though no beauty, had (once she shed her enormous excess weight) a strongly physical—and physically unfulfilled—presence, adding to both her appeal and her pathos. Everything else, though, Miss Caldwell has, and she manages even the ventriloquizing monologues prodigiously.

There is also a superb supporting cast. Karen Kay Cody is heartbreakingly funny as the simpleton Sophie; Jay Hunter Morris is so good as Tony that he emerges as a perfect parody of the likes of Gary Lakes; and Audra McDonald has all the vulnerability, attitude, determination, and insecurity Sharon calls for. As Manny, David Loud is as consummate a straight man as he is an accompanist; and Michael Friel moves scenery with the stolidity of an inveterate stagehand. Décor by Michael McGarty, costumes by Jane Greenwood, and lighting by Brian MacDevitt are all impeccable.

Master Class, adroitly directed by Leonard Foglia, is funny, touching, and accomplished. At one point, our heroine exclaims, "An aria without a cabaletta is like sex without the orgasm." McNally's play is a bit like that, too. But on a Broadway starved for nonmusical theater of merit, it is a very big step in the right direction.

Racing Demon

Lincoln Center Theater finally has a winner in *Racing Demon*. If the late, unlamented *Sacrilege* showed us how not to write a controversial play about church and religion, David Hare's Shavian spellbinder is an exemplary how-to. For this internecine combat of contrasting Christianities in the arena of the Church of England is as riveting as a boxing match and as intellectually stimulating as an Oxford Union debate. Also theater so damned good that Hare in the hereafter will be consigned to hell, where—as we hear—conversation is infinitely livelier than in the other place. There are four artfully interwoven problems: What to do about a clergyman whose socialist leanings and religious doubts make him a potential liability? What to do about another ecclesiastic, whom a yellow journalist exposes as a homosexual? What to do about a marriage wherein the pastoral displaces the connubial? And above all, how to handle a driven, lower-class curate whose demonic zeal proves as ruinous to the public-school coziness of his fellow churchmen as to the love a spirited and sensible young woman bears him? The play has humor, suspense, exuberance, and pathos; though placed in an Anglican framework, it is more pope's nose than curate's egg.

When you glimpse the Spartanly pared-down but enormously suggestive scenery by Bob Crowley, the poetic projections by Wendall K. Harrington, the incisive lighting by Mark Henderson, and breathtaking direction by Richard Eyre, you worry about a sprawling cast's and potentially parochial text's ability to keep up. Rest assured: all fears are promptly allayed.

What is exhilarating about the writing is that every character in this vast array is a human being, foolish and fallible, but believable and pardonable. Side with whomever you choose; all but the journalist have a portion of justice and heaps of humanity going for them. In their clashes, theater catches life on the wing, whether soaring or broken. Miss it at a peril to your entertainment as a theatergoer, your education as an existential learner, your soul as a sentient and rational being.

I am at a loss, though, about how to describe this large, flawless cast. I've no space to analyze each individual excellence, and a mere litany of names wearies the reader. Let me say that when often irritating actors such as Josef Sommer and Michael Cumpsty, and ever delightful ones such as Brian Murray and George N. Martin, merge in magnificence, something has happened that, from Broadway to Canterbury, can pass for a miracle.

King Lear

Forced to name the world's greatest play, I suppose I'd pick *King Lear*. Forced to name the actor I'd least want to see starred, I'd choose, ahead even of Macaulay Culkin and Matthew Broderick, F. Murray Abraham. But until the Public's current production, I would not have thought a director could reduce this towering masterpiece to the mess Adrian Hall has perpetrated. We are told here that the most shattering tragedy is, in fact, a farce. Clearly, Hall took the line about "this great stage of fools" literally.

One can see playing the opening scene in a light vein, but with Cordelia's repudiation, the proceedings should darken. This is impossible if Lear is played as a cross between a clownish snake-oil salesman and a churlish shyster by an actor who seems at most 50 and is in great physical shape. Abraham (accent on the last syllable), with beady eyes shiftily straddling a bulbous nose, speaks with an accent redolent of the fish market, in a voice that shuttles between the contemptuously patronizing and the querulously whiny. This is not even a comic king; it is someone you wouldn't buy a used heroic couplet from. And I haven't even mentioned his oozy self-adulation.

This Lear is father to three plainly unrelated daughters. Goneril (Margaret Gibson) has a spurious British accent and does the young Maggie Thatcher; Regan (Elizabeth Marvel) is a ditsy, affected New York debutante; Cordelia (Brienin Bryant), self-righteous and lachrymose, speaks something like black English under a finishing-school veneer. We also get an effetely English, patently unsavory Edmund (Jared Harris); a provincial-rep Gloucester (Thomas Hill); a bespectacled, book-toting, grad-studentish Albany (Arnold Schultz); a Cornwall (Ezra Knight) who, except for his dreadlocks, is a dead ringer in looks and manner for the pretrial O. J. Simpson; and a slopy-browed, receding-chinned, snarly Kent (John Woodson)—the one righteous man done as an Ozark ogre.

As a sometimes frontally nude Edgar, Rob Campbell, an engaging actor, tries hard, but is dragged down by the company he must keep. As the Fool, Jeffrey Wright (late the sassy black hospital orderly of *Angels in America*) wears one orthopedic boot and twists himself—when he can remember—into a stunted shape. He delivers his lines with a street-English intonation and an astounding humorlessness, managing to be at once flippant and leaden. Oswald is turned by Francis Jue into an Asian hustler.

Dare one blame Eugene Lee for his low-budget set? A metallic staircase zigzags up from near stage center, a sterile platform leads off to our right, a sawed-off center-stage barrel is covered with a tablelike plank, a column with a kind of steel railing allows Lear to practice his kicking on it, paint is peeling from the walls, there is a rough-hewn throne and a portable chair. Oddest is a small fenced-in enclosure, suitable for keeping one or two geese, with casters to wheel Lear out on.

Catherine Zuber's costumes are from a medieval Gap and suffer from severe depression: they have frayed edges even when they are supposedly brand-new. Some of Lear's men wear ski masks or stockings over their heads, though no bank to rob is in sight. Natasha Katz's lighting is exhibitionistic, as when torches are brought on in broad daylight: natural-looking light turns *Caligari*-ish in midscene: and (this, of course, is also Hall's doing) every scene change is accompanied by thunder and lightning, making the necessary storm on the heath a wan anticlimax.

The hovel on the heath is a shallow, rectangular trap, in which the characters, squatting, seem to enjoy a communal bowel movement. The same trap later becomes the cell to which the captured Lear and Cordelia are escorted. She steps into it, but, apparently finding it unsuitable, steps out again, whereupon the captives are led offstage to other, presumably more than three-foot-deep quarters. Audience laughter seldom ceases, becoming loudest when Abraham tosses off some of his great speeches as if they were throwaway remarks. The time is neither quite now nor quite the past—possibly never.

As if to compensate for so much nothing, Hall throws in the odd, completely irrelevant *coup de théâtre*. When the Fool should have long since vanished, he suddenly reappears with a gaping wound in his middle, to be hoisted sky-high, dangled for a bit head down, then incongruously lowered and forgotten about. Another time, Hall has the cast give Oswald a thorough dunking in that sawed-off water barrel, whose presence until then was the play's most patent mystery. This production, by the way, is a feast for foot fetishists. At any time, one or another cast member may remove a piece of footwear or two for no apparent reason. Thus Goneril will appear fully dressed while her husband, in a nightgown, is barefoot. Next, Regan (who is a lot crazier than her father) is barefoot while her husband is fully shod. She then remains shoeless even on the battlefield, whereas Goneril is bereft of footgear only when, as a cadaver, she is carted about the stage hither and yon.

There are many other hilarious surprises. When Gloucester is blinded, he is promptly provided with a leather cap from which hangs a decorous veil hiding his bleeding sockets; though elsewhere the blood flows freely, the veil remains as pristine as a bride's. Two musicians wander in and out of the action playing Richard Cumming's nondescript music on various, somewhat bizarre instruments (waterphone, conch). The program reveals that F. Murray Abraham is "the voice of Merrill Lynch." In fraternal reciprocity, Merrill Lynch must be the voice of King Lear.

Rent

In September 1914, Puccini got wind of an abridged version of *La Bohème* to be mounted in Lucca, and promptly wrote his publisher, "I beg you not to give them the opera. You will do me a real favor." How would he have felt about a version called *Rent*, which updates the Giacosa-Illica libretto, transplants the action to the East Village, and keeps only a few bars of his music, strummed on a guitar—just enough to put the rest of the score to shame? Well, with the copyright lapsed, it would not matter what he felt.

Jonathan Larson, who wrote both words and music, died at 35 of an aortic aneurysm upon returning from the final dress rehearsal a month ago. This is doubly sad when you consider that the gifted young man was groping his way to a unified personal style that this uneven, scattershot show does not yet achieve. For although *Rent* profits from the *Bohème* infrastructure, it is also hampered by it, as the author is obliged to think up clever parallels or disheveled variations that invite unfavorable comparison with the original. Still, even this partial success holds a genuine promise cut off from fulfillment.

The poet Rodolfo becomes Roger, the punk rocker; the painter Marcello, Mark Cohen, a filmmaker brandishing his camcorder. The philosopher Colline is now Tom Collins, a black mechanic of some sort; the musician Schaunard is Angel Schunard, a Hispanic transvestite and street drummer who succors the mugged Collins and becomes his lover. Mimi is still Mimi but is now a performer in an S&M nightclub, and a junkie afflicted with AIDS. Roger, Collins, and Schunard are all HIV-positive. Benny (i.e., Benoit), the landlord, is a homeboy gone yuppie, full of bohemian-unfriendly schemes, and a rival for Mimi's favors. Maureen (Musetta), a performance artist, has left Mark for a black lesbian lawyer, Joanne.

There are all sorts of approximations of the opera but also a few radical departures. Thus it is Angel who dies of AIDS, whereas Mimi merely seems to die. Her fever breaks, and she revives to join the rest of the cast in the finale, "There is no future, there is no past. / I live each moment as my last." This copout makes a mockery not only of logic but also of death and Jonathan Larson's own tragedy. It is, however, not the only thing that doesn't make sense in *Rent*. Let us, however, judge the show on its own terms. The music is both eclectic and erratic as it tries to embrace every form of pop. It is most successful in some ensemble numbers and in tributes to (or takeoffs on?) show tunes, such as "Tango: Maureen" and "Santa Fe," a fantasy about starting a restaurant in that city. Also in Maureen's performance-art number, "Over the Moon," which Idina Menzel performs with infectious comic brio. Other fine performers include Wilson Jermaine Heredia (Angel), Taye Diggs (Benny), and Jesse L. Martin (Collins), with the rest of the cast of fifteen mostly pleasant or better. Only Anthony Rapp, as a smarmy Mark, and Daphne Rubin-Vega, as an inconsequential Mimi, disappoint.

Michael Greif's staging, despite inventive moments, does not quite keep the action that sprawls over a large and inflexible stage in proper control, and Marlies Yearby's rudimentary choreography is no help at all. There are savvy and sassy costumes (by Angela Wendt) and scenery (by Paul Clay) to which Blake Burba's lighting does not do full justice. The five-piece band led by Tim Weil is in fine fettle. *Rent*, which opened just as *La Bohème* celebrated its centenary, will probably prove less perdurable but is not without its quirkily perky charm.

Floyd Collins

You would think that the story of Floyd Collins, a spelunker trapped deep underground, and the efforts to rescue him would work fine in the movies—as was demonstrated by Billy Wilder's powerful *Ace in the Hole*. But surely not as a stage musical! *Floyd Collins*, with music and lyrics by Adam Guettel, and book, additional lyrics, and direction by Tina Landau, shows otherwise. This is *the* original and daring musical of our day, concerned with saying something in words and music, not merely bringing in da noise or paying the rent.

Following with reasonable but unslavish fidelity the events in Barren County from January 30 to February 16, 1925—the subterranean engulfment of Floyd Collins, eager to discover a lucrative tourist attraction near his old Kentucky farm, and the ensuing rescue operations that turned into a media circus—the musical finds a smashing meeting place for suspense, comedy, and social criticism. Also for fact and fantasy, wry humor, and stoic endurance. "Something for everybody" can easily denote a cynical commercial potboiler; in the case of *Floyd Collins*, it designates a truly national work and a rare case of high art, generally elitist by nature, proving itself genuinely democratic.

Take, first, the music. Adam Guettel is the grandson of Richard and son of Mary Rodgers, a third-generation musical-comedy man. But don't look for echoes of *Oklahoma!* or *Once Upon a Mattress* here. Better yet, don't look for similarities to Sondheim, Lloyd Webber, or Boublil and Schönberg—the tripartite division of contemporary musical theater, as painful as the partition of Poland. Here, starting appropriately with bluegrass, adding Tin Pan Alley when the rescue operation becomes a sideshow, and pushing through to the use of music as authentic mood-painting as in modern opera, we have something that will not be easily and confiningly pinned down, yet cannot be dismissed as magpie eclecticism. It is not always tuneful in, say, the Kern or Puccini mode, as today's opera can no longer be, either; but it finds a personal amalgam of melody, rhythm, and arrangement that transcends expectation and subserves the action.

The lyrics, likewise, are neither dazzlingly clever à la Sondheim, nor sweetly predictable à la so many other Americans, nor yet defiantly prosaic à la sundry Brits. They display a happy openness to all sorts of possibilities, with an emphasis on the functional: how best to tell the story, how best to develop character, how best to get a point across. If the songs resemble anything, it is Louis Kahn or Alvar Aalto. Schelling called architecture frozen music; here we have music as melting architecture: not gaudy, but perhaps a touch Gaudí.

The book, too, is remarkable. It manages to convey both underground horror and the frenzy above; both the agonizing crawl of time below and the deadly urgency above ground. Using a cast of thirteen (and some doubling) and the standard length for a two-act musical, Tina Landau has given us a portrait of America where disaster becomes a spectator sport and drama can as easily hurtle into tragedy as slide into farce. And by being her own director, she was able to write as much with the staging in mind as to direct with the script at heart. Here everyone is a winner.

Well, perhaps not the character of Nellie Collins, Floyd's teched sister. Whether it is the role or its interpreter, Theresa McCarthy, something about Nellie is hard to take: she is less the elemental voice of feeling, as she may have been intended, than a somewhat cloddish clown. But everyone else hits the bull's-eye: Christopher

Innvar as the unidealized, nakedly human Floyd, Don Chastain as his profoundly ambiguous father, Cass Morgan as his staid but solicitous stepmother, Jason Danieley as his stalwart yet eventually discouraged brother, Martin Moran as the initially exploitative but subsequently engaged reporter, Michael Mulheren as the bullying entrepreneur in charge of digging the shaft, and all the exemplary others.

Add to this a set by James Schuette that is both ingenious and simple, costumes by Melina Root that command respect without attracting undue attention, and lighting by Scott Zielinski that conjures up darkness as compellingly as daylight. Dan Moses Schreier's sound and Bruce Coughlin's orchestrations, along with Ted Sperling's sensitive conducting of the versatile eight-piece band, make further first-rate contributions. Unlike several other overtouted and underachieving current musicals, *Floyd Collins* reestablishes America's sovereignty in a genre it created, but has since lost hold of: it is the modern musical's true and exhilarating ace in the hole.

A Midsummer Night's Dream

Will the enchanted forest, so crucial a character in *A Midsummer Night's Dream*, ever be recalled from banishment? Since Peter Brook in his famous (or notorious) production turned both Athens and its surrounding woods into an all-white gymnasium, deforestation—indeed, defoliation—has been the thing, as if based on some newly discovered Shakespeare defolio. Adrian Noble, in his Royal Shakespeare Company production, designed by Anthony Ward and now visiting here, has incarnadined Brook's gym, making the white one red. Otherwise, it's all almost identical, except for there being no trapeze but, as in a bedroom farce, more doors. These, by the way, can sink into or rise from the floor, with Oberon and Puck perched on them—possibly the most interesting feature of a generally earthbound production.

Well, no; there is also the giant red umbrella that descends to provide inside it a round scarlet bed, which then mounts with Titania and Bottom, and leaves them there, presumably enjoying a flying fornication. Later on, each of the four Athenian lovers gets his or her individual laundry bag for a bit of like levitation. Moreover, much of the scenery consists of giant lightbulbs hanging, like pears without their tree, all over the air. If only it were that easy to suspend our disbelief as well.

Take the business of having some of the mechanicals (artisans)—in outrageous wigs and noses, but otherwise in the same clown garb—double as Titania's fairies: economical, but perhaps a bit too vulgarly deconstructivist. Among the many candidates for the authorship of Shakespeare's plays, the Ringling Brothers seem least convincing. Yet the circusy scenes with the mechanicals are often genuinely comic here, but, at times, a bit forced, attenuated, flat. Also crude.

The crudeness, however, is not limited to these hapless thespians. How do you feel about an Oberon who debags Puck to reveal his comic underwear? The very same Puck who, earlier, kissed him passionately on the mouth? And what about a Philostrate played as a mincing queen? Why provoke those nasty double entendres on fairy tales?

Other things are no less odd. It has become not infrequent to have the actors playing Theseus and Hippolyta double as Oberon and Titania. But then, to make a point, shouldn't the actors change a little more than part of their costume? I can see the human and fairy rulers being made alike or different, but why something in between and not quite either? Well, perhaps Hippolyta wouldn't, like bare-legged Titania supine before the standing Bottom, play footsie with his genitalia. But then again, sweet Hermia kicks Demetrius smack in the balls.

The Athenian lovers come off worst. All four of them are unsightly, Hermia and Lysander particularly so: and only Emily Raymond, as Helena (an actorproof part), is at all amusing. Flute (Mark Letheren), in drag, may be the prettiest mortal maiden around. The lovers are played as charmlessly as can be, with lower-class accents and mannerisms. Much of their acting is slithering around on their knees, although backs and behinds, too, often double as feet. And the cutesiness! When Demetrius defiantly declares to Lysander. "I'll go with thee cheek by jowl," the two fellows exit like professional tango dancers, cheeks glued together. And much of the lovers' comedy depends on those many doors—former trees, no doubt, for which one can't see the forest.

There remains some pleasure in hearing Shakespeare out of British mouths, even if only the imposing Alex Jennings (Theseus/Oberon) speaks his lines poetically. The gifted and comely Lindsay

Duncan has been directed to portray a snooty, self-absorbed Hippolyta, and a less-than-delightful Titania, which is a titanic disaster. Barry Lynch, a solid Irish actor, is a big lummox of a Puck, then doubles as the effete Philostrate, well enough if you want that sort of thing. The mechanicals—led by the giant economy-size Bottom of Desmond Barrit, and including John Kane (Peter Brook's Puck) as Quince, are funny, but it is a sobering fact that the Starveling of Robert Gillespie, when playing the wordless Moonshine, gets the biggest laughs of all.

Probably the worst thing about this production is Anthony Ward's costuming, especially the hideous shoes (slippers?) worn by the lovers. Probably the nicest, besides Alex Jennings, is the music of Ilona Sekacz, except when she lifts a passage (unintentionally, I think) from one of today's most popular musicals.

The King and I

The original 1951 production of *The King and I* was a wonderful thing, but the current revival, based on an Australian production, is in many ways as good, in some ways less impressive, and in one way even better. In any case, it is a judicious blend of the original and some rethinking: part revival, part new birth. If you were reborn, wouldn't you want to emerge a bit different?

Gertrude Lawrence was elegant, charming, and beautifully poised as the widowed schoolteacher Anna Leonowens. Donna Murphy is, on top of all that, deeply moving. Of course, the story itself is inherently touching, as it follows the deepening relationship between Anna and the ornery but very human king to its heart-wrenchingly bittersweet conclusion. Miss Murphy, however, is poignant in her own right, with her memories of a happy marriage cut short by death, her problems with asserting female dignity in a fiercely patriarchal society, her need to be recognized as a gentlewoman and not just an underpaid servant.

Miss Murphy manages to be convincingly British, sings consummately, and never stops acting. By acting, I mean entering into a character's body and soul, becoming that individual inside and out, and reinventing her story by engaging it, incident by incident, entirely afresh. Hers is a performance, above all, of the sort of warmth sorely needed this snowy April.

He that plays the king stands in the long shadow of Yul Brynner, but Lou Diamond Phillips succeeds in playing him otherwise—a noteworthy achievement. His is a more boyish king, more impetuous than deliberate, whose efforts to understand and improve himself are wrung from an even bumpier conflict. This is a winning performance, forcefully sung and bouncily affecting, properly mellow in the end.

Among the hearty supporting performances, note especially those of Randall Duk Kim, as the prime minister; Tae-won Kim, as the head wife; and Guy Paul, as the British envoy. Little Kelly Jordan Bit, as the fan-dancing princess, is enchanting. The somewhat weaker links in the cast are the doomed lovers, played by Jose Llana and Joohee Choi, but it must be said that the staging has not been of help to them.

Most of Jerome Robbins's stunning dances have been retained, with some not entirely felicitous changes, and there is evocative additional choreography by Lar Lubovitch. The direction, by Christopher Renshaw, is generally effective; I don't know whether it is he or Lubovitch who introduced some darling touches into the March of the Siamese Children, or who it was that somewhat diminished the "Getting to Know You" number. But what with splendid dancers in the Uncle Thomas ballet and elsewhere, and some irresistible kiddies of whom even the tiniest lustily sings, the show seldom flags.

Nothing but admiration is due the Australian design team. Brian Thomson's scenery is sumptuous without excess, and shifts with exemplary fluidity. The night sky alone, so often a star-studded cliché, is novel and magical here. Roger Kirk's costumes are at once airy and substantial, ornate yet never overdone. Nigel Levings's fighting is a living, swirling organism. And the additional orchestrations by Bruce Coughlin (late of the fine *Floyd Collins*) savvily supplement the original ones.

But let us pay final tribute to Rodgers and Hammerstein, whose memorable book and score have become even lovelier and more lucent with the passage of 45 years. I never thought I would say this about a musical, but in a production such as this, *The King and I* is the equal of all but the supreme operatic masterpieces.

A Funny Thing Happened on the Way to the Forum

Some gloomy things happened on the way to the revival of *A Funny Thing Happened on the Way to the Forum*. One of our wittiest, sexiest, smartest, and most songful musicals has undergone a sea change from high to ebb tide. Some of the old felicities are still there, but an essential string is untuned, some crucial tesserae are missing from the mosaic of merrymaking—Thalia, the comic muse, has averted her face from the proceedings.

The original 1962 staging by George Abbott and the choreographer Jack Cole had a marvelously bawdy, lustily heterosexual character, with male and female flesh palpably yearning for each other and the air thick with Plautine bawdry. The cast comprised several mature, even elderly comedians, their Borscht Belt rowdiness as blissfully chomped on as a down-in-the-mouth stogie. Take Zero Mostel, whose Pseudolus I described at the time as "pungent, fatty, succulent, infinitely malleable… the memorial of (at least) twelve Caesars rolled into one, carved out of goat cheese and lecherous as the goats it came from." This fellow, after many accumulated years of slavery, craved his liberty as hotly as he panted for the courtesans in Lycus's next-door establishment. That round face and round body joined the bulging eyes in one ball of beady concupiscence. Nathan Lane, the currently slimmed-down pseudo-Pseudolus, is too young, too hyper, too campy—and largely unconvincing as the womanizing Pseudolus.

As Hysterium, his fellow slave and castrato co-conspirator, we once had Jack Gilford, an older actor with a meltingly melancholy face, oozing comic plangency, and, in drag, scaling vertiginous heights of absurdity. Mark Linn-Baker is too chipper, not properly hysterical, almost believable in female disguise. Where is the tart savor of Gilfordian chopped liver in the voice, where the innate sweetness peeking through layers of downtroddenness? As Senex, the pussywhipped oldster, we had David Burns, the archetype of overripe, innuendo-mongering Catskill savvy; now, young Lewis J. Stadlen rasps up a storm, but must we recruit our geezers from among the artful whippersnappers?

Ernie Sabella, however, offers a zesty tub of a Lycus, a pumped-up pimp of full-bodied farce. Even so, John Carradine's 1962 dourly cadaverous procurer was a more dazzlingly original creation. As the formidable termagant Domina, Ruth Kobart was huge, hatchet-faced, and horrific; compared with her, Mary Testa is a mere soubrette. But the usually lithe Cris Groenendaal provides an exemplarily strutting, vainglorious hulk of a Miles Gloriosus, puffed up with ludicrous grandeur. And exquisitely befuddled as Raymond Walburn's Erronius was in the original, the emaciated William Duell, in his different way, is equally droll.

George Abbott made the young lovers, despite the madcap maelstrom around them, obviously in love, with a grace that commanded our empathy and had us rooting for their nuptials; Preshy Marker and Brian Davies contributed a duly lyrical strain. The current Philia, Jessica Boevers, looks goony and acts goofy: Jim Stanek, the new Hero, is nearer the mark, but a silly wig and sillier staging hobble him. Jerry Zaks's direction swamps the romance with farce. And the gorgeous courtesans? The twins do not convey twins, the giantess is the size of one of the other girls, and none of them is remotely as stunning as Lucienne Bridou was back then. Even the all-purpose male trio, the Proteans, though nimble and versatile, prove flimsy in their martial mode.

Most of the singing passes muster, although Jonathan Tunick's orchestrations are brassy and acidulous even where the original ones, by Irwin Kostal and Sid Ramin, were ingratiating. Several songs in Stephen Sondheim's ear-entrancing score—one of his two or three best—suffer accordingly, and the frisky "Pretty Little Picture" is, unaccountably, cut altogether. Sad to say, even the incomparable Tony Walton, whose first Broadway assignment was designing the 1962 production, has tried too hard to compete with himself, and cutesiness sneaks in, with the courtesans' mourning garb worthy of Frederick's of Hollywood. But Paul Gallo's controlledly brash lighting nicely conjures up orange sunbursts and pomegranate nightfalls.

Rob Marshall's choreography, like Zaks's direction, has spots of inspired tomfoolery but is frenetically overzealous, with choreographic and directorial gags bordering on hysteria. It is like an illusionist who—not content with producing one elegant white rabbit—lets his top hat sprout an entire motley warren, thus turning magic into mere mass production.

What remains indestructible is the book by Burt Shevelove and Larry Gelbart, arguably the most urbane and literate musical-comedy text ever conceived. But much of this sophisticated comedy gets

swallowed up by the sight gags, and the often less-than-spot-on
delivery by a would-be ensemble frequently on the spot. Rather
like the emperor Augustus upbraiding his dead general, Quintilius
Varus, for losing him an army in the Teuton forests, I say to Jerry
Zaks, "Give me back my legions of joyous moments!"

A Delicate Balance

In my 1966 review of Edward Albee's *A Delicate Balance*, I pointed
out that in stage works nothing much need happen, but that Shaw,
for example, "fills his nothingness with incisive speculation…;
Beckett raises nothingness to fierce, tragicomic heights. But the
nothingness—perhaps more accurately nothinginess—of Albee's
plays is petty, self-indulgent, stationary. Albee's nothing is as dull
as anything."

    A Delicate Balance, a Pulitzer Prize-winning lucubration in three
acts, concerns Tobias and Agnes, an affluent, middle-aged, suburban Wasp couple; Claire, Agnes's alcoholic younger sister, who,
to everyone's annoyance, lives with them; Julia, their 36-year-old
daughter, who stays with them whenever one of her marriages
breaks up, as the fourth one just did; and their best friends, Harry
and Edna, who, when a nameless terror suddenly grips them, decide to move in with Agnes and Tobias, possibly in perpetuity. To
say that people are not seized by "the Fear" in the middle of their
mundane activities, and, if so seized, do not insist on moving in
with their friends forever, and, if undertaking such a *démarche*,
would roundly be sent packing is beside the point. Albee does not
write about people: he writes about humanoid constructs of his
agenda-addled brain. You can call these puppets symbols, fantasies,
or paper dolls, depending on your tolerance for three-dollar bills.

    To fill out the gaps in the pseudo-action, Albee comes up with
riffs. One such is Claire's disquisition on whether she is "an alcoholic" or "a alcoholic." Another is Tobias's reminiscing about his
unhappy relationship with a cat he once had—good for three and
a half pages of maundering text. Yet another is Claire's two-page
account of trying to buy a topless bathing suit in October. And so
on. Albee fancies himself and his characters to be great talkers—in
paragraphs, no less—unlike ordinary mortals who, it seems, speak
in sentences, if that. In witness whereof, Agnes opens the play with

an interminable monologue, artfully interlarded with little asides from both her and Tobias. It is built up on a sentence that, unfortunately for Albee's vaunt, does not parse. (I have shown in greater detail in one of my books how tenuous Albee's grasp of grammar and syntax is.)

There are funny moments in *A Delicate Balance* whenever the famed Albeean bitchy repartee takes over. Claire gets most of the good and nasty lines, but others also receive their fair share. If the point is—as it seems to be—to show how obnoxious these people are, the play certainly comes off. In other respects, Albee is the playwright with the longest eclipse: between *Who's Afraid of Virginia Woolf?* (1962) and *Three Tall Women* (1994), both important, everything he wrote is either poor or pitiful.

Gerald Gutierrez has directed with his usual suavity, and Rosemary Harris, Mary Beth Hurt, Elizabeth Wilson, and John Carter expertly convey both the storm and the teapot. George Grizzard is, if possible, even finer, far surpassing Hume Cronyn's performance in the premiere. But, for all her masterly timing and dry-martini delivery, Elaine Stritch is way too old to play Agnes's younger sister (a part very well handled in 1966 by Rosemary Murphy), and her search for a topless swimsuit emerges somewhere between ludicrous and obscene. But her balancing of a tumbler is delicate indeed.

Buried Child

Buried Child is San Shepard's best play. It is what the French call *misérabiliste* theater, but as good of its kind as they come, as much of a classic as *Christina's World* or a George Price cartoon. The central concept of a rural American family going down the drain because of—literally—a skeleton in the closet may be a bit schematic and the symbolism-cum-absurdism a tad dragged in by the cat. Even so, the flamboyant blend of the comic and the horrific, the verbally teasing and visually terrifying—in short, the hair-and-hackle-raising humor—takes you to a Shepard country where, laughing and shuddering, you never know when you'll be rolling in the aisle or scared out of your wits.

It is useless to try to retell the plot, minimalist yet convoluted, but sense can be made of the seemingly preposterous: Shepard gives us his family's and his country's history as reflected in a fun-house mirror, the very distortions grinning their way to the core of an insidiously incisive truth. The couch-bound grandfather (James Gammon), cursing his family and world as he revels in his filth; the mild-mannered near-idiot son (Terry Kinney) who keeps bringing in things that grow or fester outside; the one-legged and violent elder son (Leo Burmester) who practices petty viciousness on other people; the grandmother (Lois Smith) who berates everyone and hangs out with an addled priest (Jim Mohr); the grandson (Jim True) who escaped to the city, returning years later with his saxophone and a girlfriend (Kellie Overbey) who wants out of this madhouse in which none of the family recognize her boyfriend—all of these compel us to join their metaphysical staggers between farce and melodrama.

Gary Sinise has directed this Steppenwolf production with the trademark Chicago athleticism whose physicality sometimes detracts from the deeper meaning; he also introduces non sequiturs such as Grandma's leaving white-haired and returning a flaming redhead. But he does keep the mayhem spinning, even if the finish is less devastating than it might be. In the remarkable cast, only Jim True strikes me as too dopey a beanpole for what is, after all, the nearest thing to an authorial alter ego.

The set by Robert Brill, costumes by Allison Reeds, and lighting by Kevin Rigdon are fittingly, frighteningly good. And to think that it took Shepard's masterpiece 18 years to reach Broadway! But at least it gets there in style.

The Beckett Festival

Under the unassuming surface, the four great initial plays of Samuel Beckett embrace the fundamental themes of existence and, like no others in English since Shakespeare's, wrestle them to the ground. For each of mankind's major defeats—by faith, love, society, and mortality—Beckett conjures up a tremendous theatrical master image that, supported by subsidiary images and dialogue, achieves a reduction to the absurd.

Yet this tragic vision is endured with smiles, laughter, and poetry. His epitaphs for humanity are concise, lyrical, and memorable, like the magisterial funerary epigrams of *The Greek Anthology*, making this Irish heir to Shakespeare also kin to the poet Callimachus. The later plays, by comparison—whatever their minimalist virtues—are anticlimactic, as if *King Lear* were followed by *Titus Andronicus*.

It was a splendid idea for Lincoln Center to import a revival of *The Beckett Festival* from Dublin's Gate Theatre. Here, if you were lucky enough to get in, you could enjoy a fine overview of Beckett's entire theatrical *oeuvrc*, nineteen works in all. I myself write this after seeing three of the four supreme plays, with *Endgame* yet to come. In her revelatory book about his formative years, *The World of Samuel Beckett, 1906–1946*, Lois Gordon refers to S.B. as "the man who would create the definitive literary forms of our time." I would merely substitute "characteristic" for "definitive" and say amen. The man who married Kafka to Joyce pretty much did it all.

More radiantly than ever, *Waiting for Godot*, that lapidary masterpiece, seems to contain within it the seeds of works to come. The two tramps whiling away their endless stationary wait for the mysterious and perhaps imaginary Godot foreshadow not only subsequent Beckett characters but also the people and situations in Stoppard, Pinter, Albee, Mamet, and countless others to follow.

Vladimir (Didi) and Estragon (Gogo) are archetypes but are given all-too-human form. Vaudeville comics as well as doomed mortals, they epitomize respectively the intellectual and the common man. Didi's chief problems center on his penis, the cerebral fellow's Achilles' heel; Gogo's, on his feet and shoes, the workingman's, let's say, Achilles' foot. The one's main trouble is on the sensory-sensual plane; the other's undoing is the tiredness and constriction that subvert spiritual evolution. Each, however reluctantly, needs the other. So, in their way, do Pozzo and Lucky, the master and slave, who pass by on consecutive days with their roles all but reversed yet scarcely making a difference. They are the upper class and underclass locked in fruitless conflict. And there is also the little boy with messages from Godot that may be mere products of childish fancy, if not something worse.

In his program note, Gerry Dukes correctly stresses Beckett's efforts to "generalize" the play, to set it "wherever you happen to be" in a stripped-down, desolate landscape. Walter Asmus, the German director who has worked with Beckett, has here been seduced into making Didi and Gogo demotically Irish, and Pozzo aristocratically English, thereby giving the play a sociopolitical specificity Beckett labored to avoid. Otherwise, the looks, rhythms, and acting leave little to be desired.

Barry McGovern's Didi and Johnny Murphy's Gogo are as neatly differentiated individuals as they are a compelling comic symbiosis. They fill up the large, near-empty stage with their bustling existences that tragicomically crumble under the load of all that emptiness. They make you laugh without letting you forget that the closest sound to a guffaw is a sob. Much the same goes for Alan Stanford and Stephen Brennan as Pozzo and Lucky, although the towering Stanford's Oxonian snuffle may be a mite too broad. All four combine to convey lives that, whether they head for the vacuity of the scenery or the congestion of the auditorium, will come to nothing. Godot, who is God, will never show.

Things fare less well with *Happy Days*, where Rosaleen Linehan, accomplished actress though she is, lets down the heroine, Winnie—buried to her waist in Act One, to her neck in Act Two. Here is the middleaged wife trapped in her marriage to Willie, ex-lover turned mentally estranged and physically enfeebled spouse, who inhabits a hole on the other side of the sandstone in which Winnie is stuck. When visible at all, he reads and occasionally quotes from the paper, barely and smugly responding to Winnie's attempts at conversation. In the end, he undertakes a maneuver whose ambiguity leaves both Winnie and us with a crushingly unanswered question.

The superb Winnies I have seen—Ruth White, Madeleine Renaud, Irene Worth—all conveyed the spontaneously mindless babble of the heroine, her cheerful and then cheerless resignation, with a mettlesome benightedness as her sole support. The games she invents for herself, the gallantly time-killing stratagems and broken recollections of poetry and romance, pass the days she calls happy as she sinks ever deeper into helplessness.

Those earlier Winnies were sublime in their basic frivolity that wrested consolation from sand and stone, engulfment and indifference. Miss Linehan—with the indubitable collusion of her famous director, Kerel Reisz—gives us a rather more actorish, sophisticated, almost glamorous Winnie, too well endowed for a mere Everywoman. Her line readings are too cannily artful, her resources replenished by some Swiss bank account of the soul. In the small, foolproof part of Willie, Barry McGovern is fine. So much, in any case, for marital bliss.

In *Krapp's Last Tape*, an old man listens to autobiographical recordings, his annual account of each bygone year. The play is about senescence, loneliness, the uselessness of living in the past, with perhaps a sideswipe at the blessings of technology. The memories evoked are filial, amatory, and literary, but all meager and unsustaining. Forty minutes of futility, then, with small pleasures in food, drink, and the sound of words.

Krapp, at 69, listens to the tape memorializing his 39th year. Significantly, he remarks, "Hard to believe I was ever as bad as that"—even though this was when he made summer love with his girl in a boat and sold seventeen copies of his book, on which he proudly commented, "Getting known." Yet about this and other banner years, he concludes, "No, I wouldn't want them back." Now he revels in stretching out a word: "*Spooool*," which he calls the "happiest moment of the past half-million."

David Kelly, who created this role at the 1959 Irish premiere, is reprising it 37 years later: I wonder what goes through his head. His young voice on the spool sounds wonderfully brash, but he may be a little too senile as the 69er, whose anger on looking back—"Once wasn't enough for you?"—seems not borne out by the performance. "The fire in me now" may not demand a conflagration, but at least a few more sparks.

Skylight

After World War II, new British playwrights burst forth like gangbusters. It was like a bicycle race; first a whole pack, then a *peloton*, and finally two cyclists out front: Tom Stoppard and now David Hare. With the others declining, drying up, or dead, the race remains to these two.

Hare came from behind. *Slag, Knuckle,* and *Teeth 'n' Smiles* showed great promise but had something slightly limiting about them. Other plays—*Plenty, A Map of the World, Fanshen*—were politicized to the verge of propaganda. Still, in *Plenty* and again in *The Secret Rapture*, Hare was fighting his way through to making his characters as interesting as his ideas, albeit with uncertain results. But with *Racing Demon* and now *Skylight* he has written first-rate drama in which the humanist concern for individuals and the socialist concern for the world do more than intertwine: they fuse.

Skylight is the story of Kyra Hollis, who as a young girl escaped her respectable but stodgy provincial background and started out as a waitress in a London restaurant, where she promptly caught the eye of the owner Tom Sergeant and his wife, Alice. Tom, considerably older than Kyra, had worked his way up from the ranker ranks to end up as a wealthy restaurateur. Soon Kyra became, as it were, a member of the Sergeant family—almost literally, as she and Tom conducted a six-year affair behind Alice's back. Everyone was happy, including the two Sergeant children, until Alice found out.

Kyra left, and Alice, who developed cancer, made Tom's life an expiatory hell. To assuage her suffering, Tom built her a sumptuous sickroom with all comforts and a magnificent skylight. Three years have passed without communication between Tom and Kyra; Alice has died, as has Kyra's lawyer father. The Sergeant daughter is in college: the son, Edward, is 18 and adrift. Kyra lives in a shabby London suburb and teaches underprivileged kids in a similar one at the other end of the city. Even during her long daily bus trips, she is reasonably content.

The past irrupts. First Edward, then Tom comes calling of a winter evening. With Tom, it turns into a long night of sex and disputation. He wants Kyra back and cannot conceive of her enjoying her present life, about which he waxes wonderfully sardonic. She defends her new existence and cause. The debate grows in intensity and scope: Is fulfillment found in giving or taking? Where is the proper border between self and selflessness? The ensuing agon is fierce, funny, and intellectually challenging. As written, directed, and acted here, it goes from absorbing to overpowering.

Two opposite philosophies of life, incisively argued, are couched in flesh-and-blood characters who, rebedding and reconsidering each other, fight all the better. The dialogue glints and flashes, prickles with witty barbs and bitter sagacity, and cuts to the bone. The disputants touch on the biggest issues, yet keep them snugly within their human containers: the embattled ideas do not spill over into disembodied shadowboxing in an ideological fog. Everything is as concrete as the cooking and eating that keep coming to the fore, yet encapsulates the oldest, most consuming conflicts.

Richard Eyre's staging is consummate: thoroughly thought out, but always at the service of naturalness and universality. Lia Williams's Kyra is as complex as she is endearing: perceptive, quirky, impulsive, and wise. She stands before us in the nakedness of her honesty, the dignity of her compassion. In the generous hands of a superb actress, she tickles our mind even as she skewers our heart. As Tom, Michael Gambon is intense, commanding, and possessed of an almost frighteningly projectile diction. A spellbinding monolith, he lacks only grace of aspect and movement. I wish he could portray force without verging on brutishness: be a little less Charles Laughton or Leo McKern, a little more Trevor Howard or John Mills. Christian Camargo is an entirely winsome Edward.

John Gunter's fine set has a diaphanous back wall, suggestive of Alice's skylight. And what does that stand for? It is open to multiple interpretations, like Hare's entire play. It compels us to look beyond, to search for meanings in a work that abounds in them.

Full Gallop

When, last season, Manhattan Theatre Club did not transfer *Full Gallop* from its limited engagement to an open-ended run, I thought they had taken leave of their senses. But here it finally is, as funny, charming, madcap, and irresistible as it was before, and as it would be on any number of visits. This is the monodrama—I mean mono-farce—about Diana Vreeland, the fearsome fashion arbiter, who for decades wielded style-making power from behind her desks at first *Harper's Bazaar* and then *Vogue*. A whirlwind bearing aloft talented models, designers, and photographers, she was a scintillating wit and fabulous character in her own right and wrong.

The play by Mark Hampton and Mary Louise Wilson, who stars in it, takes place not long after Vreeland's summary dismissal from *Vogue*, in her spectacularly cluttered Park Avenue living-room. It covers the hours between her rejection of a job as a consultant to the Costume Institute offered her on the phone by the Met's curator Theodore Rousseau ("Why is everybody trying to put me in a museum?" she growls, and "I don't care if they've got the Shroud of Turin!") and her return call to Rousseau, in which she accepts with the proviso "You'll have to renovate the clothes: nobody gives a damn about authentic if they're ugly." We are granted an hour and three quarters with a fabled *monstre sacré* in her demonic digs (splendidly designed by James Noone) as we listen to her recollect a chicly checkered past; pass canny judgment on people and fashions and life; conduct uproarious dialogues with her skeptical French secretary, Yvonne, over the intercom; and hobnob telephonically with the luminaries of international society.

As sublimely performed by Miss Wilson—whose makeup, utterance, and demeanor fit Vreeland to a T—this is the highest hilarity, the Everest of camp. The actress displays exquisite timing, teasing gestures, devastating inflections, and murderous facial play. Hear Miss Wilson say, "You can't destroy Europe; you can't even nick it," or "We allowed a splash of bad taste—no taste is what I am against," and you will feel transported into Thalia's lap. Nicholas Martin's pinpoint-accurate staging, discreetly omnipresent, supplies the final sheen. I don't know how much of this is actual Vreeland and how much authorial invention; if the latter, it is, in Anatole France's words, a story truer than the truth. I can promise you two laughs a minute, and broad smiles in between.

Fit to Be Tied; *The Vagina Monologues*

The overrated Nicky Silver turns utterly meretricious, meaningless, and contemptible in *Fit to Be Tied*. What could be more distasteful than a contrived, superficial farce riding on outlandish sight gags and hit-or-miss one-liners that cheaply indulges homosexual (and occasionally heterosexual) fantasies, then tries to legitimize itself by coyly, pussyfootingly invoking AIDS?

It is hard to review this nauseating concoction without the kinds of pejoratives that make the perversely curious want to rush to catch it. Say that a play is creepy, prurient, awash in childishly smutty jokes, and you might as well hire out as its publicist. Yet a farce about a superrich kid with a crazy and sex-crazed mother married to the boy's crass stepfather is already suspect. If the mother runs away to go live with the boy, whom she both stiflingly coddles and casually betrays by bedding his love object, the mess thickens.

Concoct then a situation wherein the boy's lover, with whom the boy has difficulties consummating the sex act, nevertheless ends up in a sunny ménage à trois with the boy and his mother while the stepfather's inept attempts to reclaim his wife are joyously spurned, and the stench becomes overpowering. Especially when the lover is an angel in the Radio City Christmas Show, and sports angelic drag even when the boy ties him up in his clumsy "first foray" into sadomasochism, observing, "How hard can it be?" Mother rings doorbell, boy locks tied-up lover into closet and explains tardy response to ringing with "I was masturbating." "That is so darling!" exclaims Mom.

Silver is a vest-pocket clone of Tony Kushner, himself hardly coat-pocket-size. A pox on all pubescently maladjusted playwrights populating America with grotesque angels because they cannot manage rounded human beings. There are no consistent, never mind true, characters here, and don't even think of sensible plotting. If all else fails, in goes a witless parody of O'Neill, the boy having played the addicted mother in a high-school production of *Long Day's Journey Into Night*. Now the lover is following son and mother around the apartment with a video camera, ostensibly making a movie of the O'Neill play. Absurd? Absurdist? Derivative? Demented? Take your pick.

Or just how amused are you by this typical line: "You are looking at me," says our hero's bibulous mother, "like I'm Lee Remick in *Days of Wine and Roses*." Even Jean Smart's smart delivery cannot disguise that this easy allusion, recognized, is meant to make the spectator feel devilishly—or angelically—with-it. That's what Nicky Silver is about: half-baked one-upmanship, facile inversion, smirking wallows in dimestore depravity, and salvos of quips of which one in twenty hits a target. Not all that is Silver glitters. The production values are excellent. Only the play sucks.

The Vagina Monologues is Eve Ensler's survey of how women feel about their vaginas. Some of it is indeed monologues, some of it is Q&A read off cards by Miss Ensler, seated on a bar chair in front of a screen on which red light is sometimes projected. Most of the monologues are routine stuff, but some of the answers to questions are at least bizarre: "If your vagina could talk, what would it say?" "Where's Brian?" Asked to describe the smell of their organ, women answer, "Somewhere between fish and lilies" or "The South Pacific" or "Paloma Picasso." For redeeming social content, Miss Ensler traveled to Bosnia to research the effect of civil war on vaginas. Some of her Bosnian informants were among the clamorously enthusiastic audience.

I tend to mistrust a playwright-screenwriter-actress who, speaking in her own person, says "I had to lay down," "astrologer" for "astronomer," and, after years of research, "clitoris" with the accent on the second syllable. But I found enlightening the replication of some twenty types of female moans during intercourse, and the information that "they love vaginas in Pittsburgh."

This Is Our Youth

Once in a blue, or perhaps indigo, moon, a play and production manage to come together in a perfect, gemlike whole. Such is the case of Kenneth Lonergan's tongue-in-cheek charmer *This Is Our Youth*, as presented by the consistently worthy New Group. It concerns some very young people on the Upper West Side in 1982, lost in a mist of substance abuse and sexual anomie and squirming like fish in a leaky aquarium.

Dennis Ziegler is a pusher connected to a whole network of young dealers and clients, and is, of course, a druggie himself. He has a hectic but seemingly satisfying life of snorting coke and screwing around to his heartless heart's content. To his pad comes an old school pal, Warren Straub, a bit of a nerd, who has made off with his father's 15,000 smackers in a plastic bag and his own precious collection of antique toys in a large suitcase. He hopes to move in with the chum he hero-worships and away from the dad he hates.

But Dennis browbeats him when he does not patronize him, while Wallace tries lamely to ingratiate himself, committing gaffe after laughable gaffe. The interaction between them is deliriously funny, slightly pitiful, and furiously lifelike. When Dennis goes off with a girlfriend, Warren is left with her sidekick, Jessica Goldman, whom he has coveted from afar. Jessica, confused and defensive, does not know what to make of the good-looking but timid and bumbling Warren. Their interplay, a stumbling mating dance, is riotous yet also touching, and ends on a note of winsomely absurd hilarity in which Father's cash plays a prominent but ambiguous role.

You'll have to find out about Act Two for yourself; it, too, is often uproarious, though in the end a mood of overarching melancholy credibly yet somewhat studiedly takes over. But even in its lesser moments, this is a play to reckon with, and an audience of both young and old (myself included) boisterously lapped it up. My program crawls with quotable lines, but merely reproducing them would not convey their full humor or poignancy.

For this, you must hear them against Allen Moyer's letter-perfect mess of a set, see them in Eric Becker's whimsically incisive costumes. You must catch the superb direction of Mark Brokaw, who elicited dead-accurate bopping movements, exquisitely offbeat timing, and bizarrely authentic inflections from all concerned. Josh

Hamilton's Dennis is bursting with precarious bravado, spouting hilarious venom over the phone at countless associates, patsies, and girlfriends and playing every kind of bullying game with the puppyish Warren. Wonderful as Hamilton is, Mark Ruffalo's Warren is even more so. Ruffalo can make such pitiful buzzwords as "What's up?" and "Whatever" balloon with comic pathos, and his every naïvely hopeful or ludicrously indignant utterance takes on the heartfelt resonance of a toy drum.

No less irresistible is the Jessica of Missy Yager. With the face of a heroically coping rag doll, and (risibly) dressed to kill, she cannot make a pas that isn't faux or a sound that doesn't want to be hugged. Insecure yet trying to be totally hip, she splits your sides when she doesn't wring your heart. Please do not consider the following trivial, but I feel duty-bound to hail perfection wherever I find it, whether in the caryatids of a Greek temple or Kenneth Lonergan's ear for this juvenile-grandiose dialogue. So I must pay homage to Miss Yager's legs, by far the most beautiful I have seen in years and flawlessly sculptural from every angle.

Chicago

It was a gamble to transfer the Encores! Production of *Chicago* to the larger and costlier venue of Broadway. But since *Chicago* is about women who kill their men and the mercenary lawyer who gets them off, gambling seems like the merest peccadillo. Especially when, as here, it pays off. Back in 1975, this Fred Ebb-John Kander-Bob Fosse musical opened in the shadow of *A Chorus Line*, and though easily as good, reaped the deficit of the reviewers having exhausted their supply of encomiums. Also, amorality, at least officially, was not yet in. In those days, a jury would have frowned on O. J.'s behavior. But the show did have it all: Gwen Verdon, who suggested the idea to Fosse; Chita Rivera; Jerry Orbach; and the rest. Yet, miraculously, here it is again, with all the trimmings.

In the leads, we have Ann Reinking (a sometime Fosse dancer and girlfriend), who also choreographed in the Fosse manner; Bebe Neuwirth (who won a Tony in Fosse's *Sweet Charity*); and James Naughton, who in laid-back sleaziness is second to none. Then there is Joel Grey as the lover-killing Miss Reinking's milquetoasty husband, Marcia Lewis as the most affably corrupt of prison matrons, and D. Sabella as a double-bottomed newspaperwoman. Further, six murderesses of the chorus—most of the action takes place in jail—are all terrific, but Denise Faye and Leigh Zimmerman are especially so. And there are some deft chorus boys too.

Mostly, the show concerns the rivalry between the ex-chorine Roxie (Reinking) and the vaudevillian Velma (Neuwirth) for the services of the supershyster Billy Flynn (Naughton) and tabloid publicity. There is not much plot but lots of hokum in front of a steeply raked bandstand on which perch thirteen musicians expertly conducted by Rob Fisher. There are also a couple of ladders, some chairs, and a very sparingly used elevator. The rest is magic.

Minimalism prevails. William Ivey Long's scanty black costumes scarcely change, John Lee Beatty's clever bandbox set stays put; only Ken Billington's moody lighting seems to keep getting moodier. When Joel Grey does his one number, the complaint of a man nobody notices, he dons a pair of Mickey Mouse white gloves; the effect is overwhelming, as if he had put on papal robes. And when he wiggles his white-gloved hands, it is as if a bevy of Busby Berkeley maenads had whirled onstage. Small things make huge marks; understatement is all.

Miss Reinking is suavely slinky with a demureness that oozes sex, and every male tongue hangs out; Miss Neuwirth does a scissors kick or two while maintaining her come-hither brand of snootiness, and trousers fill up with warrior ants. Miss Reinking's large come-on gestures remain sweetly unassuming—just a willow gently waving in the breeze. Miss Neuwirth's studiedly tiny steps are an invitation to any man to scoop her up and carry her off. And Naughton doles out dearly bought legal strategy like alms to an importunate beggar.

All is concise, calibrated, calculated, but nothing is stinted on. Every bosom, pelvis, and long leg is in business to keep the women in the audience identifying, the men panting. Bob Fosse, were he with us still, could have made it tougher, meaner yet; but, whether in Heaven or the other place, he cannot be displeased. The dialogue crackles, the score delights, the dancing bedazzles: if Chicago in the twenties was like this, it was more fun than Periclean Athens. I only wish Tina Paul's Hungarian were better, and Ann Reinking's hairdo less severe; but I would be happy to personally coach the one and tousle the other…

The Last Night of Ballyhoo

In *The Last Night of Ballyhoo*, Alfred Uhry returns to the Atlanta Jewish milieu of his *Driving Miss Daisy*, but though the play is polished to looking-glass smoothness, funny and sentimental in artful fusion, it never attains the luminous humanity or calm transcendence of the earlier work. Of course, except in a few brief flashes, it doesn't try to: with this feel-goodish crowd-pleaser, Uhry settles for contrivance where there could be revelation.

Adolph Freitag—in the Atlanta of 1939, with Hitler a distant rumble—is a prosperous bedding manufacturer, having inherited the business from his more gifted brother, whose widow, Reba, shares his nice house. So, too, does Boo Levy, his widowed sister, whose bumbling husband was carried along by the Freitags, and whose flighty daughter, the gawky Lala, has joined them upon washing out of college for emotional reasons.

Reba's daughter, the enlightened and very shiksaish-looking Sunny, is a successful junior at Wellesley and comes home only for vacations. Both the Freitags and the Levys are assimilated German Jews; into their midst comes Joe Farkas, a bright young New Yorker whom Adolph has hired as an assistant. Joe is "the other kind," a passionately up-front Jew from the East, whom these Westernized Jews have problems with, though not nearly so much as he with them.

Ballyhoo approaches: a great Atlanta Jewish festival that ends with a big dance, for which the wallflowerish Lala desperately seeks a date, and her mother moves heaven and earth to find her one. At first Lala makes a play for Joe, but he falls for the visiting Sunny, and she for him. I won't go on, but you can tell that this material lends itself to tragicomedy, serious comedy, or the light comedy Uhry chooses to make it. The first act, more witty than sticky, works well enough on that level. But in Act Two, Uhry gets progressively more intramurally Jewish, as various forms of Judaism duke it out, and also more saccharine and, finally, all gooily religious. At this point he lost me, though not the ecstatic audience.

It is all highly competent, well crafted, and utterly facile. With clever direction from Ron Lagomarsino, solid décor by John Lee Beatty, incisive costuming by Jane Greenwood, and the caressing lighting of Kenneth Posner, *The Last Night of Ballyhoo* gets all the needed trimmings; and then, what a meat-and-potatoes cast! As the edgily overprotective Boo, capable of volcanic fire for her daughter and polar ice for all others, Dana Ivey gives another of her bravura performances, taking comedy to spectacular peaks and precipices but also managing some subdued, achingly felt moments. As the down-to-earth, unflappable Reba, Celia Weston gives a superbly modulated performance of exquisitely timed hilarity. And as the wise, melancholy-tinged but playful Adolph, Terry Beaver is irresistible, perfectly realizing what may be the hardest assignment.

Paul Rudd and Arija Bareikis, as Joe and Sunny, are properly intense, sensitive, and vulnerable; as the more farcical couple, Lala and Peachy (the funny fellow she hooks or is hooked by), Jessica Hecht and Stephen Largay may be a bit broad, but that's how they are written. The ending is both too sweet and too parochial, but then, the entire play is preaching to the converted—or is it the unconverted?

The Changeling

Robert Woodruff has achieved the impossible. He has taken one of the greatest English plays, Middleton and Rowley's *The Changeling*, and made it unbearable even before it begins. In the program, by way of introduction, he quotes an irrelevant passage from a trashy modern novel and tells us that he has cut the play but added scenes from Webster's *The White Devil*—which is like improving *Hamlet* with a few scenes from *Doctor Faustus*. From the program synopsis, we can deduce further damnable changes, and the addition of four female lunatics and one male one, the latter perhaps—in emulation of Renaissance painting—a sneaked-in self-portrait.

The director foisted this travesty on the already beleaguered people of Israel, where he first staged it, and has brought along the Israeli choreographer with whose inane dance prologue the production begins. The set and to some extent the dance are steals from Cheek by Jowl's misbegotten *Duchess of Malfi*, with some ideas stolen from that vulgar British director Steven Berkoff thrown in. At the end of the dance—part flamenco, part tap, part climbing on chairs—the female asylum inmates have epileptic seizures, are stripped, and are locked into a row of phone-booth-like cells upstage. This much rubbish, and the play proper hasn't even started yet!

When it does, we, see a black actor, his hair dyed blond, making his way between rows of ropes strung across the stage, a notion cribbed from Richard Foreman. Stealing from three such abject sources is worse than thievery, it's stupidity. Then to hear Marin Hinkle recite Beatrice's lines like a schoolgirl regurgitating her lesson; Thom Christopher declaim Vermandero's lines with a gauntlet on one hand (a proleptic tribute to Michael Jackson?); and Christopher McCann turn DeFlores, one of drama's greatest villains, into a mincing pipsqueak... Well, after *un mauvais quart d'heure* of this, I ran for my sanity, pursued by something more foul than the hounds of hell: Robert Woodruff's wholesale butchery of a work that, according to T. S. Eliot, "stands above every tragic play of its time, except those of Shakespeare." Already a fixture in Chicago, Woodruff should take over directing its stockyards.

One Flea Spare

Naomi Wallace, the author of *One Flea Spare*, is a very confused young woman. For one thing, she is still a Marxist well after the collapse of Marxism. For another, she has taken her title from a wonderful poem by John Donne, "The Flea," specifically from the line "Oh stay, three lives in one flea spare," meaning, "Spare a flea that has sucked your blood and mine and thus united us." But by itself, *one* flea spare could mean, at best, "one extra flea," which has no demonstrable bearing on the play. Finally, she has written a piece that is not only pretentious and boring but also empty, pointless, and totally preposterous.

The great London plague of 1665 makes for a lively background, and Miss Wallace has done some research. She has clearly read Defoe's *A Journal of the Plague Year*, the relevant parts of Samuel Pepys's diary, and some modern historians. But homework does not a stage work make. Her story concerns an affluent elderly couple, William and Darcy Snelgrave, whose servants have died of the plague and who are now stuck in their boarded-up home for a month of quarantine with two separate intruders (a likely story!): a 12-year-old girl, Morse, presumed to be the daughter of Sir Nevill and Lady Elizabeth Braithwaite, plague victims; and Bunce, a disaffected young merchant sailor, pressed into one navy after another and looking for a new life. On guard outside the house is Kabe, a rascally watchman.

The plot is as simplistic as it is simple. The authoritarian, patriarchal William has a prurient, closet-gay fascination with Bunce that takes on a sadistic form: Darcy, who after two years of marriage was badly burned all over, and so lost her husband's sexual favors forever, is rekindled by Bunce. He has a permanent wound in his side into which she sensually sticks her finger. Later, he sticks a finger into some other part of hers; still later, they copulate in front of the tied-up and blindfolded William.

The precocious and flirtatious Morse—the daughter of a Braithwaite servant—has fun with Bunce as with all others, and after William dies of something unspecified, and Darcy comes down with the plague, helps the old woman commit suicide. Kabe is the common man, manipulative and unscrupulous, just what he needs to be to survive the plague and that worse scourge, the ruling class. He may, in his dallying with Morse, be a pedophile, but poor folk take their furtive pleasures where they can.

Morse, who represents the author's poetic, feminist, and Marxist sides, comes off best: she inherits the world. Bunce, the good proletarian, comes off second-best, achieving his emancipation at last. Darcy, though upper-class, is at least a woman, and so gets some sort of fulfillment in the end. For William, the rich male chauvinist, there is only humiliation and death from, as it were, political obsolescence. He embodies the Marxist message, for which Miss Wallace is hailed as a political playwright as well as a supremely poetic one. Kabe, the lord of misrule, illustrates the play's second epigraph, from Brecht: "Corruption is our only hope," a truly edifying motto.

But this sophomoric, sex-and-scatology-obsessed work needs psychoanalysis more than interpretation. As for the author's highly touted poetry, chiefly spouted by Morse and Darcy (note that both women have masculine names), here are some samples: "My head is full. Of ocean. And the shells are sliding back and forth in my ears." "I am filled. With angels." "The bird had a song like a long, long spoon and we could sip at it like jam." "I can smell your heart... It's sweet. It's rotting in your chest." This stuff can go on for whole paragraphs. With wildly poetic punctuation: "A horse on fire. In full gallop. It was almost. Beautiful. It would have been. Beautiful. But for the smell."

Miss Wallace's grammar is atrocious, full of things such as "phenomena" (singular) and "I skulked the city." Her characters keep saying "Sir Braithwaite" for "Sir Nevill" (some knowledge of England, that!). Ron Daniels's direction can do nothing to help, and even such able actors as Dianne Wiest and Jon De Vries come to grief. No one sounds properly British except little Mischa Barton, who plays Morse; she, however, cannot begin to act the part. And to think that *One Flea Spare* has won three prestigious awards! I don't know which is scarier—if the other candidates were better but lost out, or if this was really the best of the lot.

How I Learned to Drive

Paula Vogel's *How I Learned to Drive* benefits from an original slant: child molestation as an act of consenting partners, with the child as a willing participant. Miss Vogel acknowledges her debt to Nabokov's Lolita. She has written a memory play about a pedophile and his big-breasted niece by marriage, Uncle Peck and Li'l Bit, names a trifle too apt to ring true. The driving lessons Uncle Peck gives Li'l Bit over the years are a slow, careful—even caring—seduction. When did U.P.'s pursuit begin? Was it the only one of its kind? What were L.B.'s reactions? How did they change over the years? Was the thing even consummated? How did it affect L.B.'s later life? What was the rest of the girl's family—Mom, Grandma, Grandpa—like?

The play takes all this up in circuitous, nonconsecutive, jigsaw-puzzle fashion, no doubt reflecting the nonlinear workings of the freewheeling memory. Or is this time-tripping with much gear-shifting from reverse to forward and back a mere trick to create suspense, where interest should focus on analysis instead? Is it legitimate to treat the rest of the family as caricatures? Is it fair to introduce a casual sequence of U.P. teaching a male nephew (unseen) how to fish just to raise further troubling, unanswered questions? Does an ancillary episode involving the adult L.B. with a high-school student mean that because of all this, she, too... ? The head spins.

A play has every right not to answer the questions it raises—most works of art don't. But just how many unknowns is an equation entitled to? At which point does writing become algebra? Thus Miss Vogel uses the topography and chronology of her own life for L.B.'s story; is this done merely to anchor fiction more firmly in reality, or are we nudged into speculating about her self-proclaimed lesbianism, even if we accept her asseveration that this is not autobiography?

In any case, Mark Brokaw has directed inventively in Narelle Sissons's rather too schematic set. The supporting trio—Michael Showalter, Johanna Day, and Kerry O'Malley—does all anyone can, and the two leads excel. David Morse is an utterly disarming U.P., cunning pedophile and self-deluded good old boy in warmhearted blend; Mary-Louise Parker dons several ages from 11 to 35 with the skill of a quick-change artist and remains physically and emotionally truthful. Whatever its shortcomings, the play sticks more in your gut than in your craw.

Barrymore

Barrymore, by William Luce, gives you a chance to experience Christopher Plummer, the greatest living actor in the English language. It is a quasi-monodrama in which the legendary thespian, a month from his rendezvous with death, prepares to put on *Richard III* once more in a rented hall. Sometimes he spars with his unseen, sardonic prompter in the wings (well intoned by Michael Mastro); for the rest, he gloriously indulges himself. He does stagger through a pungent bit of Richard; mostly though, he sings popular ditties, recites risqué limericks, executes a few dapper dance steps, tells racy anecdotes, impersonates his siblings Lionel and Ethel, delivers snatches of *Hamlet* and other Shakespeareana, banters with the audience, and relives his soaring and plummeting career, his glamorous and clownish life.

I have no idea how much of this is Barrymore and how much Luce, but I do know that it is all plummily pluperfect Plummer. On what other actor today have the gods lavished such gifts, bestowing equally the requisites of heroic tragedian, masterly mountebank, and matinee idol? His diction can cut glass; his voice, in its chamois mode, can polish mirrors. His vocalizing bestrides the octaves, dazzles or darkens, insinuates or thunders, and, at every turn, turns mere verbiage into symphonic music. Add to this uncanny timing that espouses every joyous tremor, every wistful modulation of the soul.

And then the movements, bearing, demeanor. Though subverted by booze, this Barrymore is still an old lion, springy and sportive, ready to pounce on every passing one-liner or wring tears from licking his private wounds in public. The mode is somewhere between Gielgud and Olivier, with the Olympian poetry of the one and the protean swagger of the other, yet imitating neither. In this acting, form and content are indissolubly wedded, and style is slyly conscripted into concealing style. Thus humdrum material emerges as angelic descant laced with heady distillates of deviltry. Under Gene Saks's lusty direction, this is theater it would cost you far too much to miss.

The Hairy Ape

Theater, like other arts, would be doomed without innovation. But innovation ought to know its place, which is at the horizon, advancing into uncharted territories. It is not by moving backward, by mucking around with the works of the past, that anything new and valid is achieved. The archetypal no-talent in the theater is usually a failed creator who sets him or herself up as a director, laying his cuckoo's eggs in the nests of other, better-singing birds. His or her name may be Peter Sellars or Richard Schechner or, as in the present case, Elizabeth LeCompte (Schechner's ex-assistant director) or hundreds of others worldwide, yet the procedure is always the same: not imaginatively reliving the classics but arrogantly relieving yourself on them.

The sorry thing about this wretched phenomenon is not so much that some unfortunates practice it in some hole in the wall in SoHo, TriBeCa, or Wroclaw, but that there are misguided powers funding them (e.g., Catharine Stimpson and the MacArthur Foundation's "genius" award to LeCompte), trendy exploiters transferring them to more visible venues (e.g., the current producer, Frederick Zollo), and the solidly bourgeois audience supine and sheeplike enough to embrace and empower them out of sheer mindless manipulability.

What's horrible is that this so-called The Hairy Ape has virtually nothing to do with Eugene O'Neill's play, which it distorts and debases in every conceivable and inconceivable way. What you get at the uptown Selwyn Theater is Willem Dafoe (about whom more anon) and the six nonentities from the downtown Wooster Group clambering up and down and jumping all over the tilting jungle-gym set of Jim Clayburgh while John Lurie's music moans in the background, irrelevant TV sets (the Sellars legacy) display balderdash, and numerous microphones used by the cast do their damnedest to outblare the rest. But don't think for a moment that the mikes are used for communication: they are whispered, howled, or rattled into at breakneck speed, the voices sometimes trisected into shrill cacophony. For acting, the most you get is clown costumes and shoes being waved about, or handheld rods maniacally banged on the steel girders. As if this weren't durance enough, there is a bank of assault lights glaring into our eyes, though not quite enough to blind us to the absurdity of the proceedings.

It is clear from Don Shewey's approbatory article in the Sunday Times that Miss L. doesn't give a tinker's damn about the play. Rather, during lengthy watching of another of her productions from backstage, "she became mesmerized by the rear of Jim Clayburgh's industrial-looking steel-frame set." As Shewey quotes her, "I always thought maybe we could do a sea play on it, because it looked like a boat to me. When I read *Hairy Ape*, I thought it was perfect for that." She goes on about how the language suggested rap to her, so she turned the performers into rappers. Call it a baboon's rear-view reading of O'Neill.

The irony of it is that in his limited range but great rage, Dafoe is an interesting actor, his neurosis, or some other kind of frenzy, barely contained. It works for the parts he plays in the movies and it is with Hollywood's filthy lucre that he finances the work of his life companion, Miss L. On the strength of his name, she then raises additional funds and sells tickets. The 57 uptown performances are pre-sold, but don't despair: there is a solid trickle of walkouts throughout this 90-minute, intermissionless ordeal, and the escapees may bequeath their stubs to you. And don't fret about missing part of the show: before a cageful of gibbering, hairy or hairless apes, 45 minutes is just as illuminating as 90.

A Doll's House

Seldom was directorial advice more pregnant than Noël Coward's to a Method actor: "Don't just do something, stand there!" I wonder what Sir Noël would have said to Janet McTeer as she fidgets and fusses with her hair, squirms and squeals, burbles and blusters through the role of Nora in Ibsen's *A Doll's House*? (In America, the play should be titled *A Doll House*, as that toy is called here.) She lets her hands flutter like Tibetan prayer wheels in a gale, outcoos a turtle dove in heat, and flings herself about as if playing racquetball with her own six-foot-plus body. This is what is known nowadays as rethinking the classics.

In this interpretation of Ibsen's admittedly somewhat creakily contrived but humane and influential drama, which Miss McTeer evolved with her director, Anthony Page, there are two putatively significant innovations. First, the marriage of sweet little Nora and patriarchally overbearing Torvald Helmer is perceived as going gangbusters sexually. At any moment, the pair will fly into passionate clinches—1879 Norway miraculously transported to 1997 Hollywood—and we wonder how long it will be before the nude copulation scene. Second, the actress projects from the start a deep-seated but repressed discontent with her marriage: her busyness is overcompensation for being patronized as a less-than-equal.

Interesting, but what is gained? Ibsen's aim was to show what was stiflingly wrong with the marriages of his era, not how sexual slavery can keep an independent-minded woman from striking out on her own. And if Nora was so basically self-aware and clear-sighted, would she have naïvely forged her father's signature, even in a good cause, without awareness of the consequences? This generous but foolish act was intended by Ibsen to show the dangers of women's being overprotected and undereducated.

It is true that in the last quarter, when the drama heats up and the star stops inventing perpetual motion, things become gripping. Yet even then, can we really feel that Nora's leaving Torvald and her children is something tragic but inevitable rather than a much needed rest cure for a husband whose wife suffers from Saint Vitus's dance? On the other hand, Owen Teale so overplays Torvald's unthinking complacency, complete with a déclassé regional accent, that Nora's desertion for a parlously uncertain future comes across less as feminist self-realization than as search for a mate with a commensurate I.Q.

Except for a wretched wig, John Carlisle's Dr. Rank satisfies. I do, however, have problems with Peter Gowen's befuddled, almost yokelish Krogstad: perhaps he is puzzled by various cast members' differing pronunciations of his name. If she weren't overgroomed and over-rouged, Jan Maxwell would be a first-rate Kristine Linde, the rare case where the only American—in a supporting part, at that—outshines the visitors from England.

Frank McGuinness's "new version" of the play is, happily, not all that new, though expressions such as "Little Miss Stubbornshoes" may strike us as a trifle transatlantic. But there is nothing about this highly-touted British production that is smashing, even if Miss McTeer does smash the tambourine with which, after conspiratorially winking at us, she danced her etymologically misjudged tarantella. The term is derived from the town of Taranto, not, like so much of her performance, from the bite of a tarantula.

Sympathetic Magic; An American Daughter

It has always been Lanford Wilson's distinction to know about the things of this world. While other playwrights plowed their little acres—family clashes, love triangles, showbiz shenanigans, and whatnot—Wilson uncovered with each new play new areas of human activity and sensibility. One never knew whether he was cannily taking crash courses in this or that calling, was making lightning excursions into this or that idiosyncratic region, or had simply been everywhere and experienced everything.

The plays, of course, weren't equally successful artistically or commercially. But even the least of them in quality or duration took us where we had never been before; immersed us in bizarre occupations and unorthodox relationships, defiantly generous or spectacularly wasted lives; and opened our eyes and ears to the eccentric choreography and bewitching cacophony of existence. Of none of his works is this more true than his latest, *Sympathetic Magic*.

Consider merely the dramatis personae. Liz Barnard is an anthropologist who has worked much in Africa and is now studying the West Coast gangs for similar behavior, while also observing striking changes in her own body. Her elder child, Don, is the Episcopal minister at an outlying Bay Area church, most of whose parishioners are poor, and many sick with AIDS. He himself is homosexual; his choirmaster ex-lover, Pauly, waves his sexuality about as if it were a baton.

Liz's younger child, by another husband, is Barbara, a gifted sculptress whose current breakthrough show launches a stellar career. She has been living with Ian, a fine young astronomer and popular university professor who, with his somewhat bumpkin-ish colleague Mickey, stumbles upon a sensational discovery at the farthest galactic horizon. Meanwhile, the chairman of their department, Carl Conklin White—a dapper, smooth-talking, cheerily glacial fellow—snatches up this startling find in a potentially panic-producing way that could also deprive his two subordinates of the credit due them.

So we are hurled into the worlds of anthropology, astronomy, religion, and art. Shamans and statuary, academic maneuvering and clerical politics, the art market and choir practice with rank amateurs are made palpable and, better yet, comprehensible. So, too, are relationships, both homo- and heterosexual, both thriving and threatened. There is also the generational clash, centering on Susan, Liz's attractive young secretary. Overhanging all are the eternal opposites, science and faith, in a wrestling match not entirely unlike a lovers' quarrel, which we also get.

Such plenty would be of scant use if inexpertly handled, the front teeth biting off more than the molars can chew. It would be lost on a writer who can deal with drama but lacks humor, is high on ideas but fumbling with people. Here, though, is Lanford Wilson encompassing it all, always landing, however daring the leap, on the balls of elastic feet. He shies away from nothing, giving you even one of the most complicated and terrifying fights ever, chillingly staged by that master B. H. Barry. The rest is guided by the most empathetic of directors, Marshall W Mason, with whom, incredibly, Wilson is collaborating for the fiftieth time.

Though Dana Millican's Susan is a shade too callow, the cast is a tearproof ensemble: Tanya Berezin, David Bishins, Herb Foster, Ellen Lancaster, Jeff McCarthy, Jordan Mott, and David Pittu seem to be playing themselves in an exceptionally well-made documentary. John Lee Beatty's set is as versatile as it is simple, Laura Crow's costumes have that subdued San Francisco elegance, and Dennis Parichy's lighting captures the essence of several environments. All this at the most handmaidenly service of the author, who makes the mundane numinous, and miracles seem natural. *Sympathetic Magic* is the rare play you want, like some pieces of music, to promptly start da capo.

A warning, however, is called for. Wilson's play is so chock-full of ideas, incidents, witty, or poetic lines, scientific and philosophical argument, that you must attend very carefully with all your wits about you. Though the play is only a little over two hours in length, it feels like much more. This may prove draining, but it is worth it. It's like a vigorous workout in a mental gym; after you rest up from it, you will find your intellectual faculties racing as after no show currently on the boards. *Sympathetic Magic* is truly what is says it is, a play about the universe, universal.

Having first written about her own experiences (the right way to begin), Wendy Wasserstein has progressed to the realms of the imagination (the smart way to continue). In *An American Daughter*, she serves up the prominent physician and teacher Lyssa Dent Hughes, wife of the wry sociology prof Walter Abrahmson and daughter of the conservative Republican senator from Indiana Alan Hughes. There is also Lyssa's best friend from way back in Miss Porter's classes, the oncologist Judith B. Kaufman, who is black, Jewish, divorced, and tormented by her apparent infertility, a problem she could easily have resolved by now.

Nominated by the president for surgeon general, Lyssa is interviewed both by the flashy feminist writer Quincy Quince (a name that, even as an Anglicization, is hard to swallow) and, in a pre-interview, by TV's high-powered Timber Tucker (another name I don't buy). Hanging around is a family friend, the homosexual columnist turned screenwriter Morrow McCarthy, whose quaint moniker serves as peg for prêt-à-porter puns. All three of these media types radiate a cockiness not uncommon to the territory.

Senator Hughes has a fourth wife, nicknamed Chubby, which, of course, she isn't. Hubby Walter jocularly brings up Lyssa's always managing to muster good reasons for avoiding jury duty, which Morrow mischievously elaborates on with a reference to a misplaced summons in the presence of Timber Tucker. This gets pounced on during the TV special, and some innocent remarks about her mother, too, get the nominee into trouble. How little it takes to bring down a worthy candidate in hypersensitive and hypocritical America!

Miss W. valiantly juggles with several genres: drawing-room comedy, comedy of manners, political satire, problem play, and even domestic-infidelity drama. But she is not that much of a prestidigitator: some of the flying balls plop; others, attached to her hands by rubber bands, boomerang into her face. Lyssa seems intended as an allusion to someone in current politics, most likely Hillary Clinton, whom Kate Nelligan rather resembles, but tenuous parallels are enervating. The humor, too, turns imprecise, as when the senator regrets having given his daughter such role models as Eleanor Roosevelt and Florence Nightingale: "I should have found you heroines that are more sensible—like Arianna Huffington and Amy Fisher," which is both anachronistic and out of character.

Characters remain underdeveloped. More needs to be done with Dr. Kaufman, whose ill-judged despair defies even Lynne Thigpen's powerful talent. And someone less miscast than Peter Riegert—the perennial sophomore as college professor—would still find the role of Walter underwritten. Hal Holbrook does fill the senator's gaps with his substantial presence, and who could light up both her cigarette and her role (as Chubby) better than Penny Fuller with a demure "I only started again last month, to celebrate the twentieth anniversary of my quitting"?

Conversely, Elizabeth Marvel is unable to get beyond Quincy's irritating smugness, and Cotter Smith's Tucker could use a bit of Charlie Rose's surplus oiliness or Barbara Walters's ersatz solicitude. But Bruce Norris is a flawless Morrow, and Peter Benson gets a congressional spin doctor smack on the condescending nose.

Only the writing lacks sharp detail. Dr. Kaufman's attempted suicide and casual recovery ring false. What adolescents would, like the Abrahmson kids, stay rigorously out of sight? What attempted adultery rocks the marital boat no more than a lapping wave? All this seems even more unreal against John Lee Beatty's inviting living room, Jane Greenwood's meticulous costuming, and Pat Collins's cozy lighting. Add Daniel Sullivan's life-enhancing direction and Kate Nelligan's magisterially calibrated Lyssa, and you wonder how, amid such parenting attention, *Daughter* can look so orphaned.

Titanic

Although raising the *Titanic* has proved impossible, the sunken liner keeps popping up in various guises. Most recently a news story revealed that the killer iceberg had made not one large gash, but six small ones. Soon we are getting a two-studio supermovie on the subject. In between comes *Titanic*, the musical, which generated a flurry of rumors and news releases about mechanical difficulties that turned the onstage vessel into the unsinkable Molly Brown. So one approached the show (book by Peter Stone, score by Maury Yeston) with a bit of a sinking feeling.

There are to be experienced (1) lavish, spectacular, and imaginative sets by Stewart Laing; (2) fairly lavish, not very tasteful costumes of the touring-opera-company kind—one woman's hat comes straight out of *The Insect Comedy*—also by Stewart Laing; (3) a cast of 43, which, doubling up, can seem to be legions; and (4) an earnest but hopelessly mediocre show.

The question imposes itself: can any musical do justice to the enormousness and enormity of this tragedy, which recklessly killed over 1,500 people—roughly ten times as many as the Oklahoma City bombing? Musical comedy has proved itself able to become serious and tackle the death of its hero or heroine, but only by allowing other important characters to prosper. I do not, however, think it equipped to deal with an immense calamity, even if it had a better book and score than we get here.

Consider: a novel or a movie can encompass more, delve deeper, depict people and events in greater, truer detail. Even a fine poem, such as Hardy's "The Convergence of the Twain," can render the metaphysical essence of this disaster. It may well be that an opera by a gifted composer, using the vast resources of modern operatic music, could also wrestle the subject down.

Musical comedy, however, thrives on catchy tunes and clever lyrics, leaving too little time in between for the book to tell much of a story. (The unions, which charge time-and-a-half after eleven, don't help either.) Well then, aren't hummable tunes, jaunty lyrics, and showbiz choreography in such a context artistically inadequate and morally suspect? And what of the facile ironies of characters saying things like "This will be my last trip" to the laughing delight of know-it-all spectators? And when you also consider that the show cannot fully come to grips with the factual information needed, impatience grows. Personally, I do not blame the authors for not succeeding, only for thinking that they could.

Yeston's music for his first major production, *Nine*, had virtually no weak numbers, *Grand Hotel* was rather hit or miss, and *Titanic* is almost all miss. The only tolerable numbers are those not integral to the story, such as a dance number by the ship's orchestra and a piano ballad sung and played by the bandleader. Yeston also writes the lyrics here, and they are nothing to run up the mainmast and salute. As for the Peter Stone book, in trying to focus on as many as fifteen or twenty characters, it achieves roundedness for none. Four performers stand out nonetheless: John Cunningham as the captain, Brian d'Arcy James as a stoker, Henry Stram as

George Widener, and especially Allan Corduner as a steward. The rest, including some very talented people, merely get—dare I say it?—submerged.

Even when, on the heavily tilting deck, Isidor Straus and Ida, his 40-years wife who elects to die with him, sing a final reaffirmation of their love, the thing miscarries. Everyone else is out of sight; there are no rushing crowds or roaring water; and the song, "Still," chirps away across artful stillness. There is, however, one touching sequence when four portholes of the sinking ship frame successively different quartets of heads speaking their farewells.

Richard Jones's staging, with the help of good design, including Paul Gallo's lighting, is intermittently resourceful, as in the handling of the crow's nest, of a scene in daring perspective on a staircase, and of the simultaneous action on several decks. Still, the most memorable moment in the show is when the furniture starts sliding—first a serving table on casters, finally even a grand piano. But that is not the sort of thing a big musical wants to be remembered by.

Jekyll & Hyde

Mediocrity, thy name is Leslie Bricusse, unless it be Frank Wildhorn. They are the co-authors of *Jekyll & Hyde*, another musical that in evolving form—and two separate albums—has been around for years. Robert Louis Stevenson's was, of course, a great story, even if it took Hollywood's two movie versions to insert the sex that the author had neglected to put in. To be sure, the movies, like the present musical, are vulgarizations of the novella—"monstrous, abominable, atrocious, criminal, foul, vile, youth-depraving," Vladimir Nabokov called them, yet even he complained that Stevenson, by chastely omitting specific guilty pleasures, displayed a certain artistic weakness.

However, the book Bricusse supplies is no improvement: the people Hyde kills are, for the most part, morally wanting, making the beast appear almost a justicer. His are not mere acts of gratuitous evil, except perhaps the killing of Lucy, the prostitute who yearns for Jekyll but has an affair with Hyde.

Philosophy, to be sure, is kept to a minimum in the show; but neither, alas, is the erotic potential given its due. There is Jekyll's blonde fiancée, Emma, played and sung exquisitely by Christiane Noll, and Hyde's paramour, Lucy, sung superbly but acted rather pallidly by Linda Eder. Yet not even when she and Hyde embrace is there anything to incur so much as an R rating. The minor characters are stick figures often incorrectly observed: there cannot be such a thing as "the fourteenth bishop of Basingstoke," any more than a Victorian solicitor would speak of "a lifetime of aggravations." Even the hypodermics substituted for the original's potions strike a needlessly anachronistic note. Though hardly "youth-depraving," this book is maturity-deprived.

Frank Wildhorn provides two kinds of songs: soft and loud. The soft ones are accompanied by enervating tinkles from the orchestra; the loud ones call forth all the resources of unleashed electronics. Two or three of them can pass muster. But Bricusse is heavy-handed: thus every conceivable rhyme for *heart* gets trotted out in due time, with the single exception of *fart*. And Wildhorn is too enamored of his middling inventions, and revels in repetition.

As the dual protagonist, Robert Cuccioli works hard and efficiently, but without the necessary star quality. The supporting cast—except for the ladies and Barrie Ingham, who is British—is rather inept, and cannot even (any more than Cuccioli or Eder can) muster a British accent for sorely needed authenticity. Robin Phillips has redirected the show to good effect and co-designed the functional sets with the ubiquitous James Noone. The big scene-stealer is Beverly Emmons's brashly ostentatious lighting, which turns the show into a discotheque or MTV. But perhaps it needed it: this is, after all, a *Jekyll & Hyde* for today's kiddies.

Gross Indecency: The Three Trials of Oscar Wilde

If the chief drama critic of the *Times* had not gushed about Moisés Kaufman's *Gross Indecency: The Three Trials of Oscar Wilde*, which he somewhat belatedly caught Off Off Broadway, it most likely would not have marched on to an open-ended Off Broadway engagement. Would that have been a great loss? For those of us who know and care about Wilde, hardly. There is a certain cleverness in Kaufman's docudrama but also an annoying cuteness and, in Act Two, an even more annoying sentimentality, neither of which Wilde's story needs. His life went from high comedy to tragedy in one of the most dazzling examples the world of letters has produced. As Vyvyan Holland aptly put it in his autobiography, *Son of Oscar Wilde*, "It was a cruel irony that Oscar Wilde should have been singled out by fate to suffer for all the countless artists who, both before and since his day, have shared his weakness."

What weakness? Either that his flagrantly homosexual lifestyle provoked the wrath of a puritanical and hypocritical society in a country where homosexuality was almost as widespread as in ancient Greece; or that, through sundry pusillanimous strategic errors, Wilde bungled his own defense. And yet it took a great deal of daring and not a little strength to become what W. H. Auden has called "the patron saint of the Homintern," and start, directly or indirectly, the slow process leading to gay liberation and acceptance.

The three trials of Oscar Wilde (as one of H. Montgomery Hyde's books—the annotated transcript of those trials, and the primary source of Kaufman's play—is called) are a lesson in how easily things could have gone another way, with who knows what momentous consequences. No wonder the case has fascinated so many, as witness the number of plays, movies, and especially books about Wilde. Kaufman appears to have read them all, which is part of his trouble. Even if we needed the chorus of young men seated at a long, book-laden table just below the lip of the stage (true, they also assume some important roles, at times even joining the stage action), must we have them hold aloft whichever book the play is quoting from, and loudly proclaim it? Couldn't this—less cutesily and self-servingly—have gone into footnotes in a future printed text? What good is it to learn that this is from a letter of Lord Alfred Douglas, that from the recollections of Frank Harris or Robert Sherard, when the theatergoer has neither interest in the source nor ability to determine its trustworthiness?

Kaufman's direction may pass muster, but not his cast of mostly young, inexperienced if not downright untalented American actors, straining with unequal success to reproduce the accents of diverse British regions and classes, whose clash contributes to the societal drama underlying the personal one. (Some of these accents are even ill-chosen: Edward Carson, importantly, was Irish; Frank Harris, American.) Wilde's wit and wisdom shine splendidly throughout, but do we want a bewigged young man doing Queen Victoria in falsetto and similar burlesque elements? And then there is the acting of Kaufman's company, too young even to suggest some of the elders portrayed.

The greatest failings are those of the two thespians playing Wilde and Douglas. It is imperative in a docudrama to make these famous figures look and behave as we know from countless photographs and contemporary accounts. Thus, Wilde was large and imposing and, though profuse in dandified preciosity, physically powerful—how else could he have survived the rigors of hard labor in England's inhuman jails? Michael Emerson, however, is slight and (unlike Wilde) campy, intoning with a fruity, rubato-riddled singsong, with much eyeball-popping and rolling and a plethora of effete mannerisms. And none of his lineaments correspond to Wilde's.

Bill Dawes, a wooden actor, has neither Douglas's languid good looks nor his maniacal ferocity, let alone his aristocratic hauteur: his use of his hands is particularly inept. The others, though less important, arc scarcely better, and when the genuinely older but flimsy Queensberry (Robert Blumenfeld) snarls about trashing someone, he comes across as a paper pit bull.

Granted, *Gross Indecency* is a shoestring production, but its designers could have shown a little compensatory ingenuity. In any case, though, Wilde the man, artist, and victim was so complex a figure, enmeshed in such complicated social and legal circumstances, that no mere play can do him and them full justice. Even so, Kaufman should not have allowed Michael Emerson to turn Wilde macabrely maudlin in Act Two and fail throughout to show his unflagging kindness and, to quote Frank Harris, his "great charm... rarer among men than even goodness."

Personally, I would suggest that you could spend your money better on a good biography. But if that is too much effort, *Gross Indecency* will do, especially if it should lead to further study. Wilde deserves no less, and will amply repay such added investment.

As Bees in Honey Drown

The Drama Dept. (that abridgement presumably meant to suggest depth) offers, third time around, *As Bees in Honey Drown*, by its artistic director, Douglas Carter Beane. In this smart-ass farandole, Alexa Vere de Veer, a swinging millionairess who is actually a consummate con woman, hires Evan Wyler, a successful first-time novelist, to ghostwrite her autobiography with an eye to a future movie version. Evan (whose real name is Wollenstein, as Alexa's is Gelb) is sucked in, hook, line, and sexual preference, forgetting even his homosexuality as he falls into bed and love with Alexa.

She, in turn, offers him luxuries *Sunset Boulevard* style, although, because she scorns credit cards and carries only cash, it is soon Evan's card that must carry the burden of their joint extravagances. By reimbursement time, she vanishes. Shocked and hurt, Evan pursues her by tracking down her past victims, male and female. As you may have guessed, true love is revealed to exist only between men.

Alexa's way of testing Evan's literary prowess is to put to him this poser: "If you absolutely had to sleep with one of the Three Stooges, which one would it be?" To her query "You do love men?" Evan responds, "No. I don't love anyone. I sleep with men." When Evan tells Alexa's gay ex, "I slept with her, and I'm gay," he replies, "What do you want? Frequent-flyer miles?" which doesn't strike me as pertinent. The pithy quintessence of Beane's wit is this exchange: "Jewish?" "Close—Catholic." You can tell the level of sophistication by someone's pronouncing George Grosz to rhyme with *gauche*. Gross!

Most of the acting under Mark Brokaw's alert direction is fine, though Sandra Daley is weak in several parts. Josh Hamilton and J. Smith-Cameron are good in the leads, but the best work comes from Cynthia Nixon, Mark Nelson, and especially T. Scott Cunningham, in several smaller roles each. I understand that this sort of multiple casting saves money, but being ubiquitous these days, it begins to smack of undue archness. Here it fits in only too well: Mr. Beane is so full of beans, he drowns in them.

Les Danaïdes

Lincoln Center Festival 97's first offering, the Romanian Silviu Purcarete's *Les Danaïdes*, is hardly the "Reconstruction of Aeschylus's Lost Tetralogy" it purports to be. Instead, it is an elaborate commercial for the white suitcases the 50 Danaïds make multiple use of, which I wouldn't be surprised to find purchasable through Mr. Purcarete. These perspicuously unsoilable Purcarriers are compact and lightweight, yet hold the damnedest variety of goods, and are extraordinarily manipulable. They can be quickly piled up in a number of enticing abstract configurations, but they can also become anything from pedestals to barricades, from makeup tables to sacrificial altars. They are sturdy enough to stand or sleep on, and you can even produce a perplexing domino effect with them, valuable as a political allegory. In the larger, trunk size, they can serve as habitat for the bare-breasted but bearded woman, no doubt double-jointed, who for no good reason except packageability portrays Danaos, the father of the Danaïds. You can just hear Purcarete purring with ill-gotten delight.

Purcarete has evolved a perky choreography for the 50 fleeing Danaïds and, to somewhat less pleasing effect, for the 50 sons of Egyptos, their pursuing cousins, who would carry them off. This is often spectacular but has little to do with Aeschylus, reconstructed or unreconstructed. The gods in Aeschylus's *Suppliants* and other plays are stern but ultimately just and conciliatory. In Purcarete, they are perfidious and perverse: cackling, sneering, malicious creeps. And they quote Aristotle, Nietzsche, Corneille, and Schopenhauer, which no self-respecting Greek god, however gifted with foresight, would have deigned to do.

The ceaseless to-and-fro effectively deflects attention from Aeschylus, whose text is insufficient to the director's purpose. Purcarete does, however, exhibit further visual inventiveness, especially in his lighting, which achieves interesting trompe l'oeil effects. Stefania Cenean's costumes for the women are resourcefully self-transforming; for the men, somewhat crude, almost comical. But the pertinacious Purcarete persists in pushing toward tragedy, though there is enough evidence to believe that the trilogy (not really a tetralogy) ended with Aphrodite providing a redemptive outcome.

But Purcarete wants his gods pernicious, and has them playing peculiar games on what seem to be luminescent gaming tables, one with moving sailboats, another with building blocks, prefiguring human suffering. Yet why the hermaphroditic King Danaos, father to the princesses? Not only is Purcarete not pertinent here, but he is also downright impertinent. The actors perform in French, once spoken flawlessly by Romanians but imperfect among Purcarete's younger performers. Worse, though, are some of the English supertitles, hard-to-read and ungrammatical—e.g., "You are looking at he who heard your pleas." And the uncredited translator keeps calling Ares, the god of war, Aries, the ram, with goatish obtuseness. But perhaps such purblindness is emblematic of Purcarete's efforts.

I wish, however, Mr. Purcarete would inform us where those highly practical and mighty purty Purcarriers are to be purchased. I would get the small one for me and the trunk for him, and pack him off in it to perdition.

More Stately Mansions

Eugene O'Neill wanted the huge, unfinished manuscript of *More Stately Mansions* destroyed in case of his death. Instead, his widow gave it to the Swedish theater director and O'Neill expert Karl Ragnar Gierow to adapt. In 1967, a Broadway version partly based on this, with a superior cast headed by Ingrid Bergman, proved a superior sort of mess. Now the New York Theatre Workshop, with the help of a Flemish director, Ivo van Hove, and his designer, Jan Versweyveld, has done what O'Neill wished, though not quite in the way he intended. With a ludicrous production, they have reduced *Mansions* to rubble.

The Flemish version underlying this production was, apparently, a hit throughout Holland, but what do those folks know about late O'Neill, and how awed are they by van Hove, a bogus magus in the Peter Sellars mold, but without even the latter's pinchbeck panache? *More Stately Mansions* was, like the finished *A Touch of the Poet*, part of a projected eleven-play family chronicle tracing the disintegration, as O'Neill saw it, of moral values in America during the nineteenth and twentieth centuries. These plays were to be realistic in style, like the great completed final masterpieces for which the playwright set aside the cycle, and on which his fame largely rests.

Without any warrant, van Hove has turned *Mansions* into a piece of expressionism, such as O'Neill briefly experimented with in a much earlier phase—and a piece of senseless, vapid pseudo-expressionism at that, such as not even the immature O'Neill would have perpetrated. The story of an industrial family between 1832 and 1840, during which time a son is torn between his possessive, fantastical mother and his grasping upstart wife, between being a writer and a greedy capitalist, has been trivialized into an olla podrida of cheap theatrics.

Thus the mother opens with a soliloquy rattled off at tongue-twister speed, reducing it to near gibberish. Pretty soon we have people getting down on all fours, pulling at each other's mouths or nipples, and talking in a kind of falsetto baby-talk. One character wears period costume, while the others sport more or less outlandish contemporary garb, on a bare set lined with an assortment of irrelevant modern chairs. The backdrop features first an abstraction vaguely reminiscent of a map of Australia, and then is replaced by what looks like a UPS parcel with a painted red window, and a red door glued to it.

The actors' delivery shuttles between very loud and nearly inaudible; the acting styles range from quasi-naturalistic to clumsily stylized. Besides being misdirected, the actors lack all grace and charm. Performers run around gratuitously barefoot. All this I gleaned from the first, 75-minute act. Alas, I denied myself two others roughly as long, featuring unused pianos, vintage sewing machines, and nude wallowings.

In a program note, the director remarks that there is no "singular way" of staging O'Neill's plays. Of course, he means *single*, not singular, but he speaks truer than he knows. What he has contrived is not just singular, it's downright queer. But to the bored, the ignorant, the disaffected, bizarreness is its own best justification. Indeed, only the bizarre passes for genuine art, even if at the expense of a dead master, unable to defend himself against total misrepresentation.

There exists today a hapless coalition of reviewers and audiences grooving on this sort of balderdash, out of a mixture of jadedness, illiteracy, mindlessness, and hatred of finer things beyond its reach. I urge true lovers of theater to stand up and be counted against such pernicious nonsense. They will have to buck the tide of vociferous phonies reviling them as retrograde fuddy-duddies—a small price indeed for the kingdom of Heaven.

Side Show

The story of Siamese twins must at least skirt tragedy, no matter how you slice it, and not them. The historical English-born Siamese twins Daisy and Violet Hilton, who during the twenties and thirties went from a freak show to vaudeville fame but ended up as a supermarket bagger and checkout girl in Charlotte, North Carolina, has many tragic elements, and a new Broadway musical tries to tackle them. (A recent Off Broadway one on the same subject was campy.) But musical comedy perforce has problems with tragedy, and *Side Show* is no exception.

The musical, though it calls its heroines by their rightful names, freely deviates from fact, which it is entitled to do. It does show them rise from freak show to vaudeville, as they did, thanks here to the ambiguous ministrations of an entrepreneur, Terry Connor, and a song-and-dance coach, Buddy Foster. They also have a sort of bodyguard, Jake, a stalwart black man secretly in love with Violet, who is presented as a shrinking violet tacitly pining for Buddy. The ambitious Daisy wants to become a star and yearns not so secretly for Terry. But whereas Buddy might marry Violet for the wrong reasons, Terry, though he craves Daisy, cravenly abstains.

That is about as much as you need to know, and not much less than is known to Henry Krieger, the composer, and Bill Russell, the librettist-lyricist. For they are finally at a loss as to how to deal with their material when it reaches dramatic—if not tragic—heights, as evidenced by something like three mutually contradictory endings, which still leave us hanging. Russell's lyrics, seldom less than serviceable but scarcely more than that, cannot fully rise to the occasion. Ditto for Krieger's music, which does nicely enough in Act One but falters in Act Two of this ambitious score, whose quasi-operatic aspirations merely underscore its caducity.

Yet all is far from lost. When you tally up *Side Show*'s credits and debits, you end up, if not exactly in the black, at least in a becoming Oxford gray. There are enough good songs to make the weak ones overlookable, with splendid orchestrations by Harold Wheeler and arrangements by David Chase, who also conducts. There is wonderful scenery from Robin Wagner done with mostly modest means, an object lesson in how good taste and whimsical inventiveness can outshine lavish bedizening.

And apropos outshining, Brian MaeDevitt's inspired lighting savvily balances starkness and gaudiness, knowing full well how to make painting turn into sculpture. Thanks to Wagner and MacDevitt, space becomes palpable, whether as confining reality or alluring, deceptive infinity. Gregg Barnes's costumes, deftly juggling the flashy, comic, and elegant, never cease to surprise and delight. A choreographer-director new to Broadway, Robert Longbottom, though not coming up with anything startlingly new, manages to make the old feet fresh and idiomatic: with a name that bespeaks *ars longa*, may he enjoy more than a *vita brevis*.

The cast carries the show with panache and poignance. Alice Ripley (Violet) and Emily Skinner (Daisy) are able, first of all, to be both similar and very different as called for. They also act, sing, and dance compellingly, getting every requisite laugh and tear. On top of that, though not artificially conjoined, they maintain their Siamese twinhood flawlessly through taxing maneuvers. Jeff Mc-Carthy (Terry) and Hugh Panaro, (Buddy) must also prestidigitate: they have to keep basically unlikable characters from losing audience sympathy, and come off handsomely. Norm Lewis provides a nobly sung and acted Jake, and Ken Jennings, despite or perhaps because of a freakish voice, makes quite a freak-show boss. The supporting cast, in multiple roles, keeps up admirably.

There are some effective production numbers. In one, a vaudeville routine, the twins become a kind of double Cleopatra discovered in her funerary monument by a bunch of loony pith-helmeted explorers. She/they come(s) to life, and dance(s), sailing down the Nile with two rows of horny ancient-Egyptian swains. The choreography for the intertwined sisters drolly suggests a many-limbed Hindu deity in some Indian ritual, and it is genuinely amusing, even while also oddly lyrical.

Later, there is an impressive number in which the torn Terry fantasizes a separated and sexy Daisy, with whom he indulges in a sensual dance, only to waken to the truth of being alone and miserable. In still another showstopper, Terry, Buddy, and the girls are hoisted into a carnival ride, a heart-shaped tunnel of love created with a heart-stopping strobe effect. Amid much visual splendor, Terry and Daisy kiss passionately, but once they return to reality, all hopes are crushed.

There are echoes of past shows here—*Dreamgirls*, *The Ziegfeld Follies*, and *Merrily We Roll Along* come to mind—which may or may not bother you. Like the twins, you will most likely be of two minds. But such duality should help you understand what it is like to be inexorably twinned and all too cumbrously twained.

The Scarlet Pimpernel

I have seen bad musicals, stupid musicals, and odious musicals; what I had not seen is a musical that on top of all the above is also totally demented. But that is what *The Scarlet Pimpernel* is. At any given moment, you don't know whether to laugh (at such incompetence), cry (for the future of the musical), or faint dead away (from sheer disbelief). It is a case of, to quote Saroyan, no foundation all the way down the line, an inaptitude that, like some horrible disease, has infected both show and production from top to bottom, or, more accurately, bottom to bottom.

Frank Wildhorn is essentially a pop composer, seated not so much at the piano as at the meat grinder, churning out endless vermiform lengths of elevator, cocktail-lounge, skating-rink, and beauty-pageant music. In them, the same trite phrases are repeated over and over, giving Chinese water torture ferocious competition. His *Jekyll & Hyde* was bad enough, but his latest effort, *The Scarlet Pimpernel*, is a quantum leap into the flaming ninth circle of the orchestra pit. To the inane, flat-footed, blunted-from-overuse lyrics of Nan Knighton, who also wrote the ludicrous book, we get melody that is a rock slide on the path of musical theater.

Baroness Orczy's underlying novel may well be pure hokum, but at least it is pure; what has been concocted here has no consistency of any kind, except perhaps that of mush. Bits of the Orczy original jostle references to paranoia and Mme. Tussaud; punch-drunk jabs at romance stumble over cobbled-together and abandoned lumps of farce, and the height of wit is Sir Percy's repeated mispronunciation of Chauvelin as "shovel-in." But then, this is a production where even the measly guillotine looks more like an overgrown cigar cutter. Indeed, all of the worthy Andrew Jackness's décor emerges jerry-built, clichéd, or improbable (like an all-purpose open-field backdrop), and the no-less-respectable Jane Greenwood's costumes look uncharacteristically cheap in both materials and taste.

Natasha Katz, the dependable lighting designer, comes up here with a string of luminescent platitudes. The choreography, credited to Adam Pelty, is as minimal in invention as in scope. Rick Sordelet's swordplay should be moldering in Errol Flynn's grave. Worst of all, Peter Hunt strikes me as a wholly played-out director, lacking a single new idea, and making the old ones look more than tired—moribund. He could not even impose a system of pronunciation: bits of British and soupçons of French accents pop up sporadically, only to retreat hastily into American.

As the Pimpernel, Douglas Sills sings tolerably but seems much more at ease in the effetely foppish scenes than in the heroic or romantic ones. As the fair, beleaguered Marguerite, Christine Andreas—alas, no longer fresh as a daisy—sings decently but does not convey stardom at the Comédie Française or any other special distinction. As the evil Chauvelin, Terrence Mann recycles his Inspector Javert with a few bonus pouts and leers. With his billiard-ball eyes, flaring nostrils, and super-retractable lips extruding acres of teeth, he comes across as an extremely soulful horse. In the nondescript supporting cast, the Armand of Gilles Chiasson impresses with his total lack of charisma, and David Cromwell with the impartiality with which he ruins both Robespierre and the Prince of Wales. As the jailer calling out the names of aristocrats for the scaffold, Don Mayo gives out a French so inscrutable you wonder how anyone made it into the tumbrels.

Frank Wildhorn does, however, know how to market his wares. For *Jekyll*, he made three concept recordings, toured the hinterlands for years, and developed a breed of groupies known as Jekkies, who have seen the show 50 times. He aims at ignorant young audiences for whom musical history starts with *Les Miz* and Peabo Bryson and Céline Dion are the Adam and Eve of song styling. Such fledgling fans spread the virus to older know-nothings, and a hit results. I have no doubt that *Pimpernel*, with two preshow CDs and a giant advance, will generate its own Pimpies, and likewise lumber on unchecked.

The Lion King

Come to *The Lion King* with two pairs of eyes, one ear, and half a brain. You will be bombarded by some of the most beautiful and spectacular sights theater can offer from before and behind, so eyes in the back of the head will come in handy. You will be harangued by second-rate standard-show music and lyrics by Elton John and Tim Rice, and also by Lebo M's stirring African chants and ululations, to which your active ear should be cocked. Finally, you will be subjected to a well-worn, simplistic children's tale about a lion cub's hard road to adulthood and the throne of the animal kingdom, usurped by his wicked uncle in cahoots with some murderously laughing hyenas.

Kiddies, of course, will delightedly swallow it whole, unless they are tiny and flappable. But this is the one such show adults will feast on, too, mostly because of the wonders wrought by Julie Taymor, who designed and directed this cornucopia of dazzlements. First, the animals, large and small, re-created with unparalleled imagination, underpropped by costumes that artfully blend realism and fantasy: the prancing giraffes and leaping antelopes, the nodding elephant and barreling warthog, keep you marveling even during the story's stodgiest galumphing.

Puppetry from East and West is put to superlative use, yet the actors, singers, and dancers are accorded enough humanity to ply their anthropomorphic skills. And Taymor has found ways to transmute the strictly cartoonish bravura of the big-screen *Lion King* onto a stage you would have thought inhospitable to such things as a stampede of wildebeests, so that nothing is lost in translation. Garth Fagan's choreography (with the possible exception of amorous couples in the sky—though even that can be aesthetically defended) becomes an integral sharer in this convocation of the arts, to which solo and choral song adds riveting finishing touches.

Minor cavils are possible. The extraordinary Tsidii Le Loka's getup does not quite register as a baboon until she belatedly moons us, and the buzzards are a bit too pretty to be fearsome. But sustained by Richard Hudson's scenery and Donald Holder's lighting, the spectacle rightfully earns that most abused of epithets: *magical*. Just the way hanging plants descend like a benison and tall grasses sprout up like magic carpeting mobilizes scenic dimensions that are too often held in abeyance.

And what an array of versatile, well-drilled performers: as the reigning but soon-to-be-murdered lion king Mufasa, Samuel E. Wright easefully combines regality and tenderness. Geoff Hoyle's Zazu is the most endearingly dithering avuncular hornbill, and you couldn't ask for more bumblingly bestial hyenas than the dynamic trio of Tracy Nicole Chapman, Stanley Wayne Mathis, and Kevin Cahoon. The wind-breaking warthog of Tom Alan Robbins is adorable, warts and all, and compared with Max Casella's euphoric meerkat, the entire cast of another indestructible musical is mere cats. That prodigious actor John Vickery cunningly camps up Scar, the cruel but cowardly lion, so as to differ from Jeremy Irons in the movie. He is also delectably reminiscent of the late Cyril Ritchard—and what more welcome avatar?

As the young Simba, the lively Scott Irby-Ranniar is too much a New York street urchin; as his girl chum, young Nala, Kajuana Shuford is more credible. As the grown Simba and Nala, Jason Raize and Heather Headley neither shine nor sabotage, while the rest staunchly hold their own as swelling chorales and sinuous dancing intoxicate the senses. The book by Roger Allers and Irene Mecchi recycles the screenplay's puns and apothegms, but also adds some theatrical and megalopolitan jokes, e.g., a reference to "a shower curtain from the Guggenheim." The hyenas fail to make "a cub sandwich" of young Simba, but we, young and old, have *The Lion King* to make a heavenly hero sandwich of.

Benita Canova (Gnostic Eroticism)

Richard Foreman has been running his Ontological-Hysteric Theatre for years, though lately it is content to go by the more modest moniker of Ontological. If I had to choose which epithet to drop, I would have picked the other one, hysteria being much more the specialty of the house. The group's latest offering is *Benita Canova (Gnostic Eroticism)*, supposedly based on the paintings of Balthus—no more in evidence than Gnostic Eroticism, whatever that might be.

We get scenes from an unlikely brothel featuring alleged schoolgirls, all of whom look to have repeated every grade at least once. Three of them get to speak Foreman's nonsense, under Foreman's weird direction, in Foreman's tacky décor. Three others merely mill around, laughing, screaming, or milling. The heroine wears a yellow Jewish star, though there is no mention of a time or place that would justify it. The others have it in for her, for unclear reasons. The madam is a transvestite, played by the sometime playwright David Greenspan, who makes as little sense as the girls do. The only customer seems to be a gorilla, but even he gets to enjoy Benita's favors only when he dies.

Benita's chief rival speaks with an affected accent that sounds like a hillbilly's idea of Mrs. Astor's 400. There is also the character called The Sly One, who doesn't seem particularly sly, but is distinctly overweight. There are numerous illiterate references to a "modus oper-andus," which made me want to shout "di! di!," but I bit my tongue. The dialogue crackles, or at least cracks, as when Benita announces "My mirror has a big crack in it," and proceeds to moon us. But not really: in Gnostic Eroticism you don't get to see flesh, except Mr. Greenspan's unimpressive genitals. But back to the dialogue, which is profoundly metaphysical, as in, "Of course we are losing touch with reality—that's our one point of contact with reality."

The downtown audience, suckers for Gnostic Eroticism, grooved on this; slumming uptown types seemed baffled but intent. I, for one, was happy to leave the Ontological Theatre, muttering to my-self "On to the logical," though even that is in shortening supply.

Ragtime: The Musical

A mosaic made of tesserae, usually tells a story. A crazy quilt, made of rags, does not. *Ragtime*, the novel, tried to be both. It inter-wove the stories of three groups—Wasp, black, and Jewish immi-grant—against a background of early-twentieth-century America: eccentric, bumptious, chaotic. *Ragtime: The Musical* attempts to be mostly mosaic: connect, make sense, tell a story. But also keep some of the eccentricities and extremes—Evelyn Nesbit, Harry Houdini, J. P. Morgan, Henry Ford, Emma Goldman—visible in the inter-stices. What E. L. Doctorow just about managed in the greater space of the novel, the show can't carry off: it is a mosaic that keeps slip-ping into a crazy quilt.

Doctorow had the bold, gallant idea of writing in a style equivalent to ragtime. The simple, declarative sentences avoid hypotaxis. But they do, syncopatedly, tell about the Wasp family with generic names (Father, Mother, etc.). Intercut with this are references to famous or notorious individuals, as well as grand generalizations; this, in a way, represents the stride bass. To be sure, Doctorow is eventually forced to relax so rigid a schema, but its spirit hangs in.

There is an allegorical purpose. The beautiful Wasp Mother, wid-owed, marries the formerly penniless Jewish immigrant Tateh (not a name, merely Yiddish for Daddy), now a successful filmmaker and self-styled Baron Ashkenazy. Her Little Boy and his Little Girl become affectionate siblings, even potential spouses. And there is another, tiny, black child in this new family.

This is Coalhouse Walker III. He is the illegitimate son of Coalhouse Walker Jr., a jazz pianist who impregnated and abandoned a young girl, Sarah. She hid her newborn in the soil of the Wasp family's garden. Mother discovered it, and adopted both Sarah and her child while Father was off with Admiral Peary seeking the North Pole. Then Coalhouse came looking for Sarah, but she wouldn't leave her attic room to meet him. Yet, after many a Sunday call from her suitor, she finally relented, and a wedding was in the offing when disaster struck. Their child is the third ingredient in Doctorow's melting pot; the musical ends as Tateh, Mother, and the three kids go off happily into the sunset or to California, which is pretty much the same thing.

In between comes the tragedy of Coalhouse, an updating of the famous novella by Heinrich von Kleist, *Michael Kohlhaas*, about a horse trader whom "the sense of justice turned into a robber and murderer." Coalhouse merely turns killer when racist bullies wreck his beloved Model T Ford and indirectly cause Sarah's violent death. This makes him the leader of a small band of murderous rebels.

Such a basically serious, yet also sardonic, work demands a deft book-writer, and Terrence McNally, who did well with *Kiss of the Spider Woman*, has done so again here. He lopped and chopped skillfully, and preserved all the essentials except the ironic tone. He came up with the device of having characters relate their further experiences in the third person, an alienation effect that fits in with Eugene Lee's scenic concept. Lee combines unrealistic towers on the sides of the stage with a wooden stage floor that can sprout a bit of a garden here, some boardwalk there. A life-size living room contrasts nicely with a miniature house, a full-size segment of a ship downstage with the entire ship in miniature upstage. Three-dimensional pieces fuse with computerized background images as construction smoothly embraces projection. Atlantic City is especially ravishing.

But there are oddities. Why, for instance, is Evelyn Nesbit's red velvet swing neither red nor especially velvety? Why do we switch to vaudeville for the shooting of her famous lover, the architect Stanford White, by her crazy millionaire husband, Harry K. Thaw? Why does the otherwise apt director, Frank Galati, cast a typical chorus boy as the sturdy White, and a White look-alike as the measly Thaw? Why is the murder trial turned into a burlesque sketch, and Evelyn herself into a Marilyn Monroe parody?

Elsewhere Galati's staging is persuasive, especially as abetted by

Graciela Daniele's choreography, which arises imperceptibly from the stage movement and, equally inconspicuously, subsides back into it. Add to this the jaunty costumes of Santo Loquasto, ever so slightly tongue-in-cheek, and the always painterly lighting of Jules Fisher and Peggy Eisenhauer, and you have quite a spectacle.

Stephen Flaherty has composed three very catchy ragtime numbers, but they get reprised irritatingly often: an entire song cannot act as a leitmotiv. In between, there are ballads and anthems that lack distinction and, even more, wit. Nor does his regular collaborator, Lynn Ahrens, do any better with the lyrics: they are serviceable but pedestrian, with a sprinkling of the bizarre that barely masks the commonplace. However, William David Brohn's clever orchestrations help us across many a barren spot.

Brian Stokes Mitchell would be a first-rate Coalhouse were he not too dapper and too pale. Unlike Doctorow's older, heavier, and darker-skinned man, this Coalhouse could have driven past the racist firemen without being taken for a black. As the brittle and girlish Sarah, Audra McDonald, a barreling powerhouse of a woman and singer, is all wrong, especially when she tries to act girlish with mincing steps that look like some kind of hopscotch. Mark Jacoby's ploddingly sedulous quality almost works for Father yet is finally too simplistic.

But Marin Mazzie is an altogether satisfying Mother, even with an anachronistic coating of feminism imposed on her. (Other anachronisms include a new line for Peary's black assistant.) Peter Friedman's Tateh, perhaps a shade too farcical, is nevertheless endearing; Jim Corti is a credible Houdini, and Judy Kaye a good-as-gold Emma Goldman. Steven Sutcliffe nicely conveys Mother's Younger Brother's smartness as well as benightedness; Lynnette Perry, whose part is unfortunately decimated, was probably misdirected into making Evelyn Marilyn. The children are apt enough for us to forgive their staying the same age throughout.

The restored and fused Apollo and Lyric Theaters have yielded the lovely and comfortable Ford Center for the Performing Arts; may there be many Tauruses in its future, and the fewest possible Edsels.

The Capeman;
Shopping and Fucking

The outlaw as hero is a ticklish topic, he works best when he is an honest little guy greatly wronged by the ruling class, like Kleist's Michael Kohlhaas or his American cousin, Coalhouse Walker, who already loses something by his persecutors being merely volunteer firemen. He may also score by robbing the rich to succor the poor, but Robin Hood gains a lot by being a medieval legend rather than a modern-day reality. Significantly, Billy the Kid comes off best in Eugene Loring's ballet, where the bullets are only notes in Aaron Copland's music.

But with Salvador Agrón, a.k.a. *The Capeman*, the problem intensifies. He is fact, not fiction; at age 16, he cold-bloodedly killed two young men he mistakenly thought were members of a rival gang: apprehended, he spewed out words of ugly, remorseless defiance. True, he acquired education in jail and wrote a memoir, but in the seven years left to him after release, he accomplished nothing—not so much as a bird shelter or a volume of uplifting doggerel. The only reason Paul Simon could have chosen Agrón as subject for his putative conquest of Broadway is a befuddled liberal notion of seeing him as the hapless victim of a materialistic society. Moreover, Simon, known for his leanings toward exotic musical cultures (Africa, Brazil), here chose to embrace Puerto Rico.

Could anyone have escaped hearing about the legions of directors, choreographers, transient play doctors, and famous friends who had input into the musical *The Capeman*, whose protracted birth pangs far exceeded those required to produce real-life septuplets? Alas, Paul Simon and Derek Walcott's musical may well be the most ridiculous mouse ever birthed by parturient mountains. Or, rather, more sinister than ridiculous: *The Capeman* is as much a moral fiasco as an artistic failure.

Agrón and the Vampires, a street gang led by the Umbrella Man, are shown early on shoplifting threads in a comic scene in which the hard-sell storekeepers are portrayed as grotesque capitalists, whereas the thieving youths are fun-loving con artists, apotheosized when Sal raises his arms to reveal the scarlet lining of his stolen cape as if it were the rainbow of the Covenant encircling Mount Ararat. Conversely, as the *Times* critic complained, "the pivotal stabbing… almost passes unnoticed," but didn't he realize this was meant to minimize our hero's tragic flaw: what are two little slayings in the greater schema of an $11 million Paul Simon musical?

It might help, of course, if the show showed signs of talent. Paul Simon's Latino music, even crossbred with doo-wop, carries monotony to maniacal lengths, each song about as individual as a machine-chopped slice of chorizo. The lyrics seamlessly blend Paul Simon's pop and Derek Walcott's Homeric sensibilities: but then, why shouldn't the over-inflated troubadour and the over-rated laureate of P.C. mesh serendipitously? On the one hand, the relentlessly repeated, "I was born in Puerto Rico," which is pure Simon; on the other, the no less gratingly reiterated, "Time is an endless ocean of tears," which is profoundest Walcott. And either bard could have delivered himself of the divine distich, "The barrio was just another reservation, / But the day of the revolution is coming fast" or the searing platitude, "I wrote these pages not with ink but with blood."

The reference to the reservation is triggered by Salvador's epistolary prison romance with a desert-dwelling Indian hippie, a presumably fact-based but incoherent episode that the authors throw in like a tomahawk but that lands in their faces like a boomerang. Even the tired device of showing us three Agróns crisscrossing one another—the child Salvi, the youth Sal, and the man Salvador—is enough to give agronomy a bad name.

There is little a performer can do with such threadbare material. Two popular purveyors of Latin song, the salsa king Marc Anthony and Puerto Rico's "internationally renowned singer-composer" Ednita Nazario, as Sal and his mother, Esmeralda, are further hampered by not being actors. As the middle-aged Salvador, Ruben Blades puts on his best Mount Rushmore face and moves as if in cement shoes, thereby indicating the gravity of the occasion. The only, performer who registers at all is the Umbrella Man of Renoly Santiago. Even more surprising is that neither Mark Morris, the credited choreographer, nor the sundry uncredited ones, could enliven things with some infectious dancing.

The Capeman has one thing going for it: Bob Crowley's décor. But some of the sets are too good, with their odd worm's-eye-view perspective, their contrasts of splashy Puerto Rican colors with drab Hell's Kitchen monochrome, and their winsome use of miniatures—especially a prison scene with domino-playing dummies seen vertically rather than horizontally. But such inventive embellishment, like the cape on a juvenile murderer, merely stress the exiguity under the panoply.

A no less sorry spectacle is Mark Ravenhill's hugely hyped import *Shopping and Fucking*, which may herald the advent of the author as title-writer. This paltry contrivance depends entirely on its title, after which Ravenhill is all downhill. We get the shambling pursuit of five sordid London lowlifes, one of whom, a 30-year-old homosexual druggie, has purchased two young derelicts, one male, one female, in a supermarket for £20—overpriced if you ask me. He lives with them, in his shabby quarters, in a lopsided ménage à trois. During a stay in a detox, or somewhere else, he picks up an underage male hustler, while his previous wards embark on drug pushing and phone sex. *S & F* can boast only the gratuitously graphic representation of sadomasochist buggery and anilingus.

Ravenhill has garbled such influences as Mike Leigh, David Mamet, and watered-down Joe Orton, and thrown together disjointed scenes of denatured dialogue that veers from the subliterate to the sublimely pretentious. Take this utterance of a pretend TV producer and certifiable drug lord: "Some say there is nothing. There is chaos. We are born into chaos, we exist in chaos, and finally we are released from chaos. But this is… no. This is too painful. This is too awful to contemplate. This we deny."

By way of a little heterosexual window dressing, the one female in this quinsied quincunx is made at one point—pointlessly—to strip to her waist. Were she not played by an actress I used to abhor as Jennifer Dundas, now Jennifer Dundas Lowe, I would feel sorry for the indignities she has incurred here. The show has two directors and two lighting designers, which does not make up for not having one playwright.

The Beauty Queen of Leenane

The first play by the wildly successful young Irish playwright Martin McDonagh to reach us is *The Beauty Queen of Leenane*, and it disappoints. The authentically Irish cast—Anna Manahan, Marie Mullen, Brían F. O'Byrne, and Tom Murphy—three of them from the original production, could not be better. Neither could the original director, Garry Hynes, of Galway's Druid Theater. But the play, despite traces of talent, is lopsided: a hybrid that cannot command full credence or compassion from its viewers. Its being part of a trilogy is no excuse.

Granted, blending farce and melodrama is no easy matter. It harks back to O'Casey, who himself had problems with it. We can believe the hate-filled symbiosis of 40-year-old Maureen, the desperate spinster, and her mean-spirited mother, Mag, who doesn't want to go into a home. But that in tiny Leenane, where everybody knows everybody, Pato Dooley and Maureen should not have found each other in twenty years is hard to swallow. So, too, is the Hardyesque device of the fatally undelivered letter, and its speciously contrived causes and consequences. And even if the now sane Maureen had a breakdown fifteen years ago, would she still be hallucinating?

What truly doesn't work is the mechanistic manipulation of our feelings; improbability paradoxically combined with predictability. It is, moreover, hard to care about benighted people, who can pass muster in farce, when the play veers into would-be tragedy. To the prolific McDonagh: better luck next time.

Art; Cabaret

Some aspects of modern art beg to be satirized. When Kasimir Malevich painted his *White on White*, Ad Reinhardt perpetrated his "all black" paintings, and Yves Klein, *le Monochrome*, executed his all-blue panels, the results invited skeptical irony. One need not be a yahoo to view these products—and some of the minimalist art they spawned—as nonsense. There comes a point when the experts and collectors must be defied in a chorus of "That's enough!" At such time, *philistine* becomes an honorific, and the cognoscenti deserve a taste of the jawbones of an ass.

So I sympathize with Yasmina Reza's *Art* which was the hit of Paris in 1995 and of London in 1996, and won awards in both cities. The plot is simple. Serge spends 200,000 francs on a five-by-four painting by the renowned Antrios that is all white except for some diagonal scratches. His friend Marc, who fancies Flemish painting, considers this Antrios shit, and Serge's purchase of it an insult to their friendship. He tries to enlist the third of our musketeers, Yvan, to side with him. Yvan, an overemotional and insecure young man, seems to go along with Marc's tirades. But confronted with Serge and the painting, he does what he does best: he wavers.

As the friends argue in circles and increasing vehemence, other problems surface: Yvan's doubts about his impending wedding, which his friends urge him to call off. Even the wording of the wedding invitation has stirred up interfamilial virulence. Serge reveals his contempt for Paula, Marc's wife, which gives rise to fury just short of fisticuffs. Everyone has frenzied outbursts. Again and again, the rage returns to the painting, which Serge now protectively removes, now provokingly redisplays. The scene shifts from one friend's apartment to another's, although the set—three white walls with slightly differing ornamentation—stays the same. But evenings to be spent in comradely outings are ruined: the painting threatens to turn good friends into bitter enemies.

Reza's cunning dialogue has been fluently Englished by Christopher Hampton; even so, it requires high-powered actors to animate it, and happily, it gets them. As Marc, Alan Alda puts to insidious use his ability to pester with polish. His urbanely crinkly face oozes disapproval; his querulous voice is like a fingernail at a scab. Victor Garber's dapper Serge harbors under the facade of a convivial man-about-town a defensive arrogance expressed with mounting bile. As Yvan, Alfred Molina is pure perfection. This Brit not only sounds as American as apple pie but also manages to look more French than a briard. He blows his top in a gorgeously Mount St. Helensian monologue, but he is equally splendid in his equivocations or as, with head swiveling like a tennis spectator's, he dumbly follows the challenges buzzing past him. His incomprehension is epic: other actors need something to be funny with; Molina can be a riot doing nothing.

The set by Mark Thompson is not so monochromatic as it appears at first, though it too is mostly white on white; his costumes are the last word in dark, contemporary chic. Hugh Vanstone's lighting delights in these contrasting blacks and whites. Matthew Warchus has directed sparely but tellingly. Take the long silence as three frazzled men keep reaching, from nearer or farther positions, for a plate of olives on a coffee table. This nervous nibbling becomes a dazzling piece of choreography, yet no less natural and ludicrous than most of our quotidian rituals.

I am not sure the author's ending, apt as it is, wholly persuades. But then, like the rest of the play—and like so much modern art—it is a Rorschach test, but one that is, unlike other tests, a joy to take.

The 100 intermissionless minutes feel elegantly right: anything more would be markedly less.

I have scant use for site-specific stagings. Theater should free us from limiting literalness: A play about coal miners does not call for performing underground; a drama about psychotics needs no cast of certified psychos in a genuine madhouse. The stage is privileged to deal in illusions, allowing us to gaze deeper and see more clearly from the outside looking in than we ever could mired in the mêlée. So I question converting the Henry Miller Theatre into the Kit Kat Klub for *Cabaret*, complete with poorer sight lines, buttock-bruising wooden chairs, and tables for overpriced and distracting drinks.

Otherwise, the Roundabout is to be roundly applauded for re-creating Sam Mendes's 1993 London production, even if with some diminishment. Robert Brill resuscitates a two-tiered set, part jungle gym, part bulb-bordered and crooked picture frame around the band, part plain platform with minimal and easily removable furniture backed by three ominous doors. All very functional but also eyecatching. Joe Masteroff's refurbished book emphasizes the squalor of 1930 Berlin nightlife and the bisexuality of Clifford, the writer hero. Peggy Eisenhauer and Mike Baldassari's razzle-dazzle lighting caps the razzmatazz, though I wonder whether William Ivey Long's suitably tawdry costumes need be so bedraggled: the chorines' stockings feature more holes than a Swiss cheese, more runs than Mickey Mantle could amass at his apogee.

Mendes, aided by Rob Marshall as co-director and choreographer, confirms his directorial reputation with the nightclub scenes but does less for the goings-on at Fräulein Schneider's boardinghouse. This is partly because nightclub-site-specificity thwarts boardinghouse specificity, but partly also because the writing does not allow for much character development in either the Sally Bowles-Clifford Bradshaw central affair or the secondary romance of Fräulein Schneider and Herr Schultz, her greengrocer suitor.

The major performances are all at least a mite off. Natasha Richardson is—at last!—an authentically British Sally Bowles, but she is stolid, blatant, lacking in girlish vulnerability. Both Mary Louise Wilson (Schneider) and Ron Rifkin (Schultz) have accent problems, and the delightful Miss Wilson plays a bit too much for comedy, the good Mr. Rifkin a bit too little. John Benjamin Hickey, though aptly ambiguous sexually, comes up short on whatever would draw Sally to him. As the sinister, leering Emcee, Alan Cumming (repeating his London role) is just fine except in his song "I Don't Care Much"—a questionable number written for the movie version.

The supporting cast—notably Denis O'Hare, Fred Rose, and Michele Pawk—delivers staunchly, and Mendes's idea of making the chorines double as members of the onstage band is terrific, including that final touch when they appear wearing identical Louise Brooksian Lulu wigs. Such double duty is quite an accomplishment: whether they lend a whiff of George Grosz to the orchestra or twist themselves into Marshall's burlesque choreography, these young ladies rate unstinting kudos. Shortcomings notwithstanding, this revival of the Masteroff-Kander-Ebb *Cabaret* has enough to satisfy all but the most fastidious—the kind that wouldn't stoop to a Broadway musical in the first place.

The Chairs

Eugène Ionesco was dogged by the fear of death, with which many of his plays are impregnated. But life, too, could be frightening. In a memoir, he writes: "Torn to pieces between the horror of living and the horror of dying." The tragic farce *The Chairs* concerns a nonagenarian couple, caretakers of an abandoned tower on an isolated island surrounded by stagnant water. They are ready to die, and have invited everyone conceivable to hear the Old Man's testament, which he, unskilled with words, has hired the Orator to deliver for him. The guests—all invisible presences—start coming. The Old Man chats them up while the Old Woman knocks herself out dragging in seating for them. The stage fills up with more and more empty chairs.

The Emperor himself shows up—invisibly. By this time, the accumulated chairs have become a barrier separating the couple. At last, the (visible) Orator arrives to render the apologia. But he proves a deaf-mute, burbling nonsense sounds, then scribbling meaningless messages on a board. Meanwhile, the oldsters have jumped to their separate watery graves from opposite windows. To the audible murmurs of an unseen crowd, the Orator departs. Only the chairs, jiggling slightly, remain.

The exact meaning of every detail is debatable, but the outline is clear enough. We live in terrifying isolation, companioned mostly by imaginary others. We cannot even voice our final justification. The Emperor (God) to whom it is to be presented does not exist, and the Orator (writer, historian, advocate) cannot impart it in speech or writing. The triumphant reality is that of the chairs— dumb objects proliferating all around. "The theme of the play is nothingness," Ionesco has written; "to give unreality to reality one must give reality to the unreal, until... nothingness can be heard, is made concrete." To the French critic Claude Bonnefoy, Ionesco summed up, "Total absence: chairs without people."

But around this skeleton there is much embroidery: memories, observations, philosophizing—all of it distorted to the point of absurdity. So it was right to have Martin Crimp adapt the play to today's concerns, and without changing anything substantive make the skewed topical references and preposterous puns more current than 1952 (the play's date) and more English than French, Some few changes seem ill-founded, though. Thus the Old Woman's name, Semiramis, laden with antiquity and myth, becomes Anna-Rosetta. Anna-Rosetta who?

The production, much more elaborate than previous ones, is often inspired. It adds an evocative first set, viewing the couple from the water-girt outside; it arranges the many requisite doors in two tiers, so that chairs can also tumble from above; it diversifies the shape and period of the chairs to ecumenical effect. On top of the Quay Brothers' ingenious scenery, Paul Anderson's lighting and Paul Arditti's sounds are good and eerie. Simon McBurney's staging admirably fulfills Ionesco's wish for "a real ballet with the chairs."

Geraldine McEwan's Old Woman may be a bit too singsongy, and does not quite live up to Joan Plowright's masterly performance in the London and New York premieres. But Richard Briers's would-be debonair, self-satisfied yet insecure dotard could not be more appropriately laughable or pitiful. I disapprove of the Emperor's unjustifiably visible gloves and a gratuitous final transformation by the Orator; otherwise this production incises itself indelibly on those privileged to view it.

The Judas Kiss

The exquisite irony of it! A century after his fall from grace into penal servitude, penniless exile, and premature death, Oscar Wilde is more famous and fêted than in all his years of glitter and glory. Does even a month go by without a new book, movie, or play about him, or at the very least an article of critical reappraisal? The man and his works, whom the powers that were and the public at large had condemned to instant oblivion, resurface to an insistent afterlife of endless fascination. Oscar has won: too bad he couldn't live to see it.

Among the latest tributes are the film *Wilde* and David Hare's play *The Judas Kiss*, the one rehearsing the known facts, the other trying to forge ahead. Hare invents what might have gone on at the Cadogan Hotel just before Wilde's arrest, about which a good deal is known. Also what happened in Naples—after Wilde's release and reunion with Lord Alfred Douglas (his beloved Bosie)—about which nothing very reliable is known. The play imagines what their last night and dawn together may have been.

Hare must be given credit for his omissions: he has resisted rehashing all those echoing epigrams, the stuff the cognoscenti never tire of rehearing and that reduces neophytes to helpless guffaws. As the play moves into its more revelatory second act in Italy, and Hare improvises even more freely than in the first, the end of the long affair comes into sardonic, often witty, and intermittently philosophical focus. There are some nice patches of dialogue, with Bosie acting the rather devious straight man to Oscar's now more subdued and rueful but still not unstinging sallies and wry reflections on the follies of the world and the frailty of relationships.

Act One, however familiar (even from John Betjeman's 1937 poem, which sums up the events in a mere 36 lines), manages at any rate a certain sense of urgency. Act Two has all the interesting ideas but remains static, despite some nude cavorting by Bosie with a young Neapolitan fisherman implausibly named Galileo. The able director, Richard Eyre, does his level best, but with Wilde mostly collapsed in an armchair, Galileo crouching befuddled on the bed, and Bosie scurrying skittishly but aimlessly about, things resist enlivening. It's all rather like a staged Socratic dialogue, only a little less platonic. Some of the facile jokes apropos Galileo ("See stars, did you?") and uncharacteristically raunchy lingo ("We can't live on cock!") may delight the groundlings, but are unworthy of Hare and Eyre, let alone Wilde.

Casting Liam Neeson as Wilde is a calamity. Though Oscar, by all accounts, was not effeminate, Neeson is too butch for a longshoreman. He is enormous, with a caveman's backward-sloping brow, a hawklike proboscis, and a lumbering walk. His voice is roughhewn, often a growl; his attempt at a Wildean coiffure misfires and makes him look more like a Dutch burgher or Puritan divine. When he tries for the occasional airy flippancy or minuetish caper, he is best described by the Marquess of Queensberry's card deposited at Wilde's club: "posing as a sodomite."

Against this giant, tiny Tom Hollander's frizzy-haired pixie of a Douglas is equally wrong. Here the playwright, too, falsifies, substituting for the character's imperious rages and poseurish languors a sniveling, subaltern whininess. And I seriously doubt whether Robert Ross—Wilde's most solicitous friend—was as fussily schoolmarmish as the script, rather than the capable Peter Capaldi, makes him out to be.

There are moments when the acting—as often as not of such minor characters as a hotel employee amusingly embodied by Alex Walkinshaw—takes off and the dialogue provides something to bite into. Bob Crowley's sets, though more restrained than usual, are not without allure, especially as lighted by Mark Henderson. But sorely lacking for me is the drama so well anticipated by John Webster's lines: "Thou hast led me like an heathen sacrifice, / With music and the fatal pomp of flowers, / To mine eternal ruin."

Follies

I shamefacedly admit that, like some colleagues, I did not in 1971 recognize the greatness of *Follies*. I now see that *Follies* is the kind of show irresistible to anyone who has lived long enough to fathom the meaning of aging, lost youth, mortality, and the magnificent though Pyrrhic victory of not going gentle into that good night. The show potently accumulates meaning from all our losses, from all our gallant last-ditch stands. Never mind Flo Ziegfeld, and mourn for two incomparable stars whose luster the show now subsumes: Alexis Smith and Lee Remick. Were there ever two more maturely beautiful women on our stages, more ladylike and sexy, more aglitter yet accessible, more totally theatrical and not the least bit stagy? Where are you now, Alexis and Lee, you two marvelous Phyllises of the 1971 premiere and the 1985 concert revival? You are built into the accruing glory that is *Follies*, as surely as Daphne lives in the olive tree, as Andromeda lights up the sky.

Do not for a moment think the Paper Mill Playhouse, in Millburn, New Jersey, peddles some nice but provincial, reflected-glory production for memory-chewing old-timers but small beer for newcomers. This staging has Broadway luminously written all over it, and the sooner it gets there, the better.

You remember the story, don't you? An old Ziegfeldish producer, Dimitri Weismann, throws a farewell party to past glory in the ruins of his old theater, now being torn down to become a parking lot. Entertainers and showgirls of his famed extravaganzas, along with the men they loved and/or married, show up for a final fling, and old loves reblossom among the ruins, wrecked spouses try to rebuild crumbling marriages or start new ones. The past and the present briefly co-exist in a striking double exposure: we see the two principal couples, Phyllis and Ben, Sally and Buddy, as well as various individuals as they were then and as they are now. The stage is aswirl with intermingling ghosts: those whose ghostly presence haunts the present, and those whose ghastly present bemoans and grasps at happiness past.

If there was a flaw in the original, Hal Prince production, it was that James Goldman's brilliantly conceived book allowed too much dialogue to slow down the vibrant life in Stephen Sondheim's score and Michael Bennett's choreography. The Millburn revival prunes verbiage to a muscular terseness, and gives full vent to eloquent dancing and a score of twenty hit numbers, outsparkling one another; but not really outsparkling—sharing their radiance, rather like the Milky Way.

Much depends on the right cast, and here we have seven great luminaries of yore: Kaye Ballard, Eddie Bracken, Donna McKechnie, Ann Miller, Liliane Montevecchi (less solipsistic than usual), Phyllis Newman, and Donald Saddler. They act, sing, and dance with untarnishable bravura and mastery that should speak equally loud to established fans and astounded new audiences.

But the newer or new performers mostly hold their own. It would be hard to find fault with Jo Ann Cunningham, Michael Gruber, Vahan Khanzadian, Natalie Mosco, Carol Skarimbas, and several others. Especially impressive is the Phyllis of Dee Hoty, who ably wears the mantle of Alexis Smith and Lee Remick, than which there is no higher praise. For the London revival, Phyllis's terrific number. "The Story of Lucy and Jessie," was dropped for Diana Rigg, who couldn't dance it, and replaced by "Ah, but Underneath," nice but overshadowed by earlier striptease numbers in *Pal Joey* and *Gypsy*. For the elegant Miss Hoty, the original should be restored.

Two further problems are the actors playing Ben and Buddy, the former collegiate stage-door Johnnies who married Phyllis and Sally, respectively. Ben, a writer, was initially Sally's lover, and Buddy, a super-salesman, must now watch Ben and Sally gravitate toward each other again. The sophisticated Ben should be played by the current Buddy, Tony Roberts, whose lack of dancing skills makes him less fit for a part calling for a hoofer like Dick Van Dyke. And that fine singer Laurence Guittard does not fully convey the rivenness of Ben. So their deeply human opposites, Donna McKechnie and Dee Hoty, are not matched.

Michael Anania has designed very good sets, though they do not quite equal the evocative eeriness of Boris Aronson's originals. Gregg Barnes's costumes are suitably grand, Mark Stanley's lighting incandesces, and Jerry Mitchell comes as close to Michael Bennett as any rethinking choreographer can come to what was perfection. Robert Johanson's staging keeps it all beautifully astir, and Jim Coleman and Toni Helm take ample care of the musical end. Which brings us back to Sondheim, whose supreme masterpiece this is—a kind of *King Lear* of musical comedy. In a just and wiser world, it is not *Les Miz*, *Phantom*, and *Cats* that would be forever; instead, there would be one sold-out theater playing *Follies* always. *Always.*

The Dying Gaul

I approached *The Dying Gaul* with unhappy memories of Craig Lucas's other plays but, to my astonishment, found this one tightly constructed—not just grabbing our attention but also keeping it.

Robert, the semiautobiographical protagonist, has lost his long-time lover to AIDS and is offering a script based on the relationship to Jeffrey, a film producer, in his Hollywood office. Jeffrey, though married to Elaine and a father, is really bisexual, but has until now satisfied his same-sex needs in fly-by-night encounters with inferiors on the sly. Unbeknown to him, Elaine is not fooled. Falling suddenly and passionately for Robert, he offers him a million for his screenplay, and wants only a small rewrite: turning the central gay relationship into a straight one. Robert is deeply shocked but, with promises of future freedom, grudgingly starts revising.

He also becomes Jeffrey's lover and a frequent visitor at Jeffrey and Elaine's home. The wife, sensing danger of losing her husband, finds Robert in a chat room on the Internet. (Improbable but not impossible given some strong clues she has.) Robert and Elaine become cyberpals, and Elaine resorts to a cheap trick. Without quite saying so, she implies that she is Robert's dead lover come back in this form to guide and protect. When Robert ascertains that the friend is not his therapist, Foss, playing games, he begins to fall: who else could know so many intimate things about him?

The play now turns wildly melodramatic, though still less so than *Cymbeline*, and not without a few shreds of credibility remaining. A good part of its efficacy comes from the staging by Mark Brokaw, probably the best young director around.

Except for the Foss of Robert Emmet Lunney, who hasn't much to work with, the other parts are handsomely done. Tony Goldwyn may make his bisexuality a trifle too obvious as an otherwise spirited Jeffrey, but Linda Emond is paradigmatic as a plain woman unfulfilled in her marriage yet hell-bent to hang in—until she finds out more than she wants. Tim Hopper is a fine Robert but ought to be as good-looking as Craig Lucas to make Jeffrey's instant infatuation believable.

I am not sure, though, that Jeffrey would use language as crass as "I want to suck you until there's not a drop of juice left," "What is that warm eight-inch dick doing right now?" and more of the like. For the rest, Lucas's dialogue is crisp and effective. Amid Allen Moyer's minimal yet suggestive scenery and Christopher Akerlind's caressing lighting, the lure of Los Angeles permeates the proceedings. *The Dying Gaul* is a famous late-Roman statue, but I shan't burden you with its relevance here, now that an unjustly carping *Times* review has caused the dying of the entire show with galling haste.

Side Man

Whatever points the Roundabout loses for its Shavian charade, it recoups for rescuing *Side Man* from vanishing with its brief downtown run. Warren Leight's comedy-drama is about the itinerant jazz musicians known as sidemen, who, during the big-band era, provided the needed backup. They could play anything asked of them, and were on the road most of the time, except when—regularly—they hit the unemployment line. It is all seen through the memory of Clifford, who at 30 remembers the doomed marriage of Gene, his trumpet-player father, and Terry, his mother, driven to drink and hysteria by her husband's neglect of everything but his precious horn.

There are three themes: the unhappy marriage that, from early childhood on, the son who loves both his parents tries to keep together; the jocular camaraderie of the sidemen, with their devil-may-care living and loving; and the passion of all concerned for a music condemned to fall victim to downward-changing tastes. Gene's friends and colleagues are the drug-addicted Jonesy, the lisping and nerdish Ziggy, and the womanizing Al. At their favorite hangout, the Rainbow Lounge, they spar with the waitress, the tough but likable Patsy, who beds trumpet player after trumpet player, waiting on all but waiting long for none. The play roams freely between 1953, when Gene and Terry met, married, and were briefly a couple; and 1985, when, split wide apart, Terry has been going through suicide attempts and hospitalizations and Gene has become more and more besotted with his music and blindly staggers on.

Leight knows this world inside out, and he writes in a Hemingwayesque style unusual in drama. "No more nonets and tentets," Clifford sums up about the jazzmen. "No more 60 weeks on the road. No more jam sessions till dawn in the Cincinnati zoo. When they go, that'll be it... a 50-year blip on the screen." The elegiac tone is laced with wry humor and concludes with the ironic stage image of the music coming up as the lights fade forever on this brave old world.

Michael Mayer has again directed consummately in the larger Broadway house without noticeable loss of intimacy. One sequence will stay in every memory: three horn players listening to the tape of a dead fourth one, as music soars to the rafters and burrows into their beings. The three friends' faces and fingers twitch along with the blue notes while Kenneth Posner's lighting, which has worked miracles all along, sculpts this trio of votaries into a monument to unanimous, enraptured surrender.

Frank Wood offers an unforgettable portrait of Gene, who makes his son "wonder how he could sense everything while he was blowing, and almost nothing when he wasn't." As Clifford, Robert Sella superbly draws you into his web of humor, intelligence, and compassion for his embattled parents; when his patience finally shatters, we too are shaken to our very foundations. Angelica Tom is a splendidly unsentimental Patsy, and as the other three horn players, Michael Mastro, Kevin Geer, and Joseph Lyle Taylor couldn't be bettered. Too bad that Wendy Makkena is nowhere near up to the unavailable Edie Falco she replaced as Terry: she does not age convincingly, she overdoes the lower-class accent, and she does not get you in the gut. Even so, *Side Man* is a must.

Twelfth Night

Nicholas Hytner seems to have directed not *Twelfth Night* but its subtitle, *What You Will*. He has staged a production in which anything goes, although Jeanine Tesori's music, going from inappropriate to intolerable, hardly evokes Cole Porter. Like the costumes, speech, and acting, it ranges meretriciously all over time and place, whether to capture the kudos of young, know-nothing audiences or out of sheer anomie, I lack the psychiatric credentials to determine.

Shakespeare having set the action fantastically on the seacoast of Illyria, a country that no longer existed, Hytner decided to go him one better by driving the actors to wading, diving, tumbling into the sundry pools with which the stage is littered. On top of that, an arbitrary thunderstorm elicits near-inundation from above. All this comes as a prodigal act of supererogation: merely confronted with Shakespeare's poetic diction and iambic pentameter, few cast members manage to keep their heads above water. Yet what finally sinks the production is not so much its lagoons as its lacunae—in logic, literacy, and common sense.

Not quite a total loss, though. There are a few sound, waterproof elements, and the last ten or so minutes, when Hytner shakes off whatever demons from Peter Brook to Peter Sellars had him hagridden, are quite lovely. Let's start with the great Bob Crowley's fabulous folly of a set.

From Monet's lily ponds to the Zuider Zee, from Venice to Xanadu, everything is here in ever-shifting perspective. From miniature swimming pools to far-meandering piers made of planking. Suddenly sprouting palazzos, a baroque lighthouse seen variously from afar and nearby, and innumerable suspended lights that rise by modern magic, all is there except that useful modicum of consistency.

Conversely, Catherine Zuber's costumes fail even aesthetically.

They jumble periods and continents as if shuffling playing cards, but even taken one by one, they belong in the circus, burlesque, or a male strip joint. Countess Olivia appears in progressively tawdrier and skimpier attire until, emerging from a pool in drenched white garb, she looks all but naked. Duke Orsino, not content with steadily keeping his chest bared, strips to a jockstrap for a dip; even when he goes formally wooing, he lets a third of his gold-chain-bedizened pectorals hang out. The rest of the fashions extend from Armani to Zouave.

On the other hand, Natasha Katz's lighting is the cat's meow from lyrical to dazzling, although here, too, there is a certain arbitrariness about when light ripples reflected from the waves will gambol on the backdrop, and when not. Still, if lightbulbs were tulip bulbs, Holland would be eclipsed. Joey McKneely's dances are relaxingly inoffensive; and there are three fine performances, all by older actors.

Max Wright offers, with exquisite timing, not the conventional whippersnapper of an Aguecheek, but a middle-aged, thinning-haired stumblebum, a withering and blundering much-defeated hoper-against-hope, as touching as he is entertaining. As his mentor and nemesis, the drunken Sir Toby, Brian Murray is irresistible. Whether bloatedly grandiose or delectably deflated, he exudes roguish, anarchic life, embattled or embottled, able to charm (since there are no birds out of the trees) fish out of the seas. Philip Bosco goes well beyond any Malvolio known to me in variety and depth. Starting as a typical pompous, snootily nasal bureaucrat, he fatuously melts into a prancing, senescence-defying swain easily led by the nose. The stages by which he tries to rejuvenate himself are delineated with perfection, yet the result is more than just laughable—all too human. Moving in his downfall, sadly dilapidated in his disgrace, Bosco delivers a threateningly Parthian shot that should leave no one unshuddering.

Among the younger actors, Amy Hill is a perky and properly pesky Maria, though the part does not call for a Rosie-and-Roseanne clone. Julio Monge is a suitably virile Antonio if a Puerto Rican accent does not disgruntle your ears; as the other sea captain, Paul O'Brien is hearteningly straightforward.

David Patrick Kelly is an assured singing clown if you want a proletarian rather than a poetic Feste. After them, though, it is the deluge. Paul Rudd's insufferable Orsino just manages to be, in his better moments, merely obnoxious. Lolling around like an affected lounge lizard, mouthing words as if they were pastilles, preening and posturing as if auditioning for a Calvin Klein ad, he confuses Illyria with Chippendale's.

As Viola, Helen Hunt is as bad as it gets. She wears a permanently befuddled expression, scrunches up her eyes as though under a barrage of grapefruits, and always leads with her head as if to butt her lines into an enemy goal. Her delivery is a tuneless singsong, and whereas some Violas have trouble passing for a boy, this one has problems reminding us she's a woman. No less ludicrous is the Olivia of Kyra Sedgwick, though here the heavy directorial hand is more guiltily evident. She behaves largely like a sideshow freak, with double-jointed contortions, unhinged crouches and leaps, grimaces unlimited, and fishwifely squeals and yelps—and this, mind you, from a supposedly frosty, aristocratic beauty in unthawable mourning. In a production in which unlikely and painfully protracted smoochings proliferate, her near-rape of Sebastian takes the cake—if not the ale as well.

A sorry spectacle, too, is Rick Stear's Sebastian. Granted, he looks condignly mistakable for his sister, and tries, I imagine, to sound subduedly like her; he still gives a waterlogged performance. "Let me sleep," he says at one point, and he does so pretty much throughout. Skipp Sudduth's Fabian, outrageously costumed, mistakes grossness for comedy. And gross is the word for the musical prelude and entr'acte, in which the already jarring music competes with the blaring boogie and salsa bands of the Midsummer Night Swing in the plaza to which exiting ballet and concertgoers are rudely subjected.

But in the last ten or fifteen minutes, a sea change takes place. Non-verse-speakers do not exactly wax adept but cease to be grating, everyone acts normal, movements turn apt and comely, actors are tastefully deployed across the vast playing area, and lights and shadows assume added meaning as winners are highlighted and losers slink away.

Collected Stories

When Donald Margulies writes at the top of his form, he is as good as any playwright going: *Sight Unseen* belongs in every anthology of American drama. *Collected Stories* is not quite that powerful, but even second-best Margulies is something to sink your teeth into and chew on for a long time after. If only this year's revival at the Lucille Lortel came within shouting distance of last year's premiere at the Manhattan Theatre Club.

The problem begins with the star. Uta Hagen always struck me as the poor man's idea of an actress in the grand style: the gestures, the vocal gymnastics, the regal manner, but not the heart—or soul—of the matter. At 79, she is a prodigy of youthful energy in hoisting a hefty bundle of old tricks. A good acting teacher, her manner of performing is didactic, overemphatic (even in cutenesses), demonstrative rather than internalized.

Here she is Ruth Steiner, a successful short-story writer and creative-writing teacher, in her Greenwich Village apartment giving a tutorial to a promising but overawed graduate student, Lisa Morrison. In six scenes, we observe their growing relationship. Lisa insinuates herself into Ruth's life by becoming her secretarial assistant, then disciple and protégée, and finally friendly rival, as she in turn publishes a volume of acclaimed short stories. She even surpasses her mentor by publishing a novel, one that appropriates Ruth's lengthy love affair with Delmore Schwartz, so secret and sacred to Ruth that she herself never wrote about it.

But Ruth made two mistakes. She taught Lisa that a fiction writer must take her material wherever she finds it, and she gave her a detailed, though incomplete, account of her years with the much older, disintegrating poet. Without permission. Lisa has turned this into a novel; Ruth feels betrayed as writer, teacher, and friend. Their showdown is the impassioned climactic scene.

In trying to make his play more comic and dramatic, Margulies sometimes overplays his hand. The opening, as Ruth shouts instructions to Lisa beneath her window and the girl mishears everything, makes no sense, given a third-floor apartment on a quiet Village street. Next, Lisa talks less like a Columbia grad student writer than like a bubblehead ("Oh, my God, that makes like so much sense!"), and Ruth is too crusty-quirky by half, though three quarters of that is in the performance. Miss Hagen forces her voice into squeaks and growls, and slurs out enough schwas to dumbfound a phoneticist.

Yet the play becomes gripping, despite matching exaggeration by the Lisa of Lorca Simons, an unsuccessful Brooke Shields clone, and mighty overdirection by William Carden, a former Hagen student, now artistic director of her HB Playwrights Foundation & Theatre. In fact, most of the collaborators on this production are part of the

HB cottage industry, and on the night I attended, even the claqueurs seemed to be HB products. The tacky and unimaginative scenery is by Ray Recht, HBPF's resident designer: would the artistic Ruth have such execrable motel furniture, and would her beloved books lie strewn about like the dead on a battlefield? And must the poles holding up the set be so nakedly exposed, and a cliché backdrop of neighboring brick façades distract our eyes from the actors?

But Margulies's writing scores undeterred, as, for example, in the scene where Lisa reads from her novel to an enthusiastic crowd at the Y. Her prose is cleverly reminiscent of that by another Morrison, Toni, as it hovers between the true and the trashy, to the delight of the assembled culture vultures. Again, in the concluding agon, the playwright gives each woman strong arguments, and neither triumphs, forcing us to sort out the rights and wrongs of the case for ourselves.

Alas, even the ill-chosen piano music between scenes is overloud and irritating. And when you recall last year's fine MTC version, you wish this seedy revival had never happened.

Cymbeline

Shakespeare's *Cymbeline* does not lack for distinguished naysayers. Dr. Johnson refused to "waste criticism upon [its] unresisting imbecility." Shaw perceived it as "for the most part stagy trash of the lowest melodramatic order," and even such a modern scholar as Derek Traversi found it "a strangely incoherent and incomplete performance."

The plot has three strands. First, the refusal of Imogen, the English King Cymbeline's daughter, to marry the cloddish Cloten, son of her wicked, scheming stepmother; her secret marriage to the consequently banished commoner Posthumus; and the many ordeals before the spouses are happily reunited. Second, the story of the king's two sons, whom Belarius, an unjustly banished lord, abducted as toddlers, to live as hunters in a Welsh mountain cave, and how the trio, through heroism in war, found their way back into royal grace. Third, Cymbeline's refusal to pay tribute to Rome, and his victorious war against it, into which most of the play's characters are variously drawn.

But the most famous aspects of the play are two. The banished

Posthumus's wager with Iachimo, an Italian gentleman, that the latter could not seduce his wife, and the low trick—hiding in a trunk in Imogen's bedchamber—whereby Iachimo makes it look that he succeeded: and the scene where Imogen, in a drugged sleep and presumed dead, is buried next to the decapitated Cloten, who is wearing Posthumus's clothes and lacks that useful identifier, a head. She wakes, thinks the trunk her husband's, and despairs. (Clearly, a heroine with a trunk problem.) This scene is hardest to stage, and the test of any production. Andrei Serban's Central Park mounting roundly flunks that test.

The scene is played, like just about everything here, for belly laughs. The slow dragging on of Cloten's corpse, its clumsy burial under a few scattered flowers (with Imogen not rating even that much cover), Imogen's mistaking the cadaver amid comic screams and with leaps befitting a demented springbok, are naturally taken by the audience as a huge joke. But this, like so much else here, is selling Shakespeare short.

Too bad. Entering the Delacorte Theater, we are greeted by the delightful scenery of Mark Wendland. A grove of superb trees frames a lush oval lawn, with a pit of inviting white sand at its center, and therein a plinth to sit or stand on. Bordering this to our left is a picturesque river suitable for wading; in the back, the illuminated Belvedere Castle and all the Central Park trees. As ravishingly lighted by Michael Chybowski—with swirling mists to dance on the light beams—a fairy-tale wonderland is conjured up. Marina Draghici's costumes generally enhance the enchantment; bizarre but cannily persuasive. The only false notes are Cloten's mop of flaming punk hair and Elizabeth Swados's music: okay when it merely pings, no way when it swings into extended action.

Cymbeline, though by no means a tragedy, as its first editors would have had it, is a tragicomic romance in which Jupiter and his eagle appear, and laughter and horror chase each other to a conciliatory finish. To turn it into lumbering burlesque may tickle the groundlings, but does not, as Serban put it in a recent interview, enable them "to see life on a cosmic as well as social level." He has the daffy idea of making Iachimo turn into Jupiter with a slightly different delivery and a shogun costume, to show that he was not a villain but a divine instrument to make Posthumus appreciate Imogen more. Yet how much more appreciation than exile for her sake is needed? And though Jupiter might change himself into a swan or bull to indulge his Clintonian appetites, it is unlikely he would turn devil's advocate just to enable Liev Schreiber, as Iachimo, to give us a Mandy Patinkin impersonation. The Iachimo-Jupiter combo, even with a river at hand, does not wash.

That river perhaps taking a miscue from the current watery *Twelfth Night* overacts ferociously. A busybody of water, it is everyone's wading pool and doubles, with a plank across it, as Imogen's precarious water bed. This makes Iachimo's quasi rape into a hip-deep dip and his jotted-down survey of the nonexistent bedroom furniture around Imogen sheer nonsense. Water sports abound, and, on a rather cool night, I worried when half the cast, as the Roman army, had to stay semi-submerged for a nasty quarter-hour or so. I worried even more when Stephanie Roth Haberle, seven and a half months pregnant and romping about as Imogen, threatened to turn the stage from gymnasium into gynaeceum, and have us all partake of her premature parturition.

Almost all performances badly misfire, some apparently even without the benefit of Serban's misdirection. Thus Robert Stanton not only cretinizes Cloten but also updates him by four centuries. Jarringly playing the mother of the chalky-pale Stanton is the black actress Hazelle Goodman, who camps atrociously and vainly struggles to sound Shakespearean. Philip Goodwin turns Pisanio into a bandy-legged, slow-witted, shambling clown. As Imogen, Haberle, when not airborne, grimaces and strikes overzealous attitudes; Michael Hall, her Posthumus, is all posturing and rant. Frank Raiter dodders identically in two different roles, and Jacob Smith, though quite nice as the Child, is pushed by Serban (who invented the part) into the most inappropriate situations, turning him into a nuisance.

In these circumstances, passable acting by George Morfogen, Herb Foster, and especially Liev Schreiber looms larger than it is. But there is also unimpeachable work from Randall Duk Kim as Belarius, the charming Mia Yoo in the tiny part of Helen, and, above all, Thom Sesma, who makes Caius Lucius, the Roman general, a commanding and compelling figure. At times, when Serban's visual sense holds up, we get pleasant groupings and fetching bits of choreography. At others, as during the laughable stick fights devised by J. Steven White, poseurish pictorialism turns infantile.

A few seasons ago, at the Public, we had Joanne Akerlaitis's *Cymbeline* with bicycles; last spring, at BAM, Adrian Noble and the Royal Shakespeare Company brought us their drably pedestrian one; and now this gaudy gallimaufry. Amid such a clash of *Cymbelines*, the

play's status remains a problem that I, for one, am in no hurry to
see resolved.

Communicating Doors

A devislishly cunning prestidigitator, this Alan Ayckbourn! In most
of his works, he plays brain-teasing games with time, space, and
personality, which dizzyingly reverse themselves in his cat's-cra-
dling hands. In *Communicating Doors* (1994), the forty-ninth of
his 53 plays, he combines three genres: the drawing-room comedy,
the thriller, and the time-tripping fantasy. He manages to get them
roisterously into one another's hair, exactly as entangled as he wants
them at any skittish moment.

We are in the same Regal Hotel suite in 2018, 1998, and 1978. In
the civil-war-torn London of the future, Poopay, a dominatrix, has
been summoned to the suite, ostensibly to provide the old, dying
Reece with a last thrill. Reece is terrified of his sinister business
partner, Julian, and really wants Poopay only to witness his signed
confession. In it, he tells how, with Julian as his executioner, he
contrived the demise of his second wife, Ruella, in 1998, and how,
in 1978, he married his first wife, Jessica, largely for her money, only
to have Julian, in due time, dispatch her too. When Julian cottons
on to Reece's game in 2018, Poopay's life also may be forfeit.

But this is no standard hotel suite. Its communicating doors to
the next suite are a whirling time machine with which first Ruella,
then Poopay, can time-travel, though each of them can only go
twenty years back and forth. What the two women—wary a while,
then chummily conspiratorial—struggle to achieve is to change history: to undo two murders, which, given Jessica's initial obtuseness,
and Reece and Julian's deadly schemes, takes some doing. Not to
mention that history is not overeager to turn into Silly Putty.

Don't expect me to go into the plot's elaborate machinery, both
trippy and tricky, but know that, except for defying subsequent
rational explanation, all works absorbingly while you watch. In Ian
Watson's charming book, *Conversations With Ayckbourn* (revised
1988), the playwright tells his interviewer, "When you warp time
on stage, you're warping time for an audience as well as for the
actors." Sure enough, we get drolly and anxiously involved in the
revolving doors of time. For wouldn't we all want to dip into the

past to rewrite our roles in it? Is it fair that the first draft should also be the final one?

Of course, none of this would work if our author weren't as line-by-line funny as he is overarchingly clever, if David Gallo hadn't designed a titillating set that Donald Holder has bespangled with mischievous lights, if Jess Goldstein hadn't cheekily dressed the characters to kill and be killed, and if Christopher Ashley's direction didn't so neatly espouse both thrills and spills, climaxing in a balcony scene to make Romeo and Cyrano envious. And if the actors didn't connect as niftily as those communicating doors.

Mary-Louise Parker's Poopay goes well beyond the whore with the heart of gold into the dominatrix with the soul of sunshine. Poopay ("It's French for doll," she proudly lets on) comes on as a platinum-bobbed, Cockney, black-leather barbed doll. Soon, though, her wig comes off and her carapace cracks to reveal a scared little girl. But she quickly grows into a woman of action, the cracking whip dropped for crackling wit, as wry humor and daredevil resourcefulness elevate her to heroic status. She is ably assisted by the Ruella of Patricia Hodges, a ballsy sophisticate, and the Jessica of Candy Buckley, a ditsy millionairess. They evolve into a beguilingly spunky trio, with Miss Parker rightly the mistress of revels. Few women, and no men, will leave without failing in love with her.

David McCallum provides the Regal Hotel with a house dick consistently dickheaded through five decades, and prodigally eliciting laughter. Just the knowing way in which he misreads the women's alliance as "lesbianic" is worth a good roar. Gerrit Graham is a suitably hissable Julian, and only Tom Beckett is not quite up to the many sides and ages of Reece. No matter: this canny concoction soars as Ayckbourn remains unfailingly airborne.

Wit

Can a play be made out of the last hours of a professor of literature dying of ovarian cancer? A play that hinges on a close reading of Donne's *Holy Sonnets*? That, without slighting its seriousness, sees the comedy in dying? No? Think again: Margaret Edson, with her firstling *Wit*, has managed it, and more.

Vivian Bearing, Ph.D., is a tough, brilliant, and witty professor of

English at an unnamed university. Diagnosed with ovarian cancer in its final stage, she becomes a prized patient at the University Hospital. She is given eight months of intensive chemotherapy, a slim chance of reprieve, and an excellent opportunity to provide medicos with ruthless experimentation. The play is a battle of wits: the dubious know-how of the physicians against the wit (in both the modern sense and the old one of wisdom) of Vivian supported by Donne's metaphysical poetry.

We meet Vivian Bearing as an inpatient, her hairless head in a red baseball cap, her body in a hospital gown, her feet bare. In and out of bed, she enacts or narrates the battle for life, and the scarcely less scary battle of the Ph.D. vs. the M.D. There is head doctor Kelekian, who might as well be Dr. Overbearing, to whom Vivian Bearing is just a guinea pig. There is his assistant, young Dr. Posner, who once took a course on Donne with Bearing and obtained a hard-won A-minus. But the humanities have left him with scant respect for humanity, buried under the inhumanities of medicine. And then there is nurse Susie Monahan, a well-meaning airhead. Asked whether a shot is a soporific, she replies, "I don't know about that, but it sure makes you sleep." Yet it is she who redeems the hospital gang from total lack of empathy.

For example, inpatient Bearing is routinely questioned by Dr. Posner: "What do you do for exercise?" Answer, "Pace." "Are you having sexual relations?" Answer, "Not at the moment." And so on. She reflects, "Having a former student give you a pelvic exam was thoroughly degrading." And further: "I wish I had given him an A." But *Wit* is about a lot more. About academia, both students and teachers, including such purblind scholars as Dr. Ashford, whose research assistant Vivian once was. About fathers and daughters. About the profound difference between having and not having a sense of humor. About the not unprofound one between *can* and *may*. About the consolations of a life dedicated to the study of poetry.

And about something greater yet. In his *Fifth Prebend Sermon*, Donne says, "Though there be a difference between *timor* and *terror* [fear and terror], yet the difference is not so great but that both may befall a good man." *Wit* may not provide an airtight answer to the fear of dying, but it does arm you against the terror of hospitals and their torturers. It is a dazzling and humane play you will remember till your dying day, and especially then, thanks also to a near-flawless production.

First, Kathleen Chalfant, a Vivian of power and vulnerability,

commanding intelligence and compelling irony. Visualize the dedication of an actress shaving her head for a role, not to mention
further heroism I won't reveal here. Imagine overwhelming effects
by the subtlest vocal emphases or a roll of the eyeballs. Picture
a perfect amalgam of armored intellect and naked feeling. When
Chalfant gallantly removes her cap, her glabrous head radiates a
glorious halo. And, last but not least, she does not, like most people,
mispronounce the word joust.

Add a supporting cast in which all, and Alec Phoenix in particular, shine; lighting by Michael Chybowski to stir the soul; sparing
but bone-chilling sound by David Van Tieghem; capital direction
by Derek Anson Jones, etc., etc. And don't miss the final irony:
Margaret Edson teaches elementary school in Atlanta. For this play
alone, she should be handed the Harvard English department.

Matthew Bourne's Swan Lake

Perhaps the greatest ballet of all time, Ivanov and Petipa's *Swan Lake*,
to Tchaikovsky's music, has for over a century been the apotheosis of
death-defying, romantic, heterosexual love. Through trial and error,
Prince Siegfried wins the love of Odette, queen of the swans—girls
cygnified by a wicked sorcerer—and after some lapses and tribulations is united with her in life or death, depending on tinkerings
with the choreography. The great prima ballerina Galina Ulanova described *Swan Lake* as "the most beautiful ballet you could imagine."
But could you also imagine it as a danced homosexual melodrama
with semi-nude male swans, a seedy nightclub scene, the outing of
a closeted homosexual prince, a palace ball with a pistol-toting final
shootout, an insane-asylum sequence, and similar absurdities?

You couldn't. But the choreographer Matthew Bourne could, in
what is now, all too aptly, touted as *Matthew Bourne's Swan Lake*.
Not even poor, closeted-homosexual Pyotr Ilyich would claim it as
his. The set, by Lez Brotherston, suitably suggests an ornate, tiled
bathhouse, inhabited by a mama's-boy princeling who grows up
into a mother-dominated prince. The story, with flashbacks and
wet-dream sequences, tells about his fatal affair with what now adds
new meaning to the term *swan queen*, and ends in a way open to
various interpretations.

The homosexualization of great heterosexual love stories proceeds apace. *Romeo and Juliet* has been converted into *R&J* with a four schoolboy cast; there have been several all-male *As You Like It*s (and please, don't tell us again about Shakespeare using boy actors—under duress); etc. Most of this, characteristically, of British origin. I have no objection to homosexual ballets, whether campy or not, as long as they are new and so conceived; they should not, like cuckoos' eggs, be smuggled into the nests of other birds, notably swans.

Moreover, among the many rethinkings of *Swan Lake* I have seen (most notably Balanchine's), none was as choreographically impoverished as Bourne's. I wonder whether we are now to look forward to *Sleeping Beauty* with an Aurelius, *Giselle* with a Gilbert, and *Les Sylphides* with all-male sylphs.

This said, the music is still lovely even in David Cullen's orchestration; some of the Brotherston scenery and costumes, however inapposite, impress; and there is solid dancing from the entire company, headed by Adam Cooper in what used to be the Odette/Odile role but turns now, in Act Two, into a black-clad bisexual ruffian, servicing equally the prince, the queen mother, and sundry others. The most ineffectually effete choreography comes, expectably, in the second-act numbers where men still dance with women, a veritable embarrassment of glitches. My personal advice to Matthew Boume is "Go jump in a lake"; to the spectator, Alexander Pope's "Yet let not each gay turn thy rapture move."

Corpus Christi

I hope I need not rehearse for you the melodrama that preceded the coming of Terrence McNally's *Corpus Christi*, a retelling of the Christ story in modern Texas terms, with Jesus and his disciples a group of young homosexuals, and Jesus and Judas lovers? Death threats, cancellation, reinstatement—the preproduction story roughly parallels that of its protagonist.

Well, *Corpus Christi* (named after the Texas town where McNally was raised and most of the action takes place) is neither as good as its author probably thinks it is, nor as bad as its assailants have, sight unseen, proclaimed it.

It falls between two stools, or, more accurately, tries to sit on both simultaneously. It could have been a story about a cult in modern Texas and let certain parallels gradually suggest themselves (Play

A). Or it could have been a Bible story in contemporary language, with a special angle (Play B). Instead, it shuttles between A and B, doing full justice to neither.

Personally, I prefer Play A, where McNally can be sassy, irreverently witty, and mischievous to his heart's content. There is plenty of that here, as when young Jesus, haunted by the sound of the cross being nailed together, asks Mary, "Do you ever hear hammering?" and she answers, "Your father is a carpenter. Of course I hear hammering." Or when God, after conversing with his son, announces He is leaving, at which Jesus remonstrates, "You are supposed to be everywhere all the time," and is told, "That is a very big misunderstanding."

But there is also what can only happen in Play B, notably a crucifixion that is both literal and campy, painful and irritating. Also other things that don't wash in Texas terms, and the dichotomy hurts. And then there is the homosexual element, undoubtedly disturbing to the orthodox but presented tastefully, without sensationalism. This much freedom must be granted a serious playwright and, though it may elicit all sorts of subsequent criticism, does not warrant prejudging, bomb threats, and wholesale demonstrations.

The scenery is designed with clever minimalism by Loy Arcenas and is inspiredly lit by Brian MacDevitt. David Van Tieghem and Drew McVety have provided vivid sound and delicate music (mostly for solo violin or guitar), and Joe Mantello has directed fluidly and understatedly. The actors, for the most part, do not get much of a chance, but some of them do well enough with what they are given. Michael Hall's Peter amusingly doubles as the Virgin Mary, and McVety not only makes nice music but also enacts an amusingly easygoing Matthew. I have my doubts about Anson Mount's too bland Jesus and Josh Lucas's too grubby Judas; the others remain a pleasant enough blur.

Killer Joe

Poor plays are unfortunately the staple of our theater and *Killer Joe* is as poor as they come. But it is also something worse than that: obnoxious. Written by Tracy Letts, an actor (always a danger sign), it revels in the stupidity or brutishness of four of its characters and the calculating evil of the fifth. Among them, they commit or cause to be committed five murders (including matricide and uxoricide) for money that only one of them desperately needs. Yet we are to laugh all the way at either the dumbness or the nastiness, and view the entire thing as a hoot.

It certainly deserves to be hooted, rather than applauded and cheered as it was when I attended, proving that audiences can be as derailed as playwrights. This is a trailertrash play, a genre of which we've had a fair number, but sprinkled with some Sam Shepard for ostensible cachet, as if much of Shepard weren't a lost cause, too.

In a twinkling, the Smith family in their trailer on the outskirts of Dallas decide to have father Ansel's ex-wife, Adele, now living with one Rex, offed for her $50,000 insurance, for which purpose son Chris has enlisted Killer Joe Cooper, a police detective specializing in such jobs. His fee is 25 grand; the rest, divided among drug-pushing Chris; his younger sister, the sleepwalking Dottie who dreams of modeling; old man Ansel; and his considerably younger second wife, Sharla, would leave them a measly $6,250 each.

It is not clear what sins merited Adele's expendability, but the deal is off when Joe demands payment up front. But then, having met the 20-year-old virgin Dottie, he proposes a "retainer," which means staying on as the strangely abstracted girl's lover. I will spare you the lurid developments, but will mention that the play has more loose ends and inconsistencies than you can count without an abacus, and that its crude sexuality, coarse humor, and sensationalistic violence form an unholy ménage à trois, An occasional line does hit home, e.g., "A normal person is just someone you don't know real well." More often, though, we get things like Ansel's comment on Sharla's spraying perfume on her crotch, "When you've done fumigating the Gates of Hell…"

On George Xenos's aptly observed set, and under Wilson Millam's suitably trashy direction, Amanda Plummer (Sharla) is acutely believable, and Sarah Paulson (Dottie) manages even to be touching in places. Mike Shannon (Chris) goes heavy on the mutter and mumble, and Marc A. Nelson (Ansel) is rather colorless. Scott Glenn is a properly sinister Joe, but would the character be quite that smooth, sophisticated, and laid-back?

What amazes me is that *Killer Joe* has scored in both Edinburgh and London, and been translated into seven languages. Does this betoken widespread stultification, or is it that Europeans gloat with schadenfreude each time America is presented as thoroughly abysmal?

Footloose

Impossible though it is to finger the worst musical ever—the competition is too fierce—no list of the ten worst should forgo *Footloose*. If there is anything worse than a kick in the teeth or testicles, it is the kick in the intelligence this show provides. Of course, not even *Footloose* can manage consistent imbecility; some high points are merely inept, insipid, and indescribably boring, But idiocy never lags far behind.

Footloose is based on a dismal little 1984 movie that tried to cash in on a vogue of films for teenagers, and boasted at least a magnetic performance from Kevin Bacon. Written by Dean Pitchford, writer of the musical *Carrie*, often cited as the all-time worst (but only, of course, before *Footloose*), this was the simpleminded story of Ren, a high-school youth from Chicago who moves with his mother to the burg of Bomont. Here the autocratic Reverend Shaw Moore—upon the death of his son in a car accident following a late-night dance—has instituted a curfew for teens and a ban on all dancing, which seemed absurd even in 1984. Ren manages to mobilize the town's youth, confounds Moore and his city council cohorts, and dancing comes back to Bomont.

The musical's book, by Pitchford and Walter Bobbie, is situated "in the recent past," which must mean something between the Middle Ages and Mesopotamia. It edulcorates even the paltry screenplay, so that, for instance, Ariel Moore, the minister's rebellious daughter, barks louder than she beds, and the story must now seem, to both young and old, rather like an attempt to defang *Winnie the Pooh*. The score, by Tom Snow and Pitchford, which seamlessly incorporates songs from the movie by similar no-talents, is without exception verbally maladroit and musically banal, and, even when performed by the gifted Dee Hoty and Catherine Cox, irredeemable.

Walter Bobbie, the co-author and director, has one indisputable talent—for riding on the coattails of his choreographer. When that happens to be someone like Ann Reinking (as in *Chicago*), his work looks good; when, as here, a newcomer named A. C. Ciulla, from the wonderful world of nightclubs and TV, the result, both directorially and choreographically, is catastrophic. There is not a single original touch to be discerned anywhere, and everything is either hysterical or listless as it lunges or sashays from commonplace to commoner place.

John Lee Beatty is a fine set designer, but here he must have either worked in his sleep or been told to make it all into a heartland community-center production for the proper down-home look. Money could not have been at issue, as *Footloose* enjoys some of the most deep-pocketed producers around. Toni-Leslie James, never a first-rate costumer, here looks downright cut-rate. Ken Billington's always variable lighting here mistakes vulgarity for vitality. But the worst thing is, save the abovementioned exceptions, the cast.

Jeremy Kushnier, an import from Manitoba, is not so much Kevin as Canadian bacon, and could no more galvanize Bomont into dirty dancing than Galvani could have electrified his famous frogs into a tarantella. Jennifer Laura Thompson is as unprepossessing as ungifted in the role of the high-school vamp Ariel, and can pass for a teenager only if umpteen qualifies. In fact, when you look at the stage, you notice with horror the absence of a single attractive young person of either sex.

If *Footloose* were presented at Radio City Music Hall or Madison Square Garden (two of the producers), it might just pass with the other schlock that there beguiles the benighted. On Broadway, it is sickening. Do not be fooled if it has a run: its presenters have drummed up a sizable advance sale and are loaded enough to throw good millions after bad. The Reverend Shaw Moore asks in the pulpit, "if Whitman were alive today, what song would he hear America singing?" I don't know, but if it were *Footloose*, Walt would have to drop dead twice.

The Ride Down Mt. Morgan

Arthur Miller's *The Ride Down Mt. Morgan* has been riding around for some years (London, Williamstown) before landing at the Public. The play is doused in the scent of desperation, only slightly less acrid than cheap perfume. Miller, the son of naturalism, has tried before to cut his ties to realism, but some umbilical cords are made of steel. Here now is a work awash in dreams, nightmares, and fantasies, straining doggedly to be antirealist.

Lyman Felt, a failed writer wildly successful as an insurance magnate, has led a double life for a decade. In New York City, he is married to Theo(dora), a Protestant minister's daughter, somewhat starchy, with a similarly proper grown daughter, Bessie. In Elmira, he has a Jewish wife, Leah, also in insurance, and a 9-year-old son, Ben. One snowy night in Elmira, he drives his car down a steep, icy road closed to traffic (he removed the barrier), has a near-fatal accident, and is slowly recovering in a hospital bed under the steadily watchful eye of a nurse—there's antirealism for you.

When Leah got pregnant and ready to abort, Lyman promised her wedding bells, and she had Ben. Pretending to be divorced, he eventually married her. Now the two wives and daughter (we're spared the boy) meet at his bedside in both Lyman's fantasies and in reality, in scenes deliberately confusing. David Esbjornson's staging is calculatedly unrealistic, with overlappings and double exposure, characters appearing in odd places including the air, and Lyman popping in and out of his bed, which itself keeps changing its position. Brian MacDevitt's lighting projects abstract designs on the backdrop, or picks out characters frozen in square patches of light. Elizabeth Hope Clancy's costumes peel away quickly in dream scenes. John Arnone's scenery replaces the curtain with a Mondrianesque design of chrome rods, and employs ever-shifting white drapes to change the stage configuration.

But except for expatiating on Lyman's lust and his rationalizations for having two wives, the play accomplishes little. True, there is some breast-beating for Lyman, and orgies of round-robin recrimination, the staple of Millerian dramaturgy. Yet we do not even get a clear sense of how the wives differ, and actually see Theo in a lusty sexual situation, which is more than we get from the supposedly earthier, sensual Leah. And we cannot conceive how Lyman manages to keep his spouses separate and ignorant: Elmira is hardly at the antipodes, and long sojourns in those not especially Arcadian purlieus seem unjustifiable by business other than monkey.

If the wives remain sketchy, Bessie, Tom, and Nurse Logan are mere stick figures. But Miller can write effective lines—e.g., "The problem is not honesty, but how much you hurt others with it" and "Why does anyone stay together once they realize who they are with? "—atrocious grammar notwithstanding. But these must be balanced against such stuff as, "Leah smelled like a pink, bright cantaloupe, and when she smiled, the clothes seemed to be dropping off her" and "I walk in the valley of your thighs," and still more such senescent masturbation.

Frances Conroy, though a replacement, makes Theo almost believable, but Meg Gibson's Leah contributes little that might drive a man to bigamy. As for Patrick Stewart, he reminds me of those

Englishwomen whose accents get them telephone-answering jobs
with snobbish American firms. He seems to shout and growl even
on the rare occasions when he speaks softly, his beady eyes and
clotted voice contributing to the shiftiness of his acting. His Lyman
is about as credible as the hair on his head; but, of course, *Star Trek*
can confer greatness on anyone.

Electra

David Leveax's inspiration for staging the *Electra* of Sophocles was
a little girl in a Sarajevo documentary struck dumb by the death of
her brother. But who in this production displays what Leveaux calls
that "inconsolable silence"? Pylades is (rather awkwardly) written
as a non-speaking part, and the two silent members of the three-
woman Chorus are no little girls, and quite marginal besides. The
Chorus leader and, of course, Electra talk a blue streak. And here
there is no murderous mortar fire, and no war. As that subtle classical scholar Bernard Knox has shown, this is family, not societal,
drama; in this, unlike in other Sophoclean plays, the polis does not
exist. The violence is intramural.

Apropos intramural, Johan Engels's set is part dilapidated palace
façade with fire escapes leading nowhere, and part adjoining sand-
lot with broken-down salon chairs inexplicably scattered about. In
the middle is a mystery Thing. Propped up at one end by a broken-
off marble Ionian capital is a long, slanting wooden board, suggesting a collapsed catafalque. Nonchalantly draped around its head in
artfully flowing folds is a dirty old sheet, which Woman 3 will later
throw on as a shawl.

Still later, when Orestes and Pylades go about their bloody errand, she makes up the Thing as a bed, with that sheet nicely folded
down for, I presume, the royal corpses to slide in comfortably. At
other times, the Thing is a combination horse and trampoline for
Electra's gymnastics.

Mycenae, we gather, is afflicted with creeping mutism, but those
who speak display no consistent accent. Electra is veddy British,
Clytemnestra and Orestes vestigially so, Chrysothemis mid-Atlantic, the Tutor (here called Servant) stage-American, Aegisthus
street American, and Woman 1 gutter-American. Further, the two
female mutes act not at all shell-shocked: they solicitously hug or

support Electra, crawl with her when she crawls, but never say boo. Often, however, they circle around her, like jackals wanting to make sure their dinner is indeed dead.

Sophocles writes glorious poetry and poetic prose to which Frank McGuinness's translation does splendid, actable justice. But some actors declaim it with that incipient sob that used to be the sine qua non of the grand style, while others trundle along prosily. Electra recites, rants, whimpers, or rails sarcastically for yocks. As Zoë Wanamaker plays her, she is part Madwoman of Chaillot wearing her father's tattered clothes, part Ursula the pigwoman from *Bartholomew Fair*, and two parts Gelsomina from *La Strada*. If her balding-hedgehog hairdo were blonde, she would, with hopping gait and clownish mannerisms, be a fair caricature of Giulietta Masina. An actress possessed of a large bag of tricks, she is dead set on not sparing us a single one.

As Clytemnestra, Claire Bloom, wearing Johan Engels's Jezebel red, looks great but gives a routine performance. Michael Cumpsty's Orestes is a confused, grandstanding jock, intoning his lines with stentorian plangency. Marin Hinkle's Chrysothemis is a skittish teenager with a whiny singsong, and Stephen Spinella's old tutor sounds a bit too fruity, and walks, gestures, and hefts Electra like no graybeard ever. Pat Carroll's huge Woman 1 looks and sounds like the Platonic idea of a fishwife; as Woman 2, Mirjana Jokovic is reduced to a jittery scaredy-cat. Myra Lucretia Taylor is, quite offensively, turned into a black mammy as Woman 3, who also makes the beds. Daniel Oreskes, costumed as a Mycenaean Tom Wolfe, is a crude Aegisthus; Ivan Stamenov, the Pylades, is gotten up as a Greek fisher-boy catamite for Anglophone tourists, which may be why he keeps timorously mum.

When, finally, someone pushes aside the ostensibly heavy back-wall gate like an easily sliding door, to reveal an operettaish white staircase in near-two-dimensional cross section, the production at last fully acknowledges its flatness.

Parade

Parade is a dark musical, a topic much discussed currently. The 1913–1915 case of Leo Frank, a Brooklyn-born Jew lynched, despite his innocence, by an anti-northern and anti-Semitic Georgia mob for the murder of a 13-year-old girl, is about as dark as a subject can get; the murders in *Sweeney Todd* are essentially comic, almost like those in *Arsenic and Old Lace*; and in *South Pacific*, a tragic death is canceled out by a happy ending. The illegal execution of a guiltless man, whose death sentence the governor of the state had already overturned, however, is truly tragic and nowise sugarcoated in the show.

Now, why shouldn't what is rather too loosely called "musical comedy" by some embrace a darker subject as long as it is handled with intelligence, skill, and, wherever possible, humor? This is not a monochromatically somber piece, but a suspenseful slice of unvarnished life, mixing anguish and grief with smiles and laughs, and graced with exceptional production values.

Religious or racial prejudice and xenophobia are not likely to go away as long as human nature is what it is. There are and will be other Leo Franks of one kind or another, guilty of nothing more than being outsiders and lacking charisma. *Parade* rates an A for courage and professionalism, and is superior, even as sheer entertainment, to the crudeness of a *Scarlet Pimpernel* and the ineptitude of a *Footloose*.

I concede that the score by the young and promising Jason Robert Brown seldom rises above the serviceable. It is not derivative and does advance the plot; it does not, however, meet the higher demands of, say, the final duet for Leo and his wife, Lucille, where transcendence is called for. But the book by Alfred Uhry, the gifted playwright and expert on Atlanta Jewish life, is consistently apt and gripping. It gamely tackles a complex and sprawling subject, neither oversimplifying nor forfeiting cohesiveness. It enlightens without preachment, and lets the dramatic or ironic prose merge seamlessly with the musical numbers.

Next, *Parade*, named after the Confederate Memorial Day parade that frames the action, boasts a wonderfully stimulating physical production. The sets by Riccardo Hernández are richly evocative and find the proper blend of realism and stylization, of solidity and fluidity, of Here and Beyond. Note especially that mighty, overarching oak, whose brooding presence keeps growing in ominous import. Judith Dolan's costumes are suitably understated and nicely in period, and Howell Binkley's lighting adds subtle ironies of its own.

Whoever plays Leo Frank faces the awesome task of having to be winning without obvious charm, manly despite his mousiness, and a star performer in a role that, except for its length, has none of the splashy attributes of a star vehicle. I cannot think of anyone else nowadays able to carry this off with such shining modesty, such exemplary avoidance of mannerism, such unswerving conviction and convincingness as Brent Carver. He is matched every step of the way by the Lucille of Carolee Carmello. She plays a modern-day Joan of Arc without a scintilla of false—or even inapposite real— glamour, and infuses seeming ordinariness with enough lambent faith and dauntless determination to move a good-size mountain, if not budge human stupidity.

If I mention no further names it is because they are too numerous and form an ensemble that should not be fractured. But glory be to the two guiding lights: Harold Prince (direction) and Patricia Birch (choreography). They have fused speech and song, movement and dance, incisive detail and all-encompassing panorama into as compact a whole as is dramatically possible. *Parade*, which could have been a millstone, emerges as a milestone.

The Iphigenia Cycle

Staging Greek drama in today's theater is virtually impossible, except for JoAnne Akalaitis, for whom it is totally so. But then, she's not much better at anything else. You have to hand it to her, though: few have parlayed a greater lack of talent into such unlimited opportunities to evenhandedly ruin whatever they touch. This has nothing to do with Miss A.'s supposedly advanced, innovative approach, and everything to do with today's lack of standards, whereby whatever is different is automatically saluted. You'd think it easy to distinguish between the good and the merely new ("Enter the Tour de France on a unicycle? How ingenious!"), but, alas, it no longer is.

Miss A. brings us *The Iphigenia Cycle*—i.e., *Iphigenia at Aulis* and *Iphigenia in Tauris*, in that order. Euripides wrote *Aulis* some years later, independently from the earlier drama, but okay, why not advert to the order in which the story unfolds and combine the two works? Not if you have a tin ear and glass eyes. You begin by picking actors who have either no ability or no proper training, and pay no attention to their unsightliness. You make sure that a white daughter has a black mother, and that the Chorus is given stylized and synchronized movements, while the principals act naturalistically with no unifying principle. Then you choose a pedestrian transla-tion (by Nicholas Rudall), and let everyone speak with whatever accents the multiethnic backgrounds provide.

You add a nonsensical set of dainty white bleachers (by Paul Steinberg) and the most asinine costumes (by Doey Luthi—some moniker!) one has seen in donkey's years. Why, for example, would the Chorus wield candy-colored umbrellas opened for no visible or audible reason, and as arbitrarily laid aside? Why would Agamem-non sport the flimsiest of bathrobes over a Gap shirt and military pants and boots? Why would Clytemnestra, in a ghastly orange coatdress, drag a baby around the battlefield, especially if that baby is Orestes, who, in a few years' time, will kill her to avenge his mur-dered father? Why would she stand by like a lump when outrage requires some kind of action?

Again, why would the zombified Achilles sport a Patrick Stew-art unhairdo, a black rubber outfit with a football player's pads and tight-fitting sheer black sleeves, and, as sole weapon, a nickel-plated croquet mallet? Why would Iphigenia be a dippy debutante, complete with slouch and singsong, a white sheath stressing her beanpolishness, and huge white bath shoes to give Manolo Blahnik nightmares? Why would Menelaos affect punk hair dyed platinum? Why would the bottom of those bleachers be outlined with fluo-rescent lights (by the usually fine Jennifer Tipton)? Why would the nondescript music of Bruce Odland turn to demented banging all through the intermission?

But this is only half of it; I left after *Aulis*, Minoan bulls couldn't have dragged me back to *Tauris*, where, I'm told, things really went hog-wild. But even if Miss Akalaitis (whom her detractors unjustly call Alka Seltzer, a drug meant to settle, not turn, stomachs), had set things in a hall of mirrors, each with a lipstick-scrawled STOP ME BEFORE I KILL AGAIN!, nothing would deter the demented from rehiring her.

You're a Good Man, Charlie Brown

Comic strips do not naturally translate into Broadway musicals, and indeed, *You're a Good Man, Charlie Brown*, based on *Peanuts*, started life Off Broadway in 1967, amassing an impressive run. A good musical, these days, being as hard to find as a good man, it's not surprising that this nugatory nugget should re-emerge as a somewhat fancier Broadway offering. Clark Gesner, who wrote the book, lyrics, and music, never had a comparable success, but even one such whopper ain't peanuts.

The present revival is a curious hybrid, half delightful, half let-down: the question is whether half a bird in hand is worth one in the bush. Clearly, if an adult cast of six is to animate a half-dozen popular cartoon figures—three little boys, two little girls, and one super-dog—they have to be expert performers as well as something even more important: able to dig up the buried child (or dog) in themselves, not as easy as it sounds. Three cast members can; three fail.

Kristin Chenoweth, as Sally Brown, replacing another character in the original version, is something you won't often encounter: perfection. Without stooping to caricature, the actress looks, sounds, walks, breathes sassy, precocious little-girlhood, solemnly sure of her worth and exercising her superiority with serene lofti-ness. You do not have to be a parent, or even a man, to want to wrap her in tissue paper and take her home with you. Her love is Linus Van Pelt, he of the famed security blanket. Linus is incarnated by B. D. Wong, no stripling but a veteran actor who can gaze and chatter as ingenuously as if born yesterday. Yet he is also the thinker of the gang, manifestly sucking his wisdom out of his thumb.

Roger Bart, tall, clean-cut, frat-boyish, would not seem to be the likeliest Snoopy, especially not without a dog mask, tail, and other such appurtenances. But it just goes to show that a dog's Bart can be as good as his bite: the actor is the essence of dogginess from the optimistic expectancy in his eyes to the bounce in his cavortings. When he hunkers down for a siesta, his limbs jellify into sensuous bonelessness, and his growls melt into blissfully dying burbles. His fantasizing himself as that flying ace, the Red Baron, is as airy-hairy as caninely possible, and he is equally at home in the pilot seat of a Fokker triplane as surveying the world from the top of his doghouse.

Lucy Van Pelt, the pint-size termagant with the gargantuan ego, requires a particularly fine actress to bring out the Xanthippe-adoring Socrates in all of us. Alas, the stringbeany Ilana Levine weilds no such magic. Her tormenting of brother Linus and uncouth attempts to vamp Schroeder are technically correctly executed, but we never forget that this is acting, and by an adult at that. As Schroeder, the Beethoven-obsessed keyboard belaborer, Stanley Wayne Mathis, good as he was in *Jelly's Last Jam* and *The Lion King*, would not appear to be the obvious choice. And sure enough, his Schroeder is only obvious, not choice. He conveys no genuine childlikeness, and when he infuses his singing with *St. Louis Woman*-ish soul, the spirit of Ludwig Van is betrayed.

The crowning fiasco, however, is the Charlie of Anthony Rapp. In the vastly overrated *Rent*, he was, in my view, the greatest irritant, but he was doubtless cast here as bait for the *Rent* fans. His straining to portray a lovable loser only emphasizes his basic smarminess. Hard as it is to define charm, I can define its opposite in two words: Anthony Rapp.

Clark Gesner's music and lyrics never rise above the functional, but at least they are that. The book is better, thanks to the original "Peanuts" vendor, Charles Schulz. The best song is Sally's "My New Philosophy," which, like other good things here, is new and by Andrew Lippa. Nobody does cartoonish scenery better than David Gallo, whose dizzying cleverness transcends into arch-clever dizzyingness for the Red Baron flying sequence. Kenneth Posner's lighting is not a whit less ingenious, and not for a moment witless. Michael Krass's costumes seem to be cut from not cloth but smiles, and Michael Mayer's direction tirelessly whips these ex-drawings into exciting stage life.

Death of a Salesman

If the pen cannot give a tragic hero sufficient weight, perhaps the scales can. The first and superb Willy Loman was Lee J. Cobb, of great talent and considerable avoirdupois to make his fall reverberant. He contributed in no small measure to the success of Arthur Miller's *Death of a Salesman*, which returns to Broadway with Brian

Dennehy, a potent actor weighing even more than Cobb and twice as much as our last Willy, Dustin Hoffman.

Miller put his finger on our prime weakness: a gullibility to the wiles of salesmanship. "I sell, therefore I am" is the neo-Cartesian maxim Willy is meant to embody and explicate. Rightly, Miller embeds this value system in a business, social, and family context, but the interaction of the elements is achieved more by contrivance than by a sense of the inevitable. Moreover, the language tends to lack the poetic heightening tragedy requires. What are we to make of "Nobody dast blame this man. A salesman is got to dream, boy. It comes with the territory"? The original production also owed a lot to Elia Kazan's rapturous staging.

Robert Falls's mounting is very different. For starters, there is no cityscape, and Richard Woodbury's alternately thunderous and jazzy music is far from the fluty and elegiac one Miller stipulated and Alex North delivered in 1949. Falls has made minor adjustments in the text, but Mark Wendland's décor departs radically from Jo Mielziner's original. It is much less realistic, with more black, empty space, a busy turntable, translucent sliding panels. Falls adds oblique lighting (by Michael Philippi) that casts venetian-blind shadows, enhanced and echoing sound, overlapping dialogue, characters in consecutive scenes simultaneously visible, and a Loman house more fluidly expressionist with fewer details.

This does not, of course, elicit more tragedy, though it makes the melodrama, which the play essentially is, spookier, more hallucinatory, startling. But the cards are too neatly stacked against a Willy hurtling out of control; his heroically struggling wife, Linda; and his elder and sensitive son, Biff, as opposed to the younger, happy-go-lucky Happy. Opportunities let slip, hopes for the future dashed, attempts at family rapprochement regularly misfiring, and one of the unlikelier cases of kleptomania are just a few of the Lomans' problems.

Yet most of the acting is splendid. Dennehy is a man truly at the end of his tether, letting us in on every step of his decline via naïve optimism, disregard of reality, aging, and capitalist callousness. He is a bull slowly wrestled down in some terrible tauromachy. Elizabeth Franz, after a bit too much tremolo and head-waggling, settles into a quietly and thoroughly moving Linda. Kevin Anderson welds Biff's duality as unmoored drifter and canny *raisonneur* into a totally believable and heartrending amalgam. Only Ted Koch's Happy is a bit lacking in the necessary dumb appeal. In the competent supporting cast, Howard Witt's Charley is outstanding. This *Salesman* is a hard but efficacious sell.

The Mineola Twins

Paula Vogel's not-quite-new *The Mineola Twins* (originally *The Minnesota Twins*) is neither top- nor bottom-drawer Vogel, though it is written in good part from her drawers. The mind and the crotch have harmoniously collaborated in this her most openly lesbian play, and what emerges is more than a campy piece in which three women play six parts, three of them male.

It is about sisterhood—literally and figuratively—and how very different, indeed antithetical, women may bond together despite their animosities, and what they can give to, as well as get from, one another's male offspring. It proclaims sisterhood beautiful even at its most acrimonious, and that someday, though not quite yet, all women may live in peace together despite divergent sexualities and warring ideologies.

Fundamentally, it is the story of how the twins Myrna and Myra, from a middle-class home in Mineola, fared through the Eisenhower, Nixon, and Bush eras. It is about the internecine hatred of these near-identical opposites: Myrna, conventional, bourgeois, reactionary; Myra, rebellious, promiscuous, radical. And yet somehow alike. All through high school, young womanhood, and early middle age, they—sometimes bitterly, sometimes cheerfully—detest each other (including stealing each other's sons and lovers) while also being joined at deeper than skin, or even bone, level.

Vogel writes farce here, and the jokes come thick and fast. They are based on true knowledge of the periods chronicled—of their mores, mentalities, media, language, and artifacts. Many of the gags are recycled or ersatz, often fished out of waters depleted by too many anglers. Some, however, mocking old bromides and rituals (especially sexual ones), manage to squeeze fresh laughs out of old fallacies, old prejudices that can still use a swift kick in the behind to speed them along their all-too-foot-dragging way.

What helps the play enormously is the letter-perfect production. Joe Mantello, a passable actor, is rapidly developing into an unsurpassable director of a type of (usually homosexual) comedy, to which he brings steady sophistication, resourcefulness, and effervescence. I suspect that a good quarter of *Mineola* is Mantello. But there are also bubbly contributions from the sets of Robert Brill and Scott Pask, the costumes of Jess Goldstein, the lighting of Kevin Adams, and the sound of David Van Tieghem.

And then there's the acting. As the twins, Swoosie Kurtz lets her exemplary facial play, timing, inflection, and body language perform double miracles in antipodal roles, and make clear her mastery of every term in the comedian's lexicon. She is expertly supported, especially in a hilarious male part, by Mo Gaffney, whom I have always viewed as Kathy Najimy's better half, and who, on her own, is two whole lots of fun. And playing a pair of opposed sisters' totally reversed sons, Mandy Siegfried proves herself a young comedienne who'll duly knock them dead from Mineola to Minnesota. *The Mineola Twins* may be satire listing toward sitcom, but for once I understood why people around me were laughing.

Annie Get Your Gun; *Not About Nightingales*

Who would have thought it possible to even dislike Bernadette Peters? Yet her Annie Oakley in the revival of *Annie Get Your Gun* is something to elicit potshots from the most pacific spectator. It is a mixture of miscasting and misdirecting, but also terrible miscalculation on the actress's part. When Frank Butler sings to Annie, "A doll I can carry / The girl that I marry / Must be," it is the sort of thing one tells a ragamuffin bordering on virago. Miss Peters, however, is petite, cute, and cuddly, just an iota short (or long) of Jon-Benet Ramsey. Her drawl is a farrago of southern, Texan, and Brooklynese, issuing slowly, with many a ritard, rubato, and tremolo in both speech and song. But the matinee audience around me, looking duly papered, responded with nonstop multiple orgasms.

Too bad that the show has two choreographers, Graciela Daniele and Jeff Calhoun, and no director, although the former is listed in that capacity. Even the dances look like leftovers from *Ragtime* (Daniele) and *The Will Rogers Follies* (Calhoun). And they are often out of character, as when the large and virile Frank, seated on the floor, latches on to the leg of the last boy in a chorus line and is dragged comically across the stage.

A total overhaul was deemed necessary out of deference to Indians and feminists. Peter Stone was brought in for that purpose: the "I'm an Indian Too" and "I'm a Bad, Bad Man" numbers were accordingly omitted, other excisions and changes were made (replacing ethnic humor with equally dubious big-boob jokes), and a new concept was imposed. We now get Buffalo Bill's Wild West Show performing a play-within-a-play about Frank and Annie, a tired and tiresome device that undercuts the story's immediacy and emotional impact. Thus, to fit the concept, the production opens gratuitously with "There's No Business Like Show Business" in tacky Lake Tahoe style; by the time the song is reprised in the appropriate places, it no longer surprises and delights.

The admirable Tony Walton's sets are pleasant but unduly constricted by being obliged to represent a play-within-a-play. Conversely, William Ivey Long's costumes are excessive and inappropriate. Most surprising, Miss Peters, in somewhat ragged voice, delivers her songs as if they were unconnected nightclub numbers. But then, I can't say much for Bruce Coughlin's arrangements either.

Tom Wopat is a solidly likable, no-nonsense Frank Butler, honestly acted and decently sung. As his assistant, Valerie Wright is the stock comic sourpuss. Ron Holgate is a plausible Buffalo Bill, but Gregory Zaragoza, a genuine scion of the Pima tribe, is a Sitting Bull turned out of P.C. reverence into a wooden Indian Custer would have demolished like a sitting duck. As the male half of the secondary couple, Andrew Palermo sings winningly and dances with spectacular airiness, but his slight stature causes problems.

The laughs are there, all right, many of them added by Stone, and the Irving Berlin score remains indestructible. Still, anyone who listens to a cast recording with the indomitable Ethel Merman or the playful Mary Martin will get a better idea of what this show can be. Miss Peters's Annie, like this *Annie Get Your Gun*, misfires.

It is not often that a lost early work of a playwright is exhumed smelling like roses rather than of corpse. That, however, is the case of the remarkable *Not About Nightingales* (1938), the fourth play by Tennessee Williams, for whose re-emergence Vanessa Redgrave's snooping deserves our first round of applause. Many more must go to the play at the Circle in the Square, which should become a place of pilgrimage not only for faithful Williams fans but also for anyone looking for powerful theater resoundingly mounted.

Though Tennessee vehemently denied it, this prison play is

melodrama, but even that lowly genre, elevated by a nascent genius, can prove as intellectually stimulating as it is viscerally gripping. It is the unsettling work the 27-year-old dramatist submitted to the socially conscious Group Theater, which curtly rejected it. Reflect on what talent was required to flesh out so many characters—Inmates, guards, prison employees, and the warden—on the basis of a mere magazine article about a scandal in a Pennsylvania prison. Twenty-five prisoners, thought to be the ringleaders of a hunger strike caused by appalling food, were confined to a punitive boiler room whose temperature could go up to 200 degrees. Four of the men were found dead, roasted alive. Tom Williams, as he was then known, had not done actual time in jail, but his early home life felt like incarceration.

The play shuttles between the prison block—where a number of diverse prisoners roister, quarrel, and struggle to survive under the draconian regime of a psychopathic prison warden, Boss Whalen—and the warden's office and waiting room. Here an intelligent, self-taught inmate, Jim Allison, works as a file clerk, unjustly called a stoolie by his fellow prisoners although he strives to help them. Whalen plays a cat-and-mouse game with Jim, but an even nastier one with Eva, the desperate young woman happy to find employment as his secretary, even though his attentions to her are far from benevolent. Eva and Jim attempt a brief, foiled love affair.

Expecting something conventional along the lines of the then-popular prison movies, I was stunned and excited to find something incomparably finer—more touching, humane, humorous, and impassioned. Also a bit self-consciously poetic and symbolic, a double-edged sword Williams kept honing all his life. What he wrote here lends itself splendidly to both small and thunderously big performances—none bigger than Corin Redgrave's grotesque yet scary Boss Whalen. Scarcely less sharp, in this AngloAmerican production, is the superb work of such British and American actors as Finbar Lynch, Sherri Parker Lee, and James Black—indeed of the entire cast, a perfectly homogenous ensemble, working in Richard Hoover's masterly set that puts this hostile space to exemplary use.

Stupendous is the word for Trevor Nunn's direction, the kind you see only a few times in a life of theatergoing. Even if you shun so-called depressing plays, you'd better catch this one, unless you want regrets for the rest of your days.

Closer

Patrick Marber's *Closer* is a sad, savvy, often funny play that casts a steely, unblinking gaze at the world of relationships and lets you come to your own conclusions. It is rather like that scar on young Alice's thigh: of a strange shape, clumsily made, and for which she and others offer various explanations, none of which may be true. But it is there, and something it betokens may never have healed.

There are four characters, sufficient for this wistful merry-go-round. Alice, who has heedlessly walked in front of a taxi, has had her leg injured just below that old scar. Dan, a young obituary writer, passing by, has brought her to the hospital. While they wait for a doctor to show up, they banter and fall in love. A middle-aged doctor, Larry, hurrying by, notices only because Alice is pretty, but, being a dermatologist, can offer only skin-deep comfort. Which is how most comfort is.

Time passes rapidly in *Closer*. After a considerable lapse, we are in the studio of the somewhat older Anna, a photographer taking pictures of Dan. It's for the book jacket of his forthcoming novel, the story of himself and Alice, with whom he is now living. Yet here he is instantly craving Anna, who, although seemingly aloof and even mildly sarcastic, is not unresponsive. Alice, arriving to pick up Dan, rightly suspects that there has been some hanky-panky.

The next scene takes place on the Internet, and is both visually and comedically highly stimulating, but that is as much as I can tell you about it. From here on, as several years go by, everyone ends up sexually and emotionally involved with everyone else, each trying vainly to get closer to the other. Marber tells his story in short, staccato scenes in which the unsaid talks as loudly as the said. The dialogue is almost entirely stichomythic, the occasional speech still not much longer than a few lines. There are frequent pauses, but not of the Pinteresque variety—more like skipped heartbeats.

There are many ways of interpreting this play. Is it on the Anouilhesque theme of how innocence and the rare ability to love never goes unpunished in this world? Is it about how no relationship lasts, and how everyone ends up alone or with somebody else in a worse kind of aloneness? Or is it about the noose of time tightening around everyone's neck, closer and closer? Or is this the Eliotian theme about our not being able to bear very much reality, and that the truth ultimately kills? Early on, the obituarist Dan, asked by

Alice, "Do you like it… in a dying business?" answers, "It's a living."
And how is the loving business? Perpetually dying. But always only
for one partner; there is no shared *Liebestod*.

Closer, this acutely observed, wise play, is directed by its author
the way he has written it: with a scalpel. He has elicited a semi-abstract unit set from Vicki Mortimer that is adaptable through minimal changes to both the specifics and the ambiguities of each situation. Her costumes are similarly evocative, and Hugh Vanstone's
lighting artfully fills in the elliptic scenery. Paddy Cunneen's music
is brash and raw, like the emotions. And the acting is just fine.

Although Ciarán Hinds, as Larry, may be a bit excessively unwinning, he conveys well the weaknesses of a strong man. Rupert
Graves gets the volatile, puppyish but nevertheless hurtful mischievousness of Dan perfectly, and Natasha Richardson splendidly balances coolness and passion, irony and pain. As for Alice: no one
could capture the intermingled aggressiveness and vulnerability of
youth with more empathy than Anna Friel. *Closer* does not merely
hold your attention; it burrows into you.

True, we have three very fine American plays, rather unusually,
currently on our boards (*Wit*, *Side Man*, and *This Is Our Youth*),
but why is it that good straight plays come so much more readily
from Britain? Is it tradition, education, culture, subsidies, more and
cheaper theater, or what? Someone should investigate.

The Iceman Cometh

We owe England a lot for rediscovering some of our shows for us:
the wonderful *Not About Nightingales* and now that absolute masterpiece *The Iceman Cometh*. And while we are on debts, let's not
overlook O'Neill's debt to Ibsen: Hickey, the antihero of *Iceman*,
cometh out of Gregers Werle in *The Wild Duck*. But O'Neill took
Ibsen's conceit and ran with it, in his own idiosyncratic and idiomatic direction, even farther than the Norwegian.

This masterwork of American and world theater needs little more
summary than *Hamlet*. You all know that it is a long but riveting
play about hopeless drunks in Harry Hope's saloon downtown—or
even farther down, in hell—who survive on a mix of rotgut and
pipe dreams, the opium of the messes. They believe they'll someday
resume the lives they've flunked out of, and they wait, like fallen

angels, for the gates of Heaven to reopen. Well, a couple of them know better, and one of them merely awaits someone's approval of his projected suicide.

What none of them wants is the truth: that their aspirations are totally delusory, and that they'll never take a step out of the artificial paradise of booze and woozy palaver. And then there is Hickey, the supersalesman, who drops in periodically to join in the factitious fun. But now something grave has happened to him, and he resolves to prod these moles out into the world to realize their pipe dreams. They fail, just as he expected they would. But the result is not what he wished for: instead of being freed from their sense of false hope and guilt, they feel squashed; even the whiskey has gone flat. Until, that is…

However well you may know *Iceman*, you must see this wondrous production, staged by Howard Davies with consummate artistry. On a terrific set by Bob Crowley, magisterially half-lit by Mark Henderson, these lost souls enact a comedy-drama whose relevance extends to the soberest souls among us. The staging is splendidly pictorial and tirelessly resourceful, and the actors, including five repeaters from the London cast, perform this comic nightmare like an intoxicating dream. The 255 minutes (which include two intermissions) go by rather too quickly, but never fear: the memories will last you long enough to recoup the fairly steep ticket price a hundredfold.

The cast is, mostly, superb. Tony Danza is a trifle too obvious as the bartender-pimp, Michael Emerson tries to do too much with Willie, and Richard Riehle does too little with McGloin. But the others are just about perfect, and please pay special attention to what Paul Giamatti, Jeff Weiss, and Katie Finneran do with what could have been lesser roles. And now for Kevin Spacey.

We have had the masterly Hickey of Jason Robards in 1956. His was a poetic, charismatic, almost balletic Hickey—until the final, painful scene, all lyricism, laughs, and razzle-dazzle. Now comes the equally great but antithetical Spacey, as a Hickey who, by the time we meet him, is ice-cold, sinisterly charming, radiating a diabolic beauty. His speech sounds like the blandishments of a solicitous kindergarten teacher one moment, like distant machinegun fire the next. On the move, he is a panther in pants; when still, a coiled cobra. His gaze is by turns encouraging, enigmatic, unendurable. It is a performance to make every nonactor want to take up acting and every actor want to give up in despair.

There is a marvelous, unjustly neglected barroom poem by Kenneth Patchen about (among other things) his mother's meeting with God: "She said it was like a fog coming over her face / And light was everywhere and a soft voice saying / You can stop crying now." That is the mood in which you'll leave this show.

Le Cid

Among the more unusual casting methods is that used by Declan Donnellan for his production of *Le Cid*, Corneille's tragicomic masterpiece of 1636, which has just visited BAM. Based on a Spanish play about Iberia's semi-legendary eleventh-century hero, *Le Cid* tells of Rodrigo Diaz, known as El Cid (the boss), a soldier of fortune who was equally willing to fight for or against the Moors but finally proved most useful to Spain and Charlton Heston.

The play concerns the love of Chimène and Don Rodrigue, and how the latter, to avenge an insult to his father, kills his beloved's father in a duel. Whereupon Chimène, though still in love with him, clamors for his head. But because of his valiant routing of the Moors, who paid him less than the king of Castile, our heroic mercenary earns the royal accolade. The most the king is willing to grant Chimène is for a volunteer, Don Sanche, to fight Rodrigue in a duel as her champion. But what chance has poor Sanche when the lady herself derides him mercilessly, rooting for his adversary? Yet all ends well enough for everybody except Pierre Corneille, whose masterwork is travestied here by Donnellan & Co.

Using a French cast speaking French, Donnellan, who is said to be as fluent in French as he is flaky in directing, picked most of his male actors by their torsos, to which he strips them on a slender pretext. Thus Rodrigue is played by William Nadylam, a black actor with broad shoulders and a wasp waist—a perfectly triangular torso. Other male actors who peel for Donnellan display torsos that are milky white, smooth, and elongated, or white and darkly hairy, achieving a delightfully dappled effect. Don Gomès, killed early by Rodrigue, is nevertheless kept on throughout on the sidelines, hovering as a semi-nude ghost, and even, in a particularly inventive touch, becoming his daughter's dresser, clothing and shoeing her.

Ah, yes, not to be accused of homoeroticism, Donnellan has Chimène plead with the king barefoot and seemingly nude under her father's military greatcoat. When she removes it, she too—but much more briefly—displays shapely, understated breasts and over-sized panties, lest she outstrip the bare-chested males. Similarly, when the Infanta unaccountably sheds her dress amid the court of Castille, she is allowed to keep on her slip, lest the appeal become excessively heterosexual. She must, however, brandish a ubiquitous cigarette, which turns her into a chain-smoking harridan.

The staging consists mostly of parading about forward, back-ward, and sideways, as in close-order drill. Unlike Corneille, who keeps the duels offstage, Donnellan has the adversaries shadow-fencing in stop-motion from opposite sides of the stage, while between them the next scene weaves awkwardly, in and out. The courtiers are given various squeals and squawks, with occasional flamenco dancing or guitar playing to obscure the words. When Rodrigue—the ramrod-stiff and blank-voiced Nadylam—is to re-port about his glorious naval victory, he is made to sit in the king's chair while the king and court crouch or squat at his feet, and min-gy surtitles translate about every third or fourth line of eloquent verse into drab prose.

Declan Donnellan practices directing as antithetically and abu-sively to the author's intentions as perversely possible, reaping ku-dos from benighted reviewers and audiences alike. This was the case with every production of Cheek by Jowl, which he ran with his designer and companion Nick Ormerod. Cheek by Jowl disbanded when the pair split up, leaving behind something best described as mere Cheek. Thus the set for *Le Cid* consists of three chairs and nothing else, yet earns one Philippe Marioge design credit! This kind of theater and its success augur the Declan of the West.

The Civil War

There are two ways to be beyond criticism: being above it or being below it. Shakespeare, for example, was above being shot down by the fusillades of even such eminent marksmen as Voltaire and Tol-stoy. Others, however, are so firmly entrenched in the lowest public taste that they are as invulnerable to criticism as low-flying stealth bombers to detection by radar. Such a one is Frank Wildhorn, who, with the opening of *The Civil War*, has three shows simultaneously dumbing down Broadway.

A genuine education, if such a thing were widely available, might teach people that artistic value is not to be measured by the number and volume of standing and yowling ovations. Critics, to be sure, are often wrong—especially those who reflect the majority taste. But the under- or miseducated public is wrong even more often. Yes, good folk knew enough to enjoy Dickens; they also know enough to love Judith Krantz, Danielle Steel, and Stephen King. The only real test is the slow but true test of time. By dint of being drilled, bullied, shamed—and, yes, even taught—the public eventually accepts Shakespeare. Even so, as Georg Kaiser has the goddess Athena declare in his drama *Pygmalion*, "The populace / Would sooner stone a genius than perceive him."

But the populace is perfectly pleased to anoint Wildhorn instantly as Messiah to the Unwashed. And when it comes to commercial savvy, he is indeed a genius. To be sure, as head of a popular division of Atlantic Records, he is well placed to peddle all sorts of advance concept recordings of his gestating shows and to engage pop celebrities as his recording "artists." Beyond that, he picks subjects of timely or proven popular appeal, e.g., *Jekyll and Hyde*, *The Scarlet Pimpernel*, and now *The Civil War*.

The good news is that the show does not use all the numbers Wildhorn has contrived for evolving versions of his opus; the bad news is that he does use 23, plus three reprises. These songs have only ghostly pseudo-tunes stretched out ad nauseam and uncannily resembling one another, revealing the two chief instruments for which Wildhorn composes: the meat grinder and the cookie cutter. Of course, someone who, like him, has churned out pop songs for years has or acquires a certain facility, but facility is not the same as felicity.

As this essentially bookless show's book writer, Gregory Boyd, explains, the show tunes of the great theater composers were the pop music of the day, and so we get here "country, pop, gospel, folk, r&b, and rock." What he does not say is that the Gershwins, Porter, Berlin, Rodgers, etc., though influenced by jazz, were good enough not to imitate but be imitated by the pack. And in no case would they have stooped to some of today's musically and verbally monotonous genres.

But there is further confusion here. Wildhorn and his unimpressive orchestrator, Kim Scharnberg, attempt to reconcile contemporary and period musical idioms, and come up with a hybrid that is neither fish nor fowl. Even their striving for variety—following up a thunderous march with a soulful guitar number—proves formulaic if not, indeed, disjointed. It all comes down to a personal style; which Wildhorn doesn't have, unless you consider generic banality a style.

Jack Murphy's lyrics do not help. This, for instance, from "Virginia": "There was a land… / A land to pleasure the eyes / Where the old was new / And the foolish wise." What does this seemingly clever paradox mean? At most, it describes the Wildhornian modus operandi. Or take this much-reprised bit sung by a slave couple about to be "sold apart": "If prayin' were horses all of us would ride / And ever I'd be by your side." Aside from rhythmic clunkiness, what sort of trope is this? Who but an Attila the Hun or Genghis Khan would conceive marital bliss as riding side by side? Or what of the following, from the war profiteer's song, "Greenback": "Get it any way that you can / Lie, cheat, sugar sweet / Elite, Easy Street…" What does the inept switch from verbs to not especially apposite nouns accomplish except an indigestible glut of rhymes on eat?

The book is all songs and vignettes, with the odd crumb of action or smidgen of spoken words. In itself, this could pass if it weren't so schematic. We are told that much of what is sung or spoken was assembled from Lincoln and Whitman, Sojourner Truth, and Frederick Douglass, as well as contemporary letters, headlines, and diaries. But bear in mind that the heedlessly pieced-together patchwork quilt can be as displeasing as homogenous sludge. Any show that can use the drab voice of David M. Lutken to drone out Lincoln's most powerful utterances is tone-deaf.

Even the portrayal of the Union Army, Confederate Army, and slave population, each played by seven actors, displays something reductive in its pat symmetry, and neither Jerry Zaks's direction nor Luis Perez's musical staging rises above the serviceable.

On the credit side, though, there are some splendid projections by the evidently inexhaustible Wendall K. Harrington, intensely dramatic lighting by Paul Gallo, suggestive scenery by Douglas W. Schmidt, and nicely restrained costuming from William Ivey Long. And there are some fine performances, vocal or histrionic, or both. I was particularly taken with Michel Bell, Lawrence Clayton, Cheryl Freeman, Carpathia Jenkins, Keith Bryon Kirk, and Irene Molloy, with several others behind only because of less ample opportunities. Gene Miller, though, as the Confederate captain, showed (possibly temporary) vocal strain. Leo Burmester simply reprised his performance in *Les Misérables*, although the show's most rousing number, "How Many Devils?" derives from the same source.

The Civil War has been treated successfully in only one musical, *Shenandoah* (not much superior, to my mind), which the authors of *The Civil War* do not mention in the record booklet, though they list a couple of obscure others. So this very choice of theme in these days of Bosnia, Kosovo, etc., etc. is shrewd enough. And when that war's 620,000 dead are evoked—along with the names of famous battles and their casualty numbers projected on the backdrop—unearned emotions are instantly elicited. Yet from any serious artistic standpoint, Wildhorn's musical merely augments the casualty list to 620,001. Still, as I mentioned earlier, criticism is powerless here, and the loudest sound you'll soon be hearing is wild Wildhorn laughter all the way to the bank.

bash: latterday plays

Loathsome is the word for Neil Labute. His two movies, *In the Company of Men* and *Your Friends and Neighbors*, are loathsome. His current bill of short stage works, collectively titled *bash: latterday plays* (LaBute doesn't use capitals) is no less loathsome. In both movies, nice women (one of them deaf) are viciously abused by delighting men, couples do nothing but cheat and fight, men double-cross one another or brag, as one doctor did, that he had the best sex of his life gang-raping a boy in high school.

Mind you, one can have a grim, misanthropic view of the world, but are there really in it only pathetic victims and ruthless, sadistic creeps? The worst thing about labute (to accord him the spelling he deserves) is that throughout his films and plays you cannot miss the gloating tone, the smirk on the author's face. Yet, so insensitively thrill-seeking are critics and audiences that LaBute garners rave reviews and full houses.

The three playlets in *bash* are monologues. In *medea redux*, the speaker is a young woman who at 13 was seduced by her teacher. Pregnant, she was abandoned by him, but "anyways, billie, that's my son, billie, 'william,' whatever… was born… he's great, and umm, without getting all shitty about it, i give birth and a bunch a years pass, okay?" The woman is talking into a tape recorder and also to us. Is she in a police station? In her kitchen? Or simply in the world according to LaBute?

She traces her seducer to a Phoenix school, and a correspondence develops. When Billie is 14, she takes him to meet his since married but otherwise childless father in a motel. The man loves children, we are told, and falls in love with the kid. When he leaves for a moment, the woman, as premeditated, kills her boy in his bath (Medea with a touch of Clytemnestra). Now she visualizes in tranquillity the tearful father screaming against the cosmos, although "there's never an answer," as she remarks and takes another puff on her cigarette.

In the second playlet, a man whose job seems threatened by downsizing lets his infant daughter asphyxiate in the hope that he will be kept on for compassionate reasons, only to find out there was no question of dismissal—it was all a practical joke by a friend of his. *iphigenia in orem* (Utah) is the pretentious title.

The third and longest play comprises the parallel monologues of a pair of affianced Mormon juniors who improbably attend Catholic Boston College. They alternate telling about a big dance they drove to in New York City with two other B.C. couples. While the girls, tired, snooze in their room at the Plaza, our hero and his two male cronies wander into Central Park and follow a middle-aged homosexual into a public toilet, where they beat him to death or at least grave permanent damage. Then they return to the Plaza and resume their "normal" lives with their insipid girlfriends.

This item is called *a gaggle of saints*. Since all the characters are adherents of Mormonism, which LaBute converted to while on scholarship at Brigham Young University, he subtitles his opus *latterday plays*, with a pun on the Latter-Day Saints and our sad, postmodern world. The Mormons were good to him, so he repays them by making all his murderers Mormons.

The cheap trick LaBute uses throughout is to make his characters stupid twits whose speech is numbingly banal, awash in verbal detritus. Then, in the middle of it, there will be either some totally improbably high-falutin poeticism, or some staggering enormity delivered with utter blandness. As if this weren't enough, he doesn't give a rap about placing his characters in a recognizable context. Where were that 13-year-old's parents all along, during pregnancy, birthing, and after? How did she bring up Billie without the help, for fourteen years, of that supposedly child-loving teacher father? Or, in the second play, how come the male child-murderer's wife accepts his deed without demur? Crib deaths regularly lead to dissolution of the marriage. Again, how do the gay-bashers escape scot-free, untroubled even by their conscience? Is the world full of LaButes?

You may think it poor form to give away this much plot and subvert surprise. But there are really no surprises in these works: just imagine the worst and multiply by ten. Still, in case you can't do the math, someone must spell out a warning. Rely on the chief critic of the *Times*, and you'll read in his lengthy encomium that *bash* is "informed with an earnest, probing moralism as fierce as that of Nathaniel Hawthorne."

Actually, if you want to understand LaBute, you had better seek out Dinitia Smith's article in the *Times* of June 23. There you will learn about LaBute's hatred for his truck-driver father. It surfaces in all three playlets, where fathers bring death. Even as we're told in lip-smacking detail about the ghastly fate of the hapless homosexual, we are informed twice that he reminded the assailant of his father. But at no point is there any sense of the author's awareness of what he is gleefully blurting out. It may be of further Freudian interest that the basher first indulges in some erotic foreplay with his victim. Also to be gleaned from this article, curiously captioned "A Filmmaker's Faith in God, If Not in Men," is how inarticulate and subliterate our author really is. Would any decent speaker of English say, "There is a reaction to my father in terms of the severity of my male characters"? Again, "In the past my work was mostly black… This one broaches into the territory of beige." To say nothing of the ignorant use of *parameters* for perimeters. Finally, we gather that Mrs. LaBute is a family therapist. If she can keep her spouse's problems confined to his plays and movies, she must be a helluva good one.

To broach into the actual production, its design is suitably minimal, although Joe Mantello's direction is at times too clever by half. In the third play, Paul Rudd overacts shamelessly, as is his wont; in the second, Ron Eldard is, except for a few minor excesses, entirely persuasive. The best work comes from Calista Flockhart, whose timings and inflections are unerringly on target, no matter what preposterous demands are inflicted on her. Still, if your reason for going is not so much relish of nastiness as wanting to see Ally Mc-Beal in the flesh, be forewarned: there is very little flesh on dem bones.

Contact

Contact is billed as "a dance play by Susan Stroman and John Weidman," with what little there is of play mostly by Weidman and the variety and plenitude of the dancing all Stroman. Its two shorter pieces and concluding longer one are of uneven merit but never without interest.

The theme, we have been told, is "swing" in its sundry significances. The first item, "Swinging," is an interpretation of Fragonard's famous painting (circa 1768), and starts with a nobleman lolling over the remnants of a picnic and looking up at his lady love soaring ever higher on a swing propelled by a manservant. Charming at first, it becomes coarse and ends with a switcheroo unconvincingly meant to herald the Revolution. Stroman, not a classical choreographer, is somewhat schematic here, though not without a scintilla of winsomeness.

"Did You Move?" takes place in a 1954 Queens Italian restaurant, where a brutish, possibly mafioso client all but immobilizes his repressed wife. During his rather lengthy absences at a buffet (Why, when there is waiter service?), the wife dances rapturously, first solo, then with a complaisant headwaiter. Stroman does better here, and has in Karen Ziemba a gifted and adorable protagonist. But again, Weidman's scenario seems manipulatively unpleasant, and Stroman is not entirely at home in the *Gaîté Parisienne* mode.

But in the long third piece, "Contact," Stroman transcends mere "musical staging," to which some would limit her, and offers a swing-dancing piece worthy of the best contemporary choreographers. The story is both repetitive and predictable, but Stroman makes it emotionally involving and choreographically absorbing. An alcoholic and suicidal ad executive finds himself in a dive where a sleek girl in yellow is the cynosure of all the rowdy dancers. He is fascinated but, despite the encouragement of the Bartender (the droll Jason Antoon) and come-hither looks from the girl herself, too shy to make contact.

Back home, he almost hangs himself, but the tenant downstairs, who has been telephonically protesting his bare and noise-making floors, brings up a carpet ad out of the Yellow Pages—and turns out to be the girl in yellow, barefoot, hair down, in sleepwear, now even more enchanting. Boyd Gaines, a delightful actor and inspired amateur dancer, performs with aplomb. Backed up by a terrific ensemble, Deborah Yates triumphs as the girl in yellow; as dancer, actress, woman, she is every man's dream and headed for a manifest career.

The recorded music is eclectic but serviceable; the sets are tasteful and evocative; the William Ivey Long costumes and Peter Kaczorowski lighting all you could ask for. A somewhat spotty evening, then, whose highlights, however, are high indeed.

Dame Edna: The Royal Tour

Hats off—from berets to toques, from homburgs to pillboxes—to *Dame Edna: The Royal Tour*. Other performers have invented running stage personas for themselves like Australia's Barry Humphries and his Dame Edna Everage, but have they been this amusing? I am prepared to declare him the funniest man in today's theater. Also the funniest woman.

Humphries has many strengths. He is a great improviser who plays with his audience as if it were a beach ball. Picking out a few patsies in the house, he starts a dialogue with one or another, drops then returns to this one or that, summons some of them up onstage. But in sundry ways, the rest of us are also included. Much of it is insult comedy, but, as he/she keeps saying, meant in the nicest possible way. With Dame Edna, you simply kiss the knife she/he sticks into you.

Further, we have here a master/mistress of movement and facial expression whose silences are as funny as the words. Like all good comics, Edna has studied up on her venue, and the sly topical references to persons living or wishing they were dead are deadly accurate. Again, Edna is gloriously incorrect politically, and chooses targets with awesomely apposite impudence. Her timing, including throwaway lines, is a nonpareil, and her worst nonsense makes canny sense.

There is also the structure of the show. It starts out with funny shtick serving as building blocks, but the blocks become airborne balls miraculously multiplying. It turns more manic as it romps ahead, the leitmotifs juggled with not only dexterity but also mnemonic prowess, as Dame Edna remembers the names and histories of her audience victims and keeps weaving them into a tapestry as sumptuous as *The Lady with the Unicorn*, and much funnier. There is wit to spare, so I could give away free samples with impunity, except that there was not enough time between jokes to write anything down.

Edna also sings and dances, backed up by a pianist doubling as Polaroid photographer, and the Ednaettes, two attractive dancers. Let me add that the Dame herself has terrific legs—as, I'm sure, has her show.

An Experiment With an Air Pump

The larking good news is that the Manhattan Theatre Club has two fine plays on right now. On Stage One, we get Shelagh Stephenson's *An Experiment With an Air Pump*, which deals with two groups of people in the same house in 1799 and 1999. One of the latter is descended from the former, and something strange connects the two groups. "Aha," you say, "she got that from Tom Stoppard's *Arcadia*." Yes, and she makes no bones about it. In 1799, the younger generation is staging a homemade play wherein one girl represents Arcadia; could an homage be plainer? But haven't playwrights been borrowing from one another at least since the new kid on the block cannibalized Thomas Kyd? Moreover, if there can be in music variations on a theme by Corelli, why not variations in drama on a theme by Stoppard?

Stephenson does a good job, which is what matters. Her play concerns stubborn problems: head versus heart, art versus science, the souring of love in marriage, the tantalizing survival of the past, and the transience or persistence of both fame and infamy. I just said that Stephenson makes no bones about something; but she does have the 1999ers discover under their house a set of bones from a hasty 1799 burial, and thereby hangs a heartbreaking tale the moderns cannot decipher.

In the Newcastle home of Dr. Joseph and the erudite but unfulfilled Susannah Fenwick live also their daughters, Maria and Harriet. Two young scientists, the ruthless Armstrong and the principled Roget (future father of the thesaurus) are regular guests. For it is here that the playwright imagines the famous Newcastle Literary and Philosophical Society to have met, and she has much fun inventing absurd titles for their papers. In 1999, the house is being sold by a descendant of the Fenwicks, Ellen, a geneticist wooed by a company experimenting with human pre-embryos, and her husband, Tom, a lit-prof. victim of downsizing, leery of putting down embryos.

In 1799, we hear people rioting outside for cheaper fish prices, even as the Fenwick circle hopes for better centuries to come. In 1999, Tom and Phil, a repairman, regret the selling of the house to a corporation, while Ellen has doubts about the biological-engineering job offered by Kate, a younger colleague, a scientist as heartless now as Armstrong was back then. Tom, tortured by unemployment, is even more skeptical about that job. Outer and inner turmoil cross over the centuries in chiastic form; the new millennium, foreseen in 1799 and accosted in 1999, holds out scant chiliastic promise.

The play's title derives from a famous old painting (shown on-stage) depicting a group watching a scientific experiment; the onstage events both mirror and acridly reverse the painted situation. Stephenson's writing is literate yet straightforward, as when Tom exclaims, "I am going to sail into the twenty-first century as a middle-aged redundant man supported by a younger, sexier wife who works at the cutting edge of technology. Maybe there's a sort of poetic justice to it." If the justice in *Air Pump* is only poetic, the poetry is decidedly just, as in the simple but poignant 1799 toast "to a future we dream about but cannot know."

The comedy in 1799 circles around Harriet's silly play, with the girl smarting from writerly inadequacy and hopelessly wanting to be a doctor. Also around the awkward letters from and to her Indian-army fiancé read out by Maria before a moving curtain, behind which scenes and epochs change. The sadness is in Susannah's frustration and the dread fate that befalls Isobel, the Fenwicks' Scottish maid, a highly intelligent, hunchbacked autodidact. Out of all these threads, the author weaves a carpet whose figures we must detect if we are to discern the patterns of time and history, and our own share in them.

Christopher Duva's Roger, Jason Butler Harner's Armstrong and Phil, Ana Reeder's Harriet and Kate, and Clea Lewis's Maria (if you don't mind her looks of an anorectic Bette Midler) are all good. Even better are Daniel Gerroll's Joseph and Tom, Linda Emond's Susannah and Ellen, and Seana Kofoed's Isobel. The play has discreetly dextrous staging by Doug Hughes, masterly décor by John Lee Beatty, subtle costumes by Catherine Zuber, telling music by

David Van Tieghem, and lighting by Brian MacDevitt to take your breath away.

Dinner With Friends

Slowly but surely, Donald Margulies is establishing himself as one of our leading playwrights. Four of his plays are of prime importance: *The Loman Family Picnic, Sight Unseen, Collected Stories,* and now the wonderful *Dinner With Friends*.

Two married couples have been best friends for years. In their Connecticut home, Karen and Gabe, international food writers, are giving a dinner for Beth and Tom, which he doesn't attend. It emerges from the heartbroken Beth that he has left her for another woman, Nancy. Gabe and Karen are almost as crushed, having expected "to grow old and fat together, the four of us." When Tom shows up at his home in the next scene, late at night, he is enraged that Beth broke the news of their breakup in his absence. Late as it is, he rushes over to his friends in the next scene to present his side of the story.

Act Two begins with another dinner, twelve and a half years earlier, in a summer house on Martha's Vineyard, where Karen and Gabe are introducing Beth to Tom. Then we skip to five months after the events of Act One, as Beth reveals to Karen, on the summer-house patio, that she has fallen in love with an old friend whom she intends to marry. Rather than share in Beth's happiness, a shocked—and envious—Karen does everything to dissuade Beth, who justifiably resents her meddling. Later that day, in a Manhattan bar, Tom, a lawyer, tells Gabe about his happiness with Nancy, to which Gabe reacts sourly.

Still later that night, Gabe and Karen are going to bed in the Vineyard house, and discuss the Tom-and-Beth situation, as well as their own by-now-uneventful marriage, in which they soldier on without much passion and with some misgivings, clinging to it like the shipwrecked to their raft.

From this already you can gather that there is skillful construction here, as well as keen psychological insight. Thus Tom and Beth end their aforementioned angry confrontation by hungrily enacting the beast with two backs. Thus Tom's racing over to his friends to justify himself has an additional motive: Karen's fabulous lemon-almond polenta cake that Beth tells him was a comfort to her and whose leftovers he's dying to taste. Thus the strength and weakness of a stagnant marriage are emblematized in the ritual of folding a bedspread in perfect harmony but with robotic emotional detachment.

Margulies is a master of observing what might seem old hat with fresh eyes, hearing it with fresh ears. When the jealousy-racked Karen wonders about Beth's longstanding infidelity, "We saw them practically every weekend in those days; when would she have had time for an affair?" Gabe answers, "I don't know, during the week?" This is funny, especially as Matthew Arkin delivers it, but with an underscoring of wistfulness. Throughout, this ostensibly contented pair give off an aroma of envy as their opposite numbers cut loose from the time "when practical matters begin to outweigh abandon."

Take Beth's confession that during some stupid action movie she refused to fondle Tom's crotch:

KAREN: "Was this before or after the girlfriend?"
BETH: "Must've been after."
KAREN: "That's right, one more nail in the old coffin."
BETH: "You got it."
GABE: "See that? One lousy hand job, you could've saved your marriage."
KAREN: "Gabe!"

You can feel that Karen's exclamation is only partly concern for Beth's feelings.

Daniel Sullivan's inventive direction helps immeasurably, as does Neil Patel's perfect-pitch set design. Matthew Arkin superbly lets Gabe's doubts peck through his certainties; Lisa Emery does Karen's edginess on the threshold of hysteria splendidly. As Beth, Julie White again proves herself a complete comedienne down to those little inchoate noises that convey seismic tremors; as Tom, Kevin Kilner goes from likable to ludicrous without skipping a beat. *Dinner With Friends* is entertainment as succulent as it is sobering.

Marie Christine; In the Blood

When Michael John LaChuisa works in musical comedy—notably in *Hello Again*, but also elsewhere—he is on safe ground. But he has written that there are no significant differences between the musical and opera, and he has ambitions in that direction, as his current *Marie Christine* strongly suggests. Unfortunately, it is an unholy mess that tosses more unrelated and indigestible things *into* the pot than, if they were tossed out, an entire kitchen sink could hold.

LaChiusa wrote the work for Audra McDonald, as a retelling of the Medea story set in turn-of-last-century New Orleans and Chicago. Two things prove immediately and glaringly wrong with his book—or is it libretto? He often cannot find proper new equivalents for the mythical tale: the daughters of Pelias are reduced from 50 to 2, and their killing of their father becomes a brief danced hugger-mugger, too opaque for the uninitiated. The book is so episodic and disjointed, in so many clashing styles, that it suspends more goodwill than disbelief.

The mise-en-scène, by the director-choreographer Graciela Daniele, is equally untidy and confusing. Christopher Barreca's set is a round arena behind which stretches a steeply raked platform, half of which sometimes turns into a set of stairs. Behind it, lampposts may waddle in; above, chandeliers may do a round dance. To the left of the arena is a pie-slice-shaped set of bleachers, where supporting players and chorus members may sit when they're not seated in the auditorium. This is all very grand, but cohabits poorly with supposedly intimate scenes in private rooms, which one stick of furniture surfacing through a trap door sheepishly tries to convey.

The lighting, by Jules Fisher and Peggy Eisenhauer, is meant to help situate us but often grandly overshoots the mark as it tries to project the misadventures of the Creole beauty Marie Christine with the fickle sea captain Dante Keyes from Chicago onto a cosmic, mythical plane. Her voodoo (or *voudon*) skills are underscored by a drummer, perched high above stage right, who periodically beats out a devil's tattoo.

Presently, a new clashing element obtrudes: a Chicago brothel run by the madam Magdalena, a favorite hangout of Boss Gates's gang. Here Dante, Gates's protégé is stumping for political office, and also performs a love dance with Gates's daughter Helena, for whom he is dumping Marie Christine. In this dance, the now pathetically pursuing Marie joins in with unintended overtones of a ménage à trois.

Magdalena unwieldily intrudes. In the brothel, she provides crass comic relief, reducing the show to a stale Wildhornish musical. Then she reappears as a supposedly serious character (King Aegeus, in drag, no less) who, in exchange for being made fertile by

Marie's magic, promises to get Marie's little boys back to her within a month if only she will yield them up to their father, Dante, who ferociously claims them. How she would manage that we're not told, and Mary Testa's camping as Magdalena drags the show further down. The ineptly conceived murder of the boys is resoundingly anticlimactic.

And the score? In trying to be operatic, LaChiusa, whose lyrics are serviceable, comes up with music that tends to be thwartingly dissonant, indeed chaotic. When it deigns to turn up a melody, it is simplistic and has-beenish. And what pretentiousness! Thus one of Marie's brothers sings a totally out-of-place setting of Jules Laforgue's poem "Complainte de Lord Pierrot" in what might as well be Swahili. No wonder Marie promptly stabs him to death.

Audra McDonald is a fine singing actress who, as Marie Christine, does everything vocally and histrionically possible to keep us involved. Anthony Crivello's Dante is less impressive, and the rest are a mixed bag. But Toni-Leslie James's costumes are apt and, when required, elegant, and Jonathan Tunick's orchestrations toil valiantly. But such peripheral virtues can no more hold this patchy show together than Band-Aids could Apsyrtus, the chopped-up brother whom the mythic Medea threw in the path of her pursuers. The many previous retellings of the Medea story all strove to tell us more about the troubled heroine; only *Marie Christine* is content to tell us less.

Suzan-Lori Parks's plays have been eccentric, attitudinizing, overambitious. So were her statements about them—e.g., this, in *Bomb* magazine: "My plays are like these [Oberammergau] passion plays where the community comes together to re-enact the passion of whomever." The passion of whomever was there all right, but closer to the Ontological-Hysterical than to Oberammergau.

In her latest, *In the Blood*, Parks has her characters clumsily voice their interior monologues in spotlighted "confessions," and Hester La Negrita's five young bastards, always near starvation under a megalopolitan bridge, are played by the same adult actors who portray their fathers and Hester's various tormentors. These include the black preacher, father of her youngest; an unfeeling white doctor; a white girlfriend who dragged Hester into drugs and porn exhibitions; and a callous black welfare lady who got Hester involved in a threesome with her husband.

The thrust here isn't so much antiracist as pro-feminist, and Hester herself, whose knowledge of the alphabet stops at the letter A, is Parks's take on Hester Prynne. The play itself is Parks's updating of *The Scarlet Letter*, as, upon seeing it, you might easily not have guessed. Hester is somewhat shiftless, but she does provide food for her children (we're not told how) while denying it to herself (we're not told how she survives).

Nevertheless, the good news is that the stylization largely works, and that a recognizably human story is told. As Hester, Charlayne Woodard gives an affecting performance, unaffected even when she is forced to deliver over-poetic lines. However down-and-out and ragged, this Hester maintains a lambent dignity. Rob Campbell, Gail Grate, Bruce MacVittie, and Deirdre O'Connell do justice to their widely divergent dual roles, and only Reggie Montgomery hams it up under David Esbjornson's otherwise acceptable direction. If Parks's next play marks an advance similar to the one *In the Blood* does over its predecessors, it should be eagerly anticipated.*

---

*P.S. 2005: No advance. Parks has been getting steadily worse—downright abominable.

Criticism from
the 2000s

Minnelli on Minnelli

On nobody's shoulders has celebrity weighed more heavily than on Liza Minnelli's. Trying to live up to two famous and gifted parents with your own rather modest endowments is no easy task, and having to watch your mother going to pieces must also take its toll. In paying tribute to her father via the music in his films, Liza, with *Minnelli on Minnelli*, is also seeking redemption for herself. She is a performer whose chief diet is audience adulation, and what is partly a tribute to Dad's movies is also partly Daughter's comeback from alcoholism, overweight, and an overlong absence from regular performing.

Undeniably, someone or something fills up the Palace stage. It is not so much the now chubby Betty Boop face, the tubby torso that Bob Mackie's artful, and sometimes even tasteful, costumes toil to disguise. Nor is it the voice, although it can still, despite some frayed edges, belt out a song punchily, even if dentures (?) put an extra h after the s's and an extra y after the t's. It is certainly not the dancing, done mostly by a clutch of agile chorus boys who sometimes, in one of showbiz's oldest tricks, wheel Liza about on a chair with casters, which here takes on symbolic dimensions.

What is patently, pleadingly, hungrily on view at the Palace is a giant Need that handily earns a capital N. This Need cries "LOVE ME!" from all its wide-open pores, sneaks an entwined sob and laugh into every spoken word, and is a huge vacuum cleaner sucking up every sliver of adoration the audience lets drop. It is an epic, an epochal Need that lets this petite waif out-orphan all Annies,

out-hunger all Oliver Twists. It is too big even for a Vincente Minnelli movie, and clamors for D. W. Griffith. It has inherited all the
wrong things: Vincente's looks and voice, Judy's judgment and self-
control; yet, quavering but undaunted, it can swallow an entire vast
auditorium and still remain unglutted, needy.

Although John Arnone's scenery is routine stuff, Howell Binkley's lighting doubles heroically as sculpture and architecture, and
several wizards have contributed musical, vocal, and dance arrangements. You will not leave without feeling something, though
whether it is admiration, compassion, embarrassment, or sadness
is very hard to assess.

The Wild Party

Manhattan Theatre Club offers the first installment of a unique phenomenon: two major musicals, soon to be concurrent, both derived
from a narrative poem by Joseph Moncure March, *The Wild Party*.
At MTC, *The Wild Party* has book, music, and lyrics by Andrew
Lippa, remembered favorably for his additional songs and arrangements for the recent *You're a Good Man, Charlie Brown*.

The problem with this show about a wild party given in 1929 by a
pair of vaudevillians, a clown and a dancer whose crumbling affair
is to be revivified by a bacchanal, is that a stage work cannot readily
proceed from one thing to another in linear fashion like a poem: it
has to keep the populous partiers in simultaneous sight, occupied
with this or that. Cinematically put, you have to shoot at once in
close-up and with a wide-angle lens. Theatrical history is littered
with the corpses of attempts at this sort of thing.

Matters are further complicated by the period. The music has to
be jazz-age but also, to avoid pastiche, contemporary. Moreover,
new song lyrics have to blend in with the original's narrative verse,
preserved in unavoidable spoken passages. Most troubling, both
the old poem and the new lyrics tend toward the level of "Let me
drown in females foreign, / Let me dangle from a limb; / Teach
me how to put my oar in, / But don't you dare to teach me how to
swim." Or, worse yet, "Like a member of the pack, / I ramble; / Like
a ledger in the black, / I gamble."

The story comes down to a quadrangle. The clown, Burrs,
bored after a three-year cohabitation, cannot let go of the dancer,

Queenie, who, though unhappy, cannot overcome inertia and leave. He still brutalizes, she still endures. The party guests include Kate, an ex-whore risen in station, and her escort, the spiffy Mr. Black, actually a club doorman, who promptly goes for Queenie, as she, by and by, does for him. Kate vainly tries to seduce Burrs, who's jealously eager to recapture Queenie. It all ends in curiously unaffecting bloodshed.

Lippa's music, though idiomatic, is not rich in melody, depending largely on rhythm and harmony. Yet after periods of waffling, it can achieve moments of moody or sprightly tunefulness, even if mostly in novelty numbers rather than in integrated, character-developing ones. Typical is the bouncy lesbian's ironic "An Old-Fashioned Love Story," zestily delivered by Alix Korey.

David Gallo has designed an open platform with jazzy floor patterns that can split into two to five unequal, jagged sections on which groups or individuals are suggestively stranded. In the zigzagging gaps between sections, processions of revelers can parade in hectic merriment. The platform is surrounded on three sides by facades of buildings ominously leaning toward center stage: a few sticks of furniture create, as the floor reconfigures itself, different constellations.

Kenneth Posner's lighting throws additional jazzy patterns on the floor, catches groups in skewering lateral beams, or encloses individuals in a cage of light as sheaves of separate white or colored rays hurtle from above. Martin Pakledinaz's costuming is jauntily fantastical, but here a prevailing inconsistency becomes objectified as the initially weirdly expressionist costumes turn bohemianly realistic. Consistently fine are Michael Gibson's orchestrations: bluesy, funky, boisterous, or dwindling to single melancholy instruments, always firmly supportive of the action.

Under Gabriel Barre's intelligent direction, the ensemble work is solid and the four principals realize their less-than-ample opportunities. Julia Murney's Queenie is a compelling flapper fatale, Brian d'Arcy James's Burrs, as described, "a very scary clown"; both sing winningly. As Mr. Black, Taye Diggs is by turns restrained and commanding, but the show is stolen by the ebullient Idina Menzel's Kate, a veritable geyser of vitality. Mark Dendy's choreography is better in acrobatic solos than in unified group numbers, which lack diversity; Lawrence Keigwin's acrobatic dancing, though, is exhilarating. The excitement is mostly in the production values; even so, this *Wild Party* never bogs down for too long.

The Tale of the Allergist's Wife

As the poet Horace observed, parturient mountains can give birth to a ridiculous mouse. More rarely, the reverse occurs. This is not quite the case of Charles Busch's *The Tale of the Allergist's Wife*, yet who would have expected from a campy downtown playwright a nicely structured, intelligently funny, satirically relevant uptown comedy? It has only two defects. The minor one is that Rilke is not buried in Germany, as here averred, but in Switzerland; the major one, that Busch could not think of a good ending.

The retired but still overactive allergist Dr. Ira Taub is married to Marjorie, an immobilized nervous wreck since the death of her therapist. To be sure, her troubles run deep. She has read all the right books, attended every conceivable concert, lecture, and exhibition, and is an expert on German literature and, especially, Hermann Hesse, whose *Siddhartha* is her favorite. But this has only marginalized Marjorie: a failed novelist, she cannot gain entry into the artistic and intellectual life she craves. She is not helped by Ira, who, though devoted, has little time for her or Hesse: still less by her kvetching Jewish mother, Frieda, preoccupied with her bowel movements and indifferent to her daughter's inertia. Not to mention that, in the Bronx River Road days, Frieda always favored her other children.

So now the elegantly furnished (by Santo Loquasto) Upper West Side apartment of the Taubs is a battleground: Marjorie, hysterically snapping at Ira and Frieda, cannot find peace even in her ability to quote Kafka and Cocteau. When her mother is at the door, she wishes it were Simone de Beauvoir. Well, one fine day it almost is. In comes Lee Green, ostensibly having rung the wrong bell. This fabulously dressed (by Ann Roth), youngish woman is in fact Lillian Greenblatt, a long-ago neighbor, whose many lives have included bonding in the Village with Kerouac, Baldwin, and Andy; sleeping with Günter Grass (how much closer to German literature can you get?); working for Chanel in Paris; acting in a Fassbinder movie; sitting at dinner between Kissinger and Princess Di; and reading all of Hesse, including *Magister Ludi*.

This last made me suspicious: I doubt if anybody, Hesse included, ever finished reading *Magister Ludi*. And, sure enough, Lee is not quite what she seems to be. More of this witty, civilized play I cannot reveal, except that it needs a better ending. But not to despair: "Old I may be," says Hesse's Govinda to Siddhartha, "but I shall never stop seeking."

If you seek an ideal cast, look no further. Linda Lavin, for whom the admiring Busch wrote Marjorie as, he says, a kind of King Lear, is that and more: Lady Macbeth, Willy Loman, Lydia Languish, and, better yet, herself at her dizzying best. As the befuddled Ira, Tony Roberts is—well, I'll say it—adorable. As the mother and mother-in-law from Gehenna, Shirl Bernheim is it, from aleph to omega. For Lee, Michele Lee is in every way as perfect as her last name. And as Mohammed the doorman, Anil Kumar is what I've always longed for: no doorman of mine has ever been able to discuss Nadine Gordimer with me.

Having already praised Santo Loquasto and Ann Roth, let me add merely that Christopher Akerlind's lighting supplies delicious touches—note just what the chandelier does during scene changes. And Lynne Meadow has directed with the comic know-how of one who has digested everything from *Demian* to *Damn Yankees*. As for Charles Busch, he could have supplied generations of similarly named politicians with a full complement of humor.

The Noise of Time

In the past two centuries, an ultraconservative spirit decried all innovation in the arts with suspicion and derision. Under the subsequent dispensation, anything new and different was hailed with blind enthusiasm, irrespective of its utter meaninglessness: one must not be the last to salute a potential classic. Of the two forms of delinquency, the second is by far the worse. Opposition forces the innovator to strive harder, resort to subtlety to circumvent intolerance. Mindless salivating at novelty merely encourages phonies to peddle their inanities to unwarranted Pavlovian acclaim.

Such is the case of the Theatre de Complicite's *The Noise of Time*, a piece of sheer pretension, ineptitude, and emptiness that elicited deafening audience ovations and two glowing features plus two rave reviews from our newspaper of record. It confirms my belief that were you to put a pair of copulating dogs on the stage, you, too, could, with the inevitable hype, pass for as great an artist as the charlatan, lunatic, or imbecile Simon McBurney, guiding light (or chief obfuscator) of Complicite, who conceived and staged this piece. It purports to shed light on the life of Dmitri Shostakovich, on how we hear music, on the place of the artist in history, on the somber meanings of the composer's fifteenth and last quartet, and, for all I know, on the price of eggs.

To be sure, McBurney pulled one clever stunt: the last 35 minutes or so of this 80-minute farrago are taken up by the excellent Emerson String Quartet's rendition of the Quartet No. 15, well worthy of applause. Especially so if you consider that the Emersons had to play in near darkness, standing, perambulating, or sitting too far apart for eye contact, and finally seated on a platform in two rows facing the audience, thus going from strolling gypsy musicians to artful posers for a publicity photograph. For much less money, you could have caught an evening of the Emerson's recent five-part traversal of the complete quartets, played, in chronological order, in full view and with unimpeded hearing.

For in the sparsely lit *The Noise of Time*, there is neither full view nor unimpeded hearing, to say nothing of sense. Those who know that the loudspeakers' oft-referred-to Slava is Mstislav Rostropovich, that the composer's bombastic wartime Seventh Symphony was broadcast on an NBC national hookup (we hear scratchy shreds of it), that the young Dmitri was a movie-theater pianist once caught in a cinema fire, that Stalin & Co. made the artist's life miserable, etc., will learn nothing new from garbled references here. The others will be left in an even greater dark than prevails onstage. The four nonspeaking performers enact mostly inscrutable maneuvers, carrying about women's garments or obsolete radios, transporting numerous lonescoan chairs on and off, dismantling a cello, gesticulating wildly or careering about, and making nuisances of themselves in front of a backdrop alternating photographs of the composer with sheet music, ocean waves, and meaningless abstractions. They even undermine the Emerson's playing by hovering about, pretending to read the sheet music, or carrying around that deconstructed cello.

The loudspeakers blare out disconnected fragments (some of them in Russian) from an old, screechy, spotlighted radio, including bits of announcers' pontifications, snatches from Shostakovich's letters, random bursts of his Seventh Symphony, references to the cosmonaut Yuri Gagarin's singing a Shostakovich patriotic ditty in outer space, frequent salvos of applause, and lots of static. This may or may not be the noise of time (Aleksandr Blok's definition of history), but it certainly is the cacophony of fraud. The locus, for six performances, was the auditorium of the John Jay College of Criminal Justice, perpetrating on this occasion a hoax verging on the indictable.

Aida

Shakespeare could imagine nothing worse than the rude mechanicals' offering for Duke Theseus' wedding, *Pyramus and Thisby*, now far surpassed by *Pyramids and Disney*, or, as they presume to call it, *Aida*. In its earlier incarnation as *Elaborate Lives* (Atlanta, 1998), it featured a functional pyramid, which had to be scrapped for malfunctioning. I myself would have kept the pyramid, however dysfunctional, and scrapped the show.

The new version, clearly a project by committee, has a book by the schlockmistress Linda Woolverton, the precious playwright David Henry Hwang, and the deep social thinker Robert Falls, who also directed. It avers to have been "suggested by the opera," which, if consulted, could only have suggested, "Get lost!" What *Rent* did to *La bohème*, *Aida* the musical does to *Aida* the opera in spades. Not least ludicrous is the happy ending, brazenly purloined from *One Touch of Venus*, whose dorky hero, having lost the goddess herself, hooks up with her human double at a museum. Here, in a museum prologue and epilogue, the present-day reincarnations of Radames and Aida, after stalking each other around the Egyptian collection, lock into a closing clinch.

As heralded by stinkers like *Saturday Night Fever* and *The Civil War*, the undignifiedly Disneyfied *Aida* is that new kind of musical in which nothing much works. But if it can reach the mightiest of target audiences, the ear-brain-and-taste-impaired, it can, borne aloft by Disney's deep pockets, run at least as forever as *Cats*.

Elton John has concocted a score wherein everything sounds the same—i.e., tuneless, without even enough theatrical savvy to make the particular tunelessness appropriate to the character who mouths it. For the first-act finale, though, he reached for something grander, "The Gods Love Nubia," a sort of hymn or anthem for Aida and her fellow Nubian slaves in an Egyptian internment camp, on whose evidence the gods don't give an old-fashioned rap for Nubia. The arrangers and orchestrators—Paull Bogaev (who also conducts), Steve Margoshes, and Guy Babylon (slightly east of Suez)—have supplied Sir Elton's music with a disco-from-hell beat that manages to make it, to coin a phrase, worse than it sounds. Tim Rice's lyrics, some of which I tried to take down but my hand balked, wallow, perfectly matched, in the same trough as the tunes.

Aida is Heather Headley, ex-lioness from *The Lion King*, a tall, angular young woman whose acting consists of feral scowls, whose speaking voice is an ominous growl, and whose singing is a confrontational blend of bellowing and caterwauling. It appears that you can take the girl out of *The Lion King* but not the lioness out of the girl. As Amneris, her rival in love, Sherie René Scott, chooses or is directed to impersonate—as Ben Brantley aptly noted—Tori Spelling on *Beverly Hills 90210*.

The Radames, Adam Pascal (formerly of *Rent*), boasts of not having had a single singing or acting lesson, which proves incontestable, and that he has ignored the Puccini and Verdi originals so as not to "taint his ideas"—an unnecessary precaution, as he seems free from anything resembling those. The supporting players, who might have made modest contributions, abstained-perhaps from an excess of modesty.

Robert Falls's direction being no help, and Wayne Cilento's MTV-ish choreography being one part Egyptian fresco and nine parts fiasco, it's all up to the production values. Natasha Katz does some impressive and novel things with her lighting, but Bob Crowley's costumes and sets, with two exceptions, are a disaster. Palm trees are fetchingly mirrored in the Nile, and a vertical swimming pool amusingly displays fliers as swimmers. For the rest, the gifted Crowley now seems to think that a production should adapt to him rather than vice versa. His decor would be the pride of one of our classier automobile showrooms; his costumes are Las Vegas Ruritanian, except for a fashion show put on for Amneris by her handmaidens as runway models, which is straight out of Pharaoh Ziegfeld's Nilotic wet dreams.

It is rumored that the true inspiration for *Aida* was Disney's search for an excuse to market a black doll. If it does not make Headleyan sounds to frighten little children, it should be a huge success.

Copenhagen

Plays such as *Benefactors*, a shattering drama, and *Noises Off*, an incomparable farce—not to mention the dazzling novel *Headlong*—have established Michael Frayn as a major writer. So it is with infinite regret that I must confess to finding his current *Copenhagen* more admirable than compelling, more awesome than satisfying. *Copenhagen* is both a rare and sorely needed political play and an even rarer, and potentially deeper, play of ideas. The question of what might have happened had Hitler possessed the atom bomb, and the roles of the Danish physicist Niels Bohr and his German disciple Werner Heisenberg in the Allies' having it and the Nazis not, are matters of uncommon interest. Why Heisenberg sought out in occupied Denmark his former master and later partner in quantum mechanics, uncertainty principle, complementarity theory, particle physics, and atomic fission is certainly of political, historical, moral, and philosophical interest, lacking only, at least as presented here, in dramatic interest.

To me, at any rate—who already as a student cared little for math and not a particle about physics (though I loved the Latin hexameters of Lucretius on the nature of things)—all this talk about atoms and electrons, photons and neutrons, uranium and plutonium, fission and heavy water is heavy going. My awe at Frayn's exhaustive research into a hermetic field (his background is in philosophy), his effort to penetrate the mystery of a historic meeting on which so much may have hinged but about which we know so little, and his noble attempt at a parallel (perhaps even connection) between the enigmatic behaviors of particles and human beings is nothing short of boundless. Alas, respect is not tantamount to absorption.

Which is not to say that much about *Copenhagen* is not provocative and watchable. Take Peter J. Davison's design and Mark Henderson and Michael Lincoln's lighting. Take Michael Blakemore's direction, which goes as far as conceivable in humanizing abstraction, in embodying the near-disembodied. Philip Bosco as Bohr, Blair Brown as Mrs. Bohr (personifying the enlightened non-scientist's and patriotic Dane's views), and Michael Cumpsty as Heisenberg perform wonders in nudging ideas toward palpable life. Observing the actors' way with such difficult memorization and tricky interplay is no mean spectacle.

Ultimately, though, I prefer Friedrich Dürremnatt's handling of much the same topic in *The Physicists*, either in the acting version of 1960 or in the revised, more literary version of 1980. Not that this quasi-absurdist play was any more flesh-and-blood than Frayn's; it was, however, more accessible and theatrical.

The Green Bird;
The Wild Party!

The enchanting surprise of the month, if not the season, is *The Green Bird*, the 1765 fairy-tale comedy by Carlo Gozzi. As translated by Albert Bermel and Ted Emery (with added prose by Eric Overmyer and lyrics by David Suehsdorf), choreographed by Daniel Ezralow, and graced with funky pastiche music by Elliot Goldenthal, this is sheer delight, made sheerer by Christine Jones's sets, Constance Hoffman's costumes, Donald Holder's lights, and especially Julie Taymor's masks, puppets, and staging.

Forgive my clobbering you with so many names, but credit must be given where it is due. In compensation, I'll spare you the complicated plot wherein orphaned twins, Barberina and Renzo, flee their plebeian foster parents, Truffaldino and Smeraldina, to search for their true parents, King Tartaglia and his hapless queen, Ninetta, whom the wicked queen mother, Tartagliona, has imprisoned beneath the royal toilets. Tartagliona's sidekick is the evil soothsayer Brighella (all these are commedia dell'arte names), and that is only half the cast. It also includes a talking giant sculptured head, a beautiful female statue that comes to life, a sorceress's garden and an ogre, mountain, tigerish monsters, singing apples, and dancing waters. And, of course, the eponymous Green Bird, fluttering frolicsomely.

If you think this is kiddie stuff, think again. It is really for adults, although children will get enough of it to enjoy it, too. It is as much social satire as fairy story, as much comedy of manners as giddy farce. The adapters have sneaked in funny contemporary references without disrespect to Gozzi's honored bones, and a cast that looks equally good with and without masks act, up enough of a storm for a banquet set of teacups. Everyone here is delicious, but I must single out Didi Conn's pungent Smeraldina, Derek Smith's hilarious Tartaglia, Edward Hibbert's most waspish queen Tartagliona, and Andrew Weems's quick-change artistry in a passel of roles. Also Lee

Lewis, for being the loveliest of statues that ever came to life, and possibly even of those that didn't. Though more modest in scale than Miss Taymor's other triumph, the song of the *Bird* is sweeter, smarter, and subtler than the roar of the Lion.

What a fiasco, this second, Broadway version of *The Wild Party!* It makes the middling Off Broadway one look, in retrospect, like a masterpiece. (Had Andrew Lippa's version opened second, it might still be running.) From music and lyrics by Michael John LaChiusa, and a book by him and George C. Wolfe, we get a second take on the trashy late-twenties narrative poem by Joseph Moncure March, doggerel that should have been let lie by both.

The two versions are fairly different, but not enough to make us seek out the moldering original poem. This much is true of both *WPII* and *WPI*: Burrs, the ominous clown, and Queenie, the promiscuous showgirl, are sparring spouses; to bring about peace, they give a party to which they invite all the demimondains they know. *WPII* conceives this as a vaudeville entertainment with placards heralding each scene, further cheapening the cheesy proceedings.

WPI at least had some semblance of a story line; *WPII* is almost all random incidents that refuse to mesh. In both versions, a courtesan named Kate brings along a somewhat mysterious Mr. Black who becomes involved with Queenie, while Burrs fools around with Kate; finally, a gun is pulled, and someone gets killed. Both versions also feature a comic lesbian, but only this one has two comic Jews, Gold and Goldberg, two would-be producers. And here, Burrs is a blackface clown; in *WPI* he was a whiteface one.

WPII does have an asset in Eartha Kitt, but what this amazing crone prodigy contributes is her own story unrelated to the show. As Burrs, Mandy Patinkin does some super-creepy things with grating falsetto and clumsy audience participation. He is as diabolic as he is over-the-top—call it deviled ham. The excellent Tonya Pinkins is hamstrung by her role as Kate, and the macho Black, cast in *WPI* as a sexy black, is here an effete ephebe. As Queenie, Toni Collette, in an anachronistic Monroe wig, works hard and deserves our sympathy.

WPI had terrific sets and lighting, nowhere near matched here. Lamest of all is George C. Wolfe's direction, followed closely by Joey McKneely's choreography. LaChiusa's songs come off quite well as pastiche, although one misses some sort of ballad. All in all, I cannot imagine the most desperate gate-crasher wanting to be caught dead at this party.

Jitney

Jitney is the revised version of August Wilson's first play, the start of what became a ten-part series, still in progress, about African-American lives, one play per decade. Here the seventies are viewed through the goings-on in the office of a gypsy-cab company in the Pittsburgh of 1977. There are five drivers, including Becker, the owner, each with his own problems. Youngblood, a Vietnam vet, is having troubles with his woman, Rena, their small son, and the house he wants to buy for them. Fielding is an alcoholic, unable to stop drinking even on the job. Turnbo, a malicious gossip, is always fomenting dissension. Doub, the *raisonneur*, has a hard time keeping the others in line.

Boss Becker has a son, Booster, about to be released after twenty years in jail for a crime of passion, which also caused his mother's death from grief. He has cut his son off, and wants nothing to do with him. Moreover, the entire block the car service is on is to be razed forthwith. Rena suspects Youngblood of cheating on her and of stealing the household money. Only Shealy, the numbers runner, and Philmore, doorman at the nearby hotel, are relatively problem-free. If this sounds like melodrama to you, be advised: whatever it is, it is so vividly written, acted, and directed (by Marion McClinton, a Wilson specialist) that it keeps you steadily amused, concerned, and moved.

Where all performers are flawless, suffice it to list them: Willis Burks II, Paul Butler, Anthony Chisholm, Leo V. Finnie III, Stephen McKinley Henderson (who looks a lot like Wilson), Barry Shabaka Henley, Russell Hornsby, Carl Lumbly, and Michole Briana White. The lovers' quarrels between Hornsby and White, and the father-son confrontation between Butler and Lumbly, are among the strongest scenes you can see anywhere today. Add an atypical but incisive set by David Gallo, unerring costumes by Susan Hilferty, and pointed lighting by Donald Holder, and you may wonder how *Jitney* could have eluded Broadway, which—with the meter, I hope, still running—should be its next and lasting destination.

The Laramie Project

After Moisés Kaufman's clumsy and ostentatious *Gross Indecency*, about Oscar Wilde, my expectations for his new docudrama were pretty low. To my surprise, *The Laramie Project* is a terrific piece of theater, history, and life in the heartless heartlands. It concerns the horrific death of young Matthew Shepard at the hands of two very young Laramie gay-bashers, Which filled the world with sorrow and indignation a couple of years ago. Kaufman and his company, Tectonic Theater Project, traveled six times to Laramie over a year and a half, conducted hundreds of interviews and workshops, and pieced together the story of this crime that could have occurred in many places but that coming from such a relatively conflict-free state as Wyoming resounded even more shatteringly.

I hope that you know the shameful and shocking story, but even if you have extensive knowledge, you will be held in rapt attention by this in-depth examination of just about every aspect of the background and foreground of the event, as seen and heard through the eyes and mouths of numerous witnesses, neighbors, indifferent or impassioned fellow citizens, media persons, family members, direct and indirect participants. There emerges a mosaic as moving and important as any you will see on the walls of the churches of the world.

In a little over two and a half hours (including two short breathers), we get to know every nook and cranny of Laramie before, during, and after the Shepard tragedy, and so much more besides: how smart or stupid, compassionate or cruel, noble or ignoble some very ordinary—as well as some extraordinary—people can be. And beyond that, how closely compounded and confused the ordinary and the extraordinary can be within a single person. All this in the characters' own words and, as superbly enacted by eight actors in a multiplicity of roles, with their own gestures, facial expressions, intonations, pauses, tears, and laughter.

Yes, laughter too; for in the self-contradictory convolutions of human thought and action, the funny can, innocently or not, co-exist with the most tragic. Accordingly, *The Laramie Project* has some dazzlingly humorous moments that relieve—but never cancel out—the dreadful injustice that was done here. Guilty of this murder is a very large portion of humanity, however far away as the crow—but not the mud—flies. For which of us, in one way or another, has not been a wolf—or, rather, much worse than this noble animal—to his fellow man?

Both the individual pieces and their assemblage here are nothing short of stunning, in both senses of the word. I name the eight good actors who, as researchers, collaborated with Kaufman and his assistant, Leigh Fondakowski: Stephen Belber, Amanda Gronich, Mercedes Herrero, John McAdams, Andy Paris (the only one who sometimes overacts a bit), Greg Pierotti, Barbara Pitts, and Kelli Simpkins, not forgetting Robert Brill (set), Moe Schell (costumes), Betsy Adams (lighting), and the highly evocative music of Peter Golub. Nowadays, when every piece of dreck receives standing ovations from foolish and self-important theatergoers, you should not miss a theatrical and human event that deserves standing up for, with applause or, better yet, silently, taking an important lesson profoundly to heart.

Proof; Don Carlos

Manhattan Theater Club does it again! David Auburn's *Proof* is what *Copenhagen* ought to be: a play about scientists whose science matters less than their humanity. Here, those of us who want their dramatic characters to be real people need not feel excluded. Robert, a world-famous mathematician who went crazy; Catherine, his mathematically brilliant but too-depressed-to-work daughter: Hal, a young math teacher going through Robert's hundred-plus confused notebooks; and Claire, Robert's older daughter and a successful actuary, are above all fascinating individuals. Robert isn't any less human even for being, through most of the play, dead. All four—whether loving, hating, encouraging or impeding one another—are intensely alive, complex, funny, human.

The very first scene in *Proof* is masterly: a birthday dialogue between father and daughter, in which Catherine, alive, is barely living, and her celebrated father is sparklingly trying to rouse her into action although he is (I hate to give it away but must) dead—Catherine's fantasy. Yet this mysterious, droll, and electrifying scene is really exposition in disguise: something generally a bore, but here so splendidly reconceived as to fascinate—as indeed all of *Proof* does.

So here we have Robert, the near-genius mathematician who

went mad and eventually died, and Catherine, who gave up a potentially great mathematical career to look after him and, in the process, let herself run down, perhaps irreversibly. Here, too, is Claire, the narrowly practical daughter, who wants to save Catherine from what may be incipient madness by dragging her from Chicago to New York and supervising her life—benignly as she sees it, but horribly as Catherine does. And here is Hal, revering Robert's work and secretly in love with Catherine, fumbling and bungling everything. Out of this curious quartet, Auburn creates emotionally and intellectually enveloping music.

The performances are perfect: Larry Bryggman's lovable but exasperating Robert; Johanna Day's officious yet well-meaning Claire; Ben Shenkman's clumsy but gradually maturing Hal. As for Mary-Louise Parker, her Catherine is a performance of genius. Is there another young actress as manifold, incisive, sexy, and effortlessly overpowering? Add to this Daniel Sullivan's superb direction and the classy production values (by John Lee Beatty, Jess Goldstein, and Pat Collins), and it all spells J-O-Y. Instead of taking up more time reading, you are urged to run and get your tickets immediately.

What the Royal Shakespeare Company has done to Schiller's *Don Carlos* (1787) is worse than deconstruction: wanton destruction. Let's start with one example of Robert David Macdonald's flatfooted translation. Schiller's Queen Elizabeth says of the rustic Aranjuez surroundings: "Hier grüsst mich meine ländliche Natur, / Die Busenfreundin meiner jungen Jahre," which I approximate with: "Here I am greeted by my country nature, / The boon companion of my younger years." MacDonald contrives: "What I find here is nature still unspoilt. / The way it was when I was still a child"—prosaic and platitudinous, with total loss of Schiller's imagery.

Next, the admittedly long play was cut to shreds, though given this mounting, it is still overlong. Gale Edwards, the Australian director and current London hotshot, further prosified the production with inapt modern dress by Sue Wilmington, stale décor by Peter J. Davison, and gross music by Gary Yershon. The drama is about the repressively totalitarian, Catholic values of 1568 Spain clashing with the liberal-humanitarian ideals of Prince Carlos and his gallant friend the Marquis of Posa. It requires the austere costumes and forbidding backgrounds against which freedom—political, moral, sexual—rebels. In silly modern dress, nothing makes sense.

Further, Edwards has Carlos (Rupert Penry-Jones) epigonous-ly aping early Brando-James Dean acting, hurling himself about like a boomerang, howling like an aborigine in the outback, grab-bing people unceremoniously by the neck, or dispensing loutishly chummy kisses. The others perform just as problematically and are, confusingly, in many cases black. This bespeaks a progressive, enlightened court, hardly stifling and revolt-inducing. The crazed, druggy Carlos would not have been handed over to the Inquisi-tion, merely sent to rehab, and not plotted against by Princess Eboli played as a Spice Girl formerly known as Princess. I felt sorry only for John Woodvine as King Philip, a solid actor vulgarly misdirected by Miss Edwards, who similarly mucked up the current *Jesus Christ Superstar*. She should be sent back to Australia to train kangaroos to jump through hoops.

Macbeth

Dustin Hoffman used to tell a story (apocryphal, no doubt) about John Wayne's essaying the lead in a stage production of *Macbeth*. In no time, the audience erupted in guffaws. Angered, the Duke marched downstage and bellowed, "Listen, I didn't write this crap!" The good news about Kelsey Grammer's version of *Macbeth* is that it wasn't funny. The bad news is that it would have been better if it had been, rather than what it was: dull.

Clearly contrived on the cheap and in haste, this production, since closed, turned "the Scottish play" into a skittish play, and, worse yet, a sottish play. It sprinted (actually huffed and puffed) through the text in under two hours, either to make the *Guinness Book of Records* or to emulate Tom Stoppard's *The 15-Minute Ham-let*. The words were spoken not only trippingly on the tongue but also without much thought or feeling allowed to get in their way. When more emotion was needed, the volume was turned up, or the elocution became more orotund. Sometimes, especially by Gram-mer, the relentless rush was encroached on by misplaced caesuras or unwarranted pauses, producing a vocal arrhythmia without sig-nificant deceleration, let alone significance.

The text, though Shakespeare's shortest, was somewhat cut, and played without intermission, sanctioned perhaps by Malcolm's "We shall not spend a large expense of time" and Macduff's "Gentle heavens, cut short all intermission," however different their context. This may have helpfully covered up some of the (to rephrase Proust) intermittences of the art, but it also increased the sense of hugger-mugger. The set-and-costume designer, Timothy O'Brien, had made everything black (Ad Reinhardt would have rejoiced), except white tops for the Macbeths on ceremonial occasions and blue-gray for Lady Macduff and her children. This could have worked (see below) if variety had been achieved elsewhere. It would also have worked to keep the period vaguely modern (see below again) if this had been consistent. But Terry Hands, the director, began with an invented longish battle sequence with distinctly medieval broadswords and even some visored helmets, only to drop the helmets, but not the swords, as the costumes o'erleaped a handful of centuries.

The mostly empty stage nevertheless featured a drawbridgelike staircase and a similarly retractable catwalk, but Hands's lighting was more elaborate and did create some striking effects. Other things, though, were badly garbled. One wonders, for instance, why the witches, two of whom were already played by blacks, had their faces blackly besmeared like mud wrestlers, though all they wrestled with was their lines, Myra Lucretia Taylor even managing to make hers incomprehensible. The supporting cast, which had some name recognition, did not offer a single noteworthy performance.

More disturbing was that Diane Venora, a usually fine Shakespearean (her Gertrude managed to survive even Andrei Serban's stage *Hamlet* and Michael Almereyda's movie one) was a clichéd Lady Macbeth. Looking unduly matronly, moving foursquarely (poor blocking from Hands), and delivering her lines with rote histrionics, she sadly sank to her co-star's level. Kelsey Grammer was not awful, merely unpoetic, untragic, uninteresting. Shakespeare somewhat cavalierly stinted on showing us much of Macbeth's initial positive sides, save his martial prowess, so that his corruption through vaulting ambition does not readily make us feel the loss of a good man. Hence it helps if the actor is a fine figure of a man, of noble countenance and with a beautiful speaking voice. Grammer can't claim any of this. He conscientiously delivered the words and went through the prescribed motions, but there was nothing noble about his visage, virtuosic in his movements, arresting about his voice. He could not make even the greatest verses sing.

B. H. Barry had worked out some scary dueling sequences with those heavy swords, for which the actors deserve medals for bravery. But what sort of coronation banquet is given for only two invited guests, and without the ghostly Banquo either visible or adequately suggested? The witches' cauldron was of thermos size for Weird Sisters traveling light; the Sisters themselves impersonating the awesome prophesying apparitions as they circled Macbeth in a ring-around-the-rosy. Macbeth twice got the better of Macduff in their climactic duel—even knocked him down once—and could easily have finished him off were it not that the witches appeared (unsolicited by the text) and did him in. Could it have been, given that Macduff was played by a black actor, racial solidarity? Malcolm, looking rather like funny little Teller of Penn and Teller, did not hold much promise for running post-Macbeth Scotland.

Meanwhile, New Haven's international Festival of Arts and Ideas imported intact a highly successful Royal Shakespeare Company production of *Macbeth* (also now closed), running about ten minutes longer than the New York one but hardly dawdling. Its likewise black sets and costumes were by Stephen Brimson Lewis, inventively lighted by Tim Mitchell. It had live musicians, performing rousing Japanese-flavored music by Adrian Lee that beat Colin Towns's canned score for the Grammer version, though it did at times become too raucous. These costumes, too, were modern, but more aptly devised and with more relief from straight black.

Here, too, there was a kind of drawbridge, albeit a traditional one, from behind which a golden glow bathed the Macbeths at their coronation. There were some stirring *coups de théâtre*, as when the witches were heard from under the banqueting table, which they crashingly overturned as they emerged. The ghostly presences were faces pressed from behind against a black rubber backdrop, molding themselves into creepy high relief. The cauldron here, too, was modest but not diminutive, and there was something interesting suspended from above that could have been clouds, branches, or abstract sculpture. The witches had powerful voices but rather odd, tomboyish costumes. Hard as it must be to get small British children away for a tour, it was unfortunate that Lady Maccluff seemed to have only one boy to represent "all my pretty ones," especially since Fleance was played here by a boy who could have done some doubling.

But the grossest violation of the text by the RSC involved the porter. Played by an atypically young man, and haranguing the audience like Dame Edna, he launched on a spoof of Bill Clinton, interpolating into the "equivocator" passage references to Arkansas and some of the notorious Monica doubletalk. Otherwise, this was a good production, even if Antony Sher, the Macbeth, looked rather plebeian, not unlike Bob Hoskins. He made up for it by being a most accomplished actor, with a sardonic glitter in his darting eyes, a way of exuding intensity even when perfectly still, a voice suffused with streetwise cunning, and a coiled-spring quality hovering between mockery and menace. But he did go astray with the "Tomorrow and tomorrow" soliloquy, which he declaimed too artificially.

Harriet Walter was a wonderful Lady Macbeth: a faintly neurotic society hostess with aristocratic hauteur that did not quite conceal traces of hysteria. Her gaze was haughty, her manipulation of Macbeth rather grande dame-ish as she nudged and shamed her somewhat less classy husband upward. This worked much more chillingly than the usual frenzied exhortation of a power-hungry climber, and made the unraveled sleepwalking scene, by contrast, even more pathetic. The others contributed handsomely under Gregory Doran's generally sound direction. A final cavil, though, about Macduff's fighting Macbeth's broadsword with a wooden pole, particularly bizarre after Macduff's plea, "Within my sword's length set him." A case of pole-vaulting ambition?

Finally, what set this production many lengths ahead of Grammer's American *Macbeth* was its Britishness. British English, however it may have sounded in Shakespeare's day, has acquired a poetry-enhancing speech melody that tuneless, flat American cannot match. Great acting can compensate to an extent, but the New York production had none of that, with the master of Dunsinane little better than an inane dunce.

Spinning Into Butter

Rebecca Gilman's *Spinning Into Butter* is a brave, honest, intelligent, and important play, which mitigates its being only intermittently well-written. It concerns racism by the educated white, liberal woman dean of a small Vermont college but also reverse racism by a Puerto Rican student who aggressively puts the would-be helpful dean, Sarah Daniels, on the defensive. It reveals the hypocrisy of various types of whites who claim to be concerned anti-racists—a

couple of other quite insensitive deans, a Wasp senior who organiz-
es a Students for Tolerance group from self-serving motives—but
it ultimately also attacks political correctness, the no-win situation
into which the fictional Belmont College, like so much of America,
has steered itself.

We see here characters so concerned with doing the politically
correct thing that they neglect doing the humanly right one, which
is to engage in any sort of dialogue with the black student who has
been getting anonymous, threatening hate letters. When Sarah, at
play's end, reaches out to him, the promise of future understanding
is guardedly adumbrated.

The play has at least two triumphs. The major one is a twenty-
minute monologue in which Sarah—with great candor, insight, and
unsparingness—relates and analyzes the history of her racism, in
a way that must buttonhole, disturb, and set to constructive thinking every unclenched spectator. If the writing were on this level
throughout, the play would be a surefire winner.

The minor triumph is twofold. When Sarah tells Ross, the truly
liberal fine-arts prof and her former lover, that she hates Toni Morrison, and makes out a case for why "her books suck," and again
later, when she tells the fellow deans, "So what if she won the Nobel
Prize'? So did Pearl S. Buck." It takes considerable courage in this
p.c. society to attack this most overrated bad writer full blast. And
where a lesser playwright would have written "Pearl Buck," that
mock-conscientious "Pearl S. Buck" augurs the master.

There are, however, flaws. The protocol and procedures of a college are oversimplified and even distorted; the circumstances of
Sarah's dismissal are a bit forced; the salt-of-the-earth, blue-collar,
white campus cop is idealized, though Gilman says that idealization
is a form of patronization; the lone art professor is not representative of the faculty; the nonpresence of the college president is a defi-
nite minus, though I can see how Gilman wanted to be economical—one set, small cast—to facilitate inexpensive productions.

Daniel Sullivan, one of our best directors, has perhaps improved
the play by exacting certain rewrites, but has not given it quite the
visually indelible and psychologically incisive direction he is famous for. The students enter a dean's office far too casually, and
throw themselves and their belongings about rather too imperi-
ously. The door of the office is left open by too many who enter,
although this is to set up a crucial instance when Sarah, quite improbably, manages to hide behind this opened door. And Sullivan

has cast the supporting roles less than flawlessly: though Daniel Jenkins's Ross isn't bad, think what, say, Daniel Gerroll could have done with the part.

John Lee Beatty's set is pertinent, especially what we see of the campus through a window; Jess Goldstein's costumes, perhaps a shade too stylish for Sarah, are cogent; and Brian MacDevitt's lighting is, as always, wonderfully dramatic.

Hope Davis has hitherto, in films and plays, always been miscast as the sweet, lovely ingenue. I suspected that, as Sarah, she would at last be good. I was wrong: she is much more than that, marvelous. Her outbursts of warmth and sudden frosts, enthusiasms, and anxieties, little victories and not-so-small defeats must be carefully calibrated. She must never ring false, do too much, lose our sympathy. Miss Davis does all this flawlessly, sometimes even sublimely.

Spinning Into Butter is a play that, lapses and all, demands to be experienced, reflected upon, and, if possible, digested. To avoid it is not only to cheat oneself as a theatergoer; it is also, more gravely, to shirk an opportunity to think about serious matters involvedly.

Gore Vidal's The Best Man

Because of last year's unrelated but identically titled movie, *The Best Man* had to become *Gore Vidal's The Best Man*, which is just as well considering that Vidal is the best thing about it. It is his best play, and one of his shrewdest pieces of writing, holding up well even in an imperfect production.

The play takes place in two Philadelphia hotel suites during a 1960 political convention in which two candidates for the presidential nomination are running neck and neck. Secretary of State Russell is a Harvard-educated Rhode Island liberal, refined and honorable; supposedly Mafia-busting senator Cantwell (note his name!) is a man of the people, adept at dirty tricks and mouthing phrases like "Let the best man win." Both hope for the endorsement of the wily but likable ex-president, Art Hockstader, who keeps them in suspense. A triangle play in a sense, though with love replaced by politics.

Vidal, who himself ran unsuccessfully for political office, is a senatorial scion and presidential kinsman; he knows the political scene with slightly jaundiced intimacy, and has loosely modeled his three principals on Stevenson, Nixon, and Truman. He has deftly surrounded them with wives, campaign managers, a few ancillary figures, and a swaggering horde of reporters and delegates. The piece is a political whirligig but also a play of ideas, about the politics of life as much as the life of politics, which also includes insights into two very different marriages. Basically a wry comedy, it has serious overtones and philosophical implications.

Cantwell has acquired hospital records of a long-past nervous breakdown of Russell's, with which, unless the latter bows out of the race, he threatens to ruin him. Then an old grudge-bearing Army buddy of Cantwell's shows up and offers Russell a homosexual scandal from the senator's service days, usable as a potent counterweapon. Despite urgings to the contrary, Russell shies back from dirty pool, yet may be forced into playing it.

Russell has also been a hefty womanizer (a touch of Kennedy in this Stevenson), so that his wife, Alice, has left him, but she has now come back to support his candidacy. Cantwell and his dizzy wife, Mabel, play lovey-dovey Papa and Mama Bear with each other as it they knew Osborne's *Look Back in Anger*, which, like most other cultural things, they don't. Needless to tell you whose side Vidal is on, but he has written juicy roles for all concerned. And wit is plentiful, edged with sadness: Hockstader is dying by inches.

The writing squeezes all sorts of good things out of this material: surprises, reversals, pungent character sketches, satire, worldly wisdom. It is all (including shady sex in the White House) as timely as four decades ago but, to be sure, not so much because of oracular prescience as because the carnival never really changes, in Philadelphia or Washington as in New Orleans or Rio. But that does not mean that reminders of this sadly comical sameness should not be issued periodically, especially if they are well crafted and witty.

Unfortunately, Ethan McSweeny's direction is not up to snuff. When it is not simply plodding, it seems to have goaded the good Christine Ebersole into caricaturing Mabel Cantwell, and has not curbed the funny but excessive Elizabeth Ashley (as the chairman of the Women's Division) from helicoptering over the top. It has also allowed Jonathan Hadary, as the weaselly Marcus, to become even more precariously mannered than he usually is, which constitutes a woeful wonder.

As Russell, Spalding Gray does little to dispel our notion of him as a monologuist rather than an actor, but he carries himself with dignity even if with undernourished passion. As Cantwell, Chris

Noth tends to be rather one-note, but at least the note is Well chosen and sees him through. Better than either is the Hockstader of Charles Durning, one of our canniest actors, who scores with the minimum of effort or emphasis.

Good work, too, from Michael Learned as an Alice Russell whose hauteur is not frigidity, whose repressed longing is not played for pathos. Mark Blum and Jordan Lage, as the rival campaign managers, get every ounce of vitality out of their supporting roles. Add John Arnone's cleverly stylized set, skillffilly suggesting two different suites plus a convention hall, even if neither Arnone nor the director quite succeeds in conveying three different rooms within the same suite. Theoni V. Aldredge's costumes exhibit her trusty savoir faire, though one of Mabel's may be too droll to be true. Howell Binkley's lighting, David Van Tieghem's sounds, and Walter Cronkite's voice complete the compelling picture. Whatever reservations you may have about this production, boredom will not be one of them.

The Full Monty

The musical version of *The Full Monty* is rather like the near-proverbial glass of water that, depending on your point of view, may be half full or half empty. Looked at from below—way below—from the vantage point of *Footloose* and *Saturday Night Fever*, it will seem easily, or easefully, half full. Seen from above, say, from the level of *Oklahoma!* and *Follies*, it is incontestably half empty.

To be sure, in an age of Frank Wildhorn musicals, wild-carded or shoehorned into the running, *The Full Monty* deserves sympathetic attention. Although yet another adaptation of a movie—in this case the endearing little British film of the same title—it has a pure source, which it does not excessively pollute. You will recall that tale of blue-collar unemployment in the north of England, where an unlikely handful of out-of-work steelworkers, idle since the closing of the mills, takes a leaf from a traveling Chippendale's show, male striptease to which the town's wives and daughters are riotously flocking.

The group, which includes a mama's boy fatso and the men's better-educated but now similarly jobless factory foreman, wonders how to rival, with unsexy bodies and without showbiz know-how, the professional stripper-dancers. But as it turns out, the pros strip

only to the G-string; the amateurs, however, will bare everything—
or, as they say in England but not in Buffalo, whereto the musical
transposes the action, the full monty.

It might be supposed that poverty and desperation in Sheffield
and Buffalo are, apart from semantic differences, pretty much the
same. But a small, British, nonmusical working-class movie is very
different from a lavish Broadway musical. It thrives on the quaint
regional dialect, the class differences (as between worker and foreman), and the passion for soccer that allows for frenzied shenanigans. The unemployed Buffalonians, however great their love of
the Bills, do not stage earnest but clumsy football matches with
comic results.

The looks of such a film can be touchingly drab; the actors can
appear endearingly amateurish. The Broadway musical must have
sets to fill a large stage, choreography to lift the hearts, songs sung
and danced to with expertise by an attractive cast to justify the
steep ticket prices. Amateurishness meant to be felt for rather than
merely laughed at is just about the hardest thing for a Broadway
musical to tackle. That the show works even as well as it does is
more of an achievement than most people will realize.

The credit for that goes partly to Terrence McNally, the adapter,
who has done a workmanlike job but for some facile jokes and the
sneaking in of an overtly homosexual element that while pleasing
some may alienate others. It was smart to pick a pop composer,
David Yazbek, a newcomer to Broadway. The music sounds like
most of today's rock: simplistic, with the first few songs seemingly
hammering in a mere four or five notes, but just what the younger
audiences, which the show needs, will feel at home with. Yazbek's
lyrics are rather better.

The general smartness is attributable largely to the director, Jack
O'Brien, a canny treader of fine lines. Thus John Arnone's clever
sets, jazzily lighted by Howell Binkley, are on the cusp between
showy and unpretentious; Robert Morgan's costumes are likably
trashy; and Jerry Mitchell's choreography is inventive yet, by and
large, not beyond the reach of determined amateurs. Above all,
O'Brien keeps the show moving nimbly, provides delightful directorial grace notes, and has cast impeccably.

Patrick Wilson is a well-sung (that is the word) and down-to-
earth leading man, and Lisa Datz and Emily Skinner play two very
different but equally persuasive wives. Romain Frugé expertly merges the comic and the touching. Since all the actors in this show do

so well and blend into a seamless ensemble, I will not dumbfound you with a further long list of names, but must single out André De Shields for his quicksilver dancing and moving performance.

For all this, *Monty* is not memorable. To revert to that half-filled glass of water, it is hard to say whom it satisfies: those parched for good musicals may need something more to quench their thirst; those not especially thirsty may seek a brew headier than water to quaff.

Class Act

Class Act is a cute little musical that Linda Kline and Lonny Price have contrived from the songs of the late Edward Kleban, whose dream was to write Broadway musicals. A cantankerous individual, not good at collaboration, Kleban died relatively young. Lightning struck only once: he wrote the lyrics for *A Chorus Line*. But he wanted his music to be as successful as his words, which did not come to pass.

The show is narrated by the dead Kleban, usually a tiresome device but here quite effective, as he is nimbly enacted and sassily sung by Price, he of the comically rabbinical looks, who is also the show's director and coauthor. We see Ed mostly as a student in the tightly knit BMI Musical Theater Workshop presided over by the legendary, sharp-tongued Lehman Engel. Here Ed first made some noise, a female fellow student or two, and a fairly general nuisance of himself. Still, the story of the workshop class (hence the show's title) and Kleban's subsequent half-life in show business—John Gielgud's firing him from the revival of *Irene*, etc.—makes for an entertaining evening, studded with pleasant enough Kleban songs.

For anyone knowledgeable or curious about the frantic ups and downs of Broadway hopefuls, the show has many a droll reminder or revelation; others, less interested in such peripeties, may be somewhat less amused. Yet the songs, though seldom outstanding, are enjoyable, and the cast is solid. Especially good are Randy Graff, as the philandering Ed's longtime biologist girlfriend who finally walks, and the dependably hilarious Jonathan Freeman, as Lehman Engel. Good work, too, from Nancy Kathryn Anderson, Carolee Carmello, Julia Murney, and Ray Wills, all in multiple roles, with Wills particularly funny as Marvin Hamlisch, composer of the music for *A Chorus Line*. Only David Hibbard does not quite get the quiddity of that show's guiding force, Michael Bennett.

There is also an inexpensive but utilitarian set by James Noone, niftily tongue-in-cheek costuming by Carrie Robbins, and engaging choreography by Scott Wise and Marguerite Derricks. Price's staging brings it all bouncily together.

Comic Potential

Alan Ayckbourn's *Comic Potential* (1999) is—I thought so when I saw it in London, again when I read it, again when I reviewed it here (February 7, 2000), and most recently when I reexperienced it at the Manhattan Theatre Club—one of the finest plays of all my theatergoing decades. It is a riotous farce, a tremulously exquisite love story, a superb satire on television and other human follies, a wise and serious drama full of playfully tossed-off profundities about sundry aspects of life and art, and an irresistible evening in the theater. If you are going to see only one play in your life, make it this one.

It is a play about the future, when television has sunk even lower than it has now, and actors are replaced by actoids—a sort of performing robot programmed to deliver cheap comedy and melodrama proficiently and economically for idiot consumption. We are watching a cheesy hospital serial being enacted by such actoids, one of whom, playing a nurse, interpolates unprogrammed laughter into her role, considerably annoying Chandler Tate, a once-famous film-comedy director, now a drunk reduced to helming this tripe. He spars with two amiable lesbians, Trudi the technician and Prim the programmer, in the control booth.

The surgeon actoid announces, "I'm going to remove the temporary pluster cust and umputate just above the unkle;' which is described by Trudi as "random AU subrogation," a common robotic defect. But the nurse's laughter is something else: the machine beginning to become human.

In comes the man-eating harridan and staff tyrant Carla Pepperbloom, the TV's regional director, to supervise and undercut the proceedings. She promptly bullies everyone, and, noting the nurse's inchoate independence, proposes to have her melted down, as is done with any defective or overused actoid. But with Carla comes Adam Trainsmith, unwealthy but talented young nephew of Lester Trainsmith, the American billionaire who controls global television and artificial intelligence, a youth she hopes to seduce. Adam wants to meet his idol, Chandler, and also learn how to break into TV comedy writing. Left briefly alone with the nurse, whose serial number is JCF31333, and whom he calls Jacie Triplethree, he begins talking to her and finds her capable of intelligent original responses.

At first interested only in writing a farce for Jacie—in her comic potential—Adam gradually falls in love with her. She, treated for the first time as a human being, blossoms into a fine and loving but confused one. Adam runs off with her, as everyone pursues the scandalous fugitive couple. With delightful humor, tinged with equally delightful seriousness, Adam teaches Jacie, and she, in turn, teaches him. It is a twist on the Pygmalion story, with Galatea giving back as much as she receives—or more.

What evolves is hilarious, touching, suspenseful, sagacious, and magisterially written. There is much that is smashingly funny, and as much that is incisive and profound. Take Prim's warning to Adam about falling for an actoid: "Every time you speak to it, you trigger some response. It pulls it out of its memory bank and blurts it back at you. That's all it's doing." To which Adam: "Maybe that's all any of us do." Or take the love-smitten and terrified Jacie telling Prim she wants to be melted down: "I'm unstable. I no longer control my feelings." Whereat Prim: "If that was a criterion, we'd all be melted down."

Or this, when Jacie, deeply perturbed, wonders: "Why me?... Am I so unique?" Chandler responds: "Forget unique. The road to stardom is strewn with the forgotten bodies of people who were told—usually by some stupid critic—and, worse still, *believed* they were unique." (But he promptly contradicts his own precept.) At the risk of proving a stupid critic, I declare *Comic Potential* unique.

The American production, wonderfully designed by John Lee Beatty, Jane Greenwood, and Brian MacDevitt, is not quite so well directed by John Tillinger as it was in England by the author. Nor is the supporting cast—with the exception of Peter Michael Goetz's terrific Robert Altman impersonation, as Chandler—up to the Brits. But all this is unimportant; what matters is that Janie Dee has come over to re-create her prize-winning performance as Jacie.

We have read so much about legendary actresses, past and present, missing whose creations of this or that great role leaves us permanently deprived. Such a spectacular achievement is Miss Dee's. To miss Janie as Jacie—perfectly blended and, after who knows how many performances in Britain, still as fresh as a daisy—would be criminal; at the very least, an act of reckless spiritual self-deprivation. The fineness of detail, the range of emotion, the inventiveness and total rightness of the smallest gesture and the tiniest intonational shading—but also of the most broadly farcical (yet still impeccably judged) or the most heartrendingly poignant (yet not one jot overdone) effect leaves one pleasurably gasping. I am not sure that I have ever seen its equal, but I am certain I have never seen, nor ever will see, its superior.

Seussical

The people behind *Seussical* the musical aimed at an audience from 7 to 77. They may have got the more infantile 7 and the senile 77; they didn't get what lies between. A potentially amiable show became something that only (see the ads) Rosie O'Donnell and Liz Smith could love. Here and there a bit of talent, an idea or two, make their mark; the rest is all militantly cheerful, mercilessly whimsical murk.

Just about everything went wrong, starting with the music of Stephen Flaherty, the lyrics of Lynn Ahrens, and the book by both perpetrators, with Eric Idle as accessory. By picking bits from several Dr. Seuss books, they came up with a patchwork instead of a story line; by retaining some of Dr. Seuss's writing and grafting onto it their inferior own, they achieved further destabilization. Rather than speak the sooth, or the Seuss, they speak with worse than forked—at the very least trifurcating—tongues: they speak mishmash, about as faithful to Seuss as Messalina was to the emperor Claudius.

There are two kinds of songs: the generic and the simplistic, with only the *Lion King*-ish "Solla Sollew" and the eclectic "Havin' a Hunch" showing signs of at least borrowed life. The choreography, by Kathleen Marshall, is similarly uninspired, hurtling from cute to desperate without passing Go. Kathleen's brother, the genuinely talented Rob Marshall, was brought in to revise Frank Galati's direction (Galati was the worst possible choice for a cute show), but true redirecting would have required not a director but a dam builder.

The producers seem to have scapegoated Catherine Zuber's costumes and Eugene Lee's sets for their fiasco in Boston. Zuber, apparently, stuck too close to Seuss, which strikes me as correct. They brought in William Ivey Long, a specialist in sophistication, and his costumes now look like a nightmare cross between Arcimboldo and Vegas. Lee, who excels at the stark or structural, was another wrong choice. The clever Tony Walton, brought in to brighten things up, could not quite remove the *ereal* from funereal. Natasha Katz, usually splendid, turns stage and auditorium into one huge dance hall, but a Roseland by any other name is still a Roseland.

The concept and casting of the characters is the final catastrophe. As the Cat in the Hat, the charmless David Shiner, a somber clown, is miscast; minus the menace, he is a shiner in the eye of the show. Kevin Chamberlin does what can be done with a Horton made to look less like an elephant than like an elephant hunter. As the wife of the Mayor of Whoville, the able Alice Playten is saddled with a poor part and poorer Mayor. As their son, Anthony Blair Hall is too big for a Who child and too small for a Tom Hanks look-alike. At least Michele Pawk, however mannered, infuses much-needed sass into Mayzie LaBird.

The rest, men and women alike, seem to have been chosen for their lack of appeal, mistaken for humor. Janine LaManna, as Gertrude McFuzz, is a cuckoo hatched in a songbird's nest. The Bird Girls are a trio of trying grotesques. Most bizarre is hefty Sharon Wilkins, the least of the red-hot mamas, as the Sour Kangaroo, whose credibility requires a quantum leap of faith. Her baby is a hand puppet, for which she is totally unable to ventriloquize a voice. The minor characters and chorus members perform with the grinning despair with which slave workers in a Siberian salt mine would strain to improve their lot. *Seussical* may be a woozical, or a Whosical, but a musical it's not.

The Play About the Baby

Even the title of Edward Albee's *The Play About the Baby* is grossly misleading; it should be *The Play About Nothing*. If ever there was desperation—a large, thudding slab of desperation—on a stage, this is it. An older couple, not married, called Man and Woman, come to where Boy and Girl live, make love, and have a baby. Eventually the elders walk off with it, after convincing Boy and Girl that there never was a baby. Actually, what there never was is a play.

What goes on for nearly two hours is the woolliest, phoniest, most pretentious woolgathering this side of the world's biggest sheep-shearing festival. Albee simply throws anything and everything into the pot, pell-mell, with the most brazen and relentless repetitions, as if a silly remark, clotted paragraph, or outlandish jest—even an entire scene—repeated twice, thrice, or more thereby became compelling. Disconnected, pointless, smart-ass anecdotes; semantic discussions; and song-and-dance fragments are stirred together in wantonly clashing fashion. Puny, unrewarding variations are played on irrelevant statements. The players address the audience in ceaseless windy monologues; even the disjointed dialogue sounds like monologuizing. Much of it is crude and tasteless, unconvincingly heterosexual or suggestively homosexual, often gloatingly self-contradictory and, ultimately, nonsensical while pretending to be deeply meaningful. This so-called play isn't merely awful; it's offal.

Albee has written three good plays and a couple of tolerable ones; the rest are worthless. When I was associate editor of the Mid-Century Book Society, I proposed Albee's first volume of plays for a selection. From Berlin, W. H. Auden, one of the editors, wrote me: "I am afraid I must say No to *The* [*sic*] *Zoo Story*. I can well believe that on the stage it is effective, but read cold on the printed page it seems *too* irrational." Well, Albee has come a long way since: he can now write plays that would seem too irrational scribbled on an outhouse wall, too inept for the puppet stage. It is a shame to see two fine actors (Marian Seldes and Brian Murray) and a passable one (Kathleen Early) make fools of themselves; David Burtka is too untalented even to be counted. I thought that after *The Man Who Had Three Arms*, Albee could sink no lower. I was wrong.

A Skull in Connemara

In *A Skull in Connemara*, the young Irish playwright Martin McDonagh mashes together bits of absurdism and Artaudian theater of cruelty, then sprinkles them with some powdered Synge. This need not necessarily spell fiasco, but the jokes turn sour, the plot and dialogue are studiedly outrageous, and you don't give a farthing for any of the characters, and so the work, whatever its commercial value, is artistically nil.

Mick Dowd, in his fifties, has for a profession digging up Leenane's dead after a number of years and dumping them in a nearby lake to make room for newer arrivals. This work is done discreetly by night, with the full approval of Father Welsh or Walsh, as none of his parishioners knows his name for sure. The play opens in Mick's humble cottage, where seventyish Maryjohnny Rafferty drops in regularly for some poteen. Talk is about nothing much— e.g., whether it is still August or already September. We gather that seven years ago Mick did jail time after his drunken driving killed his wife, Oona.

The villagers suspect Mick of cracking Oona's skull with a hammer, then making it look like a car accident. This suspicion is revived in conversation with Mairtin Hanlon, Maryjohnny's twentyish and loutish grandson, arriving with the news that Father Welsh, or Walsh, has appointed him assistant gravediggerupper. The next scene is in the graveyard, where Mick and Mairtin are exhuming skulls and bones and collecting them in a sack. They are mostly taunting each other until Thomas, Mairtin's elder brother and Leenane's grandiose but inept policeman, shows up for some three-way taunting.

An asthmatic, Thomas alternatingly smokes and sucks on an inhaler. Mairtin is twice pushed into an open grave and pelted with loose earth; Thomas narrates the unsolved case of an enormously fat villager found nude and dead before his TV, with only a jar of jam and a lettuce in his huge fridge. Mick allows how, "If it was the height of summer, and he wasn't expecting any visitors, it might well explain the stark naked." After a meditative pause, Thomas opines, "It might explain the stark naked, ay. It might not explain the complete absence of food in his six-foot fridge! Eh?"

Spirited discussions develop about whether more people drown in septic tanks or are run over by combine harvesters, and whether drowning in one's wee is worse than choking on sick. Another debate develops about whether young Mairtin got into trouble by cooking alive a cat or a hamster. Thomas, who cannot tell the difference between circumstantial and hearsay evidence, is nevertheless a stickler for facts: "Cooking cats, ay. No. A hamster it was. MICK: It's the same difference, sure. THOMAS: Pardon me? MICK: It's the same difference, I said. THOMAS: It's not the same difference at all, sure. A cat is one thing. A hamster is another." When Mick wonders whether this is "worth the argue," Thomas launches on a speech climaxing with, "Things like that are the difference between solving or not solving an entire case, sure." Meanwhile, Mairtin has gone off to see Father Welsh, or Walsh, to verify whether what Mick told him is true: that people are buried with their willies snipped off lest they offend the Lord. Then Mick discovers, horrified, that Oona is missing from her grave.

The entire next scene, in Mick's cottage, is punctuated by Mick and Mairtin, armed with wooden mallets, drunkenly smashing the disinterred skulls and bones on the parlor table, so as to facilitate their disposal. One of the mallets eventually gets used on a living head.

The actors—Kevin Tighe, Zouanne LeRoy, Christopher Carley, and Christopher Evan Welch (not Walch)—perform this stuff as if they believed it. David Gallo's set features headstones hanging from the ceiling, and Gordon Edelstein's direction is no less topsy-turvy. As I was leaving, a stranger remarked that he did not envy me my job. By the way, don't sit in the front rows, to avoid flying bone fragments. The play, unfortunately, cannot be avoided from any row.

Ten Unknowns

Jon Robin Baitz is one of our most stimulating playwrights, but just possibly the most uneven. Some of his plays even veer, from act to act, from antic to anticlimax. Yet you must hand it to him: he doesn't repeat himself. Even at his least good, he finds new ways of being bad.

Ten Unknowns is, in my view, an equation with too many unknowns. The biggest of them is what the piece is trying to say as it ends in a shaggy-dog-drawing story. I can't explain that *drawing* without giving away too much, so let's just call it shaggy dog. A once-promising WPA painter, Malcolm Raphelson, went to Mexico to assist Diego Rivera and remained there. In a ramshackle home-cum-studio, he drinks mescal, enjoys Mexican movies and radio, and avoids people and painting.

It is 1992, and Trevor Fabricant, a SoHo art dealer who has been supporting him, shows up *chez* Malcolm, which has no telephone. The year before, Trevor sent his boyfriend, Judd Sturgess, a gifted but drug-addicted young art-school graduate, to be Mal's assistant and spurrer-on. And indeed, Malcolm has started painting again in a new, very different style, which Trevor hopes to present in a New York retrospective. But the oddball painter won't even show him his new paintings. Judd, too, seems to have slacked off, except during bitter quarrels with Mal.

Meanwhile, the 72-year-old artist has run into an attractive 30-year-old grad student from San Francisco, Julia Bryant, trying to do field work on the glass frog, a dying or extinct species. Monolingual, untraveled, and rather lost, Julia is taken in by Malcolm and becomes the catalyst for a not wholly unpredictable revelation. The interaction among these four characters is the stuff of this sometimes overheated, sometimes lethargic play, alternatingly pointed and pointless.

When I eventually read the text, I realized how dazzling Daniel Sullivan's direction and everybody's performance was. Threadbareness was gorgeously glossed over by Donald Sutherland's quirkily fascinating Malcolm, Justin Kirk's amusingly embittered Judd, Julianna Margulies's impressionable yet resilient Julia, and Denis O'Hare's infuriating but droll Trevor. Much of the dialogue has people talking over or under one another, a tricky and trying business director and cast have managed expertly.

An atmospheric set by Ralph Funicello, telling costumes by Jess Goldstein, and moody lighting by Pat Collins help considerably. But there is something unfulfilled about this intermittently sparkly but ultimately uncommunicative work.

Lobby Hero

Soon after making the year's best movie, *You Can Count On Me*, Kenneth Lonergan delights us with his irrepressible *Lobby Hero*, confirming him as a comic wizard. To have written those and the unforgettable *This Is Our Youth* would have lasted many authors a lifetime, but with Lonergan we get the feeling of a life force just getting into full swing.

The antic center of the new play is Jeff, an amiably shiftless young man on the night watch as security guard at a generic East Side high-rise. The captain in charge of this and other buildings, William, is barely older and meticulous, doing scrupulous late-night checkups on the watchfulness of his staff. Jeff, who is a kidder, and

William, who is superconscientious, engage in bizarrely dialectic duologues. William warns Jeff that one day he'll "wake up in a lobby just like this one, except everyone's gonna be calling you Pops," and that listening to William's admonishments would have saved this "callous, careless kind of joke-telling, sit-on-my-ass-my-whole-life type of person" from becoming a "doddering useless old unemployed Pops doorman."

WILLIAM: Okay. Keep laughing, Jeff. 'Cause the joker laughs last. And the joker's gonna laugh last at *you.*

JEFF: What do you mean, like the Joker from *Batman?*

WILLIAM: No… I just mean—like, you know, like the generic joker. Like the laughing figure of Fate, or whatever you want to call it.

JEFF: Oh, sure, *that* joker. Everyone's terrified of *him.*"

There is something a bit skewed, a bit loopy about Lonergan people who wend their way through life widdershins, and Lonergan talk that is really front-stoop (or lobby) philosophizing. So, too, we get Bill, the cocky veteran policeman, and Dawn, his insecure rookie partner who doesn't know her own strength. Though Dawn is sleeping with Bill, a married father, he also has sessions with the call girl in 22J while his unsuspecting partner is made to cool her heels in the lobby. While Dawn may be in trouble for having hit an attacking drunk too hard in the eye, William wrestles with the problem of providing his unstable brother, involved in the killing of a nurse, with a fake alibi.

The interaction of Jeff, William, Bill, and Dawn becomes a deliciously discordant string quartet in Lonergan's hands, especially after Jeff reveals to Dawn what Bill is really up to in 22J. As Jeff prattles on to the hurt and seething Dawn, who bids him to shut up, he replies: "Sure. I'd be glad to. Why don't you say something for a few seconds and then I'll say something back and we'll go on like that. I'm a goddamn security guard, for Christ's sake. I'm lonely as shit. I'll shut up. I'd *love* to hear somebody else talk." But she won't respond as he importunes her about "illicit kind of behind-the-scenes, in-the-back-of-the-squad-car-type romances."

I confess to being a sucker for these slightly bumbling, sweetly pathetic Lonergan shenanigans, and for a play in which all the characters are sympathetic screwups. Especially Dawn, a particularly lovable loser, whom Heather Burns, despite some shrillness, plays enchantingly. Tate Donovan is fine as an only slightly crooked cop, and Glenn Fitzgerald is winning as the frustrated doorman full

of ingenuous guile. Best is Dion Graham as the Captain, William, baffled between dutifulness and brotherly devotion. Mark Brokaw has directed with delicate compassion in Allen Moyer's bitingly realistic set. *Lobby Hero* ends in an understatedly touching gesture, fraught with that insidiously lingering Lonerganian resonance.

The Invention of Love

The Invention of Love is Tom Stoppard's most literary play yet. Ostensibly, it is about A. E. Housman's unrequited love for the heterosexual Moses Jackson, and about Housman's more nearly fulfilled passion for scholarship. Also about how the pessimistic poet of *The Shropshire Lad* coexisted in the same man with the fanatically finicky editor of Latin texts and scourge of other editors past and present. But it is mostly about Tom Stoppard's wit, erudition, gift for persiflage, ability to bone up on any subject, dramatic flair, and even greater talent for intellectual debate along with skill in blending disparate elements into a provocative, daedally tangled web, flashes of lightning from which further dazzle an audience, and further blind it.

Having been too clever by half in several of his plays, Stoppard has lately managed to be too clever by three quarters. The result is remarkable but not really a play, if by *play* we mean something that can be followed by an audience with a standard education and average intelligence. By *followed*, I do not mean getting the general drift, but catching at least a good part of the allusions, quotations, parodistic references, wordplay, and other fine points, for fine points are Stoppard's stock-in-trade. Plot and characterization are not completely lacking but are minimal in importance.

Even the title is almost irrelevant. It refers to the fact that before Catullus and his poems to Lesbia, there was really no such thing as love poetry in the fullest sense, and that the romantic elegy was the invention of a later poet, Propertius. But even though these things figure as part of the discussions in the play, they are not nearly so important as debates about minor points of textual criticism; one-upmanship among scholars; jokes about the afterlife in Hades or Elysium; the problems of homosexuality; the difference between someone like Housman, who represses his sexual instincts, and Oscar Wilde, who flagrantly indulges them. Both men come to grief, but the question remains: which is the greater—or, perhaps, better—grief?

You are likely to know enough about Wilde, Ruskin, and Walter Pater, who figure prominently; if you read the program notes assiduously, you will also get a sense of Benjamin Jowett, Mark Pattison, W. T. Stead, Henry Labouchère, Frank Harris, and Jerome K. Jerome. Still, even I, knowing enough about them, as well as something about Pollard and Postgate, could not get the full impact and import of the play until I subsequently read it, wishing I had done so beforehand.

This is not to equate *The Invention of Love* with the likes of *The Play About the Baby*, which is pure flimflam, signifying nothing; there is no doubt that Stoppard's play, unlike Albee's, is not sheer smug mystification. But whether you say too little or too much, whether or not on the strength of your name you can get away with murder, the fact remains that it helps to take the audience into account. As the old Housman remarks in the play, "I have been practicing a popular style of lecture at Cambridge as yet confused with memories of University College"—his previous job in London—"but it's based on noticing that there are students present."

It seems to me that lengthy discussions of specific disputed words in the works of Horace, Catullus, and Propertius—as to, say, whether *freti* or *feri* was what the poet wrote—do not belong in a play, even if the scene is academia. Or is it? There are three somehow related boat trips: Oxford undergraduates rowing on the Cherwell, meeting up with the underworld boatman Charon ferrying souls to their final destination, and, later, the journalist-novelist Jerome K. Jerome and friends rowing past Reading gaol, where Wilde was imprisoned. There are reciprocally relevant discussions among Oxford dons and stars of the London popular press. Few of the finer points are anywhere near perspicuous, yet drama is not an abstruse poem by some *poeta doctus*. And where does Stoppard get off quoting Latin and Greek verse (to be sure, with translations following) when he himself, in an interview in the *Lincoln Center Theater Review*, misuses *fortuitous* in a way revealing simultaneous insensitivity to Latin and English?

This said, there is fine acting from 19 actors in 24 roles, ably headed by Richard Easton (old Housman) and Robert Sean Leonard (young Housman). Indeed, their scene together, like the scene in which Moses Jackson cottons on to his friend's true feelings about him, are theater in the best sense. Jack O'Brien has directed with his usual savoir faire, Bob Crowley's sets and costumes have his customary éclat, and Brian MacDevitt's lighting may be more triumphal than ever. But if there is anything more troubling than fast food that leaves you hungry, it is a feast that does the same.

Follies

When Stephen Sondheim's *Follies* arrived in 1971, we critics were pretty obtuse about it. It now emerges as one of our finest musicals and should be on the top-ten list of even those people who, like me, don't believe in list-making.

That original production had the benefit of Harold Prince and Michael Bennett's co-direction and the latter's choreography, of Florence Klotz's eye-popping costumes, and Boris Aronson's magnificent ruin of a set. And, of course, 22 Sondheim songs, each worthy of a musical-comedy hall of fame, if such a thing existed. They stand up even in the crippled current revival of the Roundabout production.

You may have seen the Paper Mill Playhouse revival of 1998, which was appreciably better, but because of some ugly behind-the-scenes politics did not make it to Broadway. That need not stop you from seeing this one; *Follies* has enough life to survive even in a half-alive revival.

The first problem with this mounting is its lack of opulence. Yes, costs have skyrocketed, but the Paper Mill surmounted that hurdle. A show about a fabulous party given by a Ziegfeld-like producer in his about-to-be-demolished theater, reuniting surviving cast members from all his shows one last time—not to mention the ghosts of showgirls past and the incarnate memories of some of these performers' younger selves—has to be lavish. And beyond the glitter of opulence, it must also glow with the burnish of remembrance, light up with the luster of nostalgia. Mark Thompson's décor is serviceable, Hugh Vanstone's lighting better than that, and the veteran Theoni V. Aldredge's costuming honorable. Still, lacking is some of the glory that was greasepaint, some of the grandeur that was roaming down memory lane.

The cast has its sparklers. The part of the sophisticated Phyllis, twice indelibly incarnated in the beauty and talent of Alexis Smith and Lee Remick, has a condign incumbent in Blythe Danner; if her voice has its limitations, her acting and loveliness have none. No less impressive are Polly Bergen, as the ultimate survivor, Carlotta, whose anthem to durability, "I'm Still Here," ranks with the best; and Joan Roberts, the original Laurey from *Oklahoma!*, as an endearingly enduring Heidi. There are winning contributions by other beloved old-timers: Betty Garrett, Donald Saddler, Marge Champion, and Louis Zorich.

But Matthew Warchus has never directed musicals, and it shows: he does not trust the power of a great song delivered with absolute simplicity. As a director of plays, he believes that everything needs to be acted. So he casts the fine actress Judith Ivey as Sally and obliges her to act out redundantly "Losing My Mind" with distracting superimposed histrionics. He has similarly undercut Miss Danner's "The Story of Lucy and Jessie" with supererogatory gestures. And because Treat Williams is not a dancer, he has made him instead run around kicking over chairs during "The Right Girl," undermining his singing and distorting his characterization.

He has also made some poor casting choices. That Gregory Harrison played a similar part badly in *Steel Pier* is no reason to let him louse up Ben with his charmlessness. To cast Lauren Ward as anything but an ugly duckling is a mistake; to cast her as Young Sally, a catastrophe. Even the tiny role of Kevin could profit from someone more appealing than Stephen Campanella.

But Warchus's chief failings are not knowing where to place singers for optimum efficacy and not even exploiting the full potential of the scenery. And allowing the mediocre Kathleen Marshall to come up with even less than her customary choreography.

For all that, it would be folly to pass up the indestructible *Follies*. From every one of its splendidly orchestrated songs (by Jonathan Tunick), Stephen Sondheim proclaims "I'm Still Here," while James Goldman's far from flawless book nevertheless captures the ability of theater to make us—with art or artifice, truth or trickery—however briefly, partakers of immortality.

The Producers

Advance raves can be counterproductive. The unanimous word on *The Producers* was superlative, arousing in some of us unfillable expectations. Sure enough, at a late preview, people around me wallowed in gusts of guffaws while I chuckled fitfully.

Mel Brooks always struck me as half crudely funny and half merely crude. His 1968 film, *The Producers*, found me only sporadically tickled, despite my love for Zero Mostel and early Gene Wilder. I was not even greatly taken with the now-legendary production number "Springtime for Hitler," which struck me as forced, and still does to some extent in the musical adaptation, even though Susan Stroman has staged it riotously, William Ivey Long costumed it uproariously, Robin Wagner designed it mischievously, and Peter Kaczorowski lighted it, well, lightsomely.

As you may recall, the shady producer Max Bialystock and his "creative" accountant and bumbling sidekick Leo (short for Leopold) Bloom aim to cash in on a scam that hinges on an instant Broadway flop. They produce to this effect *Springtime for Hitler*, an abysmal musical by Franz Liebkind, an unhinged neo-Nazi pigeon breeder and sub-zero author, meant to give offense to all. Instead, the show is an immediate smash, with Max and Leo, whose ruse backfires, headed for jail. As a grandiose production number on Broadway—with the passage of time having made Nazi jokes less disturbing and audiences less discerning—the show within the show couldn't help being a hit, which makes the eponymous producers into even bigger fools than intended.

The book still has the naughty-schoolboy humor—if that is to your taste—and Brooks has added sixteen new songs to the movie's two. It has been his lifelong ambition to write words and music for a Broadway musical, and, by Jove, he has done it. The score is always workmanlike in its lyrics, and if the tunes have a slightly recycled sound, they are nevertheless melodious and at times even rousing. And what you get from Miss Stroman's choreography and direction is, of course, well above what flounders in today's surrounding musicals.

The production values dazzle, as, for example, in hilarious things done with pigeons, walkers, and balls and chains, which I wouldn't dream of revealing here. Just when you thought that Nathan Lane had shot his considerable wad, he is Max to the max; here he is giving off more funny faces, deftly daft moves, and athletically hurled throwaway lines than a Christmas tree has sparklers, and singing with the sweetness of a dying swan. Though a trifle less assured, Matthew Broderick's Leo is endearingly artful and songful enough to make us believe that every Joycean dog will have his Bloomsday.

And what a pleasure to have back Cady Huffman of the endless legs—and scarcely shorter looks and talent—even if her makeup here leaves something to be differently desired.

Everyone is on the mark. The gay jokes—worn rather thin in 33 years—are nevertheless spiffily executed by Gary Beach, Roger Bart, and others, cheekily abetted by the winking costumes. Brad Oscar exudes goofy gusto as Liebkind; Ray Wills and Peter Marinos make pleasing contributions, although the miking throughout is annoyingly obstreperous. That there is enough to Brooks to electrify the many and divert the few brooks no denying. But for full flotation, sit with your expectations left, unlike life jackets, uninflated.

The Credeaux Canvas

The Credeaux Canvas is the third recent play about painters, and I was prepared to resent it. Instead, it turned out the best of the lot, better even than most plays about non-painters. Keith Bunin's serious comedy concerns three friends in their twenties in an East Village attic apartment shared by Winston, a gifted art student, and Jamie, a low-level real-estate agent. For the past six months, Amelia, a struggling chanteuse, has moved in as Jamie's lover. Jamie's wealthy art-dealer father has just died, leaving his son nothing except sudden despair begetting a vengeful, foolhardy scheme.

For an art-school thesis, Winston has been copying, brilliantly, a still life by the great, obscure dead painter Jean-Paul Credeaux, who is soon to be discovered, especially as more and more of his nudes keep surfacing. The plan is for Winston to paint a Credeaux nude—with Amelia posing—supposedly inherited by Jamie from his father, to be sold to Tess, a rich widow client of the father and already the proud possessor of a genuine Credeaux still life. She is stubbornly and stupidly sure of her own expertise and never consults experts: the fake Credeaux should make the young people's fortune.

Winston and Amelia very reluctantly go along with the scheme, which brings much farce and drama to three young lives. Among other things, Amelia, nervous about posing in the nude, is emboldened when Winston, too, strips to paint her, which soon leads to a hectic love triangle. (The nude scene is played so naturally by the two gifted actors that the spectators take it easily in their stride.) The plot twists this way and that over a four-year span, sometimes slightly straining belief but never relaxing its hold on the attention.

Bunin writes dialogue that is charming, funny, at times deliberately awkward, full of headlong starts and tongue-tied stops, rather in the delightful mode of Kenneth Lonergan. You feel empathetic anxiety for the characters even as you laugh and rejoice with them, however amoral or harebrained their meanderings. It is a dance on the razor's edge that requires expert production, which from the sure-footed direction of Michael Mayer and the nifty design team of Derek McLane, Michael Krass, and Kenneth Posner, it gets in spades.

The acting is perfect. Glenn Howerton's Jamie hovers wonderfully between crazy self-assurance in intrigue and pathetic fragility in love. Lee Pace's Winston is near-horizontally laid-back one moment, jack-in-the-boxishly resurgent the next—now with a bumbling stammer, now with torrential volubility. As Amelia, Annie Parisse is prodigious, playing virtually four different women in one. She negotiates the transitions with total ease, absolute credibility, and irresistible appeal. As the silly but not so stupid Tess, E. Katherine Kerr contributes a bravura cameo. Can you ask for more?

Topdog/Underdog

Whether she knows it or not, Suzan-Lori Parks is a Pinter disciple. In a recent *Times* interview, she declared, "I'm less interested in meaning—whatever that word means, I'm not quite sure, I keep meaning to look up 'meaning'—than in doing." Sure enough, her new play, *Topdog/Underdog*, is chock-full of doing, and perfectly devoid of meaning.

Two black brothers, Lincoln and Booth, share a seedy furnished room. The topdog, Lincoln, in costume and whiteface, impersonates Honest Abe in a sideshow, for customers playing Booth to shoot at. His younger bro, underdog Booth, lives by shoplifting and practices three-card monte (which the author misspells), in the hope that older bro and he will resume this former activity and get rich. Two thirds of the play is about practicing and discussing the playing-card hustle; the rest is about Lincoln losing his job, Booth losing his girl, the amazing Grace, and about nastily comic power plays ending in absurd melodrama. It is beautifully played by Don

Cheadle and Jeffrey Wright, and smartly staged by George C. Wolfe. If ever a production wagged the dog, *Topdog/Underdog* is it. But it is only fair that, after a *Full Monty*, we should get an empty one.

In the aforementioned interview, Ms. Parks—who is 38, a Mount Holyoke graduate, and a professor of playwriting at Cal Arts—cites her recent discovery and study of Shakespeare: "That's a writer I want to emulate. Great characters, great stories, great language. When you think of Shakespeare, you don't think of meaning. You think of Richard II: 'Let's sit on the ground and sing [*Richard II, The Musical*?] sad stories of the death of kings.' Whoa, here's the king sitting on the ground! My heart's breaking! That's the kind of play I want to write." Whoa! Find me the Shakespearean emulation in *Topdog/Underdog* or, failing that, *any* Shakespeare study unconcerned with meaning.

The Seagull

The old quandary: are Chekhov's plays comedies, as he claimed, or dramas, as Stanislavsky & Co. staged them? In Chekhov, according to the great poet Anna Akhmatova, "everybody's situation is hopeless. If one looks too closely, all one sees is cockroaches in the cabbage soup." But here is the critic Stanley Kauffmann: "Chekhov stubbornly tells the truth about us, but of all great writers, he is the gentlest." These are not irreconcilable views. Truth, however gently expressed, cuts deep; cockroaches do not deter starvelings from the soup. Chekhov's greatness lies precisely in seeing both sides of a coin: even if it makes scant difference whether it comes up heads or tails, spinning through the air it sure does glisten.

The star-studded Public Theater production of *The Seagull* at the Delacorte has generated unprecedented ticket demand, with people sleeping out in Central Park to be first on line. Granted, these folks are more star- than theater-struck; typically, I overheard one young woman gush, "I hear it's, like, *such* a good play." Still, even the wrong reason is good enough if it brings people to Chekhov.

Mike Nichols has certainly assembled a stellar—which is not to say heaven-sent—cast. What made the Moscow Art Theater (or any other) great was its ensemble acting. Rare enough nowadays, it is in this production nonexistent. From poor musicals, people are said to emerge humming the sets; here, too, most hummable is the scenery. And not just the décor of Bob Crowley, who planted rows of oh-so-Russian birches for a backdrop, but also what that even greater designer, Nature, provides (though for the later, indoor scenes, a back wall to stave off the overwhelming outdoors would have helped).

Nichols steers a middle path between the groundlings' craving for horseplay and the higher-minded theatergoer's need for nuance and authenticity. Crowley's costumes are credible, as is some of the hair styling. Thus, for instance, Marcia Gay Harden is Masha until she opens her mouth, when she becomes Marcia, with contemporary New York speech and demeanor. Similarly, though Christopher Walken is an amusing Sorin, nothing about him suggests a retired civil servant bemoaning the full life he feels cheated out of; if anything, Walken suggests more past gallivanting than Larry Pine's rather too subdued doctor Dorn. Pine underplays, Walken caricatures.

Or take Konstantin, who, in the British production for which this fluent Tom Stoppard version was commissioned, was the handsome and appealing Dominic West. Here it is the capable but chubby, homely, charmless Philip Seymour Hoffman, more muzhik than poet. No wonder Nina prefers the writer Trigorin, who, besides being famous, is played by the charismatic Kevin Kline with commendable restraint. But what a ninny of a Nina: Natalie Portman, in the first three acts, comes across as an all-American 13-year-old; in Act IV—with Nina destroyed, despairing, and semi-demented—she may attain 15. Unmoving, she also seems undernourished, though nowhere near so as Stephen Spinella, whose Medvedenko would waft off on the first gust of Russian wind, straight to Siberia.

Two admittedly easier lesser roles are handled best: John Goodman is a terrific Shamrayev, and Debra Monk a persuasive Polina. And then there is the highly accomplished but overcute or overdirected Meryl Streep: just because she can do a cartwheel doesn't mean Arkadina would do one. Altogether, Nichols courts comedic stunts: staggers, stumbles, pratfalls, leaps, jigs, bodies hurtling at bodies. Some of this works; much of it feels either facile or gratuitous—or both.

Mark Bennett's music is apt, and Jennifer Tipton's lighting spoton. The production is not shameful, but this sublime play deserves better: more sour cream in the borscht, and fewer cockroaches.

Urinetown, the Musical

When Greg Kotis, co-author with Mark Hollmann of *Urinetown, the Musical*, found himself down and out in Paris and unable to afford a public toilet, he conceived the idea for this show. In it, the population of a city is compelled by law to urinate in "public amenities," the fee going to the private Urine Good Corporation, headed by the ruthless capitalist Caldwell B. Cladwell. The excuse is a prolonged drought and water shortage, and anyone caught by the ferocious police force relieving himself in the bushes will be sent for draconian punishment to a place called Urinetown. There are long lines at the amenities, with many of the queuers unable to pay but hoping for a gratis pee.

Fantasies are fine as long as they have an inner logic and a compelling symbolic value. Here, absolutely nothing makes sense, and self-contradictions proliferate like bunny rabbits, to which Cladwell, who manipulates both the legislature and the police, compares the poor in the show's best song. We can suspend disbelief when the puritanical Deputy in *Measure for Measure* makes fornication a capital offense, or when Peter Pan teaches the children to fly, i.e., escape in dreams parental authority. But controlling urination—with defecation slurred over in a single line of a single lyric—makes no sense even on the fantasy level. Especially not when the police force is run by the dreaded Officer Lockstock, who is also the comic narrator making sophomoric jokes about musical comedy (in whose silliness he implicates both the show's creators and its audience).

So much for Kotis's book. Hollmann's music is parody, mostly of Brecht-Weill's *Mahagonny* and Blitzstein's *The Cradle Will Rock*—sometimes more copy than spoof—but comprising also *faux* gospel, *faux* Sondheim, *faux Les Miz*, and *faux* whatever. The Hollmann-Kotis lyrics have a die-hard whimsicality that would do credit to a frat show, which *Urinetown* basically is.

The romantic subplot involves Bobby Strong, the reluctant assistant to the pitiless Penelope Pennywise, supervisor of Amenity No. 9, described as "the poorest, filthiest urinal in town," and Hope Cladwell, the nabob's daughter fresh from college, soon to be taken hostage by the insurgent poor, led by Bobby. How these poor nearly hang her while Bobby, trying to negotiate with Cladwell, is instead captured and sent off to Urinetown, whence no one returns, is for you to find out, should you still have the desire to do so.

The originality of *Urinetown*, if it has any, lies in the equal con-tempt for the rich and the poor, and in what would be a tragic end-ing if persiflage could yield pathos. But if anything makes a show ridiculous rather than entertaining, it is an anything-goes attitude: the thrown-in kitchen sink always lands with a thud. Yet the audi-ence with whom I earlier viewed this show Off Broadway (to which it had been elevated after its premiere in the Fringe Festival) was lapping it up, as was the Broadway one at a late preview. Mencken was right to comment about the American public's lack of intel-ligence proving all too profitable; its lack of good taste should pay off nearly as well as a pee-fee.

John Carrafa's choreography is similarly pan-parodic, and John Rando has directed with random cleverness. The acting is perfectly geared to the campy material, with John Cullum (Cladwell), Nan-cy Opel (Pennywise), and Jeff McCarthy (Lockstock) the happiest campers. Hunter Foster and Jennifer Laura Thompson are dedicat-edly ludicrous lovers, and Spencer Kayden, as orphaned Little Sally, plays this ersatz Annie as if—to quote the show's favorite plati-tude—there were no tomorrow. Part of *Urinetown* is indeed *Annie* with no "Tomorrow," but most of it is *Mahagonny* with far too much alienation effect.

The Late Henry Moss

Sam Shepard writes three kinds of plays. Some are naturalistic, with perhaps a touch of the bizarre; some are part realistic, part fantastic or arcane; some are totally nutty, such as *States of Shock*. They fall into three periods: the early one, fascinating though uneven; the middle, mostly effective (*Curse of the Starving Class, Buried Child, Fool for Love, True West*); and the late, starting with *A Lie of the Mind* (1985), very much inferior.

The Late Henry Moss is, alas, late Sam Shepard, unable to find its form or convey its meaning. It rehashes the heavily belabored Shepard topics: ferocious fighting between brothers; problems with a difficult or impossible father (present or absent), life in the des-ert as opposed to life in the city, sex as a violent physical conflict, unexplained occurrences with contradictory explanations whirling around them.

Ray Moss, a younger brother about whose life we find out nothing, has arrived in a New Mexican adobe hut where his older brother, Earl, has been keeping a three-day vigil over the already stinking body of their dead father, Henry. We learn that Henry was a drunk in poor physical shape, but also terrifying and seemingly indestructible. Also that when the brothers were children, Henry used to beat their mother, whereupon she would lock him out of the house, eliciting even worse explosions. When the going got too rough, Earl, instead of interceding, got into his jalopy and was gone for seven unaccounted-for years, though we don't learn much about the following years, either. We discover that Esteban, who lives in a neighboring trailer, regularly brought the boozing Henry soup and other food, which he mostly ignored.

How did Henry survive? Ray discovers that his father had a girl-friend, Conchalla Lupina, a fellow drunk he met in jail, who is earth mother, whore, superwoman, and angel of life and death—"a man could die in her arms and thank the saints." Back when Henry was alive, she declared him dead, which he sometimes anxiously believed, sometimes vehemently denied.

As a symbol, Conchalla is as confusing as everything else here, the language foremost. Esteban sometimes speaks in faulty, His-panicized English; at other times, his English is prosaic but flawless. Ray can sound like a lowlife, a solid bourgeois (somewhat dense), or an inspired poet. Taxi, the driver Henry summons from Albuquer-que to ferry him and Conchalla on a fishing trip to the mountains, is part voluble stooge, part sweet reasonableness itself.

And the structure? We get two major flashbacks while Ray freezes on a small platform downstage left. The first is justified as Taxi's narrative of the fishing excursion; the second just occurs, out of nowhere. At play's end, the brothers are back in their opening position, repeating the first two lines of the initial dialogue. Amid all the ruckus at one point, Esteban is calmly preparing a menudo, on whose stench Ray acridly comments, and which, according to the stage directions, the audience is supposed to smell. (We were spared this; perhaps the smell of the play was deemed sufficient.) As opposed to such literalism, we get a pit musician accompany-ing the action with highly stylized music, and a door opening and closing by itself.

The play is directed by Joseph Chaikin, Shepard's pal and some-time co-author, slowly and uninventively. Chaikin, who is partially disabled by a stroke, has cast as Taxi a somewhat similarly disabled actor, which does not jibe with his character and creates further confusion. Ethan Hawke is tolerable as Ray, but the able Arliss Howard is a bit too slight to make a suitable adversary as Earl. My heart went out to him during a brutal fight, dazzlingly devised by B. H. Barry, in which Ray wipes up the floor with him, and then supererogatorily makes him wipe the same floor with a rag. Sheila Tousey gets Conchalla's toughness, but not her appeal. Guy Boyd is a bit weak as Henry, Jose Perez fine as Esteban in this generally well-designed production.

Well, perhaps the clue is in Earl's observation "People are always making up stuff," and Ray's remark "People will believe anything." The former may apply to Shepard, the latter to the audience.

Dance of Death

In the spirit of fairness, I guess, one must do unto Strindberg as one did unto Ibsen. On the heels of last week's mangling of *Hedda Gabler*, we get a not dissimilarly debased Strindberg masterpiece, complete with two British stars and a prominent British director to add cachet to the deconstruction, plus the now customary young monolingual American playwright to provide what is called, rather grandly, an adaptation.

Dance of Death spans three days in the 25-year-old marriage of Captain Edgar (no last name), commander of a tiny island off the Swedish coast, and his wife, Alice, a onetime actress, who live in a tower, formerly a prison. The marriage was and is a battlefield. Edgar drinks heavily, is constantly broke, offends everyone, and brutalizes Alice. She lacerates him with stinging ironies (at which he is no piker, either), and does her best to sour his existence; they have no friends, their children are away on the mainland, although Edgar adores his daughter, whom each parent uses as a weapon against the other; the unpaid servants keep quitting, the couple's credit is shot, and the larder is empty.

Now along comes Kurt, Alice's cousin, back from years in America, to take over as the island's quarantine officer. Both Edgar and Alice woo him as an ally in their internecine skirmishing. Kurt introduced Edgar to Alice; Edgar, however, was instrumental in Kurt's ex-wife's snatching custody of their beloved children. Kurt's uneasy loyalties are divided as he becomes the sounding board in turn of one spouse and then the other. Dance music from a party given by the army medical officer—to which the spouses were not invited—drifts tauntingly into their ears; later, there is a storm, which this production overdoes like so much else.

As Edgar, Sir Ian McKellen, an epigone of the great knights who by now have mostly died out of the English theater, endeavors to maintain their tradition but gives a performance far too mannered, posturing, and languidly spoken, his words emerging slowly and stickily, like gum pulled from his mouth. The usually admirable Helen Mirren, as Alice, matches McKellen in attitudinizing demeanor and affected speech, and both—no doubt on Sean Mathias's directorial prompting—play as much as possible, and beyond, for belly laughs. We miss the full oppressive sense of a mutually destructive love-hate. David Strathairn, as Kurt, owning neither the speech melody nor the elaborate trickery of the wily Brits, is even more lost than the part calls for.

Santo Loquasto's two-level set has epic sweep, the costumes displaying his customary savvy; Natasha Katz's lighting can be aptly splashy or sparing. Richard Greenberg's adaptation comprises some cuts, a few cutenesses (e.g., "He gets so puffed up, there isn't room for the room"), an occasional clinker (e.g., "that's not the worst implication of the situation"), and not a few annoyingly anachronistic modernisms, such as the oft-repeated "bottom-feeders," which others have rendered as "trash" (Meyer), "scum" (Sprinchorn), or "rabble" (Carlson). Nevertheless, the play's gargoylishly grimacing grandeur cannot be wholly obliterated.

Homebody/Kabul

The trouble with Tony Kushner and his new play *Homebody/Kabul* is that he chews more than he can bite off. The problem with Afghanistan is, Allah knows, great enough, but Kushner goes at it so obliquely, elliptically, and deviously that all his wordy, windy overelaboration (after much cutting, the play still runs three hours 40 minutes) only further obscures the tiny kernel of plot. Logic, in his hands, becomes logorrhea; illumination is bypassed for obfuscation; character is merely an excuse: anyone in the play can turn profound or simpleminded, eloquent or inarticulate, to suit Kushner's hunger for effect.

The work started as a monologue, a rather sesquipedalian, somewhat dithering Englishwoman's reverie about Kabul based on a 1965 guidebook to that city. Large chunks of that book are read aloud by the woman, identified only as Homebody. She has not been to Afghanistan, but she has bought ten Afghan hats (*pacoolis*), and distributed them among the guests at a party, which thus (or as Kushner has it, "thusly") became an uncharacteristic success.

So the monologue, which is Act One, is eighteen pages of history and geography read from the guidebook, interlarded with senescent musings about such things as the differently colored antidepressants she and her husband use, and how she sometimes pops his yellow and red pills instead of her green and creamy-white ones, so as to understand him better. From her party, and her husband's work in computers spanning space and time, her thoughts drift to "that galaxy so far away, exhaling protean scads of infinitely irreducible fiery data in the form of energy pulses and streams of slicing, shearing, unseeable light—does that nebula know it nebulates? Most likely not. So my husband. It knows nothing, its nature is to stellate and constellate and nebulate and add its heft and vortices and frequencies to the Universal Drift, unselfconsciously effusing, effusing, gaseously effusing," etc. Whereas she cannot tell her "simple tale without supersaturating my narrative with maddeningly infuriating or more probably irritating synchitic exegeses. Synchitic exegeses. Jesus." That "Jesus" at least we can understand, even if it is there only to echo "exegeses."

To start a play of well-nigh four hours with an eighteen-page monologue is already exasperating enough, especially since Homebody becomes in Act Two, rather unconvincingly, the unseen wife of an English computer expert, improbably named Milton Ceiling. With their drone of a daughter, Priscilla, they have traveled to Kabul, where Mrs. Ceiling (i.e., Homebody) has mysteriously disappeared. The official explanation is that she was torn to bits by ten West-hating fanatics, and that her body, or its dismembered parts, cannot be found. This is lengthily expounded by Dr. Qari Shah in medical jargon that passes comprehension—a full page of stuff like "After dislocation of the humerus from the glenohumeral joint, there was separation and consequent calamitous exsanguination from the humeral stump," etc.

It later appears that Mrs. Ceiling may not be dead, but has converted to Islam so as to replace a first wife, Mahala, of whom Dr. Qari Shah has tired, and who would have Milton and Priscilla smuggle her out of Kabul and into London. Mahala is half crazy, and speaks in a mixture of Socratic epigrams and hogwash, often in fluent French, sometimes in Farsi. Languages and jargons are Kushner's obsession, what with long segments of dialogue in Dari or Pashto (which Kushner had translated for him) usually spoken without translation. (In the manuscript, translations are provided, but that's no help to the audience.)

The aim is to bamboozle, astound, and arouse our masochistic wonderment. When they do speak English, the Afghans sound either like Oxonians or, more often, like bunglers in pidgin, with thick accents for heightened incomprehensibility. Frequently several persons speak simultaneously in different tongues, to assure total inscrutability, except for Priscilla, whose profuse *fucks* and *fuckings* provide oases of accessibility. Kabul might as well be Babel, from which, appropriately for Kushner, we derive the word *babble*.

The plot, insofar as it exists, concerns Priscilla's search for her mother, dead or alive, with a guide who is a philosophical Tajik poet writing his poems in Esperanto (we duly get a sample), sheaves of which he foists on Priscilla to deliver to someone in London— except that these poems may really be encoded messages from a spy posing as poet. Meanwhile, Milton, who never leaves his hotel room, gets drunk with Quango Twistleton (a name partly derived from P. G. Wodehouse), who is some kind of semiofficial go-between for the British and Afghans. From alcohol they progress (oh so slowly) to opium, thence to heroin, allowing their language to get boozily baroque and even less penetrable. But Quango lusts for Priscilla, who reluctantly agrees to trade her bod for a document allowing Mahala to exit Afghanistan and, in return, lead Pris to her missing (or dead) mother, however unlikely such a resolution may be in a shaggy-mom story.

And all this, except by Yusef Bulos, rather dubiously enacted— but whom do we blame: the author, the actors, the director (the Brit Declan Donnellan), whose steady chum (Nick Ormerod) designed the provocative set, gorgeously lighted by Brian MacDevitt? Out of each three-hour half of *Angels in America*, 40 or 45 minutes are salvageable; out of Kushner's current gaseous effusing, considerably less. But then, it is not easy to tack two endless acts on a mere preexisting monologue, however overlong.

Elaine Stritch at Liberty

True style is the seamless blend of the natural and the artful, which is what Elaine Stritch, with a constructional assist from John Lahr and a directorial one from George C. Wolfe, consummately delivers in *Elaine Stritch at Liberty*. Here the persons unseen are as present as the one seen, and the protagonist's life, onstage and off, proves rich enough in adventure and misadventure, achievement and setback, fallibility and triumph, to fill the biggest stage, fulfill the most exacting expectations.

First, there is the cogent fusion of narration and song. Stritch's storytelling and singing are not separate entities; they flow into each other almost imperceptibly. The blend is possible because, by her merrily mercurial delivery, Stritch can make speech sing, just as her speechlike naturalness in singing makes song feel like self-baring conversation. It is all varicolored wool melding into a single tapestry.

Next, the mastery of emphasis, rhythm, and pause. Stritch can wax almost grotesquely histrionic, yet carry it off with conspiratorial facial play, infectious body language. Hyperbole becomes not hamming but metaphor. Sudden changes—from loud to soft, lento to presto, or vice versa—keep us on our toes, increasingly aware that the tempo is the message, that acceleration and retardation are the music of living. And those pauses that might give Pinter envious pause are the interstices wherein thought can catch up with the meaning of action.

Finally, there is that barstool, the show's sole prop, enhancing the speaker's eloquence. Confidently perching or restoratively leaning on it, emphatically plunking it down or cannily relocating it, blithely ignoring it or stymiedly crumpling up over it, Stritch makes the high chair embody moods, objectify states of being. Everything here is finely conceived, calibrated, communicated. It is in this net of calculation that truth is captured, even as the crafty machinations of the camera yield, in the right hands, the unarguable spontaneity of the snapshot.

The Goat, or Who Is Sylvia?

We read in Guido Ruggiero's *The Boundaries of Eros: Sex Crime and Sexuality in Renaissance Venice*: "The Signori were not the least interested in masturbation except as it related to intercourse with a goat." So they should have found Edward Albee's latest caper (from *capra*, Latin for goat) of genuine interest. Still, as a young woman leaving *The Goat, or Who Is Sylvia?* explained to her escort, "This is a metaphor." But for what? Pederasty? Pedophilia? Pediatrics?

One problem with the play is that it makes no sense. Martin, a famous and happily married architect, tolerant of his teenage son's homosexuality, has just turned 50. While shopping for a farm in upstate New York, he sees a goat making googoo eyes at him, falls in love with her (it's a she-goat, nothing queer about Martin), has an affair with her, and names her Sylvia. This last may be a tad de trop.

Poor Martin gets no sympathy from his oldest friend, Ross, who betrays him to his wife, Stevie; from his gay son, Billy, who does, however, end up kissing him passionately on the lips; or from Stevie, who goes around smashing whatever is breakable in their living room and making beastly jokes about Martin's paramour.

Now, for a metaphor to work, it must first function on the literal level, but one melting caprine glance does not usually induce zoophilia in a 50-year-old enjoying good sex with his attractive wife. The author compounds his error by having Stevie perform an offstage act well beyond a female amateur's capacity. An even bigger mistake is Albee's dialogue, which slipperily shuttles between the farcical and the portentous, inducing gales of laughter in the most inappropriate places. Especially irksome are three perennial Albee tics, here reaching their culmination. One is semantic one-upmanship, whereby characters continually and gratuitously correct one another's grammar and metaphors. Another is needless repetition of obvious things, because the hearer was preoccupied, deaf, or just thick. The third is relentless use of obscenity for cheap laughs.

Jeffrey Carlson is adequate as Billy, the somewhat goatishly named gay son; as Ross, the meddling friend, Stephen Rowe is rather poor. Bill Pullman and Mercedes Ruehl do wonders for the hapless spouses, all to no avail. Most amazing to me was having overheard one producer say Albee's previous work, *The Play About the Baby*, was put on to obtain the rights to the "much better" *Goat*. Can it be that producers cannot tell much better from equally bad?

Oklahoma!

The good news is that *Oklahoma!*, which is to the modern musical what *Oedipus Rex* is to Greek drama, is back. The not-so-good news is that London's Royal National Theatre production, which was touted as the wonder of wonders, seems to have lost something in transit: checking my feet, I found my socks still on.

"A much darker version" was the trumpeted hype, and though there may be a shade or two of darkening, this in itself is not a virtue. Definitely deserving, however, are Anthony Ward's transporting sets and costumes (barring an unfortunate toy train), fervidly lit by David Hersey; the Robert Russell Bennett orchestrations artfully refurbished by William David Brohn and David Krane; sizable parts of Trevor Nunn's direction and Susan Stroman's choreography; and much of the performing.

That's a lot, but there remains the problem inherent in all revivals of beloved classics: at what point does rethinking become thoughtlessness? The exact demarcation line is hard to find and harder to cleave to. Take the dances: Stroman's are often strikingly inventive, tumultuously acrobatic, and provocatively spicy; but now and again, one misses the simpler, folksier, more heartfelt approach of Agnes de Mille. In the attempt to be more earthily realistic, for example, the title number has become a plausible post-wedding party but a far less rousing communal ode to the Oklahoma Territory.

Nunn's direction starts with some breathtaking *coups de théâtre*, and further bright touches periodically pop up in alternation with less felicitous ones. The more complex interpretation of Jud Fry, bitingly sung and unsettlingly acted by Shuler Hensley, is to be hailed; the coarsening of Ali Hakim, redoubled by Aasif Mandvi's lack of charm, is to be deplored.

Patrick Wilson is a winning Curly in singing, acting, bearing, and looks, and one wonders wherein may have lain Hugh Jackman's widely affirmed superiority in London. Andrea Martin squeezes every last drop of bonhomie and deviltry out of Aunt Eller. Justin Bohon is the sweetest of Will Parkers, and dances entrancingly. Jessica Boevers is a pleasant enough Ado Annie, and the minor roles are flavorously taken.

The real problem is the chief import from London, Josefina Gabrielle as Laurey. Perhaps because she has been too long at it and grown too mature for the part, or because she is much more dancer than singer (unprecedentedly, she does her own dancing in the dream ballet), or because Nunn wanted her more tomboy than girly-girl, she emerges more contrived and unspontaneous, more starchily unfeminine. And, whoever is to blame, there is scant electricity between her and Curly.

Even so, the songs are there in the old, blessed profusion, the primary and secondary love triangles continue to triangulate, and the land continues to lure us city slickers. So take a leaf from Huck Finn in his urge "to light out for the Territory ahead of the rest," and discover that as with the Post Office, *Oklahoma!* is OK with you.

Private Lives

If you have sat through as many *Private Lives* as I—and, most likely, you have—the question "Why that again?" might legitimately arise. But be advised; Howard Davies's staging, with this cast and these trappings, will have you watching a different play: hardly the same, but just as delicious.

There have been some great Amandas, but never anything like that of Lindsay Duncan. For starters, she is so damnably attractive that not leaping onstage requires serious self-restraint. But then, consider her miracles of timing, wonders of inflection, inexhaustible varieties of expression. Also a range of movements from slinky pussycat to stalking panther; sudden changes of voice from seductive purr to skewering hiss; and an array of silences from pregnant pause to coquettish sulk. Note further a repertoire of sinuous body twists, suggestive lip curls, and a gaze that can puncture frontally, sideswipe smilingly, or reverse inward into enigmatic reverie. I have always avoided the phrase "to die for"; for this performance, I can no more resist it than I can the woman herself.

Elyot is usually played with Noël Coward's own silkily acid understatement. Alan Rickman, with a long repertoire of villains behind him, plays the sophisticated bon vivant with a smooth façade, under which there lurks a tragicomic clown with raw nerves and rough edges, straining to convert sarcasm into socially acceptable irony. This is not a slippery, world-weary cynic but a self-muzzled attack dog, a barely catnapping volcano. And all the more sexually challenging to the right woman—or the wrong one.

And who could be more devastatingly wrong than Emma Fielding's superb Sibyl, not the usual dithering ingenue but a flaunter of maidenly ingenuousness, a truculent wielder of ravenous innocence? Only the Victor of Adam Godley is ordinary (except for his ears), but manages to make ordinariness jaggedly droll. As a labor-shirking—or is it xenophobic?—French maid, Alex Belcourt contributes a saucy vignette.

Davies has slowed down the Coward tempo from volatile volubility to fragmented fury and Pinteresquely creeping deviousness. That makes the second act drag a bit, but lends biting novelty to the other two. Caparisoned in Tim Hatley's stylishly sly scenery, Jenny Beavan's sassy costumes, and Peter Mumford's mercurial lighting, this *Private Lives* is a public benefaction: two hours that can irradiate a lifetime. I only wish Rickman would not throw away the line about whose yacht is anchored just offstage.

House and *Garden*

Alan Ayckbourn, author of some 60 mostly memorable plays, has also reinvented space and time, geometry and chronometry. What in lesser hands might be mere gimmickry becomes, in his, genius. That word is usually invoked posthumously, but why begrudge it to a living artist who time and again has given us so much pleasure and pabulum rather than the usual Pablum?

What the masters of comedy (and few, if any, American playwrights) have always known is that comedy is only one face of the coin whose obverse is tragedy. The characters in Ayckbourn's twin plays, *House* and *Garden*, are funny all right, but each of them carries inside, or causes in others, a goodly share of sadness and dejection. *House* and *Garden* unfold simultaneously to the minute in an English country house and the lower, unrulier part of its garden, and when any one of the fourteen characters leaves the stage in one play, it is usually to go onstage in the other.

Thus *House* and *Garden* can be performed only in adjoining theaters, and require split-second timing not only from the often frantically shuttling (backstage or through the lobby) performers but also, and first of all, from the author. Do not assume, however, that this is merely a cute tour de force; it is, aside from much laugh-out-loud fun, also a serious demonstration of the idea that what happens to people in contiguous but separated places gravely affects, perhaps even radically changes, their tragicomical lives.

The "upstairs" characters are the prosperous Platts, businessman Teddy and homemaker Trish, and their brilliant 17-year-old, A-student daughter, Sally. Also the neighboring Maces, naïve Dr. Giles and unbalanced Joanna, and their small-time-journalist son, Jake, in love with Sally, who may or may not reciprocate. The "downstairs" folk are the surly and taciturn Platt gardener, who cohabits with both the silly Platt housekeeper and her slatternly chambermaid daughter. Also a neighboring caterer, Barry Love, always bullying and berating his eager but fumbling wife, Lindy. These two are erecting a maypole and tent for the annual garden fest to delight the local children.

In the house, there is to be a luncheon party, to which a minor, non-Anglophone French movie actress, Lucille Cadeau, is invited (as a second choice) to open the subsequent festivities. She is chauffeured and guarded by a fierce female agent, who is to deliver her promptly afterward to a very posh nearby rehab center. Also invited to lunch is a long-ago schoolmate of Teddy's, Gavin Ryng-Mayne, a snobbish novelist-playboy and political hobnobber, who will presumably deliver the prime minister's invitation to Teddy to stand for Parliament.

In the course of an August Saturday, one illicit affair will end and another begin, while some dalliances will lead to frustration. One person will become totally unhinged, two will cut marital moorings, and some will be embroiled in various rowdy or ridiculous messes. Even a stentorian dog and some underfoot children will add to the midsummer madness. Tangled nets will be woven, Gordian knots cut through. Even that Gavin always introduces himself as "Ryng-Mayne with a y" (modestly passing over a second y in silence) can give rise to a hilarious exchange.

Under John Tillinger's endlessly inventive direction, everyone in the cast is at least good (which includes plausible British accents and fluent French from Lucille), with some performances truly outstanding. Take Jan Maxwell's Trish, who when she pretends that her cheating husband does not exist sends comic shudders (a special kind) up and down our spines. And Nicholas Woodeson's Teddy and Olga Sosnovska's Lucille, who must gambol with each other across a language barrier and through a sidesplitting mishap, always thrillingly daffy. Further, Ellen Parker, who makes the sweetly helpless and hapless Lindy a wistful joy. Again, no one in the theater or even in an asylum can do hysteria better than Veanne Cox (Joanna); Daniel Gerroll's Gavin makes cool sophistication or condescending hauteur roll off his tongue like champagne off a duck's back.

The sets, costumes, and lighting are dazzlingly handled by John Lee Beatty, Jane Greenwood, and Duane Schuler, respectively, and even the water, whether as a highly unpredictable fountain or a dependably British downpour, contributes handsomely to the clockwork chaos. See the plays preferably in alphabetical order and on the same day, but such is Ayckbourn's mastery that each can stand on its own legs as securely as the actors can run on theirs.

The Exonerated

Docudramas can take liberties with the truth in subtle, sometimes unintentional ways. But I have no reason to disbelieve Jessica Blank and Erik Jensen that the vast majority of *The Exonerated* is "as it was said two, five, ten, and twenty years ago by the actual participants." These are six people who spent from 2 to 22 years on death row, were then found innocent, and eventually were set free. Besides interviewing them, Blank and Jensen "spent countless hours in dusty courthouse record rooms" unearthing how these things came to pass. Mistaken for law students, the pair were allowed to proceed. "With a few exceptions, each word spoken... comes from the public record."

The ten seated actors, with scripts—which, however, they barely use—enact the six victims as well as various family members and officials. What they say is moving not only because it is horrible and true but also because of how simply yet powerfully it is expressed. Six decent but not initially extraordinary persons are transmuted by injustice, suffering, and endurance into speakers of something very close to poetry. We shudder to think how much of their lives was wrongfully annihilated by the state, with frequently delayed releases even after innocence was established, and not a penny in compensation. The equally guiltless husband of one woman was executed; she vows to be his living memorial. Whatever you may think of the death penalty, or of our system of justice, the play should make you think—and feel—some more.

Under Bob Balaban's direction, the ten actors are unerring. They are Charles Brown, David Brown Jr., Jill Clayburgh, Richard Dreyfuss, Sara Gilbert, Bruce Kronenberg, Phillip Levy, Curtis McClarin, Jay O. Sanders, and April Yvette Thompson. Honor to them all.

Movin' Out

Twyla Tharp's second try at a Broadway musical is worse than her first, *Singin' in the Rain*, in 1985. It would, of course, help if *Movin' Out* were set to music rather than to Billy Joel, but we are used to street noise and can tune out this tuneless stuff without too much effort. As for the words, they largely get lost on their own, and can be dismissed as dialogue snippets overheard on the subway. That leaves the dancing, which, if we are to believe the program, tells a story, something Tharp apparently cannot do. When, afterward, I read in the synopsis something about Long Islanders during the Vietnam era, this came as news to me. If you had told me it was about Carnaby Street during the Mod heyday, I would have believed it just as much.

In Act One, the choreography is very tired indeed, rehashing not only Tharp's clichés but also some other people's. Still, resist the urge to flee, because Act Two is better, at moments even quite good: finally, there is some invention here, though more for the men than for the women, whose chief function is to be tossed about. The dancers are on target: the fetching Elizabeth Parkinson is wonderfully various, Ashley Tuttle a dream on pointe, and John Selya simply overwhelming; only Keith Roberts rather annoys.

Working on a shoestring, Santo Loquasto (set) and Suzy Benzinger (costumes) did not knock themselves out. Donald Holder tried harder on the lighting, to no avail. If you have foreign visitors who speak no English, this is the show for them.

Hollywood Arms

Plays about passion are profuse and easy: heterosexual or homosexual, interracial or senescent, kinky or chaste. What is difficult and rare is a play about affection, which is what Carrie Hamilton and Carol Burnett's *Hollywood Arms* is. Authentic affection: not syrupy or sentimental, posturing or feelgoodish, gussied up for theatrical effect. *Hollywood Arms* is about real people who fight or let one another down, jab and jeer, needle and explode, but also, when need be, help. People who are sarcastic or pathetic failures, impoverished and disappointed. But also people who, disguised or tucked away, have locked up from everyday use a fund of genuine affection for one another. Something like good, inherited crockery, replacing the paper plates on special occasions, something precious and precarious, hauled out however chipped, and however in danger of further chipping.

Hollywood Arms is about a dysfunctional family that has migrated to Hollywood in hope of success and ease. Actually, it was only Louise, the young mother, who left her own mother, Nanny, and her little daughter, Helen, behind in the sticks, while she hoped to become another Louella Parsons, or at least a writer of movie-star profiles. Though Louise, with scant success, is not ready for them, Nanny and Helen descend on her in her seedy apartment house, the Hollywood Arms, sometimes also visited by Louise's ex-husband, Jody, a decent weakling, tubercular and alcoholic, peddling coupons when not hospitalized.

Louise has a lover she loves, Nick, but he is married. She also has a sweet, solicitous suitor, Bill, whom she does not love. Because he has steady employment, Nanny keeps nagging Louise to marry him, however lovelessly, for a meal ticket. When Louise gets pregnant by Nick, she yields to Bill's pleading, at the cost of becoming alcoholic herself. There is also the good-natured landlady, Dixie, single mother to the precocious and bratty Malcolm, Helen's playmate. On the roof, with a view of the City of Angels, the kids play their fantasy games, and here, too, much later, will come Helen's illegitimate sister, Alice, for air and dreams.

The not exactly unwobbling pivot of all this is Nanny, a stubborn, sardonically wisecracking, drolly hypochondriacal matriarch without portfolio—i.e., with too few people to boss around. But to Louise, Helen, Jody, and Bill, she is a bit of a tyrant, albeit a grouchily benevolent one, and very funny to boot. We see these people at two crucial stages in their lives: in 1941 and again in 1951, when Helen, who is really Carol Burnett, begins a New York theatrical career.

The play is a comedy-drama, a comedy that almost imperceptibly, and never totally, becomes serious. As comedy, too, it is unusual. Unlike most recent comedies that campily feed off their characters' stupidities, here, despite assorted failings, no one is dumb and an easy butt for jokes. The humor is not in dim-wittedness and one-upmanship but in warmly portrayed everyday fallibility, in comic outbursts during which ordinary people give off funny or funny-sad sparks that keep both the farcical and the maudlin at bay.

That Linda Lavin is a fabulous Nanny you don't need me to tell you, but this always remarkable actress manages here to surpass even the stiff competition of her own previous triumphs, squeezing every last drop out of her part without the slightest trace of ham or plea for sympathy. Scarcely less admirable is the Louise of Michele Pawk, who lends great heft to a humdrum character, making her intensely human and profoundly moving. Donna Lynne Champlin is unswervingly straightforward as the grown Helen, and Sara Niemietz makes little Helen lovable with never an iota of cuteness. Amazing, too, is the Malcolm of Nicolas King, a child actor with timing to make old pros envious. Frank Wood is an honestly unembellished Jody, and Patrick Clear a restrainedly sympathetic Bill. Leslie Hendrix and Emily Graham-Handley lend savvy support, as do the impeccable décor of Walt Spangler, Judith Dolan's incisive costumes, and Howell Binkley's empathetic lighting. Robert Lindsey Nassif's accompanying music also adds distinctly to our pleasure.

But *Hollywood Arms* has yet another form of invaluable affection, that of Harold Prince for the characters and their story. You will never see more feelingful insight, more self-effacing love for their quirks, foibles, and kindnesses, from a director for his stage children, big and small. If only this thoroughly endearing play and production could have been seen by Burnett's daughter and co-author, Carrie Hamilton, dead before even the Goodman Theatre premiere. One fervently hopes that the joy of such a true creation accompanied her on her final journey.

La Bohème;
Dance of the Vampires

Little did Puccini suspect that his *La Bohème*, adapted from the play Henri Murger adapted from his novel circa 1850, would continue to be readapted ad infinitum, if not ad nauseam. Joe Papp produced an English version starring Linda Ronstadt, Jonathan Larson slapped *Rent* on us, and Baz Luhrmann has now revived his 1990 Australian Opera mounting on Broadway.

Those of us subjected to Baz's *Romeo + Juliet* and *Moulin Rouge* had reason to fear the worst; what we get is merely quirky and unremarkable. Performed in Italian with combined sur- and subtitles in an uncredited 1957 English vernacular updating, it sports references to an MG, a Rolls-Royce, and Marlon Brando. That the opera's third act, with its customs office, had to be relocated to the Franco-Belgian border, whither the tubercular and penniless Mimi could hardly have dragged herself, is the least of its problems. More problematic, in this computerized age, is the old-fashioned décor (by Mrs. Luhrmann, a.k.a. Catherine Martin), relying on wagons moved slowly by stagehands in full audience view. The orchestra, to fit into a Broadway pit, was reduced by Nicholas Kitsopoulos's orchestration; the conductor, Constantine Kitsopoulos, provides the requisite musical-comedy background.

So we get an array of young singers (nice idea), who presumably compensate with youth and acting for less powerful voices. The buzzword, or Bazword, is accessibility, for luring young non-operatic audiences to opera, dumbing-down not excluded. Thus the preface to the text informs us that to avoid anachronism, "the entomology [*sic*] of the slang" was carefully checked. Unchecked, however, were things like rendering "Addio senza rancor" in the titles as "Goodbye without regret," which may be more accessible than rancor, but makes no sense.

Visual innovations include a Café Momus and environs as neon-lit as Times Square; an exaggeratedly cramped bohemian attic fronted by a huge red sign that reads L'AMOUR, presumably to explicate what the show is about; handheld spotlights for, say, the firelight from the stove; a building with edgily exposed girders; an onstage balcony featuring scantily clad female and male whores; a vintage bemedaled military overcoat for Schaunard; and the British sugar daddy Alcindoro singing, for added verismo, in English.

The music still sounds seductive, and the alternating cast I caught sang almost as well as it looked. Ekaterina Solovyeva was an accomplished Mimi, and David Miller a personable Rodolfo. Chloe Wright was a full-throated and full-bodied Musetta, and Ben Davis, aside from some stiffness, satisfied as Marcello. The rest coped respectably enough. For the seasoned operagoer, here is a modest curiosity; for the rock-bound neophyte, a challenge to see if the show, like Musetta's shoe, really fits.

Dance of the Vampires is based on a film by Roman Polanski and a German book and lyrics by Michael Kunze, but with English lyrics and music by Jim Steinman, and an English book by Kunze,

Steinman, and David Ives. If you want to know how many cooks it takes to spoil a brew, this is it, although here the very recipe was sickening. Camp needs to be truly funny and flawlessly executed. Not so with this clumsily contrived claptrap, which does not even relish what it is parodying—another missing prerequisite. There is something bloodless about these bloodsuckers, toothless about these fangs.

To give you some idea of how low the show stoops, its Transylvanian village is called Lower Belabartòkovitch. Professor Abronsius, the chief, albeit clumsy, vampire killer, travels with a transfusion apparatus but doesn't administer to the neediest—the show—which flickers forlornly, like a dying Sylvania lightbulb in search of a Trans.

Perhaps the biggest disappointment is Michael Crawford, who feebly rehashes his *Phantom of the Opera* performance and can't even muster a convincing Lower Belalugosian accent. As Sarah, the heroine, Mandy Gonzalez fails in acting, singing, and looks. Wasted are the acting talents of René Auberjonois and Mark Price, and the fine singing of Max von Essen.

The gifted David Gallo has devised scenery that, more expensive than impressive, shuttles between the ghoulish and the garish. Costumes and lighting do what they can, but neither John Carrafa's haphazard choreography nor John Rando's hit-or-miss direction—to say nothing of Steinman's music, mere vamping—can make what's dead undead.

Take Me Out

Baseball has always bored me. It is to Richard Greenberg's credit that he has made it—or at least its locker rooms—interesting. In *Take Me Out*, he has also written some rhapsodic paeans to the game. If only he could have done as much for the theater.

Take Me Out is genus boulevard comedy–melodrama, species gay. And why not, so long as it entertains, which it unremittingly does, although cleverness, which is Greenberg's element, is never the whole story. To be sure, young men in the audience are rocked and racked with laughter, to the point where a mere "So?" from one of the characters elicits guffaws that register on the Richter scale. Credibility, however, lags well behind.

We get here baseball characters whose speech is literate to the point of literariness, as when Kippy, the play's narrator and short-stop for the Empires (read Yankees), proclaims, "So now we start the Kafkaesque portion of the evening. Well, Kafka-lite, anyway… Dekaf-ka." Kippy seldom stops short of the professorial, but the others have their arias, too—even the brutish Shane. Brought in from double-A Utica as a closer (his only talent), he doesn't even know which state he was born in but makes speeches that only Dostoyevsky's disinherited were previously heirs to.

This is at least preferable to a play in which people spoke like real baseball players, though Greenberg does include a couple of meatheads, plus a pair of Latinos who palaver in Spanish, and a Japanese import who speaks nothing but Japanese until it suits Greenberg otherwise. As a result, the play tends to devolve into so many skits.

The central figure, Darren Lemming (suggested by Derek Jeter) is nothing short of mythic. Half black, he is one who "even in base-ball, one of the few realms of American life in which people of color are routinely adulated by people of pallor," as Kippy tells us, "was something special." An almost superhumanly gifted and privileged being, he can publicly declare his homosexuality and privately com-pare himself to God. Significantly, though, Greenberg finesses two *scènes à faire*: the press conference in which Darren outs himself, and the confession of Kippy, married and a paterfamilias, that he is in love with Darren. Conversely, there is an abundance of shower and locker-room scenes with male frontal nudity, so that, if only a song were introduced, one could feel blissfully transported to Off Broadway's *Naked Boys Singing!*

What truly distinguishes the show is the acting and directing. Daniel Sunjata's Darren exudes devilish self-assurance and perfect timing enough to make you believe he is Superman. As his accoun-tant, a caricatural gay man tacitly enamored of him, Denis O'Hare gives a spectacular performance. He prestidigitates with limbs and torso as if they were made of Indian clubs, and tremulously con-veys Greenberg's profound cuteness and cute profundities. Superb, too, is Frederick Weller's touchingly animal Shane, with the others scarcely behind in ensemble acting. No one can stage this kind of play better than Joe Mantello, especially when supported by the canny set of Scott Pask, apt costumes of Jess Goldstein, and blazing lights of Kevin Adams.

Nine

The good news about the revival of *Nine* is that the director, David Leveaux, dares to make it different from the Tommy Tune original. The bad news is that most of the differences don't work. You'll recall that the book is Arthur Kopit's version of Mario Fratti's version of Fellini's *8 ½*, with music and lyrics by Maury Yeston. The master film director Guido Contini is desperate for a new script idea that won't come; his marriage to Luisa is on the rocks; his glamorous leading lady and ex-lover, Claudia, has retired to Paris with a new man; his sexually grasping mistress, Carla, is getting a divorce dreaded by him; his producer, Liliane La Fleur, justifiably impatient, is on his back; and more women than he can handle are eager to get on their backs for him.

Everyone converges on a spa near Venice where Guido and Luisa hoped for some peace together. There ensues a roundelay of sex and jealousy and demands on Guido, interspersed with memories of his dead mother and the 9-year-old Guido's discovery of erotics through the fat slut Saraghina.

The lyrics are engaging, the music lilting, the story serviceable. Scott Pask's arid set is steel panels, runways, and a spiral staircase, with a bathetic Botticelli mural for backdrop, but no Venice. Vicki Mortimer's costumes are a well-meaning hodgepodge, Jonathan Butterell's choreography will just do, and only Brian MacDevitt's lighting is, as usual, exquisite.

The cast is mostly good. Antonio Banderas's Guido, barely intelligible, overdoes childishness at the expense of charisma. Mary Stuart Masterson, however, is a winningly sung and persuasively long-suffering Luisa; a near-nude Jane Krakowski pleases as Carla and shows exceptional spunk singing while being hoisted sky-high upside down. The ageless Chita Rivera proves undauntably compelling as Liliane, but the talented Laura Benanti is miscast as Claudia: in no way does she suggest Cardinale, the Ur-Claudia, or any other Italian sex goddess. The remaining women are fine, as is William Ullrich's plucky little Guido.

And the innovations? Omission of "The Germans Are Coming" (why?); a Carla who, in Guido's imagination, descends from the sky (why not?); and a cast at times awash in ankle-high water (why on earth?). Still, *Nine* gives more tuneful musical than anything else around.

Talking Heads

"Critics," wrote Alan Bennett, "should be searched for certain adjectives at the door of the theatre—'irreverent,' 'probing,' and (above all) 'satirical.'" So I'll refrain from calling *Talking Heads*, two Bennett evenings of three monologues each, irreverent or satirical. But I can't quite forgo "probing," for in each of these penetrant character sketches, one main and several ancillary figures are—all right, not probed, but sweetly, humorously, compassionately apprehended. With an uncanny sense of detail, and with sympathy for their foibles, pity for their failures, and joy in their Pyrrhic victories, Bennett conjures up struggling creatures of riveting genuineness, and grants them their all too often overlooked heroism, writ small but felt deep.

The personages are a zealous antiques dealer who makes the blunder of a lifetime, a nosy meddler and compulsive complaint-letter writer who is fulfilled in prison, an atheistic and alcoholic vicar's wife who finds happiness bedding an Indian grocer, an earnestly self-deluded skin-flick actress spouting soulful platitudes, a mentally disturbed mama's boy and closeted homosexual with selectively sharp insights, and a woman who forms a bizarre but satisfying relationship with her elderly chiropodist. For all their denuding self-exposure, they are clothed in the author's sheltering tactfulness.

The excellent actors are Brenda Wehle, Christine Ebersole, Kathleen Chalfant, Valerie Mahaffey (adorable but not always audible), Daniel Davis (so good we should see much more of him), and the authentic, inimitable Briton Lynn Redgrave. But the five Americans also manage highly creditable regional or class accents. Michael Engler's incisive direction, Rachel Hauck's smartly stripped-down set, Candice Donnelly's shrewd costuming, Chris Parry's unfussy lighting, Wendall K. Harrington's helpful projections, and Michael Roth's tongue-in-cheek music contribute handsomely. One question remains: is Bennett imitating life, or is life imitating Alan Bennett?

Gypsy; *Salome: The Reading*

High among top-notch American musicals is the Styne-Sond-heim-Laurents *Gypsy*, though no show (*Nine*, for recent example) is wholly foolproof. We have seen some inferior *Gypsy*s, of which the current revival was rumored to be one. But there seems to have been enough last-minute repair work to make this *Gypsy* stand favorable comparison with the legendary original. The alleged drawbacks—the scenery and Mama Rose—have been brought up to snuff and, in the case of Bernadette Peters, well beyond.

Most Mama Roses have been too butch or brash (Bette Midler, Tyne Daly, and even Ethel Merman), too sophisticated (Angela Lansbury), or too ladylike (Betty Buckley). It remained for Peters to achieve the perfect blend of fanaticism and femininity, of monster and victim. Here for once is a demonic stage mother who can also convey sexiness, pathos, and charm. We understand now how she could enslave a man, make children her thralls, breach hearts and barriers, and steal restaurant flatware with puckish style. Also what made her what she is—desperate to attain vicariously through a daughter what her background prevented her from becoming herself.

Much credit must go to the direction of Sam Mendes and the additional choreography of Jerry Mitchell, who retained most of Jerome Robbins's dazzling originals and added a few winning touches of his own. Mendes, among much else, came up with a smaller proscenium arch within the actual proscenium, allowing us to see, as Baby June and Baby Louise perform, the wings where Rose and Herbie empathize (Rose even—very movingly and slightly frighteningly—duplicating her daughters' turns).

There is much distinguished acting. John Dossett is easily the most convincing Herbie yet: finely calibrated and thoroughly believable. Tammy Blanchard is a satisfactory Louise, especially in her scene with Tulsa (a winning David Burtka), but who can equal the definitive Louise of Crista Moore? Dainty June is competently handled by Kate Reinders, although the squeals of Heather Tepe's Baby June are a bit too high for non-canine ears. Addison Timlin touchingly conveys Baby Louise's shyness and awkwardness with economy and finesse remarkable in a child actor. As the strippers, Heather Lee, Kate Buddeke, and Julie Halston (neatly doubling as Miss Cratchitt) hit the mark.

Anthony Ward's sets and costumes will do nicely, though seeing stagehands at work adds a Brechtian touch made not enough or too much of. Jules Fisher and Peggy Eisenhauer supply inconspicuously incisive lighting, and even the little lamb is a perfect little lamb. It is good to have *Gypsy* back: an old friend one doesn't wish to be separated from for too long.

Estelle Parsons, the director of *Salome: The Reading*, explains in a program note that a mere reading is corroborated by Oscar Wilde's having actually written *Salome* "to be read for the beauty of the language." To be read for that, perhaps, but staged for a good deal more. Wilde wrote it in French for Sarah Bernhardt, not one to stint on production values. Readings belong in a concert hall; in a theater, the play needs all the help it can get. And indeed, this production has embryonic scenery, costumes, lighting, and music, and some vestigial action.

Still, if beauty of language is your selling point, it would help if your cast could manage acceptable stage English rather than low-rent New Yorkese—Al Pacino's included (not to mention his mis-pronunciations: *mien* as a disyllable, *exquisite* misstressed, and so on). The Italian for salami is *salame*; that for ham might as well be Salome, at least in this reading. Pacino has played Herod before, and the part does lend itself to some excess, which is what he now looks for in a role. He'll do anything for a cheap laugh, perhaps confusing *buffo* with *boffo*, relishing sudden leaps from hangdog schlemiel to heaven-storming ranter, from grotesque wiggleworm to fire-breathing basilisk—enough imploding pauses, demented stares, and wheedling singsong for six characters in search of a straitjacket. Did Al never hear Hamlet's admonishment to the actors not to out-herod Herod, an act punishable by whipping?

Marisa Tomei at least gets one thing right: her princess is a spoiled teenager, but, a tolerable belly dance notwithstanding (no seven veils, alas), she does not sound the depths of repressed sexuality run amok. David Strathairn is hamstrung by Jokanaan, a part that is mostly invective; sensibly, he is not all roar, but neither does he soar. The most intelligent performance is the restrained Herodias of Dianne Wiest, unfortunately too refined for her surroundings. Most ludicrous, next to Pacino, is the comedy team of Captain (Chris Messina) and Page (Timothy Doyle), the one a baby roaring for his rattle, the other a female impersonator petulant about being deprived of his drag.

Long Day's Journey Into Night; I Am My Own Wife

There can be little doubt that America's favorite dramatic subject is the dysfunctional family. It stretches from *The Glass Menagerie* to *The Skin of Our Teeth*, from *Death of a Salesman* to *The Fifth of July*. Equally clearly, its grandest specimen is *Long Day's Journey Into Night*, which rightly earns its frequent revivals, however few—if any—of them can do full justice to this long and devilishly demanding Eugene O'Neill masterpiece.

Broadway's most recent tussles with it—the disastrous Jonathan Miller–directed and Jack Lemmon–starring abridgment in 1986 and the routine, lackluster version with Colleen Dewhurst and Jason Robards two years later—cried out for better to come. Yet is there a more unlikely family than beefy Brian Dennehy as James Tyrone, the aging matinee-idol father; British grande dame Vanessa Redgrave as the naïve, convent-bred Mary Tyrone; loutish Philip Seymour Hoffman as the handsome-wastrel elder son, Jamie; and the totally different—what family is *he* from?—Robert Sean Leonard as Edmund, the poetry-writing tubercular younger son, the author's self-portrait?

Each of these parts is an actor's plum, and even the peripheral Irish maid, Cathleen, is at least a raisin, which Fiana Toibin performs in the sensible traditional fashion. But that quartet of loving and resentful, wounding and forgiveness-begging infighters—sometimes funny, sometimes pathetic, and ultimately tragic—is now a car with unaligned wheels lurching ahead on a bumpy road.

Can you really see the colossal Dennehy, with his blunt-to-blustering overdrive, as a once-promising, lofty Shakespearean selling out into a dashingly swashbuckling Monte Cristo? In his final, drunken confession scene, he does score some points, but too few, too late. Sadly one recalls the first and finest James Tyrone, Fredric March, a magnificently poetic wreck of a man. Vanessa Redgrave's Mary Tyrone is weird and fluttery, by turns childish and hysterical, untrustworthily unpredictable from the start. It is admittedly hard to convey the dichotomy of this lovable but ruinous character, best captured in my view by Martha Henry, Constance Cummings, and Geraldine Fitzgerald. The highly accomplished Redgrave gets some details right, but the overarching mental unstableness she exudes is so excessive as to make one wonder whether she is playing or being unhinged.

Robert Sean Leonard, genuine talent notwithstanding, has prematurely developed an RSL persona, or groove, into which he slips with disquieting predictability. As for Philip Seymour Hoffman, he comes nearest the mark, but Jason Robards, the original Jamie, set the standard here for a lyrically beautiful loser, for which this actor is physically unqualified.

Santo Loquasto, like others before him, has designed a faithful replica of the O'Neills' New London shabby-genteel cottage, but this has the disadvantage of precluding a more exposed staircase allowing for Mary's final, shattering descent. His costumes are suitable. Brian MacDevitt's lighting is, as always, beyond reproach. Robert Falls has directed effectively until the end; with Mary flouncing in from the rear and fluttering all over the place, the conclusion is even flatter than the absence of that symbolic descent would predicate. Still, the grandeur of O'Neill's achievement is hard to expunge, and not a little of it survives, however hampered, here.

Charlotte Von Mahlsdorf, really Lothar Berfelde (1928–2002), was a German museum curator and transvestite, whose fascinating autobiography, *Ich bin meine eigene Frau*, has been dramatized by Doug Wright, who has retitled it *I Am My Own Wife*. From childhood, Lothar thought of himself as a girl, and was tormented by his brutal, wife-beating father, understood by his hapless mother, and sheltered successively by an enlightened great uncle and a lesbian aunt.

The memoir chronicles Lothar's adventures and often narrow escapes under Nazism and Communism, the odd jobs that trained him for collector- and curatorship, and his adjustment to transvestism and homosexuality. The persecution of Jews and homosexuals is compellingly conveyed in terse and shattering vignettes. Equally powerful are evocations of aerial bombardments and other horrors of war.

And, of course, fond reminiscences of gay joints and the doings in the gay netherworld. Much of this doesn't translate into one-man (or any) theater; least of all the arduous but spellbinding transformation of a disintegrating mansion into a charming museum, achieved by Charlotte's two hands without outside help.

Act One, more Charlotte than Doug, works handily; Act Two, which is more Doug as interviewer, condenser, imaginer, and fabricator, is less interesting and annoyingly self-serving. But Jefferson Mays—with mediocre German pronunciation, a good German accent in English, and very fine performing that involves quick character and voice changes—does yeoman's service. Derek McLane's décor, David Lander's lighting, and Moisés Kaufman's staging contribute handsomely. "My motive was always to preserve something," Charlotte wrote, "not for myself but for posterity."

The Persians

I have always considered Aeschylus and Sophocles great dramatic poets, but Euripides the first poetic dramatist able to command a modern stage. The National Actors Theatre has happily proved me wrong with Aeschylus's *The Persians* (472 B.C.), which held my attention for its 80 propulsive minutes. Ellen McLaughlin's version is both literate and actable, if a bit overinfused with contemporary antiwar relevance. Ethan McSweeny has turned the chorus into seven Persian counselors who mostly talk individually, and only rarely in concert or in repetitions. Just once in the end do they, effectively, sing. (Michael Roth has composed some persuasively archaic-sounding music.)

McSweeny gives them arresting moves and actions, and all speak well enough, although only Herb Foster distinguishes himself through looks, demeanor, and delivery. The minimal but inventive scenery, by James Noone, serves well, as do Jess Goldstein's costumes (modern, but with an overlay of old Persian) and Kevin Adams's unfussily resourceful lighting.

The Persians, though enemies, are treated fairly by the Athenian playwright, who himself once fought them at Marathon. Roberta Maxwell brings sovereign presence of speech and bearing to Atossa, widow of Darius and mother of Xerxes, but she might have been a little warmer in compassion for her defeated son. Michael Stuhlbarg is a suitably chastened Xerxes, and Len Cariou is properly ghostly as Darius's minatory ghost. Good work by Brennan Brown as the shattered messenger who relates the terrible fiasco at Salamis, albeit with a rather too New Yorky accent. Altogether, American English lacks the melody that both classical Greek and modern British can stunningly supply.

INDEX OF PLAYS REVIEWED